Professional Active Server Pages 3.0

Richard Anderson, Chris Blexrud, Andrea Chiarelli, Daniel Denault, Alex Homer, Dino Esposito, Brian Francis, Matthew Gibbs, Bill Kropog, Craig McQueen, George Reilly, Simon Robinson, John Schenken, Dean Sonderegger, Dave Sussman

Wrox Press Ltd. ®

Professional Active Server Pages 3.0

Published by Wrox Press Ltd. Arden House, 1102 Warwick Rd, Birmingham, B27 6BH
Printed in USA
ISBN 1-861002-6-10

Trademark Acknowledgements

Wrox has endeavored to provide trademark information about all the companies and products mentioned in this book by the appropriate use of capitals. However, Wrox cannot guarantee the accuracy of this information.

Credits

Authors
Richard Anderson
Chris Blexrud
Andrea Chiarelli
Daniel Denault
Alex Homer
Dino Esposito
Brian Francis
Matthew Gibbs
Bill Kropog
Craig McQueen
George Reilly
Simon Robinson
John Schenken
Dean Sonderegger
Dave Sussman

Additional Material
Matthew Bortniker
Charles Campbell
James M. Conard
Richard Harrison
Keith Stanislaw
Kent Tegels

Managing Editor
Chris Hindley

Editors
Craig A. Berry
Dan Maharry
Lisa Stephenson
Adrian Young

Development Editor
Liz Toy

Index
Andrew Criddle

Project Manager
Sophie Edwards

Technical Reviewers
Matt Bullock
Chad DePue
Andrew Enfield
Alexander Haneng
Robert Howard
Shawn Jackson
Jeff Johnson
Stephen Kaufman
Brad Kingsley
Ajoy Krishnamoorthy
Dave Navarro
Robert Oliver
Matthew Reynolds
Ulrich Schwanitz
Steven Smith
Kevin Spencer
Andrew Stopford
William Storey
Adwait Ullal

Design/Layout
Tom Bartlett
Mark Burdett
William Fallon
Jonathan Jones
John McNulty

Illustrations
William Fallon
Jonathan Jones

Cover
Chris Morris
Concept by Third Wave

About the Authors

Richard Anderson

Richard Anderson is an established software developer who has worked with Microsoft technologies for nearly 10 years. He works for a small yet globally known software house in Peterborough (England), where he currently holds the position of "Research and Development Manager". What that means is that he plays with lots of great new technologies, and then tells people how they work, ensuring they are correctly understood and adopted correctly and successfully in new applications. He also writes applications too, and is responsible for mentoring and managing C++ and VB developers. Richard can be contacted via his private email account `rja@arpsolutions.demon.co.uk`.

Chris Blexrud

Chris Blexrud, MCSD, is a consultant for Born Information Services, Inc. (`http://www.born.com`), a Microsoft Solution Provider. Chris's main areas of expertise are in Microsoft technologies such as ASP, VB, COM/DCOM, MTS, COM+, and various BackOffice products. When Chris is not developing business solutions, he enjoys snowmobiling and hunting in northern Minnesota and spending time with family and friends. Chris can be reached at `chris.blexrud@born.com`.

Andrea Chiarelli

Andrea Chiarelli is an independent consultant with experience in software design and training. He holds a degree in Computer Science and a Master in Software Engineering, works for software companies and training centers in Tuscany (Italy) and is a regular contributor to Computer Programming, an Italian programming magazine. His experience spans from database design to multimedia software developing. In recent years he's specialized in designing Internet and Intranet systems developing Web-based applications and interfacing databases to the Web primarily using Active Server Pages technology.

Daniel Denault

Daniel Denault is a developer and network administrator developing Internet applications and doing high security network configuration designs and installations in the behavioral healthcare industry. Dan Denault is also an independant consultant. These applications are developed using the following technologies Customized ActiveX controls, ActiveX DLL's, Active Server Pages, Word and Excel OLE automation, JavaScript, VBScript, DHTML, IIS, and SQL Server 7.0. Daniel Denault can be contacted at `admin@csopgh.com`.

Dino Esposito

Dino is a free-lance consultant based in Rome, Italy. He specializes in scripting and COM development and worked for Andersen Consulting focusing on development of Web-based applications.

He loves writing and is a contributing editor to Microsoft Internet Developer for which runs the Cutting Edge column. He regularly contributes also to Microsoft Systems Journal, MSDN News, Windows Developer's Journal. Get in touch with Dino at `dinoe@wrox.com`.

Brian Francis

Brian Francis is the Technical Evangelist for NCR's Retail Self Service Solutions. From his office in Duluth, Georgia, Brian is responsible for enlightening NCR and their customers in the technologies and tools used for Self Service Applications. Brian also uses the tools he evangelizes in developing solutions for NCR's customers. He has worked extensively with Wrox Press as a technical reviewer and has also co-authored on a number of projects.

Matthew Gibbs

Matthew is a Microsoft IIS team member, specializing in the IIS and ASP help desk. Matthew regularly talks on all of the IIS 'gotchas' and work-arounds.

Alex Homer

Alex came to writing computer books through an unusual route, including tractor driver, warehouse manager, garden products buyer, glue sales specialist, and double-glazing salesman. With this wide-ranging commercial and practical background, and a love of anything that could be taken to pieces, computers were a natural progression. Now, when not writing books for Wrox, he spends his spare time sticking together bits of code for his wife's software company (Stonebroom Software - `http://www.stonebroom.com`) or just looking out of the window at the delightfully idyllic and rural surroundings of the Peak District in Derbyshire, England.

Bill Kropog

Bill Kropog is a full-time consultant for a Web and software development firm in New Orleans, Louisiana. Bill specializes in finding new and creative ways to display and manipulate data with Active Server Pages. He uses Visual InterDev 6.0 for most of what he develops, with frequent hops into Visual Basic 6.0. He also creates most of the graphics he uses in his projects (Corel Xara 2.0 and Adobe PhotoShop 5.0), making him a well-rounded developer. XML is the latest thing on Bill's plate, and, being a former journalist, he'd like to develop XML-based standards for online publications to make it easier to share news and to bring ordinary journalists into the online world.

Craig McQueen

Craig is a Principal Consultant at Sage Information Consultants, Inc. His role at Sage is to guide clients in their adoption of Internet technologies into their existing business. Recently, he led an e-commerce implementation of Site Server at a major consumer electronics company. Previous to consulting, Craig led the development of two small retail Internet products: InContext WebAnalyzer and InContent FlashSite.

Craig has a Master of Science degree from the University of Toronto where he specialized in Human-Computer Interaction.

George Reilly

George V. Reilly has been a member of the IIS/ASP development team since shortly before ASP 1.0 shipped at the end of 1996. Nowadays he is responsible for IIS performance. He has been doing his best to write tight code since he discovered the BBC Micro in his native Dublin, Ireland in 1982. In retrospect, he has a hard time believing that he found enough time to co-write "Beginning ATL COM Programming", Wrox Press, 1998.

Simon Robinson

Simon Robinson lives in Lancaster, UK, where he shares a house with some students. He first encountered serious programming when doing his PhD in physics. He would program in FORTRAN when his supervisor was watching (physics lecturers like FORTRAN) and C when he wasn't. The experience of programming was enough to put him off computers for life, and he tried to pursue a career as a sports massage therapist instead until he realized how much money was in programming and wasn't in sports massage. He then spent a year writing some very good cardiac risk assessment software but he and his business partner never got round to selling it to anyone. Finally, driven by a strange lack of money, he looked for a–whisper the word quietly–job. Which somehow ended up–after a year of his working for Lucent Technologies in Welwyn Garden City–leading to him writing books about computers. You can visit Simon's web site at `http://www.simonrobinson.com/`

John Schenken

John Schenken is currently Software Test Lead on the Visual Basic Server Enterprise Team for Microsoft. He was previously Test Lead for the Microsoft Script Debugger that shipped with Windows NT Option pack and is still responsible for it in Windows 2000. He has a computer science degree from Texas A & M university. He has programming experience involving MSMQ, SMTP, NT Event Log, NT Perf Counters, ASP, business objects and ADO (basically wide experience writing end-to-end web applications involving business objects).

Dean Sonderegger

Dean is responsible for the technology and development of products at Ultraprise Corporation based in Sterling, Virginia. He's worked with Active Server Pages since its inception and specializes in internet-based commercial application development. The majority of his spare time is spent chasing his two sons Crawford and Jordan, or with his lovely wife Karen.

David Sussman

David has spent most of his professional life as a developer, starting with Unix and C, in the days when the Internet was only used for Usenet newsgroups. He then switched to Microsoft development languages, and spent several years moaning about the lack of pointers in Visual Basic. Like Alex, he lives in a quiet, rural village, this time in Oxfordshire. He spends his spare time convincing himself that he'll get off his backside and get fit. He never does.

N
W

Table of Contents

Introduction

They say that everyone can remember exactly where they were, and what they were doing, when one of those major events in history occurred. It could be when President Kennedy was shot, it could be the day that Elvis Presley died, or it could just be something less historic and much closer to home – such as the first time you saw 'Doom'.

One of our colleagues firmly believes that the introduction of Microsoft's **Active Server Pages** (**ASP**) technology, or **Denali** as it was called then, was one such important event. He backs this up by remembering exactly what he was doing at the time. He'd just finished work on a book about Web database connectivity techniques, ending with the jewel-in-the-crown at that time–the **Internet Database Connector** (**IDC**). The rapid addition of an extra chapter before going to press, to cover this exciting new ASP technology, was the order of the day. In fact that single chapter was probably the reason for most of the book's sales, because suddenly every developer wanted to be 'into' ASP.

All this sounds like it was a long time ago, and we have all become quite blasé about Active Server Pages and whole range of techniques that have built up around it. But (at the time of writing) this was less than three years ago. Yet here we are, with version 3.0 of ASP just released, and with a feature set, performance and capabilities that leave the original version 1.0 standing in the dust.

What Is This Book About?

This book is about **Active Server Pages 3.0**, as included with **Windows 2000**. However, because ASP is now a core part of so many Web-oriented features within Windows, this book covers a far wider area than just how ASP works. ASP is maturing all the time to encompass more integration with other Windows services and software, and so there are many other areas that impinge directly on the use and performance of ASP.

In particular this involves the Windows operating system itself, including the new security features of Windows 2000, and the Internet server software that comes with Windows 2000 – Internet Information Server (IIS). On top of this are the other less obvious services, which also have a direct or indirect effect on the way that ASP works. These include COM+, the various Internet service administration tools, and – indirectly – the many other services and installed software packages that either provide additional functionality to ASP, or which have interfaces that are available for use in ASP.

In fact, this is really where ASP comes into its own, and why it has become such an integral part of working with Windows on the Internet. ASP introduced the concept of using ActiveX interfaces or discreet component objects (separate controls that provide a COM interface) within Web scripts, rather than running external executable programs as had previously been the norm in other Web scripting languages (such as Perl).

This integration with COM and ActiveX means that ASP can effectively access anything on the Web server, or a connected network, which provides a suitable interface. From this alone, a huge market has grown up for components and objects that implement or encapsulate specific functions. More than that, almost all installed software and services in Windows either include a set of specific ActiveX components, or directly exposes a COM interface, to allow ASP to access it.

So, as well as chapters all about the roots of ASP, the base object structure, and how it's used, you'll also see chapters that demonstrate the many different ways that ASP integrates seamlessly with other software and services in Windows. One of the most obvious of these is access to data in a relational database or other type of data store (such as Active Directory), and you'll see several chapters devoted to these topics.

We'll also explore the intimate relationship between Internet Information Server and COM and the new COM+, and see how ASP has changed the way that it hosts and executes external components to provide better performance and scalability. This also affects the way that components are designed and built, and we'll be exploring this topic in some depth as well.

Who Is This Book For?

When Active Server Pages was first introduced, we produced a book covering that initial version from the point of view of a beginner to the technology. Fair enough, because at that point everyone was a beginner. However, the runaway success of ASP means that this is no longer the case. There are many millions of knowledgeable and active ASP developers out there who want hard-core technical coverage of ASP in its new version.

Then, when version 2.0 of ASP was released, we produced a separate beginner's guide, and this is also the case with version 3.0. This book is the *professional-level* version, and is aimed at two categories of developers. Firstly, it is designed to satisfy the needs of those who are already well practiced in the skills of ASP and server-side Web application development. Secondly, it will be a useful and fast-track guide to those who are less familiar with ASP, but have a server-side Web application development background – perhaps in the use of Perl, IDC, etc. For newcomers to Web applications and dynamic Web page creation, we recommend you look at *Beginning Active Server Pages 3.0* (ISBN 1-861003-38-2) first.

Version 3.0 of ASP in itself is not an earth-shattering upgrade. In fact, ASP is reaching the point where there isn't much more that can be done with it. However, the wish lists of most developers should be fulfilled with the new version. There are many subtle changes to the way that it works, in the scripting engines that are included, in the Web server (IIS) itself and in the administration tools. There are also some fundamental changes in the IIS/COM(+) relationship, which it's important that you grasp. If you didn't really do much with COM and MTS in version 2.0 of ASP (a lot of people managed to ignore them), then now is the time to get to grips with them and start building pages and components to integrate with it.

What Does This Book Cover?

Conceptually, this book is divided into several sections. This allows us to cover widely differing ASP-related topics in an orderly sequence, and helps you to grasp the basics of the way that ASP works before going on to learn about higher-level features that depend on these core topics.

- Section 1 is all about **ASP Basics**. It describes the **changes to ASP** in version 3.0, the **ASP Object Model**, and all the basic concepts required for using ASP script and external components.
- Section 2 covers **ActiveX Data Objects** (**ADO**) and **data access issues in general** – including XML. ADO is now the standard communication technology for all Microsoft applications, and its use is almost uncontested in ASP.
- Section 3 introduces the issues involved in **building components for use with ASP**, and understanding how COM and COM+ change the component environment.
- Section 4 is all about **integrating ASP with BackOffice applications** such as Microsoft Message Queue Server, Collaborative Data Objects and Microsoft Exchange, Active Directory, etc.
- Section 5 moves on to look at how ASP is used in the enterprise. It examines issues of **security, performance, scalability**, etc.
- Section 6 contains a great deal of useful **reference material** in the form of **appendices** and **tables**.

You don't have to read the whole book from cover to cover, or in any particular order. However, if you are coming to ASP from another Web development environment, you will certainly want to cover sections one and two in some depth to get a firm grasp on the fundamentals and see how they relate to other Web-development development languages and techniques.

On the other hand, those battle-hardened ASP veterans amongst you may prefer to look through Chapter 1 to see what's new and what's changed in version 3.0, before skipping from chapter to chapter to see how these changes affect you. Of course, if you prefer to lay in the bath and read it from cover to cover, then please don't let us stop you. But I bet your arms soon get tired.

What Do I Need To Use This Book?

You always know when you get to this point in a book what it's going to say. Yes, you need to have Active Server Pages installed to be able to use this book to the full. However, let's take a slightly more scientific approach than that. The requirements are:

Hardware

A machine with Windows 2000 installed to act as a Web server. Preferably this should be Windows 2000 Server or better. However, Internet Information Server and most of the associated services (with some exceptions) are included with Windows 2000 Professional (which replaces Windows NT Workstation). For Windows 2000 Server, you should aim for a machine with at least a 233MHz processor, and at least 128MB of RAM (256MB is better). For Windows 2000 Professional, you can get away with 64MB of RAM, though 128MB makes it smoother and more relaxing to use. You can run Internet Information Server 5.0 with ASP 3.0 on a Windows 9x machine, however we are concentrating in this book only on Windows 2000.

A client machine connected to the Windows 2000 machine via TCP/IP. While you can develop directly on the Web server, it's usually better to use a separate client machine. All you need is something capable of running a Web browser. The browser we are using predominantly is Internet Explorer 5.0 (IE5), though you can use another if you prefer. However, some examples that take advantage of IE5-specific features will probably fail to work on other browsers. The network between the machines should include TCP/IP amongst the active protocols. In fact, you only need TCP/IP– the rest can be disabled or uninstalled when working with ASP.

> **If you are working on a corporate network, be sure to check with your system administrator before changing the network protocol installation or setup.**

Non-Microsoft Platforms

As Active Server Pages has gained popularity within the Web-development community, the limitation of running only on a Windows platform has been seen as a problem. Two companies have moved to spread the coverage of ASP on other platforms and operating systems:

- The best known of these is **Chili!ASP** (`http://www.chilisoft.com`) which is functionally equivalent to ASP. It utilizes the same development tools and functionality as ASP but runs on Netscape, Lotus Go, as well as NT 4.0-based Web servers.
- The second ASP look-alike is Halcyon Software's **Instant ASP** (`http://www.halcyonsoft.com`), which runs on a whole range of Web server, application server, and operating system platforms. This includes Windows NT, Sun, Novell, AIX, AS/400, S/390, Apple, OS/2, Linux, Apache, Netscape, Websphere, and more.

We aren't covering these environments directly in this book, as we are concentrating on ASP 3.0 running on Internet Information Server version 5 and Windows 2000 Server. However, the knowledge you gain will apply to the other ASP-like environments as well, though you will need to confirm the actual range of coverage and compatibility on your chosen platform and operating system from the relevant supplier.

Software

Almost all of the software you'll need is included in a full installation of Windows 2000 Server. After the main OS installation has completed, and you reboot the server, Internet Explorer fires up with a page entitled Windows 2000 Configure Your Server:

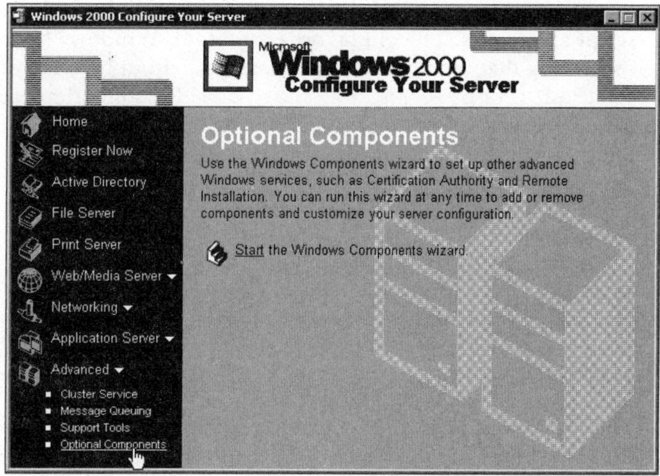

You can use this page to install the extra services and applications that you want to run on the server. You'll need to select the Advanced option and then Optional Components in the left-hand menu, then Start the Windows Components Wizard in the right-hand window to install IIS and the other Web-related software such as the Indexing Services, Clustering Services, Message Queuing Services, etc. If you want to install Active Directory, you must also first install and set up DNS from this page, then select the Active Directory option. There are Wizards that will step you through each of the processes, and they generally make the whole task very simple.

There are other items of software that you may like to install as you use this book. There are several server components that we include with the sample files, or which we provide links to so that you can download them from the original source. The sample files you'll see used in this book can all be downloaded from our own Web sites at:

```
http://webdev.wrox.co.uk/books/2610
http://www.wrox.com/Store/Details.asp?Code=2610
```

Development Tools

Probably the most obvious development tool for working with ASP is Microsoft's own **Visual Studio** package; or just **Visual InterDev** (one of the components of Visual Studio) on its own. Visual InterDev, especially in the latest version, provides a whole range of editing, debugging and code building tools. There are also many Wizards to help you get the job done more quickly.

As well as Visual InterDev, Visual Studio contains **Visual Basic** and **Visual C++**, both of which are ideal for building your own Active Server Components for use in your Web applications. You can also build Active Server Components using any other COM-enabled language such as other C++ development environments, Delphi, J++, PowerBuilder, etc.

Other companies also provide tools to build ASP pages and complete Web applications, including **Drumbeat** (`http://www.elementalsw.com`), **Fusion 3.0** (`http://www.netobjects.com`), **HAHTSite** (`http://www.haht.com`), **Cold Fusion** (`http://www.allaire.com`), **XBuilder** (`http://www.signmeup.com`) and many others.

If you are a hardened keyboard hacker, and don't like anything to get in the way of writing code your way, you might prefer to use a simple text editor to create ASP pages instead. You can even build them using a pure HTML page creation tool (such as Microsoft FrontPage), and then insert your ASP script afterwards. The old favorite ASP tool, Windows NotePad, will do quite nicely, though something that includes line numbers (to help in locating errors) is more useful. We've been using TextPad© (`http://www.textpad.com`) for some time, and find it a great improvement over NotePad. Not only do you get a multiple document interface with line numbers and macros, but many other useful options and add-ins as well.

There are other tools and add-ins that we use for specific tasks, particularly load testing and performance measurement, and you'll find these described in several places throughout the book. For a useful list of the various tools that are available, take a look at the Tools page at the 15 Seconds Web site (`http://www.15seconds.com/tool/default.htm`).

Conventions

We use a number of different styles of text and layout in the book to help differentiate between the different kinds of information. Here are examples of the styles we use and an explanation of what they mean.

Bullets appear indented, with each new bullet marked as follows:

- **Important Words** are in a bold type font.
- Words that appear on the screen, such as menu options, are in a similar font to the one used on screen, for example the File | New... menu. The levels of a cascading menu are separated by a pipe character (|).
- Keys that you press on the keyboard, like *Ctrl* and *Enter*, are in italics.

Code has several styles. If it's a word that we're talking about in the text, such as a `For...Next` loop or a file name like `Default.asp`, we'll use `this font`. If it's a block of code that is new, important or relevant to the current discussion, it will be presented like this:

```
<%
   Response.Write "Professional ASP 3.0"
%>
```

Sometimes, you'll see code in a mixture of styles, like this:

```
<%
   Response.Write "Professional ASP 3.0"
   Response.Write "...enjoy the book"
%>
```

The code with a white background is code we've already looked at, or that has little to do with the matter at hand.

Advice, hints, background information, references and extra details appear in an italicized, indented font like this.

> **These boxes hold important, not-to-be forgotten, mission-critical details that are directly relevant to the surrounding text.**

Tell Us What You Think

We've tried to make this book as accurate and enjoyable as possible, but what really matters is what the book actually does for you. Please let us know your views, either by returning the reply card in the back of the book, or by contacting us via e-mail at `feedback@wrox.com`.

All the source code for all the examples in this book is available for download at the Wrox Press Web site at `www.wrox.com` or at `webdev.wrox.co.uk`. You'll find more information about COM at a related Web site, `www.comdeveloper.com`.

We've made every effort to make sure that there are no errors in the text or the code. However, to err is human and as such we recognize the need to keep you informed of any mistakes as they're spotted and corrected. Errata sheets are available for all our books at `www.wrox.com`. If you find an error that hasn't already been reported, please let us know.

Our Web site acts as a focus for other information and support, including the code from all our books, sample chapters, previews of forthcoming titles, and articles and opinion on related topics.

Customer Support

This book introduces a totally comprehensive and unique support system. Wrox now has a commitment to supporting you not just while you read the book, but once you start developing applications as well. We provide you with a forum where you can put your questions to the authors, reviewers and fellow industry professionals. You have the choice of how to receive this information; you can either enroll onto one of several mailing lists, or you can just browse the online forums and newsgroups for an answer.

Go to `p2p.wrox.com`. You'll find three different lists, each tailored to a specific support issue:

- **Errata**
  You find something wrong with the book, or you just think something has been badly or misleading explained then leave your message here. You'll still receive our customary quick reply, but you'll also have the advantage that every author will be able to see your problem at once and help deal with it.

- **Code Clinic**
  You've read the book, and you're sat at home or work developing your own application, it doesn't work in the way you think it should. Post your code here for advice and supports from our authors and from people in the same position as yourself.

- **How to?**
  Something you think the book should have talked about, something you'd just like to know more about, a completely baffling problem with no solution, then this is your forum. If you're developing an application at work then chances are there's someone out there who's already done the same as you, and has a solution to your problem here.

Enroll now; it's all part of our free support system. For more instructions on how to enroll, please see the Appendix H at the back of this book.

N
W

1

ASP Fundamentals

Microsoft's **Active Server Pages** technology has now reached version 3.0. To many people, it has now become the natural and even the quintessential way to build dynamic Web pages, entire sites, and Web-based applications on a Windows server platform. The appearance of the `.asp` file extension in the browser's address bar has become as accepted by visitors as the `.pl` or `.cgi` extensions that also indicate a dynamically created page. In fact, for Web programmers working with Microsoft operating systems, ASP is becoming less an exciting new technology, and more a way of life.

This shift of perspective denotes a technology that is approaching maturity, and ASP is certainly doing that. The number of applications that depend on it, and tools that help you to work with it, is growing daily. There are also more and more third-party developers producing a whole range of add-ins, ActiveX server components, and even 'do-it-yourself' Web site kits that are all based on or use ASP. And we've almost stopped noticing the odd name that Microsoft christened it with. Now ASP has become a recognized term in the industry, and few people even bother to use the expanded form Active Server Pages.

Therefore, this is a book about a new version of a maturing technology. What does that mean to you, the reader? It means that we'll expect you to be reasonably familiar with what ASP consists of, what it can do, and how to use it. Our aim is not to start at the beginning, but to show you how the new version has changed and what it can do that previous versions could not.

> *If you want a basic introduction to the previous version of ASP, try Beginning Active Server Pages 2.0 by Brian Francis, John Kauffman, Juan T Llibre, David Sussman and Chris Ullman, ISBN 1861001347, from Wrox.*

That doesn't mean that you have to be an ASP expert to read this book, however. All we expect is that you have an understanding of the fundamental ways that the Web works, and some knowledge of a scripting language such as VBScript or JavaScript.

This means that we can look into ASP in a more searching and technical way. It will allow you to obtain a better understanding of what's going on under the hood, and help you take your ASP code to a higher level. While there may not be many fundamental changes to the core of ASP in version 3.0, there are plenty of exciting ways that you can use it.

Therefore, in this first chapter we'll be looking at:

- What (very briefly) is ASP about
- How ASP connects with IIS
- Set-up issues and management
- The ASP 3.0 Object Model in overview
- The concept of Object Context
- What's new in ASP version 3.0

One important difference in the approach we're taking in this chapter is that we'll base our investigation of the structure of ASP on the idea of the **context** of an ASP page or application, rather than thinking of the individual ASP objects in isolation. However, to start off, we'll have a quick run around ASP itself to make sure you understand the fundamental concepts.

The Origins of ASP

In this part of the chapter, we'll look briefly at where ASP came from, and why it has rapidly gained popularity with the Web developer community. We'll start with a look at the foundations of the Web, and the growth in dynamic Web pages. We'll see how ASP compares with many of the other technologies that can provide this dynamism, and from this we'll hopefully gain an insight into where it's going. We'll also look at the growth of **Web applications**, as opposed to just dynamic **Web sites**.

The Beginnings of HTML

The **World Wide Web** (WWW) grew out of experiments that were carried out at the CERN laboratories in Switzerland. Tim Berners-Lee, along with a team of developers, took time out to investigate and build a way of transmitting information in a format that became known as **Hypertext Transport Protocol**, or just **HTTP**. Using a markup language designed for simplicity and with a flexible structure, **Hypertext Markup Language** (**HTML**), allowed text and graphics to be displayed in a Web browser or other suitably enabled application. Certain parts of the document could become hyperlinks, which – when clicked – caused a different page or a different section of the same page to be displayed.

> *A markup language is simply a series of elements, each delimited with special characters, that define how text or other items enclosed within the elements should be displayed. For example `<EM>This is some Emphasized text</EM>`. HTML is a markup language broadly based on the **Standard Generalized Markup Language** (SGML). SGML is a way of describing languages, and is not itself a language used to create pages.*

From these simple beginnings, extra features were added to build version 4.0 of HTML that we use today. These extra features provided for more flexible text styling (such as the `<FONT>` element), and more control over the final layout of the page (such as the use of tables and frames).

One thing that all these early pages lacked was any kind of **dynamic** content. This wasn't a problem at the time, because the reason for the development of HTML was to display and transmit information (particularly technical and scientific information) between disparate computers, networks and operating systems. The standardization of documents as just simple text and markup, with images or other non-text content in separate files, meant that they could be freely transmitted across any kind of network. And, because the format of the information was fixed and the 'meaning' of each element was defined in HTML, it was relatively easy to implement a 'reader' or browser application in any programming language, on any platform or operating system.

As far as serving up these pages of information, text files and graphics can be delivered to the user by a **Web Server** application, which simply reads them from disk and converts the output to the correct HTTP protocol for transmission across the network. At the client or user end, the browser takes the incoming stream and converts it into a page that can be displayed.

The great strength of HTML and HTTP, besides universality, is that the document can contain information about the meaning of the content, and the way that the writer intended it to be perceived. It can be read by applications that don't actually display it visually: for example, blind people can use a special application that converts it into speech. Alternatively, the content can be displayed in special ways to make it more accessible to people with poor sight, or other types of disability – hence the generic term **user agent**, rather than 'browser', that is often used in technical circles.

The Beginnings of Dynamic Pages

However, new types of document content – especially those designed to allow users to enter information into a page (such as HTML form controls like `<INPUT>`) – made it necessary to develop applications that could read this information and make use of it. It also became obvious that delivering content that was extracted from another application, especially a database of some kind, required a new approach. The need to rewrite text-based pages each time was certainly not the ideal way to provide up-to-the-minute information.

Instead, it became normal practice for the Web server to expose an interface that other applications could connect to. Through this interface, custom executable applications could receive the information sent from the client, including details of the page request they made by clicking a hyperlink or typing a URL into their browser. The application could then create a response to the client internally, rather than reading a text and markup file from the server's disk. From these early beginnings have grown a whole range of ways to create pages on the fly, in response to user requests or changing information.

The interface used for these applications is still available, and is called the **Common Gateway Interface** (**CGI**) – a standard that can be implemented in any language, including C. It was from these applications that the use of a `cgi-bin` directory grew (the '`bin`' part meaning binary code rather than text). Early applications were actually compiled programs, usually written in C or C++. However, it became plain that having to know about C programming, and recompile an executable each time you wanted to make a minor change to the text or markup that it created, were limiting the use of the CGI and dynamic pages.

Instead, a way of creating the page using a scripting language was developed. This language is the **Practical Extraction and Reporting Language**, or **Perl** as it's better known, and it allows information creators to write code in a language rather like a simplified version of C or C++. Within the Perl script, you 'write' the text and markup output to be sent to the browser using the `stdin` and `stdout` ('standard in' and 'standard out') functions that communicate with the Web server via the CGI.

Perl is still a popular language on the Web, especially in Unix- or Linux-based systems. However, it isn't easy to get to grips with, especially for Web developers who have no prior knowledge of C or C++. Instead, new scripting languages are appearing that make it easier to build pages. We'll look briefly at how these make the developer's life easier next.

Server-side Scripting Techniques

For a script to work with a Web server there needs to be some kind of intermediate application, or add-in, to connect the two. It has to be able to accept a request from the user, read and interpret the appropriate server-based script file, and then create the output page and communicate it to the Web server where it is sent as the response to the client.

In some cases, the task is divided up into two sections:

- One application or add-in handles the communication to and from the Web server (generally via the CGI)
- The other handles interpreting and executing the script

This is the case in ASP, where the scripting engine used is the same as that used in other environments.

Perl was the first popular server-side scripting language, but many others have appeared since. On Unix and Linux-based systems, and the variants of this genre, a new language called **PHP** (Personal Home Page) is becoming popular. There are also languages aimed specifically at certain types of user: for example, TCL is designed to make complex mathematical calculations easier in a scientific environment.

Microsoft's Dynamic Page Creation Technologies

Microsoft introduced their Web server software with Windows NT 3.51. **Internet Information Server** (**IIS**) 1.0 was a fairly standard offering as far as features went, and it supported CGI. However, Microsoft added another interface to allow executables written in compiled languages like C and C++ to operate more efficiently. This is the **Internet Server Application Programming Interface**, or **ISAPI**. It provides much broader access to the Web server than the simple `stdin` and `stdout` functions, upon which traditional Perl engines and many other technologies depend.

Since then both Microsoft and other third-party developers have produced applications that connect to IIS through ISAPI. This is how ASP connects to IIS, as well as the other Microsoft server-side dynamic techniques. Before ASP, the most common one in use was the **Internet Database Connector** (**IDC**). This opened up a whole new world to Web developers using Microsoft platforms, making it easy to create dynamic pages that used data from a database. In particular, it introduced the idea of a **template**, which contained the boilerplate text and markup into which the results from a database query could be inserted.

Other Microsoft server-side page creation techniques that have come (and generally gone again) are **dbWeb** and **OLEISAPI**. In fact, **dbWeb** was an implementation of OLEISAPI, and to many people only went as far as proving the unsuitability of this technique for real-world use. OLEISAPI is a specific use of COM objects to communicate with IIS through a special version of the ISAPI interface. The Web server software calls a single specific function within a COM object and provides details of the user's request as parameters. The COM object simply returns the text and markup of the page as a string, which is then sent to the client as the response.

OLEISAPI opened up dynamic Web page creation to COM objects, providing programmers with the opportunity to create dynamic pages though a compiled ActiveX DLL. However, the specific implementation and data communication technique that it uses is not efficient or scalable enough for anything other than minor tasks and Intranet work (as opposed to high-volume Internet sites). It also suffers from the drawback that each change to the page text and markup requires a recompilation of the DLL.

The following diagram gives some indication of how all the technologies we've discussed so far are related:

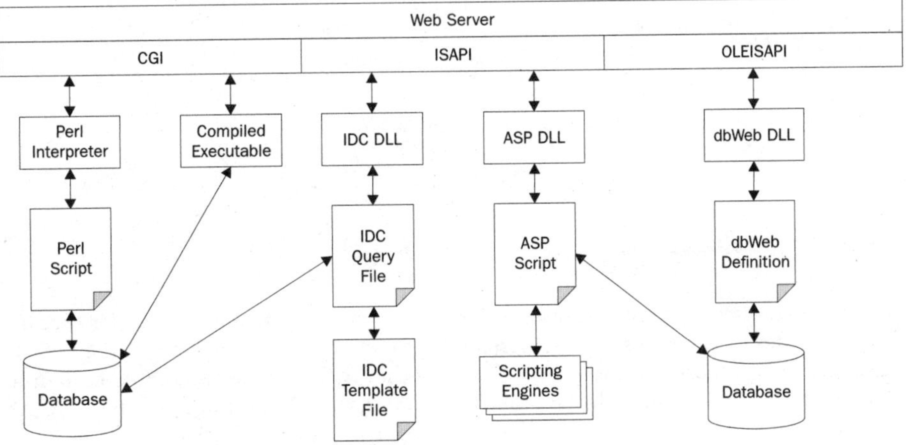

Comparing Dynamic Web Page Creation Methods

Making comparisons between dynamic page creation techniques is both a difficult and politically sensitive task. However, it's important to appreciate the differences in the way that the various interfaces, and the applications that connect to them, work. The two major concerns when creating applications that interface with a Web server are their effect on the stability of the Web server itself, and the efficiency with which they can handle multiple and concurrent page requests. These two issues are connected, in that they are mutually exclusive.

Compiled executable applications (not DLLs) that use CGI and ISAPI generally run **out-of-process** on the Web server machine. This means that they run as a separate application, in a separate memory space from the Web server application. The operating system manages them as separate processes, and prevents them from accessing memory outside their own allocation.

So, if an out-of-process application fails, it will not affect the Web server. Similarly, if it contains an error that causes it to attempt to write directly to the memory allocated to the Web server, it will be halted with a General Protection Error. Out-of-process applications can also be terminated on command by the user or the operating system, when the code is unloaded from memory automatically.

Because running out-of process means that any requirement to access the Web server's memory is forbidden, any values that are required or output that is generated can't be passed directly to the Web server. Instead, a cross-process call must be made, which is several times slower than accessing memory within the same process. There is also a latency imposed by the load and unload time for the executable file.

The converse applies to **in-process** applications, which are generally DLLs (rather than executables) that use the ISAPI or OLEISAPI interfaces. They can access values in the Web server's memory directly, because they run within the same memory space as the Web server. This provides very fast access and response. However, a failure or error in the code can bring down the Web server as well. For example, if code in the DLL writes directly to an area of memory that contains the Web server's operating code it can cause the Web server to fail.

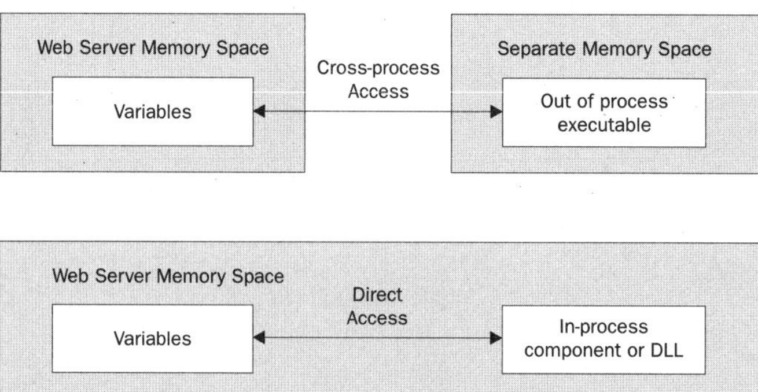

Examples of out-of-process applications are **Perl** script interpreters and `.exe` files that use the ISAPI interface. Examples of in-process components are **dbWeb**, **IDC**, and our technology of interest in this book, **ASP**. However, there is a lot more to the way that ASP and IIS interconnect than just this. So, we'll now promptly forget about all the other techniques, and delve a little deeper into ASP.

How ASP Connects with IIS

ASP itself consists purely of a single DLL named `asp.dll`, which is installed by default into your `Winnt\System32\inetsrv` directory. As we briefly indicated earlier, this DLL is responsible for taking an ASP page (indicated by the `.asp` file extension) and parsing it for any server-side script content. This script is passed to the appropriate scripting engine, and the results of executing the script are combined with any boilerplate text and HTML in the ASP page. The complete page is then sent to the Web server, where it is passed on to the client that originally requested it.

All About Application Mappings

To understand more about this process, we need to look at the way that **application mappings** work in Windows 2000. For each Web site set up on the machine under IIS, there is a root directory on the server. The **Default** Web site that is created when you install IIS is usually `C:\InetPub\WWWRoot`, unless you change the path during installation. For this directory, and certain other directories within it (which we'll discuss in detail later), there is a set of properties that define how that directory behaves with respect to IIS.

To see this, open the Internet Services Manager from the Administrative Tools section of your Start menu. This runs the Microsoft Management Console (MMC) to display the entire Internet Information Services tree for IIS:

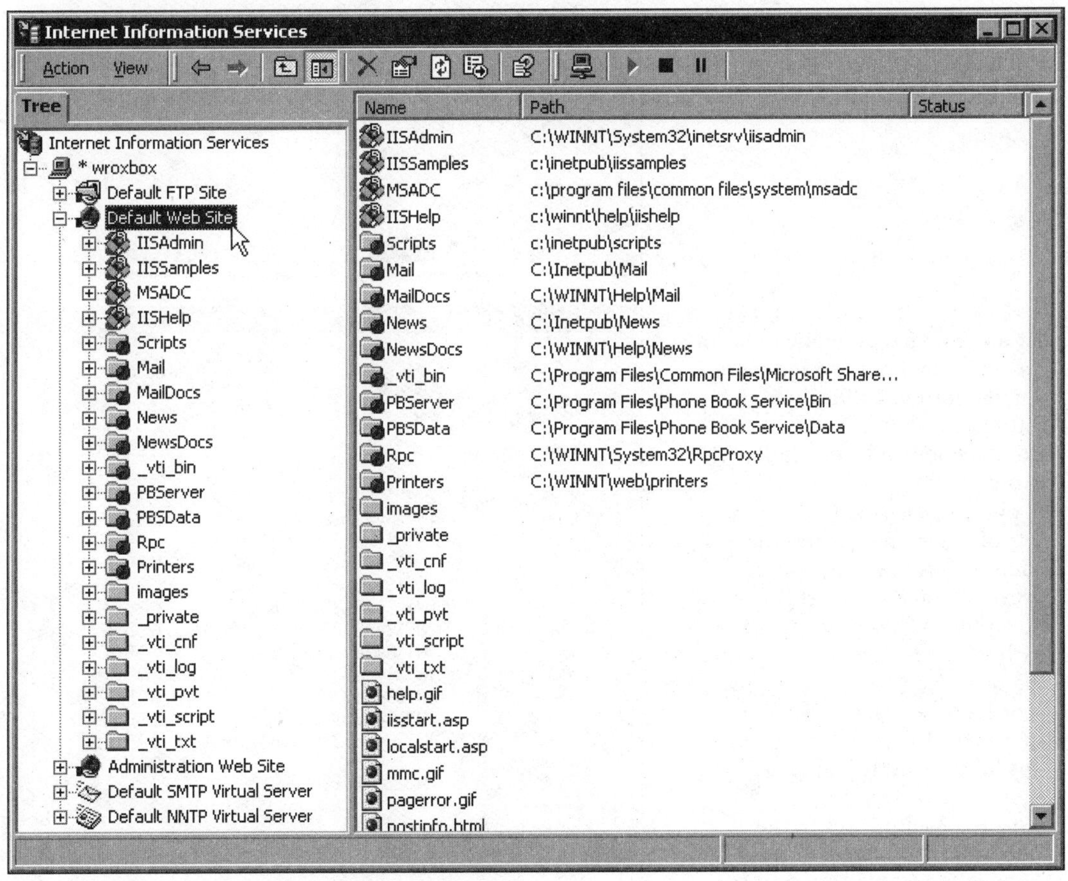

Right-click on the Default Web Site entry and select Properties, then the Home Directory page:

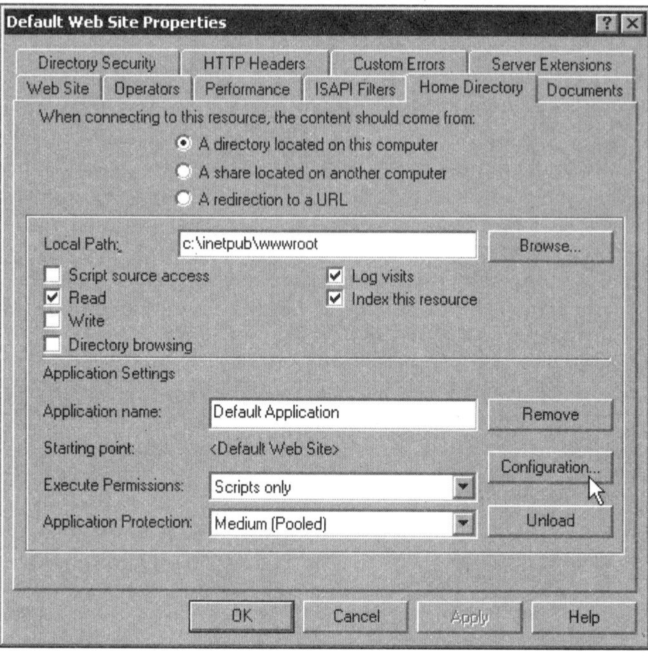

You can see that the default site is set up as a **virtual application**. In the lower half of the page there is a name for the application and settings for the Execute Permissions and Application Protection. IIS uses virtual applications as a way of isolating sets of pages and the instances of components that they use, to prevent a failure from bringing down the Web server. As we saw earlier, this is done by executing the pages and components out-of-process, in a separate memory space. We'll discover more about this later on in this chapter.

For the meantime, click the Configuration button to open the Application Configuration dialog. In the App Mappings tab, you can see the way that IIS links each type of file (using the file extension) with a specific DLL:

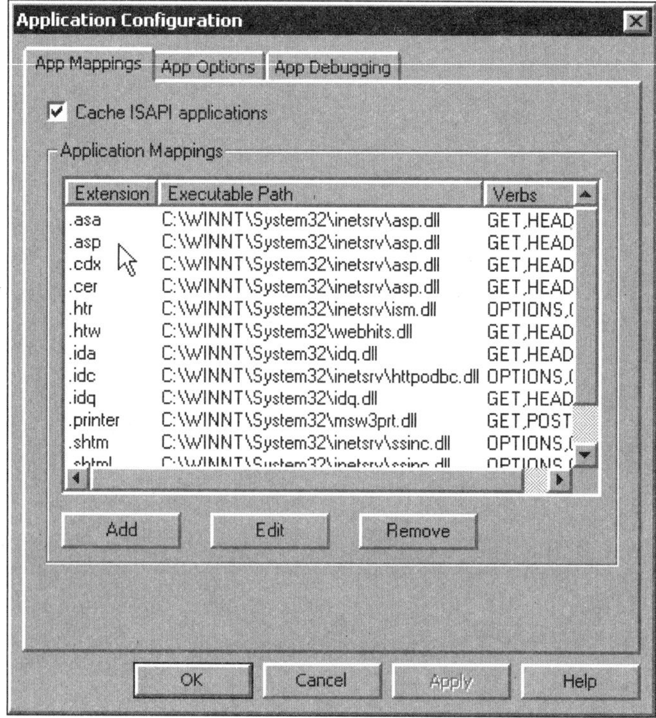

Any pages that have the `.asp` file extension – amongst others that we'll meet later – are sent to the `asp.dll` for processing. Pages with a file extension that is *not* mapped – for example `.html` and `.htm` for HTML pages, and `.xml` for XML files – are simply loaded from disk and sent directly to the client.

> *You might like to have a look at the other file types in this page. The* `.ida`, `.idc` *and* `.idq` *file extensions are used by IDC templates and query files. So, an IDC query page (*`.idc`*) will be sent to the DLL* `httpodbc.dll` *for processing. As you can guess from its name, it uses ODBC to execute a SQL statement that returns a set of records for inclusion in the page. Likewise, the* `.shtm`, `.shtml` *and* `.stm` *file extensions are mapped to a DLL named* `ssinc.dll`*. These file types are traditionally used for files that require* ***server-side include*** *(SSI) processing. We'll meet some examples of this later in the book.*

While you have the Application Configuration and Properties dialogs open, you might want to have a quick explore. We'll be using these dialogs and their settings in various places throughout the book, and it will help you to get a feel for where they are located – just don't change any settings for the moment, unless you're sure that you know what you're doing.

Processing an ASP File

We now know how an ASP page gets to the ASP DLL ready for interpretation and execution. So, what does ASP do with it when it gets there?

The first step is to decide if there is any ASP server-side code that needs to be executed. If not, it can simply inform IIS of this fact, and allow IIS to send the page to the client. In fact, this is a new feature of Windows 2000 that allows you to use the `.asp` file extension for all your pages – including those that contain no server-side script code – without sacrificing performance.

When ASP receives a page from IIS that does contain server-side script code, it parses it line-by-line. Anything that is not server-side script, or does not require server intervention by ASP, is sent back to IIS, and onwards from there to the client. As each section of script is reached, it is passed to the appropriate scripting engine. The results from the scripting engine are then inserted at the appropriate points into the page as it is sent to IIS.

> *In previous versions of IIS and ASP, all pages with the* `.asp` *file extension were parsed line-by-line, even if they contained no ASP server-side code. This is obviously a lot slower that allowing IIS to stream them directly from disk to the client.*

To make the operation more efficient, ASP also caches the compiled code that the scripting engine creates, ready for use when the page is called again. This code is not the same thing as the output that is sent to the client. The client sees the result of executing the script code after it has been interpreted, syntax checked and compiled. It's only the compiled code that is cached on the server, and this is discarded whenever the original source file is changed.

Identifying Server-Side Script Sections

The ASP interpreter identifies server-side script that is delimited in one of two ways.

Using <% %> Script Delimiters

The most common of these uses the characters `<%` and `%>` to delimit script sections:

```
<HTML>
<BODY>
This is text and HTML that <B>will not</B> be executed, and is passed to the
client.
<%
REM This is server-side script code that will be interpreted and executed by ASP
%>
</BODY>
</HTML>
```

This technique is also used where we need to insert the values of variables, or short script statements, into the rest of the text and HTML in the returned page:

```
<HTML>
<%
intResult = 7 + 6 - 1
strTheSum = "seven plus six minus one"
%>
<BODY>
The result of calculating <% = strTheSum %> is <% = CStr(intResult) %>
</BODY>
</HTML>
```

This produces 'The result of calculating seven plus six minus one is 12'.

Using the <SCRIPT> Element

When writing script that is executed within a browser, we use the `<SCRIPT>` element. This can also be used server-side, providing that we include the special `RUNAT` attribute, and set the value to `"SERVER"`:

```
<HTML>
<BODY>
This is text and HTML that <B>will not</B> be executed, and is passed to the
client.
<SCRIPT RUNAT="SERVER">
  REM This is server-side script code that will be interpreted and executed by ASP
</SCRIPT>
</BODY>
</HTML>
```

It's important to realize that an ASP page can contain both server-side and client-side script. The client-side script (which can contain `RUNAT="CLIENT"` or omit the `RUNAT` attribute) is ignored by the ASP interpreter. It is passed to the client just as though this were a normal HTML page with the `.htm` or `.html` file extension:

```
<HTML>
<BODY>
This is text and HTML that <B>will not</B> be executed, and is passed to the
client.
```

```
<SCRIPT RUNAT="SERVER">
  REM This is server-side script code that will be interpreted and executed by ASP
</SCRIPT>
<SCRIPT>
<!--
  REM This is client-side script code that will be executed within the client
  REM browser.
-->
</SCRIPT>
</BODY>
</HTML>
```

Including Separate Script Files

It's also possible to include separate files that contain script code, making it easy to write generic functions that are then available to other pages. This way, changes to the script are automatically reflected in all the pages the next time that they are executed. To include a separate script file, we use the SRC attribute of the <SCRIPT> element to specify a relative, physical, or virtual path and file name:

```
<SCRIPT RUNAT="SERVER" SRC="/myscripts/script106.inc"></SCRIPT>
```

The separate file must contain only valid script code, and cannot contain ordinary page content such as text or HTML. If we use this technique, no other code can be placed within this <SCRIPT> element – it must be empty. To add other script to the page, use another <SCRIPT> element, or the <%..%> script-delimiters.

We can also include text from files that contain script, or HTML and text, by using a ***Server-Side Include*** *(SSI) instruction. We'll look at these in more detail in Chapter 4.*

Defining the Scripting Language

ASP comes complete with two scripting engines, which are installed by default, namely **VBScript** and **JScript**. These are the same scripting engines that are used by other applications, for example Microsoft's Internet Explorer Web browsers and the Windows Scripting Host. The current versions included with Windows 2000 are version 5.0, though newer software may update these. Other scripting engines are available, such as TCL and PerlScript (an ActiveX script interpreter and not the traditional CGI-based Perl).

So, we have to tell ASP which scripting engine to use with our ASP page. The usual way is to define it in the special context declaration element, which must be the first line of the file and can only occur once. This element is denoted by having an 'at' character (@) after the opening ASP code delimiters:

```
<%@LANGUAGE="language_name"%>
```

This declaration element can also contain other instructions, as you'll see later in the chapter. To define a page as being coded in VBScript, we use:

```
<%@LANGUAGE="VBScript"%>
```

And for JScript we use:

```
<%@LANGUAGE="JScript"%>
```

After this, all the code in this page that is within <%...%> sections will be passed to the scripting engine identified in the declaration element. This is the only way to specify the scripting language for code delimited this way.

However, in the <SCRIPT> element, we can identify the scripting language for each section separately, and have more than one language per page if required:

```
<%@LANGUAGE="VBScript"%>
<HTML>
<BODY>
This is text and HTML that <B>will not</B> be executed, and is passed to the
client.

<SCRIPT RUNAT="SERVER" LANGUAGE="VBScript">
  REM This is server-side VBScript code
</SCRIPT>

<SCRIPT RUNAT="SERVER" LANGUAGE="JScript">
  // This is server-side JScript code
</SCRIPT>

<!-- the next two script sections define script code stored in separate -->
<!-- files, which is included into the script element by ASP at runtime -->
<SCRIPT RUNAT="SERVER" LANGUAGE="VBScript" SRC="/myscripts/scr106.inc"></SCRIPT>
<SCRIPT RUNAT="SERVER" LANGUAGE="JScript" SRC="/myscripts/scr106.inc"></SCRIPT>

<%
  REM This is server-side VBScript code because the default language for the page
  REM is set as VBScript in the declaration element at the start of the page.
%>
</BODY>
</HTML>
```

There's no need to hide your script code inside a 'comment' element, as you would do client-side, because as it is executed, the code is removed from the page and replaced with just the results. When you view an ASP page on the client (by selecting View Source in your browser), you see only text, HTML and any client-side script code. All server-side script has been executed, and only the *result* is sent to the client.

The Default Scripting Language

If you omit the language declaration from the ASP page or an individual <SCRIPT> element, ASP will use the default scripting engine. This is VBScript when you first install IIS, but you can change it as required for the whole of a Web site, or for individual virtual applications within a site.

In the same Application Configuration dialog that we met earlier in this chapter, there's a tab for App Options. It contains a text box where the default language is set:

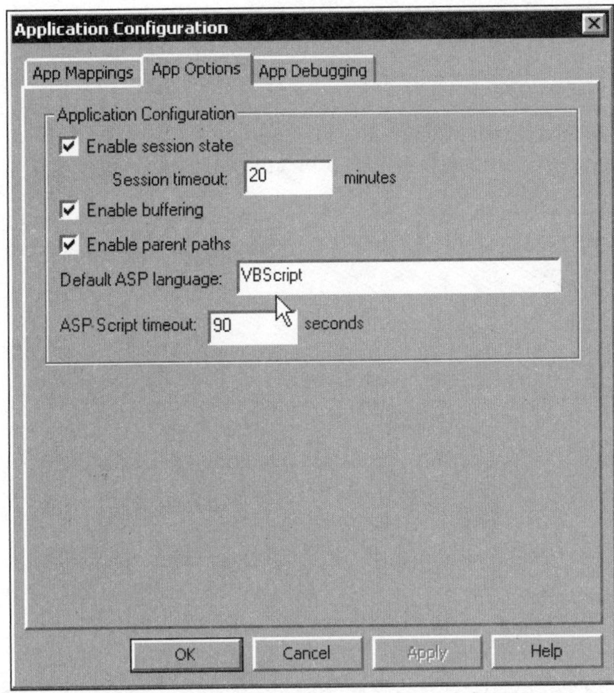

The default language can also be changed by editing the value in the `IIS:` section of Active Directory. All the settings you see in the Internet Services Manager MMC snap-in are stored in Active Directory in Windows 2000. They can be read or edited providing you have the appropriate permissions. We'll be looking in more detail at Active Directory later in the book.

Other than that, choose the language to suit your own personal preferences. If you know one language best, you can stick to it. Because all your ASP code is executed on the server, there are no browser compatibility issues to worry about. If you're proficient in both VBScript and JScript, or in another language altogether, then choose the one that best suits the task in hand. However, as their feature sets converge more and more with each release (for example VBScript 5.0 now supports regular expressions), the choice is often VBScript. Its more relaxed attitude to case and syntax, and the simpler structure of multiple statements, generally make it easier to use.

Scripting Performance Issues

Web servers generally have plenty of spare processor cycles available (except on the busiest of sites) because the main task they have is loading pages from disk and sending them to the client. Therefore, each page request results in the processor waiting for the disk to respond. These spare cycles mean that ASP scripts can usually be executed with very little overall hit on performance. And as many hits will be on pages where a compiled version of the script code is available, only the execution of this script needs to take place.

Of course, as the number of requests, and hence the server load, increases, the effect of having to parse and execute each ASP page takes its toll. It's wise, therefore, to squeeze as much performance as possible from the ASP interpreter. Here are some useful tips.

Avoid Mixing Scripting Languages on the Same Page

For this, ASP has to load both scripting engines, one after the other, and send the relevant code to each one to be executed. This slows the process down and increases memory usage. It also has the side effect that, if you write code that is executed sequentially (i.e. rather than a series of functions or subroutines that are called from another section of code), you may get sections executed in a different order from that in which they appear in the page.

For example, the following code may not produce the results you expect – you can't guarantee that the results of the JScript code will appear first or third in the page:

```
<%@LANGUAGE="JScript"%>
<HTML>
<BODY>
<SCRIPT RUNAT="SERVER" LANGUAGE="JScript">
  Response.Write('First<BR>')
</SCRIPT>
<SCRIPT RUNAT="SERVER" LANGUAGE="VBScript">
  Response.Write "Second<BR>"
</SCRIPT>
<%
  Response.Write('Third<BR>')  // JScript is the default in this page
%>
</BODY>
</HTML>
```

Avoid Excessive Context Switching Between Script and Other Content

Each time ASP finds a script section, it has to execute it, send the results to IIS, and go back to interpreting the page again. So, using the `Response.Write` statement (which simply creates text to send to the client, rather like a `Print` command) can make your page more efficient. For example, this extract of VBScript:

```
<BODY>
<%
intResult = 7 + 6 - 1
strTheSum = "seven plus six minus one"
Response.Write "The result of calculating " & strTheSum & " is " & _
               CStr(intResult)
%>
</BODY>
```

Would be more efficient than this one:

```
<%
intResult = 7 + 6 - 1
strTheSum = "seven plus six minus one"
%>
<BODY>
The result of calculating <% = strTheSum %> is <% = CStr(intResult) %>
</BODY>
```

Build a Separate Component

If you have to do huge amounts of calculation within a page, or run script that is excessively complex, then it's often a good idea to build a component and install it on the Web server. Components are usually compiled executable code, and are far more efficient to instantiate and use than interpreted ASP script code. We'll look at building components in detail later in the book.

Set-up Issues and Management

ASP is installed automatically with IIS 5.0, and the setup program makes most of the decisions about configuration for you. It automatically sets up a Default Web site based on the machine's primary IP address, and binds it to that address. This means that you can access the Web site using the machine name (on a local network) or with the URL of the machine:

```
http://sunspot                          <- access the default Web site over a LAN
http://sunspot.stonebroom.com           <- access the default Web site globally
```

Remember that IIS 5.0 is more than just a Web server that provides the WWW service over HTTP. It also provides services to support FTP (File Transfer Protocol), SMTP (Simple Mail Transfer Protocol) and a RADIUS server to allow remote authentication of users, plus a host of built-in features for managing security, user authentication, etc.

Installing Internet Information Services

IIS is not installed by default when you install Windows 2000 Server, as not all servers are intended for use as a Web server. However, once the Windows 2000 installation process is complete, the Windows 2000 Configure Server page is opened in Internet Explorer. This is where you begin the installation of IIS and the associated applications and services.

If you have already installed Windows 2000 without IIS, you can open this page from the Start *menu, at* Programs | Administrative Tools | Configure Server.

Select the Advanced option and click Optional Components:

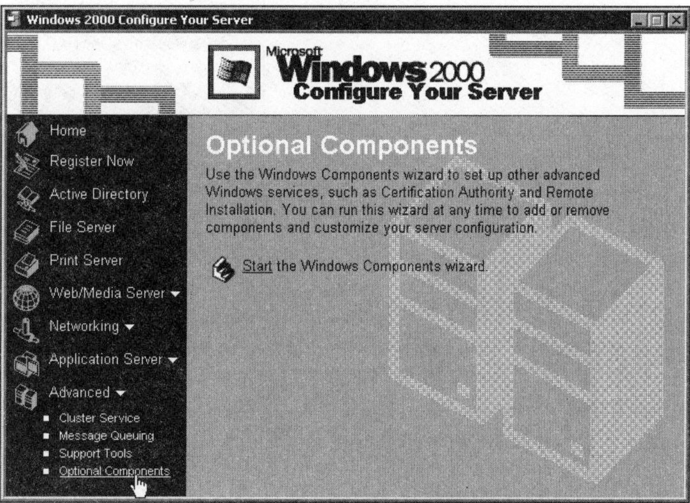

In the right-hand page, click the link to Start the Windows Components wizard. This opens a dialog (rather like that of the NT4 Option Pack) showing a list of the components that are available for installation.

You can also get at this dialog using Add/Remove Programs in the Control Panel.

Select the Internet Information Services (IIS) option, and click the Details button:

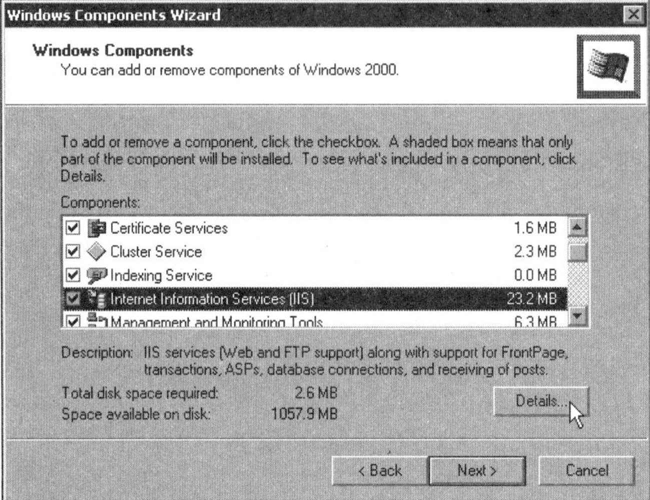

This displays a list of the sub-components for IIS 5.0. Most are already checked by default, including the FTP and WWW (World Wide Web Server) services:

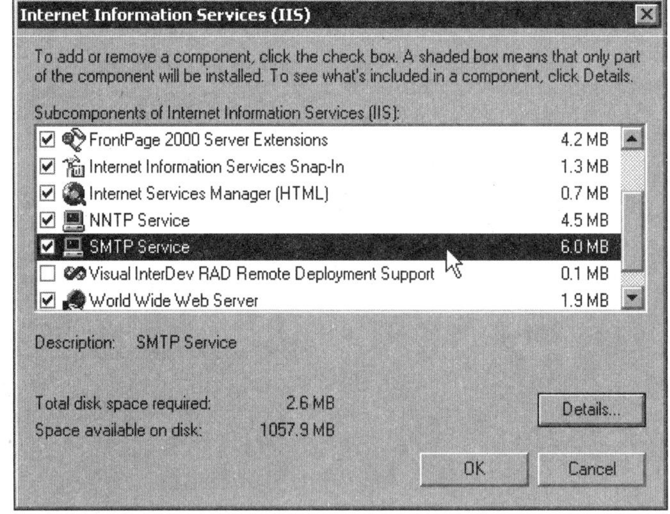

It's worth installing all (or most) of the subcomponents on machines where you intend to experiment with ASP. This makes the documentation for the subcomponents available as well – useful if you're exploring ASP and planning to build applications that use the other Windows services.

Once setup is complete, you can use the Services dialog (Start | Programs | Administrative Tools | Services) to turn off the subcomponent services that you don't need at the moment, thus reducing the load on your server.

If you intend to provide email services via IIS, be sure to select the SMTP Service option. This also installs various files that are useful for building mail-enabled ASP applications, as you'll see later in the book. The NNTP Service (Network News Transfer Protocol) is used to provide a 'newsgroups' feature, and can be installed if you wish:

Make sure you leave the Internet Information Services Manager Snap-In checked, as this is what allows you to manage the Web server in the MMC via the Internet Services Manager option on your Start menu. You can also install the FrontPage 2000 Server Extensions if you will be using Visual InterDev or FrontPage to access pages hosted on this server.

The only information you really need to provide for IIS during setup is the path to the default Web and FTP sites. The setup program suggests you use \InetPub\WWWRoot and \InetPub\FTPRoot, and you'll probably only want to change the drive if you have more than one available. It's worth putting them on a different physical drive from the one that contains your Windows system files, to provide faster access to the files.

Other Useful Windows Components

Back in the main Windows Components Wizard dialog, you can choose other Windows services that you want to install. In this book, we'll be using Message Queuing Services (MSMQ) and the Microsoft Indexing Service (what was Index Server in the NT4 Option Pack). You might like to install these now, using the default options for each one. A useful tool that can be installed from the Windows Components Wizard dialog is the Microsoft Script Debugger. We'll look at this in chapter 7, and see how it makes debugging our pages much easier. However, be sure that you don't install Script Debugger on a public or 'production' server, only on your test or development servers.

Once you've installed IIS, you can begin using it straight away. A default page is installed indicating that the site is under construction. There's also a page that describes the features and use of IIS, and has links to the various management applications. This page is at `http://server_name_or_url/localstart.asp`, and is loaded only when there is no Default.asp or Default.htm page in the root of your site:

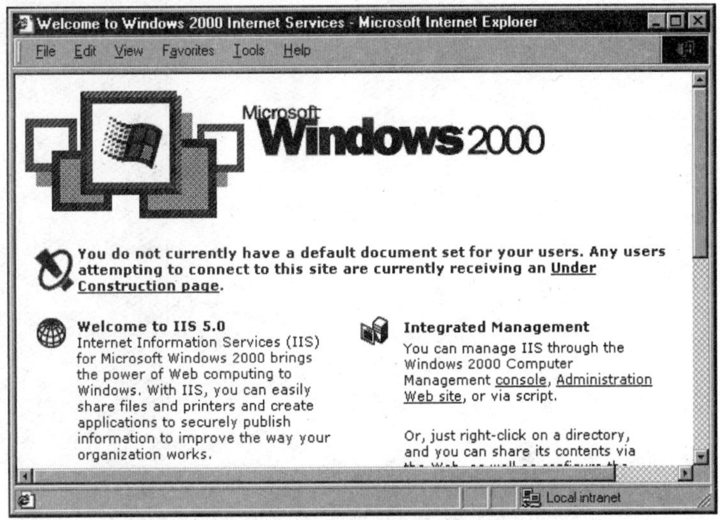

Remember that you have to access ASP pages using the HTTP protocol. If you view the contents of the Web directories in Explorer, either on the same machine as the Web server or over a LAN, you can't load them by double-clicking on them. You must type the URL of the machine (starting with `http://`) into the address box of your browser.

IIS Management Tools

As well as installing various services, the Windows Components Wizard allows you to install several tools that are used to manage IIS. We've mentioned one of these already – the Internet Services Manager, a snap-in for the Microsoft Management Console (MMC). There is also a set of HTML pages that can be used to manage IIS, which is an optional subcomponent in the Windows 2000 installation.

These pages and the Internet Services Manager can both provide remote management features. The one difference is that the Internet Services Manager requires installation on the remote machine, whereas the HTML administration pages only need the remote machine to have a browser installed (preferably IE4 or higher for best results).

The HTML Version of Internet Services Manager

The HTML administration pages provide a really neat way to manage IIS remotely, and are quick and efficient. On the server, you can open them by selecting Internet Services Manager (HTML) from the Start menu. Here, we're viewing the contents of the Default Web site:

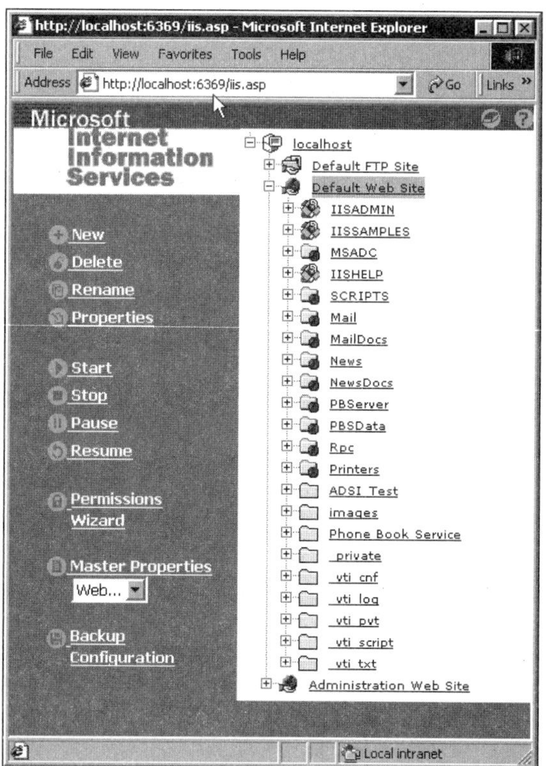

*Notice that the URL of the page includes a **port number**, in this case 6369. The setup program generates a random port number between 1000 and 9999, and allocates it to the Administration Web Site that it creates when the HTML administration pages are installed. You have to specify this port in the URL, and it is automatically added to the Start menu entry. This acts as a rudimentary security measure, preventing access by users who don't know the port number.*

To access your HTML administration pages from a remote machine, you need to know your own port number. This can be obtained from the Properties dialog for the Administration Web Site. The TCP Port number is shown in the Web Site page of the dialog:

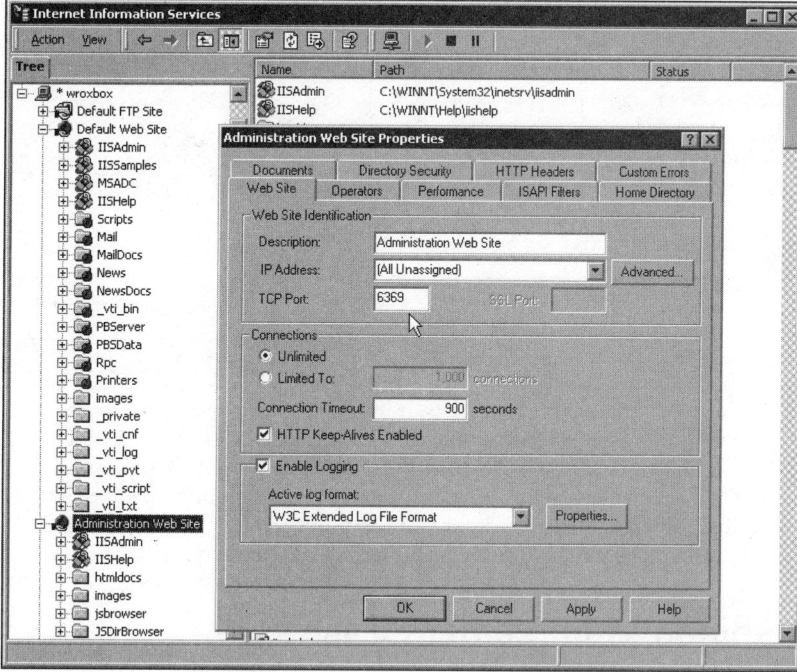

However, that's not all. By default, the pages can only be loaded into a browser that's installed on the Web server. This is because there are **IP restrictions** set up as well. In the Administration Web Site, select the IISADMIN virtual application, and open the Properties dialog for this application. Then, in the Directory Security page, select the Edit button in the IP address and domain name restrictions section:

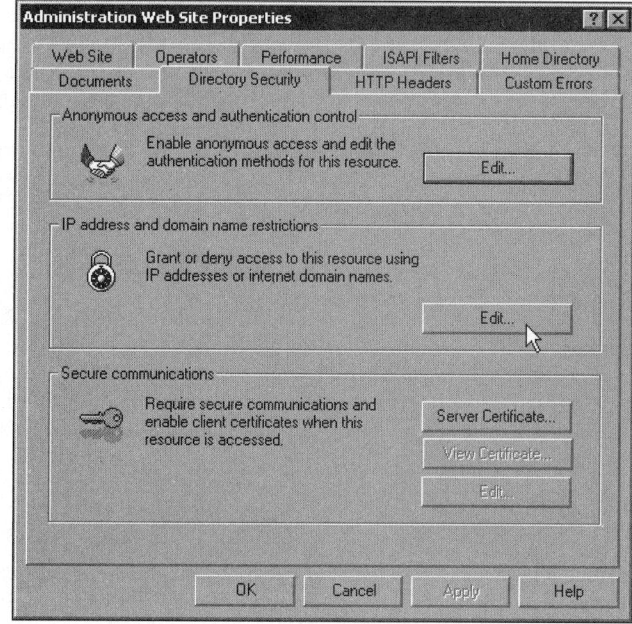

This opens a dialog where you can see the restriction. Only IP address 127.0.0.1 (the local server) can access this page, even if the correct port number is included in requests from other IP addresses:

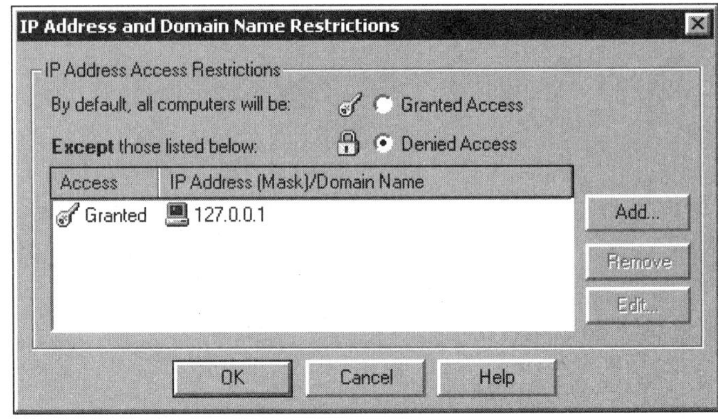

You need to change this, either by removing the restrictions (a risky option if you're connected to the Internet), or – better – by adding your own IP address to the list. This can be the IP address of your remote machine on the LAN, or the IP address of your proxy server or ISP if you connect over the Net. However, for the best level of security, you should consider setting up a secure directory for this application using certificates, and accessing it over `https` (http secure) rather than `http` – i.e. using SSL or similar. We look at these topics in more detail later in the book.

Common Management Tasks

The default configuration of IIS is generally right for most uses. However, you can modify the way that ASP works with IIS in a variety of ways once you start to build your site. We saw a couple of examples of the Properties dialog pages for the Default Web site earlier on, and if you're used to using ASP 2.0 on IIS 4, you'll find most of it is comfortingly familiar. Many of the changes involve better captioning of the dialog controls to make the meaning of the settings clearer.

The settings in the Properties dialog that you're most likely to need to change are shown in the following screenshots. In most cases, you can specify these settings for a complete Web site by opening the Properties dialog for the site, or for individual directories within the site by opening the Properties dialog for that directory.

The Home Directory Tab

The Home Directory tab is the main one where you change the way that the files in this site or directory behave. Notice that the top section of the dialog allows you to specify where the user's request should be directed. It can be a directory on the local machine, a shared directory on a remote machine, or even a URL. This last option allows you to automatically redirect visitors to another machine.

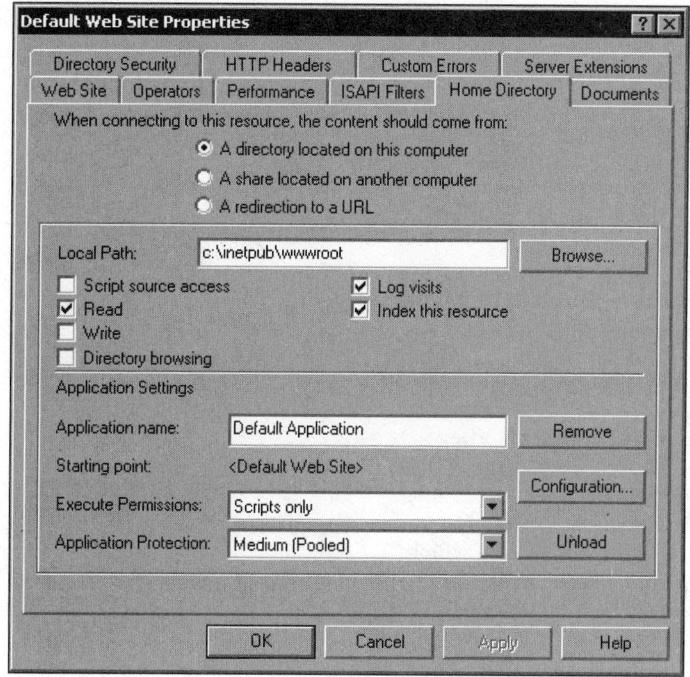

The central section of the dialog contains the settings that control what features are enabled for this site or directory. We can turn on and off Read and Write permission, browsing of the directory (when there is no default Web page in it), indexing of the page by the Microsoft Indexing Service, and logging of users and visits. We can also enable access to the source files; something new in Windows 2000 and designed for use with remote editing technologies like Distributed Authoring and Versioning (DAV). We'll look at DAV in more detail later on.

The lower section of the page is where we set up a virtual application. The Default Web Site (shown here) is automatically installed as a virtual application, as are many of the other directories that are created by the setup program for administration purposes or use by other services. We'll take a more detailed look at virtual applications later, as we start to use Active Server Components in our pages.

The Web Site Tab

The Web Site tab is used to identify the Web site to the outside world, manage the number of concurrent connections and control access logging.

The top section specifies the IP address and TCP port of the site. For the Default site, the Web service will respond to all IP addresses that are available for the server (if there are multiple network adapters or multiple addresses on one network adapter), unless they are assigned to another site. The default port for WWW access is port 80, as set up in the screenshot. Using this port number means that visitors don't have to specify the port number in their request.

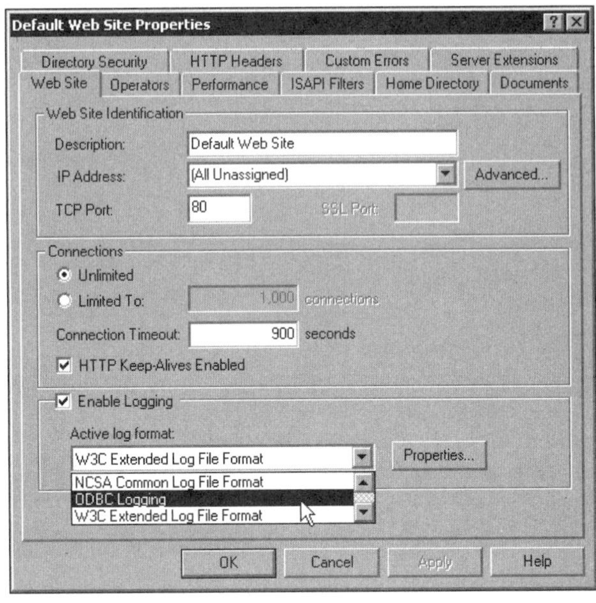

The central section of the dialog controls the number of concurrent connections that will be accepted, and the timeout after which any long-running ASP scripts will be terminated if they've not finished executing. It also allows us to specify whether to use HTTP Keep-Alives, which provide better performance for browsers that support them by keeping connections open for multiple requests.

The lower section of this dialog is where we set up the kind of access logging we want. The default is W3C Extended Log File Format, and we can use the Properties button to open a dialog where we specify in detail the information we want to record. To log to a database, you need to select the ODBC Logging option and provide an ODBC **System Data Source Name** (a System DSN, see Chapter 8) for the database table we want to use.

The Documents Tab

The Documents tab is much simpler than the previous two. It's used to specify the filenames of the default pages that are displayed if the user accesses a directory without specifying a filename. For example, if the settings shown in the following screenshot are in place, a request for `http://stonebroom.com` will result in the page `http://stonebroom.com/Default.asp` being sent back to the user:

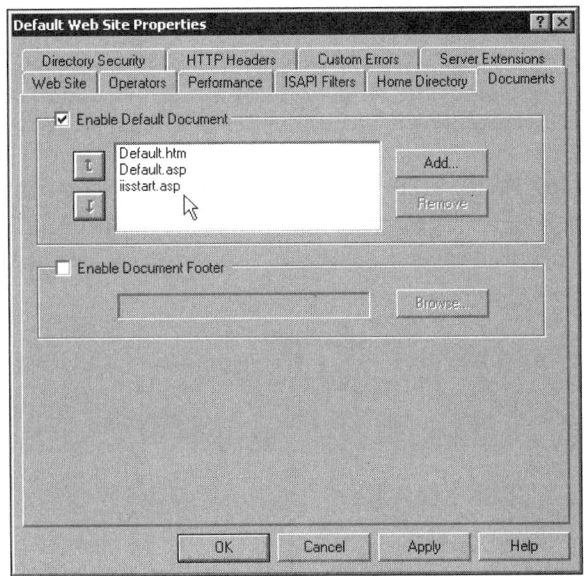

In Windows 2000, unlike earlier versions, the setup program places `Default.asp` first in the list, followed by `Default.htm`. This is because an `.asp` page that contains no ASP script can be processed almost as quickly as a pure HTML one – hence the recommendation from Microsoft to use the `.asp` file extension for all pages.

The check box below the list of documents allows us to specify the name of a text or ASP file that will be added to the end of each response, and so forms a standard footer for all the pages we send from this site or directory.

The HTTP Headers Tab

We'll be exploring what HTTP headers are, and how and why we use them, in detail in the next chapter. However, take a look at the HTTP Headers tab now, as this gives you a feel for the kinds of things that they can do, and shows you where to find the controls to change them.

The top section of this dialog is used to set the expiration date and time for each document in this site or directory. After this, any cached copies of the page in a browser or proxy server cache will become invalid and will not be displayed. This allows us to control how long a cached page 'lasts' before the user must load a new one from our server.

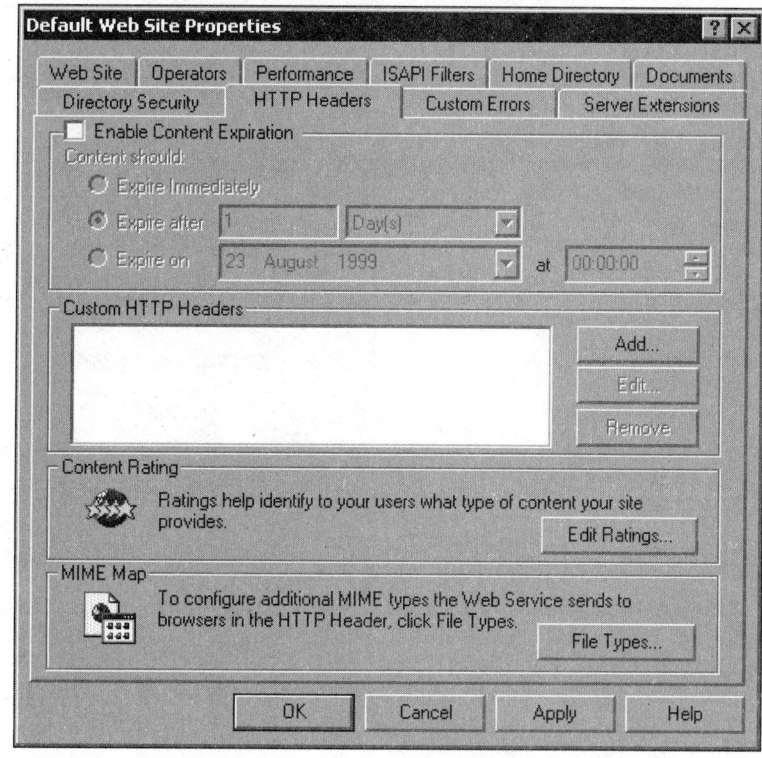

The central section of the dialog allows us to add custom HTTP headers to the response for all pages we send back from this site or directory. These are generally used with custom client applications, or for special custom data management tasks.

The two lower sections of this dialog allow us to set the Content Rating of the pages for this site or directory, and the MIME type headers that our server sends to the client. Content ratings are used to describe the content of the page in terms of sex, violence, bad language, etc. MIME type headers are used to indicate to the client what type of data to expect from our server.

The Server Extensions Tab

The final tab we're looking at here is the Server Extensions page. One of the exciting new features in IIS 5 is the addition of **Distributed Authoring and Versioning (DAV)**. While it's not quite fully implemented in Windows 2000, DAV will eventually provide a robust environment to allow users to edit documents that are stored on the Web server within their browser. This extends the current features provided by Microsoft's Visual InterDev and FrontPage tools, by allowing non-Web documents to be edited as well, for example Word documents or Excel spreadsheets. For an Intranet environment, these features will provide a far more flexible and interactive system for users.

DAV uses a set of software extensions that reside on the Web server, similar to the FrontPage Extensions that we use to enable InterDev and FrontPage to access and upload files to the server. We'll look at DAV in a lot more detail later in the book, but for the meantime have a look at the Server Extensions page in the Properties dialog:

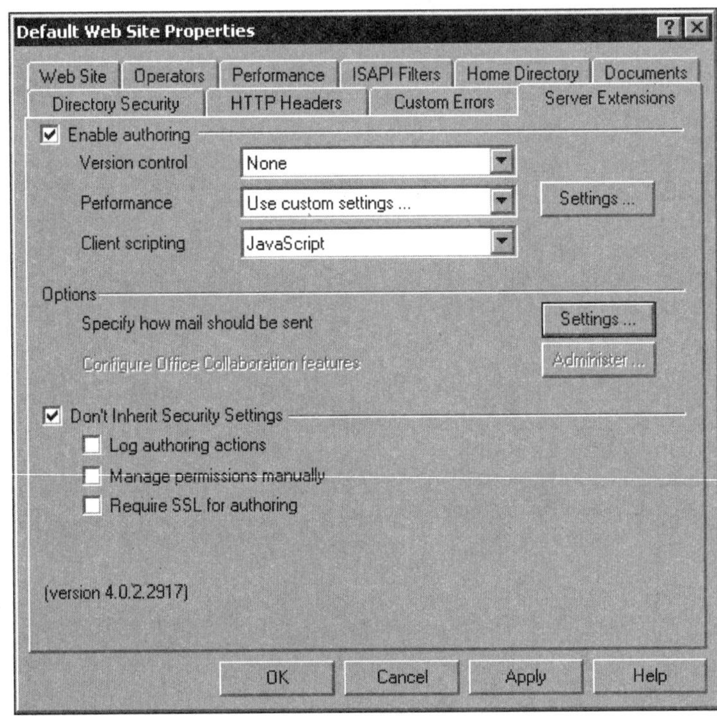

This page allows us to control the authoring and version control features that will be enabled for this virtual application. That includes specifying the way that the extensions will be used in terms of the number of page editing hits (to fine-tune the server and control page caching to give the best performance). We can also provide the default setting to send email from the page when using DAV, and set the security limitations to protect the content.

The ASP 3.0 Object Model In Overview

Before we dive headlong into the details of ASP from a programming point of view, we'll have a brief look at the ASP object model. This is important because, if you haven't already done so with ASP 2.0, you need to start thinking about the way that ASP exposes the pages it executes as individual **Context objects**.

The Concept of Object Context

In version 1.0, we all thought of ASP as an exciting new way to add some dynamic content to our Web pages. We used it to read data from databases, or manipulate the values sent from the browser as the contents of a Web page `<FORM>`. With ASP 2.0, a lot of this changed quite dramatically. The addition of **Microsoft Transaction Server (MTS)**, with its ability to handle multiple concurrent component instances and provide improved scalability, meant that the whole concept of how a dynamic Web page works 'under the covers' changed.

On top of that, MTS allows us to use transactions that are distributed across multiple components, applications and services. For example, an ASP page could update a local database while sending a message to a remote server via the **Message Queue Service** (formerly MSMQ). If any one part of the total transaction failed, the whole thing was rolled back to restore the system to its previous state.

MTS, and the growth of component usage, led to the development of **Web applications** using ASP, as opposed to simple individual dynamic pages. Inside components that are instantiated by ASP script, the **context** of the ASP page is available. The context includes all the intrinsic ASP objects (which we'll meet in a while), so we can use it to get information about the user's request and create a suitable response.

Because this context encompasses the entire ASP object model, it allows programmers to exert much more control over the complex processes that ASP and the components it uses carry out. While we generally thought of the 'root' of the object model as being the Request, Response, and other intrinsic objects, the reality is (and has been since ASP 2.0) that the root is actually an object known as the ObjectContext object.

Referencing the ASP Page Context

In ASP 1.0, the only way to reference the context was through an event that ASP raises each time it starts to execute an ASP page: `OnStartPage`. This event provides as a parameter the ObjectContext object for the ASP page. Within a component, we can capture a reference to this in a global variable, for use in our code. For example this VB code segment stores the context in a local variable named `objContext`:

```
Dim objContext

Public Sub OnStartPage(theContext As ScriptingContext)
  Set objContext = theContext
End Sub

Public Sub DoSomething()
  ...
  objContext.Response.Write "This is some text written into the page"
  ...
End Sub
```

As you can see from the code above, the object context in ASP 1.0 was of type `ScriptingContext`, an object type defined in the ASP DLL and available to code that created a reference to the file `asp.dll`. However, it soon became obvious that to control transactions and provide efficient out-of-process execution of components (which is one of the tasks that MTS managed in ASP 2.0), things had to be done differently. The page context had to be made available explicitly, without the need to hold a reference to it from the start of each page.

So, in ASP 2.0, Microsoft introduced the **ObjectContext** object. However, because the `ScriptingContext` was still available through the `OnStartPage` event, many component authors shunned the ObjectContext object in favor of backward compatibility – even at the risk of reduced performance efficiency. Now, with ASP 3.0, the time has come to make the change. In Windows 2000, MTS has disappeared into the operating system as part of the evolving COM+ technology, and it's used by default for every component that you instantiate in ASP, unless you explicitly decide to avoid it.

Referencing the ObjectContext Object

Since ASP 2.0, it's been possible to obtain a reference to the current page context through the `GetObjectContext` method that ASP makes available. This means that we no longer have to store the reference to the context throughout a page, and we can just get it whenever required:

```
Set objLocalContext = GetObjectContext

objLocalContext.Response.Write "This is some text written into the page"
```

This allows our objects to become **stateless** – in other words, they don't need to hold references to any values or objects once we've finished executing a particular method. If you haven't used ASP 2.0 and MTS before, this might seem a little esoteric a concept to grasp. However, it is vitally important. We'll be looking at the whole issue in a great deal of detail later in the book, so it's worth understanding the fundamental concepts from the start.

The Intrinsic ASP Objects

Having shown how ASP provides a 'root' object in the form of the `ObjectContext` object, we can see how the other intrinsic objects build upon it to provide the access we need to the client's requests, the responses we create, and the other objects that make scripting easier.

> *The original ScriptingContext object is still there, and the `OnStartPage` event is still available, but is now obsolete. You should only use it for pages that will be executed on IIS 3.0 with ASP 1.0, or where absolute backward compatibility is required.*

The two main intrinsic objects provided by ASP map directly to the two actions that your clients carry out when accessing the Web server. The other four are used to provide extra functions that are useful in scripting. Each provides a range of collections, properties and methods that are described in detail in later chapters:

- The **Request** object makes available to our script all the information that the client provides when requesting a page or submitting a form. This includes the HTTP variables that identify the browser and the user, the cookies that they have stored on their browser for this domain, and any values appended to the URL, either as a query string or in HTML controls in a `<FORM>` section of the page. It also provides us with access to any certificate that they may be using through **Secure Sockets Layer** (**SSL**) or other encrypted communication protocol, and properties that help us to manage the connection.

- The **Response** object is used to access the response that we are creating to send back to the client. It makes available to our script the HTTP variables that identify our server and its capabilities, information about the content we're sending to the browser, and any new cookies that will be stored on their browser for this domain. It also provides a series of methods that we can use to create output, such as the ubiquitous `Response.Write` method.
- The **Application** object is created when the ASP DLL is loaded in response to the first request for an ASP page. It provides a repository for storing variables and object references that are available to all the pages, which any visitor can open.
- A unique **Session** object is created for each visitor when they first request an ASP page from the Web site or Web application, and it remains available until the default timeout period (or the timeout period determined by the script) expires. It provides a repository for storing variables and object references that are available only to the pages that this visitor opens during the lifetime of the session.
- The **Server** object provides us with a series of methods and properties that are useful in scripting with ASP. The most obvious is the `Server.CreateObject` method, which allows us to properly instantiate other COM objects on the server within the context of the current page or session. There are also methods to translate strings into the correct format for use in URLs and in HTML, by converting non-legal characters to the correct legal equivalent.
- The **ASPError** object is a new object in ASP 3.0, and is available through the `GetLastError` method of the `Server` object. It provides a range of detailed information about the last error that occurred in ASP.

We can think of these objects as forming a hierarchy based on the ObjectContext object, though it is perhaps more useful to visualize them in relation to the process of receiving and responding to a client request. This diagram attempts to make the relationship between ASP and the process of creating and serving ASP pages clearer:

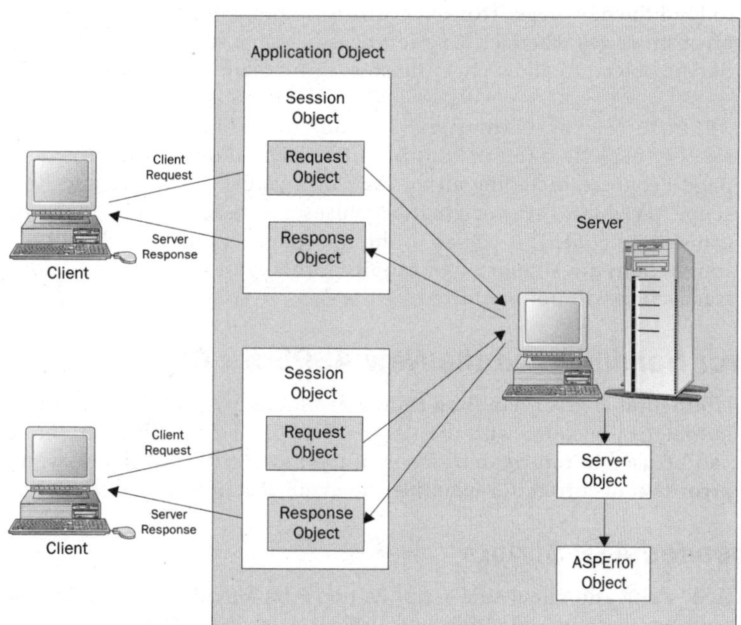

We'll be looking in detail at each of the objects, and the way that we use them, throughout the next few chapters.

What's New in ASP Version 3.0

If you're already familiar with ASP 2.0, and are looking for a concise list of what has actually changed in version 3.0, you'll find the information below. If you're reasonably new to ASP, you may wish to skip this section and continue with the next chapter, where we take an ordered view of the various ASP objects and their use.

ASP 3.0 New Features Summary

These are the new, or substantially changed and improved, features which have been added to ASP in version 3.0.

Scriptless ASP

As we mentioned earlier, ASP is now much faster at processing `.asp` pages that don't contain any script. If you are creating a site or Web application where the files may eventually use ASP, you can assign these files the `.asp` file extensions, regardless of whether they contain server-side script or only static (HTML and text) content.

New Flow Control Capabilities

Up to now, if you wanted to transfer execution to another page in ASP, you had to use the `Response.Redirect` statement. This works by sending a response to the client that instructs them to load the new page. However, this is both expensive, with a round-trip to the client, and can cause error messages when a proxy server is in use at the client end. ASP 3.0 adds two new methods to the Server object, to allow page transfers to be made on the server without requiring a new client request.

`Server.Transfer` transfers execution to another page, while `Server.Execute` will execute another page then return control to the original one. Inside the new page you can access the original page's context, including all the ASP objects like Response and Request, but you lose access to page scope variables. If the original page uses a transaction flag (in the opening `<%@ ... %>` element), the transaction context is passed to the new page. If the second ASP file's transaction flag indicates that transactions are supported or required, then an existing transaction will be used and a new transaction will not be started.

Error Handling and the New ASPError Object

Configurable error handling is now available, by providing a single custom ASP page that is automatically called with the `Server.Transfer` method. In that page, `Server.GetLastError` can be used to return an instance of the new ASPError object, which contains more details about the error that occurred, for example the error description and the relevant line number.

Encoded ASP Scripts

ASP script and client-side script can now be encoded using BASE64 encryption, and higher levels of encryption are planned for future releases of ASP. (Note that this feature is implemented by the VBScript 5.0 and JScript 5.0 scripting engines, and so requires these to be present at the point that the script is executed.) Encoded scripts are decoded at run time by the script engine, so there's no need for a separate utility. Although not a secure encryption method, it does prevent casual users from browsing or copying scripts.

A New Way to Include Script Files

Rather than using the `<!-- #include ... -->` element to force IIS to server-side include a file containing script code, ASP 3.0 can do the 'including' itself. The `<SCRIPT>` element can be used with `RUNAT="SERVER"` and `SRC="file_path_and_name"` attributes to include server-based text files containing script code. A relative physical path or a virtual path can be used in the SRC attribute:

```
<SCRIPT LANGUAGE="language" RUNAT="SERVER" SRC="path_and_filename"></SCRIPT>
```

Server Scriptlets

ASP 3.0 supports a powerful new scripting technology called **server scriptlets**. These are XML-formatted text files that are hosted on the server and are available to ASP as normal COM objects (i.e. Active Server Components). This makes it much easier to implement (or just prototype) your Web application's business logic script procedures as reusable components, as well as using them in other COM compliant programs.

Performance-Enhanced Active Server Components

Many of the Active Server Components that come with ASP have been improved to provide better performance or extra functionality. One example is the new Browser Capabilities component. In addition, there are some new components, such as the XML Parser that allows applications to handle XML formatted data on the server. Closer integration between ADO and XML is also provided (through the new version 2.5 of ADO that ships with Windows 2000), which opens up new opportunities for storing and retrieving data from a data store in XML format.

Performance

A great deal of work has been done to improve performance and scalability of ASP and IIS. This includes self-tuning features in ASP, which detect blocking situations and automatically increase the number of available process threads. ASP now senses when requests that are executing are blocked by external resources, and automatically provides more threads to simultaneously execute additional requests and to continue normal processing. If the CPU becomes overloaded, however, ASP reduces the number of available threads, to minimize the thread switching that occurs when too many non-blocking requests are executing simultaneously.

Changes from ASP Version 2.0

These are the features that have been changed or updated from version 2.0.

Buffering is On by Default

ASP has offered optional output buffering for some time. Since IIS 4.0, this has provided much faster script execution, as well as the ability to control the output that is streamed to the browser. In ASP 3.0, this improved performance has been reflected by changing the default setting of the `Response.Buffer` property to `True`, so that buffering is on by default. This means that the final output will be sent to the client only at the completion of processing, or when the script calls the `Response.Flush` or `Response.End` methods.

Note that you should turn buffering of – by setting the `Response.Buffer` property to `False` – when sending XML formatted output to the client to allow the XML parser to start work on it as it is received. You may also want to use `Response.Flush` to send sections of very large pages, so that the user sees some output arrive quickly.

Changes to Response.IsClientConnected

The `Response.IsClientConnected` property can now be read before any content is sent to the client. In ASP 2.0, this only returned accurate information after at least some content had been sent. This resolves the problem of IIS responding to every client request, even though the client might have moved to another page or site. Also, if the client is no longer connected after 3 seconds, the complete output that has been created on the server is dumped.

Query Strings with Default Documents

If a user accesses a site without providing the name of the page they require, the default document (if one exists) will be sent back to the client. However, if they provided a query string appended to the URL, this was ignored in previous versions of ASP. In IIS 5.0 with ASP 3.0, it is passed to the default page. For example, if the default page in a directory that has the URL `http://www.wrox.com/store/` is `default.asp`, then both the following will send the name/value pair `code=1274` to the `default.asp` page:

```
http://www.wrox.com/store/?code=1274
http://www.wrox.com/store/default.asp?code=1274
```

Server-side Include File Security

Server-side include files are often used for sensitive information, such as database connection strings or other access details. A virtual path (i.e. the URL rather than the full physical disk file path) could be used to specify these files, and in this situation, previous versions of ASP did not check the user's credentials against the security settings for the file. In other words, the authenticated user or anonymous Web server account was not compared to the access control list (ACL) entries for the file. In ASP 3.0 on IIS 5.0, these credentials are now checked, and can be used to prevent unauthorized access.

Configurable Entries Moved to the Metabase

In IIS 5.0, the registry entries for ProcessorThreadMax and ErrorsToNTLog have been moved into the metabase. All configurable parameters for ASP can be modified in the metabase via Active Directory and the Active Directory Service Interface (ADSI).

Behavior of Both-Threaded Objects in Applications

For best performance in ASP, where there are often multiple concurrent requests, components should be **Both-Threaded** (Single Threaded Apartment (STA) and Multi-Threaded Apartment (MTA)) *and* support the COM Free-Threaded Marshaller (FTM). Both-Threaded COM objects that do not support the Free-Threaded Marshaller will fail if stored in the ASP Application state object.

Earlier Release of COM Objects

In IIS 5.0, instantiated objects or components are now released earlier. In IIS 4.0, COM objects were only released when ASP finished processing a page. In IIS 5.0, if a COM object does not use the `OnEndPage` method, and the reference count for the object reaches zero, then the object is released before processing completes.

ASP Allows Out-of-Process Components by Default

Custom local server components can now be instantiated from IIS without changing any metabase settings. The metabase property AspAllowOutOfProcComponents that controls local server instantiation, now has a default value of 1. In earlier versions of IIS, it was 0.

COM Object Security

IIS uses the new **cloaking** feature provided by COM+ so that local server applications instantiated from ASP can run in the security context of the originating client. In previous versions, the security context assigned to the local server COM object depended on the identity of the calling process.

Components Run Out-of-Process By Default

In earlier versions of ASP, all components created within the context of an ASP page ran **in-process** by default, i.e. within the memory space of the Web server. In IIS 4.0, the ability to create a virtual application allowed components to be run **out-of-process**. In IIS 5.0 and ASP 3.0, components are now instantiated **out-of-process** by default.

To better fine-tune the component performance to Web server protection trade-off, you can now choose from the three options for Application Protection in the Properties dialog for a virtual application:

- **Low (IIS Process)**
  All application executables and components for ASP virtual applications with this setting are run in the process (i.e. the memory space) of the Web server executable (`Inetinfo.exe`). Hence, the Web server is at risk if any one of the executables or components should fail. However, this provides the fastest and least resource-intensive application execution option.

- **Medium (Pooled)** – Default
  All application executables and components from all ASP virtual applications with this setting are run in the process (i.e. the memory space) of a single shared instance of `DLLHost.exe`. This protects the Web server executable (`Inetinfo.exe`) from the risk of any one of the executables or components failing. However, one failed executable or component can cause the `DLLHost.exe` process to fail, and with it all the other hosted executables and components.

- **High (Isolated)**
  All application executables and components for an ASP virtual application with this setting are run in the process (i.e. the memory space) of a single instance of `DLLHost.exe`, but each ASP application has its own instance of `DLLHost.exe` which is exclusive to that application. This protects the Web server executable (`Inetinfo.exe`) from the risk of any one of the executables or components failing, and protects the virtual application from risk if an executable or component from another virtual application should fail. Microsoft suggests that a maximum of ten isolated virtual applications should be hosted on any one Web server.

The recommended configuration is to run mission-critical applications in their own processes – i.e. **High (Isolated)** – and all remaining applications in a shared, pooled process – i.e. **Medium (Pooled)**. It is also possible to set the **Execute Permissions** for the scripts and components that make up each virtual application. The three options are:

- **None** – No scripts or executables can be run in this virtual application. In effect, this provides a quick and easy way to disable an application if required.
- **Scripts only** – Allows only script files, such as ASP, IDC or others to run in this virtual application. Executables cannot be run.
- **Scripts and Executables** – Allows any script or executable to run within this virtual application.

What's New in VBScript 5.0

The features that are available in ASP include those provided by the scripting engines, which means that improvements there are also available in ASP. The changes to VBScript are as follows.

Using Classes in Script

The full Visual Basic `Class` model is implemented, with the obvious exception of events in ASP server-side scripting. You can create classes within your script, which make their properties and methods available to the remainder of the code in your page. For example:

```
Class MyClass

  Private m_HalfValue                     'local variable to hold value of HalfValue

  Public Property Let HalfValue(vData)  'executed to set the HalfValue property
    If vData > 0 Then m_HalfValue = vData
  End Property

  Public Property Get HalfValue()        'executed to return the HalfValue property
    HalfValue = m_HalfValue
  End Property

  Public Function GetResult()            'implements the GetResult method
    GetResult = m_HalfValue * 2
  End Function

End Class

Set objThis = New MyClass

objThis.HalfValue = 21

Response.Write "Value of HalfValue property is " & objThis.HalfValue & "<BR>"
Response.Write "Result of GetResult method is " & objThis.GetResult & "<BR>"
...
```

This produces the result:

```
Value of HalfValue property is 21
Result of GetResult method is 42
```

The With Construct

The `With` construct is now supported, allowing more compact scripts to be written where the code accesses several properties or methods of one object:

```
...
Set objThis = Server.CreateObject("This.Object")

With objThis
```

```
    .Property1 = "This value"
    .Property2 = "Another value"
    TheResult = .SomeMethod
End With
...
```

String Evaluation

The `Eval` function (long available in JavaScript and JScript) is now supported in VBScript 5.0. This allows you to build a string containing script code that evaluates to `True` or `False`, and then execute it to obtain a result:

```
...
datYourBirthday = Request.Form("Birthday")
strScript = "datYourBirthday = Date()"

If Eval(strScript) Then
   Response.Write "Happy Birthday!"
Else
   Response.Write "Have a nice day!"
End If
...
```

Statement Execution

The new `Execute` function allows script code in a string to be executed in much the same way as the `Eval` function, but without returning a result as is usually the case with the `Eval` statement. It can be used to dynamically create procedures that are executed later in the code For example:

```
...
strCheckBirthday = "Sub CheckBirthday(datYourBirthday)" & vbCrlf _
                 & "  If Eval(datYourBirthday = Date()) Then" & vbCrlf _
                 & "    Response.Write ""Happy Birthday!""" & vbCrlf _
                 & "  Else" & vbCrlf _
                 & "    Response.Write ""Have a nice day!""" & vbCrlf _
                 & "  End If" & vbCrlf _
                 & "End Sub" & vbCrlf
Execute strCheckBirthday
CheckBirthday(Date())
...
```

Either a carriage return (as shown) or a colon character `':'` can be used to delimit the individual statements within the string.

Setting Locales

The new `SetLocale` method can be used to change the current locale of the script engine. This enables it to properly display special locale-specific characters, such as those with accents or from a different character set:

```
strCurrentLocale = GetLocale
SetLocale("en-gb")
```

Regular Expressions

VBScript 5.0 now supports regular expressions (again, long available in JavaScript, JScript and other languages). The RegExp object is used to create and execute a regular expression. For example:

```
strTarget = "test testing tested attest late start"
Set objRegExp = New RegExp                        'create a regular expression

objRegExp.Pattern = "test*"                       'set the search pattern
objRegExp.IgnoreCase = False                      'set the case sensitivity
objRegExp.Global = True                           'set the scope

Set colMatches = objRegExp.Execute(strTarget)     'execute the search

For Each Match in colMatches                      'iterate the colMatches collection
  Response.Write "Match found at position " & Match.FirstIndex & ". "
  Response.Write "Matched value is '" & Match.Value & "'.<BR>"
Next
```

This produces the result:

```
Match found at position 0. Matched value is 'test'.
Match found at position 5. Matched value is 'test'.
Match found at position 13. Matched value is 'test'.
Match found at position 22. Matched value is 'test'.
```

Setting Event Handlers in Client-side VBScript

While not applying directly to ASP scripting techniques, this new feature is useful when writing client-side VBScript. You can now assign a reference to a function or subroutine to an event dynamically. For example, given a function named MyFunction(), you can assign it to a button's onClick event using:

```
Function MyFunction()
   ...
   'Function implementation code here
   ...
End Function
...
Set objCmdButton = document.all("cmdButton")
Set objCmdButton.onClick = GetRef("MyFunction")
```

This provides similar functionality to that existing in JavaScript and JScript, where functions can be assigned as properties of an object dynamically.

On Error Goto 0 in VBScript

Although this technique was not documented previously, it does in fact work in existing versions of VBScript (as those of you with a VB background and an inquisitive mind will have already discovered. It is now documented, and can be used to 'turn off' custom error handling in a page after an On Error Resume Next has been executed. The result is that any subsequent errors will raise a browser-level or server-level error and the appropriate dialog/response.

What's New In JScript 5.0

The only change to JScript is the long-awaited introduction of proper error handling.

Exception Handling

The Java-style `try` and `catch` constructs are now supported in JScript 5.0. For example:

```
function GetSomeKindOfIndexThingy() {

  try {
    // If an exception occurs during the execution of this
    // block of code, processing of this entire block will
    // be aborted and will resume with the first statement in its
    // associated catch block.
    var objSomething = Server.CreateObject("SomeComponent");
    var intIndex = objSomething.getSomeIndex();
    return intIndex;
  }

  catch (exception) {
    // This code will execute when *any* exception occurs during the
    // execution of this function
    alert('Oh dear, the object didn't expect you to do that');
  }

}
```

The built-in JScript `Error` object has three properties that define the last run-time error. We can use these in a `catch` block to get more information about the error:

```
alert(Error.number);  // Gives the numeric value of the error number
// AND the result with 0xFFFF to get a 'normal' error number in ASP

alert(Error.description);  // Gives an error desciption as a string
```

If you want to throw your own errors, you can raise an error (or **exception**) with a custom **exception object**. However there is no built-in exception object, so you have to define a constructor for one yourself:

```
// Define our own Exception object
function MyException(intNumber, strDescription, strInfo) {
  this.Number = intNumber;                // Set the Number property
  this.Description = strDescription;      // Set the Description property
  this.CustomInfo = strInfo;              // Set some 'information' property
}
```

An object like this can then be used to raise custom exceptions within our pages, by using the `throw` keyword and then examining the type of exception in the `catch` block:

```
function GetSomeKindOfIndexThingy() {
  try {
    var objSomething = Server.CreateObject("SomeComponent");
    var intIndex = objSomething.getSomeIndex();
    if (intIndex == 0) {
      // Create a new MyException object
      theException = new MyException(0x6F1, "Zero index not permitted",
                                     "Index_Err");
      throw theException;
    }
    return intIndex;
  }

  catch (objException) {
    if (objException instanceof MyException) {
      // This is one of our custom exception objects
      if (objException.Category == "Index_Err") {
         alert('Index Error: ' + objException.Description);
      else
         alert('Undefined custom error: ' + objException.Description);
      }
      else
        // Not "our" exception, so display it and raise to next higher routine
        alert(Error.Description + ' (' + Error.Number + ')');
        throw exception;
    }
  }
}
```

Other New Features

A couple of other features have been made available in IIS 5.0.

Distributed Authoring and Versioning (DAV)

This standard, created by the Internet Engineering Task Force (IETF) and now in version 1.0, allows authors in several locations to concurrently build and maintain Web pages and other documents. It is designed to provide upload and download access, and control versions so that the process can be properly managed. Internet Explorer contains features that integrate with DAV in IIS 5.0. However, in the IETF standard, and in the current release of IIS 5.0, the versioning capabilities are not yet implemented.

Referencing Type Libraries

In the past, it has been common practice to use a server-side include file to add constants from a type library (such as scripting objects, ADO or MSMQ) to an ASP page. This is necessary, as ASP does not create a reference to the type library or component DLL as does, for example, Visual Basic. In IIS 5.0, you no longer need to use include files for constants. Instead, you can access the type library of a component directly using a new HTML comment-style element, placed in the `<HEAD>` section of the page:

```
<!-- METADATA TYPE="typelib" FILE="c:\WinNT\System32\scrrun.dll" -->
```

This makes all the constants in the specified file available within the current ASP page. (Although this is slated as being new in IIS 5.0, it was working but undocumented in IIS 4.0.)

FTP Download Restarts

The FTP service now (at last, some would say) provides a restart facility for downloads. If a file download stops part way through – perhaps because of a dropped connection at the user end – it can be resumed from that point. This means that failed file downloads do not require the client to download the entire file all over again.

HTTP Compression

IIS now automatically implements compression of the HTTP data stream for static and dynamically generated files, and caches compressed static files as well. This gives faster response and reduces network loading when communicating with suitably equipped clients.

Summary

In this chapter, we've very briefly looked at many of the major topics that you need to be aware of when working with ASP 3.0. We've purposely taken the point of view of the experienced Web developer, assuming that you either have previous experience of ASP through using an earlier version, or at least you know how the Web works when clients and servers interact.

By now, you should have a good overall view of what ASP 3.0 offers – both in terms of the existing features in earlier versions, and the new features that are available in version 3.0. If you feel that you don't fully understand the concepts of the ASP object model, or the way that context is used to allow access to this object model from other sources, then don't worry about it. Providing you have a broad understanding of the topics we've covered here, you will easily be able to follow the rest of the chapters in this section, which cover it all in more detail.

In fact, in the next chapter, we'll be looking at the two main objects, Request and Response. We'll move on to explore the other objects in subsequent chapters. Then, to complete this section of the book, we'll look at how we use Active Server Components in our pages, including the scripting objects made available through the VBScript and JScript scripting engines. Finally, in Chapter 7, we look at error handling (much improved in ASP 3.0), and how you can debug your ASP pages.

This chapter, then, covered the following wide-ranging but important topics:

- What (very briefly) is ASP
- How ASP connects with IIS
- Set-up issues and management
- The ASP 3.0 Object Model in overview
- The concept of Object Context
- What's new in ASP version 3.0

So, why hesitate? Dive into Chapter 2, now and start learning about client requests and server responses.

N
W

2

Handling Requests and Responses

Having looked at the fundamental aspects of setting up and using ASP in the previous chapter, and having overviewed the intrinsic objects that it provides, we move on in this chapter to take a closer look at the two objects that you'll use most often. The exchanges that takes place between a browser (or other user agent) and the Web server during a request and response are accessed and managed in ASP through two intrinsic objects, appropriately named the **Request** and **Response** objects.

Almost all of the tasks that we carry out in an ASP page will depend on access to these two objects, and the way we use them can affect both the efficiency and the robustness of our pages. Of course, their major uses are to access values that the user sends to our server, either from a `<FORM>` section of an HTML page or appended to the URL as a query string, and to create the appropriate output to return to the user. And they share many common factors: for example both can be used to work with the cookies that are stored on a client machine.

So rather than just subdividing the chapter into two distinct sections (one for each object), we'll first look at it from the point of view of the conversation between the client and our server, and then examine the individual objects. This will make it easier to see how they are related, and help you to understand the details of this vital interaction.

Therefore, we'll be looking at:

- How the client and server interact to deliver a Web page or other resource
- The Request and Response objects in detail, and what's common between them
- How we access values from forms and in the query string

- How we read and create cookies to be stored on the client
- What server variables are, and how we access and modify HTTP headers
- How various other items, such as client certificates, are represented

We'll start with an overview of the interaction between the client browser (or 'user agent') and our ASP Web server.

Client and Server Interaction

When a browser or other user agent accesses our Web site to request a page, a conversation takes place between the client application and the Web server. We're going to take a close look at this here, because understanding what goes on helps you to grasp the fundamentals of using the ASP Request and Response objects, and this in turn will help you to get the most from using ASP.

> *To save repetition, we'll generally be using the term 'browser' for the remainder of this chapter – and throughout the book – but remember that this is not the only application that might access your Web pages. As well as the special client-side programs designed for use by those whose sight is impaired, or who have other difficulties using a conventional browser, there are also many specialist applications that might load pages from your site. Obvious examples are the* ***robots*** *used by search engines to access sites on the Web. The more accurate term for all these, including normal Web browsers, is* ***user agent****.*

The Page Request Conversation

When a browser requests a page from our Web site, it obviously has to tell our server which page it wants. It does this by using the domain name of our server to make a connection, and then providing the full path and name of the page in the request. Why the full path and name? Well, remember that the Web is a **stateless** environment, unless you take some action to create a session that identifies each client (we'll see how ASP can do this in the next chapter).

This means that every time the server finishes sending a page to a client, the client is promptly forgotten by the server. So, when they request the next page, it's just like a new visitor has arrived. The server has no idea which client this is, so it can't make reasoned judgments about which page they loaded last time, and therefore can't provide a page using a relative path. Thus, even if your page contains a relative link, such as:

```
<A HREF="Download.asp">Next Page</A>
```

the browser will automatically build up the complete URL of the new page using the current page's domain and path, or perhaps a `<BASE>` element in the `<HEAD>` section of page which tells the browser what the base URL of all links on a page is, for example:

```
<BASE HREF="http://www.wrox.com/Store">
```

You can see this for yourself if you look at the status bar of your browser while the pointer is over a link on a page. The current page's path and the base or current domain are combined with the name of the required page:

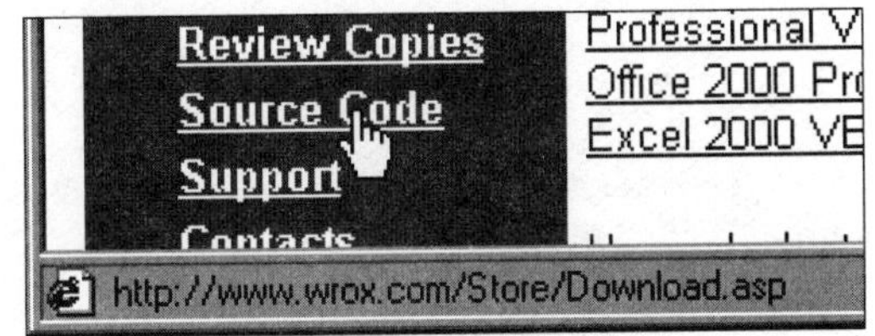

The Client Request in Detail

The full path and name combination for the page required is only one of the values that the browser sends to our Web server when requesting a page. The browser's request can also contain a host of information about the browser and the client system on which it's running. The actual content will vary from browser to browser, and very little may be supplied by other applications such as search engine robots. However, to see what may be there, the following is the content of a request from Internet Explorer 5.0 for the page `http://www.wrox.com/Store/Download.asp`:

```
7/8/99 10:27:16 Sent  GET /Store/Download.asp HTTP/1.1
Accept: application/msword, application/vnd.ms-excel, application/vnd.ms-
powerpoint, image/gif, image/x-xbitmap, image/jpeg, image/pjpeg, application/x-
comet, */*
Accept-Language: en-us
Encoding: gzip, deflate
Referer: http://www.wrox.com/main_menu.asp
Cookie: VisitCount=2&LASTDATE=6%2F4%2F99+10%3A10%3A13+AM
User-Agent: Mozilla/4.0 (compatible; MSIE 5.0; Windows 98)
Host: 212.250.238.67
Connection: Keep-Alive
```

As you can see, there is information about the user agent, such as the default language and details of the user connection. There is also a list of the types of file or 'applications' that it will accept. These are **MIME-types**, about which we'll see more later on. As well as several types of image file, the browser will accept various Microsoft Office file types. The 'standard' file types such as `text/html` and `text/text` are not listed here. They are represented by the `*/*`, which allows the server to send any type of file for the browser to try and interpret itself or through a plug-in application.

The `Cookie:` entry contains a cookie that is stored on the client and is valid for this domain. The `Referer:` entry (yes it is spelt wrongly) will only appear if the request is being made in response to clicking a link, rather than typing a URL into the address bar of the browser, and it contains the complete URL of the page containing that link.

The `Host:` entry contains the IP address or name of the client machine. However, this is not reliable enough to use to accurately identify the client, as they may be connecting through an ISP that dynamically allocates IP addresses, or through a proxy server where the IP address is that of the proxy and not of the actual client.

The Server Response in Detail

In response to the request above, and providing that the requested page is available to the browser anonymously (i.e. the user doesn't have to provide a username and password to access it), the following is sent from our Web server to the client:

```
7/8/99 10:27:16 Received   HTTP/1.1 200 OK
Server: Microsoft-IIS/5.0
Connection: Keep-Alive
```

```
Date: Thu, 8 Jul 1999 10:27:16 GMT
Content-Type: text/html
Accept-Ranges: bytes
Content-Length: 2946
Last-Modified: Thu, 8 Jul 1999 10:27:16 GMT
Cookie: VisitCount=3&LASTDATE=7%2F8%2F99+10%3A27%3A16+AM
<HTML>
... rest of page ...
</HTML>
```

You can see that our server identifies itself to the client with the software type and version. The first line indicates the HTTP protocol that it's using and contains the **status** return code. The text message `200 OK` means that the request has been accepted and is being satisfied. Next come details of the page that is being returned. This includes the MIME-type (`Content-Type:`), the size (in bytes), the date it was last modified, and the cookie to store back on the client. The remainder of the response contains the stream of bytes that make up the page.

In some cases, the server will be unable to send back a page in response to a request, perhaps because the page doesn't exist or the client doesn't have the relevant permissions to access it. We'll look in detail at security issues in a later section of the book. For now, the response that might be returned if the page doesn't exist (for example the user typed an incorrect URL into the address box of their browser) would start off with:

```
7/8/99 14:27:16 Received   HTTP/1.1 404 Not Found
Server: Microsoft-IIS/5.0
...
```

Here, the status code and message indicate that the page the client requested could not be located. The browser can use this information to display an appropriate message to the user (as is the case in IE5, when it typically overrides the server's default response with a 'helpful' error page), or it can display a default message that the server could create (depending on the server's settings).

So, having seen what goes on under the hood, let's move on to look at how this translates into the values that are provided by the ASP Request and Response objects.

The ASP Request and Response Objects

The details of the client request and the server response are made available in ASP through the intrinsic Request and Response objects:

- The Request object makes available to our script all the information that the client provides when requesting a page or submitting a form. This includes the HTTP variables that identify the browser and the user; the cookies that they have stored on their browser for this domain; and any values appended to the URL as a query string or in HTML controls in a `<FORM>` section of the page. It also provides us with access to any certificate that they may be using through **Secure Sockets Layer (SSL)** or other encrypted communication protocol, and properties that help us to manage the connection.
- The Response object is used to access the response that we are creating to send back to the client. It makes available to our script the HTTP variables that identify our server and its capabilities, information about the content we are sending to the browser, and any new cookies that will be stored on their browser for this domain. It also provides a series of methods that we can use to create output, such as the ubiquitous `Response.Write` method.

In this section, we'll first summarize the members of the Request and Response object. Then we'll go on to explore the usual tasks that we apply them to, and see how to work with the various members of each object in more detail.

The ASP Request Object Members Summary

This section gives brief descriptions of all the members of the Request object.

The Request Object's Collections

The Request object provides five collections that we can use to access all kinds of information about the client's request to our Web server. The collections are:

Collection Name	Description
`ClientCertificate`	A collection of the values of all the fields or entries in the client certificate that the user presented to our server when accessing a page or resource. Each member is read-only.
`Cookies`	A collection of the values of all the cookies sent from the user's system along with their request. Only cookies valid for the domain containing the resource are sent to the server. Each member is read-only.
`Form`	A collection of the values of all the HTML control elements in the `<FORM>` section that was submitted as the request, where the value of the `METHOD` attribute is `POST`. Each member is read-only.
`QueryString`	A collection of all the name/value pairs appended to the URL in the user's request, or the values of all the HTML control elements in the `<FORM>` section that was submitted as the request where the value of the `METHOD` attribute is `GET` or the attribute is omitted. Each member is read-only.
`ServerVariables`	A collection of all the HTTP header values sent from the client with their request, plus the values of several environment variables for the Web server. Each member is read-only.

The Request Object's Property

The single property of the Request object provides information about the number of bytes in the user's request. It is rarely used in ASP pages, as we are usually more concerned with the specific values than the entire request string:

Property	Description
`TotalBytes`	Read-only. Returns the total number of bytes in the body of the request sent by the client.

The Request Object's Method

The single Request method allows us to access the complete content of the part of a user's request that is POSTed to our server from a <FORM> section of a Web page:

Method	Description
BinaryRead(*count*)	Retrieves *count* bytes of data from the client's request when the data is sent to the server as part of a POST request. It returns a Variant array (or SafeArray). This method *cannot* be used successfully if the ASP code has already referenced the Request.Form collection. Likewise, the Request.Form collection *cannot* be successfully accessed if you have used the BinaryRead method.

The ASP Response Object Members Summary

This section summarizes all the members of the Response object, with a brief description of each one.

The Response Object's Collection

The Response object provides a single collection that we can use to set the values of any cookies that we wish to place on the client system. It is the direct equivalent of the Request.Cookies collection:

Collection Name	Description
Cookies	A collection containing the values of all the cookies that will be sent back to the client in the current response. The collection is write only.

The Response Object's Properties

The Response object also provides a range of properties that we can read (in most cases) and modify to tailor our response as required – these are set by the server, so we don't have to set them ourselves. Note that the syntax used when setting some of the properties (as shown below) is different from what you would normally expect. The properties are:

Property	Description
Buffer = True|False	Read/write. *Boolean.* Specifies if the output created by an ASP page will be held in the IIS buffer until all of the server scripts in the current page have been processed, or until the Flush or End method is called. It must be set before any output is sent to IIS, including HTTP header information, so it should be the first line of the .asp file after the <%@LANGUAGE=..%> statement. Buffering is on (True) by default in ASP 3.0, whereas it was off (False) by default in earlier versions.

Property	Description
`CacheControl "`*setting*`"`	Read/write. *String.* Set this property to `"Public"` to allow proxy servers to cache the page, or `"Private"` to prevent proxy caching taking place.
`Charset = "`*value*`"`	Read/write. *String.* Appends the name of the character set (for example, `ISO-LATIN-7`) to the `HTTP Content-Type` header created by the server for each response.
`ContentType="`*MIME-type*`"`	Read/write. *String.* Specifies the HTTP content type for the response, as a standard MIME-type (such as `"text/xml"` or `"image/gif"`). If omitted, the MIME-type `"text/html"` is used. The content type tells the browser what type of content to expect.
`Expires` *minutes*	Read/write. *Number.* Specifies the length of time in minutes that a page is valid for. If the user returns to the same page before it expires, the cached version is displayed. After that period, it expires, and will not be held in a private (user) or public (proxy) cache.
`ExpiresAbsolute #`*date[time]*`#`	Read/write. *Date/Time.* Specifies the absolute date and time when a page will expire and no longer be valid. If the user returns to the same page before it expires, the cached version is displayed. After that time, it expires, and should not be held in a private (user) or public (proxy) cache.
`IsClientConnected`	Read-only. *Boolean.* Returns an indication of whether the client is still connected to and loading the page from the server. Can be used to end processing (with the `Response.End` method) if a client moves to another page before the current one has finished executing.
`PICS("`*PICS-label-string*`")`	Write only. *String.* Creates a `PICS` header and adds it to the HTTP headers in the response. `PICS` headers define the content of the page in terms of violence, sex, bad language, etc.
`Status = "`*code message*`"`	Read/write. *String.* Specifies the status value and message that will be sent to the client in the HTTP headers of the response to indicate an error or successful processing of the page. Examples are `"200 OK"` and `"404 Not Found"`.

The Response Object's Methods

Finally, the Response object provides a set of methods that allows us to directly manipulate the content of the page that we are creating on the server for return to the client. They are:

Method	Description
`AddHeader("`*name*`", "`*content*`")`	Creates a custom HTTP header using the *name* and *content* values and adds it to the response. Will *not* replace an existing header of the same name. Once a header has been added, it cannot be removed. Must be used before any page content (i.e. text and HTML) is sent to the client.
`AppendToLog("`*string*`")`	Adds a string to the end of the Web server log entry for this request when `W3C Extended Log File Format` is in use. Requires at least the `URI Stem` value to be selected in the `Extended Properties` page for the site containing the page.
`BinaryWrite(`*SafeArray*`)`	Writes the content of a Variant-type *SafeArray* to the current HTTP output stream without any character conversion. Useful for writing non-string information, such as binary data required by a custom application or the bytes to make up an image file.
`Clear()`	Erases any existing buffered page content from the IIS response buffer when `Response.Buffer` is `True`. Does *not* erase HTTP response headers. Can be used to abort a partly completed page.
`End()`	Stops ASP from processing the page script and returns the currently created content, then aborts any further processing of this page.
`Flush()`	Sends all currently buffered page content in the IIS buffer to the client when `Response.Buffer` is `True`. Can be used to send parts of a long page to the client individually.
`Redirect("`*url*`")`	Instructs the browser to load the page in the string *url* parameter by sending a `"302 Object Moved"` HTTP header in the response.
`Write("`*string*`")`	Writes the specified *string* to the current HTTP response stream and IIS buffer, so that it becomes part of the returned page.

In the code samples that you can download for this book, you'll find a series of pages that demonstrate how you can work with the properties, methods and collections provided by the Request and Response objects. You'll find these with all the example pages for the remainder of this chapter, in the `Chapter02` subdirectory of the download from the Wrox Web site.

Working with Form and QueryString Collections

All the values that a user provides when filling in a <FORM> on the page, or which are appended to the end of the URL in the browser's **Address** bar, are made available to our ASP scripts through two collections: the `Form` and `QueryString` collection. These provide an easy way for us to access any value within our ASP code.

General Techniques for Accessing ASP Collections

Most of the ASP collections are just like the normal collections that you meet in Visual Basic. In effect, they are an array of values, but one that can be accessed using a text string key (which is not case sensitive) as well as an integer index. So, if our client-side Web page contains a <FORM> like this:

```
<FORM ACTION="show_request.asp" METHOD="POST">
  FirstName: <INPUT TYPE="TEXT" NAME="FirstName">
  LastName: <INPUT TYPE="TEXT" NAME="LastName">
  <INPUT TYPE="SUBMIT" VALUE="Send">
</FORM>
```

We can access the values that are entered into the controls by accessing the ASP `Form` collection:

```
strFirstName = Request.Form("FirstName")
strLastName = Request.Form("LastName")
```

We can also use the integer index of the control on the form, where the range of indexes starts at one for the first control defined in the HTML, and continues in the order of the control definitions:

```
strFirstName = Request.Form(1)
strLastName = Request.Form(2)
```

However this second (integer index) technique is not recommended, because if the order of the controls in the HTML is changed, or a new one is inserted, the ASP code will pick up the wrong values. What's more, it can be confusing to someone reading the code

Accessing the Entire Set of Collection Values

It's also possible to collect the entire set of values from the form into a single string variable by just referencing the collection, and without providing a key or index:

```
strAllFormContent = Request.Form
```

If our text boxes contain the values **Priscilla** and **Descartes**, the `Request.Form` statement will return the string:

```
FirstName=Priscilla&LastName=Descartes
```

Notice that the values are provided in **name/value** pairs (i.e. *control_name=control_value*), and each name/value pair is separated from the others with an ampersand (&) character. If you intend to pass the contents of the form to a separate executable application or DLL that expects this standard format for the values, you will find this technique useful. However, in general, we'll access the contents of the collection using a text key that is the name of the control on the form.

Iterating Through an ASP Collection

There are two ways to iterate through all the members of an ASP collection, in the same way as we can do for ordinary VB collections. Each collection provides a `Count` property, which returns the number of items in the collection. We can use this to iterate through the collection by using an integer index:

```
For intLoop = 1 To Request.Form.Count
  Response.Write Request.Form(intLoop) & "<BR>"
Next
```

If the two text boxes on our previous form contain the values Priscilla and Descartes, this gives the result:

```
Priscilla
Descartes
```

However, a better method is to use the `For Each...Next` construct:

```
For Each objItem In Request.Form
  Response.Write objItem & " = " & Request.Form(objItem) & "<BR>"
Next
```

This has the added advantage of allowing us to access the name of the control as well as the value. If the two text boxes on our previous form contain the values Priscilla and Descartes, the code above gives this result:

```
FirstName = Priscilla
LastName = Descartes
```

Note that some browsers may not return the values in a <FORM> to ASP in the same order that they appear on the page.

Multiple Value Collection Members

In some cases, an individual member of an ASP collection may be made up of more than one value. This occurs when several controls have the same `NAME` attribute defined in the HTML, for example:

```
<FORM ACTION="show_request.asp" METHOD="POST">
  <INPUT TYPE="TEXT" NAME="OtherHobby">
  <INPUT TYPE="TEXT" NAME="OtherHobby">
  <INPUT TYPE="TEXT" NAME="OtherHobby">
  <INPUT TYPE="SUBMIT" VALUE="Send">
</FORM>
```

This will create an entry in the `Form` collection under the key `"OtherHobby"`. However, it will contain the values from all three text boxes. If the user leaves one or more of them blank in the page when submitting it, the values returned are empty strings. If the user has entered Gardening and Mountaineering in the first and third text boxes, and left the second one empty, accessing `Request.Form("OtherHobby")` in our ASP code will return the string:

```
Gardening, , Mountaineering
```

To be able to access individual values in this case, we can use the rather convoluted code:

```
For Each objItem In Request.Form

  If Request.Form(objItem).Count > 1 Then    'More than one value in this item

    Response.Write objItem & ":<BR>"
    For intLoop = 1 To Request.Form(objItem).Count
      Response.Write "Subkey " & intLoop & " value = " _
                   & Request.Form(objItem)(intLoop) & "<BR>"
    Next

  Else

    Response.Write objItem & " = " & Request.Form(objItem) & "<BR>"

  End If

Next
```

For the previous example of a form containing three `OtherHobby` controls, this returns:

```
OtherHobby:
Subkey 1 value = Gardening
Subkey 2 value =
Subkey 3 value = Mountaineering
```

However, it's rare that you would give several text boxes the same name, so this technique should rarely be required.

HTML Radio or Option Button Controls

Nevertheless, there are situations where you do need to give several controls the same `NAME` attribute in the HTML. A common one is when you're dealing with radio (or option) buttons. For example:

```
<FORM ACTION="show_request.asp" METHOD="POST">
  I live in:
  <INPUT TYPE="RADIO" NAME="Country" VALUE="AM"> America<BR>
  <INPUT TYPE="RADIO" NAME="Country" VALUE="EU"> Europe<BR>
  <INPUT TYPE="RADIO" NAME="Country" VALUE="AS"> Asia<BR>
  <INPUT TYPE="RADIO" NAME="Country" VALUE="*"> Elsewhere<P>
  <INPUT TYPE="SUBMIT" VALUE="Send">
</FORM>
```

As the user can only select one of the options (that's why we give them all the same name) we will only get one value returned. The browser only sends the value of the selected control, so if the user of this form had selected Europe we would get just this single entry when iterating through the values in the `Form` collection:

```
Country = EU
```

This works because we have provided a different `VALUE` attribute for each of the controls, which reflects the name of the country or area for each one. If we omit the `VALUE` attribute, the browser just returns `on` for the value, so we would get:

```
Country = on
```

This isn't much use, so you should always use the `VALUE` attribute for radio-type controls where there are more than one with the same name.

HTML Checkbox Controls

When the HTML source of a form contains check box controls, they will usually be given unique names. For example:

```
<FORM ACTION="show_request.asp" METHOD="POST">
  I enjoy:
  <INPUT TYPE="CHECKBOX" NAME="Reading" CHECKED> Reading  
  <INPUT TYPE="CHECKBOX" NAME="Eating"> Eating  
  <INPUT TYPE="CHECKBOX" NAME="Sleeping"> Sleeping
  <INPUT TYPE="SUBMIT" VALUE="Send">
</FORM>
```

In this case, if just the first and third check boxes are checked (ticked) when the form is submitted, we get the following values when we iterate through the `Form` collection:

```
Reading = on
Sleeping = on
```

However, if we provide a `VALUE` for a check box we get this value sent to the server in place of the string `on`. For example, take this form:

```
<FORM ACTION="show_request.asp" METHOD="POST">
  I enjoy:
  <INPUT TYPE="CHECKBOX" VALUE="Hobby025" NAME="Hobby" CHECKED> Swimming  
  <INPUT TYPE="CHECKBOX" VALUE="Hobby003" NAME="Hobby" CHECKED> Reading  
  <INPUT TYPE="CHECKBOX" VALUE="Hobby068" NAME="Hobby"> Eating  
  <INPUT TYPE="CHECKBOX" VALUE="Hobby010" NAME="Hobby"> Sleeping
  <INPUT TYPE="SUBMIT" VALUE="Send">
</FORM>
```

When submitted with all except the third check box ticked, produces the following in the `Request.Form` collection:

```
Hobby = Hobby025, Hobby003, Hobby010
```

If we use the more complex version of the collection iteration code we described earlier (which displays each sub-key separately) we get this result:

```
Hobby:
Subkey 1 value = Hobby025
Subkey 2 value = Hobby003
Subkey 3 value = Hobby010
```

Notice that in both cases, an un-ticked check box does not return any value at all. There is no spurious comma in the first result, and no empty value in the second one. This is unlike the results that we obtained from the equivalent test using text boxes, where each text box returned a value – even if left blank. It is the browser that produces this behavior, and you need to be aware of it when you come to access the collections in your ASP code.

One awkward side effect of this is that, when we use check boxes, the index of the value bears no relation to the position of the controls in the original HTML. The fourth check box in our example above is shown as sub-key number three, because the third control was not checked when the form was submitted.

HTML List Controls

The HTML <SELECT> element, used to create standard and drop-down list boxes, presents its values in an interesting mixture of ways. The following form creates a list box containing five values which a user can select. Because we've included the MULTIPLE attribute, they can select more than one item by holding down the *Shift* or *Ctrl* keys while clicking:

```
<FORM ACTION="show_request.asp" METHOD="POST">
  <SELECT NAME="Hobby" SIZE="5" MULTIPLE>
    <OPTION VALUE="Hobby001">Programming
    <OPTION VALUE="Hobby025">Swimming
    <OPTION VALUE="Hobby003">Reading
    <OPTION VALUE="Hobby068">Eating
    <OPTION VALUE="Hobby010">Sleeping
  </SELECT><P>
  <INPUT TYPE="SUBMIT" VALUE="Send">
</FORM>
```

This is what the page looks like, showing three items selected:

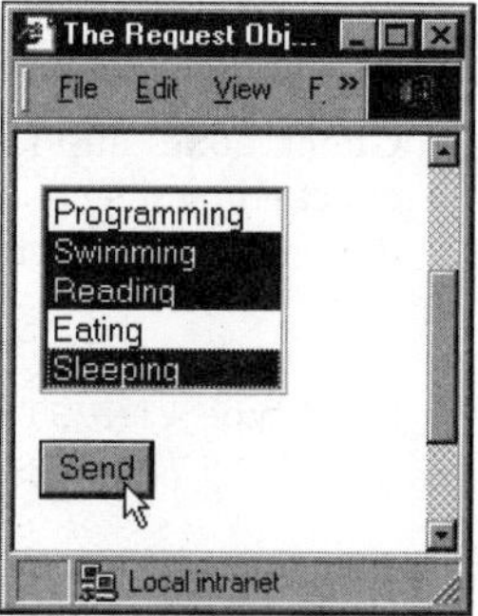

This particular case returns a single entry in the Form collection for this control. It consists of the selected values (from the VALUE attributes of the individual <OPTION> elements), delimited with commas:

```
Hobby = Hobby025, Hobby003, Hobby010
```

If we use our more complex version of the collection iteration code (which displays each sub-key separately) we get this:

```
Hobby:
Subkey 1 value = Hobby025
Subkey 2 value = Hobby003
Subkey 3 value = Hobby010
```

This follows the same conventions as the example with multiple check boxes with the same name. In fact, you can think of a SELECT list as being much like a list of check boxes where you select (rather than check) the appropriate ones.

However, list boxes also have implied values. If we omit the VALUE attributes from the <OPTION> elements, we get the text of the selected options returned instead. The Request.Form collection will contain an entry like this:

```
Hobby = Swimming, Reading, Sleeping
```

And, likewise, the more complex version of the collection iteration code will return:

```
Hobby:
Subkey 1 value = Swimming
Subkey 2 value = Reading
Subkey 3 value = Sleeping
```

Of course, if only a single item is selected, we get a result containing just that item: either `Hobby = Hobby025` if we have provided a `VALUE` attribute for the selected `<OPTION>` element, or `Hobby = Swimming` if not.

> *This behavior allows us to either get the displayed text by default (i.e. with no `VALUE`) or some alternative. The latter is very useful in cases where we want to display one thing (say, a descriptive string) and transmit something completely different (say, a short code that corresponds to the descriptive string).*

HTML Submit and Image Controls

Check boxes and radio buttons are examples of **Boolean** controls, in that they just return `on` if checked or selected. Unlike text boxes and most other HTML controls, the browser doesn't include the value of the control if it isn't checked or selected.

There is one other type of Boolean control that is used regularly, namely HTML buttons. These can be of type `<INPUT TYPE="SUBMIT">`, `<INPUT TYPE="RESET">`, `<INPUT TYPE="IMAGE">`, `<INPUT TYPE="BUTTON">`, and `<BUTTON>..</BUTTON>`.

The `BUTTON`-type controls never return a value, as they have no direct effect on a form. Even if you use one to call the `submit` method of a form, the browser will not include a value for any `BUTTON`-type controls in the request. Likewise, the value of an `<INPUT TYPE="RESET">` button is never sent to the server.

However, input button controls of type `SUBMIT` and `IMAGE` actually do submit the form to the server, and their `VALUE` attribute is included with the values of other controls on the form, provided we include a `NAME` attribute in the HTML definition. For example, this form might be part of a Wizard-style Web application, allowing the user to step through each page or cancel the process part way through:

```
<FORM ACTION="show_request.asp" METHOD="POST">
  <INPUT TYPE="SUBMIT" NAME="btnSubmit" VALUE="Next">
  <INPUT TYPE="SUBMIT" NAME="btnSubmit" VALUE="Previous">
  <INPUT TYPE="SUBMIT" NAME="btnSubmit" VALUE="Cancel">
</FORM>
```

We can include more than one `SUBMIT` button on a form, and in this case we should give each one a unique `VALUE` attribute, as shown above. When this form is submitted, our iteration through the values in the `Request.Form` collection will produce one value, depending on which button was used to submit the form. If the user clicks the Previous button, we'll get just:

```
btnSubmit = Previous
```

Therefore, we can query the `Request.Form` collection to decide which page to display next, for example:

```
Select Case Request.Form("btnSubmit")

  Case "Next"
    Response.Redirect "page_3.asp"

  Case "Previous"
    Response.Redirect "page_1.asp"

  Case "Cancel"
    Response.Redirect "main_menu.asp"

End Select
```

Likewise, we can use different `NAME` attributes for each button if we wish, and select on the name of the control whose value is included in the `Form` collection. This is useful when using buttons that don't have an integral caption, but instead a use a text caption that's placed next to them:

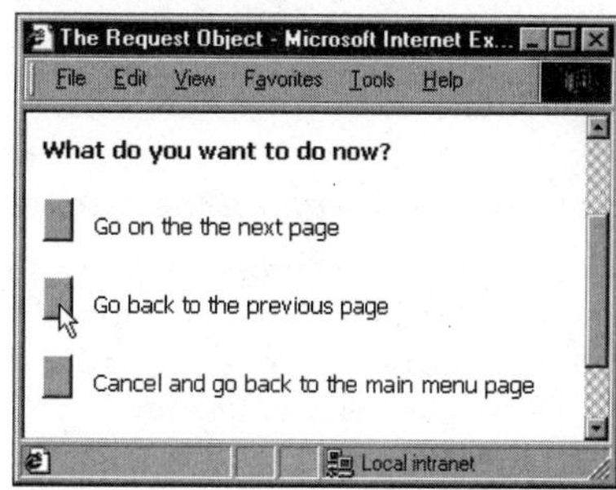

This screenshot is produced by the following code:

```
<FORM ACTION="show_request.asp" METHOD="POST">

  <B>What do you want to do now?</B><P>

  <INPUT TYPE="SUBMIT" NAME="btnNext" VALUE="   ">
  Go on the the next page<P>

  <INPUT TYPE="SUBMIT" NAME="btnPrevious" VALUE="   ">
  Go back to the previous page<P>

  <INPUT TYPE="SUBMIT" NAME="btnCancel" VALUE="   ">
  Cancel and go back to the main menu page<P>

</FORM>
```

In the ASP page that receives this form data, we can check which button name provided a value to see which was clicked:

```
If Len(Request.Form("btnNext"))     Then Response.Redirect "page_3.asp"
If Len(Request.Form("btnPrevious")) Then Response.Redirect "page_1.asp"
If Len(Request.Form("btnCancel"))   Then Response.Redirect "main_menu.asp"
```

This works because querying an ASP collection on a key that doesn't exist returns an empty string. In other words, if the second (previous page) button was clicked, the value of `Request.Form("btnNext")` is an empty string, so the length will be zero rather than producing an error. And when the second button is clicked, the value of this item in the `Form` collection, `Request.Form("btnPrevious")`, will be `"   "` and the length will be greater than zero.

Using the Request Collections Efficiently

Accessing an ASP collection to retrieve values is an expensive process in terms of computing resources, because the operation involves a search through the relevant collection. This is far slower than accessing a normal local variable. Therefore, if you intend to refer to a value from a collection more than once in your page, you should consider storing it in a local variable. For example:

```
strTitle = Request.Form("Title")
strFirstName = Request.Form("FirstName")
strLastName = Request.Form("LastName")

If Len(strTitle) Then strTitle = strTitle & " "

If strFirstName = "" Then
  strFullName = strTitle & " " & strLastName
ElseIf Len(strFirstName) = 1 Then
  strFullName = strTitle & strFirstName & ". " & strLastName
Else
  strFullName = strTitle & strFirstName & " " & strLastName
End If
```

Searching Through All the Request Collections

In some cases, you may know the key name of a value that will arrive in the Request collections, but not exactly which collection it will arrive in. For example, if you have several pages (or different sections of a page) that send a value to the same ASP script, it might appear in either the `Form` or the `QueryString` collection.

> *We'll be looking at the difference between the* `Form` *and* `QueryString` *collections in detail later on in this chapter.*

To see why a value might appear in different collections, consider the case where you use an `<A>` hyperlink element to request a page. In this case, the only way to add a value to the request (without some awkward client-side scripting) is to append it to the URL. However, the same value might also appear in a `<FORM>` on another page, or in a different part of the same page:

```
...
<FORM ACTION="process_page.asp" METHOD="POST">
  <INPUT TYPE="SUBMIT" NAME="page" VALUE="Next">
  <INPUT TYPE="SUBMIT" NAME="page" VALUE="Previous">
  <INPUT TYPE="SUBMIT" NAME="page" VALUE="Help">
</FORM>
...
...
For help go to the <A HREF="process_page.asp?page=Help">Help Page</A>
...
```

In this case, clicking the Help button on the form will send the name/value pair "`page=Help`" in the `Request.Form` collection. However, clicking the `<A>` hyperlink will also send the name/value pair "`page=Help`", but this time in the `QueryString` collection. To access the value here, we use a special feature of the ASP Request object:

```
strPage = Request("page")
```

This searches through all the collections in the order `QueryString`, `Form`, `Cookies`, `ClientCertificate`, `ServerVariables`, until it finds the first matching value name. However, this technique is far less efficient than accessing the appropriate collection directly, and somewhat unsafe unless you can be absolutely sure that the value cannot appear in another collection.

For example, we may wish to collect the name of the Web server that satisfies the client request using the `Request.ServerVariables` collection entry for "`SERVER_NAME`", which appears in every request. However, if any of the other collections contain a value named "`server_name`" (remember that key names are not case-sensitive), we'll get that value instead when using `Request("server_name")`. We can guard against this difficult to trace error by using the full syntax of `Request.ServerVariables("server_name")`.

In short, use the 'search all collections' technique with extreme caution, and only when no other technique will provide the result you need.

Accessing the Other Collections

In this section of the chapter, we've been concentrating on the `Form` collection. This is probably the one that you'll use the most. However, all these techniques apply equally well to all the other collections. That includes those provided by the Request object (i.e. `Form`, `QueryString`, `Cookies`, `ServerVariables` and `ClientCertificate`), and the `Cookies` collection provided by the Response object (and to the collections provided by other objects that we'll meet in the next couple of chapters).

We'll see how values get into the `QueryString` collection shortly, and the advantages and disadvantages that this poses. However, in the meantime, the two `Cookies` collections have an extra feature designed to make working with cookies easier. We'll look at this topic next.

Accessing and Updating the Cookies Collections

Cookies are rather more complex animals than the values that we find in the other ASP collections such as `Form` and `ServerVariables`. Cookies are small chunks of text that are stored on the client's system by their browser, and are sent to the server with every request for a page from the domain to which they apply.

ASP makes using cookies easy. We can retrieve the values of all the cookies sent with a request from the Request object's `Cookies` collection, and create or modify cookies to send back to the user with the Response object's `Cookies` collection.

Cookies contain information that can be structured in two ways. **Single value** cookies expose their values to our code through a normal ASP-like collection. However, each member of the collection can also itself be a collection. Cookies that contain this type of information are usually called **multiple-value** cookies.

Creating a single value cookie is as easy as this:

```
Response.Cookies("item-name") = "item-value"
```

To create a cookie containing multiple values, we use:

```
Response.Cookies("item-name")("sub-item-name") = "sub-item-value"
```

And to set the domain and path to which a cookie applies, and it's expiry date, we use:

```
Response.Cookies("item-name").domain = "domain-url"
Response.Cookies("item-name").path = "virtual-path"
Response.Cookies("item-name").expires = #date#
```

Normally, the client only sends cookies to the server with requests for pages that are in the same directory as the one that created the cookie. By setting the `path` property of a cookie, we can specify where on our site that cookie is valid, and will be sent with requests for pages. You need to set the `path` to "/" to have the cookie sent with page requests for the entire site.

If the Expires property is not set, the cookie will be destroyed when the user closes the current browser instance.

Note that we have to create cookies before we send any other output to the browser, because they are part of the HTTP headers for the page.

> **In ASP 3.0 buffering is enabled by default, and so no output is sent until we specifically do this with `Response.Flush` or the end of the page is reached. This means that code to create cookies can come anywhere in the page, as long as it's executed before any other output is flushed to the client.**

To read the values of existing cookies, we use the `Request.Cookies` collection. We can access each one individually using the same syntax as we did to create them:

```
strSingleValue = Request.Cookies("item-name")
strSubItemValue = Request.Cookies("item-name")("sub-item-name")
```

Note that the `Request.Cookies` collection (like all other Request collections) is **read-only**. The `Response.Cookies` collection is **write only** – we can in fact access a list of the cookie names from this collection, but not their values.

Iterating Through the Cookies Collections

To make it easier to work with the `Cookies` collections, there's an extra property named `HasKeys`. This returns `True` if the cookie we're accessing is itself a collection, i.e. it is a multiple-value cookie. Using the `HasKeys` property, we can iterate through the complete `Request.Cookies` collection to obtain a list of all the cookies and their values:

```
For Each objItem In Request.Cookies

  If Request.Cookies(objItem).HasKeys Then
    'Use another For Each to iterate all subkeys
    For Each objItemKey in Request.Cookies(objItem)
      Response.Write objItem & "(" & objItemKey & ") = " _
                     & Request.Cookies(objItem)(objItemKey) & "<BR>"
    Next

  Else
    'Print out the cookie string as normal
    Response.Write objItem & " = " & Request.Cookies(objItem) & "<BR>"

  End If

Next
```

This is similar to the convoluted code we used to extract multiple values from the `Request.Form` *collection earlier on, but here we use the* `HasKeys` *property to see if each item is a collection, whereas in the* `Form` *example we had to query the* `Request.Form(item_name).Count` *property. This is because the* ***members*** *of the* `Form` *collection (and all other collections except* `Cookies`*) are never true collections. ASP just does some 'behind the scenes' magic to retrieve the values of a multiple-item collection entry individually.*

The Difference Between Forms and QueryStrings

Having examined in some depth the techniques for accessing the various ASP collections, we need to solve another issue. What is the difference between the `Form` and `QueryString` collections? If you're used to using ASP, you'll no doubt already be aware of the differences, but it's worth reiterating them with reference to the way HTTP works.

There are just two common methods for requesting a page or resource from a Web server over HTTP. You can `GET` the resource directly, or you can `POST` values to a resource. The `GET` method is the default, as you can see if you look at this line taken from the example HTTP request we looked at early in this chapter:

```
7/8/99 10:27:16 Sent  GET /Store/Download.asp HTTP/1.1
```

If we append one or more name/value pair to the URL of the page we're requesting, they become the **query string** for the request, and are exposed to our ASP page in the `QueryString` collection. Clicking on a hyperlink in a Web page, email message or other document, typing an address into the Address bar of a browser and hitting *Return*, or clicking one of the Links or Favorites buttons in the browser all use the `GET` method.

> **Therefore, the only way to send values to ASP from any of these actions is through the `QueryString` collection, by appending them to the URL.**

The values appear in the `Request.QueryString` collection, and are accessed, in the same way as the `Form` collection examples we looked at earlier. The URL and query string combination:

```
http://mysite.com/process_page.asp?FirstName=Priscilla&LastName=Descartes
```

Provides values in the `QueryString` collection that we can access as:

```
strFirstName = Request.QueryString("FirstName") 'Returns "Priscilla"
strLastName = Request.QueryString("LastName")   'Returns "Descartes"
strRaw = Request.QueryString 'Returns "FirstName=Priscilla&LastName=Descartes"
```

The GET and POST Methods of a FORM

When we use a `<FORM>` section on a page, we can set a value for the HTML `METHOD` attribute of the opening `FORM` tag to either `"GET"` or `"POST"`. The default if omitted is `"GET"`. No doubt you can see where we're going here. If we use `"GET"` or omit the attribute, the browser bundles up the values in all the controls on the form into a query string, and appends it to the URL of the page being requested.

When this request arrives at our Web server, it is exposed through the ASP `Request.QueryString` collection. However, if we set the `METHOD` attribute to `"POST"` instead, the browser wraps the values up within the HTTP headers it sends to the server, and they are exposed to ASP via the `Request.Form` collection.

In general, you should use the `POST` method in all your HTML forms. There are limits imposed by the browser and server on the length of a URL string, so appending a long query string can cause an overflow and some of the values may be truncated. Also, the query string appears in the Address bar of the browser, and in all saved links and favorites. This is not only ugly, but it exposes values that you might not want to be made quite this visible in the HTTP request as it passes over the Web, or as it appears in your and other en-route server's log files. Values within the HTTP request headers are far less visible, and do not appear in log files.

One minor point to be aware of is that with the `POST` method, the values in a form aren't persisted. When the user reloads a `<FORM>`, the values are blank and have to be re-entered. However, when appended to a URL that is stored as a link or favorite, they *are* persisted, and so they will appear in all requests for that URL/query string combination. This might be an advantage or a disadvantage, depending on your application (some browsers can automatically persist values in a form on the client to some extent).

One other point is that the URL/query string combination cannot contain any ***spaces*** *or other* ***illegal characters****, otherwise Navigator and some other browsers will complain. Illegal characters are those that are used to delimit parts of the URL and query string, for example* '/', ':', '?' *and* '&'. *(Internet Explorer automatically converts spaces to the correct format, a plus sign* '+', *but can't cope with other illegal characters). The ASP Server object provides the* `URLEncode` *method for handling this conversion, which we'll examine in more detail in Chapter 4.*

Viewing the Contents of Requests and Responses

We've purposely stuck to theory so far, with no practical examples, because the topics we've been discussing are in most cases intimately entwined. However we've provided a series of sample pages for this chapter that demonstrate most of the features of the Request and Response objects. With the theory we've covered, you'll be able to see how these pages work, and modify and experiment with them.

The code samples for this and all other chapters are available for download from the Wrox Press Web site.

You must first install the samples on your Web server, in a subdirectory within the `WWWRoot` directory. Then access the `Chapter02` subdirectory of the samples with your browser, using:

```
http://your_server_name_or_IP/subdirectory_name/Chapter02/Default.asp
```

where `your_server_name_or_IP/subdirectory_name` *is the local path to where you installed the download.*

Viewing the Request Object Members

This provides a menu containing options to examine the Request and Response objects. Select the **Request object** first:

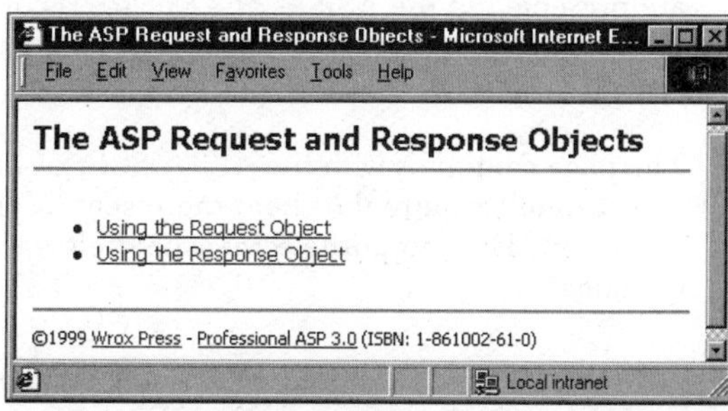

This displays a simple HTML form containing some preset values – you can edit these as you wish. Then click the **Submit** button:

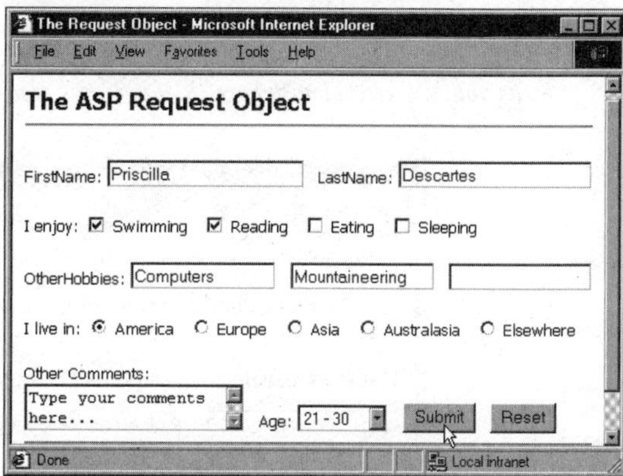

This opens a page that displays the entire contents of the request from the collections and the `TotalBytes` property of the Request object. The first screenshot here shows the `Form`, `QueryString` and `Cookies` collections:

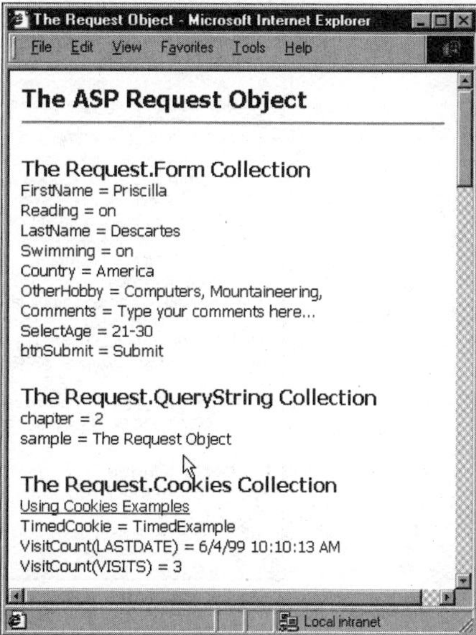

Note that you may well have different values in your page for the `Cookies` collection, and the other collections as well if you edited the values in the HTML controls on the form page:

You can see from the **Form Collection** section how the values from the HTML controls on the form are presented in the ASP `Request.Form` collection. You might like to examine and experiment with the original `<FORM>` page, named `request_form.asp`, to see the HTML that creates the form and how this relates to the values.

The page continues with the `ClientCertificate` collection, which is empty here because our server didn't require the client to present a certificate. Under that is the `ServerVariables` collection. The composite screenshot below shows just a few of the useful values that this collection contains.

> *You'll find a list of all the* `ServerVariables` *collection members, with a description of the values, in the Appendices of this book. However, you will recognize many of them from our previous discussion of the HTTP headers that are sent from the client when requesting a page. Our Web server also adds several values of its own to the collection when the request is received – as you can see below where the page was created by IIS 5.0 running on a server named* **wroxbox***:*

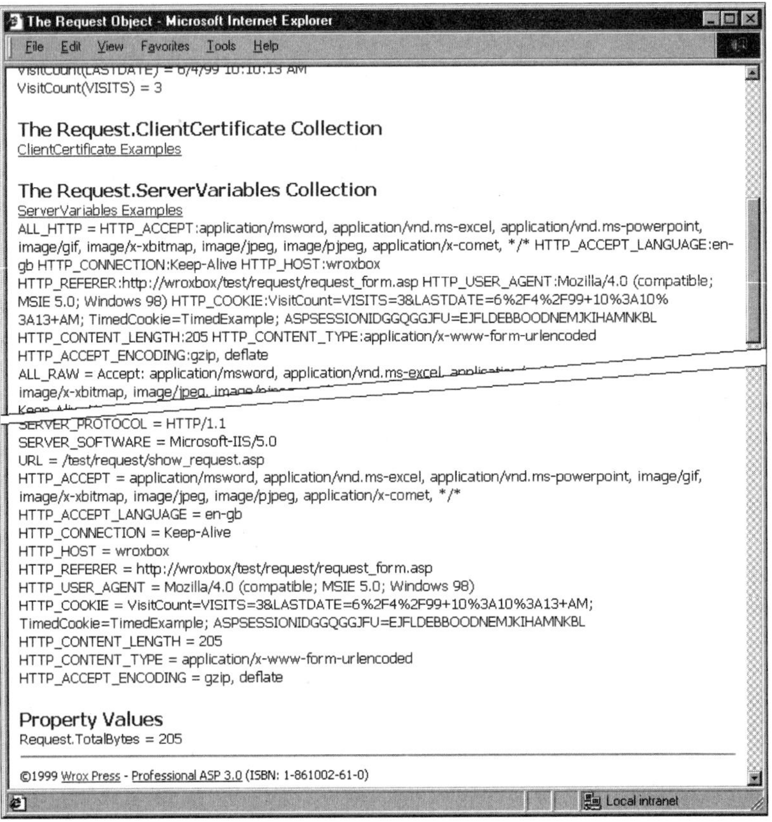

How This Page Works

To create this page, we used exactly the same code as we saw earlier in the chapter, in the discussion of the `Form` collection and how we access its values. For example, we iterate through all the collections (except `Request.Cookies`) using:

```
For Each objItem In Request.collection_name

  Response.Write objItem & " = " & Request.collection_name(objItem) & "<BR>"

Next
```

To iterate through the `Cookies` collection we use:

```
For Each objItem In Request.Cookies

  If Request.Cookies(objItem).HasKeys Then
    'Use another For...Each to iterate all keys of dictionary
    For Each objItemKey in Request.Cookies(objItem)
      Response.Write objItem & "(" & objItemKey & ") = " _
                       & Request.Cookies(objItem)(objItemKey) & "<BR>"
    Next

  Else
    'Print out the cookie string as normal
    Response.Write objItem & " = " & Request.Cookies(objItem) & "<BR>"

  End If

Next
```

To get the `TotalBytes` property, we simply use:

```
Request.TotalBytes = <% = Request.TotalBytes %><P>
```

You'll notice that there are values present in two collections that don't come directly from the HTML controls on the form. The `QueryString` collection contains two values named chapter and sample:

The Request.QueryString Collection
chapter = 2
sample = The Request Object

To create these two values in the request, we appended a string to the URL of the `ACTION` attribute of the form. This is quite acceptable, and works just like it would if appended to the `HREF` attribute of an `<A>` element. The query string values appear in the `QueryString` collection, and the `POST`ed form control values appear in the `Form` collection:

```
<FORM ACTION="show_request.asp?chapter=2&sample=The+Request+Object" METHOD="POST">
```

To prevent non-IE browsers from raising an error, we had to replace the spaces in the query string with a plus sign '+'. You'll see more about this when we look at the `URLEncode` method of the Server object in a Chapter 4.

Creating Cookies Client-side

To make sure that at least some values appear in the Request.Cookies collection, we added some *client-side* script code to the original <FORM> page, request_form.asp. This creates the multi-value cookie named VisitCount. The other cookie is one that was created by another page at some time, and already existed on our browser. You may well see other different ones:

The Request.Cookies Collection
Using Cookies Examples
TimedCookie = TimedExample
VisitCount(LASTDATE) = 6/4/99 10:10:13 AM
VisitCount(VISITS) = 3

This is the client-side code, which simply sets the cookie property of the document object as the form page is loading:

```
<SCRIPT LANGUAGE="JavaScript">
<!--
document.cookie = 'VisitCount=VISITS=3&LASTDATE=6%2F4%2F99+10%3A10%3A13+AM';
//-->
</SCRIPT>
```

Again, we had to encode the content so that it would be properly transmitted to the server—the same rules apply as with query strings appended to a URL. You'll see more details when we look at the URLEncode *method of the* Server *object in a Chapter 4.*

Viewing the Response Object Members

Go back to the original Default.asp page in the Chapter02 samples directory, and this time select the Response Object link. The page that appears shows the contents of the Response object collection and properties, and provides links to all of the Response object's methods.

Here it is, in Netscape Communicator 4.61 for a change (and to prove that we're using pure server-side and cross-platform compatible techniques). Note that because the Cookies collection is write only for the Response object, we can only display the names of the cookies and not the values. Again, you may get no cookies, or different cookies from us, when you view the page:

The various Response properties indicate information that will be used to create the HTTP headers that are sent to the client with the rest of the page (the HTML and text content). Several of these, and all of the Response object's methods, are hyperlinks that allow you to open another page, which demonstrates these in use. We'll come back to these pages in a while.

How This Page Works

The property values in the page are created simply by reading the corresponding property, and inserting it into the page. For those that are hyperlinks, we enclose them in an <A> element:

```
<A HREF="headers/expiretest_form.asp">Response.CacheControl</A>
   = <% = Response.CacheControl %><BR>
```

The links to each method are just plain <A> hyperlink elements. The only complicated part of the page is the `Response.Cookies` collection. Normally we would only access cookies to read the values in the `Request.Cookies` collection. When accessing the `Response.Cookies` collection, we have to complete all references to it before we send any output back to the client. So, right at the top of the page, we iterate through the collection to create the HTML for the page in a local string variable:

```
strCookies = ""
'We can only read the key names and not the values because
'the Response.Cookies collection is 'write only'
For Each objItem In Response.Cookies

  If Response.Cookies(objItem).HasKeys Then
    'Use another For Each to iterate all subkeys
    For Each objItemKey in Response.Cookies(objItem)
      strCookies = strCookies & objItem & "(" & objItemKey & ")<BR>"
    Next

  Else
    'print out the cookie string as normal
    strCookies = strCookies & objItem & "<BR>"
  End If

Next
```

Then we insert the result at the appropriate point in the page:

```
<P><DIV CLASS="subhead">The Response.Cookies Collection</DIV>
<I><A HREF="cookies/setcookies.asp">Response.Cookies</A>
is a write-only collection so the values cannot be displayed</I><BR>
<% = strCookies %>
```

Using Cookies in ASP

Several of the collections, properties and methods displayed in the pages we've just been looking at above have hyperlinks to other pages that demonstrate individual features of the Request and Response objects in more detail. We'll work through these in the remainder of the chapter, as we examine the various techniques that these collections, methods and properties make available to our ASP code.

We saw how to create and read cookies using the `Request.Cookies` and `Response.Cookies` collections earlier in this chapter. The sample page that opens when you click the Cookies link in either of the two pages shown above contains some ASP code that sets the values of three cookies, and displays in the page the code that it executed:

When we click the link to the Show Cookies page, the contents of the cookies are displayed. We so this by iterating through the `Request.Cookies` collection, in exactly the same way as we did in the previous pages:

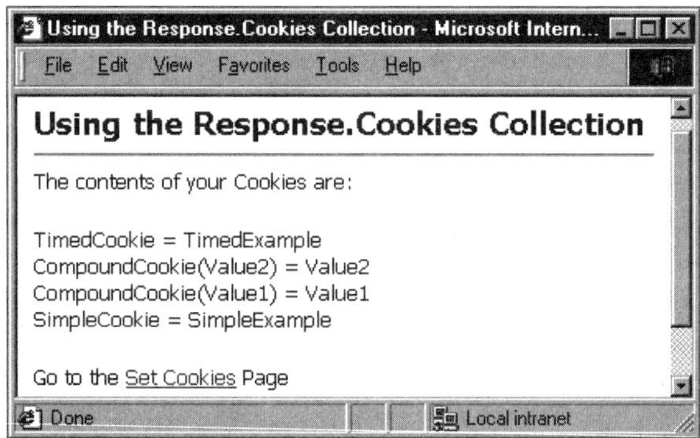

This screenshot shows the result of running the code that set the cookie values you saw previously – you may also see other cookies that are already stored on your system. However, if you now close the browser down and reopen it, then run just the page that displays the cookies, all but the TimedCookie have disappeared. That's because only this one has an expiry date set – the others are automatically removed when the browser is closed.

Storing a User's Details in Cookies

This means that we can use cookies to store both values that we want to be discarded when the browser is closed (such as users' logon details) and values that we want to persist between a user's visits to our site. In each case, the values in the cookies are made available to ASP with each page request from that user's browser.

However, remember that cookies are only sent to the server with requests for pages that are within the same virtual path as that set in the cookie, i.e. the value of `path` and any pages within (or below) this virtual path. The default, if a value for `path` is not specifically set in the cookie, is the virtual path of the page where the cookie was created. To have a cookie sent to all pages in a site, we just use `Path = "/"`.

Here's an example of storing a user's logon details from a custom Login page in a cookie. Because we haven't supplied an `Expires` value, the cookie will only exist until they next close their browser:

```
...
Response.Cookies("User")("UID") = "<% = Request("UserName") %>"
Response.Cookies("User")("PWD") = "<% = Request("Password") %>"
Response.Cookies("User").Path = "/adminstuff" 'Only applies to admin pages
...
```

Now, in each page that the user requests from the `adminstuff` directory or its sub-directories, we can look for this cookie. If it's not there, we can redirect the user to our logon page:

```
...
If (Request.Cookies("User")("UID") <> "alexhomer") _
    Or (Request.Cookies("User")("PWD") <> "secret") Then

  Response.Redirect "login.asp?UserName=" & Request.Cookies("User")("UID")

End If
...
```

Because we placed the user name from the cookie in the query string of the `Response.Redirect` URL, we can use it in the `login.asp` page if they make an error in the password and we wish to save them retyping the user name:

```
<FORM ACTION="check_user.asp" METHOD="POST">
  <INPUT TYPE="TEXT" NAME="UserName"
         VALUE="<% = Request.QueryString("UserName")%>"><P>
  <INPUT TYPE="TEXT" NAME="Password"><P>
  <INPUT TYPE="SUBMIT" VALUE="Login">
</FORM>
```

Modifying Existing Cookies

One of the 'gotchas' with using ASP to modify cookies that already exist is that you can't change just one value of a multiple-value cookie. When you update a cookie in the `Response.Cookies` collection, any existing values are lost. We might create a cookie using:

```
Response.Cookies("VisitCount")("StartDate") = dtmStart
Response.Cookies("VisitCount")("LastDate") = Now
Response.Cookies("VisitCount")("Visits") = CStr(intVisits)
Response.Cookies("VisitCount").Path = "/"   'Apply to entire site
Response.Cookies("VisitCount").Expires = DateAdd("m", 3, Now)
```

If we want to update the `Visits` and `LastDate` values, we have to collect any values that are not going to change and rewrite the entire cookie:

```
datStart = Request.Cookies("VisitCount")("StartDate")
intVisits = Request.Cookies("VisitCount")("Visits")
Response.Cookies("VisitCount")("StartDate") = dtmStart
Response.Cookies("VisitCount")("LastDate") = Now
Response.Cookies("VisitCount")("Visits") = CStr(intVisits)
Response.Cookies("VisitCount").Path = "/"
Response.Cookies("VisitCount").Expires = DateAdd("m", 3, Now + 1)
```

And, as with almost all of the other Response methods and properties, we have to do it *before* we write any content (i.e. the opening `<HTML>` tag or any text or other HTML) to the response.

Using the ServerVariables Collection

One of the collections we looked at briefly when we viewed the contents of the Request object was the `ServerVariables` collection. This contains a combination of values that represent the HTTP headers sent from the client to our server with the page request, and values provided by the Web server itself when the request is received. To show some of the ways of using values from the `ServerVariables` collection, click the ServerVariables Examples link in the Request object page (`show_request.asp`) to open another menu page:

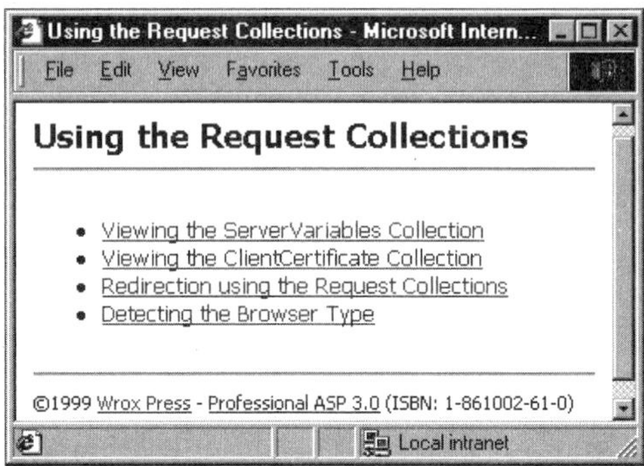

The first option on this menu displays a subset of the more useful values from the `ServerVariables` collection:

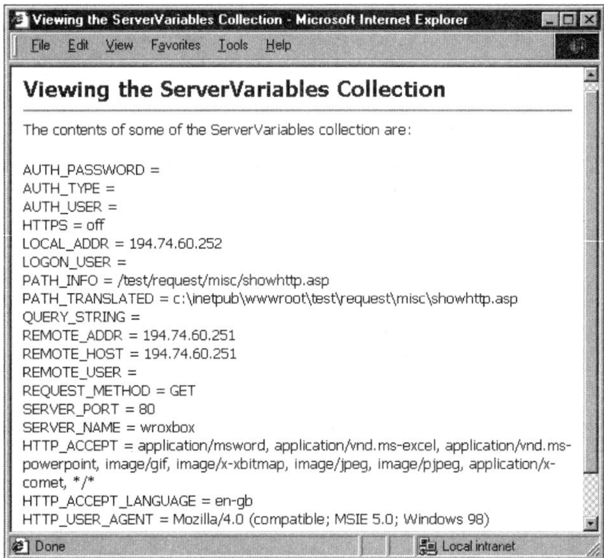

Self-Referencing Pages

The values returned in the `ServerVariables` collection include details of our Web server and path information of the current page. All these are useful when we want to create pages that work no matter where they are located. For example, to create a **self-referencing page**, where the page calls itself again to carry out another task, we could use:

```
<FORM ACTION="<% = Request.ServerVariables("PATH_INFO") %>" METHOD="POST">
```

The same effect is obtained with the HTTP `"SCRIPT_NAME"` value:

```
<FORM ACTION="<% = Request.ServerVariables("SCRIPT_NAME") %>" METHOD="POST">
```

To open a different page with an <A> element, we could use:

```
...
<%
strFullPath = Request.ServerVariables("PATH_INFO")
'Strip off the file name
strPathOnly = Left(strFullPath, InStrRev(strFullPath, "/"))
strNextPage = strPathOnly & "pages/next_page.asp"
%>
...
<A HREF="<% = strNextPage %>">Next Page</A>
...
```

Both these examples will work, even if the name or location of the original page is changed, because it uses the path information of the current page (the second one will fail if the name of the separate target page is changed, of course).

Alternatively, if we want to automatically build URLs for submission to a search engine, for example, we can collect several of the `ServerVariables` values:

```
strFullURL = "http://" & Request.ServerVariables("LOCAL_ADDR") _
             & ":" & Request.ServerVariables("SERVER_PORT") _
             & Request.ServerVariables("PATH_INFO")
```

This creates the complete URL including the port number (in case this is not the standard value of 80). For example, the result could be
`http://194.74.60.254:1768/thispath/thispage.asp`.

Detecting the Browser Version

Another useful value in the `ServerVariables` collection is the user agent string for our visitor's browser. In the Detecting the Browser Type page (`browsertype.asp`), we are using the `"HTTP_USER_AGENT"` value from the `ServerVariables` collection to retrieve the user agent string, and some script to parse this and look for a manufacturer name and browser version:

```
<%
strUA = Request.ServerVariables("HTTP_USER_AGENT")
Response.Write "The User Agent string is <B>" & strUA & "</B><P>"

If InStr(strUA, "MSIE") Then

  Response.Write "To upgrade your browser go to " _
                 & "<A HREF=" & Chr(34) & "http://www.microsoft.com/ie/" _
                 & Chr(34) & ">http://www.microsoft.com/ie/</A></P>"
  intVersion = CInt(Mid(strUA, InStr(strUA, "MSIE") + 5, 1))

  If intVersion >= 4 Then
    Response.Write "You can use Microsoft Dynamic HTML"
  End If

Else

  If InStr(strUA, "Mozilla") Then

    If InStr(strUA, "compatible;") = 0 Then

      Response.Write "Your browser is probably Navigator. You can " _
                     & "download the latest version of Navigator from " _
                     & "<A HREF=" & Chr(34) & "http://home.netscape.com/download/" _
                     & Chr(34) & ">http://home.netscape.com/download/</A></P>"
      intVersion = CInt(Mid(strUA, InStr(strUA, "/") + 1, 1))
```

```
        If intVersion >= 4 Then
          Response.Write "You can probably use Netscape Dynamic HTML"
        End If

      Else

        strVersion = Mid(strUA, InStr(strUA, "compatible;") + 12)
        strProduct = Left(strVersion, InStr(strVersion, " "))
        Response.Write "Your browser is Navigator-compatible. You can " _
                   & "search for the manufacturer using a search engine, such as " _
                   & "<A HREF=" & Chr(34) _
                   & "http://www.altavista.digital.com/cgi-bin/query?q=" _
                   & strProduct _
                   & Chr(34) & ">http://www.altavista.com/</A></P>"

      End If

    End If

  End If
  %>
```

Our results with Internet Explorer 5.0 and Navigator 4.61 are shown below. For other makes of browser, you get a link to automatically start a search at the AltaVista Web site for the manufacturer name:

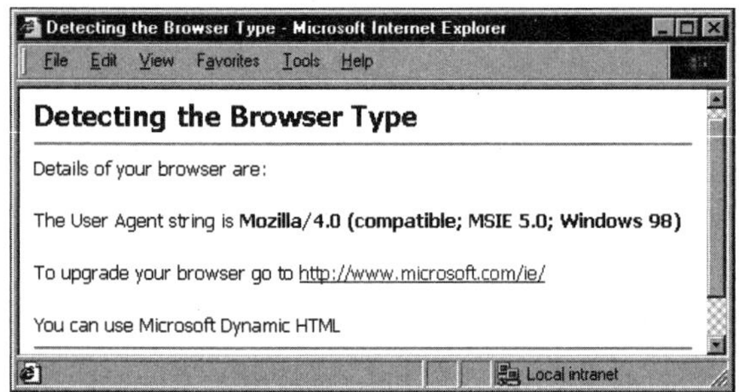

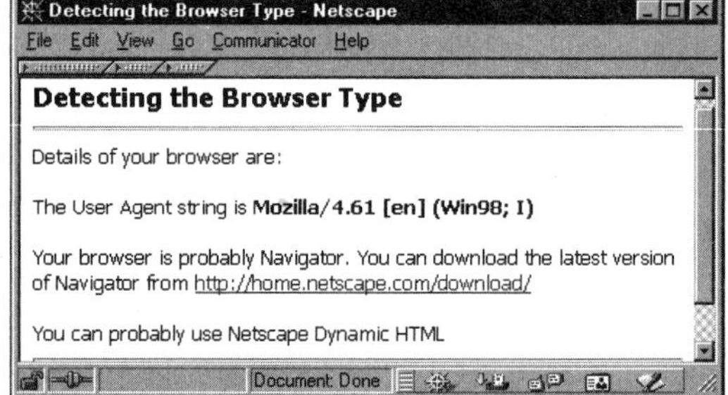

Note that Netscape does not provide a manufacturer name in the user agent string, so you can never be absolutely sure that a browser actually is *Navigator.*

Detecting the Browser Language

One other useful `ServerVariables` value is "`HTTP_ACCEPT_LANGUAGE`". This contains a language code, which was selected when the browser was installed or is hard-coded into the user's locale-specific version. Examples of language codes are `en-us` (English, United States), `de-at` (German, Austrian) and `es-pe` (Spanish, Peru).

A language code can also be generic and omit the dialect identifier: for example the bulk of our Web site visitors at Wrox have just `en` (English) as the language code.

So, we can detect the language code and load an appropriate locale-specific, language-specific or geographically specific version of our pages automatically.

```
strLocale = LCase(Left(Request.ServerVariables("HTTP_ACCEPT_LANGUAGE"), 2))

Select Case strLocale
   Case "en": Response.Redirect "http://uk_site.co.uk/"
   Case "de": Response.Redirect "http://de_site.co.de/"
   Case "fr": Response.Redirect "http://fr_site.co.fr/"
   '... etc
   Case Else: Response.Redirect "http://us_site1.com/"
End Select
```

Or for dialect-specific redirection:

```
strLocale = LCase(Request.ServerVariables("HTTP_ACCEPT_LANGUAGE"))

Select Case strLocale

   Case "en-gb": Response.Redirect "http://uk_site.co.uk/"
   Case "en-us": Response.Redirect "http://us_site.com/"
   Case "es-pe": Response.Redirect "http://es_site2.co.pe/"
   '... etc
   Case Else: Response.Redirect "http://us_site1.com/"

End Select
```

Other Useful ServerVariables Values

We can access and use any of the members of the `ServerVariables` collection to control the way that our ASP pages react to a request. We can check if a visitor accessed our site through the default port 80 or a different one. In this example we look for access through port 443, the port for Secure Sockets Layer (SSL) access (and other protocols), and redirect them to an appropriate page:

```
If Request.ServerVariables("SERVER_PORT") = "443" Then
  Response.Redirect "/securesite/default.asp"   'Secure user
Else
  Response.Redirect "/normalsite/default.asp"   'Non-secure user
End If
```

If we force our users to log on and be authenticated by our server (rather than allowing them anonymous access under the Web server's `IUSR` account (we'll deal with this in more detail in later chapters), we can query the user name. This allows us to see which user we are dealing with, and tailor the page for that user. For example, this code will only display administration links to the user named `Administrator`:

```
...
<A HREF="dispcnfg.asp">Change Display Configuration</A><BR>
<A HREF="dispcolr.asp">Change Display Colors</A><BR>
<A HREF="keyboard.asp">Change Keyboard Configuration</A><BR>
<%
If Request.ServerVariables("AUTH_USER") _
   = UCase(Request.ServerVariables("SERVER_NAME")) & "\Administrator" Then
%>
   <A HREF="allusers.asp">Administer All Users</A><BR>
   <A HREF="usrlogon.asp">Administer Logon Information</A>
<%
End If
%>
...
```

Note that ASP doesn't fill the `ServerVariables` collection until you access one of the members. The first access to a member of the collection causes IIS to get them all. Only use the `ServerVariables` collection when it's necessary.

Other Request and Response Techniques

To finish this chapter, we'll look at several useful techniques for working with the ASP Request and Response objects. This includes:

- Managing connections, buffering and page redirection
- Manipulating the HTTP headers, caching and expiring pages
- Working with client certificates
- Creating custom log file messages

Managing Connections, Buffering and Redirection

A useful feature of ASP is the ability to redirect users from one ASP page to another (ASP or HTML) page, or to another resource (such as a ZIP file or text file). While this appears to be transparent to the user, in fact it is the browser that's doing the work. When we use the `Response.Redirect` method to load a new page, we're actually sending a specific HTTP header back to the client. The header is:

```
HTTP/1.1 302 Object Moved
Location /newpath/newpage.asp
```

The browser reads the header information, and loads the page indicated by the `Location` value. This is functionally equivalent to using a client-side HTML `<META>` element in a Web page, such as:

```
<META HTTP-EQUIV="REFRESH" CONTENT="0;URL=/newpath/newpage.asp">
```

One problem with this is that a proxy server located between our server and the user may provide its own custom message containing a link to the new page rather than loading it directly, and the browser might do the same depending on the make and version. This removes the supposed transparency, and can make it cumbersome for users to surf your site if they keep getting error messages.

We can't use the `Redirect` method after sending any page content, such as text or HTML. However, one way that seems to limit the 'proxy server effect' is to make sure that *no* output (including HTTP headers) has been sent to the client first. In ASP 2.0, we had to turn on buffering and then use the `Clear` method to empty the buffer:

```
Response.Buffer = True

'Some condition to select the appropriate page:
If Request.ServerVariables("SERVER_PORT") = 1856 Then
  strNewPage = "/newpath/this_page.asp"
Else
  strNewPage = "/newpath/the_other_page.asp"
End If

Response.Clear
Response.Redirect strNewPage
```

In ASP 3.0 buffering is on (`True`) by default, so the first line can be omitted. However it does no harm, and ensures that our page will still work if transferred to an ASP 2.0 environment at some point.

> *Rather than using this type of HTTP Header redirection, a new feature in ASP 3.0 allows us to switch execution to another page through the `Transfer` method of the `Server` object. We'll be looking at this in detail in Chapter 4.*

ASP Page Buffering

As we've just seen, ASP 3.0 in IIS 5.0 has page buffering turned on by default, whereas it was off by default in earlier versions. Microsoft tells us that buffering provides much more efficient page delivery in IIS 5.0, which is why the default has been changed. In most cases, this doesn't affect us. However, if we have a very large page, or one that takes a while to be built by ASP or other server-side code and components, we can **flush** sections to the client as they are completed:

```
...
... Code to create first part of the page
...
Response.Flush
...
... Code to create next part of page
...
Response.Flush
...
```

At some point before the end of a page where we wish to stop execution of the code, we can call the `End` method to flush all the current content to the client and halt any further processing:

```
...
If strUserName = "" Then Response.End   'No name so stop execution
...
... Code to use UserName value
...
```

If we're creating output that is buffered, and has not been sent to the client, we can change our mind and delete it again, using the `Clear` method:

```
...
... Code to create first part of the page
...
If strUserName = "" Then Response.Clear
...
... Code to create a new version of this part of the page
...
```

There are two sample pages demonstrating buffering and redirection, which you can load from the main Response Object page (`show_response.asp`). The first Response.Redirect example page, named `redirect.asp`, writes some content into the buffered page, clears the buffer, then redirects to another page:

```
For intLoop = 1 To 1000000
  Response.Write "."
Next

Response.Clear
Response.Redirect "show_redirect.asp"
Response.End
```

The target page, `show_response.asp`, does the same thing, but redirects back to the main Response Object page. Because the pages are buffered, and all output must be cleared before redirection, there's no visible output in the browser. However, you can see each of the redirections taking place by watching the status bar of your browser:

The second example page, `usebuffer.asp`, is opened from the Response.Flush link in the main Request Object page. It simply iterates through each character of a string, flushing them one at a time to the client with a delay in between. OK, so it's a highly inefficient use of a Web server and ASP, but it demonstrates the point:

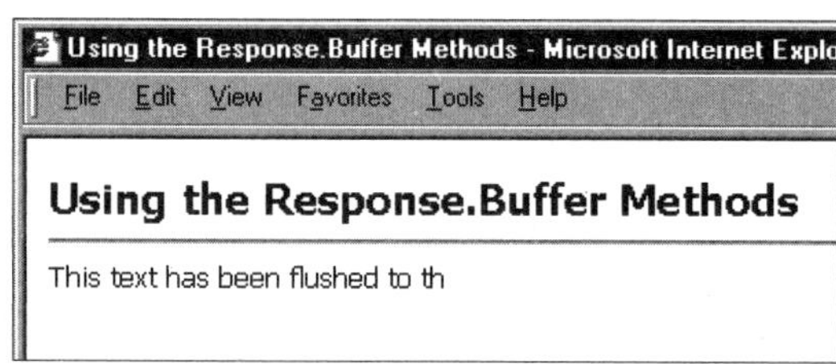

Here's the minimal ASP code required. Notice that we flush each character to the browser individually, because otherwise it will be buffered until the page is complete:

```
strText = "This text has been flushed to the browser using " & _
          "<B>Response.Flush</B><P>"

For intChar = 1 To Len(strText)

  For intWrite = 1 To 100000
  Next

  Response.Write Mid(strText, intChar, 1)
  Response.Flush

Next
```

The Response.IsClientConnected Property

The `IsClientConnected` property was introduced in ASP 2.0, but was somewhat unreliable in that you had to send some output to the client before it returned an accurate result. This has been fixed in ASP 3.0, and it can now be used freely.

`IsClientConnected` is a useful way to see if the user is still connected to our server and loading the page that ASP is creating. If not, we're wasting the server's resources creating it, as the buffer contents will just be dumped by IIS. So, for pages that require a lot of calculation time or heavy resource use, it's worth checking at each stage whether our visitor has gone off to look at the latest Dilbert cartoon instead of sitting patiently waiting to load the remainder of our page:

```
...
... Code to create first part of the page
...
If Response.IsClientConnected Then
  Response.Flush
Else
  Response.End
End If
...
... Code to create next part of page
...
```

Manipulating the HTTP Headers

We've seen in several places how ASP can create or modify the HTTP headers that are sent to the client in response to a page request. There are several properties and methods available in the Response object that help us do this. There are header methods for:

- Controlling caching and expiration
- Creating status and custom HTTP headers
- Specifying the MIME type or content type
- Adding PICS labels

We'll look briefly at each one next. Several of the properties and methods that we describe can be examined by opening the main **Response Object** page (`show_response.asp`) and clicking on the relevant property or method name:

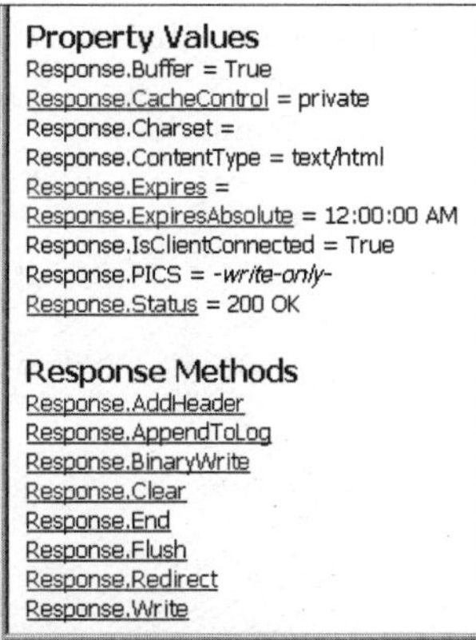

Caching and Expiring ASP Pages

The user's browser, and any proxy servers between them and our server, can **cache** HTML and ASP-generated pages. When the user next requests the page, the browser sends a 'last modified' request to our server (with an `HTTP-If-MODIFIED-SINCE` header containing the date of the cached version) asking if the page has been updated since then.

If it hasn't, our server responds with the status code and message "`304 Not Modified`", and the browser uses the cached version to save dragging another copy of the same page across the network. If there is a modified version of the page available, this is sent together with the "`200 OK`" status code and message.

The Response.CacheControl Property

Other things can affect this process, however. Any proxy servers within the network route used by the page, generally at the client end, can be instructed not to cache a page by setting the Response.CacheControl property to Private. This is the default for an ASP page in ASP 3.0, and is especially useful where a page has been tailored to an individual visitor. It prevents other users on the same network as the proxy server from getting the same page. When the value of the CacheControl property is set to Public, proxy servers are permitted to cache the page. Note that some proxy servers may perform differently, or even ignore or over-ride this header.

In Internet Explorer 4, it was possible to get spurious This page has expired messages when proxy caching was enabled. We've provided a page (expiretest_form.asp) that you can experiment with on your network through your own proxy server, to examine the effects of this property. You can display it by clicking the Response.CacheControl link in the main Response Object page:

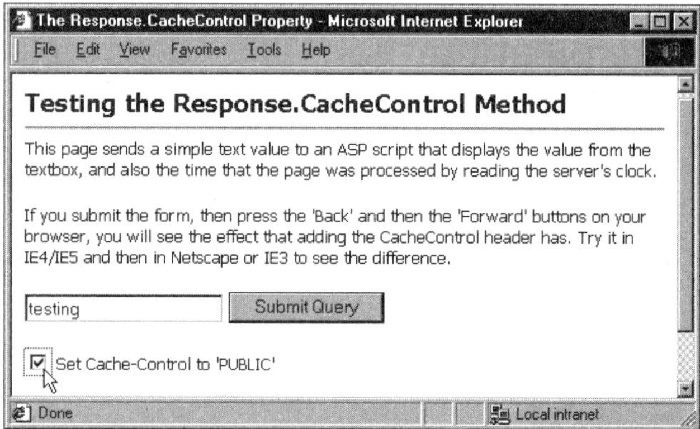

This page is submitted to the page **expiretest_result.asp**, which sets the Response.CacheControl property and then inserts the values and the time that the script was executed into the page:

```
<%
If Request.Form("public") = "on" Then   'Cache-Control check box was ticked
  Response.CacheControl = "Public"
Else
  Response.CacheControl = "Private"
End If
%>

<HTML>
...
Cache-Control is: <B><% = Response.CacheControl %></B><P>
Value in text box is: <B><% Response.Write Request.Form("textbox") %>
</B><P>Script was executed at:<B>
<%
Response.Write Right("0" & Hour(Now),2) & ":" & Right("0" & Minute(Now),2) _
               & ":" & Right("0" & Second(Now),2)
%></B>
```

By clicking the Back and Forward buttons on your browser, you can see if it is automatically re-executed, or whether the cached copy is used. The outcome varies with different browsers:

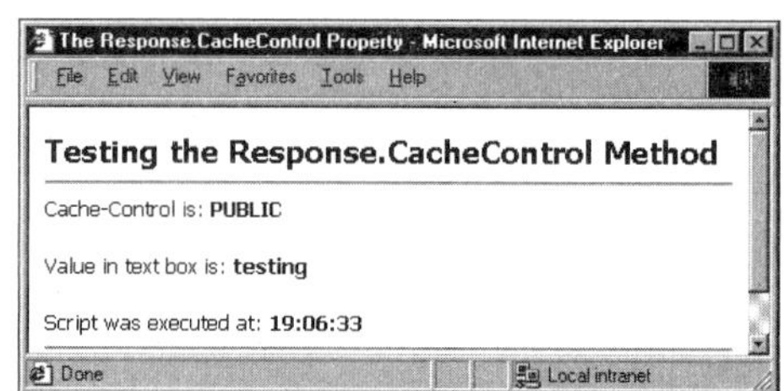

The Response.Expires and Response.ExpiresAbsolute Properties

The two properties that control how long a page is cached for are the Response object's `Expires` and `ExpiresAbsolute` properties. `Response.Expires` defines how long the page will remain valid for before it should be discarded from the cache, in terms of a number of minutes from when it was created. The `ExpiresAbsolute` property sets the absolute date and time at which it will expire.

We provide a sample page named `addheaders_form.asp` that demonstrates these properties in use. In the main **Response Object** page, click the link for either of the above properties:

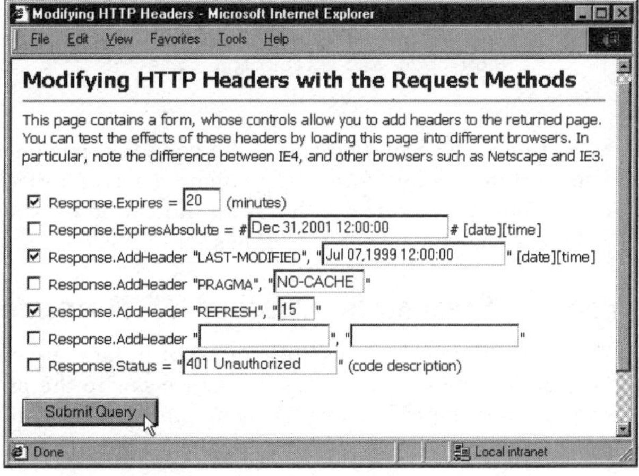

In this page, we can add our own custom HTTP headers, and set some of the various properties that affect the HTTP headers of the response. When we click the **Submit** button, the page `show_headers.asp` adds the selected headers to the return stream and then displays the code it has run to do this. It also displays the time of execution, so that we can check if a page is being cached or re-executed:

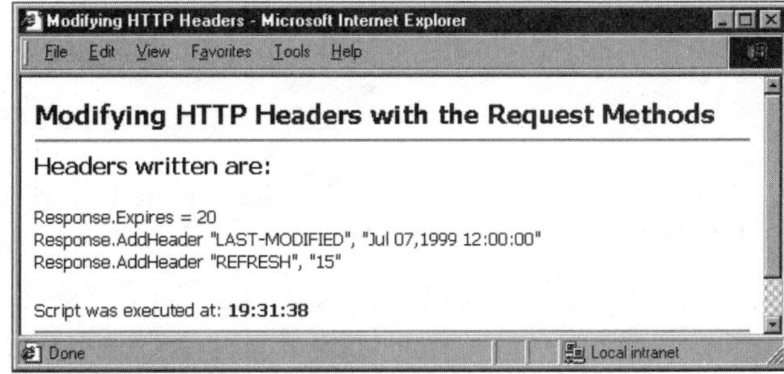

The code in the `show_headers.asp` page that creates and adds the HTTP headers looks like this:

```
<%
' Write HTTP headers before any other output
If Request.Form("expires") = "on" Then _
   Response.Expires = Request.Form("expires_value")

If Request.Form("expiresabs") = "on" Then _
   Response.ExpiresAbsolute = Request.Form("expiresabs_value")

If Request.Form("lastmod") = "on" Then _
   Response.AddHeader "LAST-MODIFIED", CStr(Request.Form("lastmod_value"))

If Request.Form("pragma") = "on" Then _
   Response.AddHeader "PRAGMA", CStr(Request.Form("pragma_value"))

If Request.Form("refresh") = "on" Then _
   Response.AddHeader "REFRESH", CStr(Request.Form("refresh_value"))
```

```
If Request.Form("addheader") = "on" And Len(Request.Form("addheader_name")) Then _
   Response.AddHeader CStr(Request.Form("addheader_name")), _
                      CStr(Request.Form("addheader_value"))

If Request.Form("status") = "on" Then _
   Response.Status = Request.Form("status_value")
%>

<HTML>
...
...Show code and execution time
...
```

The remainder simply displays the code that has been executed and the execution time. You'll notice the custom header "PRAGMA" (which we haven't discussed so far) is included in the page. Some (older) proxy servers use this as an indication of whether a page should be cached. The default is to cache a page unless the HTTP header "PRAGMA=NO-CACHE" is received.

Creating Status and Custom HTTP Headers

We can create our own status codes, or in fact any custom header we like, using the AddHeader method of the Response object – as we saw in the previous example page. This method expects two arguments: the HTTP header name and a string containing the value or values to allocate to it. As an example, the following code adds the REFRESH header to a page:

```
Response.AddHeader "REFRESH", "60;URL=newpath/newpage.asp"
```

This is equivalent to a client-side <META> element:

```
<META HTTP-EQUIV="REFRESH" CONTENT="60;URL=newpath/newpage.asp">
```

Alternatively, we can use the AddHeader method in conjunction with the Status property, to force the browser to load a new page:

```
Response.Status = "302 Object Moved"
Response.AddHeader "Location", "newpath/newpage.asp"
```

This is the equivalent of using the Response.Redirect method:

```
Response.Redirect "newpath/newpage.asp"
```

The Response.Status property can be used to send any status message we require, for example adding the lines:

```
Response.Status = "401 Unauthorized"
Response.Addheader "WWW-Authenticate", "BASIC"
```

Forces the browser to display a username/password dialog, and use BASIC authentication to send them back to the server. (We'll be looking at authentication methods later in the book).

MIME-Types and Content Types

The `Response.ContentType` property is useful when we want to send the browser a string of values that are dynamically created, and which themselves provide the browser with no direct indication of the content type – as a file extension would if it were a disk file. The default for all ASP-generated pages, unless we specify otherwise, is `"text/html"`. This type of content identifier is referred to as a **MIME-type** (MIME stands for either **Multi-purpose Internet Multimedia Extension** or Multi-purpose Internet **Mail** Extension – usually depending on the context).

If, for example, the stream we're sending to the client is a picture generated by reading binary values from a database, we need to add the appropriate `CONTENT-TYPE` header *before* sending any content:

```
Response.ContentType "image/jpeg"
```

If we are creating an XML file from a database, we use the MIME-type `"text/xml"`, and if we're creating a text file to be displayed in a text editor or stored as a disk file on the client, we use `"text/text"`.

Adding PICS Labels

The `Response.Pics` property simply adds a **PICS** (Platform for Internet Content System) label to the page, in much the same way as we would normally do with a `<META>` tag:

```
QUOT = Chr(34)

strPicsLabel = "(PICS-1.0 " & QUOT & "http://www.rsac.org/ratingsv01.html" _
               & QUOT & " l gen true comment " & QUOT _
               & "RSACi North America Server" & QUOT & " for " & QUOT _
               & "http://yoursite.com" & QUOT & " on " & QUOT _
               & "1999.08.01T03:04-0500" & QUOT & " r (n 0 s 0 v 2 l 3))"

Response.Pics(strPicsLabel)
```

This adds a PICS label that looks like the following:

```
(PICS-1.0 "http://www.rsac.org/ratingsv01.html" l gen true comment "RSACi
North America Server" for "http://yoursite.com" on "1999.08.01T03:04-0500"
r (n 0 s 0 v 2 l 3))
```

For more information about PICS, and the way you define the content of your page in regard to its suitability for young people and other visitors, check out `http://www.rsac.org/`.

Defining Headers in Internet Services Manager

We showed in Chapter 1 how each Web site and directory in IIS 5.0 has properties set in the Internet Services Manager (MMC snap-in) application. These define the HTTP headers sent to the client with all requests for resources from that site or directory. This provides an alternative to setting them with ASP script code in each page.

Right-click a Web site or directory and select Properties. In the HTTP Headers tab of this dialog, you can set content expiration to a time period or absolute date, define custom headers, create PICS content rating labels, and define content types through a MIME-types map:

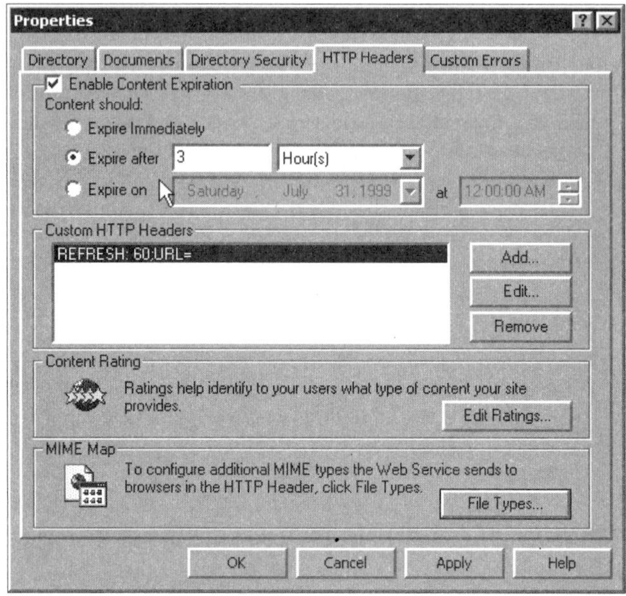

In the screenshot above, you can see that we've created a custom `REFRESH` HTTP header that will be applied to all pages loaded from this directory. So, each one will automatically be reloaded (refreshed) once a minute (ideal for the latest baseball scores but a bit heavy on your server perhaps!). This is what the Edit dialog for this custom header looks like:

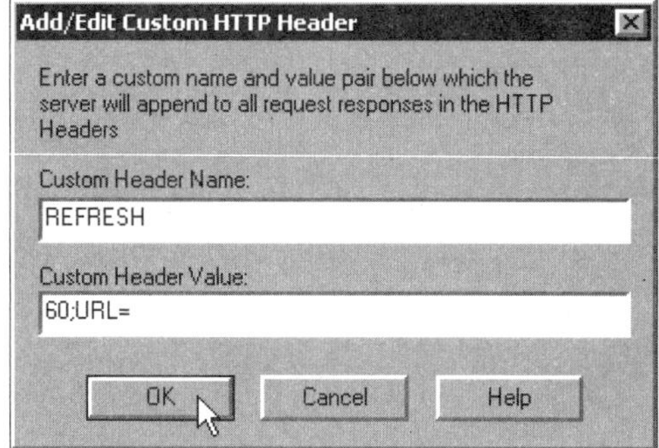

To add custom content type mappings to the MIME map, we just have to add them to the list by clicking the File Types button in the main Properties dialog:

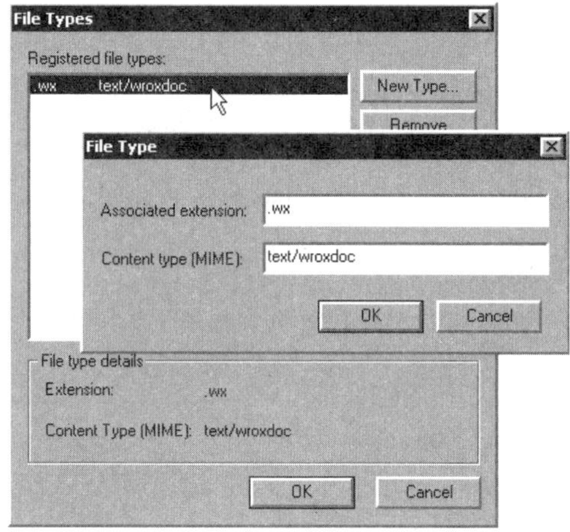

> **When you start experimenting with HTTP headers, you'll soon find out that not all browsers behave in the same way. In fact, many browsers react to different HTTP headers in different ways, making it sometimes quite difficult to reliably establish a useful overall policy.**

Working with Client Certificates

If we set up a secure Web site or a secure section of a site, we can install a digital server certificate and use it to allow visitors to authenticate (i.e. positively identify) our server using the details that are encrypted into that certificate. Each time they request a page in such a site or directory, our server will send a copy of our certificate. The browser can examine this to ensure that we really are who we say we are.

In the same way, we can set up our server to demand that the user provides us with a valid digital client certificate when they access that site or directory. They obtain these certificates from a variety of sources, such as Verisign (`http://www.verisign.com`) or Thawte Consulting (`http://www.thawte.com`). We'll look at this process in detail in later chapter 25

These scenarios use values from the Request object's **ClientCertificate** collection. In the sample code for this chapter, we've included a page that shows some of the ways of using values from this collection.

Click the ClientCertificate Examples link in the main Request Object page (`show_request.asp`) to open the Using the Request Collections menu. In this page, select the Viewing the ClientCertificate Collection link to open a page that displays the contents of a client certificate sent to the server with the page request.

This page is named `showcert.asp`, and all it does is iterate through the `ClientCertificate` collection displaying all the values it contains – with the time-honored code we've used so often before. The only differences here are that we're building an HTML table to hold the results, and truncating each one at 60 characters:

```
<TABLE CELLPADDING=0 CELLSPACING=0>
<%
For Each keyItem In Request.ClientCertificate()
  strItemValue = Request.ClientCertificate(keyItem)
  If Len(strItemValue) > 90 Then strItemValue = Left(strItemValue, 60) & ".. etc."
  Response.Write "<TR><TD>" & keyItem & " = " & strItemValue & "</TD></TR>"
Next
%>
</TABLE>
```

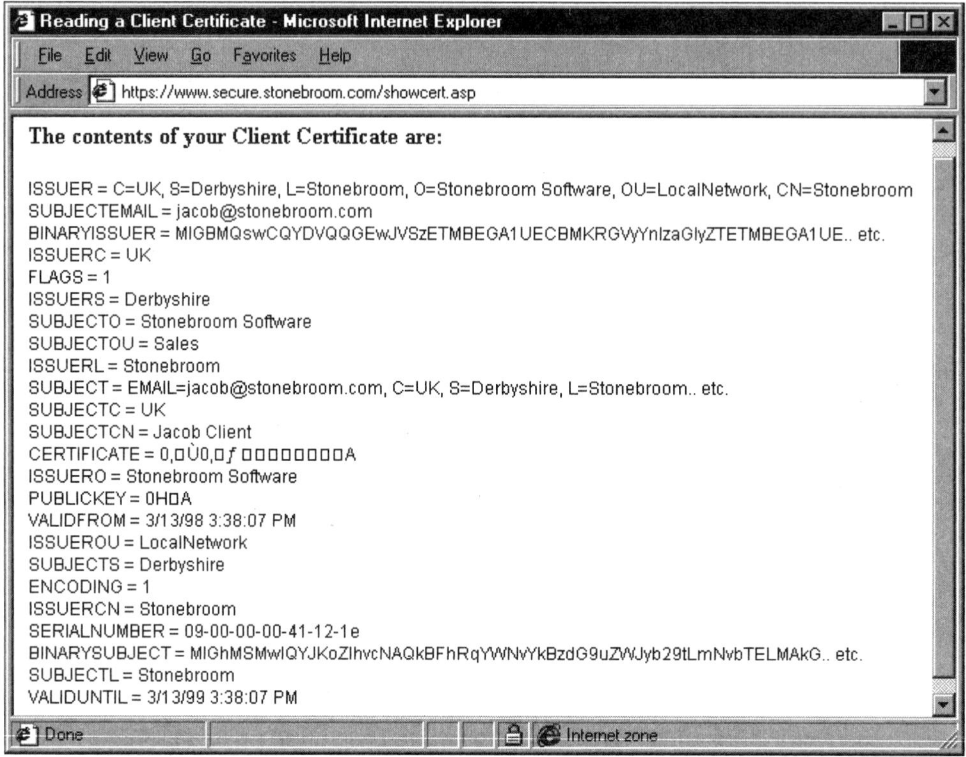

However, to get any results on your system, you'll have to set up a secure site or directory.

Redirection Using Client Certificates

Once we have forced all our visitors to a site or a section of the site to present their client certificate, we can use the information it contains to tailor the pages we create to that user. For example, we can use the `Organization` entry in their certificate to automatically redirect our own employees to a specific section of the site, and other visitors to a different one:

```
If Request.ClientCertificate("SubjectO") = "Wrox Press Inc" Then
   Response.Redirect "/wrox_staff/default.asp"   'Wrox staff site
Else
   Response.Redirect "/public/Default.asp"       'Normal public site
End If
```

Alternatively, we could use the `Country` entry to redirect visitors to an appropriate site:

```
Select Case Request.ClientCertificate("SubjectC")
   Case "UK": Response.Redirect "https://uk_site.co.uk/"
   Case "DE": Response.Redirect "https://de_site.co.de/"
   Case "FR": Response.Redirect "https://fr_site.co.fr/"
   '... etc.
   Case Else: Response.Redirect "https://us_site.com/"
End Select
```

Reading and Writing Binary Data

Two methods provide binary data access to the HTTP stream sent from the browser to the server, and the return stream from the server to the browser. The `Request.BinaryRead` method takes a parameter that specifies the number of bytes to read, and returns a Variant-type array containing those bytes drawn from the `POST` section of the request (i.e. the data that would be presented in the ASP `Form` collection). This code reads the first 64 bytes of the data:

```
varContent = Request.BinaryRead(64)
```

If we use `BinaryRead`, we cannot access the ASP `Request.Form` collection afterwards. Likewise, once we have referred to the ASP `Request.Form` collection in any way, the `BinaryRead` method cannot be used.

It's also possible to write binary data into the response stream we're creating in ASP, by using the `BinaryWrite` method. We provide it with a `Variant`-type array of the bytes we want to write to the client:

```
Response.BinaryWrite(varContent)
```

These methods are rarely used, except when creating non-HTML resources from (say) a database. An example of where you might see it used is when we read the set of bytes that make up an image file from a database, and send it to the client using the `BinaryWrite` method.

Creating Custom Log Messages

If we have set up our server to log requests to a text file in the W3C Extended Log File Format, we can use the `Response.AppendToLog` method to add a message string to the end of entries in the log file. This is useful if we want to store some value or message for a particular page, or when a specific condition arises in the script.

For example, we might like to record an employee's department number when they order more than some specific number of items through our Intranet 'stationary order' application:

```
...
If intItemCount > 25 Then
   Response.AppendToLog "Large order from '" & strDept & "' department."
End If
...
```

Setting Up Extended Logging

To use the `AppendToLog` method, you must have W3C Extended Log File Format page hit logging active. This is set up for a Web site in the Web Site tab of the Properties dialog for the site. Turn on the Enable Logging check box, choose the W3C Extended Log File Format, and click the Properties button:

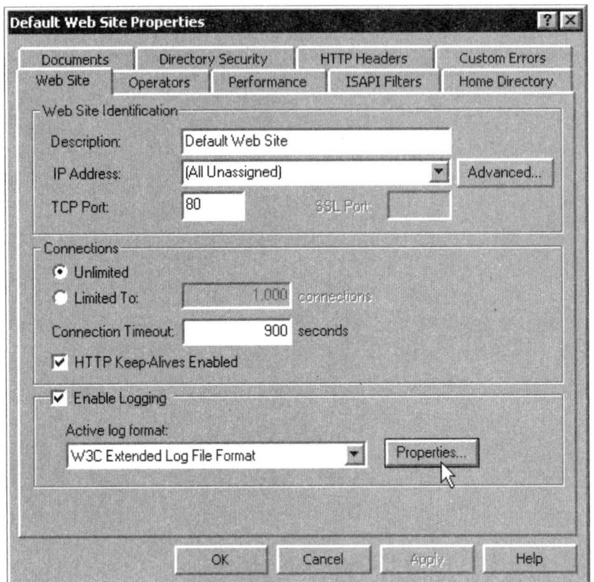

In the Extended Logging Properties dialog that appears, we can select which items we want to include in the log file. Make sure that URI Stem is checked, or the `AppendToLog` method will fail:

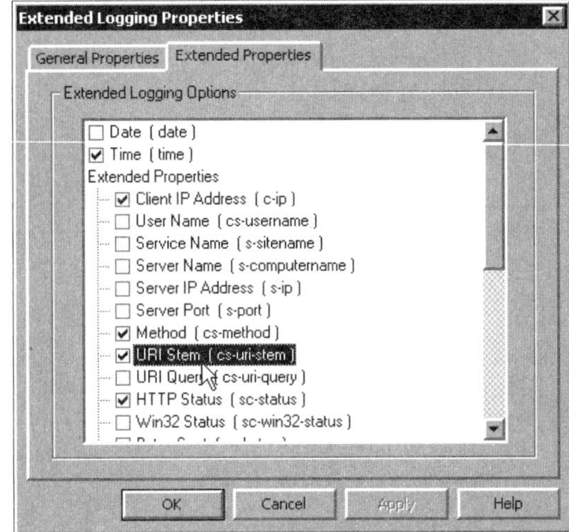

We've provided with a simple page that attempts to write an entry into the log file. You can open it from the `AppendToLog` method link in the main Request Object page (`show_request.asp`). All this page does is create a simple string containing the current date and time, and execute the `AppendToLog` method:

```
strToAppend = "Page executed on " & Now
Response.AppendToLog strToAppend
```

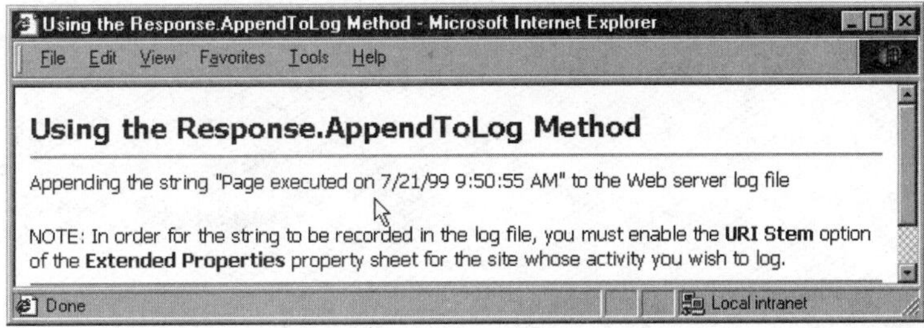

Summary

In this chapter, we've started our investigation of Active Server Pages 3.0, and we've seen how it works hand in hand with Internet Information Server 5.0 to provide an easy-to-use and efficient way of creating dynamic Web pages and Web applications. Of course, there is still a lot more to see – we've only covered two of the integral ASP objects in this chapter.

The objects we looked at are the Request and Response objects, which together allow us to access and work with the values that are part of the client/server conversation that goes on whenever a user requests and loads a page or resource from our Web site. As the well-chosen names of the objects imply, the Request object provides access to the complete content of the user's request, while the Response object allows us to create and modify the response that our server sends back.

Each of these objects exposes various parts of the conversation through collections and properties, and provides various methods that can be used to retrieve or modify individual sections. It might help you to understand exactly what's happening if you think of them as being tools to disassemble requests and use the pieces to build responses. This will help you to appreciate how the various methods affect the client, the server, and the page that we're creating.

The topics we covered are:

- How the client and server interact to deliver a dynamic page
- The Request and Response objects in detail, and what's common between them
- How we access values from forms and in the query string
- How we read and create cookies to be stored on the client
- What server variables are, and how we access and modify HTTP headers
- How various other items, such as client certificates, are represented

While this alone gives you enough ammunition to start blasting dynamic pages out from your site, there is a lot more to go at yet. We'll obviously be using these objects throughout the book, as we continue to explore the capabilities of ASP and show you how to get the best from it. In the next chapter, the journey continues with an investigation of user sessions and applications and the two ASP objects that provide access to them.

N
W

3

ASP Applications and Sessions

Having seen in the previous chapter how ASP provides us with ways to access a client request and generate an appropriate response, we'll move on to look at two more of the objects that are part of ASP. These are the **Application** and **Session** objects. They are not directly concerned with managing requests and responses, but more with managing the environment in which our ASP pages run.

One of the common problems associated with building Web sites or Web applications is the lack of **state** when using the HTTP protocol. State provides us with the ability to associate variable values, objects, and other resources with a specific user, and have them available to any routines within our applications – something that we take for granted when we write ordinary client-based applications in a programming language like Visual Basic or C++. However, the Web doesn't provide this capability. We'll see why, and how we get round this problem, in the course of this chapter.

There are also issues of terminology and technology to deal with here. We've been quite freely discussing 'Web applications' so far in this book, without really understanding or defining exactly what they are. We've also talked about 'user sessions' without fully describing what we mean by this. Both have been intentional omissions, because they are intimately tied up with the ASP concept of **applications** and **sessions**. And, as you'll expect by now, these map pretty directly to the ASP Application and Session objects.

So, this chapter explores:

- What Web applications are, and how they relate to the ASP Application object
- What user sessions are, and how they relate to the ASP Session object
- How ASP creates and manages applications and sessions automatically for us
- The features that are provided by the Application and Session objects
- How we put the Application and Session objects to work in our ASP pages

However, we'll start with a look at the thorny issue of state, because this is really at the heart of it all.

Managing State on the Web

If you think that visitors' comments such as "Just look at the state of that Web site!" reflect the problems that we as Web developers face in managing **state**, then perhaps you should be working in marketing rather than programming! However, the concept of state is something that many developers have never given a thought to until they start transferring their applications to the Web. The Web, as we've said, is a **stateless** environment. So let's explore what this means, and see the ways that we can avoid the problems that it creates.

So What Exactly is State?

In a normal single-user program, such as when we build an executable application (for example, an `.exe` file using Visual Basic) we take for granted the fact that we can declare a global (or `Public`) variable and then access it from anywhere in our code. All the time the application is running, the value remains valid and accessible.

When we move to a traditional client-server solution, such as one where a client-based application accesses a server-based database engine, each client makes a connection to the server and the database application. This connection is normally established by **authenticating** the user.

> **Authentication is typically a combination of identifying users through a user-name and then making them present a password to prove that they are a valid user.**

Once authenticated, a connection is established between the client and the server-based application, which remains in force all the time the client is using the application. This is what happens when you log onto your local Windows 2000 server. At any time, the administrator can view the active user connections using the Active Directory Users and Computers utility (click Directory Management in the Administrative Tools section of your Start menu). Much the same occurs with, for example, Microsoft SQL Server.

This permanent connection means that it's easy to identify each user when they send instructions or requests to the server. Likewise, the response or any other information can be directed back to the user at any time, through the persistent connection. More to the point, the server can store values and information about each client easily, and match that to the respective client when it's needed. And, of course, the server application can host global variables that can be accessed on behalf of any user, as and when required.

This ability to identify each client's request, and hold values in memory that are related to just that user, provides **state**. You can think of it as representing the values and context of the application's and user's internal variables throughout the life of the application or a user connection.

Why is State So Important?

If we intend to create some type of Web-based **application** that interacts with users (rather than just a Web site that displays individual pages), it must be able to provide individual state for each user. This might be as simple as remembering their name, or as complex as storing object references or recordsets that are different for each user. If we can't do that, we can't reasonably expect to do anything that requires more than one ASP page, as the variables and other references in that page are all destroyed when the page is finished executing. When the user requests the next page, we've lost all the information that they've already provided.

So, it's pretty obvious that we need to find a way to persist state for each of our visitors. It would also be very useful to be able to store values that are global to all users. An obvious example is a Web-style visitor or page-hit counter. There's not much point in giving each user their own counter – they usually want to see the total number of visitors, not just the number of times that they've visited. The number of visitors needs to be stored with **application-level state**, rather than **user-level state**.

This isn't a problem that's just arisen – it's been around for as long as commercial sites have inhabited the Web, and even before then – so there are many traditional solutions for storing state on the Web. Webmasters want to know things like whether you've ever visited their site before. If so, how many times and how often? And what other sites do you regularly visit, so that they can better target their advertising? All these things require a way to store information about users in between the page requests they make in one visit, and between each visit.

How we Create State on the Web

One of the usual ways of providing state between page requests and site visits is through **cookies**. We saw in the previous chapter how we can use these to store values on the client's machine, which are sent along with each page request to the domain for which the cookie is valid. By examining and updating these cookies with ASP, we can, to some extent, achieve a persistence of state. We can use the information they contain to identify the user, and then link that user to an appropriate set of stored values.

For example, we could detect a user request and see if it contains a specific cookie for our site. If not, we allocate the user an identifier of some type, say a number, and store it in the cookie with a long `Expires` time. Then each time they visit us, we can detect the cookie and update the information it contains. At the same time, we can collect data on the number and duration of visits and store it on our server for future reference.

However, what happens if the user moves to another computer, or deletes the cookie, or if their browser refuses to accept the cookie we send to them? In that case, we can't maintain state because we won't be able to identify them next time. Still, there are so many cookies flying around the Web now that most people just accept them, and forget they're there. If you turn on the Warn before accepting cookies option in your browser then surf a few large sites, you'll see what I mean.

Anonymous vs. Authenticated Visitors

If we decide that cookies are a bit too haphazard a solution, we can use more direct methods. The most obvious, and the one implemented by many sites, is to pop up a login dialog – either when you first hit the site as a whole, or at a page where authentication is required. You have to register first, to obtain a username/password combination of some type that allows you to access the appropriate pages.

This authenticates you as a known and valid user, at which point a cookie can be placed on your system to hold either the login details, or just a 'key' to indicate that you have been identified. Meanwhile, your details can be stored permanently on the server ready for when you come back again. While you have the cookie on your browser, you can navigate the site freely because you've been authenticated.

If there's no `Expires` date in the cookie, it dies when you close your browser, and you have to login and be authenticated again on the next visit. And of course, if you refuse to accept the cookie or delete it, you just get the login dialog again. This way, you can't access the site without being identified, and hence your usage patterns can be detected and stored for the marketing people and accountants to play with afterwards.

Internet Information Server, in hand with the Windows 2000 integral security features, can provide even stronger and more secure authentication if required, by forcing users to log on to the Web server just like they would log on to their own network. However, this only works with Internet Explorer 3 and above browsers. IIS can also use BASIC authentication to allow Web server 'logins' to be accomplished using non-Microsoft browsers.

No More Anonymous Visitors

When we use ASP on our IIS Web server, we get an automated system for tracking users during the current session (i.e. until they go off to another site or close their browser). Later in this chapter, we'll be seeing how we can use this feature both to identify visitors, and to store information locally for that user, to provide the **state** we're looking for. Here, we'll briefly see how it works in comparison to the solutions we've been discussing.

ASP and IIS together provide the concept of a user **session**, which we interact with through the ASP Session object. A new and separate Session object is created for each individual visitor when they first access an ASP page on our server. A session identifier number is allocated to the session, and a cookie containing a specially encrypted version of the session identifier is sent to the client.

The `Path` of the cookie (see the previous chapter for a description of cookie properties) is set to the path of the root of the ASP application running on our server. This will probably be the root of the Default Web site (i.e. `"/"`), but it may be another value – as you'll see later. No `Expires` value is provided in the cookie, so it will expire when the browser is closed.

Every time that this user accesses an ASP page, ASP looks for this cookie. It's named `ASPSESSIONID`*xxxxxxxx*, where each *x* is an alphabetic character. If you look at the screenshots of the `ServerVariables` collection shown in Chapter 2, you can see it in the HTTP Headers – here it is with the ASP cookie highlighted:

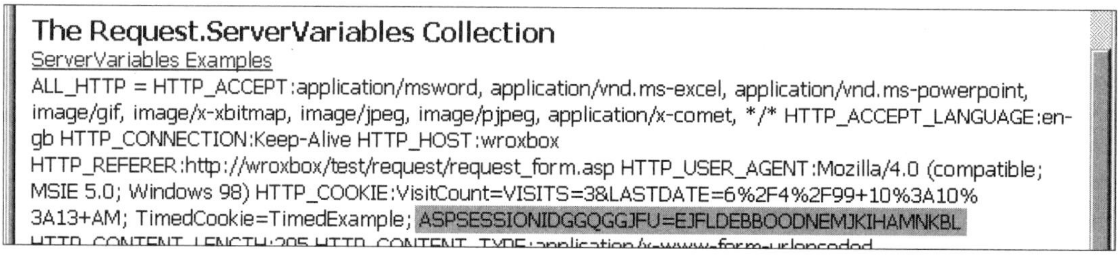

The Request.ServerVariables Collection

ServerVariables Examples

ALL_HTTP = HTTP_ACCEPT:application/msword, application/vnd.ms-excel, application/vnd.ms-powerpoint, image/gif, image/x-xbitmap, image/jpeg, image/pjpeg, application/x-comet, */* HTTP_ACCEPT_LANGUAGE:en-gb HTTP_CONNECTION:Keep-Alive HTTP_HOST:wroxbox HTTP_REFERER:http://wroxbox/test/request/request_form.asp HTTP_USER_AGENT:Mozilla/4.0 (compatible; MSIE 5.0; Windows 98) HTTP_COOKIE:VisitCount=VISITS=3&LASTDATE=6%2F4%2F99+10%3A10%3A13+AM; TimedCookie=TimedExample; ASPSESSIONIDGGQGGJFU=EJFLDEBBOODNEMJKIHAMNKBL

However, this cookie doesn't appear in the `Request.Cookies` or `Response.Cookies` collections – ASP hides it from us. But it's still there on the browser, and ASP looks for it with each ASP page request. The value that this cookie contains identifies the session for this user. Therefore, a reference to the appropriate Session object (which has been held in memory and still contains all the values that it did during the previous page requests) can be handed over to the script in the ASP page.

Of course, as we discovered earlier, this process fails if the client browser doesn't accept or support cookies. In this case, no ASP session can be created and the automatic maintenance of state doesn't happen for this visitor.

What is a Web Application?

In previous chapters, we've used the term **Web application** rather loosely, to indicate something that isn't really a Web site, but isn't a 'proper' application (in the traditional or conventional sense) either. In other words, we've thought of it as a set of Web pages and other resources that are designed to carry out some kind of task, to achieve a result. It sort of implies that there is a pre-defined route through the pages, where the user makes decisions or provides information to enable the task to be achieved.

An example is an on-line store, where you go through an iterative process of viewing and selecting goods to purchase, then step through a set of pages that collect the information required to charge you with the cost and ship the order. Alternatively, it might be a 'software upgrade Wizard' that steers you through the process of downloading and installing new software, or perhaps an Intranet-based application that creates price quotations or sales reports.

All this is in contrast to a 'normal' Web **site**, where you generally use a series of menus or navigation bars to roam around the site on no pre-defined route. However, there is a lot more to a Web application than just controlled navigation. The two things that are generally acceptable for freely roaming through a Web site – **statelessness** and **anonymity** – are generally not acceptable for a Web application.

What are ASP Applications?

While the above is a reasonable definition of the generic term 'Web application', it's unfortunately not good enough to use when we are talking about **ASP applications**. Asking what a 'Web application' is invites a subjective answer, while asking what an 'ASP application' is requires a technical explanation. The term 'application' in ASP has a specific meaning of it's own, and it's vital that you understand the concept before we move on to look at how they are implemented in practice.

ASP applications are associated with two main topics:

- The provision of global scope, through a globally accessible variable storage area
- The integration with IIS through COM+, which allows us to better manage components

We'll look at these topics next. The second one involves other ASP objects that we haven't explored in detail yet, so the coverage will be fairly general. We'll be looking at this topic in more depth in the next chapter, however, when we meet the ASP `Server` object.

Providing Global Scope for a Web Application

ASP provides an Application object, which roughly equates to the Session object we discussed earlier. However, this is at the **application-level** rather than the **user-level**. In other words, it is global not to an individual user, but to all users of the application – its scope does not limit it to access by an individual user. This is a similar concept to a global or `Public` variable in a normal compiled executable application. The Application object can be used to store variables and information (i.e. **state**) in a global context, and these values can be accessed by script running in any ASP page within the application, regardless of which visitor requested it.

However, this doesn't answer the main question – what is an ASP application? For this, we need to look under the hood of ASP.

When a user requests an ASP page, IIS creates a **context** for it (as we saw in Chapter 1) by instantiating the `asp.dll` that implements ASP. The page is parsed for server-side script, and instances of the appropriate scripting engine(s) are instantiated to execute the script.

The initial event of instantiating `asp.dll` causes an ASP application to be started, and an Application object is created. Immediately after this occurs, a user session is started for this user, and their individual Session object is created. The single Application object then remains in scope (i.e. instantiated and available) as more sessions are started. Immediately after the last remaining active session ends, the application ends, and the Application object is destroyed. Therefore, while there are visitors to the site with active sessions, there will be a single Application object available to all these users.

The Default ASP Application

When IIS and ASP are installed in Windows 2000, a Default Web site is created. This is configured as an ASP application, which involves several settings in the Properties dialog for the root folder of the site (by default this is `C:\InetPub\WWWRoot`). This is the dialog for our default Web site:

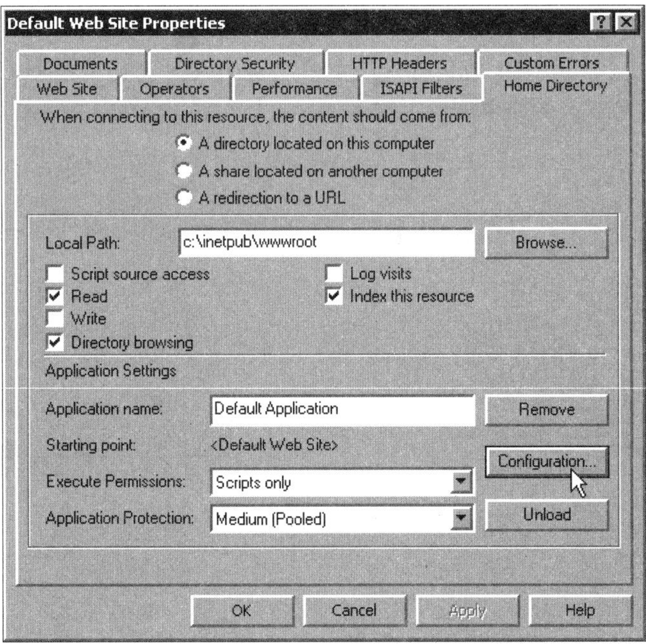

One of the things actively involved with ASP applications is a file named **global.asa**. This file is used to tailor the way that the application behaves. It is placed in the root directory of the application, and applies to all sub-directories of that directory. So, when placed in the root of the entire Web site, it defines the whole site as being part of the default ASP application.

We'll see what this file looks like, and how we use it, in the later section of this chapter on Application and Session events. For the meantime, it's enough to know that it's there.

ASP Virtual Applications

As well as the default application created during setup, we can create our own ASP **virtual application** in any sub-directory of the Web site. This application also includes all the sub-directories of the directory we define as the 'application directory'. However, this directory and the sub-folders are also part of the default application, and they share the global space created by the default Application object.

What this means in reality is that all the variables stored in the default application are also available within the application in a sub-directory. However, if an ASP page in the sub-directory application writes a value in its Application object that has the same name as an existing one in the default (root) application, the original value is no longer available within the sub-directory application. But, in other applications or ASP pages, the original value is maintained, because the root application cannot see the variables in the sub-directory application.

Think of it in terms of variables in a subroutine or function. If we define a variable `intMyValue` as being `Public` or global, we can access it from within any subroutine or function. However, if we then declare a local variable with the same name, any references within the subroutine or function to that variable will be to the local copy. The original value can no longer be accessed. When the subroutine or function ends, the local copy is destroyed and the original value of the global variable remains:

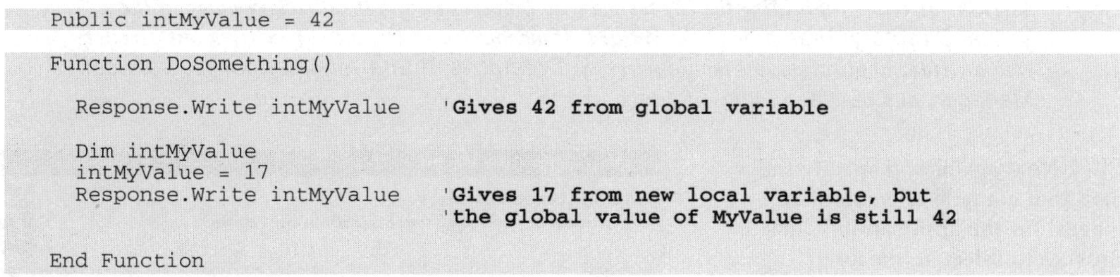

```
Public intMyValue = 42

Function DoSomething()

  Response.Write intMyValue    'Gives 42 from global variable

  Dim intMyValue
  intMyValue = 17
  Response.Write intMyValue    'Gives 17 from new local variable, but
                               'the global value of MyValue is still 42

End Function
```

Creating Your Own ASP Virtual Applications

To create a new virtual application, we can use the Internet Services Manager application or the equivalent HTML Web Manager pages.

In Internet Services Manager, right-click on the directory that you wish to create the new virtual application in, and select New, then Virtual Directory:

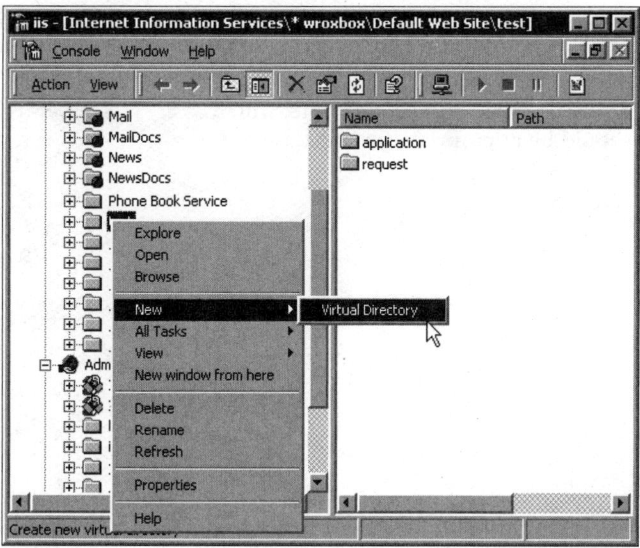

This starts the New Virtual Directory Wizard, the opening screen of which provides information about what the Wizard will do. Click Next, and in the second page type a name (or **alias**) for the new virtual application. This, combined with the path of the directory selected in Internet Services Manager, will become the URL of the application:

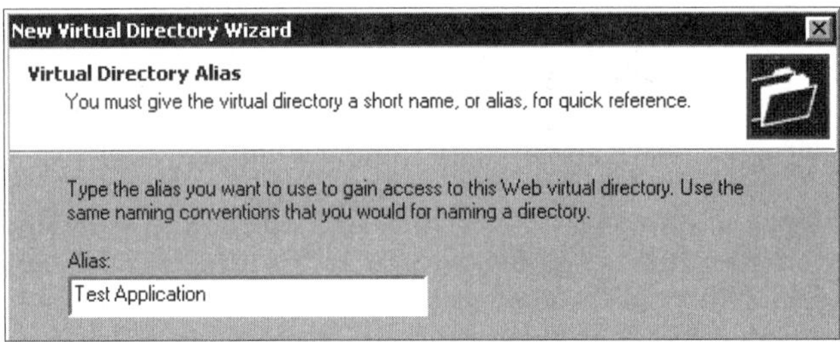

To convert an existing directory into an application with the same name as the directory, we just select the directory containing the one we want to convert and use the directory name in the Virtual Directory Alias *page of the Wizard. If we wanted to convert our existing test directory into a virtual application, we would select the* Default Web Site *entry in* Internet Services Manager*, and provide an alias of* 'test'*.*

Click Next again, and specify the path that contains the content (pages) for the application. Click Browse to select an existing directory. This is the directory that the new virtual application will point to:

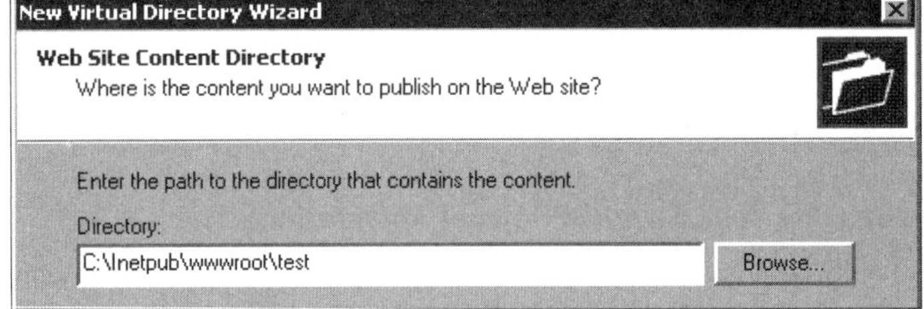

Click Next to open the Access Permissions page, and select the permissions you want to give to all users of this application. The default is Read and Run Scripts, which should be appropriate for most uses:

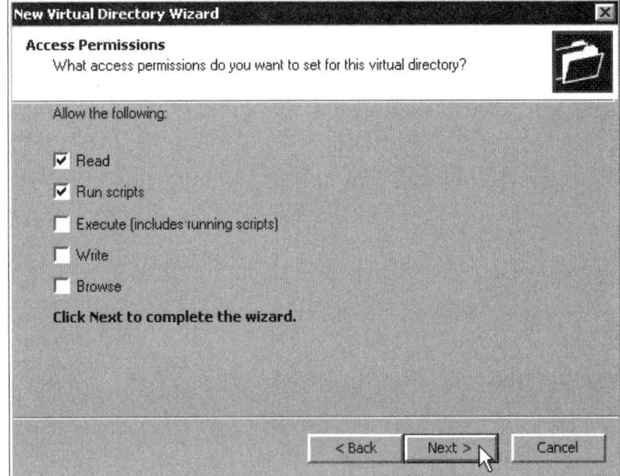

Only select Execute *if you intend to write custom compiled CGI applications that will be executed directly by the user: for example an* `.exe` *file that the user executes by specifying its name in the URL of their request, such as* `http://mysite.com/.../Test Application/create_user.exe?user=JJones`.

Click Next and the Wizard creates the virtual application. In the following screenshot, you can see it in the left-hand list, with an icon that represents an open box containing some indecipherable stuff:

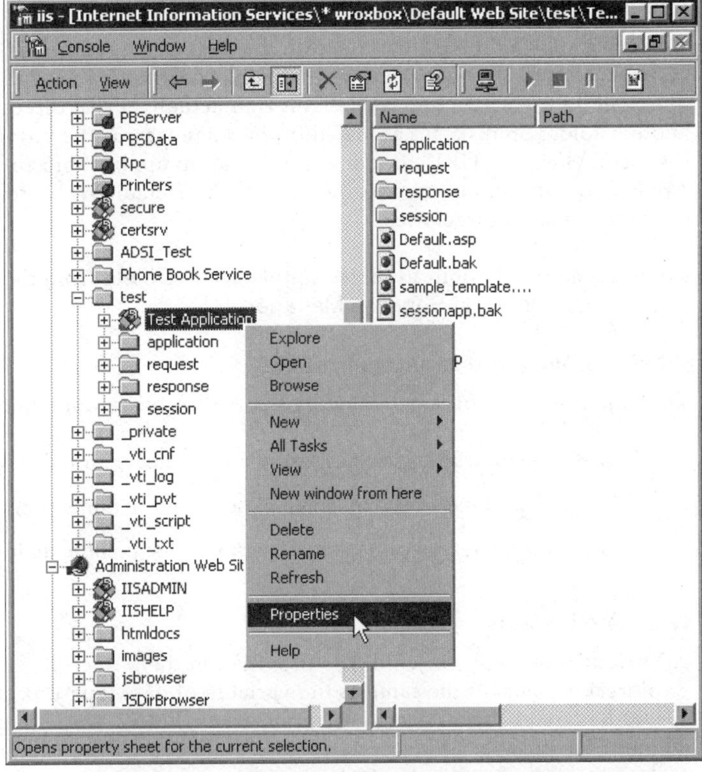

If we now right-click the new application and select Properties, we can see the settings that the Wizard has chosen. The Local Path, access permissions and Application Settings can be changed here if required. You'll also see a Remove button, which we can use to remove the virtual application:

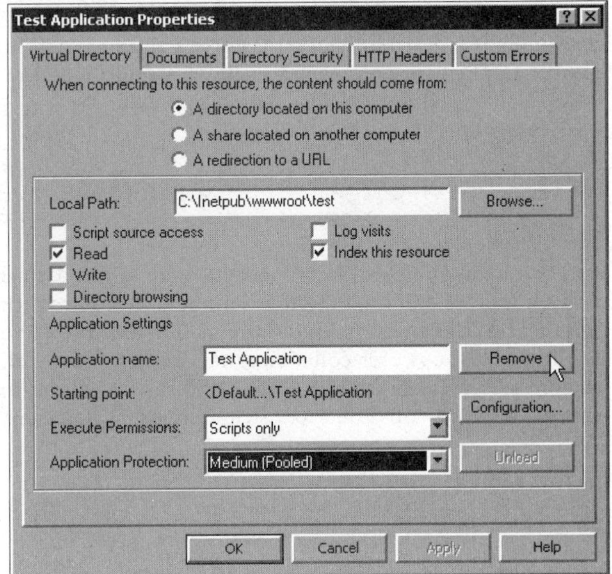

Removing Virtual Applications

However, clicking the Remove button doesn't actually remove the entry in Internet Services Manager. Instead, it converts the existing virtual application into a **virtual directory**. This has a 'folder' icon with a blue ball on it – which indicates that it isn't actually a real directory in the Web site, but a *redirection* to another folder on disk. It's accessed in the same way as the virtual application from which it was created (i.e. using the same URL), but does not act as an application. In other words, it doesn't support its own Application object, but inherits the one for the Default Web site, or for another application within this directory's parent directories.

To delete a virtual application, we simply select Delete from the right-click shortcut menu for the application in Internet Services Manager.

What Can We Store in an Application?

The global storage space provided by the ASP Application object can be used to store:

- Simple variables, such as strings and numbers (stored as Variants like all ASP script variables)
- Variant-type arrays, made up of one or more dimensions
- Variable references (again as Variants) that point to an instance of a COM object

What Are Variants?

A **Variant** is the only variable type provided in the VBScript scripting engine for ASP (and Internet Explorer). It behaves the same as the variable of data type `Variant` that can be specifically defined in Visual Basic and Visual Basic for Applications (VBA). While they don't offer the most efficient use of memory for variable storage, and require extra processing compared to the more usual base data types such as String or Integer, Variants do offer many benefits.

Internally, the Variant data type stores values as individual subtypes. However, they automatically handle implicit type conversion, allowing code such as this to be used:

```
strString = "30"
intInteger = 12

Response.Write strString & intInteger   'Writes 3012 in the resulting page
Response.Write strString + intInteger   'Writes 42 in the resulting page
```

Implicit data type conversion permits us to ignore that the value of HTML text and list controls are strings, and we can treat them as numbers if required (providing that the strings do contain a valid number). We can also freely do things like use the VBScript `Len` method to check the length of a value in the `Request.Form` collection that doesn't exist, without getting an error. (The `Len` function attempts to convert the value from the `Request.Form` call into a string – if the value is missing, `Empty` is returned, which converted to a string yields "", and hence the length is zero.)

VBScript Data Types and Conversions

We can also do explicit data-type conversion. In VBScript, the `VarType` method returns an integer indicating the subtype that Variant is currently holding:

```
Select Case VarType(varMyValue)

  Case 0 : Response.Write "Empty (uninitialized)"
  Case 1 : Response.Write "Null (no valid data)"
  Case 2 : Response.Write "Integer"
  Case 3 : Response.Write "Long integer"
  Case 4 : Response.Write "Single-precision floating-point number"
  Case 5 : Response.Write "Double-precision floating-point number"
  Case 6 : Response.Write "Currency"
  Case 7 : Response.Write "Date"
  Case 8 : Response.Write "String"
  Case 9 : Response.Write "Automation Object reference"
  Case 10 : Response.Write "Error"
  Case 11 : Response.Write "Boolean"
  Case 12 : Response.Write "Variant (used only with items in arrays of Variants)"
  Case 13 : Response.Write "Data-access object"
  Case 17 : Response.Write "Byte"
  Case 8192 : Response.Write "Variant Array"

End Select
```

Alternatively, there are functions that return a `Boolean` result for specific subtypes: `IsArray`, `IsDate`, `IsEmpty`, `IsNull`, `IsNumeric` and `IsObject`. Once we know the data subtype, we can convert it to a different Variant subtype if the data it contains is appropriate. This is useful both for clarity in our code, and to check that variables contain legal values – illegal conversion attempts will result in a run-time error:

```
blnBoolean = CBool(varVariant)     'Converts to a Variant of subtype Boolean
bytByte = CByte(varVariant)        'Converts to a Variant of subtype Byte
curCurrency = CCur(varVariant)     'Converts to a Variant of subtype Currency
dtmDate = CDate(varVariant)        'Converts to a Variant of subtype Date
dblDouble = CDbl(varVariant)       'Converts to a Variant of subtype Double
intInteger = CInt(varVariant)      'Converts to a Variant of subtype Integer
lngLong = CLng(varVariant)         'Converts to a Variant of subtype Long
sngSingle = CSng(varVariant)       'Converts to a Variant of subtype Single
strString = CStr(varVariant)       'Converts to a Variant of subtype String
```

JScript Data Types and Conversions

In JScript, the outward behavior of other variable types is similar to VBScript, but there is no concept of a Variant as an object. Instead, all values are objects, and may be one of only six data types:

- `undefined` – has the single value "`undefined`" and is used to indicate that the variable in question has not been declared and created, or has not had any value assigned to it if created implicitly. Similar to the VBScript `Empty`.
- `Null` – The variable does not contain a valid value. Similar to the VBScript `Nothing`.
- `Boolean`
- `String`
- `Number`
- `Object`

JScript provides a `typeof` function that returns the data type as a string, for example:

```
strString = '30';
intInteger = 12;

Response.Write(typeof(strString));    // Writes 'string' in the resulting page
Response.Write(typeof(intInteger));   // Writes 'number' in the resulting page
```

Each data type also has the `toString` method, which returns the value of the variable converted to a string, and the `valueOf` method, which returns the value of the variable as its original data type.

JScript Concatenation and Addition Issues

JScript differs from VBScript in many ways, not least because there is no '`&`' concatenation operator available. Instead, when the addition operator is used, it checks the variable data types to decide what to do. If both are numbers, the result is addition of the numbers. If one or both are strings, the result is concatenation of the strings:

```
strString = '30';
intInteger = 12;

Response.Write(intInteger + intInteger);  // Writes 24 in the resulting page
Response.Write(strString  + intInteger);  // Writes 3012 in the resulting page
Response.Write(intInteger + strString);   // Writes 1230 in the resulting page
```

One thing to watch if you have more than two values to add is the order of execution. The following lines of code demonstrate this:

```
intInteger = 12;
Response.Write(intInteger + intInteger + "<P>");           // Result is '24<P>'
Response.Write("<P>" + intInteger + intInteger + "</P>");
                                                           // Result is '<P>1212</P>'
```

In the first case, the two numbers are added and then the result is converted to a string and concatenated with the `"<P>"` string. In the second case, the first operation is a concatenation of a string and a number, so the number is converted to a string at this point. From then on, all the operations are concatenations. To get round this problem, we can use parentheses to force the first operation to be the addition of the two numbers:

```
Response.Write("<P>" + (intInteger + intInteger) + "</P>");
                                                    // result is '<P>24</P>'
```

Managing Components in a Web Application

The second main aspect of using virtual applications in ASP is the ability to better manage the use of components that we instantiate and execute within our script code. We're going to hold off from a detailed description of how this works, and why it is so useful, until the section of the book on ASP components.

What we want to look at very briefly here is the way that the settings we make in the Properties dialog (in Internet Services Manager) for a virtual application affect what happens when we use components in ASP pages, that are within the application.

At the bottom of the Home Directory page of the Properties dialog for a virtual application, there are two combo boxes marked Execute Permissions and Application Protection:

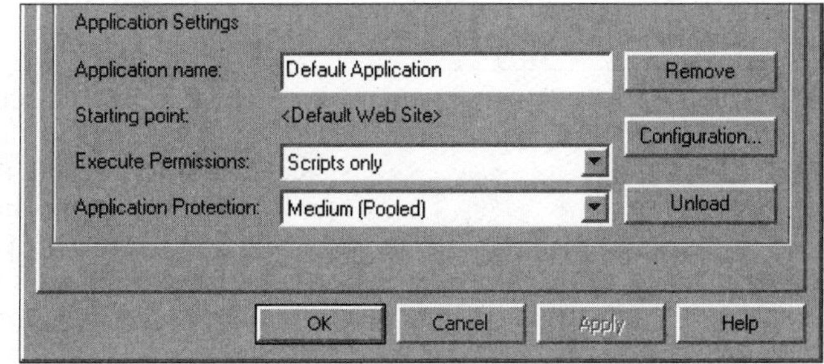

Application Protection and Execution Settings

While we won't be looking at how we create instances of components within a Web page until the next chapter, it's worth listing these options here, as you will probably want to set them when you create your application. The Execute Permissions options are:

Execute Permission	Description
None	No scripts or executables can be run in this virtual application. In effect, this provides a quick and easy way to disable an application if required.
Scripts Only	Allows only script files (such as ASP, IDC or others) to run in this virtual application. Executables cannot be run.
Scripts and Executables	Allows any script or executable to run within this virtual application.

While the Execute Permission options control the type of execution that can take place in the virtual application, the Application Protection options affect the way that executables and components are run. We've already discussed the available options in Chapter 1, but here they are again:

Application Protection	Description
Low (IIS Process)	All application executables and components for ASP virtual applications with this setting are run in the process (i.e. the memory space) of the Web server executable (`Inetinfo.exe`). Hence the Web server is at risk if any one of the executables or components should fail. This provides the fastest and least resource-intensive application execution option.
Medium (Pooled)	(Default) All application executables and components from all ASP virtual applications with this setting are run in the process (i.e. the memory space) of a single shared instance of `DLLHost.exe`. This protects the Web server executable (`Inetinfo.exe`) from the risk of any one of the executables or components failing. However, one failed executable or component can cause the `DLLHost.exe` process to fail, and with it all the other hosted executables and components.

Table Continued on Following Page

Application Protection	Description
High (Isolated)	All application executables and components for an ASP virtual application with this setting are run in the process (i.e. the memory space) of a single instance of `DLLHost.exe`, but each ASP application has its own instance of `DLLHost.exe` that is exclusive to that application. This protects the Web server executable (`Inetinfo.exe`) from the risk of any one of the executables or components failing, and protects the virtual application from risk if an executable or component from another virtual application should fail. Microsoft suggests that a maximum of ten isolated virtual applications should be hosted on any one Web server.

Microsoft recommends a configuration where mission-critical applications run in their own processes – i.e. **High (Isolated)** – and all remaining applications in a shared, pooled process – i.e. **Medium (Pooled)**.

So, having looked at what ASP applications involve, we'll now move on to examine ASP sessions in more detail.

What are ASP Sessions?

ASP sessions introduce the next level of granularity in a Web application. The ASP Application object can be used to store state (i.e. simple variables, objects, arrays, etc.) that is global and accessible to all the users that are 'running the application'. In other words, all the ASP code executed in response to all visitors' requests within this application has access to these values (providing that they have a valid session established, as we'll see shortly).

However, in many cases this is not enough. We need to be able to store values that are specific to each visitor, without having to go through the process of assigning them names that indicate which visitor they belong to. For example, we don't really want to clutter up our application's global space with a heap of values like:

```
MikeJones003PrefFGColor = "darkblue"
MikeJones003PrefBGColor = "white"
MikeJones003PrefLinkColor = "green"
PriscillaDelores001PrefFGColor = "red"
PriscillaDelores001PrefBGColor = "darkgrey"
...
etc.
```

As well as being a load on systems resources, and requiring some clever code to access the correct one for each user, it has another disadvantage. The application exists all the time that there are visitors, which means that the application's global storage area will need to grow and grow, unless we take steps to remove values as users leave the site. All kinds of difficulties start to cloud the issue.

Providing User-Level Scope in a Web Application

Instead of using a global variable store, it would be great to give each visitor their own private variable storage space – but one that is globally available to all the pages that just this particular visitor loads. That way, we can use the same name for each variable, making our ASP code much simpler to implement. The same code would work transparently for each visitor because it would access that visitor's own private storage area:

```
PrefFGColor = "darkblue"
PrefBGColor = "white"
PrefLinkColor = "green"
```

That's where the Session object comes in.

What Can We Store in a Session?

This ability to store values that are global to a specific visitor, but private as far as other visitors are concerned, makes ASP sessions very useful. We can use them to store the same types of values that we do in an ASP Application object, namely:

- Simple variables, such as strings and numbers (stored as `Variants` like all ASP script variables)
- Variant arrays, made up of one or more dimensions
- Variable references (again as Variants) that point to an instance of a COM object

Problems with Sessions

So, sessions provide a great way to store values that are specific to each user. However, there are a couple of pitfalls to watch out for:

- Remember that some browsers and Web servers are case sensitive as far as URLs, paths and filenames are concerned (for example Navigator and Unix/Linux-based servers). If you place hyperlinks to a URL in a page, and they are not exactly the same case, they are *not* treated as being the same in these browsers. Likewise, if the path or filename case is not identical, it is treated as a different directory or file by the browser. This is not important as far as locating the resource on the server is concerned, because IIS is not case-sensitive. So it will accept any mix of upper case and lower case, and return a file with the same letters in a different combination of case. However, if a cookie has a path specified, and it is different to the path specified in a hyperlink in terms of case, the browser may not return it to the server along with a page requested from that directory. This means a user session that depends on that cookie will not be located, and the Session object will not be in scope (i.e. any values in it will not be available). Hence, it's a good idea to stick to all lower case, or an obvious mix of letter case, in all your directory and page names.
- In previous version of IIS and ASP, there were also some minor bug-associated problems with nested applications. Sometimes, when the user left a nested ASP virtual application and returned to the default ASP application level, any global variables with the same name as local variables that they had defined within the nested application failed to reappear. Also, when the session was intentionally terminated, using the `Session.Abandon` method (which we'll meet shortly), any code in the `global.asa` file failed to execute. These have been fixed in ASP 3.0.
- Remember that sessions depend on cookies. Visitors that have cookies disabled, or whose browser doesn't support them, won't get a session started and so will not have access to a Session object.

Disabling Sessions

Even though this wonderful environment where state is available might seem like a gift horse, you should be prepared to don your orthodontic hat and do some looking in mouths. There's no free lunch here, because the server has to work harder to provide sessions and state than it would if it were just sending stateless pages. The activity of sending and decoding the session cookies, and matching them to the respective users, takes up processing cycles.

So, if we have no need for state to be maintained, we can disable sessions to save this processing. For example, on a Web site with no requirement to track visitors or hold global values for them, we can prevent a session being started either by setting properties in the Internet Services Manager application, or by adding code to individual pages where state is not required (as we'll see shortly).

To disable all sessions for the entire Web site, you can edit the properties for the Default Web site application. And to disable sessions for a specific application, you edit the properties for that virtual application. Open the Properties dialog for the appropriate application, and in the Home Directory page click the Configuration button:

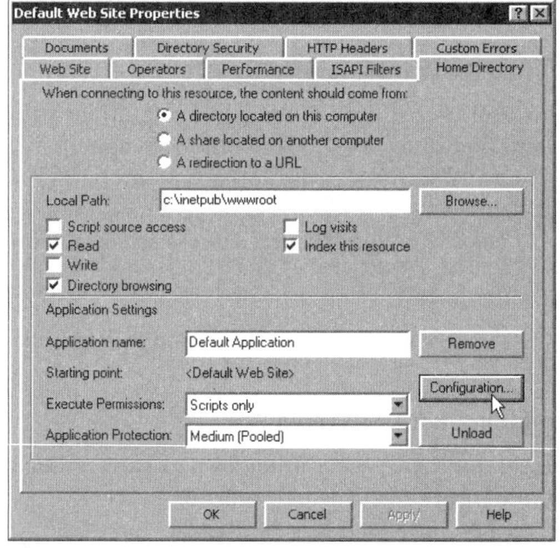

In the Configuration dialog that appears, open the App Options tab. Here, we can enable or disable sessions for the entire application (in this case the complete Default Web site), and also change the default session timeout value. In the screenshot you can see that it's set to 20 minutes. This was the default in previous versions of ASP, and allows us to maintain the same value if required (in ASP 3.0, the default is now 10 minutes):

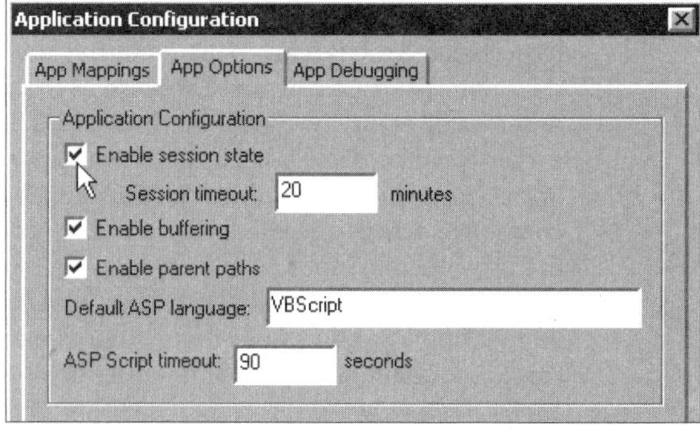

If we want to disable sessions for a specific page, while allowing them to be created and used in other pages of the same application, we can add an entry to the ASP processing directive for that particular page. It is appended to the default language statement (or can be used alone if you aren't specifying a default language):

```
<%@LANGUAGE="VBScript" ENABLESESSIONSTATE="False"%>
```

So, having primed your natural inquisitiveness with descriptions of the ASP Application and Session objects, let's move on to look at them in detail.

The ASP Application and Session Objects

The two ASP objects we've been talking about so far in this chapter, the Application and Session objects, provide us with access to the collections, methods, properties and events that ASP applications and sessions expose. In this section, we'll examine the two objects from a programming point of view.

- The Application object is created when the ASP DLL is loaded in response to the first request for an ASP page. It provides a repository for storing variables and object references that are available to all the pages that all visitors open.
- A Session object is created for each visitor when they first request an ASP page from the site, and remains available until the default timeout period (or the timeout period determined by the script) expires. It provides a repository for storing variables and object references that are available just to the pages that this visitor opens during the lifetime of the session.

The following diagram (repeated from Chapter 1) shows graphically how a user's request and our server's response sit 'within' that user's ASP session. And all sessions sit 'within' the ASP application:

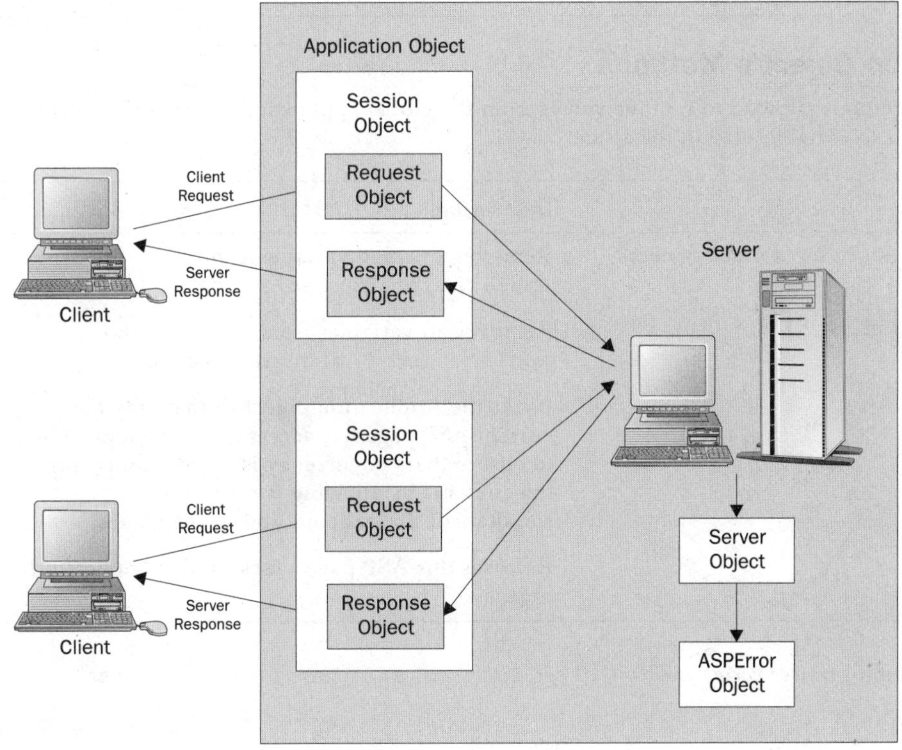

The ASP Application Object Members Summary

This section describes all the collections, methods and events of the Application object (the Application object has no properties). We'll do the same with the Session object (which does have properties) in the following section. Then we'll go on to explore the tasks that we usually apply these objects to, and show you in more detail how to work with the various members of each object.

The Application Object's Collections

The Application object provides two collections that we can use to access the variables and objects that are stored in the global application space. The collections are:

Collection Name	Description
`Contents`	A collection of all of the variables (and their values) that are stored in the Application object, and are *not* defined using an `<OBJECT>` element. This includes Variant arrays and Variant-type object instance references.
`StaticObjects`	A collection of all of the variables that are stored in the Application object by using an `<OBJECT>` element.

The Application Object's Methods

The Application methods allow us to remove values from the global application space, and control concurrent accesses to variables within the space:

Method	Description
`Contents.Remove("`*variable_name*`")`	Removes a named variable from the `Application.Contents` collection.
`Contents.RemoveAll()`	Removes all variables from the `Application.Contents` collection.
`Lock()`	Locks the Application object so that only the current ASP page has access to the contents. Used to ensure that concurrency issues do not corrupt the contents by allowing two users to simultaneously read and update the values.
`Unlock()`	Releases this ASP page's lock on the Application object.

Note you cannot *remove variables from the* `Application.StaticObjects` *collection at run-time.*

The Application Object's Events

The Application object exposes two events that occur when it starts and ends:

Event	Description
`onStart`	Occurs when the ASP application starts, before the page that the user requests is executed and before any user Session objects are created. Used to initialize variables, create objects, or run other code.
`onEnd`	Occurs when the ASP application ends. This is after the last user session has ended, and after any code in the `onEnd` event for that session has executed. All variables existing in the application are destroyed when it ends.

The ASP Session Object Members Summary

This section summarizes all the members of the Session object, with a brief description.

The Session Object's Collections

The Session object provides two collections that we can use to access the variables and objects that are stored in the user's local session space. These collections are:

Collection Name	Description
`Contents`	A collection of all of the variables and their values that are stored in this particular Session object, and are *not* defined using an `<OBJECT>` element. This includes Variant arrays and Variant-type object instance references.
`StaticObjects`	A collection of all of the variables that are stored in this particular Session object by using an `<OBJECT>` element.

The Session Object's Properties

The Session object provides four properties. They are:

Property	Description
CodePage	Read/write. *Integer.* Defines the code page that will be used to display the page content in the browser. The code page is the numeric value of the character set, and different languages and locales may use different code pages. For example, ANSI code page 1252 is used for American English and most European languages. Code page 932 is used for Japanese Kanji.
LCID	Read/write. *Integer.* Defines the locale identifier (LCID) of the page that is sent to the browser. The LCID is a standard international abbreviation that uniquely identifies the locale; for instance 2057 defines a locale where the currency symbol used is '£'. This LCID can also be used in statements such as `FormatCurrency`, where there is an optional `LCID` argument. The LCID for a page can also be set in the opening `<%@..%>` ASP processing directive and overrides the setting in the `LCID` property of the session. A list of the ASP processing directives appears later in this chapter.
SessionID	Read only. *Long.* Returns the session identifier for this session, which is generated by the server when the session is created. Unique only for the duration of the parent Application object, and so may be re-used when a new application is started.
Timeout	Read/write. *Integer.* Defines the timeout period in minutes for this Session object. If the user does not refresh or request a page within the timeout period, the session ends. Can be changed in individual pages as required. The default is 10 minutes, and shorter timeouts may be preferred on a high-usage site.

The Session Object's Methods

The Session methods allow us to remove values from the user-level session space, and terminate sessions on demand:

Method	Description
Contents.Remove("*variable_name*")	Removes a named variable from the `Session.Contents` collection.
Contents.RemoveAll()	Removes all variables from the `Session.Contents` collection.
Abandon()	Ends the current user session and destroys the current Session object once execution of this page is complete. You can still access the current session's variables in this page, even after calling the `Abandon` method. However the next ASP page that is requested by this user will start a new session, and create a new Session object (if any exist).

Note that you cannot *remove variables from the* `Session.StaticObjects` *collection at run-time.*

The Session Object's Events

The Session object exposes two events that occur when the session starts and ends:

Event	Description
`onStart`	Occurs when an ASP user session starts, before the page that the user requests is executed. Used to initialize variables, create objects, or run other code.
`onEnd`	Occurs when an ASP user session ends. This happens when the predetermined session timeout period has elapsed since that user's last page request from the application. All variables existing in the session are destroyed when it ends. It is also possible to end ASP user sessions explicitly in code using the `Abandon` method, and this event occurs when that happens.

Using Application and Session Events

The ASP Application and Session objects exhibit a characteristic that no other integral ASP object does. This is something that you wouldn't normally expect in a server-based scripting environment – the provision of **events**. However, as we saw in the previous tables of the objects' members, these are specific events that are connected with the workings of ASP sessions and applications.

Application and Session Event Handlers

ASP raises an event each time an application or session starts or ends. We can detect and react to these events by writing normal script code in a special file – `global.asa` – located in the root directory of an application (i.e. the `\InetPub\WWWRoot` directory for the Default Web site, or a folder that is defined as a virtual application). This file can also contain one or more HTML `<OBJECT>` elements, used to create component instances that will be used within that application or user's sessions.

We'll be looking at how we create component instances in more detail in Chapter 4. The following code is an example `global.asa` file that we use in our sample pages for this chapter. For the meantime, just accept the code you see for the `<OBJECT>` elements, and the lines that start with the `Set` keyword:

```
<!-- Declare instance of the ASPCounter component
     with application-level scope //-->
<OBJECT ID="ASPCounter" RUNAT="Server" SCOPE="Application"
        PROGID="MSWC.Counters">
</OBJECT>

<!-- Declare instance of the ASPContentLink component
     with session-level scope //-->
<OBJECT ID="ASPContentLink" RUNAT="Server" SCOPE="Session"
        PROGID="MSWC.NextLink">
</OBJECT>

<SCRIPT LANGUAGE="VBScript" RUNAT="Server">

Sub Application_onStart()
```

```
'Create an instance of an ADO Recordset with application-level scope
  Set Application("ADOConnection") _
     = Server.CreateObject("ADODB.Connection")
  Dim varArray(3)                                'Create a Variant array and fill it
  varArray(0) = "This is a"
  varArray(1) = "Variant array"
  varArray(2) = "stored in the"
  varArray(3) = "Application object"
  Application("Variant_Array") = varArray  'Store it in the Application
  Application("Start_Time") = CStr(Now)     'Store the date/time as a string
  Application("Visit_Count") = 0            'Set counter variable to zero

End Sub

Sub Application_onEnd()
  Set Application("ADOConnection") = Nothing
End Sub

Sub Session_onStart()

 'Create an instance of the AdRotator component with session-level scope
  Set Session("ASPAdRotator") = Server.CreateObject("MSWC.AdRotator")
  Dim varArray(3)                                'Create a Variant array and fill it
  varArray(0) = "This is a"
  varArray(1) = "Variant array"
  varArray(2) = "stored in the"
  varArray(3) = "Session object"
  Session("Variant_Array") = varArray       'Store it in the Session
  Session("Start_Time") = CStr(Now)         'Store the date/time as a string

 'We can access the contents of the Request and Response in a Session_onStart
 'event handler for the page that initiated the session. This is the *only*
 'place that the ASP page context is available like this.
 'as an example, we can get the IP address of the user:
  Session("Your_IP_Address") = Request.ServerVariables("REMOTE_ADDR")

Application.Lock                              'Prevent concurrent updates
  intVisits = Application("Visit_Count") + 1   'Increment counter variable
Application("Visit_Count") = intVisits        'Store back in Application
  Application.Unlock                           'Release lock on Application

End Sub

Sub Session_onEnd()
  Set Session("ASPAdRotator") = Nothing
End Sub

</SCRIPT>
```

As this is the `global.asa` file that we'll be using in our example pages in this chapter, you'll need to place it in the root directory of your Web site, or in a directory that you configure to be a virtual application and which contains the other sample files.

Reading and Storing Values

Note in the example above how we read and store Application and Session variables – just like we did in the Request and Response object collections. To set the values of variables:

```
Application("variable_name") = variable_value
Application("variable_name") = variant_array_variable_name
Set Application("variable_name") = object_reference
```

To retrieve the values of variables:

```
variable_value = Application("variable_name")
variant_array_variable = Application("variable_name")
Set object_reference = Application("variable_name")
```

And, of course, we can do likewise for the Session object.

You can see how we `Lock` and `Unlock` the Application object when we access it from a Session event handler, and we need to do the same if we access it from an ASP page. It's not required when we are accessing values in the Application object from code within the Application events. That's because there's only one instance of the Application object in any application, and code within its event handlers runs only when there are no active user sessions.

You can also see how a rudimentary user session counter is implemented. It uses an application-level variable named `Visit_Count`, which is incremented as each new session is started.

And we're not limited to simply storing values in the Application or Session objects either. For example, our own Web Developer Web site at `http://webdev.wrox.co.uk` has a `global.asa` file that writes an entry into a database on the server, with details taken from the `Request.ServerVariables` collection, each time a new session is started. This provides a rudimentary way to count the number of individual visitors we get, and collect some basic information about them.

Creating Variant Arrays

One topic that we haven't discussed – and which we should describe as it's a very useful technique – is the way we can create and use a Variant array to store values in the Session and Application objects. A Variant data type, as we saw earlier, can contain an **array**, rather than just a single value.

> *An array is simply a long row of binary values stored in a specific order in a contiguous area of memory. All that's needed is to arrange for the Variant to point to the first item, and give it information on the size and structure – the scripting engine looks after all that for us anyway.*

We can create an array with one, two, or more dimensions within a Variant variable. We can then assign this to an application-level or user session-level variable, and make the whole array available as appropriate. The code above demonstrated the technique for a simple one-dimension array:

```
Dim varArray(3)
varArray(0) = "This is a"
varArray(1) = "Variant array"
varArray(2) = "stored in the"
varArray(3) = "Session object"
Session("Variant_Array") = varArray
```

When Do Applications and Sessions Start and End?

We mentioned this topic when looking at how ASP applications and session work. To summarize briefly in more down-to-earth terms:

- An application *starts* when the first user requests an ASP page that is within the application scope – i.e. the default root directory of the Web site, or a user-defined virtual application within a subdirectory of the site. This occurs before any user sessions start.

- A session *starts* when any user first requests an ASP page within the default application or a virtual application (if they do not already have an active session).
- A session *ends* when that user has not loaded an ASP page within the timeout period specified for the session. The timeout can be set in script code using the `Session.Timeout` property, set individually for each application in its Properties dialog, or set by changing the default in the IIS metabase via the `IIS:` section of Active Directory. A session also ends after a page containing a call to the `Session.Abandon` method finishes executing.
- An application *ends* immediately after the last active session within that application ends.

The ASP Processing Directive

As we saw in Chapter 1, we can add a **processing directive** to an ASP page. There, we used it to define the default scripting language for the page. However, the processing directive can contain more than one item if required. The keywords that can be used in this statement are:

Directive Keyword	Description
`LANGUAGE="`*language_name*`"`	Sets the default scripting language for the page, as we saw in Chapter 1. For example `<%@LANGUAGE="VBScript"%>`
`ENABLESESSIONSTATE="True"|"False"`	When set to `"True"` prevents a session cookie from being sent to the browser, and so no new Session object will be created and any existing session content will not be available.
`CODEPAGE="`*code_page*`"`	Sets the code page for the page, as discussed earlier in this chapter. For example, `<%@CODEPAGE="1252"%>`
`LCID="`*locale_identifier*`"`	Sets the locale identifier for the page, as discussed earlier in this chapter. For example, `<%@LCID="2057"%>`
`TRANSACTION="`*transaction_type*`"`	Specifies that the page file will run under a transaction context. Legal values are: `"Required"`: the script will run within an existing transaction if one is available, or start a new transaction if not. `"Requires_New"`: the script will always initiate a new transaction. `"Supported"`: the script will run within an existing transaction if one is available, but will *not* start a new transaction. `"Not_Supported"`: the script will not run within any existing transaction, and will not initiate a new transaction. *We look at transactions in more detail in Chapter 18.*

Only one processing directive is permitted on a page, and it should be the first line. We can include more than one of these items in our processing directive – they must be separated by a space, with *no* spaces around the equals sign, for example:

```
<%@LANGUAGE="VBScript" CODEPAGE="1252" LCID="2057"%>
```

The ASP Application Object in Action

We've provided some sample pages that demonstrate the ASP Application and Session objects in use. To use them on your system, you must place them on your Web server within a virtual application, and put the supplied `global.asa` file in the root directory of that application. The easiest way is to put the `global.asa` file we provide in the root directory of your Default Web site (by default `C:\InetPub\WWWRoot`).

> *It is a good idea to rename any existing* `global.asa` *file, say to* `global.old`*, so that you can reinstate it afterwards.*

> **All the sample files for this book can be obtained from our Web site – you'll find all the example pages for the remainder of this chapter in the `Chapter03` subdirectory of the samples.**

The `Default.asp` page in the `Chapter03` samples subdirectory is a simple menu that allows you to run the Application and Session example pages:

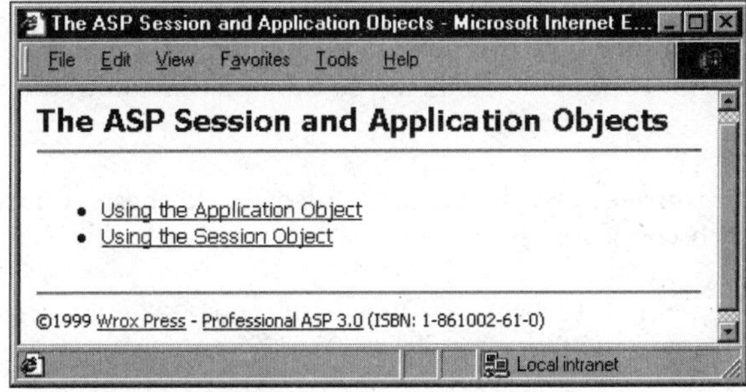

Displaying the Contents of the Application Collections

Click the first link to open the Application Object sample page, named `show_application.asp`. This displays the contents of the current Application object for this virtual application:

You'll notice how the ASPCounter object is a member of the `StaticObjects` collection (it's defined with an `<OBJECT>` element), but the rest (instantiated with `Server.CreateObject`) are members of the `Contents` collection:

You can see the values that we placed into these collections using our example `global.asa` page, which we saw earlier:

```
<!-- Declare instance of the ASPCounter component with
     application-level scope //-->
<OBJECT ID="ASPCounter" RUNAT="Server" SCOPE="Application"
        PROGID="MSWC.Counters">
</OBJECT>
...
...
<SCRIPT LANGUAGE="VBScript" RUNAT="Server">

Sub Application_onStart()

  'Create an instance of an ADO Connection with application-level scope
  Set Application("ADOConnection") = Server.CreateObject("ADODB.Connection")
  Dim varArray(3)                           'Create a Variant array and fill it
  varArray(0) = "This is a"
  varArray(1) = "Variant array"
  varArray(2) = "stored in the"
  varArray(3) = "Application object"
  Application("Variant_Array") = varArray   'Store it in the Application
  Application("Start_Time") = CStr(Now)     'Store the date/time as a string
  Application("Visit_Count") = 0            'Set counter variable to zero

End Sub
...
...
</SCRIPT>
```

The Code to Iterate the Contents Collection

To iterate through the `Contents` collection, we use a `For Each...Next` construct. However, each item in the collection can be a simple Variant-type variable, a Variant array, or a reference to an object. Because we need to handle each type of value differently, we have to examine each one to see what type it is.

We could do this using the `VarType` function in VBScript. However, we decided to use the `IsObject` and `IsArray` functions instead:

```
For Each objItem in Application.Contents

  If IsObject(Application.Contents(objItem)) Then
    Response.Write "Object reference: '" & objItem & "'<BR>"

  ElseIf IsArray(Application.Contents(objItem)) Then
    Response.Write "Array: '" & objItem & "' contents are:<BR>"
    varArray = Application.Contents(objItem)

   'Note: the following only works with a one-dimensional array
    For intLoop = 0 To UBound(varArray)
      Response.Write "  Index(" & intLoop & ") = " & _
                     varArray(intLoop) & "<BR>"
    Next

  Else
    Response.Write "Variable: '" & objItem & "' = " _
                   & Application.Contents(objItem) & "<BR>"

  End If

Next
```

Notice how we retrieve the array from the Session object. We assign it to a local (Variant) variable using:

```
varArray = Application.Contents(objItem)
```

The size of the array (the number of elements) can be found using the `UBound` function, so we can iterate through it with this as the terminating condition:

```
For intLoop = 0 To UBound(varArray)
...
```

This example expects a one-dimensional array, and will only display the contents of such an array. You can edit the code to cope with more dimensions if required, for example:

```
For intLoop = 0 To UBound(varArray)

  intNumberOfDimensions = UBound(varArray, 1)

  For intDimension = 0 To intNumberOfDimensions
    Response.Write "  Index(" & intLoop & ") = " _
                   & varArray(intLoop, intDimension)
  Next

  Response.Write "<BR>"

Next
```

The Code to Iterate the StaticObjects Collection

The `StaticObjects` collection contains all the object references that are declared in `global.asa` by using an `<OBJECT>` element. We iterate this array with more simple code, because we know that each entry should be an object variable. We output the name of the object (as originally defined in its `ID` attribute):

```
For Each objItem in Application.StaticObjects

  If IsObject(Application.StaticObjects(objItem)) Then
    Response.Write "&lt;OBJECT&gt; element: ID='" & objItem & "'<BR>"
  End if

Next
```

Adding Values to the Contents Collection

We can add values to the Application object at runtime in any ASP page in just the same way as we did in the `global.asa` page's script code. The sample page allows us to add a new Variant value to the Application object, and it has a name and value already suggested – you can edit these if you wish:

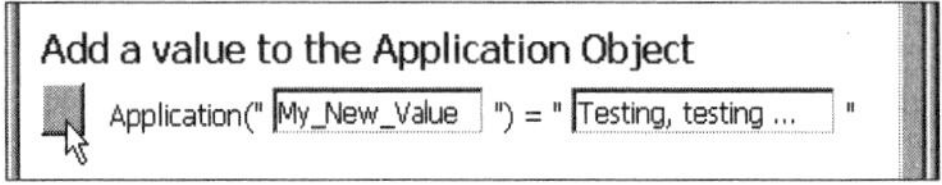

Clicking the button reloads this page, adding the value to the `Application.Contents` collection and displaying it in the list:

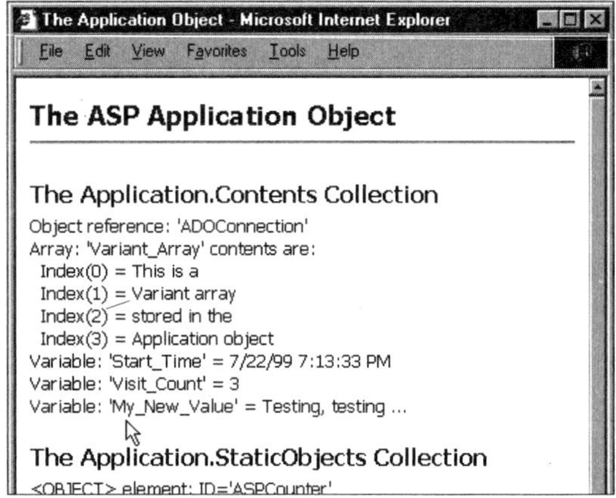

The Code to Add New Contents Entries

All the buttons and other HTML controls are placed on a form in the sample page. The `ACTION` is set to the path of the current page, so it's reloaded when the form is submitted. The `METHOD` is `"POST"`, so that the values in the controls will appear in the `Request.Form` collection. We saw both of these techniques in the previous chapter:

```
<FORM ACTION="<% = Request.ServerVariables("SCRIPT_NAME") %>" METHOD="POST">
```

The buttons on the form are all normal HTML `INPUT` controls, with the same (three non-breaking spaces) caption but with different names. For example, the code to create the first button (to add values to the Application object) is:

```
<INPUT TYPE="SUBMIT" NAME="cmdAdd" VALUE="   ">
```

When the page is reloaded, we can check the Request.Form collection to see which SUBMIT button was clicked, and carry out the appropriate action. In the case of the button to add a value to the Application object, which is named cmdAdd in the HTML <INPUT> element that creates it, we use:

```
If Len(Request.Form("cmdAdd")) Then
  strVarName = Request.Form("txtVarName")
  strVarValue = Request.Form("txtVarValue")
  Application.Lock
  Application(strVarName) = strVarValue
  Application.Unlock
End If
```

Notice how we use the Application.Lock and Application.Unlock methods to ensure that the value is not corrupted by access from two users concurrently. This is unlikely to happen when we are just setting it to a particular value, as opposed to reading it and then updating it with a value that's dependent on the value we just read. However, it's wise to always use the Lock and Unlock methods.

Removing Values From the Contents Collection

At the bottom of the sample page are two buttons that allow us to remove values from the Application.Contents collection. The first removes a single named value from the collection, and the drop-down list box displays a list of the names of the values in the Contents collection (remember, we can't remove values from the StaticObjects collection because they are, as the name suggests, *static*):

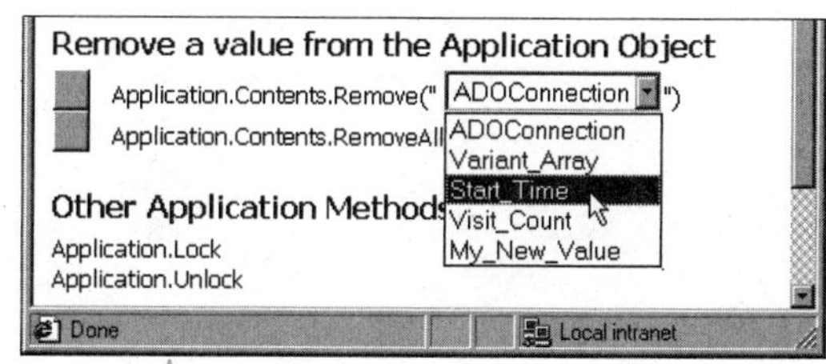

The list is created as the ASP page is executing by iterating through the Contents collection as we did before. But this time, we collect just the names of each item and place them into <OPTION> elements within the <SELECT> list element:

```
...
<SELECT NAME="lstRemove" SIZE="1">
<%
For Each objItem in Application.Contents
  Response.Write "<OPTION>" & objItem & "</OPTION>"
Next
%>
</SELECT>
...
```

When viewed in the browser, after execution of the ASP code, the result is:

```
<SELECT NAME="lstRemove" SIZE="1">
  <OPTION>ADOConnection</OPTION>
  <OPTION>Variant_Array</OPTION>
  <OPTION>Start_Time</OPTION>
  <OPTION>Visit_Count</OPTION>
  <OPTION>My_New_Value</OPTION>
</SELECT>
```

Removing a Single Value

When we click the button to remove a single value, the form is again submitted to the same page, but this time we look for the `SUBMIT` button named `cmdRemoveThis`. If it exists (i.e. this button was clicked) we use the value from the list box in a call to the `Remove` method of the `Application.Contents` collection:

```
If Len(Request.Form("cmdRemoveThis")) Then
  strToRemove = Request.Form("lstRemove")
  Application.Lock
  Application.Contents.Remove(strToRemove)
  Application.Unlock
End If
```

Notice that this is a method of the `Contents` collection, not the Application object. The syntax is `Application.Contents.Remove`, and not `Application.Remove`.

Here's the result, with the `Start_Time` value removed from the `Contents` collection:

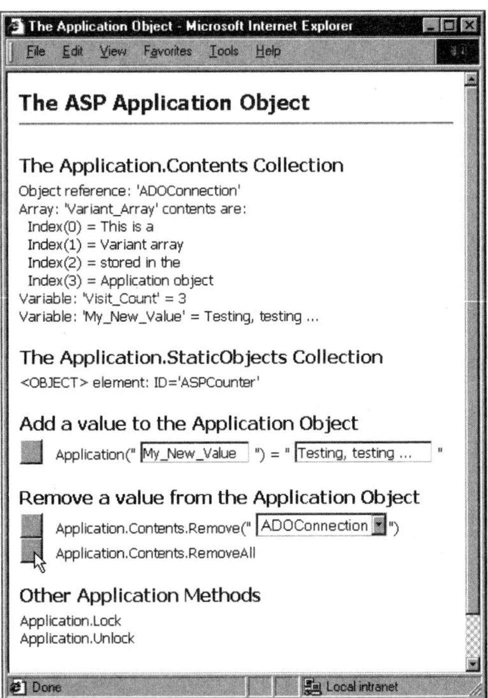

Removing All the Values

If the last of the three `SUBMIT`-type buttons is clicked (as shown in the previous screenshot), the code in the page detects that this button, named `cmdRemoveAll` was clicked. It executes the `RemoveAll` method of the `Application.Contents` collection:

```
If Len(Request.Form("cmdRemoveAll")) Then
  Application.Lock
  Application.Contents.RemoveAll
  Application.Unlock
End If
```

Again, notice that this is a method of the `Contents` *collection, not the* `Application`*. The syntax is* `Application.Contents.RemoveAll`*, not* `Application.RemoveAll`*.*

Here's the result, with all the values removed from the `Contents` collection (remember that we can't remove items from the `StaticObjects` collection at run-time):

The ASP Session Object in Action

The second of our sample pages, `show_session.asp`, demonstrates how we can use the Session object. You can open it by going back to the opening menu page (`Default.asp`) in the `Chapter03` samples subdirectory.

Displaying and Updating the Session Collections

The Session Object example page looks similar to the one for the Application Object that we've just been using. It iterates through the `Contents` and `StaticObjects` collections of the Session object, displaying their names and (where possible) their values. If you compare these values with the Application Object page, you'll see the differences.

You can also see the extra value for the IP address of the client. This was collected from the `Request.ServerVariables` collection by code in `global.asa` when the session started. This page also displays the values of the four Session properties:

Here are the relevant sections of the `global.asa` file that we use in our example – those that add the default values to the session that you see in the screenshot above:

```
...
<!-- declare instance of the ASPContentLink component with
     session-level scope //-->
<OBJECT ID="ASPContentLink" RUNAT="Server" SCOPE="Session"
        PROGID="MSWC.NextLink">
</OBJECT>

<SCRIPT LANGUAGE="VBScript" RUNAT="Server">
...
...
Sub Session_onStart()

  'Create an instance of the AdRotator component with session-level scope
  Set Session("ASPAdRotator") = Server.CreateObject("MSWC.AdRotator")
  Dim varArray(3)                           'Create a Variant array and fill it
  varArray(0) = "This is a"
  varArray(1) = "Variant array"
  varArray(2) = "stored in the"
  varArray(3) = "Session object"
  Session("Variant_Array") = varArray       'Store it in the Session
  Session("Start_Time") = CStr(Now)         'Store the date/time as a string
```

```
    'We can access the contents of the Request and Response in a Session_onStart
    'event handler for the page that initiated the session. This is the *only*
    'place that the ASP page context is available like this.
    'as an example, we can get the IP address of the user:
    Session("Your_IP_Address") = Request.ServerVariables("REMOTE_ADDR")

    Application.Lock                               'Prevent concurrent updates
    intVisits = Application("Visit_Count") + 1     'Increment counter variable
    Application("Visit_Count") = intVisits         'Store back in Application
    Application.Unlock                             'Release lock on Application

  End Sub
  ...
  ...
  </SCRIPT>
```

The code to iterate through the `Contents` and `StaticObjects` collections is the same as what we used in the **Application Object** example page earlier, except that it (of course) references the `Session.Contents` and `Session.StaticObjects` collections rather than the `Application.Contents` and `Application.StaticObjects` collections.

Near the bottom of the page are buttons to add values to, and remove them from, the `Session.Contents` collection. These work in exactly the same way as the equivalents in the **Application Object** example page, except that they too access the `Session.Contents` collection – and its `Remove` and `RemoveAll` methods. So, we won't be repeating the code or explanations here.

Terminating a User Session

At the bottom of the **Session Object** page is a button that terminates the current user session, by calling the `Abandon` method of their Session object. This is on the same form as the rest of the HTML controls, and is named `cmdAbandon`. When the form is submitted to this page again, we look for this value in the `Request.Form` collection (as we did in the **Application Object** example). If we find it, we redirect the user to a different page:

```
If Len(Request.Form("cmdAbandon")) Then
  Response.Clear
  Response.Redirect "abandon.asp"
  Response.End
End If
```

The new page, named `abandon.asp`, is quite simple. Besides the text and HTML to create the messages, the only code is this:

```
<% Session.Abandon %>
```

The remainder of the page is a form containing just a single `SUBMIT` button. Notice how we use the value for the URL of the referring page (`HTTP_REFERER`) from the `Request.ServerVariables` collection to ensure that the previous page (our **Session Object** example page) is reloaded:

```
<FORM ACTION="<% = Request.ServerVariables("HTTP_REFERER") %>" METHOD="POST">

  <P><DIV CLASS="subhead">Your Session Has Been Terminated</DIV>

  A new <B>Session</B> will be started when you load another<BR>
  ASP page. It will contain any values that are defined in<BR>
  the <B>global.asa</B> file for this application.<P>

  <INPUT TYPE="SUBMIT" NAME="cmdOK" VALUE="   ">
    Return to the previous page<P>

</FORM>
```

This is the result. At this point the current user session has been terminated (abandoned) and the user cannot reference the contents of the original Session collections or properties:

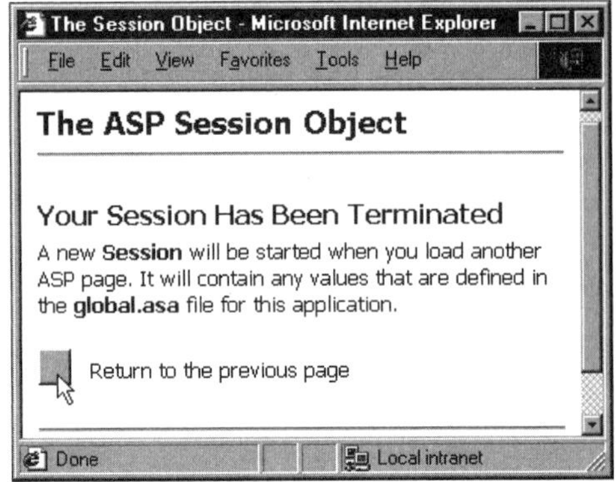

However, bear in mind this only occurs *after* the page containing the call to the `Abandon` method has *finished* executing. The user's session content can be obtained from the Session object while the page containing the `Abandon` method is still executing – even after the call to the method has been made. The session only ends when the page does.

Of course, when we go back to the Session Objects example page, which displays the session contents, we will start a new ASP session. This will have a different `Start_Time` value, and the other default session values created by executing the `Session_onStart` code in `global.asa`:

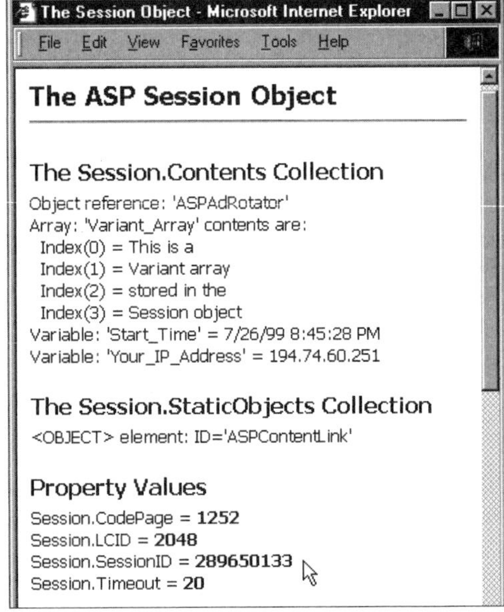

Notice that the `Session.SessionID` *property value has* not *changed. ASP tends to allocate the same session ID again, so you can't rely on this to indicate that a new session has started.*

Summary

In this chapter, we've looked at two more of the ASP intrinsic objects: the Application and Session objects. These equate to the concepts in ASP of an **application** and a user **session** (both specific terms, and not the more generic versions that we often imply when talking generally). ASP applications allow us to allocate special properties to a set of pages that define how IIS and ASP will manage these pages, and other components that they use.

However, the main reason for using ASP applications and sessions is often to obtain **state** automatically. In other words, the ability to store information and variable references that are either global and available to all pages loaded by users (i.e. in an application), or available to all pages for just a specific user (in a session). This makes it much easier to build Web applications (as in the more general terminology – applications that work on the Web, but can behave like traditional compiled applications to achieve specific tasks).

We finished up the chapter with a look at how we use the ASP Application and Session objects in detail, through a couple of sample pages. These pages demonstrate all the techniques that are available with the two objects we've been studying.

So, this chapter covered:

- What Web applications are, and how they relate to the ASP Application object
- What user sessions are, and how they relate to the ASP Session object
- How ASP creates and manages applications and sessions automatically for us
- The features that are provided by the Application and Session objects
- How we put the Application and Session objects to work in our ASP pages

In the next chapter, we move on to another of the ASP intrinsic objects – the `Server` object and it's there that we'll find most of the exciting new features of ASP 3.0.

N
W

4

Server Processes and the ASP Server Object

In the previous chapters, we've examined some of the intrinsic objects that are implemented within ASP. In particular, we've looked at the Request and Response objects that provide us with access to the client's request and our server's response, and the Session and Application objects that allow us to manage state and values that are global, or local to a specific client. There is one more major object that's part of ASP – the **Server** object. This chapter is devoted to the background and use of this object.

The Server object provides us with a way of extending the capabilities of our ASP pages, by instantiating and using other external objects and components within our server-side script. In fact, many would say that this object is *the* major factor for the growth in popularity of ASP. The introduction of the Server object makes a lot of sense, because it means that ASP itself does not have to incorporate all the features that we might want. It allows us to call on other applications and components to do the work that they are specifically designed for.

This also fits in nicely with the overall aims of building applications that are made up of individual objects, rather than the 'do-everything' monoliths that we're so used to seeing eat up space on our hard disks. The whole world is moving towards the concept of componentization and 'plug and play' – not only in the computing world, but in every walk of life. These days, when your car or TV breaks down, it's likely that the mechanic or engineer will simply pull out the faulty part and plug a new one in. Even car workshops and TV repairmen are becoming object-oriented.

However, IIS also supports the more traditional ways of using external objects and interacting with the server's environment. With one particular exception these are not really part of ASP, but they are often very useful and have been better integrated with ASP through some new features of the Server object. We'll briefly review these while we're looking at the whole issue of the server's role in ASP and componentization. Then we'll go on to look at the ASP Server object in detail.

So, in this chapter, we'll see:

- The background and use of traditional server-side include (SSI) directives
- What the ASP Server object is designed to achieve, and how it compares with SSI
- How we use the Server object to instantiate and work with external components and applications
- How we use the Server object to execute encapsulated scripts, or other ASP pages
- How we use the Server object to manage errors that occur in our scripts
- How we use the Server object to perform format conversions for HTML or HTTP compatibility

The Server object is part of a process of handling errors in ASP pages that is new in IIS 5.0 and ASP 3.0. We'll see how it works in this chapter, although there is a separate chapter (Chapter 7) devoted to a whole range of debugging and error handling topics. The discussion of error handling in this chapter will therefore be brief, and limited to the ways that the Server object is directly involved in the process.

Server-Side Processing in Dynamic Pages

As far as server-side processing is concerned, ASP is a relatively new technology for producing dynamic Web pages. What do we mean by dynamic pages? Well forget all about the advances in client-side functionality for a moment. We're not talking about things like client-side scripting, Java Applets, Dynamic HTML or ActiveX controls. What we mean by a dynamic page is a page that is specifically created by the server in response to a client request, and which may be different each time, depending on a variety of circumstances.

As a simple example, it might just be a page that contains the current date and time. The page will obviously display a different value each time the page is requested, because the date and time will depend on the server's clock, or on a resource that provides the date and time (for example a separate server or a feed from a standard clock on the Internet). Of course, our dynamic pages will be more complex than this, perhaps displaying the current values of some records from a database or a summary of waiting email messages on a mail server. What's important is that the server isn't just reading a plain HTML page or text file from disk and sending it to the client – it's actually having to do some work itself to create the page.

The Internet Server Application Programming Interface

In Chapter 1, we looked at some of the ways that dynamic pages can be created. The traditional technique is through an interface to the Web server known as the **Internet Server Application Programming Interface**, or **ISAPI**.

The ISAPI can be used to execute other applications, and these applications can read the values of the client's request and create the Web server's response through the 'C'-style `stdin` and `stdout` stream functions. All the ISAPI application has to do is write the text and HTML that make up the resulting page to the Web server's output via the `stdout` function. In fact, this is actually what the ASP DLL does under the covers, though in a more object-oriented way.

Internet Information Server has supported ISAPI applications and script interpreters since its inception. It also provides a special interpreter DLL that offers another way of accessing the server's request and response, though in a more limited way. This is through **Server-Side Include** directives – so called because they are executed on the server, and the result is included in the response sent to the client. This feature is implemented in IIS through a DLL named `ssinc.dll`. By default IIS maps any pages that have the file extension `.shtml`, `.shtm` or `.stm` to this DLL. You can see the mappings by opening the Properties dialog for the Default Web site, and clicking the Configuration button in the Application Settings section:

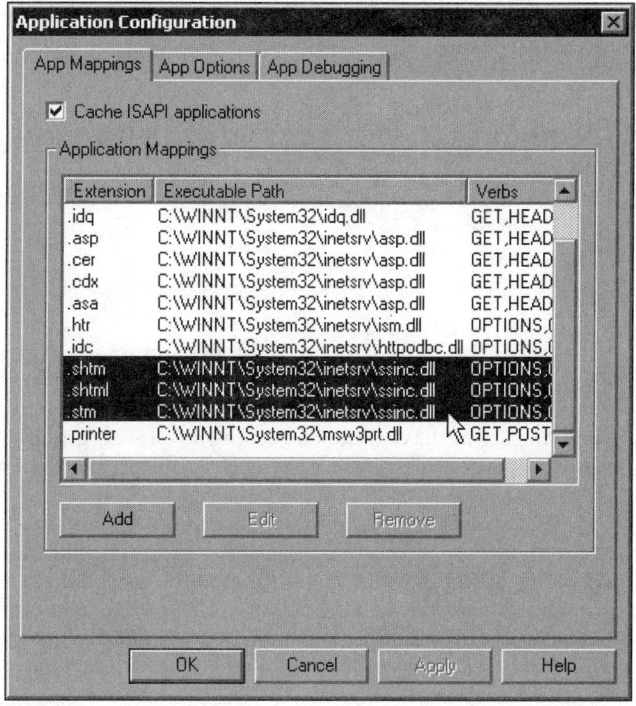

So, a page with one of these mapped extensions will be sent to the `ssinc.dll` for processing. There, any server-side include statements in the page are acted upon, and the result (if any) is inserted into the server's response and hence into the page that the client receives.

> *One interesting point is that, because these files are mapped to the `ssinc.dll` file and not to our ASP DLL (`asp.dll`), any ASP code in these pages will be ignored and sent to the client as it stands – the client will get to see the script, as it won't have been executed. However, in ASP 3.0 there is a way to avoid this, which we'll come back to later on when we look at the `Execute` and `Transfer` methods of the Server object.*

Server-Side Include (SSI) Directives

What can we do with server-side include statements, or **directives** as they're more properly known? Well, to be honest, not much – unless we decide to create our own executable files that run on the Web server, and can access the ISAPI via the `stdin` and `stdout` functions. This really means writing them in C, C++ or perhaps another language like Delphi. Visual Basic isn't really suitable for this. Besides, almost all of the things that we can do with SSI instructions can be achieved equally well from within ASP. In many ways, the SSI features of IIS are there for backward compatibility with older Web sites and Web pages that use these features.

However, there may be times when we do want to use SSI on our site rather than (or as well as) ASP. In IIS 5.0, server-side includes can be integrated with ASP pages in a site far more easily than before, so you may find them useful – especially as a way of executing operating system commands or legacy CGI applications. We'll look very briefly at the instructions that are available.

One of these, the #include directive, has been used with ASP for some time, as well as in SSI pages. In fact, this has been the cause of much confusion for ASP developers who don't have a traditional Web development background.

The Mysterious ASP #include Directive

Within an ASP page, we can use the #include instruction to insert the contents of another file into our page:

```
<!-- #include file="/scripts/usefulbits.inc" -->
```

This takes the entire content of the file and inserts it into the page, replacing the <!-- #include..--> line. It's a useful technique for inserting sections of HTML that we use over and over again in this and/or other pages, and it's also regularly used to insert sections of code. For example, if we have a file containing several script functions (or just in-line script code) that we use in several pages, we can use #include to insert this into each page where it's required.

This provides a level of componentization for our pages by separating script from content. It means that updates to the script are automatically reflected in every page that uses the 'include' file the next time it's opened by the client. Include files are also an easy way to insert information that is specific to a server, so that moving the site to another server doesn't mean having to edit all the pages that refer to the original server (obvious examples are database connection strings or links that specify a full URL or server name). And this can lead to greatly reduced maintenance costs.

For example, we could use the following as an include file named connect.inc:

```
<%
strConnect = "SERVER=myserver;DATABASE=mydb;DRIVER={SQL Server};" _
             & "UID=username;PWD=secretpassword"
%>
```

And we can then use this in any of our pages with:

```
<!-- #include file="path_to_file\connect.inc" -->
<%
...
strTheConnectionString = strConnect   'From include file
...
%>
```

Another other situation where 'include' files can be useful is when we have blocks of content that are updated at specific intervals. For example, the page that displays the list of books on the Wrox Web Developer site contains a table holding all the cover images, book titles and action buttons. The HTML and text for this table is held in a separate file, which is included in the main page with a single #include statement. Each time a new book is added to the database from which the page is constructed, the 'include' text file is completely rebuilt from that database, and written to disk as a text file:

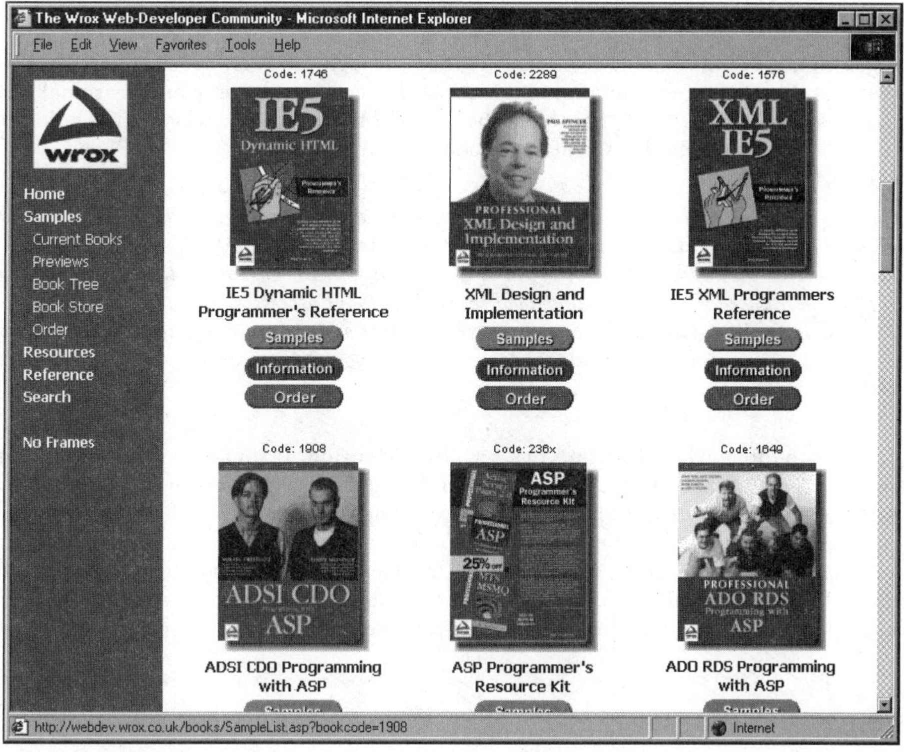

This technique vastly reduces the load on our Web server and database server, and produces a faster response for visitors to the site.

Include Files and ASP

But the `#include` instruction we use in an ASP page (i.e. a page with the `.asp` file extension) isn't actually processed like a true SSI directive. It's simply a particular instruction that ASP recognizes as it parses the file. `ssinc.dll` is used directly to carry out the SSI `#include` directive. The complete page, with the `#include` instruction replaced by the contents of the file it references, is then interpreted by ASP.

This means that ASP has no control over what happens in the `#include` statement, which is why trying to set the value of the `#include` file reference with ASP code doesn't work. For example, you may be tempted to try:

```
<%
'This will *not* work
strIncludeURL = Request.Form("FileName")
%>
...
<!-- #include file="<% = strIncludeURL %>" -->
```

This won't work because `ssinc.dll` will look for a file named `<% = strIncludeURL %>`, and won't be able to find it – even if you do have strange file-naming habits.

Security of Include Files

ASP pages on a Web server cannot be downloaded through the Web Services section of IIS to a client without the script they contain being executed. Yes, there have been occasional security holes found, such as the famous `$DATA` problem that hit all Microsoft Web servers that hold the Web content on NTFS-formatted disks. This has been fixed in IIS 5.0.

The `$DATA` problem occurred because all files on a Windows NTFS drive have a default 'value', which is the content of the file, and this is denoted by the suffix '`::$DATA`' after the filename. It was discovered that adding this to the end of a URL for an ASP page upset the script mappings in IIS, and allowed the server to download the page without processing the script within it. A fix is available for IIS4 and earlier versions, or you can just add the mappings to force IIS to execute the page as normal: i.e. add mappings for `.asp::$DATA` and `.asa::$DATA`, both pointing to the file `asp.dll`.

Include files are often given the `.inc` or `.txt` file extension. If someone discovers the path and filename of an include file on your site, they can download it without it being executed as part of an ASP page by typing the URL of the include file into the **Address** bar of their browser. To prevent this, especially where the files contain sensitive information such as a database connection string, you may wish to give them the `.asp` file extension. In this case, if a user attempts to download one, it is passed to ASP first. ASP will execute any script code in the file, and only send the results. So, say we have a connection string defined in our include file like this:

```
<%
strConnect = "SERVER=myserver;DATABASE=mydb;DRIVER={SQL Server};" _
             & "UID=username;PWD=secretpassword"
Response.Write vbCrlf   'Output a carriage return character
%>
```

The client will only receive a single carriage return and not the script code, because it's been executed on the server by ASP. If we don't include the carriage return, the browser hangs waiting for a response (although that really isn't our problem anyway – we don't intend to allow the user to access this file directly).

IIS 5.0 and Windows Access Control Lists

In IIS 5.0, Microsoft has also changed the way that server-side include files are accessed by the Web server and operating system.

In previous versions of IIS, when the `ssinc.dll` loads an include file that is referenced by a virtual URL (i.e. used `VIRTUAL="filename"`, rather than `FILE="filename"`), it circumvents Windows own security features and ignores any security settings on the file or the directory where it is stored. Now, in IIS 5.0, the account under which the current ASP or SSI page is running must have suitable permissions set in the Windows Access Control List (ACL) for the file and directory. If not, the SSI instruction will fail.

Server Side Include Directives Summary

As well as the `#include` statement that we've already looked at, there are five other server-side include directives supported by IIS (remember that, with the exception of `#include`, these cannot be executed within an ASP page):

Directive	Description

`#include`	Inserts the contents of a specified file into the response stream being sent to the client, replacing the directive. For example:
	
	`<!-- #include FILE="usefulbits.inc" -->`
	
	This inserts the contents of the file named `usefulbits.inc` into the response. The file can be described by a relative or full path and filename combination, such as `FILE="..\scripts\myscr.inc"`. It can alternatively be described using a virtual relative or absolute path using the `VIRTUAL` attribute, for example:
	
	`<!-- #include VIRTUAL="/mysite/usefulbits.inc" -->`
	
	`<!-- #include VIRTUAL="../../thisbit/usefulbits.inc" -->`

`#config`	Specifies the format that will be used for dates, times and file sizes in following directives, and the text of the generic SSI error message that is returned to the client. For example:
	
	`<!-- #config ERRMSG="SSI Processing Error" -->`
	
	Sets the SSI error message text to 'SSI Processing Error'.
	
	`<!-- #config TIMEFMT ="%A, %B %d %Y %H:%M:%S" -->`
	
	Sets the format for dates and times that are returned by following SSI directives. This example sets a format style of Saturday, August 14 1999 10:34:50. A list of the tokens that can be used in the format string is given in Appendix C.
	
	`<!-- #config SIZEFMT ="BYTES" -->`
	
	Sets the unit by which file sizes returned by following SSI directives will be calculated. This example sets the unit to bytes. The alternative value for `SIZEFMT` is `"ABBREV"`, which specifies that the size calculation will return the file size in kilobytes (KB).

`#echo`	Inserts the value of an HTTP environment variable into the response stream being sent to the client, replacing the directive. For example: `<!-- #echo VAR="SERVER_NAME" -->` Writes the name of the server that is executing the directive into the page.

Table Continued on Following Page

Directive	Description

`#exec`	Executes a program or a shell command on the server. For example:
	
	`<!-- #exec CGI="/scripts/myapp.exe?value1=this&value2=that" -->`
	
	Executes the CGI application named `myapp.exe` in the context of the Web server (i.e. with access to the request and response via the ISAPI). It will also pass the value of the query string `value1=this&value2=that` to the application. The application runs in a separate memory space from the Web server.
	
	`<!-- #exec CMD="cmd.exe /C iisreset /stop" -->`
	
	Starts an instance of the specified operating system command interpreter (in this case `cmd.exe`), and executes the command `iisreset /stop`. The `/C` parameter instructs the command interpreter to exit automatically once the command has been executed. You must add the following entry to the Windows Registry when using the `CMD` version of `#exec`:
	
	`HKEY_LOCAL_MACHINE`
	`\SYSTEM`
	`\CurrentControlSet`
	`\Services`
	`\W3SVC`
	`\Parameters`
	`\SSIEnableCmdDirective`
	
	Set the value to `1` and restart the WWW service to allow the `CMD` token to be used in the `#exec` directive. Set it to `0` to disable it and prevent unauthorized use.

`#flastmod`	Inserts the date and time that a specified file was last modified into the response stream being sent to the client, replacing the directive. For example:
	
	`<!-- #flastmod FILE="Default.asp" -->`
	
	Like the `#include` directive, the file can alternatively be defined using a `VIRTUAL` path such as:
	
	`VIRTUAL="/mysite/usefulbits.inc"`
	
	or
	
	`VIRTUAL="../thisbit/usefulbits.inc"`

Directive	Description

`#fsize`	Inserts the size of a specified file into the response stream being sent to the client, replacing the directive. For example:
	`<!-- #fsize FILE="Default.asp" -->`
	Like the `#include` directive, the file can alternatively be defined using a `VIRTUAL` path such as:
	`VIRTUAL="/mysite/usefulbits.inc"`
	or
	`VIRTUAL="../thisbit/usefulbits.inc"`

The IISRESET Utility

One of the new utilities provided with IIS 5.0 is the `iisreset.exe` program. It is useful as a command-line utility to control the Internet services running on the local or a networked computer, providing that the account used to execute the utility has Administrator privileges. It can be used to stop or start all the services in the correct order, display the service status, reboot the server machine, and enable and disable service management. For example:

```
iisreset /RESTART /TIMEOUT:30 /REBOOTONERROR
```

Will stop and restart all the Internet services in the correct sequence. If a service fails to stop or restart within the specified timeout period of 30 seconds, the server will reboot. Some of the switches can be used in a `CMD`-type `#echo` SSI directive, providing that the page has anonymous access removed and the user supplies details of a valid account that has Administrator privileges on the target server. A full description of this utility and the available command switches is in Appendix G.

The NET STOP and NET START Commands

The `net.exe` utility can be used to manage any service running on a server, either locally or from another machine, providing that the account used to execute the utility has Administrator privileges. Although not recommended for use with Internet services such as the WWW or FTP service, it is useful for stopping and starting other services (in fact, the `net` command can be used to issue a whole range of other network-related commands as well).

The syntax is `net [start | stop]` *service_name*

So, for example, we can use it to stop and start the Microsoft Indexing Service with the commands: `net stop cisvc` and `net start cisvc`. It can be used in a `CMD`-type `#echo` SSI directive, providing that the page has anonymous access removed and the user supplies details of a valid account that has Administrator privileges on the target server. We'll see an example of this shortly.

> *A full list of all the options and switches for the `net` command can be found in the Windows 2000 Help files. Select Help from the Start menu, and in the Index page of the Help window look for 'net commands'.*

An Example of Server-Side Includes In Action

We've provided some sample pages that you can use to experiment with the various server-side include statements. Open the `Chapter04` subdirectory of the samples to display the SSI Directives and the ASP Server Object main page (this is `Default.asp` in the `Chapter04` directory):

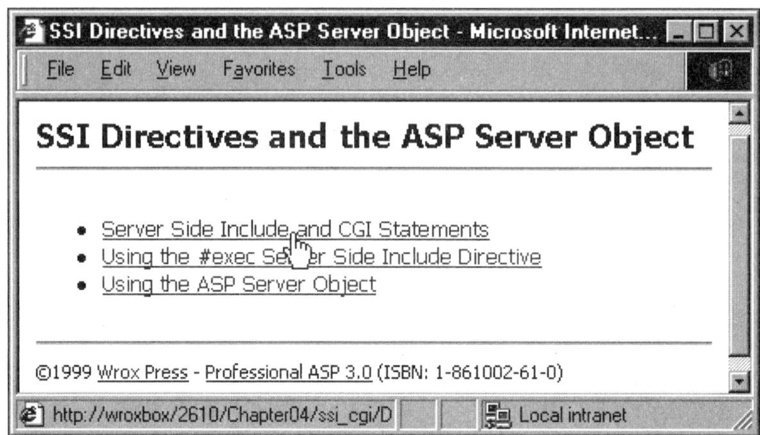

All the samples for this book can be downloaded from our Web sites. You'll find all the example pages for the remainder of this chapter in the `Chapter04` subdirectory of the samples.

Using the SSI/CGI Processing Directives

Click the link to the Server-Side Include and CGI Statements page. This opens the page named `ssi_cgi.stm`. Note the `.stm` file extension – this is *not* an ASP page. This page uses all of the SSI directives we've looked at earlier except for the `#exec` directive (which we'll see shortly). The page displays the directive it is using, followed, where appropriate, by the result:

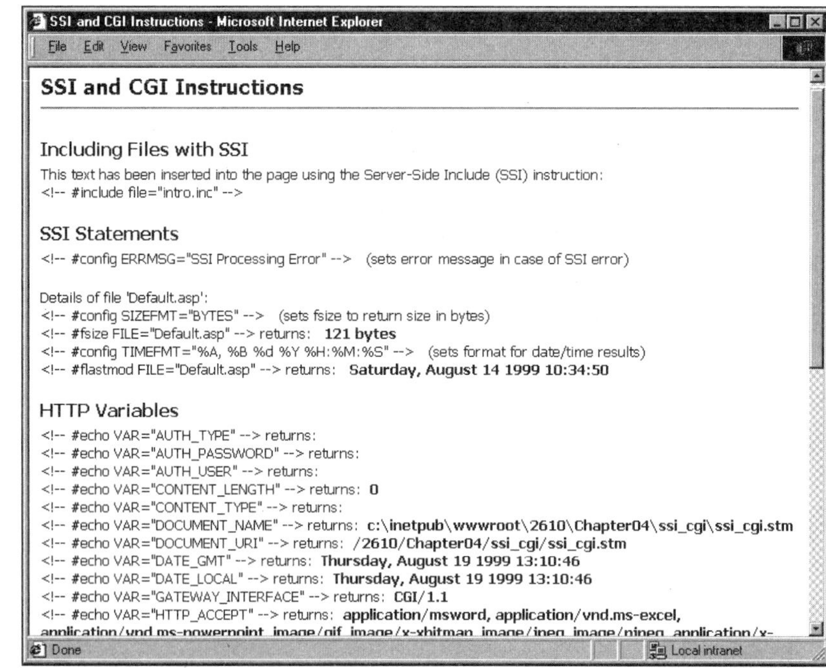

The #include Directive

The first section of the page, Including Files with SSI, displays the contents of another separate file named `intro.inc`. This is the complete content of that file:

```
<P><DIV CLASS="subhead">Including Files with SSI</DIV>
This text has been inserted into the page using the Server-Side Include (SSI)
instruction:<BR>
&lt;!-- #include file="intro.inc" --&gt;<P>
```

Notice how we have to use the HTML entities `<` and `>` to display the angle brackets in the page. If we didn't, they would be treated as parts of the comment element, and would cause the instruction within it to be executed.

The code in the main `ssi_cgi.stm` page that inserts this file into the page is simply:

```
<!-- #include file="intro.inc" -->
```

The #config, #fsize and #flastmod Directives

The next section of the page displays the size and last-modified date of a file named `Default.asp` in the same directory as this page. It uses the `#config` directive three times:

- Once to set the SSI error message
- Once to set the format for dates and times
- Once to set the format for file size calculations

It uses the `#fsize` and `#flastmod` directives to insert the values into the page:

```
<P><DIV CLASS="subhead">SSI Statements</DIV>
&lt;!-- #config ERRMSG="SSI Processing Error" --&gt;  
(sets error message in case of SSI error)<BR>
<!-- #config ERRMSG="SSI Processing Error" --><P>

Details of file 'Default.asp':<BR>
&lt;!-- #config SIZEFMT="BYTES" --&gt;  
(sets fsize to return size in bytes)<BR>
<!-- #config SIZEFMT="BYTES" -->

&lt;!-- #fsize FILE="Default.asp" --&gt;
returns:   <B><!-- #fsize FILE="Default.asp" --> bytes</B><BR>

&lt;!-- #config TIMEFMT="%A, %B %d %Y %H:%M:%S" --&gt;  
(sets format for date/time results)<BR>
<!-- #config TIMEFMT="%A, %B %d %Y %H:%M:%S" -->

&lt;!-- #flastmod FILE="Default.asp" --&gt;
returns:   <B><!-- #flastmod file="Default.asp" --></B><P>
```

The #echo Directive

The final section of the page (only some of which is visible in the screenshot) displays the contents of all the HTTP headers that can be accessed using the `#echo` directive. The code for each one is the same, with just the `VAR` attribute value changed. There is a full list of all the permissible values of the `VAR` attribute in Appendix G:

```
<DIV CLASS="subhead">HTTP Variables</DIV>
&lt;!-- #echo VAR="AUTH_TYPE" --&gt;
returns:  <B><!-- #echo var="AUTH_TYPE" --></B><BR>
&lt;!-- #echo VAR="AUTH_PASSWORD" --&gt;
returns:  <B><!-- #echo var="AUTH_PASSWORD" --></B><BR>
... etc ...
```

Using the #exec Directive

The `#exec` directive is more difficult to use than the other SSI directives, and for this reason we've separated it out into another set of pages. However, you can access the starting page shown in the next screenshot from the main ASP Server Object and SSI Directives menu, which we started from earlier on.

In that page, select the link for Using the #exec Server-Side Include Directive. This opens the SSI #exec Directive page:

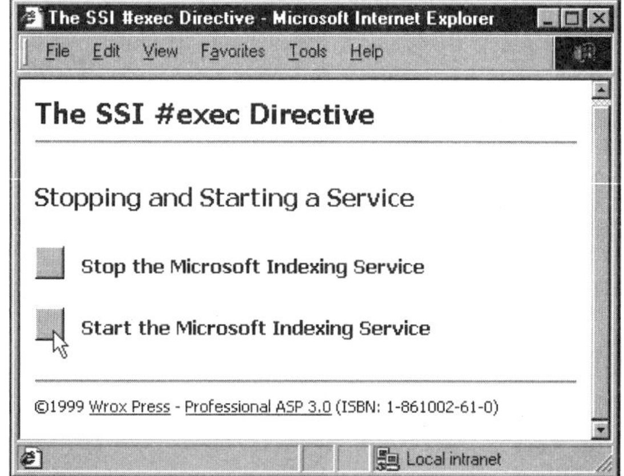

This is an ASP page named `ssi_exec.asp`. The two buttons are used to open `.stm` pages that carry out the actions described in the page, using the `#exec` directive.

Running this Sample on Your Server

However, before you can get the SSI `#exec` directive sample pages to work on your own server you must perform some configuration changes. Firstly, you will need to create the `SSIEnableCmdDirective` entry (with type `DWORD`) in the Registry on your Web server machine, under the existing key named:

```
HKEY_LOCAL_MACHINE\SYSTEM\CurrentControlSet\Services\W3SVC\Parameters
```

And then set the value to 1, as shown below:

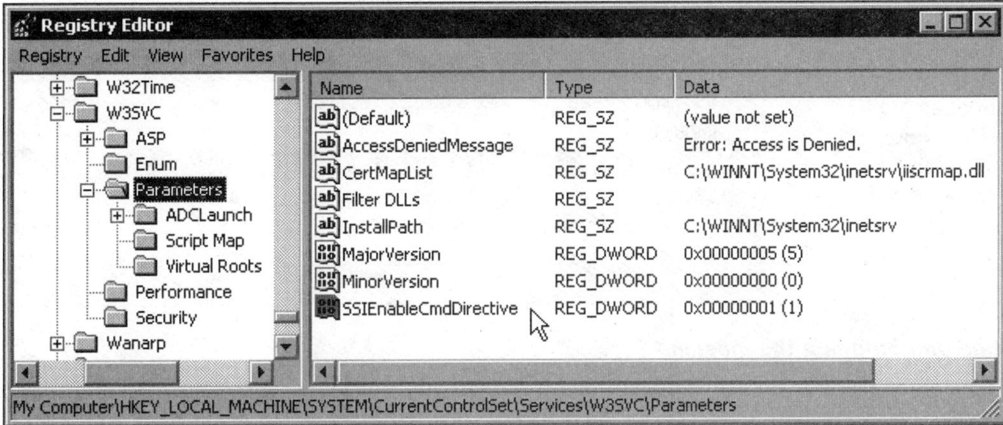

This will allow the `#exec` directive to be used with the `CMD` attribute.

Next, you have to disable anonymous access to the directory containing the `.stm` files that use `#exec`, so that the client will be forced to provide the account details of an existing account that has Administrator-level privileges. This is required for the `net` command to work.

Fire up the Internet Services Manager utility and Select the directory containing the `.stm` files that use `#exec` (in our example these are `start_cisvc.stm` and `stop_cisvc.stm` in the directory named `exec`). Then open the Properties dialog for that directory. In the Directory Security page click the Edit button in the Anonymous access and authentication control section to open the Authentication Methods dialog:

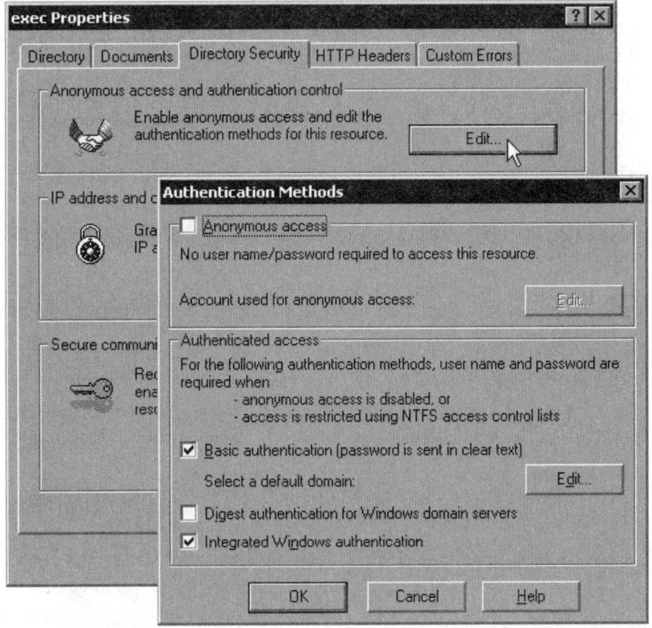

In this dialog turn *off* the Anonymous access checkbox. If you're not using Internet Explorer to access the sample pages, turn *on* the Basic authentication option to allow non-IE browsers to submit a username/password to access the pages. You'll get a warning about security; just click Yes. Now the browser will be forced to prompt for suitable account credentials, because it can't access the page anonymously.

To be able to see the results of starting and stopping the service, open the Services MMC snap-in and stop the Indexing Service:

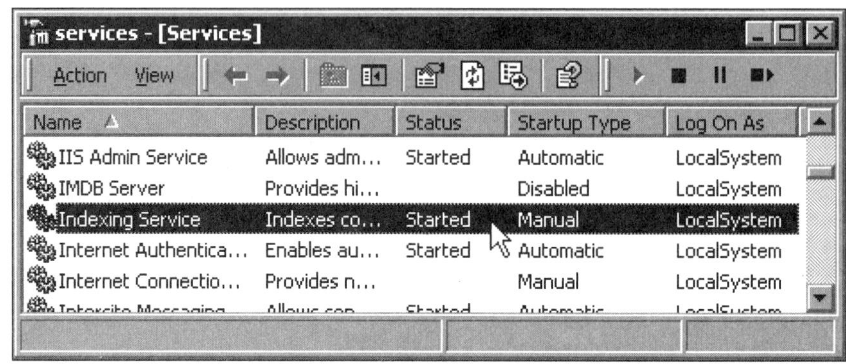

Starting and Stopping the Indexing Service

Right, we're ready to go. Click the button on the sample Web page to start the Microsoft Indexing Service.

> *The short service name for this is `cisvc` – it used to be called Microsoft Index Server but the `'ci'` bit actually refers to* content indexer.

When prompted, enter the username and password of an account on the Web server that has Administrator privileges. As the page (named `start_cisvc.stm`) opens, you'll see the delay as the `#exec` directive loads an instance of the Windows command interpreter (`cmd.exe`) and then executes the `net start` command. Once the service has started (or if it's already running) the rest of the page is displayed:

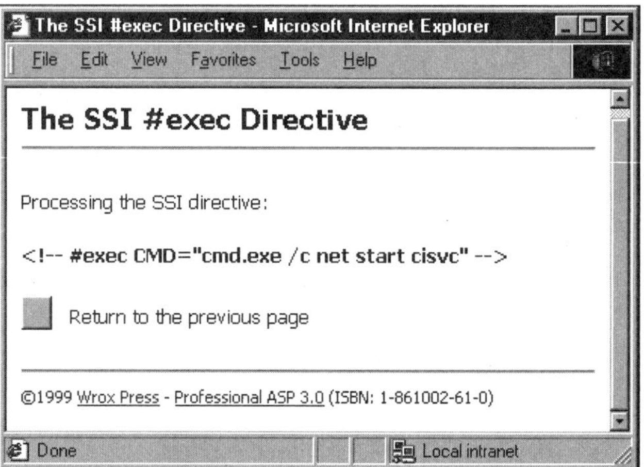

The code in this page is simple enough. You can see the `#exec` directive, with the `CMD` attribute set to `"cmd.exe /c net start cisvc"`. It's followed by a form containing the `SUBMIT` button that reloads the previous page:

```
<P>Processing the SSI directive:</P>
<P><B>&lt;!-- #exec CMD="cmd.exe /c net start cisvc" --&gt;</B></P>
<!-- #exec CMD="cmd.exe /c net start cisvc" -->

<FORM ACTION="../ssi_exec.asp">
<INPUT TYPE="SUBMIT" NAME="cmdOK" VALUE="   ">
  Return to the previous page<P>
</FORM>
```

From the previous page, you can open the other .stm page – stop_cisvc.stm – which stops the service again. The only difference is that it uses the net stop command rather than net start:

```
...
<!-- #exec CMD="cmd.exe /c net stop cisvc" -->
...
```

The ASP Server Object

As we've seen in the previous section, there's a quite a lot we can do with the traditional dynamic page instructions and directives, through server-side include pages that access the Web server via the ISAPI. However, there are some obvious limitations as well.

For example, we can retrieve the values of all the HTTP headers sent from the client with a request from the ASP Request.ServerVariables collection. It matches almost exactly the use of the SSI #echo directive, but has the major advantage that the values are returned as strings to our code. We can retrieve and manipulate these strings as we wish, whereas the #echo directive simply inserts the value into the page. Much the same argument applies with the #fsize and #flastmod directives, as we can easily get this information using script with one of the objects that is part of the VBScript and JScript scripting engines. You'll see more details of this in later chapters.

As for the #exec directive, as we've seen, it is useful – but very limited. It's really only aimed at running system commands or custom CGI applications, and neither provide our code with any real control over the process. The ASP Server object opens up a whole new way of running other applications or components that is both safer and much easier than trying to use the #exec directive. Of course, for some things (especially where we do need to execute an operating system command or a legacy CGI application) #exec is invaluable.

To begin our exploration of the Server object, we'll summarize all the methods and properties that are available and then go on to look at them in more detail.

ASP Server Object Members Summary

The Server object is designed for carrying out specific tasks on the server, in particular those that relate to the server's environment and processing activities. For this reason it has only a single property that provides information. However, there are seven methods that can be used to format data in server-specific ways, manage execution of other pages, manage execution of external objects and components, and assist in handling errors.

The Properties of the Server Object

The single property of the Server object provides access to the script timeout value for an executing ASP page:

Property	Description
`ScriptTimeout`	*Integer. Default* = `90`. Sets or returns the number of seconds that script in the page can execute for before the server aborts page execution and reports an error. This automatically halts and removes from memory pages that contain errors that may lock execution into a loop, or those that stall while waiting for a resource to become available. This prevents the server becoming overloaded with badly behaved pages. You may need to increase this value for pages that do take a long time to run.

The Methods of the Server Object

The methods of the Server object provide ways to format data, manage page execution, and create instances of other objects. In alphabetical order they are:

Method	Description
`CreateObject("`*identifier*`")`	Creates an instance of the object (a component, application or scripting object) that is identified by "*identifier*", and returns a reference to it that can be used in our code. Can be used in the `global.asa` page of a virtual application to create objects with session-level or application-level scope. The object can be identified by its ClassID such as "{clsid:BD96C556-65A3...37A9}" or by a ProgID string such as "`ADODB.Connection`".
`Execute("`*url*`")`	Stops execution of the current page and transfers control to the page specified in "*url*". The user's current environment (i.e. session state and any current transaction state) is carried over to the new page. After that page has finished execution, control passes back to the original page and execution resumes at the statement after the `Execute` method call.
`GetLastError()`	Returns a reference to an ASPError object that holds details of the last error that occurred within the ASP processing of the page. The information exposed by the ASPError object includes the file name, line number, error code, etc.
`HTMLEncode("`*string*`")`	Returns a string that is a copy of the input value "*string*" but with all non-legal HTML characters – such as '<', '>', '&' and double quotes – converted into the equivalent HTML entity – i.e. `<`, `>`, `&`, `"`, etc.

Method	Description
`MapPath("`*url*`")`	Returns the full physical path and filename of the file or resource specified in "*url*".
`Transfer("`*url*`")`	Stops execution of the current page and transfers control to the page specified in "*url*". The user's current environment (i.e. session state and any current transaction state) is carried over to the new page. Unlike the `Execute` method, execution *does not* resume in the original page, but ends when the new page has completed executing.
`URLEncode("`*string*`")`	Returns a string that is a copy of the input value "*string*" but with all characters that are not valid in a URL – such as '`?`', '`&`' and spaces – converted into the equivalent URL entity – i.e. '`%3F`', '`%26`', and '`+`'.

Creating Instances of Other Objects

In the previous chapter, we examined the ASP concept of a **virtual application**, and saw how it can be used to provide process isolation for components and other objects that we use in our ASP pages through the Application Protection setting. This followed on from a discussion in Chapter 1 of how the ASP ObjectContext object provides a context for our ASP pages to run within, and how we can use other components and objects that run within this same context.

The ASP Server object is designed to provide the features we need to create instances of these components and applications, so that we can use them to extend the capabilities of our ASP scripts. It does this by implementing a special version of the `CreateObject` method. We'll see why this is required next.

Creating Object Instances in VBScript and JScript

In Visual Basic or Visual Basic for Applications (VBA), we can create instances of objects in a variety of ways. We can use the `New` keyword to create a new object of the type specified:

```
Dim objNewObject As New MyComponent
```

However, this isn't possible in ASP with VBScript or JScript, because these scripting engines don't implement data typing. We can't declare a variable as being of any specific data type – they are all `Variants` or an equivalent type (depending on the scripting language in use).

An alternative in Visual Basic and VBA is the use of the generic `CreateObject` or `GetObject` methods. The `CreateObject` method takes as its argument a **ClassID** or (more usually) a **ProgID** string, and returns a new object of that type:

```
Set objNewObject = CreateObject("ADODB.Connection")
```

The `GetObject` method is normally used when we have a document of a specific type, and we want to create an instance of an object that can handle this type of document:

```
Set objExcel = GetObject("C:\myfiles\sales.xlw")
```

We can also specify the type of object that we want as well as a filename, which is useful if we have several objects that can handle that document type:

```
Set objExcel = GetObject("C:\myfiles\sales.xlw", "Excel.Application")
```

VBScript supports `CreateObject` and `GetObject`. JScript has `getObject`, which works like the VBScript version. JScript also implements a function that works in the same way as the VBScript `CreateObject` method, named `ActiveXObject`. However this is used in conjunction with the JScript `new` operator:

```
objNewObject = new ActiveXObject("This.Object");
```

With the exception of the Visual Basic `New` keyword, which isn't supported in VBScript or JScript, we *can* use all these techniques to create instances of objects within an ASP page. However, 'can' doesn't mean 'should', and in most cases the scripting engine object creation functions should not be used in an ASP page.

Creating Object Instances in ASP Pages

To understand why the generic scripting engine object creation methods are not ideal for use in ASP pages, consider again our earlier discussions on **context** in ASP and the ObjectContext object.

When we create an object instance within an ASP page using the generic methods of the scripting engines, that object is not instantiated within the context of the currently executing page. It doesn't get a reference to the ObjectContext object, and so cannot use this to access the context of the page, i.e. the values within that page's context.

This means that the object cannot use the intrinsic ASP objects – it can't access values in the Request, Response, Application or Session collections, or use the methods and properties that the intrinsic ASP objects expose. Neither can the object interact with any existing transactions that may be current within the context, so it can't use the ObjectContext methods to abort a transaction if something goes wrong.

Of course, you may not want to interact with the context of the page. But there are other reasons why using the generic object creation methods is generally inadvisable. IIS automatically instantiates objects within a special COM+ run-time wrapper called `dllhost.dll`, which enables the object to be properly pooled and reused within the current virtual application (remember that the Default Web site is itself a virtual application).

The settings for a virtual application, as we saw in the previous chapter, allow us to control whether objects are created in the memory space of the Web server, or separately in shared or individual out-of-process instances of `DLLHost.dll`. If we use the generic scripting engine object creation methods, this circumvents all the component isolation and scalability features that are automatically provided when the `CreateObject` method of the ASP Server object is used.

The CreateObject Method of the Server Object

To experiment with the `CreateObject` method, open the main `Chapter04` menu page of the sample, and click the link Using the ASP Server Object:

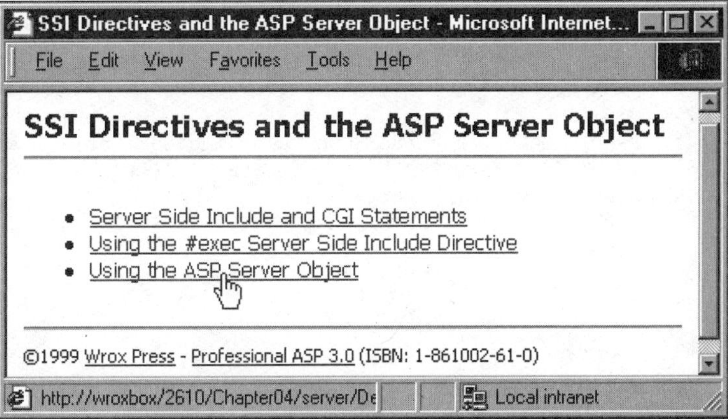

This opens a page named `show_server.asp`, which you can use to experiment with all of the Server object's methods. It also displays the value of the single Server object property, `ScriptTimeout`. The default value for this property is `90` seconds:

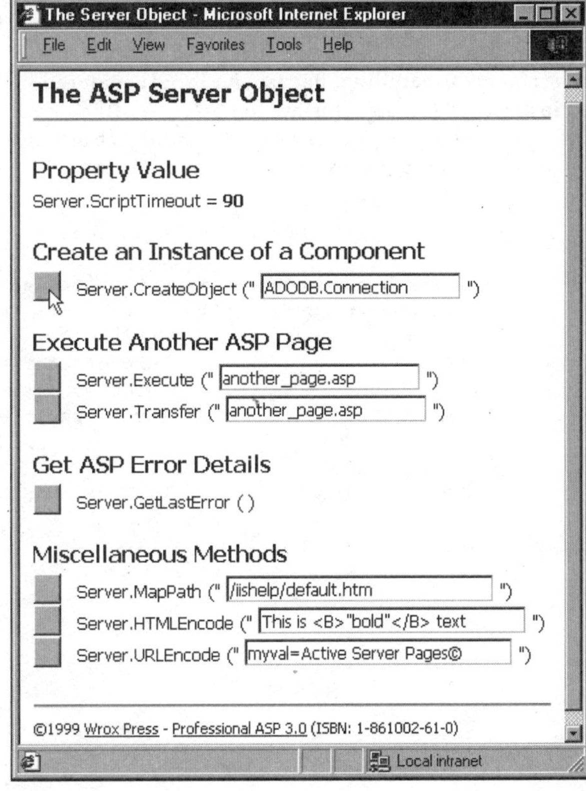

In the Create an Instance of a Component section of this page there's a text box where you can type the ProgID string of an object that you want to create within the context of the page. You can even type a numeric ClassID if you tend to have the kind of memory that stores such things. We've set the default value of his text box to the ProgID of one of the common objects from the ActiveX Data Objects library: ADODB.Connection.

Clicking the button next to Server.CreateObject submits this page back to itself, because all the controls are on a single <FORM> with the ACTION set to the path and name of this page:

```
...
<FORM ACTION="<% = Request.ServerVariables("SCRIPT_NAME") %>" METHOD="POST">

<P><DIV CLASS="subhead">Create an Instance of a Component</DIV>
<INPUT TYPE="SUBMIT" NAME="cmdCreateObject" VALUE="   ">
  Server.CreateObject ("
<INPUT TYPE="TEXT" NAME="txtProgID" SIZE="25" VALUE="ADODB.Connection">
")<P>

...

</FORM>
...
```

When the page reloads, a section of ASP code in the page, placed before the <FORM> section, looks to see which button was clicked to submit the form. If it was the button named cmdCreateObject – as in this case – the code collects the ProgID string from the text box. Then it turns off the default script error handling, in case the ProgID entered by the user is invalid, and attempts to create an instance of the object using the Server.CreateObject method. Finally, it turns the default error handling back on, checks to see if an object instance was actually created by using the IsObject function, and displays an appropriate message:

```
QUOT = Chr(34)  'Double quote character
...
'Look for a command sent from the FORM section buttons
If Len(Request.Form("cmdCreateObject")) Then
  strProgID = Request.Form("txtProgID")
  On Error Resume Next       'Turn off default error handling
  Set objObject = Server.CreateObject(strProgID)
  On Error Goto 0            'Turn default error handling back on

  If IsObject(objObject) Then
    Response.Write "<B>Results:</B><BR>Sucessfully created object with "_
                   & "ProgID of <B>" & QUOT & strProgID & QUOT & "</B><HR>"
  Else
    Response.Write "<B>Results:</B><BR>Failed to create object with " _
                   & "ProgID of <B>" & QUOT & strProgID & QUOT & "</B><HR>"
  End If

End If
...
```

Here's the result for our `ADODB.Connection` object. You can see that it was instantiated OK, and we can then go on to use it in our code:

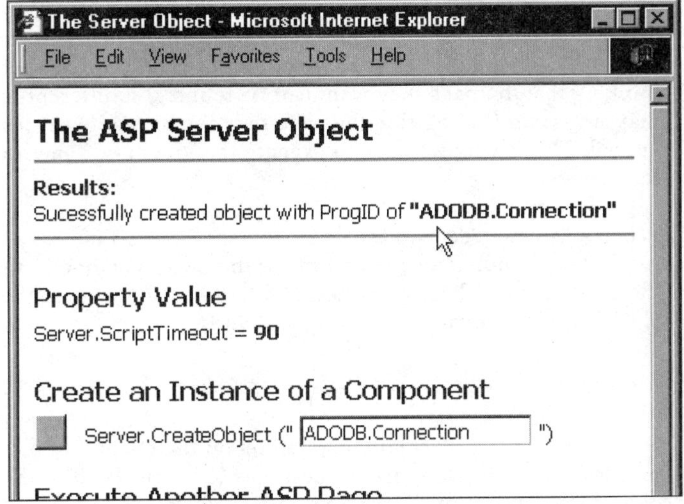

We won't be looking at how we *use* objects in this chapter. You may already be familiar with this anyway – once we have created our object instance we use it just like we would in any other situation. We call the methods and read and set the properties in exactly the same way as when using Visual Basic; or with VBScript, JScript client-side in the browser.

However, we will be looking at using objects and components in more detail in the next couple of chapters, where we investigate some of the objects that are implemented by the scripting engines, and the installable components that come as part of an IIS 5.0/ASP 3.0 installation. We'll also see some other free or commercial components in use, and discuss how we choose which ones to use in various situations. And, later in the book, we'll even show you how easy it is to build your own components for use with ASP.

Executing Other Pages

One of the most exciting new features in ASP 3.0 and IIS 5.0 is the introduction of programmable **server-side redirection**. What this means is that, finally, we can transfer control and execution of a page to another one without having to bother the client by using `Response.Redirect`. We'll see what we mean by this next.

The Problems with Client-side Redirection

ASP programmers regularly use the `Response.Redirect` statement to load a different page to the one that is currently executing. However, many don't realize that this doesn't automatically cause the server to immediately load and execute the new page. What it actually does is add an HTTP **redirection header** to the output stream being sent from the Web server to the client. This header looks something like this:

```
HTTP/1.1 302 Object Moved
Location newpage.asp
```

The standard HTTP status message in this header, 302 Object Moved, tells the browser that the resource they requested has moved. The Location header provides the address of the page they want. Of course this doesn't have to be the reality – what we're doing is fooling the browser into thinking that the page they want can be found at a different location. What is actually happening is that our server is executing the page they requested, but is telling them that the page they want has moved. This is why we have to execute the Redirect method before we send any page content to the browser.

When a browser receives the 302 Object Moved message it responds by canceling the current request and sending a new request for the page specified in the Location value. This works in just the same way as when we use a META HTTP-EQUIV tag in the <HEAD> section of the page – the HTTP header shown earlier is equivalent to:

```
<META HTTP-EQUIV="REFRESH" CONTENT="0;URL=newpage.asp">
```

So the redirection is actually happening on the client, not on our server. While this isn't generally a problem, it can cause spurious messages to be displayed if there is a proxy server in use at the client end of the connection. The proxy server will usually intercept the status message and may itself generate a page that is sent on to the client that made the original request. This is why the ubiquitous and annoying message The object you requested has been moved and can be found here is often displayed on the client when we use Response.Redirect, although proper use of buffering can usually prevent it.

When you use Response.Redirect *in IIS 4 or earlier, you should always turn on buffering at the top of your ASP page and then call* Response.Clear *before executing the* Response.Redirect *method. Of course, with page buffering being turned on by default in ASP3.0, this is not such an issue. As long as you use* Response.Clear *before executing the statement, no previously generated output will be sent to the client.*

Server-side Redirection in ASP 3.0

In ASP 3.0 and IIS 5.0, we can avoid the need to use client-side redirection in almost all cases by taking advantage of the two new Server object methods: Execute and Transfer. They cause control to be passed immediately to another page, which can be an ASP script page or any other resource – such as an HTML page, zip file, or other type of file.

The difference between them is that the Execute method 'calls' the other page, much like we call a subroutine or function in our script code. When the other page or resource has completed execution or streaming to the client, control passes back to the statement following the call to the Execute method in the original page, and execution continues from there. When we use the Transfer method, control does not pass back to the original page, and execution stops at the end of the page or resource we transferred control to.

What makes the two methods even more useful is that the current page's *context* is also passed to the target page or resource. This includes the values of all the variables in all the intrinsic ASP objects, such as the collections of the Request, Response and Session objects, and all their properties. The Application object context is also transferred, even if the page is within a different virtual application.

The result of all this is that the browser thinks that it's still receiving the original page. It has no idea that anything unusual is going on at our server. Its Address bar still shows the same URL, and (best of all) the Back, Forward and Refresh buttons work normally. When we use client-side redirection, especially with an HTML `META` element, this isn't usually the case.

Part of the context that is transferred to the new page or resource is any existing **transaction state**. While we aren't going to look at transactions in detail until a later chapter, it's worth mentioning here. The current page's context is encapsulated with the ASP `ObjectContext` object, which we discussed in Chapter 1. If we need to work with this object as part of an ongoing transaction, we can use it within the page that we transfer control to.

Using the Execute and Transfer Methods of the Server Object

You can experiment with the `Execute` and `Transfer` methods in the sample page we used earlier. The page contains the name of another file that we've provided in the samples – imaginatively named `another_page.asp` – as the default value for both methods:

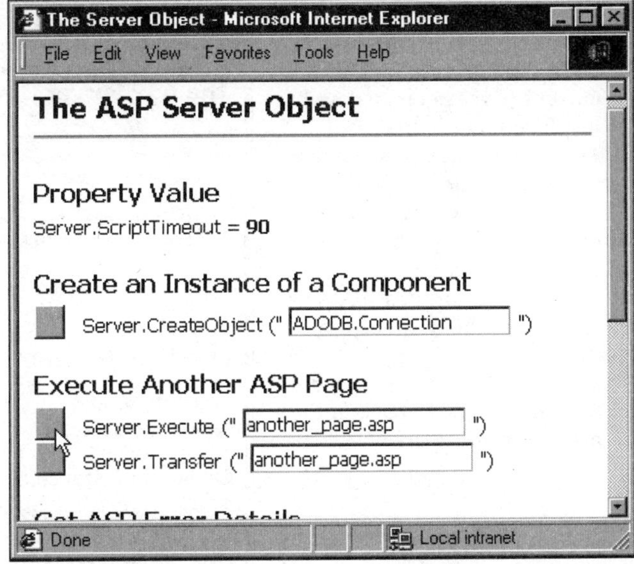

Clicking the button for the `Server.Execute` or `Server.Transfer` method submits the form that all the controls are on back to the same page, reloading it. Script code at the top of this page then looks to see which of the buttons was used to submit it. If it was one of the buttons named `cmdExecute` or `cmdTransfer`, we write the path of the current page into the output stream and then call the appropriate method. We pass to it the value from the text box associated with that button. Then we again write the path of the current page into the output stream:

```
...
If Len(Request.Form("cmdExecute")) Then
  strPath = Request.Form("txtExecPath")
  Response.Write "Currently executing the page: <B>" _
               & Request.ServerVariables("SCRIPT_NAME") & "</B><BR>"
```

```
    Server.Execute (strPath)
    Response.Write "Currently executing the page: <B>" _
                 & Request.ServerVariables("SCRIPT_NAME") & "</B><BR>"
  End If

  If Len(Request.Form("cmdTransfer")) Then
    strPath = Request.Form("txtTransferPath")
    Response.Write "Currently executing the page: <B>" _
                 & Request.ServerVariables("SCRIPT_NAME") & "</B><BR>"
    Server.Transfer (strPath)
  End If
  ...
```

When the button for the `Server.Execute` method is clicked we see the path of the current page, as created and displayed by the first `Response.Write` statement in the code shown above. This is followed by some output that comes from the page we executed, `another_page.asp`. After this comes the output from the second `Response.Write` statement that shows we are back in the original page again:

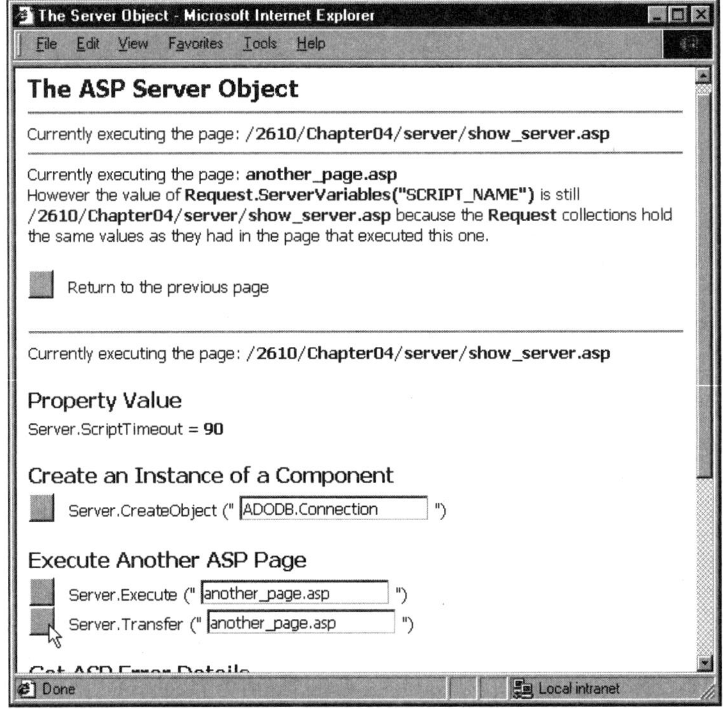

The section between the two horizontal lines in the page, which shows the currently executing page as `show_server.asp`,comes from the original page. The section between the next two horizontal lines comes from the page we executed, `another_page.asp`. This is the complete source of that page:

```
<%@ LANGUAGE=VBSCRIPT %>
<HR>
Currently executing the page: <B>another_page.asp</B><BR>
However the value of <B>Request.ServerVariables("SCRIPT_NAME")</B> is still <BR>
<B><% = Request.ServerVariables("SCRIPT_NAME") %></B>
because the <B>Request</B> collections hold<BR>
the same values as they had in the page that executed this one.<BR>
```

```
<FORM ACTION="<% = Request.ServerVariables("HTTP_REFERER") %>" METHOD="POST">
<INPUT TYPE="SUBMIT" NAME="cmdOK" VALUE="   ">
  Return to the previous page<P>
</FORM>
<HR>
```

Notice that we can't use `Request.ServerVariables("SCRIPT_NAME")` to get the path of this page as it's being executed, because the context is still that of the original page. We have to write the page name in as text – there's no way that we can get it directly from the ASP context.

The reason that we've included a button to open the previous page here is that this page can also be called using the `Server.Transfer` method, by clicking the appropriate button back in the main page. This time we see the same output up to the end of the page `another_page.asp`, but nothing else. Because we 'transferred' to this page instead of 'executing' it, control does not pass back to the original page:

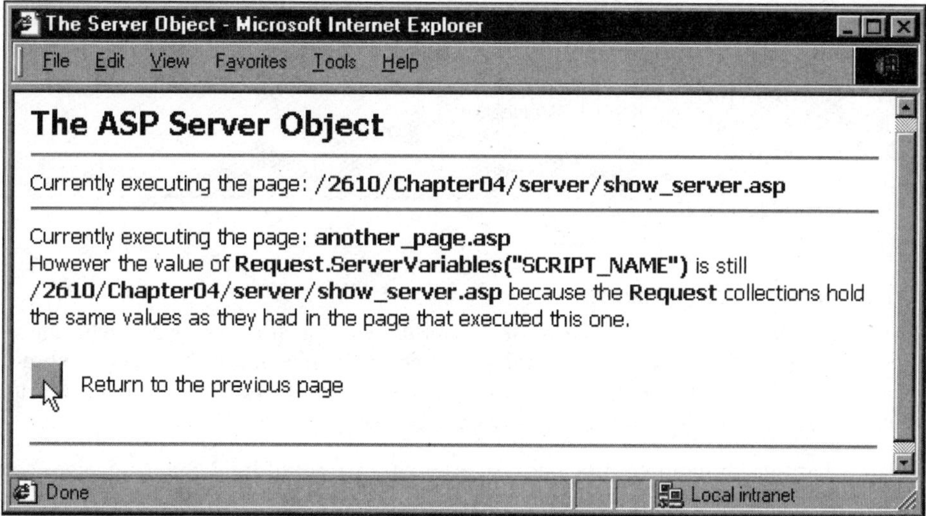

Executing SSI Pages from ASP

At last, we now have a way to use SSI directives successfully within our ASP pages if we need to. It's not something that is often required, but it can be done. The problem in the past was that, because we can't include ASP code in an SSI page (which has the `.stm`, `.shtml` or `.shtm` file extension), we can't seamlessly redirect back to the original page again. We have to add a button or link to load the original or another ASP page.

Now, with the `Server.Execute` method, we can execute an SSI page and have control returned to the original page automatically, all without the client being aware of what's going on. They just see the original ASP page load and results of executing it arrive. Any output from the SSI page is seamlessly inserted into the response stream. Alternatively, of course, we can use `Server.Transfer` if we don't want the original page to resume execution once the SSI page has completed.

To see this technique in action, type the virtual path to the CGI-SSI example page we used earlier into the text box for the `Server.Execute` method (and/or the `Server.Transfer` method if you like). The path you need is "`../ssi_cgi/ssi_cgi.stm`". After clicking the button to call the `Execute` or `Transfer` method, you'll see that the `.stm` page, complete with the results of the SSI directives, has been executed. After the content from `ssi_cgi.stm` comes the remainder of the original page, although this isn't visible in the screenshot – you'll have to scroll down to see it:

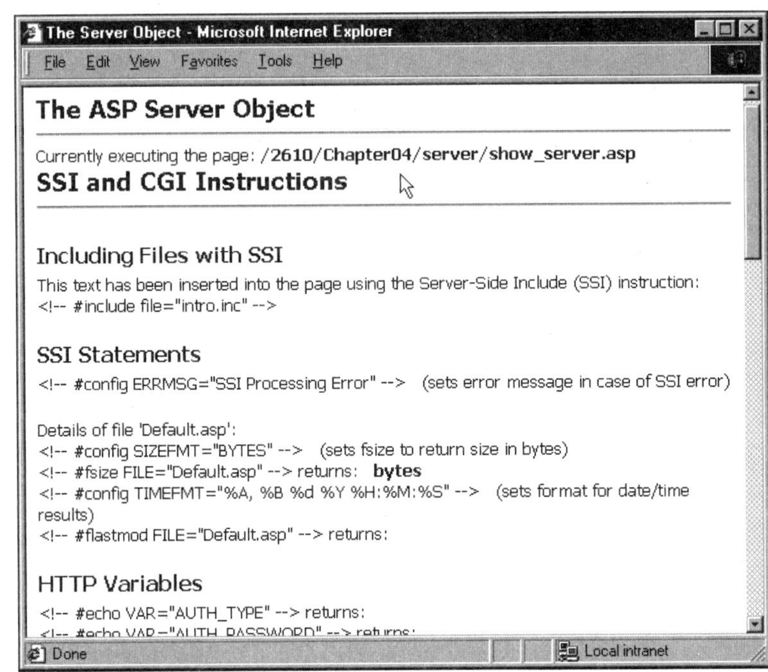

But Sadly Not the SSI #exec Directive

Sadly, the `Execute` and `Transfer` methods generally won't work successfully with the `#exec` SSI directive, because the `.stm` page containing the directive then runs within the context of the ASP page that called it. In most cases, it needs to run under a separate context that comes from referencing the page directly.

It's a shame that this limitation exists, because otherwise we could freely execute pages containing `#exec` 'invisibly', from within an ASP page, by using the `Server.Execute` method. This would have been an ideal solution for the sample pages we looked at earlier that stopped and started the Indexing Service with the `net stop` and `net start` commands.

Instead, we had to resort to old and proven methods. We simply use the `Response.Redirect` method to open the relevant page when the user clicks a button:

```
<%
'Look for a command sent from the FORM section buttons
If Len(Request.Form("cmdStop")) Then
  Response.Redirect("exec/stop_cisvc.stm")
End If

If Len(Request.Form("cmdStart")) Then
  Response.Redirect("exec/start_cisvc.stm")
End If
%>
```

You can try entering the virtual path of an SSI page that uses `#exec` into the text boxes for the `Server.Execute` and `Server.Transfer` methods in the example page. The relative virtual paths of the `#exec` example pages we used earlier are "`../ssi_cgi/exec/start_cisvc.stm`" and "`../ssi_cgi/exec/stop_cisvc.stm`".

Error Handling with the Server Object

ASP has long been criticized for its lack of 'proper' error handling.

In VBScript, there is the `On Error Resume Next` statement, which causes the script interpreter to ignore run-time errors and continue execution of the script code. The script can then check the value of the `Err.Number` property to see if an error has occurred. If so, it returns a non-zero value. In ASP 3.0, we can also use `On Error Goto 0` to 'turn back on' the default error handler. This actually worked in ASP 2.0 as well, but was not documented.

In JScript, we now have a new error handling feature as well: the 'C'-style `try` and `catch` statements. However all these error-handling techniques are implemented not by ASP or IIS, but by the scripting engines that ASP uses.

> *We're devoting a whole section of Chapter 7 to the debugging and error handling techniques that involve script and the scripting engines.*

In the meantime, the ASP and IIS development teams have got together to add a new feature that makes error handling in our ASP pages even easier. This comes in two parts: the configuration of IIS error pages, and the use of a new method and object that have been added to ASP.

The GetLastError Method of the Server Object

In ASP 3.0, the Server object has gained a new method named `GetLastError`. However, unlike with the VBScript `Err` object, we can't call this method whenever we like, just to see if an error has occurred. It can only be used successfully within an ASP custom error page – something we'll be looking at shortly. If we try and use it by turning off the default error handling (with `On Error Resume Next`) like we do with the `Err` object, the `GetLastError` method is unable to access the error details.

One thing that the `GetLastError` method does do is provide far more information about the source of and cause of an error. The `GetLastError` method creates and returns a reference to an object, new in ASP 3.0, named the **ASPError** object. This has a series of properties that return information about the most recent error that occurred before the `GetLastError` method was called.

The Properties of the ASPError Object

The ASPError object provides nine properties that describe the error that occurred, the nature and source of the error, and (where possible) return the actual code that caused it:

Property	Description
`ASPCode`	*Integer.* The error number generated by ASP/IIS, such as 0x800A0009.
`ASPDescription`	*String.* A detailed description of the error if it is ASP-related.

Table Continued on Following Page

Property	Description
`Category`	*String.* The source of the error, i.e. internal to ASP, the scripting language, or an object.
`Column`	*Integer.* The character position within the file that generated the error.
`Description`	*String.* A short description of the error.
`File`	*String.* The name of the file that was being processed when the error occurred.
`Line`	*Integer.* The number of the line within the file that generated the error.
`Number`	*Integer.* A standard COM error code.
`Source`	*String.* The actual code, where available, of the line that caused the error.

Configuring 'Single-Page' Error Handling

It might seem like the error message page that's returned to a client from the server when an error (such as 404 Not Found) occurs is generated magically within IIS, but this isn't the case. They are ordinary HTML pages, which are loaded in response to an error and sent back to the client. These are usually referred to as **custom error pages**.

However, they are set up as part of the default installation of IIS, and the name arises more because they *can* be customized as required. In fact, it was possible in earlier versions of IIS to set up custom error pages.

> *In IIS 4.0, we could specify a custom error page for each different type of HTTP protocol or server error, for each directory in any of the Web sites on our server.*

The IIS Default Error Pages

The default error pages supplied with IIS live in the `WinNT\Help` directory of the Web server. In the case of IIS 5.0 in Windows 2000, this is `WinNT\Help\iishelp\common`:

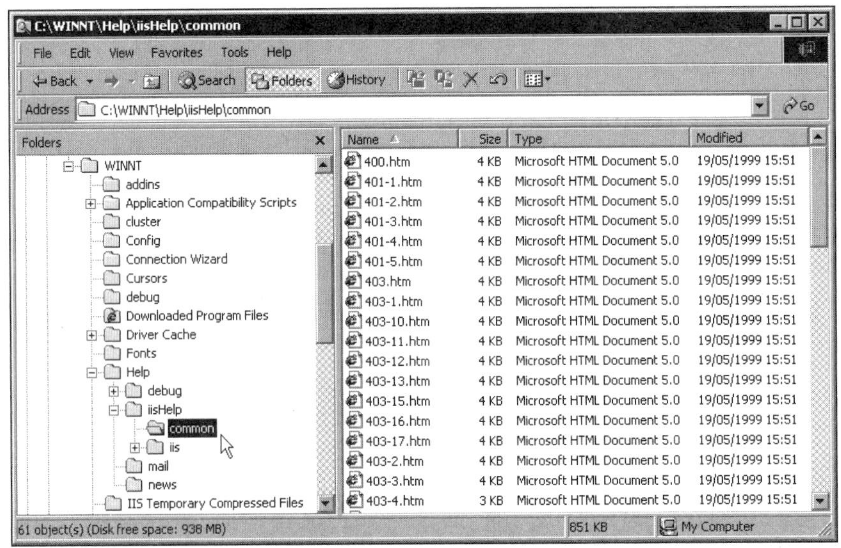

You can open any of these in a browser to see the result, or in a text editor to see the source HTML and script code. The page that is used when a 404 error occurs is `404b.htm`, and this contains a client-side script code section that can take the current document URL (retrieved from the `url` property of the `document` object) and display it in the page:

```
The page you are looking for might have been removed, had its name changed, or is
temporarily unavailable.<HR><P>Please try the following:</P>
<UL><LI>If you typed the page address in the Address bar, make sure that it is
spelled correctly.</LI>
<LI>Open the
<SCRIPT>
  <!--
    if (!((window.navigator.userAgent.indexOf("MSIE") > 0)
    && (window.navigator.appVersion.charAt(0) == "2"))) {
      Homepage();
    }
  //-->
</SCRIPT>
home page, and then look for links to the information you want.</li>
...
<SCRIPT>
function Homepage(){
<!--
  DocURL = document.URL;
  protocolIndex=DocURL.indexOf("://",4);
  serverIndex=DocURL.indexOf("/",protocolIndex + 3);
  BeginURL=DocURL.indexOf("#",1) + 1;
  urlresult=DocURL.substring(BeginURL,serverIndex);
  displayresult=DocURL.substring(protocolIndex + 3 ,serverIndex);
  document.write('<A HREF="' + urlresult + '">' + displayresult + "</a>");
}
//-->
</SCRIPT>
```

This produces the familiar page that you are probably quite used to seeing:

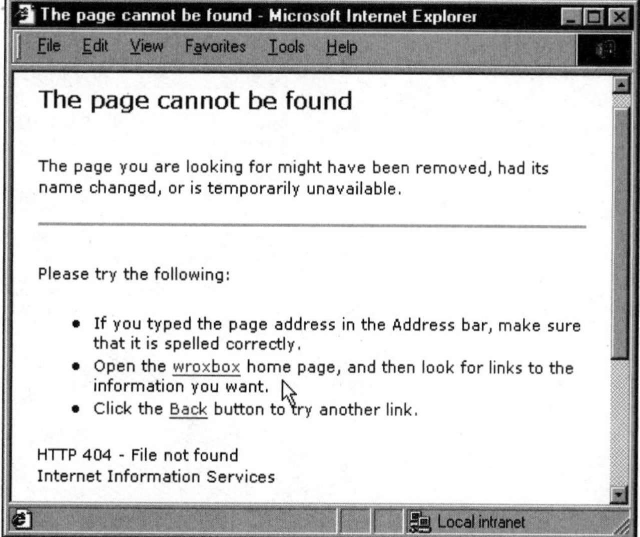

Error Page Mapping in IIS

When IIS detects an error, it sends the appropriate error page back to the client. How does it know which one to send? Obviously, the name of the page has something to do with it, but in fact, the file names are not important. The mapping between errors and error page files is done in the Custom Errors page of the Properties dialog for each directory.

In Internet Services Manager, right-click on the directory for which you want to edit the mappings, and select Properties. If you're setting up the sample files that we provide on your own server, select the `server` subdirectory within the `Chapter04` directory:

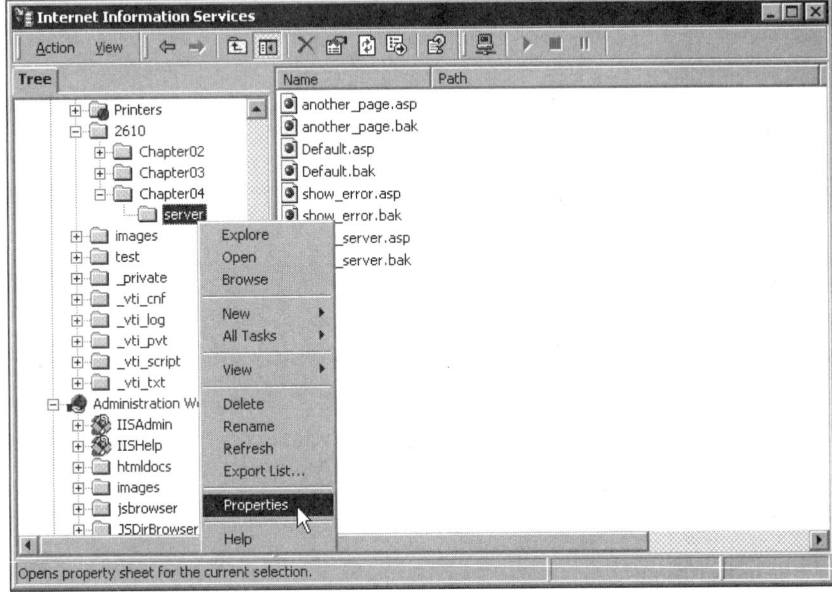

In the Custom Errors page of the Properties dialog is a list of the default mappings set up when IIS is installed (unless, of course you've already changed any):

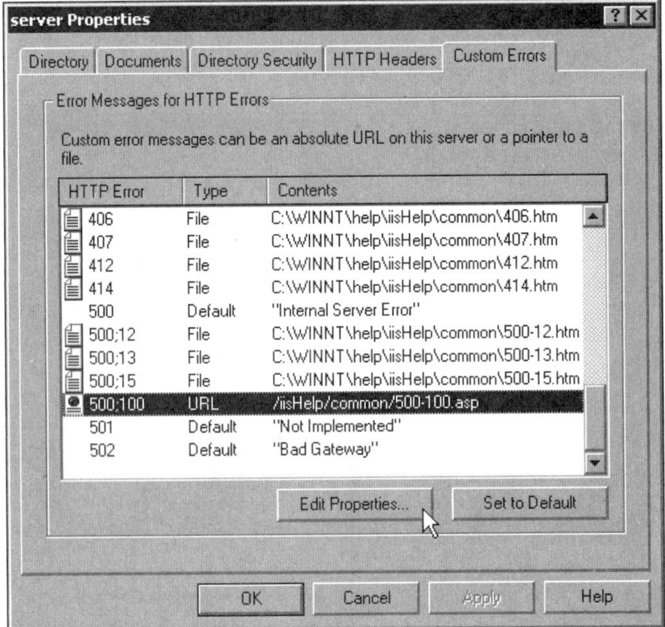

Near the bottom of the list is an entry for the HTTP error 500:100. Type 500 errors are those that are generated by ASP, and you can see that some are already mapped to error pages. These are the generic errors such as Invalid Application, Server Shutting Down, etc. However, the 500:100 error occurs specifically when ASP loads a page that contains a syntax error, or in which a run-time error occurs. The default mapping shown in the list indicates that the page named `500-100.asp` will be executed when such an error occurs for a file in this directory.

So, here's the rub. The message that we see when an ASP error occurs is not only an ordinary Web page – it's an ordinary *ASP* Web page (i.e. it has the `.asp` file extension). You're probably miles ahead of me already, but what this means is that we can edit the mapping to point to a different page instead if we wish.

Specifying a Custom Error Page

Click the Edit Properties button in the Custom Errors page to open the Error Mapping Properties dialog. Select URL in the Message Type drop-down list, and type the full virtual path to your own custom error page:

The value shown in the screenshot points to a custom error page that we've created for use with our sample pages. You may have to use a different path depending on where you installed the sample files.

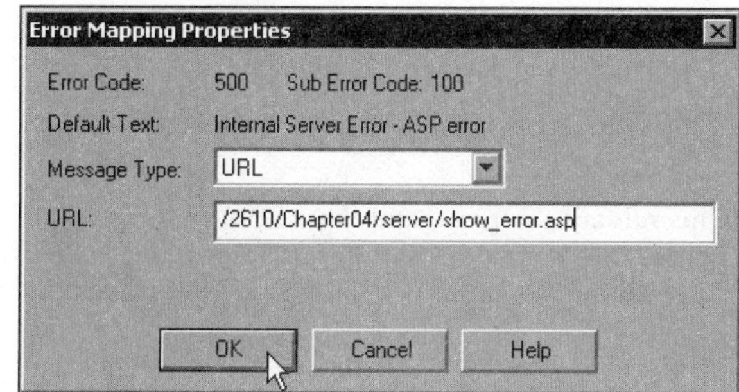

Now our custom error page will be opened whenever an error of type 500:100 occurs. The other two options for Message Type are:

- Default: where we can simply enter a short text message rather than specifying a page that is to be sent to the client
- File: where we specify the physical path to an HTML error page

When we select File, the page we specify is loaded by IIS in the same way as when we load a file by double-clicking on it in Windows Explorer. This means that we can't use this option for an ASP page, because in this situation any script in it will not be executed.

Using the GetLastError Method and the ASPError Object

We have now configured IIS to load our own custom error page when an ASP-related error occurs in any page within the directory where we edited the error mapping properties. This means that, in effect, we now have a 'proper' script error trap set up, because an ASP run-time error in any of the pages in this directory will fire up our custom error page.

In fact IIS does this internally through the `Server.Transfer` method, which means that we'll have access to the complete context in which the original page was running as well. We can get at that vital script context, and so we can make decisions about what to do based on the error that occurred. On top of this, the ASPError object can be retrieved within the custom error page, so we can find out all about the error that caused the error page to be loaded.

> *It is possible to do something similar in IIS 4.0 by editing the error mapping properties. However, there is only the generic 500 error ("Internal Server Error") available in the mappings. On top of that, the context of the page is not transferred when the custom error page is loaded, so it's difficult to do anything other than provide a non-specific error message.*

You can see the ASPError object in action from the ASP Server Object sample page we've been using in the previous examples. Click the button for Server.GetLastError():

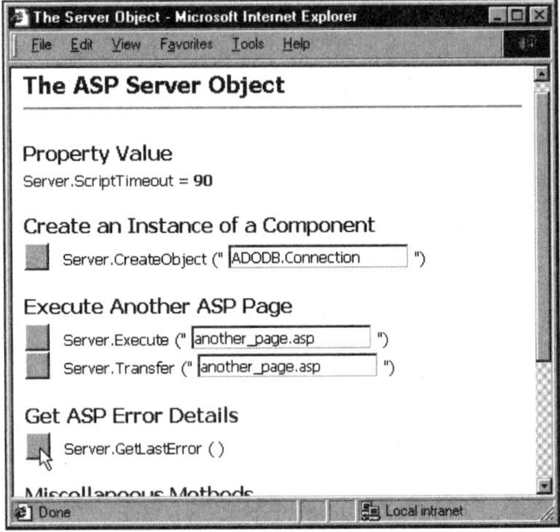

This reloads the page, and the ASP script within it looks to see which button was clicked to submit the form. If it was the button for Server.GetLastError(), which is named `cmdGetError`, we execute some simple code that we know will always cause a run-time script error:

```
...
If Len(Request.Form("cmdGetError")) Then
   Dim arrThis(3)
   arrThis(4) = "Causes an error"
End If
...
```

Because we earlier configured the error page mappings for this directory to load our own custom error page, this is opened as soon as the error occurs (via the `Server.Transfer` method working invisibly in the background):

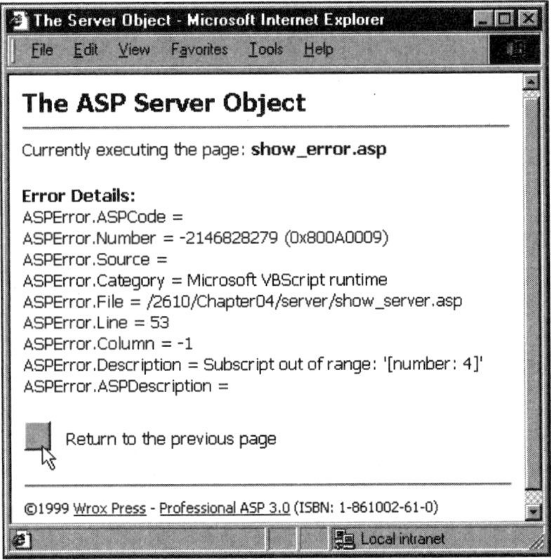

What the Sample Error Page Code Does

Our custom error page displays the values of all of the ASPError object properties. It also behaves properly by using the `Response.Status` method to send back an HTTP header status message to the client indicating that an error occurred. Then it gets a reference to the ASPError object using the `GetLastError` method, so that it can access the error details:

```
...
<%
Response.Status = "500 Internal Server Error"
Set objASPError = Server.GetLastError()
%>
Currently executing the page: <B>show_error.asp</B><P>
<B>Error Details:</B><BR>

ASPError.ASPCode = <% = objASPError.ASPCode %><BR>
ASPError.Number = <% = objASPError.Number %>
                  (0x<% = Hex(objASPError.Number) %>)<BR>
ASPError.Source = <% = Server.HTMLEncode(objASPError.Source) %><BR>
ASPError.Category = <% = objASPError.Category %><BR>
ASPError.File = <% = objASPError.File %><BR>
ASPError.Line = <% = objASPError.Line %><BR>
ASPError.Column = <% = objASPError.Column %><BR>
ASPError.Description = <% = objASPError.Description %><BR>
ASPError.ASPDescription = <% = objASPError.ASPDescription %>

<FORM ACTION="<% = Request.ServerVariables("HTTP_REFERER") %>" METHOD="POST">
<INPUT TYPE="SUBMIT" NAME="cmdOK" VALUE="   ">
  Return to the previous page<P>
</FORM>
...
```

One point to note is that if a scripting or ASP error occurs within your custom error page, IIS will just return a generic message that corresponds to the error code 500:100. This could be the scripting engine's own error message, or just the rather curt message Internal Server Error. It doesn't reload the custom error page repeatedly.

Remember that the full context of the page that contained the error is passed to our custom error page. This means that we can still use the values stored in any of the intrinsic ASP object collections or properties. For example, if we retrieve the `HTTP_REFERER` value from the `Request.ServerVariables` collection, it will reflect the URL of the page that called our original page (i.e. the page before the one where the error occurred). It doesn't change when the server transfers execution to our error page, and so will not contain the URL of the page that was executing when the error occurred.

Likewise, the `SCRIPT_NAME` value will be the name of the page that contained the error, and not the error page URL. You can confirm this by checking the URL in the Address bar of your browser when an error page has been loaded. However, the values stored in script variables within the original page are *not* available in the custom error page.

If the original ASP page is likely to be running within a transaction (i.e. it contains an `<%@TRANSACTION="..."%>` directive at the top of the page), we should also consider whether we need to take some action within our page to abort the transaction. For example we may need to call the `SetAbort` method of the intrinsic `ObjectContext` object:

```
ObjectContext.SetAbort    'Fail the transaction if an ASP error occurs
```

We'll be looking at the whole topic of transactions later in the book, when we examine the role that ASP plays within them.

Using the Properties of the ASPError Object

There are a few points worth noting about the ASPError object's properties:

- There should always be a value for the `Number` property, even if no error has occurred (if you call `GetLastError` and query this property in your ASP page, it will be zero if no error has occurred). Generally, for ASP script run-time errors, the `Number` property returns hexadecimal `0x800A0000` plus the standard scripting engine error code. Hence, our example returned `0x800A0009` for a Subscript out of range error, because the VBScript error code for this type of error is `9`.
- When an error *has* occurred, there will always be a value for the `Category` and `Description` properties.
- The `ASPCode` property value is generated by IIS, and will be empty for most script errors. It is more likely to appear for errors involving the use of external components.
- The `ASPDescription` property value is generated by the ASP pre-processor (rather than the script engine currently in use), and will again be empty for most script errors. It is most likely to appear for errors such as invalid method calls to the ASP intrinsic objects.
- The `File`, `Source`, `Line` and `Column` properties are only set if the details are available when the error occurs. For a run-time error, the `File` and `Line` properties are usually valid, but the `Column` property often returns `-1`. The `Source` (code) is only returned when the error is a syntax error that prevents the page being *processed* by ASP (rather than a run-time error that prevents it being *executed*). Generally in these cases, the `Line` and `Column` properties will be valid as well. If you write the value of the `Source` property into the page, it's wise to `HTMLEncode` it first, as shown in the code example earlier – just in case it contains any non-legal HTML characters. We'll be looking in detail at the `HTMLEncode` method later in this chapter.

Getting Path Information with the Server Object

Often when we work with files stored in our Web site, we need to be able to get the actual physical path for those files, rather than using the virtual path or URL by which they are normally referenced within other pages. An example is where we use the `FileSystemObject` (which we'll meet in the next chapter) to read and write files that are outside the `InetPub\WWWRoot` folder of the Web site. Alternatively, when we are creating our own custom components, or using commercial components that have to access the file system, we often need to provide them with a physical path to a file.

The MapPath Method of the Server Object

The HTTP header variables that we can extract from the `Request.ServerVariables` collection do contain the physical path to the current file – in the `DOCUMENT_NAME` and `PATH_TRANSLATED` headers. However, the Server object provides a method called `MapPath`, which we can use to get the physical path of *any* file for which we can provide a valid virtual path. You can see the `MapPath` method in action and experiment with it in the sample page we've been using so far.

Near the bottom of the page, in the **Miscellaneous Methods** section, is a button that executes the `Server.MapPath` method and provides it with the value in the text box next to the button. We've set this to `/iishelp/default.htm` in the page's source code, because this file should be automatically installed on your machine. You can type the URL of a different page if you wish:

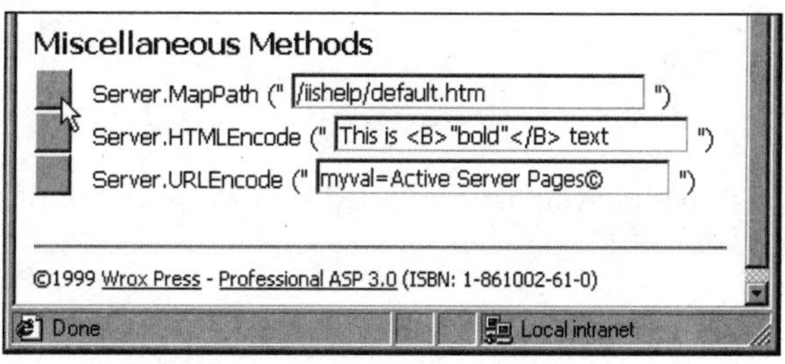

Clicking the button reloads this page, executing the method and displaying the result at the top. The rest of the original page is then shown below it so that you can have another go:

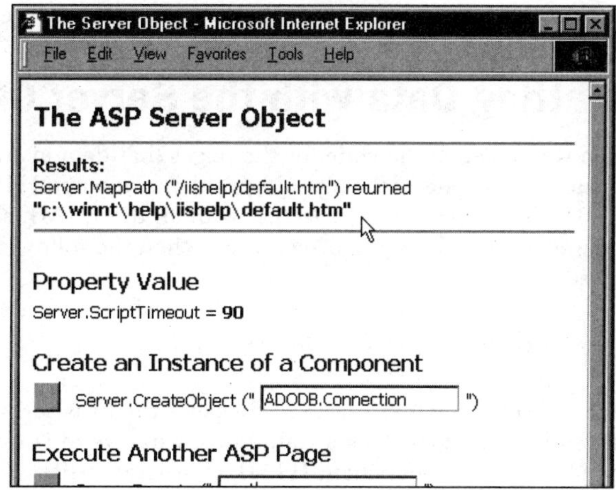

What the Sample Page Code Does

The code to carry out the process you see here is much the same as we've used in the similar sample files earlier.

In the ASP script section at the top of the page we test for the name of the button that was clicked to submit the form. In this case, it will be `cmdMapPath`, and we simply pass the value in the matching text box named `txtMapPath` to the `Server.MapPath` method and display the result:

```
If Len(Request.Form("cmdMapPath")) Then
   strValue = Request.Form("txtMapPath")
   Response.Write "<B>Results:</B><BR>Server.MapPath (" & QUOT & strValue _
                & QUOT & ") returned <B>" & QUOT & Server.MapPath(strValue) _
                & QUOT & "</B><HR>"
End If
```

MapPath and Virtual Application Directories

Notice the result we get from the `MapPath` method for the file `/iishelp/default.htm`. It is outside the Web server directories, and in the `help` directory of the main `winnt` directory. This neatly demonstrates how useful the `MapPath` method is.

When we have a URL for a file within the default Web site directories, the path part of the URL will often be the same as the physical path. For example, you might have a file stored on the Web server in:

```
C:\InetPub\WWWRoot\yourfiles\thisfile.asp
```

Providing you have installed your Web root in the default directory during setup, this will have a URL of:

```
http://yoursite.com/yourfiles/thisfile.asp
```

However, the IIS Help files are installed in a **virtual** directory outside the default Web site root, and so there is no direct correlation between the URL used to access them and the physical path. Only by using the `Server.MapPath` method can we get the true physical path.

Formatting Data with the Server Object

When we looked at the code for the pages that demonstrate the SSI directives earlier in his chapter, we came across one of the age-old problems of using HTML. How do we display HTML code in an HTML page? If we use it 'as is' (i.e. with all the HTML characters in place), it is interpreted and rendered as HTML by the browser. So when the following extract from an HTML page is viewed in a browser:

```
This is the syntax of a <TABLE> element:
```

it won't display the text `<TABLE>` because the browser will recognize it as an opening tag of a table, and render it as such. To get round this, we have to convert all characters that are not legal or valid in HTML into the equivalent HTML **character entity**. The most common ones we usually have to contend with are:

Character	HTML Entity Equivalent	Character	HTML Entity Equivalent
<	`<`	>	`>`
&	`&`	"	`"`
©	`©`	®	`®`

The opening ampersand and closing semi-colon in all of the entries are part of the standard way of denoting an entity in languages like HTML that are based on the rules of SGML (Standardized General Markup Language).

Numeric HTML Entity Equivalent Strings

Notice that the last of the examples, the registered trademark symbol, is a numeric value preceded with the '#' character, rather than a text abbreviation of the meaning (like `copy` for the copyright symbol). All characters with an ANSI code value greater than 126 can be represented in HTML as the ANSI code of the character in decimal, prefixed with `&#` and suffixed with a semi-colon. So the ½ (one half) character has an entity equivalent of `½`.

In fact you may care to use numeric entity equivalent strings in preference to some of the less universally supported text entity strings. An example is the trademark character (™), which has an entity equivalent string of `™` – but not all browsers (for example Navigator) recognize this and they will display the entity string in the page. Instead, using `™` works fine in all browsers.

The HTMLEncode Method of the Server Object

The need to convert HTML to text that is valid for display, without it being treated as HTML and rendered by the browser, means that we have to perform an encoding of the non-valid characters into the equivalent HTML entity strings. To manage this conversion, the Server object provides the `HTMLEncode` method. You can experiment with this in the ASP Server Object sample page that we supply.

Simply enter some text into the appropriate text box and click the button. We've provided some default text that is actually HTML:

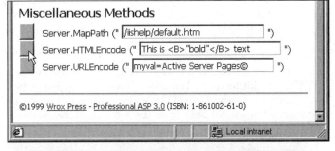

The result is again shown at the top of the page as it is reloaded. In this case, the `HTMLEncode` method has converted the angle brackets into `<` and `>` and the double-quote characters into `"`:

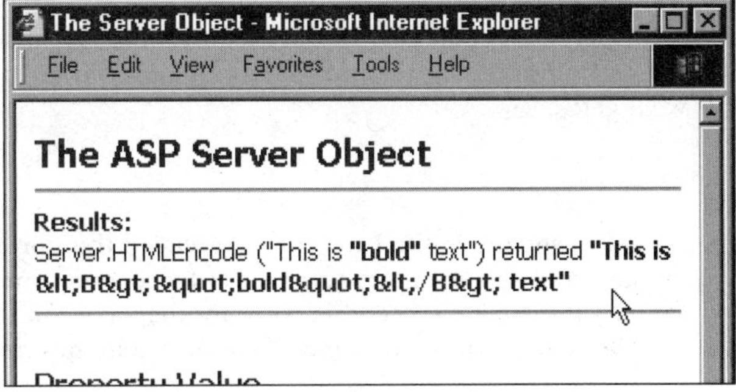

What the Sample Page Code Does

There are a couple of interesting points about the result that we get here.

Firstly, notice that within the brackets after the method name we've lost the `<B>` tags, but gained a bold section of text instead. What's happened is that when we display the original value in the page, it's being rendered as HTML – so the `<B>` tags disappear from view and their content is displayed in bold text.

We can get round this easily enough. In fact, this is just the situation that the HTMLEncode method is designed for. At present our sample code writes out the original value like this:

```
...
Response.Write "Server.HTMLEncode (" & QUOT & strValue & QUOT & ") returned"
...
```

What we can do is apply the HTMLEncode method to the value we are writing out:

```
...
strResult = Server.HTMLEncode(strValue)
Response.Write "Server.HTMLEncode (" & QUOT & strResult  & QUOT & ") returned"
...
```

This gives us a more useful result:

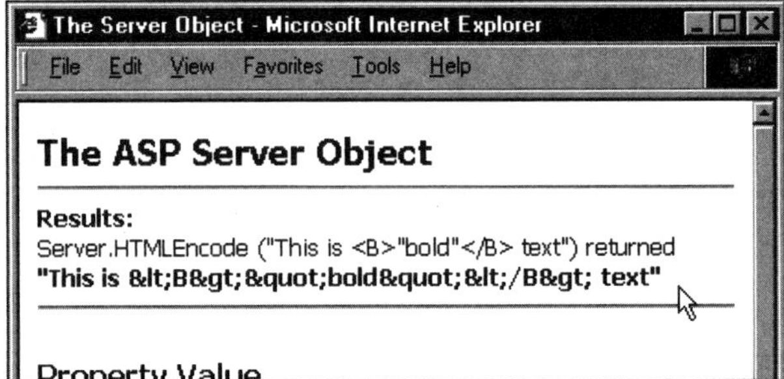

And that's by no means the whole story. We've solved the problem of how to display HTML using HTML without having it rendered. But what happens when we want to display the results of the HTMLEncode method in HTML without having it processed and rendered? To see the problem, consider what we got back from the HTMLEncode method:

```
This is &lt;B&gt;&quot;bold&quot;&lt;/B&gt; text
```

We can't display this in an HTML page as it stands, because the HTML character entities will be processed and rendered by the browser and displayed as the entity replacement character. In other words we'll get:

```
This is <B>"bold"</B> text
```

We won't get to see the entities that have replaced the non-valid HTML characters. To get round this, we apply the Server.HTMLEncode method a second time. This converts the ampersands (&) into `&` and so this time we get what we want displayed in the page. The complete code for this part of the sample page (with the first modification we mentioned above) is:

```
If Len(Request.Form("cmdHTMLEncode")) Then
   strValue = Request.Form("txtHTMLEncode")   'Get the value from the text box
   strResult = Server.HTMLEncode(strValue)    'HTMLEncode to convert <, > and "
   strDisplay = Server.HTMLEncode(strResult) 'Then again to convert & to &amp;
   Response.Write "<B>Results:</B><BR>Server.HTMLEncode (" & QUOT & strResult _
                  & QUOT & ") returned <B>" & QUOT & strDisplay & QUOT _
                  & "</B><HR>"
End If
```

HTMLEncode and Default Values for HTML Controls

We've seen how the HTMLEncode method is useful when we want to display HTML code in an HTML page without it being processed and rendered as HTML. OK, so you're unlikely to come across this situation in most of your 'normal' ASP pages – unless you have data in your database or other data source that contains HTML, which you want to display as text.

But one place where HTMLEncode is really valuable is when we preset the value of text-type HTML controls in our pages by setting the VALUE attribute. As an example, look at the source of the sample page we've been using to experiment with the HTMLEncode method. The HTML that creates the text box where you enter the value to be encoded is defined like this in the HTML:

```
...
<INPUT TYPE="TEXT" NAME="txtHTMLEncode" SIZE="35"
       VALUE="This is <B>&quot;bold&quot;</B> text">
...
```

This is 'manually-encoded' rather than using the Server.HTMLEncode method (perhaps we should say it has been WroxAuthor.Encoded, i.e. encoded by a Wrox author object!). We also only bothered to encode the double-quote characters and not the angle brackets. Why? Well, if we hadn't done this, the code would read:

```
       VALUE="This is <B>"bold"</B> text">
```

While the angle brackets don't cause a problem in this situation, the un-encoded double-quotes do. The actual value placed in the text box will be "This is <B>" – i.e. it will be truncated at the second double-quote character. So, when we create pages that preset the value of controls, we should always consider using HTMLEncode to prevent values being truncated:

```
<%
strValue = Request.Form("txtSomeValue")
%>
...
<INPUT TYPE="TEXT" NAME="txtSomeValue" .
       VALUE="<% = Server.HTMLEncode("strValue") %>">
...
```

When the browser sends the value of a control that has been HTML-encoded to our server, however, it automatically reverses the encoding. This means that the value is available in the original format within the Request collections.

Formatting Data for URLs

There is another situation where we often need to convert a text string into another format for use in our Web pages. Modern Web servers and operating systems all quite happily support file names that contain spaces, (although this isn't really a wise practice for Web pages). But it is possible that a URL we want to use could contain space characters, and since the syntax of a URL for use over HTTP doesn't allow for spaces (and several other characters) we have a problem.

A more common situation also raises its ugly head. When we send values to our server as members of the `QueryString` collection, they are appended to the end of the URL after a question mark character '`?`'. This might occur for the values in a `<FORM>` that has its `METHOD` set to `"GET"`, or which has the `METHOD` attribute omitted altogether. Alternatively, it may be values that we append directly to the URL, possibly in an `<A>` element:

```
<A HREF="http://myserver.com/mypage.asp?title=Instant JScript">
         Instant JScript</A>
```

Some browsers (such as Internet Explorer) can cope with this, as they automatically perform the conversion necessary before they send the HTTP request to the server. However, most other browsers don't do this, and the result is that the URL is usually truncated at the first space or non-legal character. So in Navigator, the link shown above would request the page `http://myserver.com/mypage.asp?title=Instant`. On the server, the missing part of the `title` name/value pair could cause the code to fail.

To stay within the limitations of the HTTP protocol definition, we have to make sure that certain characters are removed from any string that is used as a URL in an HTTP request. The non-legal characters are all those with an ANSI code above 126 and certain others with ANSI codes below this.

Characters with an ANSI code above 126 must be replaced by a percent sign (`%`), followed by the ANSI code in hexadecimal. So, the copyright character (©) becomes `%A9`. The characters with ANSI code below 126 that are not legal in a URL, together with their legal replacements, are:

Character	HTTP/URL Replacement	Character	HTTP/URL Replacement
space	+	\	%5C
'	%27	]	%5D
!	%21	^	%5E
#	%23	`	%60
$	%24	{	%7B
%	%25	|	%7C
&	%26	}	%7D
(	%28	+	%2B
)	%29	<	%3C
/	%2F	=	%3D
:	%3A	>	%3E
;	%3B	Chr(10)	*ignored*
[	%5B	Chr(13)	%0D

The URLEncode Method of the Server Object

It will probably come as no surprise to know that the Server object provides a method that we can use to convert any string into a format that is suitable for, and legal within, an HTTP URL. You can experiment with this method – named `URLEncode` – using our sample page:

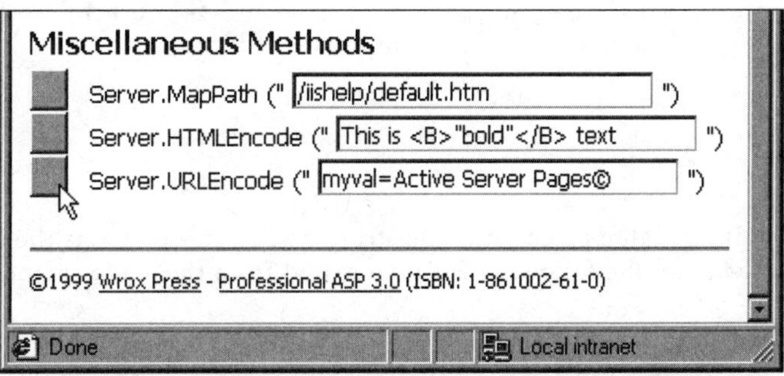

Here, our page proposes a value that we know is not legal as a URL, because it contains spaces and a character with an ANSI code above 126. The result of applying the `URLEncode` method to this value is that all the spaces are replaced by a plus sign, and the copyright symbol is replaced by `%A9`:

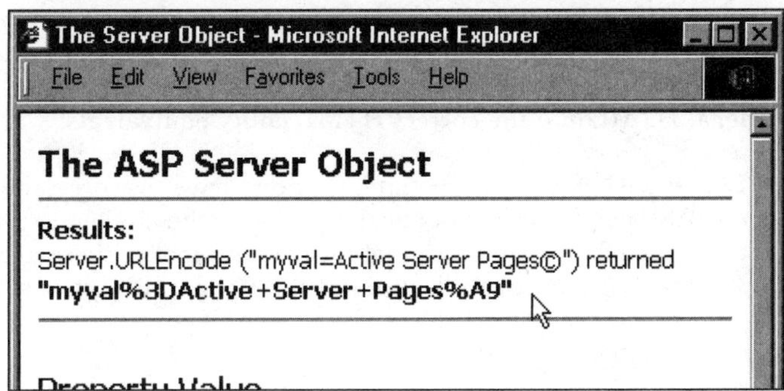

What the Sample Page Code Does

The code in the sample page that carries out this function is, as you'll expect, remarkably simple. We just check to see if the button for the `URLEncode` method was clicked, and if so, pass the value of the appropriate text box to the `Server.URLEncode` method and display the result:

```
If Len(Request.Form("cmdURLEncode")) Then
   strValue = Request.Form("txtURLEncode")
   Response.Write "<B>Results:</B><BR>Server.URLEncode (" & QUOT & strValue _
                  & QUOT & ") returned <B>" & QUOT & Server.URLEncode(strValue) _
                  & QUOT & "</B><HR>"
End If
```

URLEncode with HTML Anchors and Other Links

The most common use of the `URLEncode` method is when we are writing the values of `<A>` elements or other links into our pages with ASP. For example, if we build a set of links that contain values from a database in the query strings, we should always apply the `Server.URLEncode` method to the strings first:

```
<%
strValue = Request.Form("txtSomeValue")

'Create the full URL for the link as an HTTP-legal string
strURL = "http://mysite.com/books.asp?title=" & Server.URLEncode("strValue")
```

```
'Make sure we don't have any non-legal HTML characters in the page text
strLink = Server.HTMLEncode("strValue")
%>
...
<A HREF="<% = strURL %>"><% = strValue %></A>
...
```

If the value placed into the string `strValue` contains the book title `"Active Server Pages©"`, we will get the following HTML created from this code segment:

```
<A HREF=" http://mysite.com/books.asp?title=Active+Server+Pages%A9">
Active Server Pages&copy;</A>
```

Notice how we apply not only the `Server.URLEncode` method to build a legal URL string, but also apply the `Server.HTMLEncode` method to the text of the link to ensure that we convert any non-legal HTML into the correct HTML entity equivalents.

Like the `HTMLEncode` method, we don't have to worry about decoding the URL-encoded values in our ASP pages. IIS automatically performs the conversion of URL-encoded strings sent in the HTTP request back into their original format, and makes them available as such in the `QueryString` and `ServerVariables` collections of the Request object.

Summary

In this chapter, we've looked at some of the issues that are involved in providing dynamic content for our Web pages, through the various processes that take place on the Web server. Some of these are not directly connected with ASP itself, though a broad understanding of what is going on helps us to understand how the basic processes work (or sometimes don't work, as the case may be).

We examined how IIS supports traditional server-side include directives – some of which may still be useful, especially if you're building administration pages. In particular, the `#exec` directive is useful for both executing system commands and integrating legacy applications. We also looked at one particular server-side include directive, the `#include` statement, to understand the issues involved in using this within our ASP pages.

The bulk of this chapter was devoted, however, to the ASP Server object. This provides us with ways to manage server-side processes from within our ASP pages. It can create instances of other objects, applications or components within the correct context of the Web server and ASP. It also provides a series of methods that allow us to execute other pages or resources, and format information in the correct way for use in our ASP scripts and pages.

The Server object also brings with it a new ASP intrinsic object, the ASPError object, and a way of using this to provide better error handling for our scripts. We can now provide 'proper' script error handling on a directory-by-directory basis, and get better information about what went wrong – when it inevitably does.

So, the topics we covered are:

- The background and use of traditional server-side include (SSI) directives
- What the ASP Server object is designed to achieve, and how it compares with SSI
- How we use the Server object to instantiate and work with external components and applications
- How we use the Server object to execute encapsulated scripts, or other ASP pages
- How we use the Server object to manage errors that occur in our scripts
- How we use the Server object to perform format conversions for HTML or HTTP compatibility

This completes our study of the intrinsic ASP objects, and in the next chapter we move on to see how we can extend the capabilities of our pages. By taking advantage of the Server object's ability to create instances of other objects and components, we can build pages that can do almost anything except make the coffee. And with the advances in operating systems and embedded computing systems that we keep hearing about, maybe ASP will soon be able to make the coffee as well!

N
W

5

The Scripting Runtime Library Objects

In the previous chapter, we saw how Active Server Pages can use instances of objects that are already defined on the server so that we can take advantage of the methods and properties that they provide to extend the capabilities of our ASP pages. There are a whole range of objects that we can use, ranging from the scripting objects and installable components that come with a standard IIS/ASP installation, to those that we build ourselves or buy in from other vendors. And, like so much to do with the Internet, there are even free ones available from various Web sites that you can download and use in your own pages.

The objects we'll take a look at in this chapter are those provided by the ASP scripting environment, often referred to as the **Scripting Runtime Library** objects. They are exposed to our code through the scripting engine that we're using, and will perform various useful tasks along with our ASP script code.

There is a second category of components that is generally referred to as **Active Server Components**. These are usually implemented by separate ActiveX DLLs or other files. We'll be looking at these in the next chapter.

Of course, we also need to look at how we actually get these objects into our pages. We saw how the Server object provides a method to instantiate objects in the previous chapter. We'll be exploring this topic further here.

So, in this chapter, we'll see:

- What the scripting engines we use offer in the way of scripting objects
- How we create instances of scripting objects and other components
- A summary of the features and members of the scripting objects
- How we can use the scripting objects in our own code

We'll start with a look at what scripting objects actually are.

What are Scripting Objects?

In the previous chapters, we explored the **object model** for Active Server Pages.

> *An object model is basically a way of understanding how the various parts of the system are related.*

The ASP object model provides a structure that we can use to manipulate the different elements in the HTTP requests and responses, and the ASP environment as a whole. For example we saw how we can find out the values of any cookies sent from the browser by looking in the `Cookies` collection, which is part of the ASP Request object.

The scripting languages we use also have an object model. However, this model is for the objects that the scripting languages provide, as opposed to the objects like Request and Response that are provided directly by the ASP DLL. The scripting objects are provided by the **Microsoft Scripting Runtime Library** (`scrrun.dll`), which is installed with the default **Active Scripting** script engines.

Different Types of Objects and Components

Don't be confused by the words 'object' and 'component', and the range of various such items that seem to be available as part of ASP. They are all accessible in the same way – through COM – as we'll see in this and the next chapter. Conceptually, we can divide them into four groups:

- **Intrinsic ASP objects** such as `ObjectContext`, Request, Response, Application, Session, Server and ASPError. We examined these in Chapters 2 to 4.
- **Scripting objects** that are made available through the Scripting Runtime Library. These are Dictionary, `FileSystem` and `TextStream`. This chapter is devoted to these objects.
- **Installable components** are those provided by Microsoft in a standard installation of IIS 5.0 and ASP 3.0. We'll look at these in the next chapter.
- **Other components** that we either buy from independent vendors, find on the Web, or create ourselves. There are also some supplied with other Windows services or products, such as Windows Scripting Host. We've provided a list of some of them in the Appendices to this book, and we devote a whole section to building your own components later on.

The VBScript and JScript Scripting Objects

Microsoft provides three main objects as part of the Scripting Runtime Library:

- The **Dictionary** object provides a useful storage object that we can use to store values, accessed and referenced by their name rather than by index, as would be the case in a normal array. For example, it's ideal for storing the name/value pairs that we retrieve from the ASP Request object.
- The **FileSystemObject** object provides us with access to the underlying file system on the server (or on the client in IE5 when used in conjunction with a special type of page named a **Hypertext Application** or **HTA**). We can use the FileSystemObject object to iterate through the machine's local and networked drives, folders and files.
- The **TextStream** object provides access to files stored on disk, and is used in conjunction with the FileSystemObject object. It can read from or write to text (sequential) files. It can only be instantiated via the FileSystemObject object, so you might prefer to think of it as a child of that object.

The FileSystemObject object acts as 'parent' for a series of other objects and collections that we use to interact with the file system. It exposes three collections of objects – the Drives, Folders and Files collections – each of which is a collection of the appropriate Drive, Folder or File objects. These handle iterating and referencing the drives, folders (directories) and files on disk:

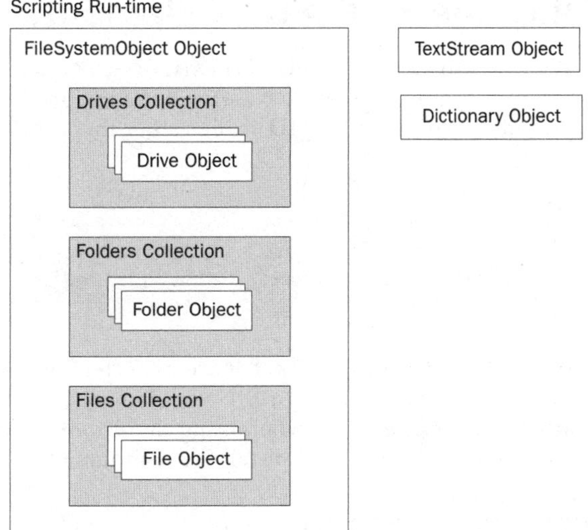

In the remainder of this chapter, we'll look at each of these objects and collections in turn and see how they can be used. However, we first need to make sure that you understand the different ways that instances of objects and components can be created or **instantiated**. This is the subject of the next section.

Creating Instances of Objects and Components

We create instances of the Scripting Runtime Library objects in exactly the same way as we do with any other objects and components. We can use the special `CreateObject` method that is exposed by the intrinsic ASP Server object (which ensures that the objects are created properly within the context of the current page), or we can use an `<OBJECT>` element. We'll look at both methods, and see which is appropriate depending on the requirements of the page.

Using the Server.CreateObject Method

As we saw in the previous chapter, when we looked at the Server object, a component or other object instance can be created from its **ProgID**:

```
<%
Dim objThis
Set objThis = Server.CreateObject("ADODB.Connection")
%>
```

The 'official' format for a ProgID string is "*vendor.component.version*", where the vendor name and component version are optional. Usually the ProgID will only include the first two sections (as in the example above). Few vendors place a version number on the ProgID, because this would prevent new versions that are backward compatible from using the same ProgID, and hence require ASP pages to be changed to use the new version.

Using the <OBJECT> Element

We can also use the standard HTML `<OBJECT>` element to create an instance of a component on the server by adding the `RUNAT` parameter and specifying the value `"SERVER"`. Again, it's usual to provide the object's ProgID string rather than the numeric ClassID:

```
<OBJECT ID="objThis" RUNAT="SERVER"
        PROGID="This.Object">
  <PARAM NAME="param1" VALUE="value1">
  <PARAM NAME="param2" VALUE="value2">
</OBJECT>
```

If the object has properties that are exposed for use in our script, we can set them within the `<OBJECT>` element using `<PARAM>` elements, just like we would in an HTML page. A `CODEBASE` attribute is not required when using the `<OBJECT>` element in ASP, because the server will never attempt to download and install the component or object if it's not already available.

Specifying a ClassID

Alternatively, we can specify the **ClassID** of the object or component we want to create. This is useful when we don't know for sure what other components may be installed on the target machine – particularly when we're instantiating components on the client, in a page in a browser for example.

In theory, component ProgIDs (the text "*vendor.component*" strings) should not conflict with each other, as they should all be unique. However, this is not a bulletproof approach. There may be a vendor in Northern China with the same name as one in the Isles of Scilly – there's always a chance that they might choose the same ProgID. On the other hand, valid ClassIDs are always unique, so there's no chance that this can happen when we use a ClassID to identify the component.

If we decide to use the ClassID of the object or component, we place it in a CLASSID attribute rather then a PROGID attribute:

```
<OBJECT ID="objThis" RUNAT="SERVER"
        CLASSID="clsid:892D6DA7-E0F9-11D2-B2E9-00105A42AF30">
  <PARAM NAME="param1" VALUE="value1">
  <PARAM NAME="param2" VALUE="value2">
</OBJECT>
```

But when we come to instantiating objects on our own server, we should be aware of what actually *is* installed in the way of objects and components. So when we create instances of objects in our ASP code, we can safely use the ProgID string. This is why the ClassID is rarely used in ASP pages. However, as all the ProgID is used for is to look up the CLSID, you can substitute the ClassID of a component or object for the ProgID if you wish.

Setting the Scope of Object Instances

By default, all object and component instances created in an ASP page (whether with the Server.CreateObject method or an <OBJECT> element) have **page scope**. This means that they exist only as long as the page is executing in ASP, and they are destroyed automatically after the current page has completed and the results have been sent to the client.

However, if we place the <OBJECT> declaration in the global.asa file that exists in the root directory of our Web site or virtual application, we can specify that an object or component should have **application** or **session scope** instead.

Creating Objects with Application-Level Scope

We can create an object with application-level scope by setting the SCOPE attribute to "APPLICATION":

```
<OBJECT ID="objThis" RUNAT="SERVER" PROGID="This.Object"
        SCOPE="APPLICATION">
</OBJECT>
```

The object instance will be created as soon as the application starts, i.e. as soon as the first user requests a page from the directories that are part of that virtual application. For the default Web site, this will be any directory on the site. The object instance then stays in existence until the application ends, which occurs immediately after the last user session has ended. At this point the object is destroyed. However, while it exists, it can be referenced and used by any user in any page that is within the appropriate virtual application or Web site directories.

Creating Objects with Session-Level Scope

If we want to create an instance of an object that is available to a single user, but which remains in scope across all the pages that they access, we can create an object with session-level scope. We do this by setting the SCOPE attribute to "SESSION":

```
<OBJECT ID="objThis" RUNAT="SERVER" PROGID="This.Object"
        SCOPE="SESSION">
</OBJECT>
```

The object will be created as soon as it is referenced – that is, referenced by code in a page that the user loads from the virtual application or Web site (one where the `global.asa` file holding this `<OBJECT>` declaration resides). When this user's session expires and is destroyed, the object instance it references is also destroyed.

What about Scope and State?

While it might seem like a good idea to create object instances globally, or in the global context of a user session, there are a couple of issues to consider with this practice. One of the prime reasons for doing this may be to be able to use the object to preserve **state** between user requests. In other words, we might set a few properties in our object, which are common to all the pages we use it in. This would seem to be a good idea as it saves creating a fresh instance and setting the properties each time.

In fact, Microsoft suggests that this is generally a bad idea, and is a hangover from traditional program design thinking. On the Web, the biggest issue we have to face up to is how our server – and the Web applications and dynamic pages that it provides – will cope with the (hopefully) millions of visitors that the site will get. Having instances of components hanging around in memory ready for a page request from a specific user is not the most efficient use of resources – not when there could be several hundred simultaneous users browsing the site.

Instead, Windows 2000 provides new COM+ Runtime features that can handle component creation, caching and usage in ways specifically designed to maximize throughput while minimizing server resource usage. Instead of us making half-baked decisions based on guesswork, about which object instances to store where and for how long, we're better off letting the operating system do it for us.

In other words, create the instance of the object within the page where you need to use it, and let it die when the page ends. COM+ will pick up the pieces and look after all the complexity involved in the background automatically. If you want to find out more about how it does this, take a look at Chapter 14, where we explore the topics of component creation in more detail.

Of course, in some situations we may still require an object to have application-level or session-level scope, particularly if we do need to hold state between page requests. We do this in one of the examples that you'll meet for the Dictionary object later on.

The Difference Between Server.CreateObject and <OBJECT>

The `Server.CreateObject` method creates an instance of the object immediately. In most cases this is what we want to happen. However, the `<OBJECT>` element only creates an instance of the object it specifies when we first reference that object. So, if we stop using the object in our code, it won't get created.

This might be useful if your code only uses the object under certain circumstances – depending perhaps on the value of some request parameter. It can save server resources if the object is not required.

However, you can do the same by only executing the `Server.CreateObject` method if you actually require the object to be created. The only circumstance where `<OBJECT>` helps is if you remove the calls to the object from your code and forget to remove the `Server.CreateObject` line – but that's just sloppy programming anyway!

Finally, remember that you can remove objects from a Session or Application if they were created using the `Server.CreateObject` method. You can't do this if they were created using an `<OBJECT>` element.

Component Threading Model Issues

One other issue that we should consider when we use objects or components in our pages is the way that the object behaves in respect to multiple requests for that object. In fact, this is one of the most complex topics to understand in ASP. The **threading model** of a component, combined with the scope that it is created in, affects the performance and capabilities of the component and the application or ASP page that instantiates it.

> *__Threads__ are system objects that are executed by the processor to carry out the task defined by the component code. Each can be thought of as a single set of binary instructions. In a multi-threaded environment like Windows, there can be many threads active at time.*

There are actually five threading models (including the new **Neutral-threading** model introduced in Windows 2000):

- **Single-threaded** – Only one process at a time can use the component
- **Apartment-threaded** – Several processes can use the component, but only on a single specified thread
- **Neutral-threaded** – Several processes can use the component, and can use any one of a specific set of threads
- **Multiple-** (or **Free-**) **threaded** – Several processes can use the component, and these processes can run on different threads
- **Both-threaded** – The object can behave as both an apartment-threaded and a free threaded object

> *We won't be attempting to explain the technical details of threading models here – we'll be covering them later in the book.*

Apartment-threaded components (such as we can create ourselves with Visual Basic or as XML script components) will generally perform well with `Page`-level scope, and are acceptable with Session-level scope. In fact, at `Page`-level, they will probably out-perform Both-threaded components, due to the lower processing overheads.

The new Windows 2000 Neutral-threading model provides even better performance – though at the moment there are few such components and suitable development tools available.

If you need Session-level components, aim to use Both-threaded ones if they're available. And if you need Application-level scope, you should always use Both-threaded components.

However, Microsoft recommends avoiding giving any components Session-level scope, and even more so Application-level scope, unless it's absolutely necessary. Causing component instances to remain active for longer periods than are required for `Page`-level scope components often provides no benefit over the object brokering features that COM+ can provide.

Referencing Object Type Libraries

In previous versions of ASP, one annoying factor when using objects or components in our scripts was that the public constants (if any) defined within the component were not available in ASP. This meant that we had to declare them (or an equivalent) ourselves, and specify the appropriate values.

For example, when we used the ActiveX Database Object (ADO) component (which we'll meet and examine in detail in Chapter 8) in earlier versions of ASP, we had to add the declarations of the pre-defined constants used in the `Open` method of a recordset:

```
Const adOpenKeyset = &H0001
Const adLockPessimistic = &H0003
Const adCmdTable = &H0002
...
rs.Open "Contact", "DSN=GlobalExampleData;UID=examples;Password=;", _
         adOpenKeyset, adLockPessimistic, adCmdTable
...
```

An alternative in the case of ADO is to use the `#include` directive to insert a file named `adovbs.inc` into the page. This is supplied with IIS/ASP and contains all the predefined constants for ADO. We just have to make sure that we use the latest version if we update the code, and check that it's available to all the pages that require it.

In IIS 5.0, there is a far better way. We can instead add a **reference** to the type library for the component or object, by using the `METADATA` directive within an HTML comment element (in fact, this worked in IIS 4.0 but was not documented):

```
<!-- METADATA TYPE="TypeLib"
                FILE="path_and_name_of_file"
                UUID="type_library_uuid"
                VERSION="major_version_number.minor_version_number"
                LCID="locale_id"
-->
```

Where:

- ***`path_and_name_of_file`*** is the absolute physical path to a type library file (`.tlb`) or ActiveX DLL. Either this or the ***`type_library_uuid`*** parameter must be provided.
- ***`type_library_uuid`*** is the unique identifier for the type library. Either this or the ***`path_and_name_of_file`*** parameter must be provided.
- ***`major_version_number.minor_version_number`*** (optional) defines the version of the component required. If this version is not found the most recent version is used.
- ***`locale_id`*** (optional) is the locale identifier to be used. If a type library with this locale is not found, the default locale for the machine (defined during setup) will be used.

So, we can use this technique to make the intrinsic ADO pre-defined constants available in our ASP pages by using:

```
<!-- METADATA TYPE="TypeLib"
               FILE="c:\Program Files\Common Files\System\ado\msado15.dll"
-->
```

The file name `msado15.dll` *is still used for the later (i.e. 2.50) versions of the ADO component.*

If ASP is unable to load the type library, it will return an error and halt execution of the page. The possible error values are:

Error	Description
ASP 0222	Invalid type library specification
ASP 0223	Type library not found
ASP 0224	Type library cannot be loaded
ASP 0225	Type library cannot be wrapped (i.e. ASP cannot create a type library wrapper object from the type library specified)

Creating Object Instances on the Client

While we're discussing techniques for instantiating objects and components on the server in ASP, it's worth quickly reiterating the way we do the same thing in pages that run client-side within the browser. If you use ASP to create pages that contain client-side script code, or which have `<OBJECT>` elements that create client-side component instances, you will find this useful. Remember that, in many cases, the scripting Runtime objects can be instantiated and used client-side as well as in ASP on the server.

The VBScript CreateObject Method

When we use `CreateObject` on the client, we are creating instances of components or objects within the context of the browser, and they run in the same memory space as the browser (i.e. in-process) unless the object is implemented as an executable with the `.exe` file extension.

It's usual to specify the **ClassID** of the object, rather than using the string **ProgID**, as this is less likely to clash with other objects that may be installed on the client:

```
<SCRIPT LANGUAGE="VBScript">
Dim objThis
Set objThis = CreateObject("clsid:892D6DA7-E0F9-11D2-B2E9-00105A42AF30")
...
</SCRIPT>
```

However, the **ProgID** can be used if preferred, and with common objects or components (especially those that are supplied as part of the standard installation) the risk of getting the wrong component is fairly slim:

```
<SCRIPT LANGUAGE="VBScript">
Dim objThis
Set objThis = CreateObject("Scripting.Dictionary")
...
</SCRIPT>
```

The JScript ActiveXObject Method

To instantiate an object or component in JScript on the client, we have to use the `new` operator in conjunction with the `ActiveXObject` method:

```
<SCRIPT LANGUAGE="JScript">
  var objMyData = new ActiveXObject('clsid:892D6DA7-E0F9-11D2-B2E9-00105A42AF30');
</SCRIPT>
```

or

```
<SCRIPT LANGUAGE="JScript">
  var objMyData = new ActiveXObject('this.object');
</SCRIPT>
```

The <OBJECT> Element Technique

We can also use an `<OBJECT>` element to create client-side object or component instances. We need to omit the `RUNAT` attribute or set it to `"CLIENT"`. However, this attribute is ignored on the client, so setting it is usually only done to save confusion when it's used in an ASP page that may use the `<OBJECT>` element to instantiate server-side component instances as well:

```
<OBJECT ID="objThis" RUNAT="CLIENT"
        CLASSID="clsid:892D6DA7-E0F9-11D2-B2E9-00105A42AF30"
        CODEBASE="http://yourserver.com/components/mycomponent.cab">
  <PARAM NAME="param1" VALUE="value1">
  <PARAM NAME="param2" VALUE="value2">
</OBJECT>
```

Notice the presence here of the `CODEBASE` attribute, which allows the client to download and install the component from the URL specified if it is not already installed. This only works in Internet Explorer 3 and above.

> *For a full description of how to use the `<OBJECT>` element, the attributes that are permissible, and their values when used on the client, check out* http://msdn.microsoft.com/workshop/author/dhtml/reference/objects/OBJECT.asp *or look up* "<OBJECT> tags" *in the Windows 2000 Platform SDK documentation. Or try IE5 Dynamic HTML Programmer's Reference, ISBN 1-861001-74-6 from Wrox Press.*

The Scripting.Dictionary Object

Many Microsoft languages, such as Visual Basic, VBScript and JScript, provide **collections**. We can think of a collection as being like an array, but with its own built-in functionality that looks after the basic tasks of storing and manipulating the data, and sizing for the required number of elements. We don't have to worry about which row or column the data is in, we just access it using a unique key.

VBScript and JScript both offer a similar object known as the **Scripting Dictionary** (or just **Dictionary**) object. This acts like a two-dimensional array, holding the key and the related item of data together. However, in true object-oriented fashion, we can't just access the data items directly. We have to use the methods and properties supported by the Dictionary object instead.

We have provided some samples pages for this chapter that allow you to experiment with the methods and properties of the scripting Runtime objects. The samples for this chapter are in the Chapter05 *subdirectory of the download file.*

Creating and Using Dictionary Objects

We can create an instance of the Dictionary object like this:

```
' In VBScript:
Dim objMyData
Set objMyData = Server.CreateObject("Scripting.Dictionary")
```

```
// In JScript:
var objMyData = Server.CreateObject('Scripting.Dictionary');
```

```
<!-- Server-side with an OBJECT element -->
<OBJECT RUNAT="SERVER" SCOPE="PAGE" ID="objMyData"
        PROGID="Scripting.Dictionary">
</OBJECT>
```

The Dictionary object can also be used client-side in Internet Explorer.

The Dictionary Object Members Summary

Here's the full list of properties and methods for the Dictionary object.

The Dictionary Object's Properties

Property	Description
`CompareMode`	(*VBScript only*). Sets or returns the string comparison mode for the keys.
`Count`	Read only. Returns the number of key/item pairs in the Dictionary.
`Item(key)`	Sets or returns the value of the item for the specified *key*.
`Key(key)`	Sets the value of a *key*.

The Dictionary Object Methods

Method	Description
`Add(`*key, item*`)`	Adds the *key/item* pair to the Dictionary.
`Exists(`*key*`)`	Returns `True` if the specified *key* exists or `False` if not.
`Items()`	Returns an array containing all the items in a Dictionary object.
`Keys()`	Returns an array containing all the keys in a Dictionary object.
`Remove(`*key*`)`	Removes a single key/item pair specified by *key*.
`RemoveAll()`	Removes all the key/item pairs.

An error will occur if we try to add a key/item pair when that key already exists, remove a key/item pair that doesn't exist, or change the `CompareMode` *of a Dictionary object that already contains data.*

Adding Items To and Removing Items From a Dictionary

Once we've got a new (empty) dictionary, we can add items to it, retrieve them, and remove them :

```
' In VBScript:
objMyData.Add "MyKey", "MyItem"             'Add value MyItem with key MyKey
objMyData.Add "YourKey", "YourItem"         'Add value YourItem with key YourKey
blnIsThere = objMyData.Exists("MyKey"       'Returns True because the item exists
strItem = objMyData.Item("YourKey")         'Retrieve value of YourKey
strItem = objMyData.Remove("MyKey")         'Retrieve and remove YourKey
objMyData.RemoveAll                         'Remove all the items
```

To do the same in JScript, we use:

```
// In JScript:
objMyData.Add('MyKey', 'MyItem');             // Add value MyItem with key MyKey
objMyData.Add('YourKey', 'YourItem');         // Add value YourItem with key YourKey
var blnIsThere = objMyData.Exists('MyKey'); // true because the item exists
var strItem = objMyData.Item('YourKey');      // Retrieve value of YourKey
var strItem = objMyData.Remove('MyKey');      // Retrieve and remove YourKey
objMyData.RemoveAll();                        // Remove all the items
```

Changing the Value of a Key or Item

We can change the data stored in a Dictionary by changing the value of the key, or by changing the value of the item of data associated with a specific key. To change the value of the item with the key `MyKey`, we use:

```
objMyData.Item("MyKey") = "NewValue"      ' In VBScript
```

```
objMyData.Item('MyKey') = 'NewValue';    // In JScript
```

If the key we specify isn't found in the Dictionary, a new key/item pair is created with the key as `MyKey` and the item value as `NewValue`. One interesting aspect is that, if we try to retrieve an item using a key that doesn't exist, we not only get an empty string as the result (as we'd expect) but also a new key/item pair is added to the Dictionary. This has the key we specified, but with the item value left empty.

To change the value of a key, without changing the value of the corresponding item, we use the `Key` property. So, to change the value of an existing key `MyKey` to `MyNewKey`, we could use:

```
objMyData.Key("MyKey") = "MyNewKey"        ' In VBScript
```

```
objMyData.Key('MyKey') = 'MyNewKey';    // In JScript
```

If the specified key isn't found, a Runtime error is generated.

Setting the Comparison Mode

The `CompareMode` property of a dictionary is only available in VBScript –it cannot be used in JScript. It allows us to define how the comparison is made when comparing string keys. The two permissible values are `BinaryCompare` (0), which produces a binary comparison (i.e. matching is case sensitive), and `TextCompare` (1), which produces a text comparison (i.e. matching is *not* case sensitive).

Iterating Through a Dictionary

There are two methods and a property that are of particular interest when dealing with a Dictionary. These allow us to iterate through all the key/item pairs stored in it. The `Items` method returns all the items in a Dictionary as a one-dimensional array, while the `Keys` method returns all the existing key values as a one-dimensional array. To find out how many keys or items there are, we can use the `Count` property.

For example, we can retrieve all the keys and values from a Dictionary called `objMyData` using the following code. Notice that, although the `Count` property holds the number of key/item pairs in the Dictionary, VBScript and JScript arrays always starts at index zero.Therefore we have to iterate through the array using the values `0` to `Count - 1`:

```
' In VBScript:
arrKeys = objMyData.Keys                  'Get all the keys into an array
arrItems = objMyData.Items                'Get all the items into an array

For intLoop = 0 To objMyData.Count - 1   'Iterate through the array
  strThisKey = arrKeys (intLoop)          'This is the key value
  strThisItem = arrItems (intLoop)        'This is the item (data) value
Next
```

```
// In JScript:
// Get VB-style arrays using the Keys() and Items() methods
var arrKeys = new VBArray(objMyData.Keys()).toArray();
var arrItems = new VBArray(objMyData.Items()).toArray();

for (intLoop = 0; intLoop < objMyData.Count; intLoop++) {
  // Iterate through the arrays
  strThisKey = arrKeys[intLoop];          // This is the key value
  strThisItem = arrItems[intLoop];        // This is the item (data) value
}
```

Alternatively in VBScript, we can use the `For Each...Next` construct to do the same:

```
' Iterate the dictionary as a collection in VBScript
For Each objItem in arrItems
   Response.Write objItem & " = " & arrItems(objItem) & "<BR>"
Next
```

A Dictionary Object Example

We've provided a series of sample files that you can use to experiment with the various features of the Scripting Runtime Library.

The default page for this chapter's code provides a series of links to the VBScript samples that are available. You'll find that some are also available in JScript as well, and these are in the appropriate subdirectories of the `Chapter05` directory:

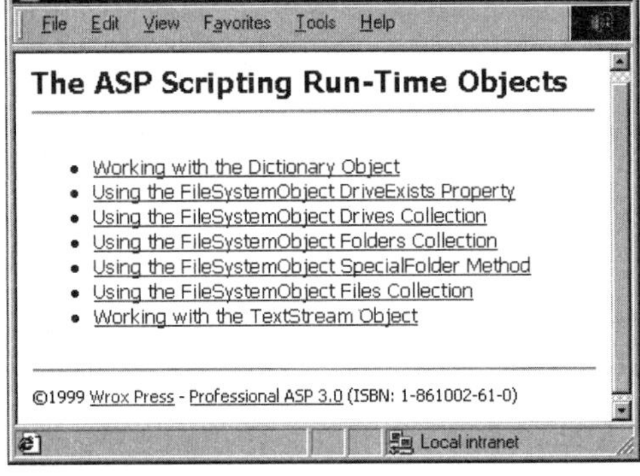

To see the Dictionary object in action, click the first link on the menu page to open the page named `show_dictionary.asp`. This page displays the contents of a dictionary object that we've provided, and controls that allow you to try out the properties and methods that it exposes:

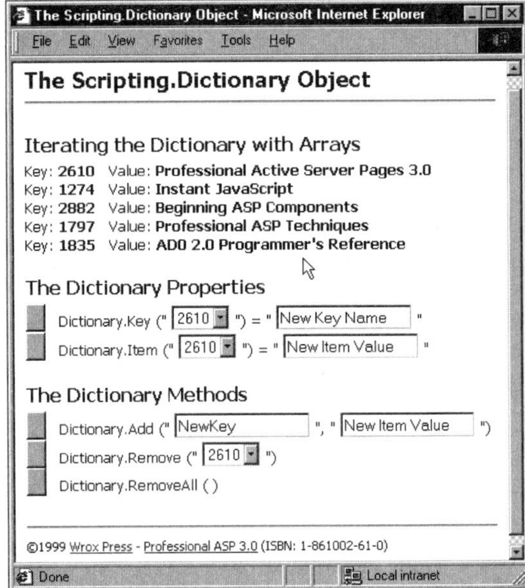

The Dictionary global.asa File

One of the files that we've supplied with the `Dictionary` object example page is a version of `global.asa`. This creates and pre-fills a `Dictionary` object that has session-level scope, so that the contents are not lost between page requests. While this is not ideal practice in general (for scalability reasons), in this example it allows you to see the effects of the properties and methods on the dictionary contents.

If you download and install the samples on your own server, you must either create a virtual application based on this `global.asa` file, or copy the contents into your existing `global.asa` file (if one does already exist) in the root folder of the Default Web site. We showed you how to create a virtual application using the Wizard in Chapter 3. However, the easiest way to create a virtual application for this example is to right-click the `dictionary` sub-folder within the `Chapter05` samples folder, and in the **Home Directory** page of the **Properties** dialog, click the **Create** button:

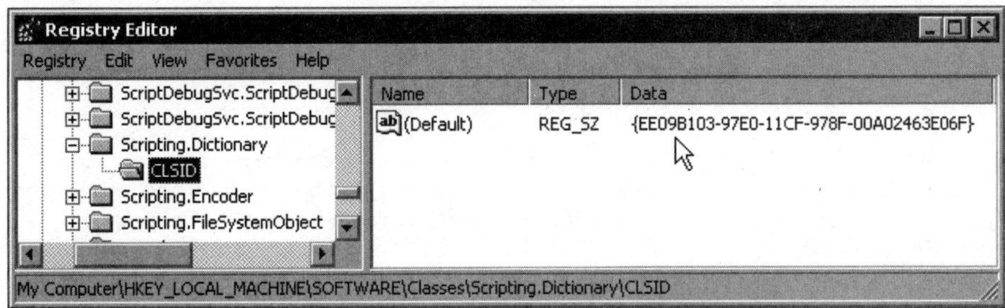

The code in our `global.asa` file uses an `<OBJECT>` element to create an instance of the `Scripting.Dictionary` object with session-level scope. Then, in the `Session_onStart` event handler, it places a series of values into the dictionary using the `Add` method, and assigns a reference to the Dictionary object to an ASP Session variable named `MyDictionary`:

```
<OBJECT ID="objBookList" RUNAT="SERVER" SCOPE="SESSION"
        PROGID="Scripting.Dictionary">
</OBJECT>

<SCRIPT LANGUAGE="VBScript" RUNAT="SERVER">

Sub Session_onStart()
  objBookList.Add "2610", "Professional Active Server Pages 3.0"
  objBookList.Add "1274", "Instant JavaScript"
  objBookList.Add "2882", "Beginning ASP Components"
  objBookList.Add "1797", "Professional ASP Techniques"
  objBookList.Add "1835", "ADO 2.0 Programmer's Reference"
  Set Session("MyDictionary") = objBookList
End Sub

</SCRIPT>
```

The Dictionary Example Page

The first task for our code in the main **Scripting.Dictionary Object** page is to get a reference to the Dictionary object that we instantiated with session-level scope. Notice that this reference is an object variable, and so we have to use the `Set` keyword in VBScript.

After this we check to see if we actually did get an object. This is always good practice, as it indicates where the problem lies if you haven't properly set up a virtual application containing our `global.asa` file. In this case you'll see our own message instead of an ASP error message (but note that we have to turn off the default error handling for this to work):

```
<%

On Error Resume Next    'turn off default error handling

' Retrieve Dictionary object from user's session
Set objMyData = Session("MyDictionary")

If IsObject(objMyData) Then   ' Found Dictionary object in Session

...

  %>

  <P><DIV CLASS="subhead">Iterating the Dictionary with Arrays</DIV>
  <%
  arrKeysArray = objMyData.Keys              'Get all the keys into an array
  arrItemsArray = objMyData.Items            'Get all the items into an array
  For intLoop = 0 To objMyData.Count - 1     'Iterate through the array
    Response.Write "Key: <B>" & arrKeysArray(intLoop) & "</B>   Value: <B>" _
                   & arrItemsArray(intLoop)& "</B><BR>"
  Next
  %>
  ...
  ... Other code and controls go here ...
  ...
  <%
Else

' Could not find Dictionary object in the session
  Response.Write "Dictionary object not available in global.asa for session"

End If
%>
```

The list of the dictionary contents shown in the page is created using the `Keys` and `Items` methods of the Dictionary object to create two arrays, and then iterating through them as we did in the code extracts shown earlier on.

The Dictionary Page Controls

Below the list of the dictionary's contents are a series of HTML controls that can be used to set some of the properties of the Dictionary object, and execute various methods. These controls are all on a `<FORM>` that has this page as the `ACTION` attribute value, so the content of the form is submitted back to this page. This is the same technique as we've used in the samples in earlier chapters.

Within the `<FORM>` section, each action to change a property or execute a method is through a button (with no caption). Any values for the property or method are placed into text boxes or lists next to the button.

The first button on the page is used to set the `Key` property of an item in the dictionary. We use a drop-down list from which you can select an existing entry on its key. The code shown below creates the controls for this part of the page. You can see that to populate the list, we've used the other technique for iterating a dictionary object – a `For Each..Next` statement:

```
...
<FORM ACTION="<% = Request.ServerVariables("SCRIPT_NAME") %>" METHOD="POST">

<P><DIV CLASS="subhead">The Dictionary Properties</DIV>
<INPUT TYPE="SUBMIT" NAME="cmdChangeKey" VALUE="   ">
  Dictionary.Key ("
<SELECT NAME="lstChangeKey" SIZE="1">
<%
For Each objItem in objMyData
  Response.Write "<OPTION>" & objItem
Next
%>
</SELECT> ") = "

<INPUT TYPE="TEXT" NAME="txtChangeKey" SIZE="15" VALUE="New Key Name"> "
<BR>
...
... Other controls go here ...
...
</FORM>
...
```

Using the Dictionary Properties and Methods

So, in the Scripting.Dictionary Object page, click the button we've just been examining to change the `Key` property of one of the existing entries:

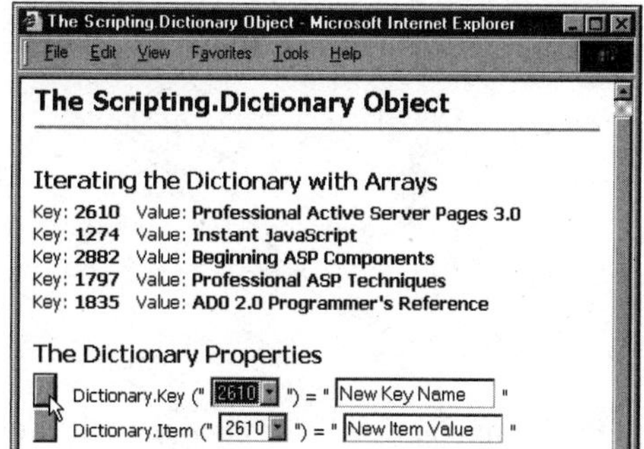

This submits the form back to this page again. The page contains a script section that looks for values in the request indicating whether a button was clicked. We can tell which button was clicked by looking for its name in the `Request.Form` collection. If we find a value for `cmdChangeKey`, we extract the values from the list and text box and use them to change the `Key` property:

```
...
'Look for a command sent from the FORM section buttons
If Len(Request.Form("cmdChangeKey")) Then
  strKeyName = Request.Form("lstChangeKey")   'Existing key from list box
  strNewKey = Request.Form("txtChangeKey")    'New key value from text box
  objMyData.Key(strKeyName) = strNewKey       'Set Key property of this item
End If
...
```

After the page has reloaded, the result can be seen in the list of the dictionary's contents:

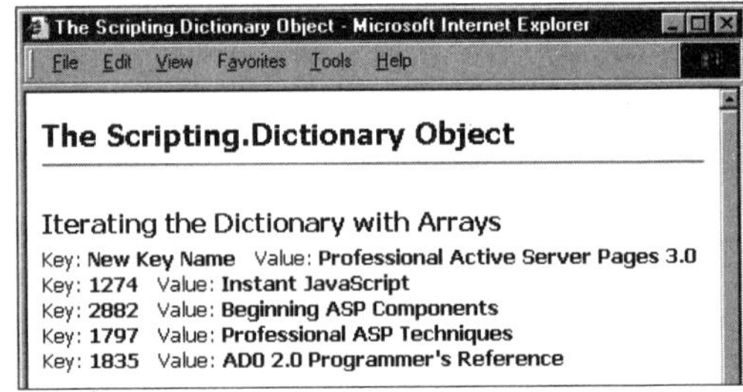

The remaining code in this page is used to set the `Item` property of an entry, or carry out the execution of one of the Dictionary object's methods. This is the code for these operations. Each section does much the same as the `Key` property code that we've already seen above. And, each time, the results are displayed in the list of the dictionary's contents:

```
  ...
  If Len(Request.Form("cmdChangeItem")) Then
    strKeyName = Request.Form("lstChangeItem")   'Existing key from list box
    strNewValue = Request.Form("txtChangeItem")  'New item value from text box
    objMyData.Item(strKeyName) = strNewValue     'Set the Item property
  End If

  If Len(Request.Form("cmdAdd")) Then
    strKeyName = Request.Form("txtAddKey")       'New key value from text box
    strItemValue = Request.Form("txtAddItem")    'New item value from text box
    objMyData.Add strKeyName, strItemValue       'Execute the Add method
  End If

  If Len(Request.Form("cmdRemove")) Then
    strKeyName = Request.Form("lstRemove")       'Existing key from list box
    objMyData.Remove strKeyName                  'Execute the Remove method
  End If

  If Len(Request.Form("cmdRemoveAll")) Then
    objMyData.RemoveAll                          'Execute the RemoveAll method
  End If
...
```

For example, if we now click the button for the `Add` method, we'll add a new item to the dictionary's contents:

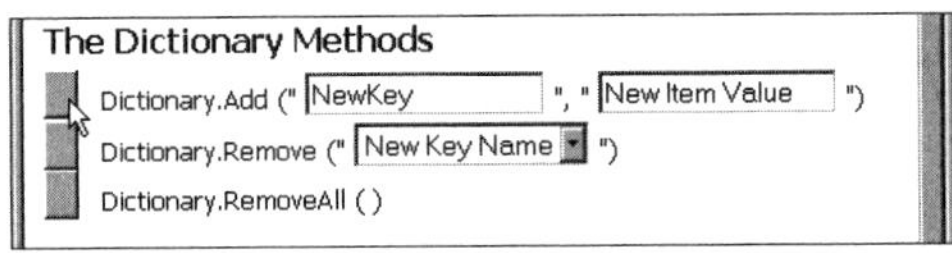

And here's the result:

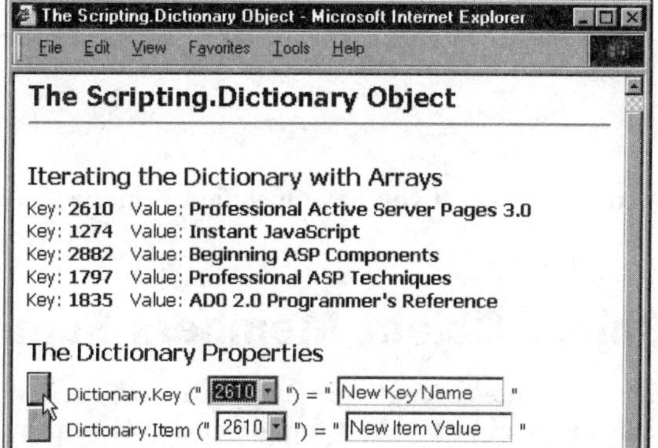

You can experiment with the properties and methods of the Dictionary object yourself using this page – and even discover which cause Dictionary object errors, and under what circumstances. For example, try adding an entry with the same key value as an existing entry.

The Scripting.FileSystemObject Object

The **FileSystemObject** object provides access to the computer's file system, allowing us to manipulate text files, folders and drives from within our code. It's one of the objects provided by the Scripting Runtime Library, and is available in VBScript and JScript for use in ASP pages on the server. It can also be used client-side in Internet Explorer 5, providing that the pages have the `.hta` file extension, to indicate that they're part of a **Hypertext Application** (HTA). In this section, we'll only be looking at how we use the FileSystemObject in ASP script on the server.

> *A Hypertext application is made up of special 'trusted' pages that contain the `<HTA:APPLICATION>` element in the `<HEAD>` section of the page, for example:*
>
> *`<HTA:APPLICATION ID="objMyApp" APPLICATIONNAME="myApp">`*
>
> *These pages can use features of the client-side scripting engines that are not usually available, amongst them the FileSystemObject and TextStream objects. For more information about Hypertext Applications, check the out the Microsoft Workshop site.*

We can create an instance of the FileSystemObject object using:

```
' In VBScript:
Dim objMyFSO
Set objMyFSO = Server.CreateObject("Scripting.FileSystemObject")
```

```
// In JScript:
var objMyFSO = Server.CreateObject('Scripting.FileSystemObject');
```

```
<!-- Server-side with an OBJECT element -->
<OBJECT RUNAT="SERVER" SCOPE="PAGE" ID="objFSO"
        PROGID="Scripting.FileSystemObject">
</OBJECT>
```

It's also useful in an ASP page to add a reference to the FileSystemObject type library to the page. This allows us to use the intrinsic constants that it defines directly, without having to substitute the numeric equivalents as you've probably done in the past. The type library for the complete scripting Runtime library can be added to any ASP page using:

```
<!-- METADATA TYPE="typelib" FILE="C:\WinNT\System32\scrrun.dll" -->
```

You must edit the `FILE` attribute value if you have installed Windows in a different folder from the default.

The FileSystemObject Object Members Summary

The FileSystemObject object provides a single property and a whole range of methods, which we use to manipulate the other subsidiary objects that it implements. We've provided a full summary here, and we'll go on to look at each of the subsidiary objects in turn later on.

The FileSystemObject's Property

The FileSystemObject object has a single property that allows us to retrieve a list of all the valid drives on the current machine:

Property	Description
`Drives`	Returns a collection of Drive objects that are available from the local machine. This includes network drives that are mapped from this machine.

The FileSystemObject's Methods

The FileSystemObject object provides a range of methods for manipulating the subsidiary objects like Drive, Folder and File. It also implements two methods for working with TextStream objects: `CreateTextFile` and `OpenTextFile`. We've divided the list of methods into three categories depending on the type of object that each is designed to work with.

Methods for Working with Drives

Method	Description
`DriveExists(`*drivespec*`)`	Returns `True` if the drive specified in *drivespec* exists, or `False` if not. The *drivespec* parameter can be a drive letter as a string or a full absolute path for a folder or file.
`GetDrive(`*drivespec*`)`	Returns a Drive object corresponding to the drive specified in *drivespec*. The format for *drivespec* can include the colon, path separator or be a network share, i.e. "`c`", "`c:`", "`c:\`" or "`\\machine\sharename`".
`GetDriveName(`*drivespec*`)`	Returns the name of the drive specified in *drivespec* as a string. The *drivespec* parameter must be an absolute path to a file or folder, or just the drive letter such as "`c:`" or just "`c`".

Methods for Working with Folders

Method	Description
`BuildPath(`*path, name*`)`	Adds the file or folder specified in *name* to the existing *path*, adding a path separator character ('\') if required.
`CopyFolder(`*source, destination, overwrite*`)`	Copies the folder or folders specified in *source* (wildcards can be included) to the folder specified in *destination*, including all the files contained in the *source* folder(s). If *source* contains wildcards or *destination* ends with a path separator character ('\'), then *destination* is assumed to be a folder into which the copied folder(s) will be placed. Otherwise it is assumed to be a full path and name for a new folder to be created. An error will occur if the *destination* folder already exists and the optional *overwrite* parameter is set to `False`. The default for *overwrite* is `True`.
`CreateFolder(`*foldername*`)`	Creates a new folder which has the path and name specified in *foldername*. An error occurs if the specified folder already exists.
`DeleteFolder(`*folderspec, force*`)`	Deletes the folder or folders specified in *folderspec* (wildcards can be included in the final component of the path) together with all their contents. If the optional *force* parameter is set to `True`, the folders will be deleted even if their read-only attribute (or that of any contained files) is set. The default for *force* is `False`.
`FolderExists (`*folderspec*`)`	Returns `True` if the folder specified in *folderspec* exists, or `False` if not. The *folderspec* parameter can contain an absolute or relative path for the folder, or just the folder name to look in the current folder.
`GetAbsolutePathName (`*pathspec*`)`	Takes a *path* that unambiguously identifies a folder and, taking into account the current folder's path, returns a full path specification for the *pathspec* folder. For example, if the current folder is "`c:\docs\sales\`" and *pathspec* is "`jan`", the returned value is "`c:\docs\sales\jan`". Wildcards and the "`..`" and "`\\`" path operators are accepted.
`GetFolder(`*folderspec*`)`	Returns a Folder object corresponding to the folder specified in *folderspec*. This can be a relative or absolute path to the required folder.
`GetParentFolderName (`*pathspec*`)`	Returns the name of the parent folder of the file or folder specified in *pathspec*. Does not check for existence of the folder.

Table Continued on Following Page

Method	Description
`GetSpecialFolder` (*folderspec*)	Returns a Folder object corresponding to one of the special Windows folders. The permissible values for *folderspec* are `WindowsFolder` (0), `SystemFolder` (1) and `TemporaryFolder` (2).
`MoveFolder` (*source*, *destination*)	Moves the folder or folders specified in *source* to the folder specified in *destination*. Wildcards can be included in *source*, but not in *destination*. If *source* contains wildcards or *destination* ends with a path separator character ('\') then *destination* is assumed to be the folder in which to place the moved folders. Otherwise it is assumed to be a full path and name for a new folder. An error will occur if the *destination* folder already exists.

Methods for Working with Files

Method	Description
`CopyFile` (*source*, *destination*, *overwrite*)	Copies the file or files specified in *source* (wildcards can be included) to the folder specified in *destination*. If *source* contains wildcards or *destination* ends with a path separator character ('\'), then *destination* is assumed to be a folder. Otherwise it is assumed to be a full path and name for the new file. An error will occur if the *destination* file already exists and the optional *overwrite* parameter is set to `False`. The default for *overwrite* is `True`.
`CreateTextFile` (*filename*, *overwrite*, *unicode*)	Creates a new text file on disk with the specified *filename*, and returns a TextStream object that refers to it. If the optional *overwrite* parameter is set to `True`, any existing file with the same path and name will be overwritten. The default for *overwrite* is `False`. If the optional *unicode* parameter is set to `True`, the content of the file will be stored as Unicode text. The default for *unicode* is `False`.
`DeleteFile` (*filespec*, *force*)	Deletes the file or files specified in *filespec* (wildcards can be included). If the optional *force* parameter is set to `True`, the file(s) will be deleted even if the Read-only attribute is set. The default for *force* is `False`.
`FileExists` (*filespec*)	Returns `True` if the file specified in *filespec* exists, or `False` if not. The *filespec* parameter can contain an absolute or relative path for the file, or just the file name to look in the current folder.
`GetBaseName` (*filespec*)	Returns just the name of a file specified in *filespec*, i.e. with the path and file extension removed.

Method	Description
GetExtensionName (*filespec*)	Returns just the file extension of a file specified in *filespec*, i.e. with the path and file name removed.
GetFile(*filespec*)	Returns a File object corresponding to the file specified in *filespec*. This can be a relative or absolute path to the required file.
GetFileName(*pathspec*)	Returns the name part of the path and filename specified in *pathspec*, or the last folder name of there is no file name. Does not check for existence of the file or folder.
GetTempName()	Returns a randomly generated file name, which can be used for performing operations that require a temporary file or folder.
MoveFile(*source*, *destination*)	Moves the file or files specified in *source* to the folder specified in *destination*. Wildcards can be included in *source* but not in *destination*. If *source* contains wildcards or *destination* ends with a path separator character ('\'), then *destination* is assumed to be a folder. Otherwise it is assumed to be a full path and name for the new file. An error will occur if the *destination* file already exists.
OpenTextFile(*filename*, *iomode*, *create*, *format*)	Creates a file named *filename*, or opens an existing file named *filename*, and returns a TextStream object that refers to it. The *filename* parameter can contain an absolute or relative path. The *iomode* parameter specifies the type of access required. The permissible values are ForReading (1 – the default), ForWriting (2), and ForAppending (8). If the *create* parameter is set to True when writing or appending to a file that does not exist, a new file will be created. The default for *create* is False. The *format* parameter specifies the format of the data to be read from or written to the file. Permissible values are TristateFalse (0 – the default) to open it as ASCII, TristateTrue (-1) to open it as Unicode, and TristateUseDefault (-2) to open it using the system default format.

***Unicode files** use two bytes to identify each character, removing the ASCII limitation of **256** available characters.*

Working with Drives

As a simple example of how we can use the FileSystemObject object, we can get a list of available drive letters using the `DriveExists` method:

```
' In VBScript:
Set objMyFSO = Server.CreateObject("Scripting.FileSystemObject")

Set objFSO = Server.CreateObject("Scripting.FileSystemObject")
For intCode = 65 To 90   'ANSI codes for 'A' to 'Z'
   strLetter = Chr(intCode)
   If objFSO.DriveExists(strLetter) Then
      Response.Write "Found drive " & strLetter & ":<BR>"
   End If
Next
```

Or in JScript:

```
// In JScript:
var objFSO = Server.CreateObject('Scripting.FileSystemObject');
for (var intCode = 65; intCode <= 90; intCode++) {
   strLetter = String.fromCharCode(intCode);
   if (objFSO.DriveExists(strLetter))
      Response.Write('Found drive ' + strLetter + ':<BR>');
}
```

The result of both these code fragments is the same. This is the page named `driveexists_vb.asp` from the sample files we supply:

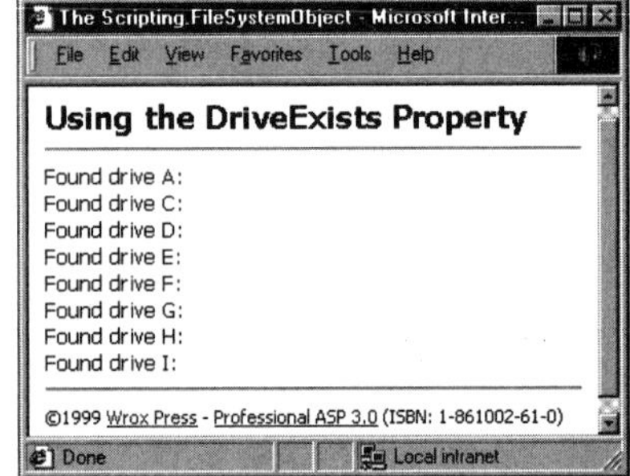

The Drive Object

As we've seen, the FileSystemObject object contains one property – `Drives` – which returns a collection consisting of all Drive objects available on the local machine. Each item in the `Drives` collection is a Drive object. The Drive object exposes these properties:

Property	Description
`AvailableSpace`	Returns the amount of space available to this user on the drive, taking into account quotas and/or other restrictions.
`DriveLetter`	Returns the drive letter of the drive.

Property	Description
DriveType	Returns the type of the drive. The values are Unknown (0), Removable (1), Fixed (2), Network (3), CDRom (4), and RamDisk (5). However, note that the current version of scrrun.dll does not include the pre-defined constant for Network, so you may have to use the decimal value 3 instead.
FileSystem	Returns the type of file system for the drive. The values include "FAT", "NTFS" and "CDFS".
FreeSpace	Returns the actual total amount of free space available on the drive.
IsReady	Returns a Boolean value indicating if the drive is ready (True) or not (False).
Path	Returns the path for the drive as a drive letter and colon, i.e. "C:".
RootFolder	Returns a Folder object representing the root folder of the drive.
SerialNumber	Returns a decimal serial number used to uniquely identify a disk volume.
ShareName	Returns the network share name for the drive if it is a networked drive.
TotalSize	Returns the total size (in bytes) of the drive.
VolumeName	Sets or returns the volume name of the drive if it is a local drive.

So, by using the Drive objects that are members of the Drives collection, we can produce a list of drives on the server far more efficiently than by checking if a drive exists for each possible drive letter – and along the way, we can get information about the drive. In VBScript, the code looks like this:

```
' In VBScript:
' Create a FileSystemObject instance
Set objFSO = Server.CreateObject("Scripting.FileSystemObject")
' Create a Drives collection
Set colDrives = objFSO.Drives

' Iterate through the Drives collection
For Each objDrive in colDrives
  Response.Write "DriveLetter: " & objDrive.DriveLetter & "<BR>"
  Response.Write "DriveType: " & objDrive.DriveType & "<BR>"

  If objDrive.DriveType = 3 Then
    If objDrive.IsReady Then
      Response.Write "Remote drive with ShareName: " & _
                     objDrive.ShareName & "<BR>"
    Else
      Response.Write "Remote drive - IsReady property returned False<BR>"
    End If
  Else
```

```
      Response.Write "FileSystem: " & objDrive.FileSystem & "<BR>"
      Response.Write "SerialNumber: " & objDrive.SerialNumber & "<BR>"
      Response.Write "Local drive with VolumeName: " & _
                     objDrive.VolumeName & "<BR>"
      Response.Write "AvailableSpace: " & objDrive.AvailableSpace & " bytes<BR>"
      Response.Write "FreeSpace: " & objDrive.FreeSpace & " bytes<BR>"
      Response.Write "TotalSize: " & objDrive.TotalSize & " bytes<P>"
    End If

  Next
```

Notice that we can't compare the `DriveType` *property to the pre-defined constant* `Network` *because (at least in the current version of* `scrrun.dll`*) this has been omitted from the type library, and hence is not available as a public constant.*

The same thing in JScript looks like this:

```
// In JScript:
// Create a FileSystemObject instance
var objFSO = Server.CreateObject('Scripting.FileSystemObject');
// Create a Drives collection
var colDrives new Enumerator(objFSO.Drives);
// Iterate through the Drives collection
for (; !colDrives.atEnd(); colDrives.moveNext()) {
  objDrive = colDrives.item();
  Response.Write('DriveLetter: ' + objDrive.DriveLetter + '<BR>');
  Response.Write('DriveType: ' + objDrive.DriveType + '<BR>');
  if (objDrive.DriveType == 3)
    if (objDrive.IsReady)
      Response.Write('Remote drive with ShareName: ' +
                     objDrive.ShareName + '<BR>')
    else
      Response.Write('Remote drive - IsReady property returned False<BR>');
  else
    Response.Write('Local drive with VolumeName: ' +
                   objDrive.VolumeName + '<BR>');
  Response.Write('FileSystem: ' + objDrive.FileSystem + '<BR>');
  Response.Write('SerialNumber: ' + objDrive.SerialNumber + '<BR>');
  Response.Write('AvailableSpace: ' + objDrive.AvailableSpace + ' bytes<BR>');
  Response.Write('FreeSpace: ' + objDrive.FreeSpace + ' bytes<BR>');
  Response.Write('TotalSize: ' + objDrive.TotalSize + ' bytes<P>');
}
```

One point to note before you run this code on your own system. If you don't have a disk in your `A:` drive or CD-ROM drive, you'll get a 'Disk Not Ready' error. You can protect the page from this by testing the `IsReady` property for *every* drive before trying to access anything other than the `DriveLetter` and `DriveType` property.

The result of the VBScript code example (when a little extra formatting is added) looks like this when run on one of our test servers. This is the page named `drivescollection_vb.asp` from the sample files we supply:

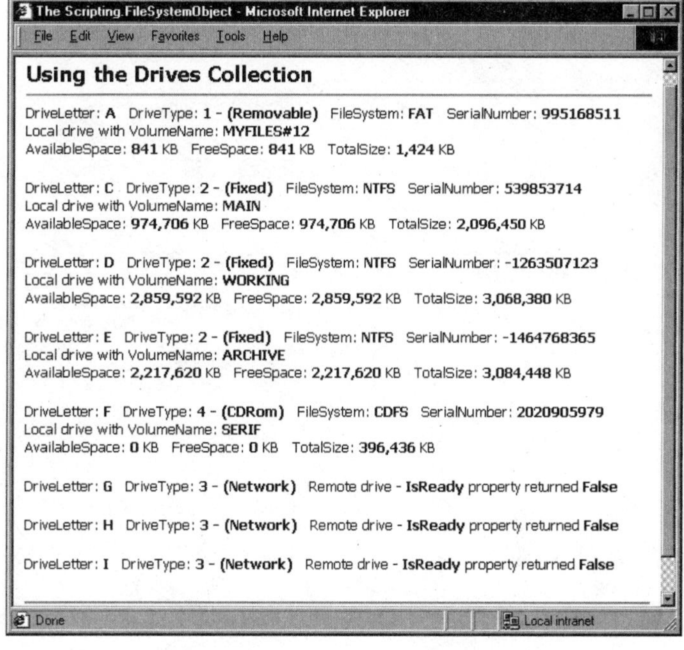

Navigating the File System

Several of the methods of the FileSystemObject can be used to get references to other objects, so that we can navigate through the file system of the server and any networked drives. In fact, the FileSystemObject object is probably one of the most complex of all the objects or components that you'll use in your ASP code (with the exception of the ActiveX Data Objects components).

The complexity comes from the extremely high level of flexibility we have in how we access different parts of the file system. For example, we can navigate from the root FileSystemObject down to a file on any drive through the various subsidiary objects. Starting from the `Drives` collection, we go to a Drive object, then to the root Folder object of that drive, then to a subfolder Folder object, then to the `Files` collection in that folder, and finally to a File object within that collection.

Alternatively, if we know which drive, file or folder we want, we can go directly to them using the `GetDrive`, `GetFolder`, `GetSpecialFolder` or `GetFile` methods. The next diagram will help you to understand the way that all the collections, objects, methods and properties that are used to navigate the file system are related:

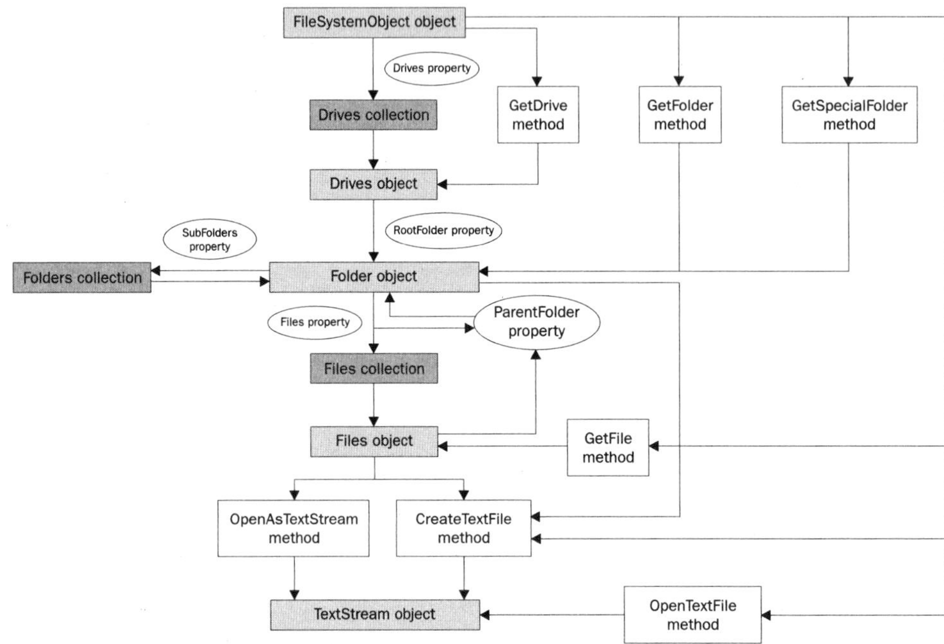

The Folder Object

The `RootFolder` property of the Drive object returns a Folder object, through which we can access all of the content of this drive. We can use the properties and methods of the Folder object to traverse directories on the drive, and to get at all the properties of this or any other folder.

The Folder Object's Properties

The Folder object provides a set of properties that we can use to get more information about the current folder, and to change the folder name:

Property	Description
`Attributes`	Returns the attributes of the folder. Can be a combination of any of the following values: `Normal` (0), `ReadOnly` (1), `Hidden` (2), `System` (4), `Volume` (name) (8), `Directory` (folder) (16), `Archive` (32), `Alias` (64) and `Compressed` (128). For example, a hidden read-only file would have the value `3`.
`DateCreated`	Returns the date and time that the folder was created.
`DateLastAccessed`	Returns the date and time that the folder was last accessed.
`DateLastModified`	Returns the date and time that the folder was last modified.
`Drive`	Returns the drive letter of the drive on which the folder resides.

Property	Description
`Files`	Returns a `Files` collection containing File objects representing all the files within this folder.
`IsRootFolder`	Returns a Boolean value indicating if the folder is the root folder of the current drive.
`Name`	Sets or returns the name of the folder.
`ParentFolder`	Returns the Folder object for the parent folder of this folder.
`Path`	Returns the absolute path of the folder, using long file names where appropriate.
`ShortName`	Returns the DOS-style 8.3 version of the folder name.
`ShortPath`	Returns the DOS-style 8.3 version of the absolute path of this folder.
`Size`	Returns the size of all files and subfolders contained in the folder.
`SubFolders`	Returns a `Folders` collection consisting of all folders contained in the folder, including hidden and system folders.
`Type`	Returns a string that is a description of the folder type (such as "Recycle Bin") if available.

The Folder Object's Methods

The Folder object provides a set of methods that can be used to copy, delete and move the current folder. They work in the same way as the `CopyFolder`, `DeleteFolder` and `MoveFolder` methods of the FileSystemObject object, but don't require a *source* parameter because the source is this folder.

Method	Description
`Copy(`*destination* `,` *overwrite*`)`	Copies this folder and all its contents to the folder specified in *destination.* If *destination* ends with a path separator character ('\') then *destination* is assumed to be a folder into which the copied folder will be placed. Otherwise it is assumed to be a full path and name for a new folder to be created. An error will occur if the *destination* folder already exists, and the optional *overwrite* parameter is set to `False`. The default for *overwrite* is `True`.
`Delete(`*force*`)`	Deletes this folder and all of its contents. If the optional *force* parameter is set to `True` the folder will be deleted, even if the Read-only attribute is set on it or on any contained files. The default for *force* is `False`.
`Move()`	Moves this folder and all its contents to the folder specified in *destination.* If *destination* ends with a path separator character ('\') then *destination* is assumed to be the folder in which to place the moved folder. Otherwise, it is assumed to be a full path and name for a new folder. An error will occur if the *destination* folder already exists.

Table Continued on Following Page

Method	Description
`CreateTextFile` (*filename, overwrite, unicode*)	Creates a new text file within this folder with the specified *filename*, and returns a TextStream object that refers to it. If the optional *overwrite* parameter is set to `True`, any existing file with the same name will be overwritten. The default for *overwrite* is `False`. If the optional *unicode* parameter is set to `True`, the content of the file will be stored as unicode text. The default for *unicode* is `False`.

We can navigate between folders using the `ParentFolder` property of the current folder, to go back towards the root of the drive. We stop when we get a folder returned for which the `IsRootFolder` property is `True`. To go down the tree, away from the root of the drive, we simply iterate through or access specific folders within the `Folders` collection that's returned by the `SubFolders` property of the current folder.

The following code iterates through all the folders in the root of drive `C:`, and displays information about each one. In VBScript, the code looks like this:

```
' In VBScript:
' Create a FileSystemObject instance
Set objFSO = Server.CreateObject("Scripting.FileSystemObject")
' Get a reference to drive C
Set objDriveC = objFSO.GetDrive("C:")
' Get a reference to the root folder
Set objRoot = objDriveC.RootFolder
' Get a reference to the Folders collection
Set colFolders = objRoot.SubFolders
' Iterate through all the folders within this folder
For Each objFolder in colFolders
  Response.Write "Name: " & objFolder.Name & "   "
  Response.Write "ShortName: " & objFolder.ShortName & "   "
  Response.Write "Type: " & objFolder.Type & "<BR>"
  Response.Write "Path: " & objFolder.Path & "   "
  Response.Write "ShortPath: " & objFolder.ShortPath & "<BR>"
  Response.Write "Created: " & objFolder.DateCreated & "   "
  Response.Write "LastModified: " & objFolder.DateLastModified & "<P>"
Next
```

The same thing in JScript looks like this:

```
// In JScript:
// Create a FileSystemObject instance
var objFSO = Server.CreateObject('Scripting.FileSystemObject');
// Get a reference to drive C
var objDriveC = objFSO.GetDrive('C:');
// Get a reference to the root folder
var objRoot = objDriveC.RootFolder;
// Get a reference to the Folders collection
var colFolders = new Enumerator(objRoot.SubFolders);
// Iterate through all the folders within this folder
```

```
for (; !colFolders.atEnd(); colFolders.moveNext()) {
    objFolder = colFolders.item();
    Response.Write('Name: ' + objFolder.Name + '   ');
    Response.Write('ShortName: ' + objFolder.ShortName + '   ');
    Response.Write('Type: ' + objFolder.Type + '<BR>');
    Response.Write('Path: ' + objFolder.Path + '   ');
    Response.Write('ShortPath: ' + objFolder.ShortPath + '<BR>');
    Response.Write('Created: ' + objFolder.DateCreated + '   ');
    Response.Write('LastModified: ' + objFolder.DateLastModified + '<P>');
}
```

And the result of the VBScript code example looks like this when run on one of our test servers. This is the page named `folderscollection_vb.asp` from the sample files we supply:

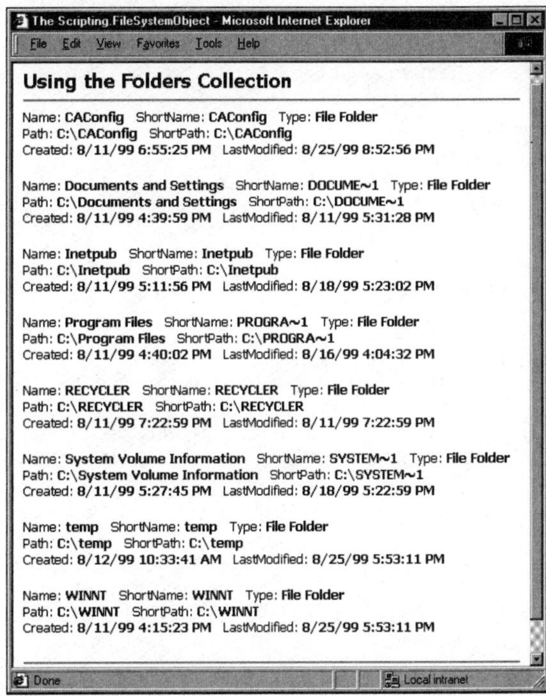

Working with Special Folders

One of the methods of the FileSystemObject object, `GetSpecialFolder`, returns the Folder object for any of three 'special folders' on the machine:

- `WindowsFolder` - the %Windows% directory, by default `WinNT` (or `Windows` on a non-NT/2000 machine)
- `SystemFolder` - the %System% directory, by default `WinNT\System32` (or `Windows\System` on a non-NT/2000 machine)
- `TemporaryFolder` - the %Temp% directory, by default `WinNT\Temp` (or `Windows\Temp` on a non-NT/2000 machine)

To get a reference to a special folder, we supply the appropriate pre-defined constant as a parameter of the `GetSpecialFolder` method:

```
' In VBScript:
Set objFSO = Server.CreateObject("Scripting.FileSystemObject")

Set objFolder = objFSO.GetSpecialFolder(WindowsFolder)
Response.Write "GetSpecialFolder(WindowsFolder) returned:<BR>"
Response.Write "Path: " & objFolder.Path & "<BR>"
Response.Write "Type: " & objFolder.Type & "<P>"

Set objFolder = objFSO.GetSpecialFolder(SystemFolder)
Response.Write "GetSpecialFolder(SystemFolder) returned:<BR>"
Response.Write "Path: " & objFolder.Path & "<BR>"
Response.Write "Type: " & objFolder.Type & "<P>"

Set objFolder = objFSO.GetSpecialFolder(TemporaryFolder)
Response.Write "GetSpecialFolder(TemporaryFolder) returned:<BR>"
Response.Write "Path: " & objFolder.Path & "<BR>"
Response.Write "Type: " & objFolder.Type & "<P>"
```

Or in JScript:

```
// In JScript:
var objFSO = Server.CreateObject('Scripting.FileSystemObject');

var objFolder = objFSO.GetSpecialFolder(WindowsFolder);
Response.Write('GetSpecialFolder(WindowsFolder) returned -  ');
Response.Write('Path: ' + objFolder.Path + '   ');
Response.Write('Type: ' + objFolder.Type + '<BR>');

var objFolder = objFSO.GetSpecialFolder(SystemFolder);
Response.Write('GetSpecialFolder(SystemFolder) returned -  ');
Response.Write('Path: ' + objFolder.Path + '   ');
Response.Write('Type: ' + objFolder.Type + '<BR>');

var objFolder = objFSO.GetSpecialFolder(TemporaryFolder);
Response.Write('GetSpecialFolder(TemporaryFolder) returned -  ');
Response.Write('Path: ' + objFolder.Path + '   ');
Response.Write('Type: ' + objFolder.Type + '<BR>');
```

The result of the VBScript code example (when a little extra formatting is added) looks like this when run on one of our test servers. This is the page named `specialfolders_vb.asp` from the sample files we supply:

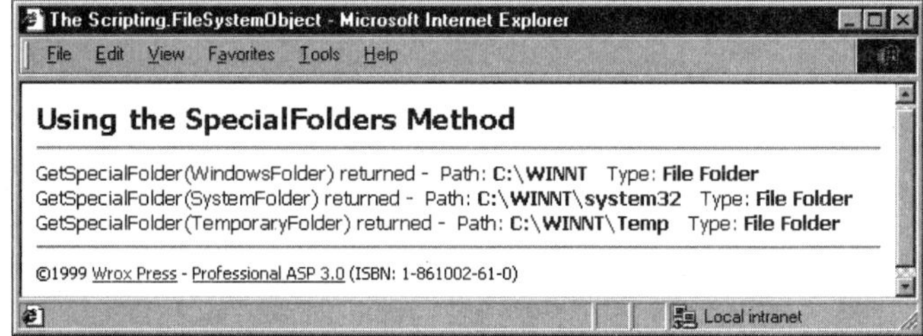

The File Object

The File object provides access to the properties of a file, and implements methods that we can use to manipulate that file. Each Folder object exposes a `Files` collection, containing File objects that correspond to the files in that folder. We can also get a File object reference directly from the FileSystemObject object, by using the `GetFile` method.

The File Object's Properties

The File object has a series of properties that are similar to the Folder object:

Property	Description
`Attributes`	Returns the attributes of the file. Can be a combination of any of the following values: `Normal` (0), `ReadOnly` (1), `Hidden` (2), `System` (4), `Volume` (name) (8), `Directory` (folder) (16), `Archive` (32), `Alias` (64) and `Compressed` (128).
`DateCreated`	Returns the date and time that the file was created.
`DateLastAccessed`	Returns the date and time that the file was last accessed.
`DateLastModified`	Returns the date and time that the file was last modified.
`Drive`	Returns a drive object representing the drive on which the file resides.
`Name`	Sets or returns the name of the file.
`ParentFolder`	Returns the Folder object for the parent folder of this file.
`Path`	Returns the absolute path of the file, using long file names where appropriate.
`ShortName`	Returns the DOS-style 8.3 version of the file name.
`ShortPath`	Returns the DOS-style 8.3 version of the absolute path of this file.
`Size`	Returns the size of the file in bytes
`Type`	Returns a string that is a description of the file type (such as "Text Document" for a `.txt` file) if available.

The File Object's Methods

Again, like the Folder object, the methods of the File object allow us to copy, delete and move the file. There's also a method that we use to open the file as a text stream:

Method	Description
`Copy(`*destination, overwrite*`)`	Copies this file to the folder specified in *destination*. If *destination* ends with a path separator character ('\'), then *destination* is assumed to be a folder into which the copied file will be placed. Otherwise it is assumed to be a full path and name for a new file to be created. An error will occur if the *destination* file already exists, and the optional *overwrite* parameter is set to `False`. The default for *overwrite* is `True`.
`Delete(`*force*`)`	Deletes this file. If the optional *force* parameter is set to `True` the file will be deleted, even if the Read-only attribute is set. The default for *force* is `False`.
`Move()`	Moves this file to the folder specified in *destination*. If *destination* ends with a path separator character ('\'), then *destination* is assumed to be the folder in which to place the moved file. Otherwise it is assumed to be a full path and name for a new file. An error will occur if the *destination* file already exists.
`CreateTextFile` `(`*filename, overwrite, unicode*`)`	Creates a new text file on disk with the specified *filename*, and returns a TextStream object that refers to it. If the optional *overwrite* parameter is set to `True`, any existing file with the same path and name will be overwritten. The default for *overwrite* is `False`. If the optional *unicode* parameter is set to `True`, the content of the file will be stored as Unicoded text. The default for *unicode* is `False`.
`OpenAsTextStream` `(`*iomode, format*`)`	Opens a specified file and returns a TextStream object that can be used to read from, write to, or append to the file. The *iomode* parameter specifies the type of access required. The permissible values are `ForReading` (`1` – the default), `ForWriting` (`2`), and `ForAppending` (`8`). The *format* parameter specifies the format of the data to be read from or written to the file. Permissible values are `TristateFalse` (`0` – the default) to open it as ASCII, `TristateTrue` (`-1`) to open it as Unicode, and `TristateUseDefault` (`-2`) to open it using the system default format.

So, given a File object, we can use the `ParentFolder` property to get a reference to the Folder object containing the file, and use this to navigate the file system. We can even use the `Drive` property to get a reference to the appropriate Drive object, and from there, the various Folder objects and their contained File objects.

Alternatively, given a Folder object and its corresponding `Files` collection, we can iterate through the collection examining each file in that folder. We can also use the methods of each of the File objects to process the file in some way – perhaps by copying, moving or deleting it. This code lists the files in the first folder on your '`C:`' drive:

```
' In VBScript:
' Create a FileSystemObject instance
Set objFSO = Server.CreateObject("Scripting.FileSystemObject")
' Get a reference to drive C
Set objDriveC = objFSO.GetDrive("C:")
' Get a reference to the root folder
Set objRoot = objDriveC.RootFolder
' Get a reference to the SubFolders collection
Set objFolders = objRoot.SubFolders

' Get a reference to the first folder in the SubFolders collection
For Each objFolder In objFolders
  Set objFolder1 = objFolders.Item((objFolder.Name))
  Exit For
Next

' Iterate through all the files in this folder
For Each objFile in objFolder1.Files
  Response.Write "Name: " & objFile.Name & "   "
  Response.Write "ShortName: " & objFile.ShortName & "   "
  Response.Write "Size: " & objFile.Size & " bytes    "
  Response.Write "Type: " & objFile.Type & "<BR>"
  Response.Write "Path: " & objFile.Path & "   "
  Response.Write "ShortPath: " & objFile.ShortPath & "<BR>"
  Response.Write "Created: " & objFile.DateCreated & "   "
  Response.Write "LastModified: " & objFile.DateLastModified & "<P>"
Next
```

Notice that we can't use a numeric index to reference an item in a `Folders` or `Files` collection, so we have to use a trick of iterating up to the first item in the collection with a `For Each...Next` statement and then using the `Name` property of that item. We also have to use nested parentheses to force it to be passed by value (as a string) to the `Item` method of the `Folders` collection.

The same thing in JScript looks like this:

```
// In JScript:
// Create a FileSystemObject instance
var objFSO = Server.CreateObject('Scripting.FileSystemObject');
// Get a reference to drive C
var objDriveC = objFSO.GetDrive('C:');
// Get a reference to the root folder
var objRoot = objDriveC.RootFolder;
// Get a reference to the first folder in the SubFolders collection
var colAllFolders = new Enumerator(objRoot.SubFolders);
var objFolder1 = colAllFolders.item();
// Get a reference to the Files collection for this folder
var colFiles = new Enumerator(objFolder1.Files);

// Iterate through all the files in this collection
for (; !colFiles.atEnd(); colFiles.moveNext()) {
  objFile = colFiles.item()
```

```
    Response.Write('Name: ' + objFile.Name + '   ');
    Response.Write('ShortName: ' + objFile.ShortName + '   ');
    Response.Write('Size: ' + objFile.Size + ' bytes    ');
    Response.Write('Type: ' + objFile.Type + '<BR>');
    Response.Write('Path: ' + objFile.Path + '   ');
    Response.Write('ShortPath: ' + objFile.ShortPath + '<BR>');
    Response.Write('Created: ' + objFile.DateCreated + '   ');
    Response.Write('Accessed: ' + objFile.DateLastAccessed + '   ');
    Response.Write('Modified: ' + objFile.DateLastModified + '<P>');
}
```

The result of both these code fragments is the same. This is the page named `filescollection_vb.asp` from the sample files we supply:

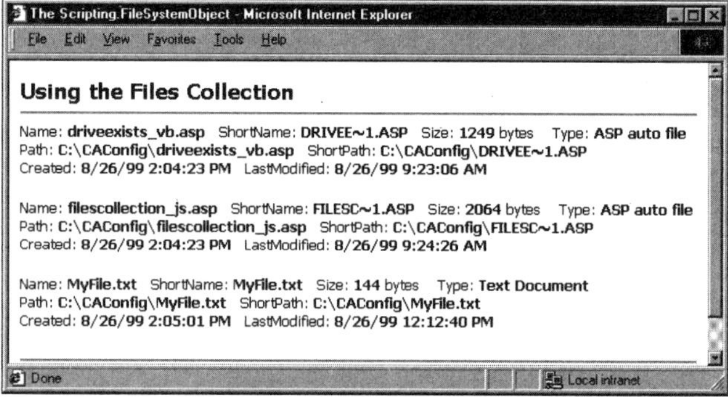

Note that the first folder on your `C:` drive could well be the same as on our –, `CAConfig`, which is empty by default. In this case, you should copy some files into it to see the results, and then delete them again afterwards.

The Scripting.TextStream Object

Several of the methods of the FileSystemObject, Folder, and File objects are concerned with creating, reading from and writing to text files via a TextStream object. You can see this object at the bottom of the FileSystemObject navigation diagram that we used earlier in this chapter.

From this, you'll gather that, although the TextStream object is defined as a separate object from the subsidiary objects of the FileSystemObject object, it is inexorably tied up with it. We have to use the FileSystemObject object or one of its subsidiary objects to be able to create a TextStream object and access the contents of a disk file.

Methods for Creating TextStream Objects

The three methods that are used to create or open a text file and return a TextStream object are:

Method	Description
`CreateTextFile` (*filename*, *overwrite*, *unicode*)	Creates a new text file on disk with the specified *filename*, and returns a TextStream object that refers to it. If the optional *overwrite* parameter is set to `True`, any existing file with the same path and name will be overwritten. The default for *overwrite* is `False`. If the optional *unicode* parameter is set to `True`, the content of the file will be stored as unicode text. The default for *unicode* is `False`.
`OpenTextFile` (*filename*, *iomode*, *create*, *format*)	Creates a file named *filename*, or opens an existing file named *filename*, and returns a TextStream object that refers to it. The *filename* parameter can contain an absolute or relative path. The *iomode* parameter specifies the type of access required. The permissible values are `ForReading` (`1` – the default), `ForWriting` (`2`), and `ForAppending` (`8`). If the *create* parameter is set to `True` when writing or appending to a file that does not exist, a new file will be created. The default for *create* is `False`. The *format* parameter specifies the format of the data to be read from or written to the file. Permissible values are `TristateFalse` (`0` – the default) to open it as ASCII, `TristateTrue` (`-1`) to open it as Unicode, and `TristateUseDefault` (`-2`) to open it using the system default format.
`OpenAsTextStream` (*iomode*, *format*)	Opens a specified file and returns a TextStream object that can be used to read from, write to, or append to the file. The *iomode* parameter specifies the type of access required. The permissible values are `ForReading` (`1` – the default), `ForWriting` (`2`), and `ForAppending` (`8`). The *format* parameter specifies the format of the data to be read from or written to the file. Permissible values are `TristateFalse` (`0` – the default) to open it as ASCII, `TristateTrue` (`-1`) to open it as Unicode, and `TristateUseDefault` (`-2`) to open it using the system default format.

The methods listed above are implemented to a varying degree in the three objects FileSystemObject, Folder and File object. This table summarizes the availability:

Method	**FileSystemObject** object	**Folder** object	**File** object
`CreateTextFile`	**Yes**	**Yes**	**Yes**
`OpenTextFile`	**Yes**	(No)	(No)
`OpenAsTextStream`	(No)	(No)	**Yes**

So we can use these methods to create a new text file, or to open an existing one. Once we've done this, we have a TextStream object reference to it, and we can manipulate the file using the methods and properties of the TextStream object.

Creating New Text Files

The `CreateTextFile` method creates a new text file, or overwrites an existing one. It returns a TextStream object that we can use to read from or write to the file.

We first create a FileSystemObject object, which we use to create a TextStream object. This example uses VBScript to create a 'normal' (i.e. not-Unicode) file named `MyFile.txt`, replacing any existing one with the same name:

```
Set objFSO = Server.CreateObject("Scripting.FileSystemObject")
Set objTStream = objFSO.CreateTextFile("C:\TextFiles\MyFile.txt", True, False)
```

To do the same in JScript we can use:

```
var objFSO = Server.CreateObject('Scripting.FileSystemObject');
var objTStream = objFSO.CreateTextFile('C:\TextFiles\MyFile.txt', true, false);
```

Once the file has been created, we can use the `objTStream` reference (which is a reference to a TextStream object) to work with the file.

Opening Existing Text Files

The `OpenTextFile` method opens an existing text file. It returns a TextStream object that we can use to read from or append data to the file.

Again, we first create a FileSystemObject object, then use it to create a TextStream object. This VBScript example opens a file named `MyFile.txt` ready to read the contents:

```
Set objFSO = Server.CreateObject("Scripting.FileSystemObject")
Set objTStream = objFSO.OpenTextFile("C:\TextFiles\MyFile.txt", ForReading)
```

The same in JScript is:

```
var objFSO = Server.CreateObject('Scripting.FileSystemObject');
var objTStream = objFSO.OpenTextFile('C:\TextFiles\MyFile.txt');
```

To open the file for writing, and create a new file if the one specified doesn't already exist, we could use:

```
' In VBScript:
Set objTStream = objFSO.OpenTextFile("C:\TextFiles\MyFile.txt", ForWriting, True)
```

```
// In JScript:
var objTStream = objFSO.OpenTextFile('C:\TextFiles\MyFile.txt', ForWriting, true);
```

If we want to open an existing Unicode file ready to append data to it, but *not* create a new file if the one specified doesn't already exist, we could use:

```
' In VBScript:
Set objTStream = objFSO.OpenTextFile("C:\TextFiles\MyFile.txt", ForAppending, _
                                     False, TristateTrue)
```

```
// In JScript:
var objTStream = objFSO.OpenTextFile('C:\TextFiles\MyFile.txt', ForAppending,
                                     false, true);
```

Opening a File Object as a TextStream Object

The `OpenAsTextStream` method of the `File` object opens the file that this object refers to and returns a TextStream object that can be used to read from, write to, or append to the file. So, given a `File` object (not a FileSystemObject in this case) named `objFileObject`, we can open it for appending as a 'normal' (i.e. not Unicode) TextStream object method like this:

```
' In VBScript:
Set objTStream = objFileObject.OpenAsTextStream(ForAppending, False)
```

```
// In JScript:
var objTStream = objFileObject.OpenTextFile(ForAppending, false);
```

Notice that we don't need a file name with this method, because it's executed against the file referenced by the `File` object. And there is no *create* parameter, because the file must already exist. If we want to start with a new empty file, we can use:

```
' In VBScript:
Set objTStream = objFileObject.OpenAsTextStream(ForWriting)
```

```
// In JScript:
var objTStream = objFileObject.OpenTextFile(ForWriting);
```

And if we just want to read from the file:

```
' In VBScript:
Set objTStream = objFileObject.OpenAsTextStream(ForReading)
```

```
// In JScript:
var objTStream = objFileObject.OpenTextFile(ForReading);
```

The TextStream Object Members Summary

The following is a full list of the properties and methods available for the TextStream object. We'll look at the important ones in detail shortly.

The TextStream Object's Properties

The TextStream properties provide information about the current position of the file pointer within the file. Notice that all the properties are *read-only*:

Property	**Description**
`AtEndOfLine`	Returns `True` if the file pointer is at the end of a line in the file.
`AtEndOfStream`	Returns `True` if the file pointer is at the end of the file.
`Column`	Returns the column number of the current character in the file starting from `1`.
`Line`	Returns the current line number in the file starting from `1`.

The `AtEndOfLine` and `AtEndOfStream` properties are only available for a file that is opened with `iomode` of `ForReading`. Referring to them otherwise causes an error to occur.

The TextStream Object's Methods

The methods of the TextStream object are:

Method	**Description**
`Close()`	Closes an open file.
`Read(`*numchars*`)`	Reads *numchars* characters from the file.
`ReadAll()`	Reads the entire file as a single string.
`ReadLine()`	Reads a line (up to a carriage return and line feed) from the file as a string.
`Skip(`*numchars*`)`	Skips and discards *numchars* characters when reading from the file.
`SkipLine()`	Skips and discards the next line when reading from the file.
`Write(`*string*`)`	Writes *string* to the file.
`WriteLine(`*string*`)`	Writes *string* (optional) and a newline character to the file.
`WriteBlankLines(`*n*`)`	Writes *n* newline characters to the file.

Writing to a Text File

Once we've created a TextStream object that refers to a file, using the `CreateTextFile`, `OpenTextFile` or `OpenAsTextStream` method with the `ForWriting` or `ForAppending` parameter, we can write to it and close it using VBScript like this:

```
' In VBScript:
objTStream.WriteLine "At last I can create files with VBScript!"
objTStream.WriteLine
objTStream.WriteLine "Here are three blank lines:"
objTStream.WriteBlankLines 3
objTStream.Write "... and this is "
objTStream.WriteLine "the last line."
objTStream.Close
```

Or using JScript:

```
// In JScript:
objTStream.WriteLine('At last I can create files with JScript!');
objTStream.WriteLine();
objTStream.WriteLine('Here are three blank lines:');
objTStream.WriteBlankLines(3);
objTStream.Write('... and this is ');
objTStream.WriteLine('the last line.');
objTStream.Close();
```

Reading from a Text File

Once we've created a TextStream object that refers to a file, using the `CreateTextFile`, `OpenTextFile` or `OpenAsTextStream` method with the `ForReading` parameter, we can read from it and close it using VBScript like this:

```
' In VBScript:
' Read one line at a time until the end of the file is reached
Do While Not objTStream.AtEndOfStream
   'Get the line number
   intLineNum = objTStream.Line
   'Format it as a 4-character string with leading zeros
   strLineNum = Right("000" & CStr(intLineNum), 4)
   'Get the text of the line from the file
   strLineText = objTStream.ReadLine
   Response.Write strLineNum & ": " & strLineText & "<BR>"
Loop
objTStream.Close
```

Or using JScript:

```
// In JScript:
// Read one line at a time until the end of the file is reached
while (! objTStream.AtEndOfStream) {
   // Get the line number
   intLineNum = objTStream.Line;
   // Format and convert to a string
   strLineNum = '000' + intLineNum.toString();
   strLineNum = substr(strLineNum, strLineNum.length - 4, 4)
   // Get the text of the line from the file
   strLineText = objTStream.ReadLine();
   Response.Write(strLineNum + ': ' + strLineText + '<BR>');
}
objTStream.Close();
```

A TextStream Object Example

To see some of the ways that we can work with text files using the TextStream object, we've provided a VBScript sample page that uses much of the code we described above. From the main `Chapter05` menu page in the sample files, select the link to Working with the TextStream Object to open the page named `show_textstream.asp`.

This page displays the text content of a file named `MyFile.txt` that's stored on disk. It's displayed in a `<TEXTAREA>` control that allows you to edit the text, and underneath this are three buttons. They are used to update (i.e. replace) the original text with the content of the `<TEXTAREA>` control, append the text to the end of the existing file contents, or rewrite the file with the original default contents:

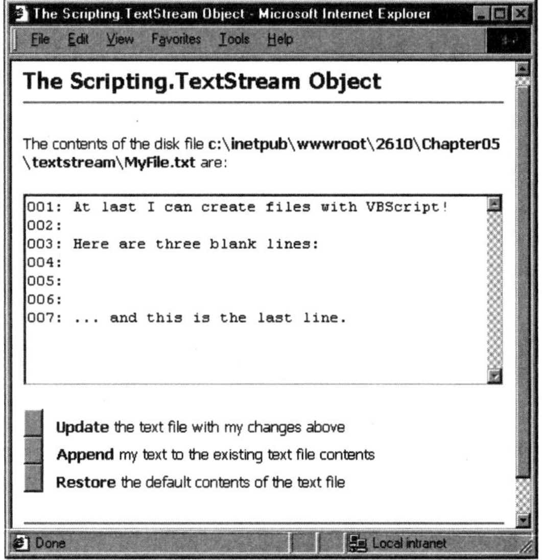

Reading the Existing Text File Contents

Each time the page is loaded, the text file is opened and the contents are read and placed into the `<TEXTAREA>` control. To start off, notice how we use the `Server.MapPath` method to get an absolute physical path of the file `MyFile.txt`, which is in the same directory as this page. Then we create our instance of the FileSystemObject:

```
<%
strTextFile = Server.MapPath("MyFile.txt") 'Get absolute the path of MyFile.txt

'Create an instance of a FileSytemObject object
Set objFSO = Server.CreateObject("Scripting.FileSystemObject")
...
```

This page, like most of the other samples for this section of the book, contains a `<FORM>` section that holds the HTML controls on the page. The `ACTION` is the current page, so the form contents are posted back to the same page.

The `<TEXTAREA>` is filled with the current contents of the text file as the page loads each time:

```
...
<FORM ACTION="<% = Request.ServerVariables("SCRIPT_NAME") %>" METHOD="POST">

The contents of the disk file <B><% = strTextFile %></B> are:<P>
<TEXTAREA NAME="txtContent" ROWS="10" COLS="50" WRAP="PHYSICAL">
<%
'open the text file as a TextStream object
Set objTStream = objFSO.OpenTextFile(strTextFile, ForReading)
'read one line at a time until the end of the file is reached
Do While Not objTStream.AtEndOfStream
   'get the line number
   intLineNum = objTStream.Line
   'format and convert to a string
   strLineNum = Right("00" & CStr(intLineNum), 3)
   'get the text of the line from the file
   strLineText = objTStream.ReadLine
   Response.Write strLineNum & ": " & strLineText & vbCrLf
Loop
objTStream.Close
%>
</TEXTAREA><P>
```

You can see how we open the text file for reading, and iterate through it reading one line at a time (rather than reading the whole file into a single string). This is because we want to add line numbers ourselves, which are not part of the text within the file. For each line we read from the file (before we read it) we retrieve and format the `Line` property to create a three-digit number. Then we write the line number and the text line from the file into the page within the `<TEXTAREA>` control.

Updating the Text File Contents

When the Update button in the page is clicked – perhaps after editing the text in the `<TEXTAREA>` control – we need to rewrite the contents of the text file using the text in the `<TEXTAREA>` control. To do this we have some ASP code in the page, before the section that creates the HTML controls, which checks the `Request.Form` collection to see which button (if any) was clicked to reload the page.

So, if the Update button was clicked, we collect the contents of the `<TEXTAREA>` control as a string, split this string into an array of separate lines of text, and open the text file ready to rewrite the content. Then we can loop through the array of lines we've just created and, providing that there is a line number, write the content of that line to the file:

```
...
'Look for a command sent from the FORM section buttons
If Len(Request.Form("cmdUpdate")) Then
  'Get contents of TEXTAREA control
  strNewText = Request.Form("txtContent")
  'Split it into an array of lines at each carriage return
  arrLines = Split(strNewText, vbCrLf)
  'Open the text file for writing, which replaces all existing content
  Set objTStream = objFSO.OpenTextFile(strTextFile, ForWriting)
  For intLine = 0 To UBound(arrLines)
```

```
      strThisLine = arrLines(intLine)
      'Write out each line in turn as long as it's got a line number
      If Len(strThisLine) > 4 Then objTStream.WriteLine Mid(strThisLine, 6)
    Next
    objTStream.Close
  End If
  ...
```

The HTML `<TEXTAREA>` *control can add extra characters to the* `Value` *that it returns, depending on the format of the content within the original HTML page and the setting of the* `WRAP` *attribute. In particular, it's worth placing the closing* `</TEXTAREA>` *tag immediately after the closing ASP script delimiter* '`%>`' *to prevent an extra carriage return being added to the contents of the control–i.e. use:*

```
%></TEXTAREA><P>
```

Rather than:

```
%>
</TEXTAREA><P>
```

Appending Content to the Text File

To append content to the existing file when the Append button is clicked, we do almost exactly the same as when we update the content. The difference is that this time we open the file for appending instead of for writing. The extra parameter added to the `OpenTextFile` method call this time prevents a new file being created if the one we specify does not already exist:

```
...
If Len(Request.Form("cmdAppend")) Then
    strNewText = Request.Form("txtContent")
  arrLines = Split(strNewText, vbCrLf)
  Set objTStream = objFSO.OpenTextFile(strTextFile, ForAppending, False)
  For intLine = 0 To UBound(arrLines)
    strThisLine = arrLines(intLine)
    If Len(strThisLine) > 4 Then objTStream.WriteLine Mid(strThisLine, 6)
  Next
  objTStream.Close
End If...
...
```

Rewriting the Default Content

Finally, the Restore button simply rewrites the text file with the original default content again. This code is the same as that we saw when we discussed how to use the TextStream methods that write to a text file:

```
...
If Len(Request.Form("cmdDefault")) Then
  'write out default contents to file
  Set objTStream = objFSO.CreateTextFile(strTextFile, True, False)
  objTStream.WriteLine "At last I can create files with VBScript!"
  objTStream.WriteLine
  objTStream.WriteLine "Here are three blank lines:"
  objTStream.WriteBlankLines 3
  objTStream.Write "... and this is "
  objTStream.WriteLine "the last line."
  objTStream.Close
End If
```

Summary

In this chapter, we've begun to see just how powerful the ability to use objects and components in our ASP pages can be. We first discussed the nature of objects and components in general, and the different types that are available. Then we moved on to concentrate on how we create instances of objects within our ASP (and client-side) script code.

Many of the objects you will use in your own pages will be 'external' components, i.e. components that are installed on the server separately from ASP. However, in this chapter, we have concentrated on the objects that are always available when we use ASP with one of the default scripting languages: VBScript or JScript. These are implemented by the Scripting Runtime Library, in the file `scrrun.dll`.

The objects are the Dictionary object, the awkwardly named FileSystemObject object, and the TextStream object.

The Dictionary object provides us with a useful way to store values that are indexed and accessed by name, rather than by a numerical index as in an array. It's ideal for storing things like the name/value pairs that we find in the intrinsic ASP Request collections.

The FileSystemObject object and the TextStream object are inexorably linked, in that we use them both to access the contents of the disk drives that are available on our server or networked (mapped) to it. The FileSystemObject object provides access to the drives, folders (directories) and files, and exposes properties and methods that we can use to get information about these, or move, copy or delete them.

A TextStream object can be created to reference any file on the system, and through it we can read and write to that file. It is treated as a text file for reading and writing, and we can even handle Unicode-format files. This combination of navigation and read/write capabilities allows us to exert complete control over the file system of the server. We can also use these objects (with limitations) in script code running on a client machine.

So, in this chapter, we looked at:

- What the scripting engines we use offer in the way of scripting objects
- How we create instances of scripting objects and other components
- A summary of the features and members of the scripting objects
- How we can use the scripting objects in our own code

In the next chapter, we'll move on from the Scripting Runtime Library objects, to look at other components that we can use in our ASP pages. This includes the installable components that are supplied with IIS/ASP, and some that you can source elsewhere.

N
W

6

Active Server Components

In the previous chapters, we've looked at two different types of objects – objects that are an intrinsic part of the **Active Server Pages Object Model**, and objects provided by the **Scripting Runtime Library**. In this chapter, we're going to take a look at a third type of object that can be used in ASP, namely **Active Server Components** (or just **server components**).

In many ways, these are like the traditional ActiveX Controls that you use in client-side script in a browser, or in a programming environment like Visual Basic. However, they are designed for execution on the server, rather than as an object running on the client.

The obvious question, then, is where these components come from. Some are provided as part of the normal ASP/IIS installation, while others are available free on the Web or as a bought-in product. In this chapter, we'll show you how useful the various components that come with ASP can be, and then look at a few examples of other components that are available. Once you're comfortable using Active Server Components, you'll have no trouble slotting other supplier's products into your ASP pages – you'll find a list of some of the third-party components that are available at the end of this chapter. And we even show you how to build your own components later in the book.

There are several components available to ASP that we won't be covering in this chapter. One of the principal uses of dynamic web site technologies is to publish information direct from a database management system or other type of data store. This, together with the requirement to collect data and store it back in a database or other data store, is what drove the original developments in server-side programming. To achieve these tasks using ASP, we take advantage of a set of components called the **ActiveX Data Objects** library, or just **ADO**. This is too big a subject to do justice to in one chapter, together with all the other components – instead we devote a whole section of this book to it, starting from Chapter 8.

In this chapter, then, we'll see:

- How **server components** differ from other types of objects that we use in ASP
- A recap of how we instantiate objects, with particular reference to server components
- The installable components that are provided with ASP 3.0 and IIS, such as the **Ad Rotator**, **Content Linking**, **Page Counter** and **Tools** components
- Some of the third-party components that are available

Scripting Objects vs. Server Components

The previous chapter demonstrated the various **scripting objects** that are made available to ASP/IIS by the Scripting Runtime Library, `scrrun.dll`. It's important not to confuse these with **server components** – the subject of this chapter.

Server components are usually implemented within their own DLL or executable file. Take for example the 'Content Linking' component that you'll meet in this chapter, which is implemented by the file `nextlink.dll`. Once this DLL is installed and registered on the server, the object it provides is available within any scripting language that ASP is set up to support.

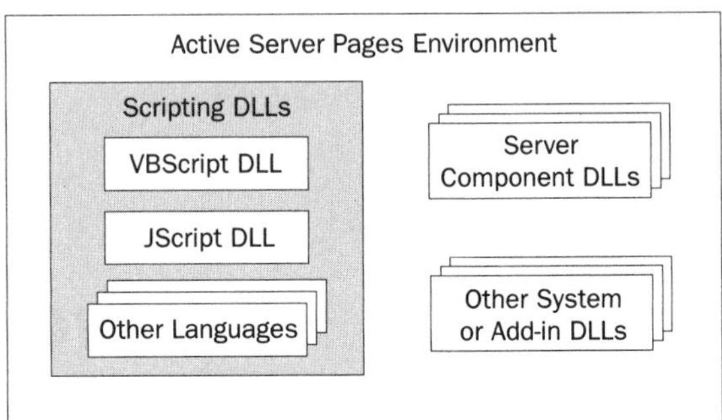

Most of the standard components supplied with ASP/IIS are aimed at specific tasks that you often need to accomplish in your website or corporate Intranet. Of course, what you ultimately want to achieve with ASP depends on the kinds of information you want to publish and the overall aims of your site. However, using pre-built components can – as you'll see – provide a head start when you come to getting the show on the road.

Using Server Components

We looked in detail in the previous chapter at how objects and components in general are instantiated in our pages. Exactly the same applies to server components as to the Scripting Runtime Library objects. The only real difference is that, unlike scripting objects, server components are usually implemented as **separate** DLLs and may require you to run a setup program or manually register the component before use, if they haven't been installed by default with ASP.

The CreateObject Method

So, to summarize, we can create an instance of an object in an ASP page using the `CreateObject` method of the intrinsic ASP `Server` object:

```
Set objThis = Server.CreateObject("this.object")      ' in VBScript
```

or

```
var objThis = Server.CreateObject('this.object');     // in JScript
```

This creates a reference to the object in the variable `objThis`, and we can then work with the object in our script. In other words, we can manipulate its properties and call its methods from our code as required.

Using an <OBJECT> Element

Alternatively, we can use a normal `<OBJECT>` element to create an instance of an object, in the same way as we would when creating an object instance in a web page on the browser. ASP supports a special implementation of the HTML `<OBJECT>` element, and we can use this to place an object in our pages. To define an instance of a component or scripting object in a normal `.asp` file, we use the syntax:

```
<OBJECT RUNAT="SERVER" SCOPE="PAGE" ID="objThis" PROGID="this.object">
</OBJECT>
```

Alternatively, we can use the `CLASSID` of the object instead of the 'friendly name' (or `PROGID`):

```
<OBJECT RUNAT="SERVER" SCOPE="PAGE" ID="objThis"
        CLASSID="CLSID:OACE4881-8305-11CF-9427-444553540000">
</OBJECT>
```

We use the `SCOPE` attribute to set the scope of the object, the options being `"SESSION"`, `"APPLICATION"` and `"PAGE"`. If we use an `<OBJECT>` element in a normal `.asp` file we have to use `"PAGE"` or omit the `SCOPE` attribute altogether, because the object will only be available within the page in which it's instantiated. However, if we place the `<OBJECT>` element in `global.asa`, we can create an object that is available throughout the current session, or globally throughout the application, by using the values `"SESSION"` or `"APPLICATION"` for the `SCOPE` attribute.

Checking for the Existence of an Object Instance

One common source of errors is attempting to create an instance of an object that isn't installed (or isn't registered), or using the wrong **ProgID** for an object in the `CreateObject` method or an `<OBJECT>` element. By default, ASP will raise an error and halt the execution of the page.

So, it's worth adding some code to your pages to check that the object was properly instantiated before attempting to access it. In VBScript, we can do this by turning off the default error handling and then using the `IsObject` function to see if our object variable does in fact reference an object:

```
'in VBScript:
...
On Error Resume Next   'turn off default error handling
Set objThis = Server.CreateObject("this.object")

If IsObject(objThis) Then
  'the CreateObject method succeeded
  On Error Goto 0     'turn the default error handling back on
  ...
  'rest of the script goes here
  ...
Else
  Response.Write "Sorry, this page cannot be accessed at present"
  Response.Flush
  Response.End
End If
...
```

In JScript, we can use the new error handling features in the JScript 5.0 scripting engine, which we examined at the end of Chapter 1:

```
// in JScript:
...
try {
   var objThis = Server.CreateObject('this.object');
   ...
   // rest of the script goes here
   ...
}

catch (exception) {
   Response.Write('Sorry, this page cannot be accessed at present');
   Response.Flush();
   Response.End();
}
...
```

The ASP/IIS Installable Components

The standard installation of ASP/IIS includes a range of server components. These are described in the IIS documentation as **installable components**, though they're all fully installed by default. It's likely that the name is just a hang over from previous versions of ASP, where some of these components had to be installed manually – a better name would probably be 'instantiable components'.

Remember, we'll be covering one specific installable component, the ADO component, in Chapter 8. You'll also find that later chapters use other components that are installed as part of a specific service or server application: for example the Collaborative Data Objects (CDO and CDONTS) components that are used to work with mail servers and email messages. In the remainder of this chapter, we'll see how we can gain extra functionality for our Web site or Intranet using the other ten general-purpose components that are described in the IIS documentation as installable components.

The ASP installable components are found in your `WinNT\System32\inetsrv\` directory in Windows 2000, and this directory is also used for the configuration files that some of the components require. In alphabetical order, we'll be exploring the following components:

- The **Ad Rotator** component is used to control the appearance of clickable images, such as adverts or banners, in a page. Using information stored in a configuration file, it can display different images based on the weightings that the configuration file specifies. It also has features to redirect clicks on adverts to the appropriate URL, and record the number of clicks for each one.
- The **Browser Capabilities** component uses the `UserAgent` string, which is sent to the server by a browser to identify that browser. It exposes a set of properties that reflect the particular browser's capabilities – for example, whether it supports scripting, cookies or Java applets.
- The **Content Linking** component is useful for providing a series of easily navigated pages that can be changed and updated without having to edit the individual pages. It takes a text file that contains the page URLs and the display order, and makes it easy to create pages that are linked together in the specified order.

- The **Content Rotator** component takes a configuration file that specifies sections of HTML, text or code that will be inserted into other pages. Depending on the weightings specified in the configuration file, it displays one of these sections of content.
- The **Counters** component can create, increment and persistently store any number of individual integer counters for use in script code.
- The **Logging Utility** component provides access to our Web server's log files, allowing the data to be read or updated from within an ASP page. It is new in Windows 2000 with IIS 5.0 and ASP 3.0.
- The **MyInfo** component provides a repository for storing name/value pairs that are accessible globally over the whole site. The data is stored in an XML-formatted text file on the server. (This differs from application scope in that the values persist outside the Web site scope).
- The **Page Counter** component keeps track of the number of times a page has been accessed, and can be used to track hits for a number of different pages.
- The **Permission Checker** component is useful for preventing script errors caused when a user attempts to access a resource for which they don't have the correct permission set up.
- The **Tools** component provides methods that you can use in your pages to check for the existence of a file, process an HTML form, and generate a random integer. There are also methods for use on the Apple Macintosh that check for the existence of a server plug-in, and check if the current user is the site owner.

*There is another component – the **Status** component – provided with IIS/ASP for use only on Personal Web Server for the Apple Macintosh. We aren't covering this component here. For more details, check out the IIS 5.0 documentation that's provided with ASP/IIS, at* http://localhost/iishelp/iis/htm/asp/comp1qt0.htm.

Using the Sample Pages

We've provided a series of sample pages that demonstrate all these components.

As usual, you can download the samples from the Wrox Web site, and run them on your own machine. You'll find the code for this chapter in the `Chapter06` *subdirectory of the download file.*

Before you run the samples, make sure that the entries that instantiate the 'global' instances of the **MyInfo** and **Counters** components are in the `global.asa` file for your Default Web Site. The code you need is in the `global.asa` file we provide with the sample files. It's also printed below – so if you prefer, you can add it to the code in your existing `global.asa` file instead of replacing the whole file:

```
<!-- declare instance of the ASP Counters component with application-level scope -
->
<OBJECT ID="objCounters" RUNAT="Server" SCOPE="Application"
PROGID="MSWC.Counters">
</OBJECT>

<!-- declare instance of the ASP MyInfo component with application-level scope -->
<OBJECT ID="objMyInfo" RUNAT="Server" SCOPE="Application" PROGID="MSWC.MyInfo">
</OBJECT>
```

The main menu page for the samples (`Default.asp`) uses the **Content Linking** component to create the links to each of the sample pages. Therefore, we'll look at this component first. You'll also find that the discussions of the **Ad Rotator** and **Counters** components follow on from each other in the next section as we use them in the same sample page.

The Content Linking Component

The **Content Linking** component is a very useful tool for sites that provide contents pages, or pages that contain a list of links to other pages on the same site. It automatically matches the URL of the currently displayed page to a list of pages stored in a text file on the server, and can allow users to browse through the list of pages in forward or reverse order. In other words, even after the visitor has clicked on a link in the contents page and is viewing one of the pages in the list, the component can still tell whereabouts that page is within the list.

And because all the details are stored in a text file, maintaining the site – and the links between the pages – becomes a matter of just editing the text file. For example, we can change the order that the pages are displayed in just by rearranging them in the content linking list file.

The Content Linking List File

The **Content Linking List file** contains a simple list of page URLs, in the order they are to be displayed. We also supply matching descriptions, which are used to display the link text in the 'contents' page, and we can add comments to each one if required. Comments help identify the links later, and aren't visible to visitors.

The file contains one line of text for each page. Each line consists of the URL, description and optional comment, separated by *Tab* characters (not spaces, otherwise it won't work) and ending with a carriage return. For example:

```
newpages.htm	New additions to our site	we update this weekly
offers.htm	Special Offers for this week	we only update this monthly
register.htm	Registration for new users
main.htm	The main forum and chat area	must be registered first
index.htm	Back to the contents page
```

Note that the target URLs must be specified as a relative virtual or physical path, such as `forum\enter.htm`. URLs that start with `http:`, `//`, or `\\` can't be used. If you want to create a menu that contains absolute URLs like these, you can build a redirection page using ASP and specify this in the content linking list file. For example, if we have a page named `redirect.asp` that contains just this code:

```
<%
'redirect the request to the site specified in the query string
Response.Clear
Response.Redirect Request.QueryString("url")
%>
```

we can use it in our content linking list file like this:

```
redirect.asp?url=http://www.cyscape.com/	CyScape BrowserHawk Web Pages
redirect.asp?url=http://www.softartisans.com/	SA fileUp Component Pages
redirect.asp?url=http://www.stonebroom.com/swindex.htm	Stonebroom RegEx Pages
```

The Content Linking Component Members

The Content Linking component provides eight methods that retrieve various entries from the content linking list file, either relative to the current page's entry or as an absolute entry using an index number. The index number of the first item is `1`.

Method	Description
`GetListCount(`*links_file*`)`	Returns the number of items in the file *links_file.*
`GetListIndex(`*links_file*`)`	Returns the index number of the current page in the file *links_file.*
`GetNextURL(`*links_file*`)`	Returns the URL of the next page in the file *links_file.*
`GetNextDescription(`*links_file*`)`	Returns the description of the next page in file *links_file.*
`GetPreviousURL(`*links_file*`)`	Returns the URL of the previous page in the file *links_file.*
`GetPreviousDescription(`*links_file*`)`	Returns the description of the previous page in file *links_file.*
`GetNthURL(`*links_file, n*`)`	Returns the URL of the *n*th page in the file *links_file.*
`GetNthDescription(`*links_file, n*`)`	Returns the description of the *n*th page in the file *links_file.*

If the current page isn't in the Content Linking List file:

- `GetListIndex` returns 0
- `GetNextURL` and `GetNextDescription` return the URL and description of the last page in the list
- `GetPreviousURL` and `GetPreviousDescription` return the URL and description of the first page in the list

Using the Content Linking Component

Once we've created our content linking file, we can add the component to our pages. Here's a typical example that iterates through all the entries in the content linking file, and creates a list of the pages as hyperlinks:

```
<% 'in VBScript:
Set objNextLink = Server.CreateObject("MSWC.Nextlink")
%>

<UL>
<%
'get the number of entries in the menu file
intCount = objNextLink.GetListCount("contlink.txt")
```

```
    'loop through the entries
    For intLoop = 1 To intCount %>
      <LI>
      <A HREF="<% = objNextLink.GetNthURL("contlink.txt", intLoop) %>">
      <% = objNextLink.GetNthDescription("contlink.txt", intLoop) %>
      </A>
    <%
    Next
    %>
    </UL>
```

This code first creates a Content Linking object. Inside the normal `<UL>` and `</UL>` tags, it uses the object's `GetListCount` method to find out how many entries there are in the Content Linking List file. It then loops through them, and for each one it places an `<LI>` tag in the page, followed by an `<A>` tag. The value for the `HREF` attribute is retrieved from the list file using the `GetNthURL` method, and the description to use as the text of the link is retrieved using the `GetNthDescription` method.

Notice here that our content list file is in the same folder as the ASP page that uses it. If it wasn't, we could provide either a relative physical path, or a full virtual path, to it like this:

```
intCount = objNextLink.GetListCount("links\contlink.txt") 'physical path
intCount = objNextLink.GetListCount("/demo/contlink.txt") 'virtual path
```

Creating a Contents Page

We've used the Content Linking component to create the menu page for the samples we provide for this chapter. The page `Default.htm` in the `Chapter06` subfolder of the samples uses the code we've seen above to create this menu:

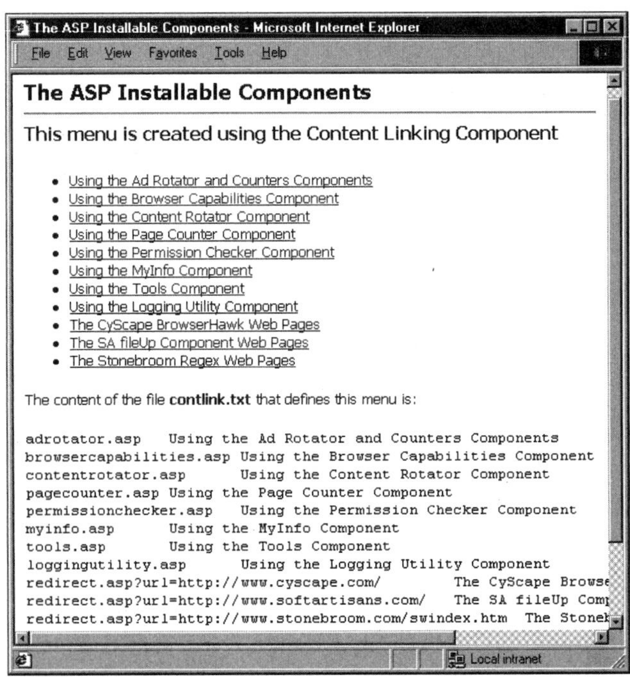

You can see that the contents of the Content Linking List File are shown in the page below the links. We've done this using the `FileSystemObject` object that we met in the previous chapter:

```
<%
'create an instance of a FileSytemObject object
Set objFSO = Server.CreateObject("Scripting.FileSystemObject")

'open the text file as a TextStream object
Set objTStream = objFSO.OpenTextFile(Server.MapPath("contlink.txt"), ForReading)
Response.Write objTStream.ReadAll   'read the whole file and put into page
objTStream.Close
%>
```

If you edit the `contlink.txt` file, you'll see the menu entries change when you next reload this page. Notice the last three entries in the file. These use the `redirect.asp` technique we described earlier to insert an absolute (rather than relative) URL into the list.

Browsing Through the Pages

When we create an instance of the Content Linking component and access one of its methods, it matches the *current* page's URL with the entries in the Content Linking List file we specify in that method call. We can use it not only to create a contents list (as we've just seen), but also to navigate between pages in the list while we've got one of them open in the browser.

This means that we can use hyperlinks or buttons to move to another page from one of the listed pages. For example, we can add Next and Back buttons to a page, because we can tell which is the next or previous item in the list by using the `GetNextURL` and `GetPreviousURL` methods. Alternatively, we can jump to any other page in the list using the `GetNthURL` method. And, of course, we can tell where we are in the list at the moment using the `GetListIndex` method.

Here's some code that adds Next and Back buttons to a page. All we have to do is place it in each of the pages listed in the Content Linking List File, or insert it with an SSI `#include` directive:

```
<!-- need a form to force Navigator to display the buttons -->
<FORM ACTION="">

<% 'in VBScript:
'create an instance of the Content Linking component
Set objNextLink = Server.CreateObject("MSWC.NextLink")
'set the content linking list file path and name
strListFile = "contlink.txt"
'get the index of the current page in the list
intThisPage = objNextLink.GetListIndex(strListFile)

If intThisPage > 1 Then  'can go back
%>
  <INPUT TYPE=BUTTON VALUE="&lt; Back"
     ONCLICK="location.href='<% = objNextLink.GetPreviousURL(strListFile) %>';"
     TITLE="Go to '<% = objNextLink.GetPreviousDescription(strListFile) %>'">
   
<%
End If
%>
```

```
<INPUT TYPE=BUTTON VALUE=" Menu " ONCLICK="location.href='Default.asp';"
       TITLE="Return to the main 'Installable Components' menu">
<%
If intThisPage < objNextLink.GetListCount(strListFile) Then  'can go forward
%>
   
  <INPUT TYPE=BUTTON VALUE="Next &gt;"
         ONCLICK="location.href='<%= objNextLink.GetNextURL(strListFile) %>';"
         TITLE="Go to '<% = objNextLink.GetNextDescription(strListFile) %>'">
<%
End If
%>
</FORM>
```

The first step is to create the Content Linking component, and then put the name of the list file into a variable so that we can use it while creating the client-side JScript code later in the page. Besides, it makes the page easier to maintain, because we only have to change it in one place if we want to use a different filename.

Now we can see where we are within the Content Linking List. The `GetListIndex` method provides the index number of the current page, starting from `1` for the first page in the list. If the current page has an index greater than `1`, we know that we can go backwards, so we include the HTML to create the **Back** button in the page. Similarly, if the current page's index is less that the number of items in the list, we can include a **Next** button. We always include a **Home** button so that the visitor can get back to the contents page easily at any time.

If you open one of the pages listed in the menu page that we've just been examining, you'll see that we've used this technique to create a set of navigation buttons on each page. The code that creates them is in the file `contlinkbuttons.inc`, which is inserted into each page with a `#include` directive:

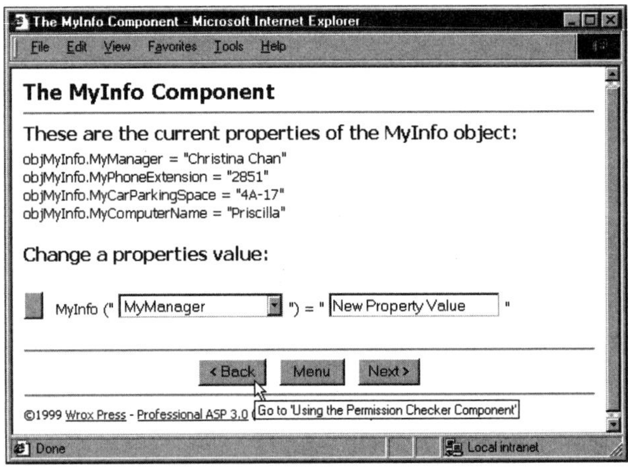

The screenshot above shows the three buttons on a page in the middle of our list. And you can see that we added one other finishing touch. We used the `GetPreviousDescription` method to get the text of the link for the previous pages, and put this into the `TITLE` attribute of the **Back** button so that it acts as a pop-up tip:

```
<INPUT TYPE=BUTTON VALUE="&lt; Back"
   ONCLICK="location.href='<% = objNextLink.GetPreviousURL(strListFile) %>';"
   TITLE="Go to '<% = objNextLink.GetPreviousDescription(strListFile) %>'">
```

We also used `GetNextDescription` to do the same thing for the **Next** button.

Jumping with JavaScript

You'll see that our navigation buttons use JavaScript (rather than VBScript) to load the new page. This provides compatibility with most modern browsers.

For example, the Back button contains the attribute:

```
ONCLICK="location.href='<% = objNextLink.GetPreviousURL(strListFile) %>';"
```

When the HTML version of the page is created by ASP, the expression inside the `<%...%>` tags is replaced with its value, so the page sent to the browser could look like this:

```
ONCLICK="location.href='permissionchecker.asp';"
```

You can also see why we chose to use a variable to hold the name of the Content Linking List file – it's cumbersome to include a third level of nested quotes inside a single statement.

> *Remember that the default language in the browser is JavaScript (or JScript in IE), not VBScript. By using JavaScript, we avoid having to provide a `LANGUAGE` argument in the `OnClick` code, as well as providing compatibility with non-IE browsers.*

The Ad Rotator Component

The **Ad Rotator** component allows an ASP page to display a different graphic each time this page is referenced from a browser. This technique is often used in sites that display advertisements – hence the component name. Every time the page is opened or re-loaded, ASP uses the information in a **rotator schedule file** to select a graphic, and insert it into the page. However, the Ad Rotator component can do more than this. We can arrange for the image to be a hyperlink rather than a static graphical picture, and even record how many users click each one of the advertisements.

Of all the components we're looking at in this chapter, the Ad Rotator is probably the most complicated to use. That's because it involves several different files. Before we look at each individual file, an overview of the process might help you to see how it all fits together.

The visitor sees one of the advertisements specified in the rotator schedule file on the page. Usually this is also a hyperlink, and clicking on it loads a **redirection file**. This is a normal ASP page, which can do things like log the user's action to a file or counter and then redirect them to the appropriate advertiser's site.

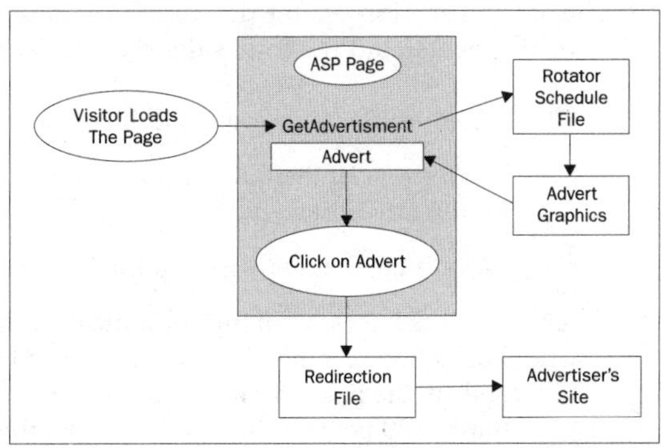

The Rotator Schedule File

The Ad Rotator component depends on the rotator schedule file to specify which advertisements or graphics are to be displayed. This file includes the names of each of the image files, the sizes they are to be displayed at, and the relative percentage of times each one should be displayed. The file is divided into two sections, which are separated by a line containing only an asterisk (`*`).

So the format of the file is:

```
REDIRECT URL
WIDTH width
HEIGHT height
BORDER border
*
adURL
adHomeURL
text
impressions
```

where:

- *URL* is the virtual path and name of the program or ASP file that implements the redirection.
- *width* and *height* define the size of the advertisement on the page in pixels. The default is `440` x `60`.
- *border* specifies the width of the border around the advertisement in pixels. The default is `1`. Use `0` for no border.

The first section is optional, and sets the default values that apply to all the advertisements in the schedule. This provides us with a way of setting these values for all images. The border thickness can alternatively be set using the Ad Rotator component's `Border` property, as we'll see shortly. If we omit one or more of these optional parameters, and don't set the object's properties explicitly, it will use its own default values. And if we omit all of these parameters, we still have to include the asterisk as the first line of the file.

The second section – after the asterisk – must exist in the file. It provides details of the individual advertisements, and the four values are repeated for each advertisement. The required entries are:

- *adURL* is the virtual path and filename of the advertisement image file.
- *adHomeURL* is the URL to jump to for this advertisement. A hyphen (`-`) indicates there is no link for this advertisement.
- *text* is the text for display if the browser doesn't support graphics.
- *impressions* is an integer indicating the relative display time or weighting for this advertisement. For example, if the file contains three advertisements, and their impressions values are set to 4, 6, and 10, the first is included in 20 percent of the returned pages, the second in 30 percent, and the third in 50 percent. It doesn't indicate the actual **time** that the advertisement will be displayed in the browser. Note that the actual occurrence of each individual advert is determined at random, and is then modified to achieve the weighting.

So, an example redirection file might look like this:

```
REDIRECT AdRotFiles/ad_redirect.asp
WIDTH 400
HEIGHT 50
*
AdRotFiles/wrox.gif
http://www.wrox.com/
Better Books from Wrox Press
3
AdRotFiles/lunar.gif
http://www.going-to-the-moon.com/store.asp
Acme Lunar Boost Supplies
1
```

The Ad Rotator Component's Members

The Ad Rotator component exposes one method and three properties. The method is:

Method	Description
`GetAdvertisement` (*schedule_file*)	Uses the information in the specified *schedule_file* to create and return a string containing the HTML required for inserting the next appropriate image into the page.

And the properties are:

Property	Description
`Border`	*Integer.* The thickness of the border around the advertisement in pixels. If not set, the value in first section of the schedule file is used.
`Clickable`	*Boolean.* Specifies whether the advertisement image should be displayed as a hyperlink. The default is `True`.
`TargetFrame`	*String.* The name of the frame in which to display the advertisers page if the user clicks the image. If omitted, the page is loaded into the current browser frame or window, replacing the page that contains the advertisement image. This property can also be set to one of the standard HTML frame identifiers: `_top`, `_new`, `_child`, `_self`, `_parent`, or `_blank`.

Using the Ad Rotator Component

The following code demonstrates the Ad Rotator component in action. After creating the component instance, we set the properties and call the `GetAdvertisement` method, specifying the relative physical path of the rotator schedule file. The HTML code returned by the component is then inserted into the page using the `Response.Write` method:

```
<%  'VBScript example
QUOT = Chr(34)
Set objAdRot = Server.CreateObject("MSWC.AdRotator")
objAdRot.Border=0                       'no border
objAdRot.Clickable=TRUE                 'is a hyperlink
objAdRot.TargetFrame="TARGET=" & QUOT & "_blank" & QUOT
                                        'load into new window named fraAdFrame
strHTML = objAdRot.GetAdvertisement("AdRotFiles\ad_schedule.txt")
Response.Write(strHTML)                 'put the HTML into the page
%>
```

The parameter for the GetAdvertisement method is the physical path and name of the rotator schedule file, relative to the current directory or the Web site root directory. In the code above, the file is in a directory named AdRotFiles, which is a subdirectory of the current directory containing the ASP page that is executing. If this file is stored in a directory named AdRotFiles that is in the root of the Web site, we would use "\AdRotFiles\MyAdFile.txt" instead.

When we call the GetAdvertisement method, it returns HTML code that we can insert into our page to create the advertisement. For the first advertisement in the example rotator schedule file that we saw earlier, we'll get this:

```
<A HREF="/AdRotFiles/AdRedirect.asp?
        url=http://www.wrox.com/&image=/AdRotFiles/AdPics/wrox.gif">
<IMG SRC="/AdRotFiles/AdPics/wrox.gif"
     ALT="Better Books from Wrox Press" WIDTH=440 HEIGHT=60 BORDER=0></A>
```

You can see that it has placed the image inside a normal <A> tag. The HREF attribute is set to the name of our redirection file, AdRedirect.asp, with the advertiser's home page URL and the image we used appended to the query string. Therefore, our redirection file will be loaded and executed on the server when the user clicks on the advertisement.

The Redirection File

The redirection file can be an ASP page, an ISAPI DLL, or a CGI application. Whichever is used, it must be able to accept and identify the advertiser's home page URL and the image name parameters sent to it in the query string. It can examine these and decide what to do next: for example, it will usually redirect the user to the URL associated with the advertisement. This is easy to do using the VBScript code:

```
Response.Redirect Request.QueryString("url")
```

However, the redirection file provides us with the opportunity to do more than this. For example, we can count the number of users that have clicked on each advertisement – which is particularly useful if we're getting paid according to the number of redirections we achieve. We could do this with the Counters component that you'll meet later in this chapter:

```
...
'get the URL of the advertiser's target page
strAdvertiserURL = Request.QueryString("url")
If Instr(strAdvertiserURL, "wrox.com") Then
  'this is an advert for the Wrox Press site
  objCounters.Increment("wrox")
  Response.Clear
```

```
      Response.Redirect strAdvertiserURL
   End If

   If Instr(strAdvertiserURL, "going-to-the-moon") Then
      'this is an advert for the Lunar Boost store
      objCounters.Increment("lunar")
      Response.Clear
      Response.Redirect strAdvertiserURL
   End If
   ...
   ..'same for other advertisers
   ...
```

As the query string contains the name of the image file, we can also refer to this in our script. If the same advertiser has three different images in the rotator file, we can track the number of responses for each one separately:

```
   ...
   If Instr(strAdvertiserURL, "wrox.com") Then
      'this is an advert for the Wrox Press site
      Select Case Request.QueryString("image")
         Case "books.gif"
            objCounters.Increment("wrox_books")
         Case "website.gif"
            objCounters.Increment("wrox_site")
         Case Else
            objCounters.Increment("wrox_other")
      End Select
      Response.Clear
      Response.Redirect strAdvertiserURL
   End If
   ...
```

A Sample Ad-Rotating Page

The sample files provided for this chapter include a demonstration of the Ad Rotator component at work. You can open it from the main ASP Installable Components menu we saw earlier. The top section of the page displays an advert that is defined in our Rotator Schedule File named `ad_schedule.txt`, which you'll find in the `AdRotFiles` subdirectory of the samples for this chapter:

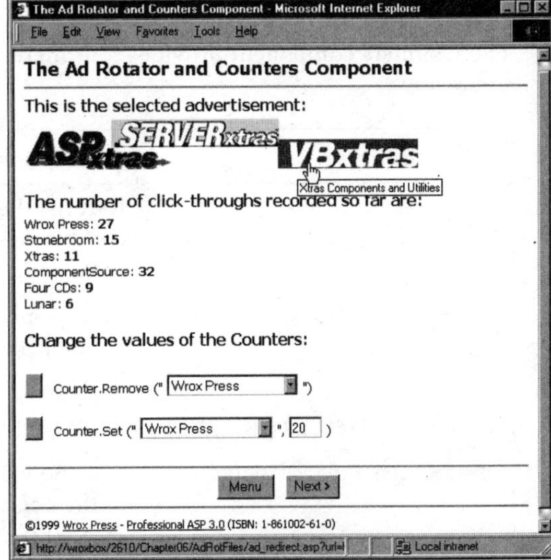

The code we've used is that which you saw earlier – we've just added a few more entries to the rotator schedule file to make it more obvious how the adverts change each time the page is loaded. If you click on one of the adverts, this runs the code in the redirection file named `ad_redirect.asp` and the appropriate advertiser's page is opened in a new window. Again, the code to do this is exactly the same as we saw earlier, when we discussed the way that the redirection file works.

You'll recall that in the redirection file, we're using instances of counters (created by the Counters component) to store the number of click-throughs for each advertiser:

```
...
If Instr(strAdvertiserURL, "wrox") Then
   objCounters.Increment("wrox")
   Response.Clear
   Response.Redirect strAdvertiserURL
End If
...
```

You can see these in the page above, the remainder of which demonstrates the Counters component in action. We'll look at this component next.

The Counters Component

The **Counters** component can be used to create, store, increment and retrieve any number of individual counters. Not to be confused with the *Page Counter Component* (discussed later in this chapter), the Counters component can be used to maintain a count of any kind of values.

A **counter** contains an integer value, which can be manipulated through the methods of the Counters component. We use the `Set` method to set the specific value of the counter and the `Get` method to retrieve it. To increase the counter value by `1` we use the `Increment` method, and to remove a counter we use the `Remove` method. All counter values are stored in a text file – `counters.txt` – which can be found in the same directory as the `counters.dll` component.

The Counters Component's Members

The Counters component provides four methods that are used to maintain the value of each counter we create:

Method	Description
`Get(`*counter_name*`)`	Returns the current value of the specified counter. If the counter has not been previously created it creates it, sets it to zero, and returns zero.
`Increment(`*counter_name*`)`	Increments the current value of the specified counter. If the counter has not been previously created it creates it and sets it to one.
`Remove(`*counter_name*`)`	Destroys the specified counter.
`Set(`*counter_name*`, `*value*`)`	Sets the value of the specified counter to the integer provided in the *value* parameter. If the counter has not been previously created it creates it and sets it to the specified value.

Using the Counters Component

There is only one copy of the `counters.txt` file, which all instances of the component access. Therefore, we should only create a single instance of the Counters component, and make it available to all the pages in our Web site. The usual way to do this is to create an application-wide instance in the `global.asa` file in the root of the Default Web Site (hence this is not really a scalable solution).

All we need is this code:

```
<!-- declare instance of the Counters component with application-level scope -->
<OBJECT ID="objCounters" RUNAT="Server" SCOPE="Application"
        PROGID="MSWC.Counters">
</OBJECT>
```

We can use the Counters component to create a new counter for any task that we need to accomplish. In the following code, we count the number of replies we get to each of three options for some given survey question. This page would be loaded in response to the user submitting a form that contains the three options – we'll assume that the options are selected by clicking `SUBMIT` buttons with the names `"cmdYes"`, `"cmdNo"` and `"cmdMaybe"` and the captions (i.e. values) `"Yes"`, `"No"` and `"Maybe"`:

```
<% 'in VBScript:
If Request.Form("cmdYes") = "Yes" Then objCounter.Increment("Response_Yes")
If Request.Form("cmdNo") = "No" Then objCounter.Increment("Response_No")
If Request.Form("cmdMaybe") = "Maybe" Then
  objCounter.Increment("Response_Maybe")
%>
```

If this is the first time that a particular response was received, a new counter will be created and initialized to `1` automatically.

Counters are not limited in scope, because the Counters object is created in `global.asa`. That means they're available to any page within the virtual application or Web site where they are created. And so our 'survey responses' counters could be used on any page of that application. Remember that the single Counters object can provide as many individual counters as required – we don't need to create more Counters object instances.

In the previous sample page for the Ad Rotator component, we saw how we can use the Counters component to store the number of click-throughs for each advertiser. We display the current values in the page using the `Get` method of the Counters component:

```
Wrox Press: <B><% = objCounters.Get("wrox") %></B><BR>
Stonebroom: <B><% = objCounters.Get("stonebroom") %></B><BR>
Xtras: <B><% = objCounters.Get("xtras") %></B><BR>
ComponentSource: <B><% = objCounters.Get("compsrc") %></B><BR>
Four CDs: <B><% = objCounters.Get("fourcds") %></B><BR>
Lunar: <B><% = objCounters.Get("lunar") %></B><BR>
```

So, the resulting page is updated to show the current values of the counters each time it loads. However, the page also contains some controls where we can call the other two methods of the Counters component – to remove a counter (effectively setting it to zero) and to set a specific value for a counter:

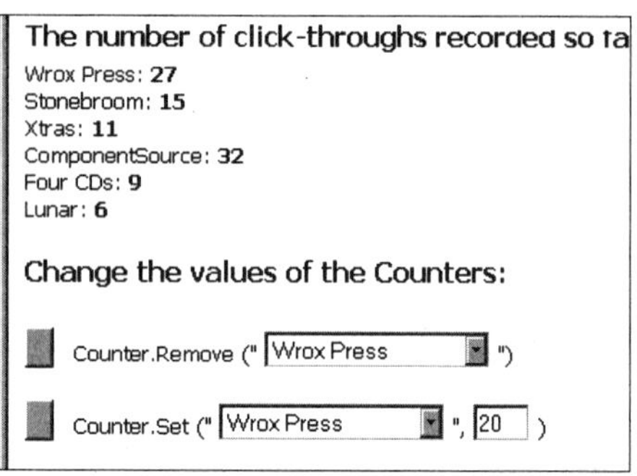

These controls are on a <FORM> that is submitted back to the same page when any of the small blank buttons are clicked – in exactly the same way as we've done in almost all the samples pages for the chapters in this part of the book. This is the HTML that creates the controls for the `Remove` method seen in the screenshot above:

```
<FORM ACTION="<% = Request.ServerVariables("SCRIPT_NAME") %>" METHOD="POST">
<INPUT TYPE="SUBMIT" NAME="cmdRemove" VALUE="   ">
  Counter.Remove ("
<SELECT NAME="lstRemove" SIZE="1">
  <OPTION VALUE="wrox">Wrox Press</OPTION>
  <OPTION VALUE="stonebroom">Stonebroom</OPTION>
  <OPTION VALUE="xtras">Xtras</OPTION>
  <OPTION VALUE="compsrc">ComponentSource</OPTION>
  <OPTION VALUE="fourcds">Four CDs</OPTION>
  <OPTION VALUE="lunar">Lunar</OPTION>
</SELECT> ")<P>
...
</FORM>
```

As the page loads, it checks to see if any of the buttons were clicked by examining the `Request.Form` collection. If it finds an entry for one of these buttons, it runs the appropriate section of code. In the case of the Remove button, this is:

```
If Len(Request.Form("cmdRemove")) Then
  strCounterName = Request.Form("lstRemove")   'get the counter name

  objCounters.Remove strCounterName
  Response.Write "Removed counter '<B>" & strCounterName & "</B>'.<P>"
End If
```

Much the same happens for the Set method – only this time we need to collect the new value from the text box as well. We check to see that it's a valid number before calling the `Set` method:

```
If Len(Request.Form("cmdSet")) Then
  strCounterName = Request.Form("lstSet")   'get the counter name
  strNewValue = Request.Form("txtSet")      'get the new value
  If IsNumeric(strNewValue) Then            'if it can be converted to a number
    intNewValue = CInt(strNewValue)         '... then convert it
```

```
    objCounters.Set strCounterName, intNewValue
    Response.Write "Set counter '<B>" & strCounterName & _
                   "</B>' to <B>" & strNewValue & "</B>.<P>"
  Else
    Response.Write "<B>'" & strNewValue & "</B>' is not a valid number.<P>"
  End If
End If
```

As you call the methods of the Counters object using the buttons in the page, you'll see a message at the top of the page when it reloads, and the new values in the counters:

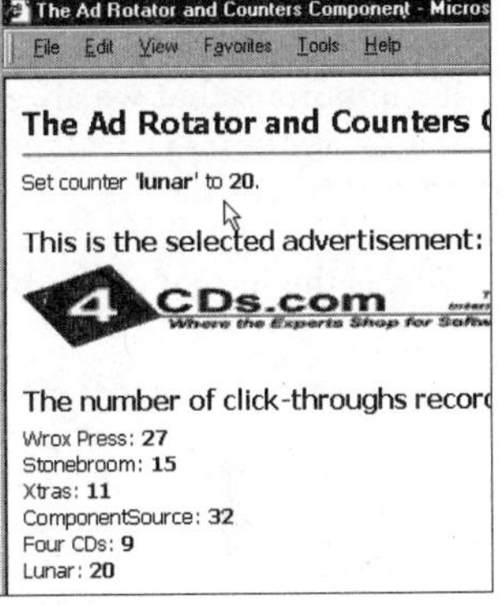

The Browser Capabilities Component

One of the problems we face when creating all kinds of web pages – not just dynamic ones that use ASP – is deciding which of the increasing range of HTML elements and other client-side techniques we should take advantage of. While it's great to be able to use all these features, such as Java applets, ActiveX controls, and the most recent HTML elements, we need to be aware that some visitors will be using browsers that just don't support them. All they might see of our carefully crafted pages is a jumble of text, images, and – even worse – the client-side script code that's supposed to make them work.

This isn't a discussion on how you should design pages to support different browsers (if you want to know more about that, try Professional ASP Techniques for Webmasters by Alex Homer, ISBN 1-861001-79-7, from Wrox). However, the **Browser Capabilities** server component provided with ASP and IIS can be used to determine which of a whole range of features a browser supports, at the point when it actually references one of our pages.

When a user requests a page from the server, the HTTP header that their browser sends includes details of the browser they're using. In HTTP-speak it's called the **user agent** string, and defines the browser's name, version, operating system and compatibility level. The Browser Capabilities component looks for this string within its own configuration file, and adopts a range of properties equivalent to that browser's features. Hence, at any time while the page is being executed, the Browser Capabilities component can provide details of which individual features are or are not supported.

In ASP 3.0, a new feature has been added to the Browser Capabilities component. By including a `METADATA` directive in our ASP page (as you'll see later), we can instruct the component to fetch a cookie from the browser, and add any values it contains to the current instance of the component as new properties. This provides a way for us to collect more user-specific information from the browser rather than just the generic browser-specific information that's available in the `browscap.ini` file. We'll come back and look at the new `METADATA` technique shortly, after we've seen how the existing browser-detection feature works.

The browscap.ini File

The Browser Capabilities component uses a server-based text file named `browscap.ini`, which must be in the same directory as the `browscap.dll` component file. The `browscap.ini` file contains the information about most current and older browser, and there's also a default section that's used when a browser's 'user agent' string doesn't match any of the ones specified in the file. So adding new information about browsers, or updating the existing information, is as easy as editing the `browscap.ini` file.

We'll look at the format of this file first. All of the entries in `browscap.ini` are optional. However, it's important that we always include the default section. If the browser in use doesn't match any in the `browscap.ini` file, and no default browser settings have been specified, all the properties are set to `"UNKNOWN"`.

This is the format of the `browscap.ini` file:

```
; we can add comments anywhere, prefaced by a semicolon like this

; entry for a specific browser
[HTTPUserAgentHeader]
parent = browserDefinition
property1 = value1
property2 = value2
...

[Default Browser Capability Settings]
defaultProperty1 = defaultValue1
defaultProperty1 = defaultValue1
...
```

The `[HTTPUserAgentHeader]` line defines the start of a section for a particular browser, and the `parent` line indicates that another definition contains more information for this browser. Then each line defines a property that we want to make available through the Browser Capabilities component, and its value for this particular browser. The `Default` section lists the properties and values that are used if the browser isn't listed in its own section, or if it is listed but not all of the properties are specified.

For example, the file contains a section containing the values for Internet Explorer 5.0 in a section headed `[IE 5.0]`. This has no `parent` line, and so the only properties it will expose (other than those defined in the default section) are those we explicitly define:

```
[IE 5.0]
browser=IE
Version=5.0
majorver=5
minorver=0
frames=TRUE
tables=TRUE
cookies=TRUE
backgroundsounds=TRUE
vbscript=TRUE
javascript=TRUE
javaapplets=TRUE
```

```
ActiveXControls=TRUE
Win16=False
beta=False
AK=False
SK=False
AOL=False
Update=False
```

This section won't match any browser, because the HTTPUserAgentHeader line is simply [IE 5.0]. However, using it as the parent, we can add the definition for IE5 browsers:

```
[Mozilla/4.0 (compatible; MSIE 5.*; Windows 95*)]
parent=IE 5.0
version=4.0
minorver=0
platform=Win95
```

Here, we've specified IE 5.0 as the parent for this browser. The properties we've explicitly provided replace, or add to, those values in its parent's definition. But it will also assume any other property values there that aren't explicitly listed in its own section.

To help with recognizing very similar versions of a browser, we can use the asterisk (*) wildcard in the HTTPUserAgentHeader line. Then:

```
[Mozilla/4.0 (compatible; MSIE 5.*; Windows 95*)]
```

will match, for example:

```
[Mozilla/4.0 (compatible; MSIE 5.0; Windows 95)]
[Mozilla/4.0 (compatible; MSIE 5.5; Windows 95 AOL)]
... etc.
```

However, wildcard matches are only used if the user agent string sent by the browser doesn't fully match an HTTPUserAgentHeader that does *not* include an asterisk. Only if this test fails will it attempt to match with wildcard HTTPUserAgentHeader values, and it will use the first one it finds in the file that does match.

Lastly, we add the default browser section:

```
[Default Browser Capability Settings]
browser=Default
Version=0.0
majorver=#0
minorver=#0
frames=False
tables=True
cookies=False
backgroundsounds=False
vbscript=False
javascript=False
javaapplets=False
activexcontrols=False
...
```

This assumes a 'worse case scenario', where the browser supports almost nothing at all. However, it's up to us to define the actual values we want to use as this base. But if we've defined some of the default properties as `True`, and we *do* get a visit from someone running a text-only browser on a green-on-black Unix terminal, they might not see our page to full effect.

Maintaining Browscap.ini

Keeping `browscap.ini` up to date with new browsers as they are released, and adding older or specialist ones that we may have to contend with, is obviously important. To make life easier, a reasonably comprehensive version of `browscap.ini` is supplied with ASP and updated ones can generally be downloaded from Microsoft's web site. However a company called **CyScape Inc** provides versions of `browscap.ini` that are often more up to date than those on the Microsoft website.

You can find the latest version of `browscap.ini` at http://www.cyscape.com/browscap/, and subscribe to a mailing list to automatically receive the newest version of the file. CyScape also manufactures a competitor to the Microsoft Browser Capabilities component, named **BrowserHawk**. We'll look at this later in the chapter. New versions of `browscap.ini` can also be obtained from http://www.asptracker.com/.

Using the Browser Capabilities Component

Having grasped how the `browscap.ini` file can provide customizable properties containing information about a particular browser, it's time to actually see the Browser Capabilities component in use. This is relatively simple – we just create an instance of it and reference its properties:

```
<% 'in VBScript:
Set objBCap = Server.CreateObject("MSWC.BrowserType")
blnVBScriptOK = objBCap.vbscript    'save the result in a variable
If blnVBScriptOK Then
  Response.Write "This browser supports VBScript"
Else
  Response.Write "This browser doesn't support VBScript"
End If
%>
```

This checks to see if the browser supports VBScript and displays an appropriate message. You can imagine how this can be modified to direct the user to different pages depending on the response given by the browser.

Of course, we can use the Browser Capabilities component's properties to do much more complex things than this. One of the favorite techniques is to load a different index page for a site depending on what features the browser supports. If our site has a set of pages using frames, and a different set that does not, we can check the browser's ability to display frames when it first hits our site and redirect it to the appropriate index page.

Using the Browser Capabilities Cookie Feature

One of the features added to the new version of the Browser Capabilities component (as well as the claimed improvement in performance), is a way of getting more information about the specific client that has loaded the page.

The information in `browscap.ini` applies to all browsers of that specific type, so the component can only report features that are common to all installations of that browser. For example it can tell you if the browser *supports* cookies, but it can't tell you if that user has disabled them in the 'options' dialog of their browser.

Likewise, when we use complex page designs, it would be nice to know what kind of connection the user has, so that we can choose appropriately-sized graphic files to send them. This allows us to provide a much richer environment if they are connected through, say, a LAN rather than a modem. It also helps if we can find out the screen resolution they are running in, and even things like the user language they've set up their browser to use, their operating system and processor type, etc.

IE5 can provide this kind of information using a default **behavior** that can be assigned to an element in a client-side page. Behaviors are new in IE5, and are not supported elsewhere. They are a way of adding extra functionality to elements in the page, which is linked to the element via the `STYLE` attribute or a CSS style sheet entry. In particular, the `clientCaps` behavior provided within IE5 can be used to provide information about the client machine and browser setup and current options.

By creating an element and linking the `clientCaps` behavior to it, we can then query that element to get the information about the client that we require. The following page from the sample files we supply – `browscap_cookie.htm` – does just that. It first defines a style that includes the `clientCaps` behavior to be applied to all elements of type `<IE:clientcaps>`. This is XML syntax, using the namespace defined for the current page in the `XMLNS` attribute of the opening `<HTML>` tag.

Then it collects a range of values from the element to which we've assigned the `clientcaps` behavior, and builds up a cookie containing these values. Finally, it assigns this cookie to the `cookie` property of the document, so that it will be sent to our server with requests for pages from this particular server directory:

```
<HTML XMLNS:IE>
<HEAD>
<STYLE>
 IE\:clientcaps {behavior:url(#default#clientcaps)}
</STYLE>
</HEAD>
<BODY ONLOAD="createCookie();">
<IE:clientcaps ID="objCCaps" />

<SCRIPT LANGUAGE="JavaScript">

function stopAllErrors() {
  return true; // prevent display of any errors
}

function createCookie() {
  window.onerror = stopAllErrors;
  var strCookie = new String();
  strCookie = 'width=' + objCCaps.width
            + '&height=' + objCCaps.height
            + '&availWidth=' + objCCaps.availWidth
            + '&availHeight=' + objCCaps.availHeight
            + '&bufferDepth=' + objCCaps.bufferDepth
            + '&colorDepth=' + objCCaps.colorDepth
            + '&javaEnabled=' + objCCaps.javaEnabled
            + '&cookieEnabled=' + objCCaps.cookieEnabled
            + '&connectionType=' + objCCaps.connectionType
            + '&platform=' + objCCaps.platform
            + '&cpuClass=' + objCCaps.cpuClass
```

```
            + '&systemLanguage=' + objCCaps.systemLanguage
            + '&userLanguage=' + objCCaps.userLanguage;
  document.cookie = 'BrowsCap=' + strCookie;
}
</SCRIPT>

</BODY>
</HTML>
```

To use the cookie, we simply insert the special METADATA directive into our ASP page:

```
<!--METADATA TYPE="Cookie" NAME="BrowsCap"
             SRC="browserCapabilities/browscap_cookie.htm"-->
```

Now, when this ASP page runs, it will automatically send the page browscap_cookie.htm to the client. The client will execute the behavior and then return the cookie, whereupon the Browser Capabilities component adds the contents of the cookie to the list of available properties for this instance of the component. We can then query them in the same way as we do the properties generated by the browscap.ini file:

```
width: <B><% = objBCap.width %></B><BR>
height: <B><% = objBCap.height %></B><BR>
... etc.
```

The Browser Capabilities sample page we provide shows both sets of values: those collected from the properties defined in browscap.ini and those from the client-side cookie page. Of course, you're not limited to collecting just the values from the clientcaps behavior in the client-side page. You can query any property of the browser using Dynamic HTML (perhaps to get the size of the browser window) or the traditional object properties like navigator.appName:

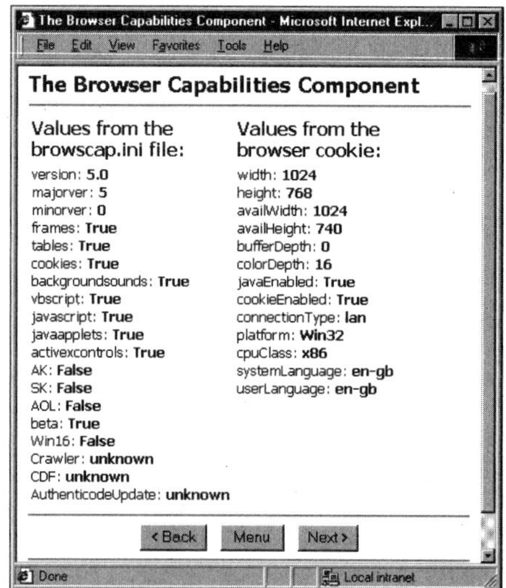

The Content Rotator Component

The **Content Rotator Component** is like a simplified version of the Ad Rotator component. We need to provide a **Content Schedule File**, which is just a text file containing different sections of text and HTML code. The Content Rotator component automatically displays one of these in our pages. We can include any number of text content entries in the schedule file, and specify the weighting that will control how often each one is included in the returned page.

The Content Rotator Schedule File

The structure of the **Content Schedule File** is much simpler than the equivalent Ad Rotator's schedule file. We just supply a list of the individual text strings we want to use, prefixed by a line that starts with two percent signs (`%%`). To set the relative weighting of each – which determines how often each will appear in the return page – we add a number to this line, and we can also append comments to it using a pair of forward slash characters:

```
%% 3 // This is the first entry in the schedule text file
For more information, mail us at
<A HREF="mailto:feedback@wrox.com">Wrox Press</A>

%% 4 // This is  a multi-line text string
<H4>Wrox Press</H4>
<UL>
  <LI> Language Primers
  <LI> Advanced Programming
  <LI> Internet Applications
</UL>

%% 2
Visit us on the <A HREF="http://www.wrox.com">World Wide Web</A>
```

This example shows three different text strings that can be used in our pages. The weightings are 3, 4 and 2, so the entries will appear on average in three out of nine, four out of nine, and two out of nine pages. Note that (like the Ad Rotator component) the actual occurrence of each individual string is determined at random, and then modified to achieve the weighting – if you load the page nine times, you may not get exactly these results.

The Content Rotator Component Members

The Content Linking Component provides just two methods that retrieve content from the Content Schedule File:

Method	Description
`GetAllContent` (*schedule_file*)	Retrieves and displays all the content strings in the *schedule_file* file.
`ChooseContent` (*schedule_file*)	Retrieves but does not display the next appropriate content string from the *schedule_file* file.

Using the Content Rotator Component

To get a specific section of text and HTML from the schedule file, we use the object's `ChooseContent` method. This retrieves an entry, in accordance with the weightings specified in the content schedule file. We can then insert it into the output stream being sent to the client using the `Response.Write` method:

```
<% 'in VBScript:
Set objMyContent = Server.CreateObject("MSWC.ContentRotator")
strContent = objMyContent.ChooseContent("ContentRotator/content_schedule.txt")
Response.Write strContent
%>
```

This code uses a schedule file in the same directory as the page. If it's stored elsewhere we have to include the path of the schedule file, which can either be a physical path relative to the Web site's root directory, or a full virtual path. For example:

```
objMyContent.ChooseContent("\content\mycontent.txt")   'relative physical path
objMyContent.ChooseContent("/demo/mycontent.txt")      'full virtual path
```

If we want to display all the content strings in the Content Schedule File, we can use the object's `GetAllContent` method. As with `ChooseContent` method, we have to supply the path of the schedule file. For example, the following code gets all the content in the content schedule file and displays it in the page. Note that this method inserts the content into the page automatically, so we don't need to use `Response.Write`. It also automatically adds a horizontal rule between each entry in the file:

```
objMyContent.GetAllContent("mycontent.txt")
```

To see the Content Rotator component in action, open the sample page we provide from the main 'ASP Installable Components' menu. This page uses the Content Schedule File we described earlier. It calls the `ChooseContent` method to place a single entry at the top of the page, then uses the `GetAllContent` method to display the entire content of the schedule file:

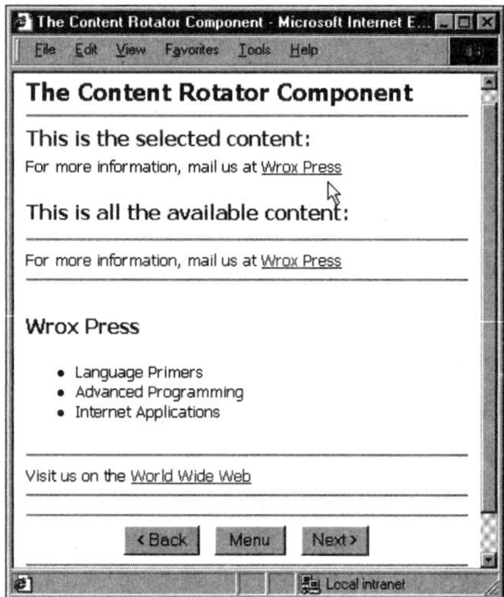

The Page Counter Component

The **Page Counter** component can be used to count how many times a particular page is accessed by our visitors. The component periodically saves its data in a text file on the server's disk – the **Hit Count Data File** – so in cases of shutdown or error, the current data is not lost.

The Page Counter Component Members

The Page Counter component provides methods for adding a hit to the hit count file, and for reading and resetting the hit-count totals:

Method	Description
`Hits([`*page_path*`])`	Returns the hit count for the page specified in *page_path*. If the optional *page_path* parameter is omitted, it returns the hit count for the current page.
`PageHit()`	Increments the hit count for the current page.
`Reset([`*page_path*`])`	Sets the hit count for the page specified in *page_path* to zero. If the optional *page_path* parameter is omitted, it sets the hit count for the current page to zero.

Using the Page Counter Component

For a change, we'll use JScript in this example to illustrate using the Page Counter component. We create the object instance with the `Server.CreateObject` method, then call the `Hits` method to get the number of hits for the current page. If it has reached five, we reset the counter back to zero and put a link in the page for our visitor to claim their prize:

```
<% // in JScript:
var objPageCount = Server.CreateObject('MSWC.PageCounter');

// increment the counter and display the current hit count
objPageCount.PageHit();
Response.Write('You are visitor number ' + objPageCount.Hits() + '<P>');

// we treat every fifth visitor as a winner
if (objPageCount.Hits() == 5) {
   objPageCount.Reset();    // reset the counter
   Response.Write('You\'re a lucky winner!<BR>');
   Response.Write('<A HREF="winner.asp">Go to our winners page</A><BR>');
}
%>
```

Notice the use of a backslash to escape the single quote in the string used in the second `Response.Write` *statement. This prevents the JScript engine from treating it as the end of the string.*

We've provided a sample page that uses the Page Counter component. However, because we use a VBScript include file in each of the sample pages, we have coded the example for this component in VBScript as well. While it's possible to mix scripting languages in an ASP page, using script inside an SSI #include file can upset the page buffering and cause unpredictable results. Although the scripting language is different, the sample page works in exactly the same way as shown above.

We've included a <FORM> section in the page that contains two buttons. Both submit the form to reload the page:

```
<FORM ACTION="<% = Request.ServerVariables("SCRIPT_NAME") %>" METHOD="POST">

<INPUT TYPE="SUBMIT" VALUE="   "> Reload this page<P>
<INPUT TYPE="SUBMIT" NAME="cmdReset" VALUE="   ">
PageCounter.Reset( )

</FORM>
```

At the start of the page, as in our other sample pages, we look for the relevant button names in the request. In this page, we're only interested in the second button, named `cmdReset`. If it was clicked, we execute the `Reset` method of our Page Counter component to reset the visit count for this page to zero:

```
'look for a command sent from the FORM section buttons
If Len(Request.Form("cmdReset")) Then objPageCount.Reset   'reset the counter
```

The code we saw earlier will then call the `PageHit` method to set the counter to `1` and display it in the page. Notice that we've used the `Hits` and `Reset` methods without providing a value for the optional parameter, so they will both operate on the current page's counter. We could, of course, use them in a different page that summarized the results for several pages.

The Permission Checker Component

The **Permission Checker** component is used to determine whether the account under which the current user is accessing our site has been granted permissions to read a particular file or access a resource (in Windows NT/2000 only, not Windows 9*x*). We can use it to tailor pages so that they only contain links to resources that the current user has permission to access. This technique is also useful for hiding restricted access pages or resources from other visitors, so that they won't know that they exist and won't be tempted to try hacking into them.

The Permission Checker Component Members

The Permission Checker component has a single method:

Method	Description
`HasAccess` (*file_path*)	Checks to see if the current user account under which the current ASP page is being executed has permission to access the page specified in *file_path*. This can be a physical or virtual path to a page, file or other resource. Returns `True` if the current account has permission to access it or `False` if not.

How the Permission Checker Component Works

Generally, unless we specify otherwise, our users will be accessing the pages anonymously, and therefore IIS will access resources on their behalf using its own Windows account. By default this is IUSR_*machinename* (for example IUSR_WROXBOX), so the Permission Checker component will check if the IUSR_*machinename* account has access to the specified page or resource.

However, by turning off the Allow Anonymous Access option in Internet Services Manager ,either for a Web site or a specific directory, we force IIS to prompt the user for the username and password of a valid user account. This account is then used to access the resources for which anonymous access is denied.

Access control is specified in the Internet Services Manager, in the Directory Security page of the Properties dialog for a site or directory. Click the Edit button in the Anonymous access and authentication control section of this dialog page to open the Authentication Methods dialog, and turn **off** the 'Anonymous access' option:

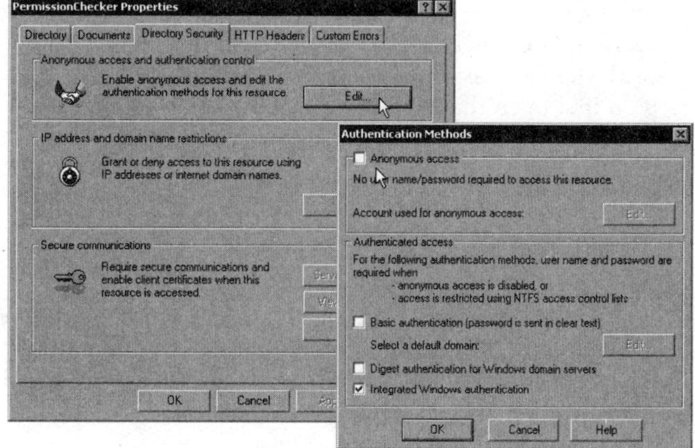

When the Permission Checker component is instantiated in a page that is accessed by a user under their own account (rather than IUSR_*machinename*), it checks to see if their account has access to the specified resource. If we disable anonymous access so that all users have to supply their account details, we can use Windows Explorer to set up specific permissions on each file or resource – in the Security page of the Properties dialog for that resource:

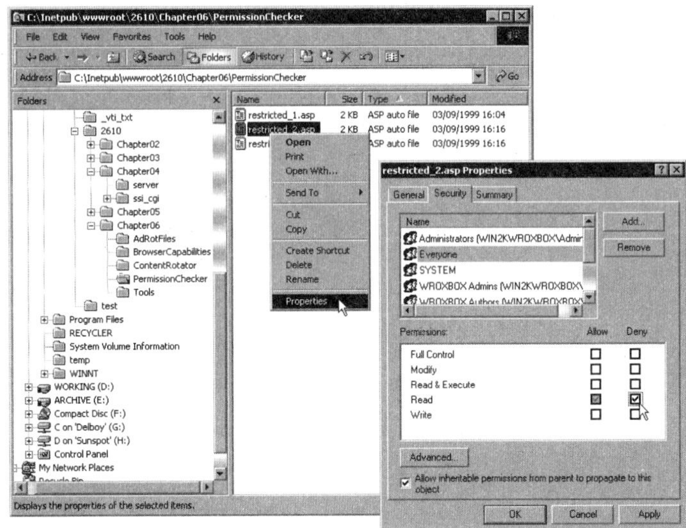

Using the Permission Checker Component

We can use the Permission Checker component to check whether the current user has permission to access any other page (anywhere on our site) with the `HasAccess` method. We've provided a series of sample pages that you can use to experiment with the Permission Checker component. When you first open the example (from the main ASP Installable Components menu), you will see three links in the page:

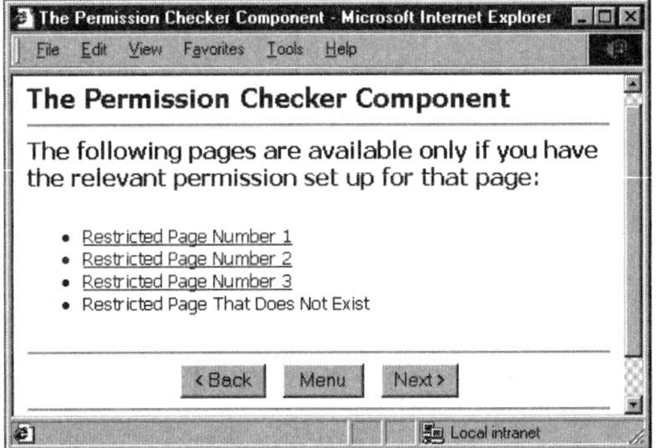

Each refers to a page in the `PermissionChecker` subdirectory of the `Chapter06` samples directory. However, the Permission Checker component is used to see if the current user has access permission for each page. The entry for each page is only a hyperlink if the user actually does have permission to access the page:

```
'create an instance of the component
Set objPermit = Server.CreateObject("MSWC.PermissionChecker")
%>
<UL>

<LI>
<% If objPermit.HasAccess("PermissionChecker/restricted_1.asp") Then %>
  <A HREF="PermissionChecker/restricted_1.asp">
<% End If %>

Restricted Page Number 1
```

```
<% If objPermit.HasAccess("PermissionChecker/restricted_1.asp") Then %>
  </A>
<% End If %>
</LI>

...
..'other page links here
...
</UL>
```

At present we have permission to access all three restricted pages, so all three entries are hyperlinks. However, the fourth link is to a page that doesn't exist (it may have been moved or deleted), and it does not appear as a hyperlink because the component can't access it using the current user's (i.e. the IUSR_*machinename*) account – or any account for that matter!

> *Note that we chose just to remove the hyperlink and leave the link text in the page. It probably makes more sense in a real-world situation to remove the complete entry for pages that are not accessible.*

If we now remove the Read (and any other) permission from the page `restricted_2.asp` in the `PermissionChecker` subdirectory (as shown in the earlier screenshots) and reload the page, the entry for the newly restricted page does not appear as a hyperlink:

- Restricted Page Number 1
- Restricted Page Number 2
- Restricted Page Number 3
- Restricted Page That Does Not Exist

The MyInfo Component

The **MyInfo** component was originally introduced with Personal Web Server, and used to keep track of personal information provided by the server administrator. However, it can be used in ASP 3.0 to provide persistent storage for name/value pairs, or almost any other type of information that can be represented as a text string. The information is stored in XML format in a text file – `myinfo.xml` – located in the `inetsrv` directory of your Web server machine. In Windows 2000, this is `WinNT\system32\inetsrv\`.

As with the Counters component, we should only create a single instance of the MyInfo component, and make it available to all the pages on our Web site. Make sure that you have this code in the `global.asa` file for your Default Web Site:

```
<!-- declare instance of the MyInfo component with application-level scope -->
<OBJECT ID="objMyInfo" RUNAT="Server" SCOPE="Application" PROGID="MSWC.MyInfo">
</OBJECT>
```

Using the MyInfo Component

The MyInfo component has no properties or methods by default. However, we can add properties to it ourselves, simply by assigning a name and value to them. For example, we can add information about our work environment and our co-workers using:

```
<% 'in VBScript:
objMyInfo.MyManager = "Christina Chan"
objMyInfo.MyPhoneExtension = "2851"
objMyInfo.MyCarParkingSpace = "4A-17"
objMyInfo.MyComputerName = "Priscilla"
%>
```

As with any component's properties, we can retrieve the values using code like this:

```
<% 'in VBScript:
strManagerName = objMyInfo.MyManager
strPhoneExtension = objMyInfo.MyPhoneExtension
strParkingSpace = objMyInfo.MyCarParkingSpace
strComputerName = objMyInfo.MyComputerName
%>
```

This is a useful way to store occasional values between page requests without requiring a user `Session` to be available. It also provides a storage area for values that might change in the future, and so any other page that uses these values will automatically pick up the changed value the next time it runs. It could be a useful way to avoid having to edit a lot of other pages!

We've provided a simple example of using the MyInfo component, which you can run from the main ASP Installable Components menu. It uses the code we've just seen to set the properties of the component, and includes a section where you can change the values of these properties:

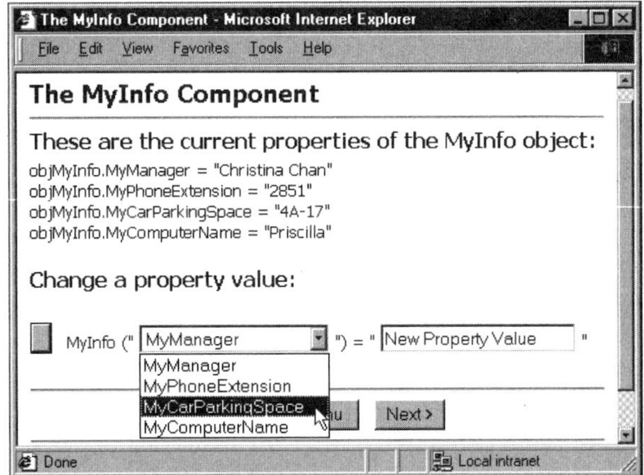

To create the properties the first time the page is opened we use a flag variable named `SetDefaultValues`, which is stored in the user's `Session` object. We set it to `"Yes"` after setting the properties to our 'default' values the first time the page is opened in each session. When the page is reloaded during the current session, the values are not reset to the defaults:

```
'an instance of the component is already created in global.asa
If Not Session("SetDefaultValues") = "Yes" Then
  'set the properties if they're not set to the default values,
  'i.e. if this is the first time that the page has been run
  'during the current user session
  objMyInfo.MyManager = "Christina Chan"
  objMyInfo.MyPhoneExtension = "2851"
  objMyInfo.MyCarParkingSpace = "4A-17"
  objMyInfo.MyComputerName = "Priscilla"
  'set a session flag to show that the default values hve been set
  Session("SetDefaultValues") = "Yes"
End If
```

As the page loads each time, we also check for a value in the request for the button that is used to change a property value. As in the other samples, this is on a <FORM> that also contains the drop-down list and text box. If we find that the button was clicked, we collect the values from the drop-down list and text box and use them to change the relevant property value:

```
'look for a command sent from the FORM section buttons
If Len(Request.Form("cmdChange")) Then
  strPropertyName = Request.Form("lstName") 'get the name of the property
  strNewValue = Request.Form("txtValue")    'get the new value for the property
  objMyInfo(strPropertyName) = strNewValue  'set the component property value
End If
```

The Tools Component

The **Tools** component provides useful methods that we can use in our pages to check for the existence of a file, process an HTML form, and generate a random integer. There are also methods for use on the Apple Macintosh that check for the existence of a server plug-in and check if the current user is the site owner.

The Tools Component Members

The Tools component provides five methods, two of which are operating system dependent:

Method	Description
`FileExists (`*relative_url*`)`	Returns `True` if the file specified in *relative_url* exists, or `False` if not. The file must be specified as a virtual relative path and filename, and must reside within the published Web site directories.
`Random()`	Generates a random integer between –32768 and 32767. Use the `Abs` function (VBScript) or `Math.abs` function (JScript) to get a positive integer between 0 and 32768. Use the `Mod` operator (VBScript) or `%` operator (JScript) to get a number within a specified range, for example: `intRand = (objTools.Random Mod 76) + 25` to get an integer between 25 and 100.
`ProcessForm (`*output_url*`,` *template_url*`, [`*insertion_point*`])`	Processes an HTML form by taking the file specified in *template_url*, and inserting into it the values from a form that has been submitted to the current page. The result is written to the file specified in *output_url*. If the optional *insertion_point* (string) parameter is specified, the component finds this string in the existing output file and inserts the new content at that point. If the *insertion_point* parameter is not specified, any existing *output_url* file is replaced with the new output.

Table Continued on Following Page

Method	Description
`Owner`	**Apple Macintosh only**. Returns `True` if the current user account is the owner of the Web site, or `False` if not.
`PluginExists (`*plugin_name*`)`	**Apple Macintosh only**. Returns `True` if the server *plugin_name* specified is installed on the machine, or `False` if not.

Using the Tools.FileExists Method

We can use the `FileExists` method to check if some file exists on our server before we allow a user to try and access it. (Note that this works in an identical manner to `FileSystemObject.FileExists`.)

In this example, the user provides the relative URL of a page that they want to open by typing it into a text box named `txtURL`. We can check if it exists before we try to redirect them to it:

```
<% // in JScript:
var objTools = Server.CreateObject('MSWC.Tools');
var strURL = Request.Form('txtURL');   // collect the page URL they entered
if (objTools.FileExists(strURL))       // see if it exists
   Server.Transfer(strURL)             // if it does, transfer to it
else                                   // or if not display a message
   Response.Write('Sorry, the page you requested does not exist');
%>
```

We've provided a sample page (using VBScript) that demonstrates all three (non-Macintosh) methods of the Tools component. As usual, you can run it from the main ASP Installable Components menu:

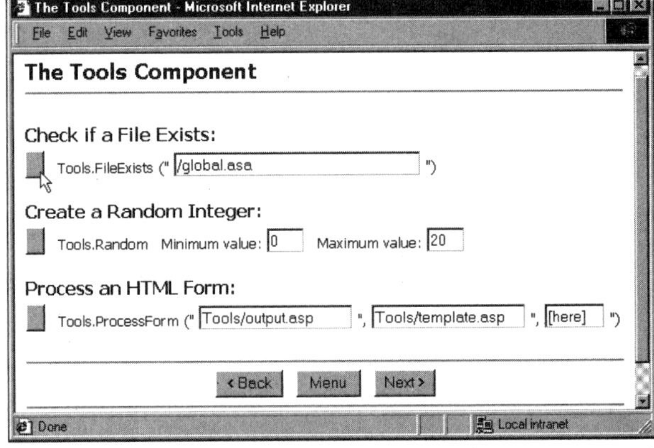

The first section of the page allows you to enter the full relative URL of a file and tells you if it exists. The default value we provide checks to see if there is a `global.asa` file in the root directory of your Web site. When the button is clicked, a message indicating whether the file was found is placed at the top of the page:

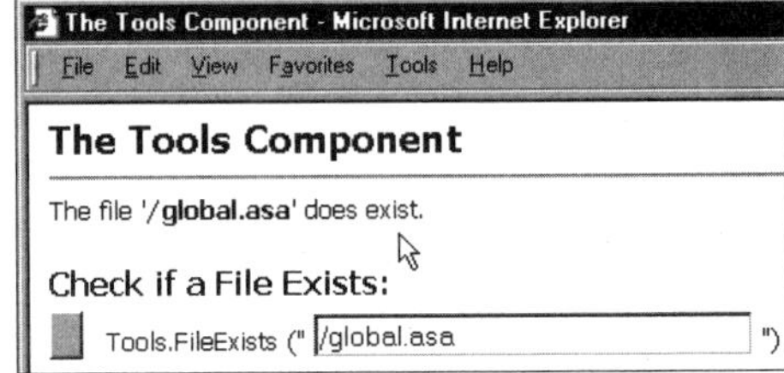

As is now becoming the norm, we place all the controls in the page on a `<FORM>` that is submitted back to this page. At the start of the page we look to see which button was clicked. If it was the one for **FileExists**, we simply call the `FileExists` method of the component and display an appropriate message:

```
'look for a command sent from the FORM section buttons
If Len(Request.Form("cmdExists")) Then
  strFile = Request.Form("txtFile")
  If objTools.FileExists(strFile) Then
    Response.Write "The file '<B>" & strFile & "</B>' does exist.<P>"
  Else
    Response.Write "The file '" & strFile & "' <B>does not</B> exist.<P>"
  End If
End If
```

Using the Tools.Random Method

Sometimes we need a random number to perform some task in our ASP pages, such as redirect a user to a random page, choose colors, or display quotations or 'tips of the day'. We can use the `Rnd` function in VBScript, but this requires us to do some extra work to convert the value into an integer within a specific range. The `Random` method of the Tools component is much easier to use, because it produces integer values directly.

The result of the `Random` method is an integer between -32768 and 32767. To get an integer within a specific range, we can use the `Abs` function of our scripting language and then take the modulus of the next highest integer. For example, to produce positive integers from 0 to 20 in VBScript we can use:

```
intRandom = Abs(objTools.Random) Mod 21
```

To get a value between, say, 50 and 100, we can use:

```
intRandom = (Abs(objTools.Random) Mod 51) + 50
```

Our sample page uses this technique to create a random number, although it does a little checking of the values entered by the user first – to ensure that they are both valid positive numbers and that they're in the correct range relative to one another:

```
If Len(Request.Form("cmdRandom")) Then
  intMin = -1   'preset to illegal values and then
  intMax = -1   'only set if a valid number is entered
  strMin = Request.Form("txtMinimum")
  strMax = Request.Form("txtMaximum")

  If IsNumeric(strMin) Then intMin = CStr(strMin)
  If IsNumeric(strMax) Then intMax = CStr(strMax)

  If (intMin >= 0) And (intMax > intMin) Then
    intRandom = (Abs(objTools.Random) Mod (intMax - intMin + 1)) + intMin
    Response.Write "Your random value is: <B>" & intRandom & "</B><P>"
  Else
    Response.Write "<B>The numbers you entered are not valid.</B><P>"
  End If

End If
```

The result is displayed at the top of the page when it reloads:

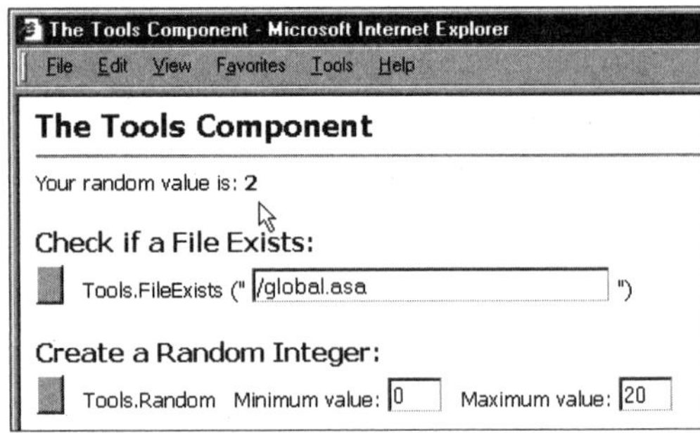

Using the Tools.ProcessForm Method

The most complex method of the Tools component is ProcessForm. It reads a template file stored on disk, inserts into it information that we create (probably from the contents of the current page's Request.Form collection), then writes the result out to disk as a file. The syntax of the method is:

```
ProcessForm (output_url, template_url, [insertion_point])
```

The template and output files are defined with relative URLs compared to the current page. The output file can be an ASP page, and if so it's processed as normal when it's opened in a browser. The template file can contain ordinary ASP code, but this is not executed – it's simply copied into the output file. However, if we place the ASP code in the template file within the special <%%..%%> delimiters, it *will* be executed as the template is being loaded. This allows any dynamically created values (such as the time and date of the process) to be inserted into the output page.

This is our sample file template.asp (in the Tools subdirectory of the Chapter06 samples):

```
This file was created by the ASP Tools component
------------------------------------------------
The content of the request was:

Output file name: <%% = Request.Form("txtOutput") %%>
Template file name: <%% = Request.Form("txtTemplate") %%>
Insertion point text: <%% = Request.Form("txtInsert") %%>

------------------------------------------------
Created <%% = Now() %%>
```

Our sample page contains controls that are preset to use this template file. They create an output file named output.asp in the same folder as the template file:

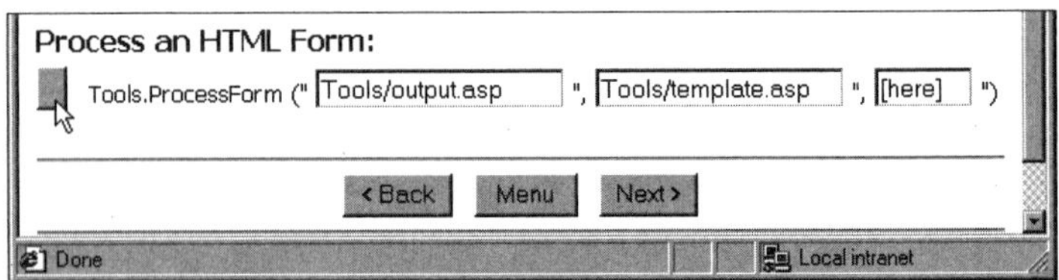

When we click the button, a section of ASP code is executed that collects the values from the text boxes and calls the `ProcessForm` method:

```
If Len(Request.Form("cmdProcess")) Then

   strTemplate = Request.Form("txtTemplate")
   strOutput = Request.Form("txtOutput")
   strInsertPoint = Request.Form("txtInsert")
   '...
   ' we display the template contents here
   '...

   'process the form contents
   objTools.ProcessForm strOutput, strTemplate, strInsertPoint

   '...
   ' we display the output file contents here
   '...

End If
```

Setting the Output File Access Permissions

If you get an MSWC.Tools error 80004005 Couldn't open output file error message, it means that IIS doesn't have permission to write to the directory you specified for the output file. The quickest way to solve this problem for the example page is to use the Security page of the Properties dialog to give the Everyone group Full Control for the `Tools` directory and the file named `output.asp` it contains:

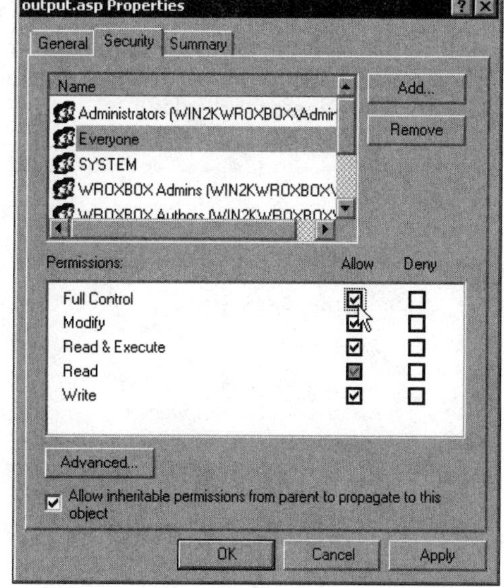

Viewing the File Contents

The next screenshot shows the result of running the code above with the default values. You can see the original template file content, and the content that the `ProcessForm` method inserted into the output file:

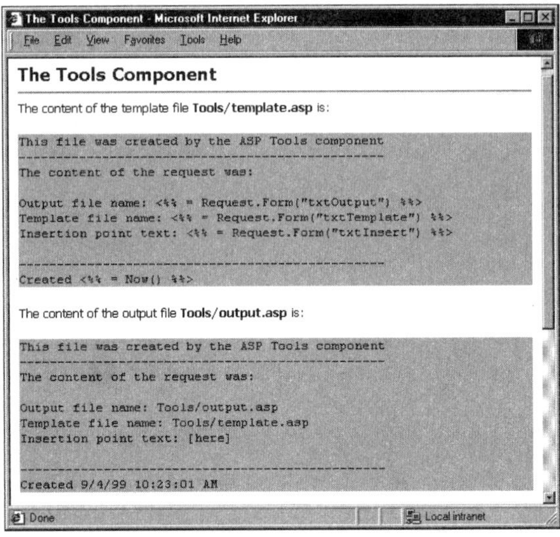

We omitted the code that displays the contents of the files from the excerpt we saw earlier. It's much the same as that we used in the main ASP Installable Components menu page, to display the contents of the **Content Linking List** file. We use instances of the FileSystemObject and TextStream objects to read the complete file into a string, and then insert it into the page (remembering to use the `Server.HTMLEncode` method so that the '<' and '>' characters are converted into their character entity equivalents for display):

```
QUOT = Chr(34)    'double-quote character
...
'use a FileSytemObject object to display the template file contents
Set objFSO = Server.CreateObject("Scripting.FileSystemObject")

Response.Write "The content of the template file <B>" & _
               strTemplate & "</B> is:"

Set objTStream = objFSO.OpenTextFile(Server.MapPath(strTemplate), ForReading)
strContent = Server.HTMLEncode(objTStream.ReadAll)    'read whole file
objTStream.Close

Response.Write "<DIV CLASS=" & QUOT & "showcode" & QUOT & "><PRE>" & _
               strContent & "</PRE></DIV>"
...
```

About the Insertion Point Parameter

The optional *insertion_point* parameter of the `ProcessForm` method can be used to insert text at a specific point in the file. The method will look for the first instance of the specified string in the output file, and then insert the new content it creates at that point. Prefixing the *insertion_point* string with an asterisk (*) places the new content before it in the output file, otherwise it is inserted after the first instance of the *insertion_point* string. If the *insertion_point* parameter is omitted, the new content replaces the entire output file.

> *Note that the insertion_point parameter was* ***not implemented*** *in early versions of the* `Tools.ProcessForm` *method.*

The Logging Utility Component

The **Logging Utility** component is new in ASP 3.0. It provides a way to access the log files generated by IIS for the Web and FTP sites that our server supports.

The Logging Utility Component Members

The Logging Utility component provides six methods that we can use to read the contents of the log files and write new records into existing log files. You'll probably recognize the similarity between these methods and those of the FileSystemObject object that we met in the previous chapter:

Method	Description
`AtEndOfLog()`	Returns `True` if all the records in the file(s) have been read when iterating through them with the `ReadLogRecord` method.
`CloseLogFiles` (*io_mode*)	Closes log files that are open. The value of *io_mode* specifies which files to close. The constant `ForReading` (`1`) closes all files that have been opened for reading, `ForWriting` (2) closes all files that have been opened for writing, and `AllOpenFiles` (32) closes all open files.
`OpenLogFile` (*filename, io_mode, service_name, service_instance, output_format*)	Opens the log file or set of log files specified in *filename*. The optional *io_mode* parameter can be `ForReading` (1 – the default) or `ForWriting` (2). The optional *service_name* and *service_instance* parameters limit the records that are returned from the file as it is read to a particular IIS service (i.e. "W3SVC" and "1"). The optional *output_format* parameter is used when writing to the file, to indicate the format to use.
`ReadFilter` (*start, end*)	Limits the records that are returned when reading from the file(s) to those within the specified date and time range. Both parameters are optional and, if omitted, the *start* is the first record in the file(s) and the *end* is the last record.
`ReadLogRecord()`	Reads the next log record from the current log file(s) opened by the `OpenLogFile` method.
`WriteLogRecord` (*logging_object*)	Writes log records from a file that has been opened for reading to a file that has been opened for writing. The parameter is an object variable referencing the Logging Utility component instance that holds the source records.

The Logging Utility component also provides twenty properties that correspond to the fields in an IIS log record:

Property	Description
`BytesReceived`	The number of bytes received from the browser as the request.
`BytesSent`	The number of bytes sent back to the browser as the response.
`ClientIP`	The IP address of the client or their host (i.e. proxy server).
`Cookie`	The contents of any cookie sent in the request.
`CustomFields`	An array of any custom headers that were added to the request.
`DateTime`	The date and time of the request as GMT.
`Method`	The operation type, such as "GET" or "POST".
`ProtocolStatus`	The status message returned to the client, i.e. "200 OK".
`ProtocolVersion`	The protocol version string, such as "HTTP/1.1".
`Referer`	The URL of the page containing the link that initiated this request if available.
`ServerIP`	The IIS machine's IP address.
`ServerName`	The machine name of the IIS server.
`ServerPort`	The port number that the request was received on, such as "80".
`ServiceName`	The service name, such as "MSFTPSVC" or "W3SVC".
`TimeTaken`	The total processing time to retrieve and create the returned page.
`URIQuery`	Any parameters in the query string appended to the URL in the request.
`URIStem`	The target URL that was requested.
`UserAgent`	The user agent string sent by the client.
`UserName`	The logon name of the user if they are not accessing the server anonymously.
`Win32Status`	The Win32 status code returned after processing the request.

Using the Logging Utility Component

The most common use of the Logging Utility component is likely to be for the custom querying of log files. The ability to write new files that are made up of selected records from an existing file means that we can summarize certain types of entry, or selectively pick out records for further investigation.

To use the `ForReading`, `ForWriting` and `AllOpenFiles` constants that are exposed by the component, remember to include a `METADATA` directive in the `<HEAD>` section of the page:

```
<!-- METADATA TYPE="typelib" FILE="C:\WINNT\system32\inetsrv\logscrpt.dll" -->
```

To iterate through the records, we just need to open the file and repeatedly call `ReadLogRecord` until `AtEndOfLog` returns `True`. In this example, we're also filtering the records, so that we get only those for the last 24 hours (i.e. from yesterday until today):

```
'create the component instance
Set objLogUtil = Server.CreateObject("MSWC.IISLog")

'open the log file for reading, for the W3SVC instance number 1
objLogUtil.OpenLogFile "extend#.log", ForReading, "W3SVC", 1

'set a filter for the last day's records only
objLogUtil.ReadFilter DateAdd("d", -1, Now), Now

'loop through the records
Do While Not objLogUtil.AtEndOfLog
   objLogUtil.ReadLogRecord      'read the next record
   Response.Write "Request received for page " & objLogUtil.URLStem & " on " _
                & objLogUtil.DateTime & " from IP address " _
                & objLogUtil.ClientIP & ".<BR>"
Loop
objLogUtil.CloseLogFiles(ForReading)    'close the file(s)
```

We've provided a sample page that demonstrates the Logging Utility component in use, which can be run from the main ASP Installable Components menu.

Make sure that you disable anonymous access in Internet Services Manager for the directory containing the sample files or for the `loggingutility.asp` file, otherwise you won't be able to access the log files. Open the Directory Security page of the Properties dialog for the `loggingutility.asp` file or the directory that contains it. Click the Edit button in the Anonymous access and authentication control section of this dialog page to open the Authentication Methods dialog, and turn **off** the Anonymous access option.

You'll also have to edit the page to change the filename of the log file to suit your machine. We turned on W3C Extended Logging in the Web Site page of the Properties dialog for the Default Web Site:

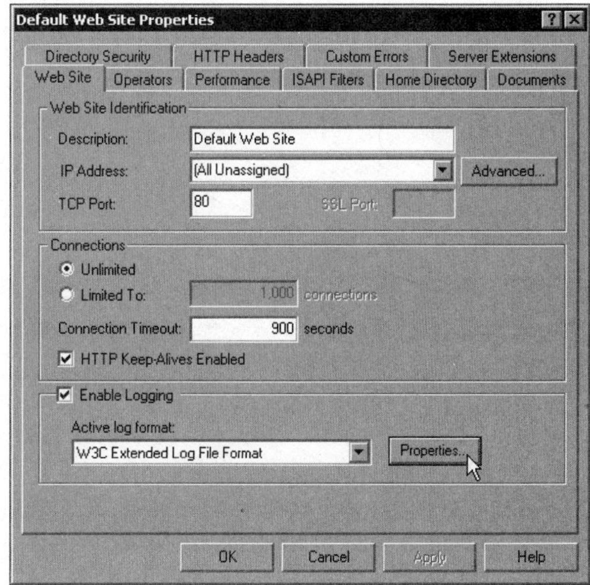

In this dialog, click the Properties button to open the Extended Logging Properties dialog. There you can find out the file name that will be used for the files. We chose the fixed-size log file option, so the file names will be `extend1.log`, `extend2.log`, etc:

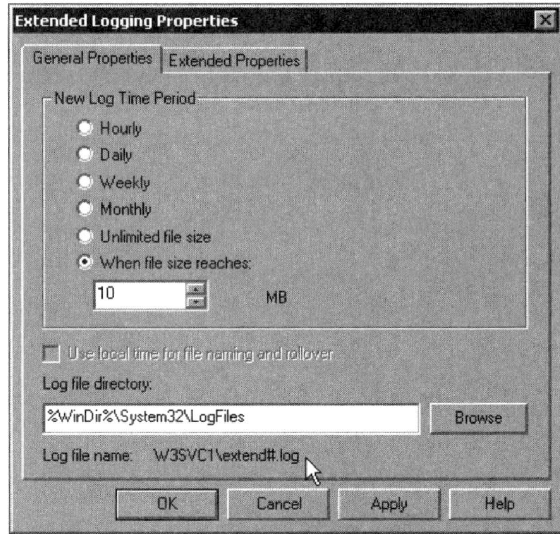

You should also open the Extended Properties page and make sure that all the values you want to log are selected:

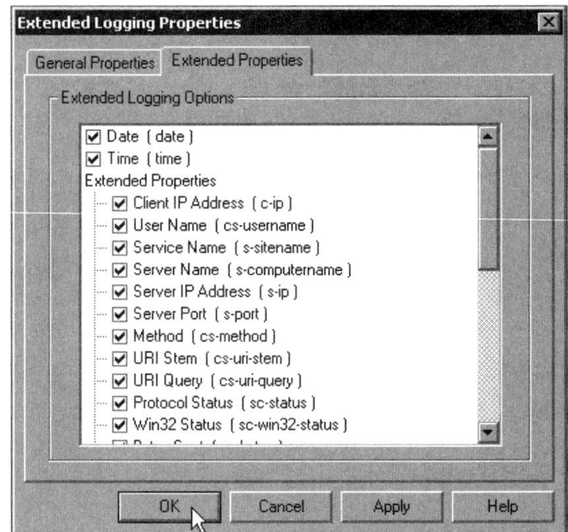

Now, you can run the sample page and see the results. We've chosen to display the values in a normal HTML table using this code:

```
<%
Set objLogUtil = Server.CreateObject("MSWC.IISLog")
objLogUtil.OpenLogFile "extend#.log", ForReading, "W3SVC", 1, 0
objLogUtil.ReadFilter DateAdd("d", -1, Now), Now
%>
<TABLE CELLPADDING="10">
<TR>
<TH>Date/Time</TH>
<TH>Client IP</TH>
<TH>Bytes Sent</TH>
<TH>Target URL</TH>
</TR>
```

```
<%
Do While Not objLogUtil.AtEndOfLog
   objLogUtil.ReadLogRecord  'read the next record
%>
<TR>
<TD><% = objLogUtil.DateTime %></TD>
<TD><% = objLogUtil.ClientIP %></TD>
<TD><% = objLogUtil.BytesSent %></TD>
<TD><% = objLogUtil.URLStem %></TD>
</TR>
<%
Loop
objLogUtil.CloseLogFiles(ForReading)
%>
```

And here's the result:

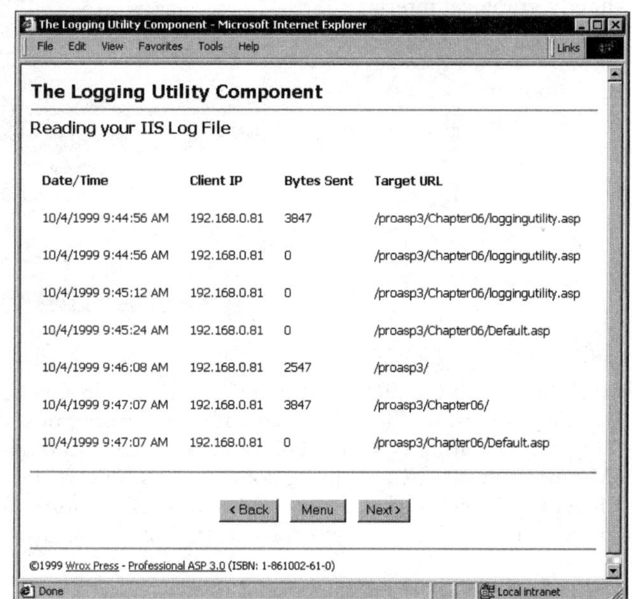

Third Party Server Components

In this section we briefly outline some of the popular commercial and free third-party server components which you can use with ASP.

Two of the common tasks you have to accomplish when developing websites are managing compatibility and uploading files to the server. We'll look at a couple of components that can help out. We'll also look at a component that can be used instead of the Microsoft sample Registry Access component (which appears to have been withdrawn from their Web site).

You'll find a comprehensive list of some of the most useful components available in Appendix G

The BrowserHawk Component

While many people are happy with the Browser Capabilities component that's supplied with IIS and ASP, it suffers from the problem that the browser definition file, `browscap.ini`, requires regular maintenance or replacement to keep up with new browser releases.

CyScape, the company that provides updated versions of `browscap.ini`, also offer their own component that carries out browser detection, both on the server and on the client. What's more, it provides a handy graphical interface that can be used to view and modify its own browser definition file:

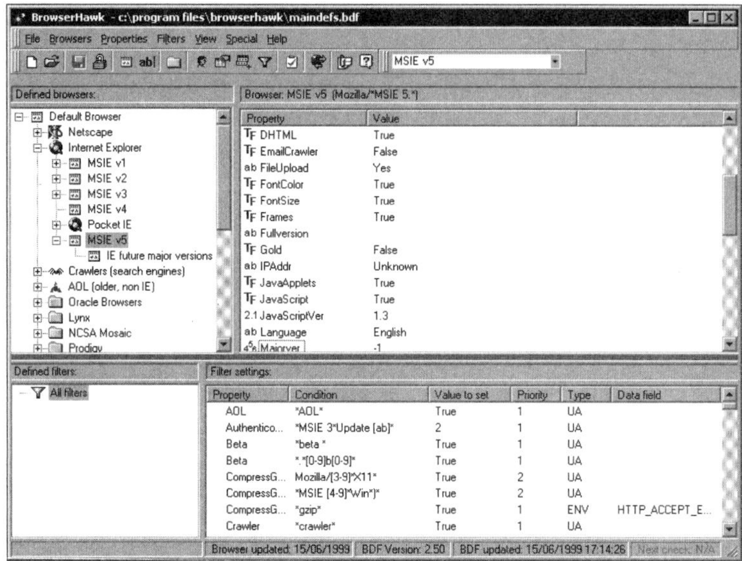

You can see that there are many more properties available for each browser type, such as Dynamic HTML, style sheets, the JavaScript version, file upload capabilities, Secure Sockets Layer support, operating system details, and language. And, like the Microsoft Browser Capabilities component, you can add your own as well. There is also a useful Wizard-style feature that helps you to add new browsers to the definition file:

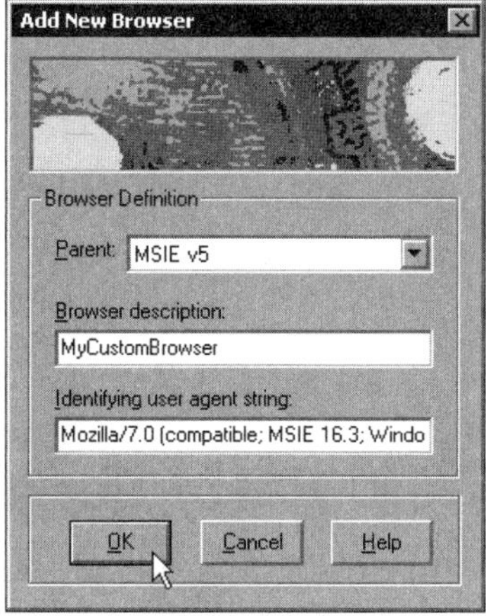

Some of the nice tricks that BrowserHawk has up its sleeve are the ability to recognize new browsers (using a special pattern-matching algorithm), and a far wider range of browsers supported by default – including Opera and WebTV. It's also easy to add new properties, using the filtering feature.

However, probably the biggest advantage with BrowserHawk is the ability to automatically check periodically for new versions of the browser definition file from the CyScape website, and merge the additions into your current definition file. This means that you don't have to keep copying the definition files to all your Web servers.

Using the BrowserHawk component is easy, as it's compatible with the MS Browser Capabilities component. All you need to do is change the ProgID in your Server.CreateObject method or <OBJECT> element that creates the component instance, from "MSWC.BrowserType" to "cyScape.browserObj":

```
Set objBCap = Server.CreateObject("cyScape.browserObj")
```

However, you should check out the BrowserHawk documentation regarding a few issues that can arise.

You can download a copy of BrowserHawk from the CyScape website at http://www.cyscape.com/. *We've included the example pages that come with BrowserHawk in the samples for this chapter so that you can see how to use it. They're in the* BrowserHawk *subdirectory of the* Chapter06 *directory.*

The SA-FileUp Component

One regular requirement on many websites is the ability to accept files that are posted from the client to the server. In IIS4.0, Microsoft provided a component known as the **Posting Acceptor** which did just that. This component is no longer included with a standard installation of IIS 5.0 and ASP 3.0, though it is included if you install Site Server Express. You can also download it from the Microsoft website at http://www.microsoft.com/windows/software/webpost/post_accept.htm.

However, many people find the Posting Acceptor both limited in features and difficult to program. One of the popular alternatives is the **SA-FileUp** component from **Software Artisans**. Unlike Posting Acceptor (which is an ISAPI filter), SA-FileUp is a true ActiveX DLL server component, and integrates easily into ASP pages. This means that the same techniques for setting security on pages and limiting user access can be used as in any other ASP pages or components. It can also be run within the MTS/COM+ out-of-process environment like any other ActiveX DLL.

A full tutorial for using SA-FileUp is provided at http://www.activeserverpages.com/upload/, so we will only show you the results here. However, we've included the example pages that come with the component in the samples for this chapter, so that you can see how to use it. They're in the SAFileUp subdirectory of the Chapter06 directory. You'll need to download a copy of SA-FileUp from the Software Artisans website at http://www.softartisans.com/.

Using the SA-FileUp Component

The sample pages provided with SA-FileUp create a simple page containing a FileUpload element and a button, using the HTML INPUT elements:

```
<FORM ACTION="safileup_response.asp"
      ENCTYPE="MULTIPART/FORM-DATA" METHOD="POST">
...
<INPUT TYPE="FILE" NAME="FILE1">
...
<INPUT TYPE="SUBMIT" NAME="SUB1" VALUE="Upload File">
...
</FORM>
```

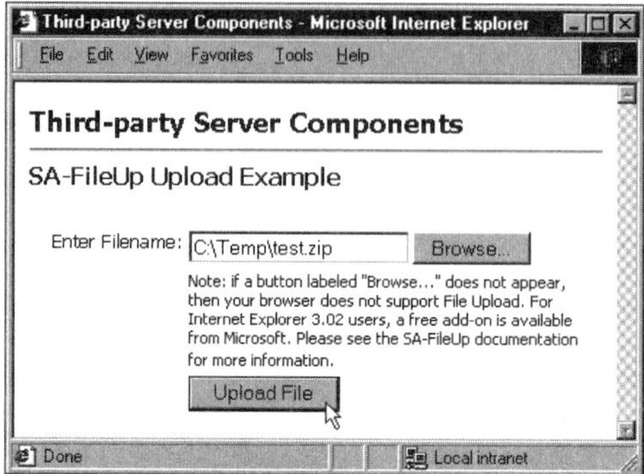

When the user submits the form, the contents are posted to the server and an ASP page there creates an instance of the component and starts the upload process. Afterwards, the component returns a series of values that describe the file that was uploaded:

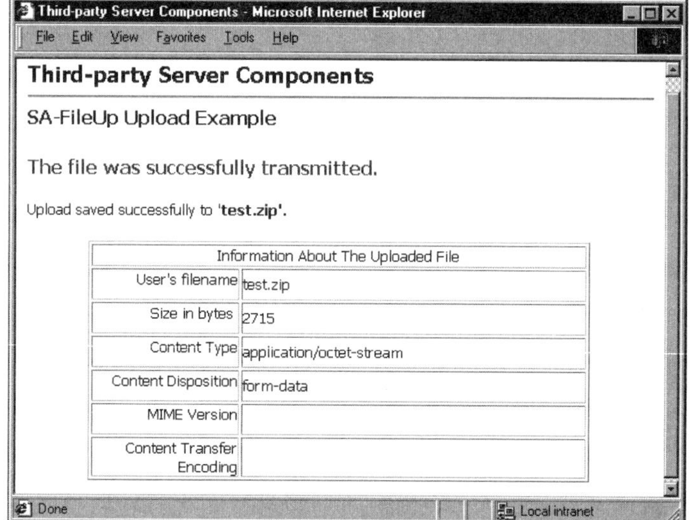

SA-FileUp fetches the file and stores it temporarily on the server, where it can be saved as a normal disk file or placed in a database as binary data. You can also control the upload process with ASP, limiting the size of the upload or even discarding it. And you can change the name and location of the uploaded file dynamically.

The RegEx Registry Access Component

One of the sample components that Microsoft provided with IIS 4.0 was capable of accessing the system Registry on the server. This is useful for checking things like which version of a particular item of software is installed, or various parameters being used by IIS or the operating system.

This component has disappeared from IIS 5.0 but there are other commercial versions available if you need this functionality. One of them is **RegEx**, which provides access to any part of the local machine's Registry, providing that the current user has sufficient permissions. Remember that in an ASP page that is accessed anonymously, the current user is the IUSR_*machinename* account.

The RegEx Component Members

The RegEx component provides four methods to read and write Registry values, and one method to access the internal component version information. Full information and documentation is provided with the component, an evaluation version of which can be downloaded from `http://www.stonebroom.com/`. The example pages that come with it are included in the samples we provide for this book, though you'll need to download the component yourself:

Method	Description
`GetRegValue` (*RegistryHive*, *SubKeyString*)	Returns the 'Default' value of a given sub-key from the Registry, or an empty string if the value cannot be accessed
`SetRegValue` (*RegistryHive*, *SubKeyString*, *NewValue*)	Creates or updates the 'Default' value within the specified sub-key, setting the data-type to `REG_SZ` (String). Returns `True` if the update is successful, or `False` otherwise.
`GetRegValueEx` (*RegistryHive*, *SubKeyString*, *ValueName*, *ValueType*)	Returns a named value from the specified sub-key, updating the variable specified in the last parameter of the method with the data-type of the returned value. Returns an empty string, and `REG_ERROR` as the data-type, if the value cannot be accessed.
`SetRegValueEx` (*RegistryHive*, *SubKeyString*, *ValueName*, *NewValue*, *ValueType*)	Creates or updates a named value within the specified sub-key, setting the data-type to that specified in the last parameter of the method. Returns `True` if the update is successful, or `False` otherwise.
`GetInternalVersionNumber()`	Returns the internal version number of the component. If it is an evaluation version, the return value will contain this information as well.

Using the RegEx Component

The RegEx component is supplied with an example application written in Visual Basic, which allows you to experiment with the methods that it exposes. This application uses the RegEx component to allow you to read and write values to any part of the system Registry, in any of the supported data types or as the default `String`-type values. A warning is displayed before any updates are made, to prevent accidental changes.

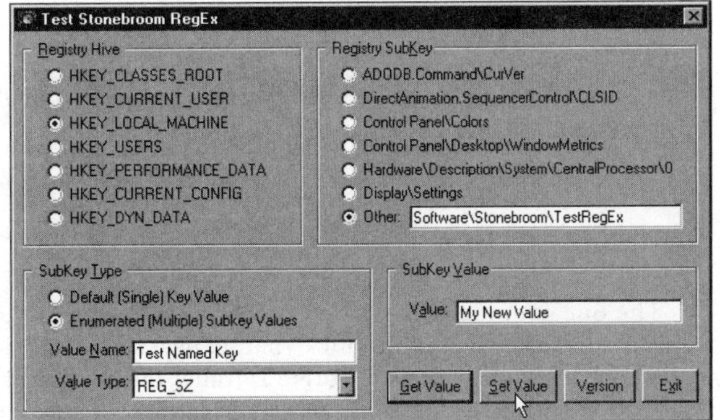

There is also a simple ASP example that displays some values from the Web server's Registry, and allows you to read and set a 'test' sub-key as well. Again, this page can be modified and used without limitation in your own applications. Here's the result when run on IIS4 on NT4:

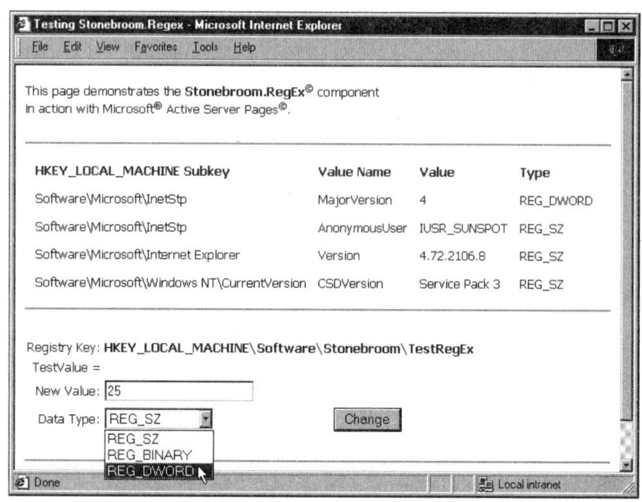

Remember that changing values in the Registry can prevent your system from running properly. You should always back up the Registry files before editing the contents.

Summary

In this chapter, we've looked at how ASP can take advantage of a whole range of server components to add extra features that aren't otherwise available. We also considered the difference between server components and the other types of objects that we use in ASP, such as the intrinsic ASP objects and the objects in the scripting runtime library.

As well as looking at the installable components that are provided with ASP 3.0 and IIS 5.0, we showed you three commercial components that provide regularly-required features. We also listed many popular components that you can download from the Web, some of which have free or shareware/evaluation versions available.

So, in this chapter we saw:

- How **server components** differ from other types of objects that we use in ASP
- A recap of how we instantiate objects, with particular reference to server components
- The installable components that are provided with ASP 3.0 and IIS, such as the **Ad Rotator**, **Content Linking**, **Page Counter** and **Tools** components
- Some of the third-party components that are available

The one component we haven't mentioned so far, however, is probably the most important. It's likely that a major requirement for dynamic pages on your site is to interface with data in databases or data stores, especially on a corporate Intranet rather than the Internet as a whole. We've devoted a whole section to just to this topic. However, before we move on to that, we'll look at one other basic topic – error handling and debugging.

7

Debugging and Error Handling

Having now covered all the basic techniques that you'll need to get started using ASP, we have one other topic to look at in this section of the book. What do you do when it all goes wrong? You know what it's like. That carefully scripted ASP page just curls up and dies, and all you get is some useless advice about clicking the Refresh button or contacting the Webmaster of the site to tell them that their page isn't working properly.

This chapter is intended to act as a help zone as well as a source of useful information. It may also be a way of preventing the need for a trip to the supermarket to buy hair-restoring products. We'll be looking in detail at how errors can arise in our scripts and pages, the different types of error that can occur, and what actually causes them. More important, we'll look at how we can prevent errors where possible, or handle them gracefully if we can't prevent them.

And then, in the section that you'll perhaps turn to first, we'll examine techniques for debugging our pages – i.e. how we find and cure errors without spending hours barking up the wrong tree and going round in circles at the same time. By the time you get to the end of this chapter, there'll be no more loud and circulatory canine activity in your IT department.

So, this chapter covers:

- The different types of errors that can occur
- How we can prevent many kinds of errors from arising
- How we can handle errors gracefully if we can't prevent them from happening
- How we go about finding and fixing script errors and other types of errors
- How we use custom error pages to get information about errors
- How we can record errors that occur to monitor our site
- Creating a custom error page and an error log file
- Provide references for on-line help

One topic that we won't be covering in this chapter is how we handle the special kinds of errors that can arise when we use ActiveX Data Objects (ADO) to access data sources from within our pages. Like many components, this implements its own error handling system, and we'll be looking at this in depth in Chapter 8. In the meantime, in this chapter, we'll start off with a look at the different types of errors that can occur–so that you can recognize them and take the appropriate action.

Different Kinds of Errors

There's a rumor going round that, deep in the darkest rain forests of Africa, work a group of programmers who never make mistakes in their code. You have to feel sorry for them, because they have never enjoyed the pleasures of having to debug a recalcitrant application that just refuses to work properly. Let's face it, debugging code is a real fun-filled activity, which tests your powers of observation and lateral thinking. So it's just a good thing that most of us 'real-world' programmers get to experience it regularly.

Of course, some would say that debugging is more about luck than judgement. OK, so the time it takes to debug a section of faulty code does depend, to some extent, on luck. It you start looking in the right place first off, you're more likely to fix the problem quickly.

But this isn't the way that debugging should be. In theory, when something fails to work, we don our sleuth's cap (the Sherlock Holmes deerstalker and pipe are optional) and track the bug down in a logical and ordered way. As a wise and experienced programmer, this is always the way you approach debugging. Only amateurs start randomly changing values in the code and adding `Response.Write` statements all over the place (kicking the server also seems to help).

However, to be able to logically track down errors in our code, we have to know some of the basics about how they can arise. More important is getting some idea of *where* they can arise, so that we can go to the right place the first time. This chapter is all about the different kinds of error that can occur, the different ways that they manifest themselves, and how we go about recording and curing them. And, just as important, we'll look at how we go about preventing them in the first place.

We'll start with a look at the different kinds of errors that can occur. If you are one of those programmers deep in the darkest rain forests of Africa you can, of course, skip straight to the next chapter.

Syntax or 'Compilation' Errors

When we first come to run some newly written code, the first type of error we usually see is the common **syntax error**. This is just what it says, an error in the syntax of the code. It's like when we use bad grammar in our writing – the recipient may not be able to figure out what we mean. And, because program compilers and interpreters (such as script engines) are far more pedantic about getting the syntax exactly right, they are more likely to complain than our mother is when she reads the letters we send her.

Syntax errors are also usually the easiest to find and cure. In most cases, the compiler or interpreter will indicate the line number and character position within that line, and often tell us what it was expecting to find there. For a simple example, if we have this code:

```
<%
Response.Write "The repayments for your loan are $" & curPayment _
          & " per " & strInterval & , due on the " & strDay & " of each "
          & strInterval & "."
%>
```

we might expect to get something like this:

```
The repayments for your loan are $124.50 per month, due on the 12th of each month.
```

What we actually get is:

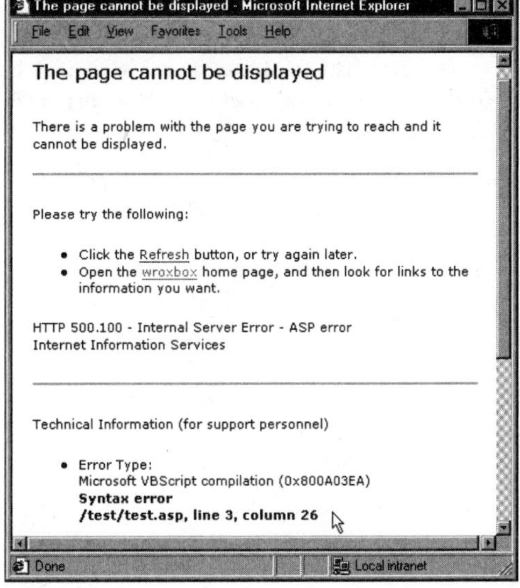

Line 3 in the file is the second line of the `Response.Write` statement. The VBScript interpreter ignores leading spaces and tabs on a line when reporting an error message, so after a bit of character counting we get to the part of the code where it's obvious that we missed out an opening double-quote character. So, we add it and run the page again. Now we get this:

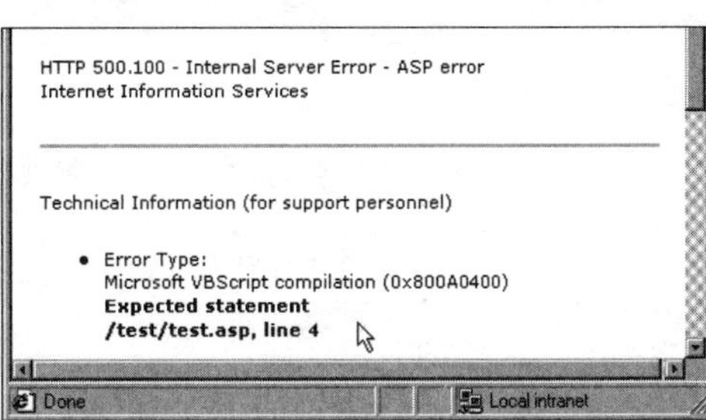

OK, so this is another easy one, even though the line where the error occurs is actually the third line not the fourth one. We left off the line-continuation character '_' from the end of the previous line. What the code should look like is:

```
<%
Response.Write "The repayments for your loan are $" & curPayment _
          & " per " & strInterval & ", due on the " & strDay & " of each " _
          & strInterval & "."
%>
```

Where Did The Error Occur?

Notice that the script interpreter simply reports where it *finds* the error, and not where the error actually is. In this case, the previous three lines are syntactically correct, and would have produced a result. It is just the fourth line that causes a problem, because it starts with an illegal character that is not part of a valid statement. The script interpreter didn't realize that we intended it to be part of the previous line.

Errors like this are common because we're usually thinking more about the text we want to output than the proper order of double-quotes, string concatenation characters ('&' in the case of VBScript), and line continuation characters.

Syntax errors that are caused by bad spelling of keyword or built-in function names, or illegal parameter lists for functions, are generally easier to spot because the error message will probably indicate the actual position of the error. For example this code is intended to write tomorrow's date into the page:

```
Response.Write DateAdd(Now(), "d", 1)
```

What we actually get is:

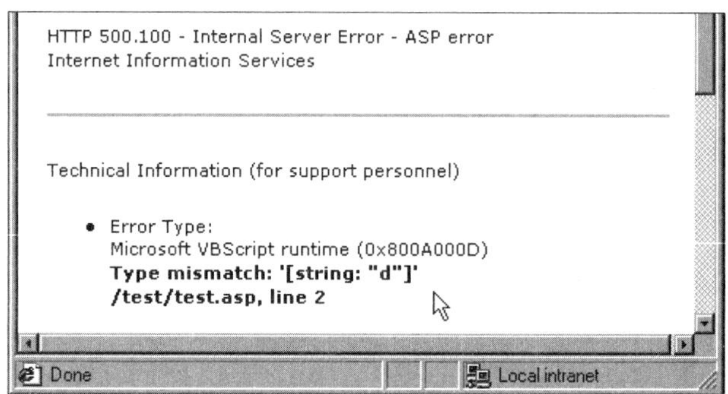

This is because the syntax of the `DateAdd` function is:

DateAdd (*interval_string, interval_number, start_date*)

So, what we should have written is:

```
Response.Write DateAdd("d", 1, Now())
```

The script interpreter has detected that we provided a `String`-type value for the second parameter when the `DateAdd` function expects an `Integer` data-type.

Code Structure and Script Constructs

Another regular source of syntax errors, and one that can sometimes prove hard to find, arises when we are building pages that use nested or complex script constructs, such as `If Then..Else..End If` or `Do While..Loop`. For example this code:

```
<%
If Len(Request.Form("cmdSet")) Then
  strCounterName = Request.Form("lstSet")
```

```
    strNewValue = Request.Form("txtSet")
    If IsNumeric(strNewValue) Then
      intNewValue = CInt(strNewValue)
      objCounters.Set strCounterName, intNewValue
      Response.Write "Set counter " & strCounterName & " to " & strNewValue
    Else
      Response.Write strNewValue & " is not a valid number"
      If Len(Request.Form("cmdRemove")) Then
        strCounterName = Request.Form("lstRemove")
        objCounters.Remove strCounterName
        Response.Write "Removed counter " & strCounterName
    End If
  End If
  %>
```

produces the error shown in the next screenshot:

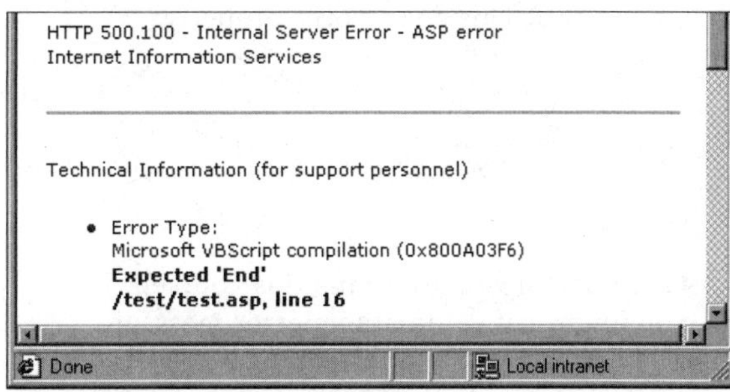

Why would we want to put an End statement in our page? However, quickly looking at the code shown earlier reveals that we missed out an End If, not an End. There should be another one at the end of the code:

```
        ...
        Response.Write "Removed counter " & strCounterName
      End If
    End If
  End If
  %>
```

In this case, it's quite easy to find because we have indented the code and the 'gap' soon catches the eye, especially as the error message is referring (roughly) to the place where it's missing. However, this is only because our code ends there. If we had another 40 lines of code within the same set of <%..%> delimiters, the error message would probably still point to the last line (line 56). And if other script constructs within the new code upset the nesting even more, the error may be identified at that position instead.

What About JScript?

If you aren't a JavaScript expert, and you really want to experience some syntax errors, switch over from VBScript to JScript. JScript is far less tolerant of lazy code writing than VBScript, and compounds the difficulties by being case sensitive for both keywords and variable names. So, this code:

```
<%
var datToday = new Date();
Response.Write(datToday.GetMonth());
%>
```

produces the familiar 'Object doesn't support this property or method' error:

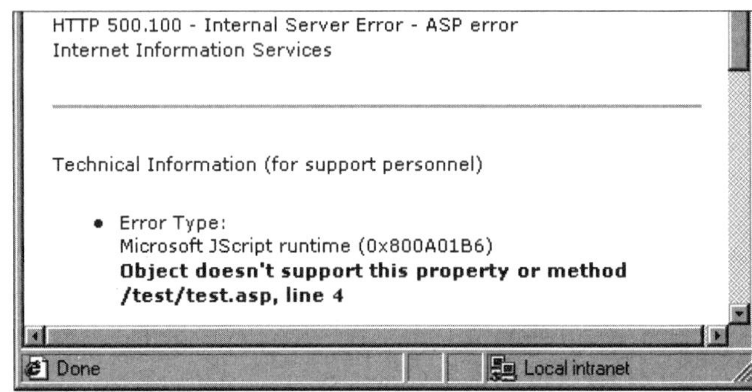
HTTP 500.100 - Internal Server Error - ASP error
Internet Information Services

Technical Information (for support personnel)

- Error Type:
Microsoft JScript runtime (0x800A01B6)
Object doesn't support this property or method
/test/test.asp, line 4

Done
Local intranet

The reason is simply that the JScript function to return the current month number is `getMonth`, not `GetMonth`. This code works properly:

```
<%
var datToday = new Date();
Response.Write(datToday.getMonth());
%>
```

Of course, if you are trying this yourself, you might not get the same error message. The first time we ran this code, we got the error shown in the next screenshot instead:

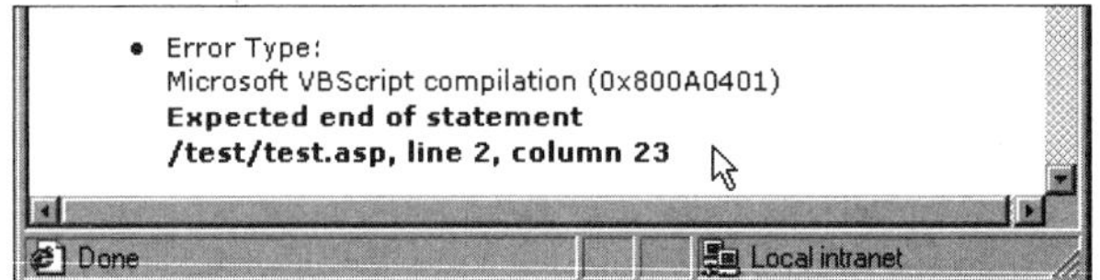
- Error Type:
Microsoft VBScript compilation (0x800A0401)
Expected end of statement
/test/test.asp, line 2, column 23

Done
Local intranet

What's wrong with line 2? Well, nothing if we were using the JScript interpreter. However, another look at the error message reveals all. This is a VBScript compilation (or syntax) error. The VBScript interpreter is parsing our JScript code, so it's no wonder we get strange error messages. We might as well be writing that letter home to our mother in Portuguese (NB: if your mother is Portuguese then substitute another language).

Mind Your Language

The reason why IIS seems to be having a bad-hair day is simply that we forgot to add the `@LANGUAGE` directive at the top of the page. The default (if we don't change it in the Registry or using Internet Services Manager) is VBScript, so the VBScript engine is used to execute code that has no `@LANGUAGE` directive. A good reason to always use one, even if we are using the default language set up for our server. If we move the pages to another server, where the default language is different, this is the kind of result we can expect.

While we haven't covered all the possible kinds of syntax error that you might come across, you should have gathered how they can arise, and how the error message isn't always as accurate as you might like. It would be nice if ASP sent us a neat display of the page showing the error, and giving a full and accurate description of it, and even asking if we want it fixed automatically.

In fact there is an application called the Microsoft Script Debugger that tries to do some of these things. We'll look at it later in this chapter, and also summarize some of the important points for avoiding syntax errors. In the meantime, we'll move on to look at the second main type of error that can arise in our pages.

Semantic or 'Runtime' Errors

Syntax errors can be annoying to find and fix, but for some real excitement in programming we need to hit the other type of error. **Semantic errors**, or **runtime errors** as they are often called, only manifest themselves when we actually execute the code in a script or other program. They identify errors in the semantics of the code – in other words errors that arise when perfectly valid code, which the compiler or interpreter has parsed and accepted, is executed. The term 'runtime error' is often used to refer to the *result* of a semantic error, in other words the error is in the semantics of the code, but it only becomes visible when the code is run.

The distinction comes from the fact that all program compilers or interpreters have to build an internal representation of the code before they can process it. This involves matching the start and end of each construct to figure out what code each one contains, and then parsing each statement to see how it should be executed. For example, if we have an `If Then..Else..End If` construct in our code, the first pass that the interpreter or compiler makes through the code collects details of which statements are within the `'Then'` part, and which are in the '`Else`' part. It has to do this to be able to tell where to go after testing the condition in the `'If'` part of the construct.

> *The only real difference between a **compiler** (such as is found in programming languages like Visual Basic and C++) and an **interpreter** (such as is used in the scripting languages like VBScript and JScript) is that a compiler doesn't attempt to execute the code. Instead, during a second pass through the source, it builds up the binary instructions or symbolic code that will be executed at runtime and writes them to a file such as an `.exe` or `.dll` file. An interpreter doesn't create a file containing the code, but simply executes each line during this phase.*

Errors that Halt Execution

So, if our code contains a semantic error we will usually get an indication of this at runtime. If we're lucky, the code will halt when the error occurs, making it easy to figure out where the error lies. For example this code declares an array that can hold six elements:

```
<%
Dim arrValues(5)   'to hold six elements, indexed from 0 to 5
arrValues(6) = "Whoops, got an error"
%>
```

If we try to read or set the value of the element with the index `6`, we get a runtime error:

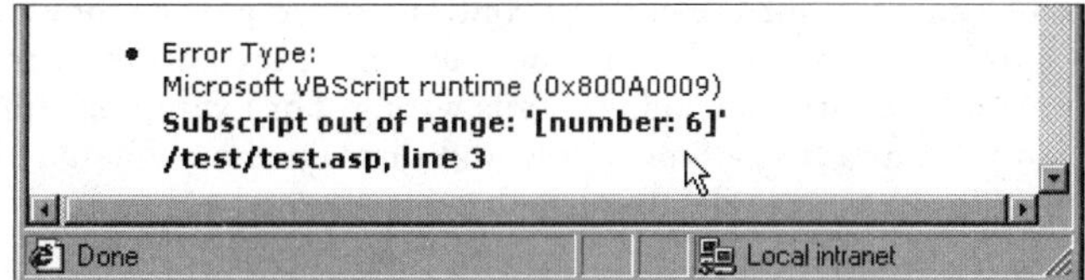

Notice that the error type here is a **runtime** (i.e. semantic) **error**, and not a **compilation** (i.e. syntax) **error**. Helpfully, the error message shows the line number and the error description, making it easy to see what went wrong. Again, this is a simple example but in more complex code it could arise where we are iterating through some values and adding them to an array:

```
<%
Dim arrValues(5)                    'to hold six elements
For intLoop = 0 To intListCount     'the number of items in some list
  arrValues(intLoop) = Request.Form("SelectedItems")(intListCount)
Next
%>
```

In this case, it might be that we've got too many items in the list, or not enough indexes in the array. Depending on the requirements of the code, you should know which of these is wrong and be able to fix it either by increasing the size of the array:

```
<%
Dim arrValues(10)                   'to hold eleven elements
For intLoop = 0 To intListCount     'the number of items in some list
  arrValues(intLoop) = Request.Form("SelectedItems")(intListCount)
Next
%>
```

or by stopping the iteration when the required number of entries have been collected from the list:

```
<%
Dim arrValues(5)                    'to hold six elements
intArrayMax = intListCount
If intArrayMax > 5 Then intArrayMax = 5
For intLoop = 0 To intArrayMax      'only add the first six items
  arrValues(intLoop) = Request.Form("SelectedItems")(intListCount)
Next
%>
```

Many other runtime errors can halt execution of the page, such as a failure to instantiate some component or object because we got the `ProgID` wrong, or because the component isn't properly installed. In these cases the result is usually the error message 'ActiveX Cannot Create Object', followed by the line number of the `Server.CreateObject` method call.

Errors that Produce the Wrong Result

We said that we might be lucky and get a runtime error that halts the execution of our code. The alternative is for the code to continue to execute as though nothing has happened, but instead produce the wrong result. These are often the hardest errors to find and solve, because we may not even be aware that something is wrong. For example, suppose we have a page that takes a user's date of birth as a `Date`-type value, and displays the elements of the date separately (maybe we intend adding them to a database as three individual entries):

```
<%
'get the value from the Request and display it
datBirthdate = Request.Form("BirthDate")
Response.Write "The value you entered is: " & datBirthdate & "<P>"

'get the individual date elements
intDay = Day(datBirthdate)
intMonth = Month(datBirthdate)
intYear = Year(datBirthdate)
```

```
'and display them
Response.Write "Day: " & CStr(intDay) & "<BR>"
Response.Write "Month: " & CStr(intMonth) & "<BR>"
Response.Write "Year: " & CStr(intYear) & "<BR>"
%>
```

Here's the result, displayed in the US date-style of *month/day/year*, and it all seems fine:

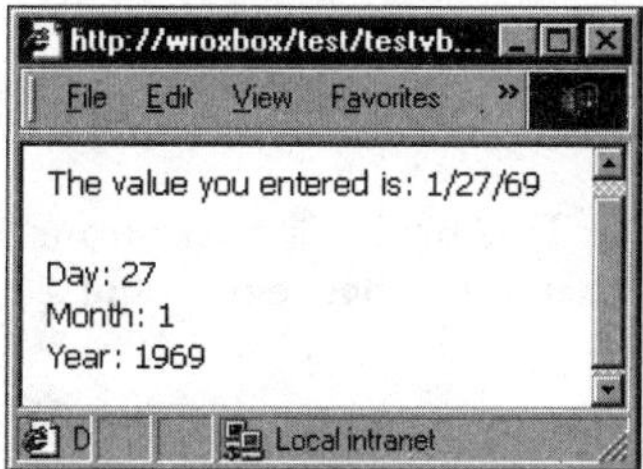

However if the user enters an invalid date, or leaves the text box on the form empty, we get a runtime error:

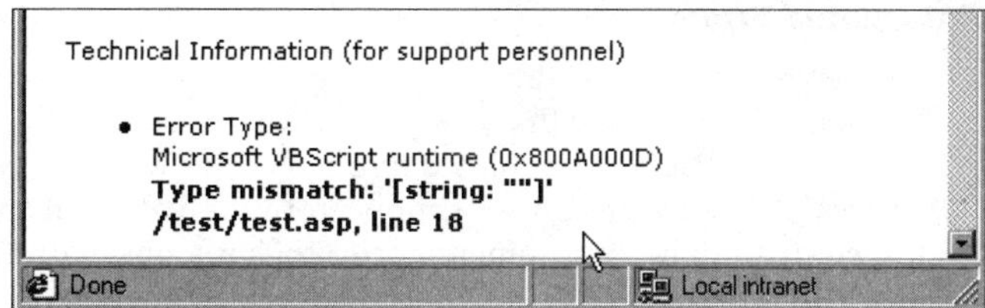

Not a JScript Expert?

This isn't a big problem as far as finding the error goes, because we can quickly see why it occurred. And the fact that it stopped our page from executing helps to track it down. However, less intuitive errors can occur. For an example, we've re-written the code in JScript. Not being a JScript expert, we've made a couple of minor errors:

```
<%
// get the value from the Request and display it
var datBirthdate = new Date(Request.Form("BirthDate"));
Response.Write("The value you entered is: " + datBirthdate + "<P>");

// get the individual date elements
intDay = datBirthdate.getDay();
intMonth = datBirthdate.getMonth();
intYear = datBirthdate.getYear();

// and display them
Response.Write("Day: " + intDay.toString() + "<BR>");
Response.Write("Month: " + intMonth.toString() + "<BR>");
Response.Write("Year: " + intYear.toString() + "<BR>");
%>
```

Here's the result. You can immediately see that something is wrong even though our code didn't stop with a runtime error. Just when is month zero?

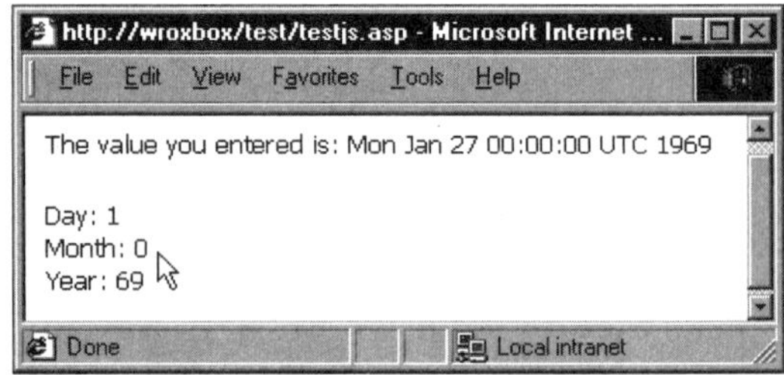

This problem arises from the fact that JScript returns the result of the `getMonth` function as a number between `0` and `11`, so we need to add one to get the correct answer:

```
intMonth = datBirthdate.getMonth() + 1;
```

Propagated Errors

This error would probably be quite obvious, even if we didn't put the original value in the page to compare the results with. However, if we are interfacing with a database system and had not seen the result as it's displayed here, we might wonder why our code was failing to update the database correctly. Even worse, if we simply store the values in the database as integer numbers, the error may not come to light until someone tries to run a query on the data.

At this point, the discovery that around one twelfth of our employees were born in month zero will probably raise a few eyebrows, and cause a few problems. And remember that it's not just all those January children that have incorrect information stored in the database, it's every employee. Now, tracking down the error could be a huge task–especially if many different applications add and modify records in the database. Never mind finding which code line the error occurred in, we've got to figure out which *application* it occurred in first.

Grasp the Day

What might not be so obvious in the code above is that we've also got the wrong *day* number. No matter what the user enters for the date, our code will obstinately only ever give values between `0` and `6` for the 'day'. The reason for this is down to assumptions made during coding, especially when converting from VBScript to JScript. In JScript, the `getDay` function returns the day of the week, not the day of the month as you might expect. It is the JScript equivalent of the VBScript `Weekday` function. The return values from `getDay` are zero for Sunday through to six for Saturday.

> *Just to make life interesting, the VBScript `Weekday` function returns `1` for Sunday through to `7` for Saturday!*

Instead, we need the `getDate` function in JScript to get the day of the month. So the correct code is:

```
...
// get the individual date elements
intDay = datBirthdate.getDate();
intMonth = datBirthdate.getMonth() + 1;
intYear = datBirthdate.getYear();
...
```

And this gives the result we want:

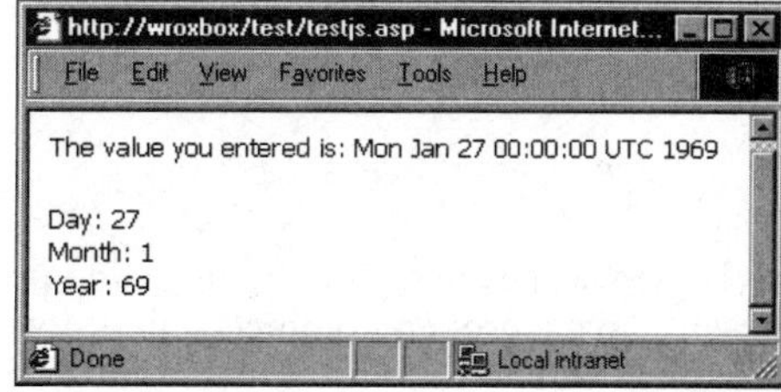

Different Kinds of Runtime Errors

The previous section of this chapter has shown you some of the issues involved in understanding how errors can arise, and some ideas on where to look for them and how to fix them. More importantly, you should now grasp the different kinds of errors that can occur, and how to differentiate between them. Remember that debugging is a lot easier if you know where to look, and what to look for. Towards the end of this chapter we'll also be looking at how to trap errors when they do occur, and even prevent them in the first place, where possible.

However, before we do that, we'll look a bit deeper into the different kinds of runtime or semantic errors that you are sure to come across at some stage. We've divided this section up into:

- Logical errors
- Script runtime errors
- ASP and SSI runtime errors
- Client-side script errors

Logical Errors

Logical errors are often the hardest to track down in our scripts, because they have a tendency to produce the wrong result without stopping the page from executing with a runtime error. It's generally only when some value goes 'out-of-bounds', as we saw with the array example earlier on, that a runtime error is raised.

In the context of errors and debugging, however, an **algorithm** doesn't mean the same as the things you learned about in school mathematics class. An algorithm in computing terms simply means a section of code that carries out a task, usually returning some result.

Numbers That Go Out Of Bounds

Typically logical errors do, however, involve numbers. This might be as in our previous example of the calculation of an array index, or it might be something else that involves a number going outside the acceptable range. For example, if we have a series of graphics named `image1.gif`, `image2.gif`, etc, we might display them with some code that chooses an image at random:

```
<%
'create a random number between 1 and 5
intRandom = CInt(Rnd() * 5) + 1
%>
<IMG SRC="<% = "image" & CStr(intRandom) & ".gif" %>">
```

This should create an `<IMG>` element in the page that specifies one of the images chosen at random, for example:

```
<IMG SRC="image3.gif">
```

However, just occasionally this code produces the filename `image6.gif`, and in this case our page will have a broken graphic symbol if we only expect to get a result between 1 and 5 inclusive. The reason is that the `CInt` function in VBScript *rounds* the value to the nearest integer. To truncate it, as we need to do in this example, we have to use the `Int` or `Fix` function instead.

Coping With Operator Precedence

Other types of logical errors involve simply getting the instructions for a calculation wrong, for example multiplying when we meant to divide. Some harder to spot errors can arise due to the execution order or **precedence** of the mathematical operators in our code, for example this code may or may not produce the correct result:

```
intResult = intValue1 * intValue2 + intValue3
```

If the values are `2`, `3` and `5` respectively, the result of this calculation is `11` because multiplication has a higher operator precedence than addition, and so is executed first. But if we intended to multiply the sum of the second two values by the first value, we would be expecting to get `16` instead. In this case, we have to use parentheses to override the default operator precedence:

```
intResult = intValue1 * (intValue2 + intValue3)
```

You'll find a precedence list for all the script operators in the VBScript 5.0 documentation under 'VBScript Basics' | 'VBScript Operators'. The JScript equivalent is found under JScript Tutorial | JScript Basics | JScript Operators. Basically, however, remember that multiplication and division come before addition and subtraction.

Managing and Formatting String Data

Taking the term in its computing sense, any construct or function that calculates a result can be thought of as an **algorithm**. For example, we might construct a string that represents a customer's name from values in a database. Without concerning ourselves here with how we extract them from the database (we'll look at this in the next section of the book), this code might do the actual string concatenation:

```
strTitle = {get from database}
strFirstName = {get from database}
strMiddleInitial = {get from database}
strLastName = {get from database}
strOther = {get from database}

strPrint = strTitle & ". " & strFirstName & " " & strMiddleInitial _
       & ". " & strLastName & " " & strOther
```

Hopefully, we'll get something like:

```
Ms. Janet C. Clarke MBNA.BSc.MechEng.
```

But not everyone is as clever as Janet is, or had parents that could think of a suitable middle name. And many people might not have a title specified, so we might get just:

```
. Alex . Homer
```

This certainly isn't a critical error in that it will cause our script to fail, or produce a runtime error. However, I might not be very impressed by a company that addressed me in this way. Instead, the code can check for the presence of each element of the name before adding it to the output string:

```
...
strPrint =""
If Len(strTitle) Then strPrint = strPrint & strTitle & ". "
If Len(strFirstName) Then strPrint = strPrint & strFirstName & " "
If Len(strMiddleInitial) Then strPrint = strPrint & strMiddleInitial & ". "
If Len(strLastName) Then strPrint = strPrint & strLastName
If Len(strOther) Then strPrint = " " & strOther
```

This ensures that spaces and delimiters (i.e. periods) are only added where there is a value for that part of the name. OK, so if we only had a value for the `strOther` string, and none of the others, we'd get a space at the start. However it's probably a highly unlikely scenario. And anyway – if we were feeling that paranoid – we could prevent it by only adding the 'other' part if we had a last name:

```
...
strPrint =""
If Len(strTitle) Then strPrint = strPrint & strTitle & ". "
If Len(strFirstName) Then strPrint = strPrint & strFirstName & " "
If Len(strMiddleInitial) Then strPrint = strPrint & strMiddleInitial & ". "
If Len(strLastName) Then
  strPrint = strPrint & strLastName
  If Len(strOther) Then strPrint = " " & strOther
End If
```

Now the worst case would be an empty string as the result, and we can always test for this possibility and abort the printing altogether:

```
...
If Len(strPrint) = 0 Then
  Response.Clear
  Response.End
End If
```

Script Runtime Errors

Script runtime errors usually arise when we try and use a function that doesn't exist, or break one of the rules of the scripting language we are using. Many errors will be syntax errors (as we discussed earlier in the chapter), but many can arise from relying on things to be available that aren't, or using values that are incompatible with the parameters for a function.

For example, we might have a form that collects a date from the user and stores it in a database or processes it in some other way. We want to make sure it is a valid date, so we use the `CDate` function before inserting it into our database:

```
<%
strData = Request.Form("TheDate")
datDate = CDate(strDate)
...
```

If the user makes a mistake filling in the form, our code produces a scripting error:

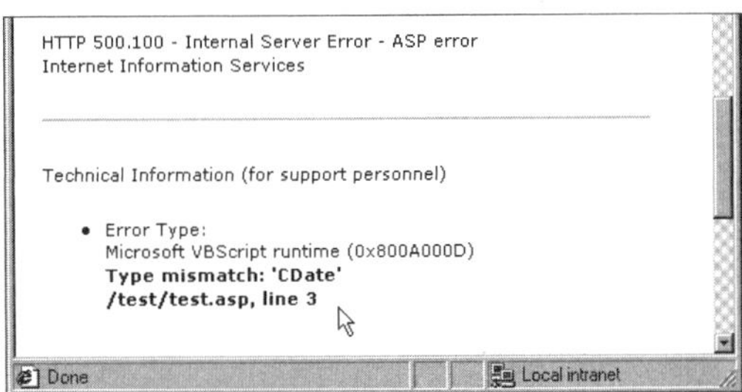

Looking at the error message, we can see that the error has been generated by the 'VBScript runtime' – the scripting engine that is executing the code. The error number is displayed in hexadecimal, and consists of (as we saw in Chapter 4) the VBScript error number with the hex value `0x800A0000` added to it. In this case, the VBScript error number is hex `0xD`, or `13` in real money.

> *The error numbers returned by most Microsoft technologies, including ASP, always consist of an 8-character hexadecimal status message. The first character is always `8`, and indicates that this status message is a **severe error** message. This is followed by two zeros, and then the service code. For VBScript and JScript errors, the service code is always "A". Finally, the last four characters are the error number in hexadecimal.*

If you check the VBScript documentation, you'll find that error `13` corresponds to the error "Type Mismatch". Of course, we already know this because the error description is also shown in the ASP error page. However, as you'll see when we look at error handling techniques later on in this chapter, being able to get the error number is often useful.

Notice also in the previous screenshot that, as in all our other error pages in this chapter so far, the server's response to the error is the HTTP status code 500.100, described as 'Internal Server Error'. In Chapter 4, when we examined the way that ASP custom error pages work, we discovered that this error is used to load the error page that we see in these screenshots. Later in this chapter we'll see how we can implement a better way of handling these errors in our own pages.

ASP and Server Side Include (SSI) Runtime Errors

Scripting errors are raised by the particular scripting engine we are using. However, the ASP DLL and the SSI DLL can also raise errors which are not connected with the scripting engine we are using. A typical SSI example is when we get the path or name wrong for the file in a `#include` directive:

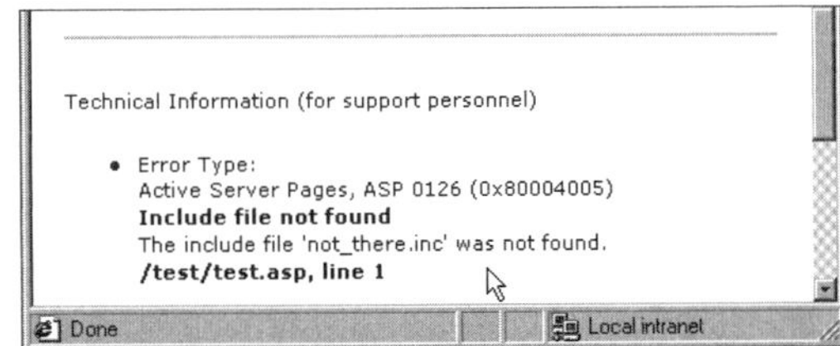

In this case, the error is raised by the SSI DLL, and not by the scripting engine or ASP. You can see that the error type is 'Active Server Pages', and the ASP internal error code is 'ASP 0126'. However, the error number is 4005 in this case, referring to a specific error defined for the Server-Side Include DLL, `ssinc.dll`.

ASP Error Codes Summary

For errors that involve a failure within the ASP DLL, the following are the common error codes that are returned. These are the codes you'll find in the `ASPCode` property of the ASPError object when an error of this type occurs:

Error Code	Error Message and Extended Information
`ASP 0100`	Out of memory. (Unable to allocate the required memory.)
`ASP 0101`	Unexpected error. (The function returned *exception_name.*)
`ASP 0102`	Expecting string input.
`ASP 0103`	Expecting numeric input.
`ASP 0104`	Operation not allowed.
`ASP 0105`	Index out of range. (An array index is out of range.)
`ASP 0106`	Type Mismatch. (A data type was encountered that cannot be handled.)
`ASP 0107`	Stack Overflow. (The quantity of data being processed is above the permitted limit.)
`ASP 0115`	Unexpected error. (A trappable error *exception_name* occurred in an external object. The script cannot continue running.)
`ASP 0177`	Server.CreateObject Failed. (Invalid ProgID.)
`ASP 0190`	Unexpected error. (A trappable error occurred while releasing an external object.)
`ASP 0191`	Unexpected error. (A trappable error occurred in the `OnStartPage` method of an external object.)
`ASP 0192`	Unexpected error. (A trappable error occurred in the `OnEndPage` method of an external object.)
`ASP 0193`	OnStartPage Failed. (An error occurred in the `OnStartPage` method of an external object.)
`ASP 0194`	OnEndPage Failed. (An error occurred in the `OnEndPage` method of an external object.)
`ASP 0240`	Script Engine Exception. (A script engine threw exception *exception_name* in *object_name* from *object_name.*
`ASP 0241`	CreateObject Exception. (The `CreateObject` of *object_name* caused exception *exception_name.*)
`ASP 0242`	Query OnStartPage Interface Exception. (The querying object *object_name*'s `OnStartPage` or `OnEndPage` method caused exception *exception_name.*

ASP errors generally arise only when there is a problem in a component or with the server itself. The most common are the `ASP 0177` error when using `Server.CreateObject`, and the dreaded `ASP 0115` error that generally indicates an error has occurred within the component's code. However, stopping and starting the Web service, or rebooting the server, will sometimes cure the latter. The former is generally caused by failure to install a component properly, or an error in the **ProgID** string that we've specified.

ASP and SSI errors are rare compared to the more common scripting errors, and there is little we can do to prevent them. They also nearly always result in the page execution being halted, so the problem tends to be immediately obvious.

Client-side Script Errors

So far, we've looked at errors from an ASP-centric perspective. This is to be expected because, after all, this is a book about ASP. However, ASP is often used to create pages that contain client-side script as well. As long as the `<SCRIPT>` elements that enclose the client-side code don't have the `RUNAT="SERVER"` attribute, ASP will ignore them and they will appear unchanged in the page that's sent to the client.

So, if we open an ASP page and get a browser error dialog displayed, it's no good starting to search our ASP code for errors. The browser doesn't see the ASP code, and so can't flag any errors. If a dialog appears on the client, it must be an error in the client-side code.

Syntax Errors

As in our ASP scripts, a syntax error in the client-side code we put into pages that we send to the browser will show up when the script is loaded on the client. Usually, this results in the page execution being halted, though the contents of the page will still load as normal (unless they are being loaded dynamically by the client-side script code). However, the user will see a dialog containing the error details, or a status bar message indicating that the page contains an error.

Modern browsers tend to hide the details of scripting errors in pages, by only displaying a small error icon in the status bar. In Internet Explorer 4 and 5, the 'normal' error dialog can be enabled in the Internet Options dialog, in the Advanced page:

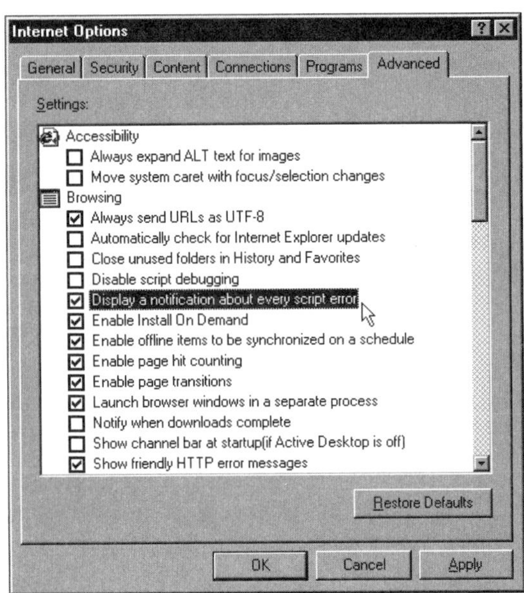

Fixing client-side errors in script code is just like fixing them server-side, and is usually easier because we often load the page directly from the server's directories just by double-clicking on it. We generally don't need to access the page via the Web server and HTTP to see the results in the browser. The only exception to this is if some server interaction is being done by the client side script, such as data-binding using RDS or loading resources such as images or XML documents dynamically with client-side code.

Runtime or Semantic Errors

As well as the usual possibility of syntax errors in client-side scripts, we often encounter runtime or semantic errors. In fact, client-side, these are often more prevalent, because we don't have the same kind of control over our script's environment as we do server-side. We can't be sure exactly what the user has running on their machine – we really only get an approximate indication on our server from things like the Browser Capabilities component.

So, it's far more likely that scripts which use client-side objects, or version-specific scripting languages and features, will fail. Otherwise, however, handling client-side errors is much the same as handling server-side ones.

Client-side Code Created on the Server

The one particular exception to the 'client-side dialog-box versus ASP error page' rule about where an error occurs is when we use ASP code running on our server to create the client-side code dynamically. For example, we might want to calculate a value in ASP and then pass it on to the script code running on the client. Probably the easiest way to do this is to insert it into the script code as a variable:

```
<%
'get the name of our server from the ServerVariables collection
strServerNameInASP = Request.ServerVariables("SERVER_NAME")
%>

<SCRIPT LANGUAGE="JScript" RUNAT="CLIENT">
<!-- hide code from older browsers
var strServerName = "<% = strServerNameInASP %>";
...
alert('Server name is: ' + strServerName);
...
// stop hiding code -->
</SCRIPT>
```

On the client, after ASP has weaved its magic with this page, all we'll get is:

```
<SCRIPT LANGUAGE="JScript" RUNAT="CLIENT">
<!-- hide code from older browsers
var strServerName = "WROXBOX";
...
alert('Server name is: + strServerName);
...
// stop hiding code -->
</SCRIPT>
```

> *We can omit the* `RUNAT="CLIENT"` *attribute, but we added it to make it clear, when looking at the ASP page, where the code will be executed.*

So, if we have a situation where we want to fill a client-side array with values from, say, a server-side database, we might use:

```
<SCRIPT LANGUAGE="JScript" RUNAT="CLIENT">
<!-- hide code from older browsers
var arrBooks = new Array(10)  // highest available index will be 9

<% 'start of ASP processing
intIndex = 0
Do While { not at the end of some recordset }
   strTitle = { get title from database record }
   Response.Write "arrBooks[" & CInt(intIndex) & "] = '" _
                 & strTitle & "';" & vbCrlf
   intIndex = intIndex + 1
   { move to next record in database }
Loop
%>
...
do something here on the client with the array of book titles
...
// stop hiding code -->
</SCRIPT>
```

This server-side ASP code will produce client-side script code that creates an array of book titles when it is executed on the client. However, it could also produce a client-side scripting error in a browser error dialog. The reason is that the array named `arrBooks` (created by the JavaScript code when it runs on the client) can only accept nine book titles, but the server-side code could easily produce more than this – depending on how many records are in the source database. What we could end up sending to the client is:

```
<SCRIPT LANGUAGE="JScript" RUNAT="CLIENT">
<!-- hide code from older browsers
var arrBooks = new Array(10)  // highest available index will be 9
arrBooks[0] = 'Instant JavaScript';
arrBooks[1] = 'Professional ASP 3.0 Programming';
arrBooks[2] = 'ADO 2.5 Programmers Reference';
...
etc
...
arrBooks[9] = 'ASP Techniques for Webmasters';
arrBooks[10] = 'ASP Programmers Reference'; // <- client-side error occurs here
arrBooks[11] = 'ADSI CDO Programming';
arrBooks[12] = 'Professional MTS and MSMQ Programming';
...
do something here on the client with the array of book titles
...
// stop hiding code -->
</SCRIPT>
```

Whether this is actually a server-side error or a client-side error is open to discussion. The important thing is that the page won't work until we fix it, either by increasing the size of the array or controlling the number of records we accept from the database.

Preventing Errors

Having seen some of the different types of errors that can occur, and gotten a feel for where to look for them, we'll move on to consider the ways that we can avoid introducing them into our code in the first place. While we can't promise to elevate your code writing to the level of zero errors, like those programmers rumored to be working in darkest Africa, you will find that many of the common techniques summarized here can help to reduce the bug count.

Good Coding Practice

Avoiding errors in our code is almost exclusively connected with good coding practice. There are lots of things we can do to reduce the likelihood of introducing errors into our pages. Probably no programmer adopts all the techniques listed here, although some take certain techniques to extremes – even to the extent that they introduce more errors by being too pedantic or concentrating too hard on one particular topic.

The things we're going to consider here are:

- Formatting and indenting code
- Being 'Explicit' about your declarations
- Convert your variables to the appropriate data types
- Using a good variable naming convention
- Encapsulating your script
- Being aware of potential error situations
- And finally, testing it!

Formatting and Indenting Code

Many VBScript programmers are lazy about the way they format the code they write. While this doesn't stop it from working, it can make it extremely difficult to see where an error is coming from. For example, in the code we looked at earlier, where there was an `End If` missing, it was quite obvious where it should have been because of the indenting of the nested constructs:

```
            objCounters.Remove strCounterName
            Response.Write "Removed counter " & strCounterName
         <--- missing 'End If' should be here
      End If
   End If
   %>
```

If your code looks like this, you won't find it easy to spot this error – or most other kinds of errors (and, yes, we have seen code that looks like this):

```
<% if Len( Request.Form("cmdSet")) then
strCounterName=Request.Form("lstSet" )
StrNewValue=Request.Form ("txtSet")
if isnumeric (strnewvalue)   then
intNewValue =cint(strnewValue)
  objCounters.Set strCounterName, intNewValue
Response.write   "Set counter "   & strCounterName &" to "& strNewValue

else
Response.write  strNEWVALUE  &" is not a valid number"
  If Len ( Request.Form ("cmdRemove")) then
strCounterName = Request.Form("lstRemove")

objCounters.Remove strCounterName
Response.write  "Removed counter "& strCounterName
end if
End IF
%>
```

Explicit Variable Declaration

VBScript supports the `Option Explicit` statement. When inserted at the beginning of a script page, it will prevent the use of variable names that have not been previously declared using the `Dim` statement (or `ReDim` for dynamic arrays). This seems to be extra effort that is not actually required, because the scripting languages allow us to create a variable on demand by simply assigning a value to it. However it can help to avoid errors, especially those hard-to-find logical errors that cause the script to produce an incorrect result.

For example we might write this code:

```
<%
'get values for calculation
strSalesTotal = Request.Form("SalesTotal")
curSalesTotal = CCur(strSalesTotal)
sngCommissionPercent = 2.5

'calculate commission payment
sngCommission = curSalesTotal * (sngComissionPercent / 100)
%>
```

As it stands, this code will execute without an error (providing that the user enters a legal value for the sales total, of course). However it will always produce a result of zero, because we misspelled the `sngCommissionPercent` variable name in the last line. The script interpreter will quite happily create a brand new variable called `sngComissionPercent`. And, as it hasn't been assigned a value, it will return zero when used in a mathematical calculation.

To prevent this kind of error, we just add the `Option Explicit` statement at the start of the code:

```
<%
Option Explicit
Dim strSalesTotal
Dim curSalesTotal
Dim sngCommissionPercent
```

```
'get values for calculation
strSalesTotal = Request.Form("SalesTotal")
curSalesTotal = CCur(strSalesTotal)
sngCommissionPercent = 2.5

'calculate commission payment
sngCommission = curSalesTotal * (sngComissionPercent / 100)
%>
```

Now the script engine will flag a syntax error when it tries to interpret the code, and indicate that the variable has not been declared:

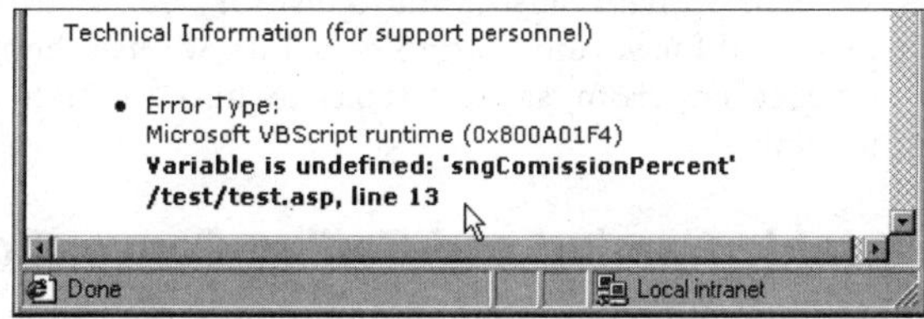

In JScript, referencing a variable that has not been declared returns "`undefined`", and so we can test for this before we attempt to use the value.

Variable DataType Conversions

Looking back at the previous code, you can see that we convert the value provided by the user into a `Currency` data type using the `CCur` function. In VBScript, there are a whole range of data-type conversion functions like this – we described them in detail back in Chapter 3:

```
blnBoolean = CBool(varVariant) 'converts to a Variant of subtype Boolean
bytByte = CByte(varVariant)    'converts to a Variant of subtype Byte
curCurrency = CCur(varVariant) 'converts to a Variant of subtype Currency
datDate = CDate(varVariant)    'converts to a Variant of subtype Date
dblDouble = CDbl(varVariant)   'converts to a Variant of subtype Double
intInteger = CInt(varVariant)  'converts to a Variant of subtype Integer
lngLong = CLng(varVariant)     'converts to a Variant of subtype Long
sngSingle = CSng(varVariant)   'converts to a Variant of subtype Single
strString = CStr(varVariant)   'converts to a Variant of subtype String
```

If a conversion cannot be accomplished, i.e. the contents of the variable are not valid for the new data type, a runtime error will occur. However if we *are* converting the value, it's likely to be because we expect it to be valid and we want to use it in our code. So detecting an invalid value is 'a good thing'.

Our earlier example could look like this if we want to treat a blank entry as zero and any other non-valid entry as a user error:

```
strSalesTotal = Request.Form("SalesTotal")
If Len(strSalesTotal) = 0 Then
   'no value entered, so assume zero
   curSalesTotal = 0
ElseIf Not IsNumeric(strSalesTotal) Then
   'not a valid number, so report an error and stop
   Response.Write "The value you entered is not a valid number."
   Response.Flush
   Response.End
```

```
Else
    'OK to convert the string value and use it
    curSalesTotal = CCur(strSalesTotal)
End If
```

In JScript all variables are objects, and have the `typeOf()` method. We can use this to discover what type of data is stored in the variable, again as we described in detail back in Chapter 3.

We will probably also want to test for "`null`" (`Null` in VBScript) to check that values have been provided for various variables before we use them in our code. This is particularly the case where we extract data from, say a database, where the fields can often contain `Null` to indicate that no data is available.

Variable Naming and Coding Conventions

Throughout this and the previous chapters, you've seen how we use a three-letter prefix for all variable names to indicate the data type that they hold. While all variables in the two scripting languages provided with ASP are of type `Variant` (or the JScript equivalent), it's useful to be able to tell from the variable name what type of data it is (or should) be storing. This can help to prevent errors as we write our code.

There are many different variable-naming conventions. The one we use is:

Data type	Prefix
`Boolean`	`bln`
`Byte`	`byt`
`Date/Time`	`dat` or `dtm`
`Collection`	`col`
`Double`	`dbl`
`Integer`	`int`
`Long`	`lng`
`Object`	`obj`
`Single`	`sng`
`String`	`str`

For a page that contains functions and subroutines, it's often useful to indicate if a variable has been declared or exists outside any function or subroutine, and hence is global to the page. For this we add the '`g`' prefix. So a globally available string variable might be named `gstrMyString`. Similarly an '`a`' prefix can be used to label arrays and array elements.

Commenting Your Code

Many programmers feel that adding comments to code not only increases development time unnecessarily, but also slows down page execution because the script interpreter has to read and then skip the comment lines each time. While there is some truth in the latter assertion, code that has no comments is often impenetrable when we come back to it in a month's time.

You should at least comment your generic functions and subroutines so that both you and others can re-use them, especially as this is now even easier to do with the new `Server.Execute` method (see Chapter 4 for more details). This is the format for commenting a re-usable routine that Microsoft recommends:

```
'****************************************************************
'Purpose: what the routine is designed to achieve
'Inputs: a list of all the parameters to the routine
'  parameter1: description, data-type, etc.
'  parameter2: description, data-type, etc.
'Returns: what data type is returned, and what it contains
'Comments: other comments about the routine, update history, etc.
'****************************************************************
```

Encapsulating Script for Code Reuse

We've just seen how we might comment our subroutines and functions to make it easier to re-use them. The principles of object-oriented programming are built round the concept of code re-use, and both the SSI `#include` directive and the new `Server.Execute` method make it easy to call functions that are stored in code libraries.

For example, if we have a series of functions that we use to calculate the tax and delivery charge payable on goods, we can insert the page containing this code into any other page using:

```
<!-- #include VIRTUAL="/library/code/online_sales/tax_and_delivery.inc" -->
```

The include file must contain start and end script delimiters, either `<SCRIPT RUNAT="SERVER">..</SCRIPT>` or `<%..%>`. Each function or subroutine should take the values it requires as parameters, and return the result as the value of the function or as an updated parameter. It should never operate on global variables, which might not be available in different pages. The code in the main page can then safely call these functions and subroutines as required.

The alternative is to use `Server.Execute` (or `Server.Transfer`) to switch execution to another page. This is useful if we have a section of ASP that creates, say, an online purchase summary for a customer. It can contain HTML to create the heading and a table, and code to calculate and fill in the values using the contents of the `Request` collections (remember that we can't pass script variables to another page using `Server.Execute` or `Server.Transfer`). Alternatively the page we `Execute` can hold functions, class definitions (in VBScript), or any other content that is designed to be reusable.

Managing Potential Error Situations

While we can code defensively to try and avoid errors, such as testing the values of variables before we try and convert or use them, there will always be some occasions where we can't prevent an error occurring. The obvious example is when we try to access a file that the user specifies, perhaps using the methods of the FileSystemObject object. We can never be really sure that the file hasn't been moved, deleted, or marked read-only – all of which could prevent our code from working.

Other similar cases may be when we come to access databases or other data stores, or files that require a specific level of permissions for the user account. In all these cases, there is a possibility that the code could fail because the access required cannot be achieved.

We can often test for a potential error like this by defensive coding. For example, we can use the `FileExists` method of the `Tools` component or of the FileSystemObject object to see if a file actually does exist before we access it, or we could use the **Permission Checker** component to see if the current user account has permission to access the requested file or resource. We can also use FileSystemObject to obtain the attributes setting of a file to see if it is read-only before attempting to delete or overwrite it.

These kinds of situations, and many more similar ones, can be potential sources of runtime errors if we don't think about what might go wrong, and how we can prevent it.

And Finally, Test It!

Yes, it seems obvious, but testing is the best defense against errors that can be propagated throughout an application and cause untold damage if not found in time. Test your pages with the kinds of values that you expect to get submitted by users, or which you might find in, say, a database that your code accesses. Also, and probably more important, check what happens with values you don't expect. Does the code prevent these from causing errors elsewhere, as well as preventing them from upsetting the routines you are testing?

Good testing techniques should encompass a range of values that includes **expected values, boundary condition values** and **out-of-bounds values**. Testing with values you expect to be passed to your pages is something you should do naturally every time. Likewise, out-of-bounds values are usually easy to defend against. For example you may decide to limit the acceptable range of values to numbers between `-100` and `+100` inclusive using:

```
If (intValue < -100) Or (intValue > 100) Then
   'not a valid value, so report an error and stop
   Response.Write "Values must be between -100 and +100 inclusive."
   Response.Flush
   Response.End
End If
```

However, remember to look out for boundary conditions. Can your routine handle `-100` and `+100`, or did you intend to limit it to values *between* these numbers? And what happens when the value is zero? Will your code come to a grinding halt with a 'Divide By Zero' error?

Handling Errors

Even after adopting defensive coding techniques, errors can still creep into our pages. This may be because our testing wasn't thorough enough, or because some other resource or service we are depending on decides to misbehave. To guard against these possibilities causing our pages to crash and burn, we can implement custom error handling in our code.

The ASP Default Error Handler

As we've seen earlier, ASP and IIS pick up most errors that occur in our pages, and an error page is generated automatically. Almost always the error is of type 500.100, and IIS uses the `Server.Transfer` method to load the default error page named `500-100.asp` and send it to the client. We saw how this works, and how we can interface it with our own custom error pages back in Chapter 4, where we examined the `Server.Transfer` method.

However, runtime scripting errors are not always raised by IIS the second they occur. When a runtime error occurs, the scripting engine looks at the context of the current execution point or statement. If we are executing a subroutine or function, the default script engine error handler **raises** the error by halting execution of the routine and going back to the code that called this routine in the first place.

There, it looks to see if any other error handler has been implemented. If not, it repeats this process again, going back to the code that called this routine. When it gets back to the main code in the page, outside any other subroutine or function, it again looks to see if any other error handler has been implemented. Only if none has been found during this process does it raise the error to ASP, which instructs IIS to transfer execution to the default error page.

VBScript Error Handling

In VBScript, we can tell the script interpreter to disregard any errors it finds, and continue execution with the next statement, using the `On Error Resume Next` statement. Once this statement has been processed, the script engine will continue executing code regardless of any errors it finds. However, this only applies to the context that the statement was executed within, in other words it doesn't apply to nested functions or subroutines.

Using On Error Resume Next

If an error occurs in a routine that doesn't itself execute the `On Error Resume Next` statement, then the error is raised to the calling context. This is repeated until either a context is found that has executed `On Error Resume Next`, or the default script error handler raises the error to ASP and IIS displays the default error page:

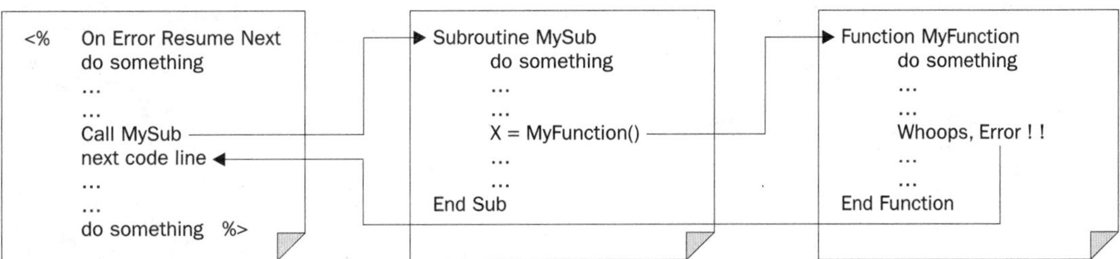

This chain of error calls means that we can create functions or subroutines that are protected from runtime errors halting execution of our code. If we place an `On Error Resume Next` statement at the start of a routine, we know that any runtime error will stop execution of that routine, but execution will continue with the calling code and not cause the page to be halted.

For example, if we need to write a string to a file we can protect against an error breaking our code by doing the file access in a separate function:

```
'creates a file named strFileName, overwriting any existing one with that name
'and writes strContent into it then closes the file
'returns True if it succeeds, or False on any error
Function WriteNewFile(strFileName, strContent)
   On Error Resume Next  'turn off the default error handler
   WriteNewFile = False  'default return value of function
```

```
    Set objFSO = CreateObject("Scripting.FileSystemObject")
    If Err.Number = 0 Then Set objFile = objFSO.CreateTextFile(strFileName, True)
    If Err.Number = 0 Then objFile.WriteLine strContent
    If Err.Number = 0 Then objFile.Close
    If Err.Number = 0 Then WriteNewFile = True
End Function
```

Notice that we check the value of the VBScript Err object's `Number` property before we attempt to execute each code statement. If it is zero we haven't had an error occur yet, so we can continue with creating and writing to the file. However if an error does occur, the script engine will simply set the values of the Err object's properties, and continue by executing the next line.

Only if we can execute every line without causing an error will the return value of the function be set to `True`. Otherwise the function will return the value `False`. We can test for this in the code that uses the function and take appropriate action.

This is only a simple example, and we may wish to use a separate function for each part of the task instead so that we can identify more accurately where the error occurred. It also makes reading the code while debugging easier. In the main part of the page we would call three separate functions instead:

```
If CreateNewFile(strFileName) Then                   'create the new file
   Response.Write "New file successfully created<BR>"
   If WriteContent(strContent) Then                  'write the content
      Response.Write "Content written to file<BR>"
   Else
      Response.Write "ERROR: Failed to write to the file<BR>"
   End If
   If CloseFile(strFileName) Then                    'close the file
      Response.Write "File closed<BR>"
   Else
      Response.Write "ERROR: Failed to close the file<BR>"
   End If
Else
   Response.Write "ERROR: Failed to create the new file<BR>"
End Function
```

Using On Error Goto 0

In ASP 2.0 (although not documented) and in ASP 3.0, we can also use the statement `On Error Goto 0` to turn the default error handling behavior back on. A runtime error occurring after executing this statement will cause the default error handler to run, checking each nested routine in the context chain until it reaches the main page code. If no other context has turned off the default error handler, execution of our page will halt and the IIS default error page will be displayed.

The VBScript Err Object

In the previous examples, we checked to see if an error had occurred, when default error handling is turned off, by examining the `Number` property of the VBScript Err object. The Err object stores information about runtime errors – here is a list of the methods and properties it provides:

Method	Description
Clear	Clears all current settings of the Err object.
Raise	Generates a runtime error.

Property	Description
Description	Sets or returns a string describing an error.
Number	(Default) Sets or returns a numeric value specifying an error.
Source	Sets or returns the name of the object that generated the error.

We can use these properties to check what kind of error occurred, for example we might want to take different action depending on the error number. Alternatively, we can use the Source and Description property values to display the error information to the user, or log it to a file.

We can also use the Err object to create an error. Why would we want to do this? Well, there are times when we might want to pass a custom error message back to the user. We can set the properties of the Err object to any value we please, then call its Raise method to raise this error. This stops execution of the code, and passes the error back up the call chain.

This example shows how we might handle an error while reading a text file on the server's disk. Notice how we use the constant vbObjectError to make sure that the error number we select doesn't conflict with an existing error number. By adding our own arbitrarily chosen number to the constant, we can be more certain that it will not conflict with the pre-defined error numbers:

```
Function ReadThisFile(strFileName)   'returns the content as a string
   On Error Resume Next
   ReadThisFile = ""   'default return value of function
   Set objFSO = CreateObject("Scripting.FileSystemObject")
   Set objFile = objFSO.OpenTextFile("strFileName", ForReading)
   Select Case Err.Number
      Case 0                'OK, take no action
      Case 50, 53           'standard file or path not found errors
         'create custom error values and raise error back up the call chain
         intErrNumber = vbObjectError + 1073      'custom error number
         strErrDescription = "The file has been deleted or moved."
         strErrSource = " ReadThisFile function"
         Err.Raise intErrNumber,  strErrSource, strErrDescription
         Exit Function
      Case Else             'some other error
         'raise the standard error back up the call chain
         Err.Raise Err.Number, Err.Source, Err.Description
         Exit Function
   End Select
   ReadThisFile = objFile.ReadAll  'we opened it OK, so return the content
   objFile.Close
End Function
```

The code that calls this function can use On Error Resume Next, and catch the error raised by this routine:

```
On Error Resume Next
strContent = ReadThisFile("myfile,txt")
If Err.Number = 0 Then
   Response.Write "File content is:<BR>" & strContent
Else
   Response.Write "Error in " & Err.Source & "<BR>" & Err.Description
End If
```

JScript Error Handling

Up until version 5.0, JScript was not renowned for its error-handling capabilities. However this all changes in version 5.0, as it has adopted an error-handling system that is very similar to Java and C++. While it's not as easy to get to grips with as the VBScript techniques, many people think that it puts JScript well ahead in the error-handling stakes.

We looked in detail at how JScript error handling works in Chapter 1, while discussing the new features in the two main scripting languages. Rather than repeat it all here, we suggest that you look back there if you skipped over it when reading that chapter.

Using IIS Error Pages

A new link in the ASP error-handling process is the provision of customizable error pages for IIS. In fact this feature was available in ASP 2.0 with IIS 4.0, but the addition of a new ASP intrinsic object, the ASPError object, makes it much easier to use and adds a whole new level of functionality.

We looked at how we set up custom error pages back in Chapter 4, when we examined the Server.Execute and Server.Transfer methods. We also described and used the ASPError object there, though in a limited way. In this section, we'll see how we can use the combination of a custom error page and the ASPError object to create a much better (and language independent) way of handling ASP errors.

We've created a custom error page using VBScript that examines the contents of the ASPError object. It builds a string containing a comprehensive report of the error and writes it to a log file on the server's disk. However, the design of the page is such that a visitor will only see a message indicating that the page isn't available, plus options to reload the previous page or go to our Home page. They won't be aware that an error has occurred.

Even though we've used VBScript to create this page, all the features it uses are available to JScript as well, so it could easily be converted to, or written from scratch in this language if you prefer.

You can download the sample files for this and the other chapters of the book from our Web site at http://www.wrox.com.

Setting Up the Custom Error Page

Before you can use the custom error page, you must set it up in Internet Services Manager (in the same way as we demonstrated in Chapter 4). Once you have installed the samples file into your `wwwroot` directory, open the Properties dialog for the `Chapter07` subdirectory. In the Custom Errors page, scroll through the list and select the entry for HTTP error '500:100'. Click the Edit Properties button and type in the URL of the custom error page `custom_error.asp`:

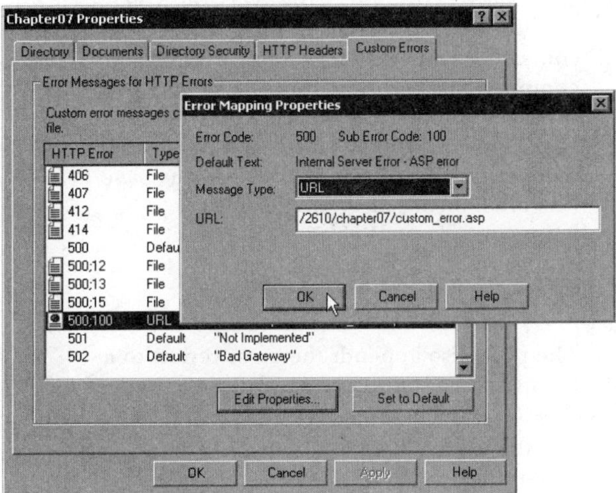

Now our custom error page will open whenever an ASP error occurs in a page in the `Chapter07` directory.

Using the Custom Error Page

Now open the `Chapter07` directory in your browser and select the link to 'Using a Custom Error Page'. This page displays a series of buttons that allow us to cause various types of error. Click the top button marked 'Load a page with a syntax error':

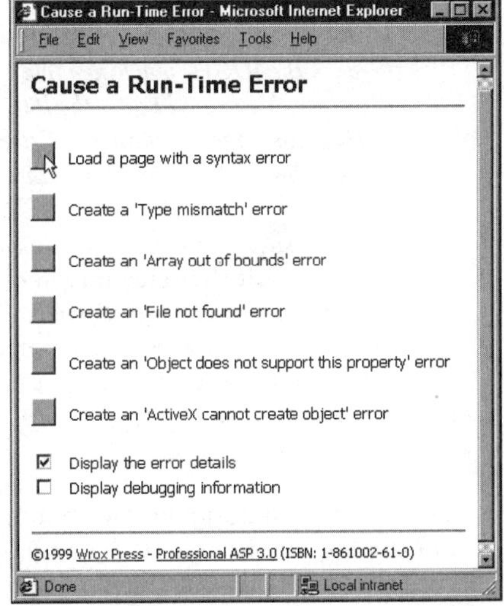

This loads a simple page named `syntax_error.asp`. However you won't see it because, as the name suggests, it contains a syntax error. ASP aborts compilation/execution of this page and transfers execution to our custom error page. This displays details of the error, and two buttons to go back to the previous page (the main menu) or to the default homepage of our Web site:

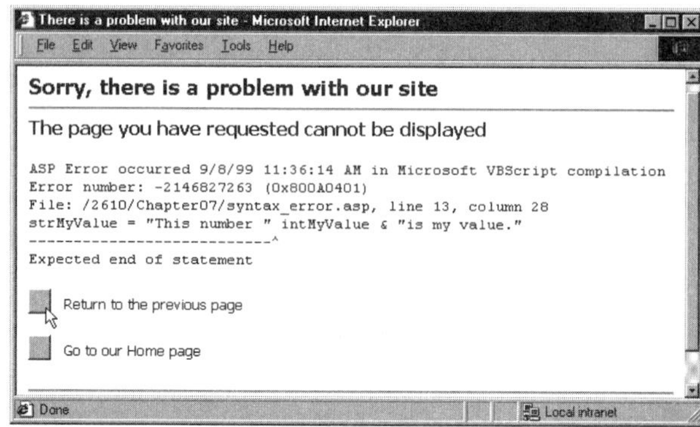

The page also appends the error report to a log file named `custom_error.log`, in the `C:\temp` folder of the server's disk. You an open it in a text editor and view it. Here, our log file has recorded several errors:

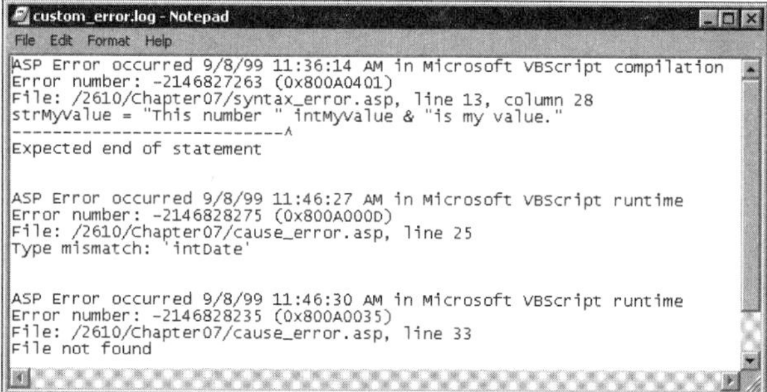

If you get a message in the page indicating that the log file could not be written it is probably because the IUSR_machinename account doesn't have permission to access the `C:\temp` directory. You should give the IUSR_machinename account Full Control of this directory while testing this page, or change the code in the `custom_error.asp` page to point to a different folder where IUSR_machinename does have Full Control.

The only reason that the error message appeared in the page is because we left the relevant checkbox ticked in the `cause_error.asp` page. If we turn this off and click the button again we don't see the error details. However they are still logged to the `custom_error.log` file on the server's disk:

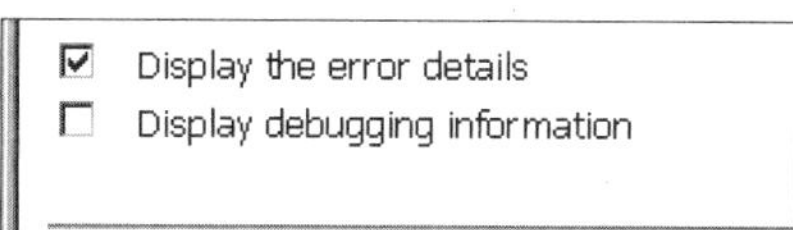

The 'Display debugging information' checkbox adds more information to the custom error page (but not the log file) to help in debugging any pages that use values from the intrinsic ASP object collections. We'll come back to this in the next section of the chapter. In the meantime, you might like to see what kind of error messages each of the other buttons on the 'Cause an Error' page creates. Notice how some provide more information than others do. In particular only the last one of the buttons provides a value for the ASP Error Code (in this case `ASP 0177`).

What the 'Cause An Error' Page Does

The page that causes the error in the first place uses the same technique as almost all our previous sample pages, with a `<FORM>` that submits values back to the same page. ASP code then looks to see which `SUBMIT` button on the form was clicked, and runs an appropriate section of code. However it also needs to see if the two checkboxes on the page were ticked, and if so it first sets one or more `Session`-level variables to indicate this:

```
<%
'see if we are going to display error and debug information
'set session variables to retrieve in the custom error page
If Len(Request.Form("chkShowError")) Then
  Session("ShowError") = "Yes"
Else
  Session("ShowError") = ""
End If
If Len(Request.Form("chkShowDebug")) Then
  Session("ShowDebug") = "Yes"
Else
  Session("ShowDebug") = ""
End If
...
```

You'll recall that, because `Server.Transfer` is used, the entire ASP context in which a page is running is passed to the custom error page by IIS when an error occurs. However the values of script variables are not, so we have to use a Session variable, or add values to the `Request.Form` or `Request.QueryString` collections to pass values to the custom error page.

After setting the Session variables, the code continues by checking to see which button was clicked. Each type of error is generated by running some suitable ASP code, with the exception of the first type – which requires us to load another page instead:

```
...
'look for a command sent from the FORM section buttons
If Len(Request.Form("cmdSyntax")) Then
   Response.Clear
   Response.Redirect "syntax_error.asp"
End If
If Len(Request.Form("cmdParamType")) Then
   intDate = "error"
   intDay = Day(intDate)
End If
If Len(Request.Form("cmdArray")) Then
   Dim arrThis(3)
   arrThis(4) = "Causes an error"
End If
If Len(Request.Form("cmdFile")) Then
   Set objFSO = Server.CreateObject("Scripting.FileSystemObject")
   Set objTStream = objFSO.OpenTextFile("does_not_exist.txt")
End If
If Len(Request.Form("cmdPageCount")) Then
   Set objPageCount = Server.CreateObject("MSWC.PageCounter")
   objPageCount.WrongProperty = 10
End If
If Len(Request.Form("cmdObject")) Then
   Set objThis = Server.CreateObject("Doesnot.Exist")
End If
%>
```

How the Custom Error Page Works

Having seen how we create the error, let's look at the custom error page. We've seen all the theory required for building a page like this in previous chapters, but we'll briefly describe the way that it works. The first step is to turn off the default error handler so that our page's code won't be interrupted by another error. Then we collect the original error details by creating a new ASPError object. Notice how we format some of the values as we go along, and convert them to suitable data types:

```
<%
'prevent any other errors from stopping execution
On Error Resume Next

'get a reference to the ASPError object
Set objASPError = Server.GetLastError()

'get the property values
strErrNumber = CStr(objASPError.Number) 'normal error code
strASPCode = objASPError.ASPCode        'ASP error code (if available)
If Len(strASPCode) Then
   strASPCode = "'" & strASPCode & "' "
Else
   strASPCode = ""
End If
strErrDescription = objASPError.Description
strASPDescription = objASPError.ASPDescription
strCategory = objASPError.Category      'type or source of error
strFileName = objASPError.File          'file path and name
strLineNum = objASPError.Line           'line number in file
strColNum = objASPError.Column          'column number in line
If IsNumeric(strColNum) Then            'if available convert to integer
   lngColNum = CLng(strColNum)
Else
   lngColNum = 0
End If
strSourceCode = objASPError.Source     'source code of line
...
```

Now we can build up an error report string. This code looks complex, but it's really only a series of nested `If Then` statements that produce nice format for the report, with no blank sections. If the error is a syntax error, the source code from the ASPError object's `Source` property will be available in our `strSourceCode` variable. We can use this with the `lngColNum` value (retrieved from the ASPError object's `Column` property) to add a marker that indicates where in the source code the error was found:

```
...
'create the error message string
strDetail = "ASP Error " & strASPCode & "occurred " & Now
If Len(strCategory) Then
   strDetail = strDetail & " in " & strCategory
End If
strDetail = strDetail & vbCrlf & "Error number: " & strErrNumber _
          & " (0x" & Hex(strErrNumber) & ")" & vbCrlf
```

```
If Len(strFileName) Then
   strDetail = strDetail & "File: " & strFileName
   If strLineNum > "0" Then
      strDetail = strDetail & ", line " & strLineNum
      If lngColNum > 0 Then
         strDetail = strDetail & ", column " & lngColNum
         If Len(strSourceCode) Then
            'got the source line so put a ^ marker in the string
            strDetail = strDetail & vbCrlf & strSourceCode & vbCrlf _
                      & String(lngColNum - 1, "-") & "^"
         End If
      End If
   End If
   strDetail = strDetail & vbCrlf
End If
strDetail = strDetail & strErrDescription & vbCrlf
If Len(strASPDescription) Then
   strDetail = strDetail & "ASP reports: " & strASPDescription & vbCrlf
End If
...
```

Logging the Error

Having created our error report in the string variable named `strDetail`, we can append it to the log file. We use the FileSystemObject object for this, just like we did in Chapter 5. If it succeeds our Boolean 'failed flag' variable will be set to `False`:

```
...
'now log error to a file. Edit the path to suit your machine.
'you need to give the IUSR_machinename permission to write and modify
'the file or directory used for the log file:
strErrorLog = "c:\temp\custom_error.log"
Set objFSO = Server.CreateObject("Scripting.FileSystemObject")
Set objTStream = objFSO.OpenTextFile(strErrorLog, 8, True)  '8 = ForAppending
If Err.Number = 0 Then objTStream.WriteLine strDetail & vbCrlf
If Err.Number = 0 Then
   objTStream.Close
   blnFailedToLog = False
Else
   blnFailedToLog = True
End If
%>
```

Jumping to Another Page

Now we are ready to create some output in the page. However, before we do, we can examine the error details to see exactly what we want to do next. For example, we can check the error type using the `Number` or any of the other properties of the ASPError object. Here, we've decided that 'Type Mismatch' errors aren't our fault, and are probably caused by the user entering bad values in text boxes. So, instead of displaying the rest of this page, we can jump to another page instead:

```
If objASPError.Number = -2146828275 Then  '0x800A000D - type mismatch
   Response.Clear
   Response.Redirect "/"                  'go to the Home page
End If
```

Whether or not you decide to do this depends on your own circumstances, and what types of errors you want to pick up and record or display. Notice that, because we don't want to pass the current page's context on to the new page, we've chosen to use a `Response.Redirect` statement rather than `Server.Transfer`.

Displaying the Error Information

Finally, we can display the error report and other information, and the buttons to return to the previous or the homepage:

```
<%
'see if the logging to file failed - if so display a message
If blnFailedToLog Then
   Response.Write "WARNING: Cannot log error to file " & strErrorLog & ".<P>"
End If

'see if we are displaying the error information
If Session("ShowError") = "Yes" Then
'use HTMLEncode in case source code contains HTML characters
%>
   <PRE><% = Server.HTMLEncode(strDetail) %></PRE>
<%
End If

'see if we are displaying the debug information
If Session("ShowDebug") = "Yes" Then Server.Transfer "debug_Request.asp"

'create the buttons to return to the previous or Home page
strReferrer = Request.ServerVariables("HTTP_REFERER")
If Len(strReferrer) Then
%>
   <FORM ACTION="<% = strReferrer %>">
   <INPUT TYPE="SUBMIT" NAME="cmdOK" VALUE="   ">
     Return to the previous page<P>
   </FORM>
<%
End If
%>
<FORM ACTION="/">
<INPUT TYPE="SUBMIT" NAME="cmdOK" VALUE="   ">
  Go to our Home page<P>
</FORM>
```

The only other point to be aware of with this code is that we can't use the `Server.Execute` method within the custom error page – or at least, if we do, it doesn't work properly. While it does transfer execution to the page we specify, it never returns to this one. This is why we use the `Server.Transfer` method to load the page that displays the debugging information. And, coincidentally, this is the topic of the next section – so read on.

Finding and Curing Errors – Debugging

Having read all the above, you are now in a position to create ASP pages that never have any errors in them. But, since theory and reality don't often exist in the same dimension, you are almost bound to find that some of your pages will fail to work first time. This is where the real fun starts, and where that Sherlock Holmes deerstalker and pipe come into play. It's time to play every developer's favorite game, **debugging**.

In this section, we'll briefly look at a tool that can make debugging much easier. **Microsoft Script Debugger** attempts to raise the level of tools support for debugging ASP and client-side script to the level enjoyed by most traditional programming environments, such as Visual Basic, Delphi and Visual C++. However, we'll start off with a look at some of the more traditional techniques that can help us to track down errors that occur in our pages.

Custom Debugging Techniques

In Chapter 2 we saw how we can use the `Response.Write` method in conjunction with the Request collections to display the contents of a collection. One of the first things to do when you have code that uses values collected from the request is to make sure that you do actually have the values you expect. It's very easy to misspell or change the name of an HTML control in a `<FORM>` page, or make a mistake client-side as you create the query string to append to a URL.

Displaying the Various Collection Contents

Therefore, when your code attempts to work with the values that the user supplied, you may not get the results you expect, or any results at all. Remember that referencing a value in the Request object's collection that doesn't exist (i.e. using `Request.Form("ThisControl")` when there isn't a control named `"ThisControl"` on the form) doesn't raise an error. You just get an empty string as the result. The same applies if you are expecting to find values stored in variables in the user's Session object, or in the global Application object.

If we create a simple page that displays the contents of all the Request object's collections, and the Session and Application objects' `Contents` and `StaticContents` collections, we can access it from any page using `Server.Execute`. All we have to do is add the following line to any ASP page to display the entire contents of the collections. You'll have to set the appropriate path to the file, of course, depending on where you place it on your server:

```
<% Server.Execute "/path_to_file/debug_Request.asp" %>
```

This is a great way to make sure that any values we expect to find in the Request, Session and Application collections actually *are* there, and contain appropriate values. We've provided a suitable file named `debug_request.asp` in the `Chapter07` subdirectory of the sample pages for this book. It's basically a combination of the `show_request.asp` page we used in Chapter 2 and the `show_application.asp` and `show_session.asp` pages we used in Chapter 3, but with all the HTML code removed. It simply iterates through all the collections placing the values into the current page.

You can see this page by running the 'Custom Error Page' example we saw in the previous section of this chapter with the checkbox marked 'Display debugging information' ticked, or open it directly from the main menu page in the `Chapter07` directory.

Displaying Intermediate Values

A second way to see what's going on in our page is to display the values of variables as the page executes. This traditional technique can't be beaten when we know roughly where the error is coming from, and which variables are 'playing up'. However, IIS 5.0 makes it a bit harder than usual to use this technique because of the change to the way page buffering is implemented.

In previous versions of ASP and IIS, page buffering was turned off by default, and few people bothered to turn it on (using `Response.Buffer = True`) unless they intended to carry out page redirection using `Response.Redirect` (see Chapter 2 for more details). Buffering considerably increases the efficiency of IIS, as it reduces the number of times that it has to switch between pages when responding to multiple requests.

However, when a runtime error that halts execution occurs, IIS automatically calls the `Response.Clear` method followed by `Server.Execute` to load the custom error page. So, any output that we've written into the page is lost. The answer is to temporarily add the line:

```
<% Response.Buffer = False %>
```

right at the top of the (original) page after the `<@LANGUAGE..>` directive. Any debugging output created by `Response.Write` statements will then appear at the top of the custom error page. Just remember to take it out again after you've finished debugging the page.

It's also sometimes useful to be able to force code to execute past an error point, and then display the values of the suspect variables. Simply add the `On Error Resume Next` statement near the beginning of the page. You can then also access the Err object (in VBScript) and display the error number, source and description.

Check Component Property Values

If we use components that have properties we set in our ASP script code, we can often track down errors by displaying all the properties (or just the suspect ones) after we've set them, and before and after we call the methods of the component. You might find that the value of a property is changed unexpectedly by the component when one of the methods is run – perhaps intentionally or perhaps because of a bug in the component. If you're as paranoid as we are, you'll never assume anything when you can't see the actual code for yourself.

Microsoft Script Debugger

When we come to more complex applications that handle 'real-life' tasks, we often need a more powerful tool to debug our ASP applications. **Microsoft Script Debugger** is a debugging tool that allows us to debug script running on the client and on the server. It can be used to debug programs written in any ActiveX-enabled scripting language, including VBScript and JScript. We can also use it to debug calls to Java applets, Java Beans and ActiveX components.

Before we take a look at the tool itself, we'll cover some introductory issues. As you've seen earlier, ASP applications can consist of two types of script – client-side script and server-side script. **Client-side script** usually consists of VBScript or JScript script statements that appear in the HTML page when it arrives at the client, and they are executed there – either when the document is loaded or in response to some event such as button click. **Server-side script**, again usually VBScript or JScript, is executed by IIS when the page is requested by the browser, but before its contents are sent to the client. In this discussion we'll take a look at server-side script debugging – the way we can debug our ASP applications. However, many of the techniques we cover can also be used client-side to debug script that runs there.

Debugging on the Server

To debug server-side script we run Script Debugger on the same computer that is running IIS. Before we can use it, however, we must enable debugging. To maximize performance, debugging is not enabled by default for ASP-based applications.

> **You should *never* enable debugging for a production application, i.e. a public site that is live and being used by others, since debugging slows down the whole application and errors can halt page execution indefinitely.**

Debugging can only be set for a **virtual application** or an entire Web site. To enable debugging open the Properties dialog for your virtual application or site and, in the Home Directory page, click the Configuration button. In the Application Debugging page of the Application Configuration dialog select 'Enable ASP server-side script debugging'. Now we are ready to debug our application.

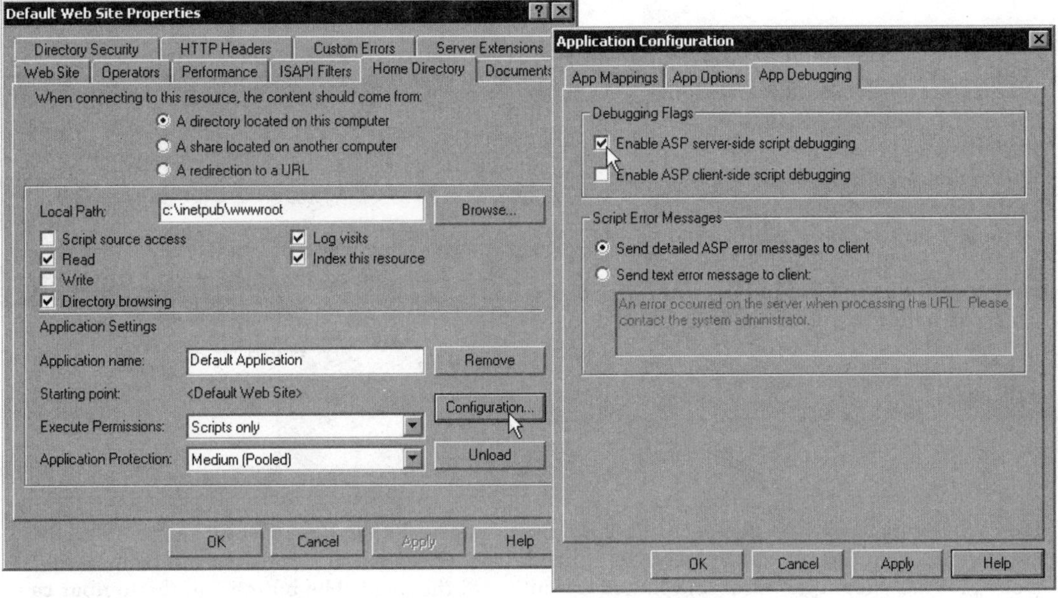

Notice that the Application Configuration dialog contains a checkbox to enable client-side script debugging. This is not implemented in IIS 5.0, and is documented as being 'reserved for future use'. The Script Error Messages section contains the text that will be sent to the client if you disable the normal `500-100.asp` custom error page.

How Server Scripts are Processed

Unlike client-side scripts, ASP-based application scripts are not event-driven. Instead, when the client requests a page from a server, the server reads the page and processes all the server script (everything inside `<%..%>` and `<SCRIPT RUNAT="SERVER"></SCRIPT>` sections). This includes script sections that are 'inline' with HTML text, such as:

```
The value of the result is: <% = strResult %>
```

The processing flow is shown on the following diagram.

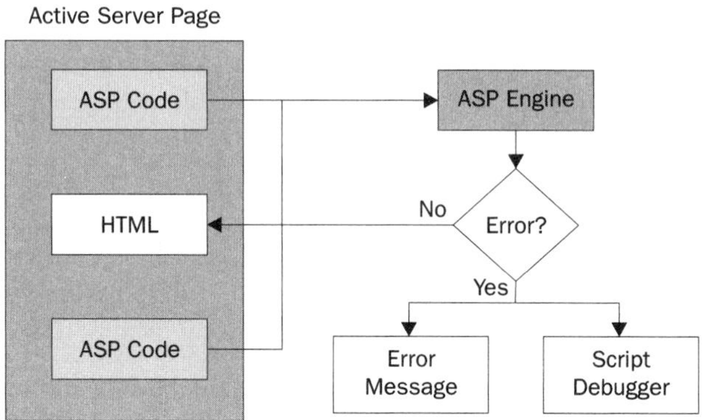

All script in the ASP page is processed when the page is loaded by IIS, so both syntax and runtime errors are caught by ASP and the scripting engine before any output is sent to the client (unless you turn off buffering or call the `Response.Flush` method).

How Script Debugger Can Help

When an error occurs, and providing that script debugging is enabled, we see a dialog appear on the server screen that describes the ASP code error. Clicking OK then opens Script Debugger on the server with a read-only copy of the current ASP page loaded, and the line where the error occurred indicated by an arrow:

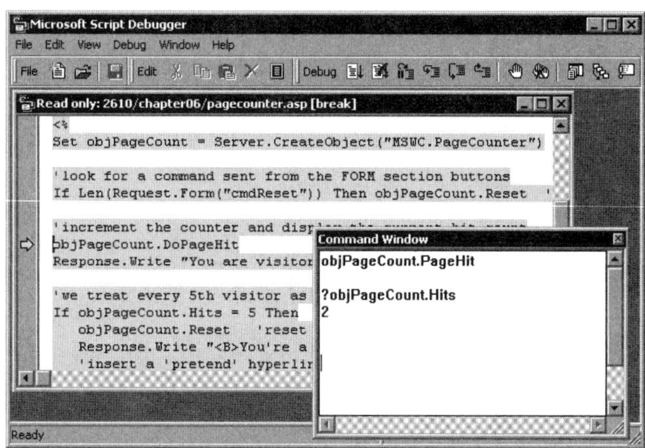

Here, the error has arisen because we got the name wrong for the **Page Counter** object's method that increments the number of page hits (`DoPageHit` instead of `PageHit`). At the moment, Script Debugger has caught the error and halted execution of the page. The buttons on the toolbar can be used (amongst other things) to continue execution, single-step through the code, or abort the processing of the page.

The button on the far right of the toolbar opens the Immediate window in Script Debugger. Here we can interact with the page, and hopefully get to see what went wrong. For example we can query or set the values of variables or component properties, and execute built-in functions and subroutines, custom functions and subroutines, and methods of objects that have been created. In the screenshot you can see that we've called the `PageHit` method of the **Page Counter** component (by its correct name this time), and then queried the `Hits` property to see what value it now holds at this point in the executing (but halted) script.

> *To see why you should never use Script Debugger on a 'public' site, try opening a page that contains a server-side ASP error from a client machine. In this case, the error message dialog appears on the server, and Script Debugger opens there. On the client, the page is stalled (i.e. does not load) until the instance of Script Debugger running on the server is closed again.*

Starting and Using Script Debugger

As well as appearing automatically when an error occurs in a page in a virtual application that has script debugging enabled, we can start script debugger manually. This can be done from the Windows 2000 Start menu (Programs | Accessories | Microsoft Script Debugger). Alternatively we can insert a `Stop` statement into our ASP code at the point where we want to open script debugger. IIS halts execution of the ASP code when the `Stop` statement is reached, starts Script Debugger, displays the current page, and indicates the current line containing the `Stop` statement.

Script Debugger can perform a range of tasks, including:

- Viewing a list of all the documents that are running or have run, from which we can select one to view and edit.
- Setting a new breakpoint in a page that's open to indicate that execution should stop at that point so that debugging can take place.
- Single-stepping through code one statement at a time, optionally executing any subroutines or functions.
- Viewing the **Call Stack**, which shows the nested subroutines or functions that have been called up to this point in the code.

Script Debugger Tips and Tricks

Here is a list of tips that can help you find errors in your scripts more easily while you are using Microsoft Script Debugger.

- If you are debugging server-side scripts, enable the Script Debugger for the ASP application they appear in. If the debugger is not enabled on the server, error messages are passed as text to the client browser and you cannot use the Script Debugger with your server-side scripts.
- Remember to disable debugging when your application is ready, otherwise you'll see server performance degradation and pages with errors will stall on the client.
- When the Script Debugger is enabled for one or more ASP applications, all server errors are passed to it including those that occur as remote clients access pages. Therefore, you should *not* enable the Script Debugger for an ASP application unless you can work on the server itself.
- If you are working in a browser that is not installed on the server, and an error is displayed within the page, there is an error in the server-side script. If an error message is displayed in a dialog box, the error is in a client-side script.
- If there is a syntax or runtime error in a `.asp` file and debugging is enabled for that ASP application, the client browser will not display the syntax error (unless the browser is running on the server). Instead, it eventually times out and displays an error indicating that it cannot open the page.
- When looking at line numbers in error messages note that if there is an error in the server-side script, the line number displayed in the error message points to the line in the `.asp` file that contains the error.

- If there is an error in the client-side script that is created by an `.asp` file, the line number does not point to the faulty line in the `.asp` file. Instead it points to the line in the HTML output of that `.asp` file where the error occurred. To see this line view the source of the HTML file in the client browser.
- Error codes for VBScript and JScript are listed in Appendix D.

Getting Help and Support for ASP

If you come up with an error that you can't cure, or something that appears to be a bug in ASP, it's nice to be able to call on outside help to solve the problem. There are many useful sources of general information about ASP on the Web, and we listed many at the end of Chapter 1. However, for specific problems, you really need some more direct assistance.

The obvious places to start are on your own machine. The documentation for ASP and IIS is quite comprehensive, and can be accessed from a browser through the URL `http://`*`yourservername`*`/iishelp/`. You should make sure that you install all the documentation for IIS when you run the Windows 2000 Additional Components setup or the main setup program (depending on which version of Windows 2000 you are installing).

There is also a full Platform SDK available from Microsoft for Windows 2000, which contains plenty of additional and peripheral information about Windows as well as covering the Internet services in Windows 2000. This also contains a full VBScript and JScript reference. The Platform SDK is available from Microsoft, and is supplied to MSDN members. The scripting references are also available separately, and can be downloaded from the Microsoft scripting site at `http://www.microsoft.com/scripting/`. You can also obtain the Script Debugger from here.

The Microsoft Developer's Network (MSDN) Web site also provides plenty of support and help, even if this information can sometimes be difficult to find. You might want to start from the Workshop site at `http://msdn.microsoft.com/workshop/`, which has a good index as well as a series of topic contents in the left-hand navigation bar.

Alternatively, the main MSDN Library at `http://msdn.microsoft.com/library/default.htm` contains articles, a knowledge base, FAQ and other support materials for IIS and ASP. The left-hand window uses a Java expanding list control to make navigation easier.

If you need help on specific topics, or want to ask other developers questions, there are some useful Newsgroups on the 'Net. Try `msnews.microsoft.com`, and subscribe to `microsoft.public.inetserver.iis`, `microsoft.public.inetserver.activeserverpages` and `microsoft.public.inetserver.iis.misc` for a start. Some ASP Web sites also provide discussion areas, forums or chat rooms for ASP topics.

Summary

In this final chapter of part one of the book we've looked at what is probably the least favorite job of most programmers. It's unlikely that all but the simplest of our scripts will work correctly first time, and as we take advantage of more and more of the features that ASP provides, the opportunity for errors to creep into our scripts increases. So, having a good basic knowledge of how errors occur, and how to find and cure them, can only be an advantage.

We looked at the different kinds of errors that can occur, and where they come from. More to the point, understanding how they are trapped and raised by the default ASP and scripting engine error handling systems helps us to track them down far more easily. As the complexity of the ASP scripting and runtime environment has increased with successive implementations of ASP, so has the number of possible error situations.

As well as looking at what errors are and where they come from, we also examined some ways that we can code defensively so as to catch problems early on, and prevent them from propagating errors or invalid data to other applications. The fewer simple mistakes you make when writing your code, the easier it is to find and cure the more obscure ones.

However, good coding practice can't prevent some kinds of errors occurring, such as those that arise when we have to depend on external resources and services. This means that providing our own custom error handling code is important, and knowing how to trap errors when they do occur and handle them gracefully makes the difference between pages that are bullet-proof and those that fall over in the slightest breeze.

Finally, we ended the chapter with a look at Microsoft Script Debugger. This useful tool can help us to find and cure runtime errors in our pages, by allowing us to pause execution and single-step through the code, while at the same time being able to view what's going on and even interact with the script.

So, this chapter covered:

- The different types of errors that may occur
- How we can prevent many kinds of errors from arising
- How we can handle errors gracefully if we can't prevent them from happening
- How we go about finding and fixing script errors and other types of errors
- How we use custom error pages to get information about errors
- How we can record errors that occur to monitor our site

In the next section of the book, we go back to working with server components. We'll look in depth at the ActiveX Data Objects (ADO) component, and see how we use it to access databases and data stores of all kinds.

N
W

8

ADO 2.5 Basics

In the first section of this book you've learned about Active Server Pages, and how they can be used to bring dynamic content to a Web site. You've seen how it's scripting that gives us the Active part of ASP, allowing us to customize our Web pages, and that it's possible to build quite a lot of power into ASP pages.

In this section we're going to look at the integration of *ASP and data*. There's really no limit to the amount of scripting you can use in your Web pages, but without data of some form you're going to reach a dead-end pretty soon. Your data might make up the actual content of the site, or indicate how the site is to be laid out, but ultimately it's data that's the important thing. If you build your Web site around a **data store**, then to change the site you only need to change the data.

ActiveX Data Objects (ADO) are the components that allow us to interact with data stores. This might mean just building a page based on some data, or a fully interactive e-commerce system. Either way, it's ADO that allows us to communicate with the data. This section will cover the major aspects of getting data to and from some data store, and the ways in which you can manipulate that data once you've got it.

We'll first be looking at what ADO is and what components it comprises, and then how we can access data stores. In the next chapter we'll take a look at some more advanced aspects of ADO, such as commands, stored procedures, and some performance tips for optimizing your applications. The next step is to look at the interaction between the Web server and the browser, and how data can be manipulated in both places. Then we'll look at a potentially huge area in data access, that of XML, examining what XML is, how it can be used to represent data, and how we can use it. Since XML leads us to the future, we'll then look at Microsoft's dream of Universal Data Access, where data doesn't just come from databases. Finally we'll look at the alternatives to the standard Microsoft databases (such as Access and SQL Server) and how ADO can be used with them.

So, to start our section on ADO, in this chapter, we are going to:

- Examine how ADO interacts with data
- See what the components of ADO are
- Show how to connect to data stores and create recordsets
- How to manipulate and change the data
- See how to handle ADO errors

Why ADO?

ADO is a fairly simple idea – the idea that you should only have *one way* to access data. It's not a new idea either, taking the best bits of existing database access technologies, and melding them together into something that's fit for today and the future. And that's quite an important thing - the future. Many of the other technologies, such as DAO and ODBC, are perfectly acceptable for the way many applications are being developed, but the rise of the Internet has brought its own problems.

In many cases, the traditional methods of data access always seemed to revolve around a 2-tier client/server system. This gave you a permanent connection to your data, and provided great facilities, such as responsive searches, easy data modification, and so on. In the Internet world, we now have to deal with the inherent stateless nature of the Web, and the potentially huge number of users that can access your site. It's no longer possible to rely on a permanent connection to your data, or guarantee the number of users, so you have to design your applications to take this into account.

So, what exactly are **OLE DB** and **ADO**? Let's answer that by way of a comparison with some existing data access technologies. If you've done any database programming before, you might be familiar with ODBC and RDO. Open DataBase Connectivity (ODBC) is an Application Programming Interface (API) to allow access to relational databases, such as Access and SQL Server. Because it is an API many programmers, especially in the Visual Basic arena, found it complex to use. Remote Data Objects (RDO) are ActiveX objects that sits on top of ODBC, giving all of the facilities of ODBC, but in an easy to use form.

We can equate OLE DB to ODBC, and ADO to RDO.

OLE DB is the underlying technology that interfaces between our programs and the source of the data.

It's quite complex, and really only used by C and C++ programmers. ADO, as the name suggests, are ActiveX objects that provides easy access to the OLE DB functionality.

You might find the terms ActiveX and COM objects used in a confusingly interchangeable way. There is essentially no difference for you as an ASP programmer because they are both based on the COM architecture, but ActiveX is a cross-platform standard for components, whereas COM is Windows specific.

Although Microsoft has introduced a new technology for accessing data, they haven't immediately written off the old ones. ODBC is still very much in force, and works hand-in-hand with OLE DB and ADO. ODBC is, in fact, not solely a Microsoft product, and is controlled by an international group, and because it is so widely used, it's not going to suddenly die. That's not the idea behind OLE DB – it's not trying to kill off existing technologies, but *advance* on them.

OLE DB and ADO Architecture

So we've given a brief explanation of what OLE DB and ADO are, but where do they fit in the overall picture of things. The diagram below shows how these two technologies sit together in relation to applications and data stores:

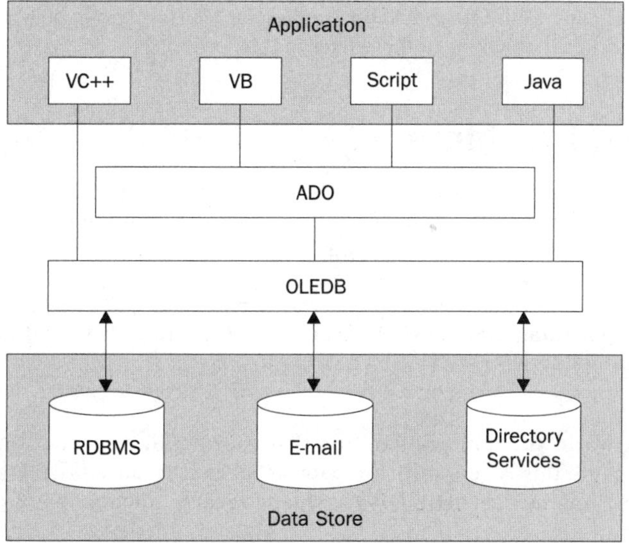

Here you can see the idea. At the top we have an application (a Web or normal application, it doesn't matter). Underneath that we have ADO and/or OLE DB, which provide access to the data. The reason we have both ADO and OLE DB is that OLE DB is the *underlying* technology. However, OLE DB was not designed to be used in all languages; so ADO sits on top of OLE DB, and provides an interface for those languages, such as Visual Basic and scripting languages, which can't access OLE DB directly. ADO also provides an easier programming interface than OLE DB, so even those languages that can use OLE DB directly, such as C++ or Java, can use ADO to simplify their data access.

The above diagram shows Microsoft programming languages, but ADO is a COM component, and can therefore be used in any COM compliant language, such as Delphi, or scripting language that supports the Active Scripting interface. So whilst ADO is not yet platform independent, it is language independent. Of course, for ASP, we'll be concentrating on VBScript and JScript, as well as showing some Visual Basic code when we use ADO in components.

So you now know that OLE DB and ADO allow access to data, but why do we need them? What's wrong with the old methods? There are two main reasons:

- The first is that OLE DB and ADO are designed to give you access to *data stores*. Note that I said 'data stores', not 'databases'. Although databases are still the most widely used form of data storage, they don't necessarily contain all of your data. Messaging systems, such as Microsoft Exchange Server, are widely used to store data; Directory Services are now starting to appear in the mainstream, and these contain data about users, machines, and so on; Web servers store huge volumes of information. The list goes on, and it seems sensible to have one way to access all of these different types of data.
- The second reason is the rise of Internet applications, and the stateless nature of the Web. The older data access methods aren't designed to handle data when they are not permanently connected to their store of data. OLE DB and ADO are designed for this – they provide disconnected recordsets, and we'll be looking at those later in this section.

Consumers and Providers

The ADO architecture diagram showed how ADO sits between the application and the actual store of the data. In the Microsoft documentation, and other sources, you'll see the terms **Consumers** and **Providers** – two obvious terms, but it's important to be clear as to exactly what they are.

> **A Provider is something that provides data, and a Consumer is something that uses (consumes) that data.**

In the programming world you'll most often find that your application is a consumer of data, but what about the provider. Well, this is generally the data store, and because OLE DB is designed to talk to a variety of data stores, you have an **OLE DB Provider** for each unique type of data store.

This idea of separate Providers is not new, but it makes programming easier. You write your program to talk to ADO or OLE DB, and OLE DB talks to the Provider. This means that you only have to learn one set of rules for accessing data, however the data is stored, and in some cases you can actually swap Providers without changing your code at all. This is what ADO and OLE DB do really well – provide a common set of programming interfaces to data stores.

To connect to your data store you have to use an OLE DB Provider. The initial set provided with ADO 2.5 are:

- Jet OLE DB 4.0 – For Microsoft Access databases
- DTS Packages – For the SQL Server Data Transformation Services
- Internet Publishing – For access to Web servers
- Indexing Service – For Index Catalogs
- Site Server Search – For the Site Server search catalog
- ODBC Drivers – For ODBC Data Sources

- OLAP Services – For the Microsoft OLAP server
- Oracle – For Oracle databases
- SQL Server – For Microsoft SQL Server databases
- Simple Provider, for simple text files
- MSDataShape – For hierarchical data
- Microsoft Directory Services – For the Windows 2000 Directory Services
- DTS Flat File – For the SQL Server Data Transformation Services flat file manager

This is just the initial list supplied by Microsoft, and depends on which services you install on your server, and what software you have installed. The Provider for Oracle for instance, requires Oracle client software to be installed on your machine.

OLE DB Providers are available from other manufacturers, for other stores of data, and you can also write your own. We'll show you a way to write a simple OLE DB Provider in Chapter 11.

To find out which Providers are installed on your system, you can use a Data Link Properties dialog. We'll show you how to use this in the Data Link section later in this chapter.

Providers and Drivers

One thing to note is the inclusion of an OLE DB Provider for ODBC, which allows OLE DB access to existing ODBC data sources. The great advantage of this is that ODBC is more widely spread than OLE DB, and there are a greater number of **ODBC Drivers** available than OLE DB Providers. This gives us instant access to legacy data systems, without the need to wait for OLE DB Providers to become available.

It's important not to get confused between Providers and Drivers. This diagram should make things clearer:

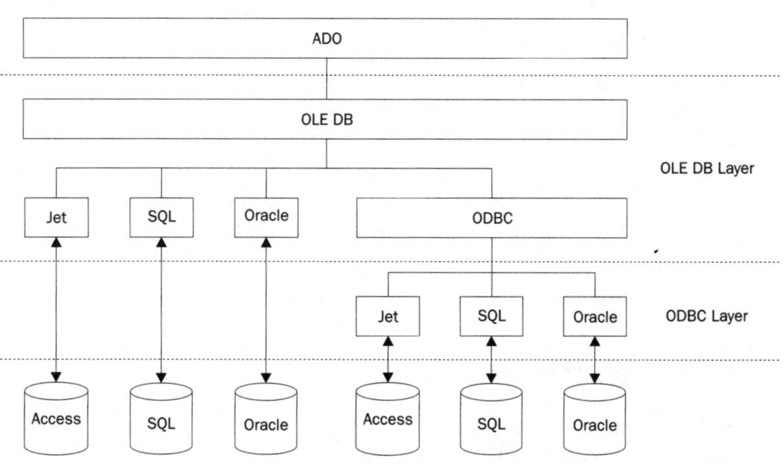

This clearly shows the divide. Providers are in the OLE DB layer, and Drivers are in the ODBC layer. If you want to use an ODBC Data Source you use the OLE DB Provider for ODBC, which in turn uses the appropriate ODBC Driver. If you don't need to use and ODBC data source, then you can use the appropriate OLE DB Provider – these are generally referred to as the **native providers**.

You can also clearly see that the use of the Provider for ODBC means an extra layer is required. For this reason, the OLE DB Provider for ODBC might be slightly slower that the native OLE DB Providers when accessing the same data.

The ADO 2.5 Object Model

The object model of ADO 2.5 is similar to previous versions, although there are two new objects. The diagram below shows the objects and their relationship to each other:

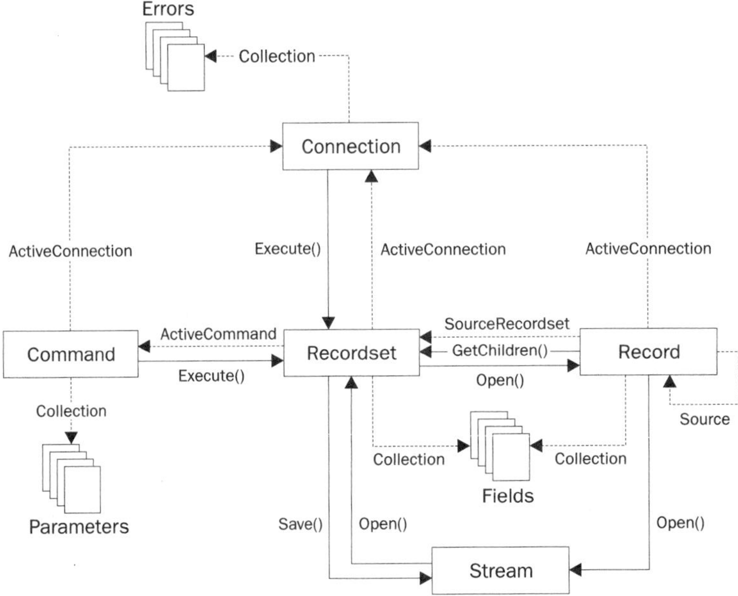

If you've used ADO before you'll see that the Stream and Record objects are new, and we will be covering them in detail in Chapters 11 and 12.

The Properties collection has been deliberately left off the above diagram, so that you can easily see the interaction between the main objects. A simplified object model showing the Properties collection is shown later in this chapter.

Let's examine these objects in a little more detail.

The Connection Object

The **Connection object** is what enables us to connect to data stores. It is through the Connection object that we can specify which OLE DB Provider we wish to use, the security details used to connect to the data store, and any other details specific to the connection to the data store.

One thing you should note is that it is not necessary to explicitly create a Connection object to connect to a data store. You can create Command, Recordset and Record objects without a Connection object, although you do need to specify the details of the connection. ADO implicitly creates a Connection object for you if you do not create one yourself. If you are going to be running several commands against a Provider, you should explicitly create a Connection as it's more efficient than letting ADO create one each time you run a command.

As well as providing the connection to a data store, the Connection object allows you to run commands against the data store. These can be constructed or stored commands (for example SQL commands or a stored procedure), and can optionally return a set of data from the store.

The Command Object

The **Command object** is designed for running commands against a data store. But hang on, I hear you say, can't the Connection object do that? Yes it can, but the Connection object has restrictions on its facilities for handling commands, whereas the Command object was specifically created for dealing with all aspects of commands. In fact, a Command object is implicitly created when you run a command from the Connection object.

Whilst other objects allow parameters to be passed to commands, you can't specify any details about the parameters. Using the Command object allows you to specify the exact details (such as data type and length) of the parameters, as well as use output parameters and return values, which accept values back from the command.

So as well as running commands and maybe getting a set of records back, you can also get additional information if it is provided by the command.

The Command object is also useful for running commands that don't return any records, such as SQL queries that insert new data or update existing data.

The Recordset Object

The **Recordset object** is probably the most commonly used object in ADO, since it is this object that contains the sets of data we extract from our data stores. We often run commands that have no data returned, such as those that add or update data, but in most cases we will probably be fetching a set of records.

The Recordset is the object that holds this set of records. It allows us to change the data (additions, updates and deletions), move around the records, filter the records so that only a subset are shown, and so on. The Recordset object also contains a Fields collection, where there is a Field object for each field (column) in the recordset.

Whether you are dealing with data in an ASP page, or using data remotely with Remote Data Services (RDS), then it's the Recordset object you'll be dealing with.

The Record Object

Versions of ADO prior to 2.5 were great at handling structured data, such as sets of records from databases, but were not designed for sets of data where the columns may be different (that is, the number of columns and data type) for each row. This isn't a problem for SQL data, but what about file and mail systems, Web servers and other such data stores? These we consider as *semi-structured*, where they are less structured than a recordset, but more structured than binary data, which usually represents text or images.

Generally, semi-structured storage follows a tree-like organization, with nodes, sub-nodes, and files. Consider a Web site, for example, where we have folders, sub-folders and files. The screenshot below shows the Web site for a machine, and in particular a virtual directory called `public`:

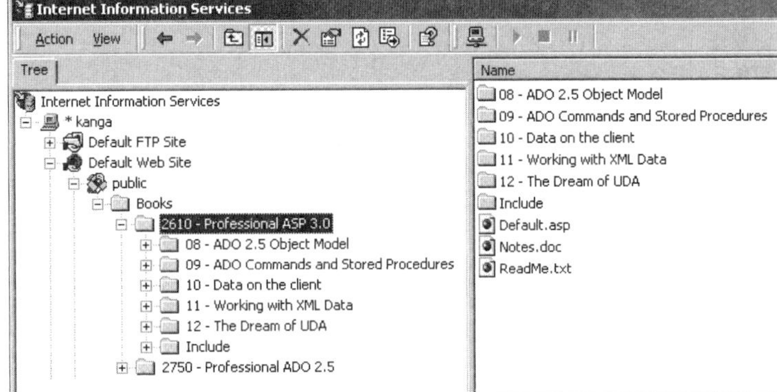

If you had to model this in ADO you might think that this fits neatly into recordsets – maybe nested ones. But look at the highlighted directory – this contains files of different types – there are several directories, an ASP file, and text file, and a Word document. You could easily imagine mapping this onto a recordset, with fields such as Name, Type, Last Access Time, and so on, but unfortunately it's not that simple. What about access permissions – these differ between files and directories. Also for the directories, you need to be able to access the files under the directory, and for files you might want to access the contents.

Because of this complexity the **Record object** was introduced. In the above situation, we have a collection of entries, with some properties that are the same. But each entry also has unique properties, so we need some other way to handle these. A collection is mapped onto a recordset, and an individual file is mapped to a record, with the properties of the file being mapped into the Fields collection.

This means that we have a recordset containing nine rows. Accessing an individual row in the recordset gives us the properties (fields) for that file, but that's all it gives us – just the properties. To access the contents of a file or directory, you need to use a Record object, which contains the unique properties of the file or directory. It's a bit difficult to get used to this concept, but don't worry – you'll see more examples of the Record object in Chapters 11 and 12.

With the initial release of Windows 2000, the only use of the Record object is with the OLE DB Provider for Internet Publishing. Once Microsoft Exchange 6.0 ships, they will be an OLE DB Provider that will offer access to the Exchange Information Store in a similar method, using recordsets and records.

The Stream Object

The **Stream object** is used to access the contents of a *node*, such as an email message, or a Web page. Using the Stream object we have access to the actual contents of a file, or resource. So, combined with the Record and Recordset objects, you can not only get access to files on a Web server, or email messages, but also access their contents. You could therefore build an email client that only uses ADO as its method to access your mail system. This may not seem a great advantage, but it does mean that you don't have to learn the API or Object Model for the mail system – one less learning curve.

> *Another use for streams is XML, where we can access a set of data (structured or semi-structured) as a stream of XML.*

The Stream object is designed to handle binary data, therefore, it can also be used to handle BLOB data, such as images or large chunks of text from databases.

Again, you'll see more examples of the Stream object in Chapters 11 and 12.

Collections

There are several collections in the ADO object library, each of which holds zero or more copies of their associated object. You can use the same structure of code to loop through the collections:

The syntax in VBScript is:

```
For Each Object In Collection
  'Do something with Object
Next
```

For example, to loop through the Fields collection of a Recordset object:

```
For Each objField In rs.Fields
  Response.Write objField.Name & "<BR>"
Next
```

If you prefer JScript, then you can use the `Enumerator` object:

```
for (objField = new Enumerator(rs.Fields);
     !objField.atEnd(); objField.moveNext())
  Response.Write(objField.item().Name + '<BR>');
```

The Fields Collection

The **Fields collection** holds **Field objects** associated with a recordset or a record. For a recordset based on structured data, such as SQL data, the fields will correspond to the columns in the data, and contain details about the column, such as its name, data type, length, and so on. You'll see plenty of examples using the Fields collection as we go through the next few chapters.

For semi-structured data, the properties of an object will correspond to the Fields. You'll see more of this in Chapter 12.

The Parameters Collection

The **Parameters collection** is used solely by the Command object, and identifies the parameters in stored commands. The most frequent use of parameters is with stored procedures in SQL databases, which allow data to be passed into and out of predefined SQL statements. The ability to have parameters that return information to ADO is useful because it allows more than just a recordset to be returned from a stored procedure. For instance, consider a complex stored procedure that updates different tables, and then returns a recordset – you could have output parameters to indicate how many updates took place.

Another good reason for using parameters is performance, especially when you only need to return a single value from a stored procedure. In this case, there is no point having a recordset created for you, just to hold this one value – it's more efficient not to return a recordset, and to return the value in an output parameter.

The Parameters collection is covered in more detail in Chapter 9.

The Errors Collection

The **Errors collection** contains details of the last ADO or OLE DB Provider error that was generated by a command, and can only be accessed through the Connection object. You might think that this is a restriction, since an explicit Connection object is not required, but you can access the implicit Connection object through the `ActiveConnection` property of the Command, Record or Recordset objects. For example:

```
For Each objError In rs.ActiveConnection.Errors
  Response.Write objError.Name & "<BR>"
Next
```

We'll look at the Errors collection in more detail later in this chapter.

The Properties Collection

The **Properties collection** was not shown on the earlier object model diagram so as to reduce confusion. Its relationship to the object model is shown below:

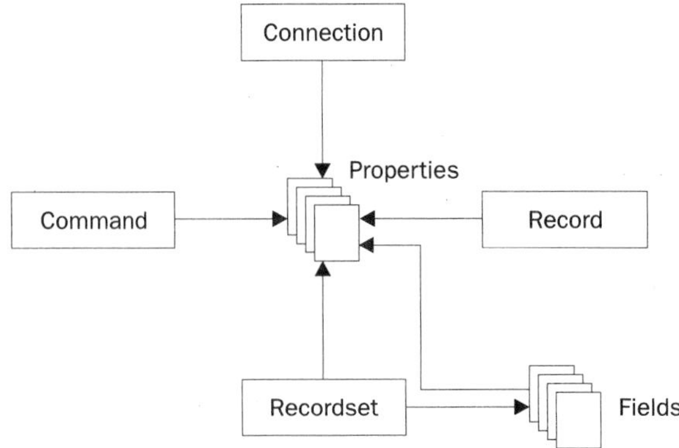

The reason we have a collection of Properties is because ADO is designed to work with many different data stores, each of which might have different facilities. By making the Properties a collection, it is dynamic, and can therefore change according to the data provider. For example, the OLE DB Provider for Jet allows us to access the Jet specific security properties:

```
Set conDB = Server.CreateObject("ADODB.Connection")
conDB.Open "DSN=Nwind"

conDB.Properties("Jet OLEDB:Database Password") = "LetMeIn"
```

None of the other Providers have this property, so it wouldn't be sensible to add this to the Connection object as a static property. By telling ADO which OLE DB Provider you are using, it can fill the Properties collection with the default values for the Provider.

We won't be covering the Properties collection in detail in this book, although there will be occasional use of it. For more information on this collection see Professional ADO 2.5 Programming *or the* ADO 2.5 Programmer's Reference, *both by Wrox Press.*

ADO Constants

When using ADO you'll find that there are predefined constants for a lot of the options, such as those that define the cursor type and lock type. When using languages such as Visual Basic or Visual C++ these constants are automatically available to you once you reference the ADO type library. In ASP this isn't the case, so you have two options.

The first method of reference the constants is to include them in your ASP file:

```
<!-- #INCLUDE FILE="adovbs.inc" -->
```

You can either copy the include file into your local directory, or reference it from the installation directory, the default of which is `C:\Program Files\Common Files\System\ado` (the above file contains the ADO constants for VBScript – for JScript, you should use `adojavas.inc`). One disadvantage of this method is that it makes your ASP page larger, since a whole host of constants are included, many of which you won't typically need.

You could create an include file of your own that contains only the constants you need but you will probably find that you keep editing this file as you take advantage of more and more functionality of ADO.

A better solution is to create a reference to the type library, which makes the constants available without having to include them in the file:

```
<!-- METADATA TYPE="typelib" FILE="C:\Program Files\Common Files\System
                                   \ado\msado15.dll" -->
```

Don't worry that the name of the DLL is `msado15.dll` *– this is the correct name and contains the latest version of ADO.*

You can either include this `METADATA` statement in each ASP file where it's required, or put it in the `global.asa` file, in which case, the constants will be available to every Web page in the application.

Connecting to Data Stores

If you need to access a data store, the first thing you'll need to do is create a *connection* to it. We mentioned earlier that you explicitly use a Connection object or let ADO implicitly create the connection for you – either way you have to know the details of the data store.

The actual method of connecting to a data store is the same for all types of store, although the actual details used to connect are different. This is not surprising, since different Providers need different types of information. Some Providers require user credentials before they allow you access to data stores, whereas others accept default security credentials.

There are several different ways you can connect to a data source:

- A **Connection String**. This is where you put the connection details in a string, or directly into the command that opens the data store. The advantage for this method is that the connection details are kept within the ASP page. The disadvantage is that if you have several pages you'll have more maintenance if you change the connection details. The way around this is to create a string variable with the connection details and have this as an ASP include file – that way you only have a single instance of the connection string, but it's kept with the rest of the ASP pages. Another common technique is to store the connection string in an Application state variable, where it can be used be all pages in the application.
- A **Data Link File**. This is a file (with a `.udl` extension) that contains the connection details. The advantage of this is that you only need a single data link file for any number of ASP pages. To create a data link file, you just create a new text file, and rename it (you'll need to make sure that Windows Explorer shows file extensions). Once renamed, you can just open it (double-click) to get the Data Link Properties dialog. Previous versions of ADO allowed data link files to be created from the New menu in Windows Explorer. We'll look at Data Link files a little later in the chapter.
- **ODBC Data Sources**, or **DSNs**. These are similar to Data Link files, but are only applicable to ODBC Data Sources. They are centralized, and to be used in an ASP page, the Data Source must be a **System Data Source**. ODBC Data Sources are created from the ODBC Data Source Administrator, which can be found in the Administrative Tools folder.

Any of these three methods is as perfectly acceptable as any other, and which you use is a matter of preference. Direct connection strings will probably be marginally faster because all of the connection details are supplied. Data link files require the details to be read from a file, and ODBC DSNs require the details to be retrieved from the registry. The speed difference is very small, but you might as well gain every advantage you can.

Connection Strings

The connection string varies depending upon the Provider, because each Provider of data might require different details.

> **One important point to note is that the OLE DB Provider for ODBC is the default – therefore if you leave off the `Provider=` section, you will automatically use ODBC.**

Listed below are some samples of connection strings for various providers, and you'll see more examples later in the book.

Microsoft Access

If using an ODBC connection, without a DSN:

```
Driver={Microsoft Access Driver (*.mdb)}; DBQ=C:\wrox\database_name.mdb
```

For the native OLE DB Provider:

```
Provider=Microsoft.Jet.OLEDB.4.0; Data Source= C:\wrox\database_name.mdb
```

The examples above show the Access database being stored in the `C:\wrox` directory. Although you might be tempted to store the database within the same directory as the Web files, don't do it, otherwise anyone can download the entire database. It's always preferable to store the database outside the Web directory, where no one externally can access it.

Microsoft SQL Server

For Microsoft SQL Server, using the Provider for ODBC:

```
Driver={SQL Server}; Server=server_name; Database=database_name; UID=user_name;
PWD=user_password
```

For example:

```
Driver={SQL Server}; Server=WATCHER; Database=pubs; UID=davids; PWD=whisky
```

For the native OLE DB Provider, the syntax is similar:

```
Provider=SQLOLEDB; Data Source=server_name; Initial Catalog=database_name; User
Id=user_name; Password=user_password
```

For example:

```
Provider=SQLOLEDB; Data Source=WATCHER; Initial Catalog=pubs; User Id=davids;
Password=whisky
```

Microsoft Indexing Service

The Indexing Service is only accessible through a native OLE DB Provider. The syntax is:

```
Provider=MSIDXS; Data Source=catalog_name
```

For example, using the `Web` catalog:

```
Provider=MSIDXS; Data Source=Web
```

ODBC Drivers

In the examples that use the OLE DB Provider for ODBC, the `Driver` is shown in curly braces. For example:

```
Driver={Microsoft Access Driver (*.mdb)}; DBQ=C:\wrox\database_name.mdb
```

The name you use should be the exact name taken from the list of drivers when creating a new data source:

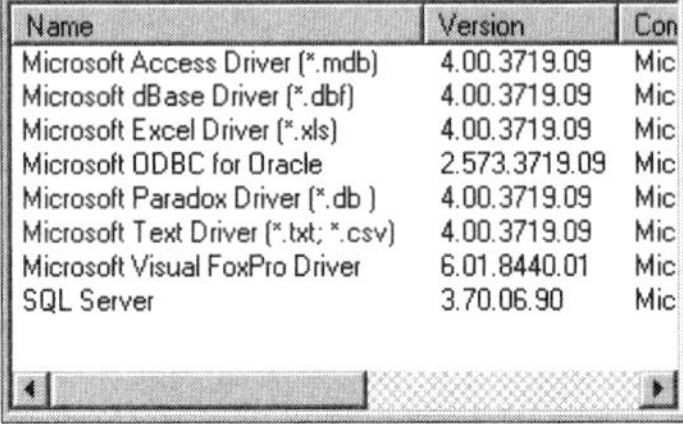

Name	Version	Con
Microsoft Access Driver (*.mdb)	4.00.3719.09	Mic
Microsoft dBase Driver (*.dbf)	4.00.3719.09	Mic
Microsoft Excel Driver (*.xls)	4.00.3719.09	Mic
Microsoft ODBC for Oracle	2.573.3719.09	Mic
Microsoft Paradox Driver (*.db)	4.00.3719.09	Mic
Microsoft Text Driver (*.txt; *.csv)	4.00.3719.09	Mic
Microsoft Visual FoxPro Driver	6.01.8440.01	Mic
SQL Server	3.70.06.90	Mic

Data Link Files

Previous versions of ADO allowed you to create a Data Link file by right-mouse clicking in a directory in Windows Explorer. This created the new file, which you could then open to get the Data Link Properties dialog box. At the time of writing Microsoft had removed this option from the right-mouse button, because they said it "confused users". They have said, however, that they will provide a registry file to re-introduce this functionality.

Remember that you can also create a Data Link file by simply creating a blank text file and renaming the extension to `.udl`.

Once you have the physical data link file, you can open it, either by double-clicking, or right-mouse clicking and selecting Open. You are then presented with the following dialog:

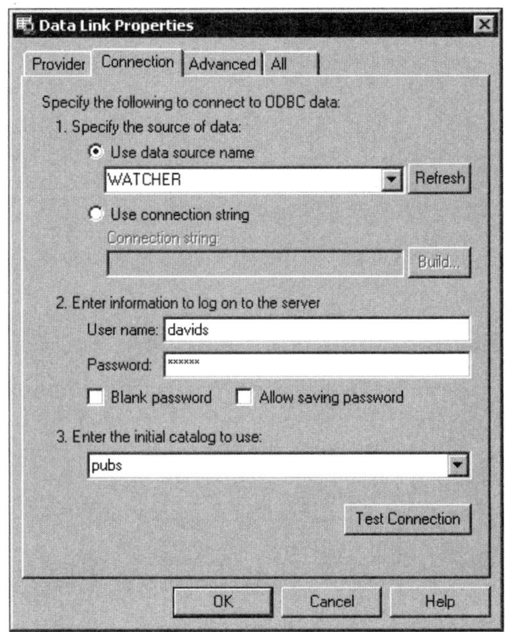

The details of this screen change depending upon the Provider selected. The example above shows the SQL Server Provider, connecting to a SQL Server called `WATCHER`, logging in as `davids` (with the password being masked), and using the `pubs` database. Note that if you select the **Allow saving password** option the password you type will be saved in plain text in the UDL file.

To change the Provider you can select the **Provider** tab:

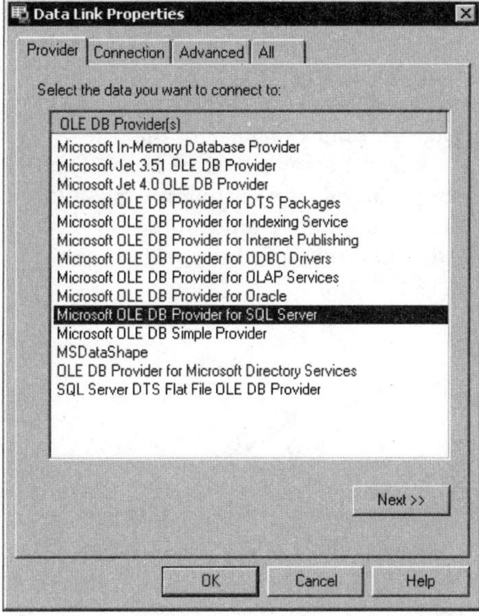

From this selection you can pick whichever Provider you need, and then press the **Next** button to fill in the appropriate connection details.

Alternatively, you can edit the file in a text editor:

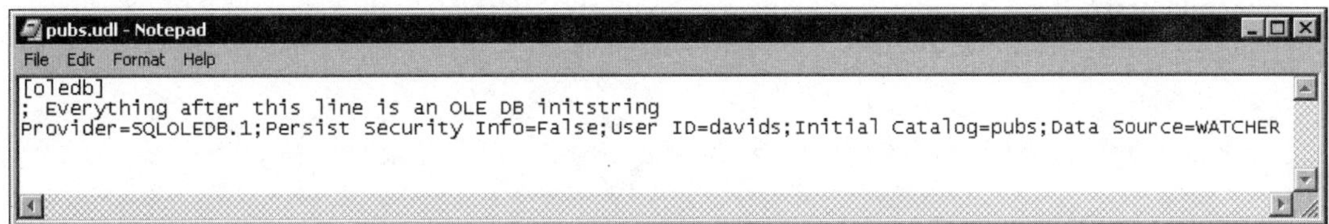

You can see that the UDL file is really just storing a connection string.

To use the data link file you simply specify the data link file when opening the connection:

```
conPubs.Open "File Name=C:\wrox\pubs.udl"
```

ODBC Data Sources

ODBC Data Sources (commonly called Data Source Names, or DSNs) are set up through the Data Sources option on the Administrative Tools menu. Previous versions of Windows had this as an applet in the Control panel. To access a DSN from an ASP page you must make sure that the DSN is set up as a System DSN. This simply involves selecting the System DSN tab on the Data Source Administrator, and then selecting the Add... button:

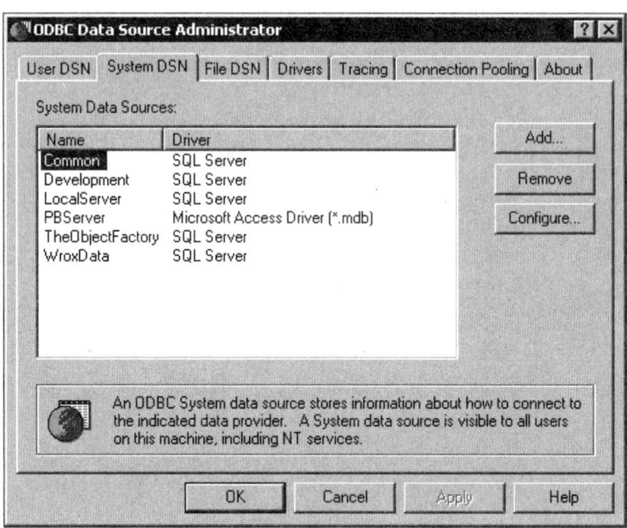

You can then pick the ODBC Driver you wish to use, and fill in the appropriate ODBC parameters.

Once a DSN is set up, you use the `DSN=` attribute of the connection string. For example:

```
conPubs.Open "DSN=pubs"
```

Using Include Files

Using include files to contain your connection strings gives you a central place to store the connection details for a number of ASP pages. To do this, simply create a new ASP file, perhaps called `Connection.asp`, and place the following in it:

```
<%
  strConn = "Provider=SQLOLEDB; Data Source=WATCHER; " & _
            "Initial Catalog=pubs; User Id=davids; Password=whisky"
%>
```

In your ASP pages, you can now add this at the top of the page:

```
<!-- #INCLUDE FILE="Connection.asp" -->
```

This saves you having to type the connection details for each ASP page, and lets you change the connection used for the entire site from one central location.

This include file is also a good place to put the `METADATA` tag for the ADO constants.

Using Connection State

Storing the connection string in an Application variable is quite a common trick too, and equally as effective as using an include file. For example, you could add the following to your `global.asa` file:

```
Sub Application_OnStart()

    strConn = "Provider=SQLOLEDB; Data Source=WATCHER; " & _
              "Initial Catalog=pubs; User Id=davids; Password=whisky

    Set Application("ConnectionString") = strConn

End Sub
```

In our ASP pages you can then use the following:

```
Set conPubs = Server.CreateObject("ADODB.Connection")

conPubs.Open Application("ConnectionString")
```

Personally, I prefer the include file method because I write lots of different samples, connecting to lots of different servers and databases. Using the Application method would mean I'd have to close my browser down every time to restart the application. You can use whichever method you prefer – there's no difference in terms of speed.

> *For most of the examples you will see in this section of the book, I will be using a* `Connection.asp`*, which contains the connection string, as an include file.*

Connection Syntax

OK, so that's the theory, how do you actually go about connecting to this store of data? Well, if using an explicit Connection object, you use the `Open` method, which has a syntax like so:

```
connection.Open [ConnectionString], [UserID], [Password], [Options]
```

The arguments are as follows:

Argument	Description
`ConnectionString`	The string containing the connection details. This can be the name of an ODBC DSN, the name of a Data Link file, or just the actual connection details.
`UserID`	The name of the user to use during the connection. This overrides any user name supplied in the connection string.

Table Continued on Following Page

Argument	Description
`Password`	The password for the user. This overrides and password details supplied in the connection string
`Options`	This can be `adAsyncConnect` to specify that the connection be established asynchronously. Omitting this parameter ensures a synchronous connection.

Connecting asynchronously is no use in an ASP environment, since scripting languages can't receive events from ADO.

Connection Examples

Let's have a look at a few examples – we'll assume that `strConn` contains a valid connection string.

To open a connection you use the `Open` method of the Connection object. For example:

```
Set conPubs = Server.CreateObject("ADODB.Connection")

conPubs.Open strConn

' Some processing

conPubs.Close
```

Alternatively, you can use the `ConnectionString` property:

```
Set conPubs = Server.CreateObject("ADODB.Connection")

conPubs.ConnectionString = strConn
conPubs.Open

' Some processing

conPubs.Close
```

There is no difference between the two, and if you use the former method, then the `ConnectionString` property is filled in for you.

It's worth noting that ADO may change the `ConnectionString` property once the connection to the data store has been established. Don't worry about this, as it's just ADO filling in some extra properties.

Connection Pooling

Connection pooling is something that tends to confuse many people, but the principle is quite simple. When you close a connection, as far as you (and ADO) are concerned, the connection is closed. Underneath the scenes however, OLE DB doesn't actually close the connection – it just places it in a **pool** of *non-active* connections. Whenever you (or anyone else) open a connection, OLE DB first checks the pool for an existing connection that exactly matches the same details. If it finds a connection in the pool you are given this connection. If no connection is in the pool, then a new connection is created for you. Connections are removed from the pool after a default period, so as not to waste server resources.

So what's the advantage of this? Well, opening a connection is one of the slowest actions you can do, therefore, connection pooling enables you to re-connect to data stores without the overhead of creating a connection. This is particularly important in Web sites, where you may have a lot of connections being opened and closed in succession.

> *For ODBC Connections, the pooling can be controlled from the ODBC Data Source Administrator. For OLE DB, Connection pooling (or Session pooling as it is sometimes called) cannot be changed.*

It is important to note that connection pooling is not *connection sharing*. A connection will only be reused once the connection has been closed by its client. Connections that are in-use (that is, have not been closed) are not reused.

Housekeeping

To take effect of connection pooling you need to make sure that your housekeeping is in order. This involves closing Connection objects as soon as possible, so that they can be returned to the pool and reused. You may think that constantly opening and closing connections is costly, but you have to consider scalability – your Web application could be used by many people, and OLE DB is pretty good at managing the connection resources.

> **The general rule is that you should open the connection as late as possible and close it as soon as possible, so the connection is open for the *shortest* period of time possible.**

Recordsets

We mentioned earlier that recordsets are the most commonly used object in ADO, and that's not really surprising. After all, they are the ones that contain the data. But, there's a lot more to recordsets than you might first think, and knowing the details of how the data is held and manipulated is important, since it allows you to make informed decisions on what type of recordset you are going to use.

Type of recordset? You mean there are different types? Indeed there are, and they differ in subtle ways, which can easily trip you up. The first thing to get to grips with is the notion of cursors.

Cursors

A **cursor** is something that confuses many people, but really it's quite simple.

> **A cursor is what manages the set of records and the current location within the recordset, the latter being handled by the current record pointer.**

But wait a minute, isn't that what the Recordset object does? Well yes, but part of what makes a recordset a recordset is its cursor. That still hasn't really answered the question of what a cursor is, so let's look at a recordset:

AU_ID	AU_LNAME	AU_FNAME	PHONE
172-32-1176	White	Bob	408 496-7223
213-46-8915	Green	Marjorie	415 986-7020
238-95-7766	Carson	Cheryl	415 548-7723
267-41-2394	O'Leary	Michael	408 286-2428
274-80-9391	Straight	Dean	415 834-2919
341-22-1782	Smith	Meander	913 843-0462

Here we have six rows and four columns. Pretty standard stuff. When you first open a recordset the current record is the first record – that's the one for `Bob White`. What is it that identifies the current record? Yep, the current **record pointer**. And what handles this pointer? You guessed it – the cursor. So when you move to the next record, or to any other record, it's the cursor that performs the move for you. When you access the fields of the current row the cursor knows which row you are on, so it can return the correct values. If you try to move beyond the end of the recordset, the cursor handles this.

A good way to think about this is to imagine the cursor as a window that can move up and down the recordset. The window is as wide and tall as a single row, so you can only see one row's worth of data at once. When you move to another record, the window moves too.

You might think this is pretty simple, but it's really important, because what you can do with the cursor is determined by the cursor type.

Cursor Types

The type of cursor identifies what functionality the cursor gives to you. There are four types of cursor:

- **Static** (`adOpenStatic`). Static cursors contain a static copy of the records; meaning that the contents of the recordset are fixed at the time the recordset is created. Any records modified, added or deleted by other users will not be visible. Movement through the recordset is allowed both forwards and backwards.

- **Forward Only** (`adOpenForwardOnly`). The default cursor type, which is identical to a Static cursor except that you can only move forwards through the recordset.
- **Dynamic** (`adOpenDynamic`). A dynamic cursor doesn't have a fixed set of records. Any changes, additions or deletions by other users will be visible in the recordset. Movement through the recordset is allowed both forwards and backwards.
- **Keyset** (`adOpenKeyset`). Keyset cursors are similar to Dynamic cursors, except that the set of records is fixed. You can see changes by other users, but new records are not visible. If other users delete records, then these will be inaccessible in the recordset. This functionality is achieved by the set of records being identified by their keys – so the keys remain, even if the records change or are deleted.

To understand these concepts it's easy to think of your cursor window again. Think of Forward-Only cursors as having your window on a ratchet – it can only go forwards. The advantage of this is that once you've gone past a record the cursor can forget completely about it, since it's never going to go back to it. A Static cursor removes the ratchet, allowing backward movement, and because you can also move back through the records, the cursor needs to keep track of these. For this reason Static cursors are slower than Forward-Only cursor.

For Keyset and Dynamic cursors your window can move forwards and backwards, but what you are looking at might change. A Keyset cursor allows you to see *changes* to the data made by other people, but doesn't allow you to see new or deleted records. So, the set of records is fixed, but not the contents. A Dynamic cursor expands on this by allowing not only the contents of the records to change, but also the set of records. So you can see new records appear, and deleted records disappear from the recordset.

The type of cursor you use depends on what you are aiming to achieve. If you simply want to look through the records, perhaps building up a table or a selection list, then a Forward-Only cursor is best. The other cursor types will work just as well, although they may be slower. This is because you cannot move backwards in a Forward-Only recordset, therefore, once you have moved past a record, ADO can forget about it.

The cursor type can have an impact of performance, especially when using server cursors. In Microsoft SQL Server 6.5 for example, both Keyset and Static cursors require a complete copy of the data to be put into the temporary database (`tempdb`). Keysets are slightly more efficient because they only copy the keys into the temporary database. For Microsoft SQL Server 7.0 this is not the case, and the performance of the various cursor types is much less different.

Cursor Location

So we've explained what a cursor is, and how it manages our data for us, but where does it live? Again the answer is one of those 'it depends' answers, because it depends upon the data store. Certain data stores, such as Microsoft SQL Server, have a **cursor service** of their own, whereas others, such as Microsoft Access, don't have a cursor service.

So when you open a recordset, you have to choose whether you want the data store to manage your cursor, or whether you want OLE DB and ADO to manage the cursor locally for you. The latter can be done because OLE DB has its own cursor service. The two options are decided by using the `CursorLocation` property of either the Connection object or the Recordset object. You set this property to one of two values:

- `adUseServer` – To let the data store manipulate the cursor
- `adUseClient` – To let ADO manipulate the cursor

You should set this property before you open the connection or recordset, like so:

```
conPubs.CursorLocation = adUseServer
conPubs.Open strConn
```

Or

```
rsAuthors.CursorLocation = adUseClient
rsAuthors.Open "authors", conPubs
```

The default cursor is server-based, and it's important to understand the difference between the two types. For a server cursor, it's the responsibility of the data store to manage the records. So, when you create a recordset using server cursors, the data store controls the movement along the records, the updating of records, and so on.

For a client cursor, the entire contents of the recordset are copied onto the client, and managed by the local client cursor service. This means that for a client cursor, opening a recordset with a large number of records takes considerably longer than the same recordset using server-based cursors. There are times when you need to use client-based cursors, and you'll see some examples of this when we look at components later in the book.

Firehose Cursors

One thing you might read about is a **firehose cursor**, and it's important to explain this because it can lead to a great improvement in performance. Firehose cursors are only relevant when connecting to Microsoft SQL Server, as it is a special type. What happens is that SQL Server creates the set of records requested by the client, and then just throws this data directly to the client, as fast as the client can receive it. There is very little cursor management by SQL Server itself, which means it can handle the data faster. What this means is that the data is returned to the client in super quick time (that's a technical term). From the client perspective they behave like Forward-Only cursors.

So why didn't I talk about firehose cursors above, when discussing the different cursor types? Because they are only specific to SQL Server, and only when using server-based cursors. There isn't a special type, and the way to get a firehose cursor is to *not* specify a cursor type.

Locking

OK, so that's explained cursors and how the data is managed. Can we get onto creating recordsets yet? I'm afraid not, as there's one topic left – that of **locking**.

Locking is how we ensure the *integrity* of our data, making sure that changes aren't overwritten. We need to avoid the classic lost update situation; where one user changes some data, and then another user changes it immediately afterwards. To manage this protection we lock records, just like we lock our house, and there are several different methods of ensuring that records are protected. We set these methods by the **lock type**.

Lock Types

The lock type determines whether, and how, records are locked when you update them. There are four types of locking:

- **Read Only** (`adLockReadOnly`). The default locking type, which means the recordset is read-only, and records cannot be modified.
- **Pessimistic** (`adLockPessimistic`). When amending a record, the provider will try to lock the record to guarantee the successful editing of the record. This is generally accomplished by locking the record as soon as editing takes place.
- **Optimistic** (`adLockOptimistic`). The record is not locked until the changes to the record are committed to the data store, by way of the `Update` method.
- **Batch Optimistic** (`adLockBatchOptimistic`). Batch optimistic locking allows multiple records to be modified, and the records are only locked when the `UpdateBatch` method is called.

When you don't need to modify any records you should always use a Read-Only recordset, so that the provider does not have to do any checks on the records. For general use, Optimistic is probably best, since the data store only locks the record for a small period of time – whilst it's actually updating the data. This reduces the resources used.

Pessimistic locking increases data integrity, but at the cost of concurrency. This is the ability of many users to view the data at once. A locked record is not available for viewing by other users, therefore concurrency is reduced. Optimistic locking locks the record for a shorter period of time and therefore increases concurrency, but there's a greater chance of the data being modified by others.

For a good discussion on concurrency and locking get hold of Inside SQL Server 7.0, by Ron Soukup and Kalen Delaney, Microsoft Press. In fact it's a great book, so go and buy it anyway - there is a great deal of valuable information in it.

Creating Recordsets

Creating a recordset is extremely easy, and is achieved by the `Open` method of the Recordset object:

```
Recordset.Open [Source], [ActiveConnection], [CursorType],
               [LockType], [Options]
```

The arguments are:

Argument	Descriptions
`Source`	The source of the data. This can be the name of a table from a database, a stored query or procedure, a SQL string, a Command object, or any other command applicable to the Provider.
`ActiveConnection`	The connection to use for the recordset. This can be a connection string or an open Connection object.
`CursorType`	The type of cursor to use. This must be one of the defined cursor types. The default is `adForwardOnly`.
`LockType`	The type of locking to use. This must be one of the defined lock types. The default is `adLockReadOnly`.
`Options`	Tells the provider what the `Source` argument is – that is, whether it is a table, a text string, and so on.

For example, to open a recordset on the `authors` table in the `pubs` database:

```
Dim rsAuthors

Set rsAuthors = Server.CreateObject("ADODB.Recordset")

rsAuthors.Open "authors", strConn

' Do something here

rsAuthors.Close
Set rsAuthors = Nothing
```

Notice that several of the arguments have been left off. In fact, all of the arguments are optional, and you could set their corresponding properties before opening the recordset:

```
Dim rsAuthors

Set rsAuthors = Server.CreateObject("ADODB.Recordset")

With rsAuthors
   .Source = "authors"
   .ActiveConnection = strConn
   .CursorType = adOpenForwardOnly
   .LockType = adLockReadOnly
   .Open
End With

' Do something here

rsAuthors.Close
Set rsAuthors = Nothing
```

Once the recordset has been opened, you are automatically placed on the first record. If there are no records in the recordset, then both the `BOF` and `EOF` properties will be `True`:

```
rsAuthors.Open "authors", strConn

If rsAuthors.BOF and rsAuthors.EOF Then
  ' Recordset is empty
End If
```

The Options *Argument*

The `Options` argument of the `Open` method allows you to specify what the command text contains. It can be one of the following `CommandTypeEnum` constants:

- `adCmdText` – To indicate a text command, such as a SQL string
- `adCmdTable` – To indicate the name of a table
- `adCmdStoredProc` – To indicate the name of a stored procedure
- `adCmdFile` – To indicate the file name of a saved recordset
- `adCmdTableDirect` –To indicate the name of a table
- `adCmdURLBind` – To indicate a URL

The difference between `adCmdTable` and `adCmdTableDirect` is small, but if you want all columns from a table, then `adCmdTableDirect` is marginally faster, as ADO performs some internal optimization.

If you don't specify the type of command then ADO has to work out what type of command is being executed, leading to a marginal overhead.

There are also two other options: `adCmdUnspecified`, indicating that no type is specified, and `adCmdUnknown`, indicating that the command type is not known. In general, you probably won't use these.

Additional Options

The `Options` argument can be one of the above constants, but you can also add in one of the following `ExecuteOptionEnum` constants:

- `adAsyncExcute` – To indicate the command should be executed asynchronously
- `adAsyncFetch` – To indicate that after the initial set of rows has been fetched, and remaining rows are fetched asynchronously
- `adAsyncFetchNonBlocking` – Similar to `adAsyncFetch`, except that the fetching of records never blocks commands
- `adExecuteNoRecords` – To indicate that the command does not return any records

Asynchronous processing means that actions happen in the background; so instead of running a command and waiting for it to finish (**synchronously**), you can run the command, and then carry on doing something else, whilst the command is executing in the background. This can be used to great advantage when building user interfaces, as you can return from the command and show the user something, whilst the data is still being fetched in the background. It is less useful to the ASP programmer when returning recordsets, since scripting languages don't support ADO events, therefore you would never know when the recordset was finished being populated. You could use asynchronous operations when dealing with commands that update, delete or insert data, and that don't return a recordset, but only if you don't care about the results.

The `adExecuteNoRecords` option on the other hand, is extremely useful. It tells ADO that the command you are executing does not return any data; therefore, there is no point in building a recordset (which would be empty anyway). This can speed up action queries, where you are running commands that update or add data.

To add one of these options you can use the `Or` statement (or its equivalent the plus (+) sign):

```
adCmdStoredProc Or adExecuteNoRecords
```

```
adCmdStoredProc + adExecuteNoRecords
```

We'll be looking at this in more detail in the next chapter, since it's more useful when dealing with commands, rather than recordsets.

Moving Through the Recordset

Once you have a recordset open you often need to loop through each record. This is where the `EOF` property really comes in to play. `EOF` becomes `True` when the end of the recordset has been reached, so you can construct a loop like this:

```
rsAuthors.Open "authors", strConn

While Not rsAuthors.EOF
  Response.Write rsAuthors("au_lname") & ", " & _
                 rsAuthors("au_fname") & "<BR>"
  rsAuthors.MoveNext
Wend
```

The above example continues the loop until the `EOF` property is `True`. The `MoveNext` method is used to move to the next record.

If your recordset allows moving backwards you can use `MovePrevious`, in which case your loop should check for `BOF`. There are also `MoveFirst` and `MoveLast` methods that move you to the first and last records in the recordset respectively:

```
  rsAuthors.Open "authors", strConn, adOpenDynamic
' Now on first record

  rsAuthors.MoveLast
' Now on last record
```

```
  rsAuthors.MovePrevious
  rsAuthors.MovePrevious
  rsAuthors.MovePrevious
' Now three rows from the end of the recordset

  rsAuthors.MoveFirst
' Back at the beginning again
```

Using the Fields Collection

The Fields collection contains a Field object for each field (column) in the recordset. The Fields collection is the default collection of the recordset, and can therefore be omitted when accessing fields, as is the case in the `While…Wend` example above. Because of this, there are several ways to access fields:

```
rsAuthors.Fields("au_lname").Value
rsAuthors("au_lname").Value
rsAuthors(1).Value
rsAuthors.Fields(1).Value
```

You can use either the field name, or its position in the collection. Using the name is preferable, as your code is more easily maintainable.

The `Value` property is the default property for a field, and can therefore also be omitted, like so:

```
rsAuthors("au_lname")
```

If you need to loop through all of the fields, you can use the `For Each` construct:

```
For Each fldAuthor In rsAuthors.Fields
  Response.Write fldAuthor.Name & " : " & _
                 fldAuthor.Value & "<BR>"
Next
```

This example prints the name and value of each field.

Bookmarks

When you are moving around the recordset you might want to retain the position of a record and then move back to it later. In a similar way to real bookmarks, a **recordset bookmark** holds a unique pointer to an individual record.

To use a bookmark you simple assign the `Bookmark` property to a variable:

```
varBkmk = rsAuthors.Bookmark
```

You can then move about the recordset, and later return to the bookmark record by performing the reverse command:

```
rsAuthors.Bookmark = varBkmk
```

Bookmarks are extremely useful when searching for records in a recordset. There's an example of this in the *Find* section, a little later in the chapter.

Note that not all recordsets support bookmarks – the `Supports` *method (discussed below) allows you to identify this.*

There is one very important point to note about bookmarks – you cannot use them across different recordsets, even if those recordsets are created from the same command. Consider the following:

```
rsAuthors.Open "authors", strConn
rsAuthorsOther.Open "authors", strConn

varBkmk = rsAuthors.Bookmark
varBkmkOther = rsAuthorsOther.Bookmark
```

Despite the fact that both recordsets are created using the same command, the bookmarks for the recordsets are *not* the same.

You can achieve interchangeable bookmarks by using the `Clone` *method, but we won't discuss that here.*

Supported Functionality

As mentioned above, not all recordsets support bookmarks. There are other recordset options that are not supported by all providers, or types of recordsets, so you can use the `Supports` method to identify these.

`Supports` takes one or more of the `CursorOptionEnum` values as its argument, and returns `True` or `False` to indicate whether the options are supported. The list of values in is quite large, and is therefore in Appendix F.

For example:

```
If rsAuthors.Supports(adBookmark) Then
' The recordset supports bookmarks
  varBkMk = rsAuthors.Bookmark
End If
```

You can combine more than one constant using `Or` or the plus sign (+):

```
If rsAuthors.Supports(adBookmark Or adFind) Then
' The recordset supports bookmarks and use of Find
End If
```

Filtering Recordsets

Filtering is a way of temporarily restricting the view of records in a recordset. This is useful if you want to only show certain records in a recordset, but you don't want to re-query the data store every time.

Filtering with a Criteria

The `Filter` property takes a variety of arguments, one of which is a criterion very much like a SQL `WHERE` clause:

```
rsAuthors.Filter = "state = 'ca'"
```

This would restrict the recordset to only show those records where `state` was `ca`. Applying this filter would place you back on the first matching record. You could loop through all of the records in the recordset, and only those records that match the criteria would be visible in the recordset.

You are not limited to single search criteria, and you can use `And` or `Or` to join multiple criteria together:

```
rsAuthors.Filter = "au_lname = 'Homer' Or au_lname = 'Francis'"
```

This would include in the filter only records where the last name was `Francis` or `Homer`.

The above examples show filter where a column matches a value, but you can use any of the following for the operator:

```
< for less than
> for greater than
<= for less than or equal to
>= for greater than or equal to
<> for not equal to
LIKE for wildcards
```

When using wildcards you can use either the `*` or the `%` character. For example:

```
rsAuthors.Filter = "au_lname LIKE 'Ho%'"
```

The `*` or `%` acts as a wildcard, matching any number of characters. So, the above example would match all records where the contents of the `au_lname` field starting with `Ho`.

You can use an empty string to reset (clear) the filter, so that all records are once again shown:

```
rsAuthors.Filter = ""
```

Filtering with a Constant

The `Filter` property can also take one of the `FilterGroupEnum` constants as its argument. These are:

- `adFilterNone` – To remove the current filter. This has the same affect as using an empty string.
- `adFilterPendingRecords` – To view only records that have changed, but have not yet been sent to the server. This is only applicable in batch update mode.
- `adFilterAffectedRecords` – To view only records affected by the last `Delete`, `Resync`, `UpdateBatch` or `CancelBatch` method call.
- `adFilterFetchedRecords` – To view records in the cache. This means the results of the last method call to retrieve records.
- `adFilterConflictingRecords` – To view records that failed to update during the last batch update.

We'll be looking at batch updating in a little while.

Filtering with Bookmarks

The last method of filtering recordsets is to use an array of bookmarks. This allows you to build up a list of records, and then at a later date apply a filter. For example:

```
  rsAuthors.Open "authors", strConn, adOpenKeyset, _
                 adLockReadOnly, adCmdTableDirect

' Save bookmark for the first record
  avarBkmk(0) = rsAuthors.Bookmark

' Move forward two records
  rsAuthors.MoveNext
  rsAuthors.MoveNext

' Save bookmark for the third record
  avarBkmk(1) = rsAuthors.Bookmark

' Move to the end and save the bookmark
  rsAuthors.MoveLast
  avarBkmk(2) = rsAuthors.Bookmark

' Now apply the filter
  rsAuthors.Filter = Array(avarBkmk(0), avarBkmk(1), avarBkmk(2))

' Now loop through the recordset
  While Not rsAuthors.EOF
    Response.Write rsAuthors("au_lname") & "<BR>"
    rsAuthors.MoveNext
  Wend
```

When you loop through the recordset at the end, there are only three records, because only three bookmarks were applied in the filter.

Notice that we can't use the `avarBkmk` array directly – you have to use the `Array` function to convert the individual bookmarks to a variant array.

Searching For Records

Searching for individual records is performed with the `Find` method. It is similar in usage to filtering with a criterion:

```
rsAuthors.Find "au_lname = 'Lloyd'"
```

The main difference is that you can only have one criterion – using `And` or `Or` is not allowed.

You can use optional arguments to specify some extra options. The full syntax is:

```
Recordset.Find Criteria, [SkipRows], [SearchDirection], [Start]
```

`SkipRows` is a number, indicating the number of rows to skip before starting the search. By default this is 0, and the search starts on the current row.

`SearchDirection` can be either `adSearchForward` to search forwards in the recordset, or `adSearchBackward` to search backwards in the recordset.

`Start` is a bookmark, identifying the position from which to start the search.

If the record you search for is found, then you are placed at that record. If the record isn't found, then you are positioned in one of two places:

- If searching forwards, then you are positioned after the end of the recordset, and `EOF` is set.
- If searching backwards, then you are positioned before the start of the recordset, and `BOF` is set.

Using Bookmarks to Save Your Position

This re-positioning when records are not found is one place where bookmarks come in handy, since you can bookmark your current position, search for a record, and if not found, move back to the saved position. For example:

```
' Save the current position
  varBkmk = rsAuthors.Bookmark

' Find the record
  rsAuthors.Find "au_lname = 'Sussman'"

' Was it found
  If Not rsAuthors.EOF Then
    Response.Write "Found: " & rsAuthors("au_lname") & ", " & _
                   rsAuthors("au_fname") &" <BR>"
  Else
    Response.Write "Not found. Moving <BR>"
    rsAuthors.Bookmark = varBkmk
  End If
```

One good reason to use `Filter` over `Find` is that you can only specify one search criterion in a `Find` statement, but `Filter` allows multiple criteria to be specified. This means that if you want to find a record with values in more than one field you cannot use `Find`. You can however, filter the records, and then remove the filter once the record has been found.

Modifying Records

Whilst a large proportion of the Web is used to just display information, the Web application is becoming more common place. In this situation, it's really no good just having read-only data. If you are building an application you nearly always need to modify existing data, or add new data, and there are several ways you can do this. In this section, we'll look at using the methods of the Recordset object to alter date, and in the next chapter we'll look at how you can use action queries to perform the same task.

Using the Recordset object's methods, you use a locking type *other than* `adLockReadOnly` to be able to change the data (assuming you have permission, or the underlying command doesn't disallow changes). Remember that the default locking type is read-only.

Adding Records

To add records to a recordset you use the `AddNew` method. There are two ways of using this. The first, and probably most widely used, is without any arguments – you simply call `AddNew`, and a new, empty record is placed at the end of the recordset. You are then free to change the data in the fields before calling the `Update` method to save your changes:

```
With rsAuthors
  .Open "authors", strConn, adOpenDynamic, _
        adLockOptimistic, adCmdTableDirect

  .AddNew
    .Fields("au_id") = "123-12-1234"
    .Fields("au_lname") = "Lloyd"
    .Fields("au_fname") = "Janine"
    .Fields("contract") = 0
  .Update

End With
```

This simply adds a new record, setting the four mandatory fields.

An alternative way is to use the optional arguments of the `AddNew` method, which are two arrays – one of the field names and one of the field values:

```
With rsAuthors
  .Open "authors", strConn, adOpenDynamic, _
        adLockOptimistic, adCmdTableDirect

  .AddNew Array("au_id", "au_lname", "au_fname", "contract"), _
          Array("123-12-1234", "Lloyd", "Janine", 0)

End With
```

This method doesn't require a call to the `Update` method.

Editing Records

Editing records is similar to the first method of inserting records – the difference being that you don't need to call the AddNew method:

```
strSQL = "SELECT * FROM authors" & _
         " WHERE au_lname='Lloyd'"

With rsAuthors
  .Open strSQL, strConn, adOpenDynamic, _
        adLockOptimistic, adCmdText

  .Fields("contract") = 1
  .Update

End With
```

This simply sets the contract field of the current record (in this case the first record, since we've just opened the recordset) to 1.

Deleting Records

To delete records you call the Delete method. Which records are deleted depends upon the optional argument, which can be one of the AffectEnum constants:

- adAffectCurrent – To indicate only the current record is deleted. This is the default action.
- adAffectGroup – To indicate that all records matching the current filter are deleted.
- adAffectAll – To indicate all records in the recordset are deleted.
- adAffectAllChapters – To indicate that records in all chapters are deleted.

At its simplest, you can just do this:

```
rsAuthors.Delete
```

This will delete the current record. If you have a Filter in place and you wish to delete all records that match the filter, then you can just add the appropriate constant:

```
rsAuthors.Delete adAffectGroup
```

Auto-Increment Fields

One of the problems that people always encounter with ADO when adding new records is that of auto-increment, or identity fields. These fields are numeric fields that are automatically updated by the database server, and are generally used to provide a unique field for each row. When the database contains multiple-tables, which is most of the time, then this unique field is often used as a foreign key in related tables. Therefore, when you add a new record you often need to find out this value.

For example, consider a table with two fields – an `ID` fields which as an auto-increment field (an `IDENTITY` field in SQL Server or an `AutoNumber` in Access), and a text field called `Name`. Now consider the following code to add a record to this table:

```
With rsData
    .Open "tblTest", adOpenDynamic, adLockOptimistic, adCmdTableDirect
    .AddNew
    .Fields("Name") = "Janine"
    .Update

    intID = .Fields("ID")
End With
```

This may seem trivial, but whether you can obtain this value after adding a new record depends upon the cursor type, the lock type, and whether or not the `ID` field is indexed. The table below lists which combinations of these allow retrieval of the value of the newly inserted ID field. Any combinations not shown mean that the value will not be returned:

Provider	Target	Indexed	Cursor Location	Cursor Type	Lock Type
ODBC	Access 97	Yes	Server	Keyset	Pessimistic Optimistic
	Access 2000	Yes	Server	Keyset	Pessimistic Optimistic
		No	Client	All	Pessimistic Optimistic
	SQL Server 6.5	Yes	Server	Keyset	Pessimistic Optimistic
	SQL Server 7	Yes	Server	Keyset	Pessimistic Optimistic
			Client	All	Pessimistic Optimistic
		No	Client	All	Pessimistic Optimistic
Jet 4.0	Access 97	Yes	Server	All	All
	Access 2000	Yes	Server	All	All
		No	Client	All	Pessimistic Optimistic

Provider	Target	Indexed	Cursor Location	Cursor Type	Lock Type
SQL OLE DB	SQL Server 6.5 SQL Server 7.0	Yes	Server	Keyset	Pessimistic Optimistic
			Client	All	Pessimistic Optimistic
		No	Client	All	Pessimistic Optimistic

This clearly shows that you must use the right combination to ensure you can obtain the correct value for the ID field. If you don't then you will get 0, and empty value, or NULL, depending upon the combination.

We'll look at another way of retrieving `IDENTITY` fields from SQL Server in the next chapter, when we deal with stored procedures.

Managing Errors

When dealing with data stores there is always the possibility of errors – security problems, trying to update a record that someone else has deleted, and so on. You can never guarantee that everything is going to work perfectly, so you have to build in some form of error control.

In Chapter 7 we looked at general error handling in ASP pages, but now we are dealing with data stores, we have to consider extra code to handle this too. Let's first look at the Errors collection before moving on to examine how that can be fitted into the new ASP 3.0 error handling structure.

The Errors Collection

The Errors collection contains an **Error object** for each error that occurred during a single ADO command. The reason we have a collection is that multiple errors may occur during a command, and the OLE DB Provider needs a way to inform the client that more that one error has occurred.

There are two important points to note about the Errors collection:

- Each time an ADO command is run, if an error occurs, the Errors collection is cleared and filled with the new details. However, if no error occurred, then the Errors collection is not touched. Therefore, the collection may contain errors even though the ADO command completed successfully.
- The OLE DB Provider may fill the Errors collection with informational messages or warnings, which will have an error number of 0. Therefore you cannot just check the number of errors in the collection and assume that an error has occurred. For instance, using the Provider for ODBC to connect to SQL Server you may get 'errors' informing you that the default database has been changed.

If you flick back to the object model near the beginning of this chapter, you'll notice that the Errors collection is only accessible from the Connection object. How then, you might wonder, can you access this if you haven't explicitly created a Connection object? Well, the Recordset object has an `ActiveConnection` property, which contains the Connection object for the current Recordset. This means that you can get to the Errors collection like so:

```
rsAuthors.ActiveConnection.Errors
```

Since we want to see all errors that occur, you really need to loop through the collection:

```
For Each errAuthors In rsAuthors.ActiveConnection.Errors
  'Display error
Next
```

To display some sensible error information you need to know exactly what's stored in this collection. The Error object contains the following properties:

Property	Description
`Number`	The ADO error number
`NativeError`	The error number from the data provider
`SQLState`	The 5 digit SQL state code for the error, when connecting to SQL databases
`Source`	The object that generated the error
`Description`	Descriptive text of the error

This means that your loop can now become:

```
For Each errAuthors In rsAuthors.ActiveConnection.Errors

  Response.Write "Number: " & errAuthors.Number & _
                 "<BR>NativeError: " & errAuthors.NativeError & _
                 "<BR>SQLState: " & errAuthors.SQLState & _
                 "<BR>Source: " & errAuthors.Source & _
                 "<BR>Description: " & errAuthors.Description & _
                 "<P>"
Next
```

ADO Errors in ASP Pages

In the Chapters 4 and 7 we examined ASP errors, and how they can be handled in a clean and neat way. One of the new features of ASP 3.0 is the advanced objects of the custom error pages, but this really falls down with ADO, because of one simple point – the script variables are not passed into the custom error page. This means that there's no way to examine the Errors collection.

So, we have a situation where you have to provide your own error handling. If you are using JScript as your server-side programming language then you have the new try/catch feature, but VBScript is still stuck in the dark ages with its error handling. At the moment the best way to check for errors is to use the `On Error Resume Next` statement, and then after each line of ADO code that could potentially raise an error, check the Errors collection. Something like this:

```
<%
  On Error Resume Next

  Dim rsAuthors
  Dim strSQL

  Set rsAuthors = Server.CreateObject("ADODB.Recordset")

  strSQL = "SELECT MissingColumn1, MissingColumn2, au_lname, au_fname " & _
           " FROM authors"

  rsAuthors.Open strSQL, strConn, adOpenDynamic, adLockOptimistic, adCmdText

  If CheckForErrors (rsAuthors.ActiveConnection) = False Then
    While Not rsAuthors.EOF
      Response.Write rsAuthors("au_lname") & ", " & _
                     rsAuthors("au_fname") & "<BR>"
      rsAuthors.MoveNext
    Wend
  End If

  rsAuthors.Close
  Set rsAuthors = Nothing

%>
```

Here we use the `CheckForErrors` routine to see if there are any errors. This would look like:

```
Function CheckForErrors(objConn)

  Dim objError    ' Error object

' Errors means the count will be greater than 0
  If objConn.Errors.Count > 0 Then

  ' Loop through the errors
    For Each objError in objConn.Errors

    ' Errors with number 0 are informational
      If objError.Number <> 0 Then
         Response.Write "<TABLE BORDER=1>" & _
                        "<TR><TD>Error Property</TD><TD>Contents</TD>" & _
                        "</TR><TR><TD>Number</TD><TD>" & objError.Number & _
                        "</TD></TR><TR><TD>NativeError</TD><TD>" & _
                        objError.NativeError & "</TD></TR>" & _
                        "<TR><TD>SQLState</TD><TD>" & objError.SQLState & _
                        "</TD></TR><TR><TD>Source</TD><TD>" & _
```

```
                    objError.Source & "</TD></TR>" & _
                    "<TR><TD>Description</TD><TD>" & _
                    objError.Description & "</TD></TR></TABLE><P>"
            CheckForErrors = True
          End If

        Next

      Else
        CheckForErrors = False
      End If

    End Function
```

This routine simply checks to see if there are any errors, and if so, creates a table for each error, giving the following result:

Error Property	Contents
Number	-2147217900
NativeError	207
SQLState	42S22
Source	Microsoft OLE DB Provider for SQL Server
Description	Invalid column name 'MissingColumn1'.

Error Property	Contents
Number	-2147217900
NativeError	207
SQLState	42S22
Source	Microsoft OLE DB Provider for SQL Server
Description	Invalid column name 'MissingColumn2'.

Whilst this isn't the most technical solution, it's really about the best we can do with VBScript. The real downside is that you have to check for errors yourself.

Summary

We've covered a lot of ground in this chapter, but it's been an important grounding in the fundamentals of ADO. What you've seen so far might well be the largest part of ADO you use, since we've covered the most important topics:

- How ADO fits into ASP
- The fundamentals of recordset structure
- How to access some basic data stores, and manipulate the data from them
- How to manage data access errors

Although these techniques will be used over and over again, they really are just the tip of the ADO iceberg. Now comes the time to expand on the basic knowledge and look at the Command object, to see how the use of some advanced features can improve performance and maintainability of your ASP pages.

N
W

9

Connections, Commands And Procedures

In the previous chapter, we looked at the basics of ADO, concerning ourselves mainly with the Recordset object and the manipulation of data. In most of the examples, we obtained data by simply specifying the name of a database table, but as you've seen from the object model, ADO has other objects that allow data to be accessed.

In this chapter we are going to look at some of these in more detail. In particular, we shall examine:

- The Connection object, and how it can be used to retrieve data and run commands
- The Command object, why it is necessary, and what facilities it has
- How to run stored procedures, especially those that require parameters
- Some simple optimization techniques for improving ADO performance
- What Data Shaping is, and how it can be used

Like the Recordset object, we're not going to cover all of the methods and properties of the objects involved. Instead, we're going to cover the most important topics, and those methods and properties that are most applicable for an ASP developer.

The Connection Object

We mentioned in the previous chapter that the Connection object is what gives us a connection to the data store, but that's not all the Connection object does. As well as storing details of the connection (such as the type of data store and the features it supports), we can use the connection to run commands.

These commands can be action queries, such as updates, inserts or deletes, as well as commands that return a recordset. You might wonder what use this is, since we have the Recordset object, but it's all part of the flexibility of ADO, that allows you to use whichever object is the most convenient, and most suited to the task in hand.

The commands run from the Connection object are generally action queries, but it's useful to know that you can get recordsets returned too.

Returning a Recordset

To return a recordset from the Connection object you use the `Execute` method. The syntax of this method is:

```
Connection.Execute CommandText, [RecordsAffected], [Options]
```

The arguments are:

Argument	Description
`CommandText`	The text of the command to execute. This is the same as the `Source` of the Recordset `Open` method, and can also represent an existing Command object.
`RecordsAffected`	A variable into which is placed the number of records affected by the command.
`Options`	The command options, which can be one or more of the values from the `CommandTypeEnum` or `ExecuteOptionEnum` constants, as detailed in the previous chapter.

The `Execute` method optionally returns a recordset, in which case you simply assign the Recordset variable as the return value. For example:

```
Set conPubs = Server.CreateObject("ADODB.Connection")

conPubs.Open strConn

Set rsAuthors = conPubs.Execute ("Authors")
```

You might wonder what the difference is between using the `Execute` method of the Connection object and the `Open` method of the Recordset object. It may not seem that there's much difference, but remember that with the `Open` method of the Recordset you have the ability to change the cursor type and lock type of the resulting recordset. These options are not available for the `Execute` method of the connection, so you will always get a forward-only, read-only recordset.

Action Commands

If you are running action commands, such as a SQL UPDATE statement, then you can use the RecordsAffected argument to find out how many records were affected by the command. For example:

```
Dim strSQL As String
Dim lngRecs As Long

strSQL = "UPDATE Titles SET Price = Price * 1.10" & _
         " WHERE Type='Business'"

conPubs.Execute strSQL, lngRecs, adCmdText

Response.Write lngRecs & " records were updated."
```

This updates the price for all business books by 10%. Once the Execute command has completed, the number of titles affected by the update will be available in lngRecs – this is the RecordsAffected argument.

Notice that we've specified adCmdText for the options of this command – this tells ADO that the command text is a text command. Whilst this isn't strictly necessary, it does allow ADO to know ahead of time what sort of command is being executed, and therefore improves performance. Remember that this value can be one or more of the values from the CommandTypeEnum values.

No Recordset Returned

If no recordset is being returned, as in the example above, then it's also best to add another option to the Execute statement:

```
conPubs.Execute strSQL, lngRecs, adCmdText + adExecuteNoRecords
```

Using adExecuteNoRecords tells ADO that the command being executed does not return any records. ADO therefore doesn't bother building a recordset. If you omit this option then ADO builds an empty recordset, which is clearly a waste of time, so adding the option will speed up the statement.

The Command Object

The Command object is designed specifically to deal with commands of any sort, but especially those that require parameters. Like the Connection object, the Command object can run both commands that return recordsets as well as those that don't. In fact, if your command doesn't have parameters, then it really doesn't matter whether you use a Connection, a Command, or a Recordset.

Returning Recordsets

For a recordset-returning command you would use the `Execute` method. However, unlike the Connection object, you do not specify the command text in the `Execute` method itself – you have to use the `CommandText` property:

```
Set cmdAuthors = Server.CreateObject("ADODB.Command")

cmdAuthors.CommandText = "Authors"

Set rsAuthors = cmdAuthors.Execute
```

This is the simplest way to tell the Command object to run a simple command that returns a read-only recordset.

The `Execute` method also has some optional arguments:

Argument	Description
`RecordsAffected`	A variable into which is placed the number of records affected by the command.
`Parameters`	An array of parameter values.
`Options`	The command options. This is similar to the `Options` of the Recordset `Open` method.

The `RecordsAffected` and `Options` are as previously explained, although you can set the command type by using the `CommandType` property:

```
Set cmdAuthors = Server.CreateObject("ADODB.Command")

cmdAuthors.CommandText = "Authors"
cmdAuthors.CommandType = adCmdTable

Set rsAuthors = cmdAuthors.Execute
```

You can also set this on the `Execute` line itself – if you're not setting the other arguments though, you must still include the commas for them:

```
Set rsAuthors = cmdAuthors.Execute(, , adCmdTable)
```

We'll look at the use of the `Parameters` argument a little later in the chapter, when we deal with stored procedures and parameters.

Changing the Cursor Type

One important thing to note about recordsets that are returned from the `Execute` method is that they have the default cursor and lock types. This means they are forward-only, read-only recordsets. There's no way to change this using the `Execute` method, but there is a way around this problem.

If you need to use a command, and require a different cursor or lock type, then you should use the `Open` method of the Recordset, but use the Command as the source of the Recordset. For example:

```
cmdAuthors.ActiveConnection = strConn
cmdAuthors.CommandText = "Authors"
cmdAuthors.CommandType = adCmdTable

rsAuthors.Open cmdAuthors, , adOpenDynamic, adLockOptimistic
```

Notice that the connection details on the `Open` line have been omitted, because the connection is set in the Command. The connection details could also have been set in the `ActiveConnection` property of the Command before it is opened.

Action Commands

For **action** commands, such as those that update data without returning any records, the procedure is similar – you just leave off the bits that set the recordset:

```
Set cmdUpdate = Server.CreateObject("ADODB.Command")

strSQL = "UPDATE Titles SET Price = Price * 1.10" & " WHERE Type='Business'"

cmdUpdate.ActiveConnection = strConn
cmdUpdate.CommandText = sSQL
cmdUpdate.CommandType = adCmdText

cmdUpdate.Execute , , adExecuteNoRecords
```

Notice that we set the command type in one place and then add any extra options in the `Execute` line. This runs the `UPDATE` command and ensures that no recordset is created.

Stored Procedures

The use of **stored procedures** is the one area where the Command object comes into its own. A stored procedure (or stored query as it's sometimes called) is a predefined SQL query stored on the database.

So why should we create and use a stored procedure instead of just creating a SQL string on the fly, as in the example shown above? Well, there are several reasons:

- A stored procedure is compiled by the database. This produces an **execution plan**, so the database knows exactly what it's going to do. This makes the execution of the procedure faster.
- Stored procedures are often cached by the database, thus making them faster to run, as they don't have to be read from disk. Not all databases support this caching mechanism – Microsoft Access doesn't, but SQL Server does.

- You can make your data a little bit more secure by specifying that your database tables can be modified only by stored procedures. This means that potentially dangerous SQL operations generated on the fly may not be performed.
- You avoid cluttering your ASP code with lengthy SQL statements. This makes the ASP code easier to maintain.
- You can keep all of the SQL code together, on the server.
- You can use output parameters in a stored procedure, which allows you to return both a recordset and other values.

> **As a general rule, stored procedures will nearly always be quicker than their equivalent SQL statements.**

To use a stored procedure you just put the name of the stored procedure as the command text, and set the type accordingly. For example, consider the previous example of updating book prices. If we created a stored procedure on SQL Server, it might look like this:

```
CREATE PROCEDURE usp_UpdatePrices
AS
    UPDATE Titles
    SET    Price = Price * 1.10
    WHERE  Type='Business'
```

For a Microsoft Access database you can create a simple update query to do the same task:

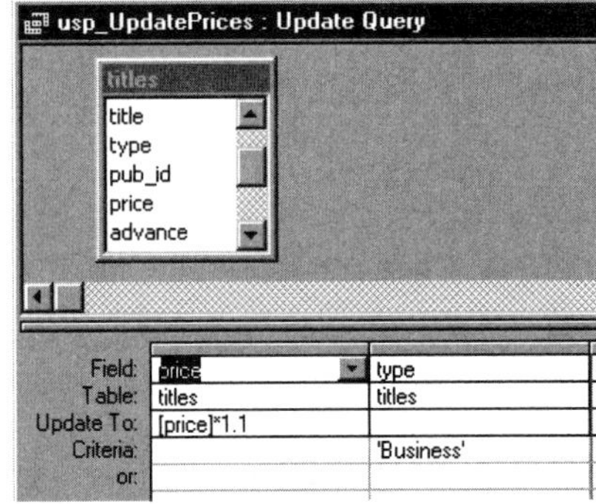

To run this stored procedure from an ASP page, you'd simply use the following code:

```
Set cmdUpdate = Server.CreateObject("ADODB.Command")

cmdUpdate.ActiveConnection = strConn
cmdUpdate.CommandText = "usp_UpdatePrices"
cmdUpdate.CommandType = adCmdStoredProc

cmdUpdate.Execute , , adExecuteNoRecords
```

This simply runs the stored procedure. No recordset is returned, because we are only updating data – remember, there's no point creating a recordset unless one is needed.

As it stands though, this procedure isn't very flexible since it only deals with one book type. What would be better would be a procedure that allows us to select the book type so we don't have to create a procedure for each book type. And while we're at it, we might as well remove the fixed 10% update, and allow this to be flexible too. So, how do we achieve this – simple, with parameters.

Parameters

Parameters to stored procedures are just like parameters (or arguments, depending on your preferred term) to procedures and functions. These allow values to be passed into a function, and then the function can use the value. Stored procedures in SQL Server (and other databases, including Access) both have this facility.

To allow the procedure to cope with multiple book types, and even allow the user to specify the price increase (or decrease), we need to add some parameters:

```
CREATE PROCEDURE usp_UpdatePrices
  @Type       Char(12),
  @Percent    Money

AS
    UPDATE Titles
    SET    Price = Price * (1 + @Percent / 100)
    WHERE  Type = @Type
```

The stored procedure `usp_UpdatePrices` now takes two parameters:

- One for the book type (`@Type`)
- One for the percentage change in price (`@Percent`)

Just like a VBScript function, these parameters are variables. However, unlike VBScript and other scripting languages where all the variables are variants, SQL variables all have specific types (Char, Money, etc). They must also follow the naming convention for SQL variables, which means they must start with an `@` symbol.

Notice that we've allowed the percentage to be supplied as a whole number (for example 10 for 10%), instead of it's fractional value. This just makes the procedure more intuitive to use.

The Parameters Collection

So now we have a stored procedure with parameters, how do we actually call this from ADO? You've already seen how to call stored procedures without parameters using the Command object, and that doesn't change. What changes is the use of the Parameters collection.

The Parameters collection contains a Parameter object for each parameter in the stored procedure. However, ADO doesn't automatically know what these parameters are, so you have to create them, using the `CreateParameter` method, which takes the following form:

```
Set Parameter = Command.CreateParameter (Name, [Type], [Direction],
                                         [Size], [Value])
```

The arguments are:

Argument	Descriptions
Name	The name of the parameter. This isn't the name of the parameter in the stored procedure, but the name of the parameter in the `Parameters` collection. It is, however, a good idea to use the same names.
Type	The data type of the parameter. This can be one of the `adDataType` constants, which are detailed in the appendices.
Direction	The direction of the parameter, indicating whether the parameter supplies information to the stored procedure, or whether the procedure supplies the information back to ADO. The value can be one of: ❑ `adParamInput`, the parameter is an input parameter, being sent to the stored procedure. ❑ `adParamOutput`, the parameter is an output parameter, being retrieved from the stored procedure. ❑ `adParamInputOutput`, the parameter is both an input and an output parameter. ❑ `adParamReturnValue`, the parameter holds the return status of the stored procedure.
Size	The size of the parameter. For fixed length types, such as numbers, this can be omitted.
Value	The value of the parameter.

Once the parameter is created it can be appended to the Parameters collection. For example:

```
Set parValue = cmdUpdate.CreateParameter("@Type", adVarWChar, adParamInput, _
                                          12, "Business")
cmdUpdate.Parameters.Append parValue

Set parValue = cmdUpdate.CreateParameter("@Percent", adCurrency, _
                                          adParamInput, , 10)
cmdUpdate.Parameters.Append parValue
```

There's no need to explicitly create an object to hold the parameter – the default type of Variant works well enough here. If you don't want to create a variable, you can also take a shortcut:

```
cmdUpdate.Parameters.Append = _
     cmdUpdate.CreateParameter("@Percent", adCurrency, adParamInput, , 10)
```

This uses the fact that the `CreateParameter` method returns a Parameter object, and the `Append` method accepts a Parameter object. This method is marginally faster than using a variable, but does make your lines of code longer and therefore harder to read. You can use whichever method you prefer.

You don't have to set the value of the parameter at the time you create the parameter, since once the parameter is appended to the Parameters collection it remains in the collection. You can therefore set the value any time before the command is run. For example:

```
cmdUpdate.Parameters.Append = _
      cmdUpdate.CreateParameter ("@Percent", adCurrency, adParamInput)

cmdUpdate.Parameters("@Percent") = 10
```

In the previous chapter we mentioned that there are several ways of accessing values in collections, and the Parameters collection is no different. The above example uses the name of the parameter to index into the collection, but you could equally use the index number:

```
cmdUpdate.Parameters(0) = 10
```

This sets the value of the first (collections are zero-based) parameter in the collection. The index number method is marginally faster that the name method, but obviously the name method makes your code much clearer to read.

> **One point that is important to note is that the parameters in the Parameters collection must match the order of the parameters in the stored procedure.**

Running Parameter Commands

Once the parameters have been added, the command can now be run and these parameter values will be passed into the stored procedure. So now, you can make a nice page that updates selected book types. For example, let's imagine a page called `UpdatePrices.asp`, that looks like this when run:

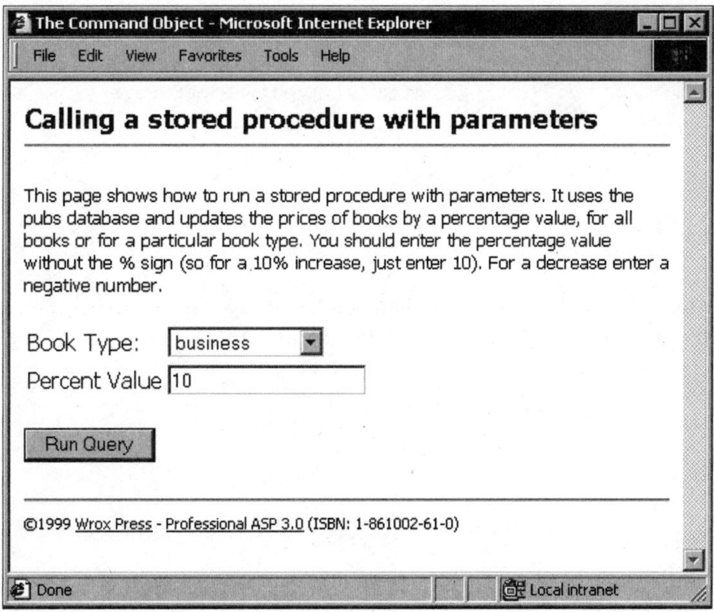

You could easily build this page dynamically, getting a list of book types from the database. The first thing we do is include the file `Connection.asp` – this contains the connection string (held in `strConn`) as well as the reference to the ADO constants, which we discussed in the previous chapter:

```
<!-- #INCLUDE FILE="../Include/Connection.asp" -->
```

Next, we can build the form (we won't show the large text body here, but it's in the sample file). The form calls the ASP file called `StoredProcedure.asp`:

```
<FORM NAME="UpdatePrices" Method="Post" ACTION="StoredProcedure.asp">
<TABLE>
  <TR>
    <TD>Book Type:</TD>
    <TD>
      <SELECT NAME="lstTypes"></TD>
```

Now we can start the ASP script, to read in the book types from the `titles` table. We use a SQL string to return only the unique book types, and then put the returned values into HTML `OPTION` tags:

```
<%
  Dim rsTypes
  Dim strSQL
  Dim strQuote

' Predefine the quote character
  strQuote = Chr(34)

' Create a recordset of the types
  Set rsTypes = Server.CreateObject("ADODB.Recordset")

  strSQL = "SELECT DISTINCT type FROM titles"
  rsTypes.Open strSQL, strConn

' Create the book types
  While Not rsTypes.EOF
    Response.Write "<OPTION VALUE=" & strQuote & _
                   rsTypes("Type") & strQuote & ">" & rsTypes("Type")
    rsTypes.MoveNext
  Wend

  rsTypes.Close
  Set rsTypes = Nothing
%>
```

Once the book types have been displayed, we can construct the remainder of our form, including a text box allowing the user to enter the percentage change:

```
      </SELECT>
    </TD>
  </TR>
  <TR>
    <TD>Percent Value</TD>
    <TD><INPUT NAME="txtPercent" TYPE="TEXT"></TD>
  </TR>
</TABLE>
<P>
<INPUT TYPE="Submit" VALUE="Run Query">
</FORM>
```

Let's now look at `StoredProcedure.asp`, the ASP page that the **Run Query** button calls. The first thing we do is declare the variables, and extract the book type and percentage from the calling form:

```
<%
  Dim cmdUpdate
  Dim lngRecs
  Dim strType
  Dim curPercent

' Get the form values
  strType = Request.Form("lstTypes")
  curPercent = Request.Form("txtPercent")
```

Now we can display some confirmation to the user of what's happening:

```
' Tell the user what's being done
  Response.Write "Updating all books" & _
                 " of type <B>" & strType & "</B>" & _
                 " by " & curPercent & "%<P>"
```

Now come the guts of the code, where we create the Command object and the parameters:

```
  Set cmdUpdate = Server.CreateObject("ADODB.Command")

' Set the properties of the command
  With cmdUpdate
    .ActiveConnection = strConn
    .CommandText = "usp_UpdatePrices"
    .CommandType = adCmdStoredProc
```

We use the shortcut method of creating and adding the parameters, using the values we've extracted from the previous page's form:

```
   ' Add the parameters
    .Parameters.Append .CreateParameter("@Type", adVarWChar, adParamInput, _
                                        12, strType)
    .Parameters.Append .CreateParameter("@Percent", adCurrency, _
                                        adParamInput, , curPercent)
```

And now we can run the stored procedure:

```
   ' Execute the command
    .Execute lngRecs, , adExecuteNoRecords
  End With
```

And just for confirmation, we can tell the user how many records were updated:

```
' And finally tell the user what's happened
  Response.Write "Procedure complete. " & lngRecs & " records were updated."

  Set cmdUpdate = Nothing
%>
```

So there we have two simple pages. The first builds a list of items to select and the second uses one of those items as a value in the update. This is the basis for many ASP pages that need to display and update data like this.

Passing Parameters as an Array

The `Parameters` collection is all very well, but it's a bit cumbersome (especially for those two fingered typists). Luckily there's a quick shortcut method, using the `Parameters` argument of the `Execute` method. For example, let's call our tame stored procedure, `usp_UpdatePrices`, but without using the `Parameters` collection.

We create the Command object and set it's properties in the same way as before:

```
Set cmdUpdate = Server.CreateObject("ADODB.Command")

' Set the properties of the command
With cmdUpdate
   .ActiveConnection = strConn
   .CommandText = "usp_UpdatePrices"
   .CommandType = adCmdStoredProc
```

But here's where the difference lies. Instead of creating parameters and adding them to the collection, we simply pass the parameters into the stored procedure via the `Execute` method:

```
   ' Execute the command
   .Execute lngRecs, Array(strType, curPercent), adExecuteNoRecords
End With
```

This utilizes the `Array` function, which turns individual variables into an array, suitable for passing into this method call. As with every shortcut, there are of course some disadvantages to this method:

- You can only use input parameters. Since you cannot specify type and direction of parameters they default to input parameters.
- This method is slower if you intend to call the stored procedure several times, since ADO will ask the data store what the parameters are, and what data types they use.

The difference in speed between the collection method and the array method is so small that it's hardly noticeable, so if you only have input parameters you can use whichever method you prefer. I actually prefer the long-winded method of the Parameters collection, because it makes it more explicit what the properties of the parameters are.

Output Parameters

We've seen that you can get the number of records affected by a command, but what if you want more information, but still don't want to return a recordset. Perhaps you want two or three values returned from a stored procedure, but don't want to go to the overhead of creating a recordset. If this is the case you can define a parameter as an **output** parameter, where the value is supplied by the stored procedure.

For example, let's consider our price update routine. Suppose we want to find out the maximum book price after the update has taken place. Our stored procedure could be changed like this:

```
CREATE PROCEDURE usp_UpdatePricesMax
  @Type       Char(12),
  @Percent    Money,
  @Max        Money        OUTPUT
AS

BEGIN
    UPDATE Titles
    SET    Price = Price * (1 + @Percent / 100)
    WHERE  Type=@Type

    SELECT @Max = MAX(Price)
    FROM   Titles
END
```

This just runs a simple `SELECT` after the update and places the value in the output parameter.

We can now change the code in `StoredProcedure.asp` accordingly to retrieve the value of `@Max`:

```
<%
  Dim cmdUpdate
  Dim lngRecs
  Dim strType
  Dim curPercent
  Dim curMax

' Get the form values
  strType = Request.Form("lstTypes")
  curPercent = Request.Form("txtPercent")

' Tell the user what's being done
  Response.Write "Updating all books" & _
                 " of type <B>" & strType & "</B>" & _
                 " by " & curPercent & "%<P>"

  Set cmdUpdate = Server.CreateObject("ADODB.Command")

' Set the properties of the command
  With cmdUpdate
    .ActiveConnection = strConn
    .CommandText = "usp_UpdatePricesMax"
    .CommandType = adCmdStoredProc
```

We simply add another parameter to the collection, but this time specifying it as an output parameter. Note that we don't give it a value. That's because the value will be supplied by the stored procedure – remember, it's an output parameter:

```
    ' Add the parameters
      .Parameters.Append .CreateParameter ("@Type", adVarWChar, adParamInput, _
                                           12, strType)
      .Parameters.Append .CreateParameter ("@Percent", adCurrency, _
                                           adParamInput, , curPercent)
      .Parameters.Append .CreateParameter ("@Max", adCurrency, adParamOutput)

    ' Execute the command
      .Execute lngRecs, , adExecuteNoRecords
```

Once the procedure is executed we can retrieve the value from the collection:

```
    ' Extract the output parameter, which the stored
    ' procedure has supplied to the parameters collection
      curMax = .Parameters("@Max")
    End With

  ' And finally tell the user what's happened
    Response.Write "Procedure complete. " & lngRecs & _
                   " records were updated.<P>"
    Response.Write "The highest price book is now " & _
                   FormatCurrency(curMax)

    Set cmdUpdate = Nothing
  %>
```

If there is more than one output parameter, then they can be accessed in the same way. You can use the Parameter name or the index number to extract the value from the collection.

Return Values

Return values from functions are handled differently from the way return values from stored procedures are handled, and this often causes confusion. In user functions, we often return a Boolean value to indicate the success or failure of a function:

```
  If SomeFunctionName() = True Then
    ' Function succeeded
```

When calling a stored procedure though, we can't use the same method, because the stored procedures are run using the `Execute` method, and this returns a recordset:

```
  Set rsAuthors = cmdAuthors.Execute
```

If we can't get a return value, how do we determine if the stored procedure executed correctly? Well, if an error occurred this would be reported, and we could handle it with the error handling code shown in the previous chapter. But what about some sort of non-fatal logic error?

For example, consider adding a new employee to the `employee` table. You don't want to stop two people with the same name being added, but you might want this situation flagged. Here's where we could use a return value, to indicate whether an employee with the same name already exists. The stored procedure might look like this:

```
CREATE PROCEDURE usp_AddEmployee
    @Emp_ID         Char(9),
    @FName          Varchar(20),
    @MInit          Char(1),
    @LName          Varchar(30),
    @Job_Id         SmallInt,
    @Job_Lvl        TinyInt,
    @Pub_ID         Char(4),
    @Hire_Date      Datetime
AS
BEGIN
    DECLARE @Exists     Int         -- Return value

    -- See if an employee with the same name exists
    IF EXISTS(SELECT *
              FROM   Employee
              WHERE  FName = @FName
              AND    MInit = @MInit
              AND    LName = @LName)
        SELECT @Exists = 1
    ELSE
        SELECT @Exists = 0

    INSERT INTO Employee (emp_id, fname, minit, lname,
                 job_id, job_lvl, pub_id, hire_date)
    VALUES (@Emp_Id, @FName, @MInit, @LName, @Job_ID,
            @Job_Lvl, @Pub_ID, @Hire_Date)

    RETURN @Exists
END
```

The first thing this procedure does is check to see if an employee with the same name exists, and sets a variable accordingly – it will be `1` if the employee exists, and `0` otherwise. The employee is then added to the table, and the `Exists` value is returned as the return value.

Notice that although we are returning a value we don't declare it as a parameter to the stored procedure.

The ASP code to call this procedure would look like:

```
<!-- #INCLUDE FILE="../Include/Connection.asp" -->
<%
  Dim cmdEmployee
  Dim lngRecs
  Dim lngAdded

  Set cmdEmployee = Server.CreateObject("ADODB.Command")

' Set the properties of the command
  With cmdEmployee
    .ActiveConnection = strConn
    .CommandText = "usp_AddEmployee"
    .CommandType = adCmdStoredProc

  ' Create the parameters
  ' Notice that the return value is the first parameter
    .Parameters.Append .CreateParameter ("RETURN_VALUE", adInteger, _
                                         adParamReturnValue)
    .Parameters.Append .CreateParameter ("@Emp_Id", adChar, adParamInput, 9)
    .Parameters.Append .CreateParameter ("@FName", adVarWChar, _
                                         adParamInput, 20)
    .Parameters.Append .CreateParameter ("@MInit", adChar, adParamInput, 1)
    .Parameters.Append .CreateParameter ("@LName", adVarWChar, _
                                         adParamInput, 30)
    .Parameters.Append .CreateParameter ("@Job_Id", adSmallInt, adParamInput)
    .Parameters.Append .CreateParameter ("@Job_Lvl", adUnsignedTinyInt, _
                                         adParamInput)
    .Parameters.Append .CreateParameter ("@Pub_ID", adChar, adParamInput, 4)
    .Parameters.Append .CreateParameter ("@Hire_Date", adDBTimeStamp, _
                                         adParamInput, 8)

  ' Set the parameter values
    .Parameters("@Emp_Id") = Request.Form("txtEmpID")
    .Parameters("@FName") = Request.Form("txtFirstName")
    .Parameters("@MInit") = Request.Form("txtInitial")
    .Parameters("@LName") = Request.Form("txtLastName")
    .Parameters("@Job_ID") = Request.Form("lstJobs")
    .Parameters("@Job_Lvl") = Request.Form("txtJobLevel")
    .Parameters("@Pub_ID") = Request.Form("lstPublisher")
    .Parameters("@Hire_Date") = Request.Form("txtHireDate")

  ' Run the stored procedure
    .Execute lngRecs, , adExecuteNoRecords

  ' Extract the return value
    lngAdded = .Parameters("RETURN_VALUE")
  End With

  Response.Write "New employee added.<P>"
  If lngAdded = 1 Then
    Response.Write "An employee with the same name already exists."
  End If

  Set cmdEmployee = Nothing
%>
```

The important thing to note is that the return value is created as the first parameter in the collection. Even though the return value doesn't appear as a parameter in the stored procedure, it is always the first `Parameter` in the `Parameters` collection.

So, just to stress this confusing point:

> **Return values from stored procedures must be declared as the first parameter in the Parameters collection, with a direction of `adParamReturnValue`.**

Using Return Values

Now this is defined we could have an initial form like this:

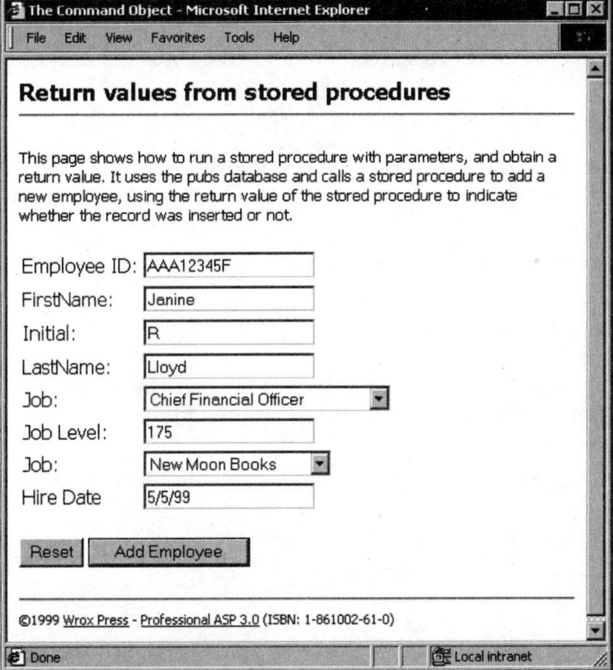

Pressing the Add Employee button would then generate:

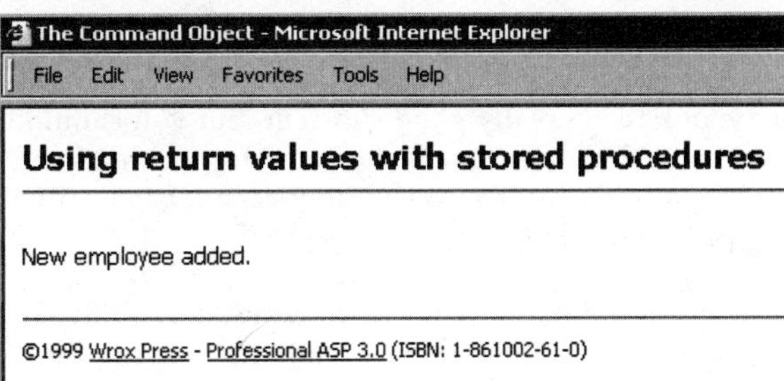

Adding the same details again (with a different employee ID) gives this:

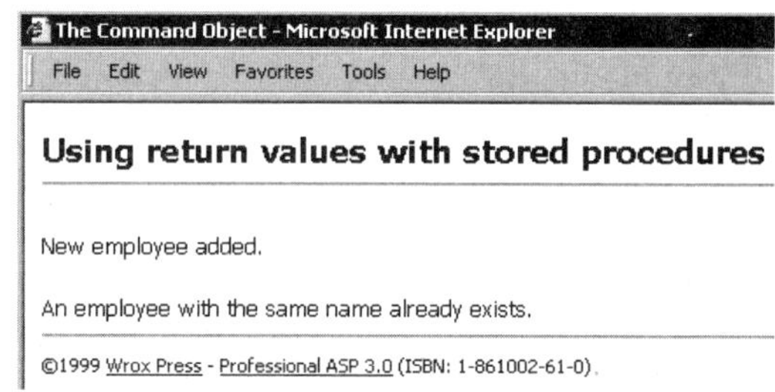

Refreshing Parameters

Instead of typing in all of the parameter details yourself, you can get ADO to do it for you, simply by calling the Refresh method. For example, let's say we've set up usp_AddEmployee with the same parameters as before. The page we use to run it is the same as before up to here:

```
With cmdEmployee
     .ActiveConnection = strConn
     .CommandText = "usp_AddEmployee"
     .CommandType = adCmdStoredProc
```

Then we'd call the Refresh method.

```
     .Parameters.Refresh
```

This tells ADO to ask the data store to provide the details of each parameter, and it creates the Parameters collection for you. You can then fill in the values:

```
     .Parameters("@Emp_Id") = Request.Form("txtEmpID")
     .Parameters("@FName") = Request.Form("txtFirstName")
     .Parameters("@MInit") = Request.Form("txtInitial")
     .Parameters("@LName") = Request.Form("txtLastName")
     .Parameters("@Job_ID") = Request.Form("lstJobs")
     .Parameters("@Job_Lvl") = Request.Form("txtJobLevel")
     .Parameters("@Pub_ID") = Request.Form("lstPublisher")
     .Parameters("@Hire_Date") = Request.Form("txtHireDate")
```

Notice that we haven't had to create any parameters, including the one for the return value.

This may look like a really good shortcut, but you should be aware that it imposes a performance penalty, since ADO must query the provider for the details of the parameters for the stored procedure. Despite this it's exceedingly useful, especially if you are having trouble getting the values for your parameters correct.

In fact, you can build a little utility to be used as a development tool, which does a refresh and then constructs the Append statements, ready for you to paste into your code. It might look something like this – an ASP page called GenerateParameters.asp:

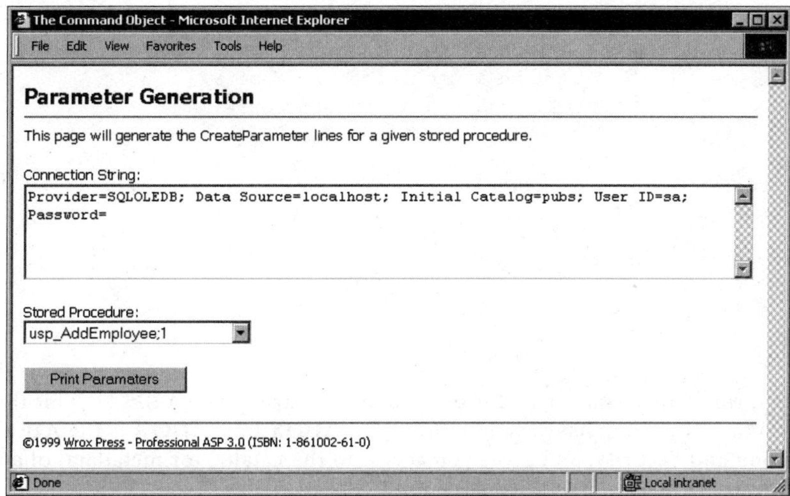

The code for this is pretty simple. The first thing to do is include the connection string, plus another file for the ADOX constants:

```
<!-- #INCLUDE FILE="../Include/Connection.asp" -->
<!-- #INCLUDE FILE="../Include/ADOX.asp" -->
```

Then we create a form, specifying that its target will be the ASP page called `PrintParameters.asp`:

```
<FORM NAME="Procedures" METHOD="Post" ACTION="PrintParameters.asp">
  Connection String:<BR>
  <TEXTAREA NAME="txtConnection" COLS="80" ROWS="5">
     <% = strConn %>
  </TEXTAREA>
  <P>
  Stored Procedure:<BR>
  <SELECT NAME="lstProcedures">
```

We then use ADOX to get a list of stored procedures from the SQL Server, and we construct a list box containing the stored procedure names:

```
<%
  Dim catPubs
  Dim procProcedure
  Dim strQuote

' Predefine the quote character
  strQuote = Chr(34)

  Set catPubs = Server.CreateObject("ADOX.Catalog")

  catPubs.ActiveConnection = strConn
```

```
    For Each procProcedure In catPubs.Procedures
        Response.Write "<OPTION VALUE=" & _
                       strQuote & procProcedure.Name & _
                       strQuote & ">" & procProcedure.Name
    Next

    Set procProcedure = Nothing
    Set catPubs = Nothing
%>
</SELECT>
<P>
<INPUT TYPE="Submit" VALUE="Print Parameters">
</FORM>
```

It's a simple form, with a TEXTAREA for the connection string, and a SELECT for the stored procedures. What you won't have seen before is the **ADOX** bits. ADOX is the **ADO Extensions for Data Definition and Security**, and gives you access to the catalog (or metadata) of a data store.

> *We're not covering ADOX in this book, but it's quite simple. More details can be found in the ADO Programmer's Reference, also from Wrox Press. Either the 2.1 version or the 2.5 version will be OK for ADOX.*

In the above example, we are using the Procedures collection, which contains a list of all stored procedures in a data store. When you press the Print Parameters button, you get the following:

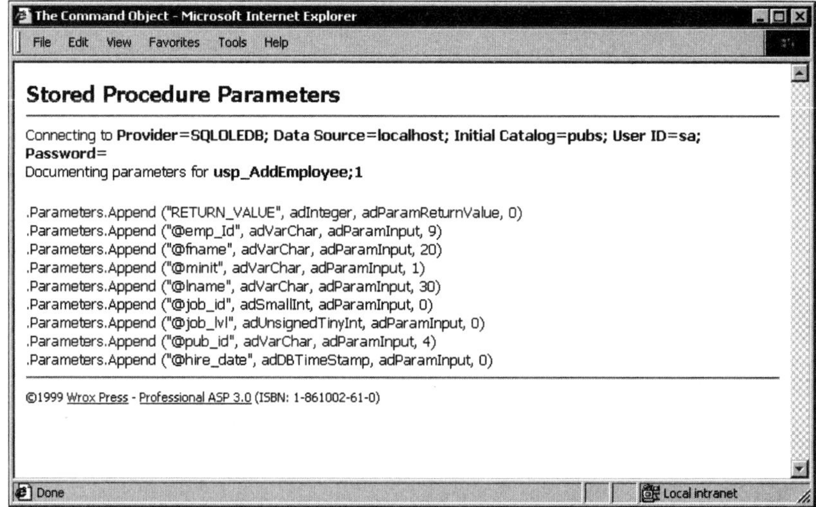

The parameter lines can simply be copied from this and pasted into your code. Easy huh! The code's not very difficult either. At the very beginning we have an include file you won't have seen before. This contains several functions that convert the ADO constants (such as data type, parameter direction and so on) into string values:

```
<!-- #INCLUDE FILE="../Include/Descriptions.asp" -->
```

Next we have a set of variables, the extraction of the user request, and the creation of the Command object:

```
<%
  Dim cmdProc
  Dim parP
  Dim strConnection
  Dim strProcedure
  Dim strQuote

' Get the connection and procedure name from the user
  strQuote = Chr(34)
  strConnection = Request.Form("txtConnection")
  strProcedure = Request.Form("lstProcedures")

' Update the user
  Response.Write "Connecting to <B>" & strConnection & "</B><BR>"
  Response.Write "Documenting parameters for <B>" & _
                 strProcedure & "</B><P><P>"

  Set cmdProc = Server.CreateObject("ADODB.Command")

' Set the properties of the command, using the name
' of the procedure that the user selected
  With cmdProc
    .ActiveConnection = strConnection
    .CommandType = adCmdStoredProc
    .CommandText = strProcedure
```

We then use the `Refresh` method to automatically fill in the `Parameters` collection:

```
    .Parameters.Refresh
```

We can now loop through the collection, writing out a string that contains the details for creating the parameter:

```
    For Each parP In .Parameters
        Response.Write ".Parameters.Append " & _
                       "(" & strQuote & parP.Name & _
                       strQuote & ", " & _
                       DataTypeDesc(parP.Type) & ", " & _
                       ParamDirectionDesc(parP.Direction) & _
                       ", " & _
                       parP.Size & ")<BR>"
    Next
  End With

  Set cmdProc = Nothing
%>
```

The functions `DataTypeDesc` and `ParamDirectionDesc` are found in the `Descriptions.asp` include file.

> *The `Descriptions.asp` include file, along with the other sample files, can be found on the supporting Web site, at `http://www.wrox.com`.*

This is a really simple technique, and shows a good use for the `Refresh` method. Well, anything that saves typing has to be good, doesn't it?

Optimization

Optimization is always a concern for every developer. After all, it hardly matters how cool your code is or what great features it uses, if your users have time to make a cup of coffee before your code responds. Database access has always been an area where optimization is an issue. Compared to many tasks, data access is relatively slow.

Because data access varies so much, it's almost impossible to come up with a fixed set of rules to optimize your database work. As is usual with these sorts of problems, the answer you'll most often get is 'it depends', because the sort of optimization you need depends on what you are trying to do.

General ADO Tips

Despite the fact that many points about optimization are dependent upon the task, there are some general areas you can look at:

- **Pick only the columns you need**
  When opening recordsets, don't automatically use a table name, or even `SELECT *`, unless you need all of the columns. Using individual column names means that you can reduce the amount of data being sent to and from the server. Even if you do need all of the columns the best performance will be achieved by naming the columns individually, since the server doesn't have to work out what the column names are.

- **Use stored procedures as much as possible**
  A stored procedure is pre-compiled and contains an already worked out execution plan. It will therefore run more quickly than a SQL statement.

- **Use stored procedures for data changes**
  This is invariably faster that using the ADO methods on the recordset.

- **Don't create a recordset unless it's required**
  When running action queries make sure you add the `adExecuteNoRecords` option, so that a recordset is not created. You can also use this technique in lookup situations when returning just a single row with one or two fields (ID values for example). In this case a stored procedure and output parameters will be quicker.

- **Use the appropriate cursor and lock modes**
  If all you are going to be doing is reading data from the recordset and displaying it on screen (creating a table, for example), then use the default forward-only, read-only recordset. The less work ADO has to do maintaining details about records and locking, the better.

Object Variables

One guaranteed way to improve performance whilst looping through recordsets is to use object variables to point to members of collections. For example, consider looping through a recordset containing Authors:

```
While Not rsAuthors.EOF
  Response.Write rsAuthors("au_fname") & " " & _
                 rsAuthors("au_lname") & "<BR>"
  rsAuthors.MoveNext
Wend
```

You can speed this code up, and make it more readable, by using the following:

```
Set FirstName = rsAuthors("au_fname")
Set LastName = rsAuthors("au_lname")

While Not rsAuthors.EOF
  Response.Write FirstName & " " & LastName & "<BR>"
  rsAuthors.MoveNext
Wend
```

Here we use two variables and set them to point to particular fields in the Fields collection of the recordset (remember that the Fields collection is the default collection). Because you're setting an object reference here you can then use the object variable instead of the actual variable, which means less work for the scripting engines, since there is less indexing into collections going on.

Cache Size

The **cache size** is the number of records that ADO reads at a time from the data store, and it defaults to 1. This means that when using server-based cursors, every time you move to another record, the record must be fetched from the data store. Increasing the size of the cache to 10, for example, would mean that records are read into the ADO buffer 10 at a time. If you access a record that is within the cache then ADO doesn't need to fetch it from the data store. Accessing a record outside the cache causes the next set of records to be read into the cache.

You can set the size of the cache by using the CacheSize property of the recordset:

```
rsAuthors.CacheSize = 10
```

You can change the cache size at any time during the life of a recordset, although the new figure only becomes effective *after* the next set of records are retrieved.

Like many performance tips, there's no set size that is best for the cache, as it varies depending upon the task in hand and the data provider. But, increasing the cache from 1 invariably increases performance.

If you want to see this in action, then use the SQL Server Profiler and watch what happens when you open a recordset using the default cache size, and compare that to what happens with an increased cache size. Not only does increasing the cache size mean ADO has less work to do, but SQL Server too.

Database Design

Don't always look to your programming to consider improvements to your data access, as you should also consider the design of the database. This isn't going to be a big discussion on database design, but there are some things you can think about when using databases for Web sites:

- **Live Data**
  When showing data to users, how important is it for that data to be up-to-date? Take a product catalog for example, how often does the catalog change? If the catalog doesn't change very often, then is there any reason to get the data from a database every time? Would a better way be to generate static HTML pages from the database, say once a week, or when the data changes.

- **Indexing**
  If you are not doing many data additions, but lots of different look ups, then consider adding indexes to your tables.

- **De-normalization**
  If your site has two distinct purposes (data maintenance and data analysis) then consider de-normalizing some tables to help with the analysis side of the operation. You could even provide separate, completely de-normalized tables for analysis that are updated on a regular basis, and to improve performance even more you could move these analysis tables to another machine.

- **Database Statistics**
  If using SQL Server 6.x then make sure you update your statistics regularly if data is being added or deleted. These statistics are used to generate query plans and can affect how queries are run. See UPDATE STATISTICS in the SQL Books Online for more details. For SQL Server 7, this task is automated for you.

These are fairly standard database design techniques, but ones you may not think about if you've got your head deep in ASP code.

Data Caching

The first thing to note is that **data caching** has nothing to do with the recordset cache size, although both can be used to improve performance. Data caching means the temporary storage of data, allowing the cache to be used, rather than re-creating the data. This is really only suitable for data that doesn't change very often, but that is accessed many times.

One of the simplest ways of caching data in ASP is to use Application and Session scoped variables. For example, imagine you have several pages on which you need to select the book type. Under normal circumstances you might consider creating an include file that contains this function:

```
<%
Function BookTypes()

   Dim rsBookTypes
   Dim strQuote

   strQuote = Chr(34)

   Set rsBookTypes = Server.CreateObject("ADODB.Recordset")
```

```
  ' Get the book types
    rsBookTypes.Open "usp_BookTypes", strConn

    Response.Write "<SELECT NAME=" & strQuote & lstBookType & strQuote & ">"
    While Not rsBookTypes.EOF
      Response.Write "<OPTION>" & rsBookTypes("Type") & "</OPTION>"
      rsBookTypes.MoveNext
    Wend

    Response.Write "</SELECT>"

    rsBookTypes.Close
    Set rsBookTypes = Nothing

End Function
%>
```

This simply calls a stored procedure to get the book types and build up a `SELECT` list. The disadvantage with this is that every time you call this function, the database is accessed. So, how about changing this function:

```
<%
Function BookTypes()

  Dim rsBookTypes
  Dim strQuote
  Dim strList

' See if the list is in the cache
  strList = Application("BookTypes")
  If strList = "" Then
  ' Not cached, so build up list and cache it
    strQuote = Chr(34)

    Set rsBookTypes = Server.CreateObject("ADODB.Recordset")

  ' Get the book types
    rsBookTypes.Open "usp_BookTypes", strConn

    strList = "<SELECT NAME=" & strQuote & lstBookType & strQuote & ">"
    While Not rsBookTypes.EOF
      strList = strList & "<OPTION>" & rsBookTypes("Type") & "</OPTION>"
      rsBookTypes.MoveNext
    Wend
    strList = strList & "</SELECT>"

    rsBookTypes.Close
    Set rsBookTypes = Nothing

  ' Cache the list
    Application("BookTypes") = strList
  End If

  BookTypes = strList

End Function
%>
```

Instead of just opening the recordset, this version of the script checks to see if there is anything stored in the Application variable `BookTypes`. If there is, then the contents of this variable are used. If not, then the recordset is opened as before. Obviously once the first person has run this routine the data will be cached, so this is only useful for data that doesn't change very often.

You could use a Session variable if you wanted to cache data on a user basis, but here you have to watch for Sessions that might expire. If this happens, then Session-level variables will die along with the session, and your code may break.

Using the Web Application Stress tool, informally called homer (probably named after Bart and not Alex), I got the following results:

Method	Page hits
Without Caching	190
With Caching	11000

That's some kind of improvement eh?

Now don't get too excited, and start caching everything like this. After all, this method is only suitable for data that is already formatted for display. And besides, my Web server is only serving me – hardly a typical Web server usage. Using WAS you can simulate multiple clients on one server, and thus give your applications a more realistic test.

The Web Application Stress tool allows you to stress test your Web pages by simulating numbers of users. It's got a simple graphical interface, and is extremely easy to use. You can find out more, and download it, from `http://homer.rte.microsoft.com/`.

Caching Objects

So what if you want to cache data that isn't formatted, so you can use it in different ways in different places? Well, you can also do this using Application or Session variables. Consider the case of book titles. You might want to use the titles in several pages – perhaps in a table showing all titles, or in a list box where the user can select an individual title, and so on. You might think that instead of caching the HTML containing the tags you could cache the recordset itself.

The simple fact is that yes, you can cache objects in both Application and Session variables, but there are two main problems:

- Objects stored in Application variables must support **Free**-threading, so they must be either Free- or Both-threaded objects. This means you cannot cache Visual Basic created components in Application variables.
- Storing Apartment-threaded objects in Session state means that the thread that created the object is the only one allowed to access it. IIS cannot, therefore, perform good thread management, because any page that tries to access this object will have to wait for the original thread to service the page. This can kill any chance of scaling your application well.

For a discussion on threading issues, refer to Chapter 16.

By default, ADO ships as an Apartment-threaded object, primarily because some of the OLEDB Providers are not thread safe. In the ADO installation directory there is a registry file that will switch ADO over to the Both-threaded model, thus allowing ADO objects to be stored safely in Application and Session objects.

So, you might think that all is well, and you can gain some sudden speed increase by all sorts of objects, but this isn't necessarily so. Many people have thought that since connecting to a data store is a relatively expensive operation, caching the Connection object would save a lot of time when reconnecting. Yes it would, but caching a Connection object means that the connection is never closed, and therefore connection pooling works less effectively. One of the ideas behind connection pooling is to reduce resources in use on the server, and caching objects in ASP state clearly doesn't reduce resources. In fact it increases them, because each time an object is cached it uses server resources. For a heavily used site this could drastically reduce the effectiveness of the Web server.

OK, so you won't store Connection objects, but how about Recordset objects, especially disconnected recordsets. Well, assuming ADO is changed from Apartment-threaded to Both-threaded, there's no reason why you can't do this, as long as you realize exactly what you are doing. Don't think it's automatically going to increase the performance of your ASP pages. Every recordset that you cache takes up server resources, both in terms of memory and ASP management, so don't even think of caching large recordsets.

Another technique is to use the `GetRows` method of a recordset, which converts the recordset into an array. Since an array doesn't suffer from the threading issues that the Recordset object does, this will be more acceptable to use in a Session level variable. However, it still uses server resources, plus you have to take into account the time taken to manipulate the array.

> **You can nearly always architect your applications so this caching technique isn't necessary.**

Data Shaping

Data shaping, or hierarchical recordsets, allows you to represent a tree-like structure or related recordsets. This is achieved by having a field in a recordset contain a recordset of its own, allowing database relationships to be expressed, and multiple recordsets to be returned in a single call. There are a couple of reasons why this is useful:

- **Performance**: When used correctly, data shaping can improve performance.
- **Convenience**: It's extremely easy to map the parent/child relationship in data shaping.

The easiest way to see what data shaping involves is to look at a diagram:

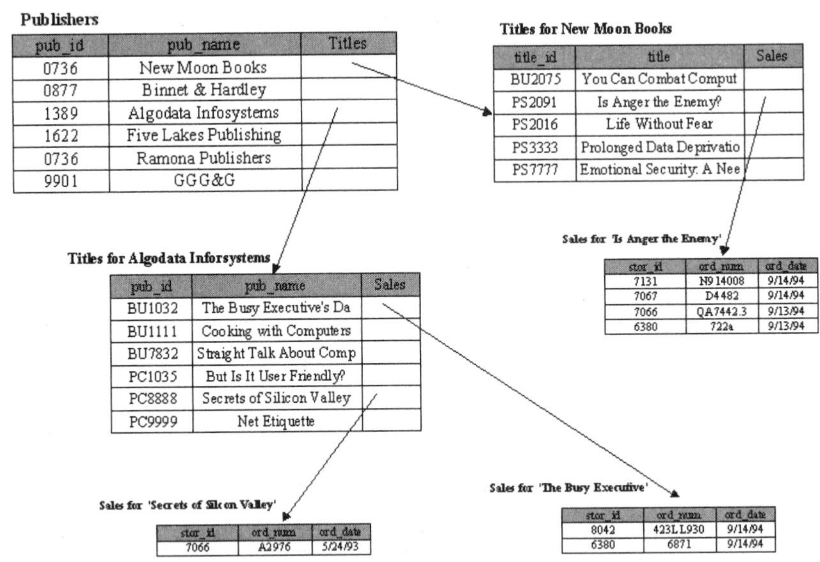

This shows a hierarchy from the `pubs` databases, showing `Publishers`, `Titles` and `Sales`.

One important point to note is that each child recordset is not a separate recordset on its own. So, in the above diagram there are not six recordsets, but only three. How come? Well, there is a recordset for each level in the hierarchy – which is `Publishers`, `Titles` and `Sales`. When you reference the Titles for a Publisher, you are actually referencing the `Titles` recordset, but ADO filters the Titles, so only those applicable to the selected Publisher are shown. This gives the impression that you have a separate recordset for each child element.

Using Data Shaping

To use data shaping you have to use the following:

- The `MSDataShape` OLEDB Provider
- A special Shape language, a superset of SQL, that allows you to construct the hierarchies

The connection string doesn't actually change that much, even though you are using a new provider. This is because you still need to get the data from somewhere. So what you do is this:

```
Provider=MSDataShape; Data Provider=SQLOLEDB; Data Source = ...
```

You use the `MSDataShape` as the `Provider`, and your normal provider becomes the `Data Provider`, with the rest of the connection string remaining the same.

The easy way to construct a connection string for data shaping is to start with your normal connection string, and append it to the end of the data shaping bits. For example, consider the following, normal connection string:

```
strConn = "Provider=SQLOLEDB; Data Source=Kanga; " & _
          " Initial Catalog=pubs; User Id=sa; Password="
```

You can create a connection string for the data shape provider like so:

```
strConn = "Provider=MSDataShape; Data=" & strConn
```

This sets the provider to be `MSDataShape`, and the `Data Provider` becomes the real source of the data. The original connections string already has the `Provider=` bits in it, so we only need to put `Data` in front of this to get the correct connection details.

The Shape Language

The shape language has its own grammar, but we won't go into the formal construction of it here – it's included in the ADO documentation. In most situations you'll be using the following command:

```
SHAPE {parent command} [AS parent alias]
APPEND ({child command} [AS child alias]
RELATE parent_column TO child_column) [AS parent_column_name]
```

The easiest way to understand this is to see an actual example, so we'll start with just `Publishers` and `Titles`:

```
SHAPE {SELECT * FROM Publishers}
APPEND ({SELECT * FROM Titles}
RELATE Pub_ID TO Pub_ID) AS rsTitles
```

The parent recordset is the first line, and the child recordset the second line. The third line indicates the two fields that provide the relationship between the parent and child. In this case both tables have a field called `Pub_ID` (the Publisher ID field). This command returns a recordset containing the publishers, and onto the end of that recordset it `APPEND`s a new column (of type `adChapter`), which contains the child recordset. The name of this column is given by the `AS` clause – in this case it will be `rsTitles`.

> *The type `adChapter` just indicates that the field contains a child recordset. Personally I think `adChild` or `adRecordset` would have been better.*

You can easily see what the fields of the parent recordset look like, by just looping through the `Fields` collection. Using the `SHAPE` command above, we get:

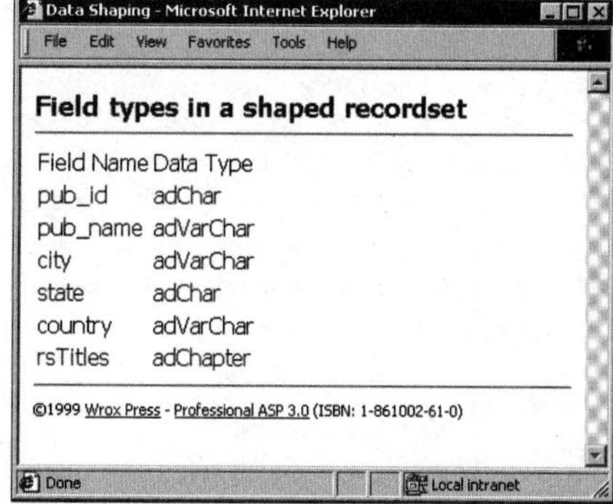

Accessing Children

We now have a recordset that is a field in another recordset, so how do we access that child recordset? Simple, we use the `Value` property of the field to set another recordset:

```
Set rsTitles = rsPublishers("rsTitles").Value
```

So you can loop through the parent records, and for each parent record obtain a recordset of the children. Here's some code that does this. We start with the usual include file and variables:

```
<!-- #INCLUDE FILE="../Include/Connection.asp" -->
<%
  Dim rsPublishers
  Dim rsTitles
  Dim strShapeConn
  Dim strShape

  Set rsPublishers = Server.CreateObject("ADODB.Recordset")
```

Now we create the connection string:

```
' Create the provider command
  strShapeConn = "Provider=MSDataShape; Data " & strConn
```

Next comes the actual shape command. This will create a parent recordset containing the Publishers, and a child recordset containing the book titles:

```
' Now the SHAPE command
  strShape = "SHAPE {SELECT * FROM Publishers}" & _
             " APPEND ({SELECT * FROM Titles}" & _
             " RELATE Pub_ID TO Pub_ID) AS rsTitles"
```

Then we open the recordset as normal:

```
' Open the shaped recordset
  rsPublishers.Open strShape, strShapeConn
```

And like normal recordsets, we can loop through the records:

```
' Loop through the publishers
  Response.Write "<UL>"
  While Not rsPublishers.EOF
    Response.Write "<LI>" & rsPublishers("Pub_Name")
```

To access the child recordset, we set a variable to point to the `Value` of the field containing the child. In this case it's `rsTitles`:

```
    ' Now the titles
    Response.Write "<UL>"
    Set rsTitles = rsPublishers("rsTitles").Value
```

The variable `rsTitles` is now a recordset, and behaves just like an ordinary one. So, we can loop through the values for this recordset, which only contains titles for the matching parent Publisher:

```
      ' Loop through the titles
      While Not rsTitles.EOF
         Response.Write "<LI>" & rsTitles("title")
         rsTitles.MoveNext
      Wend
      Response.Write "</UL>"

      ' Move to the next publisher
      rsPublishers.MoveNext
    Wend
    Response.Write "</UL>"

    rsPublishers.Close
    Set rsPublishers = Nothing
    Set rsTitles = Nothing
%>
```

This gives us a nice list of Publishers and Titles:

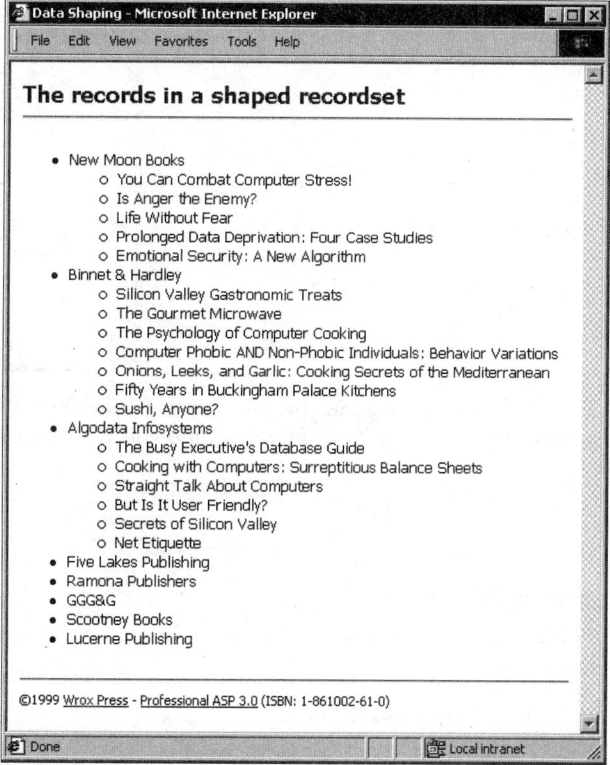

With a little bit of DHTML and some extra tags you could easily hide the titles and only show them when a publisher was selected.

Multiple Children

Data shaping would be very limited if you could only have one child per recordset, but luckily it's extremely flexible. For example, to include both the Titles and Employees for a Publisher, you could use:

```
SHAPE  {SELECT * FROM Publishers}
APPEND ({SELECT * FROM Titles}
RELATE Pub_ID TO Pub_ID) AS rsTitles,
       ({SELECT * FROM Employee}
RELATE Pub_ID TO Pub_ID) AS rsEmployees
```

You just add on any siblings to the end of the APPEND clause. This could give a result like so:

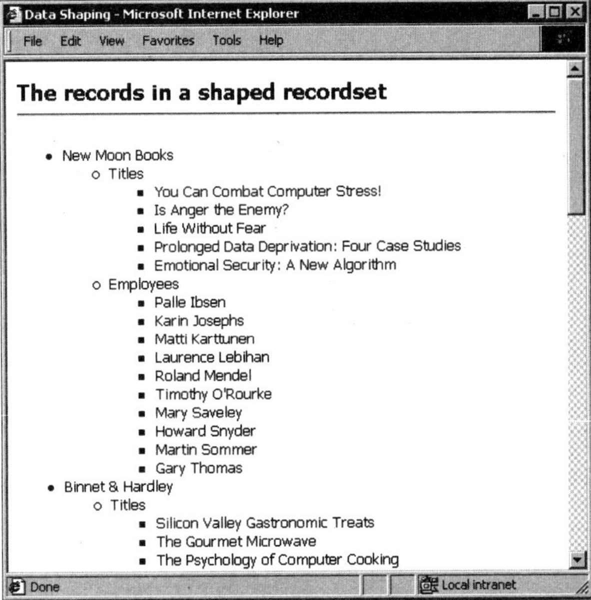

The rules of accessing the children don't change. You still use the `Value` property of the column to access the child recordset; only this time you have two children, so you have two variables:

```
Set rsTitles = rsPublishers("rsTitles").Value

Set rsEmployees = rsPublishers("rsEmployees").Value
```

GrandChildren

There is also the possibility of grandchildren, where the child recordset contains a child of its own. For example:

```
SHAPE {SELECT * FROM Publishers}
APPEND (( SHAPE {SELECT * FROM Titles}
          APPEND ({SELECT * FROM Sales}
          RELATE Title_ID TO Title_ID) AS rsSales)
RELATE Pub_ID TO Pub_ID) AS rsTitles
```

So instead of just APPENDing a SQL SELECT statement, we APPEND another SHAPE command.

Like the case with multiple children, accessing the child recordsets is the same:

```
Set rsTitles = rsPublishers("rsTitles").Value

Set rsSales = rsTitles("rsSales").Value
```

There's no theoretical limit to the number of children or grandchildren, but it's unlikely you'll want to go more than three or four levels deep.

Performance

Data shaping doesn't automatically improve performance, but when used correctly it can. The important thing to remember is how it works:

- For SELECT statements in a SHAPE command, the tables are fetched in their entirety. No optimization of the SQL is performed. Thus, if you add a WHERE clause to the parent to restrict the parent row, you still get all of the child rows. For example:

```
SHAPE {SELECT * FROM Publishers WHERE State='CA'}
APPEND ({SELECT * FROM Titles}
RELATE Pub_ID TO Pub_ID) AS rsTitles
```

  The APPEND statement returns all Titles, and not those titles for Publishers in CA. Remember, this isn't a SQL JOIN statement. The Publishers in CA and all of the Titles are fetched, and then the shape is produced.

- Although we used SQL statements, you can use stored procedures. This on its own will give a marginal improvement. However, if you use a parameterized stored procedure for the child, then the stored procedure is executed every time you access the child recordset. This means that the child recordset is not created in its entirety up front, but contains only those records from the stored procedure. The disadvantage is the extra trip to the server, but the advantage is that the data is guaranteed to be up-to-date, as it's fetched every time it's needed.

You'll see a little more about shaped recordsets in the next chapter, when we look at data on the client.

Summary

This chapter has dealt with three main topics:

- **Command objects**, and using stored procedures and parameters.
  This is an extremely important topic for the ADO programmer, since it's one area where performance can be increased without much effort. With stored procedures you have your SQL code on the server where it can be best optimized, and you have control over the data flowing into and out of those procedures.
- **Performance**
  This is just one of those issues that never goes away, and it's important to think about performance as you design your ASP applications. It's often very difficult trying to rework code to improve performance, and it's nearly always better to code for performance in the first place. The most important thing about performance is to test, test and test. Only *you* know what your system actually does, so it's important that you take responsibility for this. One great, and easy, way to test your Web site performance is to use the Web Application Stress tool.
- **Data Shaping**
  Although a less important topic than the other two, it's still worthy, as it brings ease of use to relational data. It can be used very effectively to create generic routines for nested sets of data. There's one of these routines on the sample Web site.

Although that's the end of the chapter, you'll see related bits cropping up in the next two chapters, as well as throughout the rest of the book. Now comes the time to investigate the interaction between the Web server and the browser in a little more detail. After all, having all that data is not much use unless you let people look at it.

N
W

10

ASP and Data on the Client

Data on the client – in an ASP book! Isn't that a bit of a contradiction? Not really, because I've yet to meet an ASP programmer who *only* does server-side programming. Although ASP is a server-side technology, I suspect there's really no such thing as a programmer who only programs ASP. There are however, Web developers who use it.

So, when building applications around ASP you have to consider the whole application, and that means the client too. And to get a good, responsive application, you might well need to use data on the client-side.

In this chapter we're going to look at how data can be used on the client. In particular, we'll be looking at:

- Remote Data Services, and how you get data to and from the client
- How you can bind ADO recordsets to HTML controls
- How you can use custom components to provide your data
- How you can update data on the client, and get it back to the server
- How you can get images from databases into Web pages
- How you can build table-based Web pages

There's quite a lot to cover and several different ways of achieving the same result, but it's not really very difficult.

Disconnected Recordsets

The first thing to get to grips with is the concept of disconnected data. So far in our examination of ADO we've looked at ways of obtaining recordsets, as well as how to modify the data contained in those recordsets. If you think back to when we opened a recordset, made some changes, and then closed the recordset, we retained the connection to the server during the recordset operations. That may seem fairly obvious, but remember that the Web is *stateless* in nature. If we want to use data on the client, how can it retain any connection to the server? Quite simply it can't, and this is where **disconnected recordsets** come in.

A disconnected recordset is just a normal recordset, but one that has had its connection to the server removed. The recordset then stands alone, and can act like a normal recordset, allowing updates, additions and deletions. But these changes only happen in the recordset, and are not reflected in the server because the recordset is no longer connected to the server. This isn't as disadvantageous as it sounds, since the connection to the server can be re-established and the server updated with any changes. And even if data on the server has changed, ADO gives you a way to detect these changes so you can decide which data is correct. This is called **conflict resolution**.

This disconnected recordset gives us the ability to move fully functional recordsets around between components, including between the server and the client. We'll look at how disconnected recordsets can be created in components a little later in the chapter. We won't be examining this in a great deal of detail because it's covered in Chapters 13 to 18, but we need to introduce it here so you can see how components interact with Remote Data Services.

Remote Data Services

Remote Data Services (RDS) is the name given to the set of services that allows us to handle data on the client. Now don't get worried and think we've diverted onto some new area, because RDS is part of ADO, and only comes into use when you need to transfer and use data at the client. In practice, RDS is made up from several components. A diagram makes it easier to see what they are and how they fit together:

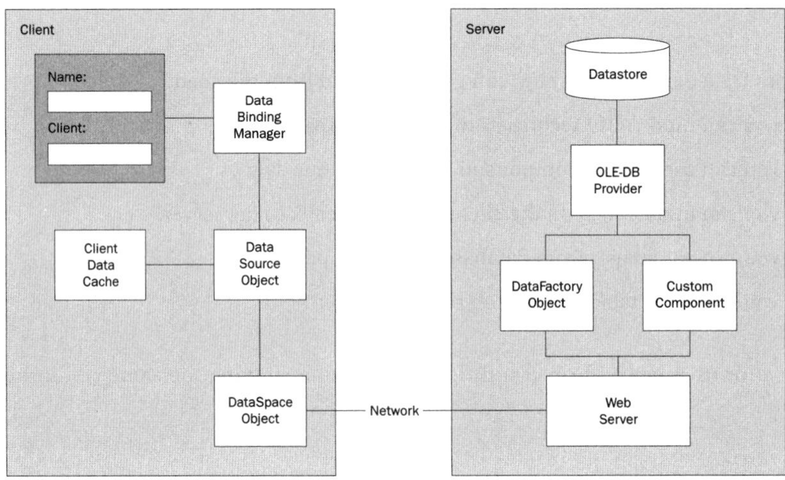

There seem to be a lot of components, but not all are used in every situation, and some aren't really part of RDS. However I've put all of the possible components on the diagram as you need to see 'the big picture'. The diagram is split into two parts, because the whole concept of using data on the client requires both some way to get it to the client, and some way to manage it once it's on the client. Let's start with the server-side.

RDS Server Components

Although I've said that RDS is for transferring and accessing data on the client, it does have some server-based components. This is necessary because there has to be some way for the data to get to the client. So, we have a set of server components that provide access to the data and then allow the data to be sent to the client. The actual sending of data is called **marshaling**.

At the very top of the diagram we have the data store, being accessed by an OLE DB Provider. This isn't explicitly part of RDS, but it does mean that any data can be used on the client with RDS as long as there is an OLE DB provider for it. From the provider, you then have two options as to how you work with the data on the server:

- The **DataFactory** is the default server-side component that provides access to data stores. It's installed as part of the server-side RDS components, and provides a way for the server to handle the sending of data to and from the client, as well as obtaining this data from the data store.
- A **Custom Component** is just a normal COM component that has methods to perform data transfer. Custom components are used when you need more functionality than DataFactory can provide. We'll see a simple example of a component in this chapter and then more complex examples later in the book.

Using these two components is the Web server, which acts as the interface between the client and the server data.

RDS Client Components

On the client-side we start at the bottom, with the **DataSpace** object. This goes hand-in-hand with the DataFactory or a custom component, and provides the client-side part of the equation. The DataSpace is a proxy object, responsible for the communication with the server, and providing the channel through which data is moved (or marshaled, as it's more commonly known). The DataSpace is a COM object that is created either in client-side script, or by using an HTML `<OBJECT>` tag. You'll see examples of this later in the chapter.

Above the DataSpace sits a **Data Source Object (DSO)**, which is responsible for storing data on the client. A DSO contains an ADO Recordset, and works together with the **Client Data Cache** to manage the data. The client data cache is simply the client cursor service managing the data on the client. A DSO meanwhile is a COM object, and, like the DataSpace, can be created either in client-side script, or by using an HTML `<OBJECT>` tag. Again, we'll be seeing examples of these later in the chapter.

Above the DSO we have the **Data Binding Manager**, whose job is to create the link between the HTML controls and the DSO. This is known as **binding**, and is performed by specifying the `DATASRC` and `DATAFLD` attributes of certain HTML controls. We'll return to these later to demonstrate how they facilitate using data on the browser.

Browser Support for RDS

It's important to understand that RDS is a Microsoft technology, and therefore only works in Microsoft browsers. In fact, RDS is only fully supported in versions 4 and above of Microsoft Internet Explorer.

When writing applications that rely on RDS, you need to be aware that the clients accessing your application might have versions of RDS different to that on the server. IE4, for example, shipped with RDS 1.5, while IE5, Office 2000 and Visual Studio 6 shipped with version 2.0. There are two ways to take care of this compatibility problem:

- Make sure all of your users upgrade to the latest version of RDS. If the clients are running Windows 2000 then they're already running the latest version, otherwise they can download it from `www.microsoft.com/data`. Version 2.5 is the latest to be released with Windows 2000, and at the same time as a downloadable package.
- Specify the Data Factory Mode when connecting to the data source. This allows you to specify which version of the RDS components you wish to use. We'll see an example of this later, under the Remoting section.

Data Source Objects

The Data Source object is a client-side object that stores and manages the data once it is on the client. Since this is the simplest way of using RDS, we'll look at these objects first.

There are several different Data Source objects, each aimed at a different sort of data:

- The **Tabular Data control (TDC)** is designed to manipulate data held in a tabular or delimited form in text files.
- The **Remote Data Service Data control** is designed to connect to OLEDB data stores, and can specify where to connect to as well as which data to return.
- The **Java DataBase Connector** is a Java applet that allows connection to data stores through the Java DataBase Control (JDBC). We're not going to be discussing the JDBC here, because it doesn't offer anything that can't be achieved by the other controls.
- The **Microsoft HTML (MSHTML)** DSO takes data marked up in HTML and uses this as the source of the data.
- The **XML** DSO uses XML data, and can be used for either well-structured or arbitrarily structured XML.

The choice of which data source object to use depends on what you are trying to do and where your data comes from. If you need to supply a small amount of data to the client, without allowing the user to update the data, then a TDC may well be suitable. The format is simple to edit and, being a text file, doesn't require any database. For data that comes from a database, and possibly needs to be updated, then the RDS data control is best. For many new sources of data you may find the XML data control a requirement. It really depends on what sort of Web application you're using, and what sort of facilities the user requires.

We'll take a look at each of these data controls in turn, and once we've examined how they can be used to get the data to the client, we'll look at how to use that data.

Tabular Data Control

The **Tabular Data Control** (TDC) is the simplest DSO, and is useful for small amounts of data that will be read-only. It's especially useful for static data that either never changes, or only changes very rarely, and that will never need to be updated from the client. For example, a TDC would be well used in providing a list of links or menu items in a page.

The TDC is created by placing an <OBJECT> tag in your HTML code. The parameter `DataURL` allows you to specify the file name containing the text data:

```
<OBJECT CLASSID="clsid:333C7BC4-460F-11D0-BC04-0080C7055A83"
        ID="dsoAuthors" WIDTH="0" HEIGHT="0">
  <PARAM NAME="DataURL" VALUE="Authors.csv">
</OBJECT>
```

As you might have guessed, the TDC only reads in data from a table, or data that are marked up in a tabular form. For example, it will work with data in Comma Separated Values (CSV) form, like so:

```
"172-32-1176","White","Bob","408 496-7223"
"213-46-8915","Green","Marjorie","415 986-7020"
"238-95-7766","Carson","Cheryl","415 548-7723"
"267-41-2394","O'Leary","Michael","408 286-2428"
"274-80-9391","Straight","Dean","415 834-2919"
"341-22-1782","Smith","Meander","913 843-0462"
"409-56-7008","Bennet","Abraham","415 658-9932"
```

The TDC is also fairly customizable. It has sixteen parameters that you can specify besides `DataURL`, either as a parameter in the object tag or in script code as demonstrated below:

Property	Data Type	Description	Default value
`AppendData`	Boolean	Identifies whether new data will replace the existing data in the DSO or be appended to the existing data.	False
`CaseSensitive`	Boolean	Indicates whether or not string comparisons are case sensitive.	True
`CharSet`	String	Indicates the character set of the data. A list of character sets is shown in the appendices.	`windows-1252`
`DataURL`	String	Indicates the URL of the source data file.	

Table Continued on Following Page

Property	Data Type	Description	Default value
EscapeChar	String	Specifies the escape character used in the source file. The escape character is placed in front of other characters to ensure they are not mistaken for the FieldDelim, RowDelim or TextQualifier.	
FieldDelim	String	Specifies the character that delimits the fields.	, (comma)
Filter	String	Sets the criteria to be used as a filter.	
FilterColumn	String	Sets the column to filter on.	
FilterValue	String	Sets the value of the column to filter on.	
Language	String	Specifies the language of the data file.	en-us
ReadyState	Long	Indicates the current state of the control. This will be one of: ❑ adcReadyStateComplete (4) if all of the data has arrived, or an error occurred ❑ adcReadyStateInteractive (3) if data is still arriving ❑ adcReadyStateLoaded (2) if the control is loaded and waiting for data to arrive This property is read only.	
RowDelim	String	Specifies the character used to delimit rows in the text file, and defaults to a carriage return.	A new line character
Sort	String	Indicates a list of column names upon which the data will be sorted. A minus sign in front of a column name indicates descending order, otherwise ascending order is used.	
SortDirection	Boolean	True if the sort is to be in ascending order, False for descending order.	
SortColumn	String	Identifies the column used for sorting.	
TextQualifier	String	Specifies the character that is used to enclose text fields, and defaults to the double quotation mark.	" (double quote)
UseHeader	Boolean	Indicates whether or not the first row of the text file contains column names.	False

The example below shows the TDC being populated by using a parameter:

```
<OBJECT CLASSID="clsid:333C7BC4-460F-11D0-BC04-0080C7055A83"
        ID="dsoAuthors" WIDTH="0" HEIGHT="0">
  <PARAM NAME="DataURL" VALUE="Authors.csv">
</OBJECT>
```

You can also get data from within client-side script. The example below shows some JScript to load the TDC with data:

```
function fillTDC()
{
    dsoAuthors.dataURL = 'authors.csv';
    dsoAuthors.Reset();
}
```

If you change the `dataURL` associated with the TDC, you must use the `Reset` method to make the new URL take effect. We'll see how this can be used in more detail when we look at data binding. The `Reset` method is the only method that the TDC has.

RDS Data Control

The **Remote Data Services Data control** provides access to normal data stores, as opposed to flat files. It's most often used to connect to SQL databases to retrieve data from tables, queries or stored procedures, and unlike the TDC, the RDS data control allows the data to be updated. We'll be showing you how to do that a little later in the chapter.

Like the TDC, you create an RDS data control with an HTML `OBJECT` tag, and the setting of the properties is performed in a similar manner.

```
<OBJECT CLASSID="clsid:BD96C556-65A3-11D0-983A-00C04FC29E33"
        ID="dsoAuthors" WIDTH="0" HEIGHT="0">
  <PARAM NAME="Connect" VALUE="Connection String">
  <PARAM NAME="Server" VALUE="Server Name ">
  <PARAM NAME="SQL" VALUE="Query Text">
</OBJECT>
```

Again, notice the use of parameters to customize the data control. The above example shows the most common set-up, but as with the TDC, there are quite a few other parameters you can specify, as follows:

Property	Data Type	Description	Default Value
Connect	String	An ADO connection string, to identify the data store.	
ExecuteOptions	Long	Indicates whether the command is executed synchronously or asynchronously. It can be one of: adcExecSync (1) for synchronous operation (the default) adcExecAsync (2) for asynchronous operation	adcExecAsync
FetchOptions	Long	Indicates how data is to be fetched. Can be one of: adcFetchUpFront (1) to fetch the data and then return control to the application adcFetchBackground (2) to fetch the first batch of data immediately, and then fetch the rest of the data in the background adcFetchAsync (3) to fetch all of the data in the background	adcFetchAsync
FilterColumn	String	Indicates which column to filter on.	
FilterCriterion	String	Indicates the criteria to use for filtering. Can be one of: < (Less Than) <= (Equal To or Less Than) = (Equal To) >= (Equal To or More Than) > (More Than) <> (Not Equal To)	
FilterValue	String	The value to filter on.	

Property	Data Type	Description	Default Value
`Handler`	String	The name and parameters of a customized data handler. This is discussed in more detail in the Security section later in the chapter.	`MSDFMAP.Handler`
`InternetTimeout`	Long	The time in milliseconds to wait before an error is generated.	300000
`ReadyState`	Long	Indicates the current state of the control. This will be one of: `adcReadyStateComplete` (4) if all of the data has arrived, or an error occurred `adcReadyStateInteractive` (3) if data is still arriving `adcReadyStateLoaded` (2) if the control is loaded and waiting for data to arrive	
`Recordset`	Recordset	Allows access to the ADO recordset underlying the control. You'll see more of this in the Data binding section. Read-only.	
`Server`	String	The name of the server on which the data resides. For security reasons this must be the same as the server that supplies the Web page. This can be a standard URL or the name of a machine (if using DCOM).	
`SortColumn`	String	The name of the column upon which to sort.	
`SortDirection`	Boolean	Indicates whether or not sorts are ascending.	
`SourceRecordset`	String	Sets the underlying recordset of the control to be an existing recordset. Write-only.	

Table Continued on Following Page

Property	Data Type	Description	Default Value
SQL	String	The SQL string used to generate the data.	
URL	String	A URL that is the source of the data.	

Asynchronous operation means that data are fetched in the background, allowing data to start being used in the Web page before all of the data have been returned. Although you often need all of the data, working asynchronously does at least let you to start processing the data. It also gives the user something to look at, and thus makes the site seem more responsive.

Like the TDC, the RDS data control can have its properties set either as PARAMETERs of the OBJECT tag, or in code. For example, the following:

```
<OBJECT CLASSID="clsid:BD96C556-65A3-11D0-983A-00C04FC29E33"
        ID="dsoAuthors" WIDTH="0" HEIGHT="0">
  <PARAM NAME="Connect" VALUE="DSN=pubs">
  <PARAM NAME="Server" VALUE="W2000">
  <PARAM NAME="SQL" VALUE="SELECT * FROM Authors">
</OBJECT>
```

Is the equivalent to:

```
<OBJECT CLASSID="clsid:BD96C556-65A3-11D0-983A-00C04FC29E33"
        ID="dsoAuthors" WIDTH="0" HEIGHT="0">
</OBJECT>

<SCRIPT LANGUAGE=JScript>

function window.onload()
{
    dsoAuthors.Connect = "DSN=pubs";
    dsoAuthors.Server = "W2000";
    dsoAuthors.SQL = "SELECT * FROM Authors";
    dsoAuthors.Refresh();
}
</SCRIPT>
```

I've used a DSN for the `Connect` *parameter because it fits into the page nicely, but this can be any valid ADO connection string.*

The URL is a new property for ADO 2.5 and it allows you to use a file as the source of the data. This file can take one of two forms; either as a recordset that has been saved with the `Recordset.Save` method, or as an ASP page which creates a recordset and then persists it to a stream. Here's what you could do:

```
<OBJECT CLASSID="clsid:BD96C556-65A3-11D0-983A-00C04FC29E33"
        ID="dsoAuthors" WIDTH="0" HEIGHT="0">
    <PARAM NAME="URL" VALUE="DataPage.asp">
</OBJECT>
```

The DataPage.asp file could contain the following VBScript code:

```
<%
  Dim rsData
  Set rsData = Server.CreateObject("ADODB.Recordset")
  rsData.Open "SELECT * FROM Authors", strConn
  rsData.Save Response, adPersistXML
  rsData.Close
  Set rsData = Nothing
%>
```

This simply creates a recordset and then uses the Save method to save the recordset in XML format to the Response object. In previous versions of ADO you could only save to a physical file, but ADO 2.5 allows us to save directly to a Stream. The result of this ASP page is a recordset in XML format. We'll be looking at the whole topic of Streams and XML data in more detail in the next chapter.

There's one really great advantage that using the URL property has over using the Connect and SQL properties – your connection details don't appear anywhere in the page that the user can see. Consider the following object definition:

```
<OBJECT CLASSID="clsid:BD96C556-65A3-11D0-983A-00C04FC29E33"
       ID="dsoAuthors" WIDTH="0" HEIGHT="0">
  <PARAM NAME="Connect" VALUE="DSN=pubs">
  <PARAM NAME="Server" VALUE="W2000">
  <PARAM NAME="SQL" VALUE="SELECT * FROM Authors">
</OBJECT>
```

The first shows the connection details. In this case we can see the DSN is named pubs, and that we are selecting all columns from the authors table. This gives hackers a potential route into your site, since they know the server name and details of the database. Now consider the URL property:

```
<OBJECT CLASSID="clsid:BD96C556-65A3-11D0-983A-00C04FC29E33"
       ID="dsoAuthors" WIDTH="0" HEIGHT="0">
    <PARAM NAME="URL" VALUE="DataPage.asp">
</OBJECT>
```

All the user sees is the URL of an ASP page, and there are no details of the server or database at all.

With the CONNECT/SQL method the user can see exactly what your connection details are, but with the URL all they see are the data. This clears up one of the security fears that people have had over using RDS.

When setting the properties of the RDS data control in script you have to use the Refresh method, like so:

```
<SCRIPT LANGUAGE=JScript>

function window.onload()
```

```
{
    dsoAuthors.URL="DataPage.asp"
    dsoAuthors.Refresh();
}
</SCRIPT>
```

This forces the data control to use the new property values, and re-fetch the data from the provider. As well as `Refresh`, the RDS data control has many other methods:

Method	Description
`Cancel`	Cancels any asynchronous operation.
`CancelUpdate`	Cancels any changes made to the data.
`CreateRecordset`	Creates an empty recordset, allowing you to create new sets of data locally.
`MoveFirst`	Moves to the first record.
`MoveLast`	Moves to the last record.
`MoveNext`	Moves to the next record.
`MovePrevious`	Moves to the previous record.
`Refresh`	Refreshes the data from the data store.
`Reset`	Applies the filter or sort criteria.
`SubmitChanges`	Sends any pending changes back to the data store.

You'll see most of these in action later in the chapter.

MSHTML Data Control

The **Microsoft HTML Data Control** is rather unusual in that it is part of IE, and it allows you to have a data source based on HTML. Although this isn't a form you'd naturally use for data storage, it could be useful if you have lots of HTML pages that do contain some form of data.

You can use this control like so:

```
<OBJECT ID="dsoAuthors" DATA="Authors.html" HEIGHT="0" WIDTH="0">
</OBJECT>
```

To be able to use the control, your HTML tags must have an `ID` attribute, as it's this that identifies the field names. For example:

```
<DIV ID="au_id">172-32-1176</DIV>
<SPAN ID="au_lname">White</SPAN>
<H1 ID="au_fname">Bob</H1>
<PRE ID="au_id">213-46-8915</PRE>
<H2 ID="au_lname">Green</H2>
<H1 ID="au_fname">Cheryl</H1>
```

You'll immediately notice something odd – this doesn't look like very nice HTML. Correct, but it's like this to illustrate a point. The HTML tag names are irrelevant – it's the `ID` that is important. The above HTML, when parsed by the MSHTML DSO, would generate two rows of data, each with three fields. You'd end up with data that looked like this:

au_id	au_lname	au_fname
172-32-1176	White	Bob
213-46-8915	Green	Cheryl

The fields are identified by the `ID` attributes. If a tag has an `ID` the same as an `ID` that already exists, then the data for that tag becomes a new row; otherwise a new field in the same row is created.

Like the controls already discussed, the MSHTML data control has a `Recordset` property, which is the only property for this control. It has no methods.

XML Data Control

You've already seen one way of including XML data into your RDS controls; using the RDS data control and the URL property to get XML data from an ASP file. The other method is to use an XML Data Island, which means using the XML tag. We'll only mention it briefly here, as the next chapter deals with XML data in more detail.

The `<XML>` tag is an IE HTML tag that acts like a data control. In many ways it's similar to using an RDS data control, but it is specifically designed for XML data. You use the tag in one of two ways.

The first way is to use the `SRC` attribute to specify the location of the data:

```
<XML ID="dsoAuthors" SRC="Authors.xml"></XML>
```

This uses the file `Authors.xml` as the source of the data.

Alternatively, you can embed the XML in the tag:

```
<XML ID="dsoAuthors">
 <Authors>
  <Author>
    <au_id>172-32-1176</au_id>
    <au_lname>White</au_lname>
    <au_fname>Johnson</au_fname>
    <phone>408 496-7223</phone>
    <contract>True</contract>
  </Author>
  <Author>
    <au_id>213-46-8915</au_id>
    <au_lname>Green</au_lname>
    <au_fname>Marjorie</au_fname>
    <phone>415 986-7020</phone>
    <contract>True</contract>
  </Author>
 </Authors>
</XML>
```

We'll be looking at this control in more detail in the next chapter.

Data Binding

So far we've used several different RDS data controls to show how you can get data to the client, but we've said nothing about what to do when it gets there. These data controls are really only responsible for the storage and management of the data, not the actual display of it. So the question is how to get the data from the data control into some HTML elements so that the user can see it.

The simplest ways of using data on the client are to bind the data to HTML. **Binding** simply means setting up a relationship between some HTML elements and the data control. The data control is responsible for managing the data and supplying the data to the HTML element, and the element displays the data on the screen.

To bind an HTML element to a data source you need to specify two attributes for it:

- DATASRC, to identify the data control that contains the data. You always put a # in front of the data source name.
- DATAFLD, to identify the field in the data control to bind to. The fields are the names identifying the columns in the data that the data control manages. So from a database, these will be the column names of a table.

For example:

```
<OBJECT CLASSID="clsid:BD96C556-65A3-11D0-983A-00C04FC29E33"
        ID="dsoAuthors" WIDTH="0" HEIGHT="0">
    <PARAM NAME="URL" VALUE="DataPage.asp">
</OBJECT>

<DIV DATASRC="#dsoAuthors" DATAFLD="au_fname"></DIV>
<DIV DATASRC="#dsoAuthors" DATAFLD="au_lname"></DIV>
```

Here we have a standard RDS data control called dsoAuthors. We create two DIV elements, and set the DATASRC attribute to point to the data control previously defined. Then we set the DATAFLD attribute to the field name – in this case it's au_fname and au_lname. That's all there is to data binding. The results would look something like this:

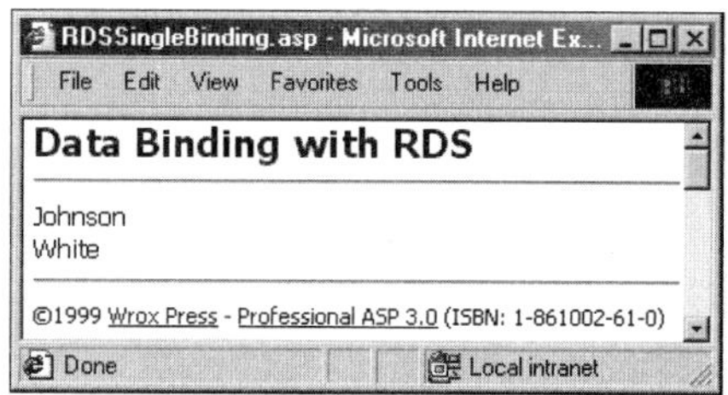

Not very exciting, but the important thing to remember is that the text output (Johnson and White) doesn't appear in the HTML at all. The HTML really only consists of what's shown above.

> **So this is what data binding is – the ability of a data control to manage data from a remote source, and for HTML elements to take that data and display it on the screen.**

There's also a third attribute – DATAFORMATAS, which can be either HTML or TEXT – to indicate how the data in the field should be formatted. This defaults to TEXT, but if you had data in HTML form, then you could get the data binding to format it for you. For example, consider the following text file:

```
Description,Image
The main Wrox logo,<IMG SRC="logos/WroxLogo.gif">
The Wrox Conferences logo,<IMG SRC="logos/WroxConferencesLogo.gif">
The ASPToday logo,<IMG SRC="logos/ASPTodayLogo.gif">
```

This will be the source file for a TDC, and contains two fields: the first is a description, and the second some HTML text to show some images. Now let's bind this to an HTML table:

```
<TABLE ID="tblData" DATASRC="#dsoLogos">
  <THEAD>
    <TR>
      <TD>Description</TD>
      <TD>Image</TD>
    </TR>
  </THEAD>
  <TBODY>
    <TR>
      <TD><SPAN DATAFLD="Description"></SPAN></TD>
      <TD><SPAN DATAFLD="Image"></SPAN></TD>
    </TR>
  </TBODY>
</TABLE>
```

Don't worry too much about the data binding here – this is known as ***tabular data binding*** *and we'll be covering it in detail in a little while. I've used it here because it illustrates the formatting better.*

Opening this in the browser gives us the following:

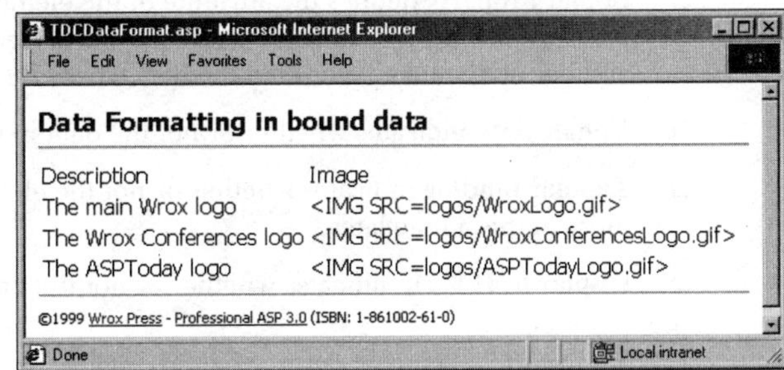

You can see that all three rows in the data file have been displayed, but the HTML is displayed as text. To view the HTML we need to use the DATAFORMATAS attribute:

```
<TD><SPAN DATAFLD="Description"></SPAN></TD>
<TD><SPAN DATAFLD="Image" DATAFORMATAS="HTML"></SPAN></TD>
```

Now when we open this in the browser we get a much better effect:

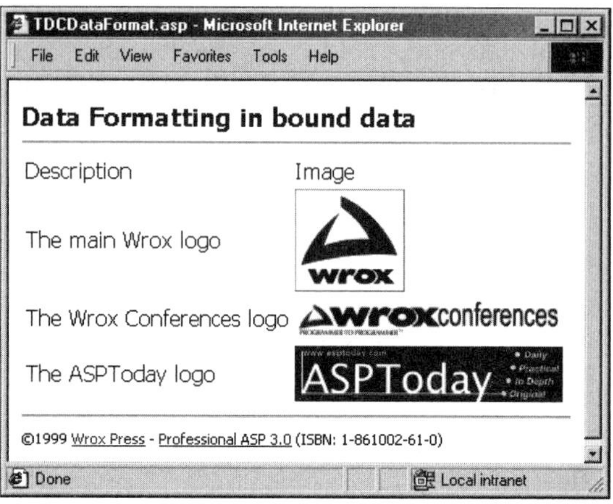

The fact that we've specified the second field to be formatted as HTML means that any HTML tags in the field are interpreted as HTML. So, our `IMG` tags become actual images. Once again the source doesn't contain any `IMG` tags, only bound data.

You can use this formatting for any field, from any data source, and any HTML tags will be interpreted. It's quite good for situations where you allow users to enter formatted text.

Elements that Support Data Binding

In the above examples we've used `<SPAN>`, `<DIV>` and `<TABLE>` tags to bind to data, but not all HTML elements support data binding. The table below details those that do. The columns in the table are:

- **HTML Element** defines the HTML element that supports data binding.
- **Bound Property** defines the attribute of the element that becomes bound to the data. For example, in our DIV tags above, the bound data was placed in the `innerText` attribute. If we used an `A` tag and bound that to a field, then the data would be placed in the `href` attribute.
- **Update data** indicates whether or not the data in the bound element can be updated.
- **Tabular binding** indicates whether or not the element allows sub-elements to be bound. You'll see more of this a little later.
- **Display as HTML** indicates whether or not the data can be formatted as HTML.

HTML Element	Bound property	Update data?	Tabular binding?	Display as HTML
`A`	`href`	No	No	No
`APPLET`	`PARAM`	Yes	No	No
`BUTTON`	`innerText` and `innerHTML`	No	No	Yes

HTML Element	Bound property	Update data?	Tabular binding?	Display as HTML
DIV	innerText and innerHTML	No	No	Yes
FRAME	src	No	No	No
IFRAME	src	No	No	No
IMG	src	No	No	No
INPUT TYPE=CHECKBOX	checked	Yes	No	No
INPUT TYPE=HIDDEN	value	Yes	No	No
INPUT TYPE=LABEL	value	Yes	No	No
INPUT TYPE=PASSWORD	value	Yes	No	No
INPUT TYPE=RADIO	checked	Yes	No	No
INPUT TYPE=TEXT	value	Yes	No	No
LABEL	innerText and innerHTML	No	No	Yes
LEGEND	innerText and innerHTML	No	No	No
MARQUEE	innerText and innerHTML	No	No	Yes
OBJECT	param	Yes	No	No
SELECT	text of selected <option> element	Yes	No	No
SPAN	innerText and innerHTML	No	No	Yes
TABLE	none	No	Yes	No
TEXTAREA	value	Yes	No	No

Single Record Binding

Single record binding is where you have only a single row of data visible at once. For example, consider the following:

```
ID:         <SPAN DATASRC="#dsoData" DATAFLD="au_id"></SPAN><BR>
First Name: <SPAN DATASRC="#dsoData" DATAFLD="au_fname"></SPAN><BR>
Last Name:  <SPAN DATASRC="#dsoData" DATAFLD="au_lname"></SPAN><BR>
Phone:      <SPAN DATASRC="#dsoData" DATAFLD="phone"></SPAN><BR>
Address:    <SPAN DATASRC="#dsoData" DATAFLD="address"></SPAN><BR>
City:       <SPAN DATASRC="#dsoData" DATAFLD="city"></SPAN><BR>
State:      <SPAN DATASRC="#dsoData" DATAFLD="state"></SPAN><BR>
Zip:        <SPAN DATASRC="#dsoData" DATAFLD="zip"></SPAN><BR>
Contact:    <SPAN DATASRC="#dsoData" DATAFLD="contract"></SPAN><BR>
```

When using single record binding each HTML element that is to be bound identifies both the source of the data (DATASRC) and the field (DATAFLD) to bind to.

The above binding gives the following results:

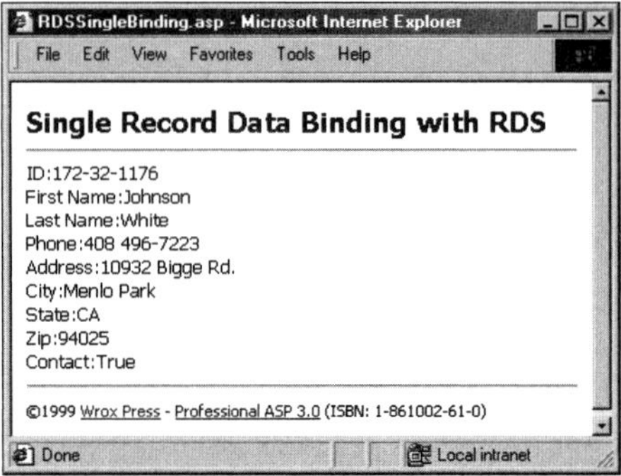

This is OK as a result, but remember that white space is ignored in HTML, so nothing is lined up neatly. Data binding has made the data easier to get to, but it hasn't made it nicer to look at. A better approach might be to use a table for alignment:

```
<TABLE ID="tblData">
  <TR><TD>ID:</TD>
      <TD><SPAN DATASRC="#dsoData" DATAFLD="au_id"></SPAN></TD></TR>
  <TR><TD>First Name:</TD>
      <TD><SPAN DATASRC="#dsoData" DATAFLD="au_fname"></SPAN></TD></TR>
  <TR><TD>Last Name:</TD>
      <TD><SPAN DATASRC="#dsoData" DATAFLD="au_lname"></SPAN></TD></TR>
  <TR><TD>Phone:</TD>
      <TD><SPAN DATASRC="#dsoData" DATAFLD="phone"></SPAN></TD></TR>
  <TR><TD>Address:</TD>
      <TD><SPAN DATASRC="#dsoData" DATAFLD="address"></SPAN></TD></TR>
  <TR><TD>City:</TD>
      <TD><SPAN DATASRC="#dsoData" DATAFLD="city"></SPAN></TD></TR>
  <TR><TD>State:</TD>
      <TD><SPAN DATASRC="#dsoData" DATAFLD="state"></SPAN></TD></TR>
  <TR><TD>Zip:</TD>
      <TD><SPAN DATASRC="#dsoData" DATAFLD="zip"></SPAN></TD></TR>
  <TR><TD>Contact:</TD>
      <TD><SPAN DATASRC="#dsoData" DATAFLD="contract"></SPAN></TD></TR>
</TABLE>
```

The HTML is not so easy to read, but it gives a much better result:

Notice that the example just shown uses SPAN elements to hold the data. If you want to be able to edit the data, then you can use INPUT elements instead. For example:

```
<TABLE ID="tblData">
 <TR><TD>ID:</TD>
  <TD>
   <INPUT TYPE="TEXT" DATASRC="#dsoData" DATAFLD="au_id"></INPUT>
  </TD>
 </TR>

. . .

</TABLE>
```

This uses an INPUT element of type TEXT. Notice that the data binding is exactly the same – it's just that the element is different.

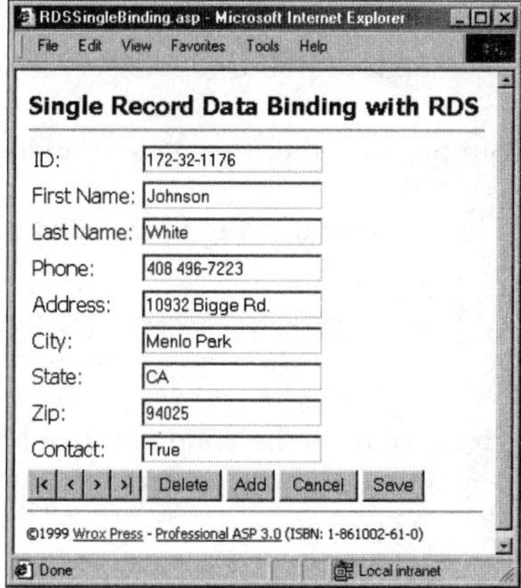

Data Navigation

Having a single record visible isn't much good unless you can get to the other records. Fortunately, the data control has a Recordset property, which is the actual ADO recordset containing the data. If you remember back to Chapter 8, the recordset has methods to move around the records:

- MoveFirst
- MoveNext
- MovePrevious
- MoveLast

For example, let's say you wanted to add some of the buttons we've used in the above screenshot on your HTML page, to give some record navigation.

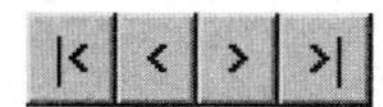

You can create these buttons like so:

```
<BUTTON ID="cmdFirst" TITLE="First Record"
    ONCLICK="dsoData.recordset.MoveFirst()"> |&lt; </BUTTON>
```

```
<BUTTON ID="cmdPrevious" TITLE="Previous Record"
    ONCLICK="if (!dsoData.recordset.BOF) dsoData.recordset.MovePrevious()">
     &lt; </BUTTON>

<BUTTON ID="cmdNext" TITLE="Next Record"
    ONCLICK="if (!dsoData.recordset.EOF) dsoData.recordset.MoveNext()">
     &gt; </BUTTON>

<BUTTON ID="cmdLast" TITLE="Last Record"
    ONCLICK="dsoData.recordset.MoveLast()"> &gt;| </BUTTON> 
```

These just make use of the movement methods of the recordset. The first and last are pretty easy – you just have to remember that the data control has a property called `Recordset`, and since that property is an object, it has methods of its own. So, this code

```
dsoData.recordset.MoveFirst()
```

Simply calls the `MoveFirst` method on the recordset that the data control is managing.

The lines for moving to the next and previous records look trickier, but are also simple:

```
if (!dsoData.recordset.BOF)
    dsoData.recordset.MovePrevious()
```

Here we have the code to move back a record, so we just check that we're not already at the beginning of the recordset by making sure the `BOF` property isn't set before performing the `MovePrevious`.

Table Binding

Table binding differs from single record binding because, instead of using a table just for alignment, we bind to the `TABLE` element. This allows us to see more than one record at a time. For example:

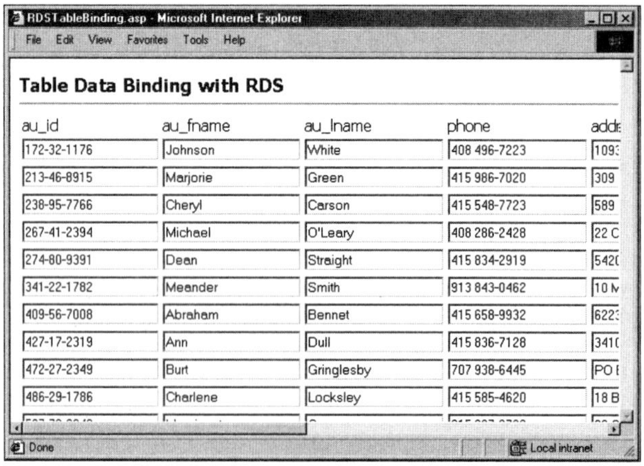

This is even easier than single record binding, and to do it you use the `DATASRC` attribute in the table, and then bind the table elements using the `DATAFLD` attribute. So, we have the table bound to the data control, and each table cell bound to an individual field.

However, looking at the table of HTML elements that can be bound, you'll see that the table cell element (TD) isn't among them. For this reason we generally use a SPAN or DIV for read-only tables, or the INPUT tag for editable tables. For example, the above screenshot was created with the following code:

```
<TABLE ID="tblData" DATASRC="#dsoData">
  <THEAD>
   <TR>
    <TD>au_id</TD>
    <TD>au_fname</TD>
    <TD>au_lname</TD>
    <TD>phone</TD>
    <TD>address</TD>
    <TD>city</TD>
    <TD>state</TD>
    <TD>zip</TD>
    <TD>contract</TD>
   </TR>
  </THEAD>
  <TBODY>
   <TR>
    <TD><INPUT TYPE="TEXT" DATAFLD="au_id"></INPUT></TD>
    <TD><INPUT TYPE="TEXT" DATAFLD="au_fname"></INPUT></TD>
    <TD><INPUT TYPE="TEXT" DATAFLD="au_lname"></INPUT></TD>
    <TD><INPUT TYPE="TEXT" DATAFLD="phone"></INPUT></TD>
    <TD><INPUT TYPE="TEXT" DATAFLD="address"></INPUT></TD>
    <TD><INPUT TYPE="TEXT" DATAFLD="city"></INPUT></TD>
    <TD><INPUT TYPE="TEXT" DATAFLD="state"></INPUT></TD>
    <TD><INPUT TYPE="TEXT" DATAFLD="zip"></INPUT></TD>
    <TD><INPUT TYPE="TEXT" DATAFLD="contract"></INPUT></TD>
   </TR>
  </TBODY>
</TABLE>
```

The TABLE element also has one other attribute useful to data binding – DATAPAGESIZE. This determines how many records are shown in the table:

```
<TABLE ID="tblData" DATASRC="#dsoData" DATAPAGESIZE="10">
```

In the above example, the table will only ever hold ten records at once. The movement methods of the recordset don't help here, because it's the table that is restricting the view of records, so you have to use two methods of the table, like so:

```
<button id="cmdPreviousPage" title="Previous Page"
    onclick="tblData.PreviousPage()">Previous Page<button>
```

```
<button id="cmdNextPage" title="Next Page"
    onclick="tblData.NextPage()">Next Page<button>
```

Dynamic Binding

All of the examples so far have shown a fixed set of records, and the bound fields have been created at design time. In my mind this doesn't lead to great code reuse or provide a flexible way to develop programs, especially since Web applications are giving the user more and more power.

The way to solve this dilemma is to create the fields in the table *dynamically*, depending on the data held in the data control. This is actually pretty easy, and depends on client-side scripting. So, let's assume we want to offer the user a choice between two tables: `authors` and `publishers`:

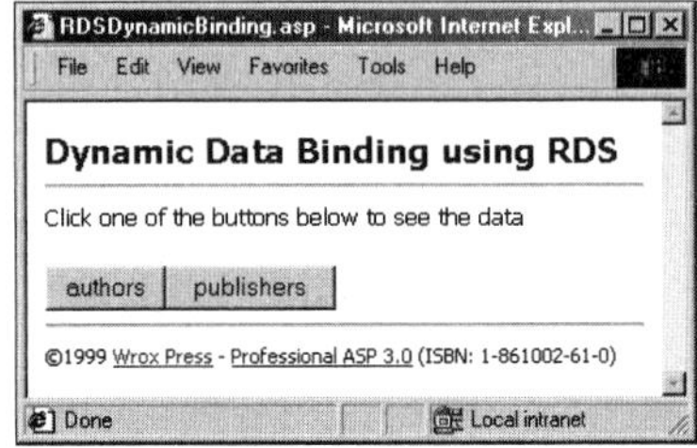

Now we don't really want to have two tables with all of their fields bound, as this would be rather cumbersome to maintain. What happens if the structure of the source data changes, or you want to add another table? The way to deal with this is to create a dummy table, and create and bind the fields dynamically, at runtime.

To start with, we have the data control:

```
<OBJECT CLASSID="clsid:BD96C556-65A3-11D0-983A-00C04FC29E33"
        ID="dsoData" HEIGHT="0" WIDTH="0"
        ONDATASETCOMPLETE="createCells()">
</OBJECT>
```

This is the RDS data control, and the only difference from previous examples is that we're not setting the parameters here, as we'll be doing that in code too. The only addition is setting the function to be run once the data has been read in by the control.

Next we need to create two buttons to identify the data:

```
<BUTTON ID="cmdAuthors"
        onclick="resetData('authors')">authors</BUTTON>
<BUTTON ID="cmdPublishers"
        onclick="resetData('publishers')">publishers</BUTTON>
```

And now the dummy table:

```
<TABLE ID="tblData">
  <THEAD><TR></TR></THEAD>
  <TBODY><TR></TR></TBODY>
</TABLE>
```

This just acts as a template. Notice that there are no cells in this table. That's because we don't know how many fields the data is going to have, so we'll create these at runtime too.

Now comes the JScript code. Let's first look at the resetData function, which sets the properties of the data control and loads the data:

```
function resetData(strTable)
{
    // reset the data
    dsoData.Connect = 'Provider=SQLOLEDB; Data Source=' +
                      '<%= Request.ServerVariables("SERVER_NAME") %>' +
                      '; Initial Catalog=pubs; User ID=sa; Password=';
    dsoData.Server = 'http://<%= Request.ServerVariables("SERVER_NAME") %>';
    dsoData.SQL = 'SELECT * FROM ' + strTable;
    dsoData.Refresh();
}
```

Although this looks slightly more complex than when we used the parameters, it's still pretty simple. Remember how the parameter names map onto properties? All we're doing here is setting those same properties, and then calling Refresh to update the data control. It probably looks worse than any previous examples because of the small bits of ASP in the code – these simply insert the name of the Web server into the properties. Using this method means that the ASP page can be moved from server to server without changing the code. The name of the table that is the source of the data is supplied to this function from the appropriate button.

Once the data has been loaded, the ondatasetcomplete event of the data control is triggered, which runs our createCells function:

```
function createCells()
{
   var fldF;
   var tblCell;

// Delete what's there already
   deleteCells();

// Now create the new cells
   for (fldF = new Enumerator(dsoData.recordset.Fields);
       !fldF.atEnd(); fldF.moveNext())
   {
// Create a new cell for the heading
   tblCell = tblData.rows[0].insertCell();
   tblCell.innerHTML = '<B>' + fldF.item().name + '</B>';

// Create a new cell for the body
   tblCell = tblData.rows[1].insertCell();
   tblCell.innerHTML = '<INPUT DATAFLD="' +
                            fldF.item().name + '"></INPUT>';
   }

// now bind to the data source
   tblData.dataSrc = '#dsoData';
}
```

Again this is pretty simple. It first deletes any existing cells (we'll look at that function in a minute), and then loops through the fields of the recordset. For each field we create a new cell in the header row (the table only has two rows – the first, 0, is the header and the second, 1, is the body). Once the cell is created we set the innerHTML property to be the field name. A similar procedure is done for a new cell in the body, but this time we make the innerHTML element hold the INPUT tag, bound to the data field. Once all of the fields are done, the table is bound to the data control.

Because this page allows you to switch between two different sets of data, you need to be able to delete the existing data:

```
function deleteCells()
{
   var intCell;
   var intCells;

// Unbind the table
   tblData.dataSrc = '';

// Delete existing cells
   intCells = tblData.rows[0].cells.length
   for (intCell = 0; intCell < intCells; ++intCell)
   {
      tblData.rows[0].deleteCell();
      tblData.rows[1].deleteCell();
   }
}

</SCRIPT>
```

This routine simply unbinds the table, and loops through the cells in the table deleting each one. Once this is run, the table only contains the empty head and body rows.

This is a fairly simple example of what can be achieved using RDS and some DHTML. You could easily turn this into an ASP include file and drop it into any application, even if the source of the data isn't going to change.

The full source code for this example, RDSDynamicBinding.asp, along with similar examples for the other data control types, is available from the Wrox Web site

Updating Data

So far you've only seen getting data onto the client, but nothing about how this data can be updated and sent back to the server. Remember that the recordset is disconnected, so how can we update data? Any changes you make to the data are part of the local records that are held by the data control, so to update the server you have to issue a special command. We don't have to do anything complex though, because the RDS data control has two methods that allow us to either cancel all of the changes we've done so far, or send all of the changes to the server.

You can create buttons for this to make it easy for the user:

```
<BUTTON ID="cmdCancelAll" TITLE="Abandon All Changes"
     ONCLICK="dsoData.CancelUpdate()">Cancel</BUTTON> 

<BUTTON ID="cmdUpdateAll" TITLE="Save All Changes"
     ONCLICK="dsoData.SubmitChanges()">Save</BUTTON>
```

The `SubmitChanges` method submits only the changed records back to the server, and the `CancelUpdate` method cancels any changes made in the local recordset.

Updating and canceling aren't the only things you might need. What if you want to add new records, or delete existing ones? Well, for these you use the normal `Delete` and `AddNew` methods of the recordset. These add or delete records in the recordset, and then when you `SubmitChanges` the data on the server is updated.

```
<BUTTON ID="cmdDelete" TITLE="Delete This Record"
     ONCLICK="dsoData.recordset.Delete()">Delete</BUTTON> 

<BUTTON ID="cmdAddNew" TITLE="Add New Record"
     ONCLICK="dsoData.recordset.AddNew()">Add</BUTTON> 
```

Conflict Resolution

One problem you may encounter due to being disconnected from the data source is that of **conflicts**. What happens if you update a record and save it to the data store, but someone else has changed the record too? Thankfully, this is catered for as part of the `SubmitChanges` method, as an error will be generated if there are any conflicts.

If one of the records fails during a call to `SubmitChanges`, then all of the records fail. This ensures that you don't get partial changes applied to the original data. You can tell which records failed by looping through the recordset and checking the `Status` property of the record. For example, instead of just calling `SubmitChanges` in the command button, you'd be better off calling your own function:

```
function updateData()
{
```

The first thing to do in this function is use the `SubmitChanges` method within a `try` block so we can handle errors:

```
  // Try and update the data
  try
  {
    // Submit the changes back to the server
    dsoData.SubmitChanges();
    dsoData.Refresh();
  }
```

If there is an error, then we can process it in the `catch` block:

```
  // RDS throws an error if the update fails
  catch (e)
  {
    var rsConflicts;
    var adRecUnmodified = 0x0000008;     // Record was not modified
    var adAffectAll = 3;                 // resync all records
    var adResyncUnderlyingValues = 1;    // Only resync underlyingValue
```

At this stage we know an error has occurred, but we don't know which one, so we resynchronize our data with the data from the data store. Using `adResyncUnderlyingValues` ensures that only the `UnderlyingValue` property of the fields is overwritten with values from the data store, meaning any changes we've made are safe (remember, our changes are held in the `Value` property). This means we can compare our values with the values in the database later on in the code:

```
    // There's been an error, so get the underlyingValues back
    // from the server to see what's changed
    dsoData.recordset.resync(adAffectAll, adResyncUnderlyingValues);
```

Next, we make a clone of the recordset, allowing us to move around the records without affecting the current position of the data control:

```
    // Clone the recordset so we don't alter the position of the original
    rsConflicts = dsoData.recordset.clone();
```

And then we can start looping through the records, checking the `Status` of each one. We only want to do something with records that have been modified:

```
    // Loop through the records in the recordset
    while (!rsConflicts.EOF)
    {
      // We're only interested in records that are modified in some way
      if (rsConflicts.status != adRecUnmodified)
      {
        // Do something with the record
      }
      rsConflicts.moveNext();
    }
  }
}
```

The `Status` can be a combination of a variety of values – these are detailed in the appendices. The sample code (`RDSConflicts.asp`) has a function included which translates these values into descriptive strings.

We know that the record has some form of conflict, but we don't know exactly why or which fields caused that conflict. So, what we need to do is loop though the fields checking the values:

```
for (fldF = new Enumerator(rsConflicts.Fields);
     !fldF.atEnd(); fldF.moveNext())
{
  if (fldF.item().originalValue != fldF.item().underlyingValue)
  {
    // Do something
  }
}
```

This is where the `UnderlyingValue` property comes into play.

The field has three values:

- `Value` is the new value; that is, the value we changed the field to
- `UnderlyingValue` is the value of the field stored in the data store
- `OriginalValue` is the value we read from the data store, but before we changed it

This means that `UnderlyingValue` will hold the value of changes made by other users, and `OriginalValue` is the value we expected the field to have. So we compare the two, and if they are different, then the field was changed by another user.

You can use all of this error information to build up a table to display if errors do occur. The sample (`RDSConflicts.asp`) produces this output:

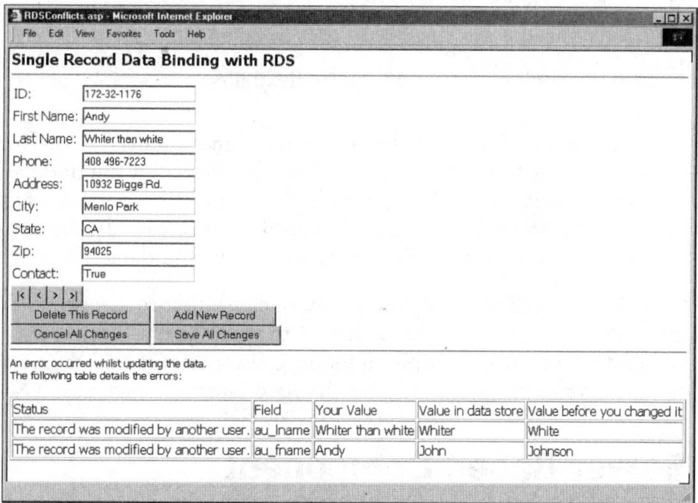

Here you can see the three different values. The original value was **Johnson**. I then changed this value to **Johns** in another window (in SQL Server Query Analyzer). In the browser window, using RDS, I then changed this to **Andy** and pressed the **Save** button. The `Resync` command loaded the value from the data store into the `UnderlyingValue` property. I also changed the last name column with similar results.

Using this method you will see the values for every field that changed. Since the `SubmitChanges` can handle changes to more than one record, you might like to add an extra column to this table to show the ID field, so you can see which record failed.

Data Transfer Between the Server and the Client

At the beginning of this chapter we showed a diagram of the RDS components, identifying which components were client-side and which were server-side. Since that diagram we've been concentrating on the client-side components – the data controls – because these are the simplest methods of using RDS. They allow the seamless transfer of data from the server to the client, and provide us with easy ways to manipulate the data in our Web pages. To get these data from the server we haven't had to do anything more than set a few properties and call the odd method or two.

The problem with the data controls is that they are relatively limited in their ability to retrieve data – there's no flexibility. For the RDS data control you have to specify connection and query details through parameters like `Connection` and `SQL`, which limits you to databases and simple queries. Also, these parameters are viewable by the user, and this may be deemed a potential security hole when using RDS. The `URL` property has partially solved this by specifying the source of the actual data, rather than where to get the data from, but this still suffers from a flaw. The user can read the URL and read the data directly, which you may not want.

The introduction of IE 5.0 has allowed easier access to XML data, and this is certainly going to be used as more XML data is made available in the future. Like the `URL` property of the RDS data control though, users will also be able to read the data directly, since the source name of the data is visible to them.

So, we have some problems.

- We need a secure way to retrieve data from a server and use it on the client
- We need a way that allows data to be updated
- We don't want to compromise flexibility

The way around these problems is to use components. A component allows us to encapsulate all of our data access functionality, including the source of the data, and ensures that the data are only exposed to Web pages. We can hide the connection details, as they'll be within the component and not exposed, so no security is compromised. We can also build our component to allow updates to the data, so we retain the flexibility of updateable data.

In addition, we have added security, because before a server-side component can be accessed from the client, we need to make a change to the registry. This ensures that only components we want can be created, and stops people uploading components and then accessing them from your server. We'll see how the registry needs to be changed later.

A Server Based Component

We're not going to examine how to create components in great detail here, since that's covered in later sections of the book, but we will show you some very simple code that could be used in a server component. This will help explain the RDS samples we'll be using.

The component starts with a constant that defines the connection details – in this case it's to SQL Server and the pubs database:

```
Private Const wroxConnection As String = "Provider=SQLOLEDB; " & _
        "Data Source=Kanga; Initial Catalog=pubs; User Id=sa; Password="
```

Then we have our first method, which will be used to supply a recordset to the client Web page. This is a standard Visual Basic function and returns a normal ADO Recordset object:

```
Public Function GetAuthors() As ADODB.Recordset

    Dim objConn As New ADODB.Connection
    Dim objRecAuthors As New ADODB.Recordset

    objConn.Open wroxConnection

    objRecAuthors.CursorLocation = adUseClient
    objRecAuthors.Open "authors", objConn, adOpenKeyset, _
                       adLockBatchOptimistic, adCmdTable

    Set objRecAuthors.ActiveConnection = Nothing
    Set GetAuthors = objRecAuthors

    Set objRecAuthors = Nothing
    objConn.Close
    Set objConn = Nothing

End Function
```

There are two important things to note here. The first is that the `CursorLocation` is set to `adUseClient`, which ensures that the client cursor engine is used. This is necessary for disconnected recordsets. The second point to note is this line:

```
Set objRecAuthors.ActiveConnection = Nothing
```

This 'disconnects' the recordset from the server, making it safe to return the recordset to our client.

The second method of our component will update the server with any changes made in the disconnected recordset. It accepts the recordset as an argument, reconnects to the data store, and then issues the `UpdateBatch` method. This sends all of the batched changes back to the server:

```
Public Function UpdateAuthors(ByRef recA As ADODB.Recordset) As Boolean

    On Error GoTo UpdateAuthors_Err

    recA.ActiveConnection = wroxConnection
    recA.UpdateBatch

    UpdateAuthors = True

UpdateAuthors_Exit:
    Exit Function

UpdateAuthors_Err:
    UpdateAuthors = False
    Resume UpdateAuthors_Exit

End Function
```

That's all there is to this component. Obviously, we've made it simple so we can quickly show you what it contains, but there's really no limit to what you can put in a component. You'll see plenty more examples of how to do this, and why you'd want to, in Chapters 13 to 18.

The DataSpace Object

The **DataSpace** object is a client-side object that's responsible for communicating with the server. Its role is to provide a way to create server-side components from the client, and allow the transfer of data between the client and the server.

Although this might sound like something complex, it's actually very simple. You create a DataSpace object in your Web page, and use the DataSpace to create your server-side components.

There are two ways to create a DataSpace object. The first is by using the `<OBJECT>` tag:

```
<OBJECT CLASSID="clsid:BD96C556-65A3-11D0-983A-00C04FC29E36"
        ID="dspDataSpace" HEIGHT="0" WIDTH="0">
</OBJECT>
```

This is exactly the same method we've used to create the other client-side RDS components – the only difference is the class ID.

The second way to create a DataSpace is to use script code. The following shows how this can be done in JScript:

```
var dspDataSpace = new ActiveXObject('RDS.DataSpace');
```

The main difference between the two methods is that when using the `<OBJECT>` tag the DataSpace object is created as the page loads. Using the script technique means that the DataSpace is created when the script is run. If you prefer to defer the object creation so that your pages load faster, then use the script technique.

Creating Server Components with the DataSpace Object

Once the DataSpace object is created, you can create server-side objects using the `CreateObject` method:

```
var = dataspace.CreateObject(ProgID, Connection)
```

`ProgID` is the ID of the object you wish to create, and *`Connection`* is the URL of the Web server. For example, imagine our Visual Basic component that provides data from the `pubs` database:

In this case our *`ProgID`* would be `WroxPubs.pubs`. Let's look at this in more detail, with a fuller example:

Creating a Component and Retrieving Data

Let's assume that our pubs class has two methods, getAuthors and setAuthors, to read and update the authors table. Before we create the component, we'll create an RDS data control to hold the data and allow data binding. Notice that there are no connection details here:

```
<OBJECT CLASSID="clsid:BD96C556-65A3-11D0-983A-00C04FC29E33"
        ID="dsoData" HEIGHT="0" WIDHTH="0">
</OBJECT>
```

You could then use the following code in your client-side script to create the server component:

```
// Create the data space
var dspDataSpace = new ActiveXObject('RDSServer.DataSpace');

// Create the custom object
var objPubs = dspDataSpace.CreateObject('WroxPubs.pubs', 'http://localhost');
```

Here we create an instance of the DataSpace object, and then use the CreateObject method to create our server-side object. We specify the name of the object and the name of the Web server. In this case we've used localhost for the Web server name, but it could be the actual name of the server. This isn't a security problem, since the user is connecting to our site anyway.

Now the variable objPubs is an instance of our WroxPubs.pubs object, and we can use its methods just like any other object:

```
// Call the method of the object to return a disconnected recordset
var rsAuthors = objPubs.getAuthors();
```

This calls the getAuthors method, which just happens to return a disconnected recordset. All we need to do now is use that recordset, so we can use an RDS data control (created with the <OBJECT> tag) to hold the recordset and allow data binding. We use the SourceRecordset property of the data control to accept the recordset we received from our component:

```
// Set the recordset to the data control
dsoData.SourceRecordset = rsAuthors;
```

At this stage the data control behaves just like it fetched the data itself. The only difference is that we've supplied the data from our component.

Updating Data Using a Component

You might wonder how we go about updating data when using the server-side component method. You can't use the SubmitChanges method of the data control, because the data control has no connection details – it doesn't know where the data came from. The recordset though, is a normal disconnected recordset that was supplied by the server component, so presumably the component knows where the data came from? Correct, so what we have to do is pass our disconnected recordset back to the server component, and it will perform the batch update for us.

To do this we first extract the recordset from the data control, and then pass this recordset as an argument to a method of the server object.

```
rsAuthors = dsoData.recordset;

objAuthors.setRecordset(rsAuthors);
```

It's pretty simple really.

Advantages of Using Server Side Components

So what's the big deal about this server-side component? Let's look at the advantages:

- There are no connection details visible to the user – which gives you a securer system. The component also has to be specially registered, so there is the added security restriction.
- You can build components in any COM compliant language. We used Visual Basic in our example because it's easy to understand, but you could use VC++ or Delphi if you wanted to. This allows you to use the language you, or your developers, are most familiar with.
- Your component isn't limited to just returning and updating recordsets. You could build in lots of logic that encapsulates things your business does as part of its data handling.
- You could encapsulate all of that conflict resolution code in the `setRecordset` method, and just return details of any errors. This means your client-side script is neater. It also means that users can't rip off your hard-worked code.

Again, the next section of the book will look at the advantages of components in more detail.

Registering Server Side Components

We mentioned earlier that you have to make a registry change before a server component can be created in a Web browser. To make your component available through RDS you must add the `ProgID` of your component to the following registry key:

```
HKEY_LOCAL_MACHINE\System\CurrentControlSet\Services\W3SVC\Parameters\
                        ADCLaunch
```

> **Warning: always be very careful when editing the registry. It's always wise to back up the registry before making any changes.**

When running `regedit`, you select the ADCLaunch key, and then from the Edit menu select New and then Key. Now type in the `ProgID` of your component. For example:

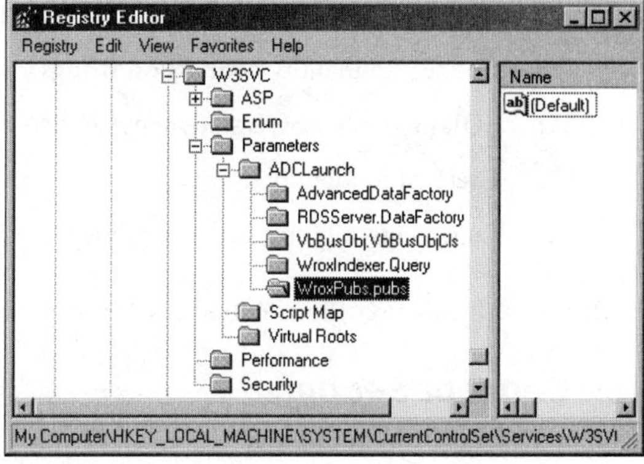

You should also consider marking your components 'safe for scripting' by doing a little more registry changing, so that IE doesn't complain when they are launched. This time there are two keys you need to add, both of which require the GUID of your component:

```
HKEY_CLASSES_ROOT\CLSID\{your_component_class_id}\
 Implemented Categories\{7DD95801-9882-11CF-9FA9-00AA006C42C4}

HKEY_CLASSES_ROOT\CLSID\{your_component_class_id}\
 Implemented Categories\{7DD95802-9882-11CF-9FA9-00AA006C42C4}
```

The best way to do this is to use the Visual Studio Package and Deployment Wizard, to create an Internet Download package. If you select the Safe for Initialization and Safe for Scripting options, the registry will be updated for you when the package is installed on the server. If you do need to get the class ID for your component, then the Wizard also creates an HTML file, in which is an `<OBJECT>` tag with the component's class ID.

Customized Handlers

RDS is a good client-side tool, and allows a great deal of data handling to be performed on the client. Most of the examples have shown the data controls using a fixed set of data, such as the `authors` table. The dynamic data binding examples, however, showed that you could allow the user to decide which data to retrieve. We did this by way of fixed buttons, limiting the data to two tables, but there's no reason why a text entry field couldn't have been provided to allow the user to enter the table name, or even to allow them to enter SQL query strings.

Of course, this expands the flexibility of RDS, but at the price of security. If you allow your users free reign to the data they'll just confuse themselves, or go hunting for that secret financial data. What you need is a way to give this flexibility, but within certain limits.

To do this you can use a **Handler**, which modifies connection strings or commands before they are executed.

The handler is a text file consisting of four parts, separated by carriage returns:

- **Connect** to identify connection strings
- **SQL** to identify SQL statements and commands
- **UserList** to identify users
- **Logs** to identify logging capabilities

By default this text file is called `Msdfmap.ini`, and it is installed in your default windows directory.

The Connect Section

The Connect section allows you to override connection string and access details, and is identified by one of two entries:

- `[connect default]` to indicate the details for the default connection
- `[connect` *`ConnectionName`*`]` to indicate the details for the connection named *`ConnectionName`*

Within the section you have two name/value pairs:

Name	Description
`Connect`	The connection string to use instead of the supplied one
`Access`	The access rights to use against this connection. Can be one of: ❑ `NoAccess` which means no access is allowed to the data source ❑ `ReadOnly` for read-only access ❑ `ReadWrite` for read and write access

For example:

```
[connect PubsDatabase]
Connect="DSN=Otherpubs; UID=GuestUser; PWD=JustAGuest"
Access=ReadOnly
```

This means that if the connection string of a data control ever equals `PubsDatabase`, the user will be logged into the database as `GuestUser` and will have read-only permissions. So if the user does this:

```
conDB.Open "PubsDatabase"
```

then they'll actually get connected to the `Otherpubs` data source.

For the default connection, your entry could look like this:

```
[connect default]
Access=NoAccess
```

This ensures that no access is given to connections that aren't detailed in the handler text file.

The SQL Section

The SQL section allows you to override SQL strings and commands, and is identified by one of two entries:

- `[sql default]` to indicate the default SQL command
- `[sql *SQLCommandName*]` to identify a specific SQL command, such as a stored procedure or stored query

There is only one entry within this section, which is the SQL statement to replace the supplied statement. For example:

```
[sql GetAuthors]
Sql="SELECT * FROM Authors"
```

The above handler entry would allow the following to be used in an RDS data control:

```
<PARAM NAME="SQL" VALUE="GetAuthors">
```

You can also used parameterized queries in the SQL, like so:

```
[sql AuthorsByState]
sql="SELECT * FROM authors WHERE state=?"
```

In this case the command executed would be:

```
<PARAM NAME="SQL" VALUE="AuthorsByState('CA')">
```

So, although the client can see the SQL string, they actually have no idea what the real SQL being executed is.

To disable any SQL values, you can do the following:

```
[sql default]
Sql=" "
```

This has the effect of not allowing any commands against the specified connection.

The UserList Section

The UserList section allows you to specify access rights to individual users, and is identified by the same *ConnectionName* as used in the Connect section:

- `[userlist *ConnectionName*]` identifies the users for the named connection

There is only one value in this section, which is the access rights allowed for the users. The values for the access rights are the same values as shown in the Connection section.

For example:

```
[userlist PubsDatabase]
Administrator=ReadWrite
DavidS=ReadWrite
Guest=NoAccess
```

The values in here override the access values in the Connect section.

For accurate use of the `UserList` section, the server must be able to validate the users, so this depends upon the authentication scheme in place on your server. For example, if using anonymous access, then all users will connect to the server using the details of the default user specified in the IIS administration properties for the site.

The Logs Section

The Logs section allows you to specify a file name into which errors are written. Logging applies to all connections, and is identified by the `[logs]` entry. The log file is created if it doesn't exist.

This section only has one value, `err`, which specifies the log file name. For example:

```
[logs]
err=C:\Temp\DFErrors.txt
```

The log file will contain the user name, error code, and the date and time of each error.

Sample Custom Handler File

All of the above sections should be combined together in a single text file. For example:

```
[connect PubsDatabase]
Connect="DSN=Otherpubs; UID=GuestUser; PWD=JustAGuest"
Access=ReadOnly

[userlist PubsDatabase]
Administrator=ReadWrite
DavidS=ReadWrite
Guest=NoAccess

[connect default]
Access=NoAccess

[sql GetAuthors]
Sql="SELECT * FROM Authors"

[sql default]
Sql=" "

[logs]
err=C:\Temp\DFErrors.txt
```

Using Customized Handlers

You can specify the handler by using the `Handler` property of the RDS data control, and giving the name of the specific handler. The default handler is called `MSDFMAP.Handler`, and it is a component that the server-side portions of RDS use. You can write your own custom handlers (they are normal COM components), and you should consult the RDS documentation if you want to do so.

To use the default handler you can do this:

```
<OBJECT CLASSID="clsid:BD96C556-65A3-11D0-983A-00C04FC29E33"
        ID="dsoAuthors" WIDTH="0" HEIGHT="0">
  <PARAM NAME="Connect" VALUE="connection string">
  <PARAM NAME="Server" VALUE="server name ">
  <PARAM NAME="SQL" VALUE="query text">
  <PARAM NAME="Handler" VALUE="MSDFMAP.Handler">
</OBJECT>
```

This will invoke the handler, and use the default file. You can specify you own file by adding it onto the end of the `Handler` property:

```
<PARAM NAME="Handler" VALUE="MSDFMAP.Handler, MyHandler.ini">
```

The handler file always lives in the Windows directory.

Recordset Paging

When looking at the RDS data control, we saw how `DATAPAGESIZE` could be used to limit the number of rows shown in a bound table, giving us a table with a number of pages. Although this is a good and simple solution, it does have the disadvantage of having all of the data on the client machine. Our example only used a small set of records, but what happens if you want a larger set of data? Do you really want to push all of the data up to the client? After all, the user can only look at one screen full at a time.

The way around this is to introduce the concept of **paging**, where we deal with one page of data at a time, returning it and only it to the client instead of all the data. To get paging working with our data, we need to work with three more properties attached to the Recordset object:

Property	Data Type	Description	Default
`PageSize`	Long	The number of records in a page.	10
`PageCount`	Long	The total number of pages in the recordset.	
`AbsolutePage`	Long	The current page number.	

Using the `AbsolutePage` property allows us to set the record pointer to the first record in a page – thus we can move directly to pages. For example:

```
rsAuthors.AbsolutePage = 2
```

If we used the default page size of 10, then the above line would place us on the 11th record in the recordset.

It's important to note that the records in a page are not necessarily fixed: the number of records is fixed, but not the records themselves. This might sound confusing, but if you think back to Chapter 8 where we discussed cursor types, you'll remember that certain cursors are based upon the keys. The actual values aren't read until the rows are requested. Thus, if you are using paging, and other users add new rows, or delete existing ones, then the actual records in your pages might change.

It's also worth remembering that the order of records in a page is the same as the order in the recordset, and is defined by the command that generates the recordset. Records in a recordset don't have record numbers to identify their positions in the recordset.

There are several ways of incorporating paging into your application, two of which use these properties, and the third of which uses a similar method but in SQL server.

Using ASP Pages to Page Through Recordsets

The first method to look at is an extension of the RDS methods you've seen previously in this chapter. We'll use the RDS data control and the URL parameter, where we have an ASP page that returns a set of records which the RDS data control then uses. If we want to introduce paging we must make sure that this ASP page only returns a single page full of data.

Let's start by looking at the ASP page that supplies the data. We're making this flexible, so we're allowing a query string to be passed into the page containing two pieces of information:

- TABLE, to identify the table to get the data from
- PAGE, to identify the page number requested

Assuming our page is called RDSURLPagedData.asp, the query would then look something like this:

```
RDSURLPagedData.asp?TABLE=authors&PAGE=2
```

Within the ASP page, the first thing to do is create the Recordset object – that's no different from before:

```
Set rsData = Server.CreateObject("ADODB.Recordset")
```

Next we get the details requested. In addition to the table name, we also have the page number supplied to us. This is the page of data that is required:

```
' Get the requested data
strTable = CStr(Request.QueryString("TABLE"))
intPage = CInt(Request.QueryString("PAGE"))
```

Now we set the page size. We're using 10 records per page, but you could easily change this. You could even let the users set this value, and pass it into the ASP page along with the table and page number:

```
' Set the page size
rsData.PageSize = 10
rsData.CursorLocation = adUseClient
```

Now we open the recordset based upon the requested table:

```
' Open the data
rsData.Open strTable, strConn, _
            adOpenForwardOnly, adLockReadOnly, adCmdTable
```

At this stage we have a recordset full of data, but we only want a single page. So, we have to set ourselves onto the page we want using the `AbsolutePage` property. Before setting the `AbsoutePage`, we check to see that the page number requested isn't 0 and that it also isn't greater than the total number of pages. In both of these cases, we set the page to the last page, which is identified by `PageCount`:

```
' Set the page
If intPage = 0 Or intPage > rsData.PageCount Then
  rsData.AbsolutePage = rsData.PageCount
Else
  rsData.AbsolutePage = intPage
End If
```

Now we are positioned on the correct page, but of course the next problem is how we transfer just that page back to the client. What we need to do is just extract the records in this page, and to do that we use a **crafted recordset**. We create a new recordset, with the same structure as the one containing the data, and copy a page full of records into it.

Crafting a recordset is easy, and involves creating a recordset object, and setting the cursor location to be *client-based.* Then we append fields to the `Fields` collection, using the data recordset to provide the details of these fields. Once the fields have been created you simply open the recordset, without specifying any source or connection details:

```
' Create the new recordset
Set rsNew = Server.CreateObject("ADODB.Recordset")
rsNew.CursorLocation = adUseClient
For Each fldF In rsData.Fields
  rsNew.Fields.Append fldF.Name, fldF.Type, fldF.DefinedSize, fldF.Attributes
Next
rsNew.Open , , adOpenKeyset, adLockOptimistic
```

At this stage we have a new, empty recordset, so we need to copy a page of records into it. This involves cycling through the page of records, adding each one to the new recordset:

```
' Now append the data, but only the number of records in a page
For intRec = 1 To rsData.PageSize
```

```
    If Not rsData.EOF Then
      rsNew.AddNew
      For Each fldF In rsData.Fields
        rsNew.Fields(fldF.Name) = fldF.Value
      Next
      rsNew.Update
      rsData.MoveNext
    End If

  Next
```

Now we have a recordset containing just a page full of data, so we can send it back to the client:

```
  ' Send the new data back to the client
  rsNew.Save Response, adPersistXML
```

Finally, the recordsets are closed:

```
  ' And clear up
  rsData.Close
  Set rsData = Nothing

  rsNew.Close
  Set rsNew = Nothing

%>
```

So, we now have an ASP page that will return a single page of data, and all we have to do is modify the client RDS page to take this into account.

The RDS data control is created with the <OBJECT> tag, as in our previous URL example:

```
<OBJECT CLASSID="clsid:BD96C556-65A3-11D0-983A-00C04FC29E33"
        ID="dsoData" HEIGHT="0" WIDTH="0"
        ondatasetcomplete="createCells()">
</OBJECT>
```

The buttons to select the table now call a different routine, called settable:

```
<BR>
Click one of the buttons below to see the data
<P>
<BUTTON ID="cmdAuthors" onclick="setTable('authors')">authors</BUTTON>
<BUTTON ID="cmdPublishers" onclick="setTable('publishers')">publishers</BUTTON>

<TABLE ID="tblData" BORDER="1">
  <THEAD><TR></TR></THEAD>
  <TBODY><TR></TR></TBODY>
</TABLE>
```

We have some new buttons to control the paging, which call `setPage` with an argument that identifies which page to move to:

```
<BR>
<BUTTON ID="cmdFirstPage" ONCLICK="setPage('First')">First Page</BUTTON>
<BUTTON ID="cmdPreviousPage" ONCLICK="setPage('Previous')">
            Previous Page</BUTTON>
<BUTTON ID="cmdNextPage" ONCLICK="setPage('Next')">Next Page</BUTTON>
<BUTTON ID="cmdLastPage" ONCLICK="setPage('Last')">Last Page</BUTTON>
```

And now comes the scripting. We've got two global variables, to identify the table being viewed and the current page number:

```
<SCRIPT LANGUAGE=JScript>

var m_strFile;
var m_intPage = 1;
```

The routine to set the table name simply sets the page number to the first page and the table name to the defined table, before calling the routine to reset the data:

```
function setTable(strTable)
{
    m_intPage = 1;
    m_strFile = strTable;
    resetData();
}
```

Resetting the data uses much the same method as we used before, but with the addition of an addition to the URL. We now supply the page number as well as the table:

```
function resetData()
{
    // Reset the data
    dsoData.URL = 'RDSURLPagedData.asp?TABLE=' + m_sFile +
                '&PAGE=' + m_iPage;
    dsoData.Refresh();
}
```

Finally, there is the routine to change the page. This just sets the page number and resets the data:

```
function setPage(strPage)
{
    switch (strPage)
    {
    case 'first':
        m_intPage = 1;
        break;

    case 'Previous':
        m_intPage = m_intPage - 1;
        if (m_intPage == 0)
```

```
            m_intPage = 1;
          break;

        case 'Next':
          m_intPage = m_intPage + 1;
          break;

        case 'Last':
          m_intPage = 0;
          break;
        }

        resetData();
    }

    </SCRIPT>
```

The result of all of the above code is a page that looks like this:

au_id	au_lname	au_fname	phone	address	city	state	zip	contract
172-32-1176	White	Johnson	408 496-7223	10932 Bigge Rd.	Menlo Park	CA	94025	True
213-46-8915	Green	Marjorie	415 986-7020	309 63rd St. #411	Oakland	CA	94618	True
238-95-7766	Carson	Cheryl	415 548-7723	589 Darwin Ln.	Berkeley	CA	94705	True
267-41-2394	O'Leary	Michael	408 286-2428	22 Cleveland Av. #14	San Jose	CA	95128	True
274-80-9391	Straight	Dean	415 834-2919	5420 College Av.	Oakland	CA	94609	True
341-22-1782	Smith	Meander	913 843-0462	10 Mississippi Dr.	Lawrence	KS	66044	False
409-56-7008	Bennet	Abraham	415 658-9932	6223 Bateman St.	Berkeley	CA	94705	True
427-17-2319	Dull	Ann	415 836-7128	3410 Blonde St.	Palo Alto	CA	94301	True
472-27-2349	Gringlesby	Burt	707 938-6445	PO Box 792	Covelo	CA	95428	True
486-29-1786	Locksley	Charlene	415 585-4620	18 Broadway Av.	San Francisco	CA	94130	True

We do have quite a major problem with this code though, because the client has no knowledge of how many pages of data there are. We can request the last page easily enough, but when moving to the next page we can't tell when we go beyond the last page. The ASP page can tell, but we at the client can't. This means that the page number on the client just keeps increasing, even though the ASP page only displays the last page.

Using a Custom Component

One way to solve the page number problems in the previous example is to use components to provide the data instead of an ASP page. We're not going to examine this in detail here, but the concept is very similar. You'd first remove the URL details, and in the `resetData` function you'd use the `DataSpace` and `DataFactory` objects to create a custom component.

This component could contain very similar code to the ASP page, and would return a recordset containing the page of data. But because the component can return more than just a recordset we could actually keep track of the maximum number of pages, which would make our paging much more intelligent.

Using ADO Paging

Another way to cure the page numbering problem is to use a quite a well-known technique for paging. It does away with RDS data binding and builds an HTML table in an ASP page. It uses the same method of paging, but doesn't involve crafted recordsets.

Let's look at the code for `ASPPaging.asp`, and then you'll see what sort of result it produces.

To start with, there's the variables and the creation of the Recordset object.

```
<%
  Dim rsData
  Dim intPage
  Dim intTotalPages
  Dim fldF
  Dim intRec
  Dim strQuote
  Dim strScriptName

  strQuote = Chr(34)   ' The double quote character

  Set rsData = Server.CreateObject("ADODB.Recordset")
```

Then we set the page size and the cursor location:

```
  ' Set the page size
  rsData.PageSize = 10
  rsData.CursorLocation = adUseClient
```

Next we open the recordset:

```
  ' Open the data
  rsData.Open "Authors", strConn, _
              adOpenForwardOnly, adLockReadOnly, adCmdTable
```

Now we have to set the page number. Upon first display the `QueryString` may be empty, so we default to the first page. If the page is specified, we check it's not outside the bounds of acceptable pages. If it's less than the first page we set it to the first page, and if it's greater than the last page we set it to the last page:

```
  ' Get the requested data
  If Request.QueryString("PAGE") = "" Then
    intPage = 1
  Else
    ' Protect against out of range pages, in case
    ' of a user specified page number
    If intPage < 1 Then
      intPage = 1
    Else
      If intPage > rsData.PageCount Then
        intPage = rsData.PageCount
      Else
```

```
        intPage = CInt(Request.QueryString("PAGE"))
      End If
    End If
  End If
```

Then we set the absolute page number to the requested page:

```
  ' Set the page
  rsData.AbsolutePage = intPage
```

When we're in position on the correct record, we can start building the HTML table. First comes the header:

```
  ' Start building the table
  Response.Write "<TABLE BORDER=1><THEAD><TR>"
  For Each fldF In rsData.Fields
    Response.Write "<TD>" & fldF.Name & "</TD>"
  Next
  Response.Write "</TR></THEAD><TBODY>"
```

And now we can loop through the page of records, building the body of the HTML table:

```
  ' Now loop through the
  For intRec = 1 To rsData.PageSize
    If Not rsData.EOF Then
      Response.Write "<TR>"
      For Each fldF In rsData.Fields
        Response.Write "<TD>" & fldF.Value & "</TD>"
      Next
      Response.Write "</TR>"
      rsData.MoveNext
    End If
  Next
  Response.Write "</TBODY></THEAD></TABLE><P>"
```

Next come the controls to allow paging. These will simply be anchor tags, with the target pointing at the same page but with a new page number. The first page is easy, since it will always be page 1:

```
  ' Now some paging controls
  strScriptName = Request.ServerVariables("SCRIPT_NAME")
  Response.Write " <A HREF=" & strQuote & strScriptName & _
               "?PAGE=1" & strQuote & ">First Page</A>"
```

We don't want to automatically give a previous page control because we may be on the first page of data already. If so, we simply use a `SPAN` with the **Previous Page** still shown, so that the paging controls don't change position from page to page:

```
  ' Only give an active previous page if there are previous pages
  If intPage = 1 Then
    Response.Write " <SPAN>Previous Page</SPAN>"
```

```
Else
  Response.Write " <A HREF=" & strQuote & sMe & _
                "?PAGE=" & intPage - 1 & strQuote & ">Previous Page</A>"
End If
```

We apply the same technique to the **Next Page** control, as we may already be on the last page:

```
' Only give an active next page if there are more pages
If intPage = rsData.PageCount Then
  Response.Write " <SPAN>Next Page</SPAN>"
Else
  Response.Write " <A HREF=" & strQuote & strScriptName & _
                "?PAGE=" & intPage + 1 & strQuote & ">Next Page</A>"
End If
```

The last page control is simple, because it will always be the number of pages in the recordset:

```
Response.Write " <A HREF=" & strQuote & strScriptName & _
              "?PAGE=" & rsData.PageCount & strQuote & ">Last Page</A>"
```

Finally we close up the recordset:

```
  ' And clear up
  rsData.Close
  Set rsData = Nothing
%>
```

And that's it. A pretty simple paging program that gives the following result:

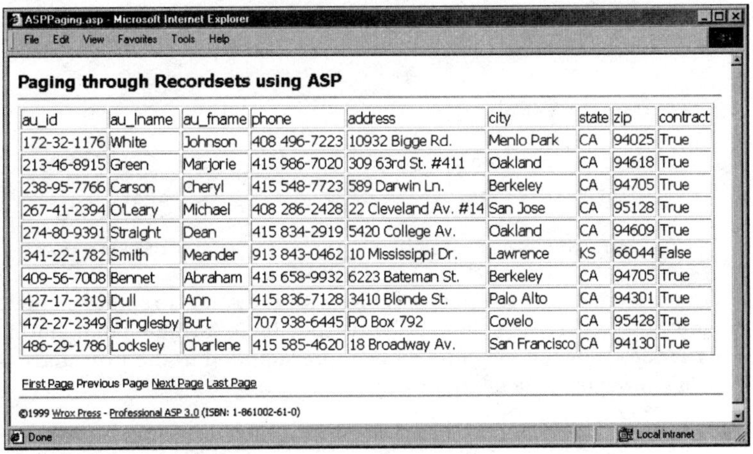

ASPPaging.asp - Microsoft Internet Explorer

File Edit View Favorites Tools Help

Paging through Recordsets using ASP

au_id	au_lname	au_fname	phone	address	city	state	zip	contract
172-32-1176	White	Johnson	408 496-7223	10932 Bigge Rd.	Menlo Park	CA	94025	True
213-46-8915	Green	Marjorie	415 986-7020	309 63rd St. #411	Oakland	CA	94618	True
238-95-7766	Carson	Cheryl	415 548-7723	589 Darwin Ln.	Berkeley	CA	94705	True
267-41-2394	O'Leary	Michael	408 286-2428	22 Cleveland Av. #14	San Jose	CA	95128	True
274-80-9391	Straight	Dean	415 834-2919	5420 College Av.	Oakland	CA	94609	True
341-22-1782	Smith	Meander	913 843-0462	10 Mississippi Dr.	Lawrence	KS	66044	False
409-56-7008	Bennet	Abraham	415 658-9932	6223 Bateman St.	Berkeley	CA	94705	True
427-17-2319	Dull	Ann	415 836-7128	3410 Blonde St.	Palo Alto	CA	94301	True
472-27-2349	Gringlesby	Burt	707 938-6445	PO Box 792	Covelo	CA	95428	True
486-29-1786	Locksley	Charlene	415 585-4620	18 Broadway Av.	San Francisco	CA	94130	True

First Page Previous Page Next Page Last Page

©1999 Wrox Press - Professional ASP 3.0 (ISBN: 1-861002-61-0)

Done Local intranet

This shows the first page of data, so you can see that the **Previous Page** control is not active.

This solution gives the user a better interface, because the controls work in a more realistic manner. However, it does still suffer from one problem that the previous paging solution suffered from – the whole recordset is opened every time a page is requested. All we've actually done is move the recordset from the client to the server. Now admittedly that's an improvement for bandwidth, but there are still more records being requested than is absolutely necessary.

Using SQL Server to Perform Recordset Paging

The final paging solution again uses a similar technique, but this time moves the page handling into SQL Server. This is a method I used to use in the dim and distant past when building 2-tier client/server solutions and it seemed worthy of re-use here. We use a SQL Server stored procedure to create a temporary table, and then return only the required records from the stored procedure. In some ways it's a bit like the solution where we crafted a recordset, only this time we're moving the crafting into SQL Server.

The main problem we have to overcome is that of selecting the records within the required page. Most relational databases don't have a concept of a record number so it's difficult to just pick the required records. The easiest solution is to duplicate the table, adding a unique, sequential record number, and then we can pick only the required records from this duplicate table. In SQL Server it's easy to use an `IDENTITY` column, but we can't rely on this from a base table because records may get deleted, which would leave gaps in our numbering. However, what we can do is create a temporary table on the fly, adding our own `IDENTITY` column, which guarantees sequential numbering.

Let's look at the stored procedure that would do this. We pass in the page required and the page size as arguments:

```
CREATE PROCEDURE usp_PagedAuthors
    @iPage          int,
    @iPageSize      int
AS
BEGIN
```

We start by disabling automatic row counts, to stop extra information being returned to the client:

```
    -- disable row counts
    SET NOCOUNT ON
```

Next come the variables:

```
    -- declare variables
    DECLARE @iStart         int         -- start record
    DECLARE @iEnd           int         -- end record
    DECLARE @iPageCount     int         -- total number of pages
```

Now we create the temporary table, with the same structure as the base table, but with the addition of an extra `IDENTITY` column. This is specific to a single table, but it would be possible to make this dynamic, allowing the table name to be supplied to the procedure. However, making it dynamic would slow the procedure down:

```
    -- create the temporary table
    CREATE TABLE #PagedAuthors
    (
        ID          int             IDENTITY,
        au_id       varchar(11)     NOT NULL ,
        au_lname    varchar(40)     NOT NULL ,
        au_fname    varchar(20)     NOT NULL ,
        phone       char(12)        NOT NULL ,
```

```
        address     varchar(40)    NULL ,
        city        varchar(20)    NULL ,
        state       char(2)        NULL ,
        zip         char(5)        NULL ,
        contract    bit            NOT NULL
)
```

When the temporary table is created, we add all of the records from the base table into it. The use of the IDENTITY column will ensure that records have unique, sequentially numbered ID fields:

```
-- populate the temporary table
INSERT INTO #PagedAuthors (au_id, au_lname, au_fname,
            phone, address, city, state, zip, contract)
SELECT    au_id, au_lname, au_fname,
          phone, address, city, state, zip, contract
FROM      authors
```

So we can work out the total number of pages:

```
-- work out how many pages there are in total
SELECT    @iPageCount = COUNT(*)
FROM      authors

SELECT    @iPageCount = CEILING(@iPageCount / @iPageSize) + 1
```

And then we can check to make sure that the requested page number is not outside the page limits:

```
-- check the page number
IF @iPage < 1
    SELECT @iPage = 1

IF @iPage > @iPageCount
    SELECT @iPage = @iPageCount
```

To select only the records from the required page, we must calculate the record numbers that identify the start and end of the page:

```
-- calculate the start and end records
SELECT @iStart = (@iPage - 1) * @iPageSize
SELECT @iEnd = @iStart + @iPageSize + 1
```

Now we can select only those records where the record number falls with the page:

```
-- select only those records that fall within our page
SELECT    au_id, au_lname, au_fname,

          phone, address, city, state, zip, contract
FROM      #PagedAuthors
WHERE     ID > @iStart
AND       ID < @iEnd
```

We can then drop the temporary table, and turn back on the record count notification:

```
    DROP TABLE #PagedAuthors

    -- turn back on record counts
    SET NOCOUNT OFF
```

To finish off, we return the total number of pages:

```
    -- Return the number of records left
    RETURN @iPageCount
END
```

So at the end of this, we have a stored procedure that returns only the selected records in a page. We now need some ASP code to take this into account.

As usual we start with the variable declarations:

```
<%
  Dim cmdAuthors
  Dim rsData
  Dim intPage
  Dim intLastPage
  Dim strQuote

  strQuote = Chr(34)
```

And like our other ASP pages, we extract the page number:

```
  ' Get the requested data
  If Request.QueryString("PAGE") = "" Then
    intPage = 1
  Else
    intPage = CInt(Request.QueryString("PAGE"))

    If intPage < 1 Then
      intPage = 1
    End If
  End If
```

Since we'll be using a stored procedure with arguments, we need two objects:

```
  ' Create the objects
  Set cmdAuthors = Server.CreateObject("ADODB.Command")
  Set rsAuthors = Server.CreateObject("ADODB.Recordset")
```

We don't need a connection object because we'll let ADO create an implicit connection for us.

Next we need to create the parameters for the stored procedure. The first is the return value, which will hold the total number of pages returned from the stored procedure. The second and third are passed to the stored procedure, and indicate the required page number and the page size respectively:

```
With cmdAuthors
  .ActiveConnection = strConn
  .CommandText = "usp_PagedAuthors"
  .CommandType = adCmdStoredProc

  .Parameters.Append .CreateParameter("RETURN_VALUE", adInteger, _
                                      adParamReturnValue)
  .Parameters.Append .CreateParameter("@iPage", adInteger, _
                                      adParamInput, 8, iPage)
  .Parameters.Append .CreateParameter("@iPageSize", adInteger, _
                                      adParamInput, 8, 10)
```

Once the parameters have been set we can run the stored procedure to return the records:

```
  Set rsData = .Execute
End With
```

Now comes the creation of the table. This is similar to our other table creation routines, except that this time the recordset only contains the required number of records, so our table can be built from the complete recordset:

```
' Create the table
' Start building the table
Response.Write "<TABLE BORDER=1><THEAD><TR>"
For Each fldF In rsData.Fields
  Response.Write "<TD>" & fldF.Name & "</TD>"
Next
Response.Write "</TR></THEAD><TBODY>"

' Now loop through the records
While Not rsData.EOF
  Response.Write "<TR>"
  For Each fldF In rsData.Fields
    Response.Write "<TD>" & fldF.Value & "</TD>"
  Next
  Response.Write "</TR>"
  rsData.MoveNext
Wend
Response.Write "</TBODY></THEAD></TABLE><P>"
```

And then come the paging controls. The first page and previous page controls are as we've seen them before:

```
' Now some paging controls
strScriptName = Request.ServerVariables("SCRIPT_NAME")
Response.Write " <A HREF=" & strQuote & strScriptName & _
               "?PAGE=1" & strQuote & ">First Page</A>"

' Only give an active previous page if there are previous pages
If intPage < = 1 Then
  Response.Write " <SPAN>Previous Page</SPAN>"
```

```
    Else
      Response.Write " <A HREF=" & strQuote & strScriptName & _
                     "?PAGE=" & intPage - 1 & strQuote & ">Previous Page</A>"
    End If
```

The next page and last page controls require the number of pages. Remember how this is the return value from the stored procedure, so we close the recordset, and then extract the value from the parameters:

```
    ' Close the recordset and extract the number of records left
    rsData.Close
    intLastPage = cmdAuthors.Parameters("RETURN_VALUE")

  ' Only give an active next page if there are more pages
    If intLastPage = intPage Then
      Response.Write " <SPAN>Next Page</SPAN>"
    Else
      Response.Write " <A HREF=" & strQuote & strScriptName & _
                     "?PAGE=" & intPage + 1 &  stQuote & ">Next Page</A>"
    End If

    Response.Write " <A HREF=" & strQuote & strScriptName & _
                   "?PAGE=" & intLastPage & strQuote & ">Last Page</A>"

    ' Clean up
    Set rsData = Nothing
    Set cmdAuthors = Nothing
%>
```

This method of paging is similar to the ASP method shown earlier, but there is still one problem. We have to create a temporary table containing all of the records from the base table. Whilst this is still a quick procedure, it could prove costly if the base table is very large. Having said that, if you are giving your users a chance to page through a recordset containing a large number of records, then you have to accept some compromises.

Data Paging Summary

So, we've seen three different methods for paging through data, but which is the best? Well, that depends on what your design constraints are.

The first method – using RDS – gives the users more responsive paging. Since all of the data is on their local machine, there is no need to return to the server for more data. However, since all of the data has to be sent to the client machine at once, the page may load slower than other pages. This is also an IE solution only, since it uses RDS. The other two methods will load quicker into the browser, but paging requires an extra trip. However, these two methods don't require any special client-side components, such as RDS, because the table is pure HTML.

The differences between the second two methods – where we create a set of records for the required page – isn't easy to spot. Some rough testing with the Microsoft Web Application Stress tool showed that the method using a crafted ADO recordset was marginally quicker, but there was very little difference. There might be a bigger difference if the SQL Server machine is a different machine than the Web server, so if you want to use either of these methods I'd make sure you do your own testing. You can get the Microsoft Web Application Stress tool from `http://homer.rte.microsoft.com/`.

Another paging solution using SQL Server was suggested to me, which used SQL Server cursors. These are similar to cursors and recordsets in ADO, in that they allow access to rows of data from a query. A cursor creates and manages a rowset in SQL Server. One of the things you can do with SQL Cursors is fetch rows starting from an absolute position in the rowset, so theoretically we could have a stored procedure that only returns a page full of rows, starting from this absolute position. Unfortunately, SQL cursors only allow access to one row at a time, therefore each row in the page would be returned as a separate recordset. On the client we'd have to use the `NextRecordset` *method to perform another trip to the server. So, whilst it seems like a good idea, it's actually less efficient that the stored procedure method shown here.*

Using Images from a Database

Images are still one area that many people are confused by and have trouble with. By far the best way to deal with images in your ASP pages is to store them in the file system rather than in a database.

However, there are people who need to access images from a database, so here's the simple way to do it, assuming the data is in a SQL Server BLOB field. Using Microsoft Access to store images has an additional problem where header information is stored in OLE Object fields. We're not going to be looking at an Access solution here.

First create an ASP file called `GetLogo.ASP`:

```
<!-- #INCLUDE FILE='../Include/Connection.asp" -->
<%
  ' Turn on buffering and set the mime type
  Response.Buffer = True
  Response.ContentType = "image/bmp"

  Dim rsLogo
  Dim strSQL
  Dim bytChunk

  strSQL = "SELECT logo FROM pub_info WHERE pub_id='" & _
            Request.QueryString("pub_id") & "'"

  ' Run the command and extract the logo
  rsLogo.Open strSQL, strConn
  bytChunk = rsLogo("logo")
  rsLogon.Close
  Set rsLogo = Nothing

  ' Write image to the browser
  Response.BinaryWrite bytChunk
  Response.End
%>
```

All this code does is accept a publisher ID and use that to query the database. The image is written to the Response stream using BinaryWrite. You could use this from another ASP page as the source of the image tag. For example:

```
<IMG SRC="GetLogo.asp?pub_id=0736">
```

Of course, you could speed this up further by using a stored procedure to return the image.

This example just returns a single image, but there's no reason why you can't have a recordset containing more than one image.

The other way to use images is to use the IMG tag and data binding, where the bound field of the IMG tag is the SRC attribute. Of course, this attribute takes a URL, so you can't bind directly to an image stored in a recordset. In fact, there's no way to use images from a recordset and place them directly into a Web page.

Summary

As we mentioned at the start of this chapter, there's no such thing as a pure ASP programmer. Here, we've concentrated on a variety of techniques for getting data to the client. We've seen that some of these use client-side scripting and RDS, whereas others use pure ASP code to generate the data.

In particular we've looked at:

- The different types of RDS data control you can use, and what sort of limitations they impose
- How you can bind HTML elements to RDS data controls to ease the coding burden and improve the user interaction with the data
- How to use the DataSpace and DataFactory to create access custom components on the server
- How you can increase the security of your Web server when using RDS
- Several different methods for introducing a paging scheme to client data

All of these topics will aid you in providing a richer user experience for your Web applications.

N
W

11

Working with XML Data

Once again you might feel that this chapter is a bit misplaced in an ASP book, but you'd be wrong. It's a fact of life that **XML (eXtensible Markup Language)** is invading our lives more and more as programmers, and I think this is 'A Good Thing'. XML has the ability to cross all sorts of boundaries, and is probably the only chance we have of obtaining a truly independent, cross-platform data transfer format.

You might think that this is a bit of a pessimistic statement, but XML *is* being adopted by almost all of the large (and small) players in the computer industry. The only time this sort of uniformity has hit everyone before was when TCP/IP was adopted as the de-facto networking protocol. XML is an international standard, is controlled by an industry standard body, has widespread support throughout the world and looks set to become one of the few single formats for a technology.

You may think this strange in a world where standards come and go like the seasons, and even single standards are fragmented by companies seeking competitive advantage. XML however, appears to be different, because it really does have wide support from many companies. Surprisingly they all seem to be really trying to achieve, and obey, this single standard. Pretty amazing really, considering the amount of petty fighting that has plagued our industry in the past.

OK, so XML is a standard that's being broadly implemented, but what has it got to do with ASP? It's simple, really. If you're using ASP to create a Web site, then the chances are pretty high that you're using a database of some sort to store data. XML is another format for storing data and one that's being increasingly used, so it's something we'll have to get used to. OK, XML is a little more than that, but read on.

In this chapter we are going to look at the following:

- Exactly what we mean by XML data
- What the Document Object Model is and how it can be used
- How ADO uses XML, and how we can use this to our advantage
- How we can make XML look nice for our users

We've already seen XML support be introduced into Internet Explorer and ADO, although support is far from full at the moment. Part of the trouble we have is that ADO and IE are evolving at different rates, so the interaction between them is less than perfect and some of the techniques you'll see in this chapter might not provide the data transfer panacea you want. At the time of writing, the integration between the two products isn't great, but both ADO and IE are continually changing. So although there are no dates for future releases, I expect ADO and IE to have a much more integrated future.

What is Extensible Markup Language?

Before we can define what XML is, it's a good idea to clarify what a markup language is. And here lies our first problem, because *language* is probably the wrong term. It's not a language in the sense that Visual Basic or C++ are languages, but it's a set of rules that define how text or documents should be marked up. OK, now we need to define what we mean by *marked up*. Marking up a document is the process of identifying certain areas of a document as having a special meaning. Still confused? OK, let's take HTML as an example, since the M in HTML stands for Markup.

We are all pretty familiar with HTML – a set of tags that identify the layout of documents. HTML contains a predefined set of tags, each with a meaning. Consider the following:

```
<BODY>
Here we have some text
<H1>This is a heading</H1>
This bit is normal text
<B>This is some bold text</B>
And finally some more normal text
</BODY>
```

Here we have some text with a few tags. To start with, we have a `<BODY>` tag, which in HTML means the start of the body of a document, and the body continues until the `</BODY>` tag is met. So here we have some meaning introduced. Within the body we have a heading, which is identified by the text within the `<H1>` and `</H1>` tags, as well as some bold text, identified between the `<B>` and `</B>` tags. Again we're introducing meaning to certain areas of the document. We've *marked* them as meaning something special.

One thing you may have noticed is that I haven't used the word *formatting*. This is deliberate, because markup and formatting aren't necessarily the same thing. The `<BODY>` tags mark an area of a document, but don't imply any formatting. The `<B>` tags however, mark an area of the document that is to appear in bold. That's because the HTML `<B>` tag is a special markup tag that implies formatting.

So, let's just refresh our memory here, to make sure it's all clear. A markup language is just a set of rules that define how we add meaning to areas of a document. That meaning might well be formatting, but this isn't the only reason to use markup.

How does XML differ from HTML?

XML takes a different view from HTML, although it still uses tags. The major difference is that XML is designed to describe the structure of text, not how it should be displayed. XML doesn't have a fixed set of tags. Consider the following:

```
<BODY>
Here we have some text
<H1>This is a heading</H1>
This bit is normal text
<B>This is some bold text</B>
And finally some more normal text
</BODY>
```

Hmm, isn't that just the same HTML? Yes it is, but only if it's in an HTML document. If you load the above into a browser then it displays the above as though it were a formatted document:

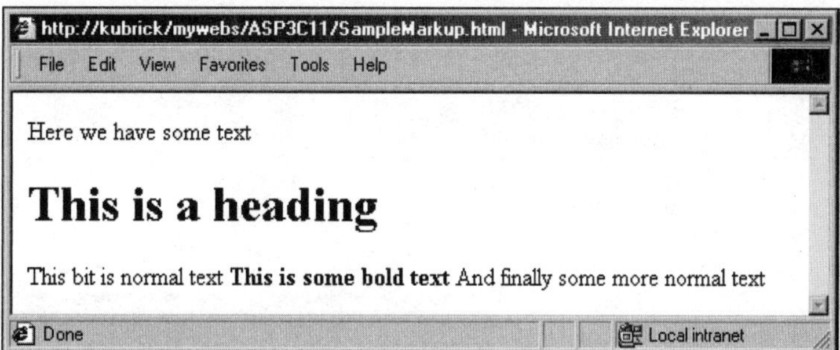

However, if the above text defines an XML document, then the tags don't mean anything. Not a damn thing. All they say is the following:

- Here's a tag called `BODY`, and inside that tag we have some text.
- Here's a tag called `H1`, and inside that tag we have some text.
- Here's a tag called `B`, and inside that tag we have some text.

You can see this quite clearly by loading the above into Internet Explorer as though it were at XML document (with a file suffix of `.xml`):

Internet Explorer interprets this XML and displays it for us. Notice it's done nothing with the XML – just displayed it. The browser knows how to interpret HTML, and displays it with all of its formatting. The browser also knows how to interpret XML, but because XML tags don't imply formatting, none is done – the tags are displayed 'as is'.

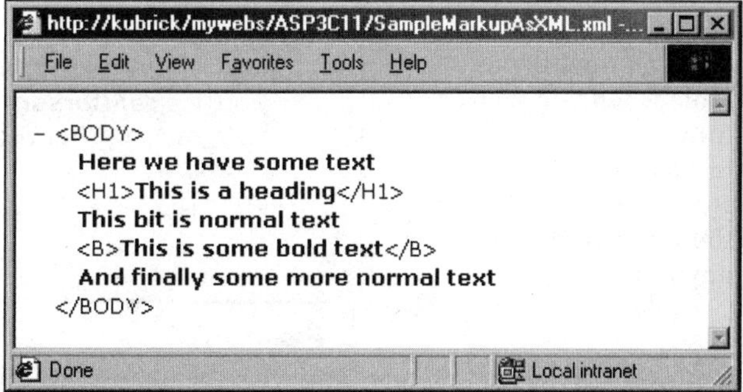

Internet Explorer does actually do a little formatting, but only to make the XML easier to read. It indents subsequent levels of tags so we see a nicely structured looking set of tags. It doesn't, however, interpret these tags.

So, what have we learned about XML so far. That it consists of tags that markup areas of the document. So what's all the fuss about XML being used for data? Well, let's have a look at another example. We saw this in use in the previous chapter, and you'll notice that the XML is more meaningful:

```
<Authors>
  <Author>
    <au_id>172-32-1176</au_id>
    <au_lname>White</au_lname>
    <au_fname>Johnson</au_fname>
  </Author>
  <Author>
    <au_id>213-46-8915</au_id>
    <au_lname>Green</au_lname>
    <au_fname>Marjorie</au_fname>
  </Author>
  <Author>
    <au_id>238-95-7766</au_id>
    <au_lname>Carson</au_lname>
    <au_fname>Cheryl</au_fname>
  </Author>
</Authors>
```

Here you can see we have several different sets of tags, and at first you might think that these tags have a meaning. After all, they have sensible names, defining a list of Authors, a single Author, and some values associated with the author. You've seen this data plenty of times in the previous chapter, and it's likely that you'd want it formatted as a table when you viewed it in a browser. But, because this is XML we still have the problem of the tags not meaning anything:

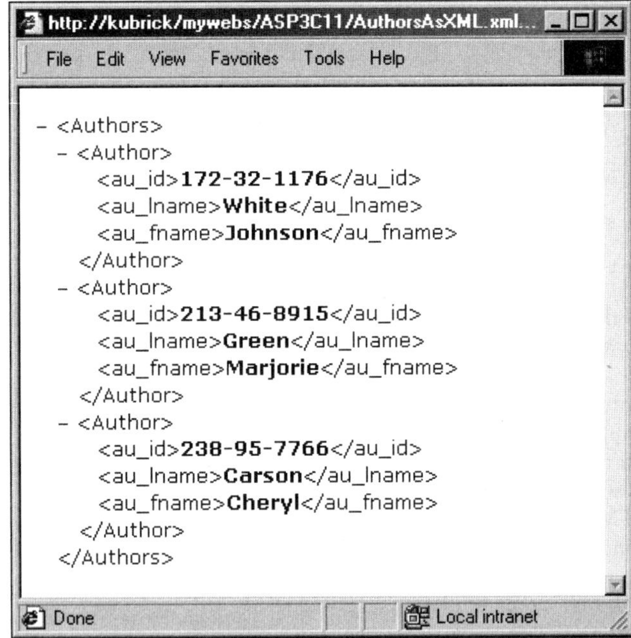

You see – IE doesn't do anything with them. So even though the tags have some meaning to us, they don't to XML. In fact there's no reason why this couldn't be shown as:

```
<HubbaHubbaHubbas>
  <HubbaHubbaHubba>
    <foo>172-32-1176</foo>
    <bar>White</bar>
    <qwerty>Johnson</qwerty>
  </HubbaHubbaHubba>
  <HubbaHubbaHubba>
    <foo>213-46-8915</foo>
    <bar>Green</bar>
    <qwerty>Marjorie</qwerty>
  </HubbaHubbaHubba>
  <HubbaHubbaHubba>
    <foo>238-95-7766</foo>
    <bar>Carson</bar>
    <qwerty>Cheryl</qwerty>
  </HubbaHubbaHubba>
</HubbaHubbaHubbas>
```

The browser again displays this as just tags:

The lesson here is that the tags can be anything you like, and it's only how we use them that give them a meaning. Of course, it's sensible to give them meaningful names to start with. After all, XML is fairly readable, so using tag names that describe the contents is common sense.

What we've seen here is that XML comprises a set of tags that describe sections of a document. In the examples using the author information, we've used XML to describe data, and we've used tag names that represent the field names of the data. So this is what I mean when I said in the introduction that XML can be used as a data interchange format. It's standard text, so can be transferred easily from machine to machine. It's not in a proprietary format, so anyone can read it, and if the tags are named sensibly, the XML data is self-describing.

So then, now you understand what XML data is, let's look at some terms, and the different ways that XML can be laid out.

Tags and Elements

We've used the name **Tag** to identify some HTML markup, such as `<B>` or `<H1>`. An **Element** is a fully formed use of those tags. Take for example:

```
<B>Some bold text and <I>italic</I> text</B>
```

This consists of two opening tags and two closing tags, but only two elements. The `B` element consists of:

```
<B>Some bold text and <I>italic</I> text</B>
```

And the `I` element consists of:

```
<I>italic</I>
```

So, an element comprises a start tag, an end tag, and the text it encloses, which can include other elements. This is a particularly important point, because it introduces the concept of **Well-formed XML** in which each opening tag *must* have a closing tag. This is very different from HTML 4.0 and earlier, where some tags don't have closing tags (`<IMG>` and `<BR>` for example) and the `<P>` tag which has been routinely misused by almost everyone (myself included).

If we are using XML to describe data, then it's possible that some fields might contain no data. In this case the tags would be empty. Empty tags in XML can be defined in one of two ways. The first is with a start and end tag, but no content:

```
<TagName></TagName>
```

The second way is to use just an opening tag, but put a slash at the end:

```
<TagName/>
```

Another part of being well-formed is that tags in XML are case sensitive, so the opening and closing tags must match in case. This means that the following is invalid XML:

```
<TAGName></tagname>
```

Root Tags

One other term to be aware of is the **Root Tag**. This is defined as the outer tag, and an XML document can have only one root. For example, let's look at the authors again:

```
<Authors>
  <Author>
    <au_id>172-32-1176</au_id>
    <au_lname>White</au_lname>
    <au_fname>Johnson</au_fname>
  </Author>
  <Author>
<au_id>213-46-8915</au_id>
    <au_lname>Green</au_lname>
    <au_fname>Marjorie</au_fname>
  </Author>
```

```
    <Author>
      <au_id>238-95-7766</au_id>
      <au_lname>Carson</au_lname>
      <au_fname>Cheryl</au_fname>
    </Author>
  </Authors>
```

Here the root tag is <Authors>. This is valid, since there's only one root tag. The following however, is invalid:

```
  <Authors>
    <Author>
      <au_id>172-32-1176</au_id>
      <au_lname>White</au_lname>
      <au_fname>Johnson</au_fname>
    </Author>
  </Authors>
  <Authors>
    <Author>
      <au_id>213-46-8915</au_id>
      <au_lname>Green</au_lname>
      <au_fname>Marjorie</au_fname>
    </Author>
    <Author>
      <au_id>238-95-7766</au_id>
      <au_lname>Carson</au_lname>
      <au_fname>Cheryl</au_fname>
    </Author>
  </Authors>
```

Here there are two tags at the top level, so this isn't valid.

The <?xml> Tag

This isn't a true XML tag, but a special tag indicating special processing instructions. The <?xml> tag is a special tag that should be the first line of each XML document, and can be used to identify version and language information. For example:

```
<?xml version="1.0"?>
```

This identifies the version of XML. The default, and current, version is 1.0. At the moment 1.0 is also the only version of XML, but having the ability to specify it in our XML documents does allow us to future proof them.

This tag is also the place where you can define the language used in the XML data. This is important if your data contains characters that aren't part of the standard English ASCII character set. You can specify the encoding used in your document by adding the `encoding` attribute to the `?xml` processing instruction:

```
<?xml version="1.0" encoding="iso-8859-1" ?>
```

A list of the most common languages and their character sets is shown below:

Language	Character Set
Unicode (8 bit)	UTF-8
Latin 1 (Western Europe, Latin America)	ISO-8859-1
Latin 2 (Central/Eastern Europe)	ISO-8859-2
Latin 3 (SE Europe)	ISO-8859-3
Latin 4 (Scandinavia/Baltic)	ISO-8859-4
Latin/Cyrillic	ISO-8859-5
Latin/Arabic	ISO-8859-6
Latin/Greek	ISO-8859-7
Latin/Hebrew	ISO-8859-8
Latin/Turkish	ISO-8859-9
Latin/Lappish/Nordic/Eskimo	ISO-8859-10
Japanese	EUC-JP or Shift_JIS

If you want to read more about the internationalization issue, then have a look at the W3Cs page on this topic – www.w3.org/International/.

Attributes

Like HTML, XML has **Attributes** to define the properties of elements, and these must also be well-formed. For attributes, this means that they MUST be enclosed in quotes. For example:

```
<BOOK ISBN="1-861002-61-0">Professional Active Server Pages 3.0</BOOK>
```

HTML allows you to get away with attributes that are unquoted, but this is invalid in XML.

Special Characters

XML has a special set of characters that cannot be used in normal XML strings. These are:

Character	Must be replaced by
&	&
<	<
>	>
"	"
'	'

For example, the following XML is invalid:

```
<BOOK>Advanced Rocket Science Dave & Al</BOOK>
```

Whereas the following is valid XML:

```
<BOOK> Advanced Rocket Science by Dave &amp; Al</BOOK>
```

Most tools that generate XML automatically convert these characters into the special counterparts, but if you are generating your own XML then you need to be aware that you must use the long form. Using these single characters in an XML document renders it invalid, and most XML processors will fail if a document contains them.

Schemas and DTDs

We've stated that XML tags don't actually mean anything and that you can give tags any name, but how do you know what sort of tags should be allowed in a document. For this you have to use either a **Document Type Definition** (**DTD**) or a **Schema**. Schemas and DTDs are the flip side of the same coin. They both specify which elements are allowed in a document, and can turn a well-formed XML document into a **valid** XML document. All this means is that as well as being correctly marked up (well-formed) it contains only the allowed elements and attributes.

We have both DTDs and schemas because somewhere along the line someone (OK, it was Microsoft) decided that DTDs were a bit stupid. A DTD is a text file that defines the structure of an XML document, but the DTD isn't itself XML – it has a completely separate syntax. This is a bit of an anomaly, and I agree with Microsoft on this front. If you're dealing with XML documents, then the structure that defines those documents should be XML too, and this is what Schemas are – XML equivalents of a DTDs.

Let's look at a typical DTD – this one's for the `authors` XML document, as generated from the `pubs` database.

```
<!ELEMENT DOCUMENT (AUTHOR+)>
<!ELEMENT AUTHOR(au_id, au_lname, au_fname, phone, address,
                    city, state, zip, contract)>
<!ELEMENT au_id (CDATA)>
<!ELEMENT au_lname (CDATA)>
<!ELEMENT au_fname (CDATA)>
<!ELEMENT phone (CDATA)>
<!ELEMENT address (CDATA)>
<!ELEMENT city (CDATA)>
<!ELEMENT state (CDATA)>
<!ELEMENT zip (CDATA)>
<!ELEMENT contract (CDATA)>
```

This is actually quite simple. It states that this document comprises 0 or more `AUTHOR` elements. The plus sign on the end of `AUTHOR` says 'one or more'. Each `AUTHOR` element is made up from nine other elements. Each of these sub-elements contains character data (`CDATA`).

There are two real flaws with DTDs:

- They aren't XML.
- You cannot specify the data types – such as integer, date, and so on – for each element. CDATA simply means that an element contains just character data, and doesn't identify the actual type of the element's contents.

Because of these reasons, Microsoft proposed Schemas to the W3C. If we convert the above DTD into a schema it would be something like:

```
<Schema ID="Author">
  <Element name="au_id"/>
  <Element name="au_lname"/>
  <Element name="au_fname"/>
  <Element name="phone"/>
  <Element name="address"/>
  <Element name="city"/>
  <Element name="state"/>
  <Element name="zip"/>
  <Element name="contract"/>
</Schema>
```

With the addition of data types we'd get:

```
<Schema ID="Author">
  <Element name="au_id" type="string"/>
  <Element name="au_lname" type="string"/>
  <Element name="au_fname" type="string"/>
  <Element name="phone" type="string"/>
  <Element name="address" type="string"/>
  <Element name="city" type="string"/>
  <Element name="state" type="string"/>
  <Element name="zip" type="string"/>
  <Element name="contract" type="boolean"/>
</Schema>
```

This schema now details not only the allowable elements, but also their data types. The CDATA of a DTD is equivalent to a string, but the schema allows other data types – the contract element for example, contains Boolean data.

It's important to note that schemas aren't a standard yet, which is why I'm not going to go into much more detail about their structure and layout, or how you use them. This chapter is really about how to use XML data in our ASP applications, and that probably means we'll be using the Microsoft XML tools. Microsoft has its own format of schemas, and some other companies use DTDs, and as yet there's not conformity. We will, however, be looking at the schema used by ADO when it generates XML a little later in the chapter.

We've had to mention them here because they are an intrinsic part of XML and you'll see schemas and DTD mentioned in other documentation. However, the way we are going to use XML data doesn't have a great deal of impact on the schema itself, so we'll leave a detailed discussion of them to another book.

> *If you're interested in this area then keep your eyes on the W3C Web site (`www.w3c.org/XML/`) for more details.*

Namespaces

One problem with XML is that you can give an element almost any name you want. Unfortunately, this means there's quite a good chance that you'll pick the same name as someone else, or even use the same name to mean different things in different XML documents. For example, consider this element:

```
<contract>Yes</contract>
```

This is taken from the `authors` table in `pubs`, and indicates that the author is a contracted author. However, what about an XML document that contains this:

```
<contract>F:/contacts/1999.doc</contract>
```

This `Contract` element identifies the document that contains the contract.

Now this isn't a problem while these two XML documents stay separated, but if you ever combine the two documents, how do you identify to which document the `contract` element belongs? This is where **namespaces** come in, as a namespace uniquely identifies the schema to which elements belong.

Namespaces are added to XML documents by defining the `xmlns` (XML Name Space) attribute in the root tag, which requires a **Uniform Resource Identifier** (**URI**). This URI is simply a name that can uniquely identify the namespace. Although any unique name can be used as a URI, you'll find that most often URLs of Web sites are used. For example, let's look at the problem of the Contract, which could hold two different types of values. If we have XML data from two different sources being combined, we might end up with this:

```
<Authors>
  <Author>
    <au_id>172-32-1176</au_id>
    <au_lname>White</au_lname>
    <au_fname>Johnson</au_fname>
    <contract>Yes</contract>
    <contract>F:/contacts/1999.doc</contract>
  </Author>
<Authors>
```

How would we differentiate the two `contract` elements? As you might have guessed, the answer is to use namespaces. So, let's add these to the XML:

```
<Authors xmlns:pubs="http://www.wrox.co.uk/ms/PubsDB"
         xmlns:wrox="http://www.wrox.co.uk/authors">
  <Author>
    <au_id>172-32-1176</au_id>
    <au_lname>White</au_lname>
    <au_fname>Johnson</au_fname>
    <pubs:contract>Yes</pubs:contract>
    <wrox:contract>F:/contacts/Johnson1999.doc</wrox:contract>
  </Author>
<Authors>
```

Here we've added the `xmlns` attributes to identify two namespaces. The structure of this is:

```
xmlns:short_name=URI
```

The *short_name* is what we use in the XML document to relate elements to tags. You'll see this used in a minute. The *URI* is just a name that will uniquely identify the namespace within the XML document. It's important to note that this URL is used purely as a unique name – the namespace doesn't actually connect to the URL or imply any connection to the Web server. It's just a way of uniquely identifying each namespace. You could put the names of your favorite cheeses in there if you like, as long as they were unique to the XML document.

In the XML elements themselves, we prefix the tag with the appropriate *short_name*, to identify which namespace the element belongs:

```
<pubs:contract>Yes</pubs:contract>
<wrox:contract>F:/contacts/1999.doc</wrox:contract>
```

So here, the first element belongs to the `pubs` namespace, and the second to the `wrox` namespace.

You can also apply namespaces to attributes. For example:

```
<Authors xmlns:pubs="http://www.wrox.co.uk/ms/PubsDB"
         xmlns:wrox="http://www.wrox.co.uk/authors">
  <Author>
    <pubs:au_id pubs:type="UID">172-32-1176</pubs:au_id>
    <au_lname>White</au_lname>
    <au_fname>Johnson</au_fname>
    <pubs:contract>Yes</pubs:contract>
    <wrox:contract>F:/contacts/Johnson1999.doc</wrox:contract>
  </Author>
</Authors>
```

Here we apply the namespace to the `type` attribute of the `au_id` element, and it uniquely separates this attribute from any other `type` attributes in the document with different, or no, namespaces.

So what's the big deal about this? Well, the namespace allows us to ensure that the data is interpreted correctly. If the XML document contains information that should be processed in some special way, or contains special information, then the namespace can identify that. It allows the XML to be distinct from any other XML that just might happen to contain the same elements or attributes.

Once again this is an area we could spend a lot of time on, but it's really outside the scope of the chapter. What we really want is for you to understand what a namespace is and what it looks like, because you'll be seeing more of them later. We won't be explicitly examining them in detail, but at least you won't be confused by what they are.

Document Object Model

The Document Object Model is an API for HTML and XML documents, and defines the logical structure of documents, and the way they can be accessed. This is really important because it defines a standard way in which we can access and manipulate the XML structure. Let's look at a simple XML document, and then how the DOM can be used.

```
<Authors>
  <Author>
    <au_id>172-32-1176</au_id>
    <au_lname>White</au_lname>
    <au_fname>Johnson</au_fname>
  </Author>
  <Author>
    <au_id>213-46-8915</au_id>
    <au_lname>Green</au_lname>
    <au_fname>Marjorie</au_fname>
  </Author>
</Authors>
```

XML documents are hierarchical by nature – that is, they always have a top-level, or root element, and then child elements. So, the above document could be represented as:

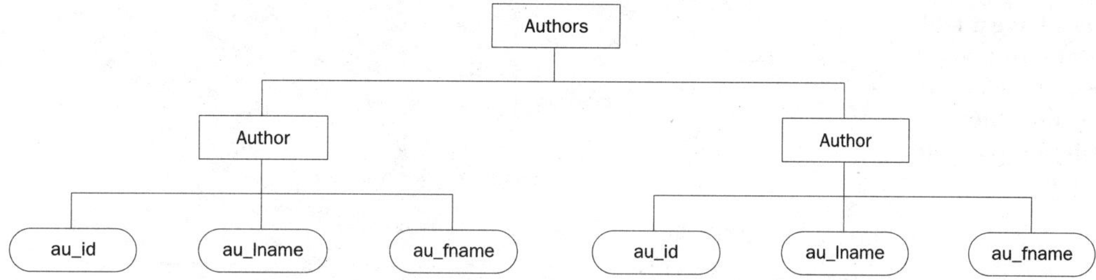

If there were more children, we would have a deeper tree. In DOM terms, these elements are also **nodes**. A node just represents a generic element in this tree-type structure.

Base Objects

To represent this hierarchical nature, the DOM provides a whole set of objects, methods and properties that allow us to manipulate the DOM. We're not going to look at them all here, but we'll cover a few to give you a flavor of the sort of things you can achieve. Let's start with the objects:

Object	Description
`Node`	A single node in the hierarchy.
`NodeList`	A collection of nodes.
`NamedNodeMap`	A collection of nodes allowing access by name as well as index.

There are a number of properties that allow traversal through the nodes:

Property	Description
`childNodes`	Returns a `NodeList` containing the children of the node.
`firstChild`	Returns the first child of the current node.
`lastChild`	Returns the last child of the current node.

Table Continued on Following Page

Property	Description
parentNode	Returns the parent node of the current node.
previousSibling	Returns the previous sibling, i.e., the previous node at the same level in the hierarchy.
nextSibling	Returns the next sibling, i.e., the next node at the same level in the hierarchy.
nodeName	The name of the node.
nodeValue	The value of the node.

This isn't a complete list, but it does gives you an idea of what's possible. For a full list check out the MSDN Online XML area, found at msdn.microsoft.com/xml/.

Let's have a look at one side of the node structure of our document with a little more detail.

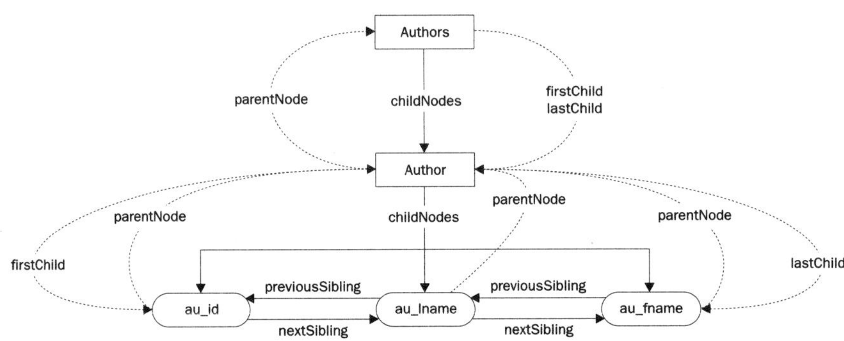

Here you can clearly see how you can use these properties to navigate around the XML DOM. The dashed lines indicate which nodes the properties point to. The children on the root node, Authors, are held in the childNodes collection. In the above case Authors only has one child, so both its firstChild and its lastChild properties point to the same node. In this case this would be childNodes(0), the only node in the collection.

The Author node however, has three children, held in a childNodes collection. The firstChild property (the same as childNodes(0)) points to the au_id node, and the lastChild property (the same as childNodes(2)) points to the au_fname node. The previousSibling and nextSibling properties point to the next node in the node collection, at the same level.

So, let's assume we have a node object called nodRoot pointing to Authors:

Code	Points to
nodRoot.childNodes(0)	Author
nodRoot.ChildNodes(0).firstChild	au_id
nodRoot.ChildNodes(0).firstChild.nextSibling	au_lname
nodRoot.ChildNodes(0).firstChild.parentNode	Author
nodRoot.ChildNodes(0).firstChild.nextSibling.parentNode	Author

You'll see more examples of this later in the chapter.

Specific DOM Objects

XML is designed to be extensible and to cater for a wide variety of documents, so there are specific objects for different types of node. Most inherit the properties and methods of the Node object, as well as adding specific methods and properties relevant to the particular node type. These objects are:

Object	Description
`Document`	The root object for an XML document.
`DocumentType`	Information about the DTD or schema associated with the XML document. Equivalent to `!DOCTYPE` in a DTD.
`DocumentFragment`	A lightweight copy of the Document, useful for temporary storage or document insertions.
`Element`	An XML element.
`Attribute` or `Attr`	An XML attribute.
`Entity`	A parsed or unparsed entity. Equivalent to `!ENTITY` in a DTD.
`EntityReference`	An entity reference.
`Notation`	A notation. Equivalent to `!NOTATION` in a DTD.
`CharacterData`	The base object for text information in a document.
`CDATASection`	Unparsed character data. Equivalent to `!CDATA` in a DTD.
`Text`	The text contents of an element or attribute node.
`Comment`	An XML comment element.
`ProcessingInstruction`	A processing instruction, as held in the `<? ?>` section.
`Implementation`	Application specific implementation details.

You probably won't use all of these, and we're not going to explain them in depth, nor their relationship to some of the XML sections, since this is really beyond the scope of this chapter. What we want to concentrate on are the basics of XML as data, and how you can use and manipulate it.

> *If you'd like to learn more about XML and the DOM then have a look at* XML IE5 Programmer's Reference from Wrox Press*, ISBN 1-861001-57-6. You should also check out Microsoft's XML area at* `http://msdn.microsoft.com/xml/` *or the W3C area at* `http://www.w3.org/DOM/`.

Traversing the DOM

Because XML is a relatively new area, many browsers don't support the handling of XML data. In fact, Internet Explorer 5.0 is really the only browser with good support for it. So, as an ASP developer, you have to decide whether you want to send the XML data to the browser, or whether you want to process the XML in your ASP pages, and send pure HTML up to the browser. Of course this depends upon your target audience, but whichever method you choose, it's useful to know how to use the DOM and how to get access to the XML objects.

So, this is just a quick section to show you how you can use the DOM to traverse through an XML document with a page called `TraverseXML.html` which you can find in the code download. We're going use IE5 here, with an **XML Data Island**. We saw these in the previous chapter when we looked at RDS, and if you remember, the data island is simply an HTML tag that acts like a data control:

```
<XML ID="dsoData" SRC="authors.xml"></XML>
```

Here we have a data island, called `dsoData`, containing the data from the XML file `authors.xml`. Since this is a data island, it doesn't actually show anything on the screen – it's just a container for the data. So, we need a way to access the data from this and display it.

To do this we're going to use a `SPAN` element. You could use one of several different element types here, but a `SPAN` is just as good as any of the others:

```
<SPAN ID="txtData"></SPAN>
```

Our aim is to use the DOM to extract the XML information from the data island, and display the data in the `SPAN`. What we need to do is start at the root node, and find any child nodes that the root has and display the details of that node. We'll display the name of the node, what type of node it is, and the value. Also, since a child node can contain child nodes of its own, we'll repeat this process, traversing down, and through the tree, until all nodes have been visited. And because this is a tree traversal operation, we'll use a recursive function to do it.

One of the pieces of information we are going to display is the node's type. This will identified by an integer, but seeing as integers aren't particularly readable, we'll convert it into a string which describes the node type. To do this we declare a global array containing the text descriptions of the node types, and use the actual node type number as its index. Right at the top of our JScript code then, we have:

```
var g_strNodeTypes = new Array('', 'ELEMENT (1)', 'ATTRIBUTE (2)',
    'TEXT (3)', 'CDATA SECTION (4)', 'ENTITY REFERENCE (5)',
    'ENTITY (6)', 'PROCESSING INSTRUCTION (7)', 'COMMENT (8)',
    'DOCUMENT (9)', 'DOCUMENT TYPE (10)', 'DOCUMENT FRAGMENT (11)',
    'NOTATION (12)');
```

Our recursive function, which we'll call `showChildNodes`, accepts an XML node, and an integer that indicates the current level of the node in the hierarchy. This just allows us to indent the output so it's easier to read:

```
function showChildNodes(nodNode, intLevel)
{
  var strNodes = '';        // string containing the node information
  var intCount = 0;         // count of the nodes
  var intNode = 0;          // current node number
  var nodAttrList;          // node list of the attributes for a node
```

We can now start building up the string, starting with the current node name, the type of the node, and the value of the node. The type is identified by an integer, and we use the previously defined array to get the description of the node type. The `getIndent` function just returns a blank string containing spaces up to the level in the tree:

```
    // Get the values for this node
    strNodes += getIndent(intLevel) + '<B>' + nodNode.nodeName
            + '</B>   Type: <B>' + g_strNodeTypes[nodNode.nodeType]
            + '</B>   Value: <B>' + nodNode.nodeValue + '</B><BR>';
```

Next we need to consider if the node has any attributes, and if so we loop through them, adding their details to the string:

```
    // Check there are some attributes
    nodAttrList = nodNode.attributes;
    if (nodAttrList != null)
    {
      intCount = nodAttrList.length;
      if (intCount > 0)
      {
        // For each attribute, display the attribute information
        for (intAttr = 0; intAttr < intCount; intAttr++)
          strNodes += getIndent(intLevel + 1) + '<B>'
                   + nodAttrList(intAttr).nodeName + '</B>   Type: <B>'
                   + g_strNodeTypes[nodAttrList(intAttr).nodeType]
                   + '</B>   Value: <B>'
                   + nodAttrList(intAttr).nodeValue + '</B><BR>';
      }
    }
```

Finally, we need to check for any child nodes, and for each child we call the same function. This allows us to repeat the same string building exercise for each node we encounter:

```
    // Check for any child nodes
    intCount = nodNode.childNodes.length;
    if (intCount > 0)
      // For each child node, display the node,
      // attributes and its child node information
      for (intNode = 0; intNode < intCount; intNode++)
        strNodes += showChildNodes(nodNode.childNodes(intNode), intLevel + 1);

    return strNodes;
  }
```

To display the output from this, we could use the following:

```
  domXMLData = dsoData
  txtData.innerHTML = showChildNodes(domXMLData, 0);
```

This just calls the function, passing in the top-level node. The output we get is:

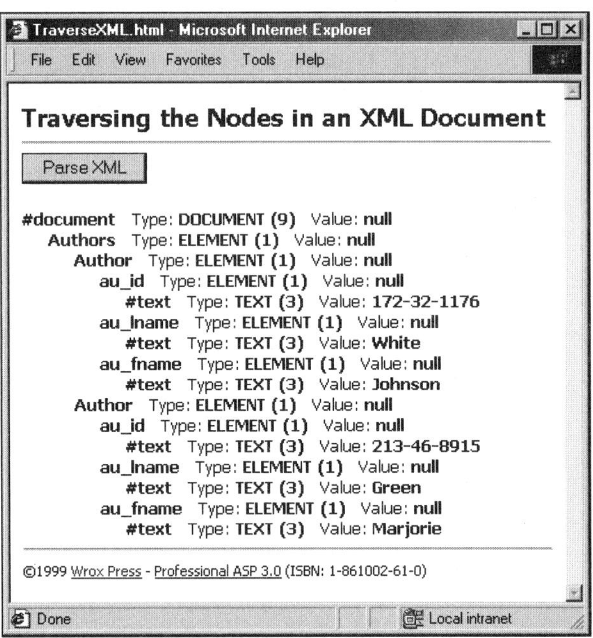

Here you can see the recursive nature of the XML DOM. At the top we have a `#Document` type node, which is an inherent parent – it's the root node of all XML documents. Notice though, that it's not actually an element – it has a type of `DOCUMENT`. So the root of the XML data is an XML document, but then under that we have the XML elements.

So, the first, or root element, is the `Authors` element. This then contains an element for each `Author` and an element for each property of the `Author`. What you also notice is that for each leaf node (i.e. node with no children) we have another node called `#text`. This contains the actual text of the node – something that confuses many people. Why does each element have a value of `null`, and its sub-element called `#text` contain the value of the node? Why not just have the value of the node contain the text? The answer is actually quite sensible, and has to do with the fact that nodes can contain other nodes, as well as containing text. If a node contained both text and other nodes, what would the value be? Would it be the text, or a pointer to the child node? This ambiguity led to the W3C specifying that the text for a node be always held in a child node, of type `TEXT`.

But hang on, I hear you cry. When we accessed the value of the node we didn't step down another level in the tree to access the child:

```
    + '</B>   Value: <B>' + nodNode.nodeValue + '</B><BR>';
```

Here we've just used the `nodeValue` property, and this is a Microsoft extension to the DOM. The W3C specification doesn't actually give a simple way to access the value of a node – you always have to traverse to the child to access the associated TEXT node. Microsoft decided that one of the most common actions would be to access the value of a node to get at the text it contains, so they introduced the `nodeValue` property. This handles the child TEXT node for us.

So, what we've had a quick look at here is what the DOM is, and shown that it stores XML data in a tree structure. Now that you understand what XML is and how it can be accessed, we need to take a look at how XML integrates with ADO and Internet Explorer.

XML in ADO and IE5

One of the greatest features about ADO 2.5 is that it allows us to access a recordset as an XML document. The advantage of this is that it provides a different way to manipulate data. You might not think that this is important, but consider the following:

- Not every programmer who deals with data knows ADO. Many are HTML and script programmers, so being able to access data through the XML DOM might be preferable to them.
- Not every programmer knows XML and the DOM, so allowing access to XML documents through a recordset means that they can stick with what they know.
- Much of what we do with data is about presentation. Data's not much good if users can't access and see it, and XML provides interesting ways to allow this.
- There is an increasing amount of content being written in XML.
- There are an increasing number of XML tools being written.

All of these add up to a persuasive argument – learn about XML.

ADO Recordsets Stored as XML

The first thing to look at when considering XML and ADO is how ADO presents its data as XML. We'll look at ways to get this XML data out of ADO in a little while, but first it's a good idea to look at the format of the XML data.

If we have a look at a section of the `authors` table converted directly from ADO, you might be a little surprised:

```
<z:row au_id="172-32-1176" au_lname="White" au_fname="Johnson"
       phone="408 496-7223" address="10932 Bigge Rd."
       city="Menlo Park" state="CA" zip="94025" contract="True" />
<z:row au_id="213-46-8915" au_lname="Green" au_fname="Marjorie"
       phone="415 986-7020" address="309 63rd St. #411"
       city="Oakland" state="CA" zip="94618" contract="True" />
<z:row au_id="238-95-7766" au_lname="Carson" au_fname="Cheryl"
       phone="415 548-7723" address="589 Darwin Ln."
       city="Berkeley" state="CA" zip="94705" contract="True" />
```

Whoa! This doesn't look like the XML we're used to. Instead of an element for each field we have an element for each row in the table, and the fields are attributes of the row element. Weird huh? One of the reasons that Microsoft used this method was the verbose nature of element-based XML documents. If you consider a large recordset converted to XML using only elements, then it's quite large. Every field has a start tag and an end tag. This way of defining data using attributes for each data item means that some of that repetition is reduced.

This is the only way XML can be extracted from ADO recordsets at the moment, although Microsoft are looking into providing some form of switching mechanism that allows the element based approach to be used. At the time of writing it's not clear whether this will be in the released version of ADO 2.5, or whether we'll have to wait for a future release.

ADO Recordset Namespace

If you're using ADO to send and retrieve XML data then you'll see a schema associated with the XML data file. The schema is embedded into the XML, at the top of the document, and it's worth looking at this a little. The first thing to note is the root element, which identifies several namespaces:

```
<xml xmlns:s="uuid:BDC6E3F0-6DA3-11d1-A2A3-00AA00C14882"
     xmlns:dt="uuid:C2F41010-65B3-11d1-A29F-00AA00C14882"
     xmlns:rs="urn:schemas-microsoft-com:rowset"
     xmlns:z="#RowsetSchema">
```

These namespaces are:

Namespace	Description
s	Identifies the URI for the schema itself.
dt	Identifies the URI for data types
rs	Identifies the rowset (recordset)
z	Identifies the individual rows

Remember what we said about namespaces earlier – they uniquely identify the XML document, or elements in it. Using namespaces ensures that the element names chosen by Microsoft are applied to the correct schema.

ADO Recordset Schema

So, we have a namespace to define the unique properties of the schema and recordset, let's look at the schema itself:

```
<s:Schema id="RowsetSchema">
  <s:ElementType name="row" content="eltOnly">
    <s:AttributeType name="au_id" rs:number="1" rs:writeunknown="true">
      <s:datatype dt:type="string" dt:maxLength="11" rs:maybenull="false" />
    </s:AttributeType>
    <s:AttributeType name="au_lname" rs:number="2" rs:writeunknown="true">
      <s:datatype dt:type="string" dt:maxLength="40" rs:maybenull="false" />
    </s:AttributeType>
    <s:AttributeType name="au_fname" rs:number="3" rs:writeunknown="true">
      <s:datatype dt:type="string" dt:maxLength="20" rs:maybenull="false" />
    </s:AttributeType>
    <s:AttributeType name="phone" rs:number="4" rs:writeunknown="true">
      <s:datatype dt:type="string" dt:maxLength="12" rs:fixedlength="true"
                  rs:maybenull="false" />
    </s:AttributeType>
    <s:AttributeType name="address" rs:number="5" rs:nullable="true"
                     rs:writeunknown="true">
      <s:datatype dt:type="string" dt:maxLength="40" />
    </s:AttributeType>
    <s:AttributeType name="city" rs:number="6" rs:nullable="true"
                     rs:writeunknown="true">
```

```
      <s:datatype dt:type="string" dt:maxLength="20" />
    </s:AttributeType>
    <s:AttributeType name="state" rs:number="7" rs:nullable="true"
                     rs:writeunknown="true">
      <s:datatype dt:type="string" dt:maxLength="2" rs:fixedlength="true" />
    </s:AttributeType>
    <s:AttributeType name="zip" rs:number="8" rs:nullable="true"
                     rs:writeunknown="true">
      <s:datatype dt:type="string" dt:maxLength="5" rs:fixedlength="true" />
    </s:AttributeType>
    <s:AttributeType name="contract" rs:number="9" rs:writeunknown="true">
      <s:datatype dt:type="boolean" dt:maxLength="2" rs:fixedlength="true"
                  rs:maybenull="false" />
    </s:AttributeType>
    <s:extends type="rs:rowbase" />
  </s:ElementType>
</s:Schema>
```

Let's look at this in more detail, so we get a good understanding of what the various pieces of it are.

The Row Element

We start with the element that identifies the schema:

```
<s:Schema id="RowsetSchema">
```

Here we have an XML element called `Schema` – the top-level element for the schema. We use the `s` namespace to uniquely identify the schema, and give the schema an attribute called `id`. This is just like giving any type of data field an ID – it identifies the field. In the schema, the ID identifies the schema itself.

Next we have the definition of an element, using the `ElementType`:

```
<s:ElementType name="row" content="eltOnly">
```

The element has two attributes. The first, `name`, just gives the element a name. In this case it's `row` – remember how the data contains one row for each row in the recordset, and the name of the element is `row`. This is the element in the schema that identifies that row. The second attribute is called `content`, and identifies what the element will hold. The possible values are:

Value	Description
`empty`	The element cannot contain any content.
`textOnly`	The element can only contain text, and not other elements.
`eltOnly`	The element can only contain other elements, and not text.
`both`	The element can contain both text and other elements.

So, what this line of the schema does is identify a row element that can only contain other elements. If you have a look at the XML data you can see this:

```
<z:row au_id="172-32-1176" au_lname="White" au_fname="Johnson"
       phone="408 496-7223" address="10932 Bigge Rd."
       city="Menlo Park" state="CA" zip="94025" contract="True" />
```

You might think that we could set the type to `empty`, since this is essentially an empty tag, but for the schema, `empty` means no content at all, including attributes.

The Field Attributes

If you look back at the XML data, you'll see that the field values are represented as attributes. So our schema must define those attributes, and there are two portions to this. The first is the definition of the attribute itself, and the second is the definition of the data type for the attribute.

To define an attribute, we have to define what it will be called – this should map to the field name of the data. We also define two other attributes. The first is a unique number for each attribute – this is the first attribute, so it's given the value of `1`. The remaining attributes are sequentially numbered. The other attribute is `writeunknown`, which identifies whether the attribute can be updated:

```
<s:AttributeType name="au_id" rs:number="1" rs:writeunknown="true">
```

`AttributeType` also has a child element to define the data type of the attribute:

```
  <s:datatype dt:type="string" dt:maxLength="11" rs:maybenull="false" />
```

This contains the data type, the maximum length of the data, and whether the attribute can contain a null value.

Other data types might contain slightly different information. For example, the contract field has the following:

```
<s:datatype dt:type="boolean" dt:maxLength="2" rs:fixedlength="true"
            rs:maybenull="false" />
```

This has the addition of an attribute to identify whether or not the data type contains fixed length data.

Data Types

When generating XML from ADO, the data types are automatically created for you, but if you intend to start authoring XML yourself, or perhaps creating schemas for some existing XML, then you might like to add support for data types. After all, this is one of the advantages schemas have over DTDs. The table below lists the data type supported by the XML-data schema:

Type	Description
`bin.base64`	A binary object
`bin.hex`	Hexadecimal octets
`boolean`	0 or 1 (0 is false, and 1 is true)
`char`	A one character length string
`date`	An ISO 8601 date, without the time. The format is yyyy-mm-dd
`dateTime`	An ISO 8601 date, optionally with the time. The format is yyyy-mm-ddThh:mm:ss
`dateTime.tz`	An ISO 8601 date, optionally with time and timezone. The format is yyyy-mm-ddThh:mm:ss-hh:mm. The timezone indicates the number of hours + or – GMT
`fixed.14.4`	Fixed with floating point number, with up to 14 digits to the left of the decimal place and up to 4 to the right
`float`	Floating point number
`int`	Integer number
`number`	Floating point number
`time`	An ISO 8601 time. The format is hh:mm:ss
`time.tz`	An ISO 8601 time with an optional timezone. The format is hh:mm:ss-hh:mm
`i1`	An 8 bit integer (1 byte)
`i2`	A 16 bit integer (2 bytes)
`i4`	A 32 bit integer (4 bytes)
`r4`	A 4 byte real number
`r8`	An 8 byte real number
`ui1`	An 8 bit unsigned integer (1 byte)
`ui2`	A 16 bit unsigned integer (2 bytes)
`ui4`	A 32 bit unsigned integer (4 bytes)
`uri`	A Universal Resource Indicator
`uuid`	A set of hex digits representing a universally unique identifier. A GUID is an example of this

The W3C also allow a set of primitive types:

Type	Description
entity	Represents the XML ENTITY type
entities	Represents the XML ENTITIES type
enumeration	Represents an enumerated type
id	Represents the XML ID type
idref	Represents the XML IDREF type
idrefs	Represents the XML IDREFS type
nmtoken	Represents the XML NMTOKEN type
nmtokens	Represents the XML NMTOKENS type
notation	Represents the XML NOTATION type
string	Represents a string type

IE Data Islands and Binding

We've already seen a few examples of XML data islands, but let's refresh our memory on how they are created, and how to bind HTML elements to them. You can create a data island with the <XML> tag in an HTML page, like so:

```
<XML ID="dsoData" SRC="authors.xml"></XML>
```

This references an external XML file as the source of the data. Alternatively you can embed the XML data within the <XML> tag:

```
<XML ID="dsoData">
 <Authors>
  <Author>
    <au_id>172-32-1176</au_id>
    <au_lname>White</au_lname>
    <au_fname>Johnson</au_fname>
  </Author>
 </Authors>
</XML>
```

We covered binding in detail in the previous chapter, and, if you remember, this can take two forms. The first option is to bind single elements, like so:

```
<INPUT TYPE="TEXT" DATASRC="#dsoData" DATAFLD="au_id"></INPUT>
```

This binds a single element to a field in the data source. The other method is to use table binding, where we bind a table to the data source, and then the elements in the table to the data fields:

```
<TABLE DATASRC="#dsoData">
  <TR>
    <TD><INPUT TYPE="TEXT" DATAFLD="au_id"></INPUT></TD>
    <TD><INPUT TYPE="TEXT" DATAFLD="au_fname"></INPUT></TD>
  </TR>
</TABLE>
```

This table would give the following result:

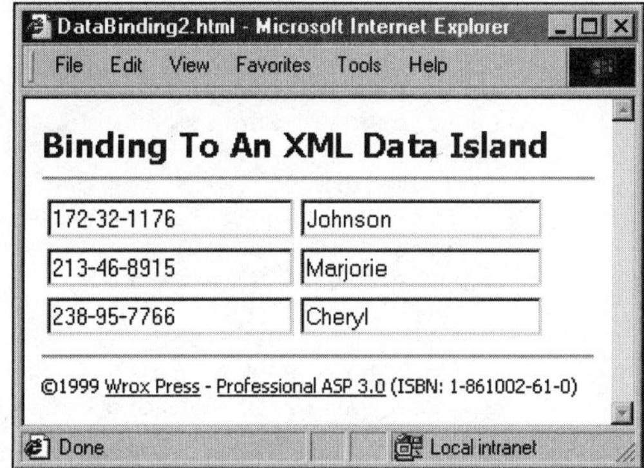

We won't go into any more detail, since we covered this simple example in the previous chapter.

Binding Hierarchical Data

All of the data we've looked at so far has been pretty simple, but you'll find a problem if you try to bind a set of XML data generated by ADO. This is because of one main reason – IE doesn't recognize schemas as a definition of the data. This means that what IE sees is this:

```
<XML>
  <s:Schema>
    . . . schema data
  </s:Schema>
  <rs:data>
    <z:row . . ./>
    <z:row . . ./>
  </rs:data>
</XML>
```

So IE sees two sets of data – the schema and the actual data. And that's not the end of our problems, because remember the data we want is held within the row. So our data is two levels deep, which means you have to do a bit of extra work.

The solution to this hierarchical binding (as demonstrated in `databinding.html`) is to use two levels of binding:

```
<TABLE ID="tblData" DATASRC="#dsoData" DATAFLD="rs:data">
<TR><TD>
 <TABLE ID="tblData" BORDER="1" DATASRC="#dsoData" DATAFLD="z:row">
  <TR>
    <TD><SPAN DATAFLD="au_id"></SPAN></TD>
    <TD><SPAN DATAFLD="au_fname"></SPAN></TD>
```

Here we bind the outer table to the element containing all of the data, and then we have an inner table bound to the row of data. The fields are then bound as before.

If you've got multiple levels of hierarchy, such as from a data shaped recordset, then you can just add more levels to the binding. For example, consider the following XML:

```
<XML ID="dsoPublishers">
<Publishers>
  <Publisher>
    <pub_id>0736</pub_id>
    <pub_name>New Moon Books</pub_name>
    <city>Boston</city>
    <state>MA</state>
    <country>USA</country>
    <title>
      <title_id>BU2075</title_id>
      <title>You Can Combat Computer Stress!</title>
      <price>$2.99</price>
      <pubdate>6/30/91</pubdate>
      <sale>
        <stor_id>7896</stor_id>
        <ord_num>X999</ord_num>
        <ord_date>2/21/93</ord_date>
        <qty>35</qty>
      </sale>
    </title>
    <employee>
      <emp_id>PDI47470M</emp_id>
      <fname>Palle</fname>
      <minit>D</minit>
      <lname>Ibsen</lname>
    </employee>
    <employee>
      <emp_id>KFJ64308F</emp_id>
      <fname>Karin</fname>
      <minit>F</minit>
      <lname>Josephs</lname>
    </employee>
   </Publisher>
</Publishers>
</XML>
```

This contains several different levels of data. First we have the publishers, then for each publisher a list of employees and a list of sales. Then for each sale, there is a list of books sold. The diagram below shows this structure:

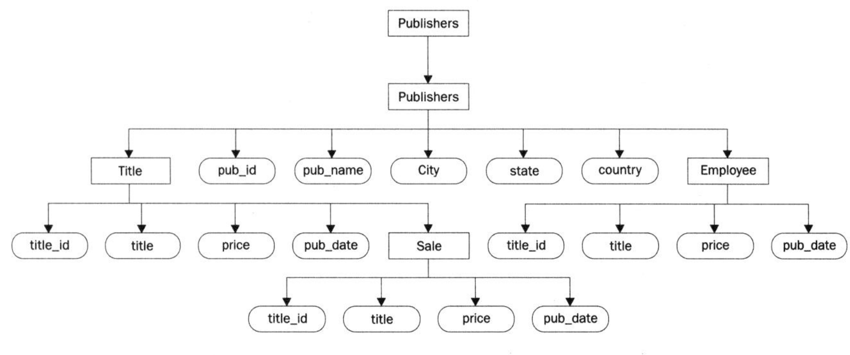

So, let's imagine that you have this hierarchical data in XML, and you want to enable it all to be viewed at once in the browser. What you're aiming to get is a top-level table containing just the publishers. For each publisher, there should be two sub-tables – one containing the employees, and one containing the sales. And for each sale, we should have another table detailing the books sold.

The only way you can bind to these multiple layers is to layer your binding. For the above XML you could do the following to give nested tables:

```
<TABLE ID="tblPublishers" DATASRC="#dsoPublishers" BORDER="1">
  <TBODY>
  <TR>
    <TD><DIV DATAFLD="pub_name"></DIV></TD>
    <TD><DIV DATAFLD="city"></DIV></TD>
    <TD><DIV DATAFLD="state"></DIV></TD>
  </TR>
  <TR>
    <TD COLSPAN=4>
      <TABLE>
        <TR>
          <TD>Titles</TD>
        </TR>
        <TR>
          <TD COLSPAN=4>
            <TABLE DATASRC="#dsoPublishers" DATAFLD="Title" BORDER="1">
              <TR>
                <TD><DIV DATAFLD="title"></DIV></TD>
                <TD><DIV DATAFLD="price"></DIV></TD>
              </TR>
              <TR>
                <TD COLSPAN=3>
                  <TABLE DATASRC="#dsoPublishers" DATAFLD="sale" BORDER="1">
                    <TR>
                      <TD><DIV DATAFLD="ord_date"></DIV></TD>
                      <TD><DIV DATAFLD="qty"></DIV></TD>
                    </TR>
                  </TABLE>
                </TD>
              </TR>
            </TABLE>
          </TD>
        </TR>
        <TR>
          <TD>Employees</TD>
        </TR>
        <TR>
          <TD COLSPAN=4>
            <TABLE DATASRC="#dsoPublishers" DATAFLD="Employee" BORDER="1">
              <TR>
                <TD><DIV DATAFLD="fname"></DIV></TD>
                <TD><DIV DATAFLD="lname"></DIV></TD>
              </TR>
            </TABLE>
          </TD>
        </TR>
      </TABLE>
    </TD>
  </TR>
  </TBODY>
</TABLE>
```

This has several bound tables, using successive levels in the XML data as the source of data. What you end up with is something like this:

Remember that all we've done is add some bound tables to the HTML – the XML data island supplies the data. Now this doesn't look too nice, but with a little bit of formatting you can achieve really good-looking results:

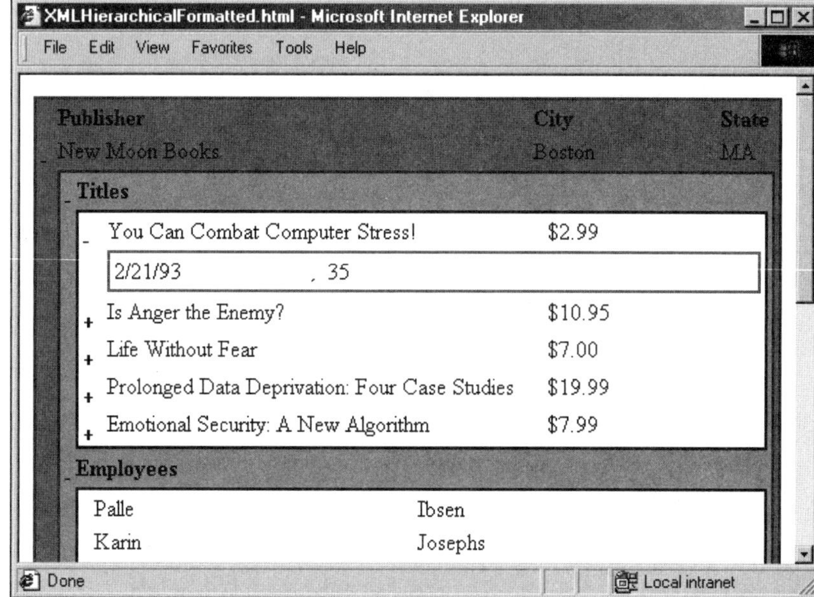

If you find your HTML binding getting a little confusing you can include the levels of the hierarchy in the `DATAFLD` attribute to make things a little clearer. For example:

```
<TABLE ID="tblPublishers" DATASRC="#dsoPublishers">
  <TABLE DATASRC="#dsoPublishers" DATAFLD="Title">
    <TABLE DATASRC="#dsoPublishers" DATAFLD="Title.sale">
  <TABLE DATASRC="#dsoPublishers" DATAFLD="Employee">
```

This doesn't change the way anything works, but it makes it clear where the `sale` field sits in the hierarchy.

Saving Recordsets as XML

Using ADO you can easily generate XML recordsets by using the `Save` method of the Recordset object, and specifying the format as `adPersistXML`. This isn't new to ADO 2.5, but what is new is the ability to persist hierarchical recordsets, and to persist them directly into other objects, such as streams and DOM objects.

This opens up all sorts of possibilities for the manipulation and transfer of data, since you're no longer just limited to creating text files containing XML data. Why is this a good thing? Well, as a programmer you want two things:

- An easy way to generate data
- A fast way to transfer data

Creating text files is easy, but slow. It involves writing the file to the disk, and then reading the data back in to manipulate it. What you need is a way to eliminate as much of the slow processing as possible. Anything that makes your life easier has to be a good thing.

Persisting ADO Recordsets to XML Files

The simplest method of converting ADO recordsets to XML is a method that's been in previous versions of ADO:

```
rsAuthors.Save "C:\temp\authors.xml"
```

There's nothing new about this, but I've included it here so that you can see how it compares to the other methods.

Persisting ADO Recordsets to a Stream

A **Stream** is simply a block of data in memory, which is not processed in any way. ADO 2.5 introduces the new Stream object, and this can be the target for saving a recordset:

```
Set rsAuthors = Server.CreateObject("ADODB.Recordset");
Set stmAuthors = Server.CreateObject("ADODB.Stream");

rsAuthors.Open "authors", strConn

rsAuthors.Save stmAuthors, adPersistXML
```

You now have a Stream object containing the XML recordset, and you can use the methods and properties of the stream to manipulate the data. For example, you can extract the XML into a string using the `ReadText` method:

```
strXMLAuthors = stmAuthors.ReadText
```

At this stage `strXMLAuthors` contains the complete XML recordset, including the schema.

Persisting ADO Recordsets to the Response Object

The other way to think of streams is to be more literal. One of the definitions my dictionary has for a stream is 'a flow or moving succession of anything'. So, let's think of a stream of data as a flow of data from one place to another. Now let's think of sending this data from our ASP page to the browser – that's a flow of data too.

The way we do this is by using a new feature of the Response object, which has built in support for Streams. So we want to pour our data into one end of the stream, and have it end up at the other end. Our end is the Response object, and the other end is the browser. Because of the integrated support for streams in the Response object, we can do this:

```
rsAuthors.Save Response, adPersistXML
```

This saves the recordset as XML directly into the Response object. The Response object then handles the sending of the data to the browser. Pretty cool huh? But what use is it? Well at time of writing it's not as much use as you'd think.

Creating XML Data Islands (or not as the case is)

It seems like this would be an ideal way to create data islands, but as I found out, it's not quite as simple as just saving the XML to the Response object. In fact, it's not really possible without going to a great deal of trouble.

The problem revolves around the fact that an XML data island is an HTML tag, with two attributes:

- `ID` – The normal HTML ID attribute, to uniquely identify elements
- `SRC` – To identify the source XML file

If creating a data island manually, you can therefore do this:

```
<XML ID="dsoData" SRC="authors.xml"></XML>
```

You can also place the XML directly between the `XML` tags, instead of using the `SRC` attribute:

```
<XML ID="dsoData">
  <Authors>
  . . .
  </Authors>
</XML>
```

This latter method seems perfect for creating a data island. For example, if we have an ASP page with the following ASP code:

```
<%
  Dim rsAuthors
  Set rsAuthors = Server.CreateObject("ADODB.Recordset")

  rsAuthors.Open "authors", strConn

  rsAuthors.Save Response, adPersistXML

  rsAuthors.Close
  Set rsAuthors = Nothing
%>
```

Then what we get in our HTML page is this:

```
<xml xmlns:s="uuid:BDC6E3F0-6DA3-11d1-A2A3-00AA00C14882"
     xmlns:dt="uuid:C2F41010-65B3-11d1-A29F-00AA00C14882"
     xmlns:rs="urn:schemas-microsoft-com:rowset"
     xmlns:z="#RowsetSchema">
 <s:Schema id="RowsetSchema">
  <s:ElementType name="row" content="eltOnly">
   <s:AttributeType name="au_id" rs:number="1" rs:writeunknown="true">
 . . .
  </s:ElementType>
 </s:Schema>
 <rs:data>
  <z:row au_id="172-32-1176" au_lname="White" au_fname="Johnson"
         phone="408 496-7223" address="10932 Bigge Rd."
         city="Menlo Park" state="CA" zip="94025" contract="True" />
  . . .
 </rs:data>
</xml>
```

I've cut out some of the data so you can see it more easily. At first this looks like a data island, but it hasn't got an ID attribute, so we wouldn't be able to bind any fields to it. This isn't too much of a problem because we can add attributes to HTML elements. We could either do this in the browser, in client-side script as the page loads, or even in the ASP code before we send the XML to the client. I won't show you how to do this because it doesn't actually solve anything.

What we have to remember is that a data island is an HTML tag, and this gives us two problems:

- The data within the XML is invalid because there are two root elements – `s:Schema` and `rs:data`.
- Any attributes that are not part of the XML tag are ignored. So all of the namespace information (the `xmlns` attributes) are ignored, which renders the XML it contains invalid.

The next logical step is to place an XML tag around our piece of ASP code, like so:

```
<XML ID="dsoAuthors">
<%
  Dim rsAuthors
  Set rsAuthors = Server.CreateObject("ADODB.Recordset")

  rsAuthors.Open "authors", strConn

  rsAuthors.Save Response, adPersistXML

  rsAuthors.Close
  Set rsAuthors = Nothing
%>
</XML>
```

This now gives us the following in the browser:

```
<XML ID="dsoAuthors">
  <xml xmlns:s="uuid:BDC6E3F0-6DA3-11d1-A2A3-00AA00C14882"
       xmlns:dt="uuid:C2F41010-65B3-11d1-A29F-00AA00C14882"
       xmlns:rs="urn:schemas-microsoft-com:rowset"
       xmlns:z="#RowsetSchema">
    <s:Schema id="RowsetSchema">
     <s:ElementType name="row" content="eltOnly">
      <s:AttributeType name="au_id" rs:number="1" rs:writeunknown="true">
    . . .
     </s:ElementType>
    </s:Schema>
    <rs:data>
     <z:row au_id="172-32-1176" au_lname="White" au_fname="Johnson"
            phone="408 496-7223" address="10932 Bigge Rd."
            city="Menlo Park" state="CA" zip="94025" contract="True" />
     . . .
    </rs:data>
  </xml>
</XML>
```

Logic dictates that this should work, but unfortunately you cannot have a tag named XML within a data island.

OK, so if we can't have the inner tag called XML why don't we rename it in our ASP code. We could load the XML into the DOM and change the nodeName property. Once again we are stumped though, because the top-level element in the DOM cannot have its name changed.

So where does this leave us? It seems that saving a recordset directly to the Response object won't let us create a data island. I suspect this is just because of the different ways that ADO and IE have evolved, and in future this will be much easier.

Don't think that it isn't possible though, because there are ways to create a data island, but they involve more than just the Recordset object. One of these is to use the DOM.

Persisting ADO Recordsets to a DOM Object

So far we've seen that you can save the recordset to a file or to the Response object. Another object that we can save a recordset to is a DOM object. Earlier in the chapter we mentioned the DOM and how it can be used to manipulate the XML. So, in our ASP code we could do this:

```
<%
  Dim rsAuthors
  Dim xmlDOM

  Set rsAuthors = Server.CreateObject("ADODB.Recordset")
  Set xmlDOM = Server.CreateObject("Microsoft.XMLDOM")

  rsAuthors.Open "authors", strConn

  rsAuthors.Save xmlDOM, adPersistXML
```

At this stage the DOM object, xmlDOM, contains the data from the recordset. This allows us to manipulate the data if we need to, before sending it to the browser. You'll see more examples of this when we look at styling, later in the chapter.

Using the DOM to Help Create a Data Island

One area where using the DOM is useful is in the creation of a data island. It's not a particularly elegant solution (many would call it a horrible hack), but it's quick, and works well. It revolves around that fact that we can access the XML from the DOM as a string:

```
rsAuthors.Save xmlDOM, adPersistXML

strXML = xmlDOM.xml
```

The variable strXML now contains the XML data. So how does this help us? Well, the problem we've had is that we can't have an <XML> tag within a data island, and we can't rename the root-level element. What we can do though, is manipulate the string:

```
strXML = "<xxx" & Mid(strXML, 5, Len(strXML) - 10) & "xxx>"
```

This relies on the fact that the XML starts with <xml and ends with xml>, so we just replace those portions of the string. It doesn't matter what you replace them with, as long as it's not XML.

So, our ASP code can now look like this:

```
<XML ID="dsoAuthors">
<%
  Dim rsAuthors
  Dim xmlDOM

  Set rsAuthors = Server.CreateObject("ADODB.Recordset")
  Set xmlDOM = Server.CreateObject("Microsoft.XMLDOM")

' Open the recordset
  rsAuthors.Open "authors", strConn

' Save it to a DOM object
  rsAuthors.Save xmlDOM, adPersistXML

' Close the recordset
  rsAuthors.Close
  Set rsAuthors = Nothing

' Extract the XMl as a string
  strXML = xmlDOM.xml

' Replace the xml tags with something else
  strXML = "<xxx" & Mid(strXML, 5, Len(strXML) - 10) & "xxx>"

' and send it back to the browser
  Response.Write strXML
%>
</XML>
```

See, I told you it was a hack! OK, it's not a great technical solution, but it does work, and fairly well. It allows us to create a data island from ASP fairly simply, and until the gap between ADO and IE closes, it's a pretty good solution.

Opening Recordsets

Since we've been given all of these great ways to save recordsets as XML, it seems natural that we have the opposite – a variety of ways to get XML into recordsets. One problem that we have to face though, is that ADO recordsets only recognize the Microsoft XML-Data schema. If your XML doesn't conform to this schema, then you cannot load it into a Recordset object. It's another of those rather annoying problems caused by a lack of flexibility in the XML support in ADO.

Opening a Recordset from an XML File

Loading a recordset from an XML file is as simple as saving it was:

```
rsAuthors.Open "authors.xml"
```

This simply opens the XML file, and parses it into a recordset. The file name you supply must be a physical path.

Opening a Recordset from the Request Object

We mentioned earlier that streams had been added to the Response object, and they've also been added to the Request. This means that you can do this sort of thing:

```
rsData.Open Request, , , , adCmdFile
```

So what good is this? Well, you combine this with the XMLHTTP object, a new object introduced in IE 5.0. XMLHTTP is designed to allow XML data to be sent to and from Web servers using the HTTP protocol. All that Microsoft has done is to wrap up some HTTP functionality into an object, to make it easy for us to use. We're not going to explain much about the XMLHTTP object, so for more information consult the IE5 documentation or the MSDN.

This object allows us to post XML from a client application to an ASP page. Here's an example of a client page that would do this:

```
<XML ID="dsoData" SRC="authors.xml"></XML>

<BUTTON ID="cmdUpdateAll" TITLE="Save All Changes"
    ONCLICK="postXML()">Save</BUTTON>


<SCRIPT LANGUAGE="JScript">

function postXML()
{
  var xmlhttp = new ActiveXObject("Microsoft.XMLHTTP");
  xmlhttp.open("POST", "XMLReadFromRequest.asp", false);
  xmlhttp.send(dsoData.XMLDocument);
}

</SCRIPT>
```

In this example, we initialize a request with the `open` method, specifying the HTTP method to use, and the URL to connect to. The final `false` indicates that asynchronous communication is not being used. We then use the send method to send the contents of the XML data island to the designated URL.

The result of this `POST` method is a stream of XML being sent to a URL. In the example above we've specified an ASP page, and the XML comes into this ASP page in the Request object, because it's a normal HTTP request. This means we can do this:

```
rsData.Open Request, , , , adCmdFile
```

Opening a Recordset from a DOM Object

Although you can save recordsets directly into XML DOM objects, you can't open recordsets directly from them. This does seem rather odd given the Stream support built into these objects, but luckily there's a way around this problem. It's a little bit convoluted, and involves a Stream object.

What you can do is save the XML from a DOM object into a Stream object, and then open the Recordset from the Stream. The result is the same, but it just involves an extra step. An example is below:

```
Set rsData = Server.CreateObject("ADODB.Recordset")
Set stmData = Server.CreateObject("ADODB.Stream")
Set domXML = Server.CreateObject("MSXML.DOMDocument")

' Open a normal recordset
rsData.Open "authors", strConn

' Save it into an XML DOM object
rsData.Save domXML, adPersistXML
rsData.Close

' Now start the process of opening the recordset based on the DOM
' First open an empty stream
stmData.Open

' Write the XML into the stream
stmData.WriteText domXML.xml

' Mark the end of the stream
stmData.SetEOS

' Reposition back to the start of the stream
stmData.Position = 0

' Open the recordset based upon the stream
rsData.Open stmData
```

It's a bit of a long-winded solution, but works well enough. Again I suspect this is one of those areas that will get better over time, and the method shown above may become redundant as better solutions are implemented within ADO.

A beneficial side effect of this is that you can easily duplicate a recordset with a modified version of this code. Listed below is a Visual Basic example, perhaps for use in a component:

```
Function DuplicateRecordset(rsData As ADODB.Recordset) As ADODB.Recordset

   Dim stmData As ADODB.Stream
   Dim rstNewData As ADODB.Recordset

   Set stmData = New ADODB.Stream
   Set rstNewData = New ADODB.Recordset

   rsData.Save stmData

   rsNewData.Open stmData

   Set DuplicateRecordset = rsNewData

End Function
```

This isn't a major piece of coding, but it might be useful if you need a copy of a recordset. Unlike cloning, where you have a single recordset and two references to it, this creates an entirely new copy of the recordset.

Styling XML with XSL

XSL stands for **eXtensible Styling Language**, and is an XML-based language to allow you to transform XML data. This transformation can be between one format of XML and another, or from XML to HTML or from XML to any type of text output.

One of the reasons for XSL is that XML is purely about data. We've already said XML tags just identify the data, unlike HTML where the tags indicate the layout. For this reason, if you want to display XML data you need to style it in some way.

XSL is actually made up of two parts – a **transformation language** and a **formatting language**, and it's the transformation half we're going to concentrate on here. Why? Simply because XSL is not yet a defined standard, which means that support for it in the major browsers is not complete. None of the major browsers support the formatting side of XSL, and many don't support the transformation side either.

When Microsoft released IE5 they built in support for XSL transformations at a level that was set by the standard at the time. Since then the standard has moved on and Microsoft have rightly decided not to update their XSL support until the standard is ratified. This means that IE5 doesn't support the formatting, but it does support a subset of the transformation language.

> *If you want to use the latest versions of XSL then there are XSL parsers available that are kept up-to-date with the standard. Although the W3C web site (`www.w3c.org`) details the current status of the XSL standard, the Web site at `www.oasis-open.org/cover/xsl.html` keeps track of the standard as well as listing software and articles on XSL.*

XSL Stylesheets

The idea behind XSL is that we have a set of rules that match elements or attributes in the XML. These rules are known as templates, and within a template you can loop through elements and attributes, apply other templates and perform other types of processing. Any text that is not part of an XSL processing instruction is output, so this is how you transform XML – by matching elements and outputting text and element values.

Let's consider the authors XML file generated from ADO that we've used earlier in this chapter. What we're going to look at is how we can transform this XML into an HTML table. We're not going to cover XSL in detail, since it's quite a large topic and outside the scope of this book, but we do want to give you an idea of what can be done with it. One of these is transforming XML into HTML.

The first thing to understand is that XSL is a form of XML, and is therefore made up of a series of tags. The top-level tag of a stylesheet is shown below:

```
<xsl:stylesheet xmlns:xsl="http://www.w3.org/TR/WD-xsl">
```

This identifies the stylesheet and the namespace, which applies to it. Since this is XML, the end of the stylesheet should have a finishing tag:

```
</xsl:stylesheet>
```

Within the stylesheet, the tags take the form of templates, which match portions of the XML document. The idea is that you match XML tags, and then you can output the values of the tags, along with other text. Let's look at a simple stylesheet to see how it works:

```
<xsl:stylesheet xmlns:xsl="http://www.w3.org/TR/WD-xsl">

<xsl:template match="/">

  <HTML>
  <BODY>

  <xsl:apply-templates select="//rs:data" />

  </BODY>
  </HTML>

</xsl:template>

<xsl:template match="//rs:data">

  <TABLE BORDER="1">
  <xsl:for-each select="z:row">
    <TR>
    <xsl:for-each select="(@*)">
      <TD>
      <xsl:value-of/>
      </TD>
    </xsl:for-each>
    </TR>
  </xsl:for-each>
  </TABLE>

</xsl:template>

</xsl:stylesheet>
```

This stylesheet converts an ADO recordset in XML into an HTML table. Let's look at in detail. We start with the stylesheet declaration:

```
<xsl:stylesheet xmlns:xsl="http://www.w3.org/TR/WD-xsl">
```

The first command is a `template` command telling us which element we should `match`. In this case we are matching the root element, denoted by the / symbol:

```
<xsl:template match="/">
```

At this stage we have started the processing of the XML tree. If we are converting this to HTML we need to output the HTML tags that start an HTML document:

```
  <HTML>
  <BODY>
```

Now we need to find the actual data. If you flick back to our examination of recordsets in XML format, you'll remember the recordset data is held under the `rs:data` element, so we use `apply-templates` to search for another template. This template will be applied, and once all processing in it has completed, processing returns to the current template:

```
<xsl:apply-templates select="//rs:data" />
```

After the inner template has been processed we can finish off our HTML document:

```
  </BODY>
  </HTML>

</xsl:template>
```

Now come the real guts of the stylesheet, where we process the data:

```
<xsl:template match="//rs:data">
```

If you'll remember, all the data is held under the `rs:data` element, and each row is held in a `z:row` element. The fields are held within attributes of the row. The first thing to do is output the `<HTML>` tag to start the table:

```
  <TABLE BORDER="1">
```

We'll need to process each row of data, since this will become a row in the HTML table. For this we use the `for-each` statement, which is much the same as a `for..each` loop in VBScript. The `select` part of the statement tells XSL which elements to loop though – in this case each `z:row`:

```
  <xsl:for-each select="z:row">
```

We are now in a row of data, so we can output the HTML row start:

```
    <TR>
```

Now we need to process the attributes, since these correspond to the fields of our recordset. Again we use the `for-each` construct, but this time our `select` is different. We want to match each attribute, no matter what it is called. In fact, if this routine is to process any set of ADO generated XML, then we won't know what the names of any rows, elements, attributes, etc. are, so we use the `*` as a wildcard. This just matches everything. To match an attribute we have to use the `@` symbol, so `@*` means match every attribute:

```
        <xsl:for-each select="(@*)">
```

Next comes the start of the HTML table cell:

```
          <TD>
```

Inside the table cell we want the value of the attribute. The `value-of` instruction tells XSL to output the value of a node, and since we are not stating anything specific to output, the value of the current node is output:

```
          <xsl:value-of/>
```

Now we hit the end of the loops, closing the tables cells, the table row, and finally the table:

```
          </TD>
        </xsl:for-each>
        </TR>
      </xsl:for-each>
      </TABLE>


    </xsl:template>

    </xsl:stylesheet>
```

Although this might not seem easy, it's not so far away from normal programming rules. It looks odd because it's all specified in XML, and the syntax is based around matching nodes in the XML, but things like the looping are pretty close to standard programming practices.

Embedded Styling

The easiest way to apply an XSL stylesheet is to specify it in the XML file. All this involves is putting the following line at the top of your XML file:

```
<?xml-stylesheet type="text/xsl href="RecordsetToTable.xsl"?>
```

For an ASP programmer this is isn't very flexible, since it means physically creating an XML file and editing it to put the stylesheet reference in.

Dynamic Styling

Instead of embedding the stylesheet into the XML you can apply it dynamically. One way of doing this is in an ASP page before sending the XML to the browser. For example:

```
<%
  Dim rsAuthors
  Dim domXML
  Dim domStyle

' Create the objects
  Set rsAuthors = Server.CreateObject("ADODB.Recordset")
  Set domXML = Server.CreateObject("Microsoft.XMLDOM")
  Set domStyle = Server.CreateObject("Microsoft.XMLDOM")

' Open the recordset
  rsAuthors.Open "authors", strConn

' Save the recordset to a DOM
  rsAuthors.Save domXML, adPersistXML
  rsAuthors.Close

' Open the stylesheet
  domStyle.Load Server.MapPath("RecordsetToTable.xsl")

' Transform the XML
  domXML.TransformNodeToObject domStyle, Response

' Tidy up
  Set rsAuthors = Nothing
  Set domXML = Nothing
  Set domStyle = Nothing
%>
```

This doesn't differ that much from some of the code you've already seen in both this and the previous chapter. Once again, we've created a recordset and persisted it into an XML DOM object. The difference is that we've then loaded the stylesheet into another XML DOM object, and used the `TransformNodeToObject` method to apply the stylesheet.

The advantage of the above method is that it sends pure HTML to the client, which is great if you need to use XML data but have to support browsers that can't process XML. If you know your users have browsers that support XML (in an Intranet for example), then you can also perform the transformation on the client.

The example below uses three data islands. The first holds the XML data, and the second two hold stylesheets – remember that they are just XML, so it's perfectly valid to do this. One stylesheet transforms the XML into a table, and the other transforms the XML into a list:

```
<XML ID="dsoAuthors" SRC="authors.xml" HEIGHT="0" WIDTH="0"></XML>
<XML ID="styleTable" SRC="RecordsetToTable.xsl"></XML>
<XML ID="styleList" SRC="RecordsetToList.xsl"></XML>
```

We then have two buttons, to call the function that will perform the styling:

```
<BUTTON ID="cmdStyleOne" onClick="applyStyle('styleTable')">Recordset</BUTTON>
<BUTTON ID="cmdStyleTwo" onClick="applyStyle('styleList')">List</BUTTON>
```

Next we have a DIV element, which is where the table or list will be shown:

```
<P>
<DIV ID="txtResult"></DIV>
```

Finally, we come to the function that performs the transformation. This uses the transformNode method of the data source to apply the selected stylesheet to the XML data. The result is displayed in the DIV element:

```
<SCRIPT LANGUAGE=JScript>

function applyStyle(sStyle)
{
  var strStyle = document.all(sStyle).XMLDocument;
  txtResult.innerHTML = dsoAuthors.transformNode(strStyle);
}

</SCRIPT>
```

This is quite a useful approach if you want to perform the transformation at the client. Although it depends on IE, it does remove the load from the Web server, and gives the user more flexibility, as they get to choose the format they view the data in.

Related Areas

There are many areas surrounding XML that are not defined standards, and are still being worked on by various committees.

- **XSL**. It's important to remember that XSL is still evolving, and has yet to be defined as a standard. Once settled it's likely that future browsers will take it into account.
- **XHTML** – Extensible HyperText Markup Language – is what HTML should have been. One great difference between HTML and XML is strictness. HTML is very loose with some of the elements not require a closing element (LI and BR for example), and attributes don't have to be enclosed in quotes. XML, on the other hand, is very strong, and requires closing tags for all elements and quote to surround all attributes. XHTML simply applies these string rules to HTML. Why? Well for a start it adds an extra degree of standardization. The other benefit is that it means XHTML files can be easily processed by an XML parser, because it conforms to XML syntax rules. XHTML relies heavily on HTML 4.01, which adds a lot of these facilities to HTML.
- **XLink and XPointer** are extensions to XML to allow linking between XML documents. XLink allows roughly the same functionality as HTML references using the <A> tag. XPointer allows links single or multiple locations of a target resource, each of which can be any section of the document. This extends the functionality of existing linking schemes, and provides a more flexible, and efficient solution.
- **Formatting Objects** is the second part of the XSL styling specification, and is designed to introduce a set of standard tags for the formatting of objects. The idea is that these will provide a display independent description of the formatting, as opposed to HTML elements which are a mix of description and layout.
- **BizTalk** is a framework designed by Microsoft as a way of using XML in a consistent way. The idea is to define a standard set of XML tags for common business scenarios. It's the start of a central repository of XML tag specifications. To find out more on BizTalk check out www.biztalk.org.

The XML Technology Preview for SQL Server

Shortly before this book was going to the printers, Microsoft released a preview of how XML data can be retrieved from SQL Server. It's called the XML Technology Preview for SQL Server, and takes the form of an ISAPI DLL, which sits between the Web server and SQL Server. This DLL converts SQL queries into XML and XML back into SQL data. The flexibility of this DLL is extremely high, and it looks to be very powerful.

This list of features include:

- Extracting XML in both row format (as used by ADO) and element format
- The ability to include a DTD with the XML data
- The ability to include a Schema with the XML data
- The ability to insert, delete and update the data via XML

We're not going to look at this in detail since it's a preview, but it's quite exciting and gives great promise for the future, and could make the use of XML data a lot easier. Just using the tool from a browser gives us the following:

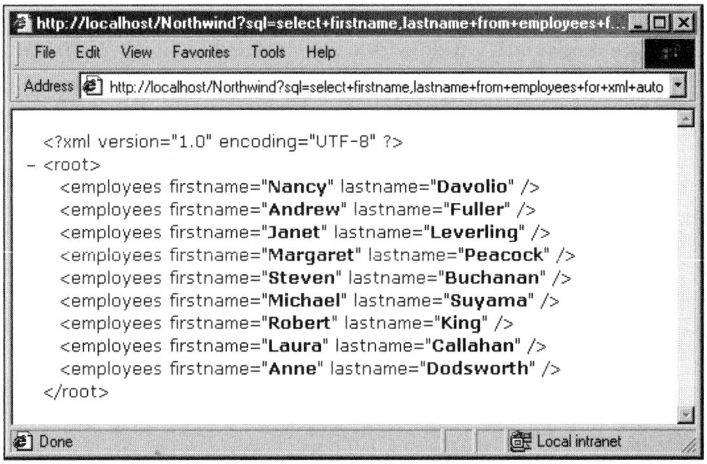

```
http://localhost/Northwind?sql=select+firstname,lastname+from+employees+f...
File  Edit  View  Favorites  Tools  Help
Address  http://localhost/Northwind?sql=select+firstname,lastname+from+employees+for+xml+auto

  <?xml version="1.0" encoding="UTF-8" ?>
- <root>
    <employees firstname="Nancy" lastname="Davolio" />
    <employees firstname="Andrew" lastname="Fuller" />
    <employees firstname="Janet" lastname="Leverling" />
    <employees firstname="Margaret" lastname="Peacock" />
    <employees firstname="Steven" lastname="Buchanan" />
    <employees firstname="Michael" lastname="Suyama" />
    <employees firstname="Robert" lastname="King" />
    <employees firstname="Laura" lastname="Callahan" />
    <employees firstname="Anne" lastname="Dodsworth" />
  </root>

Done                                   Local intranet
```

This relies on a Virtual Directory called `Northwind` being set up with the Technology Preview registration tool. This creates the virtual directory, and ensures that the new ISAPI DLL handles all requests coming into that directory. This processes the `SQL` command, sends it to SQL server, and then returns the SQL data to us, formatted as XML. If you don't like the format of the XML, and want a more traditional element based layout, then just add `,elements` to the end of your query:

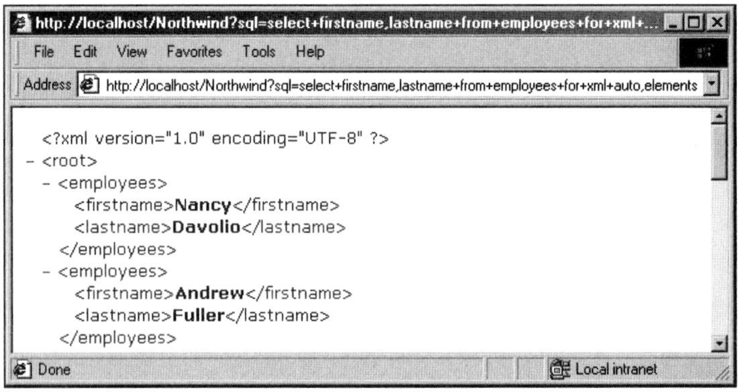

```
http://localhost/Northwind?sql=select+firstname,lastname+from+employees+for+xml+...
File  Edit  View  Favorites  Tools  Help
Address  http://localhost/Northwind?sql=select+firstname,lastname+from+employees+for+xml+auto,elements

  <?xml version="1.0" encoding="UTF-8" ?>
- <root>
  - <employees>
      <firstname>Nancy</firstname>
      <lastname>Davolio</lastname>
    </employees>
  - <employees>
      <firstname>Andrew</firstname>
      <lastname>Fuller</lastname>
    </employees>

Done                                   Local intranet
```

As you've seen earlier in the chapter, we've tried to use ADO in ASP to create data islands, but have hit many problems. This new tool from Microsoft gives us the ability to do this:

```
<XML ID="dsoData"
     SRC="http://Kanga/pubs?sql=SELECT * FROM authors FOR xml AUTO">
</XML>
```

Pretty cool huh?

We're not going to look at this in any more detail for two reasons. Firstly it's very new, and secondly it's likely to change. However, what it does give us is a peek into what we might expect from some future Microsoft technologies.

If you'd like to download a copy of the XML Technology Preview for SQL Server, it's available on the MSDN site at `msdn.microsoft.com/workshop/xml/articles/xmlsql/default.asp`. It's less than 250K, so it won't take long to get hold of.

Summary

This chapter has really been a very quick look at what is already a large area, and one that is growing daily. XML does offer huge potential for the interchange of data, and it's like that XML will start cropping up in many areas.

As an ASP programmer dealing with data, and putting together Web applications, there's no doubt that you'll start seeing XML more and more. So, in this chapter we've covered the basics of XML and what it means to you. In particular, we've looked at:

- What XML actually is, and how it relates to data
- How XML and ADO interact
- How you can use the new Stream object to transfer recordsets between ADO and XML
- How to use XSL to transform your XML data into HTML

One thing we've seen is that the integration between some of the Microsoft technologies isn't as good as it should be. In some ways this is to be expected – they are developed by different teams with different timescales – but it doesn't make our lives any easier. One of the things I've tried to do in this chapter is show you what works and what doesn't, so that you'll spend less time working this out for yourself. It is frustrating, but Microsoft are working on this integration, and I believe that it's better to wait for all of the products to work in a uniform way, than for several solutions to be thrown into the market place at once.

We've really only had time to scratch the surface of some areas, partly because it's such a huge topic, and partly because the area is still under development. But don't be under any misconceptions – XML is here to stay.

N
W

12

Universal Data Access

Universal Data Access (UDA) is the name given to Microsoft's strategy for accessing data from a wide variety of sources. Now this isn't something you need to panic about – it's not some new fangled development technique that's going to mean changing everything you do. In fact, you're probably using parts of UDA at the moment. The last few chapters have been showing you how to use ADO to access data stores, most notably relational databases, and that's just a part of UDA. Data comes in many different forms, and the idea of UDA is that you can use OLE DB and ADO to access it.

In this chapter, we're going to look at what UDA means, and why we have to be concerned with it. In particular we'll look at:

- How UDA fits into the world of the Web developer
- The OLE DB Providers that will give us access to universal data
- What semi-structured data is, and how it can be used
- How Internet Publishing could change your life
- Data stores and ASP in the wider world of the enterprise

In reality this whole chapter is about the bigger, wider world, and how we can make it smaller.

The Dream of UDA

Universal Data Access really just means the ability to access different types of data using the same technique. It's not a new idea, and is an extension of the existing ODBC technology. ODBC was designed to provide a single way to access relational databases, and became the accepted standard for cross-database access.

However successful ODBC is, it leaves itself short in one particular area – data that isn't stored in a relational database. Whilst we do have ODBC access to text files and spreadsheets, this is really just a limited foray into a much bigger area. There are increasing amounts of data being stored in documents, financial systems, mail systems, and so on, and ODBC just isn't designed to access these. There's also a lot of legacy data, which doesn't fit neatly into the relational database format.

To overcome this problem Microsoft put forward UDA as a solution. The important thing to realize is that UDA is really just the name given to something Microsoft has been aiming at for several years. If my memory is correct, I first started looking at OLE DB in 1994, which is when the first (very shaky) betas were around giving access to ODBC data. Since then Microsoft has extended the reach of OLE DB to take into account not only relational databases, but also other data providers.

With ADO 2.5 we now have access to data in many different forms, but all accessed through the same set of simple objects. This truly makes the access universal – the same technique works in a variety of languages, sometimes with very little change.

The core of UDA is OLE DB. OLE DB learns from ODBC and takes it one step further. If you remember back to our first discussion of ADO, we talked about using OLE DB Providers to access data stores. We can now look at that diagram with a little more understanding:

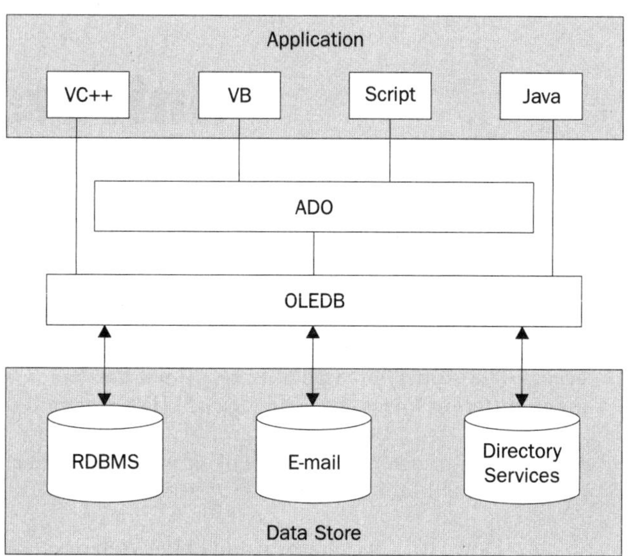

Here we see that rather than just using OLE DB to access databases, we can use it to access all sorts of different types of data. Now whilst most of your use of OLE DB will probably be relational databases, there's no reason not to think further afield.

OLE DB Providers

The only thing that limits your access to data is the availability of an OLE DB Provider. If one is available then you can use the normal OLE DB and ADO commands to get to the data. If the product vendor hasn't written a provider, then the odds are high that they're planning one for the future. It's a simple matter of business – if you want people to use your products then you have to provide easy access to the data.

OLE DB and ADO were explicitly developed to cater for multiple types of data, and for that data to be used in Web scenarios. The Web is still expanding, and ASP is becoming a more important part of the middle-tier of Web applications, so we need to take into account the different ways in which we store data for use with our Web server.

The use of OLE DB Providers allows us to expand our Web applications without having to learn new techniques. All we have to do is use a different Provider for each different type of data. There are many different types of providers, but what we want to look at here are the ones that allow access to data from sources that aren't relational databases. In particular, we'll look at the providers that allow integration of a variety of Microsoft technologies, and see how these can be used in our Web applications.

The Indexing Service

If your Web site provides access to information, then it's likely you'll want to give users some form of search ability. The **Indexing Service** integrates well with IIS, and there is an OLE DB Provider to allow read-only access to the Indexing Service catalog.

> *We're not going to be covering how to install the Indexing Service, other methods of using the Indexing Service, or its advanced capabilities.*

Anatomy of the Indexing Service

It is not much of a stretch to say that the Indexing Service is like a Database Management Server. Both hold information and allow access to that information via queries. The essential difference between Index Server and say, SQL Server, is that with SQL Server, somebody must populate the tables with data. The Indexing Service does this population for you. Understanding how exactly this process works can remain a *black-box* for most developers, however, you should understand at least the following:

- The most atomic part of Indexing Service is an **index entry**. If this were a record in a database table, it would simply be a key word and a reference to the document in which that key word was found. These records would be in one table in the database. Another table would contain all of the documents referenced by the first table, along with certain properties of those documents. These two table concepts are manifested in the Indexing Service as the **Word Lists** and **Saved Indexes.**

- With Index Server, discrete databases are known as **Catalogs.** Just as SQL Server can host multiple databases, the Indexing Service can host multiple Catalogs. Catalogs are usually tied to Internet-based services provided by the host computer. So for example, if you have a Web site and you also provide newsgroups with the NNTP service, you could have a Catalog for each. If you use virtual Web sites, each of these could have a Catalog as well.

When the service starts, it knows where to start looking for items to index, so it builds a list of files to be indexed. This activity is known as **scanning**. The items to be indexed can be anything that is stored as a file in a folder. The folder is usually configured as a virtual directory within the context of the service. This is known as **scope**.

Once the scanning process completes, the **filtering** process starts. During filtering, the Indexing Service attempts to open a candidate file. Once opened, the Indexing Service then attempts to **parse** the file apart and construct an index entry for each keyword. It also calculates other key parameters for the file. Parsing a file requires that the Indexing Service has some idea of how the file is structured. That information is collected into libraries known as **filters.** Microsoft has already developed filters for most types of content commonly found on Internet and Internet Services.

> *Vendors who use non-standard or non-Microsoft file formats also provide filters. For example, Adobe provides a filter for the PDF document standard. If you've invented your own 'file format' then you may be able to define a filter for it.*

Two more important concepts you need to understand are **characterizations** and **the document properties**.

Characterizations are, in a sense, abstracts (or executive summaries) of the document. The characterization is usually the first *n-many* characters of the renderable portions of the document. The renderable portion is generally that part of the document that is displayed (or rendered). For example, the characterization of an HTML page normally will be the content found between the `<BODY>` tags (naturally, there are painful exceptions to this). The Indexing Service allows you determine how large this characterization is. Generally speaking, the first 250 to 500 words of document should be sufficient. When returning the results of query from the Indexing Service, the characterization is the most frequently displayed information. Frequently, the beginning of the text is a good choice for display, in that it allows the user to determine quickly if this is really a document they want to drill into deeper or not.

However, a great deal of additional information about the document is also available from the Indexing Service as document properties. These properties are officially **ActiveX Document Properties**. The Indexing Service accounts for over forty such properties. The properties of most interest to those seeking to leverage the Index Service in their ASP applications, are the size of the file, date created, last accessed and last changed, and the location of the file.

The Indexing Service 3.0 vs. Index Server

If you developed ASP under IIS 3.0 or 4.0, you may have been wondering why I've been referring to Indexing Service and not **Index Server** – aren't they the same thing?

The answer to that is yes and no. The Indexing Service fulfils the same niche as Index Server – creating a searchable database of document references – but it does so differently from its predecessor. Along with this new name come some new and some changed abilities:

- Those of us who bemoaned Microsoft's decision to remove Index Server from NT Workstation under IIS 4.0 can rejoice: the Indexing Service is available under Windows 2000 Professional. In fact, in the Windows 2000 family, the familiar Start menu search option now uses Indexing Service when searching for folders or files.
- The result group is now available with the Query object. Using this method, you can ask the Indexing Service to return results grouped by a particular property.
- Additional dialects for constructing queries.

- Along with Web content, Indexing Service also maintains a Catalog for the files on the local file system. This is somewhat akin to the FastFind program in Microsoft Office.
- In previous versions of Index Server, the file system was scanned thoroughly at the start of the content indexing service. Now, when content to be indexed is placed on the new NTFS5 file system volumes, only the changed files are rescanned.
- Three new objects to assist with the upkeep of Indexing Service have joined the Query and Utility objects. These are the AdminIndexServer, the CatAdm and the ScopeAdm helper objects.

Searching the Indexing Catalog

One of the most awkward costs associated with using ADO to search the catalog is that you frequently must parse the users input to get the query to work correctly. Consider the search phrase "ASP ADO". This might mean, either:

- "Find all of the documents containing both ASP and ADO"
- "Find all of the documents containing either or ASP or ADO or both"
- "Find all of the pages containing ASP followed by ADO"

Most of the time users will assume a certain behavior, unless you make it clear that your program will do something different. And for every ten users, you may get three different expectations. Making this matter worse, simply passing "ASP ADO" in an ADO technique query generates an error:

```
Microsoft OLE DB Provider for Microsoft Indexing Service error '80040e14'
Incorrect syntax near 'ADO'. Expected '''. SQLSTATE=42000
```

Herein lies the rub of the problem. In most cases, you will need to parse the search term into individual terms and operators before including them in the SQL query. There are times that this can be a small price to pay for this feature. There are other times when it is simply not desirable. We will see how to parse phrase in more detail when we look at the SQL language under the Indexing Service.

Because the Indexing Service isn't a database, there are two main things to concern yourself with:

- The Indexing Service catalog is the `Data Source` for the connection
- The Indexing Service Provider uses extensions to the SQL language

To see how easy it is to query the Indexing Service, let's create a sample Web page. We'll start with a search form – `SearchForm.html`:

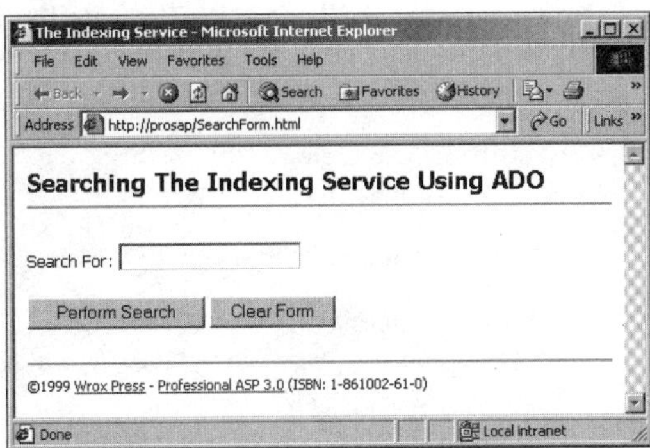

The HTML for this is quite simple:

```
<FORM Name="frmSearch" ACTION="QueryIndexServer.asp" METHOD="POST">
Search For: <INPUT TYPE="TEXT" NAME="txtSearchFor">
<P>
<INPUT TYPE="SUBMIT" VALUE="Perform Search">
<INPUT TYPE="RESET" VALUE="Clear Form">
</FORM>
```

This gives you a single text box, into which you can type your search criteria. Pressing the Perform Search button will call the ASP page `QueryIndexServer.asp`, which we'll look at now.

To start with, we include the file `Connection.asp`:

```
<%@ LANGUAGE=VBSCRIPT %>
<!-- #INCLUDE FILE="../Include/Connection.asp" -->
```

This contains the reference to the ADO type library, allowing us to use the ADO constants:

```
<!-- METADATA TYPE="typelib"
FILE="C:\Program Files\Common Files\System\ado\msado15.dll" -->
```

Next we define some CSS styles. These aren't necessary, but it allows us to format our output a little easier:

```
<HTML>
<HEAD>
<TITLE>The Indexing Service</TITLE>
<STYLE TYPE="text/css">
BODY       {font-family:Tahoma,Arial,sans-serif; font-size:10pt}
.heading   {font-family:Tahoma,Arial,sans-serif; font-size:14pt;
            font-weight:bold}
.cite      {font-family:Tahoma,Arial,sans-serif; font-size:8pt}
.document  {font-size:10pt; font-weight:bold;
            background-color:lightgrey; width:100%}
</STYLE>
</HEAD>
<BODY BGCOLOR="#FFFFFF">
<SPAN CLASS="heading">Results of search for
<I><%=Request.Form("txtSearchFor")%></I>
</SPAN><HR>
<!-------------------------------------------------------------------------->
```

Now comes the ASP code. We'll create the Recordset object and set the connection string. We'll explain the exact connection string in a little while:

```
<%
  Dim strSearch
  Dim rsSearch

  Set rsSearch = Server.CreateObject("ADODB.Recordset")

' Create the connection string
  strConn = "Provider=MSIDXS; Data Source=Web"
```

Then we construct our search string, which is a superset of the SQL language. We'll also cover that in more detail a little later:

```
' Construct the search string
  strSearch = "SELECT DocTitle, Path, FileName, Characterization, Size" & _
              " FROM SCOPE()" & _
              " WHERE CONTAINS ('" & Request.Form("txtSearchFor") & "')"
```

Next we open the recordset and loop through the records, displaying the results:

```
' Open the recordset on the search
  rsSearch.Open strSearch, strConn

' Show what's been searched for
  While Not rsSearch.EOF
    Response.Write "<SPAN CLASS='document'>" & _
                   rsSearch("DocTitle") & "</SPAN><BR>" & _
                   rsSearch("Characterization") & "<BR>" & _
                   "<A HREF='" & rsSearch("Path") & "'>" & _
                   rsSearch("FileName") & "</A>" & _
                   " (" & rsSearch("Size") & " bytes)<P>"
    rsSearch.MoveNext
  Wend

' Tidy up
  rsSearch.Close
  Set rsSearch = Nothing
%>

</BODY>
</HTML>
```

On my machine, selecting ado in the search form gives the following result (you might get different results, depending on which directories you have indexed, and the documents contained within those directories):

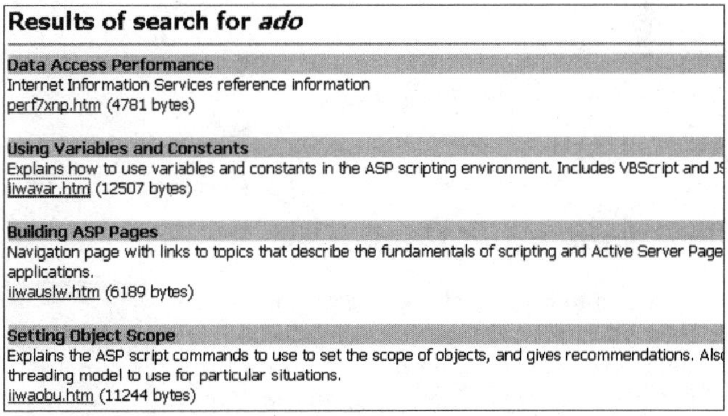

Results of search for *ado*

Data Access Performance
Internet Information Services reference information
perf7xnp.htm (4781 bytes)

Using Variables and Constants
Explains how to use variables and constants in the ASP scripting environment. Includes VBScript and J
iiwavar.htm (12507 bytes)

Building ASP Pages
Navigation page with links to topics that describe the fundamentals of scripting and Active Server Page applications.
iiwauslw.htm (6189 bytes)

Setting Object Scope
Explains the ASP script commands to use to set the scope of objects, and gives recommendations. Als threading model to use for particular situations.
iiwaobu.htm (11244 bytes)

Let's look at the two important bits of this code – the connection and the query.

Connecting to the Indexing Service with ADO

Like other ADO connection strings you've seen, the one for the Indexing Service specifies the OLE DB provider name and where the data comes from:

```
strConn = "Provider=MSIDXS; Data Source=Web"
```

The Data Source is the name of the Indexing Service catalog that you want to search. You can find the catalog names in the Computer Management Console (you can get to this by selecting the Manage item from the menu when you right-click on My Computer in Windows Explorer):

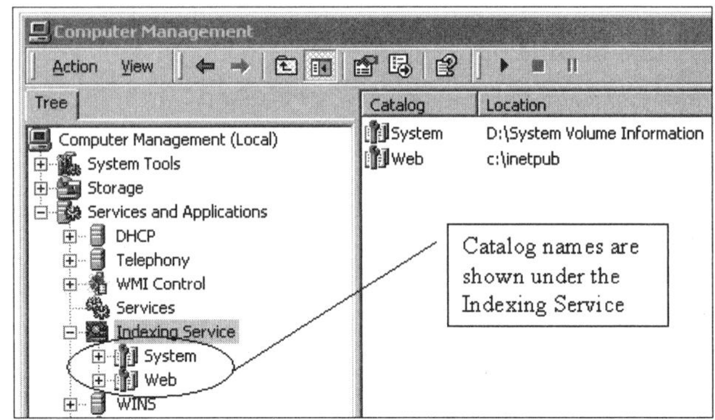

Search Strings for the Indexing Service

The search string is similar to a standard SQL query, but has special keywords. The concept is the same as searching from databases – first we pick what we want to see, then where we want to get it from, and then we add any criteria to limit the results.

We'll have a quick look at the query first, and then explain the detailed syntax.

The fields in the `SELECT` statement identify which properties are to be selected from the catalog:

```
strSearch = "SELECT DocTitle, Path, FileName, Characterization, Size" & _
```

Next comes the `FROM` clause, indicating where the data is to come from. In this case `SCOPE` with no arguments gives unlimited scope to the search, so all of the catalog entries are checked (this is explained in more detail in *The From Clause* section below):

```
" FROM SCOPE()" & _
```

And finally we need to say what we're looking for, so we use `CONTAINS` to search for documents that contain a certain string:

```
" WHERE CONTAINS ('" & Request.Form("txtSearchFor") & "')"
```

Field Names and Properties

If you're new to the Indexing Service, then you probably won't know what fields are available, but it's easy to find out because they are all listed in the Indexing Service administration tool:

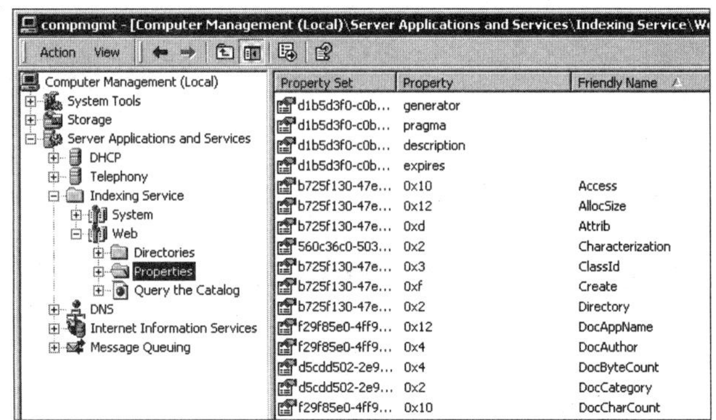

You can use the Friendly Name or the Property name as the field name.

Note that this technique only applies to the Indexing Service Provider, and not other OLE DB Providers.

Let's now look at how the Indexing Service SQL differs from the standard SQL.

The SELECT Clause

The `SELECT` clause is just a matter of selecting the field names from the list of available property names.

*You might be tempted to use `SELECT *` instead of defining individual column names. However, the OLE DB provider will throw an error if you are querying the Catalog as we do here if you try this. The * selection is only valid for Views of Indexing Service Catalogs.*

The FROM Clause

The `FROM` clause allows us to select where in the catalog the information is to come from, and is slightly different from some of the standard SQL `FROM` clauses. There are three different methods of using the `FROM` clause:

- Predefined views
- Custom views
- Using a scope

Predefined Views

The first method of selecting columns is to use a **predefined view** name – the view is just an alias for some fields. For example:

```
SELECT *
FROM   FILEINFO_ABSTRACT
```

The list of predefined views is shown below:

Predefined View	Fields/Properties
`FILEINFO`	path, FileName, size, write, attrib
`FILEINFO_ABSTRACT`	path, FileName, size, write, attrib, Characterization
`EXTENDED_FILEINFO`	path, FileName, size, write, attrib, DocTitle, DocAuthor, DocSubject, DocKeywords, Characterization
`WEBINFO`	Vpath, path, FileName, size, write, attrib, Characterization, DocTitle

Table Continued on Following Page

Predefined View	Fields/Properties
EXTENDED_WEBINFO	Vpath, path, FileName, size, Characterization, write, DocAuthor, DocSubject, DocKeywords, DocTitle
SSWEBINFO	URL, DocTitle, Rank, size, write
SSEXTENDED_WEBINFO	URL, DocTitle, Rank, HitCount, DocAuthor, Characterization, size, write

The predefined views are really just a shortcut, allowing you to select all columns from a predefined set of columns. You could equally well select the column names yourself and not use the views.

Custom Views

The second method uses a **custom created view**, and takes the same form as predefined views:

```
SELECT *
FROM   MyViewName
```

We're not going to cover the creation of custom views here: consult the Indexing Service documentation for more details.

Using a Scope

The third method is one that includes the **scope** of the search. The scope really just indicates the directories to include and the depth to go to in the search. The simplest form of this is the empty scope:

```
FROM SCOPE()
```

This states that the root of the catalog is the start for the search, and that all directories under it are to be searched. If you wish to limit the search you can add the directory names into the scope:

```
FROM SCOPE ('D:\users\davids')
```

This would only return items from the catalog in the selected directory, and any directories underneath it. If you wish to limit the search to only the selected directory, and not the subdirectories, then you can add the **traversal type**:

```
FROM SCOPE('SHALLOW TRAVERSAL OF "D:\users\davids"')
```

The traversal types are:

- `SHALLOW TRAVERSAL OF` – if you want to only search the specified paths
- `DEEP TRAVERSAL OF` – if you want to search the specified paths, plus all sub-directories

You can also specify multiple scopes:

```
FROM SCOPE('SHALLOW TRAVERSAL OF "D:\users\davids",
           'DEEP TRAVERSAL OF "D:\users\janine"')
```

If no depth is specified then a `DEEP TRAVERSAL` is the default. And you're not limited to physical paths – you can also use virtual paths in the directory. For example:

```
FROM SCOPE('DEEP TRAVERSAL OF "/ProASP")'
```

This uses the virtual path `ProASP` as the root of the search.

The WHERE Clause

As well as the standard comparisons, the `WHERE` clause has a list of predicates to cater for searching. These are:

`ARRAY` Uses logical operators to compare two arrays. This is useful for fields that have a type that is array based, such as the attributes property of a file.

`CONTAINS` Allows matching of words or phrases. For example, the following line matches documents that contain `ADO` or `RDS`:

```
WHERE CONTAINS("ADO" OR "RDS")
```

The example below matches documents where `ADO` is within 50 words of `RDS`:

```
WHERE CONTAINS("ADO" NEAR "RDS")
```

And this example matches `drink`, `drinking`, `drunk`, etc.

```
WHERE CONTAINS('FORMSOF(INFLECTIONAL, "drink")')
```

`FREETEXT` Specifies searching for the best match for the words and phrases. For example:

```
WHERE FREETEXT('programming ADO')
```

`LIKE` Uses wildcards to perform matches. For example:

```
WHERE DocAuthor LIKE 'Al%'
```

`MATCHES` Uses regular expressions to perform matches. For example:

```
WHERE MATCHES (DocAuthor, "[a-e]*"
```

This searches for all entries where the `DocAuthor` starts with any character between `a` and `e`.

`NULL` Allows matching of null values. For example:

```
WHERE DocAuthor IS NULL
```

```
WHERE DocAuthor IS NOT NULL
```

All of these selection methods give you a great deal of control over searching through catalogs with very little effort.

For more detailed information you should consult the Indexing Service documentation.

Active Directory

The OLE DB Provider for Active Directory is not new to Windows 2000, but it's only with Windows 2000 that Active Directory is fully implemented. The term you might be more familiar with is **ADSI – Active Directory Services Interface**. ADSI is the programming interface to Active Directory.

We're not going to be discussing ADSI in real detail here, because it's covered in Chapter 21. What we want to do here is give a taster of how ADSI and ADO can interact.

Active Directory is a directory service for Windows 2000 that manages the resources of a machine or a group of machines. In practice this means that there is a single source for all resource information, and the fact that there is an OLE DB Provider for Active Directory means that you can use your existing knowledge to access this resource information.

Using the OLE DB Provider is quite simple, as long as you understand a bit about Active Directory. Most of the samples show a rather strange syntax for accessing directory information – a sample query looks like this:

```
<LDAP://localhost>; ((objectClass=user));adspath;subtree
```

This lists all of the users on the local machine – not particularly intuitive is it? Luckily, there's a SQL style syntax too:

```
SELECT ADsPath, cn FROM 'LDAP://localhost' WHERE objectCategory='user'
```

This outputs exactly the same information, but is much easier to understand, certainly for someone who doesn't know much about the directory querying language.

The directory querying language is covered in the Active Directory documentation.

Paths

The first thing to understand about directory services is the need for paths to uniquely identify an ADSI object. The first part of a path identifies the directory service provider. For example:

- `LDAP`, for Lightweight Directory Access Protocol
- `WinNT`, for Windows NT
- `NDS`, for Netware Directory Services
- `NWCOMPAT`, for Netware compatibility

The second part of the path identifies the namespace, which may be different for each directory service provider. Some full examples are shown below:

```
LDAP://localhost
```

```
LDAP://webdev.wrox.co.uk/CN=WebDev,DC=Wrox,DC=co,DC=uk
```

```
WinNT://HUNDREDACRE/Tigger,Tigger
```

```
WinNT://HUNDREDACRE/DavidS
```

```
NDS://WebDev/O=Wrox/OU=Editorial/CN=DavidS
```

```
NWCOMPAT://Netware1/HPLaserJet
```

For more details on the particular syntax of your directory service you should consult the appropriate documentation.

Using the OLE DB Provider for ADS

The OLE DB Provider for ADS is installed automatically by Windows 2000, so you don't have to do anything special to use it.

Despite the complexity of paths and query strings, it's actually quite simple to access items from a directory. Let's see an example that allows the user to choose between users, groups, or all objects from a directory.

Firstly, the file `ActiveDirectory.html`, the form to allow the selection:

```
<FORM NAME="frmCategory" ACTION="ActiveDirectory.asp" METHOD="POST">
<SELECT NAME="lstCategory">
  <OPTION VALUE="user">Users</OPTION>
  <OPTION VALUE="group">Groups</OPTION>
  <OPTION VALUE="*">All Categories</OPTION>
</SELECT>
<INPUT TYPE="SUBMIT" VALUE="Run"></INPUT>
</FORM>
```

Now the ASP page that creates the results – `ActiveDirectory.asp`. First comes the creation of the Recordset and the connection string:

```
<!-- #INCLUDE FILE="../Include/RecordsetToTable.asp" -->
```

```
<%
  Dim rsUsers
  Dim strQuery
  Dim fldF

  Set rsUsers = Server.CreateObject("ADODB.Recordset")

' Set the connection string
  strConn = "Provider=ADSDSOObject"
```

Now we can build the query. We're selecting the common name and directory path from the local machine, but only selecting those objects where the category matches the one selected from the selection form:

```
' Build the query
strQuery = "SELECT cn, ADsPath FROM 'LDAP://localhost'" & _
           " WHERE objectCategory='" & _
           CStr(Request.Form("lstCategory")) & "'" & _
           " ORDER BY cn"
```

Then we open the recordset and display the results. The `RecordsetToTable` function is in the `RecordsetToTable.asp` include file, and simply converts an ADO Recordset into an HTML table:

```
' Open the recordset
rsUsers.Open strQuery, strConn

' Build a table of the details
Response.Write RecordsetToTable(rsUsers, True)

rsUsers.Close
Set rsUsers = Nothing
Set fldF = Nothing

%>
```

This simply opens a connection to the ADS provider, and then constructs a simple query, using the selected category as a filter. The results are something like this:

The Active Directory OLEBD Provider - Category = *user*

cn	ADsPath
Administrator	LDAP://localhost/CN=Administrator,CN=Users,DC=ipona,DC=demon,DC=co,DC=uk
David Sussman	LDAP://localhost/CN=David Sussman,CN=Users,DC=ipona,DC=demon,DC=co,DC=uk
Guest	LDAP://localhost/CN=Guest,CN=Users,DC=ipona,DC=demon,DC=co,DC=uk
HUNDREDACRE$	LDAP://localhost/CN=HUNDREDACRE$,CN=Users,DC=ipona,DC=demon,DC=co,DC=uk
IUSR_W2000	LDAP://localhost/CN=IUSR_W2000,CN=Users,DC=ipona,DC=demon,DC=co,DC=uk
IWAM_W2000	LDAP://localhost/CN=IWAM_W2000,CN=Users,DC=ipona,DC=demon,DC=co,DC=uk
krbtgt	LDAP://localhost/CN=krbtgt,CN=Users,DC=ipona,DC=demon,DC=co,DC=uk
SQLAgentCmdExec	LDAP://localhost/CN=SQLAgentCmdExec,CN=Users,DC=ipona,DC=demon,DC=co,DC=uk
TsInternetUser	LDAP://localhost/CN=TsInternetUser,CN=Users,DC=ipona,DC=demon,DC=co,DC=uk
VUSR_W2000	LDAP://localhost/CN=VUSR_W2000,CN=Users,DC=ipona,DC=demon,DC=co,DC=uk

This shows the Common Name (`cn`) and the unique directory path for each user held in the directory. If you have a look in the Directory Services manager you can see how this matches up:

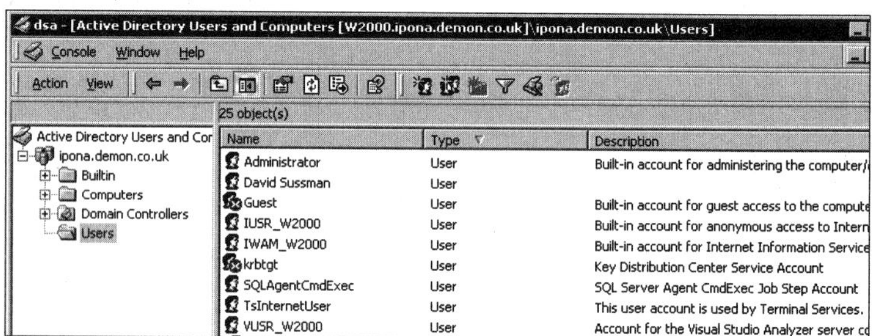

Exchange Server

Connecting to Exchange Server with ADO is something many people, myself included, have been waiting for a long time. But unfortunately at the time of writing, there's no access to Exchange Server via OLE DB and ADO. Microsoft Exchange Server 6 (code named Platinum) is in testing and there will be an OLE DB Provider available when it ships. Although there are no details yet, hopefully this will give us access to the complete Exchange store (including mailboxes, public folders, newsgroups, etc.) through ADO recordsets.

The advantage of ADO access to the Exchange directory is two-fold:

- Programmers already familiar with ADO don't have to learn another mechanism, such as CDO, for accessing Exchange data.
- Using ADO will be more convenient for certain situations, such as providing quick access to the data stores.

It's a real shame that we have to wait for this, because it will make the creation of applications that include messaging much simpler. Many Web sites already provide simple email facilities, but the Exchange Provider should open out the possibilities, and allow easier access to public folders, contact information, and so on.

Custom Providers

If you have data that cannot be accessed via an existing OLE DB Provider, then you have two options:

- Convert the data into a format that does have a provider
- Write your own OLE DB Provider

You might think the first is the simplest solution, perhaps by converting the data into a database. But if the data is from another live application, then you might have to perform this conversion frequently, which means that you're never looking at live data.

The second solution seems ominous, but that might not be the case. If your data is relatively simple, then you might be able to write your own provider in a short space of time. For example, when looking at XML data we saw that we can open an XML file as a recordset as long as the XML file followed the Microsoft schema. But what if you've got some XML data in the format of elements, like so:

```
<Authors>
  <Author>
    <au_id>172-32-1176</au_id>
    <au_lname>White</au_lname>
    <au_fname>Johnson</au_fname>
  </Author>
  <Author>
    <au_id>213-46-8915</au_id>
    <au_lname>Green</au_lname>
    <au_fname>Marjorie</au_fname>
    <phone>415 986-7020</phone>
  </Author>
</Authors>
```

You could easily convert this into the schema version, perhaps using XSL or some code with the DOM, but why not write an OLE DB Provider that reads in this data? Trust me, it's easier than you think.

The Simple Provider

This type of provider is called a simple provider, because the data is a simple text file. It could also be called the simple provider because it's simple to write. Absurdly so, in fact – a provider for this type of XML took approximately 10 minutes to write. We won't cover this in detail, but here's a rough guide of how to do it in Visual Basic.

> *For more details you should consult the OLE DB documentation. The best place to get the latest documentation is MSDN at* `http://msdn.microsoft.com:`

Creating an OLE DB Simple Provider in Visual Basic requires an ActiveX DLL project with two classes and the following references set:

- Microsoft ActiveX Data Objects 2.5 Library
- Microsoft Data Source Interfaces
- Microsoft OLE DB Simple Provider 1.5 Library
- Microsoft OLE DB Error Library

> *Plus for our provider we will also need* *Microsoft XML, version 2.0.*

One of the classes – let's call it `XMLConnection` – needs to have its Data Source Behavior property set to 1 – vbDataSource. This tells Visual Basic that this is a source of data, which is part of being an OLE DB Provider. The `GetDataMember` of this class then has to create the second class – `XMLRecordset` – which is the class that actually reads the data from the XML file.

This sounds complex, but it's actually quite simple. The following diagram shows you how it works:

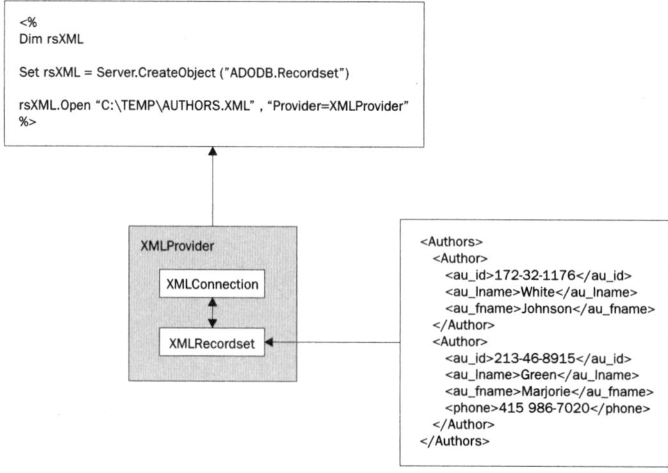

Let's look at how these two classes can be implemented.

The XMLConnection Class

The XMLConnection class provides the interface between the application and the class that actually fetches the data. Its role is to create the instance of the actual provider of the data:

```
Private Sub Class_GetDataMember(DataMember As String, Data As Object)

' XMLRecords is the name of the class that actually
' reads in the XML data from the XML file
  Dim objCustom As XMLRecords

  Set objCustom = New XMLRecords

' Call the method of the data class, passing into it the
' DataMember (field name) requested

  objCustom.processFile DataMember

  Set Data = objCustom

End Sub
```

The XMLRecordsetClass

The second class, XMLRecordset, is what actually fetches the data from the text file, and is the real guts of the provider. Writing your own simple provider means that you have to implement the functionality of the OLE DB Simple Provider, so we ensure our class does this, and sets a few global variables:

```
Implements OLEDBSimpleProvider

Private mdomColumns     As MSXML.IXMLDOMNodeList     ' List of columns
Private mdomRows        As MSXML.IXMLDOMNodeList     ' List of rows
Private mdomXML         As MSXML.DOMDocument         ' The xml to parse
```

The method to read the XML data just creates an XML DOM object and loads in the data file. It also sets a couple of object references, for later use:

```
Public Sub processFile(strCommand As String)

  Set mdomXML = New MSXML.DOMDocument

' Load the xml document
  mdomXML.Load strCommand

' Set the references to the rows and columns
  Set mdomRows = mdomXML.childNodes(0).childNodes
  Set mdomColumns = mdomXML.childNodes(0).childNodes(0).childNodes

End Sub
```

Setting the references might look rather odd, but think back to the structure of our XML data, and to the previous chapter where we looked at the DOM. The DOM document has a root node, and under that comes our XML, which has its own root node (in our sample this is `Authors`). So we use the `childNodes` property to index two levels into the tree, pointing to the first row. Each row consists of columns, so we again use `childNodes` to index one level deeper.

The `XMLRecordset` also implements several methods of the simple provider. There are three methods for the number of columns and rows:

```
Private Function OLEDBSimpleProvider_getColumnCount() As Long

  OLEDBSimpleProvider_getColumnCount = mdomColumns.length

End Function
```

```
Private Function OLEDBSimpleProvider_getEstimatedRows() As Long

  OLEDBSimpleProvider_getEstimatedRows = mdomRows.length

End Function
```

```
Private Function OLEDBSimpleProvider_getRowCount() As Long

  OLEDBSimpleProvider_getRowCount = mdomRows.length

End Function
```

And then there is the method that returns the data to the consumer:

```
Private Function OLEDBSimpleProvider_getVariant(ByVal intRow As Long, _
          ByVal intColumn As Long, ByVal format As OSPFORMAT) As Variant

  Dim varValue As Variant

  If intRow = 0 Then
     varValue = mdomColumns(intColumn - 1).nodeName
  Else
    varValue = mdomRows(intRow - 1).childNodes(intColumn - 1). _
               nodeTypedValue
  End If

  OLEDBSimpleProvider_getVariant = varValue

End Function
```

This function is automatically called when you access a particular field, so all we have to do here is return the appropriate member from the XML DOM object.

That's really all there is to it.

> *There are a few other things to do, but we're not going into detail about them here. The full code, plus a ready built version of this provider and a test program, is available from the Wrox Web site, at `http://wwww.wrox.com`.*

To use a custom OLE DB Provider it has to be registered. For the sample provider, we've supplied a `.reg` file to do this for you. If you create your own providers, then you'll need to create your own `.reg` file (or edit the registry manually) to do this for you. The OLE DB documentation for the simple provider details how to create the registry entries. Of course, if the provider is written in Visual Basic, then you'll need the Visual Basic run-time installed on the system where you intend to use the custom provider. Using the Package and Deployment Wizard will create the necessary installation files.

Semi-Structured Data

Since UDA is all about data from a variety of places, we need to cater for data that isn't truly structured. In a recordset, for example, all of the rows contain the same number of fields. Even in hierarchical recordsets, the child recordsets exhibit this same behavior. There are, however, plenty of forms of data in which the data isn't structured in this way.

Semi-structured data falls between fully structured data and binary data (such as BLOBS), in that it does have some structure, but not necessarily the same structure for each row. A mail system, for example, would be a good example of this. Consider the following:

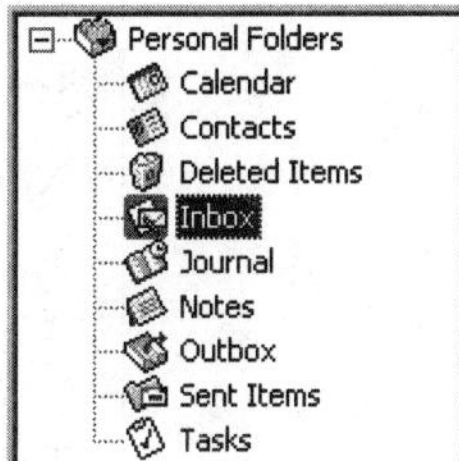

Here we have a structure of some sort. Personal Folders contains other folders, so this could be mapped as a recordset. But, each of the sub-folders stores different types of information, and therefore has different properties: the Calendar is designed for one purpose, the Contacts another. There's a perfectly good reason why this should be so, but it does complicate things if we want to represent this as a recordset. How would you have a row in a recordset with different fields from the previous row?

Semi-structured data is the answer, since it is specifically designed for this sort of situation. We could have a recordset that contains all of the common properties, and then some other object to represent the individual properties.

The Record Object

The **Record object** is what's been created to handle semi-structured storage. When thinking about this type of storage, it's a good idea to think about tree-like structures, with nodes and collections of nodes, as this makes it easy to think about the mapping onto ADO objects:

- **Nodes are modeled as Records.**
  Each node, or folder, is therefore a record. The properties for a record are those that are distinct to the node, and these become the Fields of the record.

- **Collections are modeled as Recordsets.**
  So items such as collections of folders become a recordset. Although each individual folder might not be the same as the others, it will share a set of common properties – name, last access time, etc. These common properties become the fields of the recordset.

So in the mail system shown above, Personal Folders is a record because it is a distinct node in the tree. However, it does contain sub-nodes, so it has children, and these children are a collection, and are therefore a recordset. Each row in this recordset might point to another node, so each row can be a record. This is necessary because the Contacts folder has a completely different set of properties than the Calendar folder or the Inbox. Any items that aren't nodes are handled as rows of the recordset.

In the mailbox example we'd have a recordset with 10 rows, possibly something like this:

Name	Description	Post Items As
Calendar	Calendar Comment	Appointment
Contacts	Contacts Comment	Contact
Deleted Items	Deleted Items folder	Post
Inbox	Inbox folder	Post
Journal	Journal Comment	Journal entry
Notes	Notes Comment	Note
Outbox	Outbox folder	Post
Sent Items	Sent Items folder	Post
Tasks	Tasks Comment	Task

Each of the rows would have a record associated with it, to represent the unique properties of the row.

Internet Publishing

Another new feature that is part of semi-structured data is that of **Internet Publishing**. Version 2.1 of ADO shipped with the OLE DB Provider for Internet Publishing, but it was limited in its functionality. Now, with version 2.5, the full functionality has been exposed, and it's a pretty exciting area.

Internet Publishing allows you to access Web resources from ADO, which means that you can build custom applications to manage Web sites. What's the advantage of this? Again it's the fact that if you know ADO, then you don't need to learn anything new (apart from the new objects of course), so you can use existing skills.

To see this in action let's imagine we have the following virtual Web directory:

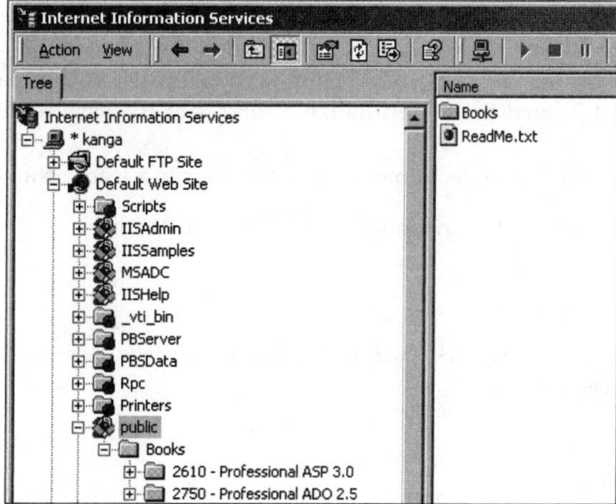

This is just a normal virtual directory – nothing special was done to set it up for use with the Internet Publisher Provider.

The Record and Recordset Objects

Many people get confused about the difference between the Record object and the Recordset object. Let's have a look at our sample Web site, but in a diagram form:

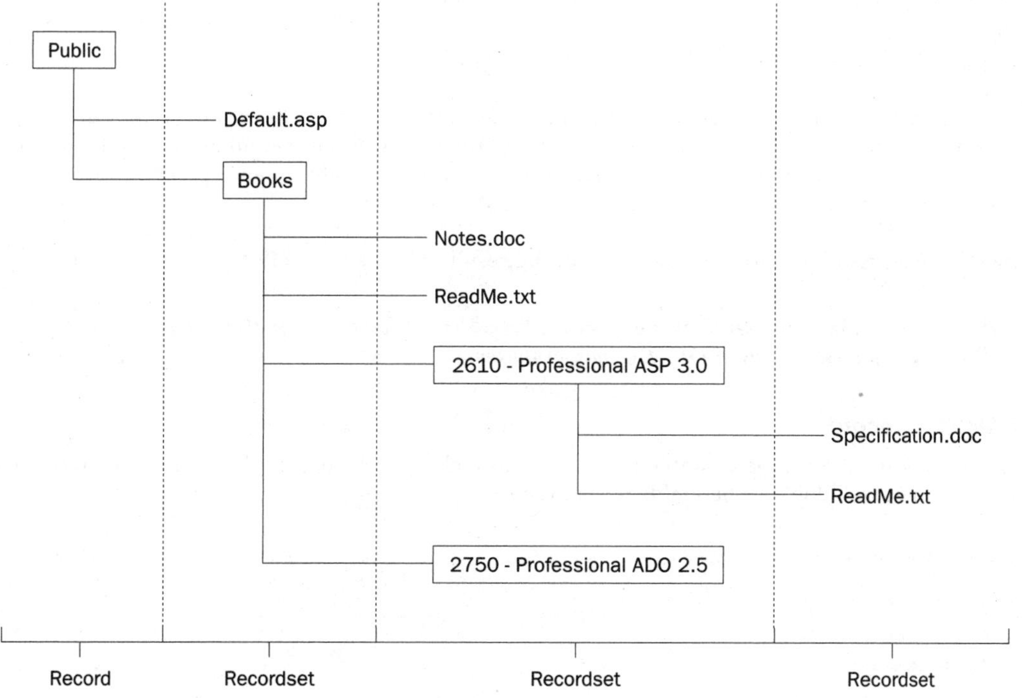

At the top of our structure we have a Record object – this represents a node in the tree. This node has children (folders and files), and these are modeled as a recordset, each row of which is either a file or a folder. If it's a folder, then it represents another node in the tree, and is therefore also a record. It's a bit hard to conceptualize at first, but it's easy to remember:

- A collection of files and folders is a Recordset
- An individual file or folder is a Record

Opening a URL

Opening a URL with the Record object is extremely easy, as you simply use the `Open` method of the Record:

```
Dim recNode

Set recNode = Server.CreateObject("ADODB.Record")

recNode.Open "public", "URL=http://localhost/"
```

This opens the `public` folder, located under the URL `//localhost/`.

There is one important point to note about this statement. The first argument identifies the file or folder, and the second argument identifies the connection string – the URL over which subsequent actions apply. This really means the scope, or root, to our operations. So further operations could be performed anywhere under this root directory. Take a look at this line of code:

```
recNode.Open "", "URL=http://localhost/public"
```

The first argument is empty, and the folder name we want to open has been moved into the connection string. Since the first argument is empty, the folder in the second argument is opened, which has exactly the same effect as the first example. However, subsequent operations are now limited – they can only be performed under the `public` directory.

So, whilst these two lines produce the same initial result, they have an effect on further actions.

> *The `Open` method has several other arguments, but we're not going to cover them in detail here. For more explanation consult the ADO documentation.*

The Fields of a Record

Let's have a look at a simple example to see this more clearly. We'll use a Record object to open a URL, and then we'll look at the Fields of that record:

```
<!-- #INCLUDE FILE="../Include/Connection.asp" -->
```

```
<%
  Dim recNode
  Dim fldNode
```

```
    Set recNode = Server.CreateObject ("ADODB.Record")

  ' Open the URL
    recNode.Open "", "URL=http://localhost/public/"

  ' Loop through the fields, showing them in a table
    Response.Write "<TABLE BORDER='1'>"
    For Each fldNode In recNode.Fields
      Response.Write "<TR><TD>" & fldNode.Name & "</TD><TD>" & _
                                  fldNode.Value & "</TD></TR>"
    Next
    Response.Write "</TABLE>"

    recNode.Close
    Set recNode = Nothing
  %>
```

This gives the following result:

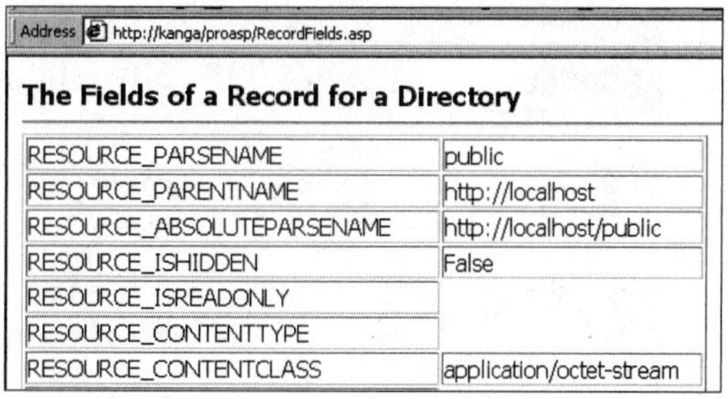

Address http://kanga/proasp/RecordFields.asp

The Fields of a Record for a Directory

RESOURCE_PARSENAME	public
RESOURCE_PARENTNAME	http://localhost
RESOURCE_ABSOLUTEPARSENAME	http://localhost/public
RESOURCE_ISHIDDEN	False
RESOURCE_ISREADONLY	
RESOURCE_CONTENTTYPE	
RESOURCE_CONTENTCLASS	application/octet-stream

What you see here is the properties of a directory mapped into the Fields collection. So, what happens if we change the `Open` line to the following:

```
  recNode.Open "readme.txt", "URL=http://localhost/public/"
```

This opens a file instead of a directory:

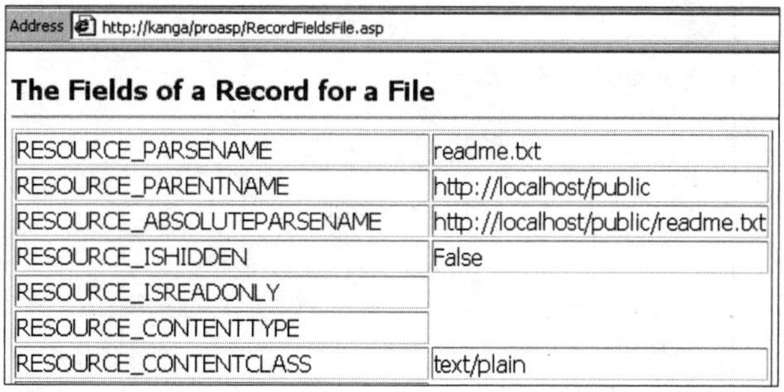

Address http://kanga/proasp/RecordFieldsFile.asp

The Fields of a Record for a File

RESOURCE_PARSENAME	readme.txt
RESOURCE_PARENTNAME	http://localhost/public
RESOURCE_ABSOLUTEPARSENAME	http://localhost/public/readme.txt
RESOURCE_ISHIDDEN	False
RESOURCE_ISREADONLY	
RESOURCE_CONTENTTYPE	
RESOURCE_CONTENTCLASS	text/plain

The same set of Fields is present, but their content is different.

The Fields of a record are listed below. Descriptions of the data types can be found in Appendix F – they are the data type constants, found under `DataTypeEnum`:

Field	Type	Description
RESOURCE_ PARSENAME	adVarWChar	The URL of the resource.
RESOURCE_ PARENTNAME	adVarWChar	The URL of the parent resource.
RESOURCE_ ABSOLUTEPARSENAME	adVarWChar	The absolute URL, including path.
RESOURCE_ ISHIDDEN	adBoolean	Indicates whether or not the resource is hidden.
RESOURCE_ ISREADONLY	adBoolean	Indicates whether or not the resource is read-only.
RESOURCE_ CONTENTTYPE	adVarWChar	The MIME type of the resource.
RESOURCE_ CONTENTCLASS	adVarWChar	The likely use of the resource.
RESOURCE_ CONTENTLANGUAGE	adVarWChar	The resource language.
RESOURCE_ CREATIONTIME	adFileTime	The time the resource was created.
RESOURCE_ LASTACCESSTIME	adFileTime	The time the resource was last accessed.
RESOURCE_ LASTWRITETIME	adFileTime	The time the resource was updated.
RESOURCE_ STREAMSIZE	adUnsignedBigInt	Size of the default Stream.
RESOURCE_ ISCOLLECTION	adBoolean	Indicates whether or not the resource is a collection – i.e. has children.
RESOURCE_ ISSTRUCTUREDDOCUMENT	adBoolean	Indicates whether or not the resource is a structured document – e.g. a Word document.
DEFAULT_ DOCUMENT	adVarWChar	The URL of the default document for a folder.
RESOURCE_ DISPLAYNAME	adVarWChar	Display name of the resource.
RESOURCE_ ISROOT	adBoolean	Indicates whether or not the resource is the root of a collection.
RESOURCE_ ISMARKEDFOROFFLINE	adBoolean	Indicates whether or not the resource is marked for offline usage.

> **You should note that `RESOURCE_CONTENTTYPE` and `RESOURCE_CONTENTCLASS` might have their values reversed. At the time of writing this was the case, but this may have been corrected for the release.**

DAV Fields

There are also some Fields that begin with `DAV:` – these are for Distributed Authoring and Versioning, and they map onto the existing Fields in the following way:

Field	DAV Field
`RESOURCE_PARSENAME`	DAV:lastpathsegment
`RESOURCE_PARENTNAME`	DAV:parentname
`RESOURCE_ABSOLUTEPARSENAME`	DAV:href
`RESOURCE_ISHIDDEN`	DAV:ishidden
`RESOURCE_ISREADONLY`	DAV:isreadonly
`RESOURCE_CONTENTTYPE`	DAV:getcontenttype
`RESOURCE_CONTENTCLASS`	DAV:getcontentclass
`RESOURCE_CONTENTLANGUAGE`	DAV:getcontentlanguage
`RESOURCE_CREATIONTIME`	DAV:creationtime
`RESOURCE_LASTACCESSTIME`	DAV:lastaccessed
`RESOURCE_LASTWRITETIME`	DAV:getlastmodified
`RESOURCE_STREAMSIZE`	DAV:getcontentlength
`RESOURCE_ISCOLLECTION`	DAV:iscollection
`RESOURCE_ISSTRUCTUREDDOCUMENT`	DAV:isstructureddocument
`DEFAULT_DOCUMENT`	DAV:defaultdocument
`RESOURCE_DISPLAYNAME`	DAV:displayname
`RESOURCE_ISROOT`	DAV:isroot
`RESOURCE_ISMARKEDFOROFFLINE`	DAV:getetag

The reason there are two sets of properties is that Internet Publishing is built on top of a protocol called **WebDAV**, and IIS 5.0 is a WebDAV server. It's therefore possible to use any WebDAV client to access IIS 5.0, so it must support the official set of DAV properties.

Web based Distributed Authoring and Versioning is discussed in more detail a little later in the chapter.

Traversing through the directories

One of the things you might need to do is obtain a list of all files and folders on a particular Web site. For example, you may be building a Web based front-end that will allow you to manage your Web site. For many sites there may only be one or two directories (advertising, e-commerce, and so on), but we now have the possibility of Web sites that are being used as a document stores. In this case they might have a fairly deep tree structure, to map onto the organization of the documents. Our sample site is like that.

Because this site has several levels to it, you can use a recursive procedure to navigate to each file and folder.

Let's see some code to show how this is done:

```
<%
  Dim intLevel
  Dim recRoot
  Dim conIPP

  Set recRoot = Server.CreateObject ("ADODB.Record")

  recRoot.Open "", "URL=http://localhost/public"

  TraverseTree recRoot

  recRoot.Close
  Set recRoot = Nothing
%>
```

```
Sub TraverseTree(recNode)

  Dim rsChildren
  Dim recChildNode

  ' Display the node name
  Response.Write FormatItem(recNode("RESOURCE_PARSENAME")) & "<BR>"

  ' Get any child nodes
  Set rsChildren = recNode.GetChildren

  ' Increase the indenting level
  intLevel = intLevel + 1

  ' Loop through the children
  While Not rsChildren.EOF

    ' Does this child contain other children
    If rsChildren("RESOURCE_ISCOLLECTION") Then
      ' Create a new child node
      Set recChildNode = Server.CreateObject("ADODB.Record")

      ' Open the new child node
      recChildNode.Open rsChildren
```

```
    ' Traverse this child
      TraverseTree recChildNode

    ' Close up
      recChildNode.Close
      Set recChildNode = Nothing
    Else
      Response.Write FormatItem(rsChildren("RESOURCE_PARSENAME")) & "<BR>"
    End If

    rsChildren.MoveNext
  Wend

' Decrease the indenting level
  intLevel = intLevel - 1

' Close the child recordset
  rsChildren.Close
  Set rsChildren = Nothing

End Sub
```

```
Function FormatItem(strItem)

  Dim strSpaces

  strSpaces = Space(intLevel * 2)
  strSpaces = Replace (strSpaces, " ", "  ")

  FormatItem = strSpaces & Replace(strItem, "%20", " ")

End Function
```

And what that gives us is the following output:

Using URLs in ADO

public
  Books
    2750 - Professional ADO 2.5
    2610 - Professional ASP 3.0
      Specification.doc
      ReadMe.txt
    ReadMe.txt
    Notes.doc
  default.asp

Let's look at the code in more detail. To start with we create a Record object – this will be the root of our tree:

```
Set recRoot = Server.CreateObject ("ADODB.Record")
```

Now we open the Record object. We are using the `localhost` as our connection, and the folder on the `localhost` we want to connect to is called `public`:

```
' Open the record based on the root node
  recRoot.Open "", "URL=http://localhost/public"
```

Then we call a routine to traverse the tree:

```
' Call the traversal routine
  TraverseTree recRoot

  recRoot.Close
  Set recRoot = Nothing
```

We've used a separate procedure to traverse the tree because the tree is recursive in nature – folders can contain other folders. So, the traversal function accepts a Record as it's starting point:

```
Sub TraverseTree(recNode)
```

We declare two variables to hold the children of this record. The recordset will hold a row for each child, and the record will hold a Folder:

```
  Dim rsChildren
  Dim recChildNode
```

We can now display the name of the record. Remember how we said that the properties of a record are mapped into the `Fields` collection – the `RESOURCE_PARSENAME` is the name of the entry:

```
' Display the node name
  Response.Write FormatItem(recNode("RESOURCE_PARSENAME")) & "<BR>"
```

We now need to see if the node has any children (folders or files), so we call the `GetChildren` method of the Record – this returns a recordset of any children:

```
' Get any child nodes
  Set rsChildren = recNode.GetChildren
```

We increase the indenting level, purely for output formatting:

```
' Increase the indenting level
  intLevel = intLevel + 1
```

And now we can loop through any children:

```
' Loop through the children
  While Not rsChildren.EOF
```

Next we need to check if this child node contains other nodes – that is, is it a folder itself? We test the `RESOURCE_ISCOLLECTION` field for this, since a node that contains other nodes is a collection:

```
' Does this child contain other children
  If rsChildren("RESOURCE_ISCOLLECTION") Then
```

If it is a collection then we create a new Record object and, using the current record pointer as the source, open the record. This gives us a new node, so we can call the `TraverseTree` routine again, using this node as the current root. This provides our recursion, as for each node (folder) we traverse again:

```
      ' Create a new child node
        Set recChildNode = Server.CreateObject("ADODB.Record")

      ' Open the new child node
        recChildNode.Open rsChildren

      ' Traverse this child
        TraverseTree recChildNode

      ' Close up
        recChildNode.Close
        Set recChildNode = Nothing
```

If the record isn't a collection we just want to display its name:

```
    Else
      Response.Write Formatitem(rsChildren("RESOURCE_PARSENAME")) & "<BR>"
    End If
```

And then we move onto the next record in the recordset:

```
    rsChildren.MoveNext
  Wend
```

We can then decrease the level in the tree and close the recordset:

```
  ' Decrease the indenting level
  intLevel = intLevel - 1

  ' Close the child recordset
  rsChildren.Close
  Set rsChildren = Nothing

End Sub
```

The `FormatItems` function just adds some non-blank spaces at the beginning of the supplied string, and then converts encoded spaces (`%20`) into spaces. This just makes the entry easier to read:

```
Function FormatItem(strItem)

  Dim strSpaces

  strSpaces = Space(intLevel * 2)
  strSpaces = Replace (strSpaces, " ", "  ")

  FormatItem = strSpaces & Replace(strItem, "%20", " ")

End Function
```

That's all there is to it. It's pretty easy if you remember these points:

- A record can contain children, so you can use the GetChildren method to return a recordset of those children
- A row in a recordset can be collection item, and can therefore be the source for a record

It's seems a bit convoluted until you get your head around it, but it's pretty easy on the whole.

Managing Resources

Not only does the record allow you access to Web resources, but it also gives you the ability to manage them too, as the following methods show:

- CopyRecord – Copies a Record, or a URL, from one location to another
- MoveRecord – Moves a Record, or a URL, from one location to another
- DeleteRecord – Deletes a Record, or a URL

You can see how, with just three methods, you could easily build a simple system to manage Web sites remotely. Here's how they work:

```
Dim recFile

Set recFile = Server.CreateObject("ADODB.Record")

recFile.Open "ReadMe.txt", "URL="http://localhost/public/Books"

recFile.CopyRecord "", "http://webdev.wrox.co.uk/public/NewReadMe.txt"
```

Although this example shows the CopyRecord method using only a source and a destination, it can take several arguments:

Argument	Description
Source	The URL of the source file. If not supplied, or an empty string, the Record object is taken as the source.
Destination	The URL of the destination file.
UserName	User name to use for connecting to the destination resource.
Password	Password to use for connecting to the destination resource.
Options	One of: - adCopyOverWrite, to overwrite an existing file or directory - adCopyNonRecursive, to only copy a directory, and not its sub-directories - adCopyAllowDataLoss, to allow the provider to use a download/upload style of copy for remote operations
Async	True to indicate asynchronous operation, False otherwise.

Being able to supply the user name and password allows you to connect to secure, remote Web sites.

> **You should be very careful when using `adCopyOverWrite` since the action is different from normal file copies – the destination will be destroyed. If copying a file and you specify a directory as a target, then the directory will be overwritten with the file.**

The `MoveRecord` method works in a similar fashion:

```
Dim recFile

Set recFile = Server.CreateObject("ADODB.Record")

recFile.Open "ReadMe.txt", "URL="http://localhost/public/Books"

recFile.MoveRecord "", "http://webdev.wrox.co.uk/public/NewReadMe.txt"
```

The arguments are the same as for `CopyRecord`, except for the `Options`:

- `adMoveOverWrite`, to overwrite an existing file or directory
- `adMoveDontUpdateLinks`, to ensure that hypertext links on the file are not updated. The default behavior is to update links if the provider is capable.
- `adMoveAllowEmulation`, to simulate the move using a download/upload and delete if `MoveRecord` fails.

Resource Security

For those of you who suddenly see this as a huge security hole, I have two familiar words – don't panic. There are two main points to realize:

- The Internet Publishing is provided as part of IIS 5.0. IIS 4 has very limited capabilities for publishing, as provided by the FrontPage Server Extensions. IIS 5.0 still supports these, but it also supports the new DAV extensions.
- Resources accessed through the OLE DB Provider for Internet Publishing are standard Web resources, you control the access in the same way as you do other Web resources.

If you ensure that there are no write or delete permissions on your site, then people cannot suddenly start messing with your files. If you do need these permissions, then you can restrict them to certain users – methods such as `MoveRecord` require access permissions, and these can be supplied as part of the method call.

So, your Web site can remain as secure as it is now. If it isn't secure, then now is a good time to start making sure it is.

The Stream Object

One thing we've not yet mentioned with regard to Web resources is how the Stream object can be used. You saw the Stream in action in the XML chapter, but you can also get the data from a Web resource. It would be fairly easy to modify our code shown above so that instead of just printing the names of the resources we print references. We could use an A tag and put in the full URL of the file, so that when the URL was clicked, the file would be loaded.

But, what if we want to have some control over the resource, rather than loading it directly into the browser. Perhaps you'd like to display it within the page. Something like this perhaps:

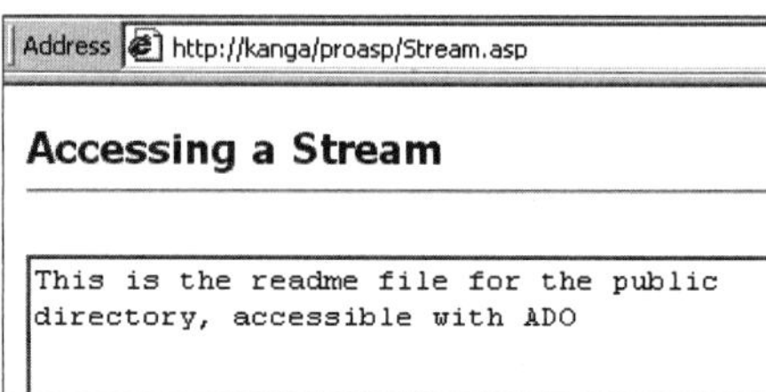

Once again this is surprisingly easy to do. As usual we start with the inclusion of the connection details, and then we start a text area, to display the contents of the file into:

```
<!-- #INCLUDE FILE="../Include/Connection.asp" -->
```

```
<TEXTAREA NAME="txtStreamContents" STYLE="width:100%; height=50%">
```

Now comes the ASP code that will read in a file. We'll first create a Stream object:

```
<%
  Dim stmData

  Set stmData = Server.CreateObject ("ADODB.Stream")
```

Then we open the Stream, specifying a file as the source of the Stream:

```
stmData.Open "URL=http://localhost/public/readme.txt", _
             adModeRead, adOpenStreamFromURL
stmData.Charset = "ascii"
```

The arguments to the Open method for a Stream specify the URL of the file to open, the access mode, and where to open the Stream from. This latter argument can be adOpenStreamFromRecord if the source of the Stream (the first argument) is a Record object. You'll see an example of this later.

Once the stream is open, we can use the ReadText method to read in the contents, and we simply display them:

```
Response.Write stmData.ReadText
```

And finally we tidy up the variables, and close the text area.

```
  stmData.Close
  Set stmData = Nothing
%>
</TEXTAREA>
```

Now I admit this isn't a particularly exciting example, and it can be achieved in other ways. But, consider the addition of a FORM object around the text area, and the addition of a couple of buttons:

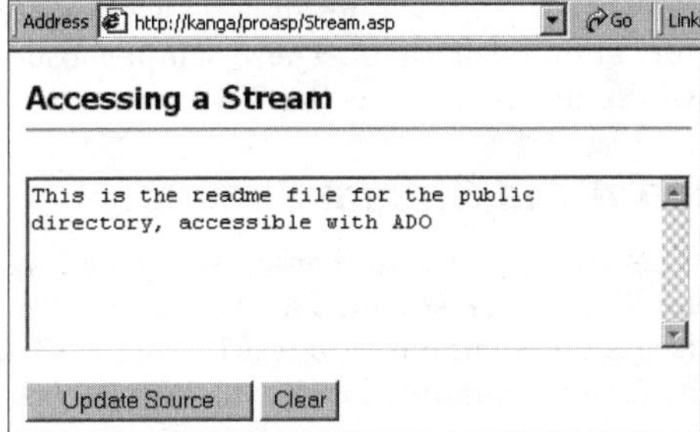

Oooh, now we can update the file – that's pretty exciting. The **Update Source** button could simply call an ASP file (`StreamUpdate.asp`), and its code is pretty simple too:

```
<!-- #INCLUDE FILE="../Include/Connection.asp" -->
```

```
<%
  Dim stmData

  Set stmData = Server.CreateObject ("ADODB.Stream")
```

After creating the Stream object, we open the file – this time using read/write permissions:

```
  With stmData
    .Open "URL=http://localhost/public/readme.txt", _
          adModeReadWrite, adOpenStreamFromURL
```

Then we move the current Stream position to the start of the Stream, and we set the end of the Stream to be the current position. This has the effect of truncating the Stream, removing its existing contents:

```
    .Position = 0

    .SetEOS
```

Then we get the text from the text area in the form of the calling ASP page and, using the `WriteText` method, we write the contents to the Stream:

```
    .WriteText Request.Form("txtStreamContents")
```

Next we tell the user what has happened:

```
    Response.Write "File updated. Current size = " & .Size
```

And finally we close the Stream:

```
    .Close
  End With

  Set stmData = Nothing
%>
```

So, with just a few lines of code we have two ASP pages that allow us to read the contents of a text file, and update them. These samples used fixed file names, but it would be fairly easy to build a form where the user selects the file name.

Record and Stream Summary

The examples we've seen in the preceding sections have shown how easy it is to manipulate resources held on a Web server. This is only the tip of the iceberg, as the possibilities it opens up are quite large. For example, as a test I wrote a Visual Basic program using only ADO that performs the same as many common FTP clients. Why? Well, there were two main reasons:

- To see how much functionality I could get from just a few ADO methods. It took longer to put together the Visual Basic drag and drop stuff, than it did to add the ADO code.
- To prove a point about the ADO functionality of the Internet Publishing Provider. It sits upon DAV, which is just HTTP. This means that you can use ADO to write remote administration programs without worry about opening up firewalls. Because it uses HTTP it will tunnel quite happily through firewalls. Of course, this means that you must make sure your Web site is secure, but at least it reduces the potential security risk.

The real guts of this technology are handled by just a few methods. You can use the `CopyRecord` and `MoveRecord` methods of the Record to move files around, and the Stream provides access to the contents of those files. You could easily write your own simple remote management tool without too much trouble.

WebDAV

We've mentioned DAV and WebDAV a few times in the preceding section, but we haven't really explained what it is. Web based **Distributed Authoring and Versions (DAV)** is what the Internet Publishing Provider is all about. As its name suggests, WebDAV is designed to allow distributed authoring of documents over the Web.

At the moment we have FrontPage and the FrontPage Server Extensions that allow editing and management of documents on remote Web servers, but this is a proprietary solution. For a few years the W3C and IETF have had a working group putting together a specification for WebDAV, and this is now a ratified standard.

WebDAV is a protocol specification, based on extensions to HTTP 1.1, and is therefore platform independent. Whilst the FrontPage solution was a good one at the time, it was a Microsoft only solution. With IIS 5.0 Microsoft has full support for WebDAV, and has been an active part of the working group.

So, what does WebDAV actually give you? Well, if we tell you that the Internet Publishing Provider is built on top of DAV, you'll see what sort of facilities you get. You have the ability to manage documents remotely, allowing editing, copying, and so on. So while you may think that Microsoft is trying to dominate the world with its own technology, what they've actually done here is bring UDA closer to reality by using an existing standard.

There are several Web servers that include WebDAV functionality, and clients are springing up in a variety of guises too. This means that you can use whatever tool you feel most familiar with, without having to compromise functionality.

WebDAV Future

WebDAV is still an evolving product, and currently the Versioning aspect is still undergoing work. This will allow true collaboration, allowing multiple editing using versioning to control the resource. Ultimately this could replace existing version control systems.

There is also other work in progress that affects WebDAV, and for more details you should consult the Web site `www.w3c.org`. Although Microsoft has made no announcements, it's likely they will update IIS sometime in the future once the Versioning side of WebDAV is ratified.

Enterprise Data

In the real world of the enterprise, Microsoft is not the only game in town. Unless the enterprise is just being formed and it has been determined that it will standardize on Microsoft-only tools and products, you can expect to see a pot-pourri of systems that your applications must interface with. Many of these systems may not even communicate on a common protocol!

Data is an enterprise's most valuable asset, and much of this data may be stored in Mainframe databases, such as Oracle and IBM's DB2, as well as non-relational databases, or even in file systems directly as groups of data files. Minicomputer systems are also abound in the enterprise, with many hosting data on Digital's (now Compaq's) VAX/VMS or Unix systems, and built around one of the Relational Database Management Systems (RDBMS) from the big four: IBM, Informix, Oracle, and Sybase.

Alternatives to Access and SQL Server

When Microsoft decided to enter the database market, it targeted SQL Server for small numbers of users – the workgroup, with small to medium data storage needs. Microsoft used SQL Server as a much needed tool to help sell their new operating system OS/2 – they needed a database or who would ever purchase the Microsoft version of OS/2, the predecessor to Windows NT. Therefore, Microsoft engineers worked with Sybase engineers to port Sybase's Unix database product to the Microsoft version of OS/2.

When Microsoft eventual targeted SQL Server for Windows NT, and took over the development from Sybase after SQL Server 4.2, it was still a workgroup-level database product. This was, in my opinion, more a marketing strategy rather than because of product performance. For whatever reason, SQL Server has been seen as a workgroup database ever since, and is only now beginning to be seen as an enterprise-level database product. Multi-processor support and better scalability has now made SQL Server 7.0 Microsoft's entry into the enterprise database market.

Microsoft's entry into the desktop database market was late, but they have eclipsed all other contenders for the desktop market. Although this section is about alternatives to Access and SQL Server, don't throw Access away quite yet. What I mean is an alternative database for Active Server Pages data access, not an alternative to the best front-end database tool in the Windows environment. I work for Informix Software, Inc. a major database vendor, but my client tool of choice is still Microsoft Access.

Today's enterprise is generally built around data stores of major database systems from IBM, Oracle, Informix or Sybase. Yes, there are others, but by no means do I mean to imply that these are the only ones you'll find in the normal enterprise. In fact, these are all Relational Database Products; much of an enterprise's data assets may not be Relational Databases at all, but in older hierarchical or CODASYL databases or in file systems. However, much of the data in older systems have been moved into RDBMS (Relational Database Management Systems), so we will be concentrating on just the major vendors.

Oracle

When Microsoft announced SQL Server 7.0, it was not long after that Oracle announced its $1,000,000.00 Microsoft SQL Server 7.0 challenge. The challenge was to show that Microsoft SQL Server 7.0 could run a specific query at least 1/100th as fast as Oracle 8 could run the same query. This has set the tone between the two software giants ever since. Oracle would like to turn its back on Microsoft's COM/DCOM and all that goes with it – instead they have chosen to concentrate on Java and CORBA as their main strategy for their distributed and Web architectures.

However, they really cannot afford to be that cavalier, Oracle does support Microsoft's DNA, COM/DCOM, OLE DB, ADO and, of course, ASP. In fact, Microsoft felt Oracle interoperability was so important that they provided an Oracle OLE DB Provider that is quite robust, and allows Oracle the same level of functionality as SQL Server 7.0. Oracle also has it Oracle Objects for OLE (OO4O) that provide ActiveX functionality. OO4O can be used from virtually any programming or scripting language including ASP.

It is relatively easy to connect to an Oracle Database using the OLE DB Provider from Microsoft, and as I have stated, the functionality is about the same level as you would find using SQL Server 7.0. However, what you will find in the real world is that most Oracle shops are still utilizing older versions of the Oracle engine such as 7.x or earlier. These present a different challenge. You will need to use an OLE DB ODBC Provider and an ODBC Driver that support that particular version of the Oracle engine. The OLE DB ODBC Provider delivers less than you would expect with the native OLE DB Provider for Oracle. This is due to the limitations of the particular ODBC Driver being used.

However, Oracle offers the widest number of platforms supported, but each platform may present different challenges. The OLE DB ODBC gateway is the easiest access method, but it also may present undesirable limitations. Like other programming tradeoffs, the developer must evaluate each compromise carefully.

IBM

IBM has five different code bases for their DB2 products – IBM developed different versions of DB2 in different locations within the company, based upon different operating systems and platforms. It has been rumored, that IBM is attempting to come up with a common code base for their very successful DB2 relational databases. This would assure consistent functionality across the DB2 product lines, thus bringing unity of functionality to the entire DB2 product line.

IBM has a major emphasis in developing a Java strategy, as well as XML integration with their database products. Their support for COM, OLE DB, and ASP has come about by collaborating with other vendors that have ported these technologies to the IBM platforms. These solutions come at a high cost at times, and are not all provided across all IBM platforms.

> *Later, we will look at Chili!Soft's ASP technology that is being ported to IBM OS/390 and AS/400 operating systems as well as other platforms.*

It has been estimated that 470 of the Fortune 500 companies have enterprise data housed in one of the IBM's mainframe environments. The SNA OLE DB provider provided with Microsoft's SNA Server provides a gateway into this data rich environment outside the DB2 environment.

The key to integrating IBM DB2 data into an ASP application is the strong support for the SQL/CLI standard within IBM.

> *ODBC is the most common SQL/CLI implementation. This has often lead to a misunderstanding with users – often users do not associate SQL/CLI's API as being ODBC. IBM finally dropped the references to CLI and just refers to CLI as ODBC.*

They may very well carry the ODBC flag since Microsoft seems to be at the end of its development in this area. IBM has the most knowledgeable CLI expert within the Standards efforts both nationally and internationally.

Informix

Informix's strategy is to be the "Standards Company." They are supporting all the major object technologies: COM/DCOM, CORBA, and Java, and they are also involved in strong efforts to integrate XML into all areas of their product line. They are the only company that has taken the total standards direction.

Informix even has its own Visual Basic tool, "Visual Basic Data Director" which helps the developer develop a successful ASP strategy. Informix supports a Native OLE DB Provider.

> *Informix's Web site,* `www.informix.com`*, has several white papers dealing with ADO access to its products.*

With the purchase of Illustra, Informix has integrated the Object Relational technology into their 9.x server line. Illustra was the commercialization of the UC Berkeley Object Relational efforts, which add rich functionality not found in other relational products.

Informix has also implemented some of the more advanced feature of the new SQL-99 Standard, and with the purchase of Red Brick, a major leader in Data Warehousing systems, they have bolstered their Data Warehouse efforts.

Cloudscape, a one-hundred percent Java SQL Database, has been purchased by Informix and rounds out their database line by providing a desktop and easily embeddable database product. The Informix Cloudscape database will provide many of the advantages of Microsoft's Access. Cloudscape will be integrated into the Informix line and will support all the interfaces supported by other Informix products, CORBA, COM, and Java. This will most likely also included ASP scripting.

Informix has provided a good platform for ASP development and the Informix database products are an industrial-strength line of databases, which are the basis for some of the industries largest database implementations. Informix databases are offered on both UNIX and Windows NT environments.

Sybase

Sybase was instrumental in the original Microsoft SQL Server development, so it is no wonder that Microsoft's SQL Server and Sybase's products are similar. However, once Microsoft and Sybase decided to go their own separate ways, their products have taken different directions.

Sybase is heavily committed to Java integration into their products. They are one of the original participants in the SQLJ standards efforts. In addition, Sybase's PowerTools produces ASP code directly, so Sybase Web-database integration is a major effort within the company.

Sybase directly supports ASP development with their tools, as well as through their ODBC and OLE DB Provider support. Sybase's support for ASP and its ASP code generation within its PowerTools product leave little doubt that the Sybase sees part of its future tied to supporting ASP efforts.

Conclusion

In conclusion, integrating information from any of the major database vendors should not be a real issue with respect to your ASP application development. All the major database vendor's support the SQL/CLI standard and the ODBC specification, and provide both directly or indirectly, through third-party support, ODBC and OLE DB Providers. Many also provide native OLE DB Providers that have proved to be as feature rich as the Microsoft OLE DB Provider for SQL Server 7.0.

SNA Server and Legacy Data Access

As I mentioned before, many enterprise data resources reside in corporate data centers on mainframes where IBM has been the market leader in mainframe technology. It has been estimated that 80% of the world's enterprise mission-critical data exists on IBM mainframes and AS/400 Systems.

Therefore, it is critical to have an integration strategy for information integration into any new application that needs to tap the enterprise's data resources and integrate well with the IBM mainframe technologies such as SNA (IBM's Networking architecture). Microsoft recognized these issues early on – Microsoft has provided a SNA (System Network Architecture) Server for a number of years. Information System professionals have depended upon IBM's SNA networks to connect terminals to mainframes but now they must integrate this information into their Web-based applications.

At the same time, most enterprises deploy separate PC networks that are also mission-critical, with such systems as the enterprise's email, document creation, workgroup databases, and discussion support systems. It has recently become more critical to tie these two systems more closely together, so that the end-user can incorporate the data stored on the host system into their correspondence, analysis and reports. It is not surprising then that these end-users use fairly simple data integration means such as:

- Copying and pasting from a terminal emulation session
- Re-entering data from printed reports
- Importing data from a text file dump that must also deal with the EBCDIC-to-ASCII file transfer conversions

EBCDIC and ASCII are both charter encoding standards. EBCDIC (Extended Binary Coded Decimal Interchange Code) is used by the IBM mainframe as it character encoded character sets. In contrast, the PC and most other systems use the ASCII (American Standard Code for Information Interchange) character encoding. Therefore, one of the main issues is conversion from one character encoding to the other.

IT professionals have demanded that there be a direct integration of the Host data, the mainframe running the database, with the PC systems. This has been a problem for many years and has been renewed because of the demands of the new wave of Internet, intranet, and extranet applications, which need to tap the mission-critical data. Data Warehouse OLAP (Online Analytical Processing or discussion support) issues have also fueled the demand for data integration as well.

Microsoft offers an easy way to tap into the enterprise's data stored on the IBM mainframe – by using Microsoft's SNA Server with its OLE DB native driver for AS400 and OS/390. This allows ASP scripts to tap into the mainframe's databases.

ASP in the Enterprise

The majority of application developed and deployed in between now and the end of 2003 will be intranet, extranet, and Internet technology based. Therefore, it makes sense to choose a middleware technology that allows for the best integration of current enterprise assets and resources into the new wave of Web-based applications that will drive the enterprise. It is not practical, or economically feasible, to move your current data assets to new platforms. It makes more sense to add additional layers that will access and leverage the enterprises current investments in technology.

Instead of using Perl on AIX, FrontPage on NT, and something else entirely on the IBM OS/390 and AS/400, you can do it all with ASP – as the glue for all the platforms with the same development tool across the board. This is a real saving and will help cut development time and effort in the process while decreasing time to market. Now you can write the application once, regardless of platform, as ASP development is not just for Windows NT and IIS. This also provides for scalability beyond what you could expect from an NT-only solution.

Chili!Soft ASP

Chili!Soft develops ASP ports for Unix and other platforms as well as supporting a wide range of Web servers. This helps ASP technology to be seen as more than just a Microsoft centric middleware strategy. For example, IBM and Chili!Soft have been working to port their ASP engine to both the AS/400 and OS/390 operating systems. This will allow ASP applications to run on the same IBM platforms that make up 80% of the enterprise's data storage. The support of ASP for Unix will also extend to the enterprise's data assets that reside on Unix based RDBMS systems, such as Oracle, Informix, DB2, Sybase, and other vendor's products.

In fact, Chili!Soft has gone one step further than Microsoft with its **Chili!Beans** technology that allows off-the-shelf Java classes and JavaBeans to become COM ASP components. If Chili!Soft is successful over the long term it will do nothing but better the ASP application development environment. Their Web site URL is `www.chilisoft.com`.

Chili!Soft Targets the ISP

The target market for the Chili!Soft product is the ISP, to provide for greater Web hosting capabilities. They believe that this will become a strong market for their technology since the acceptance of ASP in general has been growing steadily, as well as the fact that most ISPs run on UNIX, or a variant of UNIX such as Free BSD, or Linux. However, I believe that the enterprise has a definite need for the same integration of systems, and that in time, the enterprise's customers may become a strong stake holder in the Chili!Soft ASP technology.

Why Active Server Pages on Non-Microsoft Platforms?

As has been said before, most enterprises are made up of a number of different platforms and data stores. It is also just not good business to put all your eggs into the same basket. IT, like the airline industry, likes to spread the pain among several vendors. This allows for options that a single-vendor solution might not provide. A savvy IT manager does not want to be 'held hostage' by a single vendor, where there are no real competing solutions.

Beyond the above argument, most enterprises are supporting industry standards such as the ANSI/ISO SQL database language standards, the TCP/IP network protocol standards so a single-vendor specific approach is not considered an Open Standard. With the move to port ASP solutions to other platforms, ASP has a chance of becoming a *de facto* standard. Without this migration to other platforms and Web Servers, ASP will never be seen as anything other than an elegant Microsoft solution.

Chili!Soft's ASP and Distributed Object Technologies

The dramatic shift to Web-based application development has been seen as the vehicle that has made distributed application development more mainstream. The technology for distributed applications has been around for a long time, and has been used in operating systems, network operating systems, and database-engine development for some time. But distributed applications are only now finding their way into the enterprise developer's arsenal of technologies, which need to be understood and applied to develop the enterprise applications of today and the future.

There are three major directions distributed technologies are being developed: COM/DCOM, Java and CORBA. We will explore each of these technology directions and see how Chili!Soft will utilize each.

Chili!Soft ASP and COM/DCOM

Microsoft's COM is Chili!Soft ASP's native object model on both Windows NT and Unix. Chili!Soft ASP, version 3.0, now supports DCOM, and allows COM objects to appear as local COMs object even when they are distributed on another, or even several other, machines. This allows for greater distribution and load balancing.

Chili!Soft's Unix support has also extended the DCOM model to include the supported Unix platforms, thus widening the distribution environment to machines that can run heavier loads. This also means that ASP components do not have to reside on the ASP server. They can reside closer to other data assets and other data collection devices. The data collection devices could be medical instrumentation or anything equally as complex and complicated. This support for a wider distribution policy opens up a virtual limitless set of possibilities.

Chili!Soft ASP and Enterprise JavaBeans (EJB)

Sun Microsystem's new EJB, Enterprise JavaBeans, specification has been recognized as a powerful alternative to Microsoft's COM/DCOM. EJB promises to be a robust, platform independent, architecture for the creation of component-based distributed applications.

Chili!Soft ASP, version 3.0, allows the developer to immediately take advantage of the EJB Server to host transactional ASP components. The EJB Server provides many of the same services that Microsoft's MTS and COM+ provide in the COM world. The EJB Server provides such services as transaction management, life-cycle management, object persistence, thread management, as well as other services that are managed automatically.

This combination makes an excellent environment for developing industrial-strength, scalable, secure, transaction-oriented Web applications. This is an extension of what you can currently expect in the Microsoft-only ASP environment.

Chili!Soft ASP and CORBA

One of the first technologies that promised to bring true distributed application development with objects was CORBA (Common Object Request Broker Architecture) and was developed by the OMG (Object Management Group).

The OMG is moving forward in establishing CORBA as the "Middleware that's Everywhere" through its worldwide standard specifications: CORBA/IIOP, Object Services, Internet Facilities and Domain Interface specifications. With the combination of Chili!Beans technology and Java IDL, ASP developers can now use CORBA as one of their distributed application options. CORBA objects can be accessed via Chili!Beans and Java 2.0.

With Chili!Soft's approach to ASP we can see the future of ASP has been broadened considerably. More vendors, who have embraced non-Microsoft based standards and specifications, can be serviced by ASP, and this will only help it become the *de facto* standard for distributed Web application development scripting.

Summary

This chapter has looked at ADO in a wider perspective than you're probably used to. Most people, myself included, tend to stick to relational databases, but data is becoming more widely available in different forms. We therefore need to expand our horizons when talking about data, and this is what the UDA strategy has been all about.

In particular we've looked at:

- How to access a variety of different data stores from ADO
- What semi-structured data means, and how we can use the new ADO objects to access it
- What Internet Publishing means, and how you can access remote resources
- A brief overview of the wider world of the non-Microsoft enterprise

It's important to realize that what's been covered in this chapter is only the start of something bigger. Developments such as WebDAV could have a huge impact on the way we manage data on the Web, and it could prove to be a major turning point for collaboration. The current crop of Web page editing tools are very much aligned at the single author, and they leave a great deal to be desired when it comes to team work and multiple authoring.

With an increasing amount of data being published on the Web, it seems sensible (and indeed imperative) that there should be an easier way to edit, review, and publish this information. The only thing I can say is watch this space – WebDAV is going to get bigger.

Also, with companies such as Chili!Soft expanding the support for ASP across non-Microsoft platforms, ASP is quickly becoming a standard for all forms of Web-based application development in the enterprise.

This ends our discussion of data access and in the next section we will be moving on to look at how we can employ the power of components in our ASP applications.

N
W

13

Components and Web Application Architecture

Up to this point in the book, we have looked at how to use Active Server Pages to dynamically build Web pages. ASP scripting allows us to take information passed in by the browser and dynamically create an HTML (or DHTML) page to send back to the browser. When building this page, we can pull in information retrieved from databases such as SQL Server or the Microsoft Data Engine (MSDE), and add this to the HTML page to be sent back to the browser.

But ASP is more than just creating dynamic Web pages. We have the ability to tie together sets of pages into Web sites that subsequently begin to function like applications. And, thanks to the Application and Session objects, our applications can be stateful, allowing us to share information between an individual's requests to a site, and even between all the users of a site. These applications have all the power and functionality of traditional applications, along with some tremendous benefits.

As we make this transition to building larger and more scalable applications with ASP, we will want to take advantage of the technologies that allow us to do so with greater ease. If an application is truly scalable, it has the ability to handle a very large number of users with the same facility, and only slightly poorer performance, than with which it handles a very small number of users. As builders of Web sites that could be generating an income for us, the ability to support more users means more dollars in our pockets. One key way of making applications more scalable is by building them out of **components**. In this chapter and those that follow, we will take a look how to design applications out of components.

Specifically, we will look at:

- The architecture of distributed applications, including Windows DNA
- What makes up a Web application
- What are components
- A quick introduction to ActiveX and COM
- The three types of components and why we should use them
- Building Web applications out of components
- Designing a component-based Web application

To get us started, let's look at the bigger picture of application architectures.

Distributed Application Architecture

One of the key elements of any application design is the **system architecture**. The system architecture defines how the pieces of the application interact with each other, and what functionality each piece is responsible for performing. Whether we like it or not, in the Web-based world we inhabit, we are more often than not going to be building applications that exist in a **distributed** environment. In fact, the ASP applications that we have been looking at up to this point in the book are actually distributed applications.

A **distributed application** utilizes the resources of multiple machines or at least multiple process spaces, by separating the application functionality into more manageable groups of tasks that can be deployed in a wide variety of configurations. There are a number of benefits to dividing applications up into pieces, not the least of which are reusability, scalability, and manageability.

Ultimately, dividing up an application in this manner results in the creation of a series of application layers or **tiers**, each of which is responsible for an individual, or atomic, element of the application's processing.

Tiered Applications

Tiered applications can be characterized by the number of layers that information will pass through on its journey from the data tier (where it is stored in a database typically) to the presentation tier (where it is displayed to the client). Each layer generally runs on a different system, or in a different process space on the same system, than the other layers.

Two-Tier Applications (Client/Server)

Let's look briefly at the 2-tier client/server architecture. Typically, we have a user's PC for the client (front-end) and a network server that contains the database (back-end). Logic is divided between these two physical locations. Usually the client contains most of the business logic, although with the advent of stored procedures, SQL language routines allow business logic to be stored and executed on the database server:

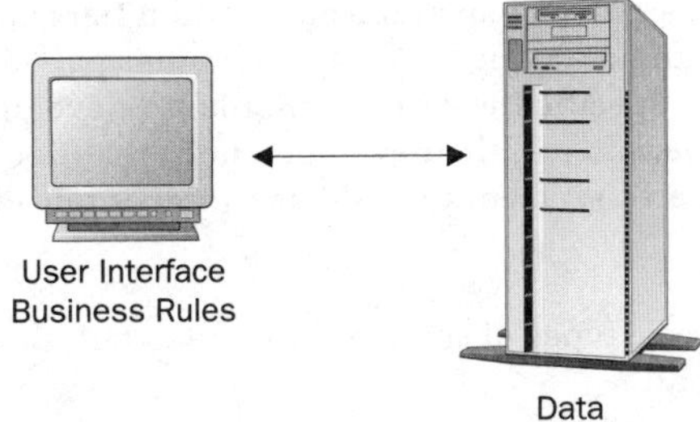

The 2-tier scenario works very well when you have a small business that only uses, or needs, a single data source. However, the goal of most businesses is to grow. As the business grows, so will the database and its requirements. Unfortunately, the 2-tier approach does not scale very well. If your business rules change then the application needs to be rebuilt and redeployed. In addition, there are factors such as the maximum number of simultaneous database connections that prevent this architecture from ever being of much value in a distributed setting with more than a few users.

Three-Tier and N-Tier Applications

Due to the limitations of the 2-tier client-server architecture, distributed applications are often divided up into three or more tiers. Components in each of these perform a specific type of processing – there's a **User Services** (Presentation) tier, a **Business Services** tier, and a **Data Services** tier in a 3-tier application.

The main distinction between this 3-tier architecture and your traditional 2-tier client-server architecture is that, with a 3-tier architecture, the business logic is separated from the user interface and the data source.

Breaking up applications into these separate tiers or sections can reduce the complexity of the overall application, and results in applications that can meet the growing needs of today's businesses. **n-tier** applications are just 3-tier applications that might further sub-divide the standard User Services, Business Services, or Data Services tiers. In any case, an application with more than two tiers can be considered an n-tier application.

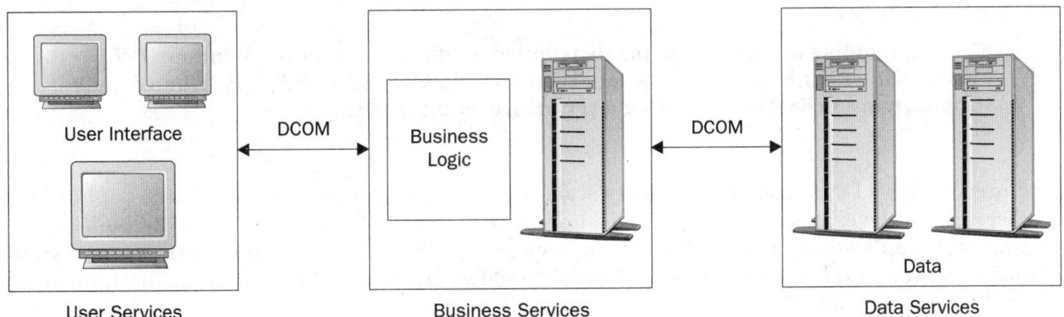

In this type of application, the client should never access the data storage system directly. If it did, it would be circumventing the business rules of the application and would thus be unable to ensure that the data on display to the client was correct.

The separation of the various aspects of an application into n tiers allows for any part of that application to be modified without having to change the other parts, allowing developers to specialize in designing and developing a specific tier or tiers. Similarly, developers can also take advantage of the development tools that specialize in the development of that tier, rather than making use of general purpose tools, which are sufficient to build an entire application but are lacking in terms of powerful features.

Before we look at the three basic types of services in more detail, there is one more variation on the n-tier theme we need to look at.

Windows DNA

Windows DNA refers to Microsoft's **Windows Distributed interNet Architecture**, and not DeoxyriboNucleic Acid. It is Microsoft's latest and greatest development model for the Windows platform, the goals of which are to:

- Provide the architecture to develop and deliver robust, scalable, networked applications on the Windows server platform
- Make both new and existing applications and data sources available to a wide range of clients, from traditional desktop applications, to Web browsers, to Internet appliances

Windows DNA is about Infrastructure

Windows DNA provides a roadmap that helps make developing distributed applications easier, because it's all about encouraging the use of already available application and operating system services to minimize the amount of infrastructure code required to create a distributed application.

Just think about all the times that you wrote hundreds of lines of code to provide transaction processing, message queuing, security, or custom database access in your applications. Now imagine all of these distributed application requirements being lifted off your shoulders. Instead, Microsoft will take care of these details for you, by providing you with a set of efficient and programmable services, leaving you to concentrate on the business requirements of the application.

> **The bottom line is that developing distributed applications with the Windows DNA model will result in higher performance, more reliable, and scalable distributed applications, delivered faster than ever before, at a lower cost.**

Before Windows DNA, usually only large-scale or enterprise applications distributed application processes. However, because of the application infrastructure, Microsoft continues to build and enhance its applications, making it easier to develop distributed applications. Soon many of your smaller network applications will be using the Windows DNA model instead of the traditional two-tier client-server model.

Windows DNA is about Interoperability

Windows DNA can interoperate with, or talk to and make use of, existing legacy systems so you can leverage and extend current technology investments. Try telling the Chief Information Officer of a medium-size manufacturing company that you want to scrap all of their existing software and hardware so you can develop new distributed applications based on the Windows DNA model.

It won't happen overnight – just like converting all companies that use Oracle database systems to Microsoft SQL Server 7.0 database systems. Microsoft has finally realized that not everyone will or can afford to convert every legacy system to run on the newest Microsoft platform. The legacy systems will remain in place, but will need to be integrated into our new applications. The evidence of this discovery can be found in the Windows DNA model, with its interoperability and support for industry standards. For example, the Windows DNA model supports the open Internet standards for HTML and XML.

The missing link between systems is DCOM, which allows applications to communicate across processes and across machine boundaries to compiled components that provide services, all the while without having to know where the service is located or how it is implemented. It allows developers to create service-based applications while using component-based development methodologies.

> *While DCOM is mainly a Windows platform service (I say mainly because DCOM has been ported over to some versions of Unix) the open Internet standards supported by the Windows DNA model ensure that you can create cross platform distributed applications.*

Windows DNA also makes provisions for the access of legacy data with its Universal Data Access (UDA) initiative, by allowing you to use the same data access library to run queries against your SQL Server and your legacy AS400 databases, for example. This is achieved by several sets of technologies all knowing how to interact with that same library, and then having the ability to access both relational and non-relational data from multiple different sources on their own system.

Windows DNA is about the Internet

When Microsoft introduced the Windows DNA architecture in September 1997, they introduced a framework for creating new Internet applications as well as integrating the Web with already existing client-server and desktop systems. The Internet is a great application platform for two main reasons:

- The Internet allows developers to create applications that are platform independent without making developers learn a new proprietary language.
- The Internet provides a flexible mechanism for deploying applications. Deployment is a major problem for lots of organizations, especially when you're talking about deploying a large-scale, enterprise application to several separated locations.

Windows DNA Services

As we've seen, Windows DNA provides a range of services that provide the necessary plumbing and infrastructure upon which we can build our application in relative ignorance.

Presentation Services

The presentation services of Windows DNA deal with how the application interacts with the user. This user can be located on the same computer, on a different computer on the same LAN, or on a computer on the other side of the world connected by the Internet. A key concept behind Windows DNA is that the accessibility of the application is not affected by the type of client that the user has. In order to provide this flexibility, Windows DNA supports a wide range of client types and a wide range of tools with which to build these presentation services.

Even though a Windows DNA application can support many different client types, we can characterize them into four distinct categories, two of which are traditional "fat-client" while the other two are "browser-based". The traditional applications are either written to take advantage of a network connection, if one is available, or written such that they simply will not function if a network connection is not present. The browser-based applications meanwhile can either be browser-neutral or tailored for a specific browser.

Internet-Enhanced Client

An **Internet-Enhanced** client is one that takes advantage of the features of DNA and can also make use of, but is not reliant upon, Internet connectivity. Take, for example, Microsoft's Office 2000 and Visual Studio. These applications support unified browsing by embedding hyperlinks from within the application, host the browser for the display of documentation written in DHTML, and provide the capability to download updates over the Internet seamlessly.

Internet-Reliant Client

An **Internet-Reliant** application is one that is written as a traditional Windows application, but which requires a network connection to a server in order to function. This type of application is generally used when the user interface of the application goes beyond what is efficiently developed using a Web-based client. It could also be an enhancement to an existing Windows application to convert it into a Windows DNA application. The primary characteristic of this type of application is that it *requires* a connection to the network in order to function, as opposed to an Internet Enhanced application, which will run on a stand-alone machine as well as on a networked one.

"Fat-client" applications can be created using any of the Windows development tools, such as Visual Basic, Visual C++, Delphi, or any other tools that will create an executable application. The reliance on a network connection can be added in several different ways. The application could link to the Windows Sockets library in order to connect to a server via TCP/IP over the local network or Internet, for example. Alternatively, it could host an embedded version of Internet Explorer to provide access to information on the network. In any case, the application interacts with (and depends on) a server somewhere on the network in order to function and won't work without a permanent link to it.

Browser-Enhanced Client

Whereas the two previous application types that we looked at are part of an executable application, the second two are browser-based applications, so called because they use HTML as their presentation mechanism. This HTML is retrieved in real time from a Web server using HTTP as a data transfer protocol. The HTML provides a user interface to the client that allows the user to interact with the application using a Web browser.

Even though HTML is a specification, different browsers often support extra functionality not found in the ratified standard. When a user interface is developed that requires the use of extensions to the HTML specification, this is known as a **Browser-Enhanced** application. For a Windows DNA application, this usually means that the user interface is targeted for delivery in Internet Explorer. With a specific browser as a delivery target, the developer can utilize technologies such as ActiveX controls, Dynamic HTML, or IE Behaviors to make the user interface more like a traditional Windows application. Even in this case, the user interface is delivered to a Web browser using the HTTP protocol from a Web server. Applications such as this are generally found on corporate intranets, where the IT department can control the target browser platform. If the application developer can expect a certain version of a browser, then they can create a Browser-Enhanced application and know that it can be executed successfully.

Browser-Reliant Client

One of the drawbacks of browser-enhanced user interfaces is that they generally require a specific browser in order for the user to work with the application. Whenever a new technology, such as a new browser version, is made available, there is usually a time lag, sometimes up to several years in length, before a large installed base of that new browser version becomes available. During that time, if the developer targets these new features, then they risk making their application unavailable to a large portion of their audience.

To avoid this problem, the developer can choose to target an earlier browser version, which will make their application accessible to wider population. These types of clients are known as **Browser-Reliant**. This may sound a bit deceiving, but the name refers to the fact that the user interface is reliant on a browser and not a specific version of that browser. It is probably not effective for a developer to develop an application that works with ALL browsers. Generally, the current standard for applications requiring a wide deployment will be a browser target of the version 3.x browsers from Netscape and Microsoft.

By targeting this browser version, the developer will have access to client-side scripting using JavaScript and the HTML 3.2 specification. It will also make the presentation compatible with all of the subsequent browsers, from both Microsoft and Netscape. With the growth in popularity of Internet Explorer following the release of version 4.0, this has also become a baseline development target for a number of developers, most notably those of corporate intranets where IE is becoming the standard.

Application Services

A Windows DNA application relies on the available application services to store and execute the core of its application logic. This business logic tier is where the application-specific processing and business rules are maintained. The Windows DNA services for developing these application components include Web services, messaging services, and component services.

Component Services

Component-based applications have been the standard method for creating applications for the better part of the last decade. From their earliest days as DDE, then OLE, OLE2, and finally today's ActiveX, component applications for the Windows platform have become widespread. It's not surprising really considering how much easier development is using components – the whole process now has a new model which consists of wiring pre-built components together to create an application. Why is this possible? Because every component has a number of publicly accessible functions that other components can discover and use. The end effect is that components are simple to reuse and allow different applications to work with each other.

To help component-based applications grow into enterprise-level applications, Microsoft added the Microsoft Transaction Server to provide services for the development, deployment, and management of component-based distributed applications. By encapsulating this plumbing into a system-level service, it freed developers from having to explicitly add this support to their applications.

With the release of Windows 2000, we saw the introduction of COM+. COM+ unifies the programming models of COM and MTS and makes it even easier to develop distributed applications by eliminating the need to handle both services individually. This allows the developer to build applications faster, easier, and ultimately cheaper by reducing the amount of code required to make use of these component services.

Messaging Services

Since not all parts of a Windows DNA application need to be located on the same computer, or even in the same physical location, it is critical that developers be able to communicate with these disparate systems. And, in the networked applications paradigm, there also needs to be a way for disconnected clients to communicate with the application. Messaging is a technology that permits this communication. Microsoft Message Queue Server (MSMQ) makes it easy to integrate applications by implementing a message delivery mechanism between applications. This allows the developer to build reliable applications that work for both connected and disconnected clients. MSMQ also offers seamless interoperability with other message queuing products, such as IBM's MQSeries.

Web Services

The application services of a Windows DNA application need a way to interact with the presentation layer on the client. In this case, that way is the Hypertext Transport Protocol, a mechanism which Microsoft's Web Server, IIS, already provides as a service for anything that cares to use it. In fact, IIS not only supports the delivery of static Web pages to a client, it can also be used to dynamically create client presentations through its integration with Active Server Pages. But you knew that already, didn't you?

Data Services

As we noted earlier, Universal Data Access is Microsoft's strategy for providing access to information across the enterprise. It provides high-performance access to a variety of information sources, including relational and non-relational data, and an easy-to-use programming interface that is both tool and language independent. UDA does not require the expensive and time-consuming movement of data into a single data store, nor does it require commitment to a single vendor's products. It is based on open industry specifications with broad industry support, and works with all major established database platforms. The two primary components that provide data services are ActiveX Data Objects (ADO) and OLE DB, both of which we've already covered in this book.

The Structure of the Web

The structure of the Web is a lattice of HTML-formatted pages, distributed from computers known as Web servers to client computers, and viewed using tools called Web browsers. At the most basic level, there is no difference between a server that has thousands of pages and a server that just has one or two. It is by linking these pages together in some form that a set of pages becomes a Web site, and by adding some additional logic, a Web site becomes a Web application.

Web Page

The basic unit of a Web interaction is the Web page itself. A Web page is a text file that is marked up using HTML. It is sent to a browser from a Web server based on a request from that browser. The browser parses the information in the HTML file, and the resulting user interface is displayed within the browser itself. The role of the Web server is to listen for a request from the client, parse the request to determine the page that the client requested, retrieve that file from the server's storage area, then transmit that file to the client. At this point, the server forgets everything about sending that file to the client, except for maybe placing an entry into a log file. It is this "connection-less" nature that gives a Web server its scalability, but in turn makes it a challenge to create meaningful applications without some additional support.

Web Site

A Web site consists of a set of related Web pages grouped together by some means. Generally, a Web site is all of the pages that exist on a server, or within a folder on that server. For example, all of the pages that are on the `www.wrox.com` server are considered part of that Web site. The correlation between the pages on a site is maintained by the links within each page on the site. The links on each page in the site will take users to other pages within the site. In this way, the pages that make up the site internally maintain the hierarchy of the site. These pages are still subject to the restriction of the Web server architecture, in that the server does not maintain information about the series of requests from a particular client. So while this related set of Web pages that make up a Web site are beginning to look more like an application, there are still some missing components.

Web Applications

Windows DNA applications are applications in the traditional sense, in that they provide a service to the user of the application. They are different in the way that they are created as well as in the components that make them up. A traditional application requires a special set of files during development, but distributes different outputs. For example, a Visual Basic application has a `.vbp` project file, multiple `.frm`, `.cls`, and `.bas` files, as well as a set of OCX components that make up the application project. Prior to the application being distributed, these files are compiled into a set of executable files for distribution and execution. The resulting executable does not require the presence of the source code files that were used to develop it.

Script-based Web applications, on the other hand, are composed of the same set of files used during development and after deployment. There is no compiled executable file produced that becomes the Web application. For example, the `.htm`, `.asp`, and `.dll` files in your Web project are the same files you deliver to your production Web server. The source code, or script, in these Web files is executed on the client or server only when a browser requests the Web page. Creating these applications builds upon the architecture of the World Wide Web, but there is some added complexity and functionality in order to have these files function as an application.

Web Application Design

In building a Web application, there are a number of new aspects of application design and development that the developer must take into consideration. While the flexibility of Windows DNA allows for a wide variety of clients accessing a wide variety of services, we will be focusing on a Web application. In a Web application, we will look at using a browser as the primary user interface. The information in our Web application will flow from server to client using the HTTP protocol. Our Application server will be Microsoft's Internet Information Server functioning as both a Web and Application server. Finally, our business and data access logic will be encapsulated within COM+ components and serve as the plumbing that links our application together.

The Browser as the User Interface

For a Web application, the user interface is presented within a Web browser. This means that the client presentation can either be Browser-Enhanced or Browser-Reliant. The type that you choose for your application should be based on the installed browser base of your target audience. If you can guarantee that most of your users will be using a particular browser level, then you should consider leveraging the features of that browser level. If there are a wide variety of browsers in use, then you may only be able to support a Browser-Reliant client presentation type. One of the advantages of using Active Server Pages to deliver the application is that it has the capability to determine with what browser the current user is accessing the application. This was covered in Chapter 6 with the Browser Capabilities component. By knowing the browser type of the current user, you can dynamically change your client presentation to support the enhanced characteristics of that browser.

HTTP as the Transport

The communication layer between the client and the server is critical to the design and implementation of the application. The HyperText Transport Protocol (HTTP) defines how the request made by the client is received and handled by the server, and then how the information is sent back to the client. Depending on the type of client presentation being supported, there can be different types of information that flow using this protocol. For the basic support of a Browser-Reliant client, the information that flows over HTTP is limited to the HTML that makes up the page, graphical images to enrich the interface presentation, information-bearing cookies, and possibly some client-side scripting to provide interactivity on the client. With an Enhanced client, special features such as Remote Data Services or COM over HTTP may also be communicated over the transport protocol. But support of these is reliant on the capabilities of the browser at the client. In either case, the HTTP protocol does not understand the concept of a persistent connection between client and server.

IIS and ASP as the Application Server

The combination of Microsoft's Internet Information Server as the Web server and Active Server Pages as the Application server provides the application component of our Web application. For Web pages and Web sites that serve up static Web pages for display, IIS can function by itself to provide the information. But when a Web application demands a dynamic display of information, we need to link the Web serving capabilities of IIS with the dynamic page generation and object integration capabilities of ASP to deliver a more robust and dynamic Web application. The scripting capabilities of ASP allow us to support business logic inside of our scripts, link with business logic components, directly access databases via ADO, and make use of data components to retrieve information.

COM+ as the Plumbing

The component-based design of Windows DNA applications is made possible by their reliance on COM+ for component services. While a fully functional application can be constructed out of ASP script and HTML, it is when the business logic and data access are separated out into components that a more robust and scalable application begins to emerge. By placing the business and data access logic inside of components that have been compiled prior to execution, the performance of the application increases. And, with the increase in performance, we have laid the path for a corresponding increase in the number of users that the application can effectively support.

Components

With all of this talk about components and component-based applications, it is important to understand just what a component is. We have seen a number of them used in ASP already in this book – remember that ADO is a set of components that support access to data sources. There are six components intrinsic to ASP 3.0 that allow a developer to access certain parts of the Web application. The concept of components is critical to the creation of scalable Web applications.

What is a Component

> **A component is an object that contains code to manipulate data from one form to another, and which provides access to that code through a well-specified set of publicly available services.**

This is a very literal definition of a component.

> **In a more practical sense, a component is an encapsulated piece of code that performs some function for an application.**

This function could be the processing of a business rule, like the computation of a sales tax, or it could be the retrieval of some information from a database for an application. The key characteristic of a component is that when it is created for use, the code for the component, as well as the information associated with the component, are packaged together. In this way, if there are multiple versions of the same component in use at one time, each one keeps its information separate from the others. There is no danger of information in one polluting the information of another.

In addition to the type of work that it performs, a component is also defined by its interface. To understand about interfaces in more detail we need to take a closer look at COM.

COM and COM+

Throughout this chapter, we have talked about components and COM rather freely. COM stands for the **Component Object Model**.

> **COM is an outgrowth of the object-oriented paradigm and is a specification that is based on a binary standard for reuse through interfaces.**

COM is an object model developed by Microsoft and implemented on all of the Windows platforms. It forms the basis for all applications developed for Windows in that nearly all interactions with the base operating system are through COM-defined interfaces. COM defines a standard for component interoperability – that is, the ability of components to interact with one another. It does not specify the language that the components are written in – it merely specifies how components need to communicate with one another and with the operating system itself. By specifying the interoperation standards that components must adhere to, it makes it easy for components created by different developers, even developers from competing companies, to work together in an application. This means that components written for COM can be reused without any dependencies from the language it was written in. It doesn't matter if an application contains components written in Visual Basic, C++, Java, or even COBOL, just as long as these components follow the COM specification.

COM+ is a set of services that combine COM with Microsoft Transaction Server (MTS) on Windows 2000 systems. MTS provides the facility to manage the lifetimes of components. Rather than having to worry about the creation and destruction of objects for their application, COM+ has the ability to manage that for us, so we can focus on implementing their business logic. With the introduction of COM+, the functionality of MTS has been merged into the operating system and is now called Microsoft Component Services. We'll take a cursory look around this in the next section, but for a more detailed discussion, you should take a look at Chapter 15.

Component Services

With the release of COM+, Microsoft Transaction Server has ceased to exist as a separate entity on Windows 2000. Its functionality is now a basic part of the operating system under the moniker "Microsoft Component Services", which should indicate that there's more under this roof than just the management of transactional services and components' lifetimes.

Along with a new name, the Component Services also offer some new functionality in the way that components are handled over MTS. As the operating system service – and not the developer – handles more and more of these features, our lives should become much simpler in the pursuit of developing robust and scalable components. Here's what's on offer.

- **Component Load Balancing (CLB)** – CLB allows multiple application servers to provide the same COM+ object for use in an application. When that object is needed, the creation request is sent first to the CLB Server which then redirects the request to an appropriate application server, based on certain criteria (like how busy and how far away from the machine running the application it is). The client application then interacts with this server for the lifetime of the component. Load balancing would be implemented at the COM class level but unfortunately, it looks like the first release of Windows 2000 will not support component load balancing. It may make an appearance as part of a Service Pack, or in a future release of Windows 200x. (I guess this will become the new OS naming convention.)

- **Queued Components** – Combines the features of COM and MSMQ to provide a way to invoke and execute components asynchronously. Processing can occur without regard to the availability or accessibility of either the sender or receiver. When a client calls a queued component, the call is made to the Queued Components recorder, which packages it as part of a message to the server and puts it in a queue. The Queued Components listener retrieves the message from the queue and passes it to the Queued Components player. The player invokes the server component and makes the same method call.

- **In-Memory Database Support** – The In-Memory Database (IMDB) is a transient, transactional database-style cache that resides in RAM memory and provides extremely fast access to data on the machine on which it resides. IMDB can be used by COM+ applications that need high-speed database lookup capabilities or applications that need to manage transient state. Data inside an IMDB can be accessed using ADO or OLE DB interfaces from a COM+ object. As with load-balanced components, the IMDB technology has not found its way into the first release of Windows 2000. It will most likely appear in a future version of Windows 200x, and will probably be enhanced based on feedback from developers.

- **Object Pooling** – Object pooling is an automatic service provided by COM+ that enables you to have instances of a component kept active in a pool, ready to be used by any client that requests the component. Once the application is running, COM+ manages the pool for you, handling the details of object activation and reuse according to the criteria you have specified. In order for components to be pooled, they need to be stateless, have no thread affinity, and be aggregatable. This means that VB components cannot be pooled, since they have a thread affinity, while properly written C++ components can.

Transaction Manager

Microsoft Component Services can function as a transaction manager for components. We will look at transactions in detail in Chapter 19. In managing a transaction for an application, Component Services will examine the components participating in the transaction to see what their transactional requirements are. Some components are quite happy to ignore whatever transaction is going on, while others want to or need to participate in a transaction. When a component is developed and deployed, the developer will set this transaction parameter for the component. Component Services will use that information to determine how the component should participate in the transaction, if at all.

Component Manager

In addition to managing components in their interactions with transactions, Component Services can also manage the components themselves. While this functionality was part of MTS, it was generally not what came to mind when looking at the features of MTS. Component Services uses the context of a COM+ component to help manage it during its lifetime.

A context is a set of run-time properties maintained for a collection of one or more objects. Each object is associated with precisely one context during its lifetime. Multiple objects can run within the same context and multiple contexts can reside within the same COM apartment. Context properties allow Component Services to provide run-time services. These properties hold state that determines how the execution environment will perform services for objects within the context.

Security Manager

Component Services provide a number of security features for your COM+ components as well. There are automatic security features, which are available without adding one line of code and are configurable administratively. Other security features can be integrated directly into the development of the component. Role-based security, which can be implemented programmatically or administratively, is the central feature of COM+ security. It allows for security down to the method level of a particular component, allowing all users to access a component, but restricting certain methods of that component to certain users.

Data-Centric Components

The bottom tier of our three-tier architecture is the data access layer. This layer is responsible for integrating with the data sources that our application needs to be able to function. These data sources could be SQL Server or Access databases, Exchange message stores, MSMQ message queues, or UNIX legacy applications. They could exist on the server itself, on some other server on the LAN, or somewhere across the Internet. The data component is not only responsible for encapsulating the access to the data, but also for making the location of that data transparent to the application as well. All that the application needs to do is instantiate and use the component – the component itself figures out the rest.

Why use them?

There are a number of reasons why data-centric components are necessary portions of a three-tier, and therefore a Windows DNA application. Obviously, without a data layer, we would only be left with a two-tier application. But seriously, there are many reasons why encapsulating data access within a component leads to a more robust application.

- **It shields the developer from the inner structure of the database**
  This encapsulation is a primary tenet of object-oriented design. If the internal workings of a component are not exposed to the developer using the component, then these inner workings can be changed, updated, enhanced, or replaced depending on the changes to the physical data store below them. It also means developers cannot circumvent security or procedures by changing rows in the database in an incorrect order, etc.

- **It provides consistent data access to different data sources**
  By encapsulating the access to disparate data sources in a common interface, developers can use similar methods to access data regardless of where the data actually resides. This means that access to data stored in a SQL Server database can be accomplished using the same methods as data stored in a flat file on a UNIX system.

- **It makes the location of the data transparent**
  With the method to physically access the database encapsulated within the component, the location of the data does not matter to the user of the component. They merely access the component, and the component makes the necessary connections to the data source to retrieve the data.

Business Components

The middle of our three tiers is the business component layer – sometimes referred to as the business logic layer or the application layer. No matter what it's called, its job is to provide the functionality for the application. This could mean managing a shopping cart for an e-commerce application, validating the benefits selection of an employee on the HR section of the intranet, or calculating the best route between two locations in a mapping application.

A business component is designed to hide the complicated interactions that a set of business rules need in order to process and also to shield the user interface designer from having to know anything about the underlying data. They simply interact with the methods of the business components to present information entered by the user and interpret the results of the component's processing.

Why use them?

Whereas data components are generally the most commonly used of the three component types in the n-tier architecture, there are also a number of compelling reasons to use business components as well. Some of these reasons are similar to, or even identical to, the reasons for using data components:

- **Business Rule Encapsulation**
  By encapsulating business rules inside a component, the developer using it does not need to worry about how the rules are actually processed. The component has a set of well-defined interfaces that the application developer will interact with. What happens inside should not matter to them, as long as the component delivers the proper results.

- **Application Reuse**
  By encapsulating business logic within components, it makes it much easier to reuse that business functionality in multiple applications. For example, a business could have one component to calculate commissions on sales. This would allow any application that needs to calculate commissions to do so using the same component. All commissions would be calculated in the exact same way, since the same component was used to calculate it.

- **Performance**
  In developing Web applications, it is very straightforward to use script to create the business rules of the application. This makes it easy to get an application up and running quickly. However, scripting not only violates the first two reasons that we have already mentioned, but it can also cause performance problems as well. Since script is interpreted every time it is run, and a component is executed from compiled code, the performance of the script cannot begin to match the performance of the compiled component.

User Interface Components

The final layer of our Web application is the user interface layer. It is in this layer that the information generated by the middle tier of the application is presented to the client. How it's presented is generally based on a template in HTML or DHTML to which dynamic information is added. In some instances, the business logic may even select which presentation template to display too.

There is a lot of debate about the encapsulation of the user interface creation code into a component. Since ASP script can be embedded within an HTML page, it is very straightforward to use ASP script to insert the dynamic values into an HTML template. If that information is part of a compiled component, then it makes it very difficult to change the presentation without recompiling the component.

Why use them?

There are a couple of occasions where a user interface component could make sense for an application. They are generally related to making repetitive tasks easier for a developer, such as displaying a menu, or where script alone cannot generate sufficient performance. For each one of these reasons, there are other, non-compiled, methods that can be used to nearly duplicate the capabilities of the component-based UI, without many of its drawbacks:

- **Repetitive Presentation**
  There are usually certain parts of a Web application that are repeated in a number of different pages – possibly with different information. A frameless Web site that is trying to replicate a framed look-and-feel generally has to recreate parts of the page over and over again. This presentation could be encapsulated into a component, which would make implementation by a developer quicker and present a more standardized appearance. However, similar functionality could be accomplished through the use of an include file containing methods capable of rendering the information to the browser.

- **Performance**
  Performance is always a big issue when it comes to building scalable Web sites. The more performance we can ring out of any aspect of the application, the better the application as a whole will perform. Encapsulating complicated presentation logic within a compiled component will allow the site to perform faster, but at the trade-off of limited flexibility to change the presentation without recompiling the component. Another method, which was covered in Chapter 3, is to store repeated HTML blocks as strings in script, and then store that script in an application-level variable. This gives the performance of compiled code without sacrificing the flexibility of ASP and HTML integration.

Component Application Design

In building a component-based application, we need to look first at how to design an application that will use components. This will include both a process for breaking the application down into its components as well as how to design the actual components themselves.

Once we're comfortable with that, we must carry on to look at several issues related to building component-based applications for the Web. Specifically, we must address the design of our components and the interfaces we choose to expose in them, how we will tie out components together and the tools we'll use to implement all of the above.

Moving to Components

As we begin to move our application from a traditional monolithic or client/server application, we need to first look at how to break the application functionality into components. This is known as **decomposition** and can be done in a number of different ways. There are many books available on various object design methodologies, so we won't go into a detailed discussion about them here. The key thing to look for in selecting, or creating, a methodology is that it fits in with your manner of doing business, and also does not radically alter your existing development processes, unless you are not happy with the way things are being done now.

There are many advocates for each methodology, but it is up to you as an application designer and developer to select the one that best meets your needs. And if you can't find one that you like, then you should feel free to take parts of existing ones and create your own. As long as you can deliver a design that not only allows you to create an effective application, but also provides a roadmap for others to understand your application, then you have an effective design methodology for yourself.

As we begin to decompose our application into components, the first step is to partition the functionality of the application into the three tiers that make up a component-based application. A good way to begin is to look at each part of the application, and determine which tier it belongs in. If you're finding it difficult to select a particular tier for a piece of the application to fit into, chances are you're not splitting it up into small enough pieces. At this point, it is time to decompose the element you are currently looking at into multiple parts, with the goal that each part will fit nicely within the presentation tier, business logic tier, or data tier.

As these components begin to fall into our design, we still need to maintain some semblance of an application in our minds.

If we don't remember to do this at this time, then when it comes time to wire the components together at the end, the chances are we will have strayed from the application design as a whole. But by keeping in mind what the final goal of the design is, then the components we end up with will readily tie together into an effective application.

Application Design

The application design is important in building a component application. Without a specified set of application requirements, it will be very difficult to create the components to support the application. In designing the overall application, there are a number of methodologies that can be used. For example, in the Use Cases approach, the application design is created by defining how the application will be used in specific instances.

Whichever method is used when we are designing a Web-based application, there are a different set of challenges that must be overcome that are not present in a traditional application. First and foremost, we as application designers have limited control over the tool that a person is using to access the application. Unless we have a tightly controlled intranet application, the chances that people will be accessing the site using different browser types and versions are quite high. This means that our application has to be designed to support this wide range of presentation types.

Internet-based applications are also usually accessed through a slow connection, such as a 33.6k or 56k modem. This has two primary implications in the design of the application:

- First, the file size of any graphical images, including those images that make up the user presentation tier, must be such that they can be transmitted quickly to the client. An application will quickly lose its usability if the person using the application is continually waiting for the application to download images. Images in a Web-based application are fine, and provide many great benefits, but if they negatively affect usability, then another method of communicating graphical information to the user must be found.
- The speed of the connection also means that every interaction with the server is going to take some perceptible length of time. This pause between interactions will have an effect on the perceived usability and performance of the application. If this delay becomes too long, or happens too frequently, then the performance of the application will be more negatively perceived. Thus, as the designer of a Web-based application, you need to be aware of the number of "round-trips" that you make between the server and the client. A system running solely over a higher-speed intranet can survive a greater number of "round-trips" than a system that relies on the public Internet in order to function.

Designing Components for the Web

In addition to some overall design concepts for Web applications, there are also some specific component design criteria that should be followed to produce an effective Web application. As applications on the Web need to be able to scale to handle large numbers of users, without causing a corresponding decrease in performance, the components used to build the application need to be able to support these requirements as well. With a Web-based application, there is also the challenge of creating an application that has the concept of a "user session," where a series of discrete user requests are treated as a single interaction with the application. Though there are multiple tools for maintaining user sessions, such as the Session object, the application designer needs to understand how the use of these tools affects the performance of the system.

Stateless Components

If you go back and look at the basic definition of an object, it is generally given as a set of code and data treated as a single unit. By combining the data with the code of the object into a single package, multiple instances of the same object can exist at the same time, and can be used to represent different pieces of information. This is a very effective design for client/server applications, where an application can create objects that represent a specific entity within the application, and then through the interface of that object, have it perform the functions of the application. Since the object itself knows about the data it contains, it can perform these functions without the need of another source to provide the data.

This also means that a particular instance of an object is explicitly tied to the data that it contains. There is no way for that object to represent itself as holding different information if it needs to participate in a different interaction. The only way for that to happen would be for the system to create a new instance of that object and load it with the required data to perform the interaction. The strength of object-based applications is that the application simply knows that it interacts with a certain type of object – the specifics about the information contained within the object is of no concern to the application. The drawback is that we now need two objects to represent our two different pieces of data.

In applications that are supporting a single user, or a limited number of users, the creation of new objects to represent new items of data will generally not degrade the performance of the system. But when we start dealing with Web applications, that are supporting hundreds or thousands of simultaneous users, the creation of multiple objects for *each* user will have serious effects on the performance of the system. Luckily, our n-tier model for Web-based applications affords us a unique opportunity to address this issue.

Since each request that a client makes of a Web server is treated as a unique connection, there is nothing binding the server to the client in between requests. This means that while the user is viewing a fully downloaded page of the application in their browser, even if they are interacting with information on that page, the server does not have to perform any processing for that particular user during that time. It is free to go off and work with other users.

But what if the first user has created some objects that are uniquely linked to that user? The server has to make sure that these objects are maintained so that the next time the user comes, they will be readily available for that user to use. This means that server resources will be tied up just waiting for the next request to come in. If you extend this out by hundreds or thousands of users, you quickly see a lot of objects sitting around, chewing up server resources, waiting for the next request to come in. So what is the solution?

If a component can be designed so that it can perform the same type of work, but yet doesn't need to maintain any information within the component to perform the work, then it could be discarded after every use. Or if the component could be developed such that COM+ could pool the component, it would just be returned to the component pool. There would be no need to hold onto a reference to that object while the user is off working with the client page. The resources that were being consumed by the object can be returned to the server. By quickly freeing up resources in this manner, the number of users that the application can support at any one time will grow dramatically.

If a component does not carry any information around within itself, it is said to be a **stateless** component. A **stateful** component therefore is one that is said to hold information internally from one client interaction to the next. There are a couple of ways of making a component stateful in your Web applications. Conversely, by not doing these things, a component can be made stateless, and thus more scalable:

- Saving a reference to a component from one page to another, by storing its reference in a Session-level variable, will cause a component to hold state.
- Setting a series of properties in a component, and then calling a method to perform some interaction, will cause the component to hold state. Passing all of the parameters to process a method as parameters will help to minimize the statefulness of a component.

Sessionless Applications

Another design criteria that we need to worry about when designing Web applications comes from the inherent stateless nature of the Web. As we mentioned earlier, once a server completes a client's request, it forgets all about that client. This means that as far as the server is concerned, that client has no past and no future with the application. Generally, an application consists of a series of steps that must be linked together in order to fulfill its tasks. If the server keeps forgetting about the client in between each step, it makes the design of the application that much more difficult.

When the application platform only supports sessionless applications, as a Web server does, we have to maintain the state of the session elswhere. There are a number of facilities that can do this for us, but each one has its effects on the scalability of the application. Step number one however is for a client to identify itself to the application each time it makes a request.

This identification could take the form of a cookie passed from the client to the server, a hidden `FORM` element that contains a unique identifier, or a parameter appended to the URL when the request is made of the server. In any case, this number must correspond to some information on the server that is unique to the client. This number can be a reference that points to an object with all of the session information in it. It could be a primary key into a database table that is holding the session information. It could also be an indication that there is other information in the request from the client, either in form fields, URL parameters, or cookies, which contain the state of the current session.

To put it succinctly, the three ways to maintain session information are:

- Storing data in the Session object
- Storing data in a database
- Passing information between pages via the Request object each time a new request is made

Each of these methods has its advantages and disadvantages. The method that you choose for your application should be based on which has the least impact on the performance, scalability, and usability of the application.

When information is stored in the Session object, it can be quickly retrieved, but it means that the information is local to that particular server only. If the application is being scaled through the use of a Web farm, then this session information will only exist on one machine within the farm. If a user wants to access their session information, then they must be directed back to that same server each time. As this prevents balancing the usage of the server based on load, it can lead to some inefficiencies in the scalability of the application. On the other hand, accessing and using the Session object is quick and it is a well-documented method of providing session information.

Storing information about a user session in a database means that multiple machines within a Web farm can access it. In this way, the client is not tied to a particular server and the Web farm can operate much more efficiently. The drawbacks of this method are that the retrieval of information from the database is orders of magnitude slower than retrieving information from the memory space on a server. There is no way to store an instantiated object within a database, as you can do in the Session object. Finally, there is no easy-to-use interface like the Session object through which to access the information.

When you use the client to store session information, you are removing the burden from the server having to maintain that information. By reducing the processing requirements of the server, you lessen the number of resources it requires, which in turn increases the number of users the server can support with the same resources. The drawbacks of this method include the lack of common interfaces to handle information passed in this manner, the strain put on the network connection in requiring that this information be passed back and forth during every request the client makes of the server, as well as relying on the client to pass you information that is vital to your application functioning correctly.

In choosing the method for maintaining the session state of an application, you need to examine each of these possibilities and choose the one that best meets the needs of your design. As with any system, you can also choose to use a hybrid that combines elements of these three choices. For example, if one part of your application is best solved by having a stateful component used by two pages, then a reference to that component can be stored in the Session object to pass it from one page to the other, and then destroyed once it is no longer needed. Note however, that you will need to abide by the component design issues involved with component scope that will be examined in Chapter 15. Meanwhile, all of the other state information about the application session could be being stored in cookies and hidden form fields. In this way, the three different methods are complementary, rather than exclusive.

Component Design

There are two key aspects to the design of a component. The interface of a component is how it communicates with the outside world, and is the only way that the outside world can work with the services provided by the component. We also need to look at where the component is physically located, which will determine how it can participate with the other components that comprise the application.

The Component Interface

The **component interface** is the mechanism by which the component interacts with the rest of the world. It is designed to provide access to the information and the functionality supported by the component. The interface is the *only* way that other components or applications can interact with the functionality within the component. The interface is comprised of the public properties and public methods of the component. Any private properties or private methods of the component will only be accessible from within the component, and therefore cannot be access via the component's interface.

We will be looking at COM and interfaces in much greater detail in the next chapter.

When designing a component's interface, we need to support the other aspects of the component design that we have already looked at. Namely, the design of the interface will directly lead to the statefulness or statelessness of the component. If we create a component interface that relies on properties being set before the component can perform any functions, then we are creating a component that is holding some internal state for some length of time. It will also require multiple calls into the component – some to set the properties, and then one to execute some action. You can see from this code sample the number of times we would have to call into the component:

```
<%
Dim obj As Server.CreateObject("MyComponent.Test")
obj.Property1 = 123
obj.Property2 = 234
obj.Property3 = "abcd"
Call obj.Method1()
Set obj = Nothing
%>
```

If we were to design this component interface such that the method call carries with it the values that it needs to perform its function, then we will have a much more stateless component. There will only be one call into the component to process the function, and no internal information will be stored within the component. If we created another method called `Method2` to achieve that, a call to it might look like this:

```
<%
Dim obj As Server.CreateObject("MyComponent.Test")
Call obj.Method2(123, 234, "abcd")
Set obj = Nothing
%>
```

As you can see, the new interface only requires one call into the component before the component can be released. This is in comparison to four calls into the component in the previous example before it could be released. And in terms of the effect on scalability, the sooner we can release a component, and let the system have its resources back, the more scalable the system will become.

Component Location

In addition to the interfaces that a component supports, the physical location of the component can also affect the scalability of the application. As our application interacts with its components, it will want to do so in the fastest and most efficient way possible. Any time wasted in creating a communication channel with a component will be more time during which the performance of the application is slightly worse than if the component was not being used. You always need to remember when trying to make applications highly scalable, to take any increase in processing time or increase in resources usage and multiply it by at least the projected number of concurrent users. Once you do that, it becomes plain to see how a minute change in resources usage or time can begin to cause serious problems.

We want to make sure that the interaction between our ASP scripts and our components, and between our components, happens in the quickest and most efficient way possible. This generally means that the component should run within the same process as the ASP application. In the next chapter, we will look at how COM+ enables you to administratively change where a component actually executes. As with all potential speed improvements, running your component in the same process as your ASP application, while faster, also makes it more likely that a problem with your component could affect your entire ASP application. When a component is run within the same process as the ASP application, then all calls into the component will be done using direct function calls. This is the fastest way to access the component.

If we run the component in a different process, then any information that is passed between the component and the application must cross the process boundary to get from the application to the component. In the Win32 environment, this is a resource and time intensive operation. It will take more system resources to make the call, and it will also require more time. This happens in both directions in the conversation between object and application as well. So any information, such as method parameters, that is passed from the application to the object will have to be marshaled across the process boundary. On the return trip, any information that the object wishes to send back to the application, such as a return value, will need to be marshaled as well.

We can also utilize the DCOM capabilities of the Win32 environment to execute our components on a different physical system than the one running the application. Even though this connection happens transparently to the application, there are still major performance penalties to be paid. Everything that was mentioned about accessing components running in a different process holds true with DCOM components but more so – the time it takes for client and server to communicate is greatly increased. This is especially true as latency increases when you move off of a LAN and onto a WAN or the Internet. You need to be very careful if you want to use DCOM components in your ASP application as a result of this.

Tying the Components Together

Once you have constructed all of the components for your application, you need a way of tying these components together. Without some sort of glue that tells the components how to interact with each other, you really don't have an application. You can use other components to serve as the glue that holds your components together, but in practice this makes constructing an application as difficult as constructing a component. One of the advantages of a component-based application is that you can quickly wire together a set of components to create your application. So to facilitate this, we can use ASP scripts as the *component glue* in our application.

On the system that is hosting your application, you will naturally need Active Server Pages installed. The system with ASP installed on it now becomes more than a Web server – it becomes your Application server. And, in order to serve your Web applications to clients, it will need to access the components that you need to build the application.

There are two types of components that can be used to build an application. Those you have custom-built and installed on the server for the application and those components already existing on the server, be they by Microsoft, yourself or some other third party.

Reusing Existing Components

When reusing existing components, you must first make sure that your use of the component does not break any other applications that are relying on the component. For example, if you were to update the component to a newer version to support your application, you could potentially be breaking an existing application that was relying on a particular version of the component. Also, if the component relies on registry settings to hold its configuration, and you change those settings to suit your application, then other applications using the component may no longer function. Note however, that none of the above should happen if you follow basic interface development guidelines.

The easiest way to see which other ASP applications are using the component is through the use of a simple text search routine, such as GREP, or the Find in Files function of Visual InterDev. Since all ASP script code is in a text format, you can simply search through all of the `.asp` files on your application server for the ProgID of the component that you are going to reuse. This will help you directly pin-point any applications using your component. You can then make provisions to test those applications when you make any changes to the component's configuration.

Installing New Components

There are a few ways to install newly created components onto your application server.

One option is to take the file containing your component – typically a `.dll` file – copy it to the server and then register it with the operating system. By doing so, sufficient information is place in the system registry to allow applications to reference the components and have the system know which component it's referring to. Installing components in this way, however, does place the onus on you to make sure that all the files the component depends upon are also present on the server. Without them, the component will be unable to function properly, and could possibly not even be registered properly.

A second way is to first build an installation program on the development machine, copy it to the application server, and then execute it. This is usually a foolproof method of ensuring that the dependencies for the component are installed properly alongside the component. One downside of this method, though, is that it requires a physical interaction with the console of the Application server. Also, if the installation program does not take into account the proper versioning of components, it can very easily overwrite a version of an existing DLL with a version that causes other applications to not execute properly, or even cause the server to crash.

A third method is through the use of a COM+ application. A COM+ application, as we mentioned earlier, consists of a set of components that the Microsoft Component Services manages as a single group. In Chapter 15, we will take a look at both how to create a COM+ application, and how to move that application from one application server to another.

Building your Components

All this talk about building components to encapsulate business logic or data access logic has hopefully laid the groundwork for you to build your own components. Well, the first thing you need to know is what tools you can use to create your components. That is one of the strongest points about COM – it is language-neutral. This means that you can create your components using nearly any language you choose. And not only are you free to select a language, you are also free to choose from a wide variety of tools with which to write your components.

Tool Selection

There are many development tools available on the market for you to create components with. The list includes:

- **Microsoft Visual C++**
  This tool creates the highest performing, lightest-weight components possible. By utilizing the Active Template Library, some of the intricacies of component creation are taken care of. But all of this performance comes at a price. This is generally considered the most difficult way of creating components and has the steepest learning curve. We will take a look at using Visual C++ in Chapters 17 and 18.

- **Microsoft Visual Basic**
  At the other end of the spectrum, Visual Basic is one of the easiest tools to use to create components. These components don't necessarily have the optimal performance that C++ components do, nor do they have their flexibility. That being said, most benchmarks have shown that a VB component, when designed and used properly, performs at about 90-95% the speed of a C++ component. What they do have is the ability to be created quickly and easily by a wide group of developers. We will be looking at creating components in Visual Basic in the next chapter.

- **Windows Scripting Components**
  Microsoft has extended the world of component creation to scripting languages as well. By adding an interface definition written using XML, we can now create components using the exact same tools and code that we use to create our ASP scripts. We'll see more of this in Chapter 16.

Component Testing

After creating a component, the most important step prior to using the component is testing it. A component needs to be tested not only to ensure that it is performing the operations that it was designed for, but that it is not adversely affecting the rest of the system. There are three types of testing that you can perform on the component.

- **Functional Testing** – This type of testing ensures that the component works as advertised. Testing of this nature is generally done by applying a set of inputs to the component for which the proper outputs are already known. The outputs generated by the component are compared with the known outputs, and any discrepancies are resolved by changing the functionality of the component.

- **Stress Testing** – To make sure that the component is not adversely affecting the systems resources, it can be tested under stress. This is usually done with a testing tool, such as WAS or WCAT, which simulates a large number of users accessing the component simultaneously. During this testing, the system resources are monitored to ensure that there is not any excessive resource utilization of the component.

- **Integration Testing** – Integration testing looks at how the component interacts with the other components that are going to be making up the application. This is done to make sure that there are no issues, such as contending for the same resources, or relying on different versions of the same DLL in order to function.

Once this testing is complete, the component is then ready for installation onto the Application server, and then for integration into the application.

An Application Design Case Study

In this chapter, we have looked at a lot of theory concerning the creation of n-tier Windows DNA applications. This theory should have covered all the bases necessary to create a component-based, scalable Web application. The problem with just theory is that it is just that – theory. It is the practical examples that the majority of us developers like to work with. Yeah sure, give me the theory, but enough already and show me how it's done!

In this section we will do just that. With all of the theory on our plate on creating a Windows DNA application, let's put it to work to actually build one. Well, that's a bit presumptuous, as we still need to look at actually coding the components of the application. So, in this section, we will see how to *design* a Web-based Windows DNA application:

- First, we will define the problem that we are going to create the application to solve. This is generally the most important, but usually the most neglected step in the design phase.
- After defining the problem, we will look at the design of the application. This design will include the component architecture and the interfaces presented by the components in the application.
- Finally, we will look at any design tradeoffs that we were forced to make and how these tradeoffs will affect the scalability and extensibility of the application.

Defining the Problem

`WhizzyBang.com`, like all small but growing Internet companies, is dealing with the administrative hassles of continually adding new employees, employees changing roles and titles, and people spread throughout the world. These challenges have made it difficult for `WhizzyBang.com` to maintain a working human resources support system without driving the poor HR employees crazy. They have decided to stop being cobbler's children, embraced the Internet as the way to do business and created a Web-based human resources information system.

This human resources system will initially need to support the following functions:

- The hiring manager is responsible for the initial creation of the employee's record.
- The human resources manager must validate the information and process the proper government paperwork for the employee.
- The employee will need to use the system to select their health care benefits. This can be used by either new employees or by existing employees.

Since the information in this application will be used by other systems as well as the human resources system, it will need to be stored in a centralized system. Other information will be required to be sent to certain agencies outside the company. The data being used by the application is stored in the following systems:

- The employee database is stored in a SQL Server 7 relational database.
- The health care selection information is stored in an Access database.
- The government paperwork is delivered to a processor via an XML-formatted e-mail transmission.

The users of this application will be located in locations throughout the country. They will all have Virtual Private Network (VPN) access to the corporate network, but this connection is only over a 128k ISDN line between the data center and the VPN provider. A VPN allows the users to dial up to the public internet and then tunnel through the corporate firewalls to reach servers within the company. The VPN is configured to allow only the HTTP protocol to pass.

The systems to run the application will be hosted at a centralized site. These systems will be dedicated to this application, but the databases that the application will access will be on separate systems. The users of the application will have Microsoft Windows 98 and 2000 workstations. The application will only be accessible when the workstations are attached to the corporate network. The application should always check for the latest version when executed by the user.

Design Implications

Now that we understand the high-level requirements of the application, we can take a look at how some of these requirements will affect the design of the application. This is critical to examine at this point. If we were to design the application, without looking at the implications of the requirements on the design, then we could design an application that was difficult or impossible to implement or use.

In looking at these design implications, we will want to understand certain aspects of the implications. First, we need to know if there are certain requirements that are mutually exclusive to one another. For example, if one requirement states that the system must be accessible by disconnected laptop users, and another states that only HTTP access is allowed, we have a dilemma. Since HTTP access is only available as a connected protocol between a client and Web server, we have two requirements that are in conflict with one another. The requirements will need to be changed in order to support the realities of the system.

In looking for design implications, we will also look at those aspects of the requirements that are very precise, such as the type of database used by the employee database. These very specific points must, by definition, be carried directly to the final design. Those requirements that are more general, such as the types of workstations used by the clients, allow us more flexibility in the design of the application.

In an initial pass at the requirements, the following can be identified as design implications:

- The workstations will support a Win32 application, but the requirement that the application be self-updating implies that a browser-based application will be easier to support. In a browser-based application, the latest version of the application is always available by the client.
- The databases that the system will access both have OLE DB providers, so we can utilize ActiveX Data Objects to interact with the database.
- The human resources manager provides a validation step to the creation of a new employee, so there needs to be a notification mechanism to tell this user that a new employee is in need of validation.
- Since the same application will be used for both new entry and update of benefits information, it should support both a guided and interactive interaction with the data.

By recognizing these implications, we can guide the design towards the path of least problems when creating the application, and away from choices that are impossible to implement. It also makes the actual design process less fraught, more straightforward and more efficient. We can always refer back to these implications, as well as the requirements, to ensure that our design is moving along the correct path.

Application Design

Now that we have established the application's requirements, and taken account of the resulting implications, we can now get to work on designing it. At this point we have a number of directions in which we can proceed with our design exercise. There are almost as many application design methodologies as there are books on Active Server Pages. The design methodology that you choose to work with may be one that is thrust upon you by your employer, one that you have used in the past, or one that you have looked at and seems interesting. However you select a design methodology, and whichever one you select, you will eventually end up at the same point – the design of an application.

You should take into account the size of the application development effort when choosing a design methodology. Are you going to be the only developer working on this application? Will you or another developer ever have to extend and enhance the application? Does your application have to integrate at the component level with other applications? These questions and others need to be asked so that you can determine if the methodology you are using is compatible with the environment your application has to work in.

For this example, we will not subscribe to a particular published methodology, such as UML or Use Cases. As a lot of developers have found, the published methodologies are great in theory, but when it comes down to actually creating an application design in the real world, the methodology that works best is usually a hybrid that meets the unique needs of the application. In our application design methodology, we will be concerned with five aspects of the design:

- **Component Architecture** – How the components in this application are partitioned across the logical tiers, and how these components work with one another.
- **Data Tier Interface** – This describes both how the data components logically integrate with the physical data stores as well as how they are accessed by other components in the component architecture.
- **Business Tier Interface** – This describes how the presentation tier accesses the business components and which data tier interfaces each component works with.
- **Presentation Logic** – This describes the various visual interfaces that the user will be interacting with in order to perform the functions specified in the application requirements.
- **Integration Architecture** – The integration architecture specifies how the components of the application will be tied together. This will cover the physical location of the components, the packaging of the components into applications, and the mechanisms that the components will use to communicate with one another.

The design methodology is primarily concerned with the interfaces of the components of the application, and how these interfaces are tied together to create the application. The interface of a component specifies the information that the component will provide based on inputs provided by a caller. The internal workings of a component are left up to the developer to implement. As long as the component interacts with its interfaces in the way specified in the design, the component can be considered a *black box*. With components designed in this way, the primary integration task is to tie the components together, which is the final step in the design.

Component Architecture

The component architecture of the WhizzyBang.com human resources application will define the components that make up that application, as well as how these components are tied together. The component architecture provides the glue between the presentation layer and the actual data. In this diagram, we can see the role that the component architecture will play in the application:

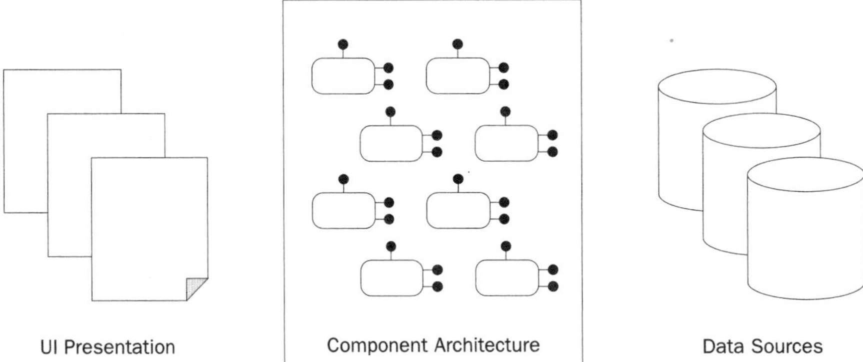

The component architecture in the application represents the business logic components as well as the data access components. These components will have their interfaces defined later, so for now we need to decide the various objects to create. Generally, object decomposition will allow you to begin with a loosely defined object and break that object into its component objects until you reach a more discrete size. First, let's take a look at the data objects.

In this application, there are three primary data sources. These three data sources are the SQL Server employee database, the Access benefits information database, and an e-mail box for sending tax information. The SQL Server database is unique in that it is used for both the retrieval of information as well as the storage of information. The employee's information is initially created by the application and stored in this database and then it is retrieved and used in the application. The information in the benefits information database is used in a read-only capacity by the application. There are no requirements in the application to write information to the benefits database. The tax information repository is exactly opposite, in that it is a write-only data source. This means that once information is written to that data store, it can no longer be retrieved by the application.

These three primary data sources can correspond initially to three objects. To begin with, we can refer to these as:

- The Employee component
- The BenefitsInfo object
- The TaxInfo object

The Employee component will be responsible for the interaction with any data inside of the employee database. Since this database contains different types of data, such as name and address information, dependent information, and benefits selection, it probably makes sense to have multiple objects to access this single physical data store. The process of breaking the Employee component up into a more granular set of objects is known as object decomposition.

In our example, we will decompose the `Employee` component into three separate objects. We will also choose an object-naming schema that will relate these three granular objects back to the original `Employee` object. The name and address information will be accessed via the `EmpInfo` object. The dependent information via the `EmpDependent` object, and the benefits information via the `EmpBenefits` object. As the `BenefitsInfo` object and the `TaxInfo` object are already somewhat granular in their nature, we will not decompose these objects into multiple objects.

The business tier of the application needs to deal with the creation and validation of an employee record and the selection or modification of employee benefits. The employee information creation section needs to enforce certain business rules on the information to ensure that the information is added correctly to the database. In this case, we can see the separation of functionality into the data object being only responsible for the access to the information, and the business logic serving as the enforcer of the business rules.

We will create three primary business objects to work with the application. The `NewEmployee` object will process the business rules related to the creation of a new employee record by the hiring manager. The `EmpValidation` object will be used by the human resources manager to validate the information related to the new hire, and then to process the proper taxation information. The final business object will be the `Benefits` object, and it will be responsible for enforcing the business rules regarding benefits for the employee.

As you can see, we have closely related the business object composition to the required functionality of the application. This allows for a closer interaction between the business rules and the presentation logic, which will reduce the number of objects needed to process a given part of the application. By reducing the number of objects that are involved in the application, we can increase the scalability of the application, since fewer resources will be needed by each application session.

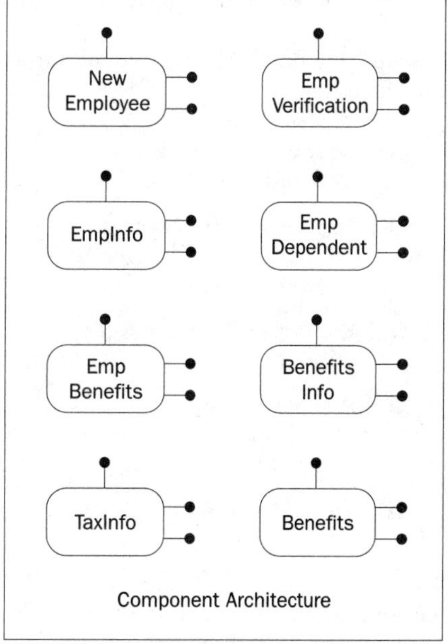

Component Architecture

You can now see that the business component architecture that connects our presentation logic with our physical data storage contains a set of eight objects. In the next two sections, we will apply the interfaces to the objects so that they can communicate with one another, and with the rest of the application.

The Data Tier Components

The data tier components are comprised of the interfaces of the five data access components. These components provide access to the data used by the application. The data interface will determine the methods in which the business components will interact with the data components to both retrieve and set information.

These components will also have an interface to the physical data itself, but the definition of this interface is not critical to our application design. The constraints of the methods of accessing the physical data, along with the specific information required to support the data tier interface, will determine how this interface to the physical data store is actually created. This physical interface is also driven by the system that the data is stored in. For the database information stored in the SQL Server employee database, this information will be accessed using the SQL Server OLE DB provider. The data for the benefits information, stored in an Access database, will be retrieved through an ODBC connection. Finally, the data transfer requirements needed by the `TaxInfo` component, since this data is transmitted via e-mail, will be performed using an SMTP mail object, like the Collaboration Data Objects (CDO).

The external interface for these components is important in that this is the manner in which the object is accessed by the rest of the application. Once this interface is defined, the business objects that need to retrieve or set business data can call through these interfaces to interact with the data that they need. The business objects will in turn expose an interface to the presentation logic.

For our five data objects, we will define the following methods to be available through their public interfaces:

- **`BenefitsInfo` object**
  `GetBenefitsForClass`, `GetBenefitInfo`, `GetBenefitOptions`
- **`EmpBenefits` object**
  `AddBenefit`, `CheckBenefitStatus`, `GetBenefitList`, `RetrieveBenefit`, `UpdateBenefit`
- **`EmpDependents` object**
  `AddDependent`, `GetDependentList`, `RetrieveDependent`, `UpdateDependent`
- **`EmpInfo` object**
  `CreateEmployee`, `DeleteEmployee`, `EmployeeStatus`, `EmployeeClass`, `IsEmployee`, `RetrieveEmployee`, `UpdateEmployee`
- **`TaxInfo` object**
  `SendTaxData`

These interfaces are defined to provide access to information stored within the data sources of the application. All will be through these objects' methods. If a business object, or a user presentation, needs to interact with the data sources to access information for display, or to update information, it must be through these methods.

The Business Tier Components

Now that we have defined how our application will be able to access data, we need to define the components that will allow the presentation logic to get access to the data in a way that is consistent with the business rules of the application. We have defined three business objects for this application – `NewEmployee`, `EmpValidation`, and `Benefits` – which correspond to the primary functional requirements of the application.

The interfaces for these components will be called by the presentation logic and will need to retrieve all the information needed for presentation by the user interface from the data tier. It will also need to define a way to update that information if it is changed by the user. The internal workings of these components will be responsible for implementing the business rules of the application. For example, it will be the responsibility of the `Benefits` component to ensure that the employee's benefits selections are valid. As with the data objects that we looked at earlier, the actual inner workings of the component are not important to us – as long as they perform the business logic processing correctly.

The three business logic components will support the following interfaces:

- **`Benefits` object**
  `AddBenefit`, `AddDependent`, `DeleteBenefit`, `DeleteDependent`, `RetrieveBenefitList`, `SetBenefit`, `UpdateDependent`
- **`EmpValidation` object**
  `GetEmployeeInfo`, `GetValidationList`, `LoginEmployee`, `SetEmpTaxInfo`, `ValidateEmployee`
- **`NewEmployee` object**
  `AddEmployee`, `CheckData`

Through the interfaces we have defined here, the presentation logic for the application must retrieve and set all of the information that it needs to function. The three-tier architecture that we have defined means that there is no direct access between the presentation logic and the data tier or the physical data itself. In this way, the presentation logic is shielded from any underlying changes in the data logic or the data structure itself. As long as the interface to the business components doesn't change, then the presentation logic doesn't need to be changed.

Presentation Logic

The presentation logic is the part of the application that actually ties into a user. This is the section of the application that generates the user interface and then receives input from the user interface based on the user's interactions. It is through the business component interface that the presentation logic communicates with the rest of the application. The user of the application will only see what is presented by the presentation logic – there will not be any direct interaction between the user and the database or the business objects.

The requirements for the application are such that the presentation layer of this application is going to be a Web application. Even though the capabilities of the client will support a Win32 executable application, there are other requirements that would make this a less-than-optimized solution. One of the requirements is for the application to always support the latest business logic. This would only be possible if every time the application requires business functionality, it requested that functionality from a central location. While this would be possible in a Win32 application that uses DCOM to communicate with components on the central server, again another application requirement prevents this solution.

Based on the analysis of all of the requirements, we have decided that the best architecture for the application is a Web-based application, where the user interface is presented as a series of dynamically generated Web pages. These Web pages will be created by a set of ASP scripts that will use COM to communicate with the business components. Each ASP page will generate one or more Web pages based on inputs by the user combined with information from the business components. The ASP scripts will be grouped into three categories – roughly corresponding to the three primary functional areas of the application.

The ASP scripts that form the presentation logic are categorized as follows:

- **New Employee Information**
  `AddEmployee.asp`, `AddEmployeeForm.asp`
- **Employee Validation**
  `DisplayValidationList.asp`, `EmployeeTaxInfoForm.asp`, `SetEmployeeTaxInfo.asp`, `ValidateEmployee.asp`, `ValidateEmployeeForm.asp`
- **Benefits Selection**
  `ChangeBenefit.asp`, `DependentList.asp`, `DisplayBenefits.asp`, `EditDependent.asp`, `EmployeeLogin.asp`, `VerifyEmployee.asp`

Now that we have defined the three layers of the application, we can take a look at how these three layers are wired together.

Integration Architecture

The integration architecture is where we tie the application together. This will specify how the interfaces of the business objects are called by the presentation logic, how the business components will call the interfaces of the data objects to get the information they need to process, and where the data components go to get the information they need. Once the integration architecture is set, the rest of the application simply becomes an implementation task. With the component nature of the application, as well as a well-defined set of interfaces, this development effort can be readily partitioned between multiple developers.

For our design exercise, we will not specify all of the integration paths, but we will look at a sampling for the application. The method for creating this integration architecture usually follows a relatively straightforward path:

- For the presentation logic, define what information is needed to be displayed, or what information the user is returning.

- For each piece of information, determine which business object and which corresponding interface is needed to either supply that information, or provide that data back to the application.
- With each business logic method, determine the physical data interaction required, and utilize the interfaces of the data components to provide that data.
- Finally, for each method of the data component objects, determine the physical data needed to support the method, and link that method to the required physical data.

For example, the `SetEmployeeTaxInfo.asp` page will need to take the taxation information entered by the human resources manager and send that information to the appropriate government agency. The business logic to perform this functionality is the `SetEmpTaxInfo` method of the `EmpValidation` object. This method will need to convert the tax information entered by the user into the appropriate format, which in this case is an XML format. It will then utilize a data object to actually transmit the information. The method to transmit this information is the `SendTaxData` method of the `TaxInfo` object. This method will need to take the information as submitted and open a physical connection to the data destination to transfer the data. In this case, the data destination is an e-mail box, so the physical connection is via an SMTP server.

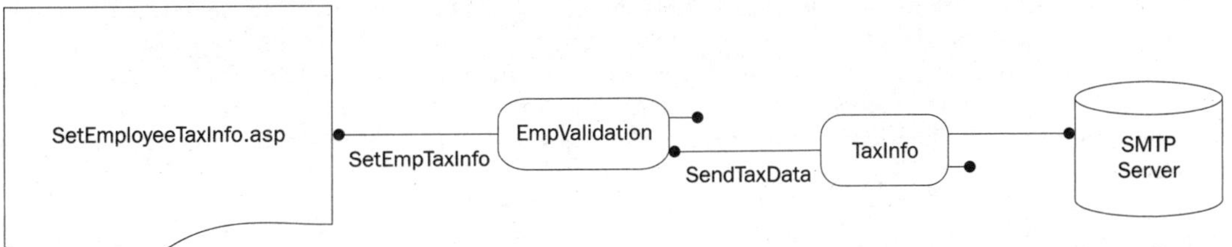

This methodology of creating the integration architecture is carried forward through every presentation logic component in the system. As more and more of the component integrations are defined, the process simply becomes a wiring up of already defined components. Once this is complete, adding new presentation functionality that is supported by existing business objects becomes a very straightforward task.

Design Tradeoffs

As we have constructed the architecture of our application, we have made a number of decisions about the design that will affect other aspects of the application. These are known as **design tradeoffs**. A design tradeoff usually involves making a choice between two possible design directions. The inputs that go into making a design trade-off include the effect on the functionality of the application, the length of time it takes to develop the application, how well the application can scale, and how easily the application can be enhanced and extended.

In creating our Web-based human resources application, we are primarily concerned with two aspects. Since the entire company will use this application, we need the application to be as scalable as possible. This means that we should be able to support multiple simultaneous users, and we should be able to increase the performance of the application by adding additional server processing power. The other aspect we are concerned with is the extendibility of the application. Since there will undoubtedly be additional functions desired by users, we want to make sure that our initial design will be able to support these additional functions. This support should be made available without requiring an extensive redesign of the application.

So let's take a look at the design for our application, and answer these two important questions about extensibility and scalability.

Can it be Extended?

The extensibility of the application can be traced to the design of the object model. We need to look and see if there are other application functions that could be implemented using the existing method calls. For example, we have the necessary business and data objects to access and edit an existing employee's information. In this way, we can add some new presentation logic to the application and, using the existing business object, add the employee information editing functionality to the application.

If we take a look at the existing data object interfaces, and look for any new business functionality that can be supported by them, we can determine any other application functionality that can be readily added. For example, the data object interface already supports the necessary interfaces to retrieve benefit information for an employee. A new business object to allow the corporate health claims processors to validate an employee's health care claims against the benefits they have selected could access this data interface.

When faced with new application requirements, the application designer should first look to the existing objects that comprise the application. Rather than diving in and immediately creating new objects, it makes sense to first look at the existing objects. When looking at these existing objects, look for the exact interfaces that you need to support your business functionality. If they don't exactly exist, chances are there are similar interfaces that you can extend and enhance. Only when you have exhausted your review of existing interfaces, should you turn to designing a new interface. Don't forget either to look ahead and bear in mind the possible future enhancements your new interface could support.

Can it Scale?

The other design question that we want to answer about our application is whether or not it can scale. Earlier in the chapter, we talked about designing components for the Web. By utilizing these design principles, we can help our application scale upwards to support more and more users. The key aspects for the scalability of object applications are related to the implementation details of the component, as well as the level of statelessness of the components.

In order to create components that can be pooled by COM+, we will need to make sure that the components used in this application are created with Visual C++. This poses a big implementation trade-off in that it generally takes longer, and requires a different developer skill to create a component using Visual C++ than it does using Visual Basic. We need to determine if the scalability afforded by C++ components outweighs the greater development time and cost over developing components in Visual Basic.

The scalability of the application is also affected by the statelessness or statefulness of the components in the application. If the design of the components is such that they have a longer lifetime, then the system will need to create a greater number of components to support more and more users. If the components can be used quickly and then discarded, then the system can function with a smaller number of components active at any one time. Since all of our components marshal all of the information necessary to perform each method with the parameters of the method, and since no information is retained from one method call to the next, we have created stateless components, which will lend to the scalability of the application.

Design Summary

We have now created the application design for our human resources application.

- The application should be built as a component-based three-tier Web application.
- It will utilize a browser-based presentation generated by ASP scripts.
- The ASP scripts will interact with a set of eight business logic components, which will support the processing of employee information, benefits information, and taxation information.
- In order for these business components to interact with the data that they need to perform their functions, they can draw from a set of three data components.
- Only these data components will interact with the actual physical data source, be it a SQL database or a SMTP mail server.

The entire application will be designed using components to support future extensibility as well as give the application the ability to scale to support a large number of users without requiring a redesign.

Summary

Web applications are quickly becoming the new application development paradigm for business in many industries. They are being used to build intranet sites to replace client/server or terminal-based applications. Consumers shopping for items on the Web are interacting with Web applications and companies that work together are now able to peer into each other's systems through a Web-based extranet. All three of these scenarios rely on the creation of Web applications that are easy to build, have robust capabilities, and are scalable to support large numbers of users. Windows DNA is the new application architecture for these types of applications for the Windows platform.

In this chapter we have seen:

- How Windows DNA allows us to build applications that are scalable and flexible
- What makes up a Web application and how you should go about designing one
- How components and Microsoft Component Services make it easier for us to build Web applications
- How you use the various pieces of the Web application architecture to create Web applications
- The three types of components and why we should use them
- A component-based application case study

In the next chapter, we will take our newly discovered knowledge about components and look at how to build a Windows DNA component using Visual Basic. Then in Chapter 15, we will then look at how to deploy it into a COM+ application, and test it to make sure that it works.

N
W

14

COM, COM+ and ASP

The **Component Object Model (COM)** is Love – well, that's what many COM gurus say, and maybe you feel just as inspired by ASP. Whilst I personally wouldn't say COM is Love, I would say it's probably one of the best technologies Microsoft has ever created. COM is certainly a technology that any serious Windows developer should understand and master, along with ASP of course. So, let's look a little closer at what all the fuss is about, try to understand why people like it so much, and determine how its relationship to ASP can help us in our development efforts.

The surprising thing about COM is that most developers and end-users are already unknowingly using it in some way, shape, or form. As an ASP developer you are using COM *all the time.* All of the ASP intrinsic objects are **COM objects**. When you use those objects you're invoking the methods of COM objects. IIS is built to a large extent using COM; indeed, just about every single Microsoft product is COM-based or enabled. If you've ever recorded an MS office macro or used VBA, you've used COM. So don't worry, COM is nothing new and it's not that difficult either.

Under Windows 2000, we've now got something called **COM+**. The '+' signifies that some important changes have been made to COM – namely the introduction of a slightly different base programming model, and the introduction of many enterprise-level **services**, such as transaction management and finite resource sharing.

So in this chapter we will be covering:

- What COM is all about
- What COM means to a developer
- How COM works
- The changes in COM+
- A simple ASP COM component written in Visual Basic

In this chapter, when I use the word COM I'm talking about details that are applicable to all versions of COM across all versions of Windows – 95, 98, NT and 2000. When I use COM+, I am speaking about details that are specific only to Windows 2000.

So What is COM, Apart from Love?

> **COM is all about a** binary level **of interoperability between clients and COM objects – in other words, how they talk to each other.**

It is **object-based** and, in a nutshell, what it achieves is the ability for somebody to package up some code into a **component**, using their preferred programming language, and then allow one or more clients to use that component and its functionality, in their preferred programming language. If the languages used are different, no problem – COM takes care of it. The client doesn't have to know how the functionality was written (what techniques or algorithms were used etc.) or what language was used; it just knows how to use it like a black box, and accesses its functionality via one or more **interfaces** – collections of related functions.

For example, do you know what language Microsoft used to write the ASP object model or ADO? Do you care? No. As long as you are aware of the available COM objects, methods and properties you can use their functionality. Those methods and properties together are known as the object's interface.

If you think of the ASP functions `CreateObject` *as* `CreateCOMObject` *and* `Server.CreateObject` *as* `Server.CreateCOMObject`*, you'll start to realize how you're already using COM.*

COM enables **location transparency** between a client and the COM objects it uses. The client and component can be running in different processes (applications) or even on different machines – once again, COM takes care of the mechanics required to bridge the distance. You use a component in the *same way*, no matter how near or far it is. COM provides the entire infrastructure to make everything work, you just focus on the important bits – writing and using components. The only requirements placed on the client and component creator are that:

- The component creator uses a programming language that can create COM components that follow the **COM specification**. For example, Visual Basic (VB) or Visual C++ (VC++).
- The client has a programming language or tool (such as Microsoft Word or ASP) that knows how to instantiate and use COM components, again, by following the rules laid down in the COM specification. Tools like Microsoft Word and ASP actually use other components to perform this creation. For example, Word uses Visual Basic for Applications (VBA) and ASP uses Active Scripting.

COM+ hasn't changed this basic model; it simply extends it with something called a ***context*** *(which we'll discuss in more detail in the next chapter), and introduces COM+ services.*

What I've just given you is a very succinct description of what COM and COM+ achieve. The basic principles are really that simple – it is Love, I guess, or is that ASP?

> *The phrase "COM object" and "COM Component" are frequently used interchangeably, and while this is not technically accurate, it's unlikely you'll be misunderstood. Strictly though they are different things: the former is an instance of the latter.*

COM is All Around you

COM is many things, and to understand all aspects of COM in detail really does take time – lots of reading and hands-on coding. On average, to become fluent and get your code right along with your understanding of COM and COM+ you probably need to allow about six months. Roughly speaking that's how long it took me to get going. However, to start to take advantage of it in your applications, and to create components in Visual Basic, only requires a few weeks given the right training. After this short amount of time you can nail down the basics and become productive with it. COM does take time to get right though, so make sure you always create a few disposable prototypes when you first start out.

We're not going to explain everything about COM in this book; it's just not possible. What we will do is give you an overview of the key elements of COM, and then give more detail on the bits that are useful to you as ASP component developers. For a more detailed introduction to COM check out these two excellent books:

- Beginning ASP Components, published by Wrox Press (ISBN 1-861002-88-2)
- VB COM, published by Wrox Press (ISBN 1-861002-13-0)

So let's take a closer look at COM. Don't worry if you find any of the details a bit scary or slightly confusing at first; they do take some time to sink in.

The Three Faces of COM(+)

COM can be broken down into three fundamental parts:

- A binary specification
- A runtime / library
- Services

Binary Specification

The COM specification defines a set of guidelines that development tools like VB follow when compiling class modules into COM components. Technologies like ASP use it to know how to create an instance of a component (COM object) and invoke its methods. For developers, this specification also defines a **consistent programming interface** across languages. What the COM specification doesn't define is how COM itself is implemented.

> *At the time of printing the COM specification was located at this URL:*
> `http://www.microsoft.com/com/resources/comdocs.asp`

All of the COM specification is defined in a language neutral fashion. It enables a client, and the COM objects it uses, to be written in different languages that support the specification – always remember, COM is a **binary specification**.

Because COM defines this **universal object-based communications medium**, it really does simplify the traditionally painful process of writing client/server applications, and having to write two APIs for different client types (e.g. one each for VC++ and VB). Trying to bend languages like VB to use functionality written in C/C++ using the `declare` statement works, but the VB programmer is often needlessly confused and forced to understand C/C++ constructs. Whilst people may argue that using the `declare` statement and other such arcane language bridging mechanisms aren't so bad, COM is a lot easier, and a much more natural and consistent way of doing things.

Runtime / Library

The COM runtime is an implementation of the COM specification and is provided with all versions of Windows. The runtime itself resides in many DLLs, although the core API is in `ole32.dll`. We use the COM runtime, and all of the functions provided in DLLs like `ole32.dll`, in our ASP developments all the time without even knowing about it – the calls are made *transparently* on our behalf.

> *The COM runtime is sometimes called the COM Library. I have a slight preference for the former term, simply because its implied context is 'during execution'. Others prefer the latter because it is also a library of functions. I'll stick to COM runtime for the most part, but expect people to use these terms interchangeably.*

A COM Client in an ASP Page

In an ASP page we use the COM runtime indirectly via the **ASP interpreter**, which in turn uses **Active Scripting** – the technology that converts VBScript, JavaScript and other scripting languages into COM calls:

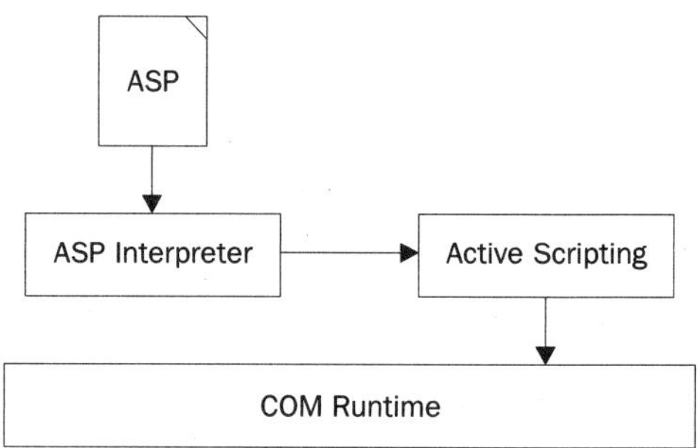

For example, when you use the `CreateObject` or `Server.CreateObject` functions in an ASP page like this:

```
Dim objConn

Set objConn = CreateObject("ADODB.Connection")
```

This code is extracted from the ASP page by the ASP interpreter and then converted by the Active Scripting engine into calls against the COM runtime. The COM runtime is the one that's actually responsible for the creation of the ADO Connection COM object.

A COM Client in VB

In VB, the same calls to the COM runtime occur when using the `New` statement. When you add ADO support to a project using the References dialog, what you're doing is telling VB about a number of COM components that you want to use. The reference you select defines these components, and then allows you to use them just like any other native VB type:

```
Dim objConn As ADODB.Connection

Set objConn = New ADODB.Connection
```

The runtime is really the useful bit of COM as far as we're concerned as developers. The COM specification is the COM bible, and it defines everything in extreme detail (should we wish to know about it), but it's the runtime that we use day in and day out.

> *With VB, the* `New` *statement will only call down into the COM runtime if the component being created is* ***not*** *within the same DLL. If the component is within the same DLL, VB doesn't need to use the COM runtime because it can directly create it.*

Services

Services are pieces of compiled code (that can only be written by Microsoft at the present time) providing significant functionality that can easily be used to enhance components. If you've used MTS before, you will have used **declarative attributes** and **declarative security**. These are two methods by which the behavior and usage of a component can be affected at runtime by an administrator.

An **attribute** in COM+ is a piece of information (metadata) that describes runtime properties for a component. You typically set these using the Component Services explorer. By associating one or more attributes with a component in this way, its runtime behavior can be affected without any need for additional programming or recompiling. This is the ultimate level of code re-use – we can leverage foundation code written by Microsoft rather than develop it ourselves. For example, in the Transactions tab for a COM+ application:

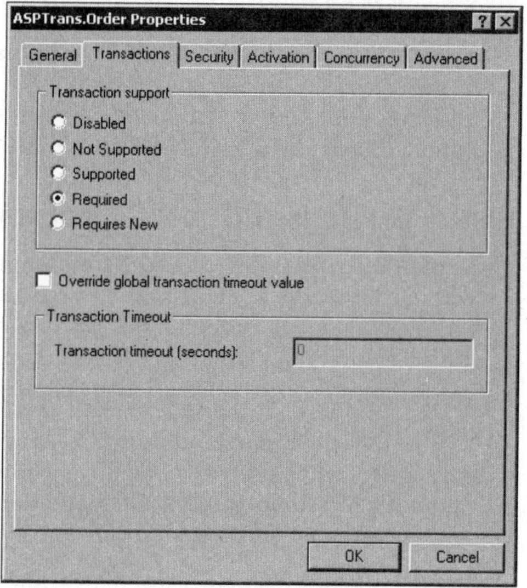

By selecting the Required option on this tab, we've told COM+ that our component wants to make use of the transaction service COM+ provides, and that each new instance of a component should take part in a transaction.

> *As we'll discuss in Chapter 19, transactions enable groups of components to perform work as one atomic unit.*

ASP Just Wouldn't be ASP Without COM

Without COM, ASP just wouldn't be so extensible or easy to use, and it probably wouldn't even exist.

Unless ASP was based on some equivalent specification/implementation you'd probably end up having to call and use different components in different ways, depending on what language was used to write them, or what company produced them. Imagine all the different approaches you'd have to understand, just to be able to invoke the methods. That's a problem C++ developers have faced for many years and still face today, even though COM does resolve the problem, because many companies have been slow to adopt COM until recently. Without COM, the amount of time you waste having to understanding the mindset of the component writer and the different APIs is a pain. Just be thankful COM provides you with an easy to use and consistent object-based programming paradigm.

At the time of writing, Microsoft estimate that 3 million developers use COM to develop COM applications that are used by over 200 million users on a daily basis. This makes COM by far the world's most successful object model.

COM Development Tools

As far as languages for writing components are concerned, the main ones on offer from Microsoft are Visual C++ and Visual Basic, both of which we'll cover both in this book.

Visual C++ does have a slight edge in terms of performance and flexibility, but that comes at a cost in needing a far greater understanding of the inner workings of COM. Once you have that understanding, using Microsoft's Active Template Library (ATL) to write components is almost as quick and easy as doing so in VB – but you have a lot more learning to do first.

Visual Basic is a Good Compromise

Visual Basic provides an excellent compromise between the need to get components written quickly, without having to spend so much time learning COM first, and the need for performance. VB also hides the majority of the COM runtime, which means you don't have to spend any time learning COM before you can create COM components. In other languages, like C++, you need a reasonable grounding in COM before being able to create COM components.

In VB, a basic understanding of COM will help you optimize your components – by understanding why things work the way they do – which is why we're introducing more about COM as we go. Although VB hides most of COM, understanding how VB maps its language constructs onto COM and knowing its COM limitations is very important.

VB is the natural progression path from ASP, especially for people who are used to working with VBScript. We'll spend a lot of time developing components using VB in this book, but we will also show you how to use C++, which has a slight resemblance to Java, and therefore JavaScript.

We'll be using Visual Basic 6.0 as our development tool, although for the topics we'll cover, there's little difference between this and version 5.0 – you can do the same things with the earlier version.

Interfaces

A lot of people in the COM world agree that the most important and powerful aspect of COM is **interface-based** programming.

> **An interface is really nothing more than a list of methods that define how something *could* be manipulated, if somebody wrote the code to implement the functionality described.**

This abstraction of **functionality** vs. **implementation** is something that has been around for years. Most people with any Object Oriented (OO) knowledge will immediately draw a very correct comparison to abstract data types (ADT).

As a real world analogy of interface-based programming, consider your TV. Its remote control provides you with an implementation of an *interface* that lets you control your TV. You don't know how the remote control works internally, but you do know that by pressing the various buttons on the control you can change the channels, increase and decrease the volume, and turn the TV on and off.

The *functionality* that remote control buttons provide can be defined by an interface (let's say `IRemoteControl`), which different remote controls can then implement. The interface for the remote control could have the following methods:

`TurnOnOff`	Turns the TV on if it's currently off, or turns the TV off if it's currently on.
`ChangeChannel`	Change to the specified channel number.
`IncreaseVolume`	Increase the sound volume.
`DecreaseVolume`	Decrease the sound volume.
`GetChannel`	Returns the currently selected channel.

If you've got three TVs in your house made by independent manufacturers, these methods could be implemented by each remote control to provide the same basic functionality, as defined by the interface. Each remote control will probably work differently internally, but you know how to use the interface (the buttons of the remote control in this case) and that's all that matters. So you know whatever TV you happen to be sitting in front of, you'll be able to change channel and watch your favorite program by using the remote control.

Internally, the implementation of the interface that the remote control exposes could communicate with the TV through another COM interface, maybe `ITelevision`. This interface would probably have similar methods to the `IRemoteControl` interface, and if every television in a house implemented the `ITelevision` interface the remote control could actually be used to control them all – ultimate control! No matter who created the television, provided the same interface was supported it could be controlled.

Components

The remote control in our example is what we call a **component** in COM. When you compile a class module contained within an ActiveX project in VB you create a component. If the project contains multiple class modules then you create multiple components.

> **A component is something that provides functionality by implementing one or more interfaces.**

Therefore, simply put, a component is a piece of functionality that is given a unique name, and packaged up and distributed in some fashion in a DLL or EXE. When you compile an ActiveX project in Visual Basic that contains four class modules, what you're creating when you hit the compile button is a **COM server** that contains four **COM components** – one for each class module. As I'll discuss in more detail shortly, what you've also created is four **COM interfaces** – one for each COM component – that are used to give people access to the methods and properties of the component (class module):

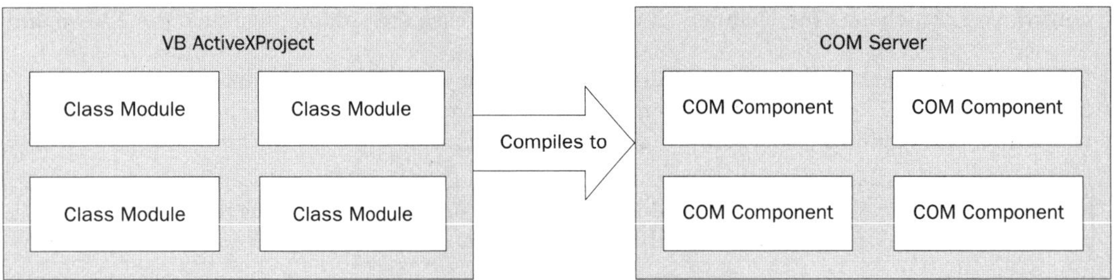

Lollypop Diagrams

A simply diagramming method is used in COM to represent the interfaces that a component supports. These **lollypop diagrams** show the interfaces extruding from the left-side of the component, which in turn is represented by the box. The name within the box is the component name. The single line sprouting from the top represents an interface called `IUnknown` that *every* component *must* implement. We'll discuss this important interface shortly.

So the lollypop diagram for our remote control example would look like this:

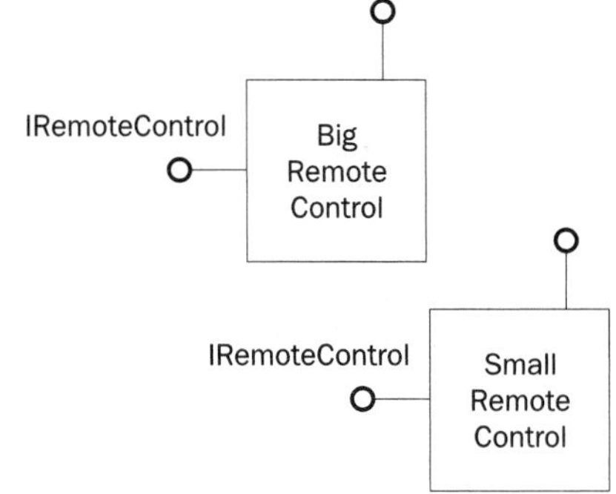

This diagram shows two components (the TVs) that provide simple channel surfing capabilities (in other words the remote control) via the `IRemoteControl` interface. It's not a complex diagram, but it clearly shows what we can do with our TVs.

> *The `IUnknown` interface is the only interface that should be shown extruding from the top of a component, so typically we don't actually label it in the diagrams.*

Default Interfaces

When you create a COM component it can have many interfaces. COM allows you to mark one interface of a component as the **default interface**, which is used by clients, such as ASP, that are not capable of selecting a specific interface themselves (we'll see why shortly).

When creating a class module in VB that's compiled into a component, you don't have any control over which interface becomes the default. The default interface *always* consists of the public methods and properties than you define as part of that class module. You can make a class module support additional interfaces by using the `Implements` keyword, but the methods of those interfaces will not by default be available to ASP.

> *When you create a public class module in an ActiveX project, the name of the interface VB creates is the class name prefixed with an underscore. So for the class module `MyTV`, the default interface will be called `_MyTV`.*

GUIDs – Unambiguous Naming of Entities

When you compile a class module and create a COM component, VB assigns a globally unique identifier called a **GUID** (pronounced goo-id) to the component. A GUID is a 128-bit number that is generated based upon the system clock and the MAC address found in your network card, and is guaranteed to be unique.

> *If you haven't got a network card a GUID will still be unique, but will only be **guaranteed** unique to your machine.*

GUIDs are the generic term used for these identifiers that *uniquely* and *unambiguously* identify entities across time and space. With 128-bits, unique GUIDs can be generated at the rate of 10 million a second until the year 5770 AD!

When a GUID is used to identify a class module it is called a **Class Identifier (CLSID)**. GUIDs are used in COM to identity lots of things, so there are various other names given to GUIDs when used in a specific context, as we will discuss shortly. These contexts include **interface identifiers (IID)**, **application identifiers (APPID)** and lots more.

Why do we need GUIDs?

So why do we need a 128-bit number to identify a component? Isn't the name we assign to our class module enough? The simple answer is no. Analysts and developers all around the world are assigning names (logical names) to their class modules every minute of the day, so there are bound to be numerous cases where the same logical names will be used by two people, especially so when people are designing applications for the same problem domain. To solve this problem a third party could assign names, but wouldn't that be a pain?

Because 128-bit numbers are pretty meaningless to the human eye and aren't particularly easy to use, a string notation is used to represent GUIDs in the registry and other places where us humans have to deal with them. Here's the CLSID (remember that's just the name of a type of GUID) used to identify (physical name) a component for the Microsoft ADO Connection component:

```
{00000293-0000-0010-8000-00AA006D2EA4}
```

This is not a Programmatic Identifier - ProgID. They are discussed later.

The Finer Points of Interfaces

As I've mentioned several times, COM is a binary specification. This binary specification covers the description of how an interface is represented in memory and accessed at runtime.

Virtual Method Tables

When you define an interface, the order of the methods, the parameters of each method and the various other attributes you define (such as the unique GUID for the interface) form the **interface signature**. When you compile a DLL or EXE containing your COM components, that signature (binary layout) is burnt (so to speak) into the created file. The information is used to build a **virtual method table (vtable)**, which is how the methods of an interface are invoked at runtime by a client. In very simple terms, you can think of a vtable as an *n*-dimensional array that contains functions, where *n* is the number of methods in an interface:

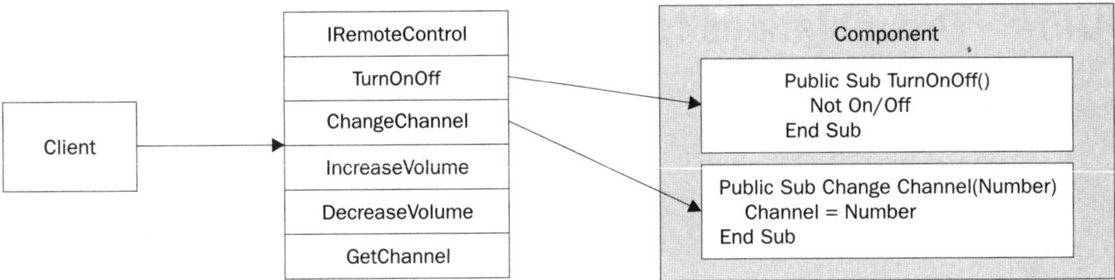

No, the array doesn't actually contain the code, but it does contain a pointer that describes where the code is actually located. So by using the vtable, we know that the entry at index 0 points us to the `TurnOnOff` method, the entry at index 1 points us to the `ChangeChannel` method and so forth.

When client code using an interface is compiled, these array indices (e.g. 0, 1, ...) are what are placed into the DLL or EXE when it's created. This is known as **early binding**. The client knows how to invoke a method in an interface by accessing a function at a given offset. The client doesn't have to query for any additional information at runtime to be able to make the call once it has an interface pointer. The interface pointer is effectively a pointer to the array of functions that we can call.

Properties are Functions

Interface methods that provide the ability to read and write an object's data (state) are termed **properties**. They are methods under the covers, as you'll see in C++, but in VB you're given the illusion that they are different. The semantics are the same, so VB is doing a good thing, but the implementation isn't, so VB introduces a level of encapsulation that can lead to a misunderstanding.

- A read only property equates to a single interface method that allows a value to be retrieved
- A write only property equates to a single method that allows the value to be updated
- A read/write property equates to two methods that allow a value to be read or updated

So, if you have four read/write properties, VB will create eight methods for reading and updating those four values.

Interface Factoring

As a general rule of thumb, interfaces usually have at least one method, and at most have 1024 (the limit stems from a limit in COM and cross-apartment marshalling). How many methods an interface has is a design issue that you decide – typically, the number is one or more, but that doesn't have to be the case. An interface can have no methods, but a typical well-designed interface will have no more than 10 or 15.

Interfaces with no methods are pretty uncommon, but they can be useful. One such application is for providing a secret handshake or signal between components and consumers, like a 'new' friend wearing a special item of clothing the first time you meet them in a crowded place so you can identify them. The interface is something a consumer can check to ensure that the component is not an imposter.

> *Factoring in this context means logically placing related methods together in a single interface. So, if I say carefully factor your interfaces, you should read that to mean paying special attention to what methods you put in different interfaces.*

Interface Guidelines

In many ways, interface design is a similar problem to user-interface design. For user-interface design we need to consider what the user will want to do through the user-interface, and figure out a user-interface that makes it easy or obvious for the user to see how to do what they want and then do it. The later part (the doing) is the most important part.

The difference is that in user-interface design we're dealing with controls, such as text boxes and radio buttons, and their layout on one or more forms. With component design, we're dealing with properties and methods, and their factoring into one or more interfaces. The better we factor the interfaces, the more usable they are for our consumers.

Like user-interface design, COM interface design is somewhat of an experience-based process. You might do it one way for one project because it suits the client base; you might do it another way because there are specific limiting or enabling technologies available. Either way, there's usually a common goal; *keep your client happy*.

We can't give you a *de facto* set of interface design guidelines for every problem you'll ever encounter, but here are some common traits of well-designed interfaces:

- **Ensure they are usable by the consumer**.
  COM has the ability to define interfaces that are language or application unfriendly – that is, they won't work. Whilst COM is designed to be a binary standard, some languages have more capabilities than others, just like some browsers have more functionality than others. COM would not be widely adopted if it limited these languages, so we have to think carefully about interface compatibility. For example, a component that is used mainly in a scripting environment like ASP should use Variants for parameters that have to be passed in, modified, and passed out. This is a feature of scripting engines, so we have to make sure our interfaces abide by these guidelines for them to work correctly in that environment.

- **The interface name (or class module) and method names are descriptive.** There is no point in calling an interface `IDoSomething` and having a method called `DoIt`. The names should be descriptive, and where possible have a clearly defined meaning in the client's problem domain.
- **The methods should be well factored, logically related, and there shouldn't be too many of them.** If you've got an interface called `IChannelSelector`, it should only contain methods that are related to changing channels. For example, if we need a method called `FineTuneChannel`, that should probably be exposed by another interface called `IChannelTuner`.
- **The same goes for properties.** They should correspond to the types of information the client is likely to be interested in.
- **Interfaces should be strongly typed.** Languages like VB and C++ are strongly typed. What this means is that variables we define are of a specific type, and only contain certain types of data, for example a number (Long, Integer etc). If somebody then tries to assign a String to that variable, the compiler will raise an error. ASP only supports weakly typed scripting languages like VBScript. With VBScript all variables are defined as Variants. This type can hold any type of data, and is happy to adapt as you use it. The benefit of an interface being strongly typed is that its use is simply more explicit – you can see what types of parameters are being used. We don't have to guess what types of data a method may or may not be able to process.
- **You should be happy to use the interface yourself** This is the golden rule that all globally successfully companies take – use your own interface, or at least be sure that if you did use it, you'd say, "great interface!"

Immutability of Interfaces

Once you've designed a COM interface and published it in some form to a client, the interface should be considered **immutable** – you shouldn't make *any* changes to it that might affect its binary representation.

Consider a description of an `IVolumeControl` interface, which has the methods `IncreaseVolume` and `DecreaseVolume`. If we released our component, and people used the remote control component in their application using our interface and all of its methods, what would happen if we decided to remove the `DecreaseVolume` method? Obviously the applications would break badly, or there would be some very annoyed neighbors. The same type of problem could also potentially occur if we change the number of parameters a method accepts, of if we change the parameter types a method uses.

So, there are a number of guidelines we should follow:

- Don't publish an interface until you're happy with it.
- If you do need to change an interface, consider leaving the existing interface alone, and creating a new interface for the additional functionality required. This is only practical if the client type supports multiple interfaces, which ASP currently doesn't.
- You can't change any part of an interface once it's published. This includes the order of methods, parameter types etc. If you do change an existing interface (which is not recommended), recompile all client applications that use it. As we've discussed, clients using early binding will have hard-coded the layout of the interface into the EXEs or DLLs, so they must be updated.

- Remember that VB hides a lot of interface information from you, so that when you modify or add public functions, subs or properties to a class module you are modifying the default interface. VB automatically creates and manages a COM interface for every public class module within an ActiveX project.

These are all good COM guidelines, but components that are written for use in ASP only have slightly more flexibility because they use late binding.

The IUnknown Interface

We've already said that every COM component implements an interface called `IUnknown`. This interface plays a pivotal role in COM and has two main purposes:

- Reference counting
- Dynamic discovery of functionality through querying for supported interfaces

QueryInterface

`QueryInterface` is the method by which the functionality of a component can be dynamically exposed and queried for at runtime. The method accepts an interface identifier (IID – another type of GUID) and, if it's supported, the requested interface is returned ready for use by the code that made the request.

In VBScript this method is called when we use the `Set` keyword. This basically says to the component, "Hey, do you support the interface this IID represents?"

```
Set RemoteControl = CreateObject("TV.RemoteControl")
```

Object Lifetimes and Reference Counting

COM allows an interface pointer to be passed around inside an application, and whilst an interface is in use, the COM object that provided the pointer must not be destroyed. Compare this to a conference call where 4 people are talking – the phone line shouldn't be disconnected by your local telecom until everybody has hung up the phone.

To track the usage of interface pointers, and therefore the object lifetime of a COM object, we use **reference counting**.

When a component is first created by the COM runtime, its 'life' begins, and the `AddRef` method on `IUnknown` is implicitly called by the component itself. `AddRef` is a simple function that increases the reference count of the component by one. The count starts at zero, and so after a component has been created, its reference count will be equal to one.

Every time the `QueryInterface` function hands out an interface pointer to a consumer, it calls `AddRef` to increase the reference count by one. Conversely, when a consumer has finished using the interface, the `Release` method is called, decrementing the count by one. If the count reaches zero, the object knows that no more consumers are using it, and so destroys itself.

A COM object is responsible for managing its own lifetime.

Whilst a very simple concept, reference counting is very powerful. However, it's a real pain in languages such as C++, as the programmer has to remember to manually call AddRef and Release. If the calls are not balanced (e.g. called an equal number of times) the object will never be destroyed. In VB and ASP we never directly call AddRef and Release, so we don't have this problem of forgetting to balance calls.

Using IDispatch – Late Binding

IDispatch is an interface that COM uses to allow methods of a component's default interface to be discovered and invoked by a client application dynamically at runtime. This type of invocation of a component's functionality is termed **late binding**, because before the method can be invoked, the component has to be asked if it supports it at runtime.

In VB, the IDispatch interface is used whenever a variable of the type Object is declared:

```
Dim objRemote as Object

Set objRemote = CreateObject("TV.RemoteControl")

objRemote.TurnOn
```

In ASP the code is almost identical, except we don't use the Object variable type and we use the ASP Server COM object to create the instance:

```
Dim objRemote

Set objRemote = Server.CreateObject("TV.RemoteControl")

objRemote.TurnOn
```

Because ASP is typeless – that is every variable defined is always a Variant – we can't request a specific interface. For example, in VB we could write the following code to access the Remote Control object's volume control interface, and then increase the volume by calling the IncreaseVolume function:

```
Dim objVolumeControl As IVolumeControl
Dim objRemote As Object

Set objRemote = CreateObject("TV.RemoteControl")
Set objVolumeControl = objRemote

objVolumeControl.IncreaseVolume
```

In ASP we cannot do this because we can't request a specific interface. All we can do is access the component's default interface. So, to achieve the same results we have to take a different approach to accessing the functionality, and indeed, design our components a little differently.

Rather than a component having multiple interfaces, we have multiple components each supporting one interface. So, if our initial design were to have one component with four interfaces, we'd have four components, each with one interface. These components can work together, and can expose each other as properties to allow navigation between the interfaces.

For example, we could have a property of the remote control object called `VolumeControl` that returns a COM object that implements the `IVolumeControl` interface (as its default interface). An ASP page could then access the methods of the interface using that returned property, so we could write code like this:

```
Dim objRemote

Set objRemote = Server.CreateObject("TV.RemoteControl")

objRemote.VolumeControl.IncreaseVolume
```

This style of code is probably quite familiar to you if you've ever used any of the Microsoft Office object models. It's not as elegant as the VB technique of using multiple interfaces, and it does require some extra work on your behalf, but it has the same net effect. Because there's a large overhead in creating multiple objects in terms of the time taken to program by the developer, you'll often find components designed for late bound clients (those that use late binding) tend to have many more methods per interface.

An alternative to using multiple objects is to return a component's non-default interface as a property, therefore avoiding the need of having multiple objects. Such practice is not guaranteed to work within a COM+ application and violates a fundamental rule of COM – an object should only ever return a single implementation of an interface.

Late binding can be more flexible under some circumstances, but has a number of drawbacks:

- It's slower than early binding. A component has to be asked if it supports a method before it can be invoked, and the `IDispatch` interface is not that efficient.
- As functionality is being queried for at runtime, it's possible that an error will occur because a method is not supported. For example, you could have spelt a method name wrong.

Generally speaking, you should always use early binding where possible, which in VB requires that you have a type library (which we'll discuss shortly).

However, we have no choice in ASP – we have to use late binding.

A Central Repository for Component Information

OK, we've talked about interfaces and components, so let's look out how components are made available, both inside and outside of VB.

The first question to ask is how do the References and Components dialogs in VB work? Where do they get the information about components? How do they know what to list? The answer is the Windows **Registry**.

The Registry currently plays a lead role in the world of COM. It's a hierarchical data store used to hold COM related information and lots more. Its role in COM+ has changed slightly – the general concept of having a 'central repository' for component information is the same, but the Registry is no longer the central repository, except for legacy components.

> *The Registry is generally never directly accessed for COM information by applications. The COM runtime provides APIs that encapsulate its usage.*

To take a closer look at the Registry, run the Registry Editor program `regedit.exe`. When it starts you'll see a number of **keys**:

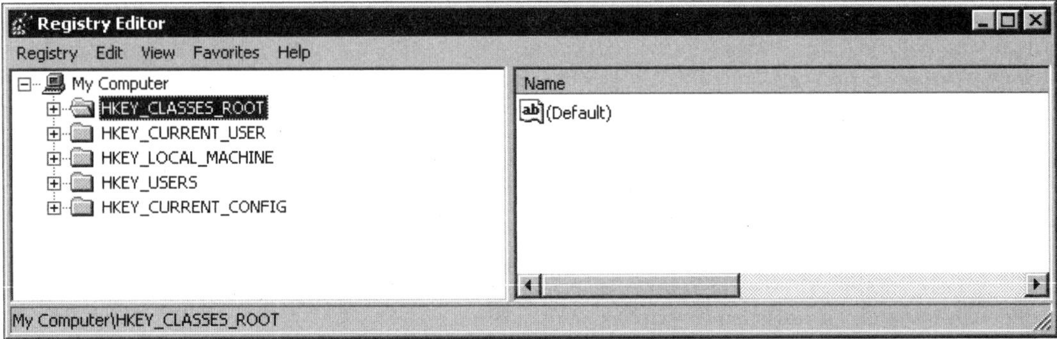

COM information is stored under the `HKEY_CLASSES_ROOT` key – known as `HKCR`. I'm not going to discuss how to use the Registry Editor or the various keys in great detail, but it's well worth having a dig around in your spare time using this tool – remembering along the way not to delete anything unless you know what you're doing!

> *For a detailed description of the Registry and its various COM related keys, check out the Richard Grimes "COM and the Registry" article at* `www.comdeveloper.com`.

When you write code that uses components and interfaces in VB, the names you use in the code are referred to as **logical** names: e.g. `SomeClass` or `IRemoteControl`. The **physical** name of components and interfaces are the CLSIDs and IIDs respectively. These identifiers (shown at the top of the picture above) are what the COM runtime uses to create components and query for interfaces, so these are what end up being compiled into your component and any applications using them.

This is important to note, because if these identifiers change for any reason your client applications will no longer work. To understand how these identifiers are created in VB we need to look at the project settings, specifically Version Compatibility.

Version Compatibility

If you bring up the Project Properties settings for an ActiveX project in VB and select the Component tab, you're presented with the following screen:

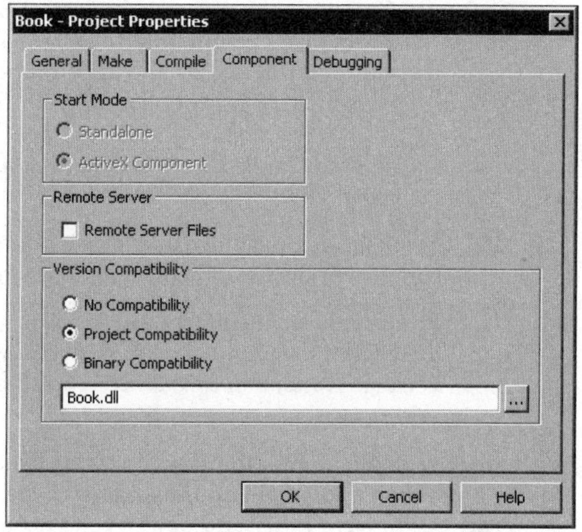

The Version Compatibility option tells VB how to manage the unique GUIDs that are assigned to components (CLSID) and interfaces (IID). Let's look at these three options.

No Compatibility

The No Compatibility option tells Visual Basic to generate a new set of GUIDs for the component's public classes, their interfaces, and type library any time you recompile the application, even if you didn't modify the interface of the component itself. This means that the component you obtain is incompatible with any existing client application that has been compiled using early binding before.

A type library is a file that describes all of the components and interface within a COM server. VB automatically creates this file and includes it as a bound resource in a COM server. When you select entries in the References dialog, it is the type library that VB uses to make the various components and interfaces available within the IDE.

Project Compatibility

The Project Compatibility option tells Visual Basic to generate a new set of GUIDs for the component's public classes and interfaces, but doesn't modify the GUID of the component's type library.

For this option to work correctly, you must provide the path to a compiled EXE or DLL. When the project is then compiled, Visual Basic reuses the GUID of the type library stored in that file. VB will also preserve the CLSIDs and the IIDs defined in a compiled reference file if you didn't change the public interface of the class modules being compiled.

Binary Compatibility

The Binary Compatibility option tells Visual Basic to always try and preserve the compatibility with a component's previous version, and to warn you if there are any changes. For each recompilation, VB tries to reuse the same CLSIDs and IIDs found in the type library specified. If the component's interface has changed, VB prompts you with three options:

- Cancel the compile so you can go back to the code editor and fix the statements that caused the incompatibility.
- Break the compatibility, and let VB create a new set of GUIDs for the type library and for all the components and interfaces exposed by the component.
- Preserve the compatibility with the previous version of the component: in this case VB will reuse all the GUIDs found in the older component, even though existing clients won't work with the newer version. This option isn't always available; for example when you've deleted a class module.

If you break the compatibility you will be asked to change the project's name – which will become the type library's name – and the name of the EXE or the DLL you're compiling to. This action permits us to have older and newer versions of the component coexist on the same machine, so that older clients can continue to work as before.

However, if you refuse to change the project's name and the EXE file name, VB will generate a new component that inherits the all CLSIDs from the older component, except for the interfaces that were found to contain incompatible definitions. This behavior helps to maintain compatibility with those clients that don't use the offending interface, but in general you should follow VB's suggestions, and agree to change the project's and executable's names.

Programmatic Identifiers

If you've used the `CreateObject` method you'll be familiar with programmatic identifiers (ProgIDs) that provide a name for creating a COM component using code like this:

```
Dim objConnection
Set objConnection = CreateObject("ADODB.Connection")
```

When you create a public class module within an ActiveX project in VB, it generates a ProgID as follows:

```
[ProjectName].[ClassModuleName]
```

ProgIDs are also sub-keys under `HKEY_CLASSES_ROOT`. What they provide is a way of looking up a CLSID at runtime from a string identifier. Using the ADO Connection component as an example, we can see that the ProgID key has a sub-key called `CLSID`. This has a default string value that is the GUID in a string format:

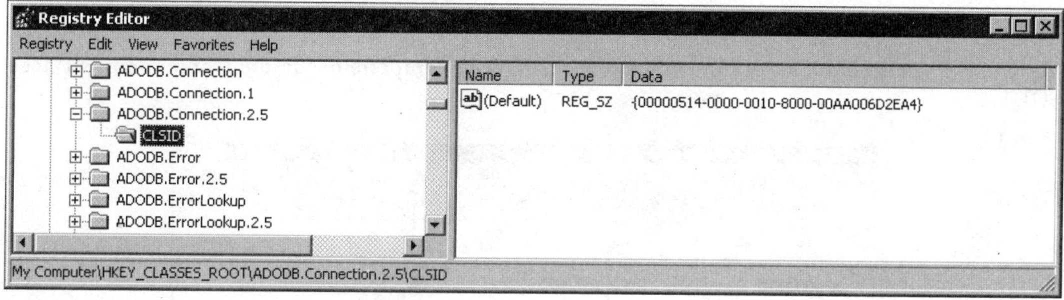

COM+ Runtime Changes

As well as providing a number of new services that can be used to increase the functionality of an application, COM+ also includes a number of changes into the basic COM runtime:

- There are now two types of components: **configured** and **non-configured**.
- The registry is no longer the main information store for component metadata; instead the COM+ catalog is the primary store.

There are also other more low level changes, which we'll look at in the next chapter.

Configured and Non-Configured Components

A **non-configured** component in COM+ is what you are creating today if you're using Windows 9x or Windows NT. They do not use any of the COM+ type services and information about them is only found in the system registry.

Configured components are described in the COM+ catalog (registration database) and make use of the COM+ services, such as the transaction support that we'll discuss in later chapters.

Configured components are the only real way forward under Windows 2000. They can only live in in-process services, and are grouped together into a **COM+ Application**. For those of you that have used MTS, a COM+ Application is basically the same thing as a package, and acts as a surrogate process for servers. For those of you who've not used MTS, you can simply think of a COM+ application as a collection of in-process COM servers that run within the address space of an executable. (`dllhost.exe`). This will be expanded upon in the next chapter.

The COM+ Catalog

In COM+ you spend a lot of time managing configured components via the Component Services GUI:

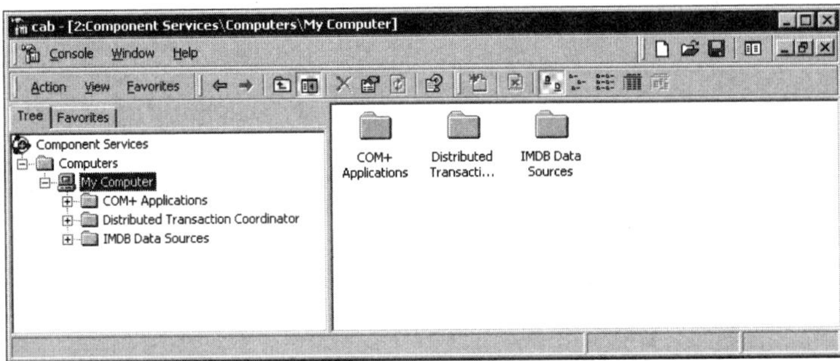

All of the component related configurations you manipulate using this GUI are stored within in the COM+ catalog, and not the Registry as with traditional COM components. The COM+ catalog provides an interface to the **registration database** (RegDB) – an optimized database that COM+ uses for activating COM+ components, much like COM uses the Registry in NT and Windows 9x.

If you've used MTS before, the COM+ catalog is the basically the same thing as the MTS catalog.

Building an ASP COM Component

We've talked enough about COM and COM+, so let's see them in action, and look at why Visual Basic is a great tool for component development by showing how quick and easy it is to whip up a DNA component.

In the spirit of DNA, we'll create a data-centric middle tier component that will enable us to retrieve a list of book titles from the `pubs` database shipped with SQL Server 7.0. The component will shield the ASP developer from the structure of the database, and enable them to retrieve, add and delete book titles. As we'll discuss in later chapters, this component is best suited for use inside of user-centric components, but for now we'll use it directly inside our ASP page.

The main ASP page will contain a view of the book titles defined within the database. It will include these fields:

- `ID` – A unique identification assigned by the creator of the title
- `Title` – The working title of the book
- `Price` – The cost of the book
- `Notes` – A brief description of the book

The main screen will look like this:

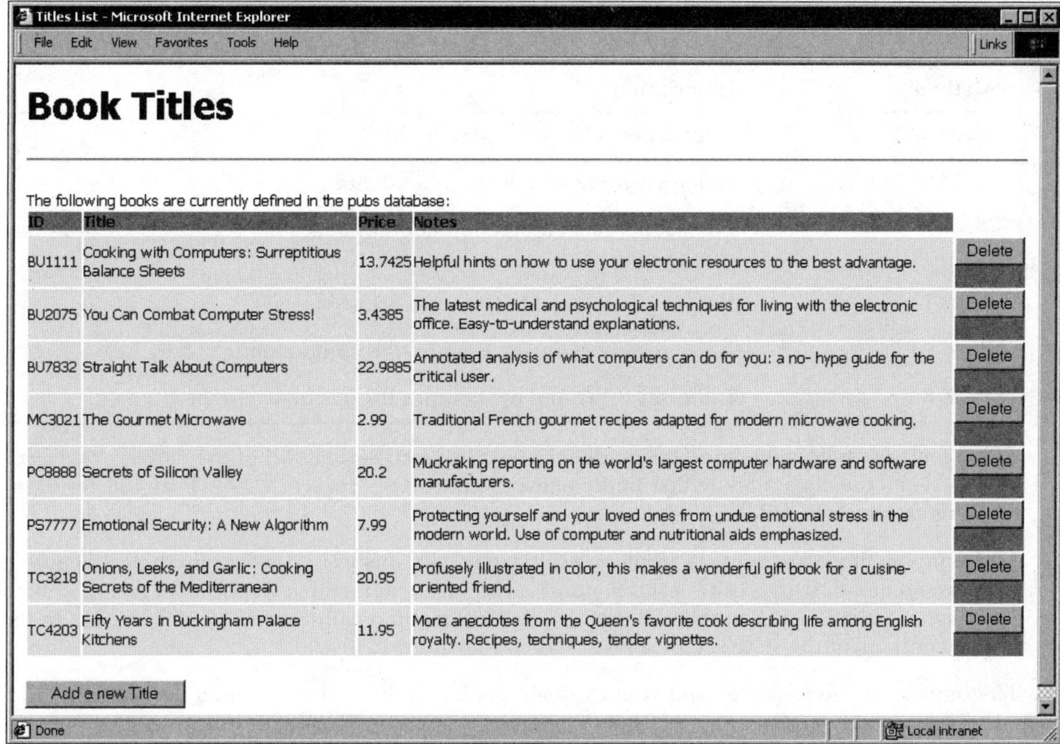

ID	Title	Price	Notes	
BU1111	Cooking with Computers: Surreptitious Balance Sheets	13.7425	Helpful hints on how to use your electronic resources to the best advantage.	Delete
BU2075	You Can Combat Computer Stress!	3.4385	The latest medical and psychological techniques for living with the electronic office. Easy-to-understand explanations.	Delete
BU7832	Straight Talk About Computers	22.9885	Annotated analysis of what computers can do for you: a no- hype guide for the critical user.	Delete
MC3021	The Gourmet Microwave	2.99	Traditional French gourmet recipes adapted for modern microwave cooking.	Delete
PC8888	Secrets of Silicon Valley	20.2	Muckraking reporting on the world's largest computer hardware and software manufacturers.	Delete
PS7777	Emotional Security: A New Algorithm	7.99	Protecting yourself and your loved ones from undue emotional stress in the modern world. Use of computer and nutritional aids emphasized.	Delete
TC3218	Onions, Leeks, and Garlic: Cooking Secrets of the Mediterranean	20.95	Profusely illustrated in color, this makes a wonderful gift book for a cuisine-oriented friend.	Delete
TC4203	Fifty Years in Buckingham Palace Kitchens	11.95	More anecdotes from the Queen's favorite cook describing life among English royalty. Recipes, techniques, tender vignettes.	Delete

Pressing the **Delete** button located at the side of any entry will delete that title. Once deleted the user is presented with a simple confirmation of deletion screen. Pressing the **Add a new Title** button will run the page `Add.asp` that allows the user to add a new title:

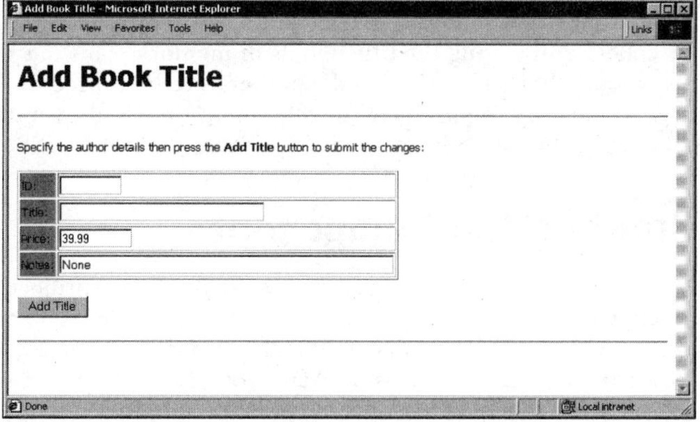

Clicking the **Add Title** button will invoke the `Add_UpdateDB.asp` page to actually perform the insertion using the component.

The Component's Interface

We'll stick with a fairly simple interface, which will provide the following methods:

Method	Description
AddTitle	Adds a new title to the database.
DeleteTitle	Deletes a title given its unique title id.
OpenTitles	Opens the data connection and initializes the recordset for titles that can be read.
NextTitle	Returns the next title from the list.
CloseTitles	Releases any resource used by the component.
IsEOF	Indicates if the end of the titles list has been reached.

These methods follow the interface guidelines we discussed earlier. All of the names are descriptive, and we'll call the class module that implements the interface, BookTitles. That will result in VB creating an interface called _BookTitles.

The component we are going to implement is stateful. By this we mean that the object is not deactivated and destroyed after each method call returns, so member variables set by one method call (such as OpenTitles) can then be used by another method call (such as NextTitle). In the case of this component the state is a database connection and recordset.

The implementation for the component will simply be a thin wrapper around the ADO database connection and Recordset objects used to access the pubs database. For example, when enumerating titles by calling NextTitle, we will simply call down into the underlying recordset object.

You may decide to take a different approach, such as enumerating all titles when OpenTitles is called, and storing the title details in memory. This has the advantage that a database connection is potentially freed earlier, and can therefore be reused and aid overall scalability. The disadvantage is that memory requirement, development time and overall complexity of the component increase as more information has to be held in memory and must be managed.

Creating the Component

Start Visual Basic and create a new ActiveX DLL project, changing the name of the default class module to BookTitles. Next, change the name of the project to Book. Because we are using ADO you also need to add a reference to the Microsoft ActiveX Data Object 2.5 Library:

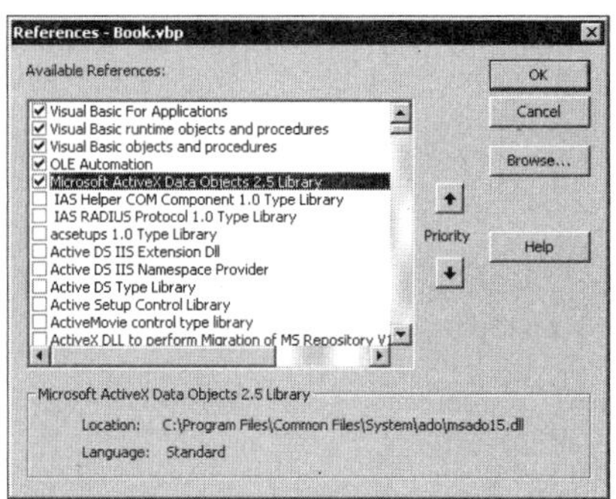

The Component's Methods

We'll now examine each of the functions you'll need to add to the `BookTitles` class module.

The OpenTitles Method

The `OpenTitles` method establishes a connection to the SQL Server 7.0 database using the `SQLOLEDB` OLE DB provider. Once a connection is established, it creates a recordset containing a list of all book titles. The default recordset `Open` parameters are used which means the recordset is not updateable:

```
Option Explicit

Private mobjConn As ADODB.Connection
Private mrsBooks As ADODB.Recordset

' Open the connection and the recordset
Public Sub OpenTitles()

  Set mobjConn = New ADODB.Connection
  Set mrsBooks = New ADODB.Recordset

  mobjConn.Open "Data Source=<SERVER_NAME>;" + _
                "Provider=SQLOLEDB;" + _
                "Initial Catalog=pubs;" + _
                "User ID=sa"

  mrsBooks.Open "SELECT * FROM Titles", mobjConn

End Sub
```

The CloseTitles Method

The `CloseTitles` method simply releases the Recordset and Connection objects that were opened in `OpenTitles`. This is called when the list of titles has been displayed so we can free the database connection as soon as possible. Releasing finite resource like database connections as soon as possible is always good practice, as shown in `list.asp`:

```
' Close the list
Public Sub CloseTitles()

' Close the record set
  If Not (mrsBooks Is Nothing) Then
     If mrsBooks.State = adStateOpen Then
        mrsBooks.Close
     End If
     Set mrsBooks= Nothing
  End If

' Close the connection
  If Not (mobjConn Is Nothing) Then
     mobjConn.Close
     Set mobjConn= Nothing
  End If

End Sub
```

The NextTitle Method

The `NextTitle` method is used to return information about the current book title, and also move the recordset cursor forward by calling `MoveNext`:

```
' Returns the next title
Public Sub NextTitle(Id As Variant, Title As Variant, Price As Variant, _
                     Notes As Variant)

' Ignore errors and more specifically null values in this demo
  On Error Resume Next

  If IsEOF = True Then
     Err.Raise vbObject + 1, "BookTitles Component", "End of cursor"
     Exit Sub
  End If

' Copy the fields back to the caller
  Id = mrsBooks.Fields("Title_id")
  Title = mrsBooks.Fields("Title")
  Price = mrsBooks.Fields("Price")
  Notes = mrsBooks.Fields("Notes")

' Move to the next title
  mrsBooks.MoveNext

End Sub
```

Notice that all of the parameters are defined as the type `Variant`. I've done this because the parameters that are passed in to the function are defined in the `List.asp` ASP page as follows:

```
<%
Dim strID
Dim strTitle
Dim curPrice
Dim strNotes

' Initialize the list
objTitles.OpenTitles

' Process each author
  While objTitles.IsEOF = False
    objTitles.NextTitle strID, strTitle, curPrice, strNotes
%>
```

The ASP interpreter (more precisely the Active Scripting engine – VBScript in this case) defines these parameters (`strID` etc.) as `Variants`. Because the `NextTitle` parameters are `ByRef` parameters, a pointer to the memory containing that `Variant` is passed into the function, so the value can be directly updated by the function.

If you tried defining the `NextTitle` function using the String and Currency types you'd get the following error:

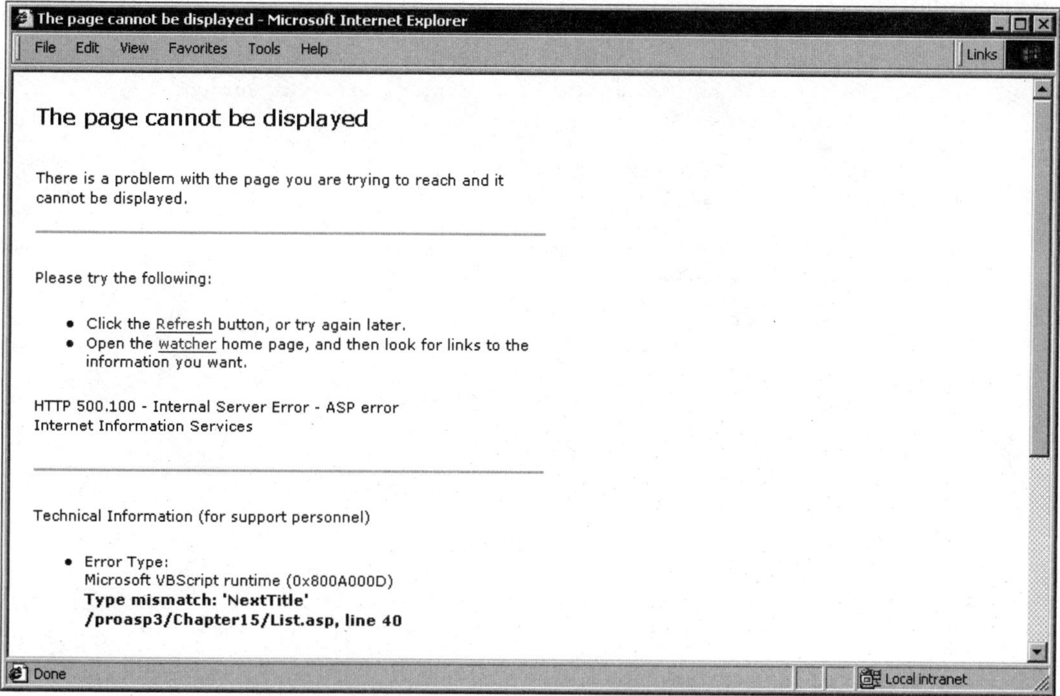

The reason this error occurs is simply because a `ByRef` parameter type must always be passed a pointer of the correct type. If we define the parameter as `ByVal`, so the parameter is passed by value, the Active Scripting engine will happily try and convert the value for us. Of course, if the conversion is not possible, then the same error will be raised.

Many commercial components that are not written with consideration to ASP have this type of problem. You'll often find yourself writing small wrappers for such components.

The IsEOF Method

The `IsEOF` function indicates if there are any more titles. This maps directly onto the `EOF` recordset property, and is used when enumerating all titles to determine if any more are available:

```
Public Function IsEOF() As Boolean

  IsEOF = mrsBooks.EOF

End Function
```

The AddTitle Method

The `AddTitle` method establishes a connection to the database and opens a dynamic recordset. This is updateable:

```
' Adds a new title to the database
Public Sub AddTitle(Id As String, Title As String, Price As Currency, _
                    Notes As String)

  Dim objConn As New ADODB.Connection
  Dim rsNewBook As New ADODB.Recordset

  objConn.Open "Data Source=<SERVER_NAME>;" + _
               "Provider=SQLOLEDB;" + _
               "Initial Catalog=pubs;" + _
               "User ID=sa"

  rsNewBook.Open "SELECT * FROM Titles", objConn, _
                 adOpenDynamic, adLockOptimistic

  rsNewBook.AddNew
    rsNewBook.Fields("Title_id") = Id
    rsNewBook.Fields("Title") = Title
    rsNewBook.Fields("Price") = Price
    rsNewBook.Fields("Notes") = Notes
  rsNewBook.Update

End Sub
```

In this code I've not reused the existing connection that `OpenTitles` *may have opened. I've done this to keep the code simple: i.e. I don't have to check if the database is already open, I just always open it. The connection and recordset are automatically released when the subroutine exits so we don't set either object to* `Nothing`.

You'll notice with this code that I've not used the parameter types of Variant. I've done this to demonstrate that you don't have to use Variants in your prototypes, provided you *don't* want to pass variables defined in ASP page variables to the function. For example, the following shows how the `Add_UpdateDB.asp` ASP page calls the function not using a variable defined within the page:

```
objTitles.AddTitle Request.Form("Id"), Request.Form("Title"), _
                   Request.Form("Price") , Request.Form("Notes")
```

Because the parameters are not defined as variables, the ASP interpreter will quite happily perform the necessary conversions for us. Why it doesn't also do this automatic conversion for variables defined on a page is strange. We can only hope that future versions of the scripting engines will support it.

The DeleteTitle Method

This method deletes the title and the associated database rows in the `Roysched`, `Sales` and `TitleAuthor` tables (necessary because of the structure of the `pubs` database shipped with SQL server). We didn't add rows to all of these tables when creating a title, but because it's possible for you to delete titles that you didn't add via the ASP UI, we have to do this to be safe:

```
' Delete a title from the database
Public Sub DeleteTitle(Id As String)

  Dim objConn As New ADODB.Connection
  Dim rsDelTitle As New ADODB.Recordset

  objConn.Open "Data Source=<SERVER_NAME>;" + _
               "Provider=SQLOLEDB;" + _
               "Initial Catalog=pubs;" + _
               "User ID=sa"

' Delete from the various tables
  objConn.Execute "DELETE FROM Roysched WHERE Title_id = '" & Id & "'", , _
                  adCmdText + adExecuteNoRecords
  objConn.Execute "DELETE FROM Sales WHERE Title_id = '" & Id & "'", , _
                  adCmdText + adExecuteNoRecords
  objConn.Execute "DELETE From TitleAuthor WHERE Title_id = '" & Id & "'", , _
                  adCmdText + adExecuteNoRecords
  objConn.Execute "DELETE FROM Titles WHERE Title_id = '" & Id & "'", , _
                  adCmdText + adExecuteNoRecords

End Sub
```

Once you've copied these functions into the VB class module, compile it to create the COM server containing the component. Once that's done we can continue on and write the ASP pages that will use the component. These are probably no different from pages you've written in the past, so we won't cover each page in great detail.

The ASP Pages for the Solution

There are a total of 4 ASP pages. These are:

- `List.asp` – Shows the complete list of book titles using the component
- `Add.asp` – Provides a simple screen for detailing information about a new title
- `Add_UpdateDB.asp` – Performs the addition of a new book title using the component and information passed from `Add.asp`
- `Delete.asp` – Performs the deletion of a book title using the component

The List.asp page

The list page is pretty typical of an ASP page that retrieves some values and displays a list. The only points worth noting are that the page is not using ADO, but rather an instance of our component:

```
<%
  Dim objTitles          ' Holds the book titles component
  Set objTitles = Server.CreateObject("Book.BookTitles")
%>
```

The immediate benefit over using ADO here is that the developer using the components doesn't have to worry about the connection details, the table names or building SQL queries.

The main bulk of the code simply enumerates from each title once the list is opened:

```
<%
  Dim strID
  Dim strTitle
  Dim curPrice
  Dim strNotes

  ' Initialize the list
  objTitles.OpenTitles

  ' Process each author
  While objTitles.IsEOF = False
    objTitles.NextTitle strID, strTitle, curPrice, strNotes
%>
```

The return data is then used to create a table with a number of rows:

```
<TR>
   <TD bgcolor="#FFFF6C"><%=strID%></TD>
   <TD bgcolor="#FFFF6C"><%=strTitle%></TD>
   <TD bgcolor="#FFFF6C"><%=curPrice%></TD>
   <TD bgcolor="#FFFF6C"><%=strNotes%></TD>
   <TD bgcolor="#3AC2EF">
      <FORM NAME="A" METHOD="POST" ACTION="Delete.asp?id=<%=strID%>">
        <INPUT TYPE="SUBMIT" VALUE="Delete" NAME="B1">
      </FORM>
   </TD>
</TR>
```

Note here that a simple form is used to provide a Delete button against each row. As we'll see next, this button invokes the ASP page `Delete.asp` when pressed and passes in the title code using the `ID` parameter.

For completeness, here's the entire page listing:

```
<%
  Dim objTitles        ' Holds the book titles component
  Set objTitles = Server.CreateObject("Book.BookTitles")
%>

<HTML>
<HEAD>
<TITLE>Titles List</TITLE>
<STYLE TYPE="text/css">
  BODY {font-family:Verdana,Tahoma,Arial,sans-serif; font-size:10pt}
  TD {font-family:Verdana,Tahoma,Arial,sans-serif; font-size:10pt}
</STYLE>
</HEAD>
<BODY BGCOLOR=WHITE>
<H1>Book Titles</H1>
<HR>
<P>The following books are currently defined in the pubs database:
```

```
<TABLE cellspacing="2" cellpadding="0">
<TR>
   <TD bgcolor="#3AC2EF"><STRONG>ID</STRONG></TD>
   <TD bgcolor="#3AC2EF"><STRONG>Title</STRONG></TD>
   <TD bgcolor="#3AC2EF"><STRONG>Price</STRONG></TD>
   <TD bgcolor="#3AC2EF"><STRONG>Notes</STRONG></TD>
</TR>
<TR>
</TR>

<%
  Dim strID
  Dim strTitle
  Dim curPrice
  Dim strNotes

  ' Initialize the list
  objTitles.OpenTitles

  ' Process each author
  While objTitles.IsEOF = False
    objTitles.NextTitle strID, strTitle, curPrice, strNotes
%>

<TR>
   <TD bgcolor="#FFFF6C"><%=strID%></TD>
   <TD bgcolor="#FFFF6C"><%=strTitle%></TD>
   <TD bgcolor="#FFFF6C"><%=curPrice%></TD>
   <TD bgcolor="#FFFF6C"><%=strNotes%></TD>
   <TD bgcolor="#3AC2EF">
      <FORM NAME="A" METHOD="POST" ACTION="Delete.asp?id=<%=strID%>">
        <INPUT TYPE="SUBMIT" VALUE="Delete" NAME="B1">
      </FORM>
   </TD>
</TR>

<%
  Wend
%>

</TABLE>
  <FORM NAME="A" METHOD="POST" ACTION="Add.asp">
    <INPUT TYPE="SUBMIT" VALUE="Add a new Title" NAME="B1">
  </FORM>

</BODY>
</HTML>
```

The Delete.asp Page

When the Delete button is pressed against a title, this page is invoked and the title is deleted using these lines of code:

```
<%
  Dim objTitles         ' Holds the book titles component
  Set objTitles = Server.CreateObject("Book.BookTitles")
  objTitles.DeleteTitle Request.QueryString("id")
%>
```

The full page is shown here, and does nothing else except provide a button to jump back to the main list. When you do jump back you might need to refresh the view to see that the title has been deleted from the list.

The full ASP page looks like this:

```
<HTML>
<HEAD>
<TITLE>Delete Book Title</TITLE>
<STYLE TYPE="text/css">
  BODY {font-family:Verdana,Tahoma,Arial,sans-serif; font-size:10pt}
  TD {font-family:Verdana,Tahoma,Arial,sans-serif; font-size:10pt}
</STYLE>
<BODY BGCOLOR=WHITE>

<H1>Delete Book Title</H1>
<HR>

<%
  Dim objTitles         ' Holds the book titles component
  Set objTitles = Server.CreateObject("Book.BookTitles")
  objTitles.DeleteTitle Request.QueryString("id")
%>

<P>
<P>Book title deleted succesfully.</P>

<FORM NAME="A" METHOD="POST" ACTION="list.asp">
   <INPUT TYPE="SUBMIT" VALUE="Back to Book Title List" NAME="B1">
</FORM>

</FORM>
</BODY>
</HTML>
```

The Add.asp Page

The Add page is simply a typical ASP form capture page. It lets the user type in the title id, name, notes and price, before passing those details to the `Add_UpdateDB.asp` ASP page:

```
<HTML>
<HEAD>
<TITLE>Add Book Title</TITLE>
```

```
<STYLE TYPE="text/css">
  BODY {font-family:Verdana,Tahoma,Arial,sans-serif; font-size:10pt}
  TD {font-family:Verdana,Tahoma,Arial,sans-serif; font-size:10pt}
</STYLE>
</HEAD>
<BODY BGCOLOR=WHITE>
<H1>Add Book Title</H1>
<HR>

<P>Specify the author details then press the <strong>Add Title</strong> button to
submit the changes:</P>
<FORM NAME="CUSTINFO" ACTION="Add_UpdateDB.asp" METHOD="POST" BORDER="1">

<TABLE border=1>
<TR>
  <TD bgcolor="#3AC2EF">ID:</TD>
  <TD> <INPUT TYPE="TEXT" NAME="id" SIZE="8" VALUE=""> </TD> </TR>
<TR>
  <TD bgcolor="#3AC2EF">Title:</TD>
  <TD> <INPUT TYPE="TEXT" NAME="title" SIZE="35" VALUE=""> </TD> </TR>
<TR>
  <TD bgcolor="#3AC2EF">Price:</TD>
  <TD><INPUT TYPE="TEXT" NAME="price" SIZE="10" VALUE="39.99"> </TD> </TR>
<TR>
  <TD bgcolor="#3AC2EF">Notes:</TD>
  <TD><INPUT TYPE="TEXT" NAME="notes" SIZE="60" VALUE="None"> </TD> </TR>
</TABLE>

<P>
<INPUT TYPE="SUBMIT" VALUE="Add Title">
<P>
<HR>
</FORM>
</BODY>
</HTML>
```

The Add_UpdateDB.asp Page

Taking the parameters passed in from Add.asp, this page adds a new book title using these two lines of code:

```
<%
  Dim objTitles          ' Holds the book titles component
  Set objTitles = Server.CreateObject("Book.BookTitles")
  objTitles.AddTitle Request.Form("Id"), Request.Form("Title"),
                     Request.Form("Price") , Request.Form("Notes")
%>
```

Once again, you can see how the developers life is made much simple using the component.

The full page looks like this:

```
<HTML>
<HEAD>
<TITLE>Add Book Title</TITLE>
<STYLE TYPE="text/css">
  BODY {font-family:Verdana,Tahoma,Arial,sans-serif; font-size:10pt}
  TD {font-family:Verdana,Tahoma,Arial,sans-serif; font-size:10pt}
</STYLE>
<BODY BGCOLOR=WHITE>

<H1>Add Book Title</H1>
<HR>

<%
Dim objTitles        ' Holds the book titles component
Set objTitles = Server.CreateObject("Book.BookTitles")
objTitles.AddTitle Request.Form("Id"), Request.Form("Title"),
Request.Form("Price") , Request.Form("Notes")
%>

<P>Book title added successfully.</P>

<FORM NAME="A" METHOD="POST" ACTION="List.asp">
   <input type="SUBMIT" value="Back to Book Title List" name="B1">
</FORM>

</FORM>
</BODY>
</HTML>
```

Summary

COM+ is a very powerful technology that is provided in the box with Windows 2000. Unless you like reinventing the wheel, you'll use it within your products for enabling clients to access your functionality via the components and interfaces that you've created.

As we've seen, creating components in VB is easy. All we really have to focus on is writing the code that implements the functionality we want our clients to use. Those clients can be ASP pages or any other COM enabled tool or programming language.

COM is designed to meet the requirements of all languages. As some languages have far more capabilities than others, you have to be aware of the limitations of the clients that might use your components. As we've seen with ASP clients, variables defined on an ASP page can only be passed to a function when that function has its parameters defined as Variants. We've also seen that ASP can only really use the default interface of a component.

In the next few chapters we're going to look a little closer at the refinements brought about by COM+ to the runtime, and look at how some of the COM+ services can be put to use.

N
W

15

COM+ Applications

As we move into the next millennium with Windows 2000 and ASP 3.0, we find that Microsoft has extended and improved the tools and technologies we have available to us developers, in aiding the development of enterprise applications. We've spent the last couple of chapters looking at how ASP and COM enable us to build Web applications. By using the powerful functions of IIS, and developing COM components using our preferred programming language, we can take Web applications far beyond a simple set of linked Web pages built from ASP script alone. We can build secure, high performance, component-based, scalable applications, designed to support business processes efficiently for large numbers of users, potentially thousands.

Probably the most significant change in Windows 2000 is that Microsoft Transaction Server has been improved and merged into the COM runtime, along with many other new features and refinements. Each of these changes can make our applications more robust and scalable than ever before.

With COM+, we build **COM+ applications** out of components, leveraging foundation **services** and code, rather than developing everything ourselves from scratch. These services give us a jump-start when developing n-tier applications based upon DNA. The applications we create can take advantage of the services and infrastructure that COM+ provides, which a typical enterprise application needs, such as transaction processing, component management, security and object pooling. Each of these services is non-trivial to implement and requires many years of development, not to mention investment. Luckily they are provided in the box with Windows 2000. All we have to do to make use of them is to use the **Component Services Explorer** to define our applications.

Component Services is the umbrella name Microsoft uses to encompasses COM, COM+ and the related technologies like Microsoft Message Queue (MSMQ).

In this chapter we'll be looking at:

- How COM+ provides us with the building blocks for creating robust and scalable component-based applications
- How to create and administer COM+ applications
- How to build components in Visual Basic that utilize the COM+ environment
- How threads and component scope affect the scalability of our sites
- How to debug COM+ components

To get started, we will look at an overview of what COM+ is, look at how it is an integral part of Windows 2000 that greatly assists and benefits us as component-based Web application developers, and understand the basic principles upon which it is built.

Microsoft Component Services (COM+)

In Chapter 13, we introduced Microsoft Component Services and COM+ as the plumbing for Windows DNA. We looked at the capabilities of COM+ as an **object broker**. As an object broker, COM+ is responsible for managing the lifetime of COM objects, and providing the plumbing that supports those objects when used inside of applications. This means that COM+ actually creates the objects, manages their use by applications, and then destroys them once they are no longer being used.

By having an object broker like COM+ manage objects throughout their lifetime, rather than needing each application to manage lifetimes individually, a more efficient use of system resources can be achieved – by careful monitoring and manipulating of the basic interaction between applications and COM objects. To achieve this, COM+ somehow needs to be involved in the application/object relationship.

Interception Basics

COM+ has the ability to inject code between an application and the COM objects (components) it is using. Later in this chapter we will see how this **interception** is implemented by COM+, but for now just imagine this process (interception) as being COM+ glue code that is invoked whenever a method or property of a COM object is used by an application. This glue code performs some initial setup processing and then invokes the real object method.

To understand the benefits and power that this interception can provide, consider a typical Web application that has multiple users accessing the same ASP page at a very frequent rate each day. Each ASP page in a component-based Web application will contain ASP script that probably performs these three basic steps:

- Creates one or more COM objects
- Uses the COM objects to generate the page
- Destroys those COM objects

If you've got say 50,000 requests for that page a day, and the page creates two COM objects, that's 100,000 COM objects that are created and destroyed. Creating and destroying a COM object does incur a degree of overhead, so it would be more efficient for the COM objects to be recycled. If we could place COM objects into a **pool** once an ASP page has finished with them, and have them taken out of the pool and re-used by another ASP page, we'd see an overall increase in performance for a Web site. The performance increase could potentially be very high if the objects used have to perform a reasonable amount of initialization each time they are created, before they can be used (such as connecting to a database and loading values). With pooling, this initialization would only have to occur once. So, with this recycling in mind, our ideal ASP script inside of our ideal ASP pages would follow these basic steps:

- Before creating a COM object, see if one already exists in a pool and reuse it. If no COM objects are available create a new one.
- Use the COM objects to generate the page.
- Return the COM objects to the pool so another page can use them.

Doesn't this recycling process sound great? Of course, in reality we can't actually implement this in ASP script for the simple reason that we can't directly access the COM runtime, as we discussed in Chapter 14. The Active Scripting engine makes the calls to the runtime on our behalf. Even if we use the COM runtime, the inherent limitations of ASP script and the Active Scripting engines actually prevent pooling anyway. Putting these limits to one side for a moment, if you could implement pooling yourself, just imagine all the complexities and issues you'd have to take into account when implementing it:

- Who would manage the pool of objects?
- When would the pool be created and destroyed?
- When would the objects in a pool be created and destroyed?
- After what period of time would you destroy objects?
- How do we manage multiple clients accessing the pool at the same time?
- How would the ASP script interact with the pool? Would the programmer creating the script have to check a pool before creating a new object and then have to remember to return a COM object to a pool?

It's hopefully clear that implementing this type of functionality in ASP script is impossible. Even if it was possible to implement the functionality, implementing it ourselves has two *very* important drawbacks that are important to understand:

- You'd have to implement all the code for object pooling yourself. That's a lot of responsibility to take on board not to mention the coding, testing, debugging and general maintenance cycle over a period of time.
- Every ASP page that used the pooling code would have to remember to correctly use the object pool, therefore placing an overhead on the programmer that is *error prone*. Programmers (like me) can be a bit forgetful and will probably forget to use the pool from time-to-time.

COM+ alleviates both of these burdens, and provides a generic infrastructure for supporting many different types of pre-written services that your components can use **transparently** – you don't have to change a single line of code to use some of them.

COM+ to the Rescue!

So how does COM+ redress these two points?

COM+ Provides Services

Firstly, it provides a number of services, such as object pooling, which you can use in your COM+ applications. You don't have to write the code to implement any of these services, which means we don't have to debug and test it, or worry about any of the other issues we discussed earlier; you simply configure your components to make use of the required services using the Component Services Explorer. As we briefly touched upon in Chapter 14, components that use these COM+ services are called **configured components**. It is this type of component from which COM+ applications are built using the Component Services Explorer.

COM+ Provides the Component/Service Interaction Transparently

Secondly, COM+ provides the infrastructure, which means we can automatically take advantage of such services *without* changing any code. Therefore, ASP script and other languages, such as VB, that are shielded from the COM+ runtime, can use these services without any significant code changes. ASP scripts, or components, don't need to be recompiled or modified to use the services, and they don't need to call low level C/C++ APIs in the COM+ runtime. Unlike COM, most of COM+ is available through COM interfaces.

Some COM+ services do impose certain programming disciplines and require small code changes if your components are going to make optimal use of them. As discussed, some services like object pooling, are unavailable to certain languages at the current time due to the inherent incompatibility between those languages and the perquisites of some COM+ services. However, the good news is that Microsoft is working towards making those services available to other languages.

> *What we are discussing in this chapter is COM+ 1.0. COM+ 2.0 promises to add many more services.*

Back to Object Pooling

With COM+ taking care of all the code and plumbing required to implement a service like object pooling, it means your code can just create a COM object as it usually does, and release it as it usually does. Behind the scenes COM+ will perform its object pooling magic using **interception**. COM+ will ensure that the object pool is checked, and try to use an existing object before creating a new one if none are available; and on the flip side it will return an object to a pool when it's no longer in use. Error prone code to implement the pooling doesn't have to be scattered throughout your application because the injection of these services into your component is done transparently.

About the Bad News (No Object Pooling for Visual Basic)

So, COM+ provides a powerful generic framework that can enhance our Web applications without the need for us to make any code changes. We use the Component Services Explorer to pick and choose the services our components use, and we don't need to recompile those components. If an administrator wants to add security to our component so only certain users can call certain methods they just use Component Services – no code changes. We don't have to worry about the security requirements of all the possible applications that might use the component; we just leave that to COM+.

Behind the scenes the COM+ runtime ensures that the services that have been configured for our components are added and used by using interception.

By now you've hopefully figured out that the word interception is very important in COM+.

The bad news, as we've mentioned, is that not all of these services can be used for components that are written in Visual Basic. Most can, but object pooling is one of the services that cannot be used. The reason will be expanded upon later in the chapter, but if you want to use that particular service you'll have to write your components in C++ as discussed in Chapter 17. You've still got plenty of other services to choose from, like transaction support and security, but to make optimal use of those you'll have to understand some of the guidelines we'll be discussing, like stateless components. We will look at the role of COM+ in managing transactions in Chapter 19.

So, let's take a closer look at how COM+ works.

COM+ Architecture

In Chapter 14 we discussed two fundamental building blocks of COM – components and interfaces. We discussed how components are effectively black boxes that provide functionality to clients via one or more interfaces. Clients do not know how the component functionality is written, but they do know that the interface is a contract upon they can rely on when using the functionality a component provides. The basic interaction between the two can be thought of like this:

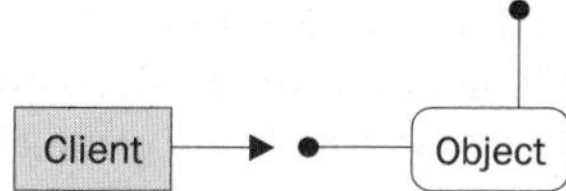

The client uses an interface of the component to achieve some task.

This diagram doesn't show any interface names as you would usually expect, simply because it is a generic diagram that can be applied to any client/object pair.

Interception – Light Weight Proxies

For COM+ to add services transparently to an object it needs to put itself between the client and an instance of a component. For example, to implement object pooling the COM+ service must intercept calls to the `Release` method of `IUnknown`. As we discussed in Chapter 14, each COM object maintains a reference count that lets an object keep track of how many outstanding clients are currently using it. When the reference count of an object goes to zero an object is responsible for destroying itself. This is obviously a bad thing for an object to do if we want it to be recycled and reused by another client, so COM+ needs to manipulate this basic lifetime cycle. In theory, the changes required are quite simple:

- The COM+ object pooling service adds an additional reference count to any component marked to be pooled when the object is created.
- Calls to the `Release` method for pooled objects are monitored. When it detects that there is *only* one outstanding reference to an object it can safely put an object back into the object pool, because it knows nobody else is using the object anymore, as it owns that reference.

Actually implementing those changes for a specific component is obviously very complicated, but COM+ makes it simple. To achieve the interception required to implement services, COM+ uses a **lightweight proxy**:

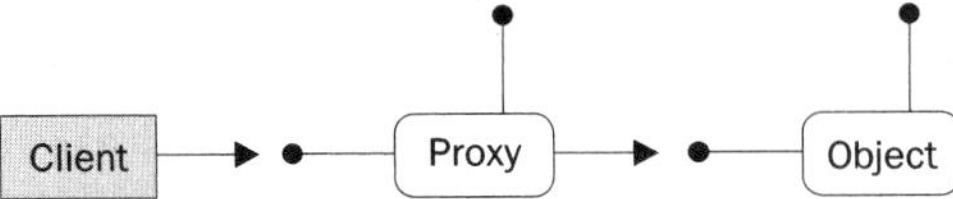

The lightweight proxy (also called an **interceptor**) is so called because it contains *just enough* code to ensure that the glue code, placed between the client and the real object, ensures that all the services the configured component wants to use, are *correctly* used at runtime.

When a client invokes a method, the glue code ensures that the runtime environment is in a suitable state before the method is actually executed, and that the original environment is restored when that method completes. For example, consider the case where the client of an object is currently involved in a transaction, but the component being called is configured to always require a new transaction. The interception glue code will ensure that the current transaction is put to one side, creates a new transaction, and then invokes the method. Any work performed in the method called will be associated with the new transaction and not the transaction that is associated with the client actually calling the component. When the method returns, the original transaction will be restored, and the transaction that was created will complete.

That was a rather simplistic description of how interception works. But, start to imagine one or more of these pre and post set-up steps being performed on your component's behalf by the COM+ runtime, and you'll start to get a good idea of what the COM+ runtime is doing, and why lightweight proxies are so important. They implement all the drudge code that is required to make the basic infrastructure plumbing work, and they save us from having to litter our code with it.

Interception may sound like an expensive process because every method of an object that is invoked by a client goes through an additional level of indirection (the glue code), but rest assured the COM+ runtime performs the operations in a very efficient manner. Quite often you'll find that the lightweight proxy is not needed if the client is using the same services as the object it creates, so there is no additional overhead. Even if the services are different, the amount of code added is only *just enough* to take into account those differences.

Contexts

COM+ tracks the runtime requirements and services an object needs by using a **context**.

> **A context is a set of runtime properties that represent the execution requirements for one or more COM+ objects.**

For example, the context would indicate to COM+ that an object is using pooling or requires a new transaction. These requirements are defined by the declarative attributes you assign to components using the Component Services Explorer, which are stored in the COM+ Catalog. These settings directly affect the properties contained within the context, and provide the COM+ runtime with the information needed to implement those services correctly for an object, or set of objects, at runtime. As we'll see later, you can also access some of these properties from within your objects.

Every COM object is associated with a *single* context when it is first created or pulled from an object pool. Once activated the context associated with an object remains the same throughout the object's lifetime, until it is returned to a pool or destroyed. The context is in effect used by COM+ to associate **out-of-band** information with an object throughout its lifetime.

> *The term out of band simply means that the data is managed by COM+ behind the scenes.*

This data is needed to apply services to a component, and without the context you would have to maintain such information yourself.

Several objects can share a context if their runtime requirements are **compatible**. I use the word *compatible* because the configuration of the component types that can share a context at runtime does not have to be identical. What algorithm COM+ uses for its context compatability test is currently un-documented. Within an object, you can obtain a reference to the context that an object is currently associated with by the `GetObjectContext` method. This returns a COM object called the **ObjectContext**. The interface returned on this object by the function is `IObjectContext`, which we'll expand on later in the chapter.

```
Set objContext = GetObjectContext()
```

Activation

The process of getting an object into a state whereby a client can use it is known as **activation**. The person creating the object is called the **activator**, and the activation process occurs when you call `CreateObject` in ASP script. A context is associated with an object during its activation.

Objects and Contexts

The relationship between an object, the object context and the context is shown here, and remains static once an object has been activated:

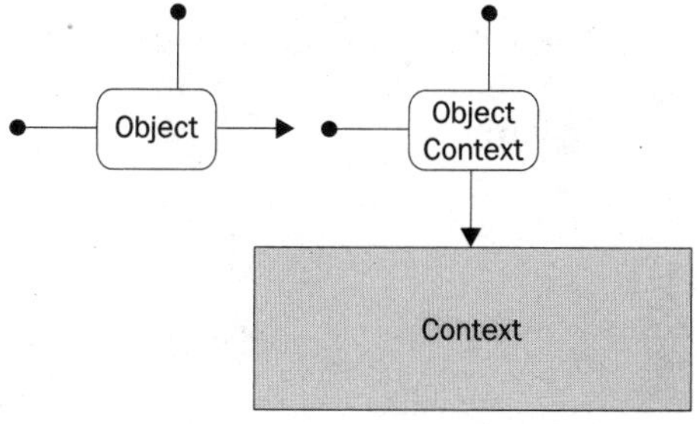

The ObjectContext is a COM object that provides access to the runtime properties held within the context that is associated with an object.

> *The name 'ObjectContext' is somewhat confusing, and don't be surprised if you find people using terms **ObjectContext** and **context object** interchangeably.*

Context Negotiation

When a COM+ object is created, the COM+ Catalog is used to determine the services a component uses. If an existing context matches the newly created object's, it will be used, if not, a new context is created:

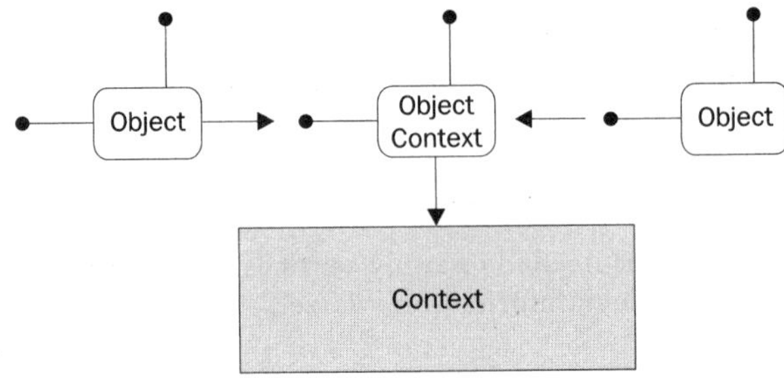

If the services required by the component mean that the context of the activator is incompatible with what it needs, a different context (and therefore ObjectContext) is used for the object:

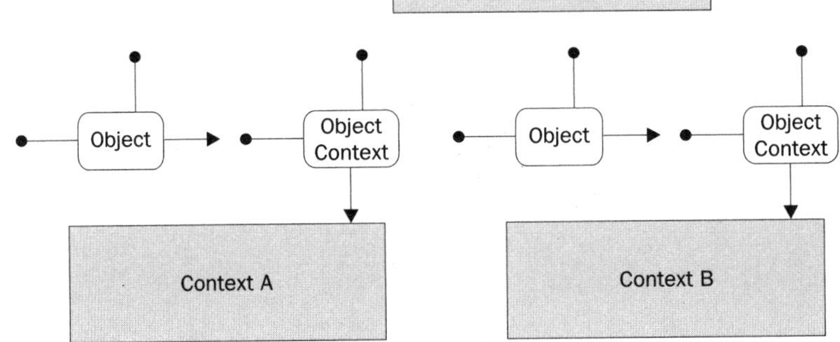

The proxy (if any) returned to the client ensures that the differences between the contexts of the activator and the object are transparently managed at runtime by the COM+ runtime, so we don't have to worry about that management in our code – client or component.

IIS and the Context

IIS uses the context to provide a COM object with access to the ASP intrinsic objects:

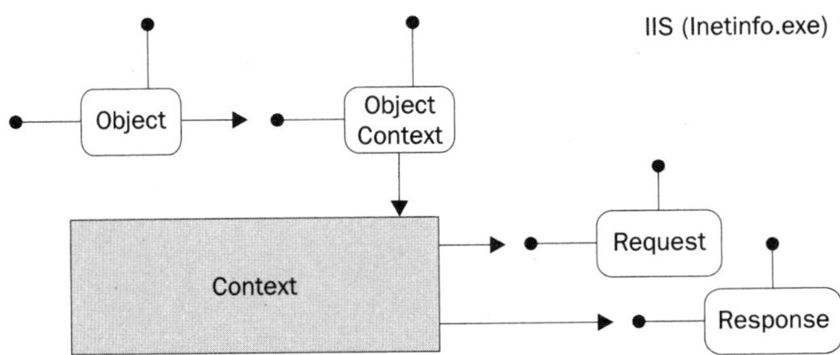

References to all of the ASP intrinsic objects (such as Request and Response) are held with the context as properties, put there by IIS. Any COM object that is associated with that context can access those properties through the ObjectContext associated with the context. Remember, the ObjectContext is a COM object that provides an interface into the context from within an object.

What this means is that a COM object can access the functionality of IIS (or any other application using the context to expose functionality) even though there is no *explicit* link or association between IIS or the object. This is, in effect, itself, a COM+ service that IIS provides to components using the COM+ infrastructure.

Interception, Contexts and COM+ Catalog – The Team Behind COM+

So far we've discuss the following key points about COM+:

- COM+ applications are built from configured components
- Configured components make use of COM+ services
- Both COM+ applications and configured components are configured using the Component Services Explorer
- The information manipulated within the Component Services Explorer is stored with the COM+ Catalog
- The COM+ runtime uses contexts and interception to ensure the runtime environment of objects correctly makes use of the services configured for a component

All of these points are new to COM+ and are not an integral part of pre-Windows 2000 COM. If you've used MTS before you simply need to redefine your terms to understand most of COM+:

- What was an MTS package is now called a COM+ application
- The services that MTS provided such as distributed transactions and security are now just called COM+ services

Component/Object Lifetimes and State

To make use of some of the services that COM+ provides, we have to re-think the programming style we are used to. For example, one service that COM+ provides is **Just-In-Time (JIT) activation** – a powerful technique for delaying the usage of server resources until they are really needed, and then ensuring they are released whilst instances of an object are not actually in use by a client.

COM+ Object Activation and Deactivation

Just-in-time (JIT) activation – the concept that a component instance is not activated until the first method of an interface is invoked – means any initialization code and resource requirements for an object are delayed until they are really needed. This means that a server's resources aren't consumed until they are absolutely needed – i.e. as a direct result of a client invoking a method on an object. This is a nice idea, because it means that a client can create a component earlier on in an application's life, and use it much later, without having to worry about resources being consumed prematurely.

By the same principle, COM+ deactivates objects as soon as possible. **As-Soon-As-Possible (ASAP) deactivation** enables COM+ to release the memory and resources consumed by the object – while allowing the client to believe that it still has a reference to the real object, without knowing that it has been destroyed. If the object can be pooled the object will be *deactivated* rather than destroyed.

But how can a client create an instance of the component early in an application's lifetime and still support JIT activations and ASAP deactivation? The answer lies in the interception mechanism we saw earlier. When a client requests an object instance, COM+ intercepts this code and, if JIT activation is enabled, instead of simply creating an instance of the object, it provides the client with a dummy proxy that the client is fooled into believing is a reference to a real object.

Then when a client actually makes a method call on the object, the proxy intercepts the call and COM+ creates a real instance of the object, which performs the necessary processing. When the method call completes the object is deactivated but the proxy remains to continue to fool the client:

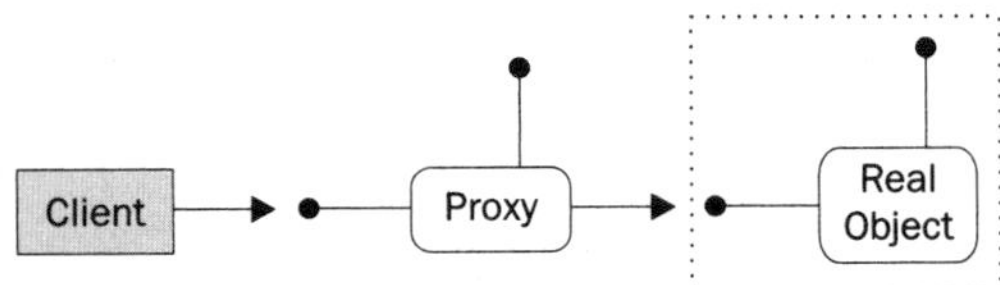

As we've already noted, the signal for JIT activation is fairly clear – it's the time at which the ASP page (or other client) makes its first method call to the object. The signal for ASAP deactivation is rather less clear. Do we deactivate immediately after a method call? To be a good transactional COM+ component that is scalable, the answer is Yes. That might sound surprising, because it will introduce a degree of overhead in that the server has to keep recreating the object, but remember, the important aspect of any application is that a server's precious resources (such as memory etc.) should be used and released quickly so that another client can then use those same resources. The only way COM+ can ensure that this happens is by deactivating an object, and destroying it, if it isn't marked to be pooled.

COM+ can efficiently create new instances of the component on demand, so the fact that objects are so frequently created and destroyed depending upon their configuration isn't actually a big overhead.

Caching Class Objects and DLLs in a COM+ Application

To achieve this efficient creating of objects, COM+ applications **cache** COM server DLLs and **class objects**.

> *Class objects are the mechanism via which COM+ objects are created. A class object is a COM object, which supports the COM interface `IClassFactory`. This interface has a method called `CreateInstance` that creates and returns a new instance of a COM+ object. There is one class object for every type of COM+ component. VB automatically creates these class objects for you.*

When a client creates an instance of a component contained within a COM+ application the following happens:

- The DLL containing the component type is loaded if it is not already in memory
- The class object for the component type is created
- COM+ asks the class object to create an instance of a new COM+ object

When a COM+ application loads a COM server (DLL) to create COM+ objects of a certain type, the DLL is kept loaded in memory until the COM+ application shuts down. If COM+ didn't perform this caching, the DLL would be unloaded when the very last object created by the class object that originated from that DLL was destroyed. The repeated creation and destruction of a single object would therefore potentially cause a DLL to be repeatedly loaded and unloaded causing disk thrashing. COM+ allows you to define the idle period at which time a COM+ application and all loaded DLLs are released:

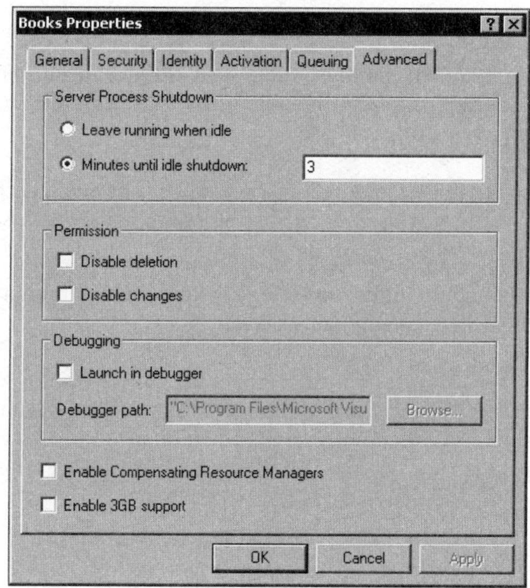

When a COM+ application creates a class object it keeps a reference to the class object until it is unloaded. This means creating an object after the first time only requires it to perform one step:

- COM+ asks the class object to create an instance of a new COM+ object

This caching improves the performance of object creation, and means that the overhead JIT activation incurs for created non-pooled objects is not so high.

JIT Activation doesn't Change COM

What we need to make very clear is that the basic rules of COM do not change to support services like JIT activation – an instance of a COM+ object is always destroyed if there are no outstanding references. However, it does change the programming approach of the client, and forces us to make our components **stateless**.

The Stateless Programming Paradigm

A COM+ component, just like any COM component, has the ability to store information internally between client interactions (method calls). A component that is doing this is said to be holding state, or is a **stateful** component. Now, if we mark this component as using JIT activation, and add the necessary calls to deactivate the object this model *dramatically* changes.

Information that is stored and manipulated by an object when a client calls it, is not available in subsequent method calls. By marking your component to use JIT activation, you've told COM+ that an object can be deactivated between method calls. What this means is that the next method call that is invoked by a client will potentially be processed by a *different* object instance.

I've used the word potentially because if an object is pooled, there is no reason why the object freed and added back to the pool wouldn't be the same object that is then re-used from the pool for the next call.

Forget OOP for JIT Components

That may take a few seconds to sink in, and you've probably read numerous texts that *incorrectly* define the stateless programming model to be something different. To put it simply the stateless programming model means two things to you as a developer:

- A client cannot depend upon the same object instance processing each method call it makes to what appears to be the same object. It can therefore not make any assumptions about the state of an object between method calls.
- An object cannot depend upon the same client calling each method it exposes. If an object is pooled, many clients will re-use the same object.

Those points are actually very simple, but the impact they have on the way you create such components and clients is significant. Forget Object Oriented Programming (OOP) with JIT components, it doesn't work. OO techniques depend upon an object having identity, behavior and most importantly state for a period of time. The last point just isn't going to happen, so code like this just won't work:

```
Dim objPerson As Richard

Set objPerson = New Richard

objPerson.Name = "Richard"
objPerson.DOB = 1972
objPerson.Title = "Developer"

objPerson.UpdateDetails
```

This is pretty typical OOP, where we set the properties of an object and then ask the object to save the changes to some type of storage medium. Can you see the problem? Well, each property access and method call will cause the COM+ runtime to create and destroy a COM object. You can't tell this is happening by looking at the code, because the creation and destruction occur within the COM+ runtime, but by the time we call the `UpdateDetails` method we are more than likely talking to a completely different object from that which we were talking to when we called the method to set the `Title` property. So what will the object save? Probably the default values you've initialized (if any) in the component's `Class_Initialize` routine.

As traditional OOP doesn't really work with COM+ JIT configured components, we have to stand back and think about a different approach for components and clients that use them. The components that don't use JIT can be programmed using the OOP techniques, but for JIT components we have to change our code to be **process-oriented**. Simply put, this means a client passes all the state necessary to process a request to an object in each method call.

Process-Oriented Objects

So for the code above to work we have to rewrite it like this:

```
Dim objPerson As Richard

Set objPerson = New Richard

objPerson.UpdateDetails "Richard", 1972, "Developer"
```

Rather than depending on state between method calls, which we now know is not the way to go, we simply pass all of the state required to perform the `UpdateDetails` process as parameters.

In ASP, two ways to achieve and stick to this stateless component design are:

- To avoid storing any information in local variables of a component
- To avoid holding onto references to that component from page-to-page

The easiest way to avoid a client inadvertently storing information inside of an object is to only present a method-based interface for the component. The component should have *no* public properties. All interaction with the component should be done through methods, and all information needed by the component to perform the work should be passed as parameters of the method calls.

Object State can be Re-Used

To review, the state of an object refers to any information that is held by the object. Typically, the state held by most objects is tied to a particular client. For example, if we had a COM object that represented the shopping cart contents of a particular user in an e-commerce application, then that object would be uniquely tied to that user. The state within that object isn't really much use to anybody else, so it cannot be re-used.

To understand why on earth you'd want to re-use the state of an object, consider a simple object that validates a list of values. Various pieces of an application create an instance of that component and use it. Now, assuming that each instance is loading those values from a database, the time taken to create the object could be fairly slow, say a few seconds. If you've got a lot of people using that particular component you could be talking about a large amount of database IO, and general overhead on an application.

By pooling such a component you could re-use the list created by one instance of component, rather than having to keep reloading it each time. This works because the state the object holds isn't specific to a particular client as in the shopping example above. So, if and when VB does support object pooling, remember that state can be re-used, and JIT is an excellent way to reduce the strain that slow-initializing objects place on a system. A perfect example of this can be found in OLE-DB, which pools database connections. Connecting to a database takes a long time and is a fairly slow process due to the authentication and general setup process, so by pooling the connection this overhead is only incurred by the first user of the Connection object. Subsequent users can simply reuse the already authenticated and setup object, provided of course that the security and connection string are compatible.

Scalable Systems keep Objects to a Minimum

I mentioned earlier that the shopping example, whereby we had an object representing the shopping cart, wasn't very scalable. To understand why, consider this system running on a large site like `amazon.com`, supporting hundreds or thousands of simultaneous users. Each user would have a corresponding COM object representing their shopping cart, which is stored in the Session object. Now, if we know the component requires 10k of memory to execute and maintain the cart, and we have an estimated 5,000 active sessions during peek times, we know that we need at least 5,000 * 10k (50,000k or around 49Mb) just for that *single* component. Although memory is a cheap resource, it's quite clear we have to consider this approach carefully.

Our tool of choice for creating components helps us achieve the other key to stateless component design. The types of components created by Visual Basic should only exist within the Page scope of an application. A reference to a VB-created component should not be stored in a Session or Application-level variable. Any attempt to do so will cause serious performance degradation of your Web server, and you can also configure ASP to generate an error message to prevent this. In this way, ASP itself promotes the use of stateless components in creating a Web application. This is all down to the threading models that our VB component is able to support.

Apartments and Threading Models

As VB ASP developers we don't have to worry too much about apartments or threading models, but they are a fundamental part of COM+ that you should be aware of. However, to understand them you need to first understand threads.

Threads

Put simply, you can think of a thread as a **lightweight process**. Unlike a process though, threads do not actually own system resources. When you start an application under Windows, such as Notepad, the operating system will create a process in which the application executes. This process will have its own address space, thus will be isolated from other processes, such that if the application goes seriously wrong, the integrity of other applications in the system is maintained.

Inside of a process you always have at least one **thread**, known as the main thread. A thread is the basic entity to which the operating allocates CPU time. So, if we have 10 processes, each with a thread that is doing some intensive work, the operating system would give each thread 10% of the overall available CPU time. A percentage of this time will actually be spent managing the thread switching, so the overall time given to your process for executing *your* code may be slightly less, say 9.5%.

A process can contain multiple threads that run concurrently. Each thread shares the system resources owned by the process, such as its virtual address space. This means that threads can execute the application's code, access global memory and other resources such as files, whilst not consuming too much additional resources.

Because threads are 'cheaper' that processes, truly scalable systems will always use a *thread-per-client*, rather than a *process-per-client*, because the resource saving is greater. Depending upon how the system is partitioned, the system might well use multiple processes for different applications, with a thread per-client. COM+ takes this approach by enabling each COM+ application to be configured to run in its own process.

COM+ also takes care of threads for you by pooling them. COM+ does this very efficiently – when the thread pool is exhausted, components will start to share threads in a round robin fashion. So if we had a thread pool size of 5, the sixth component created would share the first thread, the seventh the second and so on. Again the beauty of COM+ is that there is no need to write thread managers within your code. COM+ handles the threading for you, and languages that can't actually create or manage threads can take advantage of this functionality.

Apartments

Now that we understand what a thread is, we can begin to understand the role of an apartment:

> **An apartment is a synchronization mechanism and logical container for COM objects that provides a *thread* of execution, enabling methods of an object to be called within a process.**

When you write a COM component you need to think about how threads will access instances of it. If more than one thread can access the same object at the same time, you need to perform some type of synchronization inside of methods that will update data. If you don't then potential problems can occur.

For example, multiple threads using the same global value simultaneously could both try and manipulate the same data at the same time and lead to an inconsistent result.

Because COM is designed to let the component developer focus on writing components, it gives you the option to choose how much synchronization you want your component to take on board. If you don't want to worry about thread synchronization within methods – that is, more than one thread executing the same code at the same time – you can mark your component to run in a **Single-Threaded Apartment (STA)**.

Unlike COM+ Services, this is done from within the development tool used to create the component, rather than the Component Services Explorer. The rational behind this is quite simple: only the programmer knows if the component is thread-safe, so nobody except the programmer should define the attribute.

In COM+, apartments in many respects they have been demoted, with contexts being the main containers (so to speak) for objects now. Apartments are still important, but you should simply think of them as containers for contexts:

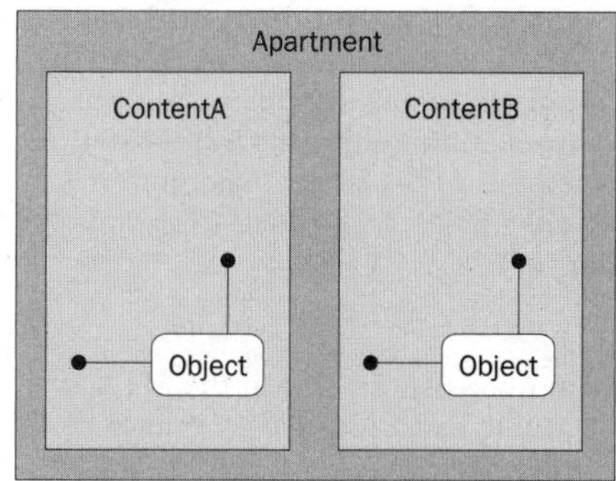

Apartments are sub-divided into one or more contexts. The number of contexts within an apartment depends upon the number of objects that are created within it, and the context requirements for those objects. By default every apartment has a **default context**. This default context is used to contain legacy non-configured components that don't use any of the services provided by COM+, e.g. those components that are not installed into a COM+ application via Component Services.

A process can contain many apartments that provide different thread-related services to objects within them. Each apartment can be associated with one or more threads depending upon the apartment type. COM+ defines three types of apartments:

- Single-Threaded Apartments
- Multi-Threaded Apartments
- Neutral-Threaded Apartments

Single-Threaded Apartments

A **Single-Threaded Apartment (STA)**, or **Apartment-Threaded** model, basically just allows only a single thread to run within each apartment. The thread is associated with the apartment throughout its lifetime. A process can contain any number of STAs.

STAs were designed for components that require call synchronisation and/or have thread affinity. The former means that the methods of an object have to be called one after the other and *never* simultaneously. The later ensures that the *same* thread always calls each method of an object throughout its lifetime.

With COM+, if a component does not have thread affinity, but requires call synchronisation, it can take advantage of performance increases by being made to use the Neutral-threading model. COM+ provides call synchronisation without having to tie component access down to a specific thread.

At the time of writing STAs are the only apartment type that VB supports.

Multiple-Threaded Apartments

By contrast, a **Multi-Threaded Apartment (MTA)** allows multiple threads to execute within the same apartment, and therefore allows multiple threads to invoke the methods of the same object instance. Unlike STAs each process can only have a single MTA:

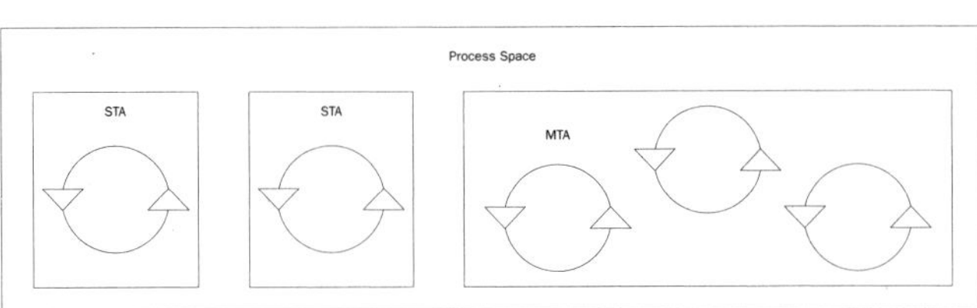

Components that run in the MTA are responsible for ensuring that they take into account the fact that they can be called by multiple threads. Access can be from different threads for each call, and potentially, calls can be made simultaneously.

Neutral-Threaded Apartments

STAs and MTAs allow an object to run in an execution environment that suits its threading capabilities, but STAs are inefficient if all an object really requires is call synchronization and not thread affinity. In this case, where the object doesn't care what thread calls it, provided only one thread ever calls the object it is happy. If we could achieve this, we potentially save an unnecessary thread switch (if the caller is on a different thread). Indeed, the caller's thread could always invoke the object's methods, provided it ensures that no other thread has called it already. This is what the new Neutral-Threaded Apartment in COM+ does.

The NTA ensures that a COM object has methods calls serialized one at a time, but any thread can make those calls. This has two major advantages:

- No cross-thread marshalling is required
- Several objects in the NTA can be active at the same time

The net result is a faster application.

The Threading Model Attribute

A COM/COM+ component signifies the threading responsibility it takes on by specifying a **threading model**. This threading model indicates to the COM runtime the type of thread scenarios the component can deal with, and directly impacts the apartment type or types the component can be created in.

There are five threading models in COM+:

- **Single-threaded** – A component instance should always be created in the main STA. The main STA is simply the first STA that is created within a process.
- **Apartment-threaded** – A component instance can be created in an STA.
- **Free-threaded** – A component instance must be created in the MTA.
- **Both-threaded** – A component instance can be created in an STA or MTA. COM+ makes the decision based upon the apartment type of the activator.
- **Neutral-threaded** – A component instance can only be created in the NTA.

Threading Models

So, COM has a rich set of threading models that enable component developers to decide how much responsibility they want to assume for handling access to their components from one or more threads. The more responsibly our components assume, the more they can potentially optimize their use, resulting in increased performance and overall scalability of the applications using them.

With VB threading models aren't really an issue; you've got two choices as of VB 6.0:

- Single – All access to *all* instances of the same component are serialized via a single thread.
- Apartment – All access to an instance of a component is serialized via a single thread, but different instances of the component can live on different threads. The thread used is static for the lifetime of the component.

The Apartment-threaded model is fine for most types of ASP component development, but, should you want to store instances of your components (objects) in the ASP Session or Applications objects, you really should use the Free- or Both-threaded models for performance reasons, which means you have to use VC++. These threading models are not available to VB because it is simply not designed for writing multi-threaded applications, and does everything in its power to shield the programmer from the concept of threads.

The Single-Threading Model

The Single-threading model *is* a **bad** thing. It stems from the early days of COM under Windows 3.1, and you really shouldn't consider using it unless the environment you're using dictates it. IIS doesn't dictate it so steer clear!

If you do use a Single-threaded component in a multi-threaded application like IIS, you are potentially making a large part of your application (anywhere that uses your component) Single-threaded. Using it means that *every* single method call, to *every* single instance of the component has to be done from the *same* thread. For example, imagine you've got 50 users accessing an ASP page or pages that uses a Single-threaded component, each page making one method call to the component. The 50th user has to wait for the 49th user's call to the object to complete before its call can be processed; the 49th user will have to wait for the 48th user's call to finish; the 48th user will have to wait for the 47th user's call to finish etc. Just reading that text was painful and slow, so imagine how the 50th user will feel waiting ages for the ASP page to be displayed in their browser!

The Single-threading model effectively tells COM your component can't cope with threads; in fact, it tells COM it has a very serious thread phobia. You want COM to serialize method calls to all instances of a component, so the component can access global or local data without having to synchronize access. If one thread reads a piece of data and updates it, another thread could do the same thing at the same time, and one of the changes will be lost.

So the bottom line is this: don't ever use components with this threading model attribute in ASP, and certainly don't ever buy a component that only supports this threading model!

The Apartment-Threading Model

The Apartment-threading model is the right choice for most ASP components. As VB supports this threading model, VB is ideally suited for writing most types of ASP components that don't require outright speed of execution, or access to operating system/SDK functions that VB cannot access. But of course if you've got skilled VC++ staff, using VC++ can be just as productive. So, when should we use VC++ instead of VB?

Well, generally speaking VB and VC are as good as each other for writing ASP components that are Apartment-threaded, but VB has some interesting implementation quirks that mean you might want to use VC++ in preference. Let's recap on what the Apartment-threading model means, and discuss how your language choice may be swayed one way or the other.

When you pick the Apartment-threading model, COM takes on the responsibility for ensuring that all access to a single instance of a component is serialized via one thread. The same thread is used to call any of the component's interface methods for the lifetime of the object. As the calling thread is always the same, the object has **thread affinity**, and can make various assumptions about the caller. It also means your VC++ components can make use of Thread Local Storage (TLS).

Put simply, Thread Local Storage is a way of effectively making a global variable unique for each thread. Rather than having to manage access to a global variable, TLS takes care of it for you.

The Apartment-threading model is the preferred threading model for most environments, so you'll also find it's the default threading model option in VC++ and VB 6.0. If we've got 50 users accessing an ASP page that uses a component with this model, each call can be processed simultaneously, so each user in theory gets an equal response time.

The Free-Threading Model

A Free-threaded object runs in a process' multi-threaded apartment (MTA). As we saw above, an application in COM+ can have only one multi-thread apartment in it. This MTA can have one or more threads within it. Any objects that are marked as Free-threaded will be created in the MTA, regardless of the apartment of the caller. Now, all of this may sound great. "Wow, multiple threads! Must mean great scalability!" This is not necessarily the case.

When a call is made from one component to another component within the same the context and apartment, the call is a direct function call. In the Win32 environment, this is a very fast process. But if a call has to be made from one context to another, or cross apartments, then a proxy needs to be created in order to make the call. The cross-apartment proxy is a lot slower due to the thread switch that is incurred.

The use of a proxy adds overhead to every function call, and slows down the system. Since a Free-threaded component will *always* be created in a Multi-threaded Apartment, even if it was created from a Single-threaded apartment, then all calls to access that component will have to be made by a proxy. This means that even though Free-threaded components sound good, they will exact a performance penalty when used in ASP script.

The Both-Threading Model

There is another type of threading model called **Both**. This is a special type of threading model in that the object can adopt the characteristics of an Apartment-threaded object as well as a Free-threaded object, depending upon the apartment type of the activator. The advantage that this threading model brings is that no matter where the component is created, it will always be created within the same apartment (excluding the NTA) as the activator. If the component is created from within a Single-threaded Apartment, then it will act like an Apartment-threaded component, and be executed in the apartment. And likewise, if it is created in a Multi-threaded apartment, it will act like a Free-threaded component and be executed in the MTA. In either case, to access this new component, proxy calls across apartments are not necessary. The only time a proxy is required is if the object is created in the NTA.

The Neutral-Threading Model

The new threading model introduced with COM+ and Windows 2000 is the **Neutral**-threading model. This is the preferred threading model for COM+ Server components. In the past, before MTS, the preferred threading model for *agile* ASP components was Both, with aggregation on the Free Threaded Marshaller.

These components, while fast and scalable, were difficult for developers to create, as they forced the developer to deal with issues such as locking and debugging multi-threaded applications. They also had to be written in a language other than VB. Neutral components are designed to be much easier to create, as COM+ has taken on the difficult parts away from us, and implemented that as part of the COM+ plumbing.

Each process has at most one Neutral-threaded apartment (NTA). Unlike the MTA and STAs, the NTA has no threads of its own. When a thread living in the MTA or an STA creates a Neutral-threaded object, it will get back a lightweight proxy to the object. This proxy will switch to the callee's object's context and not require a thread switch. In fact, no thread in the process ever needs to perform a thread switch when entering a context in the NTA. This means that all calls to a Neutral-threaded object are direct, or only require a lightweight proxy to handle cross-context management. This makes NTA objects very fast and independent of the caller's apartment. With Windows 2000, this threading model is the preferred setting for components that have no user interface.

Once VB removes the thread affinity its runtime currently has, we should see this threading model being supported by it.

ASP Components and the Apartment-Threading Model

So, our examination of the Single- and Apartment-threading models shows there is really only one choice for ASP components that are written in VB today - Apartment. As and when VB supports the Neutral-threading model that will become the preferred choice.

If the Single-threading model is used for any reason, then scalability and the potentially performance of any application is seriously comprised, as each method invoked for every component instance is serialized via one thread; this is a bottleneck.

If you're writing ASP components in VB that use the Apartment-threading model, you don't have to worry about any type of multi-threaded synchronization. You just have to remember that global state is really per-apartment state, so don't fall into the trap of thinking your component isn't working, when in fact the VB runtime is simply making your life easier.

As far as IIS is concerned, Apartment-threaded components should really only be used within an ASP. They should only be stored in the Session object with *careful* consideration, and they should never be stored in the Application object. How you use a component in IIS defines it **scope**, that is, its lifetime and availability within an IIS application. Different scopes are suited to different threading models, which include Free and Both, so let's define the scopes used within IIS, and discuss how the different threading models (include Both and Free) are best married with different scopes.

Threading Model and Scope

We have just completed a discussion about component threading models – which ones are good and which ones are not so good. We have also looked at using components within an ASP application. One aspect that we need to look at combines these two aspects, and is related to how different types of components should be used in different situations in an ASP application.

The usage and scalability of a component is directly related to where that component is used in the application. There are three domains of use, or scopes, that a component can occupy. These scopes are based on the lifetime of the component, as well as which particular clients can access the component. The three scopes are:

- Page scope
- Session scope
- Application scope

Page Scope

When you create, use, and then release all references to a component instance within a single ASP page, that component is said to have **Page scope**. If you give an object life beyond the page, by storing its reference in a Session-level or Application-level variable, then you no longer have a Page scoped object. This means that the component only exists within the scope of the page. There is no lifetime of the component beyond the life of the page. Any information that may have been contained within the component will be lost when the page is completed.

When you create a component within Page scope, this means that all calls made into the component will come from the thread that is currently processing the ASP script for the requesting user. This process is occurring within a Single-threaded Apartment inside of the ASP application. As we saw earlier, you will want to make sure that these calls are done using direct calls, since this method provides the best performance. In order to access the component using direct calls, you will need to make sure that the component is running within the same apartment as the one executing the ASP script.

If you create a Single-threaded component within the page, it can only be created on the main STA thread of the ASP application. This means that all calls to the component will have to be marshaled to cross an *apartment boundary*, in order to access the component running on the main thread.

The main thread of the application is in an STA, meaning that there can only be one execution path active at any time. When a component is being accessed that is running on this thread, it means that *nothing* else in the ASP application can be executed on that thread while the component is executing. This means that no incoming user requests can be processed if they use that thread. You will have effectively created a single-tasking Web server for many users. Doesn't sound too scalable, does it? Well, it will begin to bog down as soon as that second user tries to access it.

You will need to use a component that can be accessed using direct calls, as well as running on a thread other than the main application thread. A Free-threaded component will run inside of the MTA, so it will leave the main application thread free to continue processing. But with this component running in the MTA, and the page processing being done in one of the STAs, we have objects running in different apartments. The only way to call between them is to marshal information across the apartment boundaries. While this will not turn your Web server into a single-tasking server, it will consume more time and resources every time this component is accessed.

When we create a Free-threaded or Neutral-threaded component, we have created a component that is said to have no thread affinity. This means that the component doesn't care which thread it is executing on. It can be called from any thread. However, only a Neutral-threaded components can be called by any thread. A thread that is associated with an STA cannot call on a Free-threaded component, unless that component aggregates the Free-threaded marshaller (FTM) to avoid the proxy that COM will otherwise create.

> *The Free-threaded marshaller enables an object to have its interface pointers efficiently marshalled between apartments within the same process. When an object uses the FTM to perform this optimization, the COM+ infrastructure will ensure that any clients within the same process as the object will always directly invoke its methods - proxies will* never *be used.*

Assuming that the component does aggregate the FTM, both types of component (Free and Neutral) can be called using the thread associated with an STA. This means that the calls into the component are direct or via a fast proxy, so we will not incur any performance penalties due to marshaling.

An Apartment-threaded component will execute on the same thread that created it if the activator lives with an STA, which is the case for IIS 5.0. When an Apartment-threaded component is created within an ASP script, it will be able to execute on the same thread as the one processing the ASP script. This means that any calls to the component are done through direct calls. So in this case, an Apartment-threaded component is just as good as a Free-threaded or Neutral-threaded component. This means for us Visual Basic developers creating our components, we generally have a way to create components that work just as well, in this case, as do components created using C++.

Session Scope

When an object is created with **Session scope**, it will be available to all ASP pages that are referenced during that user's session. Each session that is created in the application will also have its own instances of Session scope objects. To create a Session scope object, you will add this entry to the global.asa file for the application:

```
<OBJECT RUNAT=Server SCOPE=Session ID=myID PROGID="objectID"></OBJECT>
```

The RUNAT=Server parameter indicates that this object is a server-side component. The SCOPE=Session indicates that this object will have Session-level scope. It will be accessible to any ASP script that is part of the application, referenced through the myID object reference.

You can also create a Session scope performance by holding onto an object reference between subsequent ASP page requests. This can be done by storing the reference to the object inside of a Session-level variable, like this:

In page1.asp:

```
<%
Dim objMyObject
Set objMyObject = Server.CreateObject("myObject.ProgID")
…use the object on the page
Set Session("myObjRef") = objMyObject
%>
```

And then in page2.asp:

```
<%
Dim objMyObject
Set objMyObject = Session("myObjRef")
…use the object on the page
%>
```

When you store an object in Session scope, this means that multiple page requests by the same user can access this object. The mechanism of processing ASP requests is such that whenever a request comes in, ASP will assign the processing of the page to a particular STA from its thread pool. So if this page request coming in also had information stored in Session-level variables, and this information includes a reference to an object, then the new page will have access to that information.

Since there can be object references stored in Session state, the environment responsible for processing the new page must be able to access these objects in the same way as the page that created them. Let's examine the five different threading models and see how they perform when stored in Session scope.

- You could store a reference to a Single-threaded object within Session scope, but given all of the performance penalties that you incur when using these types of components, why would you want to?
- If you store a Free-threaded object within Session scope, then when you use it in your next page, it will still be executing in the MTA, and the ASP script will have to use a proxy to access it. This reduces overall performance.

- When you store a Neutral-threaded component, or a Free-threaded component that aggregates the FTM, in Session scope, you are working with components that have no thread affinity. No matter what thread they run on, all calls into this component will be made using direct calls or via a lightweight proxy. Because of this, the component will cause itself to execute on the thread that is processing the new page. This gives optimal performance, and is the recommended threading model for components stored in session-scope. However, that does mean that VB is not suitable for creating a component to be stored in Session scope.

- So what happens when an Apartment-threaded component or Both-threaded component is stored in Session scope? This component has thread affinity to the STA that it was created on – it will only be able to run on this thread. It is not thread-agile like the Free-threaded FTM and Neutral-threaded components – it has one thread that it works with and no other. There are a number of threads in the ASP thread pool, with the default value of 25. So when ASP is assigning threads to incoming page requests, there is a 1 in 25 chance that the component will end up with the thread that created it. But ASP doesn't work that way.

  ASP actually examines the Session scope contents before handing the processing off to a particular thread. It is looking for any component references that may be stored there. If it finds one, it checks to see if the component has any thread affinity. So if there is an Apartment-threaded component stored there, ASP will know what particular thread this component likes. It can just hand off the request to the appropriate thread and everything will be fine. But will it?

  Remember that in an ASP application, there may be hundreds or thousands of users being served at any one time. With a limited pool of threads available to service incoming requests, chances are that a lot of these threads will be busy processing when the incoming request comes in. So what happens if one of the threads that are busy also happens to be the only thread that the component will function on? ASP can't hand off the request to another thread, since the component won't function. The only thing it can do is wait. In other words, the request will be *blocked* from processing until the needed thread becomes available.

  One can imagine a scenario where lots of clients create Session-level objects that are each locked to a particular thread. Pretty soon, the Web server can't find any threads to perform any real work on, since they are each being used by their particular client. The server will just grind to a halt and not process anything.

The only way to avoid this kind of deadlock is to only store objects that have *no thread affinity* in Session scope. This limits you to using Neutral or Both/Free-threaded objects that aggregate the FTM. Single, Apartment and Both-threaded components have affinity to a particular thread when create in IIS, so they should not be stored in Session scope.

Application Scope

An **Application scoped** object is one that can be accessed by any ASP script in the application. There is also only one instance of the object for the entire application. This object is inserted in the same way as the Session scoped object, using the <OBJECT> tag. There is one change that needs to be made for an Application scoped object:

```
<OBJECT RUNAT=Server SCOPE=Application ID=myID PROGID="objectID"></OBJECT>
```

By changing the `SCOPE` parameter to Application, there will be only one instance of this object available to all users of the application. This presents some interesting challenges when selecting a threading model for an Application scoped component. If this component is marked as using Apartment-threading, then *every* request coming into the server can only be handled by one thread. That means that only one user out of all the users accessing the site can use the object at any one time. All of the other users will have to wait until it is their turn.

The only types of objects you should store in application scope should be Free-threaded, Both-threaded or Neutral-threaded components. These components have no thread affinity, so they can be accessed by every incoming request to the application, no matter which thread is processing the request. If you are writing a Both-threaded component to use in Application scope, you must create it to aggregate on the Free Threaded Marshaller. If you use a component that does not do this, then ASP will generate an error when the component is created. Because of this, they should not be COM+ components, and they should not be registered with Component Services Explorer as the FTM causes the context to be ignored.

There are very few situations that require an Application scoped component. Maybe a page counter component should be stored at Application level, but there are alternatives to storing information that can make Application scoped components unnecessary.

Scope Alternatives

From what we have seen about component scope and components, there appear to be few choices for using components to store state between page requests, or between users in a Web application. These components can only be created using C++, and must be able to handle multiple users simultaneously. This means that they will be filled with multi-threaded code, such as critical sections and all other types of deep, complicated, low-level code. All in all, this means that they will be difficult to create, and more importantly difficult to debug.

In many cases, a better solution than creating Application or Session scoped objects, is to use Session or Application scoped *variables* that pass information to objects created at the page level. For example, you should not give an ADO Connection object Session or Application scope because the connection it creates remains open for a long time and because your script no longer takes advantage of connection pooling. You can, however, store an ODBC or OLE DB connection string in the Session or Application built-in object and access the string to set a property on the Connection object instance that you create on a single page. In this way, you store frequently used information in Session or Application state but you create the object that uses the information only when needed.

If you are still intent on using components to pass information from page-to-page, you may want to come up with a way to perform your own component serialization. This means that instead of holding onto the created component by storing a reference to it in Session scope, you store the state information that describes the component as scalar values in a Session-level variable, and then just let the component be destroyed when the page ends. When you want to use the component again on the next page, you create it using `Server.CreateObject`, and then pass it the state information that you retrieved from the Session-level variable.

Rather than look at a full code example, here is some pseudocode that describes the process:

```
<%
Dim objMyComp
Set objMyComp = Server.CreateObject("MyComp.ProgID")
….use the component
Dim vData
vData = objMyComp.SerializeMe()
Session("MyCompData") = vData
Set objMyComp = Nothing
%>
```

Then, when you want to use the component again in another page:

```
<%
Dim objMyComp
Set objMyComp = Server.CreateObject("MyComp.ProgID")
Dim vData
vData = Session("MyCompData")
objMyComp.LoadMe vData
….use the component
%>
```

The `SerializeMe` method in the component will be responsible for converting any internal state into a scalar data type that could be stored as text within a Session-level variable. The corresponding `LoadMe` method will take that same text and restore the state of the variable so that it looks identical to the way that it did just before `SerializeMe` was called.

COM+ Applications

In this chapter, we have been looking at how COM+ and Microsoft Component Services can help us developers build component-based applications. One of the primary ways that COM+ helps us do that is by providing an administration mechanism for these components as an MMC snap-in. It does this by allowing our components to be grouped together into an entity called a **COM+ application**.

> **A COM+ application is a set of COM+ configured components that, generally, perform related functions.**

In practice, you may have one or more COM+ applications that are used by your ASP application. By grouping a set of components together in a COM+ application like this, you can administer the group as a whole.

For those of you familiar with MTS packages from NT4, COM+ applications serve nearly the exact same function.

We've already seen how COM+ associates a context with each of our objects that are running in COM+ under Windows 2000. Now we will see how we can make use of this context from within our components, to extend their functionality and utilize the COM+ environment.

The ObjectContext Interface

Just as the ObjectContext is the real 'root' or gateway to the ASP intrinsic objects, we use the ObjectContext object from within our own custom components to access the runtime environment.

Before we can use the ObjectContext from within our VB component, we must first add an appropriate reference to the project, as we would any type library to define the components and interfaces we want to use in our code:

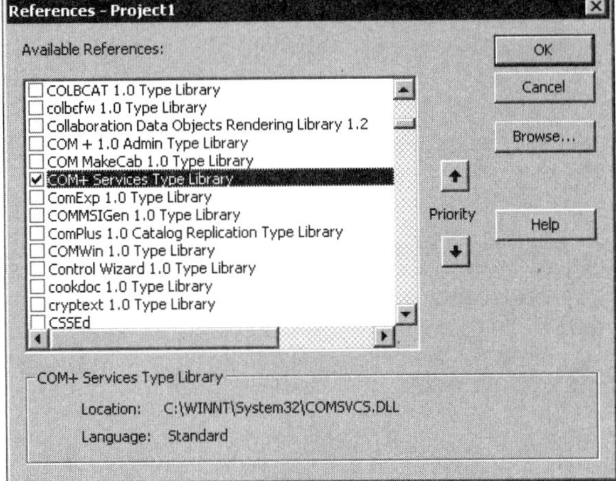

This allows us to make a reference to the context that the object is associated with, through the ObjectContext object, at runtime by using the `GetObjectContext` function:

```
Dim objContext As COMSVCS.ObjectContext

Set objContext = GetObjectContext()
```

Through this reference to the ObjectContext object, we can access the functionality of the context, just like any other COM object we use.

Controlling COM+ Resources

One of the ObjectContext object's interfaces allows our component to let COM+ know the state of the work that it is performing. If a component can explicitly tell COM+ that it is finished with its resources, then COM+ can deactivate that object sooner, and return the resources to the system, as we've discussed.

As we will see in more detail in Chapter 19 on transactions, one runtime property of the context is the so-called **Done Bit**. This is a Boolean flag that tells COM+ when an object has completed its work and can be deactivated. By setting this value to TRUE, we are basically telling COM+ that when the current method call completes, it can go ahead and deactivate the component.

To set this Done Bit to TRUE, there are two methods on the ObjectContext object that we can call:

- `SetComplete`
- `SetAbort`

Although these two methods may seem to be opposites, they both actually set the Done Bit to TRUE. The difference lies in how they affect the result of transactional work, which we'll see in Chapter 19.

To use these methods, simply execute them as member functions of the ObjectContext reference:

```
Dim objContext As COMSVCS.ObjectContext
Set objContext = GetObjectContext()
… Do some work
objContext.SetComplete ' This sets the Done Bit to TRUE
```

Referencing the ASP Intrinsic Objects

We have already seen that our COM+ objects are associated with a context and we already know that our ASP pages also have a context. What this means, in effect, is that we can use the context from our components to access the ASP intrinsic objects. As discussed, this means the context can be used as a two-way communication channel.

In order to do this, we must extend our VB components in a couple of ways:

- First, we need to access the context through the ObjectContext object, as we have seen above
- Second, we need to reference the objects from the ASP script that we want to use

Once we have these references, we can interact with the objects in the same way as if we were writing ASP script in the page. We can write script within our objects that use the same ASP intrinsic objects as the client ASP pages.

In order to reference the ASP intrinsic objects from Visual Basic, we must first tell our VB project that we are going to be using the ASP components. By doing this, VB can provide the programmer with Intellisense and other support for these components. It will also allow VB to early bind to the component, which will help to improve performance, especially when compared to a late bound client, such as the Active Scripting engine that executes the ASP script. To gain these advantages, simply add a reference to the Microsoft Active Server Pages Object Library:

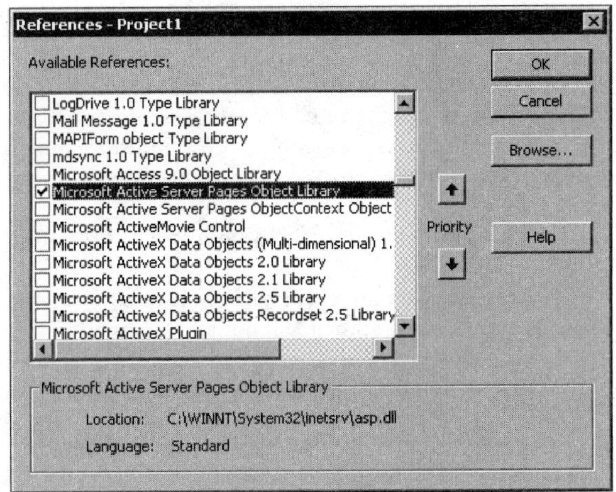

We will also need the COM+ Services Type Library *to reference the ObjectContext.*

Obtaining a Reference to the ASP Objects

Now that you have told Visual Basic that you will be using the ASP intrinsic objects in your component, the next step is to obtain a reference to them. We've already seen how to reference the ObjectContext object, so let's look at how we can use this object to obtain a reference to the ASP objects.

Remember that the ObjectContext allows access to *all* of the components in the execution environment. In order to access the component that we are interested in, we must retrieve it from the ObjectContext. So for example, if we want a reference to the ASP Response object, we will grab it from the collection of objects contained in the ObjectContext:

```
Dim objResponse As ASPTypeLibrary.Response
...
Set objResponse = objContext("Response")
```

We can retrieve each of the ASP intrinsic objects this way – all we need to do is substitute the name of the appropriate object. With the reference to the Response object stored in the local variable `objResponse`, we can now call the same methods on that object that we are used to using from VBScript in ASP files:

```
objResponse.Write "This was written by the component and not the ASP page"
```

Visual Basic COM+ Components

Let's take the component that was developed in the previous chapter, and extend it to support COM+ to makes use of the services that COM+ provides, which can help make our application more scalable. To do this, we will be making some changes to the component architecture:

- The components will be made stateless to improve scalability
- The data-access will be moved into a data-centric tier
- The presentation logic will be updated to include writing directly to ASP

In this example, we will be replicating the functionality of the example in the previous chapter, but re-architecturing it to better support the concepts we have looked at in this chapter. The functionality of the application is to support the maintenance of a list of books. The application should allow you to display the list, add to the list, and delete items from the list.

For this application, we will be using a three-tier architecture:

- The data layer will be responsible for interacting with the database. The only database interaction information that will not be contained in this layer will be the information needed to connect to the database. This is externalised from the data layer to make it easier to move the application between systems.
- The business logic tier will really be more of a user-centric component, as it will focus primarily on the interaction between the data and the presentation and contain some presentation logic in the form of ASP script. Given the simple nature of our application, there are few business rules to support, but we will maintain this layer to give us a robust application hierarchy.
- The presentation layer will be delivered using ASP script.

Component Architecture

The data component in our application supports the interaction with the database. Our database, as it was in the previous chapter, is the `pubs` database that is included with SQL Server. The data component will need to retrieve a list of titles from the database, add a title to the database, and delete a title from the database. This will give us a component interface with four methods:

- `GetTitleList` – This will return an array containing the desired information from the titles list in the database
- `AddTitleToDB` – This will take as parameters the fields to be added to a record in the title table of the database
- `DeleteTitleFromDB` – This will take as a parameter the unique ID of the title to be deleted, and remove it from the database
- `CheckTitleExists` – This will take as a parameter the unique ID of a title and return a Boolean as to whether or not that title exists

The business logic component will serve as a pass-through layer between the data layer and the presentation in the ASP pages. Since this makes for a very simplistic component, we will add a business rule that computes the lowest possible selling price for a book. The business logic component will also support methods that allow for the addition of a new title and the deletion of an existing title. The component interface will look like:

- `RetrieveTitleList` – This will return an array containing the list of titles
- `AddTitle` – This will take as parameters the information about a new title to be added to the system
- `DeleteTitle` – This will check for the existence of a particular title ID in the database, and if it exists, it will delete it

The ASP pages for this application will be identical in name and function to the ones from the example in the last chapter, though their internal workings will be slightly different to support the new component interface. We will also add a `global.asa` file to the application, which will contain the database connection string:

- `List.asp` – Shows the complete list of book titles using the component
- `Add.asp` – Provides a simple screen for detailing information about a new title
- `Add_UpdateDB.asp` – Performs the addition of a new book title using the component and information passed from `Add.asp`
- `Delete.asp` – Performs the deletion of a book title using the component

The Data Component

The data component will use ADO to retrieve the information from the `pubs` database that is stored in SQL Server. These methods will retrieve the information and return the data or an indication of success or failure to the calling object. All methods will have the database connection string passed as a parameter to the method.

Create a new ActiveX DLL project called `BookData` and name the default class `TitleData`. Add a reference to the COM+ Services Type Library and the ADO 2.5 Library. Also make sure the MTSTransactionMode for the class is set to 1-No Transactions. The default NotAnMTSObject may mean a context is not associated with the component at runtime.

The GetTitleList Method

The `GetTitleList` method will query the database for the list of titles, and return it to the calling object in an array:

```
Public Function GetTitleList(strConn As String, arTitles As Variant) As Boolean

  On Error GoTo errorGetTitleList

  Dim objConn As ADODB.Connection
  Dim rsTitles As ADODB.Recordset
  Dim strSQL As String

  Set objConn = CreateObject("ADODB.Connection")
  Set rsTitles = CreateObject("ADODB.Recordset")
  objConn.Open strConn

  strSQL = "SELECT title_id, title, price, notes FROM titles"
  rsTitles.Open strSQL, objConn, adOpenKeyset

  If Not rsTitles.EOF Then
     arTitles = rsTitles.GetRows()
  End If

  objConn.Close
  Set rsTitles = Nothing
  Set objConn = Nothing

  GetObjectContext.SetComplete
  GetTitleList = True

  Exit Function

errorGetTitleList:

  GetObjectContext.SetAbort
  GetTitleList = False
  arTitles = Err.Description

End Function
```

As you can see, this looks a lot like VBScript code that deals with databases. The primary difference is the use of the `SetAbort` and `SetComplete` methods of the ObjectContext reference. These are used to set the 'Done Bit' of the current component, which allows COM+ to know when to release the component. Rather than obtaining the reference to the ObjectContext and storing it in a local variable, we are simply grabbing it when we need it by calling the `GetObjectContext` method.

The AddTitleToDB Method

This method will take the information entered by the user about a new book title and add it to the database. The user is responsible for supplying the ID of the title, name of the title, the price of the book, and some notes about it:

```
Public Function AddTitleToDB(Id As String, Title As String, _
                             Price As Currency, Notes As String, _
                             strConn As String) As Boolean

  On Error GoTo errorAddTitle

  Dim objConn As ADODB.Connection
  Dim strSQL As String

  Set objConn = CreateObject("ADODB.Connection")
  objConn.Open strConn

  strSQL = "INSERT INTO titles (title_id, title, Price, Notes) VALUES ("
  strSQL = strSQL + "'" + Id + "',"
  strSQL = strSQL + "'" + Title + "',"
  strSQL = strSQL + "" + CStr(Price) + ","
  strSQL = strSQL + "'" + Notes + "')"

  objConn.Execute strSQL
  objConn.Close
  Set objConn = Nothing

  AddTitleToDB = True
  GetObjectContext.SetComplete
  Exit Function

errorAddTitle:

  GetObjectContext.SetAbort
  AddTitleToDB = Err.Description

End Function
```

To insert the information into the database, we will be constructing a SQL `INSERT` statement, then using the `Execute` method of the database connection object to add the information to the database. If everything worked correctly, we will call the `SetComplete` method. If there was an error, the method error handler will catch that, and then we will call `SetAbort`.

The DeleteTitleFromDB Method

When we want to delete a title from the database, we will pass this method the ID of the title, along with the database connection string. It will return a value of True if the record was deleted, or the text of the error message if it didn't work:

```
Public Function DeleteTitleFromDB(Id As String, strConn As String) As Boolean

  On Error GoTo errorDeleteTitle

  Dim objConn As ADODB.Connection
  Set objConn = CreateObject("ADODB.Connection")
  objConn.Open strConn
```

```
    objConn.Execute "DELETE FROM roysched WHERE title_id = '" & Id & "'"
    objConn.Execute "DELETE FROM sales WHERE title_id = '" & Id & "'"
    objConn.Execute "DELETE FROM titleauthor WHERE title_id = '" & Id & "'"
    objConn.Execute "DELETE FROM titles WHERE title_id = '" & Id & "'"

    objConn.Close
    Set objConn = Nothing

    DeleteTitleFromDB = True
    GetObjectContext.SetComplete
    Exit Function

  errorDeleteTitle:

    GetObjectContext.SetAbort
    DeleteTitleFromDB = Err.Description

  End Function
```

As with the example in the previous chapter, there are four tables in the `pubs` database that contain information about titles. We will need to delete information about the selected title from each one, in order for the title to be completely removed from the database. You will notice, if you haven't noticed already, that as soon as we are done with an object, like the database connection object `objConn`, we are immediately releasing the reference to that object. This will ensure that the resources are used as efficiently as possible in our application.

The CheckTitleExists Method

In order to help with some of our business rules processing, we may want to check for the existence of a title ID in the database before performing some function. To do this, we have created the `CheckTitleExists` method, which will take a title ID and return True if that title ID exists in the database:

```
  Public Function CheckTitleExists(Id As String, strConn As String) As Variant

    On Error GoTo errorCheckTitleExists

    Dim objConn As ADODB.Connection
    Dim rsTitle As ADODB.Recordset
    Dim strSQL As String

    Set objConn = CreateObject("ADODB.Connection")
    objConn.Open strConn

    strSQL = "SELECT title_id FROM titles WHERE title_id = '" & Id & "';"

    Set rsTitle = objConn.Execute(strSQL)

    If rsTitle.EOF Then
       CheckTitleExists = False
       GetObjectContext.SetAbort
       rsTitle.Close
```

```
    Else
       CheckTitleExists = True
       GetObjectContext.SetComplete
    End If

    objConn.Close

    Set rsTitle = Nothing
    Set objConn = Nothing
    Exit Function

 errorCheckTitleExists:

    GetObjectContext.SetAbort
    CheckTitleExists = Err.Description

 End Function
```

In this method, we will query the titles table of the database to see if there is a record that matches the title ID that was passed in as a parameter. If the recordset returned by the query is empty, then we know there is no matching entry. Seeing that, we will return False, and also call `SetAbort`. If the recordset is not empty, then we know we have a valid title ID, and will return True.

Business Logic Component

The business logic component in our application doesn't perform too much processing. It is primarily in place to provide the isolation layer between the user interface and the database objects. When it comes time to add business functionality to the application in the future, these components can be extended to support the new functionality, without requiring major changes to the application architecture.

Either modify the existing `Book` component or create a new ActiveX DLL project with the same names. Make sure it contains a reference to the COM+ Services Type Library and the Active Server Pages Library – this component does not need the ADO reference. Again make sure the MTSTransactionMode property of the class is set to 1–NoTransactions.

The RetrieveTitleList Method

This method will obtain a listing of all of the titles in the database, and return it to the caller in an array. It will also create a 1-dimensional array that corresponds to the other information, and contains the discounted price for each title:

```
 Public Function RetrieveTitleList(strConn As Variant, arTitles As Variant, _
                                   arDiscount As Variant) As Variant

    On Error GoTo errorRetrieveTitleList

    Dim objBookData As BookData.TitleData
    Dim blnTitlesOK As Boolean

    Set objBookData = CreateObject("BookData.TitleData")
```

```
    blnTitlesOK = objBookData.GetTitleList(CStr(strConn), arTitles)
    Set objBookData = Nothing

    If blnTitlesOK Then
       Dim intRows, intCount
       intRows = UBound(arTitles, 2)
       'arDiscount = Array(1)
       ReDim arDiscount(intRows)

       For intCount = 0 To intRows
           If IsNull(arTitles(2, intCount)) Then arTitles(2, intCount) = 0
           arDiscount(intCount) = Round((arTitles(2, intCount) * 0.65), 2)
       Next intCount

       RetrieveTitleList = "True"
       GetObjectContext.SetComplete
    Else
       RetrieveTitleList = "False - " & arTitles
       GetObjectContext.SetAbort
    End If

    Exit Function

  errorRetrieveTitleList:

    RetrieveTitleList = Err.Description

  End Function
```

This method will use the `GetTitleList` method of the database component to first retrieve the list of titles. Once it has retrieved the information, it will release the reference to the data component. It will then compute the number of rows in the array and create an array with the same number of rows. This will be used to hold the discounted price of each title. As we iterate through the array, we will check to see if the price is a Null value. If it is we will replace it with a 0. We will then compute the discounted price, and store it in the new array. Once this is completed, we will call the `SetComplete` method and return from the function.

This seems like a perfect opportunity to use the ASP intrinsic objects that we looked at earlier to make our ASP script a lot simpler. Although this logic would really be better suited to a separate component, with the simple component we have currently it is more sensible to simply add it to this business-logic component.

The RetrieveTitleListASP Method

Instead of returning just the title information, which the ASP script then converts into a table, we will take on board the constructing of this table and writing it out to the browser, directly from the component. To do this, we shall create a new method that will call the `RetrieveTitleList` method from above to obtain the array from the data component and then convert it into ASP script. This means that our component can still be used from a non-ASP client provided it uses just the `RetrieveTitleList` method:

```
Public Sub RetrieveTitleListASP(strConn As Variant)

  Dim arTitles()
  Dim arDiscount()
  Dim varResponse
  Dim intCount, intRows
  Dim objContext As COMSVCSLib.ObjectContext
  Dim objResponse As ASPTypeLibrary.Response
  Dim res

  res = RetrieveTitleList(strConn, arTitles, arDiscount)
  Set objContext = GetObjectContext

  If res = True Then

    varResponse = "<P>The following books are currently defined in the " & _
                  "pubs database:" & vbCrLf & "<TABLE CELLSPACING=""2""" & _
                  "CELLPADDING=""0"">" & vbCrLf & "<TR>" & _
                  "<TD BGCOLOR=""#3AC2EF""><STRONG>ID</STRONG></TD>" _
                  "<TD BGCOLOR=""#3AC2EF""><STRONG>Title</STRONG></TD>" & _
                  "<TD BGCOLOR=""#3AC2EF""><STRONG>Price</STRONG></TD>" & _
                  "<TD BGCOLOR=""#3AC2EF""><STRONG>Discount</STRONG></TD>" & _
                  "<TD BGCOLOR=""#3AC2EF""><STRONG>Notes</STRONG></TD>" & _
                  "<TD BGCOLOR=""#3AC2EF""></TD></TR><TR></TR>"

    intRows = UBound(arTitles, 2)
    For intCount = 0 To intRows

      varResponse = varResponse & "<TR>" & _
                    "<TD BGCOLOR=""#3AC2EF"">" & arTitles(0, intCount) & _
                    "<TD BGCOLOR=""#3AC2EF"">" & arTitles(1, intCount) & _
                    "<TD BGCOLOR=""#3AC2EF"">" & arTitles(2, intCount) & _
                    "<TD BGCOLOR=""#3AC2EF"">" & arDiscount(intCount) & _
                    "<TD BGCOLOR=""#3AC2EF"">" & arTitles(3, intCount) & _
                    "<TD BGCOLOR=""#3AC2EF"">" & _
                    "<FORM NAME=""A"" METHOD=""POST"" ACTION=""Delete.asp?id=" _
                    & arTitles(0, intCount) & """>" & _
                    "<INPUT TYPE=""SUBMIT"" VALUE=""Delete""" & _
                    "NAME=""B1"" ></FORM></TD></TR>"

    Next

    varResponse = varResponse & "</TABLE>" & vbCrLf & _
                  "<FORM NAME=""A"" METHOD=""POST"" ACTION=""Add.asp"">" & _
                  "<INPUT TYPE=""SUBMIT"" VALUE=""Add a new Title""" & _
                  " NAME=""B1"" >" & _
                  "</FORM>"

    objContext.SetComplete
 Else
    varResponse = Right(CStr(arTitles(0)), 8)
    objContext.SetAbort
 End If
```

```
    Set objResponse = objContext("Response")
    objResponse.Write varResponse

    Set objResponse = Nothing
    Set objContext = Nothing

  End Sub
```

One thing to be aware of when constructing HTML strings in a component is that string concatenation is a fairly resource heavy process so you should limit the number of strings you need to join as much as possible.

The AddTitle Method

This method will be called to add a title to the database. It will simply serve as a pass through to the data component:

```
Public Function AddTitle(Id As Variant, Title As Variant, Price As Variant, _
                         Notes As Variant, strConn As String) As Variant

  On Error GoTo errorAddTitle

  Dim objBookData As BookData.TitleData
  Set objBookData = CreateObject("BookData.TitleData")

  AddTitle = objBookData.AddTitleToDB(CStr(Id), CStr(Title), CCur(Price), _
                                      CStr(Notes), CStr(strConn))
  Set objBookData = Nothing

  If AddTitle = True Then
     GetObjectContext.SetComplete
  Else
     GetObjectContext.SetAbort
  End If

  Exit Function

errorAddTitle:

  AddTitle = "Error - " & Err.Description
  GetObjectContext.SetAbort

End Function
```

The basic steps of this component are to create the database object, call its method, then based on the results of the method either call `SetComplete` or `SetAbort` to allow COM+ to release the object. You will notice that here as well we are releasing the reference to the data object as soon as we are done with it.

The DeleteTitle Method

This method is called to delete a title from the database. We will first want to make sure that the title being deleted actually exists in the database, so we will first call the `CheckTitleExists` method. If it does, then we will call the `DeleteTitleFromDB` method of the data object. Even though the `DeleteTitleFromDB` method will work OK without the title being in the database, it will chew up unnecessary resources that could be used elsewhere:

```
Public Function DeleteTitle(Id As Variant, strConn As Variant) As Variant

   Dim objBookData As BookData.TitleData
   Set objBookData = CreateObject("BookData.TitleData")

   Dim ret As Variant
   ret = objBookData.CheckTitleExists(CStr(Id), CStr(strConn))

   If ret <> True Then
      GetObjectContext.SetAbort
      Set objBookData = Nothing
      DeleteTitle = False
      Exit Function
   End If

   DeleteTitle = objBookData.DeleteTitleFromDB(CStr(Id), CStr(strConn))
   GetObjectContext.SetComplete
   Set objBookData = Nothing

End Function
```

The ASP Pages

The ASP pages in our version of the application are nearly identical to the ones we looked at in the previous chapters. In fact, as far as the user is concerned, the only visual change to the application is that now we are displaying the discounted price of the title along with the regular price. The changes to the pages happen inside of the ASP script itself, where we are interacting with a new object model.

List.asp

This script has undergone the most dramatic changes, in that instead of interactively calling into the component to retrieve the information, we will simply call the `RetrieveTitleListASP` routine, which does all the work for us. The page has been reduced to just this:

```
<%
Dim objTitles  'Holds the book titles component
Set objTitles = Server.CreateObject("Book.BookTitles")
%>

<HTML>
<HEAD>
<TITLE>Titles List</TITLE>
<STYLE TYPE="text/css">
  BODY {font-family:Verdana,Tahoma,Arial,sans-serif; font-size:10pt}
  TD {font-family:Verdana,Tahoma,Arial,sans-serif; font-size:10pt}
</STYLE>
</HEAD>
<BODY BGCOLOR=WHITE>
<H1>Book Titles</H1>
<HR>
```

```
<%
'Write out the table
objTitles.RetrieveTitleListASP Application("ConnectionString")
Set objTitles = Nothing

%>
</BODY>
</HTML>
```

global.asa

The file that is added to our application is a global.asa file. This file is used to initialize the Application-level variable called ConnectionString. This contains the database connection string that is used by all of the components in the application:

```
<SCRIPT LANGUAGE=VBScript RUNAT=Server>

Sub Application_OnStart()
    Application.Lock
    Application("ConnectionString") = "PROVIDER=SQLOLEDB; " & _
                                      "DATA SOURCE=<SERVER_NAME>;" & _
                                      "DATABASE=pubs;USER ID=sa; PASSWORD=;"
   Application.Unlock
End Sub

</SCRIPT>
```

When you install this application on your system, you will probably need to change the DATA SOURCE parameter to point to your actual database server. Also, if you are using any kind of security on the server, you will probably want to change that as well.

The Other Pages

The only change you need to make to Delete.asp and Add_UpdateDB.asp pages are that the calls to the relevant methods on the component need to be update to pass in the connection string information:

```
objTitles.DeleteTitle Request.QueryString("id"), Application("ConnectionString")
```

And:

```
objTitles.AddTitle Request.Form("Id"), Request.Form("Title"), _
                   Request.Form("Price") , Request.Form("Notes"), _
                   Application("ConnectionString")
```

Component Services

The tool for managing your COM+ applications is the Microsoft **Component Services Explorer**. You can use this tool to create new COM+ applications, add components to applications, and set the declarative attributes for an application and its components.

COM+ applications provide the following benefits to application developers who take advantage of them:

- A method for deploying components as a pre-packaged set inside of a COM+ application.
- A method to configure a set of components as a whole. You can manipulate properties such as the security aspects of the components, load balancing settings, and transaction properties.
- COM+ applications also can contain attributes about the application that are not set at time of development, such as component synchronization properties.
- The ability to run a COM+ application within the caller's process or within a separate, isolated process.
- COM+ is responsible for the creation and management of all threads used by the components within it.
- COM+ provides access to the context, which we have looked at already.

There are two types of COM+ applications that we will be working with when creating ASP applications. They are defined by the process space in which the components of the application will be executed.

- **Server Application** – A Server application is a COM+ application whose components run inside of a dedicated process, called `dllHost.exe`. All COM+ services are available from within a Server application.
- **Library Application** – A Library application is a COM+ application that runs in the process of the client that creates it. For an ASP application, this means that it will run in the STA that is processing the current page. Library applications have better performance, but they do not support advanced COM+ features such as load-balancing and queued components.

Library applications are usually faster, since they run in the same process as IIS. Server applications provide more application stability, for if they crash, they will not take the IIS process down with them. Server applications are also easier to work with as we are testing and debugging the application, since they can be unloaded and reloaded without affecting the Web server itself.

Creating COM+ Applications

There are three steps to building and using a COM+ application:

- Component design and creation
- COM+ application creation
- COM+ application administration

We have already looked at how to perform the first step, so now we will turn our attention to the creation of a COM+ application. The components that we have already created will be grouped together to form a single COM+ application. Generally, we will take all of the components that will be used by a particular ASP application, or section of a larger ASP application, and combine these components into a single COM+ application.

The components are added to a COM+ application using the following steps:

- Create a new COM+ application, or select an existing one. Components can be added to an existing COM+ application, or you can create a new, empty application into which you can add your components.
- Add the components to the application.
- Set the declarative attributes for each component.
- If desired, export the application so it can be deployed on another system.

In addition to using the Component Services Explorer to create and set up a new COM+ application, you can also use the tool to manage existing applications. In managing a COM+ application, a system administrator can modify the properties and declarative attributes of the components that make up the application. They can also transfer the application from machine to machine, making configuration changes as they go, and then distributing the changed application back to the other machines.

Next, we will look at a step-by-step example that will show you how to create a COM+ application.

Creating a New COM+ Application

After we have written all of the code for our component, the next step will be to use Visual Basic to compile that component into a DLL. The DLL file is the executable version of the component, and will be loaded by the COM+ subsystem whenever the object is required. Assuming no errors in the code, Visual Basic will compile the component, and then register it with the operating system.

If you have a separate version of the component from Chapter 14, I recommend you unregister it first to prevent potential conflicts from arising later.

The next step is to create the COM+ application that will provide the COM+ services for our Web application. To create the COM+ application, the first step is to launch the Microsoft Component Services Explorer. The shortcut to this application is found in the Programs | Administrative Tools menu on Windows 2000:

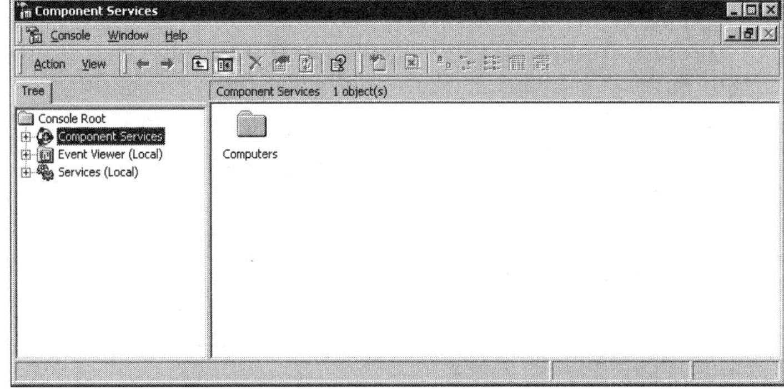

We will be creating a new COM+ Application on this computer.

To create a new COM+ application, expand the nodes until you reach the COM+ Applications folder, then select it and right-click, finally select New | Application from the context menu. This will launch the COM Application Installation Wizard that will walk you through creating the COM+ application:

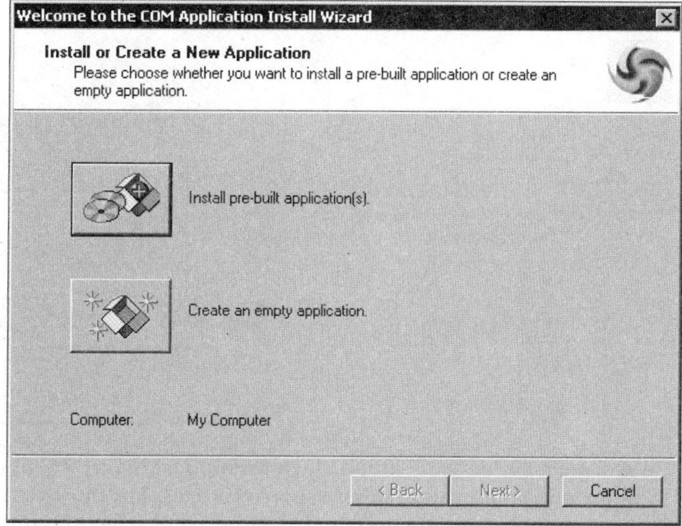

As we are creating a new application, you should select the Create an empty application choice. This will display the next step in the wizard, which asks you to configure your application. If we had created and exported a COM+ application previously, and wanted to install it on this machine, we would select the Install pre-built application(s) choice:

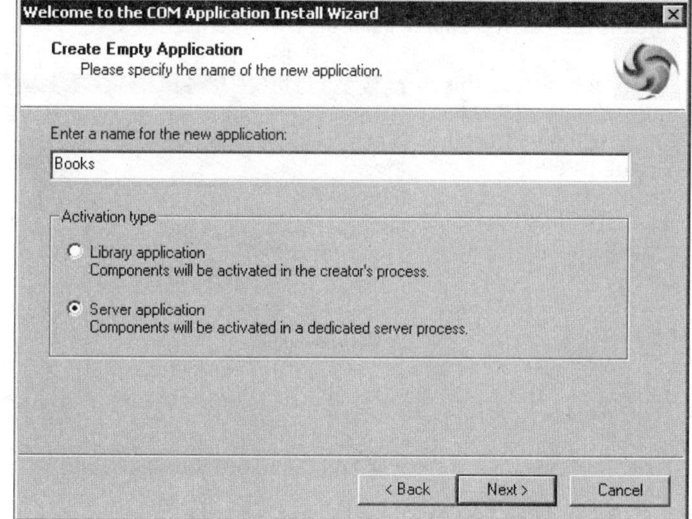

Here we can name the applications – in this example, we have chosen to name it "Books" We also need to decide whether or not to make this a Server or Library application. The default is a Server application, and we have chosen not to change that.

The next step is to determine the user identity that the application will execute under:

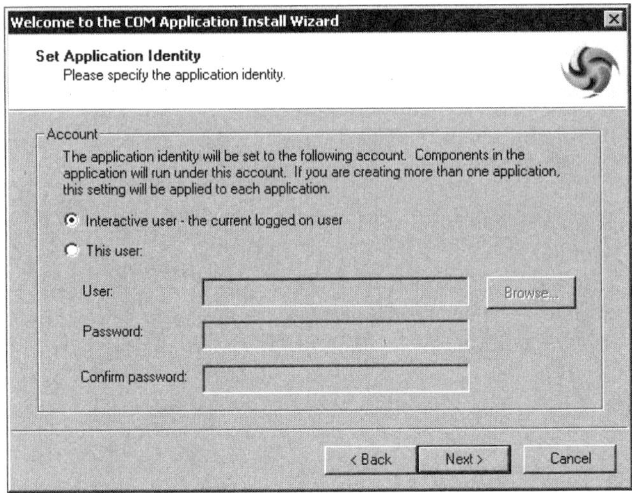

We can choose an explicit user for this application, in which case every client using this application will have the application impersonate this user. For our example, and for most of the COM+ applications that will be used with ASP, we will select the Interactive User choice. This means that the incoming user's credentials will be used for the component. Generally for an ASP application, this means the IUSR_*computername* user will be used.

After completing this step, the new COM+ application will be created:

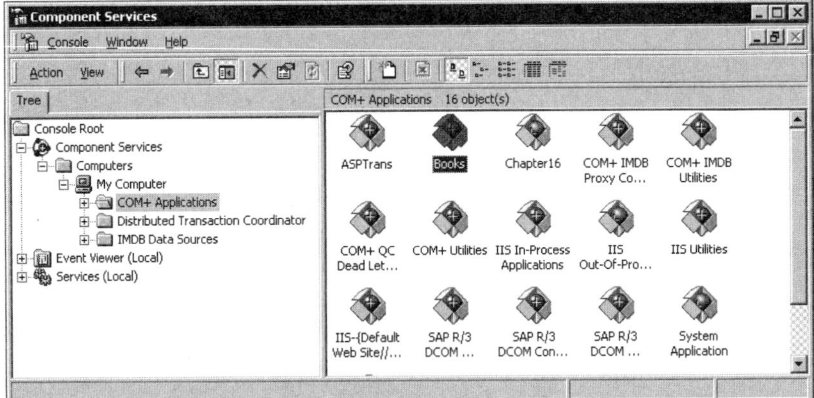

Registering Components with COM+

We can then move on to adding the components to the application. To do this, expand the application's folder to show the Components and Roles folders. Select the Components folder, which will display any components installed in the application. (At this point, it will be empty.) Right-click on the Components folder, and choose New | Component from the context menu. This will display the Component Install Wizard:

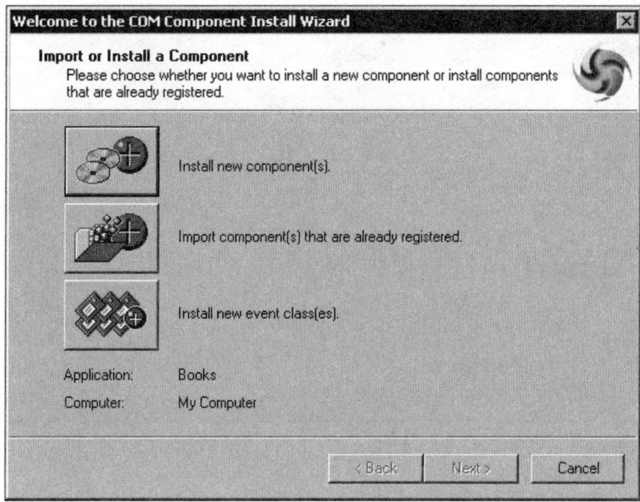

This wizard allows us to install components or event classes to our COM+ application.

COM+ Events are extensions to the COM+ programming model that support late-bound events in a COM+ application. Rather than repeatedly polling the server, the event system notifies applications that are listening whenever something important happens. We will not be looking at event classes in conjunction with ASP.

Since Visual Basic already registered the DLL for us when we compiled it, we will choose the second option:

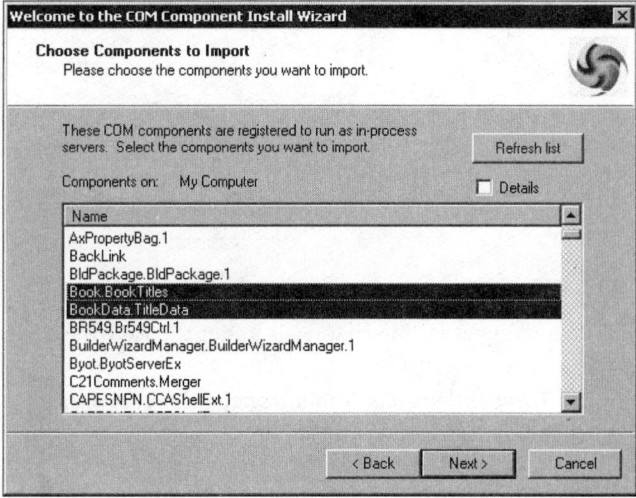

This will display a listing of all components that are registered on the system which aren't part of a COM+ application. By checking the Details checkbox, we can also see the file name and CLSID of the components. Scroll though this list until we find the components that we just created. This wizard allows us to add multiple components at one time to the application simply by selecting all of the components that we are interested in. Pressing Next will add these two components to our COM+ application:

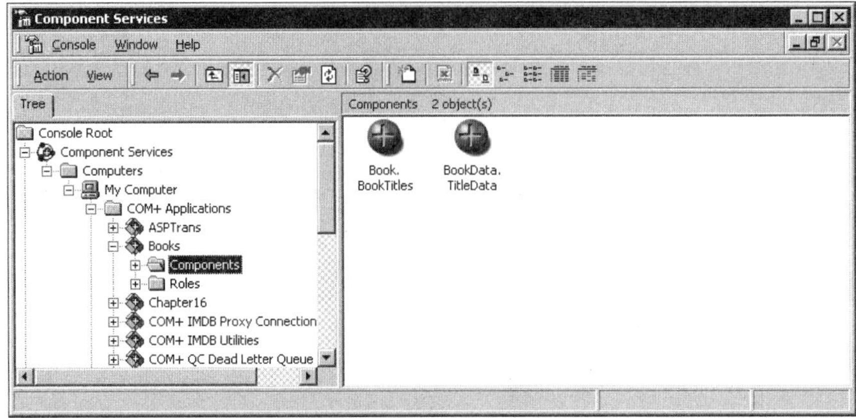

Setting Component Properties

Once you have installed the components into the COM+ application, you can modify the properties of these components as well. To display the component property page, simply select the component, right-click on it, and choose Properties:

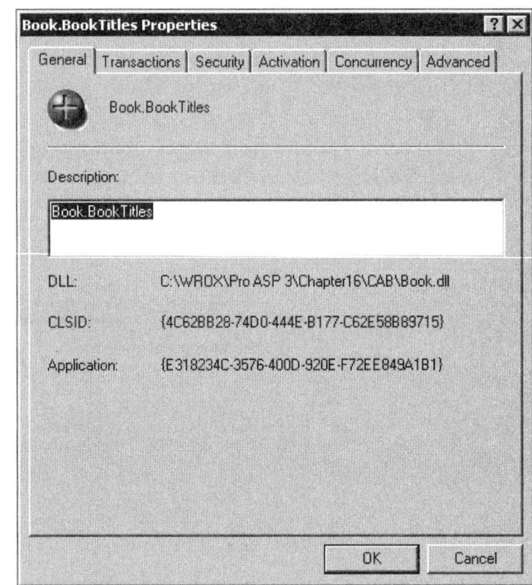

The settings that we will be looking at in this chapter is under the Activation tab.

We will be examining the Transactions *and* Concurrency *tabs in Chapter 19.*

The Activation tab contains information about how the component will be created and activated:

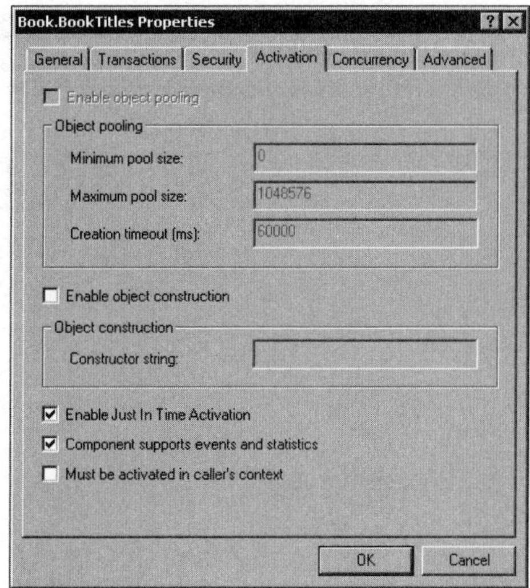

Since our component was created using Visual Basic, we are unable to use component pooling with this component. This is why the Object Pooling checkbox is disabled. Object construction allows you to administratively set a string that will get passed to the object when it was constructed. This could be used to pass in a database connection string, which would become part of the object. In our application we are passing it into every method, but we could have just as easily placed it here. Since this value is the same for all objects, it does not make the application stateful, as a traditional property value would.

By checking the Enable Just In Time Activation box, we will ensure that COM+ can activate and deactivate this component as needed automatically. Of course with a Visual Basic component, deactivation means the same as destruction. But for the creation of the component, the just in time activation means that the object won't begin to consume its full allotment of resources until it is required to.

Deploying COM+ Applications

As we mentioned in Chapter 13, we can also move our COM+ application between systems. This is a three-step process:

- First, we need to export it from the current location as an MSI file
- Next, we need to physically move the package to the target machine
- Finally, we need to install the package on the target machine

To export the COM+ application, you use the Application Export Wizard, which is launched by right-clicking on the COM+ application, and choosing Export...

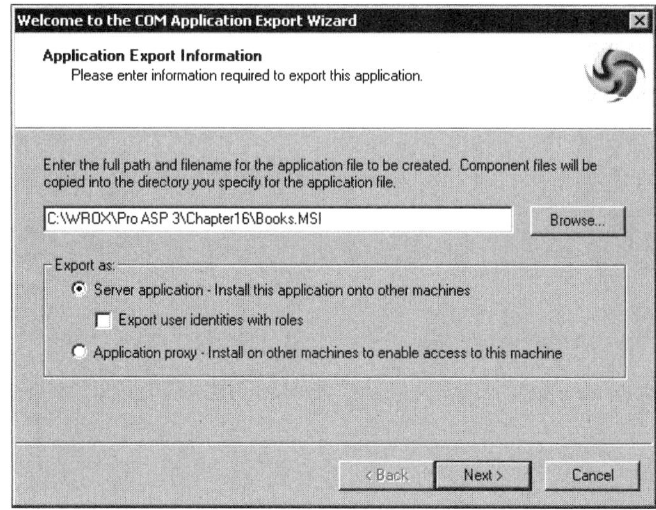

At this point we can choose to export the Server application itself or we can export an Application proxy. By exporting the Server application, we can then install the application on another machine and run the components from there. Conversely, we can export just an application proxy which, when installed on another machine, will allow clients on that remote machine to use the COM+ components on your local machine.

Installing Exported Applications

Now we have created the MSI file we can move it to the target machine and install it there. The application is installed in the same way that a new application is created. This time, instead of selecting to install a blank application, we select to install a *pre-built* application. When you choose this button from the wizard, a dialog box will appear asking you to select the MSI file to install. When you select the file, it will display a listing of the COM+ applications contained in the file:

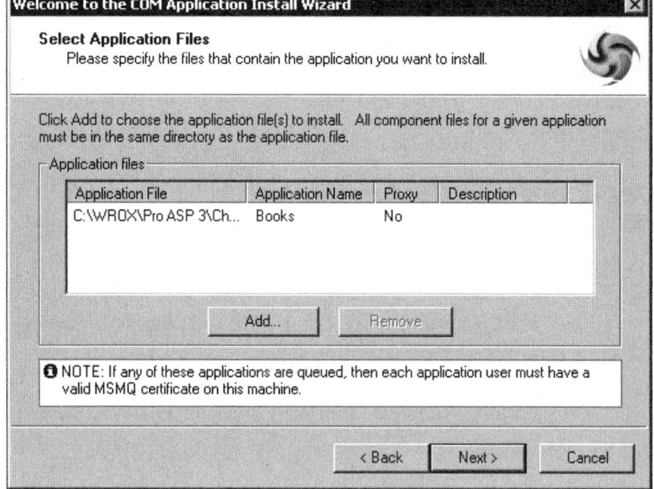

After choosing the identity of the application, which is done in the same way as for an empty application, you will be asked to choose where to install the files. The MSI file can contain path information, which can be used, or you can specify an explicit directory to install the files:

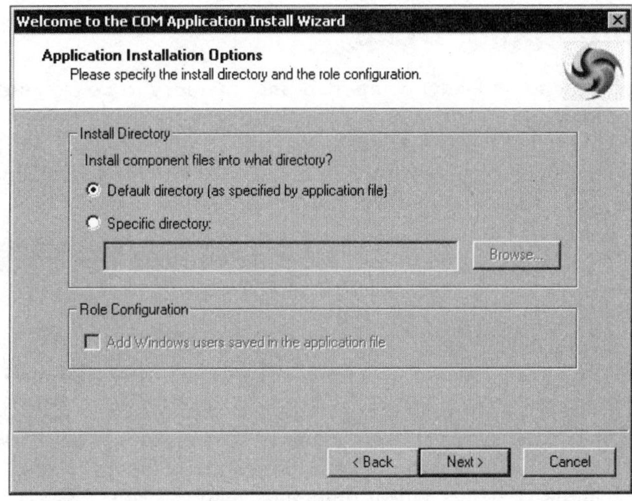

Once you click Next from this dialog, the MSI file will be installed into the directory, and your COM+ application will be created on the system. You can then use the application in the exact same way that you used it on your source machine.

Component Debugging

As good as we may be at developing components, something can always be counted on to go wrong. We therefore, need some way of working out where the bugs lie. However, unlike our ASP scripts, our components are compiled which makes it harder to find out what's really going on.

If you are developing with Visual Basic 6.0 you can establish an ASP script to use for testing your component. This will allow you to easily move back and forth between the development and testing environments.

To set this up, open the Project Properties dialog for your component and select the Debugging tab:

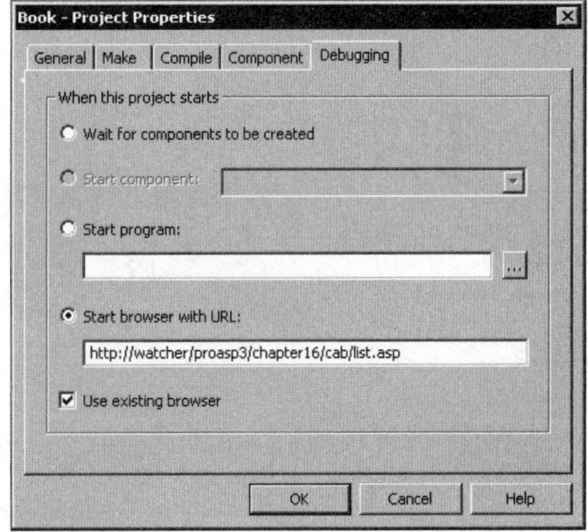

Select Start browser with URL and enter the URL for your test ASP file. If you want VB to start a new instance of the browser when the component is tested, then uncheck the Use existing browser check box.

Now you can set breakpoints in your code and simply run the project. This will launch a browser with the URL specified, but when the ASP script makes any calls to your component you can intercept them using the VB debugger and debug the project as normal.

Unlocking DLLS

When you load a component into memory to be executed in an ASP script, the system will place a lock on the DLL file. This will prevent you from deleting or altering the file while the component is loaded. After you have tested your component, you will need to make sure the component instance has been removed from memory. If you don't do this before you recompile, VB will display an error and the component will not be compiled:

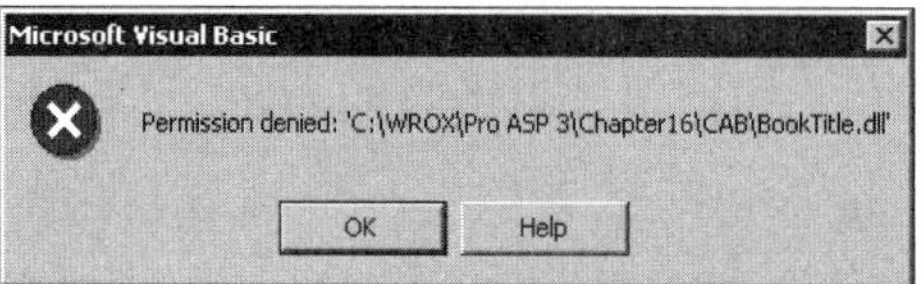

The easiest way to make sure the component has been removed from memory is to make sure the application is run in a separate memory space. This is done by selecting High (Isolated) from the Application Protection drop-down list box. Then click the Unload button in the Virtual Directory tab of the IIS Application's Properties page:

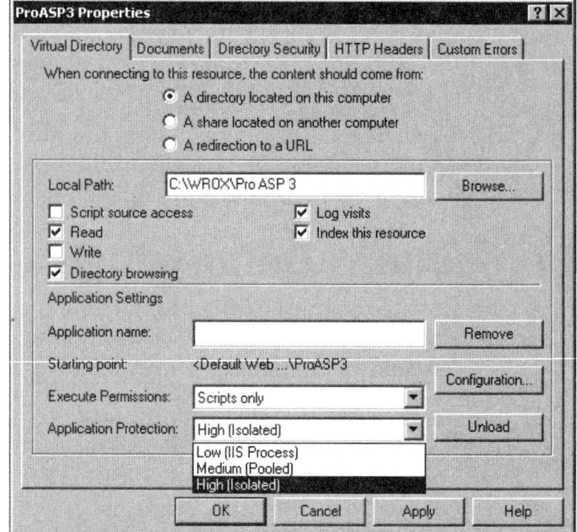

This button will only be available if you have created the COM+ application as a Server application. Since a Library application will run within the process space of IIS, you will not be able to individually unload it from memory.

If after you unload the application using the above steps you still cannot successfully recompile, the next step you can take is to use the Component Services Explorer to shut down the COM+ application. This will explicitly free it from memory:

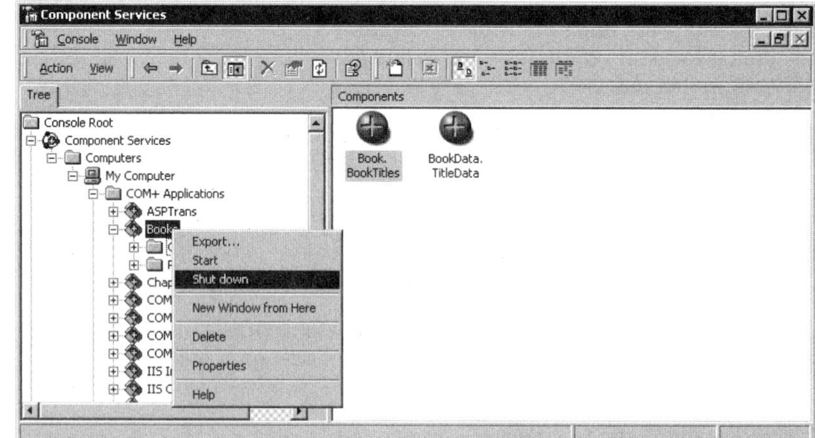

If you right-click on the name of your COM+ application, and then select **Shut down** from the context menu, the application (`dllhost.exe`) will be unloaded from memory.

If after doing this the recompile fails again, there are a few other things that may be still holding onto your COM+ application.

Visual InterDev 6 will hold onto a reference to the object in order to provide Intellisense editing capabilities. You will need to shut down VI in order to release that reference.

The last ditch effort to release the component reference is to stop and restart the Web server. To do this you can enter the following two commands at a command prompt:

- Type `net stop iisadmin /y`. This will shut down the parent service of IIS, IIS Admin. This will also shut down FTP, STMP, and any other services that are children of IIS Admin. It will unload the `inetinfo.exe` process from memory. If you type only `net stop w3svc`, to unload just the Web server, `inetinfo.exe` will not be unloaded.
- Then type `net start w3svc`. This will try to restart the Web server, and since it requires IIS Admin in order to run, that will be automatically started as well. Note that if you need access to the FTP or SMTP services, you will need to manually restart these as well.

I have also found that sometimes stopping the Protected Storage service also works.

If none of these work then a reboot will do the trick.

Summary

In this chapter, we have looked at how COM+ and the Microsoft Component Services can be used to help us create Web applications; we have seen that they free us developers from having to worry about how the components interact with the operating system. This lets us deal with supporting the business logic that is important to the application, all the while confident that the COM+ plumbing is working behind the scenes to support the application.

With component building tools such as Visual Basic, we can very easily encapsulate our application functionality, including business, presentation, and data access logic, into reusable components. Then by placing these components under the watchful eye of a COM+ application, we can let the operating system manage these components for us as we use them in our applications.

In the next chapter, we will move on to looking at how we can improve the functionality and performance of our components by writing them in C++.

N
W

16

ASP Script Components

Writing components capable of providing runtime text for ASP pages was one of the first points addressed when ASP was introduced. Three years on, we have several different solutions to the same problem, with design-time ActiveX controls (DTC) and ASP components both achieving the same purpose in completely different ways.

> *Don't confuse this DTC acronym with Distributed Transaction Coordinator.*

For one thing, DTCs are visual, working in conjunction with the authoring tool you're using to produce the runtime text in the ASP page before it's ever called. You could liken them to a sophisticated macro for Word or Excel. Once they've finished running and you've saved the page, the ASP script contains only text in place of the control. You've no need to worry either about any extra downloads the client may need to make because you've used a DTC – DTCs are development time controls only, so no extra downloads are necessary at runtime. Normally, you don't write DTCs for your own project – instead you'll use those made available by the development tool you're using. Visual InterDev, for instance, comes with a dozen or so DTCs for you to take advantage of.

As we've seen in previous chapters, ASP components are more direct and specialized, and act at runtime. They are capable of inserting code depending on runtime conditions. Such components are written in C++ or Visual Basic, and are loaded and executed on the server under the control of IIS. In using ASP components then, we directly affect the overall performance of the site itself (although not necessarily by a great deal).

In this chapter, we'll introduce you to ASP components written with script languages. Such ASP components are a special case of a more general technology called **Windows Script Components** (**WSC**), which lets you write a few types of COM objects employing only a script language such as VBScript or JScript. It's already on your machine if you're using Windows 2000 or IE 5.0, but you can also run it on IIS 4.0 on Windows NT, as well as PWS under Windows 9x.

So here we'll briefly summarize the major features of the WSC technology. You'll learn:

- The underpinnings that make writing a COM object with a script language possible
- How to write a COM object using a script language
- How to write an ASP script component
- The differences between ASP script components and other ASP components

With the theory under our hats, we'll build an example that encapsulates an HTML table to format data on the fly in a really powerful and easy-to-maintain way.

Getting Started with WSC

To reproduce everything that I'm going to cover in this chapter, you need a few binaries installed on your system. First off, point your browser to Microsoft's scripting Website at `http://msdn.microsoft.com/scripting` and get the WSC package – a self-installing file that contains:

- The binary machinery for WSC
- Documentation
- A wizard to help you write components

Note that you already have the binaries you need if you've installed Internet Explorer 5.0 or Windows 2000. You also have them with Windows 98 or Internet Explorer 4.01 (although in this latter case, you have an older version of the binaries supporting a slightly different syntax). By downloading the package from the Microsoft site you have everything fixed up.

The WSC Wizard, however, is not included with any of version of browser or operating system, and will need to be downloaded from the Microsoft scripting Web site.

A Windows Script Component

Let's start with a definition.

A Windows Script Component is a COM object written with a scripting language.

I agree that, at a first sight, this may appear to be an odd sentence. Is it really possible to write a COM object with a scripting language? There are several, quite reasonable arguments against this possibility:

- A COM object is a binary file. *VBScript and JScript do not generate binary files.*
- A COM object has a well-known binary layout. *What provides that for a script file?*
- A COM object exposes interfaces. *How is that possible with a scripting language?*
- A COM object needs registration and a CLSID. *Who deals with that?*

All these points will have a consistent and exhaustive answer in the sections to come.

Historically Speaking...

The very first attempt to componentize the Web was done in late 1997 with the release of Internet Explorer 4.0. This browser remains the only one to support **DHTML Scriptlets**, a prototype of today's Web components. A DHTML Scriptlet is basically an HTML page embedded into another one. By exploiting a special naming convention, such a child page can expose a programmable interface to the container page, allowing for methods to be called, properties to be invoked and events to be fired.

Using a DHTML Scriptlet is not that different from using an ActiveX control, but as components, they were mostly targeted at Internet Explorer and Visual Basic. In effect, they were not-really-reusable components written in a scripting language. Moreover, DHTML Scriptlets were components designed to display a user interface, rather than as a silent helper to the page being requested.

From DHTML Scriptlets to Scriptlets

Shortly after came components simply called **Scriptlets**. These were the forefathers of today's WSCs. Scriptlets were regular COM objects that you could call from within any COM-aware development tool, including Delphi, PowerBuilder, MFC and Visual Basic.

The change from DHTML Scriptlets to Scriptlets was in itself nothing special – no one really used either very much – but the way in which these new Scriptlets were written was a big departure. The structure of the component's source code had changed from a mix of HTML and script code to XML – and with reason.

A COM object is not just code. It has to expose a well-known binary layout, which means that when writing a COM object, you have at least two different categories of information to consider besides the specific code that makes it work: the implemented interfaces and the registration data. As we noted above, there's no way to carry this very particular information through a scripting language.

Microsoft had two choices. They could:

- Resort to a special naming convention to insert registration and interface information

Or

- Use a completely different syntax to write the component

They chose the latter way and used XML to specify the syntax of the component.

What changed from the Internet Explorer 4.01 Scriptlets to the current WSCs? Simply the XML schema used to store the object's additional information.

The HelloWorld WSC

A WSC file is an XML file with an extension of `.wsc`. Previously, it was `.sct`. Depending on your tolerance of yet another Hello World example, the WSC version of the infamous first program looks like this:

```
<component>

<registration progid="HelloWorld.Component"/>
<public>
   <method name="Welcome"/>
</public>

<script language="VBScript">
Function Welcome
   MsgBox "Hello, World"
End Function
</script>

</component>
```

All the information in a script component must be enclosed by the `<component>` .. `</component>` pair of tags. We also have a `<registration>`, a `<public>` and a `<script>` tag. These describe the COM object in terms of its CLSID and/or ProgID, the implemented interfaces, and its actual functionality respectively.

So now you have some idea of what a WSC file looks like, let's cover in more detail how a WSC is structured.

The Structure of a WSC

Overall, the whole structure of a WSC can be disassembled into three tiers:

- The **Descriptive tier**, which provides metadata information about the component
- The **Script tier**, which contains the script functions that make it work the way it has to
- The **Runtime tier**, given by a few binaries exposing the familiar COM layout to clients

The following figure shows the various tiers that form the source code of a WSC file.

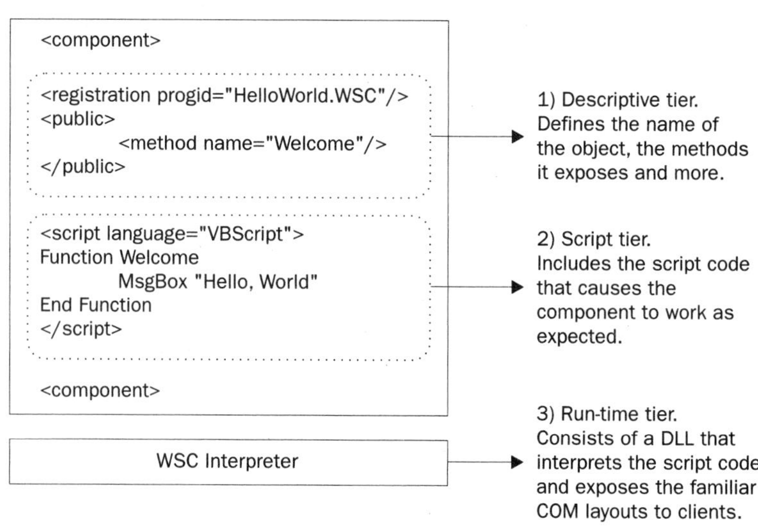

<component>
<registration progid="HelloWorld.WSC"/>
<public>
<method name="Welcome"/>
</public>
<script language="VBScript">
Function Welcome
MsgBox "Hello, World"
End Function
</script>
<component>
WSC Interpreter
1) Descriptive tier. Defines the name of the object, the methods it exposes and more.
2) Script tier. Includes the script code that causes the component to work as expected.
3) Run-time tier. Consists of a DLL that interprets the script code and exposes the familiar COM layouts to clients.

We'll start with a quick examination of these various tiers.

The Descriptive Tier

There are four basic tags that contribute to form this tier. They are:

- <registration>
- <public>
- <implements>
- <resource>

<registration>

The <registration> tag holds information to be used when adding the component to the Windows registry. Here you can specify a small description of the component if you wish, its ProgID and ClassId, and also any code that should be executed upon registration or unregistration.

For example, a freshly generated component would have a registration tag similar to:

```
<registration
    description="The first HelloWorld WSC"          <!-- optional -->
    version="1.00"                                  <!-- optional -->
    progid="HelloWorld.Component"
    classid="{6432490f-0d48-48e3-bbe7-e2e773fc843e}"
>
</registration>
```

The `description` and `version` attributes are optional, but you must specify at least one of the `progid` and `classid` attributes. If you don't then an error will occur when you try to register the component.

One sticky point here – the rules of creating a COM object, of which WSCs are one type, state that each one must have a CLSID. How, then, can a WSC do without CLSIDs? The answer is simple: they can't, and so have them automatically generated during the registration process. If you don't specify a CLSID, then the specific system utility (`regsvr32.exe`) that registers COM objects will create one for you. Note, however, that only the latest version of `regsvr32.exe` – which is distributed with Internet Explorer 5.0, Windows 2000 and the WSC package – will do this for you, or, again, the registration process will crash.

The `progid` attribute is the string you use to create an instance of the object through late binding functions such as VBScript's `CreateObject` or JScript's `ActiveXObject`. In practice, a component without a ProgID is almost unusable from within a script-based development environment. If you don't specify a ProgID, you can't create an instance of that object through `CreateObject` or `ActiveXObject`. Only Windows Script Host 2.0 lets you create an instance of a COM object having specified just its CLSID.

Executing Code During Registration and Unregistration

If needed, the facility is available to have some predefined code run when the component is registered or unregistered. Normally, the registration of a COM object from `regsvr32.exe`'s point of view is simply a matter of calling a function from within the COM object DLL. However, every WSC is registered through the same server module, `scrobj.dll`. Once invoked, it knows the name of the WSC file on behalf of which it is working, and creates all the usual registry entries for a COM object.

The DLL also looks for one of two functions (whose names are always the same) within the `<registration>` tag. Depending on whether it is registering or unregistering the component, these are `Register()` and `Unregister()`:

```
<registration
   description="This is my component"       <!-- optional -->
   version="1.00"                           <!-- optional -->
   progid="MyComp.WSC"
   classid="{e8c35060-1879-11d3-b17c-00c0dfe39736}">
<script language="VBScript">
   Function Register
      MsgBox "Registering…"       ' (e.g. generate a type-library on-the-fly)
   End Function

   Function Unregister
      MsgBox "Unregistering…"
   End Function
</script>
</registration>
```

It's up to you to specify these functions if you need them. It's not necessary to declare either of them before you register the component. You can, of course, give the functions a little more to do than pop up a message box as we've done here. You could, for example, generate the component's type library on the fly.

<public>

The `<public>` tag defines the "public" programming interface of the component. In other words, it defines the methods, properties and events the component exposes and that a client can call. The syntax is quite straightforward:

```
<public>
   <property name="MyProperty">
      <get/>
      <put/>
   </property>

   <method name="MyMethod">
      <parameter name="param1"/>
   </method>

   <event name="OnEvent">
          <parameter name="param1"/>
   </event>
</public>
```

The `name` attribute specifies the public name of each item. In the code above, the property is rendered through a variable called `MyProperty`,while the body of the method is all in a function called `MyMethod`. Both are defined in the WSC `<script>` tag. More on this later on.

Internal Names

For methods and properties you can also have an internal name. This is assigned through the internalname attribute. Basically, an internal name is the name by which you refer to the property or the method from within the WSC file.

```
<public>
   <property name="MyProperty" internalname="m_MyProperty">
      <get/>
      <put/>
   </property>
   <method name="MyMethod" internalname="DoMyMethod">
      <parameter name="param1"/>
   </method>
</public>
```

In this case, the MyProperty property is implemented through a variable called m_MyProperty. And when a client calls the method MyMethod, it is the function DoMyMethod that actually executes.

Specifying Parameters

A method can have as many parameters as it needs. The name attribute here denotes the formal name of the parameter. Also, events can have as many parameters as you want, even if some older documentation omits to state this explicitly.

Read-only and Write-only Properties

The properties you use in a WSC need neither be open to the client (i.e. available to the browser) nor read/writeable. In many case, you'll find the need for a bit more control over our clients' interaction with the component. Consider the case where your component displays the number of current sessions of your screen. This value should be read-only; it could quickly become inaccurate if a client could alter it.

Every <property> tag has two child tags: <get/> and <put/>. The former specifies a way to read the property's value and the latter a way to write to it. When someone attempts to read or write the content of the property, the appropriate one of these two procedures executes. They have a default name, which is get_ or put_ followed by the public name of the property, but this can be altered using the internalname attribute that we saw earlier. By omitting the <get> tag, you automatically make the property write-only. By omitting the <put> instead, the property becomes read-only.

Firing Events

To fire an event from within your WSC, you have to resort to calling a global WSC function called fireEvent. This takes the name of the even being fired as its first argument, and any parameters it needs as subsequent arguments.

```
fireEvent "OnEvent", dataToPass
```

<implements>

If you just need your WSC to provide methods, properties and events, then you don't need to consider the <implements> tag. Basically, this tag lets you specify the COM interfaces that your WSC will support. By default, a WSC provides automatic support for Automation and event handling interfaces. More exactly, support for these interfaces is automatically requested when you insert the <public> tag.

A COM object written with scripting languages cannot implement all the possible COM interfaces. This is something that can only be done with any degree of ease in C++ or Delphi – it can be rather complex with Visual Basic and it's simply impossible with raw script code. To work around this, a WSC needs to rely on special binary modules called **interface handlers**. Interface handlers are governed by the already mentioned `scrobj.dll`.

Interface Handlers

An interface handler (IH) is a binary module that provides support for any additional non-Automation COM interfaces.

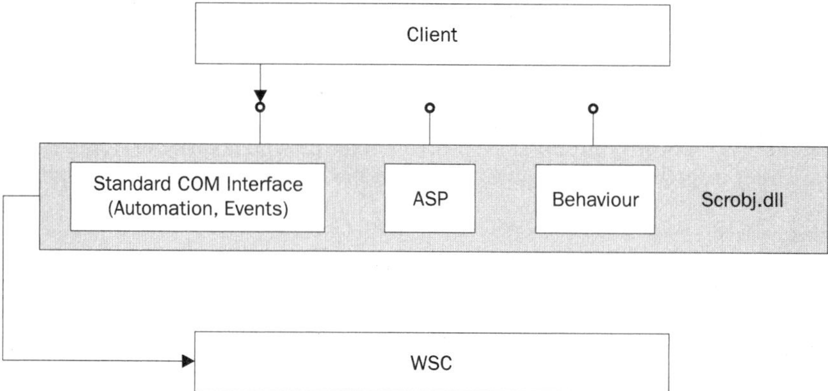

Basically, it acts as a sort of proxy between the script code in the WSC and the client application. An IH exposes to the client the standard COM layout for the given interface, and when the client attempts to call a method on the interface, the IH retrieves and executes the script code to provide that functionality.

The IHs for Automation and events are automatically loaded by `scrobj.dll` as soon as you specify a `<public>` tag. If you want to support additional interfaces, instead you need to explicitly acquire this through the `<implements>` tag. In other words, the `<implements>` tag is the way in which a WSC connects to a particular handler. The syntax is:

```
<implements type="handler" id="name"/>
```

The `type` attribute specifies the name of the interface handler, while `id` is a rarely used ID for the handler itself. In most cases, you just omit the `id` attribute. We'll cover the inner details of the WSC architecture later in this chapter.

<resource>

This tag lets you isolate within the WSC file all the basic elements (strings and numbers) that are constant in your code and that you don't want to hard-code in the script. Each of these resources is identified by an ID:

```
<resource ID="hello">Hello, world!</resource>
<resource ID="version">1.02</resource>
```

You'll use the ID to retrieve this information throughout the script code of the WSC files. The ID must be passed to a global function called getResource() to obtain the stored data:

```
<component>
   <registration progid="HelloWorld.WSC"/>
   <comment>
      Place here as many comments as you like.
   </comment>

   <resource id="hello">Hello, world!</resource>
   <public>
      <method name="Welcome"/>
   </public>
   <script language="VBScript">
      Function Welcome
         MsgBox getResource("hello")
      End Function
   </script>
</component>
```

The listing above also shows another tag in action: <comment>. As the name would suggest, any text placed between these tags will be ignored by the parser, and can be used to document the source code for the component.

Typically, you should use the <resource> tag to define any constants you want local to your script. Functionally speaking, there's no difference between using the <resource> tag and declaring a group of constants actually within your script. The <resource> tag, though, is more elegant and language-neutral.

The Script Tier

All the functions associated with the WSC's methods and properties, as well as all the helper functions, must be enclosed in one or more <script> tags. The syntax of this tag is similar but not identical to the HTML <script> tag, having only a language attribute to qualify it.

You can use any languages you want within your script components, provided that you have a proper parser installed. Microsoft only distributes two parsers – for VBScript and JScript – but third-party vendors have since made Windows Script-compatible parsers available for Perl and other languages too.

XML Compliance

Remember that, as we mentioned earlier, a WSC file is primarily an XML document – one which should comply with the XML 1.0 specification. Provided that you've followed the chapter so far, there are only two things left to do to make it so. The first is to declare it as an XML document by putting this line at the top of your file:

```
<?xml version="1.0"?>
```

However, once you've done that, you must remember to enclose all the content of any `<script>` tag you may have within a `CDATA` delimiter – just to prevent the XML parser getting confused by XML special characters, such as < or &, which it may find in your script:

```
<script language="VBScript">
<![CDATA[
Function Welcome
   MsgBox getResource("hello")
End Function
]]>
</script>
```

The Runtime Tier

To create an instance of a WSC, you normally use a function like VBScript's `CreateObject`, which takes the ProgID of the component as its first argument (and the name of the server where the component is installed as its optional second). Once called, the VBScript engine attempts to locate the name of the DLL that implements the component, taking the following steps:

- Look up the progID in the registry
- From the progID get the CLSID of the component
- Look up that CLSID in the registry
- Read the name of the executable

For WSC components, the server module is always `scrobj.dll`, located in the `Windows` directory. VBScript attempts to create an instance of the object, and while this occurs, the `scrobj.dll` is passed the CLSID of the object it's supposed to represent. At this point, the `scrobj.dll`'s core code uses this CLSID to search the registry for a WSC specific key called `ScriptletURL`. This key points to the WSC file providing the runtime code for the methods publicly available.

The WSC runtime DLL creates an instance of a fake object implementing the interfaces the WSC specifies, and returns that to the caller. Later on, when the VBScript code attempts to execute a method, it will call into this fake object, which simply extracts the right piece of code from the WSC source and executes it through the VBScript or JScript parser.

No Registration After Changes

Since the COM interface exposed to the outside world doesn't change if you add or remove properties and methods, there's no need to re-register the component after changes in the script code. For the same reason, you don't need to stop and restart the Web server after changes to a server-side script component. Everything that has to do with code execution occurs at runtime!

Available Interfaces

Remember all the objections we raised above, about writing COM objects with a scripting language? Well, you'll find the answers to all of them in the underlying runtime machinery for WSC. Client applications still find a standard COM interface, but behind the COM binary layout, the runtime engine runs script code read from a separate WSC file.

A clear consequence of this is that you always need a binary proxy for any interface you want to expose via script code. Such a proxy is what we called an interface handler. In other words, you can implement only a few COM interfaces through script code: those for which you have a valid handler.

As we're still awaiting guidelines from Microsoft on how to write them ourselves, the only handlers available at the moment are:

- Automation Handlers
- Event Handles
- ASP Handlers
- IE 5.0 Behavior Handlers

All these handlers are implemented within `scrobj.dll` – no additional file is required. The first two are automatically activated if you have a `<public>` tag. The second two require a specific `<implements>` tag:

```
<implements type="ASP" />
<implements type="Behavior" />
```

Using both `<public>` and `<implements>` tags in the same WSC is not a problem. Automation and event handlers can both co-exist with either ASP handlers or behavior handlers very well. On the other hand, you should avoid putting a behavior and an ASP component in the same WSC component: they'll clash. If you don't want to write two separate WSC files, then create a package instead!

Packages

The `<package>` tag can be found at the root of the WSC XML schema. The `<component>` tag that we've so far understood to be the root tag is in fact just a child of `<package>`, which acts as a container for multiple components to be held within a single file. The only proviso for such an arrangement is that each component in a package must be assigned a unique ID. For example:

```
<?xml version="1.0"?>
<package>

<component id="One">
<registration progid="MyComponent.One" />
<implements type="ASP" />
<public>
   <method name="DoThis" />
</public>
<script language="VBScript">
<![CDATA[
function DoThis()
   n = 1
end function
]]>
```

```
</script>
</component>

<component id="Two">
<registration progid="MyComponent.Two" />
<implements type="Behavior" />
<public>
   <method name="DoSomething"/>
</public>

<script language="VBScript">
<![CDATA[
function DoSomething()
   DoSomething = "Temporary Value"
end function
]]>
</script>
</component>

</package>
```

Writing an ASP Script Component

ASP components written in a scripting language are essentially just one particular type of Windows Script Component. They only differ from the rest in that they also have access to the ASP built-in objects – Response, Request, Session, and so on.

Of course, those objects are available only if the object is created in the IIS or PWS address space. To safely call those objects from within a piece of VBScript script code, we need someone to add references to them in the context in which the WSC `<script>` code will run. What can do this for us? The ASP interface handler!

The handler, though, is activated only if the specific WSC file requested special ASP support through the `<implements>` tag, as demonstrated in the last but one section.

The AspTable Component

Let's see now how to write a not-so-trivial component. I've called it `AspTable` because it's a sort of wrapper for the HTML `<table>` tag.

Most of the time, we use tables to display database records which may or may not have had some additional processing done to them. For example, first and last names are often concatenated and placed in the same database column.

AspTable has several useful features. It lets you:

- Add columns to the table, taking information from an ADO recordset
- Specify a dynamic expression to combine together several fields, and associate each of them with a link or an action
- Assign styles and decorative text such as headings and footnotes to certain columns

We'll be defining the following public methods in the component:

Method	Description
`SetRs(adoRS)`	Takes an ADO recordset to populate the table.
`AddColumn (heading, expr, style)`	Adds a column to the table specifying the heading, the CSS style and the expression to be evaluated for each row.
`GetText()`	Produces and inserts in the page the HTML code for the table.

Due to the way the component works, these three methods must be called in sequence for them to work correctly. So, for us to generate an HTML table from a recordset, we would first have to set the ADO recordset to work as the data source with `SetRs`, add whatever columns were needed with `AddColumn` and finally ask the component to `Response.Write` the HTML text generated with `GetText`.

AspTable also defines several public properties as follows:

Property	Description
`TableStyle`	The class name of a CSS style to apply to the entire table.
`HeaderStyle`	The class name of a CSS style to apply to all the column headings.
`Title`	HTML text to be displayed at the top of the table.
`Footnote`	HTML text to be displayed at the bottom of the table.
`ColumnCount`	Read-only property to return the current number of columns.

The component lets you display your information in a table like this:

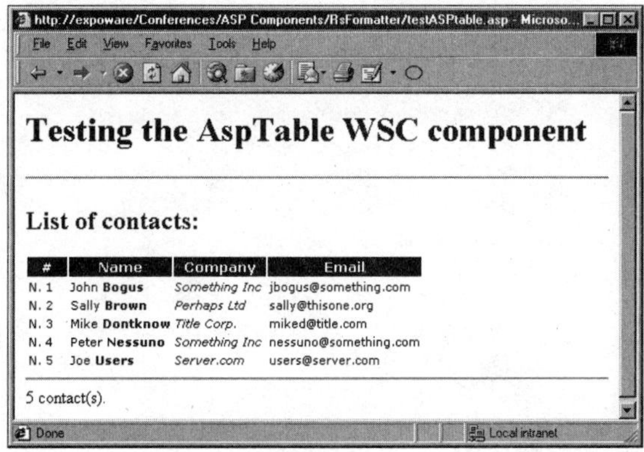

Using this component is far easier and incomparably better for maintenance and readability than having to worry about writing any HTML in order to create the table. The source code that draws the table in the figure looks just like this:

```
Set objTBL = CreateObject("AspTable.WSC")
objTBL.SetRS (rs)

objTBL.Title = "<H2>List of contacts:</H2>"
objTBL.Footnote = "<HR>%&_RECCOUNT_% contact(s).<BR>"
objTBL.TableStyle = "globTab"
objTBL.HeaderStyle = "header"

objTBL.AddColumn "#", "N. %&_RECNO_%", "num"
objTBL.AddColumn "Name", "%&FIRSTNAME% <b>%&LASTNAME%</B>", ""
objTBL.AddColumn "Company", "COMPANY", "company"
objTBL.AddColumn "Email", "EMAILADDRESS", ""

objTBL.GetText()
```

Much better than raw HTML code, don't you agree? Let's analyze the code for the component.

The following listing shows the metadata for the `AspTable` object:

```
<?XML version="1.0"?>
<component>
<registration
    description="Formats a recordset into a TABLE"
    progid="AspTable.WSC"
    version="1.00"
    classid="{33351B20-D7B0-11d2-B7C8-00C0DFE39736}" />

<public>
    <method name="GetText" />
    <method name="SetRS">
       <parameter name="rs" />
    </method>
    <method name="AddColumn">
       <parameter name="displayName" />
       <parameter name="colFormat" />
       <parameter name="className" />
    </method>
    <property name="Title" internalname="m_Title" />
    <property name="Footnote" internalname="m_Footnote" />
    <property name="TableStyle" internalname="m_TableStyle" />
    <property name="HeaderStyle" internalname="m_HeaderStyle" />
    <property name="ColumnCount">
       <get internalname="DoGetNumOfCols" />
    </property>
</public>

<implements type="ASP" />
```

Notice that all the properties are coded through internal names (actually, a matter of preference) but are exposed "as is", without the filter of a couple of `get` and `put` methods. Only the `ColumnCount` property has a `<get>` tag, since we need it to be read-only.

The Script Code for AspTable

The core of the AspTable object is the `GetText` method, which collects all the data from other methods (column information, recordset, style) and arranges a `<TABLE>` tag on the fly. Before we dive into that particular function, let's first take a look at the preliminary functions, including `SetRs` and `AddColumn` that we mentioned earlier:

```
<script language="VBScript">
<![CDATA[


'/*---------------------------------------
'// Globals
'---------------------------------------*/
Const FLDNAME_MUST_HAVE_DELIM = 1
Const FLDNAME_CAN_HAVE_DELIM = 0

Dim m_RS
Dim m_DispCols()
Dim m_NameCols()
Dim m_ClssCols()
Dim m_colCount
m_colCount=0
m_RecNo=0

'/*---------------------------------------
'// ColumnCount property
'---------------------------------------*/
Function DoGetNumOfCols()
   DoGetNumOfCols = m_colCount
End Function


'/*---------------------------------------
'// AddColumn method
'---------------------------------------*/
Function AddColumn (displayName, colFormat, className)
   m_colCount = m_colCount + 1
   ReDim Preserve m_DispCols(m_colCount)
   ReDim Preserve m_NameCols(m_colCount)
   ReDim Preserve m_ClssCols(m_colCount)

   ' Store the info
   m_DispCols(m_colCount) = displayName
   m_NameCols(m_colCount) = colFormat
   m_ClssCols(m_colCount) = className
End Function


'/*---------------------------------------
'// SetRS method
'---------------------------------------*/
Function SetRS (rs)
   Set m_RS = rs
End Function
```

Notice that any ADO recordset is fine. Remember, there's no difference between recordsets produced by a DBMS such as SQL Server, those created by any custom OLE DB data provider and those created on the fly without relying on any data source. This means that you can use the component to render *any* data.

Creating the Table

The `GetText` function follows a very simple algorithm – it builds a big string by concatenating the rows of the recordset. The real strength of this method, and subsequently of the component, is that it lets you evaluate expressions instead of the simple field content. In order words, you can assign not only the value of a field in a recordset to a column, but also a string expression that, for example, concatenates two or more fields.

This version of the component doesn't accept code in the expression but simply expands some macros. For those of you who know C/C++, this works like `sprintf`. In terms of VBScript, this can be seen as a specialized version of `Replace`:

```
'/*-----------------------------------------
'// GetText method
'-----------------------------------------*/
Function GetText()
  Dim strText

  ' Set the Title
  strText = ""
  If Len(m_Title) Then
    strText = strText + ExpandString(m_Title, FLDNAME_MUST_HAVE_DELIM) + vbCrLf
  End If

  ' Add the <TABLE> header
  strText = strText + "<TABLE class=" + m_TableStyle + ">" + vbCrLf
  strText = strText + "<TR>" + vbCrLf
  For i = 1 to m_colCount
    Dim strName
    strText = strText + "  <TH class=" + m_HeaderStyle + ">"
    strText = strText + m_DispCols(i) + "</TH>" + vbCrLf
  Next
  strText = strText + "</TR>" + vbCrLf


  ' Walk the recordset and add the <TABLE> items
  While Not m_RS.EOF
    m_RecNo = m_RecNo + 1
    strRowText  = ""

    For i = 1 to m_colCount
      Dim strClass

      ' Set the class string
      If VarType(m_ClssCols(i)) <> vbEmpty Then
        strClass = "class=" + m_ClssCols(i)
      End If
```

```
        ' Retrieve the column content
        strColumn = ExpandString(m_NameCols(i), FLDNAME_CAN_HAVE_DELIM)

        ' Format the row string
        strRowText = strRowText + "<TD " + strClass + ">" + vbCrLf
        strRowText = strRowText + strColumn + vbCrLf
        strRowText = strRowText + "</TD>" + vbCrLf
      Next

      ' Add the row to the final string to return
      strText = strText + "<TR>" + strRowText + "</TR>"

      ' Next record
      m_RS.MoveNext
    Wend

    ' Close the table
    strText = strText + "</TABLE>"


    ' Set the Footnote
    If Len(m_Footnote) Then
      strText=strText + ExpandString(m_Footnote, FLDNAME_MUST_HAVE_DELIM) + vbCrLf
    End If

    ' Closes and writes the page
    GetText = strText
    Response.Write strText
  End Function
```

The helper function `ExpandString` takes care of evaluating the string expression you want to assign to the column. It considers a field name and properly expands any string enclosed in `%` and prefixed by `&`:

```
%&FIELDNAME%
```

In addition to field names, two other macros can be used: `_RECNO_` and `_RECCOUNT_`. The former returns the current record number. The latter returns the total number of records displayed.

```
'/*----------------------------------------------
'// ExpandString helper function
'// A field name is enclosed in %&fieldname%
'// A single string 'fieldname' is also seen as field name if
'// mustHaveDelim is False/0
'----------------------------------------------*/
Function ExpandString(text, mustHaveDelim)
  SEP_ID = "%"
  FLD_ID = "&"
  FLDNAME_ID = "%&"

  newText = text
```

```
    ' Splits the string into components by %
    aTokens = split(text, SEP_ID)

    ' Single strings default to a field name. Due to this code
    ' passing 'EmployeeID' and "%&EmployeeID% is the same
    If mustHaveDelim <> 1 Then
       If UBound(aTokens)=0 Then
         newText = FLDNAME_ID & newText & SEP_ID
         aTokens(0) = FLD_ID & aTokens(0)
       End If
    End If

    ' Extracts the field names from the token array
    aFields = Filter(aTokens, FLD_ID)

    ' Process each field and replaces it in the string using
    ' the value of the current record in the recordset
    For Each field In aFields

      ' Get the real name of the field
      realName = Right(field, Len(field)-1)

      ' Get the name to replace in the string
      findName = SEP_ID & field & SEP_ID

      ' Is it a special field name such as _RECCOUNT_ or _RECNO_?
      ' If yes handle them properly, otherwise get the recordset value
      Select Case realName
        Case "_RECCOUNT_"
          rsFieldValue = m_RS.RecordCount
        Case "_RECNO_"
          rsFieldValue = m_RecNo
        Case else
          rsFieldValue = m_RS(realName)
            If VarType(rsFieldValue) = vbNull Then
            rsFieldValue = " "
          End If
      End Select

      ' Replace the strings
      newText = Replace(newText, findName, rsFieldValue)
    Next

    ExpandString = newText
  End Function
```

You can find this component – `asptable.wsc` *– and the rest of the support material in the code download for this book at the Wrox Web site.*

Now that we've got this far, all we need to do is register the component. You can do that by right-clicking the WSC file in Windows Explorer and selecting Register from the context menu that appears. Then we can call it from an ASP page. Assuming you've had no problems with registration, we'll carry on to develop a page to use our newly-created component.

Using the AspTable Object

The following page utilizes the AspTable object to display a few names taken from a database of contacts. You can find the stylesheet used here in the code download for the book.

```
<HTML>
<HEAD>
<LINK REL="stylesheet" TYPE="text/css" HREF="styles.css"/>
</HEAD>
<BODY>

<H1>Testing the AspTable WSC component</H1>
<HR>

<%
    Dim rs
    Dim sql
    Dim objTBL
```

The example database that we've used here comes as part of the code download for the book, and a system DSN called 'Contacts' should be created to point to it.

```
    ' Get the recordset
    sql = "select * from Contacts order by lastname"
    Set rs = CreateObject("ADODB.Recordset")
    rs.CursorLocation = 3                    ' adUseClient
    rs.Open sql, "DSN=Contacts"
    rs.ActiveConnection = Nothing

    Set objTBL = CreateObject("AspTable.WSC")
    objTBL.SetRS (rs)

    objTBL.Title = "<H2>List of contacts:</H2>"
    objTBL.Footnote = "<HR>%&_RECCOUNT_% contact(s).<BR>"
    objTBL.TableStyle = "globTab"
    objTBL.HeaderStyle = "header"

    objTBL.AddColumn "#", "N. %&_RECNO_%", "num"
    objTBL.AddColumn "Name", "%&FIRSTNAME% <B>%&LASTNAME%</B>", ""
    objTBL.AddColumn "Company", "COMPANY", "company"
    objTBL.AddColumn "Email", "EMAILADDRESS", ""

    objTBL.GetText()
%>

</BODY>
</HTML>
```

The recordset is obtained through a typical ADO call, and then the table is formatted by adding four columns. Notice that if the expression parameter of `AddColumn` contains just a word, then it is considered as a field name. This means that, say, the e-mail field can be displayed through `EMAILADDRESS` as well as `%&EMAILADDRESS%`. The result is in the figure below:

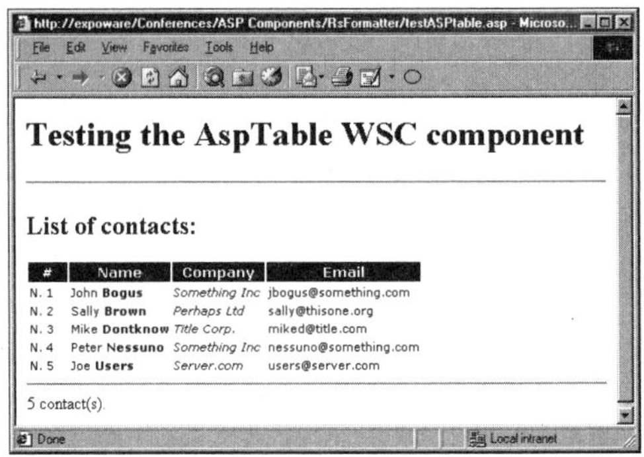

The second column concatenates the first and the last name of each contact. It also applies different formatting styles. The string expression to get this is:

```
%&FIRSTNAME% <b>%&LASTNAME%</b>
```

Changing the way in which a column is rendered, or the number of columns, is as easy as entering the following updates:

```
Set objTBL = CreateObject("AspTable.WSC")
objTBL.SetRS (rs)

objTBL.Title = "<H2>List of contacts:</H2>"
objTBL.Footnote = "<HR>%&_RECCOUNT_% contact(s).<BR>"
objTBL.TableStyle = "globTab"
objTBL.HeaderStyle = "header"

objTBL.AddColumn "#", "N. %&_RECNO_%", "num"
objTBL.AddColumn "Name", "%&FIRSTNAME% <B>%&LASTNAME%</B>", ""
objTBL.AddColumn "Keyword", "LASTNAME", ""
objTBL.AddColumn "Company", "COMPANY", "company"
str = "<A href=mailto:%&EMAILADDRESS% >%&EMAILADDRESS%</A>"
objTBL.AddColumn "Email", str, ""

objTBL.GetText()
```

And the result of this is in the next figure:

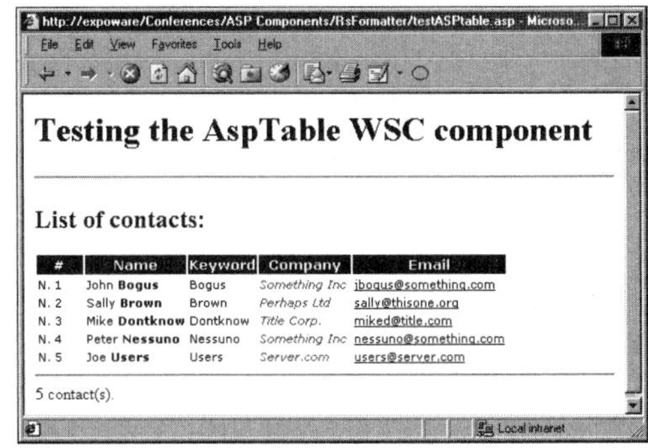

We now have a new column in the table called `Keyword`, and the e-mail addresses have been transformed into hyperlinks.

Why ASP Script Components?

To finish off this chapter, let's ponder the pros and cons of using ASP script components in your work. The obvious comparison is with compiled components, against which they have a significant plus point: WSC script files may be edited any time you like, and the changes are automatically reflected in the component when you next execute it. No more recompiling, rebooting the server to release references to the existing component, and re-registering it each time. And, once you're happy that everything is working properly, you can always use the now-proven code and/or algorithms to build a compiled version in your own choice of language. The same applies for any transactable component.

> *An ASP script component can be considered COM+-compliant. In fact, such a component can access the ObjectContext object just as any other ASP built-in object. So you can use* `SetAbort` *and* `SetComplete` *whenever needed.*

Script components also let you wrap existing business objects (components) in a standard COM interface, even if they're written in, say, Perl. By doing this, you no longer need to worry about how to write in Perl, or search for developers with the appropriate knowledge. The language neutrality of COM makes interoperability a lot easier.

Don't forget either that the componentization of code not only improves the performance of your Web site, but also helps the design and maintenance of the site by allowing you to reuse common pieces of code.

WSC-enabled pages also rank over those making use of Server-Side Include (SSI) files. Although they do essentially the same thing, ASP script components let you dynamically create the object you need, basing your decision on runtime conditions or simple input parameters. SSI doesn't allow dynamic choices: it only lets you import the file whose name is hard-coded in the source of the page.

Of course, there are some disadvantages to using ASP script components.

- Interpreted components cannot have the same performance as a compiled component, so performance is certainly not where ASP script components excel. To be fair though, performance isn't the point of using them.
- They cannot access the full Win32 API, and need a specialized COM automation object to accomplish any system-level task. Also, a scripting language is not a fully-fledged language, such as C++ or even Visual Basic for Applications (VBA) is.

Choosing the Right Tool

There's a quick and easy rule to help you choose the right tool to create your ASP components with.

> *Use Visual C++ for mission-critical, real-time components where you really need the maximum of performance on the server.*

Since the majority of server-side components perform some sort of data access, consider using C++ and raw OLE DB calls to get the most out of your machine. The combination of Visual C++, ATL templates and OLE DB interfaces is perhaps the best available today for performance. Have a look at the next chapter in this book for more on developing components with C++.

Visual Basic is also a great tool for developing components with. If you've a non-critical component to develop, then Visual Basic offers fewer development headaches than Visual C++ but the same advantages of compiled code, full Win32 access and componentization.

What about WSC then? Use them to componentize what you'd keep as raw script code in your pages. Passing through COM to create a script object adds a slight overhead, but what you get in terms of flexibility, reusability and ease of maintenance easily makes up for that.

Script Components vs VBScript Classes

One last point before we wrap up. If you plan to use VBScript 5.0 in your ASP applications, then you might consider using VBScript classes as an alternative to script components.

VBScript classes take slightly less time to be created than Windows Script Components because, unlike `CreateObject`, `New` doesn't need to pass through the COM engine and the registry to locate the files to load. The programming power is mostly the same, but with WSC you can take advantage of several different script languages rather than being tied to just VBScript.

Summary

In this chapter we've analyzed the Windows Script Component technology that is the background for ASP script components. Writing COM objects with scripting languages is not a far-fetched idea and there are, in fact, several advantages in using them. They aren't, however, the solution to everyone's woes, and are definitely not suited to every occasion.

To recap, we've looked at:

- The architecture of WSC and the role of interface handlers
- The mapping of ASP built-in objects in your page's script code
- The interaction between a client and an ASP script component
- A full example of a WSC tailored to work on an ASP page
- Advantages and disadvantages of ASP script objects

In the next chapter, we'll start of journey into the realm of high-powered components written in Visual C++.

N
W

17

Building ASP Components in C++

As we've seen so far in this section on building components, using COM Server components plays a key part in building a Web-based application. The question is not whether to build them, but rather what to build them with. One choice is Visual C++.

The C++ language raises many different emotions from people. Die-hard C++ programmers scoff at the idea of creating COM components in any other language – they feel real programmers use C++. On the other hand, Visual Basic programmers see C++ as a difficult language to learn and use, unnecessarily increasing programming time and effort. Java programmers feel they have it better than C++ programmers do, because James Gosling (the inventor of Java) took the best of many languages (including C++) to create Java. My goal in this chapter and the next is to remove the language prejudices and misconceptions surrounding C++.

This chapter will focus on issues of using the C++ language for building Server Components. It will not teach you C++. If you want to learn C++, then look up the award-winning Wrox book Beginning Visual C++ 6 by Ivor Horton, ISBN 1-861000-88-X.

In this chapter we'll look at the following:

- A brief history of C++
- Why use C++?
- Moving from VB to C++
- Introduction to ATL, STL and MFC
- Building your first C++ COM component
- Error handling and debugging

It's important to remember that you're not just building a component with C++. You have all the tools within Visual C++ available to you, making the process much easier. Let's start at the beginning by looking at the origins of C++.

The C++ Language

To make a decision on whether or not to use C++, it's important to have the facts about the language first. Let's look at the origin of C++ and where it is today.

Brief History

In the beginning there was C. C enjoyed prominence as the language of choice among programmers for producing fast, efficient code. However, there was a person named Bjarne Stroustrup who was not satisfied with just producing fast code. He wanted to introduce Object Oriented Programming to C. Starting with the core syntax of C, he added all the necessary modifications to the language to conform it to an OOP model, and C++ was the result.

Bjarne Stroustrup was the original designer and implementer of C++. However, since its inception, the language has been developed and expanded and is now a fully mature programming language. Now, C++ has been standardized by ANSI (The American National Standards Institute), BSI (The British Standards Institute), DIN (The German national standards organization), several other national standards bodies, and ISO (The International Standards Organization). The ISO standard has been finalized and was adopted by unanimous vote, Nov 14 1997. C++ is here to stay.

The C++ standard has continued to evolve over the years. C++ templates are a relatively recent extension to the language. **Templates** are mechanisms for generating functions and classes based on type parameters (templates are sometimes called "parameterized types"). By using templates, you can design a single class that operates on data of many types, instead of having to create a separate class for each type. Both the Standard Template Library (STL) and Microsoft's Active Template Library (ATL) rely on this C++ language extension.

The C++ Standard can be divided into two parts: the C++ language itself and the **C++ Standard Library**. The C++ Standard Library is relatively new to Visual C++, and in fact Microsoft only got the bugs shaken out with the release of Visual C++ 5.0. The standard library provides standard input/output, strings, containers (such as vectors, lists, and maps), non-numerical algorithms (such as sort, search, and merge), and support for numeric computation. It should be said that C/C++ contains relatively few keywords. and that most useful functionality has always come from libraries. The part of the C++ Standard Library that implements containers and algorithms is the **Standard Template Library** (**STL**).

STL is a framework of data structures (such as vectors, lists and arrays) and algorithms for searching, copying and sorting those data structures. In July 1994 the ANSI/ISO C++ standards committee voted to adopt STL as part of the C++ Standard Library. The proposal was based on generic programming and generic software library research of Alex Stepanov, Meng Lee, and David Musser. STL was created with the design goal of generality while not imposing a performance penalty.

How well does Microsoft conform to the C++ standard? Well, Microsoft ran Visual C++ against the Plum-Hall C++ conformance suite and got a score of between 92% and 93%. One of the reasons it's not 100% compliant is that it's difficult to track the standards and build a compiler at the same time. Microsoft also considers backward compatibility with existing code very important, and sometimes they have to sacrifice standards conformance to maintain this.

Why Use C++?

It is important to have good reasons to use C++ to build server components, rather than just using it to impress your boss. If you haven't used C++ before, you'll want to know why you should bother making the effort to learn it.

Performance

There are two aspects to performance: algorithm speed and machine code efficiency. An **algorithm** can be defined as the conceptual path that data takes through a system, and describes points at which it is manipulated and transformed to create a certain result. For example, an algorithm defines a process of taking a string, counting the characters in it, and returning the number of characters as the result. Algorithms are language independent, and therefore you should design your algorithm before writing your program. The first steps needed to create a fast program are well-designed algorithms that minimize the number of operations that have to occur to solve a problem. Your choice of language is the next step to having a fast program.

The best choice for performance is writing a program in assembler. This is the native language that the computer understands. However, almost no one writes an entire program in assembler, because it's extremely tedious to do. The next best choice is straight C. However, all the tools that are supplied by Visual C++ generate C++ not C, which mean that you would have to code the program manually instead of being able to use all the great generated code from the Visual C++ wizards. So, on balancing the ease of programming with performance, C++ is the best choice.

C++ performs well because it is compiled all the way down to machine code. For languages, such as VBScript and Java, code has to be interpreted by a runtime program, and the code has to be converted to machine code every time the program is run, which is not very efficient. Not only is C++ faster in that it's already compiled, the Microsoft C++ compiler has been around for many years. This means the bright compiler programmers at Microsoft have been able to put many optimizations into the compiler, so it automatically generates highly efficient machine code. Also, since C++ is, by its very nature, closer to machine code than Visual Basic is, the code generated by the C++ compiler is more efficient than Visual Basic compiled code.

Error Handling

Good error handling support makes the difference between a good program and a great program. In fact, if you make error handling one of the first things you implement, rather than the last, the entire development and testing process will go much better. However, error handling can only be as good as what the language supports.

VBScript has rudimentary error handling support. By default, you can't trap an error in VBScript – you need to call `On Error Resume Next` and then check the `Error` object every time you suspect an error has occurred.

The error handling in C++ is much better due to what is known as **exception handling**, the details of which we'll look at later on in this chapter.

Minimal Dependencies

As we just mentioned, C++ is a compiled language. This means the C++ code is converted to machine code before it's executed. As long as the code itself does not rely on any outside dynamic link libraries (DLLs), it can be moved to any other machine running the same operating system and microprocessor without requiring the installation of additional programs. To clarify, the Java language needs the Java runtime to be installed.

Making Use of Existing Code

Since C and C++ have been around for a number of years, there is a lot of existing code available. Your server component may have to use existing C/C++ code or libraries, for example, statistical libraries and C interfaces to legacy systems.

Maximizing COM Features

COM is very closely related to C++. In fact, Don Box (a leading authority on COM) titled the first chapter of his book Essential COM, "COM as a better C++". He shows how the COM specification is derived using principles from the C++ language. By understanding C++, you will have a much better understanding of COM.

Also, you cannot take advantage of all COM features in some languages. However, with C++ you can use almost all of the COM features.

When Not to Use C++

Just as it's important to know when to use C++, it is important to know when *not* to use it. Think about who will have to maintain the code in the long term. If there aren't any C++ programmers around to support it, then the developer will have to look at what programming skills are available and proceed in those languages instead.

To make changes to a C++ component you need to recompile the code in order to see the result of those changes, which can take a great deal of developing time. You can't just start Notepad, change a single line of code, and reload to get a result as you can with an ASP page. Therefore, if you're working on something where you need to make changes quickly (such as prototyping), don't use C++.

In C++, you don't get much protection from things that cause fatal errors – it's very easy to write code that will cause a component to crash. This is a trade-off that enables C++ to provide fast code. C++ will not go out of its way to check to see if anything untoward is going on in the code. It relies on the developer's skills in thinking about what kind of data is coming in, and managing the flow of the program away from possible crashes. If you are short on time for a project and you're only just starting to learn C++, it might not be a good idea to use C++. Wait until you're aware of all the C++ pitfalls and you have lots of time before testing your component. If you want to build a component quickly and easily, but are not too concerned about its speed of execution, then use Visual Basic.

Transferring ASP skills to C++

The best way to learn something new is to leverage your existing skills. Fortunately, if you're an ASP developer, you've already learned some of the skills that are required by C++. Specifically, the syntax of JScript and Object Oriented Programming concepts of ActiveX or COM will help you.

JScript

Most ASP developers have used JScript to manipulate DHTML on the browser. The syntax of JScript if very similar to C. So if you know JScript, you know basic C syntax which, of course, is a subset of C++ syntax. C++ has some additional syntax that supports object oriented programming, which is what we come to next.

Object Oriented Programming

If you have used classes in Visual Basic, any COM object or the DOM (Document Object Model) you are already familiar with the concept of Object Oriented Programming (OOP). As we mentioned earlier, the main difference between C and C++ is that C++ supports OOP.

Visual C++ Libraries

Great programmers leverage as much as they can from existing code. Programmers often purchase code that is already packaged up as libraries, and many successful companies are based on creating really good code libraries, such as Rogue Wave Software (`www.roguewave.com`).

When C was popular, code libraries were in the form of function libraries. For instance, you could purchase a math library that would have functions to perform calculus and algebra operations. Typically with a function library you have a file that you include with your code, and a library that you statically or dynamically link with.

Statically linking means the library code is physically integrated into your program. In this case, you don't have a dependency on another file but your program size can be large. Alternatively, **dynamically linking** means your program only has a stubbed version of the library, and the code is stored in a separate file, a **dynamic link library** or DLL. The DLL is not loaded into memory until a function in the DLL is called during the execution of the program. The DLL exists as a separate entity in memory, and can be accessed by many running programs simultaneously.

Then along came C++, and the function libraries changed to **class libraries**. The difference between the two is that a function library just contained a list of functions, whereas a class library is designed using the principles of OOP. For instance, you could have a class library for data structures that would include a class for a linked list. If a function library was used instead, then the linked list would have to exist separately from the functions that would operate on it. On the other hand, with a class library, a linked list and the functions that operate on it would be contained in the same class in the same file. However, as with a function library, using a class library involves including a file and linking with a static library.

Recently, there has been a shift from class libraries to template libraries. The reason for this shift is that C++ compilers have now matured to handle C++ templates properly. A template library offers a number of advantages over a class library. To use a template library, you just include a file into your program. There's no library to link with – all the library code is contained in the include file.

This might sound very inefficient, and early on it really was. It was inefficient because every file that included a template file would get a separate copy of the code, and as a result, the compiled program would be very large. However, compilers have now been optimized for templates, making this method is very efficient.

Visual C++ has three libraries at the developer's disposal: one class library (MFC) and two template libraries (ATL and STL).

Microsoft Foundation Classes (MFC)

MFC is Microsoft's class library for assisting the C++ developer. It has many different classes to support everything from implementing complex data structures to manipulating Windows and database access. So when should you use MFC in a server component? Never!

That's right – you should not have any need to use MFC in your server component. A server component does not access a Win32 Window, so you don't need these particular MFC classes. The database support is better achieved using ATL.

ATL has support for ADO and OLE DB, whereas MFC does not. STL has better data structure support than MFC. Even the most used MFC class, `CString`, has an equivalent in the standard C library. There might be the occasional MFC class that you'd like to use (such as `CSocket`), but even so, there is most likely a Win32 API you can use instead.

MFC was designed to build standalone Windows applications – not lightweight COM components. The only time you would use MFC is if you have to interface with existing code that uses MFC. Otherwise stick with ATL and STL – and your components will be smaller and faster.

Active Template Library (ATL)

You can tell that ATL is newer than MFC since it includes the word 'Active' in its name. Otherwise it would have been called the 'Microsoft Template Library'.

ATL has been designed to be a fast, easy way to create COM components while maintaining a small memory footprint. Part of the key to accomplishing this is using C++ templates for its implementation. In fact, the design of ATL follows STL in its use of templates.

C++ templates provide a type-safe way of implementing generic interfaces. Fortunately for us, Microsoft provides some wizards for generating ATL code, so you don't need to know about templates, and you don't really need to know all the details about ActiveX when building simple components. Another advantage of ATL is that there's no dependency on DLLs, which means that you don't have to ship DLLs with the application or statically link, both of which increase memory size.

As mentioned, ATL makes COM development much easier. It also has support for Data Access through OLE DB consumers and providers, and there are a few other odds and ends, such as support for building Microsoft Management Console (MMC) snap-in components.

By contrast, MFC does rely on additional runtime DLLs (or statically linking), and thus produces larger, slower code than ATL. So if you're building COM components without a user interface (such as those used with Active Server Pages), ATL is a much better choice than MFC. But what about those data structures?

Standard Template Library (STL)

The Standard Template Library is one of the most underused tools available to the Visual C++ developer. Ironically, it's also the only Visual C++ library that is a standard and cross-platform.

> *One of the reasons it isn't used much is that the Microsoft STL documentation is terrible. There are also no STL books targeted at Visual C++ programmers available. A good generic STL book is STL Tutorial and Reference Guide, by Musser and Saini.*

The reason STL is so valuable to C++ component development is that it contains many data structures and algorithms. For much of the time, the purpose of a server component is to operate on data. STL is a perfect fit for this.

Microsoft's original implementation of the STL standard first appeared in Visual C++ 4.2. Unfortunately, this implementation was so buggy that it was unusable. Some people (such as myself) got around this problem by using the Hewlett-Packard or SGI implementation of STL. Since STL is an ISO/ANSI standard, it is cross-platform (as long as the compiler supports the constructs required by STL). However, Microsoft's more recent STL implementations, which shipped with Visual C++ 5.0 and 6.0, are stable and easier to use.

STL is the perfect complement to ATL – the latter having no data structures or algorithms. Furthermore, STL and ATL have a similar implementation strategy – C++ templates – so they are perfectly compatible. And neither requires additional DLLs to be linked in, either statically or dynamically, which reduces the size of the component and it's reliance on other DLLs.

Let's look at some key STL concepts that we will use later when building a server component.

STL Iterators

When programming in C, people when often loop through data structures in one of the following two ways: using a subscript or incrementing a pointer. With two different methods of achieving the same thing, life can get confusing, and what's more, it's not possible to write a generic algorithm to handle different types. The way that STL **iterators** address this problem is best explained by illustration.

The following code shows the two standard C methods of iteration, and then the STL method of iteration. It has the simple task of counting the number of 't's in a string:

```
string          mySTLStr;
const char      *myStr;
int             tCount = 0;
int             stringLength;

mySTLStr = "test";
myStr = mySTLStr.c_str();
stringLength = strlen( myStr );

/* Iteration using a subscript. */
for ( int i = 0; i < stringLength; i++ )
    if ( myStr[i] == 't' )
        tCount++;

tCount = 0;

/* Iteration using a pointer. */
for ( const char *myPtr = myStr; *myPtr != '\0'; myPtr++ )
    if ( *myPtr == 't' )
        tCount++;

tCount = 0;

/* Iteration using an iterator. */
for(string::iterator iter = mySTLStr.begin(); iter != mySTLStr.end(); iter++ )
    if ( *iter == 't' )
        tCount++;
```

Using an iterator solves a number of problems that are encountered when using either a pointer or subscript. Both pointers and subscripts depend on the data being organized contiguously in memory, whereas iterators hide the data so that users of the data structure do not need to know how data sequences are stored. Hiding the data structure also allows the creation of generic algorithms that can work with a variety of such data structures, which are also known as containers.

For the purpose of algorithm efficiency, STL defines five classes of iterator: input, output, forward, bi-directional (that is forwards and backward) and random access. Algorithms are designed with a particular method of iteration in mind, so they can perform with maximum optimization.

Iterators are similar to pointers, in that to move to the next and previous items the increment (++) and decrement (--) operators are used respectively. Also, to get the value of an item at an iterator, the * operator is used.

STL Map

A **map** is a sorted associative container. These concentrate more on retrieving an item as quickly as possible based on a key stored with the item, rather than storing the item in a linear fashion as with sequence containers.

The STL sorted associative containers are `set`, `multiset`, `map` and `multimap`. A set is used when you have a collection of items. A map is used when you want to associate one item with another. Sorted associative containers do support traversal of the data items as a linear sequence since they use bi-directional iterators, though their fundamental purpose is keyed access.

A map container provides support for fast retrieval of data based on a separate key. This key is unique within the map. Maps have the potential to provide huge savings in storage and computing time for representing sparse data, which we'll see later in our demonstration component. The key is stored with the value in a `pair` type, and this type has two members: `first` and `second`. Retrieving `first` returns the key and `second` returns the value. An iterator of a map is of type `pair`.

We'll see examples of using `map` later in the chapter.

STL Vector

A **vector** is an example of a sequence container – other sequence containers are `deque` and `list`. They have similar functions; and the fundamental differences are in terms of performance. For example, a `deque` is similar to a `vector` except insertion and deletion at the beginning of a `deque` is much faster than with a `vector`. Different problems will need to access data in different ways. Vectors are sequence containers providing fast random access to data of varying length. Insertion and deletions are fast at the end of the sequence but slower elsewhere.

STL Algorithms

STL **algorithms** are categorized by how they affect and interact with the data structures on which they operate. The interfaces between STL algorithms and the STL data structures they operate on are STL iterators. The iterator plays an important role because it constrains how the algorithm accesses the data. Many algorithms also accept a function as part of their interface, and if this function parameter returns a `bool` value, it is referred to as a **predicate**. Using a function parameter can customize an algorithm.

Some STL algorithms allow a function to be passed as a parameter. In most cases, these functions perform a comparison and return a `bool` value. For example, a sorting algorithm would take a function as a parameter that compares two values. The function determines whether one value is less than another according to some criteria. Different functions would provide different criteria, resulting in the listing of data in different orders.

Even more interesting is passing a function object as a parameter instead of a function. A function object can contain state enabling comparison rules to exist in one place. The comparison rule used would depend on the object's state. Later in this chapter we'll see an example of a comparison function for a `sort` algorithm that's implemented this way.

Categories of STL Algorithm

STL algorithms are divided into four broad categories. Non-mutating sequence algorithms operate on data structures without changing their contents, whereas data structures are modified when operated on by mutating sequence algorithms. Various algorithms for sorting, merging and binary searching are available with sorting-related algorithms. Finally, STL has generalized numeric algorithms, for performing calculations on elements in a data structure.

- **Non-mutating sequence algorithms** do not directly change the data structure elements on which they operate. In general, they search for elements in the data structure, check for equality and count sequence elements. Examples of non-mutating algorithms are `find` and `count`. The algorithm `find` traverses a range in the data structure looking for the first iterator that equals a specified value, while the `count` algorithm counts the number of elements equal to a given value in the data structure.
- **Mutating sequence algorithms** modify the data structure elements on which they operate. These algorithms copy, replace, transform, remove and rotate elements in the container. An example of this type of algorithm is the `fill` algorithm, which puts copies of a given value in all positions of a sequence range.
- **Sorting related algorithms** sort, merge and search sequences. As well, set operations are available for sorted sequences. An example is the `merge` algorithm, which takes two sorted ranges and places the result in a range that does not overlap the input ranges.

An example of a **generalized numeric algorithm** is `accumulate`. This algorithm sums the values for a specified range in a data structure.

Iterators with Algorithms

We've already said that STL defines five classes of iterators: input, output, forward, bi-directional and random access. Algorithms are designed with a particular method of iteration in mind to ensure optimized performance.

As an example, consider the `find` algorithm, which can be used to find values in a variety of data structures. The algorithm doesn't care whether the container is a vector, list or array – the only criterion is that the data structure must support the `InputIterator`. The design of `InputIterator` guarantees the operations it supports to work efficiently – the `find` algorithm only needs the set of operations supported by `InputIterator` so `find` can work efficiently.

Some algorithms require more powerful iterators: for example `sort` requires a `RandomAccessIterator`. The trade-off for providing random access is that performance penalties are incurred for other operations, such as element insertion in the middle of a container.

Well we've had enough theory, so let's move on to creating a component.

Building Your First C++ Server Component

C++ is a standardized computer language, not owned by anyone but managed by a standards committee. STL is an extension to C++ to support data structures and algorithms, and ATL is a Microsoft-owned and maintained Template Library for making COM programming easier. Together, these technologies form an efficient way to create COM components to use within Active Server Pages.

We're now going to create a COM object using all these technologies. We will see how the Visual C++ 6.0 wizards generate a lot of the code for us, so we can focus on solving the problem rather than worrying about specific programming details.

The Problem

One of the most common ways to represent data is as a table. The columns represent a type of field and each row is a record that has values for the fields. In a text file, this table is usually represented with comma-separated values (CSV).

We are going to create a COM component that takes CSV data as input, efficiently stores it, and provides access functions to retrieve it. The data will be represented with STL data structures inside the COM component. In a later section, we'll see how to use STL algorithms for manipulating the data. In addition, in the next chapter, we will demonstrate how to store this data in a database.

For purposes of demonstration, we will assume the data is contained in a sparse table. The fields in the first row are column headings, and each succeeding row is a data record with the fields aligned with the column heading. Commas separate fields and linefeeds (`\n`) separate rows. Empty fields are represented by two commas (i.e. ,,).

The table below is an example spreadsheet table. When exported, commas will separate each of the fields.

Name	Group	Instrument
Jim Morrison	The Doors	Vocals
Keith Moon	The Who	Drums
Jimi Hendrix		Guitar & Vocals
Lenny Kravitz		Everything
Robert Plant	Led Zeppelin	Vocals

Design

The design goals for our component are to minimize storage space and minimize access time for the data. Since the data may be sparse (many empty fields) there is an opportunity to keep storage space to a minimum. Rows of the data will be accessed numerically (with a zero-based index) and columns will be accessed by name. For example, to get Keith Moon's instrument from the previous table, you would make the call `GetField( 1, "Instrument")`.

The tools used to accomplish these goals are STL's `vector` and `map` data structures. These data structures are containers; that is, they are objects containing a collection of other objects. To access objects in the collection, we will use STL iterators.

Implementation

Now that we have an idea of the functionality our component will have, we'll take the following steps to implement it:

1. Create the DLL that will contain the component
2. Create the component
3. Add properties
4. Add methods

Creating the DLL and a Component

Create a new Visual C++ project selecting ATL COM AppWizard and call it `ASPComponents`. Leave the default server type, DLL and leave the checkboxes unchecked:

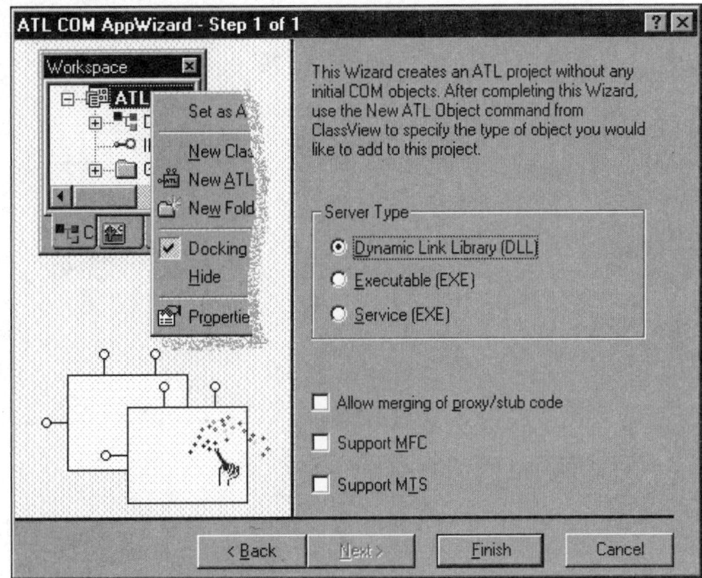

When finished, the wizard will automatically generate the shell for your components. At this point no components exist, only functions that are required by a DLL according to the COM specification. You can see these functions in `ASPComponents.cpp`. We're not going to go into the details of this file, and you don't need to change it. The Wizard will modify the file as you add components to the DLL.

Let's put a component into the DLL. Select the ClassView tab in the Workspace window. Right-click ASPComponents Classes and select New ATL Object. Then select Simple Object, and for the Short Name type `TableStorage`:

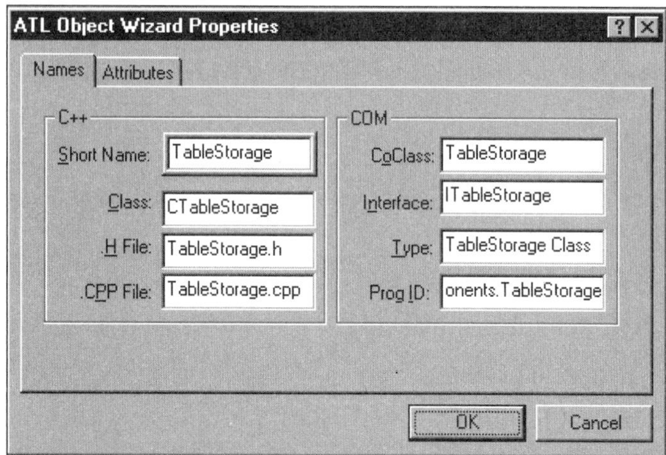

Leave the defaults on the Attributes page as shown here. Unless you plan to delve deeply into ATL, you will not need to change these options at all. A detailed description of what they all mean is beyond the scope of this book.

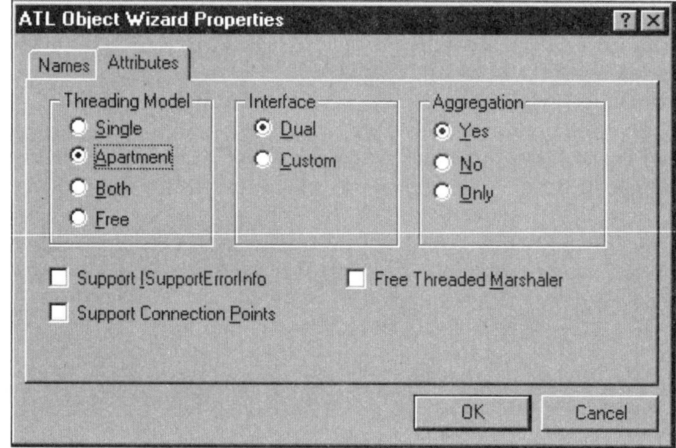

After clicking OK you will have an object to work with.

So far the Visual C++ wizard has performed all the work, and if you look in `TableStorage.h`, you'll see the ATL code that the wizard has generated. For the majority of cases, you won't need to change this code. In fact, you can go a long way without ever knowing ATL and just relying on the generated code. However, there is one change we need to make to the default settings so that the code will compile.

To reduce the size of the components, C++ exceptions are automatically turned off when the AppWizard creates an ATL component, as the C runtime library is required if exceptions are enabled. STL uses exception handling, so we need to enable it. In the Project Settings on the C/C++ property page, drop down the category box to C++ Language. Make sure that the Settings For: box is set to All Configurations, and check the checkbox that says, Enable exception handling:

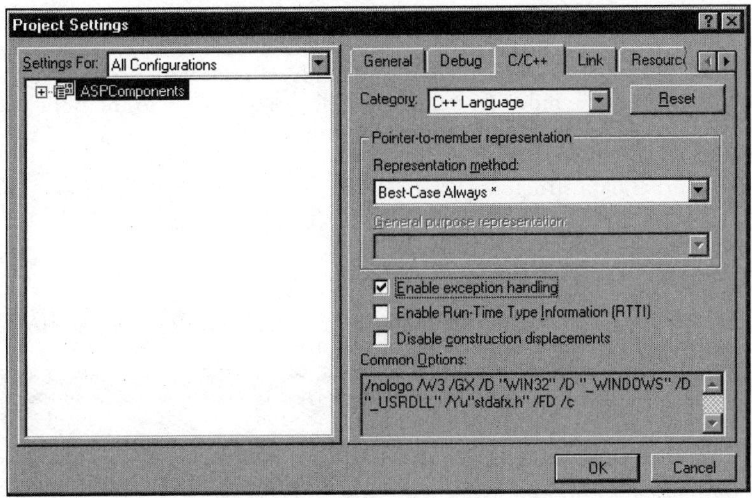

If you compile in Release mode you may get a link error. The problem occurs when a release version of an ATL project is complied with exceptions turned on. Using exceptions requires C-runtime startup code, but by default, an ATL project in release mode defines the symbol `_ATL_MIN_CRT`, which excludes the startup code. To fix this problem, go to the C/C++ preprocessor definitions and remove `_ATL_MIN_CRT`. For more information see article Q165259 in the Microsoft knowledge base.

The first piece of code we'll add sets up the STL data structures. Add the following to the beginning of `TableStorage.h`:

```
#pragma warning(disable:4786)

#include <map>
#include <vector>
#include <string>

using namespace std;

typedef map< wstring, unsigned short > COLUMN_INDEX_MAP;
typedef map< unsigned short, wstring > INDEX_FIELD_MAP;
typedef vector< INDEX_FIELD_MAP > ROW_VECTOR;
```

And add the following as protected members of `CTableStorage`:

```
protected:
    COLUMN_INDEX_MAP    m_columnIndexMap;
    ROW_VECTOR          m_rows;
```

Two `maps` and one `vector` are declared, and as you can see, the `vector` is actually a vector of one of the maps. Using the C++ command `typedef` for the maps and vector is for the programmer's convenience: it makes the code more readable and is a better description of the data type.

The COLUMN_INDEX_MAP maps a string (the name of the column) to an index. The INDEX_FIELD_MAP represents the data in each row of the table data. Since it could be a sparse row, it's implemented with a map for efficiency; empty fields will not take any space. The INDEX_FIELD_MAP maps the index from the COLUMN_INDEX_MAP to the field's value. Finally, the ROW_VECTOR contains each of the maps that represent the rows.

So now that the internal data structures are declared, we're going to expose parts of them to the outside world using properties.

Adding Properties

We are going to add two properties: the number of columns and the number of rows.

After selecting the ClassView tab in the project workspace, right-click on the ITableStorage interface. Select Add Property from the menu and fill out the dialog box as in the figure opposite. Note that we're making this a read-only property by checking only the Get Function box – i.e. you need to uncheck the Put Function box:

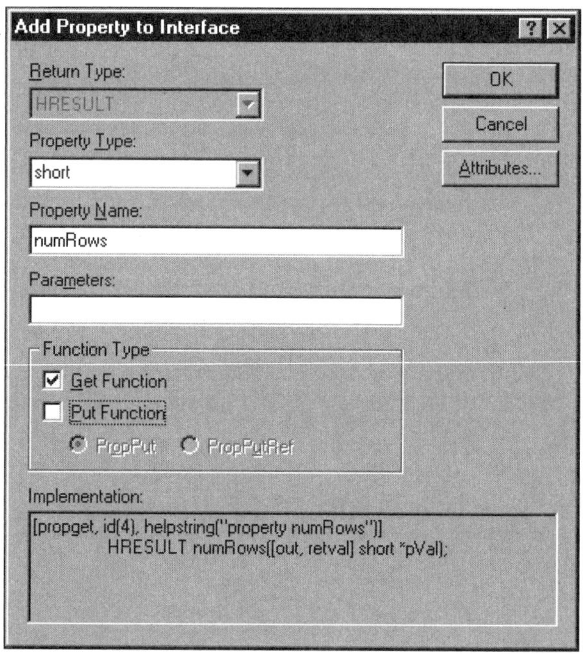

A method call get_numRows is generated that returns this property. This means you can have logic generating the property value. In this case, we're setting the property by calling the size() method of the row vector:

```
STDMETHODIMP CTableStorage::get_numRows(short *pVal)
{
    *pVal = m_rows.size();

    return S_OK;
}
```

Add another property the same way, but this time call it `numColumns`. Fill out the code as follows:

```
STDMETHODIMP CTableStorage::get_numColumns(short *pVal)
{
    *pVal = m_columnIndexMap.size();

    return S_OK;
}
```

Now we have a way of getting the number of rows and columns being stored. We just need to get some data into the component, and that's what we'll do next.

Adding Methods

At this point, we don't have a way to get any data into the internal data structures or to read them back. We're going to add four methods that will accomplish the following:

- Insert data into the data structures
- Obtain a field from the data structures
- Obtain a column name
- Sort the rows

Parsing the Data

The first method will take a comma-separated string, parse it, and insert the data into the data structures.

After selecting the ClassView tab in the project workspace, right-click on the `ITableStorage` interface. Select Add Method from the menu and fill out the dialog box as in this figure:

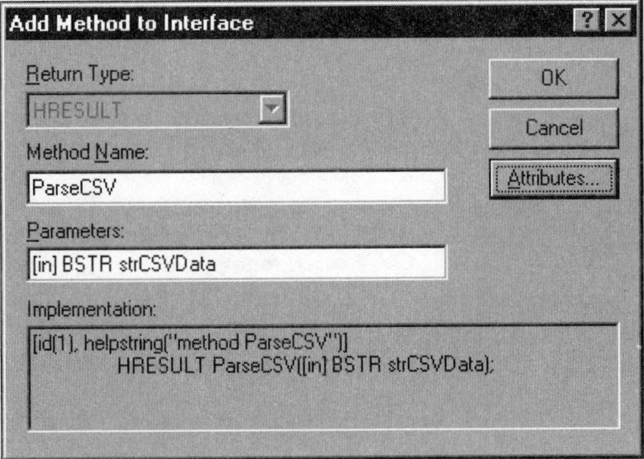

Then fill out the body of the ParseCSV method with the following code:

```
STDMETHODIMP CTableStorage::ParseCSV(BSTR strCSVData)
{
    HRESULT                          hResult = S_OK;
    wstring                          data = strCSVData;
    wstring::size_type               startPos = 0;
    wstring::size_type               endPos = 0;
    wstring                          field;
    bool                             headerRow = true;
    INDEX_FIELD_MAP                  fieldMap;
    INDEX_FIELD_MAP::size_type       fieldIndex = 0;

    // Make sure there is not any data around.
    m_rows.clear();
    m_columnIndexMap.clear();
```

The CSV data is passed in as a string parameter, and the two STL member variables are cleared to remove any data that might have been there from a previous call to the method. The rows in the string are then iterated over and parsed:

```
    endPos = data.find_first_of( L",\n", startPos );

    while ( endPos != wstring::npos )
    {
        // Obtain a field from the data.
        field = data.substr( startPos, (endPos-startPos) );
```

The first row requires special attention, because it contains the column names. Each column name is stored as a key in m_columnIndexMap, with the current size of the map as the index. When a row is processed, we use the fact that the index for the column name map is also the numerical index of the column. If the field parsed out has data, it is stored in an INDEX_FIELD_MAP:

```
        if ( headerRow )
        {
            m_columnIndexMap[field] = m_columnIndexMap.size();
        }
        else
        {
            if ( field.length() > 0 )
            {
                fieldMap[fieldIndex] = field;
            }
            fieldIndex++;
        }
```

When the end of the row is reached, the map is pushed onto the ROW_VECTOR:

```
        // Check for end of the row.
        if ( data[endPos] == L'\n' )
        {
```

```
            if ( headerRow )
            {
                headerRow = false;
            }
            else
            {
                // Start a new row.
                m_rows.push_back( fieldMap );
                fieldIndex = 0;
                fieldMap.clear();
            }
        }
        startPos = (endPos+1);
        endPos = data.find_first_of( L",\n", startPos );
    }

    return hResult;
}
```

Once all the rows are processed, the CSV data representation in the COM component minimizes storage space and has fast access because of the use of maps. Storage space is minimized because only fields that actually have values are stored, while access is fast because maps internally organize data so it can be retrieved quickly.

Accessing the Data

Now that the data is stored efficiently, we need to be able to access it.

Add a new method called `GetField` to the `ITableStorage` interface and fill out the dialog box as shown here:

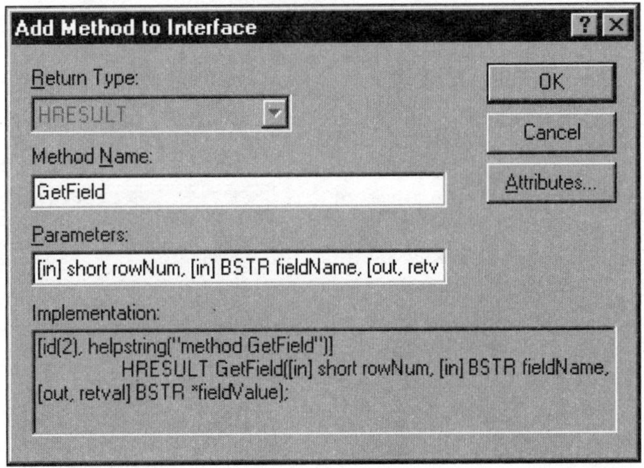

Given a row number and column name, this method will return the field's value if it exists. So change the body of the method to look like the following:

```
STDMETHODIMP CTableStorage::GetField(short rowNum, BSTR fieldName, BSTR
                                                              *fieldValue)
{
    HRESULT     hResult = E_FAIL;
```

```
        if ( rowNum < m_rows.size() )
        {
            COLUMN_INDEX_MAP::iterator    mapIter =
                                        m_columnIndexMap.find( fieldName );

            if ( mapIter != m_columnIndexMap.end() )
            {
                int    columnNum = (*mapIter).second;

                INDEX_FIELD_MAP::iterator    fieldIter =
                                        m_rows[rowNum].find( columnNum );
                CComBSTR    tempBStr( "" );

                if ( fieldIter != m_rows[rowNum].end() )
                {
                    tempBStr = (*fieldIter).second.c_str();
                    *fieldValue = tempBStr.Detach();
                    hResult = S_OK;
                }
            }
        }

        return hResult;
    }
```

The map method used to obtain a value associated with a key in a map is `find`. For `COLUMN_INDEX_MAP`, an iterator of type `pair< wstring, unsigned short >` is returned from `find`. If the key is not found, the iterator has the value of `m_columnIndexMap.end()`. If it is found, the `second` member of the returned iterator contains the value: in this case, it is the index of the column name. This index is then used as the key in the `INDEX_FIELD_MAP` for the given row to get the field value. If this is found, it's then returned through the `[out, retval]` parameter: that is, `fieldValue`.

Next we'll create a way of getting the name of a column. Add a new method called `GetColumnName` to `ITableStorage`, and fill out the dialog box as shown:

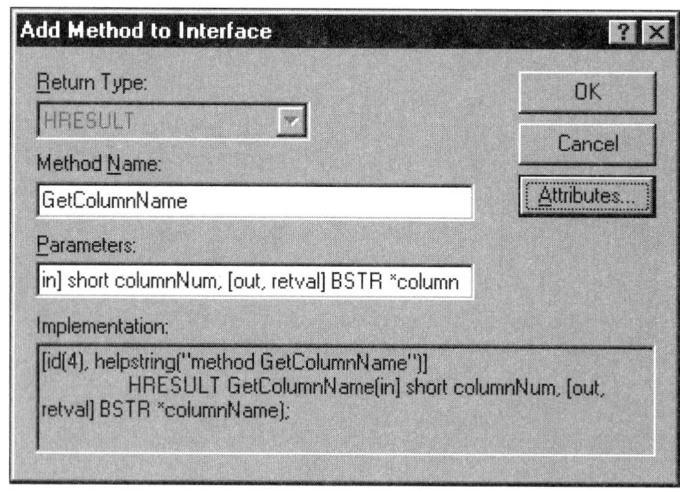

Given a column index, this method will return the column name. Change the body of the method to the following code:

```
STDMETHODIMP CTableStorage::GetColumnName(short columnNum, BSTR *columnName)
{
    HRESULT hResult = S_OK;
    bool    found = false;

    if ( columnNum < m_columnIndexMap.size() )
    {
        COLUMN_INDEX_MAP::iterator    mapIter = m_columnIndexMap.begin();

        while ( !found && (mapIter != m_columnIndexMap.end()) )
        {
            if ( (*mapIter).second == columnNum )
            {
                CComBSTR    tempBStr( (*mapIter).first.c_str() );
                *columnName = tempBStr.Detach();
                found = true;
            }
            mapIter++;
        }
    }

    if ( !found )
    {
        hResult = E_FAIL;
    }

    return hResult;
}
```

In this method, we need to do a linear search through the map, because we're actually keying on the value instead of the key. We iterate through the `m_columnIndexMap` until either the index is found or we reach the end of the map (that is, the index was not found). Notice that the `second` member of the iterator is used for comparison, since it is the value and not the key that we're looking for. If the column index is found, the column name (which is actually the key) is returned through the `[out, retval]` parameter: that is, `columnName`.

Sorting the Data

Next, let's add a method that actual does something with the data. For this, we're going to leverage the STL `sort` algorithm for sorting the rows.

Add the following line to the start of the `TableStorage.cpp` file:

```
#include <algorithm>
```

Then add a new method called `Sort` to `ITableStorage`, and configure it as in the following dialog box:

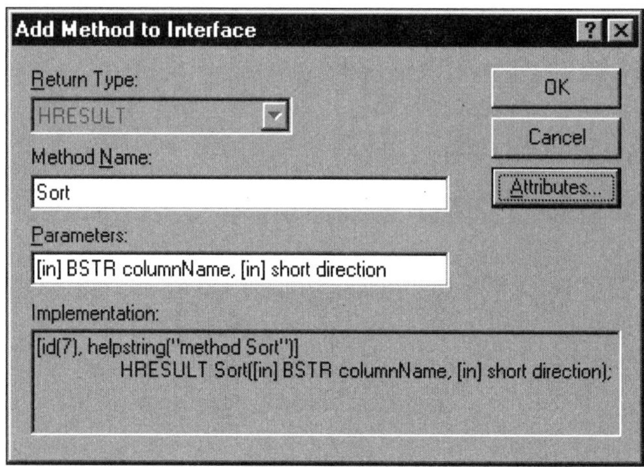

It will sort in descending order if the `direction` parameter is 0, and ascending order otherwise. Fill out the body of the `Sort` method with the following code:

```
STDMETHODIMP CTableStorage::Sort(BSTR columnName, short direction)
{
    HRESULT     hResult = S_OK;

    COLUMN_INDEX_MAP::iterator    mapIter;

    mapIter = m_columnIndexMap.find( columnName );

    if ( mapIter != m_columnIndexMap.end() )
    {
        doCompare    compareFunc( (*mapIter).second, direction );

        sort( m_rows.begin(), m_rows.end(), compareFunc );
    }
    else
    {
        hResult = E_INVALIDARG;
    }

    return hResult;
}
```

Because the `CTableStorage` data structure is a composite of STL data structures (a vector of maps), a custom comparison function needs to be provided to do the actual sorting. As well, `CTableStorage::Sort` allows the rows to be sorted on any of the columns by providing the name of the column. So that sorting can be keyed on any column with just one comparison function, a function object is used. The column to sort on is passed to the constructor of the function object – `doCompare`.

Somewhere in the file `TableStorage.cpp`, add the following function object (I put mine between the includes and the implementation of the `CTableStorage` class):

```
class doCompare : public binary_function< const INDEX_FIELD_MAP &,
                                          const INDEX_FIELD_MAP &, bool >
{
public:
    doCompare( int column, short direction ) : m_column(column),
                                               m_direction(direction) {}
    bool operator()(const INDEX_FIELD_MAP &x, const INDEX_FIELD_MAP &y)
    {
        bool    answer = false;

        INDEX_FIELD_MAP::const_iterator    valueIterX = x.find( m_column );
        INDEX_FIELD_MAP::const_iterator    valueIterY = y.find( m_column );

        if ( ((m_direction > 0) && ( (*valueIterX).second <
            (*valueIterY).second )) || ((m_direction == 0) &&
            ( (*valueIterX).second > (*valueIterY).second )) )
            {
                answer = true;
            }

        return answer;
    }
private:
    int       m_column;
    short     m_direction;
};
```

This is the declaration and implementation of the function object – `doCompare` – used for comparison during sorting. The function might look complicated – indeed, for a detailed explanation of the syntax you should look up a C++ book – but its purpose is really quite simple. It compares two rows for sorting in the order specified by the `m_direction` parameter. It takes the column number as the first parameter in the constructor and stores it in a member variable (`m_column`). Then, when it's time to do a comparison, the function object knows which column to compare.

Notice that `doCompare` derives from the STL `binary_function` template, recognizable by the strange angle bracket syntax. The Standard Template Library provides `binary_function` for convenience of creating comparison functions.

Testing

This particular component can be used from anywhere: your VB program, ASP file and even C++. Let's have a look at how you use it from an ASP.

```
<H2>TableStorage C++ Component Test Driver</H2>

<%
    Dim    objTableStorage
    Dim    csvString

    csvString = "Name, Group, Instrument" & vbLf
    csvString = csvString & "Robert Plant,Led Zeppelin,Vocals" & vbLf
    csvString = csvString & "Jim Morrison,The Doors,Vocals" & vbLf
    csvString = csvString & "Lenny Kravitz,,Everything" & vbLf
```

```
    csvString = csvString & "Keith Moon,The Who,Drums" & vbLf
    csvString = csvString & "Jimi Hendrix,,Guitar & Vocals" & vbLf

    Set objTableStorage = Server.CreateObject( "ASPComponents.TableStorage" )

    objTableStorage.ParseCSV csvString
    objTableStorage.Sort "Name", 1
%>
```

First, we create a string – `csvString` – that represents the data. A TableStorage object is then created using `Server.CreateObject`, and the string is parsed by the `ParseCSV` method. At this point the data is now in memory. We then sort the rows in ascending order by name, just for fun.

Obtaining properties is easy – just reference them:

```
<P>Number for Columns: <%=objTableStorage.numColumns %></P>
<P>Number for Rows: <%=objTableStorage.numRows%></P>
```

We can then iterate through the table to display an HTML table with the data. Notice the `On Error Resume Next`. Currently, if you try to obtain the value of a field that doesn't have a value an error is raised. We'll see a more elegant way to handle this in the next chapter.

```
<TABLE border=1>
    <TR>
<%
    On Error Resume Next
    For column = 0 to objTableStorage.numColumns - 1
%>
        <TH><%= objTableStorage.GetColumnName( column ) %></TH>
<%    Next %>

<%    For row = 0 to objTableStorage.numRows - 1 %>
        <TR>
<%        For column = 0 to objTableStorage.numColumns - 1 %>
            <TD><%= objTableStorage.GetField( row,
                              objTableStorage.GetColumnName( column ) ) %></TD>
    <%    Next %>
        </TR>
<%    Next %>

</TABLE>
```

Note that the complete code for this page, called `componentTest.asp`, can be downloaded from the Wrox Web site. The entire `ASPComponents` Visual C++ project for this chapter and the next is part of the source code for this book.

Also note that we have to specify the field name in order to get the value for a field. A more flexible interface would also allow you to provide an index to get a field value.

By running this page you should get something like the following in your browser:

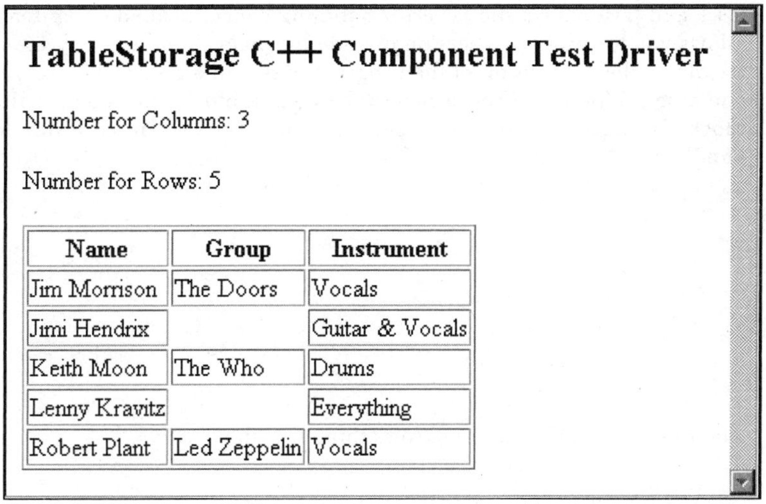

TableStorage C++ Component Test Driver

Number for Columns: 3

Number for Rows: 5

Name	Group	Instrument
Jim Morrison	The Doors	Vocals
Jimi Hendrix		Guitar & Vocals
Keith Moon	The Who	Drums
Lenny Kravitz		Everything
Robert Plant	Led Zeppelin	Vocals

Error Handling

Two important aspects of error handling are

- Ensuring that you capture all errors
- Providing an accurate description of what occurred

Proper error handling implemented early in the development process can significantly reduce the development and testing time, since bugs can be identified and fixed much faster. We're going to look at C++ exception handling for capturing errors, and using the `Error` object for returning information back to the client.

Exception Handling

Error handling can only be as good as the support the programming language provides. A typical error handling procedure consists of the following:

- Call a function
- Check the return value
- If successful, the program takes one code path, if failed it takes another

The problem with this approach is it leads to nested code that is difficult to follow. As well, there's no way to enforce programmers to check the return value. They could get lazy and not check them or simply forget to check them.

What would make more sense is to have the programming environment capture the error for you and direct the code to a predefined error handling routine. In Visual Basic you can do this with On Error Goto <your error handling function>. When an error occurs, the program will jump to the error handling function you specified. You can also signal an error from Visual Basic by calling `Err.Raise`.

C++ and Java have a similar error handling concept called **exception handling**. Exception handling allows you to "protect" a section of code by enclosing it in a `try` block. If an error occurs within the try block, then execution of the program passes to a `catch` block, where the error handling code is contained. When an error occurs in the `catch` block, the code is automatically directed to the `try` block. To signal an error you use the keyword `throw`. Here's a simple example of exception handling:

```
try
{
    myFunction( char *ptr );
}
catch( string message )
{
    sprintf( stderr, "Error occurred: %s\n", message.c_str() );
}
```

The function itself might look something like this:

```
Void myFunction( char *ptr )
{
    if ( ptr == NULL )
    {
    throw string( "Invalid pointer passed to myFunction" );
    }
    // continue processing as normal
}
```

We'll be using this style of exception handling in the Chapter 18 examples.

Once you've captured the error, the next step is to return it to the user. When the host environment for your COM object is an ASP, the best way to report an error is through the `Error` object.

The Error Object

If you disable `On Error Resume Next,` you'll get the following error when `GetField` is called on a field that doesn't have a value:

```
error '80004005'
Unspecified error

/datashaping/componenttest.asp, line 43
```

Not very helpful is it? The component needs to be able to report better information when an error occurs. It can do this using the **Error object**.

If you're creating a new ATL object, and you want to use the `Error` object, you can check the box Support ISupportErrorInfo in the ATL Object wizard properties box. This will prompt the wizard to generate the code to support the Error object.

It's also easy to manually insert the code. Just make the following modification to the include file `TableStorage.h`:

```
/////////////////////////////////////////////////////////////////////////////
// CTableStorage
class ATL_NO_VTABLE CTableStorage :
    public CComObjectRootEx<CComSingleThreadModel>,
    public CComCoClass<CTableStorage, &CLSID_TableStorage>,
    public ISupportErrorInfo,
    public IDispatchImpl<ITableStorage, &IID_ITableStorage,
&LIBID_ASPCOMPONENTSLib>
{

...

BEGIN_COM_MAP(CTableStorage)
    COM_INTERFACE_ENTRY(ITableStorage)
    COM_INTERFACE_ENTRY(IDispatch)
    COM_INTERFACE_ENTRY(ISupportErrorInfo)
END_COM_MAP()

// ITableStorage
public:
    STDMETHOD(Sort)(/*[in]*/ BSTR columnName, /*[in]*/ short direction);
    STDMETHOD(get_numColumns)(/*[out, retval]*/ short *pVal);
    STDMETHOD(get_numRows)(/*[out, retval]*/ short *pVal);
    STDMETHOD(GetColumnName)(/*[in]*/ short columnNum, /*[out, retval]*/ BSTR
*columnName);
    STDMETHOD(GetField)(/*[in]*/ short rowNum, /*[in]*/ BSTR fieldName, /*[out,
retval]*/ BSTR *fieldValue);
    STDMETHOD(ParseCSV)(/*[in]*/ BSTR strCSVData);

    // ISupportsErrorInfo
    STDMETHOD(InterfaceSupportsErrorInfo)(REFIID riid);

protected:
    COLUMN_INDEX_MAP      m_columnIndexMap;
    ROW_VECTOR            m_rows;
};

#endif //__TABLESTORAGE_H_
```

With these changes, your class will support the `ISupportErrorInfo` COM interface. However, the single method we added needs to be implemented, by inserting the following in the source file `TableStorage.cpp`:

```
STDMETHODIMP CTableStorage::InterfaceSupportsErrorInfo(REFIID riid)
{
    static const IID* arr[] =
    {
        &IID_ITableStorage
    };
```

```
        for (int i=0; i < sizeof(arr) / sizeof(arr[0]); i++)
        {
            if (InlineIsEqualGUID(*arr[i],riid))
                return S_OK;
        }
        return S_FALSE;
    }
```

Your class derives from `CComCoClass`, which has a method called `Error`: that is to say the `CTableStorage` class can use all public methods and properties defined in `CComCoClass`. Now that our class supports the error interface, we can use this method. It also you to provide all the parameters of the Error object, including error code, description and help file.

Let's change the `GetField` method to provide a more useful message. Change the end of the method to look like the this:

```
        if ( FAILED( hResult ) )
        {
            wstring    strMessage;
            wchar_t    strRow[4];

            strMessage = L"The field '";
            strMessage += fieldName;
            strMessage += L"' at row '";
            _itow( rowNum, strRow, 10 );
            strMessage += strRow;
            strMessage += L"' does not have a value.";

            Error( strMessage.c_str() );
        }
        return hResult;
```

Now you'll get something like the following error message:

ASPComponents.TableStorage.1 error '80004005'

The field ' Group' at row '1' does not have a value.

/datashaping/componenttest.asp, line 43

Not only do you get the error message we added, but you also get the `ProgId` of the component. When your component supports `ISupportErrorInfo` this information is automatically inserted for you.

Again, it's highly recommended that you put error support in your component early on in development. It will help you debug your component, and it will help users of your component with their development. Of course, if you can't figure out what's wrong from the error message, the next step is to debug the component.

Debugging

Debugging a normal executable program in Visual C++ is straightforward. You can set breakpoints and then run the program in debug mode. With a DLL, you need to do some more work: the C++ debugger has to attach to the process that is supposed to be debugged.

A DLL does not run in its own process – it runs in another process space. Therefore, you have to get the debugger to attach to the process space of the application hosting the DLL. If you are testing from Visual Basic, you need to attach to Visual Basic; if you're testing from ASP, you need to attach to the Web server process. Alternatively, with Visual Basic you can run `VB6.EXE`, open a project that uses your DLL and set breakpoints as normal.

There is a very straightforward way to setup your component for debugging. At the section of code within your component that you want to debug from, add the following line:

```
DebugBreak();
```

When the process hosting your DLL hits this line, it will stop and put up a dialog box telling you a break has been reached, asking if you want to debug the application. You press Cancel to invoke the debugger (I always get this wrong, I assume that OK means to invoke the debugger!). Provided the component is a debug version rather than a release version, when you press Cancel, Visual C++ will start up and place you at the line where you inserted the `DebugBreak()`. From there you can set additional breakpoints, watch variables and do all the other great debugging tricks.

The main problem with this method is that it is intrusive. You're changing the code in order to debug it, and you also have to be careful to avoid leaving stray `DebugBreak()`s around. If a `DebugBreak()` is encountered in production it will pop up a dialog box and lock everyone out of the Web server until OK or Cancel is pressed. That could be disastrous.

If you have used your component in an ASP, made changes and then re-compiled you may get the following error:

```
LINK : fatal error LNK1168: cannot open Debug/ASPComponents.dll for writing
Error executing link.exe.
```

Your server component runs in the process space of the Web server, and when you get this error, it means the server still has a reference to the component. More accurately, the server has a reference to the DLL in which the component is contained, so you need to have it dereference the DLL. Unfortunately to do this you need to start and stop the World Wide Web Service. If, however, your object is being run under Microsoft Transaction Server this process is much easier.

Debugging with COM+

First, make sure the activation property is set to a dedicated server process rather than a library process. This ensures the debugging will attach to the process of the component you are debugging.

In the **Project Settings** property sheet set the executable for the debug session to `dllhost.exe` and for the program arguments put `/ProcessID:` *<your process ID>*:

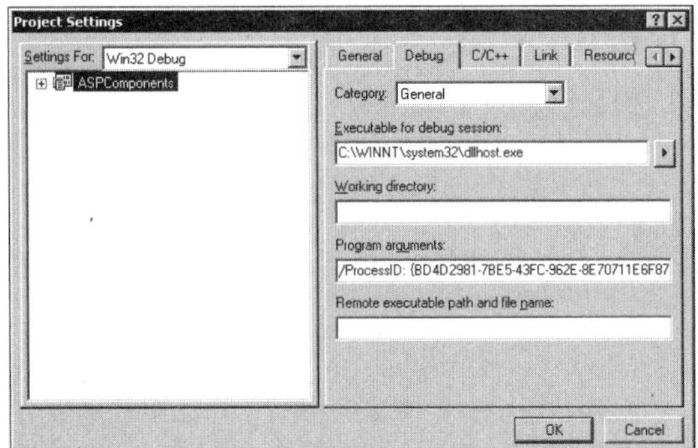

The value for your process ID can be found by right-clicking the application's icon in Component Services Explorer and selecting **Properties**:

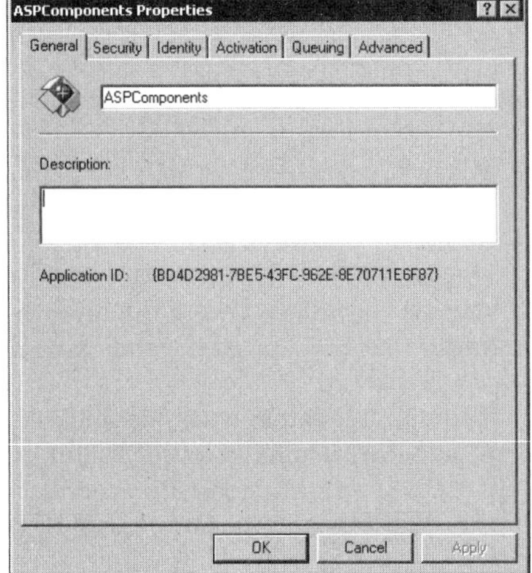

Make sure that the component is not currently in memory by shutting down the server process for the application the component is in. Otherwise you might end up using an instance of the component that the debugger is not attached to. Make sure you build a debug version of your component, set any breakpoints you want and execute the program from the build menu.

This will run the program `dllhost.exe` with the program argument instructing it to load the application that has your component. Since the debugger is attached to the COM+ process, whenever the component is accessed, the debugger has a chance to intercept the call with a breakpoint.

The other great thing about having your component in COM+ is that it will automatically put an entry in the event log if your object fails.

Summary

This chapter has introduced the origins of C++ and set the context of its relevance in developing components for ASP. You've learned about portions of C++, such as STL and ATL, that are valuable tools for creating ASP components. These tools meet the server component design goals of minimizing storage space and minimizing access time. To illustrate how to use them, we walked through creating a generic component that can be used from any application.

An important aspect of the usability of a component is the extent of its error handling. C++ exception handling provides an efficient way of capturing errors within a component. To report errors outside to a calling application, a component needs to support `ISupportErrorInfo`.

In the next chapter, we'll look at the support in Visual C++ for integrating with ASP and COM+. We'll also look at two options for Data Access from C++.

N
W

18

More C++ Component Issues

In the previous chapter we learned the basics of creating COM components in C++. Components created with those concepts are useful for in memory processing of data. However, to make a server component really powerful, it needs to interact and use other services provided with the Microsoft Platform. Specifically, the component should be able to provide data access, interface with COM+ and interact with ASP. This chapter covers the following topics.

- Using the ASP Intrinsic Interfaces
- Interfacing with COM+
- Using ADO with C++
- Using OLE DB Consumer Templates

We'll start by seeing how you can use the ASP intrinsic objects from within your C++ server component.

Interfacing with ASP

The component built in the previous chapter had no idea that it was being used within ASP. This is good if you're trying to create generic components that you want to use from any hosting environment. However, the component would be a lot more useful in your Web application if it had access to the same information that the ASP page does. In addition, it would be useful if your component could perform the same the Web-based interactions as an ASP page.

Well, thanks to the wonderful world of COM, you can do everything from a C++ component. Just as you have various objects available to you in ASP, you can also access them from your server object. Much of the work you do in ASP is through the intrinsic objects: Request, Response, Session, Application and Server. A pointer to any of these objects can be obtained through the `ScriptingContext`. So the trick is getting a pointer to the `ScriptingContext` and asking for whichever ASP intrinsic object you want.

Does that sound like a lot of work to you? Well it isn't, because Visual C++ AppWizard generates the code for you. We're going to "ASP-enable" the component created in the previous chapter. To achieve this you have two choices: you can either generate the components in this chapter and copy and paste the appropriate code into the previous component, or you can start with a fresh component and add in the code we did in the previous chapter. I'm going to take the latter option.

> **A good exercise to try is to create the shell of components using different wizard options and then using `Windiff` to see the extra code generated. `Windiff` is a program that comes with Visual C++.**

So using the `ASPComponents` Visual C++ project we created in the last chapter, insert a new ATL object. Instead of creating a Simple Object, create an ActiveX Server Component and call it `CTableStorage2`.

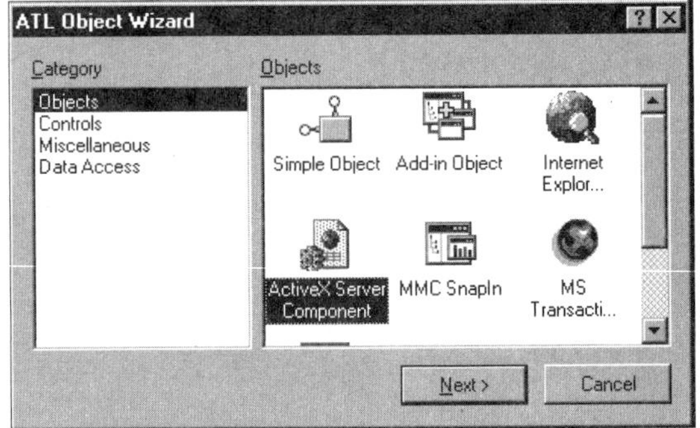

The fundamental difference between the Simple Object Wizard and the ActiveX Server Component Wizard is that the latter includes the ASP property page. In the ASP property page, select only the Response check-box. We're only going to use the Response object in our demonstration, but it's very easy to manually add any other ASP intrinsic object later if you need it.

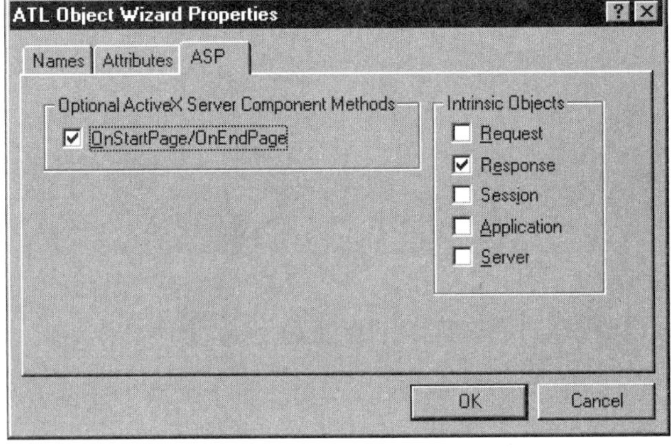

This is a demonstration of the flexibility and efficiency of Visual C++. You choose only the features you want to use, thus reducing the amount of code in your component. Of course, the downside is you need to have code for these features – they are not just part of the programming environment as they are with ASP.

Note that when you uncheck OnStartPage/OnEndPage all the intrinsic objects will be disabled. As we will see, `OnStartPage` must be called in order to obtain the intrinsic objects. The property page could have been constructed to generate `OnStartPage` and `OnEndPage` automatically if an intrinsic object is checked, but I guess it's a reminder to the developer that those dependencies exist.

Let's walk through the code that is generated when you select ActiveX Server Component. If you are ASP-enabling a component you already have, this is the code you need to insert manually.

First, in the file `TableStorage2.h` you will notice a new header file. This contains all the constants and definitions required to use the `ScriptingContext` and ASP intrinsic objects. You should never have to look in this file.

```
#include <asptlb.h>          // Active Server Pages Definitions
```

Note the use of `ScriptingContext` here rather than the more up-to-date `ObjectContext`. The ATL Wizard generated the code to use the `ScriptingContext`, and unless you really know what you're doing, you shouldn't change it.

You will see that two methods have been added: `OnStartPage` and `OnEndPage`. This gives your component a chance to do some work as soon as the ASP page creates it, and as soon as the ASP page is done with it, either through a `Set Object = Nothing` call or if the page has finished. We will look at the details of these methods later.

```
public:
    //Active Server Pages Methods
    STDMETHOD(OnStartPage)(IUnknown* IUnk);
    STDMETHOD(OnEndPage)();
```

There are some member variables added to the class. One is a pointer to the Response object. If we had checked any of the other ASP intrinsic objects there would be pointers declared for them as well. Remember that this is just a declaration of a pointer to the object, it does not actually point to the object yet.

```
private:
    CComPtr<IResponse> m_piResponse;              //Response Object
    BOOL m_bOnStartPageCalled;                    //OnStartPage successful?
```

The other member variable is a Boolean variable indicating whether or not `OnStartPage` was called successfully – we'll see in a moment why this is important. This variable is initialized to `FALSE` in the constructor, which is called when the object is first created. A constructor and destructor in C++ serve the same purpose as the Visual Basic `Class_Initialize` and `Class_Terminate` methods respectively.

```
CTableStorage2()
{
    m_bOnStartPageCalled = FALSE;
}
```

That's it for all the changes to the header file. Let's look at what the AppWizard generated for TableStorage2.cpp. The only code that the Wizard has inserted is the implementation of the methods OnStartPage and OnEndPage. Note that if you're converting the component from the last chapter, you will need to make sure that you have the line #include TableStorage2.h in ASPComponents.cpp.

The main job of OnStartPage is to get the ScriptingContext and get pointers to the ASP intrinsic objects. In this example, there's only code to get the Response Object – again, if we had checked any of the other ASP intrinsic objects, there would be code for getting pointers to them as well. Only if the pointers to ASP intrinsic objects are successfully obtained will m_bOnStartPageCalled be set to TRUE. You use this member variable to check that it is safe to use the ASP intrinsic objects:

```
STDMETHODIMP CTableStorage2::OnStartPage(IUnknown* pUnk)
{
    if(!pUnk)
        return E_POINTER;

    CComPtr<IScriptingContext> spContext;
    HRESULT hr;

    // Get the IScriptingContext Interface
    hr = pUnk->QueryInterface(IID_IScriptingContext, (void **)&spContext);
    if(FAILED(hr))
        return hr;

    // Get Response Object Pointer
    hr = spContext->get_Response(&m_piResponse);
    if(FAILED(hr))
    {
        return hr;
    }


    m_bOnStartPageCalled = TRUE;
    return S_OK;
}
```

After an ASP page is finished processing, OnEndPage is called. At this point it doesn't make sense to have pointers to ASP intrinsic objects, so the interfaces are released and m_bOnStartPageCalled is set to FALSE:

```
STDMETHODIMP CTableStorage2::OnEndPage()
{
    m_bOnStartPageCalled = FALSE;
    // Release all interfaces
    m_piResponse.Release();

    return S_OK;
}
```

Keep in mind that you can put your own code in `OnStartPage` and `OnEndPage` if you have some processing that you want to occur at the beginning and end of the object's useful life within the ASP page.

There is one other difference between a simple component and ActiveX Server Component. The `OnStartPage` and `OnEndPage` methods need to be exposed via ActiveX automation so that they can be called from outside the component. We do this by declaring them in an Interface Definition Language (IDL) file. In this case, there are two lines declaring them in `ASPComponents.idl`:

```
interface ITableStorage2 : IDispatch
{

    //Standard Server Side Component Methods
    HRESULT OnStartPage([in] IUnknown* piUnk);
    HRESULT OnEndPage();
};
```

When you compile your component, the MIDL compiler uses the IDL file to create a type library and marshaling code.

Now we are ready to use the Response object within the component. Let's add a method to use it. In the previous chapter we wrote an ASP program that generated HTML using the data stored in the component. Wouldn't it be great if the component itself generated the HTML table? The advantages that would result from this modification are better performance and encapsulation of the rendering logic.

Encapsulation has many advantages. In the above case of table generation, all the rendering code is centralized in one place, which means that any ASP page can call up the component containing the code and run it. This is obviously better than copying the same code from page to page, or writing new code. Developers can thus concentrate on high-level issues such as data access, rather than figuring out ways of iterating through the data and displaying it in a table. Calling up a component and running precompiled code is also quicker than parsing through the series of complex HTML commands.

The downside to this is that even if minor changes to the table rendering code need to be made, the component has to be recompiled. This puts design constraints on programmers when developing the components, forcing them to think carefully about which parameters they want to set when generating the table. User-modifiable features such as border size or table cell background color should be passed as parameters to the interface methods rather than hard-coded into them. It's up to the developer to ensure that component modification is reduced to a minimum. If, however, the component interface changes, then the ASP pages that use that interface have to be modified.

By this point you should have added the same methods to `ITableStorage2` as `ITableStorage` in the last chapter (e.g. `ParseCSV`, `GetField`, `GetColumnName` etc.). If not, walk through the steps we detailed in the last chapter to add them.

Now add a new method called OutputTable to ITableStorage2 and configure it as in the following dialog box:

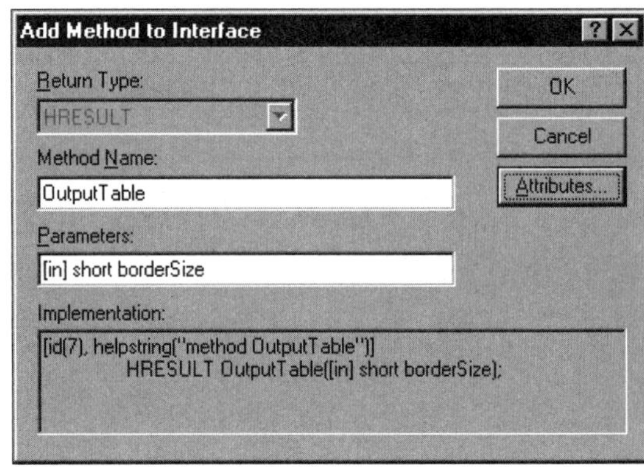

We're keeping the method simple for demonstration purposes by only allowing border size to be configured. It is very easy, though, to add other table attributes such as color and cell spacing. Let's look at the code that makes OutputTable work:

```
STDMETHODIMP CTableStorage2::OutputTable( short borderSize )
{
    HRESULT     hResult = E_FAIL;
    wstring     tempString;
    char        tableString[32];

    if ( (m_bOnStartPageCalled == TRUE) && (m_piResponse != NULL) )
    {
        sprintf( tableString, "<TABLE border=%d><TR>", borderSize );
        m_piResponse->Write( CComVariant( tableString ) );
```

First notice we put some safety checks in by making sure m_bOnStartPageCalled is TRUE and m_piResponse actually contains a pointer. One of the rules in C++ is never to assume anything! If the checks pass then we can use the Response object.

The Write method expects the string as a variant. In C++, to use a variant you actually have to specifically use a variant type. One of the easiest ways to do this is to work with the string as a character type, and then construct a variant using the CComVariant class as we've done here. The next step is to output the table columns:

```
        // Output the tables headers.
        COLUMN_INDEX_MAP::iterator    mapIter = m_columnIndexMap.begin();

        while ( mapIter != m_columnIndexMap.end() )
        {
            tempString = L"<TH>";
            tempString += (*mapIter).first.c_str();
            tempString += L"</TH>";
            m_piResponse->Write( CComVariant( tempString.c_str() ) );

            mapIter++;
        }
        m_piResponse->Write( CComVariant( "</TR>" ) );
```

The column names are stored as the key in the column map. Therefore, we iterate through the column map obtaining the column name and putting it into a table header. The string is converted to a variant as before, and sent to the browser with the `Response` object. Once the columns are output, we move on to the rows:

```
        // Output the rows.
        ROW_VECTOR::iterator        rowIter = m_rows.begin();
        INDEX_FIELD_MAP::iterator   fieldIter;

        while ( rowIter != m_rows.end() )
        {
            m_piResponse->Write( CComVariant( "<TR>" ) );

            mapIter = m_columnIndexMap.begin();

            while ( mapIter != m_columnIndexMap.end() )
            {
                tempString = L"<TD>";

                fieldIter = (*rowIter).find( (*mapIter).second );

                if ( fieldIter != (*rowIter).end() )
                {
                    tempString += (*fieldIter).second.c_str();
                }
```

Each row is an element in the `vector` data structure, so we iterate through `m_rows`. The column data has to correspond to the column heading. Remember from the previous chapter that we used a `map` for the row data to minimize storage space. Therefore, we iterate through each column name to see if a value exists for that particular row. If it does we output it, otherwise we output an empty table cell.

All that's left is to close the HTML tags and increment the iterators:

```
                tempString += L"</TD>";
                m_piResponse->Write( CComVariant( tempString.c_str() ) );

                mapIter++;
            }

            m_piResponse->Write( CComVariant( "</TR>" ) );
            rowIter++;
        }

        m_piResponse->Write( CComVariant( "</TABLE>" ) );

        hResult = S_OK;
    }
    return hResult;
}
```

To use the component, the ASP code would look like the following:

```
<H2>TableStorage C++ Component Test Driver</H2>

<%
    Dim    objTableStorage2
    Dim    csvString

    csvString = "Name, Group, Instrument" & vbNewLine
    csvString = csvString & "Robert Plant,Led Zeppelin,Vocals" & vbNewLine
    csvString = csvString & "Jim Morrison,The Doors,Vocals" & vbNewLine
    csvString = csvString & "Lenny Kravitz,,Everything" & vbNewLine
    csvString = csvString & "Keith Moon,The Who,Drums" & vbNewLine
    csvString = csvString & "Jimi Hendrix,,Guitar & Vocals" & vbNewLine

    Set objTableStorage2 = Server.CreateObject("ASPComponents.TableStorage2")

    objTableStorage2.ParseCSV csvString
    objTableStorage2.Sort "Name", 1
%>

<P>Number for Columns: <%=objTableStorage2.numColumns %></P>
<P>Number for Rows: <%=objTableStorage2.numRows%></P>

<%
    objTableStorage2.OutputTable 1
%>
```

This is very similar to the ASP code in the previous chapter, except instead of iterating through the fields to display the data we just need to call `OutputTable`. The code is cleaner and you get exactly the same result:

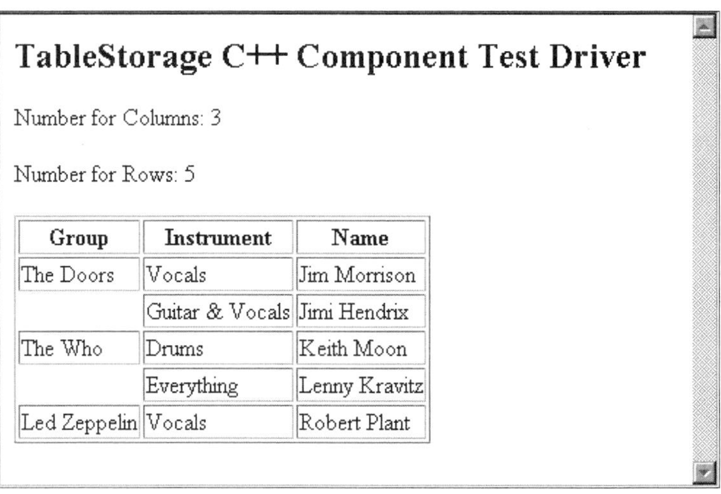

TableStorage C++ Component Test Driver

Number for Columns: 3

Number for Rows: 5

Group	Instrument	Name
The Doors	Vocals	Jim Morrison
	Guitar & Vocals	Jimi Hendrix
The Who	Drums	Keith Moon
	Everything	Lenny Kravitz
Led Zeppelin	Vocals	Robert Plant

Hey wait, that's not 'exactly' the same result – the columns are in a different order. In the C++ code, we're iterating through the columns in a different way from the ASP code. From C++, the columns will be in the order stored in the `map` data structure, which in this case is alphabetically as you can see. On the other hand, ASP code iterates through the columns in the same order that they are stored in – that is 'Name, Group, Instrument' – which is the output produced from the example in the last chapter. If you so wished, you could extend the `OutputTable` method so the user can specify the order of the columns, rather than leaving it up to the code.

Let's summarize what we have just done. A C++ server component is more useful if it can interact with the environment it's in. In this case, we showed how the C++ component can get pointers through COM to the various ASP intrinsic objects. You then have ASP's native functionality available to your component. We only looked at one ASP intrinsic object, but the others work the same way. We're going to continue to see how a C++ server component can interact with its environment by looking at COM+.

Interfacing with COM+

> **It should be noted that the Visual C++ Wizards still refer to MTS and the Visual C++ header files and static libraries still have the old "mtx" in their names. For that reason we will refer to MTS/COM+ in this section and not just to COM+.**

Visual C++ provides MTS/COM+ support in two areas: one for giving support to your project when you create it and the other to use specific components within the project.

First we'll look at giving your project MTS/COM+ support. When you compile and link your project, it becomes a DLL or EXE. To use the services of MTS/COM+ within the project you need to link in the appropriate library. The Visual C++ AppWizard can do this for you.

When you first created the project you may have noticed a Support MTS checkbox:

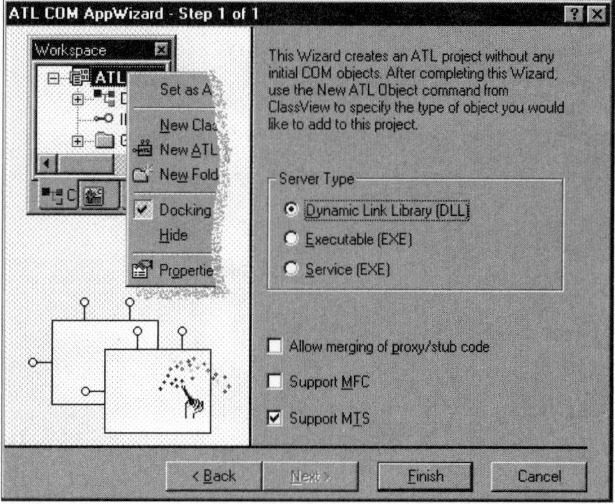

If the checkbox is checked no extra code is generated, but your project is "COM+-enabled" – the Wizard changes the project settings. Specifically, it adds the following libraries to the link line: `mtx.lib`, `mtxguid.lib` and `delayimp.lib`. So if you did not check the above check box, you can still "COM+-enable" your existing component by adding these filenames to the link line as follows:

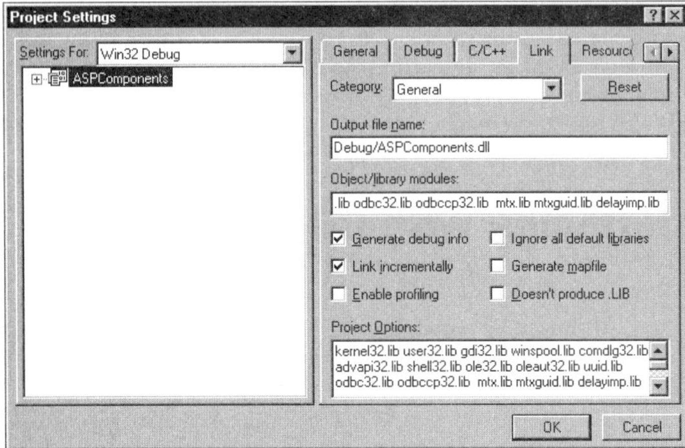

The alternative is to create a COM+-enabled component. So select MS Transaction Server Component when you add a new ATL component to your project:

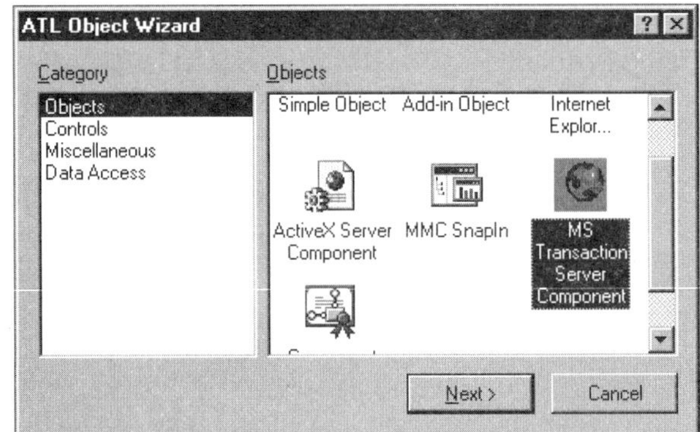

When you click on the property page you will see the following:

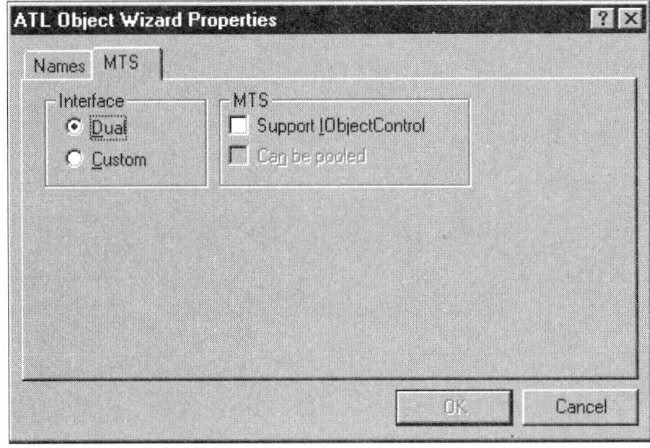

On creating the MTS/COM+ object, the Wizard does add some code to your project, so let's look at the additional code that is generated with this configuration.

First, in the header file of your new component you'll see that an include file has been added:

```
#include <mtx.h>
```

Just like the include file for ASP intrinsic objects, this file has the constants and definitions for using MTS/COM+ components within your C++ component. There is only one other change to the header file of the component:

```
DECLARE_NOT_AGGREGATABLE(CTableStorage2)
```

You cannot use an MTS/COM+ object as part of an aggregate of other objects. Therefore code is inserted to prevent this.

And that's it! As you can see, it's easy to COM+-enable your component if you didn't originally use the AppWizard to create it.

Now, if you decide to choose support for `IObjectControl`, you will have the following additional code inserted into your project. In the header file of the component, there are the following differences.

First, the component now inherits from the `IObjectControl` interface. This means that the component must implement methods defined by that interface.

```
class ATL_NO_VTABLE CTableStorage2 :
    public CComObjectRootEx<CComSingleThreadModel>,
    public CComCoClass<CTableStorage2, &CLSID_TableStorage2>,
    public ISupportErrorInfo,
    public IObjectControl,
    public IDispatchImpl<ITableStorage2, &IID_ITableStorage2,
                                                &LIBID_ASPCOMPONENTSLib>
```

Sure enough the Wizard declares the `IObjectControl` methods for you, as well as a pointer to the ObjectContext:

```
// IObjectControl
public:
    STDMETHOD(Activate)();
    STDMETHOD_(BOOL, CanBePooled)();
    STDMETHOD_(void, Deactivate)();

    CComPtr<IObjectContext> m_spObjectContext;
```

The Wizard implements the methods in the source file. The `Activate` method is called when the object is first used, and it automatically gets a pointer to the ObjectContext for you:

```
HRESULT CTableStorage2::Activate()
{
    HRESULT hr = GetObjectContext(&m_spObjectContext);
    if (SUCCEEDED(hr))
        return S_OK;
    return hr;
}
```

If you selected IObjectCocntrol support but not object pooling, the CanBePooled method will return FALSE:

```
BOOL CTableStorage2::CanBePooled()
{
    return FALSE;
}
```

We will discuss using object pooling in more detail later on.

Finally, when the object is no longer used it releases the reference to the ObjectContext:

```
void CTableStorage2::Deactivate()
{
    m_spObjectContext.Release();
}
```

There are many MTS/COM+ interfaces available to use from your server component. As well as IObjectControl, we'll examine the IObjectContext interface as well.

Transactions with IObjectContext

Each MTS/COM+ object has a context associated with it. The context is the state implicitly associated with the object, and it contains information such as the object's execution environment and the transaction that the object is participating in. The IObjectContext interface gives you access to the object's context.

With IObjectContext you can perform the following:

- Declare work complete
- Disallow temporary or permanent transaction commits
- Start new MTS/COM+ objects within the current transaction scope
- Check caller roles
- Check security
- Check on transaction state

As you saw in the previous section your component at this point already has a reference to the IObjectContext interface. We are going to implement a Clear method that removes all data from the component. Add a new method to the ITableStorage2 interface called Clear(), and don't give it any parameters. Then fill out the body of the method with the following:

```
STDMETHODIMP CTableStorage2::Clear()
{
    m_rows.clear();
    m_columnIndexMap.clear();
```

```
        if ( m_spObjectContext != NULL )
        {
            m_spObjectContext->SetComplete();
        }

        return S_OK;
    }
```

The purpose of this method is to remove all data from the component. Notice that we check to see if the ObjectContext reference actually exists. If someone wants to use your component outside of COM+ this pointer will not a have a value and will cause your component to crash if it's referenced. In this example we call the `SetComplete` method to tell COM+, "we are not holding state anymore and you can deactivate me if you wish".

Object Pooling with IObjectControl

The `IObjectControl` interface is used for object pooling, which can increase the performance of your application. A pooled object is not truly destroyed when it goes out of scope – rather it is put into a deactivated state. When a request is made for that type of object, the previous one can be used again – that is the component is recycled. The reason there is a performance increase is because not as much work needs to be performed when an object is deactivated, since it isn't completely destroyed. Similarly, not as much work is required to activate an object, since a deactivated one can be used.

Object pooling can be enabled from the MTS tab of the ATL Object Wizard properties box, during the creation of the MTS/COM+ object:

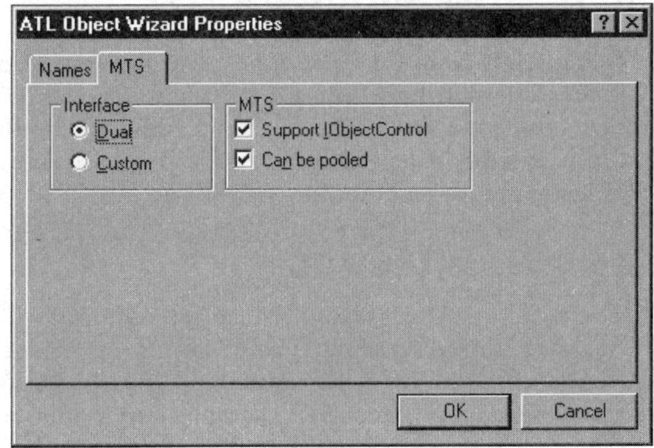

Note that the Can be pooled option is only enabled when the Support IObjectControl box is checked. Alternatively, you can change the return value of the `CanBePooled` method to `TRUE`:

```
    BOOL CTableStorage2::CanBePooled()
    {
        return TRUE;
    }
```

That's all you need to do to enable object pooling.

We have now seen how a component can interact with both ASP and COM+. The only missing capability our component needs is the ability to access persistent data – which we will look at next.

Data Access

Server components are often used to implement the business rules in a three-tier application, that is they are able to interact with databases. For data access from C++ you have two choices: ADO and OLE DB consumer templates. We've already discussed Universal Data Access (UDA) and the roles of ADO and OLE DB within it in Chapter 12.

ADO from C++ is the very same ADO you are familiar with from ASP or Visual Basic. The exact same ADO COM objects are used (such as ADODB.Recordset), you are just creating and using the ADO COM objects from a different language. However, it must be noted that there are no Visual C++ wizards for using ADO. This means you have to write all the implementation code yourself. Not only is this a manual process, but it also increases the risk of introducing errors into the code, so be careful. However, you do have the complete ADO object model available to you from C++.

An **OLE DB consumer** is something that uses the services of an OLE DB provider for accessing data. ADO is itself an example of an OLE DB consumer. From C++, you can create an application as an OLE DB consumer, thus skipping the ADO layer altogether. There are Visual C++ wizards for creating and using OLE DB consumers. This means you can walk through a wizard pointing to the database and tables you want to access, and the code will automatically be generated for you. However, since your consumer code is directed towards a specific database it may not be as flexible as using ADO.

Using ADO with C++

Using ADO from C++ combines two skill sets: understanding the ADO object model and using COM objects from within C++. You are probably already familiar with the ADO object model – that's the good news. The bad news is that currently there are no C++ class libraries or template libraries supporting ADO. Since ADO is built on COM, you use ADO as you would any other COM objects. Let's look at the steps involved.

Setting Up to Use ADO

The easiest way to use a COM component in C++ is to use the #import keyword to import the type library of the component. The #import directive generates thin C++ classes around the ADO type library and lets you manipulate the ADO objects and interfaces in a syntax close to that of VBScript and Visual Basic. Most ADO samples are written using VBScript, and #import lets you translate them to C++ with greater ease than if you tried to use ADO without the wrapper classes.

When using #import a no_namespace attribute can be used so the ADO type library contents do not have to be scoped. Unfortunately, this causes a name collision with EOF. Luckily there is another attribute called rename for problems exactly like this. So to import the ADO type library add the following lines to TableStorage2.cpp:

```
// Include the ADO type library.
#import "c:\Program Files\Common Files\System\ADO\msado15.dll" \
    no_namespace \
    rename("EOF", "adoEOF")
#include <stdio.h>
```

This line will generate an `msado15.tlh` file and an `msado15.tli` file. The `msado15.tlh` file contains forward references, smart pointer declarations and `typeinfo` declarations. The `msado15.tli` file contains implementations of compiler-generated member functions. Both files are instructive to look at, and show what is now available to you from the type library. For instance, from the `msado15.tlh` file you'll see the following smart pointer declaration for an ADO recordset:

```
_COM_SMARTPTR_TYPEDEF(_Recordset, __uuidof(_Recordset));
```

In our example later we will see how this smart pointer can then be used in code. There are also some enumerations declared in `msado15.tlh`, making ADO easier to use. Here's an example of an enumeration for cursor location:

```
enum CursorLocationEnum
{
    adUseNone = 1,
    adUseServer = 2,
    adUseClient = 3,
    adUseClientBatch = 3
};
```

As illustrated, `#import` makes using ADO more enjoyable because it automatically creates wrapper classes and type information from the type library. However, there is still the tedious job for C++ programmers of converting `VARIANT` data types returned from ADO to C/C++ data types. ADO 2.0 and Visual C++ 6.0 help solve this problem with the addition of ADO VC++ Extensions. We won't be looking at the ADO Visual C++ Extensions in this chapter – see the Visual C++ documentation for how to use them.

Also add the following macro. I like using it with ADO because it makes the code easier to read, by reducing to a minimum the amount of nested code:

```
#define SAFE_CALL( expression ) { HRESULT hr; if ( FAILED(hr=expression) ) \
    _com_issue_error( hr ); }
```

By importing the type library we can now use all of the ADO objects. Let's see how we read and write using ADO from C++. We will assume a simple database exists that looks like this.

Musicians : Table

Name	Group	Instrument
Ozzy Ozbourne	Black Sabbath	Vocals
Jim Morrison	The Doors	Vocals
Jimi Hendrix		Guitar & Vocals
Keith Moon	The Who	Drums
Lenny Kravitz		Everything
Robert Plant	Led Zeppelin	Vocals

Record: 7 of 7

We will also assume there is an ODBC connection named `MusicianDSN` set up for the database.

Reading from the Database

Start by adding a `Read` method to `ITableStorage2`. This method is going to read records from the database and insert them into the STL data structures. It takes the DSN name, username and password. Note that in the dialog box the parameters are repeated in the Implementation text box, so if you want to see a parameter and can't because it's clipped, look in the implementation.

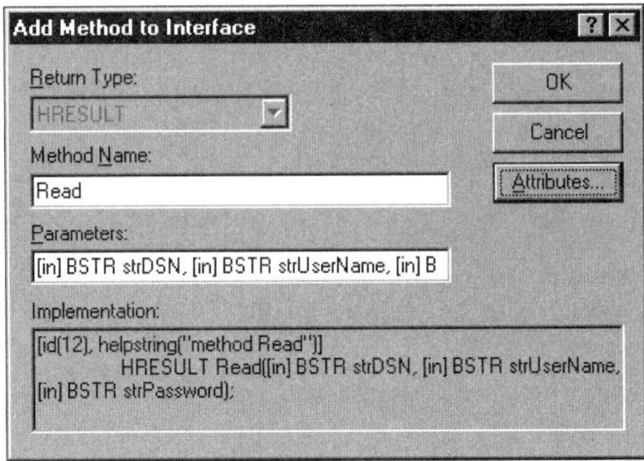

Let's walk through the implementation of the method:

```
STDMETHODIMP CTableStorage2::Read (BSTR strDSN, BSTR strUserName, BSTR
                                                       strPassword)
{
   HRESULT            hResult = S_OK;
   _ConnectionPtr     pConn( "ADODB.Connection" );  // ADO Connection object
   _RecordsetPtr      pRS("ADODB.Recordset");       // ADO Recordset object
   INDEX_FIELD_MAP    fieldMap;
   int                fieldIndex;
   wstring            fieldName;
   wstring            fieldValue;
   CComBSTR           varFieldValue;
```

First, the variables used in the method are declared. Notice how ATL smart pointers are used to create the ADO Connection and Recordset objects. We are going to use exception handling for trapping errors in the code, and therefore we start a `try` block. As well, any ADO calls are wrapped with the `SAFE_CALL` macro we declared earlier. This will throw an exception if any of the method calls return a value that indicates failure:

```
   try
   {
      // Establish a connection.
      SAFE_CALL( pConn->Open( strDSN, strUserName, strPassword, 0 ) );
```

First a connection to the database is opened. This connection is then used in the `Open` method of the Recordset object:

```
      // Open the table.
      SAFE_CALL( pRS->Open( "Musicians", pConn.GetInterfacePtr(),
                           adOpenDynamic, adLockOptimistic, adCmdTable) );
```

If we are successful to this point, we can iterate through the records in the database. First we want to make sure there is currently no data in memory:

```
        // Make sure there is no data around.
        m_rows.clear();
        m_columnIndexMap.clear();

        pRS->MoveFirst();
```

Next we need to set the column names in the STL data structure:

```
        // Create the columns first.
        for ( fieldIndex = 0; fieldIndex < pRS->Fields->Count; fieldIndex++ )
        {
            fieldName = pRS->Fields->Item[CComVariant(fieldIndex)]->Name;
            m_columnIndexMap[fieldName.c_str()] = m_columnIndexMap.size();
        }
```

We are now ready to copy data from the database to our in-memory STL data structures. We iterate through the recordset until we hit EOF. Note that a field is only inserted if it actually has a value, which saves memory:

```
        // Add data to the rows.
        while ( !pRS->adoEOF )
        {
            // Set the field values.
            for(fieldIndex = 0; fieldIndex < pRS->Fields->Count; fieldIndex++)
            {
                varValue = pRS->Fields->Item[CComVariant(fieldIndex)]->Value;

                if ( varValue.vt == VT_BSTR )
                {
                    fieldValue = _bstr_t( varValue.bstrVal );

                    if ( fieldValue.length() > 0 )
                    {
                        fieldMap[fieldIndex] = fieldValue.c_str();
                    }
                }
            }

            m_rows.push_back( fieldMap );
            fieldMap.clear();

            pRS->MoveNext();
        }

        pRS->Close();
        pConn->Close();
    }
```

Up to this point everything is in the `try` block. If any error occurs the program flow goes to the `catch` block. The details of the error message are contained in the `_com_error` variable, and I've added a helper function that will format the error details into a string. We then pass this error string to `Error` which will make it available as the `Description` property of the Error object to the client.

```
    catch ( _com_error &theErr )
    {
        string          resultMessage;

        FormatErrorMessage( theErr, resultMessage );

        Error( resultMessage.c_str() );
        hResult = E_FAIL;
    }

    return hResult;
}
```

The `FormatErrorMessage` method looks like this:

```
void CTableStorage2::FormatErrorMessage(_com_error &theErr,
                                                    string &strMessage )
{
    char          tempBuffer[64];

    strMessage =  "COM Error object\n";
    sprintf( tempBuffer, "\tCode = %0x1x\n", theErr.Error() );
    strMessage += tempBuffer;

    _bstr_t bstrDescription(theErr.Description());
    strMessage += "Description = ";
    strMessage += (LPCSTR)bstrDescription;
    strMessage += "\n";
}
```

Now that we know how to read data from a database, let's learn how to write data to it.

Writing to the Database

Add the following method to `ITableStorage2`. It will take the information in the STL data structure and write them to a database.

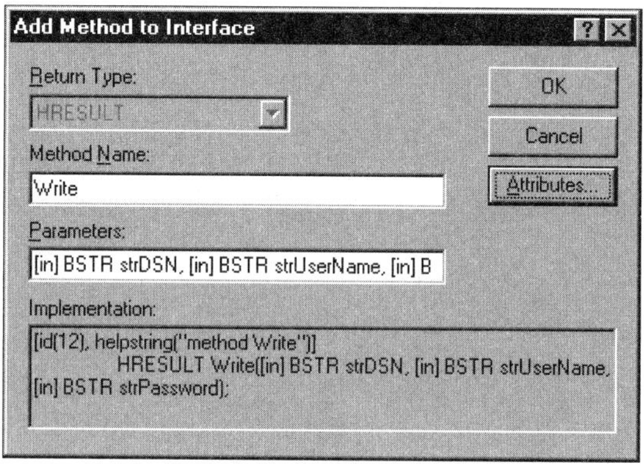

Let's look at the code for writing to the database using ADO:

```
STDMETHODIMP CTableStorage2::Write (BSTR strDSN, BSTR strUserName, BSTR
                                                                strPassword)
{
    HRESULT           hResult = S_OK;
    _ConnectionPtr    pConn( "ADODB.Connection" );
    _RecordsetPtr     pRS("ADODB.Recordset");
```

As with the Read method shown above, we declare some ADO objects. A connection is established to the database and the table is opened:

```
    try
    {
        // Establish a connection.
        SAFE_CALL( pConn->Open( strDSN, strUserName, strPassword, 0 ) );

        // Open the table.
        SAFE_CALL( pRS->Open( "Musicians", pConn.GetInterfacePtr(),
                              adOpenDynamic, adLockOptimistic, adCmdTable) );
```

At this point we are ready to write to the database. We iterated through the STL data structures in similar fashion to how we did earlier with the OutputTable method:

```
        // Output the rows.
        ROW_VECTOR::iterator          rowIter = m_rows.begin();
        INDEX_FIELD_MAP::iterator     fieldIter;
        COLUMN_INDEX_MAP::iterator     mapIter;

        while ( rowIter != m_rows.end() )
        {
            pRS->AddNew();

            mapIter = m_columnIndexMap.begin();

            // Iterate through the column names.
            while ( mapIter != m_columnIndexMap.end() )
            {
                fieldIter = (*rowIter).find( (*mapIter).second );

                // If the field has a value, add it to the database.
                if ( fieldIter != (*rowIter).end() )
                {
                    pRS->Fields->GetItem((*mapIter).first.c_str())->Value =
                        (*fieldIter).second.c_str();

                }
                mapIter++;
            }
            pRS->Update();
            rowIter++;
        }
        pRS->Close();
        pConn->Close();
    }
```

The `catch` block is exactly the same as in the `Read` method so it's not been repeated.

You should recognize the calls to ADO such as `AddNew` and `Update`, but you'll notice a couple of differences in the way they are implemented. For instance, you cannot directly use the default ADO methods. In VB you might use the following to set a field value:

```
objRS( "Name" ) = "Jimi Hendrix"
```

However, in C++ you must fully expand the method calls:

```
pRS->Fields->GetItem( "Name" )->Value = "Jimi Hendrix"
```

The other difference is that C++ does not support `Variants` very well. The above code doesn't look too bad, but I have cheated and made all the data types strings. If you had a mix of data types the code would become even messier. We will see how OLE DB consumer templates make your code cleaner.

OLE DB Consumer Templates

OLE DB consumer templates are a relatively new way to perform data access with C++. They were introduced in the Visual C++ 6.0 box as part of ATL 3.0. As mentioned in the last chapter, C++ functionality is extended through the use of libraries, and the OLE DB consumer templates library has been specifically designed for performing data access through OLE DB. This library provides:

- Access to OLE DB features
- Integration with ATL and MFC
- Binding model for database parameters and columns
- Native C/C++ data types for OLE DB programming

As well, Visual C++ has an AppWizard that generates basic OLE DB consumer code for you.

Creating an OLE DB Consumer

You have to already have your data source set up before you can create your OLE DB consumer. For our purpose we'll use the very same Access database that we used for the ADO example. So, using the ATL Object Wizard, add a new ATL object as you have done before. This time however, choose the Data Access category and select Consumer.

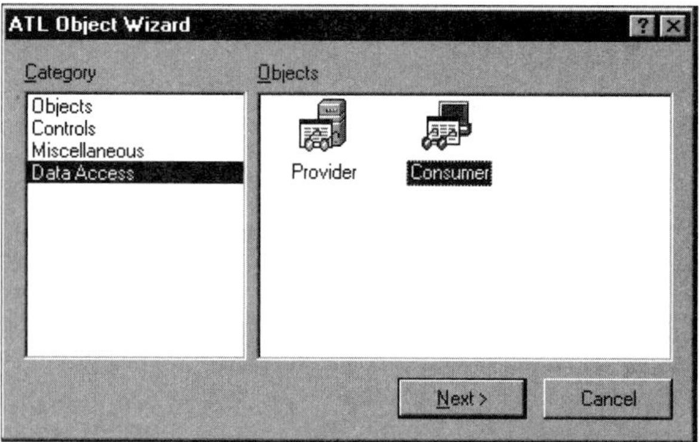

After pressing Next> you are asked for which OLE DB provider you want to use. Since I am using an ODBC driver, I need the Microsoft OLE DB Provider for ODBC Drivers.

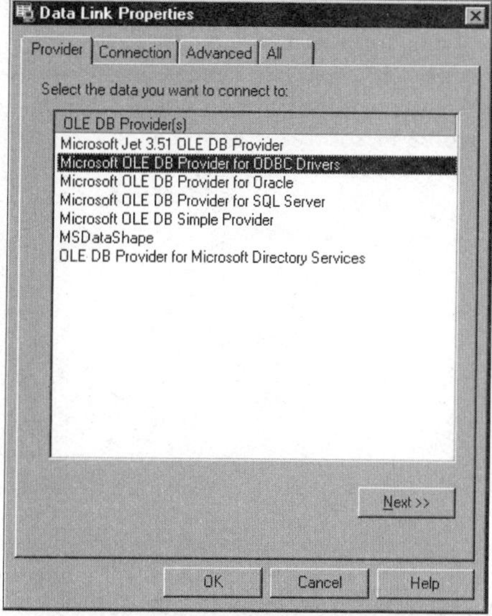

The name of the data source I'm using is `MusicianDSN` and I don't have a user name or password, although you could specify a username and password if your database requires them.

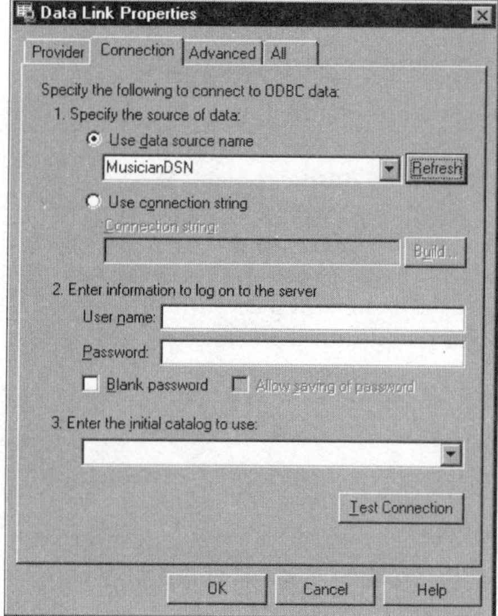

After pressing OK, you choose which table you want to use from your database.

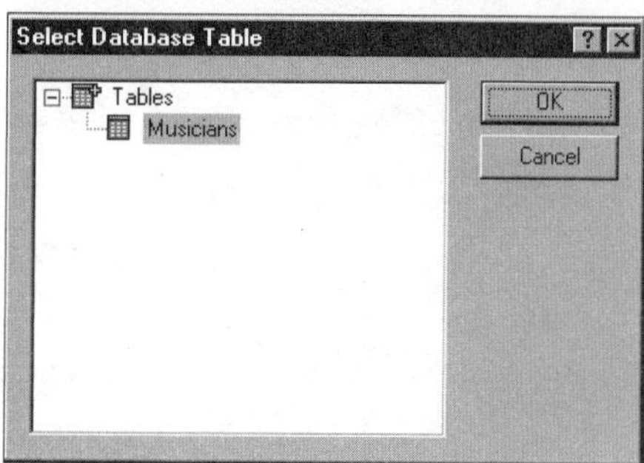

And after pressing OK again, the Wizard will automatically pick some names for you – you can change them if you want. For this example we're going to add records, so check the Insert box in the Support section.

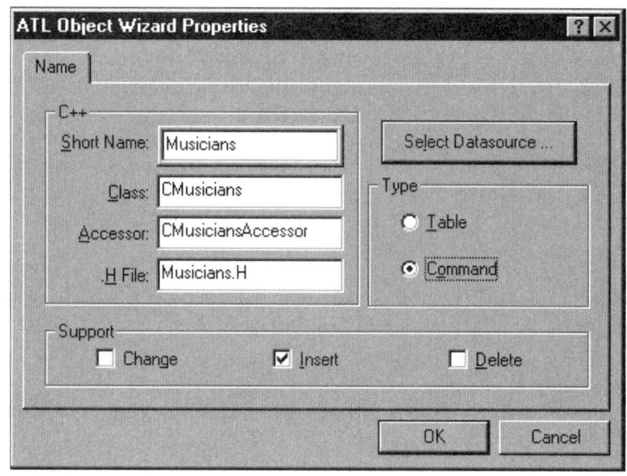

When you press OK, the Wizard will generate two classes: `CMusiciansAccessor` and `CMusicians`. These classes do all the hard work for us and hide a lot of the stuff like data type conversion that we had to do manually with ADO. We will only directly use `CMusicians`, as we will see in the next section.

Reading from the Database

Let's add a new method to `ITableStorage2` to read using our new OLE DB Consumer class. We aren't going to provide any parameters to `Read2` – the ATL Object Wizard has already hard-coded the data source name, user name and password (if you supplied them) into the `CMusicians` class.

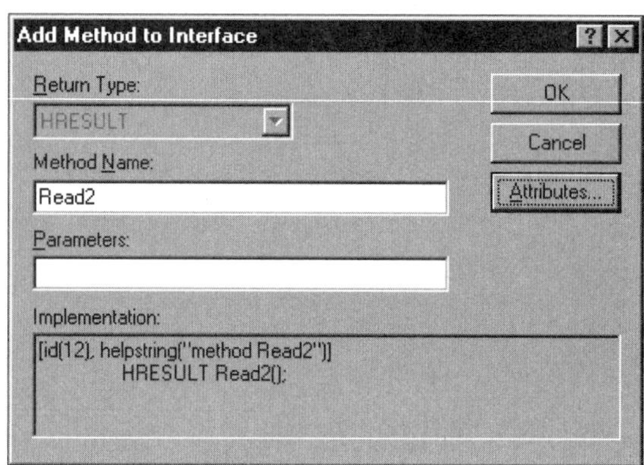

The code for the OLE DB consumer template version of the `Read2` method is much easier to follow than the ADO version:

```
STDMETHODIMP CTableStorage2::Read2()
{
    HRESULT           hResult = S_OK;
    CMusicians        theMusicians;
    INDEX_FIELD_MAP   fieldMap;

    theMusicians.Open();
```

If you haven't already done this already, include the file `Musicians.h` at the top of `TableStorage2.cpp`.

Most of the work is performed by the theMusicians object. When Open is called, a connection to the database is created and the Musicians table is opened. Next we set up the data structures. The column name map has to be manually created, which we do here:

```
    // Make sure there is not any data around.
    m_rows.clear();
    m_columnIndexMap.clear();

    // Create the columns first.
    m_columnIndexMap[L"Name"] = 0;
    m_columnIndexMap[L"Group"] = 1;
    m_columnIndexMap[L"Instrument"] = 2;
```

Next we iterate through the records. Note that with an OLE DB consumer template, instead of checking an EOF property we check the return value of MoveNext to see when we are at the end of the records. The member variables of the theMusicians object are automatically populated when MoveNext is called. Note that ClearRecord should be called before reading the next record, otherwise data from the previous record could be carried over into the next record if it has fields with NULL values:

```
    // Add data to the rows.
    while ( theMusicians.MoveNext() == S_OK )
    {
        // Set the field values.
        fieldMap[0] = _bstr_t( theMusicians.m_Name );
        fieldMap[1] = _bstr_t( theMusicians.m_Group );
        fieldMap[2] = _bstr_t( theMusicians.m_Instrument );

        m_rows.push_back( fieldMap );
        fieldMap.clear();
        theMusicians.ClearRecord();
    }

    theMusicians.Close();

    return hResult;
}
```

You'll see that the code is much cleaner to read than the corresponding code in the ADO example. Let's see if the same is true for writing records.

Writing to the Database

Add a new method to ITableStorage2 and call it Write2. Again, the database configuration information is already hard-coded in the CMusicians class, so we don't pass any parameter to Write2.

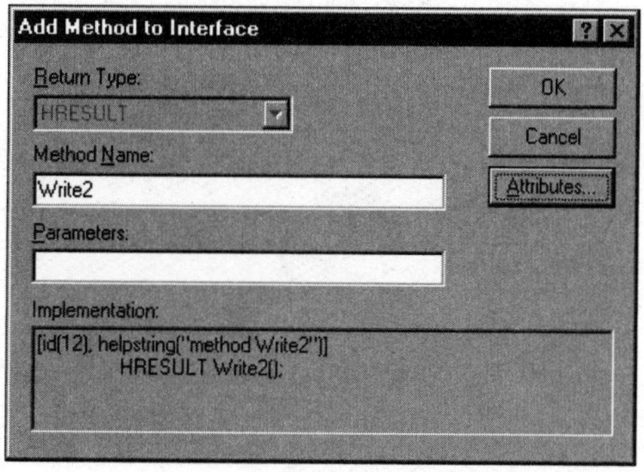

The code itself starts similar to `Read2`, and the object `theMusicians` does much of the work. We first call `Open` to connect to the database and table. To put a record in the database we populate the member variables and call `Insert`. For a new record we call `ClearRecord` to make sure there is no data hanging around from a previous record:

```
STDMETHODIMP CTableStorage2::Write2()
{
    HRESULT     hResult = S_OK;
    CMusicians     theMusicians;
    hResult = theMusicians.Open();

    // Output the rows.
    ROW_VECTOR::iterator     rowIter = m_rows.begin();

    while ( rowIter != m_rows.end() )
    {
        theMusicians.ClearRecord();

        CopyValue( theMusicians.m_Name, rowIter, L"Name" );
        CopyValue( theMusicians.m_Group, rowIter, L"Group" );
        CopyValue( theMusicians.m_Instrument, rowIter, L"Instrument" );

        theMusicians.Insert();
        rowIter++;
    }

    theMusicians.Close();

    return hResult;
}
```

You will notice I've made use of a helper method called `CopyValue`. Finding the field value in a record is a repetitive task, so creating a method to do it reduces the amount of code. This method looks like this:

```
void CTableStorage2::CopyValue( char *pBuffer, ROW_VECTOR::iterator &rowIter,
                                                              wchar_t *pFieldName )
{
    INDEX_FIELD_MAP::iterator    fieldIter;
    COLUMN_INDEX_MAP::iterator   mapIter;

    mapIter = m_columnIndexMap.find( pFieldName );
    fieldIter = (*rowIter).find( (*mapIter).second );

    // If the field has a value, add it to the database.
    if ( fieldIter != (*rowIter).end() )
    {
        USES_CONVERSION;
        strcpy( pBuffer, W2A( (*fieldIter).second.c_str()) );
    }
}
```

Which to Use: ADO or OLE DB Consumer Templates?

When you are faced with Data Access you will have to decide between ADO and OLE DB consumer templates. With ADO you can reuse your knowledge of the ADO object model. As well, it provides a bit more flexibility in that it is easier to change your code. However, ADO does not support binding to C++ data types very well, and there is no additional library or AppWizard support in Visual C++.

With OLE DB consumer templates you get both library and AppWizard support from Visual C++. This means that Visual C++ provides the basic structure of your project, and so you are able to write code faster and have less chance of introducing errors into your code. The disadvantage is you have to learn a new API for data access. However, I think that this is worth the effort if you intend to write a lot of components that require data access.

Summary

In this chapter we have taken a simple C++ server component and made it much more powerful. We have seen how you can have access to the ASP intrinsic objects. We also saw how to get access to various COM+ interfaces. Data Access was demonstrated in two ways. The ADO object model can be used from C++ but required a lot of data type conversion. The ATL Object Wizard will create an OLE DB consumer for you producing cleaner, but less flexible, code than ADO.

With all these tools in hand, you have a greater number of options when designing the architecture of your Web-based application.

N
W

19

ASP and Transacted Web Applications

In many large, mission critical applications, large numbers of tasks are performed every second. More often than not these tasks are often grouped together to accomplish a business requirement, called a **transaction**. But what happens if one task is carried out successfully and then encounters an error on the second or third related task? This error will most likely leave the system in an *inconsistent state*. This is where transaction processing becomes very important and can save the system from this inconsistent state.

Microsoft's first solution to transaction processing was bundled into a technology called **Microsoft Transaction Server (MTS)**, and now with the release of Windows 2000, Microsoft has continued to improve MTS, which has now formed part of COM+ or Component Services.

This chapter will look at the transactional features of Component Services, and see how they can be used to support transactions in applications developed on IIS.

Specifically, we will examine:

- What transaction processing is
- Why we need transaction processing
- How transaction processing works in COM+
- Transactional ASP Pages

First of all, let's take a look at what transaction processing is.

What is Transaction Processing?

Throughout this book you've been introduced to concepts involving **transaction processing**, but you may still be wondering what it really is. Transaction processing has been around since the mainframe days. You may have heard of, or have even used, products such as CICS, Tuxedo, or TopEnd. These are all examples of transaction processing systems, which provide transaction services to applications.

In order to discuss transaction processing, we must first define what a **transaction** actually is.

> **A transaction is an atomic unit of work that either fails or succeeds as a whole.**

There is no such thing as the partial completion of a transaction. Since a transaction can be made up of multiple tasks, each task in the transaction must succeed for the transaction as a *whole* to be successful. If any one part of the transaction fails, then the *entire* transaction fails.

When a transaction fails, the system returns everything back to the state it was in before the transaction was started. This process of undoing any changes is known as a **rollback**. For example, if a transaction updates two tables and fails on the third update, the system needs to "roll back" the first two updates and return itself back to its *original* state.

Maintaining Application Integrity

A critical part of any application is to ensure that any operations it performs are performed correctly. If an application were to only partially complete an operation, then the data of the application, and possibly the system, would be *inconsistent.*

For example, let's look at the potential problem of a banking application that transfers money from one account to another. If you were to transfer money out of one account, and then an error occurs before the money reached your other account, the data for the application would not be correct and would lose its **integrity** – not to mention that your money would officially cease to exist.

There are two ways to combat this:

- In the traditional programming model, the developer must anticipate any way that the operation could fail. For any point of failure, the developer must then add support to return the application to the state it was in before the operation was started. In other words, the developer has to add the code to support a *rollback* (undo) of the operation from any point that it could fail.
- The other, and much easier way, is for the operation to take place within the environment of a **transaction processing system**. The job of the transaction processing system would be to ensure that the entire transaction completes successfully or does nothing at all. If all of the tasks are completed successfully then the changes in the application are *committed* to the system, and the system can proceed to the next transaction or task. If any part of the operation does not complete successfully, which would leave the system in an invalid state, the system will rollback the changes and put the application back into its original state.

The power of the transaction processing system is that the knowledge to perform these operations is *embedded* in the system itself. The developer does not have to write code for the rollback, all the developer is required to do is inform the system if the tasks were successful. The transaction processing system takes care of the rest!

Another benefit of a transaction processing system that aids developers in building complex solutions are the ACID properties.

ACID Properties

When a transaction processing system creates a transaction, it will ensure that the transaction will have certain *characteristics*. The developers of the components that comprise the transaction are assured that these characteristics are in place – they do not need to manage these characteristics themselves. These characteristics are known as the **ACID properties**.

ACID is an acronym for:

- Atomicity
- Consistency
- Isolation
- Durability

Atomicity

The **atomicity** property identifies that the transaction is either fully completed, or not at all. Any updates a transaction might perform on a system are completed in their *entirety*. If for any reason an error occurs and the transaction is unable to complete all of its tasks, the system is returned to the state it was in before the transaction even started.

Let's return back to our bank example of transferring money from one account to another. If any errors are encountered during the process of transferring the money, the *entire* transaction is rolled back. The only way the transaction will be written to disk and the changes made permanent is if *all* parts of the transaction are successful.

To provide the ability to rollback or undo uncommitted changes, many data sources implement a logging mechanism. For example, SQL Server uses a write-ahead transaction log where changes are written to the log before they are applied or committed to the actual data pages. However, other data sources are not relational database management systems (RDBMS), and they manage uncommitted transactions completely differently. As long as the data source is able to undo any uncommitted changes if a transaction is rolled back, the technique used by a data source for managing transactions doesn't really matter.

Consistency

A transaction enforces **consistency** in the system's integrity by ensuring that at the end of any transaction the system is in a *valid state*. If the transaction completes successfully, then all changes to the system will have been properly made, and the system will be in a valid state. If any error occurs in a transaction, then any changes already made will be automatically rolled back, and the system will be returned to its original state. Since the system is assumed to be in a consistent state when the transaction was started, it will once again be in a consistent state.

Let's return to the bank example; before the accounts are altered and the money is transferred, the accounts are known to be in a valid state. If the transaction completes successfully, and the transaction is committed, then the accounts are now in a new, yet valid, state. If an error occurs the transaction will abort and return the accounts to their last known valid state.

Remember, a transaction is not responsible for enforcing data integrity, but instead is only responsible for ensuring that data is returned to a consistent state after the transaction is either committed or aborted. The burden of understanding data integrity rules, and possibly writing code to enforce them, usually falls on the shoulders of the developer who is creating the business components, so be prepared.

> *Transactions must also maintain data consistency and integrity when multiple concurrent users are accessing and modifying the same data, a concept that goes hand-in-hand with the next ACID property, isolation.*

Isolation

Transactions are performed in **isolation**, which makes them appear to be the only action that the system is executing at a given time. If there are two transactions, both performing the same function, which are running at the same time, transaction isolation will ensure that each transaction thinks it has exclusive use of the system.

> *This property is sometimes referred to as* ***serializability*** *because in order to prevent one transaction's operations from interfering with another's, requests must be serialized or sequenced so that only one request for the same data is serviced at a time.*

This is important, in that as the transaction is being executed, the state of the system may not be consistent. The transaction ensures that the system remains consistent after the transaction ends, but during an individual transaction, this may not be the case. If a transaction were not running in isolation, it could access data from the system that may not be consistent. By providing transaction isolation, this is prevented from happening.

In our bank example this means that other processes and transaction within the system will not see any of the changes made from our transaction, until it entirely completed. This is very important in case of an abort. If another process were to base a decision on the balance of an account after we remove the money from it, it would most likely be an invalid decision is the transaction was to abort. This is why the changes made by a transaction must not be visible to other parts of the system until the transaction is completed.

Isolation not only guarantees that multiple transactions cannot modify the same data at the same time, but also guarantees that changes caused by one transaction's operations will not be seen by another transaction until the changes are either committed or aborted. Concurrent transactions will be unaware of each other's partial and inconsistent changes. This means that all requests to modify or read data already involved in a transaction are blocked until the transaction completes. Most data sources, such as SQL Server and other RDBMS, implement isolation through the use of **locks**. Individual data items or sets of data are locked from concurrent access if it is involved in a transaction.

Durability

Durability means that once a transaction has been successfully completed, all of the changes it made to the system are *permanent*. There are checkpoints that prevent the system from losing information, even if the system fails. By logging the tasks a transaction performs, the state of the system can be recreated even if the hardware itself has failed. The concept of durability allows the developer to know that a completed transaction is a permanent part of the system, regardless of what happens to the system later on.

In the bank example, this means that the transfers from one account to another are permanent and will remain in the system. This may sound simple, but it is very important to be able to rely on the fact that the data will be written to disk, especially since transactions are not written to disk until they are completely committed – more on this in a moment.

All of these somewhat inter-related properties of a transaction are simply about ensuring that data involved in the transaction is managed correctly from the time a transaction begins until the time a transaction completes, be it successfully or unsuccessfully.

Distributed Transactions

Overall, transactions are pretty simplistic when all data modifications are performed against a single data source. However, as business requirements increase and applications become more complex, it is becoming increasingly common to need to access multiple databases, often at different locations. This means that distributed transactions, transactions that modify data stored in multiple numbers and types of data sources, possibly spread across any number of machines, are much more complex.

Suppose we have a transaction that requires data changes to occur in two separate databases and still require that all the properties of the ACID test be met. Basic transaction management will not suffice. There is no way to ensure that if one database server fails, the other has not already committed and become permanent. In other words, there is no way to guarantee atomicity without a way to coordinate multiple transaction processes occurring at multiple locations.

For example, a single transaction can consist of a component running on machine A, which performs a database transaction with SQL Server on machine B. Another component in the transaction could perform database transactions on an Oracle server running on machine C. These three machines, running four distinct pieces of code, can all participate within a single transaction.

Even though COM+ hides the details of distributed transactions from us, it is worthwhile to study and understand the "behind-the-scenes" architecture of distributed transactions. It's also important to remember that these ACID properties apply to all types of transactions no matter what types or number of data sources are involved in the transaction.

The Two-Phase Commit with MS DTC

Think again about our distributed transaction example above. What if the server where Oracle resides goes down? How can we guarantee atomicity? The solution comes from a protocol called **two-phase commit (2PC)** and is coordinated by the **Microsoft Distributed Transaction Coordinator (MS DTC)**.

MS DTC was first integrated into SQL Server and has now become a vital part of COM+. By adding another factor into the transaction process, MS DTC verifies all processes are ready and able to commit.

Let's explore MS DTC a little closer and see how it works. In order for the two-phase commit protocol to be coordinated, each data source in the transaction must have MS DTC installed. From these installations, the main coordinator is always going to be where the transaction originates. This main coordinator is referred to as the **Commit Coordinator** and is responsible for ensuring that the transaction either commits or aborts on all servers that are involved with the transaction. It is also the responsibility of the commit coordinator to report back to the client application whether it has successfully committed or rolled back the transaction.

The first phase in a 2PC is known as the *Prepare* phase. This is where each server carries out the instruction it receives, but buffers all writes to disk:

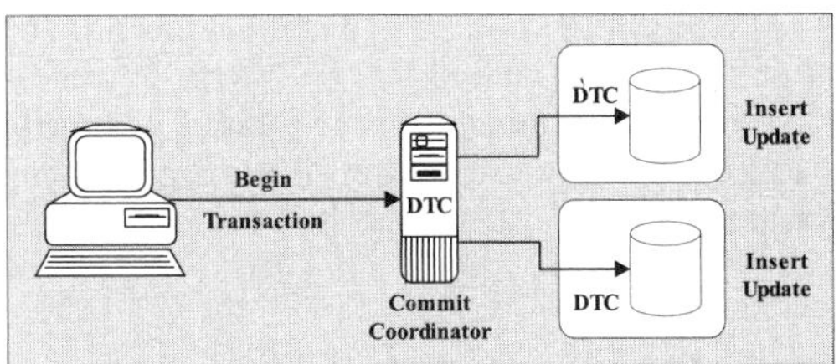

Once the server has carried out its instructions, the commit coordinator is notified about the transaction's status:

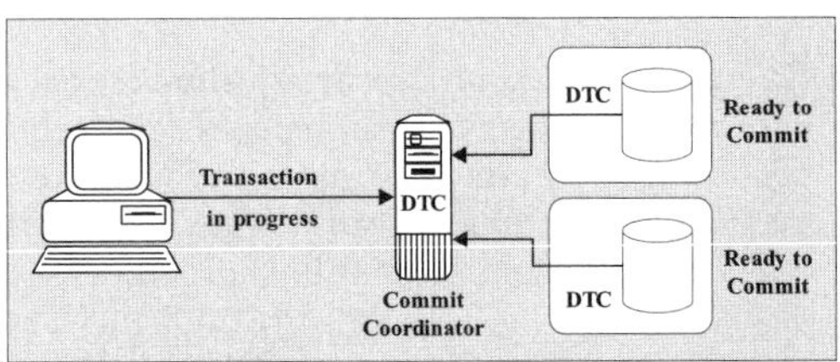

The second phase is called the *Commit* phase. If the commit coordinator receives a "ready to commit" from each data source, the transaction is committed:

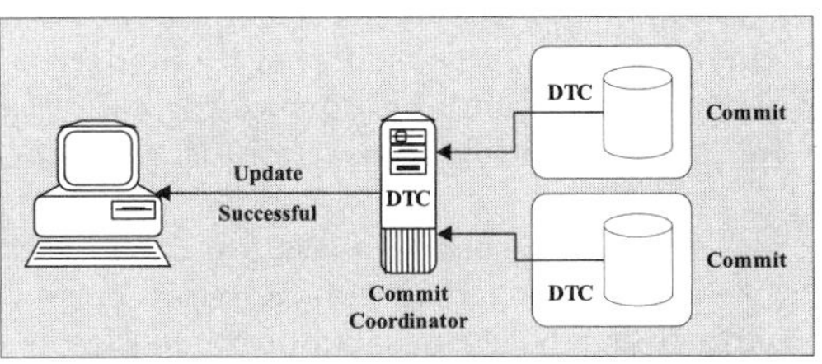

However, if one "failure" is received from any data source that is to be affected, the commit coordinator will issue a roll back and notify the client application:

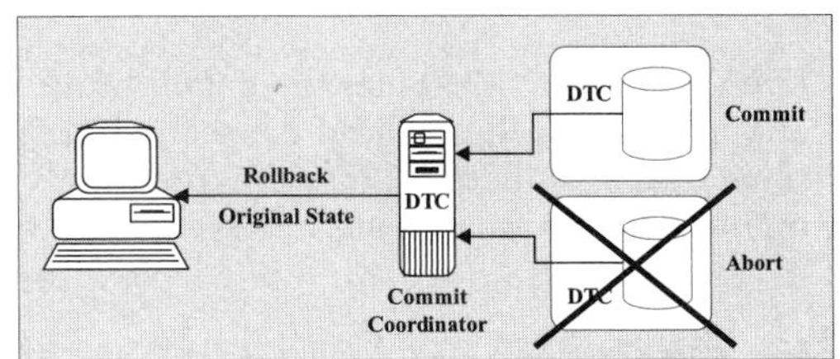

Transactional COM+ Applications

We've seen in previous chapters how COM+ provides several runtime features that simplify the development of distributed components, which in turn can be used to create scalable and maintainable ASP applications. Microsoft Transaction Server originally introduced a transaction model that was designed to simplify the development of component-based, distributed transaction processing systems. As the successor to MTS, COM+ enhances and extends MTS's powerful transaction model to provide even more flexibility and simplicity.

The COM+ transaction model eliminates the complex transaction-processing code required for distributed transactions coordinated by MS DTC. But what's even more significant, is that the COM+ transaction model *transparently* merges distributed transactions with COM+ components.

COM+ transactions, sometimes called **declarative transactions** or **automatic transactions**, are implemented through the use of declarative attributes that can be specified external to a component's implementation. All you have to do is:

- Configure your component's **Transaction Support** attribute using either the Component Services Explorer or a constant value in your component's type library
- Optionally modify your component to vote on the transaction outcome

COM+ *automatically* handles the rest of the complex and redundent details of beginning, committing and aborting transactions, by interacting with MS DTC on behalf of your component.

Since COM+ relies on MS DTC to coordinate transations, a single component can perform operations against several different types of data sources within a single COM+ transaction. When COM+ declarative transactions are used with components that leverage ADO or OLE DB for data access, the possible combinations of data sources that can be manipulated within a single transaction are endless. For example, a COM+ object could modify data in a SQL Server database, send an MSMQ message, and manipulate data from a Mainframe system all within the same COM+ transaction.

Now that we understand the benefits of COM+ transactions, let's learn how to effectively use this declarative transaction model and learn what COM+ is doing under the surface.

The Transaction Support Attribute

As I mentioned, each COM+ component's Transaction Support attribute determines how the component will participate in COM+ transactions. When a COM+ object is activated, COM+ determines both the object's Transaction Support and whether or not the creator has provided an existing transaction. Based on these two pieces of information, the COM+ runtime will either provide the object with an existing transaction, a new transaction or no transaction at all. Every COM+ object is either activated with a transaction or without one. For this reason, components that will utilize transactions are often referred to as **transactional components** and components that will not participate in transactions are called **non-transactional components**.

With COM+ there are five possible options for the Transaction Support attribute:

- **Disabled**
  When a component's Transaction Support is set to Disabled, COM+ will completely ignore the component's transactional requirements. COM+ will first attempt to activate the object within the creator's context. However, if the creator's context is unavailable or incompatible, the object will be activated within a new context. Since the object may or may not inherit the creator's context, the object may or may not share the creator's transaction.

- **Not Supported**
  When a component's Transaction Support is set to Not Supported, instances of the component will *never* participate in transactions. This setting is designed for COM+ components that do not access data sources and as a result, the component does not need the overhead of a transaction. However, an object with the Transaction Support of Not Supported will *always* be activated within a new context. This is in contrast to the Disabled attribute, which means that the object might share the context of the creator. Not Supported is the default Transaction Support level with COM+.

- **Supported**
  When a component's Transaction Support is set to Supported, instances of the component can participate within an existing transaction, but a transaction is not required and the component can execute just fine without one. It is important to remember that a Transaction Support of Supported means that transactions are only supported but not required.

- **Required**
  When a component's Transaction Support is set to Required, instances of the component will *always* execute within a transaction. Before a COM+ object is activated, COM+ will supply the object with either the creator's transaction, if one exists, or a brand new transaction. In either scenario, the component instance will *always* execute within a transaction.

- **Requires New**
  When a component's Transaction Support is set to Requires New, instances of the component will *always* be activated within a *new* transaction, created specially for this object, regardless of whether or not an existing transaction is available. This setting is designed for components that must perform work within a transaction, but whose work must be kept separate from all other transactions. When you use this setting, the COM+ object never runs inside the scope of the creator's transaction. The new transaction is completely independent of the creator's transaction.

Setting the Transaction Support

A component's Transaction Support attribute can be configured using the Component Services Explorer or a default Transaction Support setting can be specified in the component's type library. Specifying a component's Transaction Support in the component's type library is helpful because it reduces the risk of incorrectly configuring components while relieving an administrator from performing this task using the Component Services Explorer. However, it's important to remember that the Transaction Support specified in a component's type library is a *default* value that can be overridden using the Component Services Explorer.

To configure a component's Transaction Support using the Component Services Explorer, simply open a COM+ application's Component Properties dialog and from the Transactions tab, select one of the five possible Transaction Support settings:

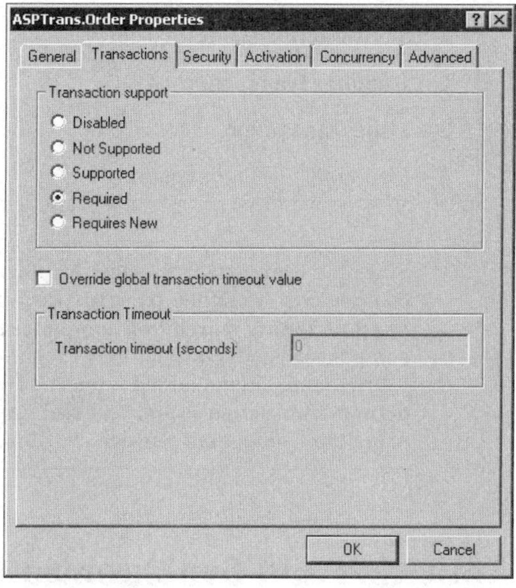

If you're using Visual C++, you can configure the default value for a component's Transaction Support in the component's type library by simply making a one-line addition to a Component's Interface Definition Language (IDL) definition. When the component is added to a COM+ application, COM+ reads the type library and automatically uses the Transaction Support setting stored in the type library as the default value.

Visual Basic 6.0 also allows developers to specify a default value for a component's Transaction Support setting by changing a class module's MTSTransactionMode property. Don't let the name of the property fool you. The MTSTransactionMode property works with both MTS and COM+. When you compile a project, Visual Basic will place the equivalent constant value for the Transaction Support setting in the component's type library:

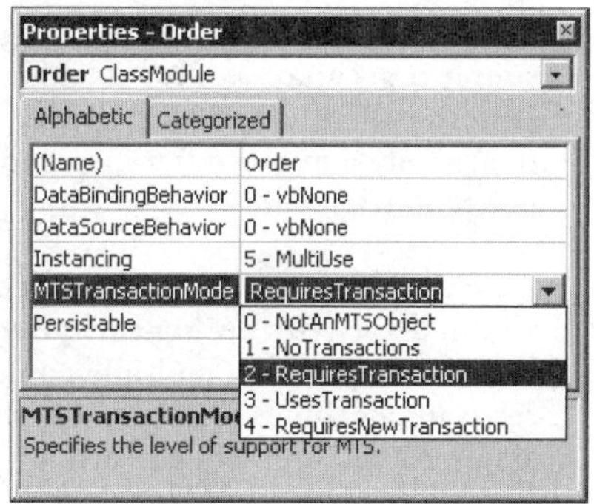

Notice that the terminology used in Visual Basic for the MTSTransactionMode values is not exactly the same as what's used in the Component Services Explorer. However, don't let this bother you. Every Transaction Support level except for Disabled (which is new for COM+) has a corresponding MTSTransactionMode setting. The following table maps the possible MTSTransactionMode values to their equivalent COM+ Transaction Support attribute:

MTSTransactionMode Property	COM+ Transaction Support Attribute
0 – NotAnMTSObject	Not Supported
1 – NoTransactions	Not Supported

Table Continued on Following Page

MTSTransactionMode Property	COM+ Transaction Support Attribute
2 – RequiresTransaction	Required
3 – UsesTransaction	Supported
4 – RequiresNewTransaction	Requires New

Since the Component Services Explorer does not read the type library when components are added from the Registered Components list, the Transaction Support setting stored in a component's type library is applied only if the component is added to a COM+ Application with the Add File dialog. Instead, COM+ components added from the Registered Components list will have the default transaction support of Not Supported until their configuration is modified using the Component Services Explorer.

Activities and Synchronizaton

When a transaction processing system provides services to multiple users, it can receive *simultaneous* calls from clients. As a result, transaction processing systems must be concerned about issues such as **multi-user concurrency, synchronization** and **thread management**. COM+ shields you from these issues and allows you to create components that execute in a multi-user distributed environment, just as you would create a component that services a single user.

COM+ accomplishes this amazing task through the use of **activities**. Within MTS, an activity was simply a group of *objects* executing on the behalf of a single client. In COM+ an activity is a group of *contexts* (which can contain one or more objects) executing on the behalf of a single client. However, this is only a minor difference and the presence of a context as the inner-most container of objects is pretty much assumed.

Activities ensure that no two objects servicing the same client can execute at the same time. Objects within an activity are **synchronized** to prevent parallel execution within the same activity. An activity can be composed of multiple contexts – containing objects – executing in separate processes or on separate machines (with a few restrictions). For these reasons, an activity is sometimes referred to as a single *logical* thread of execution.

But why is the synchronization of objects so important? Think about a scenario in which two objects executing on behalf of the same user are trying to access the same resources at the exact same time. Each object could potentially block the other object from completing its operation. This situation is known as a **deadlock**. Activities help prevent deadlocks from occurring, by only allowing one object to execute at a time, on the behalf of a single user. Additionally, activities play a role in helping COM+ manage its thread pool.

Within MTS, the synchronization of objects within an activity was enforced by linking an activity to a single *physical* thread of execution, or a Single-Threaded Apartment (STA). Objects within an activity could not execute concurrently because there was only one physical thread per activity. COM+ on the other hand, uses a sophisticated locking mechanism to enforce synchronization within an activity.

Each activity maintains a single, exclusive lock. When a method call is made on an object, and that object's context resides in an activity, COM+ first attempts to acquire the activity's lock before allowing the method call to be processed. If the lock is acquired then the call is processed by the object and the lock is not released until the method call completes. If the lock cannot be acquired, then the method call will be blocked until the lock can be acquired. Although the locking process is much more involved, from a high-level view, a single lock per activity is basically how COM+ uses logical activities to enforce synchronization of multiple contexts and thus multiple objects:

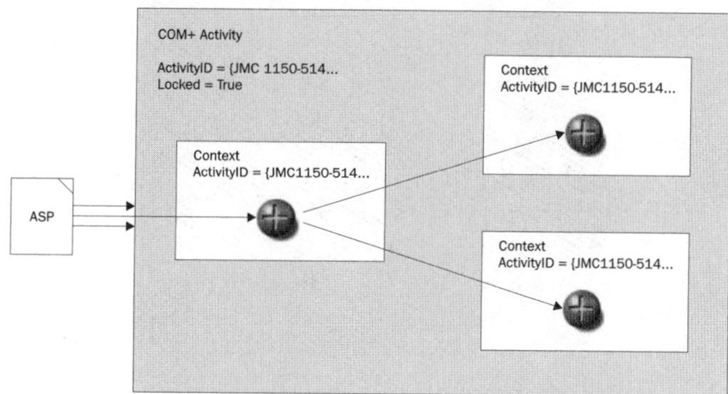

Contexts can reside in either the creator's activity, a new activity or no activity at all. However, a context cannot span multiple activities. To establish and maintain these relationships, COM+ creates a unique identifier for each activity, called an **ActivityID**, and stores the ActivityID in each context.

Activity Creation and The Synchronization Attribute

With the integration of the COM and MTS programming models, the way activities are created has also changed. With MTS, every object belonged to an activity. An activity was automatically created when a VB client created an MTS object using the `CreateObject` function or the `New` keyword (with some exceptions) or a Visual C++ client used the `CoCreateInstanceEx` function. For an object to be created within an existing activity the creator had to call the `CreateInstance` function on the ObjectContext object.

As you can imagine, this caused a lot of confusion. MTS developers had to be conscious of the logical activity boundaries and create their objects appropriately using either standard object creation techniques (`CreateObject` or `CoCreateInstanceEx`) or the ObjectContext's `CreateInstance` function.

With COM+, activities are still automatically created, but the creation of an activity is now controlled using a component's **Synchronization attribute** and is not based on how the component is instantiated. In fact, the `CreateInstance` function of the ObjectContext now functions the same as standard object creation techniques, and it is only supported for backward compatibility with MTS. Additionally, COM+ provides the ability to activate objects outside of an activity, thus avoiding the activity creation overhead and possible call blocking. This can provide performance benefits for frequently used non-transactional, 'utility' type components that, if required, implement their own locking techniques.

Just like the Transaction Support attribute, the Synchronization attribute can be configured from the Component Properties window in the Component Services Explorer:

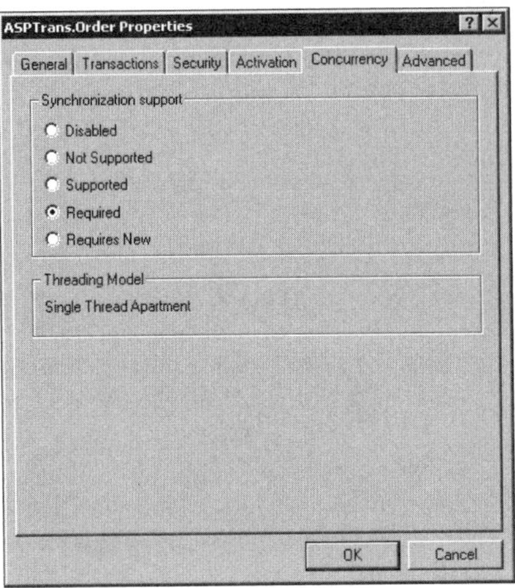

Again, there are five possible values for the Synchronization attribute:

- **Disabled**
  When a component's Synchronization attribute is set to Disabled, COM+ will completely ignore the component's synchronization requirements. Just like when the Transaction Support attribute is set to Disabled, COM+ will first attempt to activate the object within the creator's context. However, if the creator's context is unavailable or incompatible, the object will be activated within a new context. Since the object may or may not inherit the creator's context, the object may or may not share the creator's activity. You should use this setting for non-transactional components whenever possible to try to avoid the overhead of context and activity creation.

- **Not Supported**
  When a component's Synchronization attribute is set to Not Supported, an object's context will *never* reside inside an activity. However, an object with the Synchronization attribute of Not Supported will *always* be activated within a new context.

- **Supported**
  When a component's Synchronization attribute is set to Supported, an object's context may or may not reside in an activity depending on whether or not the creator's context resides in an activity. However, a component with this setting does not require an activity and can execute just fine without one.

- **Required**
  When a component's Synchronization attribute is set to Required, an object's context will *always* reside inside an activity. If the creator context resides in an activity, the new object will be activated within the creator's activity. Otherwise, COM+ will activate the object within a new context located in a brand new activity.

- **Requires New**
  When a component's Synchronization attribute is set to Requires New, an object's context will *always* be created within a new activity, regardless of the Synchronization status of the creator's context.

As you can see, the Synchronization attribute's options are very similar to those of the Transaction Support attribute. However, some synchronization options are dependent on certain values with other component attributes. In particular, components that support JIT activation or have a Transaction Support of Supported, Required, or Requires New must be activated within an activity and therefore, require a Synchronization attribute of Required or Requires New. The only time Synchronization can be set to Disabled or Not Supported is when JIT activation is disabled and the Transaction Support attribute is set to Disabled or Not Supported also. We'll discuss more about the relationship of activities to transactions in the next section.

If you think all these different configuration options sound confusing, don't worry – you're not alone. Apparently, Microsoft expected these interdependent configuration options to be confusing for developers to remember because they built validation functionality into the Component Services Explorer. If you change the JIT activation support or the Transaction Support attribute to something that's incompatible with the Synchronization attribute, the Component Services Explorer will prompt you with a nice warning message and automatically adjust the Synchronization attribute to reflect any changes:

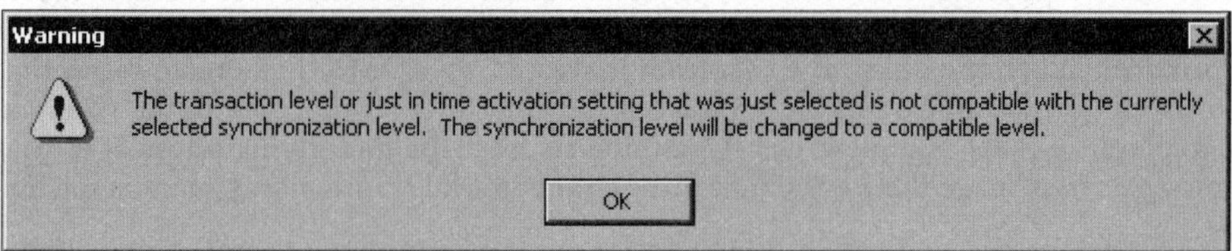

The best thing about activities is that they're totally implemented by COM+ behind the scenes. Components aren't required to perform any additional work for COM+ to provide them with automatic concurrency and synchronization services. Additionally, non-transactional components are also given the flexibility to disable the creation of activities if they wish. Nevertheless, it's important to understand the effects of changing the Synchronization attribute, and what goes on behind the scenes with activities and contexts, so you can design efficient and scalable components. Now that we have a solid understanding of the configurable attributes for transactional COM+ components, let's discuss each step of a transaction's lifetime.

Transaction Lifetimes

A COM+ transaction goes through a complex four-stage lifetime. These stages are:

1. Starting a transaction
2. Establishing and enlisting connections to Resource Managers
3. Performing operations within the transaction
4. Transaction outcome and completion

However, it is important to remember that the only requirement of components to participate in transactions is that they have a Transaction Support level of something other than Not Supported or Disabled. COM+ components can also optionally vote on the transaction outcome.

Let's take a detailed look at what's happening at each phase of a transaction's lifetime for both single and multi-object COM+ transactions.

Starting a Transaction

With the COM+ transaction model, a component does not explicitly start a COM+ transaction. Instead, COM+ automatically creates a new COM+ transaction in one of two scenarios:

- A component with a Transaction Support of Required is activated by a non-transactional client
- A component with a Transaction Support of Requires New is activated by any client

A COM+ transaction is composed of two parts:

- A **logical transaction**
- A **physical transaction**

A logical transaction, also known as a **transaction stream**, is a logical collection, or grouping, of objects that share a physical transaction. A physical transaction, on the other hand, is the underlying MS DTC transaction that coordinates the transaction outcome with data sources using the two-phase commit protocol. When the physical transaction is created by COM+, it is created with the highest level of isolation (serializable), and the transaction timeout interval specified in the Component Services Explorer. COM+ completely abstracts objects from the underlying physical transaction and instead allows us to manage the transaction through the logical transaction stream and each object's context.

It is important to note that there is always a one-to-one relationship of transaction streams to physical transactions, although, as we'll see in a minute, a logical transaction can be composed of several COM+ objects.

The first object created within a transaction stream is called the **root of the transaction**. The root of the transaction, can then optionally enlist other COM+ objects in the same transaction by instantiating COM+ components that have a Transaction Support of either Required or Supported. When an object is created in the same transaction, COM+ automatically replicates the transaction information from the root object's context to the new object's context, so COM+ can maintain the association between all objects in the transaction. This transaction information includes a GUID value called the **TransactionID**, which is also used by COM+ to identify the physical (MS DTC) transaction:

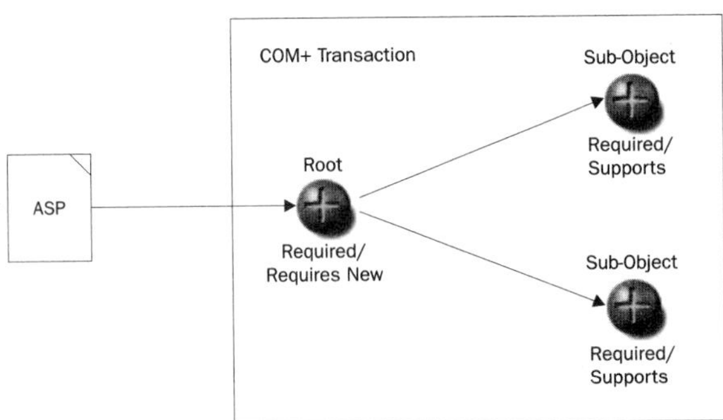

For these new objects to be enlisted in the creator's transaction they must also be created in the same activity. With MTS this meant that the root object had to create sub-objects using the `CreateInstance` method of the ObjectContext object. Now that COM+ has integrated the MTS and COM programming models, the `CreateInstance` method is no longer required and sub-objects can be created with the `CreateObject` function in Visual Basic or the `CoCreateInstance` function in Visual C++.

A COM+ transaction can never span activities, but the relationship of activities to COM+ transactions is not always one-to-one. A single activity can possibly have several COM+ transactions. If a COM+ object instantiates a COM+ component with a Transaction Support setting of Requires New, this new object will be in the same activity, but in a different COM+ transaction that is completely independent of the creator's transaction:

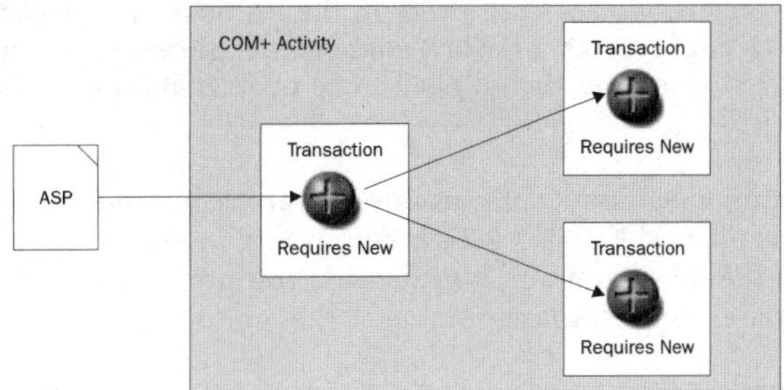

While both physical and logical transactions are typically created automatically by the COM+ runtime, COM+ also allows developers to create a COM+ object within an existing MS DTC (physical) transaction. This feature, appropriately called **Bring Your Own Transaction (BYOT),** is designed to give developers more flexibility when developing transactional components, while still leveraging COM+'s simplistic, logical transaction model. With BYOT, components can effectively use a combination of the MS DTC and the COM+ programming models to accomplish virtually any transactional task. A typical use of BYOT is to create an MS DTC transaction with different attributes, such as an isolation level lower than serializable, and then create one or more COM+ components within the physical transaction.

Establishing Connections to Resource Managers

After both the logical transaction and the underlying MS DTC (physical) transaction have been created, COM+ must ensure that all data modification operations performed by the COM+ object(s) against data sources are performed within the MS DTC (physical) transaction. Each connection to each data source must be **enlisted** or registered with the MS DTC transaction.

Once this happens, all operations are performed through the connection and monitored by the MS DTC. Although the entire enlistment process is performed by COM+ behind the scenes for each connection, it's imperative to understand the details of how this important step in a transaction's lifetime is accomplished.

A **Resource Manager** (**RM**) is the part of the database server that works with COM+ to manage durable data. So a connection to a particular data source is actually just a connection to a Resource Manager. But the COM+ transaction model adds an additional layer of software to the distributed transaction architecture called a **Resource Dispenser (RD)**.

It's important not to confuse Resource Managers and Resource Dispensers. They are two different software components in the COM+ transactional model that serve different purposes.

> **A Resource Manager is simply a system service, such as a database system, that manages durable resources in a distributed transaction.**

MS DTC coordinates transaction commitment and rollback with Resource Managers using the two-phase commit protocol. Examples of Resource Managers include: SQL Server, Oracle, and MSMQ.

> **A Resource Dispenser, on the other hand, is an in-process DLL that manages non-durable or temporary resources that reside in the Resource Dispenser's memory, such as data source connections, network connections, threads, objects, or memory blocks. These shared resources do not need to be protected from a system failure.**

Resource Dispensers can manage pools of reusable resources, automatically enlist or register them in transactions and provide a COM+ object with methods and interfaces to perform operations against these resources. One of the most common non-durable resources managed by a Resource Dispenser are connections to an underlying Resource Manager that controls persistent storage.

Don't let the terminology of "Resource Dispensers" fool you. Resource Dispensers are the same components that are always used to access resources. For example, the OLE DB Service Component always resides between a client application or object using ADO or OLE DB, and the OLE DB Provider and data source. COM+ assigns the OLE DB Service Component the role of the Resource Dispenser and the data source is the Resource Manager:

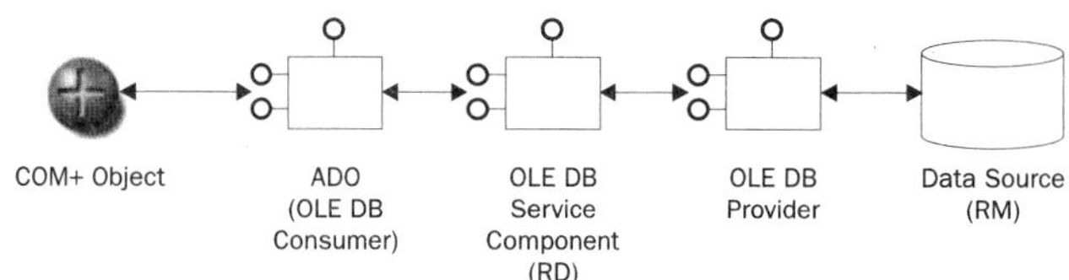

As I mentioned earlier, under this Resource Dispenser role, these software components are responsible for managing non-durable resources. But they can optionally also provide two important services:

- **Resource Pooling**
  Resource pooling provides an efficient way of dispensing non-durable resources by providing a COM+ object with a *recycled* resource instead of creating a new one. After a COM+ object is through with the resource, it is placed back into the pool where it is made available for immediate reuse by the same or another COM+ object.

  Connections to Data Sources (Resource Managers) are one of the most commonly used non-durable resources. Creating and destroying a connection to a Resource Manager is an expensive process. To efficiently provide COM+ objects with data source connections, both the ODBC Driver Manager and the OLE DB Service Component provide resource pooling of Resource Manager connections. The reusing or recycling of expensive resources is completely transparent to the COM+ object or application consuming the resource.

- **Transaction Enlistment**
  Transaction Enlistment is the process of associating or enlisting a connection to a Resource Manager with the MS DTC (physical) transaction. Once this transaction enlistment is completed, all work performed by the COM+ object through that connection will be monitored by MS DTC and will be protected within a distributed transaction. All operations will be performed as a single unit of work and the transaction as a whole will be required to conform to the ACID properties. When the logical transaction completes, MS DTC can then execute the two-phase commit protocol with all the participating Resource Managers. It is important to note that this transaction enlistment is totally optional. It is the Resource Dispenser's decision whether or not to enlist the resource in the current transaction. Transaction enlistment plays a significant role in COM+ transactions by simplifying the development of transactional COM+ components.

Thankfully, COM+ does an excellent job of hiding components from these complex details of distributed transactions. In fact, our only responsibility in this stage of a transaction's lifetime is to establish a connection to a data source just as we do normally using ADO, OLE DB or ODBC. COM+ and the Resource Dispensers are responsible for performing the complex tasks of resource pooling and transaction enlistment.

Performing Operations

Once connections have been made to the data store(s) our COM+ object can begin performing operations against the Resource Managers.

When the Resource Manager receives and processes operations against its data it takes certain measures to ensure that the transaction meets the ACID requirements. Many Resource Managers implement a logging mechanism to provide the ability to rollback uncommitted changes to fulfill the atomicity requirement. Logging mechanisms also allow a Resource Manager to ensure the durability of a transaction by being able to reapply or recover changes should an unforeseen problem occur. Locks are used to isolate a transaction's changes from affecting other transactions against the same Resource Manager. To ensure consistency, Resource Managers usually define special mechanisms or rules to protect the integrity of data.

Voting on a Transaction's Outcome

As I mentioned earlier, a transactional COM+ object's context contains a GUID value called a TransactionID, which is used to associate multiple objects within a transaction, and link the logical transaction to the underlying physical transaction. However, this is not the only information that is stored in an object's context. A transactional object's context also contains two other important pieces of information that are used to complete a transaction and vote whether or not the transaction should commit or abort. These two pieces of information are:

- **Done Bit**
  The Done Bit is a Boolean value that indicates whether or not the object should be deactivated. A value of TRUE indicates that the object has completed its work and can be deactivated, and a value of FALSE (the default) indicates that the object is not ready to be deactivated.

  The value of the Done Bit is not inspected by COM+ until a method call completes. As a result, the value of the Done Bit can be changed any number of times, as its value is only meaningful after method calls. The Done Bit is actually provided by JIT activation and, consequently, it is used the same way with non-transactional components that support JIT activation.

- **Consistency Bit**
  The Consistency Bit, sometimes called the "Happy Bit", is a Boolean value that indicates whether the COM+ object votes to **commit** or **abort** the transaction. A value of TRUE indicates the object wants to attempt to commit the transaction, and a value of FALSE indicates the object wants to force an abort of the transaction.

  The value of the Consistency Bit is only evaluated by COM+ after the object is deactivated (Done Bit is set to TRUE). As a result, the value of the Consistency Bit can be changed repeatedly, even in different method calls, because only the last value before the object is deactivated counts. COM+ initializes the Consistency Bit with a value of TRUE – meaning that COM+ is assuming the transaction wants to commit.

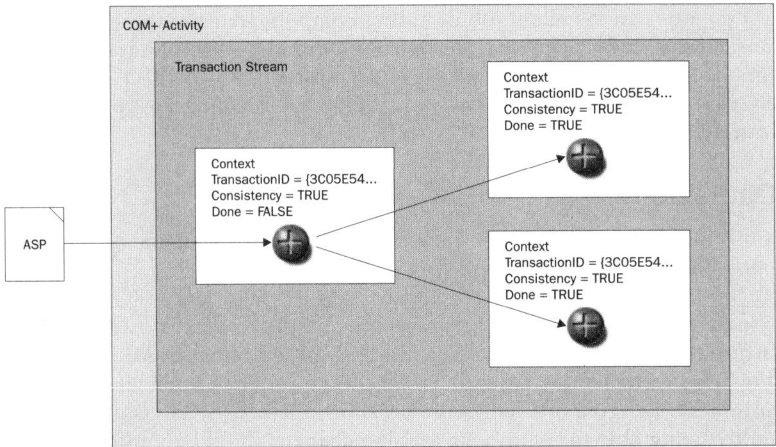

When the root of the transaction is deactivated (the Done Bit is set to TRUE for the root object's context), COM+ evaluates the Consistency Bit of each context in the transaction stream to determine the transaction outcome. The decision to attempt to commit a transaction is a unanimous decision.

If **all** objects in the transaction vote to attempt to commit the transaction, by setting the Consistency Bit of their context to TRUE, then all operations performed within the transaction will attempt to be permanently committed. However, if *any* object within the transaction votes to abort the transaction, by setting the Consistency Bit of their context to FALSE, then all the operations performed within the transaction will be rolled back. When either of these situations occur, COM+ calls down to MS DTC either to commit or abort the physical transaction. MS DTC is then responsible for coordinating the commitment or abortion of the distributed transaction with all enlisted Resource Managers through the use of the two-phase commit protocol.

The following table summarizes the outcome of a COM+ transaction with respect to the Done and Consistency Bits:

Done	Consistency	Result
TRUE	TRUE	COM+ and MS DTC will then attempt to commit the transaction.
TRUE	FALSE	COM+ and MS DTC will abort the transaction.
FALSE	TRUE	The transaction will not be committed or aborted until the root object is deactivated (Done Bit is set to TRUE).
FALSE	FALSE	The transaction will not be committed or aborted until the root object is deactivated (Done Bit is set to TRUE).

Now that you know what the values of the Done and Consistency Bits should be to commit or abort a COM+ transaction, I'm sure you're wondering how to retrieve and modify their values.

The methods of the ObjectContext (or `IObjectContext`) interface are probably the easiest way to control a COM+ transaction's outcome programmatically because they allow you to simultaneously set both the Consistency Bit and the Done Bit with a single method call. Since there are four possible combinations of values between the Consistency Bit and the Done Bit, there are also four methods defined by the ObjectContext interface. These methods are:

- `SetComplete`
- `SetAbort`
- `EnableCommit`
- `DisableCommit`

As you can see in this table, each of the ObjectContext methods maps to a unique combination of values for the Consistency and Done Bits:

ObjectContext Method	Done Bit	Consistency Bit
`SetComplete`	TRUE	TRUE
`SetAbort`	TRUE	FALSE
`EnableCommit`	FALSE	TRUE
`DisableCommit`	FALSE	FALSE

The SetComplete Method

The `SetComplete` method informs COM+ that a particular unit of work has completed successfully. `SetComplete` both forces the object to deactivate and also votes to commit the transaction by setting both the Consistency and Done Bits to TRUE. Only when `SetComplete` is called in the root object will COM+ examine the Consistency Bit in each object's context to determine the outcome of the transaction. The following code example shows how to call the `SetComplete` method:

```
Dim objContext As COMSVCSLib.ObjectContext

'Get a reference to the ObjectContext for this object
Set objContext = GetObjectContext()

'******Do some work*****

'Vote to commit the transaction
'...and deactivate the object now
objContext.SetComplete

'Release our reference to the object context
Set objContext = Nothing
```

The SetAbort Method

The `SetAbort` method notifies COM+ that the object was unsuccessful in completing its work and it wants to abort the transaction. If one or more COM+ objects in the transaction calls the `SetAbort` method, then the entire transaction will be aborted because the `SetAbort` method sets the Consistency Bit to FALSE and the Done Bit to TRUE:

```
Dim objContext As COMSVCSLib.ObjectContext

'Get a reference to the ObjectContext for this object
Set objContext = GetObjectContext()

'******Do some work*****

'Vote to abort the transaction
'...and deactivate the object now
objContext.SetAbort

'Release our reference to the object context
Set objContext = Nothing
```

The EnableCommit Method

The `EnableCommit` method notifies COM+ that the object is able to commit the transaction but the object does not want to be deactivated yet. The `EnableCommit` method accomplishes this by setting the Consistency Bit to TRUE and the Done Bit to FALSE:

```
Dim objContext As COMSVCSLib.ObjectContext

'Get a reference to the ObjectContext for this object
Set objContext = GetObjectContext()

'******Do some work*****

'Tell MTS that we can commit at any time
'...but don't deactivate the object yet
objContext.EnableCommit

'Release our reference to the object context
Set objContext = Nothing
```

The DisableCommit Method

The DisableCommit method is exactly the opposite of the EnableCommit method. The DisableCommit method notifies COM+ that the object's work is not finished and the transaction cannot currently be committed, but it does not want to be deactivated. DisableCommit sets both the Consistency and Done Bits of the object's context to FALSE. Since the object won't be deactivated, its state will be maintained across method calls:

```
Dim objContext As COMSVCSLib.ObjectContext

'Get a reference to the ObjectContext for this object
Set objContext = GetObjectContext()

'******Do some work*****

' Tell MTS that we are not ready to commit
'...and we don't want to deactivate the object yet
objContext.DisableCommit

'Release our reference to the object context
Set objContext = Nothing
```

Other Ways a Transaction can Complete

While most of the time you will explicitly control your transaction's outcome through the ObjectContext interface, you should be aware that COM+ transactions could also be completed in two additional ways:

- **Transaction Timeout**
  A transaction can end if there is no activity within the transaction for more than the configured transaction timeout value. When a transaction times out it will automatically abort. The default timeout value is 60 seconds. This value can be changed from the Options tab of the Computer Properties dialog window in the Component Services Explorer. If you are debugging transactional COM+ objects, you will definitely want to increase the transaction timeout from the 60 second default so that you will have enough time to step through a method call on a COM+ object without the transaction automatically aborting.

- **The client releases all references to the root of the transaction**
  When the client releases the last reference to the root object, COM+ *implicitly* attempts to commit the transaction. Implicit transaction commitments should always be avoided because they introduce a host of problems.

One problem with implicit commitments is that the client cannot be notified of the transaction outcome. When a root object calls the SetComplete method, COM+ attempts to commit the transaction prior to returning control to the caller. If an error occurred while committing the transaction, COM+ simply raises an error message to the client. This allows the client application to gracefully deal with the problem and possibly try the transaction again. However with implicit commitment the client is no longer connected to the root object and it consequently cannot receive error messages if the transaction cannot be committed. The client is totally unaware of the transaction outcome.

Implicit transaction commitments also leave a transaction alive longer than necessary. While a transaction is alive, it is holding precious locks to resources to ensure the isolation requirement of the ACID properties. Consequently, an open, inactive transaction could be blocking other transactions from performing operations on the same resource. This could create a performance bottleneck and severely limit an application's scalability. A much better approach is to explicitly commit or abort the transaction by calling the methods of the ObjectContext.

Transaction Lifetime Summary

While the entire process a transaction goes through in its lifetime may sound overwhelming, it's important to remember that the only requirement for your COM+ components to participate in transactions is that they are configured with the appropriate Transaction Support attribute. Many of these different techniques for committing or aborting a transaction are provided for **flexibility**. While they may be a little confusing to understand right now, they make the development of transactional, component-based systems easier.

Transactional Access to Custom Resources

You might be wondering what happens when you need transactional access to resources that don't provide a Resource Dispenser? Do you have to develop a custom Resource Dispenser and Resource Manager? Are you just out-of-luck? Thankfully with COM+ the answer to each of these questions is no.

COM+ provides a new feature called the **Compensating Resource Manager (CRM)** that provides an infrastructure that enhances COM+'s support for transaction processing.

> **Compensating Resource Managers provide an easy way to allow a non-transactional resource to participate in transactions managed by the Microsoft Distributed Transaction Coordinator (MS DTC).**

CRMs are a simpler alternative to developing a complex COM+ Resource Manager and Resource Dispenser pair, while still using the MS DTC to coordinate transactions. For example, CRMs could be developed to provide transactional access for resources such as file systems, memory or the Windows 2000 registry. Transactional COM+ components can then access these resources through the CRM's interface(s) and all operations performed by the CRM would be protected by an MS DTC transaction.

Additionally, because the MS DTC is utilized as the transaction coordinator for both the COM+ Resource Managers/Dispensers and Compensating Resource Managers, a single transaction can be composed of operations against resources using either architecture. This feature makes Compensating Resource Managers an attractive solution to providing transactional access to resources.

COM+ Transactions and IIS

Microsoft has tightly integrated the functions of IIS and COM+, which make it very easy to take advantage of transaction processing applications from within traditional Web page programming.

There are a number of different examples of the ways that the transactional features of COM+ and IIS are integrated. These include:

- Transactional Active Server Pages
- ObjectContext in ASP
- Transactional Events

A developer can use one or more of these features in their applications that use both IIS and COM+. Because of their tight integration, the developer has little work to do to fully utilize these services, in fact the ObjectContext, which wraps a transaction in COM+, is directly available to ASP pages in a transaction.

Transactional Active Server Pages

Since the integration of IIS 4.0 and MTS, developers can include ASP scripts within a transaction. These ASP pages can include calls to server components that will also participate in the same transaction. Like all transactions, if any one part of the transaction fails, then the entire transaction will be rolled back. The added advantage of transactional ASP scripts is that it makes it easy to tie multiple components together into one single transaction.

There is one issue with using transactional scripts when dealing with a transaction that aborts. The changes that were made to databases accessed with the database's Resource Manager will be automatically rolled back. However, COM+ is unable to rollback changes made within the script itself. For instance, any changes made using the script, such as changes to Session or Application variables, will not be automatically rolled back. We'll see later how to use transactional events to be notified that a transaction has aborted. When you handle this event, you can manually rollback any changes that COM+ cannot perform automatically. The reason for this limitation is because COM+ transactions can only rollback changes to services that are MS DTC compliant.

New to IIS 5.0, developers have the ability to have a transaction span multiple ASP script pages. This is available due to the addition of the new `Execute` and `Transfer` methods on the Server object.

Normally, however, all of the processing for a single transaction can be done on a single ASP page. For example, if there is an application that has one component to withdraw money from an account and one component to deposit money into an account. To transfer funds from one account to another, you would create an ASP script that uses the withdrawal component to get the funds for transfer and the deposit component to put that money in the new account. All of this functionality would be put in a transaction ASP page, so that if any part failed, all the changes would be rolled back resetting the account balances back to their initial values.

To declare a page as transactional, you use the following directive:

```
<%@ TRANSACTION = value %>
```

The possible settings for the `TRANSACTION` directive are:

- `Disabled` – Informs COM+ that the component does not wish to be involved in transactions
- `Requires_New` – Starts a new transaction, even if one already exists

- `Required` – Starts a new transaction if one does not exist, or will join an existing one
- `Supported` – Does not start a transaction, but will join one if it already exists
- `Not_Supported` – Will not join a transaction, even if one already exists

> *These values have the same effect as the settings for the Transaction Support attributes that can be set for each component using the Component Services Explorer.*

The `TRANSACTION` directive must be on the first line in the ASP page, and is usually included with the `LANGUAGE` directive. If there is anything before this in the page a script error will be generated. Just like transactions in components, if the last line of code is reached and a commit or abort has not been called, COM+ will assume a commit and write the changes to disk. Also, each object that is called by the page can and usually does use the same ObjectContext object of the ASP page to participate in the transaction.

The ObjectContext Object in Transactional ASP

When coding a transactional ASP script, you may want to be able to directly affect the outcome of the transaction the script is executing within. Just like components that are written for transactions, ASP pages can also utilize the ObjectContext object. This object has been available since the release of ASP 2.0 and provides the functionality for all of the transaction-handling routines that a developer may need. This is exactly the same object the server components participating in the transaction will be accessing, which contains the `SetAbort` and `SetComplete` methods.

The following code example displays how to instantiate a transaction with two COM objects all within a transactional Web page and invoke a method on each of them.

Notice that at the top of the page the transactional setting indicates that a transaction is required. This is what will enable the page to participate in the same transactions as the COM components. In fact the COM components will actually become part of the transaction started by the ASP page itself as long as they have a Transaction Support attribute of Required or Supported:

```
<%@ LANGUAGE=VBScript TRANSACTION=Required%>

<HTML>
<%

Dim objA
Dim objB

Set objA = Server.CreateObject("MyDll.MyClass")
Set objB = Server.CreateObject("MyDll2.MyClass2")

If Not objA.Go = 0 Then
   ObjectContext.SetAbort
ElseIf Not objB.Go = 0 Then
   ObjectContext.SetAbort
Else
   ObjectContext.SetComplete
End If
```

```
Set objA = Nothing
Set objB = Nothing

%>
</HTML>
```

As the ASP page is executed one method of each COM class is called upon. As each method is executed, the return value is evaluated to determine if the processing succeeded. If either of the methods returns a value other than zero the ASP page invokes the `SetAbort` method on the ObjectContext object and the transaction is rolled back. Otherwise the ASP page will commit the transaction and any changes will be persisted to disk.

The main point to remember from this example is that both of these method calls are brought together into the same transaction with the ASP page.

The above example could also be written so that the methods in the COM components actually call `SetComplete` or `SetAbort` internally. This would remove some of the logic from the ASP page and embed it with the rest of the logic in the COM component. The only issue with writing transactions this way is that the ASP page doesn't know if the transaction is going to be committed or aborted. However this can be worked around by implementing transaction events for IIS and COM+ to call upon.

Transaction Events

ASP pages also have the ability to listen to COM+ when a transaction is about to be committed or aborted. This is done through the use of two routines that IIS will call before COM+ commits or aborts the transaction. These methods are called `OnTransactionCommit` and `OnTransactionAbort`.

The `OnTransactionCommit` method is fired just before COM+ commits the transaction after the *Prepare* phase. As long as no parts of the transaction have aborted, the `OnTransactionCommit` routine (event) will fire and the transaction will be committed. If the transaction is aborted then the `OnTransactionAbort` event will fire:

```
<%@ LANGUAGE=VBScript TRANSACTION=Required%>

<%
Dim objA
Set objA = Server.CreateObject("MyDll.MyClass")
objA.Go
Set objA = Nothing

' Fires if the transaction commits
Sub OnTransactionCommit
  Response.Write "<HTML>"
  Response.Write "The Transaction committed."
  Response.Write "</HTML>"
End Sub
```

```
' Fires if the transaction aborts
Sub OnTransactionAbort
  Response.Write "<HTML>"
  Response.Write "The Transaction aborted."
  Response.Write "</HTML>"
End Sub
%>
```

Like most transactional ASP pages the example above starts out with by declaring that it requires a transaction. Next the script calls a method of a transactional COM object. Once the page finishes, COM+ will determine the outcome of the transaction by checking if any part of the transaction called the `SetAbort` method. If the `SetAbort` method was not called the `OnTransactionCommit` will fire and the transaction will be committed, if it was called then the `OnTransactionAbort` will be called and the transaction will be rolled back.

On-line Ordering with ASP and COM+

Now that we have gone through transactions and how they can be leveraged from ASP, let's have some fun! This section is going to start by defining a business requirement and the needs that surround it. From there this section will work through the design and implementation of a possible solution that utilizes ASP and COM+'s transactions.

The Business Need

The business need in this example is the front-end piece of an order processing system. This order processing system will generate the order for the customer and must also adjust the inventory level. It is very important that the inventory level be adjusted correctly each time an order is placed.

Since this example is comprised of two tasks, generating the order and adjusting inventory levels, it is essential that these tasks be bundled into a single transaction. This is where COM+ can help. COM+ will provide all of the plumbing work for our transaction. All that is required in our code is to tell COM+ to commit or abort the transaction.

The Design

This example can be broken down into the typical 3-tier architecture and also fits into Microsoft's DNA architecture. At a high level, the example will be an ASP user interface (UI) that looks up the various products in a SQL Server 7.0 database. However, the ASP code does not interact with the database. Instead, it utilizes a COM component to retrieve the data in the form of a disconnected recordset.

Orders are retrieved through the ASP UI, which calls upon a transactional COM component. The COM component inserts the order in to the database and also adjusts the inventory level.

Data Services

As noted above the database will reside in SQL Server 7.0. The reason for choosing SQL Server is because of its support of COM+ (DTC) transactions. SQL Server 6.5 can also be used if desired.

There are two tables in this example, one for products and the other for orders. To keep it simple let's use the names `Products` and `Orders` in a database called `ASPTransactions`:

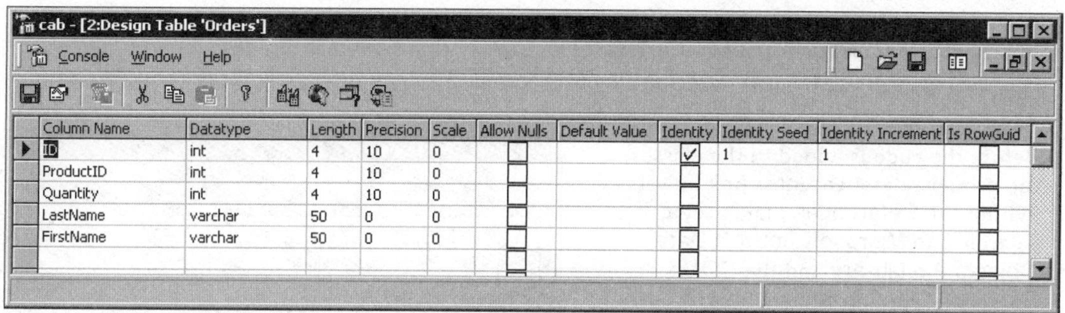

Column Name	Datatype	Length	Precision	Scale	Allow Nulls	Default Value	Identity	Identity Seed	Identity Increment	Is RowGuid
ID	int	4	10	0	☐		☑	1	1	☐
ProductID	int	4	10	0	☐		☐			☐
Quantity	int	4	10	0	☐		☐			☐
LastName	varchar	50	0	0	☐		☐			☐
FirstName	varchar	50	0	0	☐		☐			☐

You should also add some sample data into the `Products` table to be returned to the ASP page.

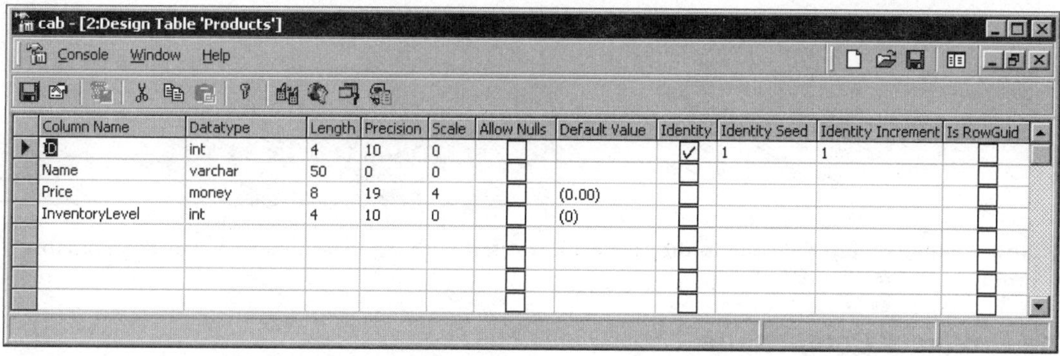

Column Name	Datatype	Length	Precision	Scale	Allow Nulls	Default Value	Identity	Identity Seed	Identity Increment	Is RowGuid
ID	int	4	10	0	☐		☑	1	1	☐
Name	varchar	50	0	0	☐		☐			☐
Price	money	8	19	4	☐	(0.00)	☐			☐
InventoryLevel	int	4	10	0	☐	(0)	☐			☐

Most applications are built upon a much more complex database design that uses stored procedures, triggers and scheduled jobs. However, this is sufficent to provide a workable example.

We have provided scripts in the downloadable source code that will create these tables for you and insert some data into the `Products` table.

Business Logic

The business logic for this example will be encapsulated in an ActiveX DLL built in Visual Basic. The DLL will contain two classes; one that provides the ability for the caller to retrieve a list of available products, and another to submit an order. The class that simply retrieves a list of products will be non-transactional, while the class that updates the tables will be transactional to make sure that either both tables are changed or neither are.

The Implementation

Let's start out by opening Visual Basic and creating a new ActiveX DLL project. Within VB, set the name of the project to `ASPTrans` and the name of the default class to `Order`. Add a second class module, and call it `Products`.

> *If you wish you can set the* MTSTransactionMode *on the* `Order` *class to* 2 – RequiresTransaction. *This will automatically set the Transaction Support attribute for the component to* Required *when it is placed into COM+. Remember that this default setting will only take effect when your component is added to a COM+ application from the* Add File *dialog.*

Before the code is added to the classes, the proper references must first be set. Within the References dialog set a reference to Microsoft ActiveX Data Objects 2.5 Library and the COM+ Services Type Library:

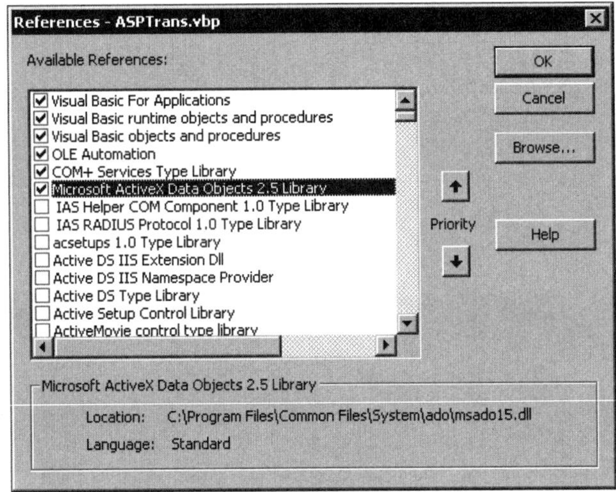

Now it's time to add the code to the classes. Let's start with the class that retrieves the available products.

The Products Component

Start by adding a function called `GetProducts` to the `Products` class. The `GetProducts` method has no parameters and will return a disconnected ADO recordset:

```
Public Function GetProducts() As ADODB.Recordset

End Function
```

Next, let's add in all of the code to handle any errors that arise, and commit or abort the transaction. One thing to note is that this function only returns data; it does not update any resources. However, we still want to use the context to inform COM+ that it can reclaim its resources:

```
Public Function GetProducts() As ADODB.Recordset

   Dim objContext As COMSVCSLib.ObjectContext

   On Error GoTo Error_Handler
```

```
    ' Get a reference to the context object
      Set objContext = GetObjectContext()

    ' Everything worked
      If Not objContext Is Nothing Then objContext.SetComplete

  Exit_Handler:

    ' Clean up
      Set objContext = Nothing
      Exit Function

  Error_Handler:

    ' An error occured
      If Not objContext Is Nothing Then objContext.SetAbort
      Resume Exit_Handler

  End Function
```

All that is left to do is to add a Recordset object, look-up the data and return it back to the caller:

```
Public Function GetProducts() As ADODB.Recordset

  Dim objContext As COMSVCSLib.ObjectContext
  Dim rsProducts As ADODB.Recordset

  On Error GoTo Error_Handler

' Get a reference to the context object
  Set objContext = GetObjectContext()
  Set rsProducts = New ADODB.Recordset

' Retreive the products
  With rsProducts
     .CursorLocation = adUseClient
     .LockType = adLockReadOnly
     .CursorType = adOpenStatic
     .Source = "SELECT * FROM Products"
     .ActiveConnection = "Provider=SQLOLEDB.1;User ID=sa;" & _
                         "Initial Catalog=ASPTransactions;"  & _
                         "Data Source=<SERVER_NAME>"
     .Open

     'Disconnect the recordset
     Set .ActiveConnection = Nothing
  End With

' Set the return value
  Set GetProducts = rsProducts

' Everything worked
  If Not objContext Is Nothing Then objContext.SetComplete
```

```
Exit_Handler:

' Clean up
  Set rsProducts = Nothing
  Set objContext = Nothing
  Exit Function

Error_Handler:

' An error occured
  If Not objContext Is Nothing Then objContext.SetAbort
  Resume Exit_Handler

End Function
```

The recently added code now completes the `GetProducts` function, which executes a normal `SELECT` to the `Products` table.

Notice that a client-side cursor is used as opposed to a server-side. A client-side cursor must be used when working with disconnected recordsets; it informs ADO to pull down all of the data at once, instead of reading a few records at a time. Once the data is retrieved the code disconnects the recordset and sets the return value for the caller.

The Order Component

Next, let's build the method to process the order from the user. This method, named `PlaceOrder`, is a normal subroutine that expects four parameters describing the order. This `PlaceOrder` is a not a function and does not have return value:

```
Public Sub PlaceOrder(strLastName As String, strFirstName As String, _
                      lngProductID As Long, lngQuantity As Long)
End Sub
```

The four parameters that `PlaceOrder` expects are the first and last name of the user, the product ID and the quantity. The `PlaceOrder` routine is going to do two primary things: add a record into the `Orders` table and adjust the inventory level for the product.

Let's again start by adding the code to handle any errors that arise and add the support for transactions. Just like the other method if an error were to occur it would be trapped in the `Error_Handler` section and the transaction will be rolled back. If an error does not arise then the transaction will be committed:

```
Public Sub PlaceOrder(strLastName As String, strFirstName As String, _
                      lngProductID As Long, lngQuantity As Long)

  Dim objContext As ObjectContext()

  On Error GoTo Error_Handler

' Get a reference to the context object
' that's running the transaction
```

```
    Set objContext = GetObjectContext()

  ' Everything worked
    If Not objContext Is Nothing Then objContext.SetComplete

  Exit_Handler:

  ' Clean up
    Set objContext = Nothing
    Exit Sub

  Error_Handler:

  ' An error occured
    If Not objContext Is Nothing Then objContext.SetAbort
    Resume Exit_Handler

  End Sub
```

Now it's time to add code to insert a record into the `Orders` table and to adjust the inventory level for the product. This can be easily done by creating an ADO Connection object and executing an `INSERT` and an `UPDATE` statement. The following code can be performed explicitly with an ADO Command object, but to keep it simple this example just uses an ADO Connection object:

```
  Public Sub PlaceOrder(strLastName As String, strFirstName As String, _
                        lngProductID As Long, lngQuantity As Long)

    Dim objContext As COMSVCSLib.ObjectContext
    Dim objConn As ADODB.Connection

    On Error GoTo Error_Handler

  ' Get a reference to the context object
  ' that's running the transaction
    Set objContext = GetObjectContext()
    Set objConn = New ADODB.Connection

  ' Add the new record to the database
    With objConn
       .ConnectionString = "Provider=SQLOLEDB.1;User ID=sa;" & _
                           "Initial Catalog=ASPTransactions;" & _
                           "Data Source=<SERVER_NAME>"
       .Open
       .Execute "INSERT INTO Orders (ProductID, Quantity, LastName, " & _
                "FirstName) VALUES(" & lngProductID & ", " & _
                lngQuantity & ", '" & strLastName & "', '" & _
                strFirstName & "')", , adExecuteNoRecords

       .Execute "UPDATE Products SET InventoryLevel = " & _
                "(SELECT InventoryLevel FROM Products " & _
                "WHERE ID = " & lngProductID & ")" & _
                " - " & lngQuantity & " WHERE ID = " & _
                lngProductID
    End With
```

```
' Everything worked
  If Not objContext Is Nothing Then objContext.SetComplete

Exit_Handler:

' Clean up
  Set objConn = Nothing
  Set objContext = Nothing
  Exit Sub

Error_Handler:

' An error occured
  If Not objContext Is Nothing Then objContext.SetAbort
  Resume Exit_Handler

End Sub
```

That's all the code that is needed for the ActiveX DLL. All that is left for the business logic is to compile the DLL and install it into a COM+ Application.

When placing the DLL into COM+ remember to adjust the Transaction Support on the `Order` component to inform COM+ that it requires a transaction when it is called upon. On the Transaction tab adjust the setting to Required:

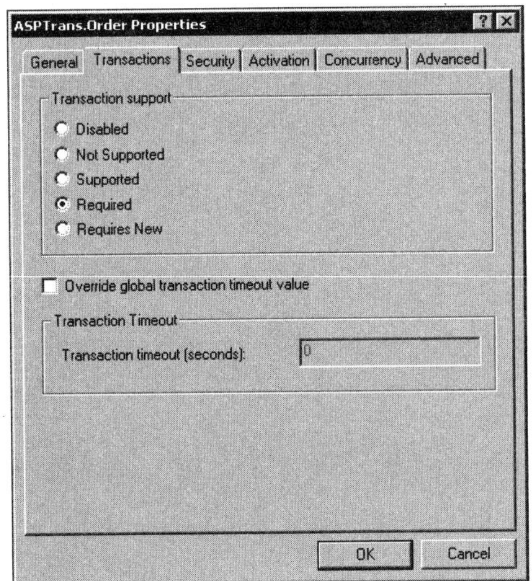

The Transaction Support attribute for the `Products` component should be configured to Not Supported because it only performs read-only operations against the database.

That completes the business logic section of the example.

The User Interface

The user interface for this example is actually quite simple. It consists of two pages: one to gather the order information from the user, and the other to submit the order and inform the user if the order has been placed successfully.

The `Orders.asp` page will display the various products to the users and allow them to generate an order. First add a form to the page that contains the order entry controls:

```
<%@ LANGUAGE=VBScript %>
<HTML>
<HEAD>
</HEAD>
<BODY>

<FORM ID="frmOrder" NAME="frmOrder" ACTION="PlaceOrder.asp" METHOD="Post">
  <BLOCKQUOTE>
  <H3>
  To generate an order enter in you first name, last name,
  the quantity, and select a product to purchase.
  </H3>
  <HR>
  <BR>

  First Name:
  <BR>
  <INPUT TYPE="TEXT" ID="txtFN" NAME="txtFN">
  <P>

  Last Name:
  <BR>
  <INPUT TYPE="TEXT" ID="txtLN" NAME="txtLN">
  <P>

  Products:
  <BR>
  <SELECT ID="optProducts" NAME="optProducts">
  </SELECT>
  <P>

  Quantity:
  <BR>
  <INPUT TYPE="TEXT" ID="txtQuantity" NAME="txtQuantity">
  <P>

  <INPUT TYPE="SUBMIT" VALUE="Place Order" ID="btnPlaceOrder"
         NAME="btnPlaceOrder">

  </BLOCKQUOTE>
</FORM>

</BODY>
</HTML>
```

Next, we have to add the code to call upon the ActiveX component and retrieve a list of products. This is done by creating an instance of the class using the `CreateObject` function from the `Server` object. Once a reference to an instance of the class is made the code can then retrieve the recordset and display its contents in a list box to the user:

```
<%@ LANGUAGE=VBScript %>
<HTML>
<HEAD>
</HEAD>
<BODY>

<FORM ID="frmOrder" NAME="frmOrder" ACTION="PlaceOrder.asp" METHOD="Post">
  <BLOCKQUOTE>
  <H3>
  To generate an order enter in you first name, last name,
  the quantity, and select a product to purchase.
  </H3>
  <HR>
  <BR>

  First Name:
  <BR>
  <INPUT TYPE="TEXT" ID="txtFN" NAME="txtFN">
  <P>

  Last Name:
  <BR>
  <INPUT TYPE="TEXT" ID="txtLN" NAME="txtLN">
  <P>

  Products:
  <BR>
  <SELECT ID="optProducts" NAME="optProducts">
  <%
    Dim objASPTrans
    Dim rsProducts
    Set objASPTrans = Server.CreateObject("ASPTrans.Products")
    Set rsProducts = objASPTrans.GetProducts

    Do Until rsProducts.EOF
       Response.Write "<OPTION VALUE=" & rsProducts("ID") & _
                      ">" & rsProducts("Name") & vbCrLf
       rsProducts.MoveNext
    Loop

    Set rsProducts = Nothing
    Set objASPTrans = Nothing
  %>
  </SELECT>
  <P>

  Quantity:
  <BR>
  <INPUT TYPE="TEXT" ID="txtQuantity" NAME="txtQuantity">
  <P>

  <INPUT TYPE="SUBMIT" VALUE="Place Order" ID="btnPlaceOrder"
         NAME="btnPlaceOrder">
  </BLOCKQUOTE>
</FORM>

</BODY>
</HTML>
```

Now that we have an ASP page to capture the user input, all that is left is to process the order. This is done through another ASP page named `PlaceOrder.asp`. `PlaceOrder.asp` is a transactional ASP page that invokes the `PlaceOrder` routine on the ActiveX DLL, which then updates the database by adding the order record and adjusting the inventory level. Let's start by adding the `PlaceOrder.asp` page, setting the `TRANSACTION` directive at the top of the page, and adding the `OnTransactionCommit` and `OnTransactionAbort` routines:

```
<%@ LANGUAGE=VBScript TRANSACTION=Required%>

<%
'Fires if the transaction commits
Sub OnTransactionCommit

End Sub

'Fires if the transaction aborts
Sub OnTransactionAbort

End Sub
%>
```

Next, fill in the transaction routines with code to inform the user of the outcome of the order request. To do this, simply enter a `Response.Write` statement within the routines:

```
<%@ LANGUAGE=VBScript TRANSACTION=Required%>

<%
'Fires if the transaction commits
Sub OnTransactionCommit
  Response.Write "<HTML>" & vbCrLf
  Response.Write "You order has been successfully placed." & vbCrLf
  Response.Write "<P>" & vbCrLf
  Response.Write "Thank you!" & vbCrLf
  Response.Write "</HTML>" & vbCrLf
End Sub

'Fires if the transaction aborts
Sub OnTransactionAbort
  Response.Write "<HTML>" & vbCrLf
  Response.Write "You order has not been placed." & vbCrLf
  Response.Write "<P>" & vbCrLf
  Response.Write "A error has occured, please try later." & vbCrLf
  Response.Write "</HTML>" & vbCrLf
End Sub
%>
```

The final piece to add to the ASP page is to read the input from the Request object and process the user's order information:

```
<%@ LANGUAGE=VBScript TRANSACTION=Required%>

<%

'Place the order
Dim objOrder
Set objOrder = Server.CreateObject("ASPTrans.Order")
objOrder.PlaceOrder Request.Form("txtLN"), _
                    Request.Form("txtFN"), _
                    Request.Form("optProducts"), _
                    Request.Form("txtQuantity")
Set objOrder = Nothing

'Fires if the transaction commits
Sub OnTransactionCommit
  Response.Write "<HTML>" & vbCrLf
  Response.Write "You order has been successfully placed." & vbCrLf
  Response.Write "<P>" & vbCrLf
  Response.Write "Thank you!" & vbCrLf
  Response.Write "</HTML>" & vbCrLf
End Sub

'Fires if the transaction aborts
Sub OnTransactionAbort
  Response.Write "<HTML>" & vbCrLf
  Response.Write "You order has not been placed." & vbCrLf
  Response.Write "<P>" & vbCrLf
  Response.Write "A error has occured, please try later." & vbCrLf
  Response.Write "</HTML>" & vbCrLf
End Sub
%>
```

Did it Really Work?

Try the example. Add a couple of orders to the system. You should be able to open SQL Server and view the records in the `Order` table:

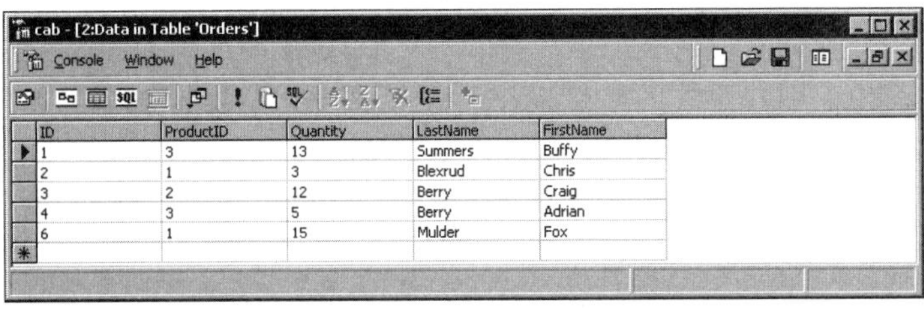

To verify the processing under a transaction, open the Component Services MMC snap-in again and select the Transaction Statistics node under the Distributed Transaction Coordinator node under the desired computer. The transaction statistics monitor listens to DTC as it commits and aborts transactions and displays a summary of the results:

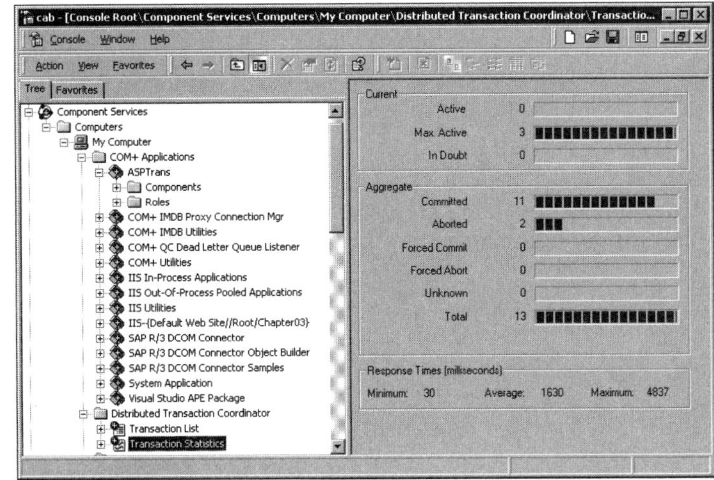

Summary

This chapter has addressed the concept of transaction processing and how it can be leveraged within an IIS application through the use of Windows 2000's Component Services (COM+).

Microsoft has provided developers with a powerful set of services which applications can be built upon. These services, such as transaction processing (DTC), allow developers to concentrate on solving business problems instead of worrying about the underlying communication between services.

In this chapter, we specifically looked at:

- What Transaction Processing is
- Why we need transactions
- How COM+ handles transaction processing
- Transactions in components
- Transactions in ASP

In the next chapter, we will move onto to another service provided by COM+, that of message queuing.

N
W

20

ASP and Message Queue Server

In the last chapter, we saw how we can add transactional abilities to our applications and components using COM+. In this chapter we are going to look at another method of increasing the scalability of our applications.

So far we have been assuming a perfect world where our server has always been available. But what happens if we can't make this assumption – does our entire system design fall apart? Obviously, not; instead we need to make use of an asynchronous communication system, more commonly referred to as **messaging** or **message queuing**.

Under a messaging scenario, instead of an application performing normal method calls and waiting for a response, the caller simply sends a 'message' to the server and proceeds as normal. Thus, messaging not only allows the client to proceed with other work, but utilizing MSMQ, the server doesn't even need to be available as the messages can be queued and processed at a later time.

In this chapter we will be looking at following aspects of messaging:

- What message queuing is
- MSMQ and its architecture
- How to administrator MSMQ
- How to interact with MSMQ using COM objects
- How to use MSMQ components in an ASP application
- How to respond to MSMQ messages asynchronously
- How to incorporate MSMQ into transactions

First though, let's get some more background on what message queuing actually is.

What is Message Queuing?

> **Message queuing is a system that allows different applications to communicate with each other using a 'store and forward' process.**

These applications can be on the same or on different physical platforms. The platforms can be located in the same room, on the same LAN, or at any locations that are electronically connected. This connection does not even need to be permanent or reliable. In addition to this, the platforms can even be running different operating systems.

This sounds like a very *heterogeneous* system. Different applications, wide geographic locations, different connection types, and different operating systems are all characteristic of the Internet-connected world that we are living in today. Being able to move data between these systems has always been a goal of those who preach about connectivity.

Technologies such as SQL, ODBC, FTP, and HTTP all provide different mechanisms for data to be moved between systems in this heterogeneous environment. The principal drawback is that these technologies are oriented to particular *types* of applications. We'd like to have an *application-neutral* technology that lets us exchange data between heterogeneous platforms as they become available. The format of the data exchanged and the rules of the platform-to-platform interaction should be left to the specific applications. The technology should simply be a *communication channel.* The fact that large numbers of systems have been created using these systems doesn't mean that there isn't a more efficient method of communication.

Messaging middleware systems are well known in the mainframe community, where they have been a fixture of high-volume transaction processing applications for years. There are a number of messaging technology products for PCs, but we will be concentrating on MSMQ as it is closely-integrated with ASP and the rest of Microsoft's development tools.

What is MSMQ

> **The basic concept of MSMQ is very simple; it is email for applications.**

Just like email messages, MSMQ messages have a **sender** and a **receiver**. The receiver, however, is a little different. The receiver of a message in MSMQ is defined by who has access to the queue (this is set by the Windows' domain security). This enables multiple receivers to respond to a *single* message in a *single* queue. In most Web applications that use MSMQ, the sender of the message is the Web server (IIS) and the receiver of the message is a custom application.

When MSMQ **messages** are comprised, they are packaged into a **container** and sent to a destination where it is persisted in a **queue** until the recipient is ready to read it. These queues are what provide MSMQ the ability to guarantee delivery of messages (store and forward), regardless of the state and reliability of the network connection.

The custom application doesn't have to be on a different machine, but it allows for greater scalability.

In most ASP applications, which utilize MSMQ, the messages are sent from ASP script or from COM components to a queue on the same server or on a different machine. Once the message is sent, the ASP script can continue processing. In the background, a different custom server-side application, usually built in a COM compliant tool such as Visual Basic or Visual C++, responds to the message and begins to process it. Another possible way to respond and process MSMQ messages is to build a SQL Server 7.0 job that uses VBScript to open the queue.

MSMQ can also communicate with other messaging systems. Level 8 Systems is developing a third-party solution to communicate with MSMQ on platforms such as Sun Solaris, HP-UNIX, OS/2, VMS, and AS/400 platforms.

Messages

As I suggested earlier, messages in MSMQ are similar to email messages. However, they are not sent to a single user or even a group of users; they are sent from a *single* application to a *single* queue on a *single* computer.

MSMQ messages are mainly comprised of three parts:

- The **Label**
- The **Body**
- The **Destination queue**

The label is very similar to the subject of an email message. Most of the time a label is used to group various type of messages together so a custom server-side application can distinguish what the message contains.

The body of a MSMQ message is very versatile. It is designed to hold anything from a String, to an array, to persistable COM objects! The actual content is not examined by the message queuing system itself and there is no explicit standard method for formatting the content of a message. This means that the format of the content can be freely determined by the two applications that are passing the message.

For example, it is possible to create an instance of Excel's Application object, load a spreadsheet and set the body of a MSMQ message to the instance of Excel. Then when the message is read, the instance of the Excel object is pulled out of it! The only requirement is that both the sender and receiver of the message must have the component registered on their system.

A message can also include implementation-specific information about, for example, who the sender and the receiver are, a timestamp saying when it was sent, and even an expiration date, after which if they are not read, they will be deleted.

MSMQ messages also contain a **Priority** attribute that determines the order in which messages are read, much like the priority level on email messages. The priority level of a message can be any integer value from 0 to 7, and determines the order in which the message is placed into a queue. Newly added messages don't always get appended to the bottom of the queue. For example a message with a priority of 6 will be place before a message with a priority of 5, the lower the number, the lower the priority. The default priority level for a MSMQ message is 3. However, a message sent to a transactional message queue will automatically assume a priority level of 0. This is due to the fact that priority levels are ignored by the transaction.

Queues

A **message queue** is where a message lives until it is picked up by the destination application. Continuing the email analogy, queues are closely related to an *inbox*. A message will stay in a queue until it expires, is read, or until the queue is purged.

There can be more than one queue in a system but as we'll see later, MSMQ supports vast hierarchies of connected systems. However, on any particular machine, a **queue manager** manages all of the queues resident on that machine. Typically, this will consist of all the queues destined to receive messages for applications on that machine. This need not always be the case. Most messaging products permit you to directly address queues hosted on remote machines provided the network administrator has configured the remote queue manager appropriately. It is up to the queue manager to determine if the destination of a message is a local queue or not. If it is local, it simply drops the message in its destination queue. If it is not local, it locates the machine where the destination queue is by using a directory server. It then negotiates the transfer of that message with the destination machine's queue manager. Once the destination queue manager receives the message, it then deposits it in the destination queue.

Each queue belongs to a single server, but one server can have multiple queues.

The main attributes of a queue are:

- **Label** – A simple string that is commonly used to define the queue
- **ID** – A GUID to defines the queue uniquely
- **TypeID** – A GUID that defines a group or type of queue

The TypeID can and will most likely be duplicated across multiple queues that perform a common task to group them together.

In addition, there are four types of queues in MSMQ 2.0:

- **Outgoing queues** are used to persist messages when a remote MSMQ server is unavailable. They are what provide MSMQ with the flexibility to operate even when another server is down. Outgoing queues are not available for use by applications – they are only used internally by MSMQ for the storing and forwarding of messages.
- **System queues** are also used internally by MSMQ and are not available to custom applications. Examples of system queues are dead-letter queues, report queues and journal queues.

- **Public queues** are the most common type of queue in MSMQ. They are the queues that can be used by custom applications to fulfill business needs. Public queues are stored in the Active Directory service, and therefore, are known to all other MSMQ servers throughout the enterprise.
- **Private queues** are similar in the fact that they are accessible from custom applications. However, they are not published in Active Directory, and so they are not available to applications outside of the local computer.

Although message queues can be created programmatically through code, they are most often created through the MSMQ section of the Computer Management snap-in. For more information on administrating MSMQ refer to the *Administering MSMQ* section below.

Why MSMQ and ASP?

So why use MSMQ? Why not just develop a simple COM component that ASP can invoke the desired functionality from through DCOM?

To answer this, consider these following questions:

- What if the server the COM object is running on isn't available?
- What if the processing takes too long, the ASP page time-out period expires and the user gives up?
- What if the processing is something that can't be done during normal hours because of table locks or processor intensity?

These questions are why services like MSMQ were developed. By using MSMQ, these questions can be dealt with in a fairly easy manner.

What if the server the COM object is running on isn't available?

If the client sends a message to MSMQ instead of directly talking to the COM object, it provides another layer of abstraction between the client and the service (COM) object. This is known as **loosely coupled** asynchronous communication.

Of course, a normal COM object can't run by itself, but a server-side executable can be developed that responds to the message and invokes the functionality on the COM object. Since the client is separated from the background, they can simply send a message and continue on processing as long as the Web server (IIS) has an MSMQ client installed.

What if the processing takes too long?

This problem is solved just like the above situation. By moving the processing to a background server process, the client doesn't have to wait until the task is completed.

What if the processing is something that can't be done during normal hours?

If the processing can't be done during normal peak hours, the task can be stored in a message queue until a scheduled server-side executable is ready to process the tasks (messages in the queue). This allows any number of messages or tasks to be stored up and run at once.

> *This is also known as batch processing.*

Speed vs. Availability

In general, messaging middleware is regarded as a technology for improving availability and scalability. This should not be confused with speed. Messaging will always be slower than a low level method of inter-process communication like sockets or named pipes. Messages, after all, eventually use those methods for their transmission. The middleware technology adds all the overhead of negotiation and notification to the basic performance of the communications protocol. How can messaging be a scalability solution if this is the case? Wouldn't we want the fastest possible communication?

Messaging middleware acknowledges that no matter how fast a technology may be, it will never be fast enough. This includes processors as well as communications. Unless a machine can handle an infinite load in zero time, you can always overwhelm it. That's where messaging middleware comes in.

First, by introducing asynchronous communications into the process, clients are freed for other tasks while awaiting a response to a message. Since queue managers place incoming messages into a buffer – the queue – the receiving server doesn't have to be fast enough to handle the heaviest possible levels of traffic. It merely needs to be 'sized' for the average amount of traffic in the system. Extra messages coming in during spikes will back up in the queue, only to be cleared when traffic eases. A system that must synchronously process messages as they arrive will fail – poor availability – while an asynchronous messaging system remains available for service.

Thus, messaging is a scalability solution in the sense that a system with asynchronous messaging can handle more traffic without failure, not in the sense that it handles lots of traffic faster.

This should illustrate the value of adding additional features to a low level protocol. Messaging middleware offers an array of features important to enterprise systems in exchange for some additional overhead:

- It improves availability
- It allows for the inclusion of occasionally disconnected computers, which basic protocols will not allow
- It allows both sender and recipient to know that a given message was received, and was received exactly once

As we go forward in this chapter, remember that raw speed is seldom the most important factor in building a scalable enterprise system.

Messaging vs. Synchronous Communication

So, should you *always* use message queuing to communicate between applications? This isn't the case either. If your business environment requires some activities be carried out synchronously, then a communication method such as DCOM is better suited to perform this type of processing. If everybody using the application is always connected to the LAN, and all of the application servers are connected over fast, local, reliable links, then messaging may not be the answer either. In addition, for many developers message queuing is a new and unfamiliar technology that they may not be willing to invest in.

A few short guidelines of when to use message queuing can help to clarify the decision to use it:

- If the application you are communicating with is not guaranteed to be running at the same time as your application
- If the message is important and will cause problems if it is lost
- If your application is not always connected to the receiver application, but still needs to be functional
- If you perform many communication tasks with other applications asynchronously, and may or may not care about their response

MSMQ Architecture

The primary parts of the MSMQ system architecture are the messages, the queues, the queue managers, and the interface that allows programs to access the information. The system operates transparently with respect to physical location. This means that an application can be sending a message to another application without having to worry about how the message actually gets there. MSMQ provides the facility for programmatically searching the set of queues available throughout a system. Once the application finds the queue it is interested in, it can send messages to it without worrying about how the message will actually get there. MSMQ handles the route taken by the message, and can (if necessary) *guarantee* that it gets to its final destination.

MSMQ's architecture is comprised of one-to-many servers and workstations that route, send, and receive messages.

Each one of these computers may or may not contain multiple message queues, and within each queue can reside multiple messages.

Server Types

MSMQ can be installed in a wide variety of sever and client installations, which can become overwhelming when getting started with MSMQ. There are four different server installations for MSMQ:

- Primary Enterprise Controller
- Primary Site Controller
- Backup Site Controller
- Router

The Primary Enterprise Controller

The **Primary Enterprise Controller (PEC)** is the *root level* in the MSMQ architecture. Every enterprise network must contain one PEC in order for MSMQ to function properly. In MSMQ 1.0 the PEC required SQL Server 6.5 or higher, but in MSMQ 2.0 SQL Server is not required because the messages and queues are stored in the Active Directory Service (ADS).

ADS comes with part of Windows 2000, however it must be added on NT4 before MSMQ 2.0 can be installed. Either version can only be installed on Windows NT 4 Server or Windows 2000 Server.

The PEC is where most of the queues are stored, especially within smaller networks. As the network size grows it may be more efficient for remote sites to hold their own queue located in a Primary Site Controller (see below).

The PEC is usually located in the main branch or headquarters of a corporation. This is because all of the other servers must be able to access the PEC to register with it (stored in ADS). If the corporation's network only consists of a small LAN, a PEC is the only server required and can be incorporated on the same server as IIS. In large enterprises, the PEC is used to store information about the location of other MSMQ servers and their queues and to route the messages between them, and is usually the only BackOffice service on the server.

The Primary Site Controller

There is usually one **Primary Site Controller (PSC)** located within a remote branch or site within a corporation's WAN. The PSC is designed for communicating with the local client on the remote LAN and coordinating any information back to the PEC. By having one PSC at each branch, it provides a single point of communication back to the PEC. This helps conserve resources, such as network communication, that are important to a remote site, especially over a slow network line.

As mentioned above, in small LAN enterprises, the PSC is not always needed; its job can be performed by the PEC.

The Backup Site Controller

The **Backup Site Controller (BSC)** is used to store a read-only copy of the information stored in the PSC. One BSC is usually installed at each site, just like the PSC, and will provide fail over support if the PSC were to fail.

A Router

As the MSMQ architecture grows in an enterprise, MSMQ **Routers** become very useful. A Router will not only help deliver messages to their destination queue, but it will also help servers with different network protocols, such as TCP/IP and IPX, communicate with one another.

MSMQ Router servers do not have local queues for storing messages. They are just designed to help determine the best route to send a message. MSMQ Router servers can also be very useful if a part of the network were to go down. The router will try to find a different path that the message can take to reach its destination.

The functionality within a MSMQ Router is also contained in the PEC and the PSC servers. Since every site is required to contain a PEC or PSC, this means that every site will contain a Router of some kind.

Client Types

The client installations are a little easier to grasp because they only have two install options:

- Dependent client
- Independent client

Independent Clients

MSMQ **Independent clients** can be installed on computers running Windows 9x, Windows NT 4, or Windows 2000. Independent clients have the ability to send and read messages to other MSMQ server queues and can also save messages in local queues.

MSMQ Independent clients are usually installed on the Application server and Web server. Since Independent clients can store messages they are not *dependent* on the MSMQ service running on the destination computer. This is very useful when a COM component or ASP script wants to send a message, but the server is not available. The Independent client will store the message locally until a MSMQ server becomes available, and forwards the message to it (store and forward).

Even though Independent clients can have local queues, they are not required to have Active Directory service or even SQL Server installed; instead the messages and queue information are persisted in files and the registry. This allows a client to have a lot of the MSMQ functionality locally without the large footprint. Independent clients also have the ability to respond to messages asynchronously by using the MSMQEvent object.

When installing an MSMQ Independent client, the installation wizard will prompt for the PEC in order for the client machine to register with it.

Dependent Clients

The MSMQ **Dependent client** is the other option for Windows 9x, NT 4, and 2000 clients. The main difference between the Independent and Dependent installation is that the Dependent client *cannot* store messages locally. Dependent clients also cannot create queues on other servers or asynchronously read messages from a queue.

Dependent clients can only send and read messages when they have access to an MSMQ server. They also do not have the functionality to receive messages because they do not have local queues.

The Dependent client is usually installed on end-user workstations, because of the small footprint that is left behind and the lack of need for end-users to respond to messages.

Site Diagram

The following is a diagram displaying the layout of a typical MSMQ installation that spans over a WAN network with a centralized LAN:

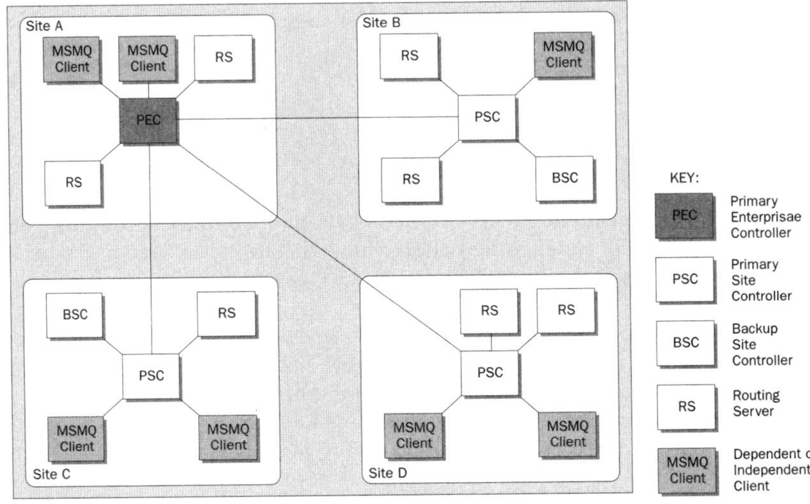

Multiple Paths

When configuring an enterprise installation of MSMQ, you determine the 'cost' of the links between two message routers. This cost can be based on any factors that you determine as relevant. Things such as speed of link, available bandwidth on link, and actual monetary usage cost of the link can go into computing the 'cost' for a link. When performing dynamic routing, MSMQ will compute the 'cheapest' link between the sender and the receiver and send the message that way. This makes the configuration of an MSMQ enterprise much simpler, as static routes do not need to be explicitly created. It also allows MSMQ to route around breaks in the network topology, thereby increasing availability of messaging services.

Delivery Options

Microsoft Message Queue Server supports three options for the delivery of messages. Each of these delivery options provides different advantages to the transmission of messages. Likewise, they each have associated trade-offs. The three types of delivery options are:

- Memory-based
- Disk-based
- Transactional-based

Memory-based Delivery

In this delivery type the message remains in the system memory as it moves from queue manager to queue manager through the message queue system. If there is a problem in the network and the queue manager that is currently processing the message cannot contact the next queue manager in the network, then the message will be held until the connection can be restored. Memory-based delivery is very fast, since the message is never transferred from system memory to disk storage. While this type of message will survive a failure in the network connection between two queue managers, it will not survive a failure of the machine that it is currently on. This is the price you must pay to get the speed advantage of memory-based delivery.

Disk-based Delivery

Alternatively, as the message moves from queue manager to queue manager, it can be written to permanent disk storage on each machine. When the message is transferred off to the next machine, it will be removed from the previous machine's disk storage as soon as the sending machine finishes its transmission. Since this message has to be written to disk on every machine that it passes through, it will take the message much longer to reach its destination than with memory-based delivery. Disk I/O, after all, is several orders of magnitude slower than RAM. The benefit here is being able to recover the message in the event of system failure. Since this delivery method means that each queue manager the message passes through writes every message sent with this delivery method to disk, a system failure would not destroy the message. This is reliant on the use of a recoverable file system, such as NTFS, for the installation of the MSMQ server.

Transactional Delivery

Finally, the progress of each message from sender to receiver can be considered a transaction. Since transactions support the ACID properties, this means that a transactional delivered message will be atomic, consistent, isolated, and durable.

To be durable, a transactional message uses the disk-based delivery method of writing every message to permanent storage as it moves through the system. The atomic characteristic means that the message will be delivered exactly one time, and in the same order it was sent.

Transactional messages use the transaction control features of COM+ to provide the transactional characteristics of the message's delivery. A notable benefit of this delivery method is that MSMQ messages can participate in transactions with database operations. This permits the creation of complex transaction rules in applications that use MSMQ.

Administering MSMQ

MSMQ 2.0, like most services in Windows 2000, is administered through MMC snap-ins. The MSMQ snap-in is located under the Computer Management snap-in:

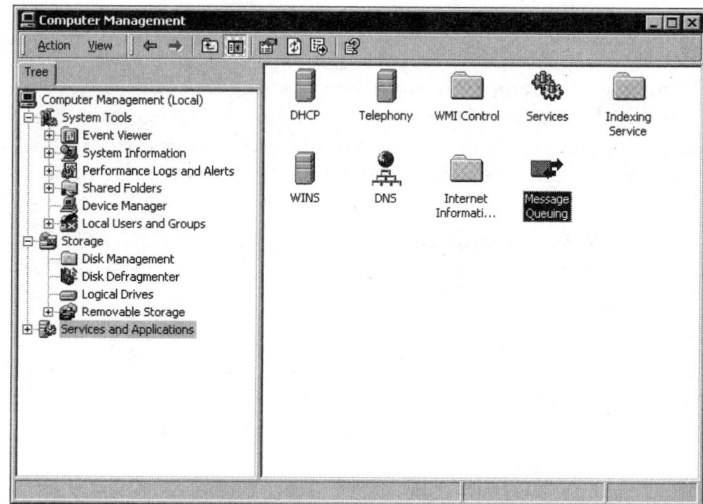

The most common task performed in MSMQ's MMC snap-in is adding a new queue. Adding a queue to an MSMQ server is very easy.

Adding a Queue

Start by opening the Computer Management snap-in and open the sub-levels under the Message Queuing node:

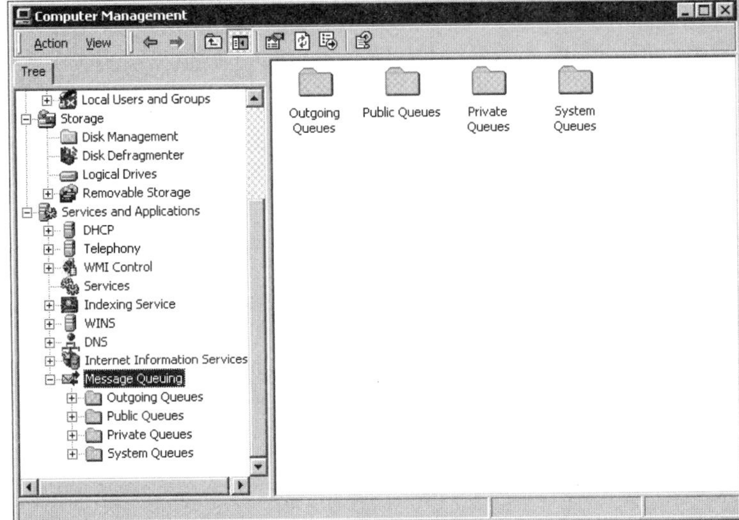

Next, right-click on the Public Queues folder and select New, then Public Queue. Now MMC should display a screen prompting for two things, the queue Name and whether or not the queue is Transactional:

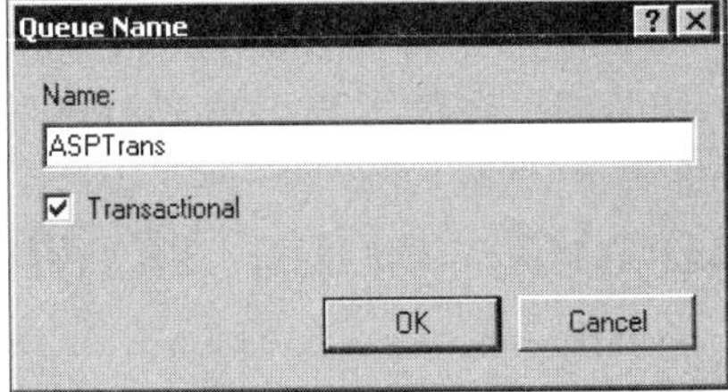

The name is a common user-friendly string that will identify the queue (Label), and the transactional setting determines if this queue will require transactions when sending and receiving messages to and from the queue. Transactions will be discussed in further detail later on in this chapter. For now, simply call the queue ASPTrans and check the transactional setting.

We'll be using this queue in our MSMQ sample at the end of the chapter.

MSMQ will now create a new Public queue called ASPTrans:

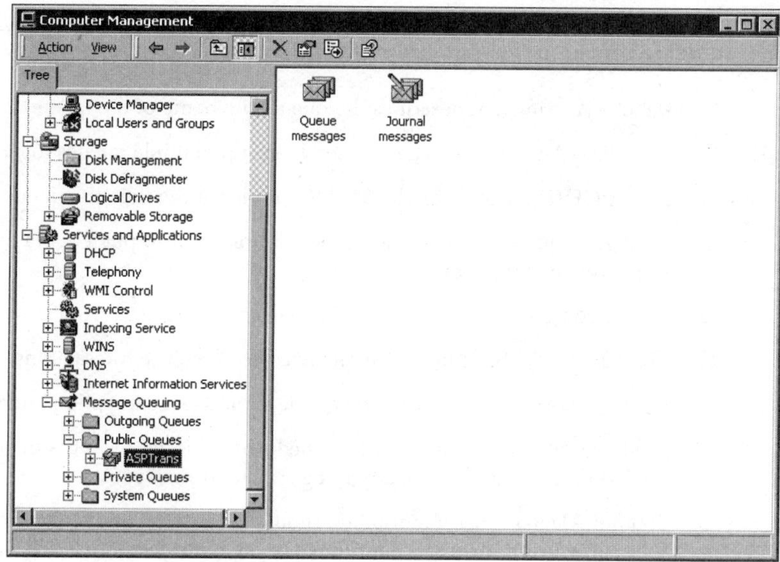

As of right now the queue is set to receive messages. Let's first take a look at the setting of a queue and what MSMQ defaults it to.

Message Queue Properties

To view the properties of an MSMQ queue, right-click on the queue in the tree on the left or on the right-pane in the MMC snap-in and select Properties. MSMQ should now display a Properties dialog box containing all of the settings for the message queue:

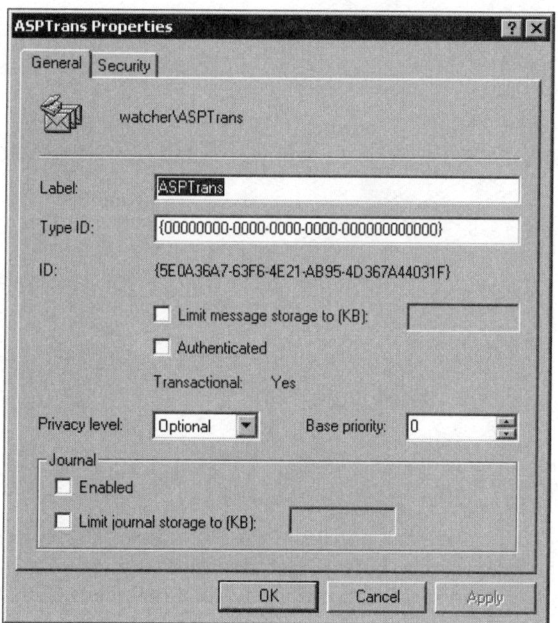

Within the Properties dialog box there are two main parts, General information and Security. The General information is comprised of the following:

- Label – A string that describes the queue (the name of the queue).
- Type ID – A GUID that can be used to group multiple queues together.
- ID – A GUID assigned by the MSMQ service at the time the queue is created.
- Limit message storage – Allows the administrator to put a quota on a queue in order to stop it from growing too large.
- Authenticated – Determines if the queue accepts client certificates.
- Transactional – Specifies if the queue is set to require transactions.
- Privacy level – Determines if the queue should use encryption and on what part of the message.
- Base priority – Determines what is the lowest priority level the queue will accept. Default is 0, however, the setting can be any integer value from 0 to 7.
- Journal – Determines if journaling should be enabled and what size it should be limited to. Journaling keeps messages after they are read, instead of deleting them.

The second part of the queue properties is Security. This is where MSMQ will look to determine who has access to read from, send to and administer a queue:

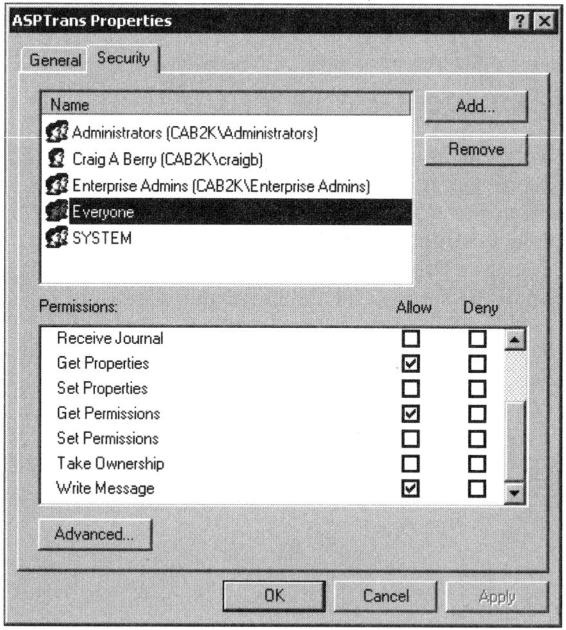

There are two entries in the Permissions area to take note of. This queue has Write Message access to everyone, but not Receive Message access. This means that a guest to a Web site has permissions to send messages, but not to read messages. This is normally what is desired unless a Web application requires users to be authenticated. Then the permissions should be tightened, the Everyone group should have its access revoked to the queue and only the desired account should be given access.

Once a message is received by a queue, it is located in the Queue messages folder under the main queue folder. The right-pane of the MMC snap-in will display any messages that are in the queue. In this screenshot there is one message that has been received with a label of Sample Message:

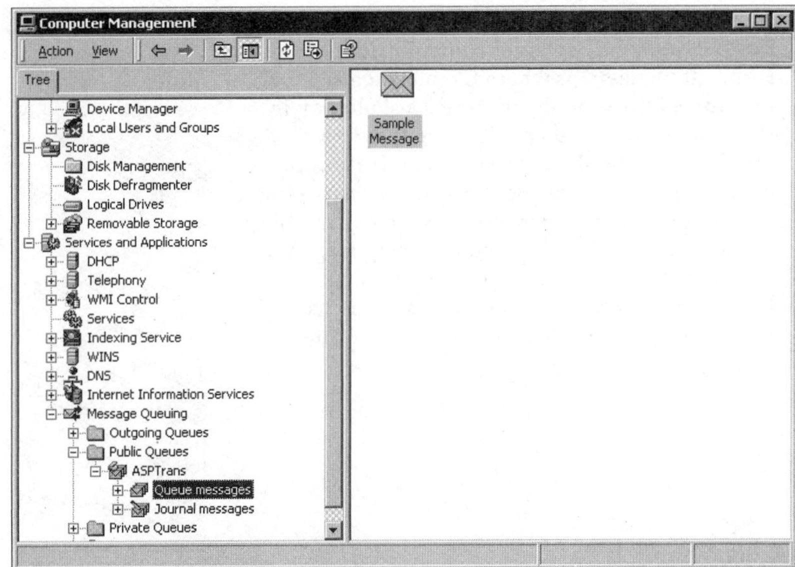

Message Properties

Just like queues, messages also have a Properties dialog box. To view the properties of a message, right-click on the desired message, and select Properties. A Properties dialog with four tabs, General, Queues, Sender and Body, will be displayed:

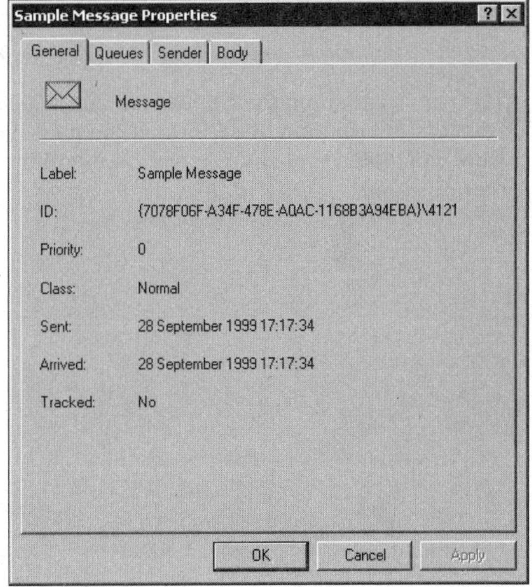

The General tab consists of basic read-only information about the queue; the Label, ID and Priority are commonly used within an application for identifying a message and its importance. The Class, Sent date, Arrived date and Tracked attributes are commonly used for auditing purposes and can also be useful for debugging.

The Queues tab displays three queues with their Format name (GUID) and common Name. The Destination queue is where the message is going to. Most of the time the messsges are already in the Destination queue by the time they are displayed in the MMC snap-in. The Response queue specifies the queue the sender is expecting a reponse in. This is used to send a comfirmation to the sender letting them know the message was received. Finally, the Administration queue is used like the Response queue, but it is automatically responded to by MSMQ when it receives the message:

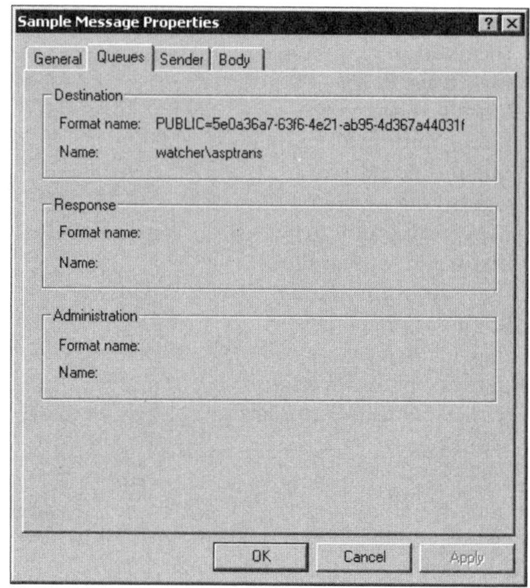

The Sender tab consists of information about the sender of the message. It contains the sender computer ID (GUID) and Pathname (computer name). The tab also contains information about the User login that sent the message; such as their login name, security identifier (SID), whether or not they Authenticated the message with a client certificate, and any Algorithm that was used.

An algorithm is used to encrypt a message for an added level of security.

The last information the Sender tab contains is Security information, describing if the messages were Encrypted and any Encryption algorithm that was used:

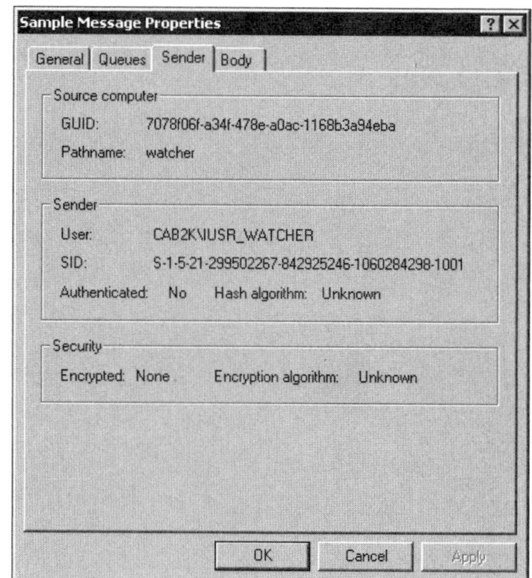

The last tab on the Message Properties dialog box is the Body. This tab is basic, but very useful. It displays the body of the message in hexidecimal form. Even though it is hard to read, you can see an ASCII version of what the message contains on the right, "T.h.i.s .i.s. .a. .s.a.m.p.l.e. .m.e.s.s.a.g.e..."

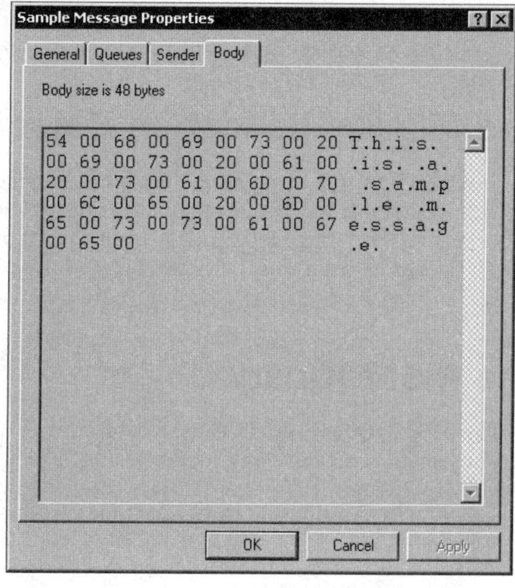

The MSMQ Object Model

Just like most BackOffice services, MSMQ has a COM API (`MQOA.DLL`), which developers can program with. MSMQ's object model is comprised of nine objects:

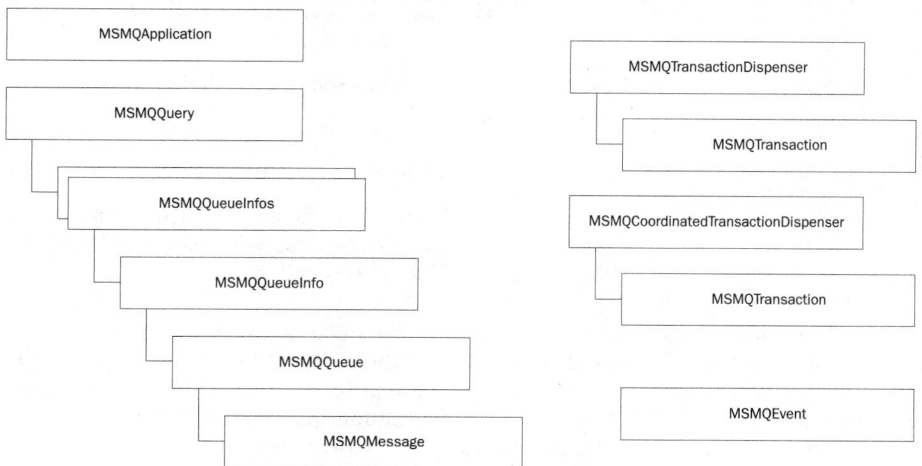

However, most ASP applications only need to utilize three of these:

- The MSMQQueueInfo object
- The MSMQQueue object
- The MSMQMessage object

Nonetheless, it is important to have a good understanding of them all when developing server-side applications to respond to and process messages.

The MSMQApplication Object

The **MSMQApplication object** is a small object that is normally not used when developing solutions with MSMQ. It has two methods: `MachineIdOfMachineName` and `RegisterCertificate`. `MachineIdOfMachineName` is used to lookup the GUID for the server name passed to it. This GUID can be used to specify the server instead of coding to the common name. `RegisterCertificate` simply registers a user's certificate in the server's Active Directory.

The MSMQQuery Object

The **MSMQQuery object** is used to provide a search for a queue given a wide variety of information. The object is actually only comprised of a single method, `LookupQueue`, that returns a collection of MSMQQueueInfo objects within a single MSMQQueueInfos object, based on the search criteria you pass to it. The syntax of this method is as follows:

```
queryObject.LookupQueue([QueueGuid] [, ServiceTypeGuid] [, Label]
                        [, CreateTime] [, ModifyTime] [, RelServiceType]
                        [, RelLabel] [, RelCreateTime] [, RelModifyTime])
```

The first five parameters specify the properties to search for in available queues:

Parameter (Optional)	Type	Value
`QueueGuid`	`String`	Identifier of queue
`ServiceTypeGuid`	`String`	Type of service provided by the queue
`Label`	`String`	Label of queue
`CreateTime`	`Variant Date`	Time when queue was created
`ModifyTime`	`Variant Date`	Time when queue properties were last set (both when the queue was created and the last time Update was called)

You can also set Boolean operators for each of these parameters (except `QueueGuid`, which makes sense when you think about it). The default value for these operators is `REL_EQ`, which simply means that the query will return a collection of queues whose properties exactly match the parameters you specify. These operators can be chosen through the last four parameters of `LookupQueue`, the names of which are simply the names of the associated property preceded by `Rel`:

Relationship Parameter	Corresponding Criteria Parameter
`RelServiceType`	`ServiceTypeGuid`
`RelLabel`	`Label`
`RelCreateTime`	`CreateTime`
`RelModifyTime`	`ModifyTime`

The possible values for these parameters are:

Relation Parameter	Means
REL_EQ	Equal To
REL_NEQ	Not Equal To
REL_LT	Less Than
REL_GT	Greater Than
REL_LE	Less Than or Equal To
REL_GE	Greater Than or Equal To
REL_NOP	Ignore this parameter

To call the `LookupQueue` method, you would do something like the following:

```
<%
Dim objQuery
Dim objQueueInfos

Set objQuery = CreateObject("MSMQ.MSMQQuery")
Set objQueueInfos = objQuery.LookupQueue(Label:="MyQueue")
```

This will return a collection of queues, all of which have a `Label` value of `MyQueue`.

If you need to differentiate between queues with the same label, you can look at the `PathName` *property in each MSMQQueueInfo object.*

The MSMQQueueInfos Collection

MSMQQueueInfos is an object that is returned from the `LookupQueue` method on the MSMQQuery object. The MSMQQueueInfos object is nothing more than a limited collection (missing the `Add`, `Remove`, `Count` methods etc.) that holds MSMQQueueInfo objects. It only has two methods: `Next` that advances the cursor to the next object in the collection, and `Reset` that sets the cursor back to the first object.

The MSMQQueueInfo Object

The **MSMQQueueInfo** object provides the functionality to create, delete and open queues located in MSMQ on a given server. This class is usually the starting point when doing any type of work with the MSMQ object model.

Opening a Queue

In order to work with a queue the `PathName` must first be set. The `PathName` property informs MSMQ what queue is desired and also tells it which machine the queue is located on:

```
<%
Dim objQueueInfo
Dim objQueue

Set objQueueInfo = Server.CreateObject("MSMQ.MSMQQueueInfo")
objQueueInfo.PathName = ".\MyQueue"

Set objQueue = objQueueInfo.Open(MQ_SEND_ACCESS, MQ_DENY_NONE)
%>
```

The code above is an example of opening a queue named `MyQueue` located on the local computer. After dimensioning a local variable, you create an instance of the MSMQQueueInfo object. The next line sets the name and location of the queue:

```
objQueueInfo.PathName = ".\MyQueue"
```

The last line opens the queue using the `Open` method:

```
Set objQueue = objQueueInfo.Open(MQ_SEND_ACCESS, MQ_DENY_NONE)
```

If the desired queue is located on a different machine replace the period with the server name (`MyServer\MyQueue`):

```
objQueue.PathName = "SomeOtherComputer\MyQueue"
```

When opening a queue, two parameters must be passed along, **Access** and **ShareMode**. Access determines what can be done with the queue. The possible values for this parameter are defined in the `MQACCESS` enumerator:

- `MQ_RECEIVE_ACCESS` (1) – The messages in the queue will be removed as they are read
- `MQ_SEND_ACCESS` (2) – Used to send messages to the queue
- `MQ_PEEK_ACCESS` (32) – Used to look (peek) at messages within the specified queue, and does not remove them

You also need to set how other people can interact with the queue when you have it open. This is controlled by the ShareMode. The setting for this parameter is dependent on the Access method you specified in the first parameter:

- If you have opened the queue for sending or peeking, then the only valid setting for this parameter is to allow others to fully interact with the queue (`MQ_DENY_NONE`)
- If you have opened the queue for receiving, then you can either allow others full access to the queue (`MQ_DENY_NONE`), or prevent others from receiving messages from the queue (`MQ_DENY_RECEIVE_SHARE`)

Even if you set this flag to one of these values, other applications can still send messages to the queue and peek at messages in it.

The `Open` routine returns a reference to an MSMQQueue object, which is where the messages are sent and received from. The MSMQQueue object is further discussed below.

Creating a Queue

Creating message queues is performed much like opening a queue, by setting the `PathName` and then calling `Create`:

```
<%
Dim objQueueInfo
Set objQueueInfo = Server.CreateObject("MSMQ.MSMQQueueInfo")

objQueueInfo.PathName = ".\MyQueue"
objQueueInfo.Create
%>
```

This creates a Public queue. In order to create a Private queue you need to precede the queue `PathName` with `PRIVATE$`:

```
objQueueInfo.PathName = ".\PRIVATE$\MyQueue"
```

If you wish to create a queue for use with transactions, you must set the first parameter of the method to `True`:

```
objQueueInfo.Create IsTransaction:=True
```

Deleting a Queue

Deleting a queue is even simpler:

```
<%
Dim objQueueInfo
Set objQueueInfo = Server.CreateObject("MSMQ.MSMQQueueInfo")

objQueueInfo.PathName = ".\MyQueue"
objQueueInfo.Delete
%>
```

The MSMQQueue Object

The **MSMQQueue object** represents a queue that has been opened through the MSMQQueueInfo object. This object provides the ability to iterate through messages within a queue in a forward-only cursor-like manner.

ASP applications that use MSMQ are mostly sending messages. However there are times when ASP pages need to open a queue and display the messages, for example administrative pages. Most MSMQ enabled applications need a server-side piece to respond to the messages as they are received and processed accordingly. This server-side piece, as described earlier, is usually a standard executable (EXE) or service that is developed in VB or VC++.

Messages can be retrieved **asynchronously** or **synchronously** from a queue. Reading messages asynchronously allows the executable to respond to a message though the use of events. MSMQ will get a reference to the code within the executable and raise events when a message arrives within the desired queue. Reading messages synchronously requires that the executable has to occasionally open the queue and look for messages on its own. This not only can take up unnecessary system resources, but can be much more difficult to program.

Within ASP pages, messages can only be retrieved synchronously, because ASP pages cannot declare a sever-side variable `WithEvents`.

> *The `WithEvents` keyword is also a mechanism for MSMQ to call into the code and raise events when a message arrives.*

This makes sense since the life of a variable in an ASP page is relatively short. However, the ability to retrieve messages asynchronously is very useful for server applications that process the messages. Accessing MSMQ messages asynchronously allows the application to wait for an event to fire when a message arrives in the queue. This allows the server-side application to not have to sit in a loop consuming resources until a message is received.

> *For more information on retrieving messages asynchronously see the section below on the MSMQEvent object.*

When retrieving messages synchronously the code execution is waiting until a message is available or the time-out expires. The following code shows how to open a queue and display the messages:

```
<%
  Dim objQueueInfo
  Dim objQueue
  Dim objMessage

' Create the queue, ignoring the error if it's already there
  Set objQueueInfo = Server.CreateObject("MSMQ.MSMQQueueInfo")
  objQueueInfo.PathName = ".\MyQueue"

' Open the queue
  Set objQueue = objQueueInfo.Open(MQ_RECEIVE_ACCESS, MQ_DENY_NONE)

' Loop through all the messages in the queue
  Set objMessage = objQueue.PeekCurrent(, , 1000)
  Do While True
     If objMessage Is Nothing Then Exit Do
     Response.Write "Message: " & objMessage.Label & "<BR>"
     Set objMessage = objQueue.PeekNext(, , 1000)
  Loop
  Response.Write "No more new messages."

' Clean up
  objQueue.Close
  Set objMessage = Nothing
  Set objQueue = Nothing
  Set objQueueInfo = Nothing

%>
```

The above code starts by using the MSMQQueue object and enters a `Do While…Loop` until the `Peek` routine of the MSMQQueue object returns `Nothing`. When this routine returns `Nothing`, it means that the time-out expires, in other words there are no more messages in the queue. In this case the time-out is set to 1000 milliseconds.

We needed to use the `PeekCurrent` method before we entered the `Do` loop to set the cursor on the first message in the queue.

The MSMQMessage Object

The **MSMQMessage object** is the heart of MSMQ. It provides the functionality that all MSMQ enabled applications take advantage of – sending and reading messages.

An `MSMQMessage` object is designed to hold a wide variety of information. In fact, the `Body` of the message can hold a String, byte array, any numeric type, or even an instance of a persistable COM object!

The `Label` of a message is a string that simply describes what the message is. It is comparable to the title of an email message.

Messages can be retrieved by opening or peeking at them. When a message is opened, it is removed from the queue once it is read. Conversely, when a message is peeked, it remains in the queue until the message expires. The opening and peeking of a message is performed in the MSMQQueue object via the `Open` and `Peek` routines, which return back a reference to the message.

The following code shows how to `Open` a message and display the `Body` and `Label`:

```
<%

Dim objQueueInfo
Dim objQueueReceive
Dim objMessage

' Open the queue
Set objQueueInfo = Server.CreateObject("MSMQQueueInfo")
objQueueInfo.PathName = ".\MyQueue"
Set objQueueReceive = objQueueInfo.Open(MQ_RECEIVE_ACCESS, MQ_DENY_NONE)

' Look for a message with a time-out of 100 ms
Set objMessage = objQueueReceive.Receive(, , , 100)

' Was there a messsage?
If Not objMessage Is Nothing Then
   'Display the contents of the message
   Response.Write objMessage.Label & " - " & objMessage.Body
Else
   'No message
   Response.Write "Nothing in the queue"
End If
```

```
' Clean up
objQueueReceive.Close
Set objQueueInfo = Nothing
Set objQueueReceive = Nothing
Set objMessage = Nothing

%>
```

The code sample above starts by opening a queue, then looking for a message within the queue, by invoking the Receive routine with a time-out of 100 milliseconds. A time-out is used to tell MSMQ when to stop waiting for a message.

When a low time-out is specified the code checks for existing messages instead of waiting for a message to be received.

To see if there was a message, we test the MSMQMessage object returned by the received function to see if it is Nothing. If the received method returned a valid message the code then displays the Label and the Body properties.

Sending a message is the most common task performed with MSMQ in ASP. To send a message, a queue is opened with send access (MQ_SEND_ACCESS) and a message is prepared, before invoking the Send routine on an MSMQMessage object:

```
<%
Dim objQueueInfo
Dim objQueueSend
Dim objMessage

'Open the queue
Set objQueueInfo = Server.CreateObject("MSMQ.MSMQQueueInfo")
objQueueInfo.PathName = ".\MyQueue"

Set objQueueSend = objQueueInfo.Open(MQ_SEND_ACCESS, MQ_DENY_NONE)

'Build/send the message
Set objMessage = Server.CreateObject("MSMQ.MSMQMessage")
objMessage.Label = "This is the label."
objMessage.Body = "This is the body."
objMessage.Send objQueueSend
objQueueSend.Close

'Clean up
Set objQueueInfo = Nothing
Set objQueueSend = Nothing
Set objMessage = Nothing
%>
```

The code example above starts out like the other sample and opens a queue, however this queue is opened with send access. Next, a message is built by creating an instance of an MSMQMessage object and setting the Label and Body properties. Finally, the message is sent by calling the Send method on the message, and passing a reference to the Destination queue as a parameter.

The MSMQEvent Object

The MSMQEvent object is a very useful object for server-side applications built in languages like VB and VC++, because it provides a mechanism for MSMQ to call into the code and fire events when messages are received in a queue (asynchronously reads). The MSMQEvent object is a very small object. In fact, it has no properties or methods; it consists of only two events:

Event	Description
`Arrived`	Used for retrieving messages asynchronously from a queue. This event will fire in the code every time the specified queue receives a message.
`ArrivedError`	Used for retrieving messages asynchronously from a queue. This event will fire in the code every time an error occurs while trying to listen for messages on a specified queue.

We'll see how we can use these events in a server-side executable later in the chapter.

The MSMQTransaction Object

The **MSMQTransaction object** is used to tell MSMQ to abort or commit a transaction that has been started by either the MSMQTransactionDispenser or MSMQCoordinatedTransactionDispenser objects by using either its `Abort` or `Commit` methods.

> *An instance of the MSMQTransaction object cannot be created using the `New` keyword or `CreateObject` function. It is created through the use of the `BeginTransaction` method on the MSMQTransactionDispenser and MSMQCoordinatedTransactionDispenser objects.*

The MSMQTransactionDispenser Objects

The **MSMQTransactionDispenser object** provides the ability to wrap multiple messages sends and receives to multiple queues in MSMQ in a transaction. Using this object is very useful for internal MSMQ transactions, but cannot contain any thing else such as SQL Server database updates or inserts. When a transaction is needed and will only contain operations within MSMQ, use an MSMQTransactionDispenser object transaction. It is much faster then the MSMQCoordinatedTransactionDispenser transaction because it does not have to deal with the overhead that the Distributed Transaction Coordinator (DTC) brings along with it.

The MSMQCoordinatedTransactionDispenser Object

The **MSMQCoordinatedTransactionDispenser object** performs a similar function to the MSMQTransactionDispenser object. However, this object provides the way to hook into the power of Microsoft Distributed Transaction Coordinator (DTC) thus giving you the power to incorporate any DTC supported data source into the transaction.

Other Ways to Access MSMQ

Beneath the COM API lies another API that is only exposed to C and C++ developers. This provides a way for experienced C/C++ developers to get to the port communication and underlying cursors.

Accessing the functionality of MSMQ at the API level is beyond the scope of this book. For more information reference Microsoft's MSDN web site (`www.msdn.Microsoft.com`) or the help/text files that accompany the MSMQ run-time.

MS DTC Transactions with MSMQ

By using DTC, transactions are not only able to encompass reads and writes to message queues, but the transaction is also able to contain any other service that supports DTC. This enables developers to write methods that modify data in a database like SQL Server (6.5 or 7.0) and send or read a message from a queue in one single transaction.

Transactions that span across multiple DTC compliant services can also be held within a transaction under COM+. This enables developers to encapsulate code into COM DLLs and place them under the control of COM+.

Although MSMQ's MSMQCoordinatedTransactionDispenser object provides a hook into the power of DTC, developers can also produce solutions that do the same thing by using transactions through COM+.

The run-time of COM+ provides the same ability that MSMQ's MSMQCoordinatedTransactionDispenser object provides. In fact, behind the scenes it is all the same, however, developing transactions through COM+ provides greater flexibility and more functionality.

Advanced MSMQ Messages

So far throughout this chapter, the code examples that work with the body of the message have contained simple String values. Now let's have some fun!

The `Body` attribute of an MSMQMessage object is actually defined to accept a value of `Variant` data type. This means the body of a message can contain a String, Date, Currency, Number, an array of bytes, or even a COM object that implements (supports) the `IDispatch` and `IPersist` (`IPersistStream` or `IPersistStorage`) interfaces.

So what does this mean? Sending Strings, Dates, and arrays in MSMQ messages is very straightforward. Simply set the body of the message to your variable:

```
objMessage.Body = strStringVariable
objMessage.Body = dtmDateVariable
objMessage.Body = curMoneyVariable
objMessage.Body = lngLongVariable
objMessage.Body = intIntegerVariable
objMessage.Body = dblDoubleVariable
objMessage.Body = arrMyArray()
```

Simple enough right? Now let's look at persisting instances of COM objects in a message.

Messaging COM Objects

New to VB6, developers are able to produce something that VC++ developers have been able to do for a long time: produce COM objects that can be persisted, via the `IPersist` interface. Even though this is done behind the scenes for us by the VB run-time, it still opens a huge window for developers who use VB to produce the business logic throughout their solution.

The `IPersist` interface provides a common interface that MSMQ can look for and call upon to have the object serialize itself. When a VB object serializes itself, it takes its internal information (variables and their values) and places them into a `PropertyBag`. The VB run-time then reads from the `PropertyBag` and serializes the data through the `IPersist` interface. This serialized binary data is what is actually stored in the body of the MSMQ message.

To build a component that supports the `IPersist` interface, start by flagging the class property Persistable to 1 – Persistable:

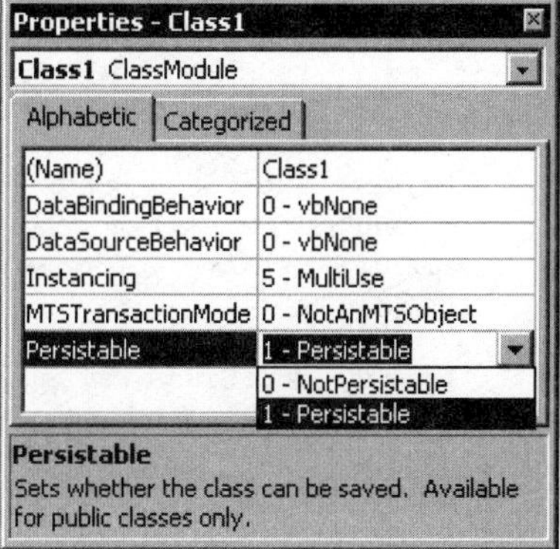

Once the Persistable flag is set, three more events will be added to the `Class` events:

- `InitProperties`
- `ReadProperties`
- `WriteProperties`

The `InitProperties` event is used to set any default values or set anything before the `ReadProperties` event fires. The `ReadProperties` and `WriteProperties` events are fairly straightforward. They provide the events to read and write the state (internal data) to a `PropertyBag` that will be stored in the MSMQMessage object.

The following code example displays how a class is written to support persistence. Notice the `Class_ReadProperties` and `Class_WriteProperties` event handlers. These are the events that the VB run-time will call when MSMQ looks for the `IPersist` interface. As noted above VB classes really don't support the `IPersist` interface. The VB run-time hides this from the VB developers and passes the calls in as class events:

```
Option Explicit

Private mstrFirstName As String
Private mstrLastName As String

Public Property Get LastName() As String
  LastName = mstrLastName
End Property

Public Property Let LastName(strNewName As String)
  mstrLastName = strNewName
End Property

Public Property Get FirstName() As String
  FirstName = mstrFirstName
End Property

Public Property Let FirstName(strNewName As String)
  mstrFirstName = strNewName
End Property

Private Sub Class_ReadProperties(PropBag As PropertyBag)
  mstrLastName = PropBag.ReadProperty("LastName")
  mstrFirstName = PropBag.ReadProperty("FirstName")
End Sub

Private Sub Class_WriteProperties(PropBag As PropertyBag)
  PropBag.WriteProperty "LastName", mstrLastName
  PropBag.WriteProperty "FirstName", mstrFirstName
End Sub
```

Now that the COM component is ready to be called upon, let's look at the code to call this class and put the internal state (`mstrFirstName` and `mstrLastName` in the `PropertyBag`) into the body of the message. From VB the code is fairly easily.

Start by creating an instance of the class and set the `FirstName` and `LastName` properties. Next, open a queue for send access. The last step is to send the message, by creating an instance of an MSMQMessage object and setting the `Label` to a string value and the value of the `Body` to the instance of the class defined above. That's it! All of the work is hidden to the consumer of the object:

```
Private Sub cmdSend_Click()

  Dim objPersist As PersistSample.Person
  Dim objQueueInfo As MSMQ.MSMQQueueInfo
  Dim objQueue As MSMQ.MSMQQueue
  Dim objMessage As MSMQ.MSMQMessage

  On Error GoTo Error_handler

' Add some state to an instance of the person class
  Set objPersist = New PersistSample.Person
  objPersist.FirstName = txtSendFN
  objPersist.LastName = txtSendLN
```

```
' Get a reference to the queue
  Set objQueueInfo = New MSMQ.MSMQQueueInfo
  objQueueInfo.PathName = ".\MyQueue"
  Set objQueue = objQueueInfo.Open(MQ_SEND_ACCESS, MQ_DENY_NONE)

' Build the message
  Set objMessage = New MSMQ.MSMQMessage
  objMessage.Label = "Person Object"
  objMessage.Body = objPersist
  objMessage.Send objQueue

' Close the queue
  objQueue.Close

Exit_handler:

  Set objMessage = Nothing
  Set objQueue = Nothing
  Set objQueueInfo = Nothing
  Exit Sub

Error_handler:

  MsgBox "Error... " & Err.Description, vbCritical, _
         Err.Source & " (" & Err.Number & ")"
  Resume Exit_handler

End Sub
```

It would make sense to say that this same type of code (altered a little for VBScript) could be used in an ASP page too. But not so! Everything will work fine until the line that puts the object into the body of the message. That line will result in an error stating:

"Cannot save an uninitialized class. You must use the global InitProperties method to initialize the class, or load the class from a PropertyBag before trying to save it."

This is a very annoying error/limitation. Even if the logic that saves the body of the message to the component is moved into the component itself, it still has the same issues. So if you want to persist COM objects in a queue then you will need to a build a component to do so.

COM+ Queued Components

With the addition of COM+, COM components can now be configured to run as **queued components**.

Queued components allow a consumer of a COM object to communicate with the object over MSMQ, without any code changes to the COM object or the consumer.

Queued components utilize four pieces called the **recorder, queue, listener** and **player**, which allow the client to communicate with the queued COM object. The recorder records the client's interaction with the object, bundles the information into an MSMQ message and sends it to the queue within MSMQ. This listener on the server responds to the message from the client's recorder and sends the message to the player. The player then reads the message and invokes the methods that the client worked with:

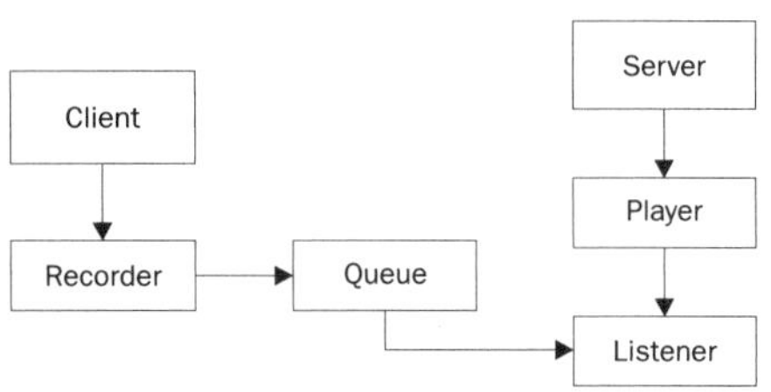

Queued components can be very useful, but they have their limitations. Since the client does not directly interact with the COM object, it cannot use parameters passed by reference or functions that have return values. However, queued components are very useful for invoking subroutines on COM objects.

To set a COM object as a queued component, simply look at the properties of the package that contains the COM object in the COM+ MMC snap-in, select the Queuing tab, and check the Queued and the Listen option:

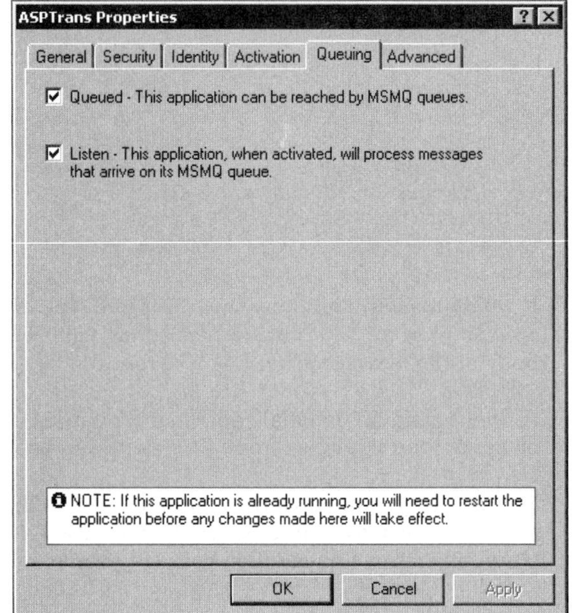

For more information on the features of queued components reference Microsoft's MSDN Web site at `www.msdn.microsoft.com` *or the text/help files that accompany the MSMQ run-time files.*

Expanding the Online Ordering Example

Now that we've seen a bit about how to use MSMQ we are going to expand our sample application from the previous chapter to also incorporate MSMQ. We will demonstrate using MSMQ in two different ways:

- Firstly, we will modify the order-placing component to send the order to a queue instead of directly updating the database.
- Secondly, we will build a server-side executable that will hang around and process messages being posted to the queue, thus actually placing the order in the database.

First we need to add some code to the component.

Adding MSMQ to the Component

We will be using the `ASPTrans` queue that we set up earlier in the chapter. You should now realize why we set it up to be transactional, as we want it to be included in the same transaction as this component.

Open the `ASPTrans` project (either from code you built in the last chapter or the downloaded source code). Before we can add any new code we need to add a reference to the MSMQ 2.0 Type Library:

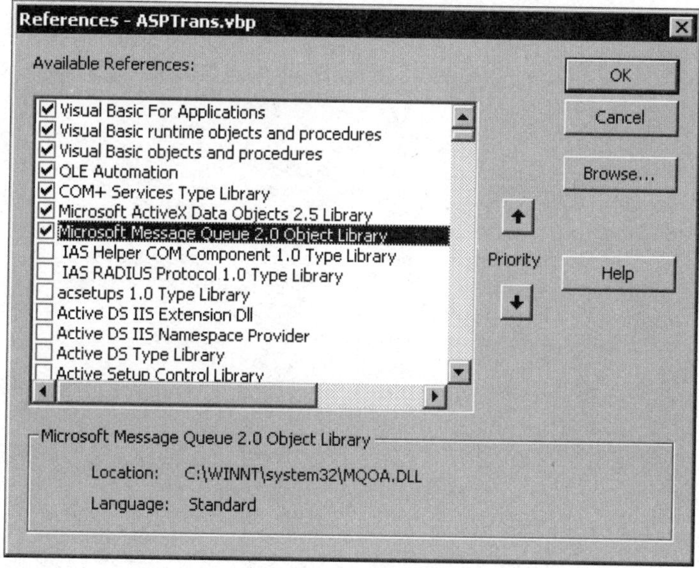

Next, we can add in the code to send a message to the `ASPTrans` queue in MSMQ. We will change the functionality of this routine so that the order is placed in a queue instead of taking place immediately.

Place this code in the `PlaceOrder` routine in the `Order` component – there is nothing in this code that we haven't already seen:

```
Public Sub PlaceOrder(strLastName As String, strFirstName As String, _
                      lngProductID As Long, lngQuantity As Long)

  Dim objContext As COMSVCSLib.ObjectContext
  Dim objQueueInfo As MSMQ.MSMQQueueInfo
  Dim objQueue As MSMQ.MSMQQueue
  Dim objMessage As MSMQ.MSMQMessage
  Dim rsOrder As ADODB.Recordset

  On Error GoTo Error_Handler

' Get a reference to the context object
' that's running the transaction
  Set objContext = COMSVCSLib.GetObjectContext
  Set objQueueInfo = New MSMQ.MSMQQueueInfo
  Set objMessage = New MSMQ.MSMQMessage
  Set rsOrder = New ADODB.Recordset

' Open the queue with send access
  With objQueueInfo
    .PathName = ".\ASPTrans"
    Set objQueue = .Open(MQ_SEND_ACCESS, MQ_DENY_NONE)
  End With

' Build and send the message
  With objMessage
    With rsOrder
      .CursorLocation = adUseClient
      .Fields.Append "FirstName", adVarChar, 50
      .Fields.Append "LastName", adVarChar, 50
      .Fields.Append "ProductID", adInteger
      .Fields.Append "Quantity", adInteger
      .Open
      .AddNew
      .Fields("FirstName") = strFirstName
      .Fields("LastName") = strLastName
      .Fields("ProductID") = lngProductID
      .Fields("Quantity") = lngQuantity
      .Update
    End With
    .Body = rsOrder
    .Send objQueue, MQ_TRANSACTIONAL
  End With

' Everything worked
  If Not objContext Is Nothing Then objContext.SetComplete
```

```
Exit_Handler:
' Clean up
  Set objMessage = Nothing
  Set objQueue = Nothing
  Set objQueueInfo = Nothing
  Set rsOrder = Nothing
  Set objContext = Nothing
  Exit Sub

Error_Handler:

' An error occured
  If Not objContext Is Nothing Then objContext.SetAbort
  Resume Exit_Handler

End Sub
```

Now if you recompile and place a new order you will see that the order has been placed into the `ASPTrans` queue:

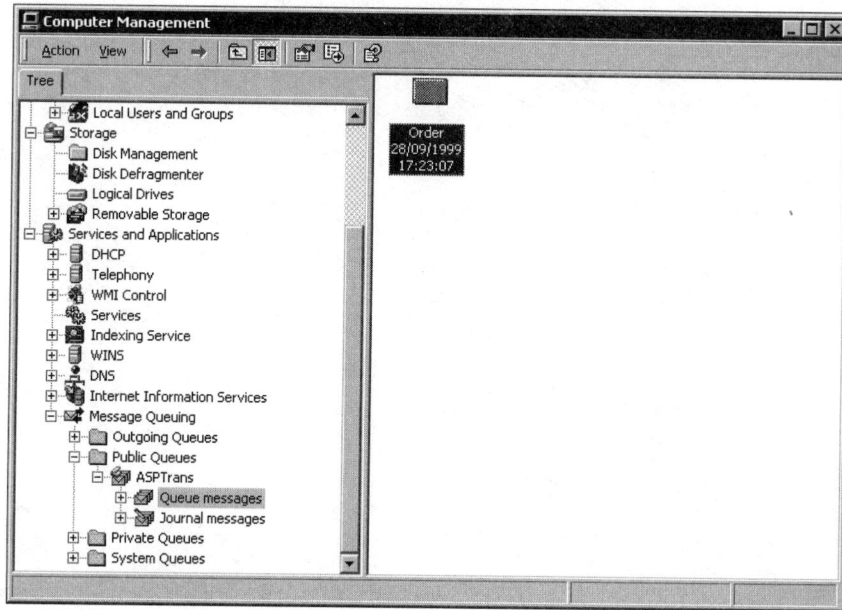

However, our order is only 50% complete. We need to process the order from the queue into the database.

Processing Queued Orders

This will be a very simple server-side standard EXE that uses the MSMQEvent object to 'listen' for orders being placed into the queue. When a message is placed we will simply use the same `INSERT` as we used previously to store the order.

Start by creating a new Visual Basic Standard EXE project and adding a reference to the MSMQ 2.0 Object Library and ActiveX Data Objects 2.5 Library.

Now, on the form within the VB project add a list box. Next, go into the code window and add the following code:

```
Option Explicit

Dim WithEvents mobjMSMQEvent As MSMQ.MSMQEvent
Dim mobjQueue As MSMQ.MSMQQueue

Private Sub Form_Load()

  Dim objQueueInfo As MSMQ.MSMQQueueInfo

' Get a reference to the queue
  Set objQueueInfo = New MSMQ.MSMQQueueInfo
  With objQueueInfo
    .PathName = ".\ASPTrans"
    Set mobjQueue = .Open(MQ_RECEIVE_ACCESS, MQ_DENY_NONE)
  End With

' Hook in the MSMQEvent class
  Set mobjMSMQEvent = New MSMQ.MSMQEvent
  mobjQueue.EnableNotification mobjMSMQEvent

  Set objQueueInfo = Nothing

End Sub

Private Sub mobjMSMQEvent_Arrived(ByVal Queue As Object, _
                                  ByVal Cursor As Long)

  Dim objMessage As MSMQ.MSMQMessage
  Dim objConn As ADODB.Connection
  Dim rsOrder As ADODB.Recordset

  Set objMessage = Queue.ReceiveCurrent
  Set objConn = New ADODB.Connection

  Set rsOrder = objMessage.Body

' Add code to process the order.
  With objConn
    .ConnectionString = "Provider=SQLOLEDB.1;User ID=sa;" & _
                        "Initial Catalog=ASPTransactions;" & _
                        "Data Source=<SERVER_NAME>"
    .Open
    .Execute "INSERT INTO Orders (ProductID, Quantity, LastName, " & _
             "FirstName) VALUES(" & rsOrder("ProductID") & ", " & _
             rsOrder("Quantity") & ", '" & rsOrder("LastName") & _
             "', '" & rsOrder("FirstName") & "')", , adExecuteNoRecords

    .Execute "UPDATE Products SET InventoryLevel = " & _
             "(SELECT InventoryLevel FROM Products " & _
             "WHERE ID = " & rsOrder("ProductID") & ")" & _
             " - " & rsOrder("Quantity") & " WHERE ID = " & _
             rsOrder("ProductID")
    .Close
  End With
```

```
    List1.AddItem "Processed, " & Chr(34) & objMessage.Label & Chr(34)

  ' Hook in the MSMQEvent class
    mobjQueue.EnableNotification mobjMSMQEvent

    Set objMessage = Nothing
    Set objConn = Nothing
    Set rsOrder = Nothing

  End Sub
```

```
  Private Sub mobjMSMQEvent_ArrivedError(ByVal Queue As Object, _
                                         ByVal ErrorCode As Long, _
                                         ByVal Cursor As Long)
  ' Something went wrong!
    MsgBox "Error accorded: " & ErrorCode

  End Sub
```

The above code starts with the `Form_Load` event and opens the `ASPTrans` queue. Next, the code sets up the `mobjMSMQEvent` object and links it to the queue. This is done by calling the `EnableNotification` method on the MSMQQueue object. Once the MSMQEvent object is linked, the only thing left to do is fulfill the `Arrived` and `ArrivedError` (optional) events.

The `Arrived` event fires every time a new message is received in the queue. Here we pull the order details out of the body of the message and enter them into our database.

Each time a message is received the `EnableNotification` method must be called again to tell MSMQ to inform the code when the next message is received. If the code fails to call the `EnableNotification`, the next message will never be seen.

Now it's time to test the code. Start by either compiling the executable or by simply running the code right within VB's development environment. You can notice that when the form's `Load` event fires the queue is opened for receive access and the MSMQEvent object is hooked-in to look for messages.

If there are any messages in the queue the VB application will respond to them right away:

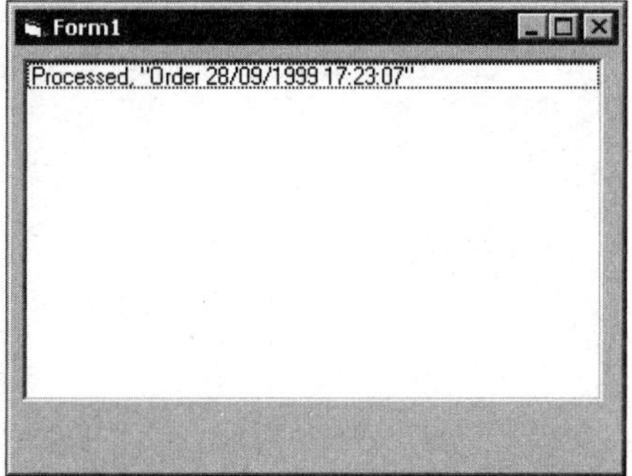

Now go back to the browser and place a few more orders. Notice that the VB application already processed them. Now stop the VB application and place several more orders. The orders are now pending as messages in the queue until the VB application is started again. Start the VB application and now the messages (orders) will be processed and the queue will be empty again.

Summary

MSMQ provides a middle layer (or common ground) that applications can use to communicate with each other in a loosely coupled asynchronous manner. Within a well-designed COM object model, MSMQ can be utilized by a wide variety of programming languages.

In this chapter, we have taken a look at the Microsoft Message Queue Server system. MSMQ allows us to communicate between applications asynchronous even when those applications are not running at the same time or the connection between applications is unreliable. The easiest way to think of it is as email for applications. The MSMQ system allows for an interconnected network of systems that can pass messages back and forth between them. The system figures out where a message needs to go, and makes sure that the message gets there. MSMQ is directly usable from ASP as well as ASP components through its COM interface.

In this chapter, we specifically looked at:

- What Message Queuing is
- What MSMQ is and its architecture
- What can be done with MSMQ
- How to administer MSMQ
- How to interact with MSMQ using COM objects
- How components can be built to interact with MSMQ
- How to use MSMQ components in an ASP application
- How to respond to MSMQ messages asynchronously
- How to incorporate MSMQ into transactions

N
W

21

Introducing ADSI and Active Directory

In this chapter, we're going to look at the **Active Directory Services Interfaces (ADSI)** and **Active Directory (AD)**, and how you can use ASP to access directory services and use the information they contain. By **directory** or **directory service** here, we really mean a specialized type of database that is designed to allow the efficient lookup of information – for example directories of network resources. Active Directory is such a directory of network resources, while ADSI is the Microsoft technology designed to access any directory at all. There are other similar technologies produced by other companies, such as Sun's JNDI, but since this is a Windows-centric book we will focus exclusively on ADSI here.

It's important not to confuse ADSI and AD, as they are fairly distinct technologies – although, since the two technologies do interact quite a bit it's convenient for us to treat them both in the same chapter. **Active Directory** is the big new directory that comes with Windows 2000. It is the directory that contains all the security and other information needed to administer domains on your local network. On the other hand, **ADSI** is a set of COM interfaces that Microsoft are pushing as the recommended means to access any directory, which implies that ADSI is also the usual means to access Active Directory. Although Active Directory is only available as part of Windows 2000 Server and Windows 2000 Advanced Server, ADSI is available for all the Microsoft 32-bit operating systems: Windows 2000 Professional, NT 4.0 and Windows 9x.

The main focus on this chapter is on ADSI, since our aim is to show you how to simply and easily access directories from ASP scripts, but due to the almost certain importance of Active Directory we will touch on some of its capabilities.

> *We'll only cover the basics of ADSI in one chapter. If you need to go into more depth you may want to refer to* Professional ADSI Programming *by Simon Robinson, also published by Wrox Press.*

So What's ADSI For

There are really two related issues here. We've already covered ADO, and seen how that technology fits in with Microsoft's Universal Data Access strategy, which we covered in depth in the second section of this book. ADO is there to give you access to any data source for which an OLE DB provider is available. But I've just now implied that in order to use directories – which are after all just another type of data source – we should use a different technology, ADSI. To understand why, we need to understand what makes directories special, and look at what ADSI can do that ADO cannot.

ADO is really a general purpose technology. In principle, Microsoft's aim is that ADO will be the way that you get to *any* data source, no matter how that data source is structured internally. There is, however, an implicit emphasis on relational data sources. There's nothing wrong with that, but it does mean that if you want to access a hierarchical data source, then ADO might not always be the best way of doing it. That's where ADSI comes in, since ADSI is specifically targeted at hierarchical data sources. If you want to start browsing around a tree-like structure, then the ADSI interfaces have been carefully designed in a way that allows you to do so very simply – that's not so easy with ADO.

Now I've talked about hierarchical data sources and directories. Are they the same thing? Well, they're similar, but not exactly the same. We'll look at the similarities first – which are to do with their tree-like structure. Later on, we'll examine those particular characteristics that distinguish directories from databases and other data sources.

> *A hierarchical data source is a set of data that is arranged in a tree-like structure, with objects containing other objects, in much the same way that folders contain files or other folders in the Windows file system – and most directories will be structured in this way too.*

In fact, the easiest way to see that is by having a quick look at the structure of Active Directory. This screenshot is taken from the program `adsvw.exe`, which is a general directory browser that is designed to look at any ADSI-compliant directory – and as we've indicated before, that includes Active Directory. `adsvw.exe` is supplied with the ADSI SDK:

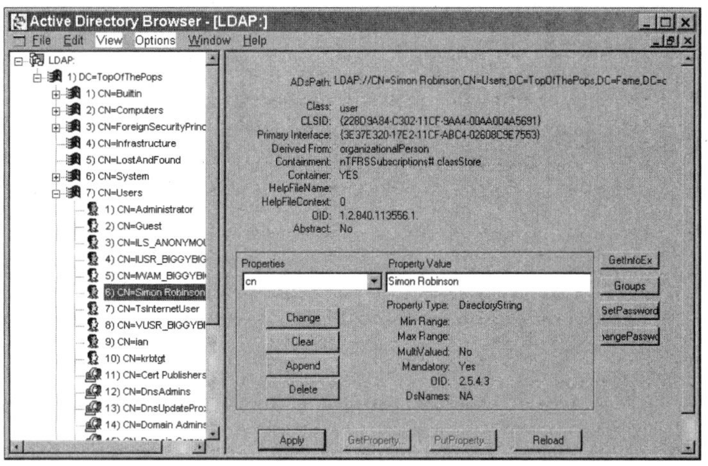

There's a lot going on in this screenshot so we're going to be referring back to it quite a lot over the next few pages. So don't worry about understanding everything in it just yet. The thing I want you to notice is that tree-like structure in the left pane of the screenshot. It's a standard tree control – and it clearly shows the hierarchical arrangement of the data in Active Directory. I've selected something named `CN=Simon Robinson` to examine. That happens to be my own user account on the local network. Its parent is something called `CN=Users`. In directory parlance, a parent-child relationship is known as **containment**. `CN=Users` is said to be a container, which contains the `CN=Simon Robinson` object. In this particular Active Directory install, `CN=Users` actually contains all the user accounts in the domain, though that won't always be the case.

The user container in turn is contained by an object called `DC=TopOfThePops`, which represents the domain itself. The `DC=TopOfThePops` is slightly misleading, since the full domain name is `DC=TopOfThePops,DC=Fame,DC=com`, corresponding to a fictitious URL of `TopOfThePops.Fame.com` (Windows 2000 supports domain names like that, though any NT 4.0 machine will only recognize the first part of the name, `TopOfThePops`). Don't worry too much about the format for these names – it's the format used by Active Directory, and you'll rapidly get used to it. `CN` stands for **Common Name**, while `DC` stands for **Domain Component**.

> *I suggest you don't worry too much about my choice of domain name for my own home network either. Well **I** liked it! Normally you would choose a name that corresponds to the DNS name of your network on the Internet. But since my Internet connection is a dial up modem, I didn't need to worry about that.*

Finally, the domain node in the tree is contained in an object called `LDAP:`. LDAP stands for **Lightweight Directory Access Protocol**. It's an industry-standard protocol for accessing directories, and the presence of this object indicates that Active Directory is compliant with LDAP. We'll say a bit more about LDAP later on.

So far all I've done is pointed out that we are storing information about a number of objects, and have arranged that information in a hierarchical manner. (By the way, I'm using the word *objects* in its everyday sense, not its technical sense, here – I'm not talking about COM objects). However, Active Directory actually provides a very good example of how the directories that you would access using ADSI are structured. Since we need to learn about Active Directory anyway, what I'm going to do next is explore Active Directory in a bit more detail – and we're going to treat what we learn about it as an example that demonstrates the typical structure of directories in general. Once we've done that, we'll be ready to learn about how to use ADSI to get at and modify the information in directories.

But first, a quick note on how to get the software you need.

What Software you Need

For this section, we will consider ADSI and Active Directory separately as their software requirements are different.

Active Directory comes with Windows 2000. If your machine is running Windows 2000 and you make it a domain controller, then you'll have Active Directory installed. If you don't you won't, period. Note that what matters is whether you have a **domain controller** running Windows 2000. If you have a Windows 2000 workstation in a domain controlled by an NT 4.0 primary domain controller, then you still won't have Active Directory.

ADSI also comes as part of the operating system with Windows 2000 (Professional or Server versions). However, it is also possible to download ADSI for NT 4.0 and Windows 9x from Microsoft's Web site. In addition, you may want the ADSI SDK in order to develop software. You need to download the SDK no matter what operating system you are running. The SDK contains various header files and documentation. It's not as essential for developing ASP clients as it would be if you were programming in VB or C++, but it does contain the `adsvw.exe` utility that we've used in our screenshots.

We're going to be using `adsvw.exe` a lot more to explore Active Directory. `adsvw.exe` is also known as the **Active Directory Browser**, but this name is a bit misleading. It's a general purpose directory browser, which we can use to examine any ADSI-compatible directory, not just Active Directory. The Active Directory Browser is quite a good tool for us to use because it itself uses ADSI to gather the information it presents to us, so we'll be seeing the information in much the same format as we'll need when we start coding up using ADSI.

As I've mentioned, `adsvw.exe` comes as part of the ADSI SDK, which you can download from Microsoft's Web site. If you don't already have it, I suggest you get a copy, as you'll find it very useful for exploring directories.

Inside Active Directory

Active Directory stores all the information needed by a domain controller to manage a domain. To that extent it is similar to the domain directory on NT 4.0 Server machines. Where it differs is that it is compliant with the LDAP standard. Since LDAP is an industry-wide standard, it is very easy to write clients that use standard APIs (including ADSI) to access Active Directory. By contrast, the corresponding database on NT 4.0 was proprietary to Microsoft. It was only possible to get limited access to the information contained using Windows API functions. In practice, it wasn't really possible to use the database as a centralized directory of network resources in the way that is possible in Active Directory.

In addition, Active Directory is much more powerful than the old NT 4.0 domain directory. It, along with the Windows 2000 operating system, supports new concepts like arranging the domains themselves in a hierarchy to form a **domain tree** – or allowing a number of independent trees to share configuration data, forming a **domain forest**. And it also allows you to store your own information in it as well as the stuff that the operating system uses.

You see, as far as the information that is stored in Active Directory is concerned, there are really two parts to it. By default Active Directory contains everything needed to manage a domain, such as computer, user and group accounts, as well as all the security permissions specifying who has access to do what. But separately, Active Directory is designed as a general purpose directory, which means that any other information that the systems administrators deem useful may be stored in it. So stuff like user accounts can appear next to details of salaries and the structure of your organization. Active Directory also has a very sophisticated security system giving administrators a fine degree of control over who is allowed to view or modify the various items of information stored.

However, what most interests us here is the overall tree structure of Active Directory, which we will use to illustrate the structure of directories in general.

Objects and Properties in Directories

The first thing we need to understand is that, whereas relational databases store their data in rows and columns inside tables, in a directory there is a much stronger concept of an object as something that we want to store information about. In the previous screenshot, we'd selected an object that was a user account. Other objects stored in Active Directory include computers, domains, and groups. Later, when we examine the WinNT ADSI provider we'll also come across objects that can be stored in other directories – like services and print queues.

Don't confuse objects in directories with the COM objects (components) that we've been using up till now. Objects in directories have nothing to do with COM. They have properties but they don't usually have methods.

In fact a directory is normally made up of nothing but objects, arranged in a hierarchical way. In turn, objects can be thought of as made up of a lot of **properties** or **attributes**.

The terms property and attribute are generally used interchangeably, so I'll swap between them in this chapter – I'll generally use whichever term adds most to the literary elegance!

But be aware that we are not talking about COM automation properties here. We are simply talking about pieces of information. A property has a name and a value. For example, the properties of my user account in Active Directory include these:

Property Name	Property Value
`CN`	`Simon Robinson`
`ADsPath`	`LDAP://CN=Simon Robinson,CN=Users,DC=TopOfThePops,DC=Fame,DC=com`
`sAMAccountName`	`simon`
`Description`	I just made up this comment and used `adsvw.exe` to set it!
`Mail`	`simon@simonrobinson.com`

Most of these should be self-explanatory. `CN`, which as I've said, stands for Common Name, is the usual name that the object is referred to. The `ADsPath` is the unique name of the object that you can use to identify it when using ADSI to access the directory. It's quite analogous to the full pathname of a file, and includes the name of the object and the names of all the objects above it in the directory hierarchy. The `sAMAccountName` is the name you supply when you log on to the domain under that account.

One important concept demonstrated by this table is that there are two parts to a property: each property has a **name** (`CN`) and a **value** (`Simon Robinson`). Well, to be more precise, it has a name and one or more values, since some properties in directories may be **multi-valued**. Think of multi-valued as being the directory way of specifying an array of values.

By the way, that table was just a small selection of attributes. If you have Active Directory installed, and you take a look at your own user account, you'll find a huge number of attributes. Many of them don't even have values set – they are just defined in case your systems administrator wants to use them.

When you are using `adsvw.exe` you can look at the different properties that each object has using the Properties *list box in the right-hand pane of the screen (as shown in the previous `adsvw.exe` screenshot). You select the appropriate property in the list box, and its value will be displayed in the neighboring text box. If you want to change the value, you can type in a new value in the text box, then hit the* Change *button below the list box. You'll also need to hit the* Apply *button to make your change permanent.*

Classes of Object

So far we've used `adsvw.exe` to look at a user account. I've hinted that there are other sorts of object around – for example objects specifying computers. The main differences between users and computers in this sense are the number and type of properties that are available for these objects. For example, if I look at this object:

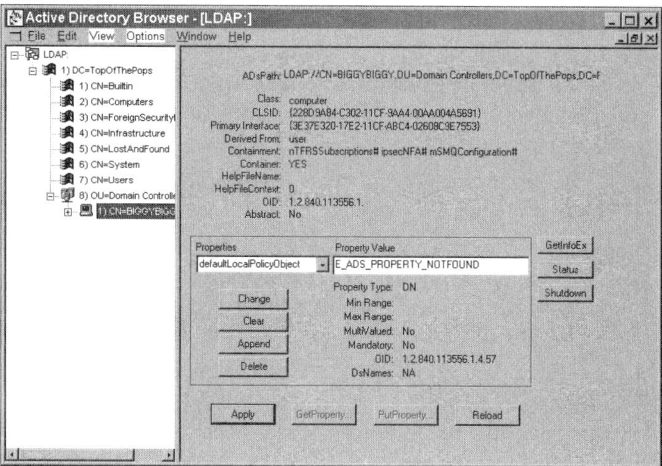

This is the object that describes my domain controller for my domain, a computer called `BIGGYBIGGY` (don't ask!). This represents a computer, and if you examine its properties, you'll see many of the same ones defined as for users. However, it also has other properties that contain information that is relevant only to a computer.

The type of object is known as its **class**. For example, in Active Directory a user is a class of object, as is a computer. Because users and computers are different classes, the sets of properties that they can have are different. In `adsvw.exe` the class of the selected object is displayed in the information at the top of the right-hand pane. You can see it in both of the previous screenshots.

So the class determines what properties may be defined for an object. More specifically, it determines the mandatory and optional properties. **Mandatory properties** are properties for which a value must be present with each instance of an object of that class. **Optional properties** are those properties for which a value may be stored, but it doesn't have to be. An object may not in general have any properties other than those that have been defined as mandatory or optional properties for that class.

Containers and Leafs

We've already mentioned that an object that can act as a parent in the directory tree to other objects is known as a container. An object that cannot do so is known as a **leaf**. Whether an object is a container or a leaf is determined by its **class**. Some classes are defined to be containers, others are leafs. For example, in Active Directory, both users and computers are containers. You can see this indicated in two of the lines of information about the objects displayed in the previous screenshots. The line `Container:` indicates whether that class of object is a container or not, and the line above, marked `Containment:` lists the names of the classes of object which this object is allowed to be a parent of.

This kind of thing is carefully defined in most directories to ensure that when users start modifying the contents of the directory, they don't damage the overall structure of the directory tree. If you attempt to create a new object and add it to the directory, you will only normally be permitted to do so if you add the object in a location which complies with all that directory's rules about what classes of object can contain what other classes of object. (Of course, there will be other checks made too – for example whether a user has sufficient security access permissions to add the object!)

The fact that a class of object is a container does not mean that it necessarily contains other objects – only that it is, in principle, allowed to do so. For example, in Active Directory, all user accounts are technically containers, but in the case of my own user account, it happens not to contain anything.

By the way, you've probably noticed quite a big analogy between directory structure and the Windows file system. Both have the same kind of hierarchical structure – folders in Windows are even sometimes called directories (the term having migrated across from Unix). In this analogy, folders in the file system would correspond to containers in directories, and files in the file system with leaf objects in directories. However, be careful in pushing the analogy too far. In the file system, folders act *only* as containers for files. They don't really have any data of their own, other than certain system attributes that Windows automatically supplies (such as creation date), and security information about who is allowed to access them. You can't store a large amount of your own text in folders in the way you would with a file. On the other hand, in directories, the containers are still directory objects in themselves, with their own sets of properties. The only difference between a container and a leaf is that a container can contain other objects too.

The Schema

We've seen how objects are defined by their class, and how this gives rise to rules that tell us what properties an object may have and whether it is a container. These rules, together with other related information such as the data type of each property (e.g. that common name is a string and is single-valued), and any restrictions on their range of values, are collectively known as the **schema**. What we haven't yet talked about is the way that the schema itself is stored in the directory. You might expect that that would be an internal detail, the implementation of which is up to the directory. To some extent, that's true; however, there is also a standard way of accessing the schema, which requires that the schema itself be stored as part of the directory.

It happens that in Active Directory, the schema is stored in a container with the `ADsPath` given by `LDAP://CN=Schema,CN=Configuration,<domain name>` where `domain name` is the name of your domain, expressed in the format we've been using for Active Directory names in our screenshots. If we examine this container, this is what we see:

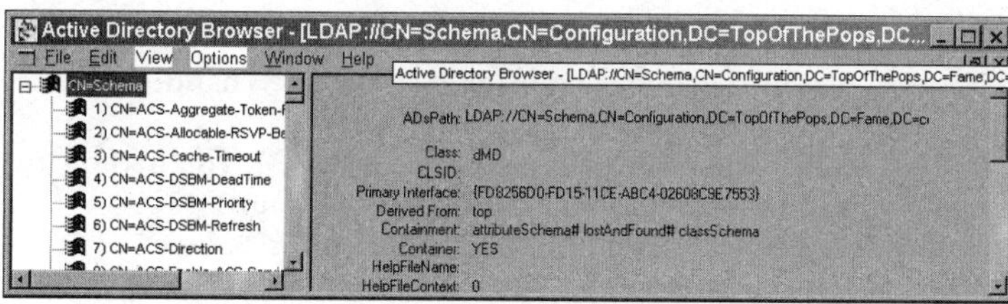

This object contains all the objects that describe the schema. As you can see from the size of that scroll bar in the tree view, that's a lot of objects – since Active Directory has a lot of classes and properties. If we scroll down a bit to find the schema entry that describes computers, this is what we find:

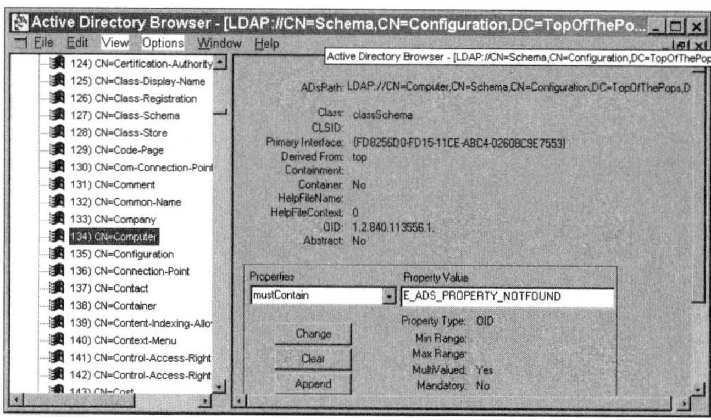

The object `CN=Computer` is the object which tells us all about how instances of the class `Computer` must behave in the directory – which is why its own class is marked as `classSchema` – it defines the schema for a certain class! Most of the other objects you can see in the tree control are `attributeSchema` objects – that is to say they give us information about a particular attribute, such as the data type for its value and whether it is multi-valued.

I've set the list box in the Properties tab to look at the property, `mustContain`. This is a multi-valued property, which lists the names of all the mandatory properties of the class computer. Another property, `mayContain`, for the same `classSchema` object, lists all the optional properties of computers.

Oddly, as indicated by the error message `E_ADS_PROPERTY_NOTFOUND` in the above screenshot, `mustContain` appears not to contain any values. On my Active Directory install, `mayContain` gives the same error message on this particular `classSchema` object. That's somewhat surprising, since we've already seen that computers do have a fair number of properties. The reason for this apparent discrepancy brings up another important concept in classes: **inheritance**.

Inheritance

It is possible for classes in directories to **derive** from each other. What does that mean?

Well, if you have had a reasonable amount of experience at COM, you'll know that it is possible for one interface to derive from another. If `InterfaceA` derives from `InterfaceB`, that means that `InterfaceA` exposes all the properties and methods defined for `InterfaceB`, as well as the additional ones defined specifically for `InterfaceA`. All COM interfaces expose the three methods `QueryInterface`, `AddRef` and `Release` simply because such interfaces are derived from `IUnknown`.

If you've done any Object Oriented programming with, for example, C++ or Java, you'll also have encountered inheritance of classes – which means the same thing. If class `ClassA` derives from `ClassB` then `ClassA` implements all the member functions and variables of `ClassB` as well as its own ones.

Well the same principle applies when we talk about inheritance of directory classes. If a class `A` inherits from another class `B`, then instances of `A` can have all the mandatory and optional properties defined in the `classSchema` object of `B` as well as those defined in the `classSchema` object for `A`. (Well – I say *can*, but in the case of the mandatory properties, *must* would be more appropriate!)

This allows us to generate new types of classes by specializing existing ones. In C++, it's even possible to have **abstract** classes, which are classes defined for the sole purpose of allowing other classes to derive from them. It is not possible to actually create any objects that are of a type given by an abstract class. C++ programmers will see that abstract classes in directories play an identical role to abstract classes in C++.

This explains one of the other bits of information that comes in that list of data at the top of the right-hand pane in `adsvw.exe`: the line marked `Derived From:`. This gives the name of the class from which the class of the object we are looking at is derived. Looking back through the previous screenshots, we can see that both `classSchema` and `dMD` (the class of the object that contains all the schema entries) are derived from a class called `top`. Computers are derived from `user` (which may sound strange but it makes sense because computers need to implement most of the same properties as users), while `user` is described from a class `organizationalPerson`, which contains more generalized information for a generic person.

In fact, in the case of Active Directory, we can go further. All objects in Active Directory (and for that matter, any LDAP-compliant directory) have an attribute called `objectClass`. This attribute is multi-valued, and its values are the names of all the classes in the inheritance tree leading down to this class. For a computer, the chain is:

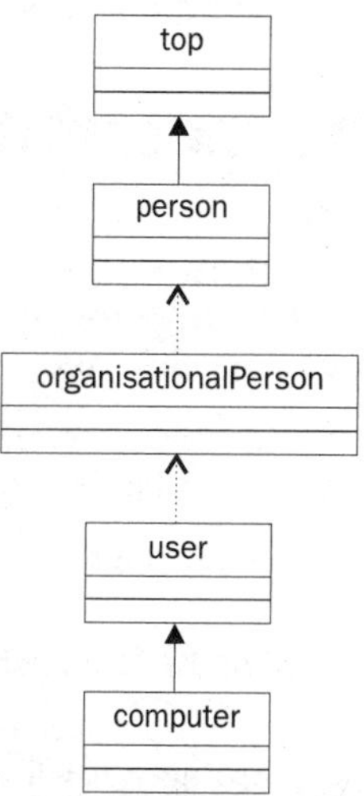

And you can see this for my domain controller, if we select the `objectClass` entry from the **Properties** list box in the Active Directory browser:

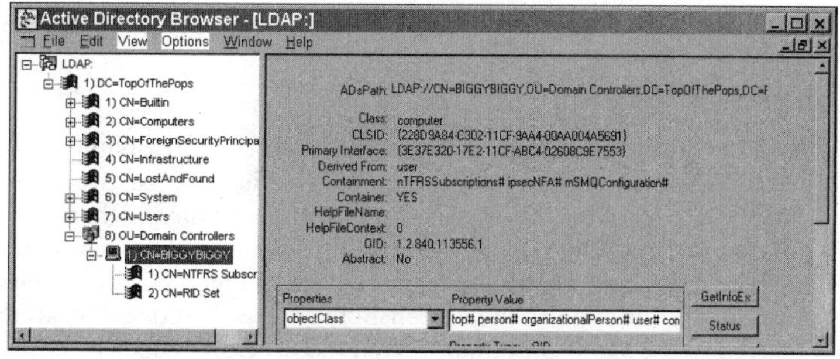

The class `top` plays an important role in Active Directory. It is a general-purpose class, and has a large number of mandatory and optional properties defined for it, which Microsoft consider as generally useful for all objects in Active Directory. All objects in any LDAP-compliant directory are derived ultimately from a class called `top`.

We've now got all the information about directory structure that we're going to need for the time being, so we're ready to talk a bit more about directories in general. Just in case you're wondering about those other fields that are listed in the screenshots, the `CLSID` is a unique GUID that is used to identify the class of the object. The line labeled `Primary Interface:` is to do with ADSI rather than Active Directory. When we come to use ADSI, we'll see that we need to create COM components to access the directory objects, one COM component for each object in the directory. Since we are using Active Server Pages we'll be exclusively using the `IDispatch` interface to talk to the COM objects. The `Primary Interface` refers to the IID of the 'real' interface for that object, i.e. the interface that we'd probably be using directly if we were coding in VB or C++ where we would avoid using `IDispatch`.

The help file name and context give help information for that class of object, and the OID is another unique identifier (the *O*bject *ID*entifier) that identifies not only the class but other information such as the name of the organization that defined the class. We won't need to concern ourselves with OIDs here.

Characteristics of Directories

We've now got a fair idea of how Active Directory is structured. Some of what we've seen is particular to Active Directory, whereas other stuff is not peculiar to Active Directory but is common to all LDAP-compliant directories. But for all of what we've just seen, the general principles, if not the implementation details, will be satisfied by most directories.

So far we've seen that a directory is a hierarchical store of information. We've also got an idea that it contains objects, which in turn have a number of attributes.

There are a number of other characteristics that are typical of most directories.

Optimized for lookup

The main purpose of a directory is to allow you to look up the information in it when you want it. Accordingly, it will usually have been implemented in a way that is optimized for read access. The expectation is that directories will be read much more often than they are written to. Active Directory is optimized in this way.

Search Facilities

All our screenshots so far showed the process of **browsing** the directory. That is to say, looking in various containers in the directory to see what's there. More commonly, we want to carry out **searches**. In a search, we are trying to find an object, where we know one or more of the object's attributes, but not the whereabouts of the object in the directory. For example, we may want to find all the user accounts where the user hasn't logged on for at least two months, in order to disable those accounts. Although in the screenshots we have seen so far, all the user accounts just happened to be stored in the same container in Active Directory, this will not necessarily the case, so we would normally need to perform a search in order to guarantee that we've found all the accounts.

Directories will usually support fairly complex search queries. Finding all user accounts that haven't logged in for two months is a fairly simple query. A more complex query might be, "Give me all the user accounts with login names beginning with 'a' where the user hasn't logged in for two months, but please do NOT return any of the accounts for domain administrators". All LDAP-compliant directories, including Active Directory, support this level of complexity in queries – which makes searching a very powerful concept.

Openness

This means that directories should be accessible through a standard set of protocols; the one being in most common use is the LDAP protocol. Having a directory accessible through open standards means that it is very easy to write client applications that can communicate with it: you don't need to learn some vendor-specific API.

Active Directory is compliant with the LDAP standards – and as you learn more about Active Directory you'll find that has quite a lot of impact on how the data is structured and accessed. There are many features of Active Directory that are there because they are a requirement of LDAP.

Transaction Processing

Many commercial databases have fairly sophisticated implementations that support transactions and rolling back transactions where operations fail. SQL Server falls into this category. The ADO interfaces include methods to support transactions, assuming the data source implements them. The reason for mentioning the topic here is that transaction processing is usually *not* considered as crucial in directories.

Replication

A common test of whether any software is useful in an enterprise environment is that it scales well – and that's just as true for directories. One of the ways that many directories (including Active Directory) support scaling is by allowing themselves to be replicated. In other words, copies of the directory are stored on several machines. In the case of Active Directory, any machine which is a domain controller will store a replica of Active Directory.

This clearly gives us the problem of ensuring that the different copies of data stored are consistent – and that could potentially lead to a huge amount of network traffic as different copies of directories try to keep up to date with each other – indeed, if we're not careful the network traffic so generated could easily destroy the very scalability that the replication was designed to allow for!

To solve this, we resort to another feature of directories. We've already mentioned that sophisticated transaction processing isn't considered a priority. Now we'll add that it's not too crucial if different replicas in a directory get out of sync. As long as updates are made eventually that is tolerated. Active Directory has been designed with this concept in mind. It is possible for replicas to contain out of date information for a short time, but the data in the replicas will after a period get synchronized with the most up-to-date version. Active Directory implements some fairly sophisticated algorithms to insure that this does happen.

Common Directories

We've now looked at what Active Directory is and what it can do. Let's have a look at some of the other directories you will commonly encounter, which you can access using ADSI.

Netscape Directory Server

This is a general purpose LDAP directory that is available from Netscape. By general purpose, I mean that you can store whatever you want in it. It's designed as a highly scalable, hierarchical data store, optimized for read access, and with a schema that – with a few restrictions due to maintaining compatibility with the LDAP standards – you can completely define yourself.

The IIS Metabase

This is the database of configuration data for Internet Information Server. It is possible to access this using ADSI, along with details of all the virtual directories on a Web site. However, the metabase is not LDAP-compliant.

The Exchange Server Directory and Site Server Membership Directory

I've grouped these together because they will both soon be merged with Active Directory, and so effectively cease to be separate directories. They are both LDAP-compliant directories. The Exchange directory stores information such as address and distribution lists for Exchange Server, while the Site Server Membership directory is used to store data that identifies people who access your Web site, for whom customized Web pages should be generated or special security provisions should apply.

Netware Directory Services

This is Novell's equivalent of Active Directory, and stores similar information concerning user accounts and resources on the network as well as security permissions. However, it is not LDAP-compliant.

WinNT

I've put this one in last, but strictly speaking it shouldn't be in this list at all. WinNT is a fictitious directory. It is a set of COM components which have registered as ADSI providers – in other words as components that allow you to access a directory through ADSI. These components then gather information from round your network concerning user and computer accounts, as well as services running on the different machines. This information is put together and presented to the client as if it were a single directory.

There are two reasons for this. Firstly, it is in recognition of the fact that many networks are still running Windows NT 4.0 domain controllers, and many may not upgrade to Windows 2000 for some time. (There was a gap of well over twelve months between the releases of ADSI and Windows 2000). Clearly it would be a shame if users on those systems were denied access to any of the facilities that Active Directory provides for accessing domain information through automation COM components and hence from scripting languages. The WinNT provider serves that purpose.

Additionally, WinNT allows access to some information that is relevant to individual machines, such as running NT services. By default, such information is not stored in the more domain-centric Active Directory.

Where Does ADSI Fit In?

If we look at how the various bits of software fit together when you (that is – a client program, typically an ASP page) attempt to access a directory using ADSI:

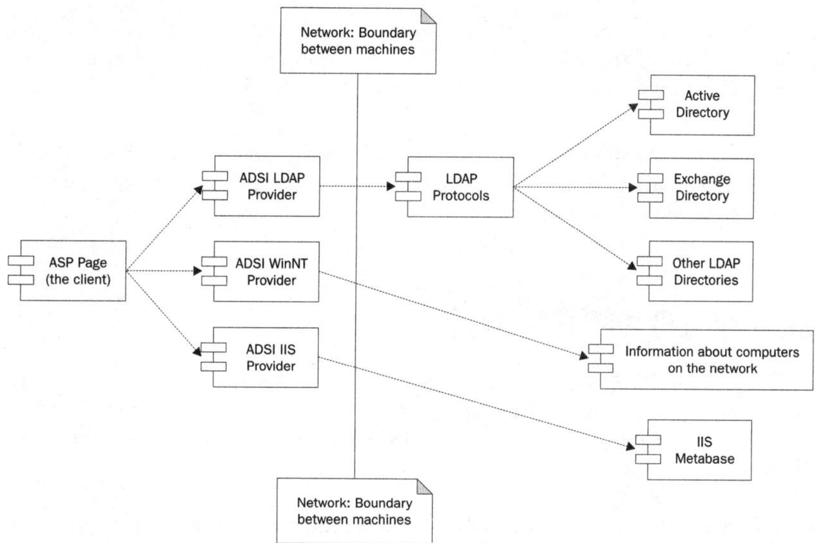

The figure above shows that ADSI comes in between the directory and you. You can think of it as a set of components that are able to translate from whatever API used by the directory you are accessing, and the standard COM-based API known as ADSI – which is therefore the only API you need to know. To that extent ADSI works in the same way as ADO.

Notice that the figure marks the likely point where you will need to go across the network – the point where communication crosses the vertical dotted line. The ADSI providers are in-process components, and so will be hosted on the same machine that your ASP page is running on. The directory service, on the other hand, may be hosted on a different machine. In the case of IIS, since we run ASP pages under IIS, IIS will definitely be on the same machine! However, this wouldn't necessarily be true if we were using ADSI from VB or C++, which is why I've shown the IIS metabase as being on the network.

ADSI, like ADO, works using a series of providers. An ADSI provider is the set of COM components that can access a particular directory or directories. When you install ADSI, you will find it comes with a number of standard providers (known as **system providers**) that have been written by Microsoft. Which providers you get depends to some extent on what software you have installed, however they normally include:

- The **LDAP Provider**, which can access any LDAP-compliant directory
- The **WinNT Provider**, which we discussed earlier and which gives access to domain information on machines in NT4-controlled domains
- The **IIS Provider**, which allows access to the IIS metabase
- The **NWCompat** and **NDS providers**, which allow access to Novell directories

You'll notice that this list quite closely matches the list of common directories that we looked at earlier.

Note that although these providers are all implemented by different components, they generally expose the same interfaces.

In this chapter we're going to be concerned with the LDAP and WinNT providers. We'll use the WinNT provider to explore the apparent directory exposed by that provider, and the LDAP provider to explore Active Directory.

> *Note that there is no separate Active Directory provider. Since Active Directory is fully LDAP-compliant, the LDAP provider serves perfectly well. That's why all the* `ADsPaths` *we've seen in Active Directory begin with* `LDAP:`*.*

Where Does LDAP Fit In?

As we've remarked, LDAP is a standard protocol for accessing directories. To that extent it is similar to ADSI – which may make you wonder (a) why there are two standards, and (b) why the diagram in the last section showed us going through first ADSI then LDAP to access Active Directory and the other LDAP directories.

LDAP is not a Microsoft standard – it is a recognized industry standard. However it is not a standard that has been designed for scripting languages. Rather it is a standard that has been designed to provide a common way that queries and other operations carried out on directories can be transmitted across the network. As such, if you read the LDAP specification itself, which you can – it's defined in Request for Comments (RFC) 2252 – you'll find it full of stuff about message formats etc. The ancillary specifications, defined in RFCs 2253-2256, contain stuff that is more relevant to a high level programmer, such as the definition of that funny `CN=whatever` format for the pathnames used by LDAP (known as **distinguished names**).

> *If you've not encountered Requests for Comments before, they are documents that appear on the Internet that suggest definitions for protocols. Eventually the suggestions made in a given RFC may be formally accepted as a standard – in which case that RFC now provides the final definition of the protocol (this has happened for the LDAP related RFCs we've mentioned). You can find a list of the RFCs at* `http://www.ietf.org/rfc/`*.*

LDAP does come with an API, which is a C-style set of function calls. This is fine if you're programming in C and C++, but not much good if you're using ASP.

By contrast, ADSI has been defined by Microsoft – and is not in any sense an industry standard. The definition of ADSI focuses on the interfaces seen by the ultimate clients – in our case the ASP pages, although the clients can also be written in C++, VB, or any other COM-aware language. There is nothing in the ADSI definitions about how communication with the actual directory service should be done, and nothing about protocols for transmitting information across the network. To that extent, ADSI is sometimes described as a **client-side API**; it is there to define the API the client uses. All the client cares about is that there is an ADSI provider available to communicate with the required directory, and how that provider actually talks to the directory is an implementation detail and is of no concern to the client.

From this description, it's not hard to see how ADSI and LDAP can fit together. On the one hand, we have a specification for an easy-to-use API for scripting clients. On the other hand we have a well-defined protocol for communicating across the network with directory services. If we can write an ADSI provider, which uses that protocol, then we will have a provider that any scripting client can use to access any directory service that answers to that protocol. That's exactly what the ADSI LDAP provider is. You can almost think of it as a component that translates from LDAP to ADSI and back. You will use the ADSI LDAP provider to access any LDAP-compliant directory, including Active Directory, the Exchange Server Directory, and Netscape Directory Server. That's why several directories are shown in the last figure as being accessed via a chain that covers both ADSI and LDAP.

Binding to our First ADSI Object

In this section we're going to start some coding. At first, we're going to use the WinNT provider. Later on we'll compare notes with Active Directory. This is partly because it will ensure that you can still run the code samples even if you are running an NT 4.0 environment, and partly because WinNT does have a simpler directory structure anyway – and that will ease our introduction to ADSI considerably. When we have some more programming experience we'll revert back to Active Directory.

So let's look at our first bit of code. To bind to an ADSI object in VBScript could hardly be simpler. You simply supply the `ADsPath` of the object to VBScript's `GetObject` method. Like this:

```
Dim objDomain
Set objDomain = GetObject("WinNT://TopOfThePops")
```

After executing this statement, `objDomain` will hold a reference to the ADSI COM component that gives us access to the object with `ADsPath` `"WinNT://TopOfThePops"`. Since I'm running a domain that NT 4.0 machines will know as `TopOfThePops`, this is the object exposed by the WinNT provider, which represents my domain.

Binding to an object works the same way, whatever provider you are using. For example, if I wanted to use Active Directory to look at my own user account, I'd do this:

```
Dim objUser
Set objUser = GetObject( _
      "LDAP://CN=Simon Robinson,CN=Users,DC=TopOfThePops,DC=Fame,DC=com")
```

In these as in all other samples, I'm putting in the `ADsPaths` and relying on the fact that I've used the directories enough to be familiar with their structures and to know what the `ADsPaths` to different objects are going to be. If you're not certain of an `ADsPath`, a good way to find out is to use `adsvw.exe` to browse through the directory. Later on, when we cover searching, we won't need to supply `ADsPaths` to locate objects, as the search will recover those for us.

Do you notice how easy it is to use the different providers? There's no need to bother about setting a connection string in the way you would with ADO. The `ADsPath` of each object always starts with the name of the provider, followed by the characters `://` so that `GetObject` is able to figure out what provider you need from the `ADsPath` alone. You'll always get a reference to the correct component provided only that you supply the correct `ADsPath`.

The precise format of the part of the ADsPath following the :// is up to the provider – and you'll notice from the examples we've seen so far that WinNT separates components with /, while LDAP separates them with commas. Also, the string in WinNT works *down* the tree from left to right, whereas the corresponding ADsPaths in LDAP work *up* the tree from left to right. Also note that the initial WinNT or LDAP is case sensitive, but subsequent parts of the string are not.

ADSI Objects and Directory Objects

Earlier I made a big fuss about the fact that you shouldn't confuse COM objects and directory objects. Yet you'll probably be aware that GetObject always gives you a reference to a COM object. So what's going on? Well what ADSI does is quite clever. You get back a reference to a COM object – a component. The component exists on your local machine, and would even be in-process if it wasn't for COM+ getting in the way in running your ASP pages. This component is not the object in the directory – but what it does is pretend to be that directory object – you could say it acts as a proxy for it. For most purposes, you can treat it as if it is the directory object itself, although we will discover there are a few circumstances where you need to be aware of the difference. So having told you to be aware of the difference between COM objects and directory objects, I'm now going to tell you that when coding up your ASP pages, you can generally treat them as if they are effectively the same thing – which is what I'll do from now on.

You still need to be aware of the distinction, however, in order to understand what's really going on in your code, but most of the time it won't affect the code you write. I'll point out the few cases where the distinction is important as we go along.

Similarly, I also made a big deal about directory object properties not being the same as automation properties on components. When we start coding you will find the difference is more apparent in this case, but a lot of the time you will see automation properties on the ADSI components which act as if they were the actual directory properties.

What with the WinNT provider pretending that it is accessing a proper directory, there's a lot of fiction going on here! But it all makes for a nice, easy-to-use, API.

Seeing the Properties of ADSI Objects

We're going to expand our little code snippet now into an ASP page that binds to the domain object in WinNT and displays out some basic information about it. The page is called DomainInfo.asp, and this is what it looks like when you run it:

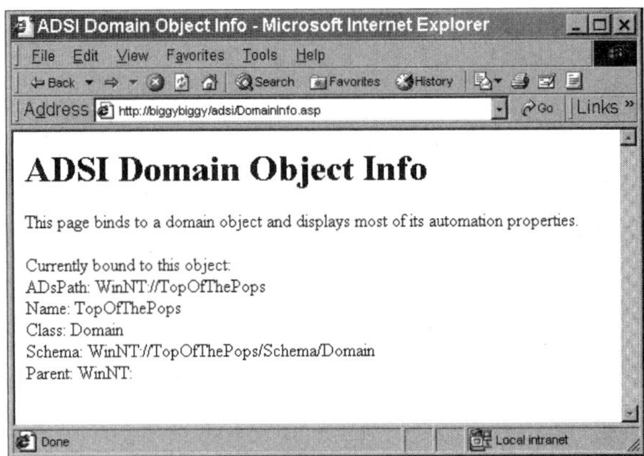

And this is the code that produced that page:

```
<%@ LANGUAGE = VBScript %>
<HTML>
<HEAD>
<TITLE> ADSI Domain Object Info </TITLE>
</HEAD>

<BODY>

<H1> ADSI Domain Object Info </H1>

This page binds to a domain object and displays most of its automation properties.
<P>

<%
On Error Resume Next

Dim objDomain
Set ojDomain = GetObject("WinNT://TopOfThePops")

Response.Write "Currently bound to this object:<BR>"
Response.Write "ADsPath: " & objDomain.ADsPath & "<BR>"
Response.Write "Name: " & objDomain.Name & "<BR>"
Response.Write "Class: " & objDomain.Class & "<BR>"
Response.Write "Schema: " & objDomain.Schema & "<BR>"
Response.Write "Parent: " & objDomain.Parent & "<BR>"
%>
```

I've tried to keep this page as simple as possible, since it's our first proper ADSI sample – so it doesn't even have any real error checking. There's an `On Error Resume Next` statement to ensure that if an error occurs the code just ploughs on regardless – if there's a problem displaying one property the code will carry on displaying all the others without any attempt to find the cause of the error.

You shouldn't have too much trouble with this code. It binds to the relevant ADSI object as we've just described, then it displays the values of some automation properties. The properties are the name and `ADsPath` of the object, as well as its class, schema and the `ADsPath` of its parent. The schema is the only property that you possibly may not recognize. It contains the `ADsPath` of the class schema object, which in turn has the details of the mandatory and optional properties of this object. The name is what in Active Directory we were referring to as the common name (`CN`). Generally speaking, `CN` is really LDAP terminology; ADSI just calls this property a `Name`.

Behind the scenes, we are using an interface called `IADs`. **All** ADSI directory objects expose this interface, which exposes a number of automation properties that give basic essential information about the object, along with some methods to get and set those properties of the directory object that have been defined in the schema.

We haven't yet used any of the methods exposed by `IADs`, but we've just demonstrated almost all its properties. (The one exception, `Guid`, gives a unique GUID that, depending on the directory, indicates either the class of the object or the particular instance – but we won't be using the `Guid` in this chapter.) Although we haven't yet encountered the `IADs` methods, I'm going to list them all here for convenience. For the time being you should regard this table as for reference – you won't understand the explanations of the methods until we've covered a few more concepts.

IADs Properties

`Name`	Stores the name of the object. For the LDAP provider this will usually be the same as the LDAP common name.
`ADsPath`	Stores the `ADsPath` of the object.
`Class`	Stores the class of the object.
`Schema`	Stores the `ADsPath` of the class schema object that describes the class of which this object is an instance.
`Parent`	Stores the `ADsPath` of the object that contains this object.
`Guid`	Stores a unique GUID that can identify the object. This property is not always implemented.

IADs Methods

`Get`	Retrieves the value of a property defined in the schema.
`GetEx`	Similar to `Get` but returns the value in a different format.
`Put`	Sets the value of a property defined in the schema.
`PutEx`	Similar to `Put` but contains more options appropriate to a multi-valued property.
`GetInfo`	Updates the cache from the directory service.
`SetInfo`	Updates the directory service from the cache.
`GetInfoEx`	Similar to `GetInfo` but allows optimization of network calls by allowing you to specify that only particular properties should be copied across.

Note that all the `IADs` *properties are read-only.*

In your dealings with ADSI you are likely to become very familiar with all these methods since they are fundamental to the process of getting and setting information on a directory object. That's why they are exposed by an interface that *must* be present on all components that represent directory objects.

Browsing a Directory: Enumerating Children of a Container

In the last section we saw how simple it was to bind to a directory object (OK, I know you're really binding to the component that wraps the directory object, but ADSI makes it look like pretty much the same thing). In this section we're going to see how easy it is to list the children of an object.

We're going to do it using another sample, which I've called `UserBrowse.asp`. This sample ASP page lists all the domain user accounts using the WinNT provider. The way that the WinNT provider exposes its data, the domain user accounts are all children of the domain object. So what we really want to do is bind to the domain object then list all of its children that happen to be of class `User`.

Here's the code that does it:

```
<%@ LANGUAGE = VBScript %>
<HTML>
<HEAD>
<TITLE> ADSI User Browser </TITLE>
</HEAD>

<BODY>

<H1> ADSI user Browser </H1>

This page binds to a domain object and lists all the user accounts in it.<P>

<%
On Error Resume Next

Dim objDomain
Set objDomain = GetObject("WinNT://TopOfThePops")

Response.Write "Domain object has ADsPath " & objDomain.ADsPath & "<BR>"

objDomain.Filter = Array("User")

Response.Write "<P>User accounts are<P>"
Response.Write "<TABLE BORDER=4>"
Response.Write "<TR><TD><STRONG>Name</STRONG></TD><TD>" & _
               "<STRONG>ADsPath</STRONG></TD</TR>"
For Each objUser In objDomain
    Response.Write "<TR><TD>"
    Response.Write objUser.Name
    Response.Write "</TD><TD>"
    Response.Write objUser.ADsPath
    Response.Write "</TD></TR>"
Next
Response.Write "</TABLE>"
%>

</BODY>
</HTML>
```

And here's the page this code produces:

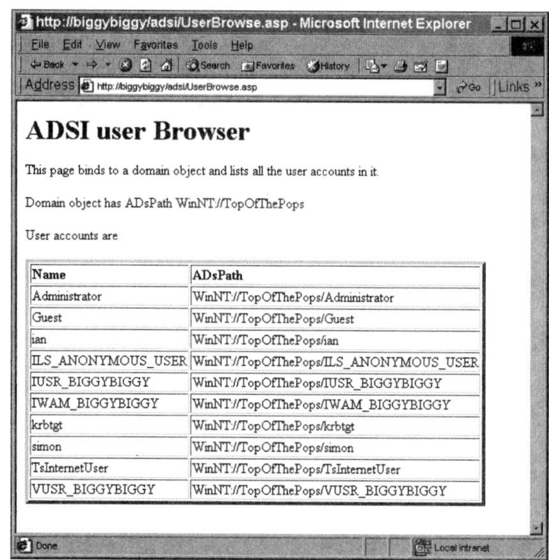

If we look at the code, we are displaying the name and `ADsPath`s of the user objects in the usual way. The interesting bit is in how we enumerate them:

```
objDomain.Filter = Array("User")

Response.Write "<P>User accounts are<P>"
Response.Write "<TABLE BORDER=4>"
Response.Write "<TR><TD><STRONG>Name</STRONG></TD><TD>" & _
               "<STRONG>ADsPath</STRONG></TD</TR>"
For Each objUser In objDomain
    Response.Write "<TR><TD>"
    Response.Write objUser.Name
    Response.Write "</TD><TD>"
    Response.Write objUser.ADsPath
    Response.Write "</TD></TR>"
Next
```

This code shows that objects, which are containers, are implemented as COM collections, so we can enumerate through their children using a `For...Each` loop.

Before we start the loop, we set a property of the domain object called `Filter`. This property contains an array of strings, and its purpose is to specify what classes of directory object we want when we enumerate over the children of this object. The reason we've set it is this. In the WinNT directory, the domain object contains not only the user accounts but also all the group accounts and computer accounts in the domain. We don't want these objects since we're interested in users, so we set the filter to indicate this. If the filter is empty, then all children will be returned.

You'll have noticed that the `Filter` is not a property defined by `IADs`. Clearly the domain object must be exposing another interface as well. The interface we are using is called `IADsContainer`, and it is implemented by all directory objects which are containers. Again, for reference, we present the complete list of properties and methods of `IADsContainer`.

IADsContainer Properties

`Filter`	The classes of children that we are interested in if we enumerate the children.
`Hints`	Similar to filter but instead of restricting the classes of children returned in an enumeration, it restricts which properties are copied across for the children, hence allowing minimization of network access.
`Count`	The number of children that satisfy the filter. Note that this property is not always implemented. For example, the WinNT provider doesn't implement it at present.

IADsContainer Methods

`MoveHere`	Moves a directory object from elsewhere in the directory to be a child of this object. You can use this method either to move objects or to rename them.
`CopyHere`	Similar to `MoveHere` except that it makes a copy of the specified directory object.
`Delete`	Deletes an object that is a child of this container from the directory.
`Create`	Creates a new directory object which is a child of this object, and which has name and class as specified in the parameters.
`GetObject`	Similar to VB's `GetObject` function, except that it can only be used to obtain a reference to an object that is a child of this container – so you only need to specify the name of the object, not its full `AdsPath`.

From this list, you can see that `IADsContainer` is the interface you need if you want to start moving objects around the directory or creating new objects. In general, you will do those sorts of operations by calling `IADsContainer` methods on the parent of the object in question. Since we've only got one chapter on ADSI, however, we won't go into how to start adding and removing directory entries.

> *Of course, the fact that the `IADsContainer` methods are exposed by a different interface from `IADs` is completely transparent to ASP code. Such code invokes the methods through `IDispatch` anyway, so it doesn't need to be aware of the fact that we are dealing with two interfaces here.*

Notice that if you want to go up rather than down the tree, then the process is slightly more complex. You need the `Parent` property of the objects – but since this only gives you an `ADsPath` rather than a reference to the object, you need to use the `ADsPath` to bind separately to the object. Something like this:

```
Dim objParent
Set objParent = GetObject(objCurrentObject.ADsPath)
```

`IADs` and `IADsContainer` are the core interfaces that you'll always keep encountering. There are a large number of other ADSI interfaces, but these are generally specialist ones that are exposed by certain types of object – and won't concern us that much at this elementary level.

Using Schema-Defined Properties

So far we've used the `IADs` automation properties to get at basic information about the object. However we've already indicated that a directory object is likely to have many more properties that have been defined in the schema. Generally speaking, you cannot access these as automation properties, since that would require whoever designed the relevant COM interfaces to have a prior knowledge of what properties the schema is going to define. This is clearly not possible since if we are to maintain directories as being open, then the ADSI interfaces need to be generically useful, not specific to certain directories. Instead, `IADs` has some methods that allow you to get or set properties by passing the name of the property as a parameter to the method. These methods are `Get`, `GetEx`, `Put` and `PutEx`. An additional bonus of doing it this way is that this allows us to enumerate through all the properties of a directory object, without having to know the names of the properties beforehand.

The following ASP page does exactly this. It binds to an object – in this case the object in WinNT that holds my account details, and uses the schema to run through all the mandatory and optional properties of that object.

Here's the page:

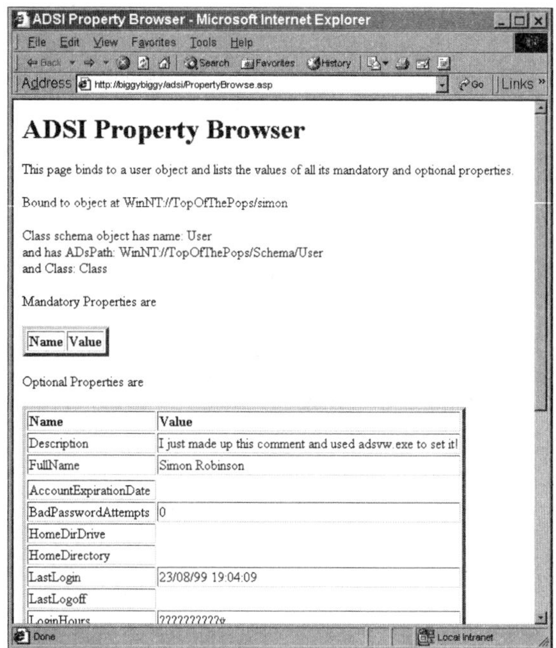

Amongst the peculiarities you'll notice are that some of the values are missing. This occurs either if the value is of a data type which is not displayable using the ANSI character set (in which case the relevant `Response.Write` line of code will raise an error), or – in the case of optional properties – if the property happens not to have a value assigned to it. The screenshot also shows that user objects in WinNT don't have any mandatory properties – the Mandatory Properties table doesn't have any entries in it.

Anyway here's the ASP code:

```
<%@ LANGUAGE = VBScript %>
<HTML>
<HEAD>
<TITLE> ADSI Property Browser </TITLE>
</HEAD>

<BODY>

<H1> ADSI Property Browser </H1>

This page binds to a user object and lists the values of all its mandatory
and optional properties.<P>

<%
On Error Resume Next

Dim objObject
Set objObject = GetObject("WinNT://TopOfThePops/Simon")
If (Err.Number <> 0) Then
    Response.Write "Failed to bind to ADSI object"
    Response.End
End If

Response.Write "Bound to object at " & objObject.ADsPath & "<P>"

' Get hold of the schema object
Dim objClassSchema
Set objClassSchema = GetObject(objObject.Schema)
If (Err.Number <> 0) Then
    Response.Write "Failed to bind to class schema object"
    Response.End
End If

Response.Write "Class schema object has name: " & objClassSchema.Name & "<BR>"
Response.Write "and has ADsPath: " & objClassSchema.ADsPath & "<BR>"
Response.Write "and Class: " & objClassSchema.Class & "<P>"

Response.Write "<P>Mandatory Properties are<P>"
Response.Write "<TABLE BORDER=4>"
Response.Write "<TR><TD><STRONG>Name</STRONG></TD><TD>" & _
               "<STRONG>Value</STRONG></TD</TR>"
For Each strProp In objClassSchema.MandatoryProperties
    Response.Write "<TR><TD>"
    Response.Write strProp
    Response.Write "</TD><TD>"
    Response.Write objObject.Get(strProp)
    Response.Write "</TD></TR>"
Next

Response.Write "</TABLE>"
Response.Write "<P>Optional Properties are<P>"
Response.Write "<TABLE BORDER=4>"
```

```
Response.Write "<TR><TD><STRONG>Name</STRONG></TD><TD>" & _
                "<STRONG>Value</STRONG></TD</TR>"
For Each strProp In objClassSchema.OptionalProperties
    Response.Write "<TR><TD>"
    Response.Write strProp
    Response.Write "</TD><TD>"
    Response.Write objObject.Get(strProp)
    Response.Write "</TD></TR>"
Next
Response.Write "</TABLE>"
%>

</BODY>
</HTML>
```

There's a bit more to this code so let's go through the new bits. First up, we bind to the user object in the normal way, though note that in this case I've taken the trouble to add a bit more sophisticated error checking.

Now it gets interesting. We need to enumerate through the mandatory and optional properties. For that we need the class schema object. So we bind to it:

```
' Get hold of the schema object
Dim objClassSchema
Set objClassSchema = GetObject(objObject.Schema)
If (Err.Number <> 0) Then
    Response.Write "Failed to bind to class schema object"
    Response.End
End If
```

Now we display the `ADsPath` of the class schema object. This stage isn't really essential, but I thought it was worth demonstrating it – just to reinforce the point that this object is a perfectly normal directory object that you can treat just like any other directory object, and it gets accessed using a perfectly normal ADSI component:

```
Response.Write "Class schema object has name: " & objClassSchema.Name & "<BR>"
Response.Write "and has ADsPath: " & objClassSchema.ADsPath & "<BR>"
Response.Write "and Class: " & objClassSchema.Class & "<P>"
```

If you have installed `adsvw.exe` you might like to use it to browse down and locate the WinNT schema objects. You'll find them in the container "`WinNT://<DomainName>/Schema`".

The next stages use a couple of new automation properties on the class schema object: `MandatoryProperties` and `OptionalProperties`. These properties contain arrays that list the names of the mandatory and optional properties. They are implemented through another interface, which we haven't met yet, `IADsClass`, which is always exposed by schema objects.

Since each string in the array is the name of one of the mandatory properties, we could display their names and values like this (this code snippet is heavily edited from the `PropertyBrowse` page listed above, to simplify it):

```
For Each strProp In objClassSchema.MandatoryProperties
    Response.Write "Name is " & strProp
    Response.Write "Value is " & objObject.Get(strProp)
Next
```

You'd similarly list all the optional properties using the OptionalProperties array.

You may wonder why we are using the automation properties named MandatoryProperties and OptionalProperties here when earlier I mentioned that Active Directory has properties named mustContain and mayContain. In fact using either name will work in Active Directory (though not in WinNT), though if you use mustContain and mayContain you'll need to use the Get method since there are no automation properties of those names, thus:

```
For Each strProp In objClassSchema.Get("mustContain")
```

This is really an issue between different standards. LDAP uses mustContain and mayContain. ADSI uses MandatoryProperties and OptionalProperties. Since we are really using the ADSI API's we're better off sticking with the ADSI way of doing it.

Get and GetEx: MultiValued Properties

Although the PropertyBrowse.asp sample looked like it would display out all the properties, it had a major flaw: it would only work for single-valued properties, and could not display multi-valued properties. The problem is with the line shown in gray:

```
For Each strProp In objClassSchema.MandatoryProperties
    Response.Write "<TR><TD>"
    Response.Write strProp
    Response.Write "</TD><TD>"
    Response.Write objObject.Get(strProp)
    Response.Write "</TD></TR>"
Next
```

This line assumes that the variable returned from the Get method is something that is printable. There are a number of reasons why this might not be the case. Get actually returns a Variant, so whether its value can be displayed depends on the type of data contained in the Variant. The property might not actually contain any values (we return an empty Variant), or the value might be in some binary format. There are also some properties that return references to other objects – for example, the nTSecurityDescriptor property of objects in Active Directory does this – although covering such attributes is beyond the scope of this chapter.

However, one reason for the contents not being printable that we need to be aware of is that the property might be multi-valued – in which case Get will return a Variant containing an array.

The possibility of multi-valued properties is the reason why IADs exposes two methods that return property values, Get and GetEx. The difference between these methods is this. Get will return the value as a Variant if there is only one value. If there is more than one value for a property, Get will return a Variant containing an array of values. GetEx will always return a Variant containing an array of values. If there happens to only be one value, then this array will only have one element in it.

Clearly which you use depends on your preference, and which method is easier in the circumstances. Mostly you'll probably use GetEx if you don't know whether a property is single or multi-valued, since with Get you won't know what format the return value is in. I chose to use Get in the PropertyBrowse.asp page since I happened to know that no multi-valued properties were present on the user object in WinNT. But if we want this page to be more generally useful then we really need it to be able to display multi-valued properties. That's what the next sample does.

One final point I should make is that you will find in some cases that properties can be obtained either using the `Get` or `GetEx` methods, or as automation properties. This occurs in cases where the designers of ADSI anticipated that certain properties would be commonly used on certain types of object, and so added interfaces that exposed those properties as automation properties. For example for a user object in WinNT, both of the following lines of code will do the same thing:

```
Response.Write objUser.Description
```

And:

```
Response.Write objUser.Get("Description")
```

The MSDN documentation for ADSI contains full details of the properties on the different providers for which it is possible to do this.

The PropertyBrowseEx Sample

This sample is similar to the `PropertyBrowse` sample but has two differences. Firstly, it uses `GetEx` rather than `Get`, so that it can display all the values of any multi-valued property, and use the same code to display single-valued properties. Secondly, instead of hard coding the `ADsPath` of the object we want to look at, it uses an HTML form to allow the user to enter the `ADsPath`. This means that we'll be able to use the same page to examine not only different objects but also objects in different directories.

This is what the page looks like when you start it out:

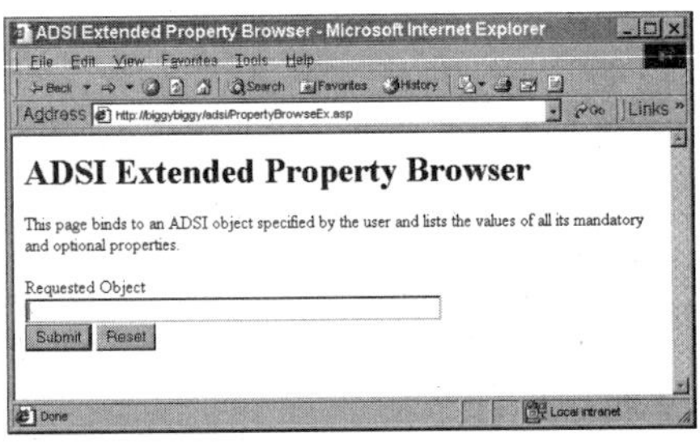

If you type in the `ADsPath` of an object and hit submit, you'll get an output pretty similar to the `PropertyBrowse` sample. For the following screenshot I've tried examining the File Service on my domain controller, `BiggyBiggy`. The file service is the NT service that is responsible for responding to requests from other computers on the network to access shared files and folders on that computer's file system. It answers to the name `lanmanserver`:

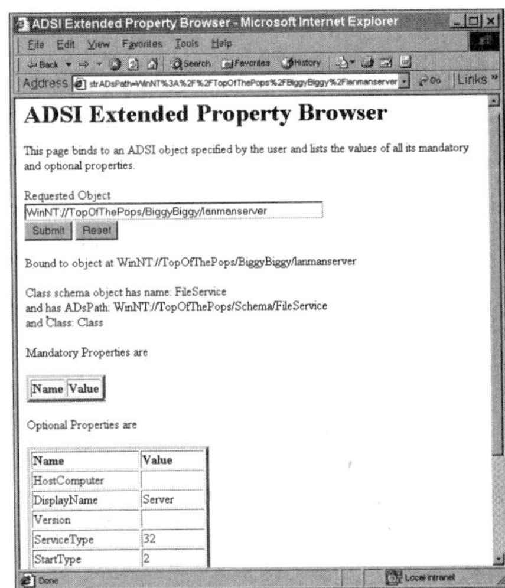

The code for this is fairly similar to the code for the `PropertyBrowse` sample, so I've just highlighted the changes. From what I've said you should be able to understand how the modified code works. Note that in the form the code takes the trouble to be user friendly by supplying the chosen `ADsPath` as a default value in the text box:

```
<%@ LANGUAGE = VBScript %>
<HTML>
<HEAD>
<TITLE> ADSI Extended Property Browser </TITLE>
</HEAD>

<BODY>

<H1> ADSI Extended Property Browser </H1>

This page binds to an ADSI object specified by the user
and lists the values of all its mandatory
and optional properties.<P>

<%
Dim strADsPath
strADsPath = Request.QueryString("strADsPath")
%>

<P>
<FORM ACTION = "PropertyBrowseEx.asp" METHOD = "GET" ID=form1 NAME=form1>
Requested Object<BR>
<INPUT TYPE="TEXT" ID=Request NAME=strADsPath SIZE=60
VALUE = <%=strADsPath%>
><BR>
<INPUT TYPE="SUBMIT" VALUE="Submit" ID=submit1 NAME=submit1>
<INPUT TYPE="RESET" VALUE="Reset" ID=reset1 NAME=reset1><BR>
</FORM>
<%
On Error Resume Next

If (strADsPath = "") Then
    Response.End
End If

Dim objObject
Set objObject = GetObject(strADsPath)
If (Err.Number <> 0) Then
    Response.Write "Failed to bind to ADSI object"
    Response.End
End If

Response.Write "Bound to object at " & oObject.ADsPath & "<P>"

' Get hold of the schema object
Dim objClassSchema
Set objClassSchema = GetObject(objObject.Schema)
If (Err.Number <> 0) Then
    Response.Write "Failed to bind to class schema object"
    Response.End
End If
```

```
Response.Write "Class schema object has name: " & objClassSchema.Name & "<BR>"
Response.Write "and has ADsPath: " & objClassSchema.ADsPath & "<BR>"
Response.Write "and Class: " & objClassSchema.Class & "<P>"

Response.Write "<P>Mandatory Properties are<P>"
Response.Write "<TABLE BORDER=4>"
Response.Write "<TR><TD><STRONG>Name</STRONG></TD><TD>" & _
               "<STRONG>Value</STRONG></TD</TR>"
For Each strProp In objClassSchema.MandatoryProperties
    Response.Write "<TR><TD>"
    Response.Write strProp
    Response.Write "</TD><TD>"
    For Each strValue In objObject.GetEx(strProp)
        Response.Write strValue & "<BR>"
    Next
    Response.Write "</TD></TR>"
Next

Response.Write "</TABLE>"
Response.Write "<P>Optional Properties are<P>"
Response.Write "<TABLE BORDER=4>"
Response.Write "<TR><TD><STRONG>Name</STRONG></TD><TD>" & _
               "<STRONG>Value</Strong></TD</TR>"
For Each strProp In objClassSchema.OptionalProperties
    Response.Write "<TR><TD>"
    Response.Write strProp
    Response.Write "</TD><TD>"
    For Each strValue in objObject.GetEx(strProp)
        Response.Write strValue & "<BR>"
    Next
    Response.Write "</TD></TR>"
Next
Response.Write "</TABLE>"

%>

</BODY>
</HTML>
```

Comparing Active Directory with the WinNT Provider

There is quite a fair bit of overlap between Active Directory and the WinNT provider – in that both to some extent give access to the same information. Stuff that is exposed through both directories includes global user, group and computer accounts in the domain. Apart from that, the WinNT provider lets you get information about local NT services and print jobs on member computers. On the other hand, Active Directory lets you get at configuration information for the domain forest, as well as any other data that systems administrators have chosen to store there.

We can see something more of the differences between WinNT and Active Directory by using both the WinNT and LDAP providers to examine data. In the following screenshots we use our `PropertyBrowseEx.asp` page to look at my user account using both providers. For both screenshots I've scrolled down past the form that specifies the `ADsPath`, so we can see more of the properties. Here's the WinNT version of my user account object:

http://biggybiggy/adsi/PropertyBrowseEx.asp?strADsPath=WinNT%...

Bound to object at WinNT://TopOfThePops/simon

Class schema object has name: User
and has ADsPath: WinNT://TopOfThePops/Schema/User
and Class: Class

Mandatory Properties are

Name	Value

Optional Properties are

Name	Value
Description	I just made up this comment and used adsvw.exe to set it!
FullName	Simon Robinson
AccountExpirationDate	
BadPasswordAttempts	0
HomeDirDrive	
HomeDirectory	
LastLogin	23/08/99 19:04:09
LastLogoff	
LoginHours	
LoginScript	
LoginWorkstations	
MaxLogins	
MaxPasswordAge	3710851

And here's the same user account but now viewed as an object in Active Directory:

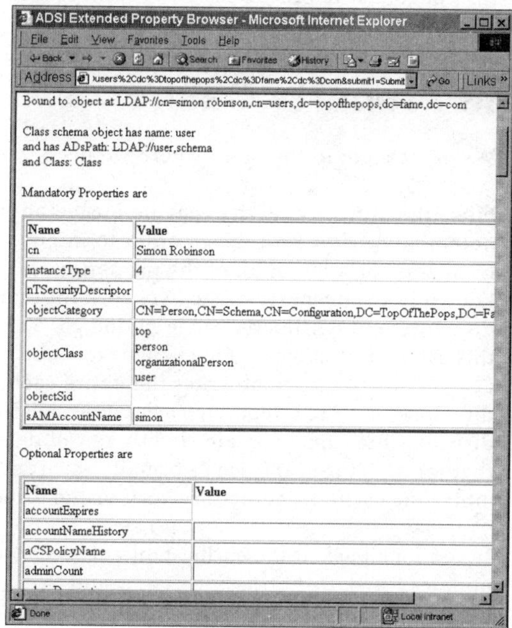

The smaller size of the scrollbar in the Active Directory screenshot shows that Active Directory is able to store many more properties for its objects than WinNT does. On the other hand, most of the optional properties have blank values – showing they are only defined in case the systems administrator wants to use those properties to store information. Also, where WinNT had no mandatory properties, Active Directory has several, including `objectClass`, which we discussed earlier. `objectClass` shows all the classes in the inheritance tree for the user class. It is also the only attribute in the screenshot that clearly shows our sample working for a multi-valued property. `objectCategory` is a property that we will come across soon when we see how to perform searching. It conveys similar information to `objectClass`, but is single valued, and is more efficient to search against. The `sAMAccountName` is just the name you use to login with, and corresponds to the `Name` of the object in the WinNT provider. `nTSecurityDescriptor` and `objectSid` contain security information about the object. Neither can be displayed since `nTSecurityDescriptor` is actually a reference to a security descriptor component, and `objectSid` is in binary format.

In general, you will find that the WinNT provider is a very basic provider, which exposes only the most elementary information about its objects. For example, it does not provide access to security descriptors. Personally, I tend to find that WinNT is easier to use if you want to do something simple with minimal coding – the larger quantity of information in Active Directory does come at a price in that it is more complex to learn to navigate your way around. If you are running on a network controlled by an NT 4.0 primary domain controller then you will of course not have access to Active Directory so you will have to use the WinNT provider. On the other hand, as we'll see when we come to cover searching, it is not possible to search using the WinNT provider – so if you are writing an ASP page that requires access to sophisticated search facilities you will have to use Active Directory.

The Property Cache

We've now got to the point where we need to introduce this important concept.

Since the directory service may be hosted anywhere on the network, accessing any one property is potentially a slow process. In order to minimize this problem, each ADSI component maintains a local copy of some or all of the properties in the corresponding directory object. This local copy is known as the **property cache**. Network traffic is minimized by copying all the properties from the directory to the property cache in one go. The client can then access those properties it needs to from this cache. If it makes some changes to some of these properties, then it can call a method (`IADs::SetInfo`) that writes the entire cache back to the directory in one go – hence updating the directory. Having a separate cache does mean there is a possibility that either the cache or the directory itself may contain slightly out-of-date values for properties – but we've already indicated that for directories this isn't normally regarded as a serious problem. The client can choose to update either the cache from the directory or the directory from the cache at any time.

If you look back at the earlier table of `IADs` methods, you'll see the three methods that handle these updates listed. `GetInfo`, `SetInfo` and `GetInfoEx`. `GetInfo` updates the entire cache from the directory, while `SetInfo` goes the other way. `GetInfoEx` can be used instead of `GetInfo` if you only want particular properties.

In general, you must always call `SetInfo` after you're done modifying the values of properties. You might expect that you should always call `GetInfo` before examining properties, but actually this is not necessary. The first time you attempt to access a property in the cache, the component will notice if the cache has not yet been initialized, and implicitly call `GetInfo` on your behalf if that's the case. You only need to explicitly call `GetInfo` if you suspect that you may be holding an out-of-date value, and want to update it.

The IADs Get, GetEx, Put and PutEx methods, as well as the automation properties, deal only with the property cache, not with the directory. So, for example, if you call Get to examine the value of a property, you will obtain the value from the cache only – although if the property cache has not yet been initialized then GetInfo will implicitly be called for you first.

> **Manipulating the property cache is the one area where you do need to be aware of the distinction between the COM components you are using, and the directory objects that you are ultimately trying to manipulate.**

Setting Values of Properties

All our examples have so far covered reading the values of properties – but writing new values is just as easy. For a single-valued property, you just use the IADs::Put method – for example if I wanted to change the description of a user account, the following code would do the trick:

```
objUser.Put "This is the new description"

'more processing

objUser.SetInfo
```

Note the call to SetInfo. We could call this method immediately after writing the change to the local cache, but it's generally more efficient to wait until you've finished making all your changes – then you only need to call SetInfo once.

You will use PutEx rather than Put if you are setting a multi-valued property. The difference is that for a multi-valued property, there are several different ways in which you might want to modify the data. You might want to add a new value to the current values, replace all the current values, or remove one or more values. Also, for any optional property, whether single or multi-valued, you may wish to clear out all the values. PutEx works in the same way as Put but takes an additional parameter to specify how you want to make the changes. We're not going to examine it in detail here, but full details are in the ADSI documentation.

Authenticating to a Directory

So far we've gone over quite a few samples, but we've tacitly relied on having sufficient security permissions to be able to execute all of them. Unfortunately, there may be a problem with that. We're dealing with ASP pages here, which means that, as often as not, our pages will be running under the Internet Guest Account. Assuming your systems administrator is even remotely good at his job, the Internet Guest Account is very unlikely to have permission to change any of the data exposed by the ADSI-compliant directories. It may not even have permission to examine very much of the data in the directories – if you've tried running any of the samples, you'll probably find we've got away with it so far but only because none of our big samples have attempted to modify or view any particularly sensitive data.

So at some point we're going to have to learn how to supply some more appropriate security credentials.

The next sample does just that. It's quite a simple example – all it does is authenticate to an ADSI object supplying an appropriate username and password. To keep things simple, this has all the machine names etc. hard-coded into it, so as with some of the previous samples, if you download it from the Wrox Press Web site, you'll need to change some of the names before you run it.

The page looks quite simple when you run it – it basically says that it worked:

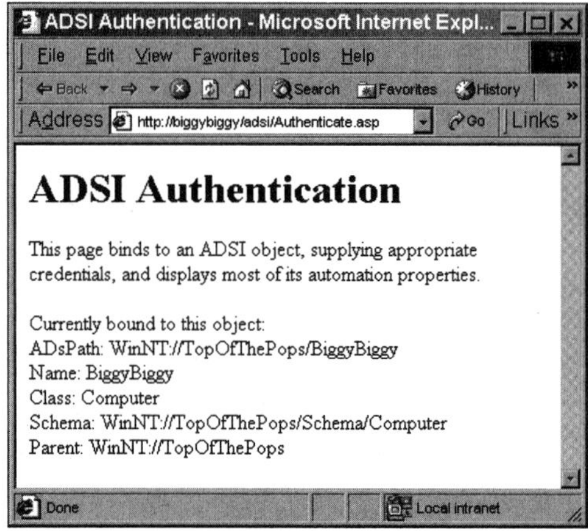

Here's the code that does the authenticating:

```
<%@ LANGUAGE = VBScript %>
<HTML>
<HEAD>
<TITLE> ADSI Authentication</TITLE>
</HEAD>

<BODY>

<H1> ADSI Authentication </H1>

This page binds to an ADSI object, supplying appropriate credentials,
 and displays most of its automation properties.
<P>

<%
On Error Resume Next
Dim ADsPath
ADsPath = "WinNT://TopOfThePops/BiggyBiggy"

' Attempt to bind while authenticating
Dim objNamespace
Set objNamespace = GetObject("WinNT:")
Dim objObjSec
Set objObjSec = objNamespace.OpenDSObject(ADsPath, "simon", _
                                          "mypassword", 1)
```

```
If Err.Number <> 0 Then
    Response.Write "Problem authenticating to the object" & "<BR>"
    Response.Write Err.description & "<BR>"
    Response.Write Err.number & "<BR>"
Else
    Response.Write "Currently bound to this object:<BR>"
    Response.Write "ADsPath: " & oObjSec.ADsPath & "<BR>"
    Response.Write "Name: " & oObjSec.Name & "<BR>"
    Response.Write "Class: " & oObjSec.Class & "<BR>"
    Response.Write "Schema: " & oObjSec.Schema & "<BR>"
    Response.Write "Parent: " & oObjSec.Parent & "<BR>"
End If
%>

</BODY>
</HTML>
```

The key lines are these ones:

```
Dim objNamespace
Set objNamespace = GetObject("WinNT:")
Dim objObjSec
Set objObjSec = objNamespace.OpenDSObject(ADsPath, "simon", _
                                          "mypassword", 1)
```

From this we see that authenticating is a two-stage process. First of all, we need to use `GetObject` to bind to the object right at the top of the directory – the object whose `ADsPath` is given by the name of the provider followed by a colon – in other words, `WinNT:` or `LDAP:` or `IIS:`. This object is known as the **namespace object**. We can then call a method exposed by the namespace object, `OpenDSObject`, to actually return a reference to the object we want. `OpenDSObject` is actually implemented through the interface `IADsOpenDSObject`, which is only exposed by namespace objects. It takes four parameters: the `ADsPath` of the required object, the username and the password for the account you wish to bind as, and an integer that indicates various flags concerning how the authentication is carried out – we'll leave it at `1` which essentially requests normal WinNT/Windows 2000 authentication.

Although this process doesn't look too complex, it's important to be aware that this is because the underlying work done by the provider to authenticate you has been effectively hidden. The provider may need to impersonate another user behind the scenes, or it may need to create a new connection. There are a large number of reasons, mostly security-related, why things may go wrong here. Some of these reasons are discussed in knowledge base articles 218497 and 158229. Because of this, you may prefer to use basic or NTLM authentication in IIS itself in order to supply the appropriate credentials rather than relying on the `OpenDSObject` *method. It's for that reason that we haven't spent much time discussing ADSI authentication in this section.*

Searching

This is the last topic we will be covering in this chapter, though it is arguably one of the most important topics in ADSI. As I mentioned earlier, one of the most important aspects of a directory is its support for complex search queries. All our ADSI samples up till now have relied on our knowing the `ADsPath` of the object we want to bind to. Searching allows us to get round that requirement – by effectively saying, "We don't know where in the directory the object we want is located, but we know something about its properties" – it might for example be a user account named 'Henry'.

In fact, although we will indirectly be using ADSI, when we come to do searching, the fact that we are using ADSI is very much hidden behind the scenes. That's because the way you search directories that are accessed via ADSI is actually not to directly use ADSI at all, but to call up some ADO objects instead. These ADO objects will internally use the services of the ADSI providers.

The reason for this is because of a restriction of scripting languages. At present, scripting languages can only talk to COM components using the `IDispatch` interface – they cannot directly call methods on other interfaces. Up till now that hasn't been a problem since all the ADSI interfaces we've needed to use are dual interfaces. Unfortunately for us, the interface that ADSI uses to perform searches is an interface called `IDirectorySearch` – and that's a custom interface. Which means it cannot be used directly from scripting clients.

This is a fairly similar situation to the case of ADO and OLE DB. When you use ADO, it's not really ADO components that are accessing the data source; it is the OLE DB components. The only reason ADO components exist is to call up the OLE DB ones on your behalf, thus solving the problem of OLE DB not being designed for use by scripting clients and hence using custom interfaces. Now we have an extra step. The ASP page must call on the services of an ADO component. The ADO component in turn calls up an OLE DB component, and finally the OLE DB component uses a special OLE DB Provider for ADSI to call up methods in the ADSI interfaces, to access the directory – or, as ADO sees it, the data source.

The process is illustrated in this diagram:

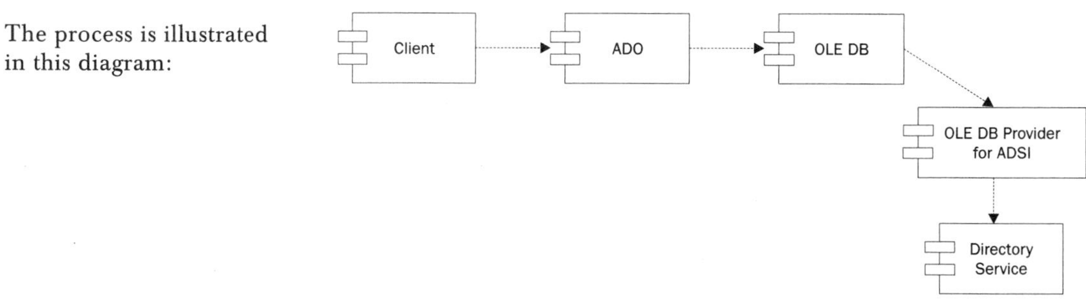

It looks complicated, but it leads to very simple client code.

There is one other point we need to be aware of when doing searching. Despite its importance in directories in general, not all ADSI providers support it. In particular, the WinNT ADSI provider doesn't – you cannot use this provider to do searches. That's because of the way the provider works – WinNT gathers its information from around the network and so there is no real back-end directory behind it with the infrastructure to support efficient searching.

The ADSI LDAP provider does allow searching, and any LDAP-compliant directory must also do so, since searching is required by the LDAP specifications. That means that we can do searches against Active Directory – so our final sample will be based on Active Directory.

The following sample demonstrates this. It's called `Search.asp`, and it uses the LDAP provider to perform a search. To keep things simple, all the search parameters have been hard coded into the page, and they request a search for all users in the directory.

Here's what the page looks like:

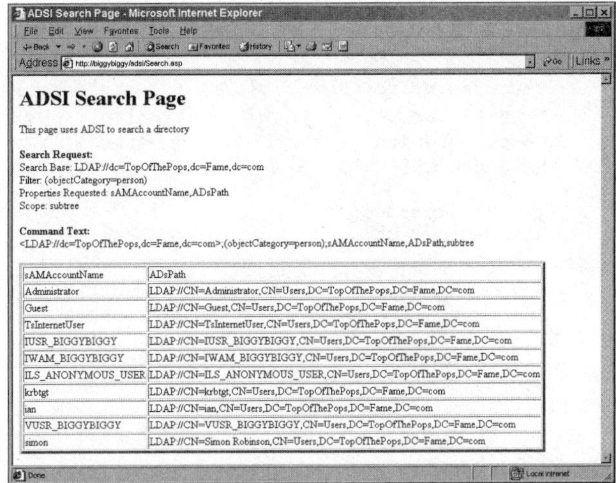

The screenshot shows that we have found all the users and displayed the `sAMAccountName` and the `ADsPath` of each one. The command text displayed just above the table is the command that is passed to ADO to generate this search result. We'll look at the syntax required for this text soon, after we've looked at the code used to generate this page. For now, you may want to note that the command text is comprised from the four strings listed at the top of the page: the search base, filter, properties requested and scope.

The code for the `Search` sample looks like this:

```
<%@ LANGUAGE = VBScript %>
<HTML>
<HEAD>
<TITLE> ADSI Search Page </TITLE>
</HEAD>

<BODY>

<H1> ADSI Search Page </H1>

This page uses ADSI to search a directory
<P>
<strong>Search Request:</STRONG><BR>

<%
```

```
On Error Resume Next

Dim strSearchBase
strSearchBase = "LDAP://dc=TopOfThePops,dc=Fame,dc=com"
Dim strFilter
strFilter = "(objectCategory=person)"
Dim strAttribs
strAttribs = "sAMAccountName,ADsPath"
Dim strScope
strScope = "subtree"

Response.Write "Search Base: " & strSearchBase & "<BR>"
Response.Write "Filter: " & strFilter & "<BR>"
Response.Write "Properties Requested: " & strAttribs & "<BR>"
Response.Write "Scope: " & strScope & "<P>"

Dim strCommandText
strCommandText = "<" & strSearchBase & ">;" _
                & strFilter & ";" & strAttribs & ";" & strScope
Response.Write "<STRONG>Command Text: </STRONG><BR>"
Response.Write Server.HTMLEncode(strCommandText) & "<P>"

Dim objConnection
Set objConnection = Server.CreateObject("ADODB.Connection")
Dim objCommand
Set objCommand = Server.CreateObject("ADODB.Command")

objConnection.Provider = "ADsDSOObject"
objConnection.Open "Active Directory Provider"
Set objCommand.ActiveConnection = objConnection
objCommand.CommandText = strCommandText

Dim objRecordset
Set objRecordset = objCommand.Execute(strCommandText)

Response.Write "<TABLE BORDER = 4><TR>"
If (Not objRecordset.EOF) Then
    For Each objField in objRecordset.Fields
        Response.Write "<TD>"
        Response.Write objField.Name
        Response.Write "</TD>"
    Next
End If
Response.Write "</TR>"

While Not objRecordset.EOF
    Response.Write "<TR>"
    For Each oField in objRecordset.Fields
        Response.Write "<TD>"
        Response.Write objField.Value
        Response.Write "</TD>"
    Next
    Response.Write "</TR>"
    objRecordset.MoveNext
Wend
Response.Write "</TR></TABLE>"
```

```
%>

</BODY>
</HTML>
```

There shouldn't be that much explaining to do here, as it's mostly standard ADO stuff, which we've already covered earlier in the book. We set up a command and pass a string to the `Execute` method of the command object. Notice that we are not directly creating any ADSI objects at all! What's new is the string that we need to pass to the ADO connection object to indicate that we want to use the OLE DB provider for ADSI, `ADsDSOObject`, and how we form the command string. Which is what we'll examine next.

Command Strings for Searching ADSI Directories

Let's go over the string we used to request a search for all users. To remind ourselves, the string was:

```
<LDAP://dc=TopOfThePops,dc=Fame,dc=com>;(objectCategory=person);
sAMAccountName,ADsPath;subtree
```

This string is composed of four parts, separated by semicolons. To understand how these parts work, let's think about the things a directory service needs to know when you request a search. There are really three things here. We need to tell the directory service:

- What we are looking for (in other words, what conditions the objects returned from the search must satisfy).
- Whereabouts in the directory we should look for them.
- When the objects are found, what attributes on them we are interested in.

In our case, what we are looking for is 'anything that's a user', whereabouts in the directory is 'anywhere', and the properties we are interested in are '`sAMAccountName` and `AdsPath`'. So far so good – all we need is a precise syntax for turning those pieces of information into something that the directory service will understand.

Let's cover the attributes requested first, as that's the easiest one. We compose a string, which we will call 'Properties Requested', which consists of a comma-separated list of the names of the attributes. Like this:

```
sAMAccountName,ADsPath
```

Next, what we are looking for. Well that's a big subject in itself. We use something called a **search filter**. How to construct search filters is a big topic, so we cover that more fully in the next section. For our particular request, we want all objects that are users. The relevant search filter is:

```
(objectCategory=person)
```

Notice that this takes the form of stating that a certain property must have a certain value. All search filters ultimately boil down to a series of conditions like this. The property we specify is `objectCategory` because in Active Directory the `objectCategory` contains information about the general type of object, so it's a convenient attribute to use for this sort of filter.

Finally, we need to specify where in the directory we want to look. For our search, we are assuming that we don't have any idea where the users might be located so we want to specify the entire directory. For other searches, you may know something about the directory structure and hence have a rough idea of where in the directory the objects can be found. Clearly, the more you can narrow down where to look, the faster the search will be.

Searches always take place in subtrees of the directory. And there are two pieces of information we need to specify the subtree: the `ADsPath` of the object at the top of the subtree, and how far down the subtree from that object we want to go. The `ADsPath` of the object at the top of the subtree is the **search base**, while how far down we want to go is the **scope**.

The search base is fairly easy to understand, since it is simply an `ADsPath`.

The scope is a string that can have one of three values:

- `subtree` – if the scope has this value, then the entire subtree below the search base will be searched.
- `onelevel` – if the scope has this value, then only those direct children of the search base will be searched. This is quite similar to enumerating the contents of a container using the `IADsContainer` methods, except we can specify a more complex search filter.
- `base` – if the scope has this value then only one object is searched: the search base. Such queries will either return no objects or one object, depending on whether the search base satisfies the search filter. It might look like there's little point in being able to perform a search with a scope of base, but there are some technical reasons to do with the LDAP specifications why it is sometimes useful.

We now have enough information to see how our command string was put together:

- The Search Base is: `LDAP://dc=TopOfThePops,dc=Fame,dc=com`

Since that is the ADsPath of the object at the root of Active Directory:

- The Search Filter is `(objectCategory=person)`

Since that tells the directory service to return all user objects:

- The Properties Required are: `sAMAccountName,ADsPath`
- The scope should be the entire subtree and so has a value of: `subtree`

The command text is formed by concatenating these four substrings like this:

```
<Search Base>;Search Filter;Properties;Scope
```

Note that the search base is enclosed in angled brackets, and semicolons are used to separate the strings. Note also that there are no extraneous spaces. My experience is that if you add any white space to make the command text easier to read, then it's a matter of chance (probably depending on where you add the white space) whether the directory service will understand your command string. So I'd suggest you don't add any!

Before we look at how to form other search requests, let's have a closer look at search filters.

Search Filters

Search filters consist of a set of conditions. Each condition says that a certain property must have a certain value, and the conditions are connected by the logical operators – AND, OR and NOT, for which the symbols used are respectively: &, | and !. It is possible to use the wildcard, *, in any of the property values, and each condition must be surrounded by round brackets (), as must the entire filter. Generally, you can use the brackets wherever you want to ensure that the logical operators are evaluated in the correct order.

So for example the filter:

```
(sAMAccountName=b*)
```

Will return all objects for which the sAMAccountName begins with b, while the filter:

```
(description=*and*)
```

Will return all objects which have a property, description, which contains the substring and somewhere in its value.

Notice that quote marks are never used to mark strings.

The unusual part of the syntax is that the logical operators & and | are written *before* the conditions to which they apply, rather than in between them. For example, if you want to specify that you are interested in all users whose sAMAccountNames begin with s, then you would write:

```
(&(sAMAccountName=s*)(objectCategory=person))
```

While if you are interested in users whose sAMAccountName begins with either s or t, then you would write:

```
(&(|(sAMAccountName=t*)(sAMAccountName=s*))(objectCategory=person))
```

The brackets ensure that the OR (|) condition is evaluated first.

This syntax is similar to the Reverse Polish syntax used by LISP and some HP calculators.

Finally, one filter you will often see is:

```
(objectClass=*)
```

This is a standard way of asking for all objects. It works because, according to the LDAP specifications, all objects must have a property called objectClass. This filter simply says that the property, objectClass, can have any value at all.

That gives us the basics of LDAP search filters. There are some more advanced things you can do with them – for example you can use custom definitions of what counts as 'equal', and there are various escape sequences used to put special characters (like round brackets) in the property values you want to test against. For more details you should refer to RFC 2254, in which LDAP search filter syntax is formally defined.

Summary

We've only introduced the very basics of ADSI and Active Directory here, but that should hopefully be enough to get you started with using ADSI to access the contents of directories. ADSI is a very powerful technology. With it you can – amongst other things – change passwords, add user accounts, stop and start NT services, manage print queues, and manage Internet Information Server itself – all from simple scripts. Many of these operations were previously the realm of Windows API functions – which meant you needed an application written in C++ to carry them out. Or if you wanted to be able to do that sort of thing from a Web page, you had to use C++ to write a component that you could call from the Web page, to perform the required operations. Now that ADSI is here, the range of tasks, particularly administrative tasks, which can be done from Web pages has once again increased considerably.

N
W

22

ASP and Collaboration Data Objects for NT Server

In the last few chapters, we've looked at how you can use Active Server Page code to interact with some of the applications and services in Microsoft Back Office. In this chapter, our focus will be on interacting with e-mail applications and services by using the **Collaboration Data Objects (CDO)**. Specifically, we will be looking at a subset of Collaboration Data Objects – **Collaboration Data Objects for Windows NT Server (CDONTS)**.

We're going to start by briefly looking at the evolution of Collaboration Data Objects, and the differences between CDO and CDONTS. We'll then investigate the intended uses for both CDO and CDONTS.

For the main part of this chapter, we'll explore the CDONTS object model, and conclude by examining some sample applications that utilize CDONTS. We'll cover CDO in depth in the next chapter.

What is CDO?

Collaboration Data Objects is the latest version of Microsoft's object library (technology) intended to provide the developer with an easy way to provide simple messaging services, as well as to be able to utilize the capabilities provided by Microsoft Exchange Server. In the MSMQ chapter, we likened MSMQ to e-mail for applications. In this chapter, we'll see that CDO really is e-mail for applications.

In CDO versions prior to 1.1, it was named OLE Messaging. With version 1.1 came the new name of Active Messaging. Now, with version 1.2, it's known as Collaboration Data Objects, or **CDO**. This object library replaces the previous versions and is shipped along with Microsoft Exchange Server 5.5, as well as being available on the Microsoft Web site. CDO is backwards compatible, so that code written using Active Messaging 1.1 requires no modifications to be able to run in a CDO setup.

With CDO, the programmer is now not only able to perform simple sending and receiving, but can also utilize Microsoft Exchange Server capabilities to provide calendaring, collaborating, and workflow functionality. Additionally, CDO can be used for either client or server applications – or both.

For programming, CDO is accessible from Visual Basic (Version 3.0 and greater), C/C++ (Microsoft Version 1.5 and above), VBScript, and Jscript. As CDO was designed for use with Exchange, there are no UI elements in the object library. However, CDO does include some rendering objects that provide the ability to generate HTML for display in a browser (as did previous versions).

Why use CDO?

As CDO is accessible from VBScript and JScript, it can be used in ASP pages to create some mail and messaging enabled Web applications. Even though most users already have a mail client, there are a number of compelling reasons to have a Web mail client.

CDO can be used to create a Web site that does not require the user to download any components (ActiveX or Plug-ins), and can allow a user to access their mailbox from any Web capable system. *Hotmail* is an example of the Web mailbox interface.

From the other side of ASP, there are a number of situations where the ability of the Web server to send mail would be a great benefit to the application. For example, the application would be able to:

- Send confirmation mail when a user orders something
- Send administrative mail to the Webmaster when a certain operation fails
- Process a database list of mail recipients and send a message to each of them

The possibilities are endless. It is for both these types of client and server scenarios that CDO was created. CDO provides the developer with a library of objects to simplify the programming and implementation of these messaging features.

What is CDO for NTS?

In many cases, a developer may not want to use the calendaring, collaboration and workflow capabilities of Exchange Server and CDO, but may just be concerned with the sending and receiving of simple mail messages. That developer is the target audience for the **Collaboration Data Objects for Windows NT Server (CDONTS)**.

> **CDONTS provides a *subset* of the functionality of CDO. It is intended to provide reliable, fast, scaleable messaging for applications that don't need to make use of the more advanced calendaring and workflow capabilities that Exchange Server and CDO provide.**

CDONTS is installed as part of the **SMTP Service**, included as an optional component for Windows 2000 Server. Since the CDONTS components are a subset of the CDO Object Library, they can be used either against the SMTP Service in Windows 2000, or against Exchange Server version 5.5 (and above, running SMTP service), without any code changes being needed. Just as CDONTS is a subset of the capabilities of CDO, the SMTP service component of Windows 2000 does not provide all the functionality that is provided in Exchange 5.5.

CDONTS is a simple object library for developers to create mail and messaging enabled applications.

As an example of the simplicity of CDONTS, let's take a quick look at what's required to be able to send a mail message using the **NewMail** object. With this object, a developer can send a piece of e-mail in as little as two lines of code:

```
Set objSendMail = CreateObject("CDONTS.NewMail")
objSendMail.Send "John@Anywhere.Com", "Jeanie@RigthHere.Com", _
                 "Greetings"," How have you been?"
```

Without yet getting into the CDONTS object hierarchy, we can tell from this example that programming for simple mail sending is a very easy task.

CDO vs. CDONTS

In writing messaging-enabled applications, you may have to decide between using CDO or CDONTS. If and when this decision needs to be made, it's important to keep in mind the intentions of each library:

- CDO is very good at leveraging Exchange Server 5.5 and supporting its more advanced features
- CDONTS is good for creating fast, large-scale, mail applications, or adding mail and messaging to an existing application

If you need to support calendars, discussions, more complex messaging, public folders or workflow management, then CDO 1.2 is the better choice. On the other hand, if you want to create an application that will just handle simple mail messages, then CDONTS is more suitable.

It is also important to note that CDONTS applications are compatible with, and will not interfere with, CDO applications. This is because CDONTS does not have any MAPI functionality itself – that is, it does not have the API support for sending and receiving e-mail. Instead, CDONTS works on Internet Information Server or on Internet Information Server in conjunction with Microsoft Exchange Server.

Note also that CDO can run either against the SMTP service included with Windows 2000, or against Exchange Server 5.5.

However, in order to upgrade from running against an IIS/SMTP platform to running against Exchange Server, you'll need to use the Exchange IMS Wizard. This wizard removes the SMTP service of Internet Information Server and replaces it with Exchange.

The next section of this chapter deals with the CDONTS Library. Although it's limited compared to the feature set of CDO, it will prove sufficient for the majority of the simple applications created using ASP. We'll then look at the additional objects provided by the CDO Library, and the differences in some of the objects between CDO to CDONTS.

CDO for Windows 2000

In addition to the CDONTS and CDO Libraries there is a third Collaboration Data Objects Library variant. Previously referred to as CDO 2.0, it is now named **CDO for Windows 2000**, which ships with all versions of Windows 2000. Functionally, this version is more capable than CDONTS, but does not support all of the messaging features and functionality that are provided by utilizing the CDO Library. Unlike the other CDO Libraries, CDO for Windows 2000 does not provide any support for MAPI protocols. As such, it is limited to only working with the SMTP or NNTP services of Windows 2000. At the time of writing, CDO for Windows 2000 is still in beta. Even so, there are some key points that can be noted.

- The first key piece of information to note about CDO for Windows 2000 is that it provides **dual interfaces**. In other words, each of the COM components included in the CDO for Windows 2000 Library implements interfaces that allow the component to be used in programming languages that support COM or Automation.

- The CDO for Windows 2000 Library has also introduced a new dependency. In order for CDO for Windows 2000 to work correctly, the Microsoft ActiveX Data Objects 2.5 (ADO) component must be installed on the system. This component is included by default in the Windows 2000 operating system, and need not be specifically installed by the user. CDO for Windows 2000 uses ADO to provide the developer with a consistent data access method for accessing and interacting with the information of which a message is composed.

- Functionally, CDO for Windows 2000 also differs from the CDO and CDONTS Libraries. In addition to the message sending and receiving capabilities, the CDO for Windows 2000 Library also adds support for event sinks. This capability allows the developer to create applications that can intercept messages and newsgroup postings arriving at the server, and access the information contained within them. Depending on the contents of the message or posting, the application may do operations such as denying the message, adding a signature or other text to the message, perform virus scans, or any number of other operations.

As mentioned earlier, the CDO for Windows 2000 Library is still in beta and its specifications may change. Because of that, we will not go into more detail on the topic, but will instead focus on the CDO and CDONTS Libraries.

The CDONTS Library

When you want to use a component, the first step is to understand its object model. Here we will go through the object model for the CDONTS component. As you can see from this diagram, the object model is pretty straightforward, and not very large:

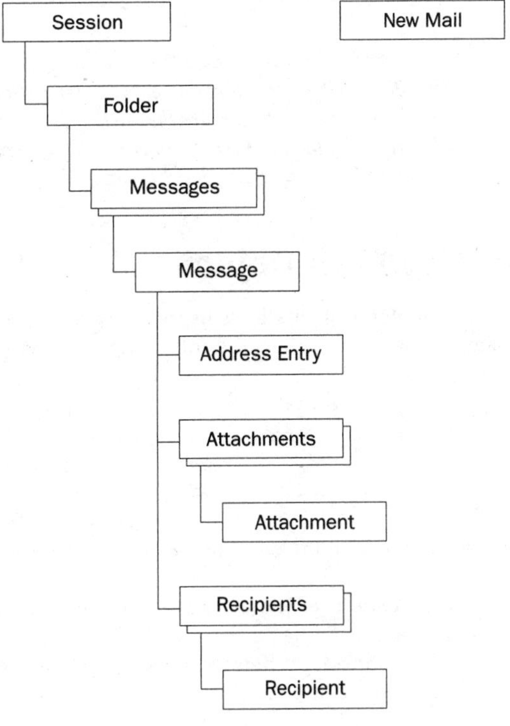

The majority of the CDONTS object model is comprised of the **Session** object and its child objects. As we've seen, an ASP Session object is created for each user that requests a page from the server, and can be used to keep track of information for that specific user. Similarly, a CDONTS Session object is created for each user logging into the mail server, and contains information specific to that user.

In addition to the Session object, CDONTS also provides the NewMail object. We'll start with the simpler NewMail object and then advance to the Session object. But first, we'll take a look at how to reference type libraries.

Referencing Type Libraries

As you program with CDONTS, you may find it useful to use constants (such as `CdoBodyFormatHTML`) instead of the value associated with them (0 for `CdoBodyFormatHTML`). To add a type library reference, you need to edit the `global.asa` file:

```
<!--METADATA TYPE="TypeLib" NAME="Microsoft CDO for NTS 1.2 Library"
          UUID="{0E064ADD-9D99-11D0-ABE5-00AA0064D470}" VERSION="1.2"-->
```

The syntax allows for File, UUID, Version, and LCID properties. The UUID is globally unique for the typelib, but consistent across installations.

Once you've added this META tag to your global.asa, you can use the CDONTS constants in your ASP pages, which relieves you from having to remember specific values. So, instead of having to know that CdoHigh evaluates to 2, you can just use the constant CdoHigh in the ASP code.

Another useful tip is to include <% Option Explicit %> at the top of all of your ASP files. Then, if you try to use a constant for which the declaration can't be found, you'll get an error when you try to execute the ASP code. If Option Explicit is not declared, then VBScript would interpret the constant as an undeclared variable and assign it value of 0 – these types of errors can be very hard to track down.

The NewMail Object

The NewMail object allows us to easily and quickly add simple mail sending capability to a Web page. As we saw earlier, the following lines will create and send a mail message:

```
Set objSendMail = CreateObject("CDONTS.NewMail")
objSendMail.Send "John@Anywhere.com", "Jeanie@RigthHere.com", _
                 "Greetings"," How have you been?"
Set objSendMail = Nothing
```

Now, we'll take a look at what is actually happening in this code.

When the code is executed, a connection is made to the SMTP service, and an SMTP message is sent to Jeanie@RightHere.com with the subject line of Greetings and the message body of How have you been? When the message is viewed, it will display as being from John@Anywhere.com.

The first step in sending a new mail message is to create an instance of the NewMail object – this is done in the first line of the code. The second line of code sends the message, composing it using the parameters of the Send method. We'll cover the Send method in more detail later in this chapter – for now, we'll just see the syntax of the method:

```
objNewMail.Send( [From] [, To] [, Subject] [, Body] [, Importance] )
```

The third line of code releases the instance of the NewMail object and frees its resources. This code does not require the developer to go through Folder or Message collections, nor does it require the user to log on.

The majority of the work in this code sample is performed in the second line – all of the important information for the message is specified in the parameters to the Send method. Alternatively, we can specify each property value for the NewMail object, as follows:

```
Set objSendMail = CreateObject("CDONTS.NewMail")
With objSendMail
  .From = "John@Anywhere.com"
  .To = "Jeanie@RightHere.com"
  .Subject = "Greetings"
  .Body = "How have you been?"
  .Send
End With
Set objSendMail = Nothing
```

These seven lines of code will create the same message as our earlier three lines of code did – they are functionally identical. The difference is that this fragment is more readable, and the reader doesn't need to know the syntax of the Send method. This code can be helpful in cases where the properties contain multiple values or are very large in size and/or length. It can also be easier to debug when it doesn't perform as expected. What you give up with this method is conciseness – when you just want to send a simple message, the parameterized Send method is the better way to go.

As mentioned earlier, there is no log on required when using the NewMail object to send mail. This does allow for anonymous mails, as well as for impersonated mailings. It's up to the developer to specify whom the mail is from. Anonymous mail can be sent by leaving the From property unspecified.

The TO, CC, BCC Properties

In the previous examples, you may have noticed that the recipients had to be fully qualified messaging addresses (Jeanie@RightHere.com).

In the realm of CDONTS, there are no such things as aliases or address books. Each of the recipients must be specified with the full SMTP address.

The NewMail object allows us to specify TO, CC, and BCC recipients for the message. For example:

```
objSendMail.To = "Jeanie@RightHere.com"
objSendMail.CC = "JeaniesBoss@RightHere.com"
objSendMail.BCC = "Steve@RightHere.com"
```

Using these properties, the message would be sent to Jeanie@RightHere.com, JeaniesBoss@RightHere.com would get a copy of the message, and Steve@RightHere.com would get a blind copy of the message.

Any recipients on the BCC line are not disclosed to the other recipients of the message, i.e. any recipients in the To or CC recipient lists will not know that a copy was sent to the BCC recipient. In the case of multiple BCC recipients, none of the BCC recipients are aware of the other recipients.

We can specify multiple names/addresses for the TO, CC, and BCC properties. To send a message to multiple recipients, simply separate the addresses with a semi-colon:

```
objSendMail.To = "John@where.com;Jack@where.com;Tina@where.com"
```

A message can only have one sender though, so the From property should never be more than one messaging address.

The Importance Property

The NewMail object exposes an `Importance` property, which allows you to set the priority/importance for the mail message. There are three different values for priority, each of which has a corresponding constant in the `CDONTS.DLL` library:

- High – `CdoHigh` or `2`
- Normal – `CdoNormal` or `1`
- Low – `CdoLow` or `0`

The default importance for a message is Normal. In order to set a message as high or low priority, we simply set the `Importance` property to `CdoHigh` or `CdoLow` respectively:

```
objSendmail.Importance = CdoHigh
```

As we saw earlier, the `Send` method also allows you to specify all the vital information for a message. In our first example, the importance wasn't specified – it is an optional parameter – but we could have specified it like this:

```
objSendMail.Send "John@Anywhere.com", "Jeanie@RigthHere.com", _
                 "Greetings"," How have you been?", CdoHigh
```

It's important to note that setting the importance of a message may not have any effect on its delivery. Although some servers have implemented functionality to speed up delivery of high importance messages, it is possible that not all of the servers along the delivery route have that functionality. Similarly, it's possible that the recipient's mail client will not visually (or otherwise) distinguish messages with varying importance.

Though there are many mail clients that do distinguish based on importance, it is not universal, and you cannot guarantee that all the recipients have a mail client with that support.

The Body of the Mail Message

The `Body` property allows you to specify the body contents of the message, which can be either plain text or HTML. For a simple, plain text body you would do the following:

```
objSendMail.Body = "How have you been?"
```

By default, all messages are plain text formatted.

Alternatively, we can send a message that has an HTML formatted body. In order to do this, we first need to change the `BodyFormat` property of the NewMail object to be `CdoBodyFormatHTML`, and then we can set the `Body` property to an HTML formatted string:

```
Dim strHTML

strHTML = "<HTML>"
strHTML = strHTML & "<HEAD>"
strHTML = strHTML & "<TITLE>Greetings</TITLE>"
strHTML = strHTML & "</HEAD>"
strHTML = strHTML & "<BODY>"
strHTML = strHTML & "<P>What a <STRONG>Wonderful</STRONG> day!</P>"
strHTML = strHTML & "</BODY>"
strHTML = strHTML & "<HTML>"

Set objSendMail = CreateObject("CDONTS.NewMail")

With objSendMail
   .From = "John@Anywhere.com"
   .To = "Jeanie@RightHere.Com"
   .BodyFormat = CdoBodyFormatHTML
   .Body = strHTML
   .Send
End With

Set objSendMail = Nothing
```

If we want to include multiple URLs in the body of our HTML message, we can make it a bit easier by using the `ContentLocation` and `ContentBase` properties. Taken together, these properties provide an absolute path for all URLs that are included in the body of the HTML message. This includes not only the URL that references the body, but also any URLs that may be within the HTML tags of the body:

- The `ContentLocation` property allows you to specify either the absolute or relative path for all of the URLs within the message body
- The `ContentBase` property allows you to specify the base path for all URLs contained within the message body

When the `ContentLocation` property is non-empty (not equal to ""), all of the URLs in the message body are interpreted as relative paths – relative to the path specified in the `ContentLocation` property. When the `ContentBase` property is also non-empty, then the `ContentLocation` path is interpreted as being relative to the path specified in the `ContentBase` property.

This can be a little confusing, so let's look at a code sample to clear things up:

```
Dim strHTML

strHTML = "<HTML>"
strHTML = strHTML & "<HEAD>"
strHTML = strHTML & "<TITLE>Greetings</TITLE>"
strHTML = strHTML & "</HEAD>"
strHTML = strHTML & "<BODY>"
strHTML = strHTML & "<P>What a <STRONG>Wonderful</STRONG> day!</P>"
strHTML = strHTML & "<IMG SRC="GreatDay.jpg">"
strHTML = strHTML & "</BODY>"
strHTML = strHTML & "<HTML>"
```

```
Set objSendMail = CreateObject("CDONTS.NewMail")

With objSendMail
  .From = "John@Anywhere.com"
  .To = "Jeanie@RightHere.com"
  .BodyFormat = CdoBodyFormatHTML
  .ContentBase = "http://www.Anywhere.com/"
  .ContentLocation = "pictures/"
  .Body = strHTML
  .Send
End With

Set objSendmail = Nothing
```

When the browser renders the `GreatDay.jpg` file, it will prefix the path with the values of the `ContentBase` and `ContentLocation` properties. So in this case, it will display the image located at `http://www.anywhere.com/pictures/GreatDay.jpg`.

We might come across a different scenario in the intranet setting. For example, some companies set up a document server that's not a Web server. Accessing this server with the http path format wouldn't work, but the `ContentBase` and `ContentLocation` properties also allow the use of UNC paths, such as:

```
objSendMail.ContentBase = "\\TheServer\"
objSendMail.ContentLocation "documents\"
```

Attachments

The NewMail object has a method to allow the addition of attachments to a message. The method is called `AttachFile`, and it has the following syntax:

```
objNewMail.AttachFile(Source [, FileName] [, EncodingMethod] )
```

Parameter	Description
`Source`	*Required.* This is the fully qualified path to the file to include as an attachment.
`FileName`	*Optional.* This caption is displayed under the attachment when it is viewed in the mail client.
`EncodingMethod`	*Optional.* The method of encoding the attachment. The default method is `UUENCODE`. Possibly encoding methods are `CdoEncodingUUencode` and `CdoEncodingBase64`.

To send a message with an attachment, we would use something like this:

```
Set objSendMail = CreateObject("CDONTS.NewMail")

With objSendMail
   .From = "John@Anywhere.com"
   .To = "Jeanie@RightHere.com"
   .Subject = "Inventory"
   .Body = "Here is the inventory report that you had requested."
   .AttachFile("c:\InventoryListing.xls", "Inventory Report")
   .Send
End with

Set objSendMail = Nothing
```

The `AttachFile` method adds the file `c:\InventoryListing.xls` as an attachment to the message. The caption for that attachment would be `Inventory Report`, and as no encoding method was specified, the attachment will be encoded using `UUENCODE`. All attachments default to encoding using `UUENCODE`, unless you either change the `MailFormat` property or specify an encoding type in the `AttachFile` method call.

The MailFormat Property

The default mail format for all messages created with the NewMail object is plain text. The `MailFormat` property allows us to choose between MIME (Multipurpose Internet Mail Extension) and plain text formatting. Plain text formatting (`CdoMailFormatText`) will format the message using RFC 822 and UUENCODE. MIME Formatting (`CdoMailFormatMIME`) will format the mail in the MIME format.

MIME formatting is designed to allow rich content messages to be transferred across mixed network and messaging environments.

To change to use the MIME format we set the `MailFormat` property like this:

```
objSendMail.MailFormat = CdoMailFormatMIME
```

We can then change the `MailFormat` back to `CdoMailFormatText` if we want to.

Any changes to the mail format will only apply to the current NewMail object. The changes will not affect the default mail format for any NewMail objects instantiated in the future, which will always be Plain Text.

As noted above, changing the `MailFormat` property will also affect the default encoding method of the message. For Plain Text formatted messages, attachments will be encoded using the UUENCODE format. For the MIME formatted messages, the attachments will be encoded using Base 64 encoding.

Also, if we specify for an attachment to be encoded using the Base 64 format, then the format for the message to which it is attached will change to be `CDOMailFormatMIME`.

Format Options

Because there are a number of encoding and formatting possibilities, you may have to decide which one is best for your use. The answer depends on the purpose of the message being sent, as well as the identity of the intended recipients of the message.

Here are some guidelines to keep in mind when choosing the formatting:

- When you're using CDONTS to just send simple administrative or informative mails to a small group, or to yourself, you'll be more concerned with the content of the message than the format. It takes a good bit of work to format the message to HTML and, in this case, you would have very little benefit from doing so. You can get the same information out of the message whether it's in HTML or Plain Text formatting, and so you should probably just use the Plain Text format.
- If you're using CDONTS to compose and send mails to a larger group, such as a mailing list or subscribers, then presentation might be more important. In this case, you would probably take the extra time to create some HTML that will show your best image. You can use Visual InterDev, FrontPage, or another HTML authoring tool to create the HTML and then just copy that into your ASP page.
- Consider the size of the message. In general, Plain Text formatting keeps messages smaller. When you use HTML formatting, you add a number of tags and other text to the message, which possibly greatly increases its size. Those bigger mails may take longer for the recipients to download. Although access speeds are up now, significantly large documents (with a number of pictures and/or attachments) may still take time and add costs in phone, ISP, and long distance charges.
- The recipient's mail client should not be left out of this decision. Although many of today's mail clients are capable of handling MIME messages, there are a number of users out there whose mail client doesn't support MIME. If you're not sure of the capabilities of the recipients' mail clients, you may want to target the lowest common denominator format. For e-mail, that format would be plain text.

Modifying Message Headers

Although the NewMail object was intended to provide a quick and easy way of sending mail messages from your ASP page, it does have some more advanced capabilities. In our first example, we saw how you can send a message by writing three lines of code:

```
Set objSendMail = CreateObject("CDONTS.NewMail")
objSendMail.Send "John@Anywhere.com", "Jeanie@lisas",
                 "Greetings"," How have you been?"
Set objSendMail = Nothing
```

If you were to open that message in Microsoft Outlook, it would look something like this:

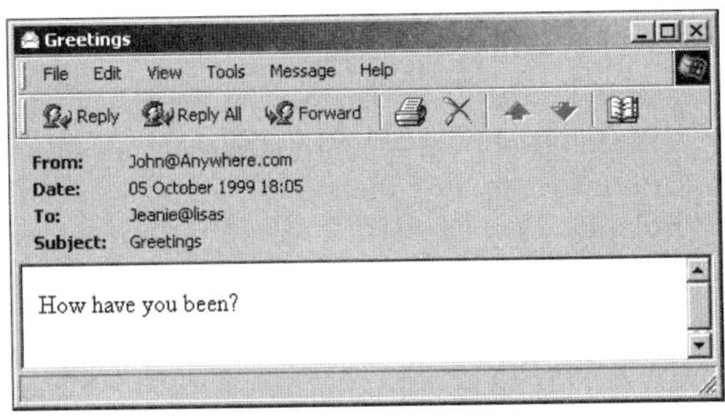

Most mail clients allow you to view the full source of the message. In Outlook 2000, when the message is opened, you can click on View | Options and then see all the message headers in the Internet Headers list box. The actual source of the message looks like this:

```
Received: from mail pickup service by MailSvr with Microsoft SMTPSVC;
         Tue, 5 Oct 1999 18:05:29 -0700
From: <John@Anywhere.com>
To: <Jeanie@lisas.com>
Subject: Greetings
Date: Tue, 5 Oct 1999 18:05:29 -0700
X-Priority: 3
X-MSMail-Priority: Normal
Importance: Normal
X-MimeOLE: Produced By Microsoft MimeOLE V5.00.2314.1300
Message-ID: <003ab5530021789@MailSvr>

How have you been?
```

You'll notice that there's much more included in the message than just the body of the message. There are a number of mail headers that are not displayed when the message is read. Most of the header information is generated based on the values set for the NewMail objects properties or as parameters on the `Send` method. The mail servers generate other information in the headers as they handle the message:

```
Received: from mail pickup service by MailSvr with Microsoft SMTPSVC;
         Tue, 5 Oct 1999 18:05:29 -0700
```

We can use the NewMail object's `Value` collection to set our own header values, and to create our own headers for the messages we send. One reason we may want to do this is that not all messaging servers are capable of interpreting some of the headers that are not automatically generated by the NewMail object. On the other hand, there may be servers that do not interpret the custom headers. In that case, the server will just ignore the headers it doesn't interpret.

For more information on these headers, such as Keywords, References, and Reply-To headers, you can look at the Standard for the Format of ARPA Internet Text Messages (STD011) at *`http://www.cis.ohio-state.edu/htbin/rfc/rfc733.html`.*

The following adds the `Keywords` header:

```
Set objSendMail = CreateObject("CDONTS.NewMail")
objSendMail.Value("Keywords") = "Greetings"
objSendMail.Send "John@Anywhere.com", "Jeanie@lisas", _
                 "Greetings"," How have you been?"
Set objSendMail = NOTHING
```

When we look again at the source for the message, we'll see that a `Keywords` header has now been added:

```
Received: from mail pickup service by MailSvr with Microsoft SMTPSVC;
         Tue, 5 Oct 1999 18:05:29 -0700
From: <John@Anywhere.com>
To: <Jeanie@lisas>
Subject: Greetings
Date: Tue, 5 Oct 1999 18:05:29 -0700
Keywords: Greetings
```

```
X-Priority: 3
X-MSMail-Priority: Normal
Importance: Normal
X-MimeOLE: Produced By Microsoft MimeOLE V5.00.2314.1300
Message-ID: <003ab5530021789@MailSvr>

How have you been?
```

The default property of the NewMail object is the `Value` collection, so the following code would have the same effect:

```
Set objSendMail = CreateObject("CDONTS.NewMail")
objSendMail("Keywords") = "Greetings"
objSendMail.Send "John@Anywhere.com", "Jeanie@lisas", _
                 "Greetings"," How have you been?"
Set objSendMail = Nothing
```

There's no limit to the number of items you can add to the `Value` collection – each one you add will just create another header for the message:

```
Set objSendMail = CreateObject("CDONTS.NewMail")
objSendMail("Reply-To") = "Jack@anywhere.com"
objSendMail("Keywords") = "Greetings"
objSendMail.Send "John@Anywhere.com", "Jeanie@lisas", _
                 "Greetings"," How have you been?"
Set objSendMail = Nothing
```

Version Property

The `Version` property of the NewMail object returns the version of the CDONTS Library that the code is executing within. The following gets a string containing the version information:

```
strCurVersion = objNewMail.Version
```

Currently, the `Version` property will return the string "`1.2`".

The Send Method

Throughout this chapter, we've used the `Send` method for the NewMail object. Using the `Send` method and listing the parameters may not be the easiest approach when it comes to readability and debugging. However, it's still useful in some applications, and it should not be overlooked completely.

Here is a list of the parameters for the `Send` method:

```
objNewMail.Send( [From] [, To] [, Subject] [, Body] [, Importance] )
```

Parameter	Description
`From`	*Optional.* String value. Address of the sender of the message
`To`	*Optional.* String value. Sets the list of `To` (primary) recipients of the message
`Subject`	*Optional.* String value. Sets the subject of the message
`Body`	*Optional.* String value. Sets the body of the message
`Importance`	*Optional.* Long value. Sets the level of importance for the message. Default is 1 (`CdoNormal`)

As you can see, each of these parameters is optional. Leaving them blank will cause the NewMail object to use its default values – all of the string parameters default to an empty string, while the `Importance` value defaults to 1 (`CdoNormal`).

In general, specifying the values as parameters is functionally no different from individually setting each property. However, one exception to this rule is that if `To` recipients lists are specified in the `Send` method as well as in the `To` property on the NewMail object, the message will be sent to all recipients on both of the lists.

The NewMail Object – Summary

Before moving on to the other objects provided by CDONTS, there are a few important points to note about the NewMail object.

- As we mentioned in the start of the chapter, the CDONTS Library supplies no user interface, and is not expected to interact with any human users. As such, none of the NewMail object's properties (other than `Version`) are intended to be read at run-time. All of the properties (again, other than `Version`) are write-only. One implication of this is that once a header or attachment is added to the message it cannot be removed. In order to remove a single recipient from a recipient list, you need to remove the entire list and only re-add the desired recipients.
- The NewMail object is not re-usable. Once the `Send` method has been called on an instance, you can't reuse that instance. If you do attempt to call the `Send` method without instantiating a new instance of the NewMail object, then you'll get a run-time error in your ASP code. Each additional message you send requires you to create a new instance of the NewMail object.
- Keep in mind that the NewMail object is separate from the other components provided by the CDONTS Library. Most of the objects are in the hierarchy under the Session object. Those objects provide a much higher lever of functionality, and allow you to create more complex applications. When you may need to do something more than simply sending an e-mail, the other objects are better used for that task.

Other CDONTS Objects

We're now going to focus on the **Session** object and all the objects that fall under it in the object model.

Your might think that the simple operation of sending a message is going to be more code intensive using the Session object than it was using the NewMail object – and you'd be right. But in exchange for more intensive coding, we gain much greater control and more capabilities.

The Session Object

The Session object contains all of the information needed for default message information, accessing the inbox/outbox, and binding to a user's mailbox. In the CDONTS Library, there are only two top-level objects: NewMail and Session. All of the user's session settings and options are stored in the Session object for each user's session. Any access to a user's messaging store is provided through the Session object. The Session object has four methods:

- `LogonSMTP`
- `Logoff`
- `GetDefaultFolder`
- `SetLocaleIDs`

The LogonSMTP Method

The `LogonSMTP` method initializes the Session object, and then binds that object to the specified mailbox. It has the following syntax:

```
objSession.LogonSMTP(DisplayName, Address)
```

Parameter	Description
`DisplayName`	*Required.* The display name for the user logged on.
`Address`	*Required.* The complete e-mail address for the user logged on.

Before a Session object can be used, it must be instantiated and the `LogonSMTP` method must be successfully executed. If you attempt to call any methods or reference any properties on the Session object before you call the `LogonSMTP` method, you'll get a `CdoE_NOT_INITIALIZED` error.

Note that there is one exception to this – you can call the `SetLocaleIDs` method before successfully calling `LogonSMTP`.

So, in order to access a user's message store, we'd use the following:

```
Dim objCurSession
Set objCurSession = CreateObject("CDONTS.Session")
objCurSession.LogonSMTP "Jack Roberts", "JackR@anywhere.com"
```

First, we create a new Session object. Then, in the last line, the session is initialized with the user's display name and messaging address settings. In addition, the session is then bound to the specified SMTP mailbox (`JackR@anywhere.com`). Once this is done, we have access to the messaging store for this user

To connect to another mailbox, we need to either create another Session object, or call the `Logoff` method and then call the `LogonSMTP` method with the new settings.

It's important to note that, although its name may imply otherwise, the `LogonSMTP` method does not perform any authentication. The method just sets properties for the Session object – they are not validated. Even if an incorrect or invalid e-mail address is specified, you won't get any errors returned. It will just initialize the values and attempt to bind to the specified mailbox – and obviously, your messages may not be delivered correctly.

The GetDefaultFolder Method

The `GetDefaultFolder` method returns the default Inbox or Outbox folder for a message store. The syntax of the method is:

```
Set objFolder = objSession.GetDefaultFolder(folderType)
```

There's only one parameter for the method – `folderType`. This can be one of two values:

- `CdoDefaultFolderInbox` (1)
- `CdoDefaultFolderOutbox` (2)

Depending on the value of `folderType`, the method will return either the default Inbox or Outbox for the current messaging store. Using CDONTS, no other folders are available through the `GetDefaultFolder` method.

The following code creates a new session and gets the Inbox folder:

```
Dim objSession
Dim objInbox
Dim collMessages

Set objSession = CreateObject ("CDONTS.Session")
objCurSelection.LogonSMTP("Jack Roberts", "JackR@anywhere.com")

Set objInbox = objSession.GetDefaultFolder(CdodefaultFolderInbox)
Set collMessages = objInbox.Messages
```

This method can be used against both the IIS platform and the IIS/Exchange Server platforms, although it's much more useful when the back-end platform is IIS/Exchange Server instead of IIS/SMTP. When Exchange Server is the back-end, this method can allow a developer programmatic access to the user's Calendar, Contacts, or other Exchange folders. We'll take a more detailed look at the folder object later in this chapter.

The SetLocaleID Method

The `SetLocaleID` method allows the programmer to specify identifiers to define the session's **locale** – the features of the environment that are based on the language, culture, and/or conventions. This can include formatting of dates and times, displaying of currency, the sorting order, and the character set that is to be used. The syntax of the method is:

```
objSession.SetLocaleIDs(CodePageID)
```

The only parameter for the method is a code page identifier – the `CodePageID` – which is a Long value.

More information and details on Code Pages can be found in the Windows 2000 documentation.

There are two key things to note about the `SetLocaleID` method. First, it must be called before the `LogonSMTP` method is executed. Second, the specified `CodePageID` is checked to ensure that it's a valid value – if not, you'll get a `CdoE_INVALID_PARAMETER` error.

The LogOff Method

Once the session is finished with, we need to end the session and log off by calling the `LogOff` method and then releasing the Session object:

```
objCurSession.LogOff
Set objCurSession = Nothing
```

The `LogOff` method will end all activity on the Session object, terminate the binding to the SMTP mailbox and will clear the settings for the Session object. It's then possible to reuse the Session object by calling the `LogonSMTP` method again.

Common Properties

Each of the objects in the Session object hierarchy have a set of properties that are common to all of the objects. These are: `Session`, `Class`, `Parent`, and `Application`.

The `Session` property returns a Session object. This is the 'root' Session object for the specified object, and it represents the session that the specified object is operating within.

The `Class` property is used to indicate the type of the object. It will return a Long value:

Value	Object Type
0	Session
2	Folder
3	Message
4	Recipient
5	Attachment
8	AddressEntry
16	Messages
17	Recipients
18	Attachments

The `Parent` property returns an object that represents the parent of the specified object. Note two unexpected values for this property:

- The value of the `Parent` property for the Session object is `Nothing`
- The Parent object for an AddressEntry object is a Message object

Lastly, the `Application` property returns a String value that is the name of the current application. When called on an object in the CDONTS Library, it will return `Collaboration Data Objects for NTS Version 1.2`.

The Session Object's Properties

In addition to the properties that all CDONTS objects have in common, the Session object exposes some specific properties for the current session. These properties and their return values are:

Property	Description
`Inbox`	*Read-only.* Folder object for the Inbox of the current session.
`Outbox`	*Read-only.* Folder object for the Outbox of the current session.
`MessageFormat`	*Read/Write.* Returns or sets the formatting/encoding of messages. Can be either `CDOMime` (MIME Messages) or `CDOText` (Plain Text Messages).
`Name`	*Read-Only.* The display name for the current session.
`Version`	*Read-Only.* The version of the CDONTS Library.

The Folder Object

The **Folder** object represents a folder or a container for the message store of the current session. Folders can contain messages, documents and forms. The standard folders are **Inbox** and **Outbox**:

- The Inbox is the delivery location for incoming mail. All mail addressed to the recipient will be delivered to the Inbox.
- The Outbox is the temporary location for outgoing mail. When a message is sent it is placed in the Outbox folder and sent when that folder is processed.

The Folder object gives us access to the contents of the specified folder. However, although we have access to the messages, the only change that we can effect is to delete entire messages. CDONTS does not allow for modifications to:

- Attachments (adding or deleting)
- Any of the TO, CC, or BCC recipient lists
- Any message properties – even properties that are writeable can't be modified

The Folder Object's Properties

As well as the common properties, the Folder object has the following properties:

Property	Description
`Name`	*Read-only*. Display name for the folder.
`Messages`	*Read-only*. Collection of messages in the folder.

The Messages Collection

The **Messages** collection is a collection of zero or more Message objects. For the Folder object, the `Messages` property returns a collection that contains all of the Message objects within that folder. In this way, we're able to access the messages in a folder. The Messages collection exposes a number of properties and methods to allow easier access to the messages, as well as ways to modify the collection of messages.

The Messages Collection's Properties

The Messages collection has two additional properties:

Property	Description
`Count`	*Read-only*. The number of Message objects in the collection.
`Item`	*Read-only*. Returns a single Message object from the Messages collection.

We can use the `Item` property to access a message in the collection. This property gives us a single `Message` object from the collection, and its syntax is:

```
colMessages.Item(index)
```

The *`index`* parameter has a value between 1 and the size of the collection. For example, if we wanted to get the first message in the collection, we would use:

```
Dim objMessage
Set objMessage = colMessages.Item(1)
```

As the `Item` property is the default property of the `Messages` collection, the following code is functionally the same:

```
Dim objMessage
Set objMessage = colMessages(1)
```

And as the `Count` property tells us the size of the collection, we can iterate through the whole collection like this:

```
For intLoop = 1 To colMessages.Count
  Set objMessage = colMessages.Item(intloop)
  ...
Next
```

The Add Method

The collection also exposes an Add method, which allows us to add new messages to the collection. When executed, the Add method will create a new Message object, add it to the collection, and then return a reference to that object. This allows us to add a message, and then modify that message and its properties without first having to locate it in the collection.

The syntax for Add is:

```
Set objMessage = colMessages.Add( [subject] [, text] [, importance] )
```

Parameter	Description
Subject	*Optional.* Subject line for the message.
Text	*Optional.* The body text for the message.
Importance	*Optional.* The importance setting for the message. The default is 1 (CdoNormal).

The following code would add a new message to the Outbox:

```
Set objOutbox = objSession.GetDefaultFolder(CdoDefaultFolderOutbox)
Set objNewMsg = objOutbox.Messages.Add

With objNewMsg
   .Text = "How are things going?"
   .Subject = "Status Needed"
   Set objRecip = .Recipients.Add(Name:="Jeanie", Type:=CdoTo, _
                                  Address:="Jeanie@anywhere.com")
   .Send
End With
```

Don't worry if you don't understand how the Recipients collection works. We'll cover that later when we look at the Message object.

The Delete Method

If you can add a message to a collection, it's also useful to be able to delete one. Your first inclination may be to call the Delete method on the Messages collection – don't. That would delete all the messages in the collection, and the action can't be undone – so take care when your code involves deleting messages.

If you want to delete only a single message from a collection, you should call the Delete method on that Message object. On the other hand, if you do want to delete all the messages in the inbox, you can use this method:

```
Set objOutbox = objSession.GetDefaultFolder(CdoDefaultFolderInbox)
objOutbox.Messages.Delete
```

The GetFirst, GetNext, GetLast, GetPrevious Methods

The messages collection also provides some methods that allow us to navigate through the messages in the collection: `GetFirst`, `GetNext`, `GetLast`, and `GetPrevious`. These methods return the first, next, last, or previous message (respectively) in the Messages collection. If any of them can't get the message, the return value is `Nothing`.

The order of messages in the collection is unknown, so we can't predict what order these methods will return messages in. When dealing with the collection of messages, you should treat the collection as being unsorted, and make no assumptions about the ordering.

The following code loops through and displays the subject line for all the messages in the inbox:

```
Set objOutbox = objSession.GetDefaultFolder(CdoDefaultFolderInbox)
Set objMsg = objOutbox.Messages.GetFirst

While objMsg Is Not Nothing
  Response.Write "Subject : " & objMsg.Subject & "<BR>"
  Set objMsg = objOutbox.Messages.GetNext
Wend
```

The Message Object

The **Message** object represents an object in the messaging store. This can be an e-mail message, a document, or a form in a folder. A Message object can be accessed through the Messages collection.

The Message Object's Properties

In addition to the common properties, the Message object has the following properties:

Property	Description
`Attachments`	Attachment object or collection of Attachment objects.
`ContentBase`	Content base header for a MIME message.
`ContentID`	Content-ID header for a MIME message.
`ContentLocation`	Content-Location header for a MIME message.
`HTMLText`	The HTML formatted message body.
`Importance`	The message's importance.
`MessageFormat`	The encoding format for the message.
`Recipients`	Recipient object or collection of Recipient objects.
`Sender`	An AddressEntry object for the user that sent the message.
`Size`	The message size, in bytes.
`Subject`	The subject of the message.
`Text`	The plain text of the message body.
`TimeReceived`	The date and time that the message was received.
`TimeSent`	The date and time that the message was sent.

We saw most of these properties when we dealt with the NewMail object, so we won't go into further details about them here.

The Delete Method

We mentioned earlier that calling the `Delete` method on the `Messages` collection would delete all the messages in that collection. If you want to delete only one message in the collection, you need to use the `Delete` method on that Message object.

For example, this deletes the first message in the inbox:

```
Set objOutbox = objSession.GetDefaultFolder(CdoDefaultFolderInbox)
Set objMsg = objOutbox.Messages.GetFirst
objMsg.Delete
```

Just like the `Delete` method on the `Messages` collection, the deletion here happens immediately and can't be undone.

The Send Method

This is similar to the `Send` method on the NewMail object. The `Send` method on a Message object will send the message to its specified recipients. We've already seen an example of this method in action, when we looked at the `Add` method of the Messages collection:

```
Set objOutbox = objSession.GetDefaultFolder(CdoDefaultFolderOutbox)
Set objNewMsg = objOutbox.Messages.Add
With objNewMsg
   .Text = "How are things going?"
   .Subject = "Status Needed"
   Set objRecip = .Recipients.Add(Name:="Jeanie", Type:=CdoTo, _
                                 Address:="Jeanie@anywhere.com")
   .Send
End With
```

The Attachments Collection

We know that a message can include attachments within itself, and CDONTS provides programmatic access to those attachments. For each Message object there's an **Attachments collection**, which will contain zero or more attachments for that message.

The collection exposes an `Item` property and a `Count` property, which we can use to iterate through all the attachments for a message:

```
Set colAttachments = objMessage.Attachments
For intLoop = 1 to colAttachments.Count
  Response.Write "Attachment : " & colAttachments.Item(intLoop).Name & _
                 "<BR>"
Next
```

In addition, the collection exposes two methods: `Add` and `Delete`. The `Delete` method has no parameters – calling it will delete all attachments from the collection, and this can't be undone.

Using the Add method, we're able to add new attachments to a message. This method has the following syntax:

```
Set objAttach = colAttachments.Add( [name] [, type] [, source] _
                                    [, ContentLocation] [, ContentBase] )
```

Parameter	Description
Name	The display name for the attachment.
Type	The attachment type. Either CdoFileData (1) or CdoEmbeddedMessage (4).
Source	The full path to the file to attach if type is CdoFileData, or a Message object if type is CdoEmbeddedMessage.
ContentLocation	MIME attachment content location header.
ContentBase	MIME attachment content base header.

For example, if we wanted to add the file C:\InventoryReport.xls to the message, our code would look like this:

```
Set colAttachments = objMessage.Attachments
colAttachments.Add ("Inventory Report", CdoFileData, "C:\InventoryReport.xls")
```

In this case, since we're not using MIME encoded messages, the ContentLocation *and* ContentBase *parameters can be omitted in the call to the* Add *method.*

The Attachment Object

For individual access to an attachment, we would use the **Attachment object**. The Attachment object represents either a file or a message that is attached to a message.

The Attachment object has the following properties:

Property	Description
ContentBase	Content-Base header value for a MIME attachment.
ContentID	Content-ID header value for a MIME attachment.
ContentLocation	Content-Location header value for a MIME attachment.
Name	Display name for the attachment.
Source	Path or location for the attachment.
Type	Attachment type. Either CdoFileData (1) or CdoEmbeddedMessage (4).

There are three methods exposed on the Attachment object.

The `Delete` method is used to delete an individual attachment from the Attachments collection for a message. This method will immediately remove the attachment from the collection, and the changes can't be undone.

The `ReadFromFile` method allows the attachment source to be loaded from a file. The syntax is:

```
objAttach.ReadFromFile(fileName)
```

The `fileName` parameter specifies the fully qualified path to the source file to load the attachment data from. This method allows us to load an attachment from a source location after the attachment object has already been created.

Finally, there's a method that allows us to save the attachment data to a file. This is the `WriteToFile` method, which had the following syntax:

```
objAttach.WriteToFile(fileName)
```

Here, the `fileName` parameter is the fully qualified path for the destination file that the attachment data is to be saved to. This method is used when you want to save the attachment to a hard drive, or to a location other than the messaging store.

The Recipients Collection

Each message has a `Recipients` property, which exposes the collection of all recipients for the message. The **Recipients collection** will contain zero or more Recipient objects. Similar to the Attachments collection, it exposes `Count` and `Item` properties.

There's also a `Delete` method – and as with the other `Delete` methods for collections, this will remove all recipients from the collection.

Adding recipients for a message is done using the `Add` method of the Recipients collection. The `Add` method has the following syntax:

```
Set objRecip = collRecips.Add( [name] [, address] [, type])
```

Parameter	Description
`Name`	Recipient's display/friendly name.
`Address`	Recipient's fully qualified messaging address.
`Type`	Type of recipient. This can be one of three values: `CdoTO`, `CdoCC`, or `CdoBCC`

The `Name`, `Address`, and `Type` parameters are the same as the `Name`, `Address`, and `Type` properties for the Recipient object (which we'll cover in the next section). If no parameters are specified, a Recipient object is still created with empty values.

This example shows the how we can add TO, CC, and BCC recipients to a message:

```
objMsg.Recipients.Add ("Jeanie", CdoTO, "Jeanie@anywhere.com")
objMsg.Recipients.Add ("JeaniesBoss", CdoCC, "JeaniesBoss@anywhere.com")
objMsg.Recipients.Add ("Jack", CdoBCC, "Jack@anywhere.com")
```

Messages in the Inbox can't be modified, so if the Add method is attempted on a message in the Inbox, you'll get an error of CdoE_No_Access.

The Recipient Object

The **Recipient object** represents a single recipient of the message. The object exposes the following properties, which map exactly to the parameters for the Add method on the Recipients collection:

Property	Description
Name	Recipient's display/friendly name.
Address	Recipient's fully qualified messaging address.
Type	Type of recipient. This can be one of three values: CdoTO, CdoCC, or CdoBCC

The Recipient object also has a Delete method, which deletes only the current Recipient object from the Recipients collection.

The AddressEntry Object

The Sender property on a Message object will return an AddressEntry object. This object contains all of the addressing information for the sender of the message, and it has the following properties:

Property	Description
Name	Sender's alias or friendly display name
Address	Senders's fully qualified messaging address.
Type	Type of address. For CDONTS, this is always "SMTP"

The Session Object – Summary

As you can see, the level of granularity and control provided by the Session object and its children is much greater than that of the NewMail object. This allows the creation of more powerful and capable applications, but it does require some more work. There's a tradeoff of between capabilities and ease of use.

Nevertheless, in this case, when you want to create that more complex application, you can still do so without too much work. CDONTS does allow you to create both simple and complex applications, and it makes both of those easier to create.

Setting Up SMPT Services

Before we can get into the details of developing applications, it's necessary to setup your server machine and configure it correctly for CDONTS.

> *Note that the name CDONTS includes* Windows NT Server. *As this implies, you'll need to have a machine running Microsoft Windows 2000 Server. In addition, for all of the following examples, you'll need to have Administrator privileges on that machine.*

You first need to verify that the SMTP service has been installed on your Windows 2000 Server machine. The easiest way to check this is to see if the Default SMTP Virtual Server node exists in your Internet Information Services Manager view. If you have the SMTP Service already installed, you'll see a view similar to this:

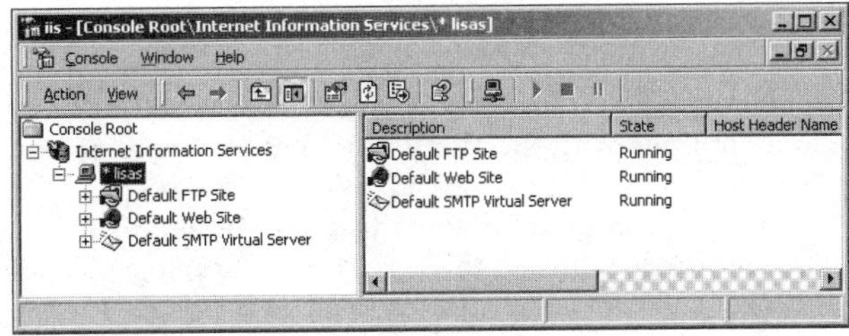

If you don't have the SMTP service installed, then you'll need to run the setup to add the Windows 2000 SMTP Service Components.

To do this, go to Control Panel and select Add/Remove Programs. When the Add/Remove Programs dialog appears, click on Add/Remove Windows Components. That will cause the Windows Components Wizard to appear:

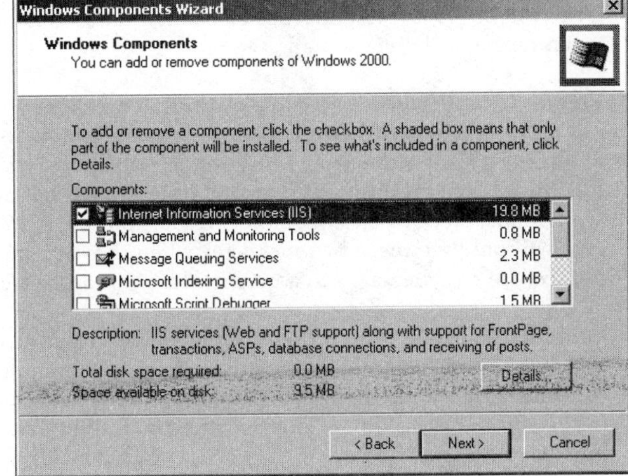

You'll need to select Internet Information Server (IIS), and then click on the Details button. That will display another dialog, which shows the subcomponents for IIS. This is where you need to check the box next to SMTP Service:

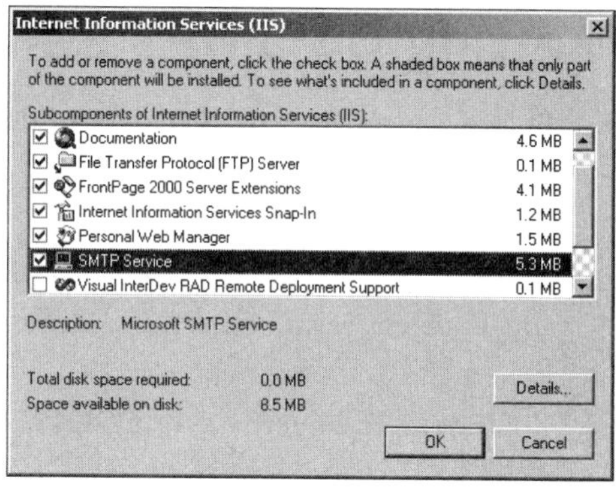

Then click OK. This returns you to the Windows Components dialog, at which point you click Next> and continue with the Windows 2000 Component setup.

You'll be prompted for some installation details for the services. For the SMTP service, you'll need to specify the location of the `MailRoot` directory. This is the location on your hard drive where the service will create directories to store messages for the Mail Queue, Mailbox, and Badmail. It's suggested that you specify a location for the `MailRoot` directory that has a large amount of disk space available.

SMTP Service Configuration

Once the SMTP Service has been installed on the machine, you need to configure the service so that it can properly deliver e-mail.

You may wonder how to setup a user's mailbox for incoming mail. Well, for the SMTP Service, it's not necessary – there's no such concept as individual user inboxes. All incoming e-mail is delivered to a central folder (the `MailRoot` folder you specified during installation), and each user's access to that folder is filtered so that they can only access the messages that are addressed to them. So, if there are five messages in the `MailRoot` folder, but only two are addressed to a specific user, then that user will only see these two messages when they log in to their SMTP session. The SMTP service will not expose any messages to a user that are not addressed to that user.

Outbound messages can be sent in two ways: either directly to a domain, or by using a smarthost mail server. If messages are delivered directly to a domain, then each message is sent only to the domain to which it was addressed. If messages are delivered through a smarthost, then every message is sent to the smarthost machine. The smarthost will then determine and execute the correct routing for the message.

Setting Up Domains

In order to do domain routing, the SMTP Service needs to have routing information for each of the possible destination domains. To provide this routing information, each domain must be added to the SMTP Service and then its properties must be configured. We can do this using the Internet Services Manager.

Expand the Default SMTP Virtual Server node, and you'll find a Domains node. This is where you can see the current list of domains, add new domains and specify their delivery settings.

To add a new domain, right-click on the node, select New, and then select Domain. This will launch the New Domain Wizard, which will guide you through the process. The first dialog asks whether the domain is Local or Remote.

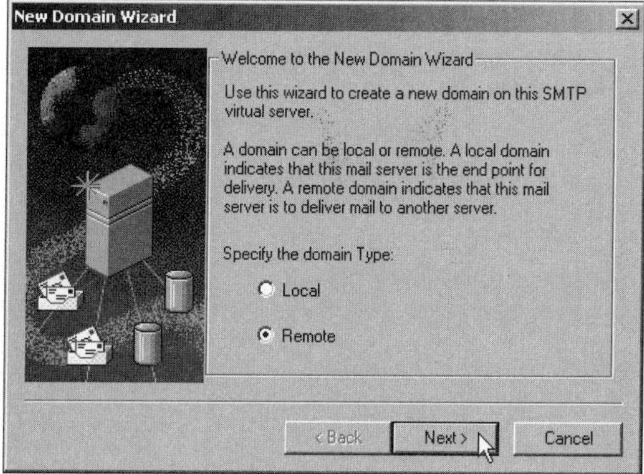

If mail sent to the domain is to be kept on the local machine, then it is a local domain. If mail sent to the domain is to be forwarded on to another mail server, then it is a remote domain. In this case, we're going to setup a Remote domain. The next dialog asks for the name of this remote domain – we'll be using Anywhere.Com.

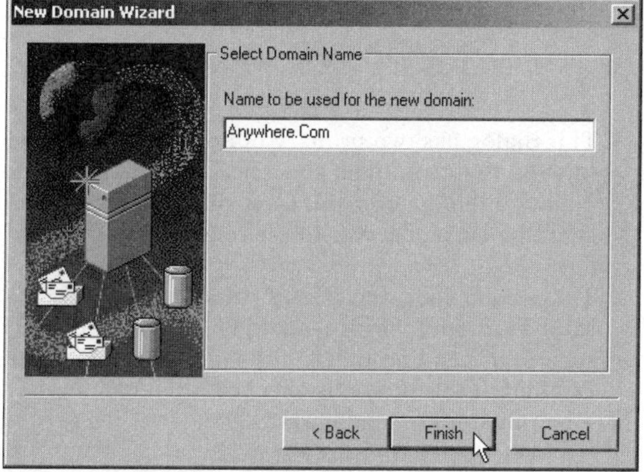

Once the name is entered and the Finish button is clicked, the new domain is created and added to the list of domains:

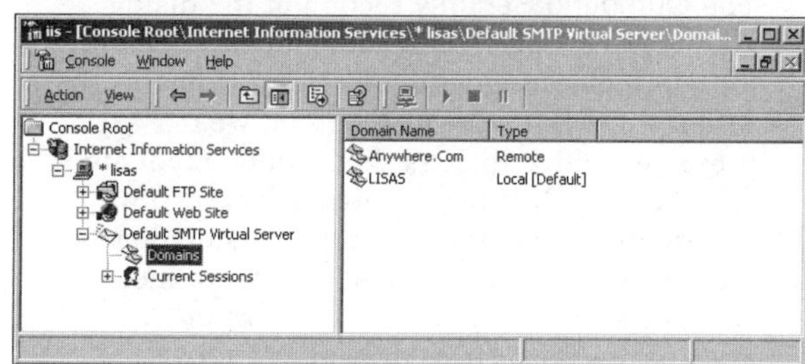

It's at this point that we must specify the routing settings for the domain. Right-click on the Anywhere.Com domain and select Properties:

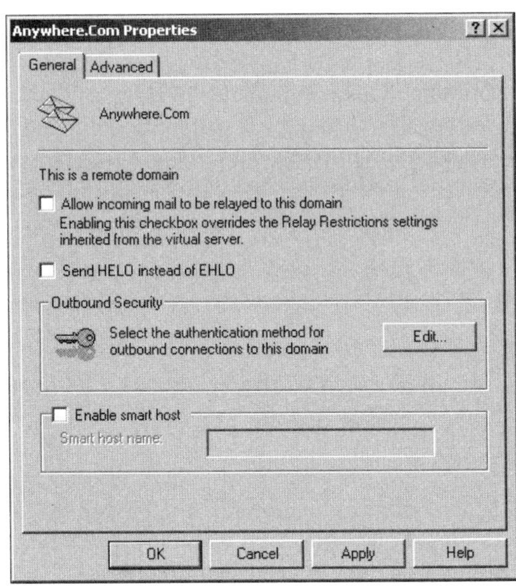

This dialog has two primary options that we can set. The first is the Allow incoming mail to be relayed to this domain checkbox. The default action of the SMTP Service is to block the relaying of mail to a remote domain. Checking this option will override that setting, and allow mail to be relayed from the current server to the remote domain.

The second checkbox, Send HELO instead of EHLO, is used when dealing with Extended Simple Mail Transport Protocol (ESMTP) servers. An SMTP client that has support for ESMTP will initiate a session by sending EHLO instead of HELO. Sending HELO indicates the client does not support ESMTP. If this option is checked, then communications to the remote domain will always – and only – be initiated by sending HELO.

The Outbound Security section of the dialog allows you to specify the authentication method for communicating with the remote domain. When we click on the Edit button, we're presented with a dialog asking which credentials are to be supplied to a receiving server. If we choose to supply credentials, they can either be sent using Basic Authentication (where the account name and password are sent in unencrypted clear text) or using Windows Security Package (where an NT account name, domain, and password are used):

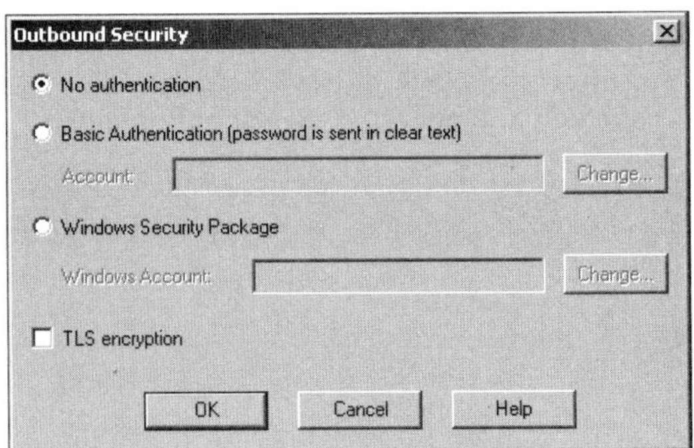

Most likely, the large majority of the destination domains will not require authentication. In that case the default of No Authentication will work. In the event that a message is returned from a domain due to an authentication requirement, then we can use the Outbound Security dialog for that domain to set the correct authentication.

SmartHost Configuration

We're going to assume that we have a smarthost machine configured. If you send messages through a smarthost, you can specify the route of messages and are able to send them over an alternate connection that may be faster or less costly than another connection/route. The smarthost will handle the routing of those messages to their final destination.

One thing to note is that when you specify a smarthost, all messages are then routed through that host, regardless of their destination domain.

For the outgoing messages, it's necessary to set the delivery and routing options. Again, we do this using the Internet Services Manager.

Launch Internet Services Manager, select the Default SMTP Virtual Server node, right-click, and select Properties. When the properties page for the service comes up, select the Delivery tab. You should see this property page:

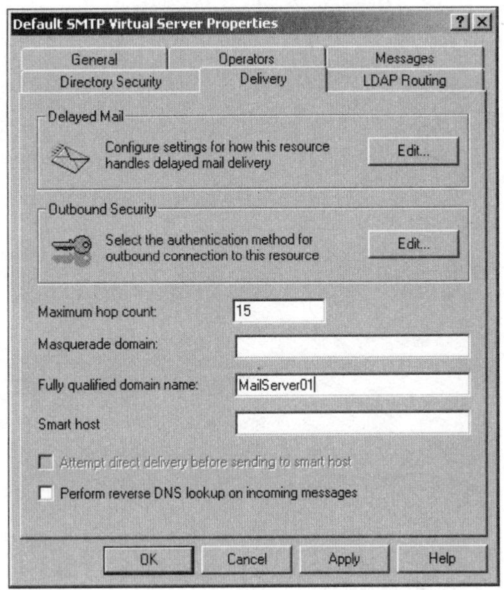

This lets you set a number of options for delivering the messages. There are a number of properties available in this dialog.

For more detailed information on the properties and their effects, look in the documentation for the SMTP Service, which is usually located at `http://<machineName>/iisHelp/iis/misc/default.asp`.

Just as there was an Outbound Security button on the properties for each domain, there's one on the Delivery tab of the SMTP Service's property page. This allows us to specify the default method of authentication to send to receiving servers. The recommended approach is to leave the security set to No Authentication and then, if messages are rejected due to requiring authentication, create a remote domain for that address and specify the correct security properties on that domain.

However, for our present purposes, we now have a correctly configured SMTP Server, and we can now move on to look at some ASP code that will make use of the service.

Using CDONTS in ASP Applications

Now that we have the SMTP Service correctly configured and able to deliver messages, we can proceed to creating some ASP applications that make use of the CDONTS Library. Our first application will allow users to send a simple e-mail message from a Web page.

> *Remember, all the code samples for this chapter are available for download from the Wrox Web site.*

SimpleMail Application

Here is the source of the ASP page that we're going to use – `SimpleMail.asp`:

```
<%@ LANGUAGE=VBScript %>
<HTML>
<HEAD>
<TITLE>Send Mail Page</TITLE><BODY>

<FONT SIZE=6><STRONG>Send Message </STRONG></FONT>

<FORM ACTION=SendMail.asp METHOD="GET" NAME=SendMail>
<TABLE BORDER=0 CELLPADDING=1 CELLSPACING=1 ID=TABLE1 WIDTH="90%">

  <TR>
    <TD><STRONG>From</STRONG></TD>
    <TD><INPUT NAME=SendFrom> <FONT SIZE=2>(required)</FONT></TD>
  </TR>
  <TR>
    <TD><STRONG>To</STRONG></TD>
    <TD><INPUT NAME=SendTo> <FONT SIZE=2>(required)</FONT></TD>
  </TR>
  <TR>
    <TD><STRONG>CC</STRONG></TD>
    <TD><INPUT NAME=SendCC></TD></TR>
  <TR>
    <TD><STRONG>BCC</STRONG></TD>
    <TD><INPUT NAME=SendBCC></TD>
  </TR>
  <TR>
    <TD><STRONG>Importance</STRONG></TD>
    <TD><SELECT ID=select1 NAME=selImportance>
          <OPTION VALUE=2>High</OPTION>
          <OPTION SELECTED VALUE=1>Normal</OPTION>
          <OPTION VALUE=0>Low</OPTION>
        </SELECT></TD>
  </TR>
  <TR>
    <TD><STRONG>Subject</STRONG></TD>
    <TD><INPUT NAME=Subject></TD></TR>
  <TR>
```

```
    <TD><STRONG>Body</STRONG></TD>
    <TD><TEXTAREA ID=TEXTAREA1 NAME=BodyText
                  STYLE="HEIGHT: 232px; WIDTH: 451px"></TEXTAREA></TD></TR>

</TABLE>

<INPUT TYPE="SUBMIT" VALUE="Send">

</FORM>

<%
If Request.QueryString("MailSent") = "True" Then
  Response.Write "Your previous message was sent.<BR><BR>"
ElseIf Request.QueryString("MailSent") = "False" Then
  Response.Write "Your previous message was <STRONG>not</STRONG> sent.<BR><BR>"
End If
%>

</BODY>
</HTML>
```

When SimpleMail.asp is viewed in the browser, we'll see the following user interface:

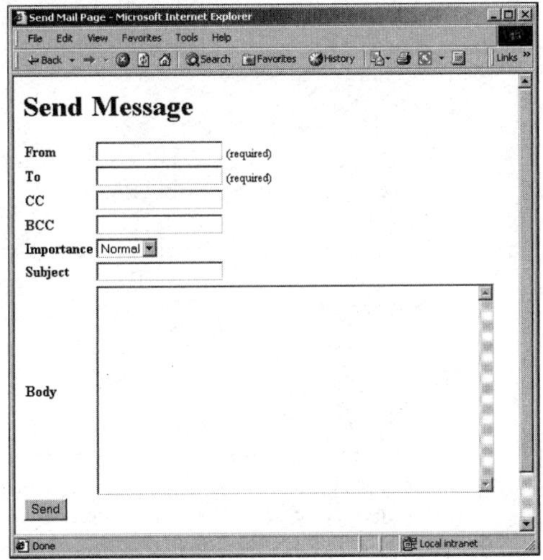

When the form is submitted, the page SendMail.asp is called, which has the following source:

```
<%@ LANGUAGE=VBScript %>
<% Option Explicit %>

<%

Dim strReferer
Dim intPos

' Get the URL of the page that referred browser to this page
strReferer = Request.ServerVariables("HTTP_Referer")
```

```
' If that referrer had a value in its query string, remove it
intPos = Instr(strReferer, "?")
If intPos > 0  Then strReferer = Left(strReferer, intPos - 1)


If (Request.QueryString("SendFrom") <> "") _
    And (Request.QueryString("SendTo")<> "") Then

  'Dimension the objSendMail variable and create a new instance of the NewMail
  'object.
  Dim objSendMail
  Set objSendMail = CreateObject("CDONTS.NewMail")

  'Set all the properties on the NewMail object using the values from the
  ' QueryString
  objSendMail.From = Request.QueryString("SendFrom")
  objSendMail.To = Request.QueryString("SendTo")
  objSendMail.Cc = Request.QueryString("SendCC")
  objSendMail.Bcc = Request.QueryString("SendBCC")
  objSendMail.Importance = Request.QueryString("SelImportance")
  objSendMail.Subject = Request.QueryString("Subject")
  objSendMail.Body = Request.QueryString("BodyText")

  'Send the message
  objSendMail.Send

  'Set the objSendMail to nothing, free its resources
  Set objSendMail = Nothing

  'Redirect the user back to the referring page and update
  ' the QueryString to indicate the message was sent.
  Response.Redirect strReferer & "?MailSent=True"

Else

  'Not all required information was provided, so the message
  ' could not be sent. Redirect the user back to the referring page
  ' and update the QueryString to indicate the message was not sent.
  Response.Redirect strReferer & "?MailSent=False"

End If

%>
```

So, having seen the source code for the pages, let's step through the application and see what it's doing. We'll look at the `SimpleMail.asp` page briefly, but our main focus for this application is the `SendMail.asp` page, which is the workhorse for the application.

SimpleMail.asp

There are a couple of features to point out in the code for the `SimpleMail.asp` page.

First, notice the dropdown that allows the user to choose the message importance from the three possible values (the `TD` tags are stripped out the make the code more readable here):

```
<SELECT ID=select1 NAME=selImportance>
          <OPTION VALUE=2>High</OPTION>
          <OPTION SELECTED VALUE=1>Normal</OPTION>
          <OPTION VALUE=0>Low</OPTION>
```

You'll see that we use the literal values for the importance value here, rather than the CDONTS Library constants. That's because those constants are available only on the server machine, and not on the client. In order to use the CDONTS constants we would have had to write our code like this (again, the TD tags were removed to make the code more readable):

```
<SELECT ID=select1 NAME=selImportance>
    <OPTION VALUE=<% =CdoHigh %>>High</OPTION>
    <OPTION SELECTED VALUE=<%=CdoNormal %> >Normal</OPTION>
    <OPTION VALUE=<% =CdoLow %>>Low</OPTION>
</SELECT>
```

This code would also require the user to have added a reference to the CDONTS Library in the global.asa for the Web project. As we mentioned earlier, placing the following META tag in the global.asa will cause IIS to load the constants from that library, and allow the developer to use the constants names instead of the literal values:

```
<!--METADATA TYPE="TypeLib" NAME="Microsoft CDO for NTS 1.2 Library"
             UUID="{0E064ADD-9D99-11D0-ABE5-00AA0064D470}" VERSION="1.2"-->
```

In this case, there's no real advantage provided by using the constants for the list box, so the sample code doesn't make use of them.

There's one more section of code in SimpleMail.asp that's worth taking a look at – the last piece of code on the page:

```
<%
If Request.QueryString("MailSent") = "True" Then
  Response.Write "Your previous message was sent.<BR><BR>"
ElseIf Request.QueryString("MailSent") = "False" Then
  Response.Write "Your previous message was <STRONG>not</STRONG> sent.<BR><BR>"
End If
%>
```

This provides a means of feedback for the user. Since the actual sending of the mail occurs in the SendMail.asp page, we need a way to let the user know whether the message was sent. We've done this by using the variable MailSent, which is passed in the QueryString.

In the case where the page is being loaded for the first time, the value of the MailSent variable is empty, so this code does nothing. The interesting cases occur when the SendMail.asp page redirects users to SimpleMail.asp, specifying a value for MailSent in the QueryString. Depending on whether that value is True or False, this code will either print out a success or a failure message on the Web page.

We'll cover the reasons why MailSent may be false in the next section, where we'll look at the code for SendMail.asp.

SendMail.asp

In this application, the `SendMail.asp` page is where the majority of the work is done. This is the page that will actually send the mail message. As you can see from its source, the page is designed so that it can be reused without modifications. Any other application/pages are able to leverage this page, and send a simple mail message by requesting the page and specifying the required information in the `QueryString`.

So let's look at the `SendMail.asp` page, starting from the top.

Design Note

The first piece of code in `SendMail.asp` has little to do with sending the message – it's mostly just an application design preference. This page was designed with the intention of making it fairly generic and useable in any Web project. `SendMail.asp` is set up so that it doesn't need to have any code in it to identify which page to redirect the browser to once it's sent the message (or failed to send the message). This is possible because the page makes use of the `ServerVariables` collection, and specifically the `HTTP_REFERER` variable value:

```
strReferer = Request.ServerVariables("HTTP_Referer")
```

This variable contains the URL of the page that referred the browser to the current page. In this application, the value will be `http://MyServer/Mail/SimpleMail.asp`. By using this variable, the programmer can be assured that – without manually modifying any code – the `SendMail.asp` page will always redirect the browser back to the page from which it was called.

As this variable contains the full URL of the referring page, it's possible there will be some `Querystring` information in that URL (for example, `http://MyServer/Mail/SimpleMail.ASP?MailSent=True`). To handle this, our code looks for a "?" and, if it finds one, it will remove the ? and all the text following it from the URL:

```
intPos = Instr(strReferer, "?")
If intPos  >0  Then strReferer = Left(strReferer, intPos - 1)
```

So, for our example, the resulting value of `strReferer` is:

```
http://MyServer/Mail/SimpleMail.asp
```

This approach lets us add the page to any Web application and use it without modifications. Any calling page need only specify the desired information in the `QueryString` when this `SendMail.asp` is referred to. After `SendMail.asp` executes its code, it will redirect the browser back to the page from which it was referred.

Verifying Sender and Receiver

Now we'll get into the meat of the code, and look at the part that deals with the message. As verification and validation are important in any application, you'll notice that the next section of code is an `If` statement, to ensure that a valid, useful message can be sent:

```
If (Request.QueryString("SendFrom") <> "") _
    And (Request.QueryString("SendTo")<> "") Then
```

This line is here to ensure that a destination address and a sender address have both been specified. Sending a message without a sender address is possible, but will result in a semi-anonymous e-mail. The term semi-anonymous is used because the sender of the e-mail will not be identified, but the server from which the message was sent can still be determined by inspecting the message headers.

In our case, we've chosen to not allow anonymous messages, and to require that a sender address be specified. As for requiring a destination address, it's no use sending a message to no one! If either of these two values is not specified, then the message will not be sent. And the `MailSent Querystring` variable will be set to `False`, indicating that no mail was sent.

> *As we discussed when looking at `SimpleMail.asp`, the `MailSent` variable is used in that page to provide some user feedback as to their sending a message.*

Sending the Message

Once we've determined that we have the required information, the first operation that needs to occur is the creation of a new instance of the NewMail object. As we noted earlier, each time you want to send a message, you need to create a new instance of the NewMail object. These lines declare a variable and then assign a newly instantiated NewMail object to that variable:

```
Dim objSendMail
Set objSendMail = CreateObject("CDONTS.NewMail")
```

Next, we need to set the appropriate properties on that mail object. For these properties, we'll be using the values that the user entered in the `SimpleMail.asp` page. These values were passed to the `SendMail.asp` page through the QueryString and so we access them using the `QueryString` collection:

```
objSendMail.From = Request.QueryString("SendFrom")
objSendMail.To = Request.QueryString("SendTo")
objSendMail.Cc = Request.QueryString("SendCC")
objSendMail.Bcc = Request.QueryString("SendBCC")
objSendMail.Importance = Request.QueryString("SelImportance")
objSendMail.Subject = Request.QueryString("Subject")
objSendMail.Body = Request.QueryString("BodyText")
```

We now have a message that can be sent to the specified recipients – all that's left to do is to send that message. We do that by simply calling the `Send` method on the NewMail object. Although the `Send` method has some optional parameters, we can leave those off in this case since we've already set the properties for the `objSendMail` object:

```
objSendMail.Send
```

> *Remember, if we do specify any recipients in the `Send` method, then the message will be sent to all the recipients specified in the `objSendMail`'s `To`, `CC`, `BCC` properties, as well as to any recipients specified in the `Send` method parameters.*

After the message has been sent, we want to clean up and release the resources for the `objSendMail` object:

```
Set objSendMail = Nothing
```

Reporting Results

Finally, when the message has been sent and `objSendMail` set to `Nothing`, the user is redirected back to the page from which they came. When this is done, there's also a value for the `MailSent` variable passed along in the QueryString, to indicate whether the mail was sent. If the `SendFrom` and `SendTo` properties were specified in the call to this page, then the message will have been sent and the value of `MailSent` will be `True`. If the `SendFrom` and/or `SendTo` values were not specified, then the message will not be sent and instead the value of `MailSent` will be `False`.

We could similarly use this method to pass back an error description, or possibly an error code – for our purposes it's sufficient to just pass on whether the message was sent or not.

Verifying the Results

Seeing as this is a mail application that only sends mail, the question may arise as to how you verify that everything worked correctly.

The simplest way of verifying that the mail was sent is for you to send it to an e-mail address to which you have access. For example, if you have a Hotmail account at `MyMailAddress@Hotmail.com`, send a message to that address and then login to hotmail to verify that the message was delivered.

Another option is to send mail to a user on the server machine. First, look in the MailRoot folder on the server machine – you'll notice X messages in the folder. Then, if the SimpleMail application exists on a server named `MailServer01`, send a test message to `User1@mailserver01`. You can then look again in the `MailRoot` folder on the `MailServer01` machine to verify that there are now X+1 messages in the folder.

The SimpleMail Application – Summary

As you can see, there's not a large amount of code needed to be able to send a simple e-mail from a web page. In the code samples we've just discussed, there are nearly as many comment lines as there are lines relating to the sending of the messages. The CDONTS Library has provided the NewMail component specifically to allow developers to do this.

The code is short – about 12 lines for the actual sending of the message – and not very difficult to understand or implement. In these simple cases, it's not unusual to spend much more time on designing the UI of the application than on implementing the functionality.

The Inbox Application

We've just seen a simple application that utilizes CDONTS and the NewMail object. Now we're going to look at a basic example of what can be done when using the Session object and the objects within its hierarchy.

This sample application will allow a user to login to their mailbox. Upon login, the user is presented with a listing of the messages in their inbox. This application makes use of three separate pages:

- `Login.asp`
- `Inbox.asp`
- `ViewMessage.asp`

We'll explore the code for each page in the order that the user encounters them.

Logging In

The first page that the user sees is the `Login.asp` page. This is a simple page where the user will enter their User/Display name and their e-mail address. The raw source of the page is:

```
<%@ LANGUAGE=VBScript %>
<HTML><HEAD>
<TITLE>Inbox login</TITLE>
</HEAD>

<BODY>
<STRONG><FONT SIZE=5>Please Login</FONT></STRONG> :

<FORM ID=LoginFrm ACTION="Inbox.asp" METHOD="GET">
<TABLE WIDTH="300" BORDER="0" CELLSPACING="1" CELLPADDING="1">
  <TR>
    <TD>User Name</TD>
    <TD><INPUT name=UserName ></TD>
  </TR>
  <TR>
    <TD>E-mail Address</TD>
    <TD><input name=UserEMail ></TD>
  </TR>
</TABLE>

<BR><BR>
<INPUT TYPE="SUBMIT" VALUE="Login" ID=submit1>

</FORM>

</BODY>
</HTML>
```

This code is fairly self-explanatory – it just takes the values and passes them along to the next page – so we'll not go into further detail about it.

When viewed in the browser, it appears like this:

Listing Messages

Similar to `SendMail.asp` in the previous sample application, `Inbox.asp` is where the majority of the work occurs in the application. Here's the source listing for the page:

```
<%@ LANGUAGE=VBScript %>
<% Option Explicit %>
<HTML>
<HEAD>
<TITLE><% =Request.QueryString("UserName") %>'s Inbox</TITLE>
</HEAD>

<BODY>
<%
Dim objInbox
Dim colMsgs
Dim strUserName
Dim strUserEMail
Dim objCurSession

' Assign the values from the query string into local variables
' since they will be needed more than once.
strUserName = Request.QueryString("UserName")
strUserEMail = Request.QueryString("UserEMail")

' Store the Session Object, User Name and Email
' in ASP session variables for possible future use.
Session("UserName") = strUserName
Session("UserEMail") = strUserEMail

' Use the values passed in to create a new session and
' initialize its variables.
Set objCurSession = Createobject("CDONTS.Session")
objCurSession.LogonSMTP strUserName, strUserEMail

'Create a Session variable to hold the user's CDONTS Session object
Set Session("CurSession") = objCurSession

' Get the Inbox Folder object
Set objInbox = objCurSession.Inbox

' Using that object, get the collection of messages in the Inbox
Set colMsgs = objInbox.Messages

' Display a greeting to the user.
Response.Write "Welcome, " & Session("UserName") & _
              ". You have " & colMsgs.Count & " messages in your inbox. <BR><BR>"

' Then, display a listing of the messages in their inbox
' Only display the table if there are some messages to display
```

```
If (colMsgs.Count > 0) then
  %>
  <TABLE BORDER=0 CELLPADDING=1 CELLSPACING=1 WIDTH=90% >

    <TR>
      <TD><STRONG>Importance</STRONG></TD>
      <TD><STRONG>From</STRONG></TD>
      <TD><STRONG>Subject</STRONG></TD>
      <TD><STRONG>Sent</STRONG></TD>
    </TR>

  <%
    Dim intLoop

    For intLoop = 1 to colMsgs.Count
  %>

    <TR>
      <TD ALIGN=MIDDLE><% ShowImportanceIcon(colMsgs(intLoop).Importance) %></TD>
      <TD><% =colMsgs(intLoop).Sender %></TD>
      <TD><A HREF="ViewMessage.ASP?MsgID=<% =intLoop %>">
          <% =colMsgs(intLoop).Subject %></A></TD>
      <TD><% =colMsgs(intLoop).TimeSent %></TD>
    </TR>

  <%
    Next

End If

%>

</TABLE>
</BODY>
</HTML>

<%
' Function to generate the correct IMG tag for the importance icon
Sub ShowImportanceIcon(intImpValue)

  Dim strIconFile

  Select Case intImpValue
    Case CdoNormal
      strIconFile = "Norm_Importance.gif"
    Case CdoHigh
      strIconFile = "High_Importance.gif"
    Case CdoLow
      strIconFile = "Low_Importance.gif"
  End Select

  Response.Write ("<IMG SRC=.\Images\" & strIconFile & ">")

End Sub

%>
```

And here's a sample of what the page would look like for a user:

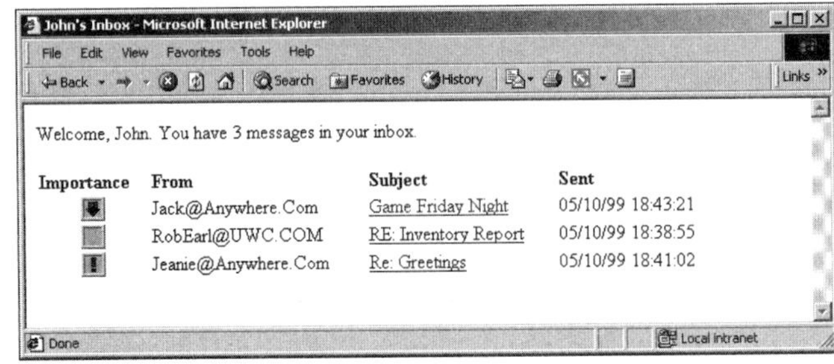

Initializing the Session Object

At the top of the page are declarations of all the variables we'll use:

```
Dim objInbox
Dim colMsgs
Dim strUserName
Dim strUserEMail
Dim objCurSession
```

Two of these variables – `strUserName` and `strUserEMail` – stand out, since they're obviously not intended to represent objects in the Session object's hierarchy. In fact, these variables are not related to the Session object at all – they're simply used to hold the `UserName` and `EMail` address values that are retrieved from the QueryString. As these values may be referenced multiple times in this page – and possibly from other pages as well – we decided to create local variables to store the values. This prevents multiple repetitive calls to the QueryString object.

Additionally, creating ASP Session objects to store the values allows the `UserName` and `EMail` values to be used by another page in the application. The usefulness of this – if it's not apparent now – will become clear later:

```
' Assign the values from the query string into local variables
' since they will be needed more than once.
strUserName = Request.QueryString("UserName")
strUserEMail = Request.QueryString("UserEMail")

' Store the Session Object, User Name and Email
' in ASP session variables for possible future use.
Session("UserName") = strUserName
Session("UserEMail") = strUserEMail
```

Once the ASP session variables are created, our next step is to create the CDONTS Session object and initialize it, using the `UserName` and `EMail` address values that were passed in:

```
Set objCurSession = Createobject("CDONTS.Session")
objCurSession.LogonSMTP strUserName,strUserEMail
```

The session is stored in an ASP session variable.

```
Set Session("CurSession") = objCurSession
```

This, like the UserName and EMail variables, allows the user's CDONTS session to be more easily accessed from another page in the Web application.

Accessing the User's Inbox

So now that the session has been created, and the user has logged in, the Session object exposes access to the user's folders. For this application, we're concerned with the Inbox. We can use the Session object's Inbox property that returns the current user's Inbox folder – we don't need to make use of the GetDefaultFolder property. Once we have the Inbox object, we're able to get the collection of messages within the Inbox. The only code required to do all of this is the following lines:

```
' Get the Inbox Folder object
Set objInbox = objCurSession.Inbox

' Using that object, get the collection of messages in the Inbox
Set colMsgs = objInbox.Messages
```

When we have the collection of message, we have access to the content of the Inbox. We can perform a number of tasks on these messages, but we can't modify them – when a message is in the Inbox, CDONTS doesn't allow modifications to it.

For this application, our next step is to provide the user with a greeting, and then display a listing of the messages in the Inbox (if any):

```
' Display a greeting to the user.
Response.Write "Welcome, " & Session("UserName") & _
            ". You have " & colMsgs.Count & " messages in your inbox. <BR><BR>"

' Then, display a listing of the messages in their inbox
' Only display the table if there are some messages to display
If (colMsgs.Count > 0) then
```

The Count property on the messages collection allows us to give the user a count of the messages in their Inbox. In addition, we use the Count property to determine if there are any messages in the Inbox to be listed on the Web page. If there are, then a simple loop will iterate through the collection and display each message's importance, sender, subject, and when it was sent.

For the most part, there's nothing especially notable in this code. There is one line that could use some more explanation though – the line that generates the text for the Subject display makes an anchor tag out of the text. It looks like this:

```
<TD><A HREF="ViewMessage.ASP?MsgID=<% =intLoop %>">
    <% =colMsgs(intLoop).Subject %></A></TD>
```

This allows the user to click on that tag and be taken to the page that will display the message. The MsgID QueryString variable indicates which of the messages is to be displayed by the ViewMessage.asp page (we'll look at this page shortly). For now, it's sufficient to note that this code generates the correct hyperlink for viewing the message.

In displaying the importance for each message, this page makes a call to a subroutine that will generate the appropriate HTML `IMG` tag for the message's importance:

```
Sub ShowImportanceIcon(intImpValue)

  Dim strIconFile

  Select Case intImpValue
    Case CdoNormal
      strIconFile = "Norm_Importance.gif"
    Case CdoHigh
      strIconFile = "High_Importance.gif"
    Case CdoLow
      strIconFile = "Low_Importance.gif"
  End Select

  Response.Write ("<IMG SRC=.\Images\" & strIconFile & ">")

End Sub
```

Depending on the value of the message's `Importance` property (which is passed into this sub as the `intImpValue` parameter), the sub will point to either the high, low, or normal importance image.

Viewing Messages

In addition to seeing what messages are in their Inbox, users may want to be able to view one or more of their messages. Our application provides a way for users to open their messages by simply clicking on them in their Inbox. For example, if we'd clicked on the message in the previous screenshot with the subject of `Game Friday Night`, we would see that message displayed like this:

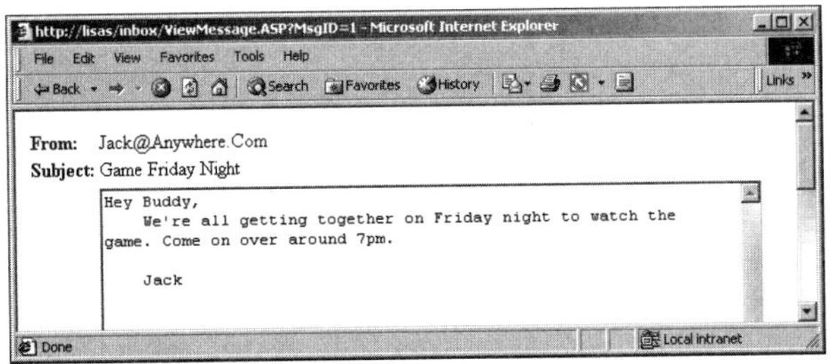

The source code for this page – `ViewMessage.asp` – is as follows:

```
<%@ LANGUAGE=VBScript %>
<HTML>
<HEAD>
</HEAD>

<BODY>
<P>
<%
Dim colMsgs
Dim objCurMessage
Dim objSession
Dim intIndex
```

```
Set objSession = Session("CurSession")
Set colMsgs = objSession.Inbox.Messages

intIndex = Request.QueryString("MsgID")

%>


<TABLE BORDER=0 CELLPADDING=1 CELLSPACING=1 WIDTH="75%">

  <TR>
    <TD><STRONG>From:</STRONG></TD>
    <TD><LABEL><% =colMsgs(intIndex).Sender %></LABEL></TD></TR>
  <TR>
    <TD><STRONG>Subject:</STRONG></TD>
    <TD><LABEL><% =colMsgs(intIndex).Subject %></LABEL></TD></TR>
  <TR>
  </TR>
  <TR>
    <TD></TD>
    <TD>
      <TEXTAREA ID=TEXTAREA1 NAME=TEXTAREA1 STYLE="HEIGHT: 390px; WIDTH: 547px">
      <% =colMsgs(intIndex).Text %>
      </TEXTAREA>
    </TD>
  </TR>
</TABLE></P>

</BODY>
</HTML>
```

At first glance, there doesn't appear to be much code necessary to display a message – that's because some of the more involved work has already been done by the `Login.asp` and `Inbox.asp` pages. The results of that work were maintained in ASP session variables, which can be easily retrieved by other pages in the application. As we said earlier, this saves us passing around the `UserName` and `UserEMail` values, as well as removing the need to keep creating new Session objects and calling `LogonSMTP` on them. All of that logon work is recalled with the following line:

```
Set objSession = Session("CurSession")
```

This assigns to the local `objSession` object the CDONTS Session object that we created and initialized in the `Inbox.asp` page. We can use this object to get back to the collection of messages in the Inbox. In this case, we are not concerned with the Inbox object, so we just get the collection of messages.

```
Set colMsgs = objSession.Inbox.Messages
```

And once we have that collection, we can access the messages contained within it. We're only concerned with one of the messages in the collection – the one the user selected for display. To determine which one that is, we use the `MsgID` variable that was passed in the QueryString.

Since we're dealing with the same collection as existed in the `Inbox.asp` page, we know the collection will be in the same order as it was there. Therefore, the index of the selected message will be the same. We'll be using the index several times in this page, so the value of `MsgID` is assigned to a local variable – `intIndex`. Our code queries the properties of the selected message, then uses the `intIndex` local variable instead of the QueryString variable `MsgID`:

```
<TR>
  <TD><STRONG>From:</STRONG></TD>
  <TD><LABEL><% =colMsgs(intIndex).Sender %></LABEL></TD></TR>
<TR>
  <TD><STRONG>Subject:</STRONG></TD>
  <TD><LABEL><% =colMsgs(intIndex).Subject %></LABEL></TD></TR>
<TR>
</TR>
<TR>
  <TD></TD>
  <TD>
    <TEXTAREA ID=TEXTAREA1 NAME=TEXTAREA1 STYLE="HEIGHT: 390px; WIDTH: 547px">
    <% =colMsgs(intIndex).Text %>
    </TEXTAREA>
  </TD>
</TR>
</TABLE>
```

An Alternative Method

We could have used another approach, and assigned the selected message's Message object to a local variable. In that case, our code would have looked like this:

```
Dim objMessage
Set objMessage = colMsgs(Request.QueryString("MsgID"))

%>

<TABLE BORDER=0 CELLPADDING=1 CELLSPACING=1 WIDTH="75%">

  <TR>
    <TD><STRONG>From:</STRONG></TD>
    <TD><LABEL><% =objMessage.Sender %></LABEL></TD></TR>
  <TR>
    <TD><STRONG>Subject:</STRONG></TD>
    <TD><LABEL><% = objMessage.Subject %></LABEL></TD></TR>
  <TR>
    <TD></TD>
    <TD><TEXTAREA ID=TEXTAREA1 NAME=TEXTAREA1 STYLE="HEIGHT: 390px;
                  WIDTH: 547px"><% = objMessage.).Text %>
</TEXTAREA></TD></TR></TABLE></P>

</BODY>
</HTML>
```

Functionally, the two methods are the same. For the same reason that we didn't request variables from the QueryString multiple times, in this example, it's a good idea to create the local Message object, instead of repeatedly getting the message from the Messages collection.

Verifying the results

The SimpleMail application was only capable of sending mail, but the Inbox application is only capable of viewing received mail. In order to verify that the Inbox application worked, it's best to utilize the SimpleMail application.

First, use SimpleMail to send a message to `Test@MailServer01` (replacing `MailServer01` with the name of your Web server). Then, login to the Inbox application with a user e-mail address of `Test@MailServer01` (again, replacing `MailServer01` with the name of your Web server). If both applications worked, you will see your test message listed.

The Inbox Application - Summary

If you specify an incorrect e-mail address on the login page, you will just not see any messages in your inbox. Since the `LogonSMTP` method does no actual validation or logging in, it allows you to have incorrect or invalid information without reporting any errors. Therefore, it's very important that the User's e-mail address is entered accurately and completely. The `UserName` is just a display name and can be incorrect, but the `UserEMail` address must be correct.

Summary

Through this chapter, we've looked at the evolution of CDONTS, its intended use, and some sample applications that make use of CDONTS. Although CDONTS has gone through some progressions in its evolution, there's still room for improvement. That CDONTS only supports SMTP mail is one of the noticeable limitations of the library. Even so, what's currently there is very useful, and greatly simplifies the addition or implementation of simple messaging capabilities for an ASP application.

Although CDONTS is limited, it's important to remember that CDONTS code is fully compatible and functional in a CDO environment. Those applications created against IIS and the SMTP Service (CDONTS) can be migrated to an IIS and Exchange platform (CDO) without any modifications.

So, in the next chapter, we'll move on to look at CDO.

N
W

23

ASP, CDO and Exchange Server

In the previous chapter, we looked at the evolution of Collaboration Data Objects, specifically focusing on the CDONTS library and its uses. As noted at the end of that chapter, the CDONTS Library is somewhat limited in its capabilities. So in order to provide more compelling, complex messaging applications we need to move up to the **CDO Library**. As the CDONTS Library is a subset of the CDO Library, it is logical that progressing to CDO gives the developer more programmatic functionality.

In this chapter, we will cover:

- The object model of CDO
- Its differences from CDONTS
- Creating a sample Mail Client application utilizing the CDO Library

The CDO Library

CDO actually provides two separate libraries:

- **The CDO Library**
  Provides the objects that are used for sending and receiving messages, as well as for programmatically accessing and manipulating the address book and folders.
- **The CDO Rendering Library**
  Provides a collection of objects that have the capability to render CDO objects in an HTML format, thus making it easier to display these objects in a browser.

For our purposes, we will focus on the CDO Library, and only briefly mention the CDO Rendering library.

First, as we did with CDONTS, we'll look at the main CDO Object Library hierarchy:

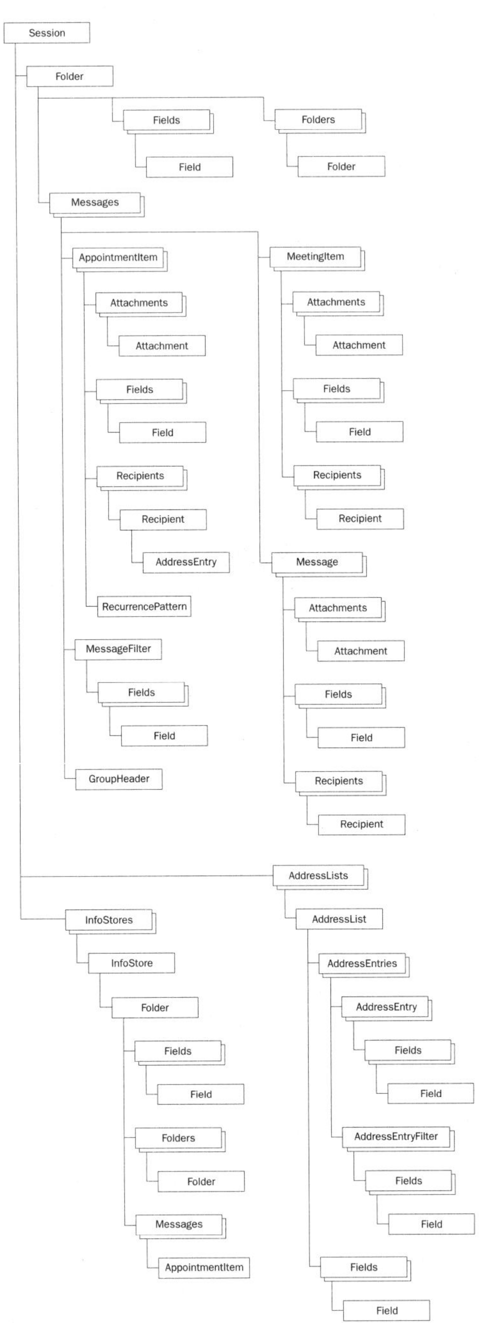

As you can see, there are many more objects in the CDO Library than are provided by CDONTS, and some of the objects shared with the CDONTS Library have more extensive properties and functionality. We'll not go into detail on all of these objects, as that's beyond the scope of this book. Instead, we'll take an in-depth look at some objects, while only viewing others from a high level.

Common/Shared Objects

As we can see from the diagram, there are several objects and collections that belong to multiple parent objects. We'll start our discussion of the CDO Library by examining these common or shared objects. If an object has a different use or behavior depending on its parent item, we'll explain that when we look at the parent item.

The Attachments Collection

The **Attachments collection** is a collection of zero or more attachments, exposed by the AppointmentItem, MeetingItem, and Message objects.

The Attachments collection provides just two properties:

Property	Description
`Count`	Returns the count of the number of items in the collection.
`Item(`*`index`*`)`	Return the attachment item at position *index* in the collection.

Additionally, just as in CDONTS, the collection supports the use of the `For Each` *VB (and VBScript) statement.*

The Attachments collection also provides an `Add` and a `Delete` method. The `Delete` method will delete *all* of the items in the collection and should be used carefully. If you only want to delete a single attachment from the collection, you should use the `Delete` method on that Attachment object instead. The deletion happens immediately and *cannot* be undone. The `Delete` method takes no parameters and would simply be used as:

```
colAttachments.Delete()
```

The `Add` method is a little more involved, as it has four parameters that the user can specify:

```
Set objAttachment = colAttachments.Add( [ name] [, position] _
                                        [, type] [, source ] )
```

Parameter	Description
`Name`	*Optional.* The caption/display name for the attachment.
`Position`	*Optional.* Character position for the attachment to appear within the body of the message.
`Type`	*Optional.* Type of attachment. Can be: `CdoFileData` (1) `CdoFileLink` (2) `CdoOle` (3) `CdoEmbeddedMessage` (4)
`Source`	*Optional.* Fully qualified path to the file containing the attachment data.

For example, if we wanted to add an Excel file (`InventoryReport.xls`) as an attachment to a message with the caption of "Inventory Report" our code would look like this:

```
Set objAttachment = colAttachments.Add("Inventory Report", 0, & _
                                       CdoFileData, "C:\Inventory.xls")
```

When adding an attachment to the collection, you can either specify all the information in the `Add` method, or you can set the properties on the resulting Attachment object. We'll look at the Attachment object itself next, and see how to add an attachment using the properties of this object.

The Attachment Object

An **Attachment object** represents a single attachment to a Message, MeetingItem, or AppointmentItem object. These attachments can be files, OLE objects, or other Message objects.

The Attachment object has the following properties:

Property	Description
`Fields`	Returns a collection of the Fields associated with the Attachment object.
`Index`	Returns the index location of the current Attachment object within the Attachments collection.
`Name`	Sets or returns the caption/display name for the attachment.
`Position`	Sets or returns the character position of the attachment within the body of the message.
`Source`	Sets or returns the fully qualified path to the file containing the attachment data.
`Type`	Sets or returns the type of attachment. Can be: `CdoFileData`, `CdoFileLink`, `CdoOle`, or `CdoEmbeddedMessage`.

You'll notice that the parameters in the `Add` method of the Attachments collection map to some of the Attachment object's properties.

We've just seen how to add an attachment by specifying all the information in the `Add` method. So here's how to add an attachment using the Attachment object's properties:

```
Set objAttachment = colAttachments.Add

With objAttachment
   .Name = "Inventory Report"
   .Position = 0
   .Type = CdoFileData
   .Source = "C:\InventoryReport.xls"
End With

objCurMessage.Update
```

You'll notice that we call the `Update` method on the Message object. This is necessary in order to commit the changes that were made to the Attachment's properties.

The Fields Collection

The **Fields collection** is a collection of one or more Field objects. Similar to the Attachments collection, the Fields collection also exposes a `Count` property, an `Item` property, an `Add` method, and a `Delete` method. The properties and the `Delete` method function in the same way as in the Attachments collection.

However, the `Add` method differs in its parameter list, as it is adding a different type of object:

```
Set objField = objFieldsColl.Add(name, Class [, value] [, PropsetID] )
```

Parameter	Description
`Name`	The name for a custom MAPI Property.
`Class`	The type of data for the Field object. Can be one of the values listed in the next table.
`Value`	*Optional.* The value of the MAPI Property.
`PropsetID`	*Optional.* The unique ID for the MAPI Property set. Similar to the ID for a Field object.

The possible values for the `Class` parameter are:

Name	Value
`CdoArray`	8192 (&H2000)
`CdoBlob`	65 (&H41)
`CdoBoolean`	11
`CdoCurrency`	6
`CdoDataObject`	13
`CdoDate`	7
`CdoDouble`	5
`CdoEmpty`	0
`CdoInteger`	2
`CdoLong`	3
`CdoNull`	1
`CdoSingle`	4
`CdoString`	8

In addition to the usual collection methods, the Fields collection also has a method for specifying the default MAPI Property set to be used.

A ***MAPI Property set*** *is a collection of* named properties, *and different sets can have different names.*

The `SetNamespace` method allows the us to specify the **Property set** (Namespace) to be used as the default. This method has the following syntax:

```
objFieldsColl.SetNamespace(PropsetID)
```

When accessing a named property, that property is within a Property set. The collection of all named properties within a Property set is called a **Namespace**.

When a property is to be added that is within the default Namespace, it is not necessary to specify the `PropsetID` on the call to the `Add` method.

The `SetNamespace` method allows you to specify the default Namespace. Any changes to the default Namespace will stay in effect until the `SetNamespace` method is called again.

So, if we wanted to create a new MAPI Property called `Display Name` that stored a String value, our code would look like:

```
objField = colFields.Add("Display Name", CdoString)
```

In this case, we've omitted the `Value` and `PropsetID` parameters. By doing so, the value of the `"Display Name"` field will be set to an empty string and will be in the default Namespace.

The Field Object

The **Field object** represents one of the MAPI Properties for a CDO object.

A **MAPI Property** is a property that describes something about the message: for example the message's sender address, the subject line of the message; and the time the message was sent.

In addition to exposing the default MAPI Properties, the Field object also allows access to custom MAPI Properties.

The Field object has the following properties:

Property	Description
`ID`	Returns the unique ID for the MAPI Property that the Field object represents.
`Index`	Returns the index location of the Field object within the Fields collection.
`Name`	Returns the name of the field.
`Type`	Returns the type of data that the object contains.
`Value`	Sets/Returns the value of the Field and its underlying MAPI Property.

The `ID` property is a 32-bit integer that contains information specifying both the MAPI Property's identifier as well as its Property type. The high-order 16-bits specify the property identifier, while its low order 16-bits specify the property type (binary, integer, etc).

There are also three methods that the Field object exposes: `Delete`, `ReadFromFile`, and `WriteToFile`:

Method	Description
`Delete`	Used to remove the current Field object from the collection of fields.
`ReadFromFile`	Used to load the value of the field from a specified file.
`WriteToFile`	Used to write the Field object's value to a file. If there is any data in the specified file, that information will be overwritten by the current data.

The syntax of the two file access methods is very similar:

```
objField.ReadFromFile(fileName)
```

Where `fileName` is the fully qualified path to the file from which to read the value for the Field object.

```
objField.WriteToFile(fileName)
```

Where, in this case, `fileName` is the fully qualified path to which to write the value of the Field object.

The Recipients Collection

The **Recipients collection** is a collection of zero or more Recipient objects. The collection is used to specify the intended recipients of a Mail object. Just like the Fields and Attachments collections, the Recipients collection exposes the `Count` property, the `Item` property, and the `Delete` method.

For the `Add` method, the syntax is:

```
Set objRecipient = objRecipColl.Add( [name] [, address] [, type] [, entryID] )
```

Parameter	Description
`Name`	*Optional.* Recipient's display/friendly name.
`Address`	*Optional.* Recipient's fully qualified messaging address.
`Type`	*Optional.* Type of recipient. Can be one of three values: `CdoTo` (1) `CdoCC` (2) `CdoBCC` (3)
`EntryID`	*Optional.* Unique ID of an AddressEntry object for the recipient.

The `Name`, `Address`, and `Type` parameters are the same as the `Name`, `Address`, and `Type` properties for the Recipient object (which we'll cover in the next section). If no parameters are specified, a Recipient object is still created with empty values. The following code example shows the adding of To, CC, and BCC recipients to a message:

```
objMsg.Recipients.Add("Jeanie", CdoTO, "Jeanie@Anywhere.com")
objMsg.Recipients.Add("JeaniesBoss", CdoCC, "JeaniesBoss@Anywhere.com")
objMsg.Recipients.Add("Jack", CdoBCC, "Jack@Anywhere.com")
```

The Recipients collection also provides an `AddMultiple` method that will create multiple Recipient objects in the collection.

The syntax of the method is:

```
collRecipeints.AddMultiple( names [, type] )
```

Parameter	Description
`Names`	Semi-colon delimited list of recipient addresses.
`Type`	*Optional.* The type of recipient. `CdoTo`, `CdoCC`, `CdoBCC`.

Note that you cannot use the `AddMultiple` *method to add more than one type of recipient at the same time.*

If you wanted to add two people to the To list and three people to the CC list, you would have to write something similar to this:

```
colRecipients.Add("Jeanie@AnyWhere.Com;JeaniesBoss@Anywhere.Com", CdoTo)
colRecipeints.Add("Jack@NoWhere.Com;Jill@Nowhere.Com;Jeanie@Nowhere.Com", _
                  CdoCC)
```

CDO provides the ability to use friendly, or **resolvable**, addresses instead of fully qualified messaging addresses. For example, we could specify the friendly name of `"Jeanie"` instead of `"Jeanie@anywhere.com"`. In order to resolve those addresses into the messaging address, the Recipients collection provides a `Resolve` method. When executed, the `Resolve` method will iterate through the entire collection of recipients and attempt to resolve each recipients address into a messaging address. Any address that can't be resolved is left as unresolved – and attempting to send a message with an unresolved address will result in an error.

Although the documentation for the method shows an optional parameter for specifying whether to display a dialog, when your application is running in ASP those dialogs are not allowed. Therefore, for our purposes, the method has no effective parameters.

The Recipients collection also provides two methods for navigating through the unresolved Recipient objects:

- The `GetFirstUnresolved` method will return the Recipient object for the first unresolved Recipient object. If there are no unresolved recipients, then it will return `Nothing`.
- The `GetNextUnresolved` method will return the next unresolved Recipient object. When there are no remaining unresolved Recipient objects, it will return `Nothing`.

In addition, the Recipients collection provides a `GetFreeBusy` method, which will return a string that indicates the free/busy times for all of the recipients in the collection. This is the combined availability for the group of recipients during a specific time frame.

The syntax of this method is:

```
strAvail = collRecipient1.GetFreeBusy(StartTime, EndTime, Interval)
```

Parameter	Description
`StartTime`	The Date/Time for the first time slot.
`EndTime`	The Date/Time for the last time slot.
`Interval`	The number of minutes for each time slot.

If we wanted to find out the availability for our meeting recipients from 9am to 2pm, in one-hour time slots, our code would look like:

```
strAvail = colRecipients.GetFreeBusy("1/1/1999 09:00", "1/1/1999 14:00", 60)
```

The resulting string has a length equal to the number of intervals between the `StartTime` and `EndTime`. Each position in the string has a value that represents the recipients availability, where possible values for the availability are:

Value	Availability
`CdoFree` (0)	Available during that time slot.
`CdoTentative` (1)	At least one of the recipients has a tentative commitment during that time slot.
`CdoBusy` (2)	At least one of the recipients has a confirmed commitment during that time slot.
`CdoOutOfOffice` (3)	At least one of the recipients is out of the office during that time slot.

In the event that two recipients have different levels of commitment during a specific time slot, the higher level will be reported. If one recipient has a tentative appointment and another is out of the office, the availability will be reported as `CdOOutOfOffice`.

The Recipient Object

The **Recipient object** represents a single recipient of the Message object.

The Recipient object exposes the following properties:

Property	Description
`Address`	The full messaging address for the recipient.
`AddressEntry`	Returns the AddressEntry object representing the recipient (details on this object are covered later in this chapter).
`AmbiguousNames`	Returns a collection of possible addresses when unable to resolve the address.
`DisplayType`	Returns the recipients display type. These are explained below.
`ID`	Returns the MAPI generated unique ID for the recipient.

Table Continued on Following Page

Property	Description
`Index`	Returns the index location of the Recipient object within the Recipients collection.
`MeetingResponseStatus`	Returns/Sets the status of the recipient's response to a meeting request.
`Name`	Returns/Sets the name of the Recipient object.
`Type`	Returns/Sets the type of recipient. One of: `CdoTo`, `CdoCC`, `CdoBCC`

The possible values for the `DisplayType` parameter are:

Display Type	Description
`CdoUser` (0)	A user in the local system.
`CdoDistList` (1)	Public distribution list.
`CdoForum` (2)	Open forum, usually a newsgroup or public folder.
`CdoAgent` (3)	Automated agent.
`CdoOrganization` (4)	Representing a large group, such as TechSupport.
`CdoPrivateDistList` (5)	A private distribution list.
`CdoRemoteUser` (6)	A user in a remote system.

And the possible values for `MeetingResponseStatus` are:

ResponseStatus	Description
`CdoResponseNone` (0)	Recipient has not responded (used by Outlook).
`CdoResponseOrganized` (1)	Recipient has not responded (used by Schedule+).
`CdoResponseTentative` (2)	Recipient has tentatively accepted the request.
`CdoResponseAccepted` (3)	Recipient has firmly accepted the request.
`CdoResponseDeclined` (4)	Recipient has declined the request.
`CdoResponseNotResponded` (5)	Recipient has not responded.

The Recipient object also exposed four methods:

- `Delete`
- `GetFreeBusy`
- `IsSameAs`
- `Resolve`

The `Delete` method will immediately and permanently remove the Recipient object from the Recipients collection.

The `GetFreeBusy` method is similar to the `GetFreeBusy` method on the Recipients collection, except that it will only get the availability for the current Recipient object.

If a message has multiple recipients and you want to check for duplicates, you can use the `IsSameAs` method to see if any two (or more) of the Recipient objects represent the same address.

The `IsSameAs` method's syntax is:

```
objRecipient.IsSameAs(objRecip2)
```

Where the `objRecip2` parameter is the Recipient object against which to compare `objRecipient`. This method will only return `True` in the event that both objects represent the same *persistent* object in the messaging system. Two Recipient objects with the same values can be considered different if they don't create the same *physical* object. So, if one object is a copy of the other, then `IsSameAs` will return `False`.

Finally, the `Resolve` method on the Recipient object works in a similar way to the `Resolve` method on the Recipients collection, except that it only attempts to resolve the address for the current Recipient object.

Again, though the documentation shows an optional parameter used to specify whether a dialog is shown, when run in an ASP environment no user interface is allowed and no dialog will be displayed.

The AddressEntries Collection

The **AddressEntries collection** is a collection that contains zero or more AddressEntry objects.

The collection has these properties:

Property	Description
`Count`	Returns the count of items in the collection.
`Filter`	Sets/Returns the AddressEntryFilter object for the collection.
`Item (`*`index, or searchValue`*`)`	Returns an AddressEntry item from the collection.

The `Filter` property will be discussed later when we look at the AddressEntryFilter object. In this section, we'll focus on the other properties.

Like the Fields, Recipients, and Attachments collections, the AddressEntries collection exposes a `Count` and `Item` property. Unlike these other collections, this is considered a *large* collection, which means that the `Count` property is not as useful or valid as it is for a small collection. Thus, the most reliable way to reference an individual AddressEntry object within the collection is to use the collection's `Get` methods, or by specifying a unique identifier.

There are four Get methods provided by the collection:

- GetFirst
- GetNext
- GetPrevious
- GetLast

These methods return the first, next, previous, and last AddressEntry object in the collection respectively. For example, if we wanted to find the AddressEntry object for the user name of "Jeanie", we could look through the collection like this:

```
Dim objAddEntry
Dim colAddEntries
Dim blnFound

blnFound = False

Set objAddEntry = colAddEntries.GetFirst

While (objAddEntry Is Not Nothing) And (Not blnFound)

   If objAddEntry.Name = "Jeanie" Then
      blnFound = True
   End if

   Set objAddEntry = colAddEntries.GetNext

Wend
```

Granted, this is not the most efficient way to locate a specific AddressEntry object. Instead, if we know that the collection is sorted based on the Name property of the object, we could use the collection's Item property and specify a search string instead of an Index. The syntax of the Item property is:

```
objAddrEntriesColl.Item(searchValue)
```

where the searchValue parameter is the string value to search for. When a search string is specified in the Item property call, the collection will return the first item found which has its current sorting property value equal to (or greater than) the string value specified in searchValue. For example, if we know that the Name property is the current sorting property, this code would return the AddressEntry object for Jeanie:

```
Set objAddEntry = colAddEntries.Item("Jeanie")
```

Knowing that you're able to search for an AddressEntry item based on the current sorting property, you're probably wondering how that sorting property is set. Well, there's a Sort method on the AddressEntries collection, which allows you to specify the sorting property to use, and which sorts the collection based on that property. The syntax is:

```
colAddEntries.Sort( [SortOrder] [, PropTag] )
```

or:

```
colAddEntries.Sort( [SortOrder] [, name] )
```

The reason that there are two possible parameter lists is that you can sort either on the default MAPI Properties, or on custom MAPI Properties. When you want to sort on a default MAPI Property, use the first syntax and specify the Property tag value for the MAPI Property to be used for the sort. If you want to sort based on a custom MAPI Property, then use the second syntax and specify the name of that property for the second parameter. For either call, the first parameter specifies the sort order, and has the possible values:

Value	Description
`CdoNone` (0)	No Sort.
`CdoAscending` (1)	*Default.* Sorts in ascending order.
`CdoDescending` (2)	Sorts in descending order.

You may also notice that both of the parameters are optional, and so the following rules apply:

- In the case that both are omitted, the collection will be resorted using the same values that were used in the last call to the `Sort` method.
- If the `SortOrder` is omitted, then the collection will be sorted in ascending order.
- If neither `PropTag` nor `name` is specified, then again the collection will be resorted using the same value that was used in the last call to the `Sort` method.

For any call to the `Sort` method, the previous sort order will not be retained. The sorts are single level sorts, and can't be nested: so for example, you cannot sort by name and address at the same time. Only one property at a time may be used as the `Sort` property for the collection.

The AddressEntry Object

An **AddressEntry object** contains all of the address information required by the messaging system. In most cases, this corresponds to a person or a distribution list that a message can be delivered to.

The AddressEntry object has these properties:

Property	Description
`Address`	The full messaging address for the AddressEntry.
`DisplayType`	Returns the AddressEntry's display type. These are explained below.
`Manager`	Returns the AddressEntry object for the manager of the user that corresponds to the current AddressEntry object.
`ID`	Returns the MAPI generated unique ID for the AddressEntry.
`Members`	Returns an AddressEntries collection for all member of a distribution list. If the current AddressEntry is not a distribution list, this returns `Nothing`.
`Name`	Returns/Sets the display name of the AddressEntry object.
`Type`	Returns/Sets the address type. Examples: SMTP, X400, etc.

The AddressEntry object also exposes five methods:

- `Delete`
- `Details`
- `GetFreeBusy`
- `IsSameAs`
- `Update`

The `Delete` method will, like the other `Delete` methods, remove the current AddressEntry object from the AddressEntries collection. The `GetFreeBusy` and `IsSameAs` methods work in the same way on the AddressEntry object as they did on the Recipient object.

The `Details` method would, if not running as an ASP application, show a dialog to display the details about the current AddressEntry object. However, as we are focusing on ASP applications, we should not use this method.

The `Update` method, on the other hand, is one that we can use in our applications. This method is used to commit changes that are made to an AddressEntry object. The syntax of the method is:

```
objAddressEntry.Update( [makePermanent] [, refreshObject] )
```

Both of the parameters for the method are optional:

- The `makePermanent` parameter specifies whether to save the changes to the address book. If the changes are not saved, they will only apply to the current AddressEntries collection. When that collection is refreshed or released, then the changes will be lost.
- The `refreshObject` parameter specifies whether to reload the property cache from the address book.

So if we wanted to update every AddressEntry in the collection to append "(Wrox)" to their display name, we would use this code:

```
For Each objAddEntry In colAddEntries
  objAddEntry.Name = objAddEntry.Name & "(Wrox)"
  objAddEntry.Update(makePermanent:=True)
Next
```

The AddressEntryFilter Object

In looking at the properties for the AddressEntries collection, we noted the `Filter` property, and saw that it set or returned an **AddressEntryFilter object**. Here, we'll look at the AddressEntryFilter object and how it affects the AddressEntries collection.

The AddressEntryFilter object is used to specify the information used when filtering an AddressEntries collection. For example, it can be used to only show the AddressEntry objects that have a remote messaging address.

The object has these properties:

Property	Description
`Address`	Returns the messaging address for the AddressEntry object that is filtered.
`Fields`	Returns a Fields collection. This contains the criteria used for filtering.
`Name`	Sets/Returns the name to use for ambiguous name filtering.
`Not`	Sets/Returns whether all conditions are negated before being added to the filter.
`Or`	Sets/Returns whether conditions are to be ORed instead of ANDed .

At first glance, you may not understand how the `Not` and `Or` properties are used – we'll cover that after first looking at the function of the object.

The key to the AddressEntryFilter object is its Fields collection. It is in this collection that we specify all of the criteria to be used for filters. We can have zero or more items in the Fields collection, and each one represents a single criterion. For example, if we wanted to add a criterion so that we only have AddressEntry items where the Home address is in CA, we would do this:

```
Dim objAddEntries
Dim objAddEntriesFilter
...
Set objAddEntriesFilter = objAddEntries.Filter
objAddEntriesFilter.Fields(CdoPR_HOME_ADDRESS_STATE_OR_PROVINCE) = "CA"
```

By default, when additional conditions (Fields) are added to the filter, they are included in an `And` clause. As such, *all* of the conditions must be met by an AddressEntry object in order for that object to be in the filtered collection. In the event that you want to filter using an `Or` clause, you need to set the `Or` property on the object. For example, to filter for all AddressEntry objects that are either in "CA" or are a remote user, then we would use this code:

```
Dim objAddEntries
Dim objAddEntriesFilter
...
Set objAddEntriesFilter = objAddEntries.Filter
objAddEntriesFilter.Or = True
objAddEntriesFilter.Fields(CdoPR_HOME_ADDRESS_STATE_OR_PROVINCE) = "CA"
objAddEntriesFilter.Fields(CdoPR_DISPLAY_TYPE) = CDO_Remote_User
```

The other property that affects how the conditions are treated is the `Not` property. If we wanted to be able to find all AddressEntry objects that are not in "CA" then our code would look like this:

```
Dim objAddEntries
Dim objAddEntriesFilter
...
Set objAddEntriesFilter = objAddEntries.Filter
objAddEntriesFilter.Not = TRUE
objAddEntriesFilter.Fields(CdoPR_HOME_ADDRESS_STATE_OR_PROVINCE) = "CA"
```

As you can see, the AddressEntryFilter object gives you great control of the AddressEntries collection. You can easily add and remove filtering criteria, allowing you to narrow down the AddressEntries collection if your application requires that capability.

When working with the object, keep in mind that releasing the object (setting it to `Nothing`) will not delete the filter for the AddressEntries collection. To remove the filter from the collection, it's necessary to set the AddressEntries collection's `Filter` property to `Nothing`.

Now we've looked at the collections and objects that can have different types of parent objects. It's clear from our discussion of these objects that they are the building blocks of messaging – it would be impossible to send messages without being able to interact with the attachments, fields, recipients, and addresses for those messages. In the next section, we move on to cover some of the higher-level CDO objects, those that use these building blocks and expand on them.

The Session Object

As with the CDONTS Library, the CDO Library is rooted with the Session object. However, just as the CDONTS Session object provides more capabilities than the NewMail object, the CDO Session object provides greater functionality than the CDONTS Session object.

The CDO Session object illustrates this point very well when you see the list of properties it provides:

Property	Description
`AddressLists`	Returns AddressLists collection for the current session.
`CurrentUser`	Returns the AddressEntry object representing the current user.
`Inbox`	Returns the Folder object representing the current user's Inbox.
`InfoStores`	Returns a collection of InfoStores for the current session/user.
`Name`	Returns the User/Display name for the current session.
`OperatingSystem`	Returns info on the current operating system – Type and Version.
`Outbox`	Returns the Folder object representing the current user's Outbox.
`OutOfOffice`	Returns True/False for whether the user's status is Out Of Office.
`OutOfOfficeText`	Returns the string of text for use in an Out Of Office response message.

The method list for the CDO Session object has also grown over that for the CDONTS Session object.

The first method on the Session object that we'll use is the `Logon` method, which is similar to the `LogonSMTP` method in CDONTS. In this case, the `Logon` method will log the user into a MAPI session, and is not limited to just SMTP servers. Before there can be any access to a CDO object, there must be a successful call to the `Logon` method. Otherwise, when there's an attempt to access an object, there will be an error of `CdoE_NOT_INITIALIZED`.

The syntax of the `Logon` method is:

```
objSession.Logon( [profileName] [, profilePassword] [, showDialog] _
                  [, newSession] [, parentWindow] [, NoMail] [, ProfileInfo] )
```

Parameter	Description
`ProfileName`	Name of the profile to use for the session.
`ProfilePassword`	The password for the specified profile.
`ShowDialog`	*Ignored in ASP code.*
`NewSession`	Specifies whether a new session is to be created or to use the current shared MAPI session.
`ParentWindow`	*Ignored in ASP code.*
`NoMail`	Specified whether the session is registered with the MAPI spooler.
`ProfileInfo`	Specified server and mailbox names to be used to create a new profile for the session.

For the `newSession` parameter, if there is no current shared MAPI session then `newSession` is ignored and a new session is created. If there is a current shared session, this parameter is used to determine whether to use that current session or to create a new session. If `newSession` is `True` and a MAPI session exists, then that session will be used. If `newSession` is `False` and a MAPI session exists, then a new session will be created.

The value specified for the `NoMail` parameter determines whether messages can be sent through spooling. If the `NoMail` parameter is `True`, then messages can only be sent through a tightly coupled message store and mail transport. When the value is `False` (the default), messages can be sent and received through the mail spooler.

To create a new session connection to the server "MailServer1" and the mailbox "Jeanie", we would use this code:

```
Dim objSession
Dim strMailbox
Dim strServer
Dim strProfileString

strMailbox = "Jeanie"
strServer = "MailServer1"
strProfileString = strServer & vbLf & strMailbox

Set objSession = CreateObject("CDO.Session")
objSession.Logon ProfileInfo:=strProfileString
```

If the logon fails for any reason, the error `CdoE_LOGON_FAILED` will be generated. Once we have succeeded in calling the `Logon` method, we have access to the objects in the hierarchy under the Session object.

The `Logoff` method is used to terminate the current MAPI session. When the user logs off, this method should be called to release the resources allocated to the Session object. It is possible to create another session by reusing the same Session object. For example, if we wanted to log off Jeanie's session and have Jack logon, we would do the following:

```
Dim objSession
Dim strMailbox
Dim strServer
Dim strProfileString

strMailbox = "Jeanie"
strServer = "MailServer1"
strProfileString = strServer & vbLf & strMailbox
...
objSession.Logoff

strProfileString = strServer & vbLF & "Jack"
objSession.Logon ProfileInfo:=strProfileString
```

However, if there is an attempt to access the Session object after the `Logoff` method has been called and before successfully calling the `Logon` method, you will get an error of `CdoE_NOT_INITIALIZED`.

There is another interesting method called `SetOption`. This is used to specify options that will affect how the CDO Rendering objects will display calendar information. By using the `SetOption` method, it is possible to affect a number of display options for the calendar:

Option	Type	Possible Values
`BusinessDayEndTime`	Time	5:00 PM
`BusinessDayStartTime`	Time	9:00 AM
`CalendarStore`	String	"Outlook"
`FirstDayOfWeek`	Long	1 (Monday) to 7 (Sunday)
`Is24HourClock`	Boolean	False
`TimeZone`	Long	One of the `CDOTmz*` constants
`WorkingDays`	Long	`CDOMonday` ... `CDOFriday`

It is important to note that the session's options are not automatically transferred to the Rendering objects, nor are the options kept in sync. The application needs to take care of setting and synchronizing all option values between the Session object and the Rendering objects.

In looking at the CDONTS objects, we sent messages by calling the `Send` method. For the CDO Library, new messages are placed in the **Outbox**. It's possible that messages in the Outbox will not be sent immediately, but in the event that it's desired to send all waiting outgoing message, we can make use of the `DeliverNow` method of the Session object. Executing this method requests that the spooler immediately deliver all of the messages that have been submitted in the current session. One side effect of this method is that any messages waiting to be delivered are also processed by the spooler.

There is also an `AddressBook` method that's designed to display a modal dialog for the user to select an address from the address book. Since we're programming in ASP, and there is no user interface allowed, this method should not be used.

Folders

The `GetDefaultFolder` method of the Session object is another one that is more functional in the CDO Library than it is in the CDONTS Library. Instead of only being able to get the Inbox or Outbox, the CDO `GetDefaultFolder` method allows access to a different number of folders. The syntax of the method is:

```
Set objFolder = objSession.GetDefaultFolder(ObjectType)
```

The single parameter, `ObjectType`, has these possible values:

ObjectType	Folder
`CdoDefaultFolderCalendar` (0)	Calendar
`CdoDefaultFolderInbox` (1)	Inbox
`CdoDefaultFolderOutbox` (2)	Outbox
`CdoDefaultFolderSentItems` (3)	Sent Items
`CdoDefaultFolderDeletedItems` (4)	Deleted Items
`CdoDefaultFolderContacts` (5)	Contacts
`CdoDefaultFolderJournal` (6)	Journal
`CdoDefaultFolderNotes` (7)	Notes
`CdoDefaultFolderTasks` (8)	Tasks

It is important to note that the Contacts, Notes, Journal, and Tasks folders are only available for Microsoft Outlook.

If only Microsoft Schedule + is in use, then attempting to reference those folders will generate a `CdoE_NOT_FOUND` error. In addition, not all of the possible message stores support all of these folder types. For example if the current session profile only has a personal message store then it may not have a Notes folder, and if you attempt to specify `CdoDefaultFolderNotes` in the call to `GetDefaultFolder` then you'll get an error of `CdoE_NO_SUPPORT`.

A notable feature in CDO (which is not in CDONTS) is that the Session object has a `GetFolder` method. This method allows you to have access to any folder in the message store, as long as that Folder's ID property is known. The syntax is:

```
Set objFolder = objSession.GetFolder(folderID [, storeID] )
```

Parameter	Description
`FolderID`	Unique ID for the desired folder
`StoreID`	*Optional.* Unique ID for the message store that contains the folder.

As it's possible for a user to have multiple message stores in one session (a personal message store and a Exchange mailbox, for example), it's necessary to be able to specify the message store from which to retrieve the Folder object. If we have a page to which we can pass in a `folderID` and a `storeID`, we could get the collection of messages in that folder:

```
Dim strFolderID
Dim srtStoreID

strFolderID = Request.QueryString("FolderID")
strStoreID = Request.QueryString("StoreID")

'Code to init objSession
If strStoreID = "" Then
   objFolder = objSession.GetFolder(strFolderID)
Else
   objFolder = objSession.GetFolder(strFolderID, strStoreID)
End If

colMessages = objFolder.Messages
```

Address Lists

In addition to accessing the messages and appointments in a message store, we also need to be able to interact with addresses. There are two methods on the Session object that interact with Addresses.

The first method, `GetAddressEntry`, is used to retrieve a specific AddressEntry object. The syntax is:

```
Set objAddressEntry = objSession.GetAddressEntry(entryID)
```

This method can be useful when the `entryID` of the desired object is known. For example, if we wanted to print the display name for the AddressEntry item with an ID of 600 we would do this:

```
Dim objSession
Dim objAddEntry

Set objAddEntry = objSession.GetAddressEntry(600)
Response.Write ("Display Name: " & objAddEntry.Name")
```

The other method available for working with addresses is the `GetAddressList` method. This method allows access to the specified AddressLists, and has the following syntax:

```
Set objAddressList = objSession.GetAddressList(ObjectType)
```

The `ObjectType` parameter specifies what AddressList to return. The possible values are:

Value	Address List Returned
`CdoAddressListsGAL` (0)	The global address list.
`CdoAddressListsPAB` (1)	The personal address book for the user/session.

The Address List Object

The `GetAddressList` method will return an AddressList item, which contains a listing of all of the addresses contained within the **address book container**. An example of an address book container would be a global address book that listed all the employees of a company. An AddressList item contains both an AddressEntries collection and a Fields collection. As both of those collections have been covered earlier in this chapter, we'll not revisit them here.

The AddressList object has these properties:

Property	Description
`AddressEntries`	Returns the AddressEntries collection representing the address list.
`Fields`	Returns one or all fields related to the AddressList.
`ID`	Returns the unique ID of the AddressList object.
`Index`	Returns the index of the current AddressList within the AddressLists collection.
`IsReadOnly`	Returns whether the current AddressList can be modified.
`Name`	Returns the name of the address book container.

In addition to the properties, the AddressList object also has an `IsSameAs` method. This method can be used to determine if two AddressLists objects were created from the same address book container. The syntax is:

```
objAddressList.IsSameAs(objAddrList2)
```

To see if our current AddressList is the same as another our code would be:

```
If objAddLists.IsSameAs(objTestAddList) Then
   Response.Write "The lists are the same"
Else
   Response.Write "The lists are different"
End if
```

InfoStores

As those familiar with Exchange will know, it's possible for a user to have more than one message store. A user may have their Exchange mailbox and also have a personal message store – each of those services is considered an **information store**. The Session object has a default InfoStore, but also provides access to other InfoStore objects through its `InfoStores` property. The syntax of that property is:

```
Set objInfoStoresColl = objSession.InfoStores
Set objOneInfoStore = objSession.InfoStores(index)
Set objOneInfoStore = objSession.InfoStores(name)
```

As you can see, you can either get the collection of all InfoStores for a session, or you can specify a specific InfoStore by identifying its `index` within the collection or its `name` property. When you work with an individual InfoStore, you can interact with its Folder object just as you interact with a Folder object off the Session object.

Now that we've been through the CDO Library hierarchy, let's look at how we make use of them in our ASP pages.

Messages

Each CDO Folder object has a `Messages` property that will return a Messages collection object. This object contains zero or more AppointmentItems, MeetingItem, Message, or GroupHeader objects. The basics of the CDO Messages collection are very similar to the CDONTS Messages collection, with the addition of a `Filter` property. Access to the objects within the collection – since it's a large collection – is best done by specifying a unique identifier or using the `Get` methods that the collection provides. The collection has the following properties:

Property	Description
`Count`	Number of objects within the collection.
`Filter`	Returns the MessageFilter object for the collection.
`Item(Z)`	Returns the object at index Z from the collection. (See below)

The next section on the CDO MessageFilter object will cover the `Filter` property and its usefulness in more detail.

The Messages Collection Item Property

For access to a single message in the collection, we can use the `Item` property. This property will give us a single Message object from the collection.

The syntax is:

```
colMessages.Item(index)
```

The value for the `index` parameter can be from 1 to the size of the collection. If we wanted to get the first message in the collection, we would use the following code:

```
Dim objMessage
Set objMessage = colMessages.Item(1)
```

As the `Item` property is the default property of the `Messages` collection, the following is functionally the same:

```
Dim objMessage
Set objMessage = colMessages(1)
```

The Add Method

The collection also exposes an Add method that allows the developer to add new messages to the collection. When executed, the Add method will create a new Message object, add it to the collection, and then return a reference to that object. This allows us to add a message and then modify its content and properties without first having to locate it in the collection.

The syntax for Add is:

```
Set objMessage = colMessages.Add( [subject] [, text] [, importance] )
```

Parameter	Description
Subject	*Optional.* Subject line for the message.
Text	*Optional.* The body text for the message.
Importance	*Optional.* The importance setting for the message. Default is CdoNormal (1).

The following code would add a new message to the Outbox:

```
Set objOutbox = objSession.GetDefaultFolder(CdoDefaultFolderOutbox)
Set objNewMsg = objOutbox.Messages.Add

With objNewMsg
  .Text = "How are things going?"
  .Subject = "Status Needed"
  Set objRecip = .Recipients.Add(Name:="Jeanie", Type:=CdoTo, _
                               Address:="Jeanie@anywhere.com")
  .Send
End With
```

The Delete Method

If you can add a message to a collection, it's also useful to be able to delete a message from the collection. Your first inclination may be to call the Delete method on the Messages collection, but like we've seen elsewhere, if you do that you delete all the messages in the collection. It's important to remember that the Delete method on the Messages collection immediately removes all of the messages from the collection and the action can't be undone, so exercise care when your code involves deleting messages.

If you want to delete only a single message from a collection, you should call the Delete method on that Message object. On the other hand, if you wanted to delete all the messages in the Inbox, you would use this code:

```
Set objOutbox = objSession.GetDefaultFolder(CdoDefaultFolderInbox)
objOutbox.Messages.Delete
```

The GetFirst, GetNext, GetLast, and GetPrevious Methods

The messages collection also provides methods to allow navigating through the messages in the collection: GetFirst, GetNext, GetLast, and GetPrevious. These methods return the first, next, last, or previous message (respectively) in the Messages collection. If any of them cannot get the message, the return value is Nothing.

The order of the messages in the collection is unknown, and so the order that these methods return messages can't be predicted. When dealing with the collection of messages, the collection should be treated as being unsorted, with no assumptions being made about the ordering.

To loop through and display the subject line for all the messages in the inbox, we would use the following code:

```
Set objOutbox = objSession.GetDefaultFolder(CdoDefaultFolderInbox)
Set objMsg = objOutbox.Messages.GetFirst

While objMsg Is Not Nothing
  Response.Write "Subject : " & objMsg.Subject & "<BR>"
  Set objMsg = objOutbox.Messages.GetNext
Wend
```

The Sort Method

One method available only in the CDO Messages collection is the `Sort` method. Using this method, we are able to sort the collection of messages based on a specific property. The Messages collection's `Sort` method is similar to the AddressEntries collection's `Sort` method, though we'll cover the details again here. The sort can be ascending or descending.

The syntax of the method is:

```
objMsgColl.Sort( [SortOrder] [, PropTag] )
objMsgColl.Sort( [SortOrder] [, name] )
```

There are two possible parameter lists so that you can sort either on the default MAPI Properties or on custom MAPI Properties. For either Property set, the first parameter specifies the sort order, and has these possible values:

Value	Description
`CdoNone` (0)	No Sort.
`CdoAscending` (1)	*Default.* Sorts in ascending order.
`CdoDescending` (2)	Sorts in descending order.

Both of the parameters are optional:

- In the case that both are omitted, the collection will be resorted using the same values that were used in the last call to the `Sort` method.
- If the `SortOrder` is omitted, then the collection will be sorted in ascending order.
- If neither `PropTag` nor `name` is specified, then again the collection will be resorted using the same value that was used in the last call to the `Sort` method.

For any call to the `Sort` method, the previous sort order will not be retained. The sorts are single level sorts, and cannot be nested. In other words, you cannot sort by name and address at the same time. Only one property at a time may be used as the `Sort` property for the collection.

The CDO MessageFilter Object

In many cases, it is desirable to be able to filter a messages collection to show only specific messages. For example, we could filter a folder to only show messages from a certain person. In order to do this filtering we make use of the **MessageFilter object**. This object contains all the information used to determine which messages to include when the collection is filtered. The object has these properties:

Property	Description
`Conversation`	Sets/Returns the filter value for the `Conversation Topic` property of the messages/objects.
`Fields`	Returns the Field collection to be used in the filtering.
`Importance`	Sets/Returns the filter value for the `Importance` property of the messages/objects.
`Not`	Specified whether the filter values are negated.
`Or`	Specified whether the filter values are Or'd (True) or And'd (False).
`Recipients`	Sets/Returns the filter value for the Recipients collection of the messages/objects.
`Sender`	Sets/Returns the filter value for the `Sender` property of the messages/objects.
`Sent`	Sets/Returns the filter value for the `Send` property of the messages/objects.
`Size`	Sets/Returns the filter value for the `Size` property of the messages/objects.
`Subject`	Sets/Returns the filter value for the `Subject` property of the messages/objects.
`Text`	Sets/Returns the filter value for the text of the messages/objects.
`TimeFirst`	Sets/Returns the filter value to be messages received on or after a date/time.
`TimeLast`	Sets/Returns the filter value to be messages received on or before a date/time.
`Type`	Sets/Returns the filter value for the `Class` property of the messages/objects.
`Unread`	Sets/Returns the filter value for the `Unread` property of the messages/objects.

As an example, if we wanted to filter the Inbox to show only those messages received from "John Smith" that are `Unread` we would use this code:

```
Dim objMsgFilter
Dim colMsgs
...
Set objMsgFilter = CreateObject("MAPI.MessageFilter")
...
Set colMsgs = objInbox.Messages
Set objMsgFilter = colMsgs.Filter
objMsgFilter.Unread = True
objMsgFilter.Sender = "John Smith"
```

You will notice that there's no need to call an `Update` method on the MessageFilter object or on the Messages collection – changes made to the MessageFilter object of the Messages collection are persisted at the time they are set. The filter is not actually applied until the collection is accessed with the `Get` methods, or iterated through using a `For…Each` loop.

The CDO Message Object

This object is similar to the Message object in the CDONTS library, but with some new properties and methods, and is accessed through a Folder object's Messages collection. The Message object can represent a mail message, a document, or a form in a folder. The properties exposed by the Message object are:

Property	Description
`Attachments`	Collection of Attachment objects representing any attachments to the message.
`Categories`	Array of strings that specify which categories have been assigned to the message.
`ConversationIndex`	If the message is in a conversation thread, this specifies the index of the message within that thread.
`ConversationTopic`	If the message is in a conversation thread, this specifies the topic of the thread.
`DeliveryReceipt`	`True` if the sender has requested a delivery receipt; `False` otherwise .
`Encrypted`	`True` if the message has been encrypted; `False` otherwise.
`Fields`	Returns the collection of Fields objects for the message.
`FolderID`	Specifies the identifier of the folder in which the folder resides.
`ID`	Specifies the identifier of the current message.
`Importance`	Specifies the importance property of the message.
`ReadReceipt`	`True` if the sender has requested a read receipt; `False` otherwise.
`Recipients`	Returns the Recipients collection for the message.
`Sender`	Returns the AddressEntry object representing the message sender.
`Sensitivity`	Sets/Returns the sensitivity property for the current message. (See below for possible values.)
`Sent`	`True` if the message has been sent or posted. `False` if the message is saved.
`Signed`	`True` if the message includes a digital signature.
`Size`	Returns the size of the message, specified in bytes.
`StoreID`	Returns the unique identifier of the message store in which the message exists.
`Subject`	Sets/Returns the subject of the message.
`Submitted`	`True` if the `Send` method has been called on the message object; `False` otherwise.

Property	Description
Text	Sets/Returns the string containing the text of the message body.
TimeCreated	Contains the date and time the message was first created.
TimeExpired	Contains the date and time the message expires and is safe to delete.
TimeLastModified	Contains the date and time the message was last saved.
TimeReceived	Contains the date and time the message was received.
TimeSent	Contains the date and time the message was sent.
Type	Sets/Returns the MAPI class of the message.
Unread	True if the message has not been read; False otherwise.

The Sensitivity property can have the following values:

Value	Description
CdoNoSensitivity (0)	Unspecified sensitivity
CdoPersonal (1)	Personal
CdoPrivate (2)	Private
CdoConfidential (3)	Confidential

Just like the CDONTS Message object, the CDO Message object has Send, IsSameAs, and Delete methods. But, in the CDO Library, the Message object has some additional methods available to us.

The CopyTo and MoveTo Methods

The CopyTo and MoveTo methods are used to copy or move the message object to another folder. This can be done within the current information store, or it can be done to a different information store.

The syntax of the method is:

```
objMessage.CopyTo(folderID [, storeID] )
objMessage.MoveTo(folderID [, storeID] )
```

Parameter	Description
folderID	Unique identifier of the destination folder for the copy operation.
storeID	Unique identifier of the destination information store for the copy operation.

In order to commit the copy or move operation, the update method must also be executed. In this example, the constant FLDR_READMAIL contains the unique ID of a folder named "Read Mail" and the constant PERSONALSTORE contains the unique ID of the user's personal information store:

```
objMessage.CopyTo(FLDR_READMAIL, PERSONALSTORE)
objMessage.Update
```

The Forward, Reply, and ReplyAll Methods

The Message object includes a number of methods intended to simplify the operation of responding to, responding to all, or forwarding a message. None of the methods have any parameters in their calls, and they all return a new Message object. All of the methods will create a new copy of the message object and any of its attachments.

For the `Reply` and `ReplyAll` methods, the correct Recipients collection is also created. For the `Forward` method, the Recipients collect has no recipients and they must be added before sending the message.

The Update Method

As we've just mentioned, in order to commit any changes that have been made to a Message object, the `Update` method must be called. This method will cause the Message to be saved to the MAPI system in its current state.

The syntax of the method is:

```
objMessage.Update( [makePermanent] [, refreshObject] )
```

The `makePermanent` parameter determines whether the changes are committed to the underlying information store. A value of `True` (default) will affect the information store, while a value of `False` will not. Meanwhile, the `refreshObject` parameter determines whether the Message object's property cache is reloaded. A value of `True` will cause the cache to refresh. The default value of `refreshObject` is `False`.

Common Properties

As for the CDONTS Library, there are some properties that are common to all of the objects in the Session object hierarchy. These are:

- `Session`
- `Class`
- `Parent`
- `Application`.

The `Session` property will return a Session object. This is the Session object that is the 'root' object for the specified object, and represents the session that the specified object is operating within.

The `Class` property will return a Long value, and is used to indicate the type of the specified object. This table shows the mapping of the `Class` property value to the type of objects:

Value	Object Type
0	Session
2	Folder
3	Message
4	Recipient
5	Attachment

Value	Object Type
8	AddressEntry
16	Messages
17	Recipients
18	Attachments

The `Parent` property will return an object that represents the parent of the specified object. Note two unexpected cases:

- The value of the `Parent` property for the Session object is `Nothing`
- The Parent object for an AddressEntry object is a Message object

Lastly, the `Application` property will return a String value that is the name of the current application. When called on the object in the CDO library, it will return: `Collaboration Data Objects for NTS Version 1.2.`

Mail Client Application

To show the CDO Library at work, we'll now look at another sample ASP application. This application, `MailClient`, will provide a Web interface that is very similar to the Outlook interface. The major differences between this application and the applications in the previous chapter, is that it makes use of the CDO Library, and utilizes Exchange Server 5.5 as the back-end.

Overview

When a user logs in, they will see a listing of their folders. When they click on a folder, they will be given a listing of the messages in that folder. Clicking on a message will open that message for the user to modify. They can then reply to the message, forward the message, or delete the message.

In order to create this application we will have six ASP pages:

- `Login.asp`
- `FolderList.asp`
- `FolderContents.asp`
- `ViewMessage.asp`
- `SearchMessages.asp`
- `Logout.asp`

Additionally we will have a frameset page (`FrameSet.asp`) that provides the user interface we require.

Server Configuration

You'll notice that the `Login.asp` page only takes a server name and a mailbox name in order to login to an Exchange mailbox. If that was all that was necessary for access to a mailbox, then this would be a very insecure application. In this case, though, the application security is handled by the Exchange Server.

For each mailbox on the server, there's a Window NT User account associated with it. When an application attempts to access a mailbox, it must provide the correct authentication information in order to do so. If an attempt is made to access that mailbox with incorrect authentication information (or none at all), the access is denied.

One side effect of this security is that Web applications need to be configured to supply the correct authentication information to the Exchange Server. By default, a Web application will not provide the correct authentication information, and even authorized users will be denied Web access to their mailboxes. This is because the default setting for an ASP applications is to allow **anonymous authentication**.

To fix this, we need to go into the Properties dialog of the ASP application and set the authentication to use NT Challenge Response. To do this, open the Properties dialog for the ASP application, and click on the Directory Security tab:

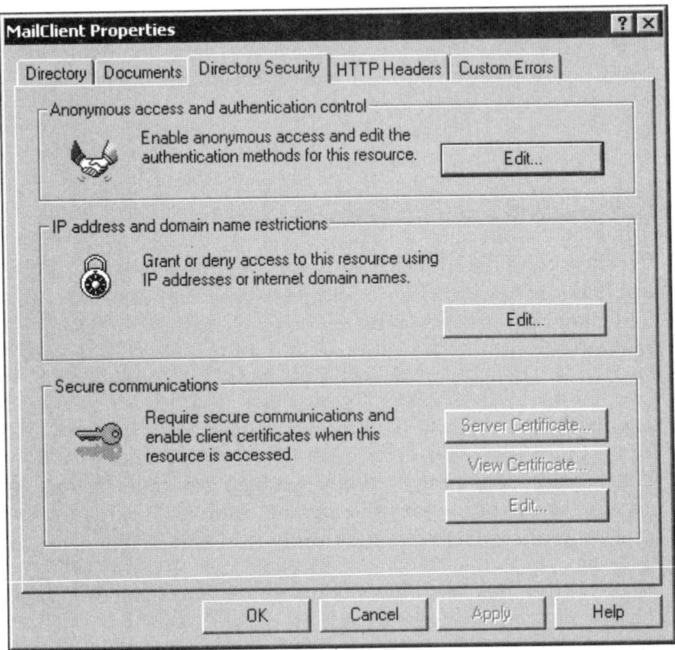

Then click on the Edit button for the Anonymous access and authentication control section. Doing so will display the Authentication Methods dialog. For our application, we need to only allow Integrated Windows authentication, so we'll uncheck the Anonymous access checkbox:

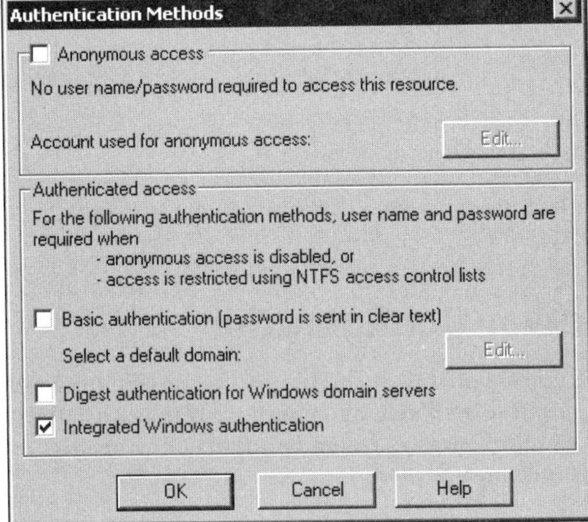

Once this is done, Netscape users may not be able to access the ASP Application, as the required authentication may not be provided.

Once the authentication is set correctly, simply click OK to the dialogs until you're back to the Internet Services Manager. The application is now configured correctly for secure interaction with the Exchange Server.

The Type Library

Before we look at any ASP, it would be a good idea to reference the CDO type library so that we can make use of the CDO constants. Place a reference to the CDO type library in either the application's `global.asa` or at the top of the `MessageList.asp`, `SendMail.asp` and `ViewMessage.asp` pages. The file is usually located at:

```
\Program Files\Common Files\System\Mapi\1033\NT\CDO.dll
```

Now that we have the application configured correctly, let's look at the pages that make up the application.

Login.asp

The first page the user will see is `Login.asp`. For this application, we'll use a `Login.asp` similar to that used for the Inbox sample application in the previous chapter. Here is the code for the page, and a screenshot of what it looks like:

```
<%@ LANGUAGE=VBScript %>
<HTML>
<TITLE>Inbox login</TITLE>
</HEAD>
<BODY>
<STRONG><FONT SIZE=5>Please Login</FONT></STRONG> :
<FORM ID=LoginFrm ACTION="FrameSet.asp" METHOD="GET">
<TABLE WIDTH="300" BORDER="0" CELLSPACING="1" CELLPADDING="1">
      <TR>
            <TD>Server Name</TD>
            <TD><INPUT TYPE="TEXT" NAME=ServerName></TD>
      </TR>
      <TR>
            <TD>Mailbox</TD>
            <TD><INPUT TYPE="TEXT" NAME=UserMailBox></TD>
      </TR>
</TABLE>

<INPUT TYPE="SUBMIT" VALUE="Login" ID=Submit1>

</FORM>
</BODY>
</HTML>
```

You'll notice that the login will request the server and mailbox name to connect to, instead of the username and password. In addition, when the form is submitted, the data will be sent to a new page called `FrameSet.asp`:

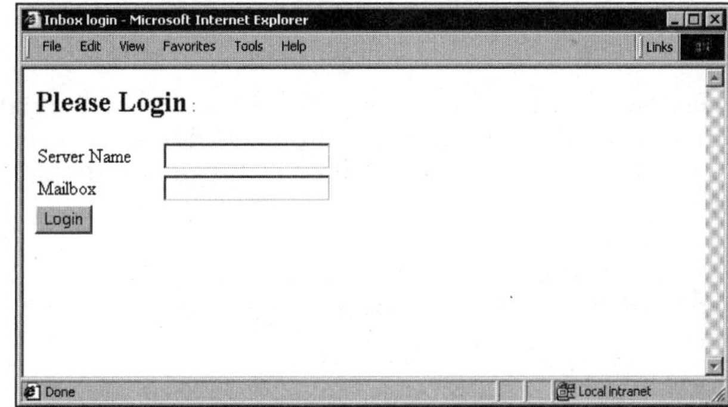

FrameSet.asp

The FrameSet.asp page creates the interface that is similar to Outlook. The key features of this page are that it has one frame to display a listing of the user's folders, and another frame that will either show the folder's contents or a message's contents. The source code for the page is:

```
<%@ LANGUAGE=VBScript %>
<% Option Explicit %>

<%
Dim objInbox
Dim colMsgs
Dim strMachineName
Dim strMailbox
Dim objCurSession

' Assign the values from the query string into local variables
' since they will be needed more than once.
strMachineName = Request.QueryString("ServerName")
strMailbox = Request.QueryString("UserMailBox")

' Use the values passed in to create a new session and
' initialize its variables.
Set objCurSession = Createobject("MAPI.Session")
objCurSession.Logon "", "", False, True, 0, True, strMachineName _
                    & vbLf & strMailbox

' Create an ASP session variable to store the current user's
' Session instance
Set Session("CurSession") = objCurSession

' Get the user's name from the session, and store it for later use.
Session("UserName") = objCurSession.CurrentUser.Name

%>

<FRAMESET ID=Inbox COLS="200, *">
   <FRAME ID="Listing" Name="Listing" SRC="FolderList.asp">
   <FRAME ID="Detail" Name="Detail" SRC="MessageList.asp">
</FRAMESET>
```

This page itself is not seen by the user – it simply creates the two frames and loads the FolderList.asp and the MessageList.asp pages into their targeted frames. FrameSet.asp does, however, execute some important ASP code.

It is in this page that the user's session is created and initialized. In the Inbox sample application, we stored the user's display name and e-mail address in Session variables. For this application, we will not need to store the values for the ServerName and Mailbox values, but we will put them in local variables for ease of access:

```
strMachineName = Request.QueryString("ServerName")
strMailbox = Request.QueryString("UserMailBox")
```

Once that's done, a new CDO Session object is created and, using the information specified on the Login page, the user is logged in to their new session. Then, that CDO Session object is stored in an ASP Session variable so that the `FolderList.asp` and `MessageList.asp` pages can access it:

```
Set objCurSession = Createobject("MAPI.Session")
objCurSession.Logon strUserName, strUserEMail
Set Session("CurSession") = objCurSession
```

It's important to notice that the session is not created with a `CDO.Session` progID, but rather with `MAPI.Session`. This is because the CDO Object Library is internally identified as "`MAPI`".

> *The reason that, when using CDONTS, we were able to use the `CDONTS.Session` progID is because the CDONTS Library is internally identified as "`CDONTS`".*

The last action that this page does is to store the `UserName` in a Session variable. Although this name is always available from the current CDO Session object, in some cases it may be useful to have quick, easy access to the `UserName` without having to first get a Session object. The following line creates the new Session variable and stores the current user's display name in that object:

```
Session("UserName") = objCurSession.CurrentUser.Name
```

The remainder of the page sets up the frameset, naming each of the frames, and then loads the folder listing page and the message listing page into their respective frames. Here is a screenshot of what the user would see in their browser upon logging in:

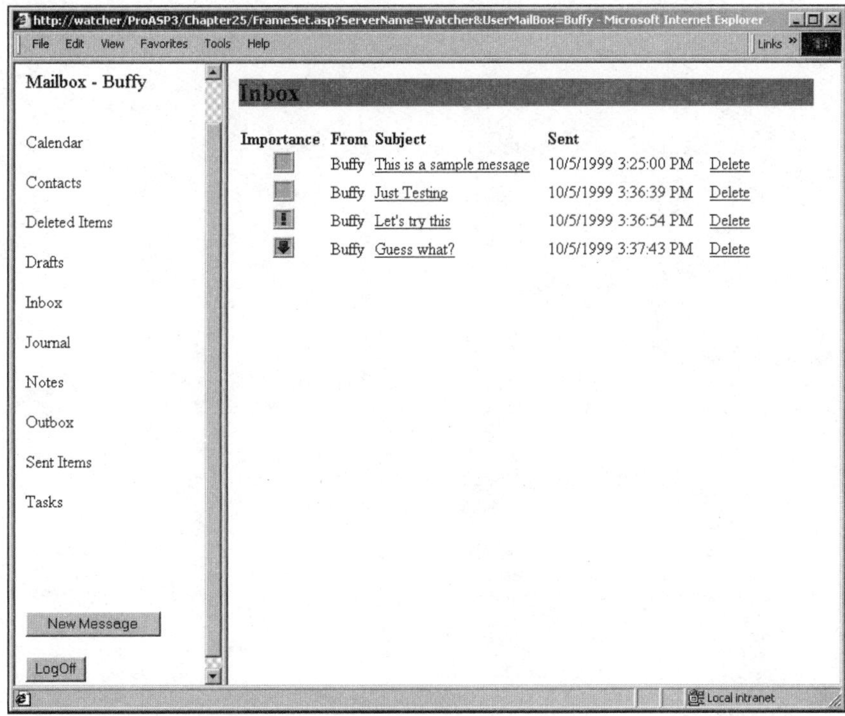

Note that the left-pane shows the folder listing (`FolderList.asp`) and the right-pane shows the contents for that folder (`MessageList.asp`). We will first look at the code behind `FolderList.asp`, and then `MessageList.asp`.

FolderList.asp

The first thing that you normally notice with a mail client is the folder hierarchy. This is normally in a tree view display (or something similar) and shows the folders that exist in the message store. For Outlook, the default folders are Inbox, Outbox, Calendar, Tasks, Journal, Notes, Sent Items, and Contacts. For our purposes, the `FolderList.asp` page will simply present the user with a list of the folders that exist in their message stores. The source code looks like this:

```
<%@ LANGUAGE=VBScript %>
<% Option Explicit %>
</HEAD>
<BODY>
<%
Dim objCurSession
Dim colFolders
Dim objFolder
Dim colStores
Dim objStore
Dim objRootFolder
Dim objInbox
Dim strFolderID

strFolderID = ""

Set objCurSession = Session("CurSession")

Set objInbox = objCurSession.Inbox

Set colStores  = objCurSession.InfoStores

For Each objStore In colStores

    If objStore.Name <> "Public Folders" Then
       Set objRootFolder = objStore.RootFolder
       Set colFolders = objRootFolder.Folders

       Response.Write "<FONT SIZE=+1>" & objStore.Name & "</FONT><BR><BR><BR>"

       For Each objFolder In colFolders
           Response.Write "<DIV STYLE=""CURSOR:HAND;COLOR:BLUE"" ID=""" & _
                          objFolder.Name & """ ONCLICK=""GoFolder()"">"
           Response.Write objFolder.Name
           Session(objFolder.Name) = objFolder.ID
           Response.Write "</DIV><BR>"
       Next
    End If

    Response.Write "<BR><BR>"

Next

%>
<BR><BR>
<INPUT TYPE=BUTTON VALUE="New Message" ID=btnNewMsg NAME=btnNewmsg>
<BR><BR>
<INPUT Type="BUTTON" VALUE="LogOff" ID=btnLogout NAME=btnLogout>
<BR>
</BODY>
</HTML>
```

```
<SCRIPT LANGUAGE=VBScript>

Sub btnLogout_OnClick()
  Window.Open "Logout.asp", "_top"
End Sub

Sub btnNewMsg_OnClick()
  Window.Open "SendMessage.asp", "Detail"
End Sub

Sub GoFolder()

  strID = Window.Event.srcElement.ID
  Window.Open "MessageList.asp?Folder=" & strID, "Detail"

End Sub

</SCRIPT>
```

As you can see, there is a certain amount of client code that is included in the page. The client code is there to allow responses to a user clicking on a folder. But before we look at the working of that code, let's first look at how the folder list is generated.

The first action to is to get the Session object and then access the collection of the user's information stores. These lines take care of that:

```
Set objCurSession = Session("CurSession")
Set colStores   = objCurSession.InfoStores
```

The first line retrieves the MAPI Session object that was stored from the `Frameset.asp` page. Then, we get the collection of information stores for that session. This will return all of the info stores for the user. These can be Public Folders, Personal Message Stores, or their Exchange Mailbox.

Once we have the collection of information stores, we look through them and list the folders contained within each InfoStore. For the Public Folders, our code is written to ignore them, as their hierarchy could be considerably large:

```
For Each objStore In colStores

    If objStore.Name <> "Public Folders" Then
       Set objRootFolder = objStore.RootFolder
       Set colFolders = objRootFolder.Folders

       Response.Write "<FONT SIZE=+1>" & objStore.Name & "</FONT><BR><BR><BR>"

       For Each objFolder In colFolders
           Response.Write "<DIV STYLE=""CURSOR:HAND;COLOR:BLUE""" & _
                          "ID=""" objFolder.Name & """ ONCLICK=""GoFolder()"">"
           Response.Write objFolder.name
           Session(objFolder.Name) = objFolder.ID
           Response.Write "</DIV><BR>"
       Next
    End If

    Response.Write "<BR><BR>"

Next
```

It's interesting to note that the code will generate `<DIV>` tags around each folder name. This is done so that we can use client side code to respond to a user clicking on a folder. The `<DIV>` tags provide the mechanism for reacting to that `click` event, and also allow us to use their `ID` property to specify the folder's name. Remember each folder has a unique ID associated with it, and when we know that ID, it is not necessary to iterate through a Folders collection in order to access that folder again. The usefulness of this will become clearer as we discuss the client code at the end of the page.

> *Unfortunately, a folder's ID is a GUID which can easily overload a query string, so in order to easily access the folder ID for a particular folder, we store the unique folder ID for each folder in a Session variable referenced by the folder's name.*

Even though the focus of this book is on ASP programming, it's not always possible (or desired) to completely avoid client-side code. In this case, the client-side code provides the substance of the user interaction. There are three functions in the client code block, and we'll look at each one individually.

The first function, `btnLogout_OnClick`, is also the simplest function. It provides the user with an easy way to log out of their mail session:

```
Sub btnLogout_OnClick()
  Window.Open "Logout.asp", "_top"
End Sub
```

When the button is clicked, the browser is directed to the `Logout.asp` page. That page will end the current MAPI Session and then redirect the browser back to the `Login.asp` page.

The next function to look at is the `btnNewMsg_OnClick` event handler. When a user wants to create a new mail message, they would click this button:

```
Sub btnNewMsg_OnClick()
  Window.Open "SendMessage.asp", "Detail"
End Sub
```

The button will then redirect the browser to the ASP page that allows the user to send a message. The `SendMessage.asp` page is detailed later in this chapter, so we'll not go into it at this point.

The last function on the page, and the most interesting one for us, is the `GoFolder` function:

```
Sub GoFolder()
  strID = Window.Event.srcElement.ID
  Window.Open "MessageList.ASP?Folder=" & strID, "Detail"
End Sub
```

This works with the `<DIV>` tags and allows us to easily select a folder and view its messages. When a user clicks on any of the Folder names, this function is called. The first line of the function will get the ID of the `<DIV>` tag that the user clicked. That ID is the name of the folder for which we want to list the messages. The second line of code in this function calls the `MessageList.asp` page and specifies the name of the folder to display. When the `MessageList.asp` page loads, it can then quickly access that Folder and display the messages within it.

Now that we see how the `FolderList.asp` page passes information to the `MessageList.asp` page, we need to look at how the `MessageList.asp` page handles that information.

MessageList.asp

Just listing the folders within a message store is not very useful to a user: they must also be able to access the messages within those folders. The `MessageList.asp` page is what provides them with that access. Here is the source code for the page:

```
<%@ LANGUAGE=VBScript %>
<% Option Explicit %>
<%
Dim strFolderID
Dim strFolderName
Dim strAction
Dim intMsgID
Dim objFolder
Dim objCurSession
Dim colMsgs

'Get the current MAPI Session object
Set objCurSession = Session("CurSession")

'Get the ID of the Folder to show the contents of
strFolderName = Request.QueryString("Folder")
strFolderID = Session(strFolderName)

' Set the action type and message ID
strAction = Request.QueryString("Action")
intMsgID = Request.QueryString("MsgID")

'If Destroy was requested make sure we are in the DeletedItems folder
' otherwise use the Inbox as the default
If strAction = "Destroy" Then
   Set objFolder = objCurSession.GetFolder(Session("Deleted Items"))
ElseIf strFolderID <> "" Then
   Set objFolder = objCurSession.GetFolder(strFolderID)
Else
   Set objFolder = objCurSession.Inbox
End If

'Get the messages within the selected folder
Set colMsgs  = objFolder.Messages

If strAction = "Delete" Then
   colMsgs(CInt(intMsgID)).MoveTo Session("Deleted Items")
ElseIf strAction = "Destroy" Then
   colMsgs(CInt(intMsgID)).Delete
End If

%>

<HTML>
<HEAD>
</HEAD>
<BODY>

<!-- Show the Title of the currently selected folder -->
<P STYLE="BACKGROUND-COLOR:GRAY">
<FONT SIZE=+2><STRONG><% =objFolder.Name %></STRONG></FONT><BR>
</P>
```

```
<%
' Then, display a listing of the messages in their inbox
' Only display the table if there are some messages to display
If (colMsgs.Count > 0) Then
%>
<TABLE BORDER=0 CELLPADDING=1 CELLSPACING=1 WIDTH=90% >

  <TR>
    <TD><STRONG>Importance</STRONG></TD>
    <TD><STRONG>From</STRONG></TD>
    <TD><STRONG>Subject</STRONG></TD>
    <TD><STRONG>Sent</STRONG></TD>
    <TD></TD>
  </TR>

<%
  Dim intLoop

  For intLoop = 1 To colMsgs.Count
%>

  <TR>
    <TD ALIGN=MIDDLE><% ShowImportanceIcon(colMsgs(intLoop).Importance) %>
    </TD>
    <TD><% =colMsgs(intLoop).Sender.Name %></TD>
    <TD><A HREF="ViewMessage.ASP?MsgID=<% =intLoop %>&Folder=
        <% =strFolderName %>"</A><% =colMsgs(intLoop).Subject %></TD>
    <TD><% =colMsgs(intLoop).TimeSent %></TD>
    <% If strFolderID = Session("Deleted Items") Then %>
      <TD><A HREF="MessageList.ASP?MsgID=<% = intLoop %>&Folder=
          <% =strFolderName %>&Action=Destroy">Destroy</A></TD>
    <% Else %>
      <TD><A HREF="MessageList.ASP?MsgID=<% = intLoop %>&Folder=
          <% =strFolderName %>&Action=Delete">Delete</A></TD>
    <% End If %>
  </TR>

<%
  Next

Else

  Response.Write "<BLOCKQUOTE>There are no items to view in this " & _
                 "folder.</BLOCKQUOTE>"

End If

%>

</BODY>
</HTML>
<%
' Function to generate the correct IMG tag for the importance icon
Sub ShowImportanceIcon(intImpValue)

  Dim strIconFile

  Select Case intImpValue
```

```
        Case CdoNormal
             strIconFile = "Norm_Importance.gif"

        Case CdoHigh
             strIconFile = "High_Importance.gif"

        Case CdoLow
             strIconFile = "Low_Importance.gif"

      End Select

      Response.Write ("<IMG SRC=.\Images\" & strIconFile & ">")

    End Sub

    %>
```

As with our other pages, the first action is to get the current MAPI Session for the user:

```
'Get the current MAPI Session object
Set objCurSession = Session("CurSession")
```

Once we have that Session object, we can then access the folders within it. On this page, we want to specifically list the contents of only one folder, the one specified in the `Folder` query string variable. First, we store the name in a local variable to make it easier to work with, and then use it to pull the folder ID out of a Session variable:

```
strFolderName = Request.QueryString("Folder")
strFolderID = Session(strFolderName)
```

Next, we determine what sort of action (if any) has been taken and set appropriate variables:

```
strAction = Request.QueryString("Action")
intMsgID = Request.QueryString("MsgID")
```

Next, we retrieve the correct Folder object. Since the logic of these pages is self-referencing, we need to makes sure we are in the correct folder when deleting objects. In addition, as it's possible that this page will be loaded with no folder specified in the query string (such as when the user first logs on), the page will default to showing the Inbox folder if no other folder is specified:

```
If strAction = "Destroy" Then
   Set objFolder = objCurSession.GetFolder(Session("Deleted Items"))
ElseIf strFolderID <> "" Then
   Set objFolder = objCurSession.GetFolder(strFolderID)
Else
   Set objFolder = objCurSession.Inbox
End If
```

Once the Folder object is obtained, the next step is to retrieve the messages that are in the folder. This is done using the Messages collection on the Folder object:

```
Set colMsgs  = objFolder.Messages
```

Next, the code checks to see if a message has been selected to be deleted or destroyed. We've made this distinction because the Delete method is irreversible – it would be better if we moved messages to the Deleted Items folder rather than destroying them immediately. Of course, when in the Deleted Items folder, we do want to get rid of them forever:

```
If strAction = "Delete" Then
   colMsgs(CInt(intMsgID)).MoveTo Session("Deleted Items")
ElseIf strAction = "Destroy"
   colMsgs(CInt(intMsgID)).Delete
End If
```

When a user clicks on the **Delete** or **Destroy** link for a message, the MessageList.asp page is reloaded with additional information specified in the query string. This code section checks for that information, and if a message has been selected to be deleted, then that specified message is deleted. The page then continues to execute, with the Messages collection having one less message in it.

At this point, all of the CDO objects contain the necessary information; next up is to generate the user's view of the folder. The first part of the interface is a title bar that indicates the current folder they are viewing:

```
<P STYLE="BACKGROUND-COLOR:GRAY">
<FONT SIZE=+2><STRONG><% =objFolder.Name %></STRONG></FONT><BR>
</P>
```

This code creates a paragraph style with a gray background to set it off from the message listing. The name of the current folder is displayed within that paragraph.

Next comes the listing of the messages that are in the folder. For this, the folder's Messages collection is used. The page first checks to see if there are any messages within the collection:

```
If (colMsgs.Count > 0) Then
```

If there are messages then it continues on to create the table that lists each message's Sender, Subject, Importance, and Time sent. Additionally, the Subject text is made into a link, allowing the user to view a message by clicking on its subject. Doing so will load the ViewMessage.asp page, specifying the ID of the message in the query string.

If there are no messages in the collection, then the page will display a message informing the user:

```
Response.Write "<BLOCKQUOTE>There are no items to view in this " & _
               "folder.</BLOCKQUOTE>"
```

The final part of the page is the ShowImportanceIcon function. Since this function was covered in the Inbox sample application, we'll not go into the details again here.

Typically, from this page the user will select a message to view. We noticed that the page generates a link pointing to ViewMessage.asp, which specifies the message ID to display. Now we will look at the ViewMessage.asp page and how it displays the selected message.

ViewMessage.asp

Any mail client must be able to display individual messages and their details to a user. The page that provides this functionality in the `MailClient` application is `ViewMessage.asp`. When a user has selected a message to view, their browser will look something like this:

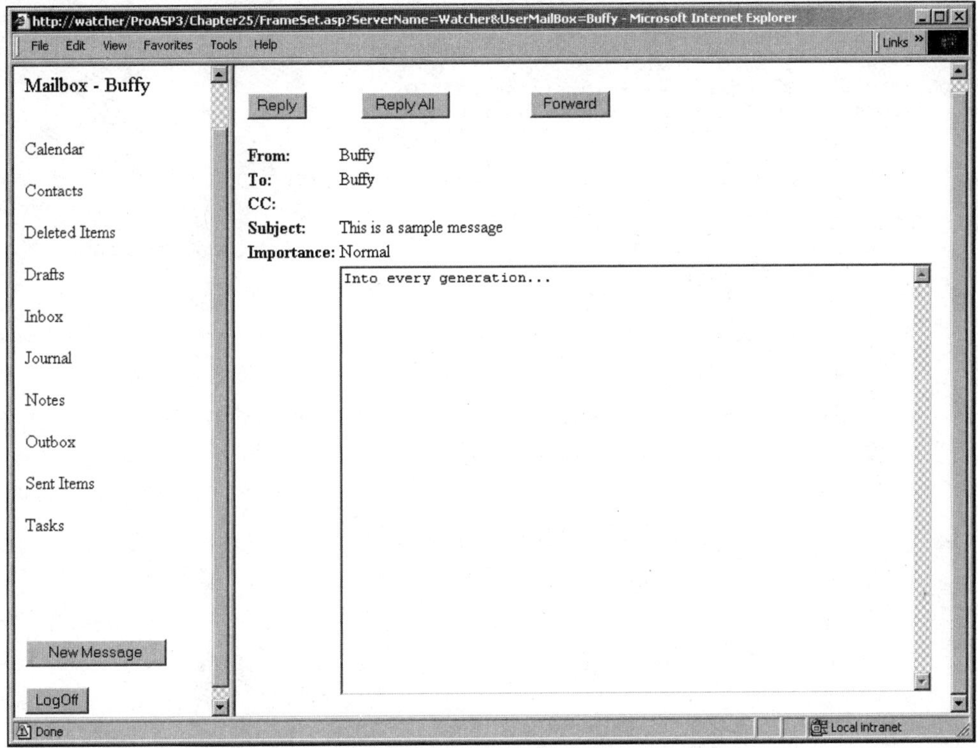

The source code for `ViewMessage.asp` is:

```
<%@ LANGUAGE=VBScript %>
<% Option Explicit %>
<HTML>
<HEAD>
</HEAD>
<BODY>
<P>
<%
Dim objMessage
Dim colRecips
Dim objRecip
Dim objFolder
Dim objSession
Dim intIndex
Dim strFolderID
Dim strFolderName
Dim strTo
Dim strCC
Dim strImportance
```

```
strTO = ""
strCC = ""

' Get the information about the message to display
strFolderName = Request.QueryString("Folder")
strFolderID = Session(strFolderName)
intIndex = CInt(Request.QueryString("MsgID"))

'Retrieve the selected message object
Set objSession = Session("CurSession")
Set objFolder = objSession.GetFolder(strFolderID)
Set objMessage = objFolder.Messages(CInt(intIndex))

'Process the recipients
Set colRecips = objMessage.Recipients

For Each objRecip In colRecips

  Select Case objRecip.Type

    Case CdoTo:
         If strTO <> "" Then
            strTo = strTo & ";" & objRecip.Name
         Else
            strTo = strTo & objRecip.Name
         End If

    Case CdoCC:
         If strCC <> "" Then
            strCC = strCC & ";" & objRecip.Name
         Else
            strCC = strCC & objRecip.Name
         End If

  End Select

Next

Select Case objMessage.Importance

  Case CdoNormal
       strImportance = "Normal"

  Case CdoHigh
       strImportance = "High"

  Case CdoLow
       strImportance = "Low"

End Select

%>

<BR>
<TABLE BORDER=0 CELLPADDING=1 CELLSPACING=1 WIDTH="400, 400, 400,*">
  <TR>
     <TD>
        <INPUT ID=btnReply NAME=btnReply TYPE=BUTTON VALUE="Reply" >
     </TD>
     <TD>
        <INPUT ID=btnReplyAll NAME=btnReplyAll TYPE=BUTTON VALUE="Reply All">
```

```
      </TD>
      <TD>
         <INPUT ID=btnForward NAME=btnForward TYPE=BUTTON VALUE="Forward">
      </TD>
   </TR>
</TABLE>
<BR>

<TABLE BORDER=0 CELLPADDING=1 CELLSPACING=1 WIDTH="75%">

   <TR>
      <TD><STRONG>From:</STRONG></TD>
      <TD><LABEL><% =objMessage.Sender %></LABEL></TD>
   </TR>
   <TR>
      <TD><STRONG>To:</STRONG></TD>
      <TD><LABEL><% =strTO %></LABEL></TD>
   </TR>
   <TR>
      <TD><STRONG>CC:</STRONG></TD>
      <TD><LABEL><% =strCC %></LABEL></TD>
   </TR>
   <TR>
      <TD><STRONG>Subject:</STRONG></TD>
      <TD><LABEL><% =objMessage.Subject %></LABEL></TD>
   </TR>
   <TR>
      <TD><STRONG>Importance:</STRONG></TD>
      <TD><LABEL><% =strImportance %></LABEL></TD>
   </TR>
   <TR>
      <TD></TD>
      <TD><TEXTAREA ID=TEXTAREA1 NAME=TEXTAREA1 STYLE="HEIGHT: 390px;
                 WIDTH: 547px"><% =objMessage.Text %>
         </TEXTAREA>
      </TD>
   </TR>
</TABLE>
</P>

</BODY>
</HTML>
<SCRIPT ID=clientEventHandlersVBS LANGUAGE=VBScript>

Sub btnReply_onclick()
  Window.Open "SendMessage.ASP?Action=Reply&MsgID=<% =intIndex %>", _
              "Detail"
End Sub

Sub btnReplyAll_onclick()
  Window.Open "SendMessage.ASP?Action=ReplyAll&MsgID=<% =intIndex %>", _
              "Detail"
End Sub

Sub btnForward_onclick()
  Window.Open "SendMessage.ASP?Action=Forward&MsgID=<% =intIndex %>", _
              "Detail"
End Sub

</SCRIPT>
```

There are two pieces of information necessary to be able to view a message: the Folder it resides in, and its position in that folder's Messages collection. Both of these details are provided in the query string, and this code retrieves it:

```
strFolderName = Request.QueryString("Folder")
strFolderID = Session(strFolderName)
intIndex = CInt(Request.QueryString("MsgID"))
```

Once that information is known, the next step is to get the collection of messages for the specified folder. First, we need to get the current MAPI Session object, and then use its `GetFolder` method to access the desired folder. Lastly, the Message object representing the desired Message is retrieved from the folder's Messages collection:

```
Set objSession = Session("CurSession")
Set objFolder = objSession.GetFolder(strFolderID)
Set objMessage = objFolder.Messages(CInt(intIndex))
```

In CDONTS, the Message object had properties for the To, CC, and BCC recipients. In CDO, all of the message's recipients are grouped into the Recipients collection. In order to generate the list of To, CC, and BCC recipients for a message, it is necessary to iterate through the Recipients collection. This code handles the generation of strings to display the To and CC recipients:

```
Set colRecips = objMessage.Recipients

For Each objRecip In colRecips

  Select Case objRecip.Type

    Case CdoTo:
         If strTO <> "" Then
            strTo = strTo & ";" & objRecip.Name
         Else
            strTo = strTo & objRecip.Name
         End If

    Case CdoCC:
         If strCC <> "" Then
            strCC = strCC & ";" & objRecip.Name
         Else
            strCC = strCC & objRecip.Name
         End If

  End Select

Next
```

For each of the Recipient objects in the collection, its `Type` property is used to determine if it is a To or a CC recipient. Recipients of type `CdoTo` have their name appended to the `strTo` string, while Recipients of type `CdoCC` have their name appended to the `strCC` string.

When all of the necessary information has been processed, the HTML is then generated. Reply, Reply All, and Forward buttons are displayed. Then, the message details and body are displayed in an HTML table.

The last code section on the page is client-side code that handles the user clicking the Reply, Reply All, or Forward buttons. This code will call the `SendMessage.asp` page, specifying the necessary information about the message and the action to be taken with the message.

SendMessage.asp

Contrary to its name, the `SendMessage.asp` page is able to do more that just send a message. The page will also handle replying to a message and forwarding a message. For example, if we had clicked the **Reply** button in the previous sample page, we would have seen this:

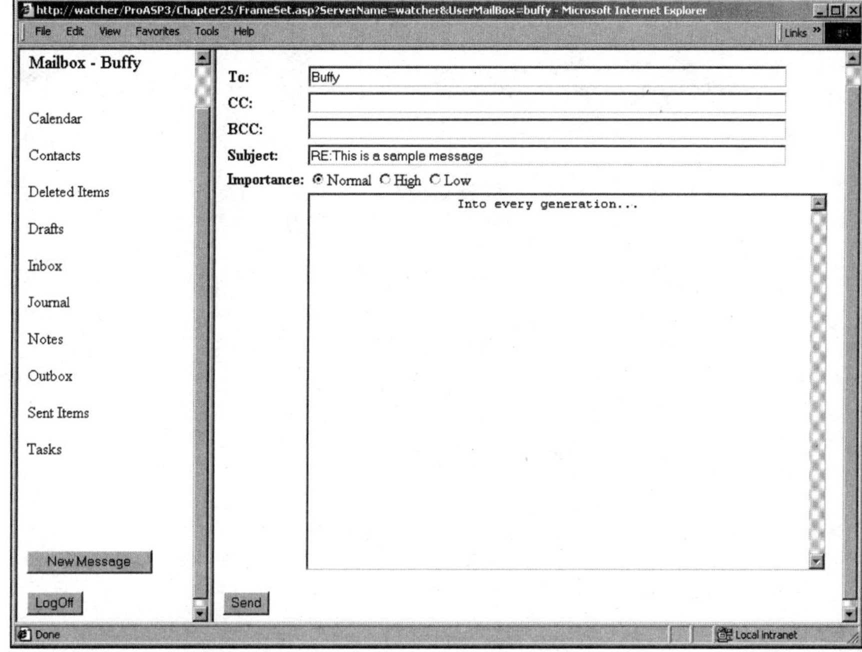

You will notice that the **To** field has been filled in with the sender of the message and that the subject has been prefixed with "**RE:**". All of the code for handling this is in the `SendMessage.asp` page. The source code is:

```
<%@ LANGUAGE=VBScript %>
<% Option Explicit %>
<HTML>
<HEAD>
</HEAD>
<BODY>
<P>
<%
Dim strAction
Dim colMsgs
Dim colRecips
Dim objRecip
Dim objCurMessage
Dim objSession
Dim intIndex
Dim strTo
Dim strCC
Dim strToList
Dim strCCList
Dim strSubject
Dim strBody
Dim strImportance
```

```
strTo=""
strCC=""
strSubject=""
strBody=""

strAction = Request.QueryString("Action")

If (strAction="Reply") or (strAction="ReplyAll") Or (strAction="Forward") Then

   Set objSession = Session("CurSession")
   Set colMsgs = objSession.Inbox.Messages

   intIndex = Request.QueryString("MsgID")

   Set objCurMessage = colMsgs(CInt(intIndex))
   Set colRecips = objCurMessage.Recipients

   For Each objRecip In colRecips

      Select Case objRecip.Type

         Case CdoTo:
              If strTo <> "" Then
                 strToList = strToList & ";" & objRecip.Name
              Else
                 strToList = strToList & objRecip.Name
              End If

         Case CdoCC:
              If strCC <> "" Then
                 strCCList = strCCList & ";" & objRecip.Name
              Else
                 strCCList = strCCList & objRecip.Name
              End If

      End Select

   Next

   strSubject = objCurMessage.Subject
   strBody = objCurMessage.Text

   Select Case strAction

      Case "Reply"
           strTo = objCurMessage.Sender.Name
           strSubject = "RE:" & strSubject

      Case "ReplyAll"
           strTo = strToList & ";" & objCurMessage.Sender.Name
           strCC = strCCList
           strSubject = "RE:" & strSubject
```

```
      Case "Forward"
           strTo = ""
           strCC = ""
           strSubject = "FW:" & strSubject

     End Select

End If

%>

<BR>
<FORM ID=SendMail ACTION="SendMail.asp" METHOD="GET">
<TABLE BORDER=0 CELLPADDING=1 CELLSPACING=1 WIDTH="75%">
  <INPUT TYPE=HIDDEN NAME=Action ID=Action VALUE="<% =strAction %>">
  <TR>
     <TD><STRONG>To:</STRONG></TD>
     <TD><INPUT TYPE=TEXT NAME=SendTo ID=SendTo SIZE=80 VALUE="<% =strTO %>">
     </TD>
  </TR>
  <TR>
     <TD><STRONG>CC:</STRONG></TD>
     <TD><INPUT TYPE=TEXT Name=SendCC ID=SendCC SIZE=80 VALUE="<% =strCC %>">
     </TD>
  </TR>
  <TR>
     <TD><STRONG>BCC:</STRONG></TD>
     <TD><INPUT TYPE=TEXT NAME=SendBCC ID=SendBCC SIZE=80 VALUE=""></TD>
  </TR>
  <TR>
     <TD><STRONG>Subject:</STRONG></TD>
     <TD><INPUT TYPE=TEXT NAME=Subject ID=Subject SIZE=80 VALUE="
         <% =strSubject %>">
     </TD>
  </TR>
  <TR>
     <TD><STRONG>Importance:</STRONG></TD>
     <TD><INPUT TYPE="RADIO" NAME=Importance VALUE="Normal" CHECKED>Normal
     <TD><INPUT TYPE="RADIO" NAME=Importance VALUE="High">High
     <TD><INPUT TYPE="RADIO" NAME=Importance VALUE="Low">Low</TD>
  </TR>
  <TR>
     <TD></TD>
     <TD> <TEXTAREA ID=BODY NAME=BODY STYLE="HEIGHT: 390px; WIDTH: 547px">
                    <% =strBody %>
          </TEXTAREA>
     </TD>
  </TR>
</TABLE>
</P>

<INPUT TYPE="SUBMIT" VALUE="Send" ID=btnSubmit NAME=btnSubmit>

</FORM>
</BODY>
</HTML>
```

Since this page is capable of handing new messages, replies, and forwards, the first step on the page is to determine which of these actions is to be performed. The action for the page to execute is passed in the query string variable `Action`:

```
strAction = Request.QueryString("Action")
```

For the simplest case of composing a new message, there's no processing for the page to do. However, for the Reply and Forward cases, there is some work needed in order to fill in the appropriate field values. For replies or forwards, the mail client will typically fill in the `To`, `CC`, `Subject`, and `Body` fields. This section of code will generate the appropriate values for the `To` and `CC` fields, based on the action (Forward, Reply, ReplyAll) to be taken. The section of code that retrieves the Message object and parses its Recipients collection is the same as for the `ViewMessage.asp` page. The code that is new to this page is:

```
strSubject = objCurMessage.Subject
strBody = objCurMessage.Text

Select Case strAction

   Case "Reply"
        strTo = objCurMessage.Sender.Name
        strSubject = "RE:" & strSubject

   Case "ReplyAll"
        strTo = strToList & ";" & objCurMessage.Sender.Name
        strCC = strCCList
        strSubject = "RE:" & strSubject

   Case "Forward"
        strTo = ""
        strCC = ""
        strSubject = "FW:" & strSubject

  End Select
```

Regardless of the action type, the message's body will not change. The To and CC lists are dependent on the action though, and this code section sets those to the correct values. Also, the correct prefix is added to the subject.

At this point, you might wonder why the `Forward`, `Reply`, or `ReplyAll` methods of the Message object were not used. Although those methods are very useful, and they do create the correct To and CC recipients, they do not provide a great benefit if you want to allow the user to edit the lists. The problem is that in order to display that information (and make it editable by the user) we would still have to parse through the Recipients collection and generate the To and CC lists. If the task was to Forward a message without any edits, then the Message object's methods would be a much better way to complete the task. In our case though, the methods did not provide any benefit.

The remainder of the page looks like the `ViewMessage.asp` page, except that the generated HTML has editable controls and is enclosed within a `<FORM>` tag. The editable input controls allow the user to modify the message before sending it. The `<FORM>` tag is used to submit all of the message information to the `SendMail.asp` page, which does the actual sending of the message.

SendMail.ASP

This page has no user interface at all. Its only purpose is to create a valid message using the information passed in, and then send that message. The source code is:

```
<%@ LANGUAGE=VBScript %>
<% Option Explicit %>
```

```
<%
Dim strToList
Dim strCCList
Dim strBCCList
Dim strSubject
Dim strBody
Dim intPos
Dim strToEntry
Dim strCCEntry
Dim strBCCEntry
Dim objCurSession
Dim objNewMessage
Dim objRecip
Dim strImportance

'Get the Required information from the QueryString
strToList = Request.QueryString("SendTO")
strCCList = Request.QueryString("SendCC")
strBCCList = Request.QueryString("SendBCC")
strSubject = Request.QueryString("Subject")
strBody = Request.QueryString("Body")
strImportance = Request.QueryString("Importance")

'First, create the new message object
Set objCurSession = Session("CurSession")
Set objNewMessage = objCurSession.Outbox.Messages.Add

objNewMessage.Subject = strSubject
objNewMessage.Text = strBody
objNewMessage.Update

'Process the To list
While strToList <> ""

  intPos = Instr(strToList, ";")
  If intPos <> 0 Then
     strToEntry = Left(strToList, intPos - 1)
     strToList = Mid(strToList, intPos + 1)
  Else
     strToEntry = strToList
     strToList = ""
  End If

  Set objRecip = objNewMessage.Recipients.Add
  objRecip.Name = strToEntry
  objRecip.Type = CdoTO
  objRecip.Resolve
  objNewMessage.Update

Wend

'Process the CC list
While strCCList <> ""
```

```
    intPos = Instr(strCCList, ";")
    If intPos <> 0 Then
       strCCEntry = Left(strCCList, intPos - 1)
       strCCList = Mid(strCCList, intPos + 1)
    Else
       strCCEntry = strCCList
       strCCList = ""
    End If

    Set objRecip = objNewMessage.Recipients.Add
    objRecip.Name = strCCEntry
    objRecip.Type = CdoCC
    objRecip.Resolve
    objNewMessage.Update

  Wend

  'Process the BCC List
  While strBCCList <> ""

    intPos = Instr(strBCCList, ";")
    If intPos <> 0 Then
       strBCCEntry = Left(strBCCList, intPos - 1)
       strBCCList = Mid(strBCCList, intPos + 1)
    Else
       strBCCentry = strBCCList
       strBCCList = ""
    End If

    Set objRecip = objNewMessage.Recipients.Add
    objRecip.Name = strBCCEntry
    objRecip.Type = CdoBCC
    objRecip.Resolve
    objNewMessage.Update

  Wend

  ' Set the importance
  Select Case strImportance

    Case "High"
         objNewMessage.Importance = CdoHigh

    Case "Low"
         objNewMessage.Importance = CdoLow

  End Select

  ' All the fields have been set, so send the message
  objNewMessage.Send

  'Then send the user back to their inbox
  Response.Redirect "MessageList.asp?Folder=Inbox"

  %>
```

All of the details for the message are specified in the query string, and the first action of the page is to retrieve those values:

```
strToList = Request.QueryString("SendTO")
strCCList = Request.QueryString("SendCC")
strBCCList = Request.QueryString("SendBCC")
strSubject = Request.QueryString("Subject")
strBody = Request.QueryString("Body")
strImportance = Request.QueryString("Importance")
```

Then, a new Message object is added to the Outbox. Since the `Subject` and `Body` properties don't need any processing, those properties are set using the values from the query string:

```
Set objCurSession = Session("CurSession")
Set objNewMessage = objCurSession.Outbox.Messages.Add

objNewMessage.Subject = strSubject
objNewMessage.Text = strBody
```

The To, CC and BCC recipients for a message do require some processing. As there's little difference, other than the recipient type, in each of the processing loops, we'll only look at the processing of the To recipients:

```
While strToList <> ""

  intPos = Instr(strToList, ";")
  If intPos <> 0 Then
     strToEntry = Left(strToList, intPos - 1)
     strToList = Mid(strToList, intPos + 1)
  Else
     strToEntry = strToList
     strToList = ""
  End If

  Set objRecip = objNewMessage.Recipients.Add
  objRecip.Name = strToEntry
  objRecip.Type = CdoTO
  objRecip.Resolve
  objNewMessage.Update

Wend
```

Each time through the loop a recipients display name will be retrieved from the list of recipients. For each display name, a new Recipient object is added to the message. Once the display `Name` and `Type` property are set on that new Recipient object, the `Resolve` method is called to get the full messaging address, then the message is updated with the new recipient. This code is the same for the To, CC, and BCC recipient lists, only differing in the `Type` property of the Recipient object.

Once all of the recipient lists have been processed, and the message's importance has been set, the last thing to do is to send the message. This is done by calling the `Send` method on the Message object:

```
objNewMessage.Send
```

Since this page has no user interface, the user is then sent back to the `MessageList.asp` page.

Logout.asp

Before we finish, we need to take a quick look at `Logout.asp`. All this page does is call the `Logoff` method of the Session object, and then load the Login page:

```
<%@ Language=VBScript %>
<HTML>
<TITLE>Inbox login</TITLE>
</HEAD>
<BODY>
<%
Dim objCurSession
Set objCurSession = Session("CurSession")

objCurSession.Logoff

Response.Redirect "Login.asp"
%>
</FORM>
</BODY>
</HTML>
```

That completes the `MailClient` application as far as we're concerned for now. There's plenty of opportunity to expand on it, by adding support for different folder type and advanced mail options.

Summary

CDO and CDONTS are both still evolving. In version 1.2, CDO has added some important HTML rendering functionality, although the possible formats that the objects generate are not extensive and cannot match the views that Outlook provides. Also, there are certain Outlook/Exchange features that are not yet included in CDO version 1.2. CDO does not provide an object for ContactItem, JournalItem, or a TaskItem. When these objects are implemented and included in CDO, it will be more suitable for creating a full application as a replacement or alternative to Outlook.

However, as you can see from going through the `MailClient` Web application, the CDO objects provide a much more granular approach to messaging. This can make the programming a little more involved than with CDONTS, but in exchange for a more a complex programming model, you gain greater control over the messaging system.

In conclusion, for a Web page that is concerned with very simple messaging and only wants to be able to send mail from an ASP application, CDONTS is the clear choice. For any ASP application that may be designed for or evolve into something more, CDO and Exchange 5.5 is definitely worth investigating.

N
W

24

Securing Your Server

So now you've built your Web applications, deployed them and are sitting back in your chair with a cup of tea and a biscuit. But have you thought of everything? What happens if the next day, some mischievous hacker mails everyone in the company with their private information having pulled it off your just-built intranet? You need to prevent these cases, not cure them.

In reality, the security of code and information over an intranet or the Internet is a priority that any Web developer should be able to offer clients or co-workers. With automated hacking tools widely available on the Internet, it's not uncommon for unskilled hackers to breach the security of a Web site. It's not really in your interest to figure out why you might get targeted by hackers, but by putting up some defense, you can at least go home at night and sleep.

However, while security set-up may be the developer's responsibility on a small-scale site, most likely it will be the joint responsibility of both developer and system administrator and both are encouraged to read this chapter thoroughly. It is crucial that both work together to achieve the highest level of security possible on their system for both employees and online customers. By working through all the aspects of your server one by one – operating system, disk access, Internet protocols, firewalls, etc – you can be pretty sure that you have a safe and secure machine.

In this chapter we will be looking at the following:

- What is security?
- Security Policies
- Securing Windows 2000
- Firewalls and proxy servers

- Securing IIS 5.0
- SQL Server 7.0 and OBJCONNC security
- ASP Application security

Note that a general administrative knowledge of Windows 2000 and its security concepts are anticipated for understanding of this chapter.

What is Security?

Among the many definitions of computer security, perhaps best is the one that describes it as the measures adopted to guard against attack, theft or unauthorized disclosure. We live in a world where DOS now stands for Disk Operating System less frequently than it does for a *denial of service* attack in which persons unknown would render a system unusable or unable to perform its primary function. Such attacks could crash an ISP or even a state-wide service area.

Such an attack may never be aimed at you. More likely, someone will try and steal – sorry, *borrow* – something from your system. Files and computer resources are all fair game, but most attackers break into servers and networks for their high-speed Internet connections, utilizing them for more barbed attacks against other networks and systems on the Internet. Why is something only the borrower will know for sure, but mostly it occurs either out of revenge against other companies or to see whether or not they can.

Within the ASP applications arena, it's the unauthorized disclosure of passwords and sensitive information that is most important to guard against, be it through the use of SSL (Secure Sockets Layer), another type of encryption or some other means. And, again, it boils down to the fact that the information is there to be pried from us is enough reason for some people to try that we need to protect our sites. Where confidential information like credit card numbers are concerned, for example on an e-commerce site, there is, of course, also the possibility of a free lunch, free stereo, holiday to the Bahamas....

Problems on the Internet with Security

There are many problems on the Internet with security, ranging from intercepting base-level packet data all the way through to accessing systems using bad passwords that are easily guessed. Even though the threat from such activity seems overwhelming, there are answers and methods that can be taken to prevent the implementation of poorly designed network security structures. AdministratrsUsers must take the extra initiative and research the Internet security features that apply specifically to their products. If precautionary steps are taken, we can have secure systems on the Internet.

One of the best ways to test your ASP Web site's security measures is to try and break into it yourself while it's still on the development server and hasn't gone live yet. Test your Web servers against denial of service attacks and test also the integrity of access level control that has been set up. You would also do well to keep up to date with those sites which detail the latest hacking tools and automated attacks. For example:

- `http://www.rootshell.com`
- `http://www.hackers.com`
- `http://www.dark-secrets.com`

Malicious Attacks/Vandalism

We've already mentioned denial of service attacks, but not online vandalism, something of an up and coming trend in recent months. The modus operandi is fairly standard – attackers will steal passwords or find some other method to get into your system and then deface your Web sites. Happily, it doesn't usually take very long to erase the 'online graffiti' and change your passwords to prevent an instant re-occurrence but the main thing is to keep your passwords under control. We'll be looking at implementing password policies on your system in the next section.

Vandals can also get into your system through FTP and telnet clients, so don't enable either service unless it is a total must. Windows 2000 users need only worry about FTP as it does not support telnet or remote console access at all unless you are using third party software. Also, if your production servers are in-house and not co-located then take the extra bit of effort to use a CD-ROM or other form of media to perform your Web site upgrades and changes. The extra effort is definitely worth it in the long run.

Impersonation\IP Spoofing

One of the biggest problems on the Internet to date is impersonation – a ploy where attackers disguise themselves as someone else, usually with access to your system. This can be a fair problem for those servers using IP-based and/or user authentication.

We'll look at the second of these later, so let's investigate the Internet Protocol - one half of TCP/IP – now. There are four layers to IP:

Layers	Description
Source Host	The machine the packet (unit of data) came from
Source Port	The port the packet came from
Destination Host	The destination of the packet
Destination Port	The destination port of the packet

The most important layer to look at when talking about impersonation is the *source host*, which defines where our pieces of information – better known as *packets* – have come from. If you can fake the source host for your packets, you can make a machine believe that they came from somewhere they did not, a technique known as **IP spoofing**. Attackers can and will use this method to fake the source host of their packets as being, or *impersonate*, a trusted machine on your network. Indeed, most denial of service attacks use this method to cover their origins.

As you can appreciate, a situation in which you cannot totally trust your own network is not a good one, but IP itself is not really to blame. It does not have much in the way of bounds checking because its sole purpose is just to provide the four layers so routers know where to send the packet.

One anti-impersonation tactic is to use a firewall to check if packets could actually have come from where they state their source host to be. Firewalls aren't infallible against IP spoofs though, but a good rule of thumb to help them out is to configure your router to drop any incoming packets that claim to be from your network. Dropping any outgoing packets which claim not to be from your network will also defend against any of your own employees attacking other networks.

Don't Become an Attacker

IP spoofing and impersonation can put your own servers at risk but it also means that your machines could become unwitting stooges in attacks on other hosts. This ruse is fairly sophisticated but the logic behind it is very simple. The single premise for this attack is that the target server can appear to be using broadcast ICMP Echo Requests, which call upon every machine on a network to ping a certain host. If an attacker can impersonate a host and send these Echo Requests to, say, both your network and another network elsewhere, then every machine on both networks will ping the impersonated host even though it did not actually request them. So, if you have 10 servers, and so does the other network, the targeted host will receive 20 uncalled-for ping packets. By repeating large sized packet broadcast ICMP Echo Requests over and over again to unwitting networks, attackers can flood and ultimately cause their targets to disconnect.

This is a denial of service attack that your network just aided in. The way around this is to make sure that your routers and machine do not respond to broadcast ICMP Echo Request, thus preventing your network's unwitting assistance in attacking other machines.

Security Policies

One thing system/network administrators should always do is keep and maintain an up-to-date security policy – an essential ingredient to keeping a user community. It's realizing that the majority of the time that the most dangerous person on your network is not one who knows what to do, but one who doesn't. Most users simply don't realize that exchanging passwords and other information they may not think sensitive could create potentially dangerous security leaks in the system and therefore the company itself.

By creating a security policy, administrators can police not only their users but themselves as well. Their users will be informed of their responsibilities to the system and the potential problems they could create if they don't adhere to the policy. Likewise, the policy should set out rules of conduct for the administrators too for them to keep. The day may come when they have to answer to someone at the company about the security details of the systems running currently.

Security policies must be set in place and enforced by the writers of the policy itself. Most policies that are written have a course of action to follow if a user fails to comply with the rules and regulations of the policy. These rules must be strictly enforced.

Anatomy of a Security Policy

When you get down to creating a policy, you'll soon realize that much more goes into a security policy than most people would expect. It's more of a specification for the entire system, covering such issues as a backup strategy, system access, maintenance, software versions, operating system versions, and log file checking.

To make it slightly easier to take in, you can split a policy into three sections:

- User requirements
- Managerial responsibilities
- Administrator's responsibilities

We'll look at each section in turn.

User Requirements

It's not a pleasant time for an administrator when a new security policy is being put in place across a system. If you err on the side of strictness, you could become Mr. Unpopular with all the users very quickly. On the other hand, if you err on the lax side of things, you've not got a policy worth the paper it's written on. The goal is to look into how you can make an effective security policy while still keeping a positive rapport with the user community.

Some of the things you need to ask yourselves are:

- Which systems do users need access to?
- What type of access will each user need? Full read/write access or the least access possible? How about people on the Internet who use the system as the anonymous user?
- What time will users to access these systems? Most security breaches take place out-of-hours so putting in restrictions based on the time of day would seem good sense.
- Do users require username and password authentication? If so, some rules on choosing passwords would be in order alongside the rules not to divulge them to anyone else or write them down in plain sight. Make plans for dial-up users accessing the system from home via modem or ISDN.
- Will users require IP-based authentication? Identifying users by their machine's IP address as well as their username and password could create an extra level of security for those areas of the system needing it.
- Do these particular users fit into a logical grouping? For example, those users in accounts needing access to finance records, those in sales needing a certain level of product info and those in supply logistics needing another type of product info.
- Will certain areas of the system that users visit require a certain level of encryption? It's not necessary to secure book information on `amazon.com`, but it's very necessary to offer an encrypted area where people can fill in their credit card information.
- Is the security model handled on an application level? At development time, it can be useful for all users, even the anonymous one, to have full read/write access to the system. Before it goes live however, this potential security hole should be addressed.

All of this information is pertinent when dealing with security. Where possible, you should try and answer each of these questions on every level. Obviously, you can't hope to answer some of them when yours is a Web-based application open to users on the Internet, but you should be able to make fairly educated guesstimates.

Managerial Responsibilities

By explaining to them what security measures are to be put in place and the security risks that can arise if they are not followed, you can place some of the responsibility for the network on the managers in your organization. There are several good reasons to do this:

- They can act as a blanket between administrators, users, and developers to alleviate the tension that can arise when implementing a security policy that everyone must follow.
- By teaching them in layman's terms what rules need to be put in place, managers can efficiently disseminate that information to the rest of the organization.
- They can and should put stipulations in place as to what will be done if rules are not followed.

Don't be remiss in discussing any and all issues with the management and pursue the fact that you must have total support with the rules and regulations you set forth for the user community.

Administrator Responsibilities

A policy would be no use if it didn't police the police and so the system administrators must also have rules, or, at the very least, procedures set out for them, including:

- What action to take if a break in occurs.
- What action to take if users violate the policy.
- How to set up new user accounts, new user group policies, file and directory permissions, etc.
- Backup strategy. What kind of backup media to use. When and what kind (full or incremental) of backup to perform. Where to store the backups and an emergency recovery plan should all go wrong.
- Hardware maintenance. How up-to-date should your servers be? When to upgrade them and what to upgrade? Bios? Network card? Other pieces of hardware?
- Software versions: if a new version, service pack, update or fix becomes available from the vendor, the administrator should be aware of it and make a reasoned decision whether or not to install it. A record should be kept of what has been installed on the servers.
- Operating system versions. As with software, any new version, upgrade or patch to the operating system needs to be rigorously tested on an isolated machine before it's applied to the live servers. The only difference is that all changes to the operating system should be even tested even harder first.
- Log files should be checked on a daily basis to see that users are doing what they're supposed to be doing. If not, action should then be taken.

Securing Windows 2000

In this section, we'll be looking at ways that we can secure our operating system to ensure that the most common attacks will not be able to affect us. We'll also take a look at a few things specifically aimed at private networks that don't apply in an Internet situation. In particular, we'll be looking at:

- Hard disk formats
- Creating Access Control Lists (ACLs)
- Subsystem removals
- Removing unneeded network services
- Restricting network access
- TCP/IP filtering

All of these things will come into play when determining how robust your network actually is. Thus the goal of this section is to build a checklist for securing our Internet sites to ensure that every precaution bar switching the machine off has been taken to prevent network security breaches.

Disk Formats

There are three different types of file system formats for disk partitions in Windows 2000 – FAT, FAT32, and NTFS – each of which has a different level of compatibility with Microsoft OSs and support for security. For the most secure site, you should immediately skip this section and choose to use the latest version of NTFS that Windows 2000 supports (NTFS 5). This has support for the following security features that FAT and FAT32 do not:

- **Access Control Lists** for objects, directories and files. ACLs contain zero or more access control entries each of which details a user's access rights to the object or file in question.
- **Disk Quotas**. Administrators can monitor and limit the amount of disk space any given user can consume. Taken another step, they can therefore prevent a server's hard drive from ever totally filling up.
- **Encrypted Files**. Taking paranoia one step further, NTFS can encrypt sensitive files and information when saved to disk.

As you can see, the NTFS files system is a much better choice when looking to set up secure Internet Web servers. Should, however, you be worried about a multi-Windows OS network or the cost of upgrading, you might do well to read on and make your own decision on how your to set your system up.

Cross-OS Compatibility

Not every version of Windows can read files saved to every type of file system, although network shares can get around this problem:

- Windows 2000 supports NTFS 5, NTFS 4, FAT32 and FAT
- Windows NT4 supports NTFS 4 and FAT
- Windows 98 supports FAT32 and FAT
- Windows 95, DOS and OS/2 support FAT only

Disk and File Capacity

Each file system also has different limits on file, disk and partition sizes it can work with as follows:

- FAT can work with partitions no greater than 2Gb in size.
- FAT32 can work with partitions up to 2Tb in size. However, a file has a maximum size of 4Gb.
- NTFS can work with partitions up to 2Tb in size and filesizes are limited only by the size of the partition. It cannot be used on floppy disks however.

Windows 2000 Security Checklist

For the rest of this section, we'll assume that you've chosen to use Windows 2000 for your Web server. That in mind, the next thing to do is construct a checklist to follow when (re)building your servers to provide a secure Internet environment. There are a number of things to look at before we even get to securing Internet Information Server itself, but before we get on with it a word of caution.

Some of the following advice does involve you making changes to the system registry and you should back it up if you are not fully aware of the ramifications of what could happen. There is no damaging content in what we are going to be doing later in this section but for safety's sake you should back it up first.

Setting The Server's Role In The Domain

When installing Windows 2000 Server on your Web-server-to-be, choose for the machine not to be a domain controller. If using Windows NT 4.0, again choose to set the box up as a standalone server rather than a Primary or Backup Domain Controller. This should remove any chance of sensitive domain information, like users and passwords, being present and thus possibly exposed to the Internet.

Disk Format

As we saw earlier, NTFS offers many more security features than FAT and FAT32 drives. If one of your server's drive partitions is already formatted as FAT or FAT32, you can convert it if you think it necessary with `convert.exe`. The procedure is very simple:

- Open a command prompt window.
- Type: `C:\>convert d: /fs:ntfs`
- Follow the onscreen prompts.

Note that you cannot reverse this procedure once it has taken place.

Partitioning Your Hard Drive

Dividing the hard drive in your Web server in to several partitions is a good idea. By putting all your Web files on an extended or logical partition, an attacker could not gain control of your primary boot partition even if he did get control of the Web site. Thus, he could not modify or compromise any system files (as they should all be on the primary boot partition).

Latest Service Packs and Hotfixes

Check to make sure you have the latest service packs and hot-fixes installed on the server according to your security policy. Make sure to review all Microsoft Security Bulletins concerning all the software installed on your server. You can find these online at `http://www.microsoft.com/security`.

NTFS 8.3 Name Generation

NTFS provides some backward compatibility with 16-bit applications by automatically generating 8.3 format filenames (e.g. `Progra~1/word.exe`) when required. However, this facility should be turned off within a secure Internet environment. To turn off NTFS 8.3 file name generation click Start, Run, type in `regedit` and edit the following key in the registry:

Registry Hive	HKEY_LOCAL_MACHINE\SYSTEM
Registry Key	\CurrentControlSet\Control\FileSystem
Name	NtfsDisable8dot3NameCreation
New Value	1

Note there is also an increase in performance after doing this.

Hiding the Last User to Have Logged On

We can also hide the username of the last user to have logged on at the server console - very handy if more than person uses it. Two keys handle this particular feature of Windows. The first to change actually stops the Windows logon box displaying the name of the last user to log on:

Registry Hive	HKEY_LOCAL_MACHINE\SOFTWARE
Registry Key	\Microsoft\Windows NT\Current Version\Winlogon
Name	DontDisplayLastUserName
New Value	1

However, the logon box will still show the default user name, which is governed by the second key to change. You can set it either to blank or to a user account that doesn't exist. This will provide a lot more security to your server if a fake username is displayed in the username box.

Registry Hive	HKEY_LOCAL_MACHINE\SOFTWARE
Registry Key	\Microsoft\Windows NT\Current Version\Winlogon
Name	DefaultUserName
New Value	Set to blank or whatever you desire.

Displaying a Legal Notice

Displaying a legal notice at logon time can be used to scare some people off and it's also a requirement for a system to gain its C2 security certificate (US-only). This is issued by the NSA's National Computer Security Center and recognizes that the server has adhered to the baseline measurement for a secure operating system. To display a legal notice at logon time, you would edit the following keys in the registry:

Registry Hive	HKEY_LOCAL_MACHINE\SOFTWARE
Registry Key	\Microsoft\Windows NT\Current Version\Winlogon
Name	LegalNoticeCaption
New Value	The title of the message box that you want to appear.

Registry Hive	HKEY_LOCAL_MACHINE\SOFTWARE
Registry Key	\Microsoft\Windows NT\Current Version\Winlogon
Name	LegalNoticeText
New Value	The text of the message box that you want to appear.

Check the Status of the Logon Screen Shutdown Button

As you may have noticed, it is initially possible to shutdown a Windows 2000 server from the logon screen without needing to log in first. Make sure that this possibility has been disabled by setting the following registry key accordingly:

Registry Hive	HKEY_LOCAL_MACHINE\SOFTWARE
Registry Key	\Microsoft\Windows NT\Current Version\Winlogon
Name	ShutdownWithoutLogon
New Value	0

Disable Anonymous Network Access

Windows 2000 also allows non-authenticated users to enumerate the users on a system. To disable this functionality we need to edit the following in the registry:

Registry Hive	HKEY_LOCAL_MACHINE\SYSTEM
Registry Key	\CurrentControlSet\Control\LSA
Name	restrictanonymous
New Value	1

Disabling Autosharing for Net Shares

Windows 2000 allows for shared network drives to be created and also auto shares all drives and creates an `ADMIN$` share on `c:\winnt`. This of course is a wonderful feature in a standard network situation but not suitable for many security reasons in a secure Internet environment. To disable this functionality we have to **create** the following key:

Registry Hive	HKEY_LOCAL_MACHINE\SYSTEM
Registry Key	\CurrentControlSet\Services\LanmanServer\Parameters
Name	AutoShareServer
Value	1

Check Permissions on the Registry for Remote Access

Windows 2000 supports access to the registry from remote locations. We'll need to use **`regedt32`** rather than `regedit` here to set the proper permissions on the following key:

Registry Hive	`HKEY_LOCAL_MACHINE\SYSTEM`
Registry Key	`\CurrentControlSet\Control\SecurePipeServers`
Name	`\winreg`

Click Security on the toolbar then select Permissions. You will notice that Administrators have full control and Backup Operators have read access. You can remove the read access if your backup software is on the local machine. You can also remove it if your remote backup software does not back up the registry.

Rename Administrator Account

When hackers try to crack your system they will commonly try to use the Administrator logon because it has the most power on the system. To circumvent this you can rename the administrator account to something else and then create a fake Administrator account and give it no access. All this is done in a few simple steps:

From the Start menu, select Programs | Administrative Tools | Computer Management
Once the dialog appears, select System Tools | Local Users and Groups | Users
You can now rename the Administrator account by selecting it and pressing `F2`.
To create a fake Administrator account, choose New User... from the Action menu and call the account Administrator:

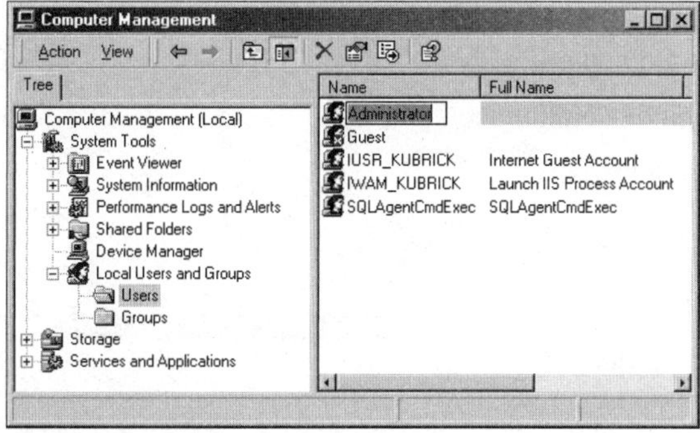

Disabling Access to Administrator Tools

There are a few tools which only administrators should be able to use. The easiest way to enforce this is by creating a new folder – for example, `c:\admintools` – copying the tools into the folder and then setting permissions on the folder so that only Administrators and the System account have control of its contents. You can find the folder's security dialog in Windows Explorer by right-clicking on the folder and selecting Properties.

Here's a list of some of the tools you ought to consider securing in this fashion. You can of course add or exclude from this list as you see fit:

- `cmd.exe` – Brings up a command prompt to run from which system tasks can be run.
- `cscript`.exe – Windows scripting host used to execute a script in a command line
- `ftp.exe` – Used to transfer files across servers and networks

- `net.exe` – Used to perform many functions within in the network
- `telnet.exe` – Used to initiate a remote console telnet session to another server
- `telnetc.exe` – Same as above
- `wscript.exe` – Windows scripting host used to execute a script in a GUI environment

Using The Microsoft Management Console

One of the greatest innovations in Windows 2000 is the use of the Management Console (MMC) to host practically every administrative application on the system. What you might not realize is that you can customize the MMC to host all your administrative tools at once, so rather than avoid confusion caused by opening various admin tools along the way, the following set of instructions creates a custom MMC session with all the required information available in one place.

- Choose Run from the Start menu, and then type `mmc /a` to bring up an MMC window and give yourself administrator's privileges
- From the Console menu, select Add/Remove Snap-in
- Click the Add button in the dialog box
- Select both Group Policy and the Event Viewer from the Add standalone snap-in dialog box, choosing on both occasions the Local Computer option
- Hit Close and then OK
- Expand the Local Computer Policy
- Expand the Computer Configuration
- Expand Windows Settings
- Expand Security Settings

Most of the following checks will be made inside this security folder:

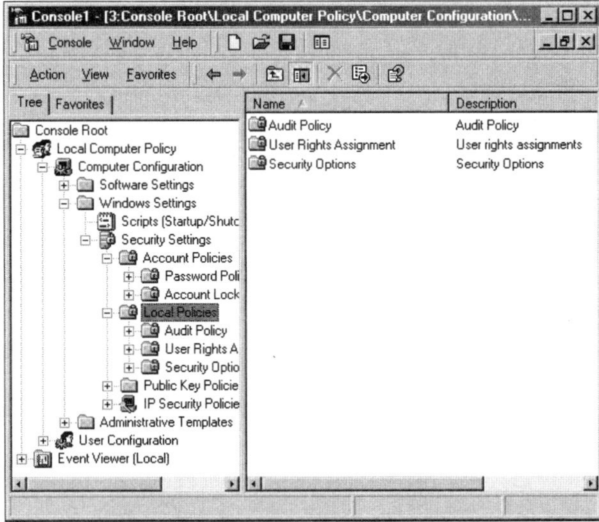

Strengthen Your Passwords

Ensuring that all passwords are at least 9 characters long will decrease the risk of someone being able to find them out as will encrypting the passwords for the domain and ensuring that they have some mix of upper and lowercase letters and numbers with a filter. You can specify each of these options and a couple of others by altering the values stored in the Password Policy folder under Account Policies.

Account Lockout Securing

It is also possible to lock out user accounts if it becomes apparent that people are trying to guess the passwords for those accounts. To enable this feature, go into the Account Lockout Policy folder and change the value for Account Lockout Count to the number of invalid password guesses you think your users may need to type their passwords correctly. You can also determine if you want to lock the account out for a certain amount of time and then re-enable it after the time limit has expired.

Limiting Access from the Network

Windows 2000 by default allows everyone to access this server from the network. This is definitely a big security risk. You can change this feature by going into the Local Policies folder then selecting the User Rights Assignment folder. Double-click the icon with the text Access this computer from the network icon and uncheck the Local Policy for Everyone box. Click the Add button and select Authenticated Users then click Add and then hit the OK button. You will be prompted to update your effective policy; choose Yes.

Auditing of Logons to the Server

To be able to write logon activity to the security event log we can go into the Audit Policy folder and change the audit account logon events and audit logon events settings. You should check that both successful and unsuccessful attempts to log on to the server are being logged. This will give a good idea of the activity that is going on when dealing with users' accounts.

Log Interval Overwrites

Depending on how much traffic your site receives and/or how many users log in to your server, you will have to decide how big a security log you should keep and when to start overwriting parts of it. Set the file size high – around 5Mb should do – for busy servers. You'll need enough space to capture the current events and keep a decent backlog of events for your site. Again, your choice of overwrite policy depends on you and your experience. A good starting point is to Overwrite events as needed.

Both settings can be made by expanding the Event Viewer snap-in, right-clicking the security log and choosing Properties.

Network Interface Security

With usernames and passwords dealt with, we need to turn our attention to our network settings and make sure they are correct and secure. There are several different ways to get to the same screen, but the simplest is to right click on the My Network Places icon on your desktop and select Properties. From the resultant dialog box, right-click Local Area Connection and select Properties again.

The only relevant protocol for Internet servers is TCP/IP, so make sure you have no network protocols installed that you don't actually need. Select Internet Protocol (TCP/IP) and then click the Properties button. You'll be presented with your machine's IP and DNS entries, but we're more interested in the WINS (Windows Internet Name Service) properties you'll find by hitting the Advanced button.

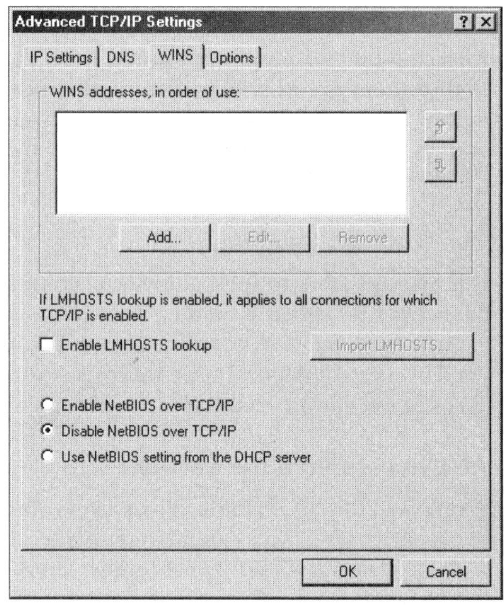

Disabling WINS

In a secure Internet environment you would not want to run WINS on the server or use it on a remote server. There have been some security issues in the past with servers running WINS and the Internet is based purely on TCP/IP anyway. Remove any WINS servers that have been defined and then uninstall WINS itself.

Disabling NetBIOS

NetBIOS is the network protocol traditionally used for Windows network communications, but which TCP/IP easily supercedes if installed. It also enables a few tools that could cause breaks in security. You can disable NetBIOS by selecting the Disable NetBIOS over TCP/IP option in the WINS settings dialog.

Disable LMHOSTS Lookup

The LMHOSTS file is used to map IP addresses to the computer names of Windows machines. So far, there have been no reports of security breaches as a direct result of enabling LMHOSTS lookup, but it's not really all that necessary, unless you can't traverse your network using IP addresses instead of computer names. You can disable LMHOSTS lookup by unselecting the relevant radio button in the WINS settings dialog.

TCP/IP Filtering

A fair number of network ports are left open by default by our server unless we tell it otherwise. Fortunately, as we know which ports are used by HTTP, FTP etc., we can shut down all but those we need on the server, even if it's already behind a firewall or proxy server. Still in the Advanced TCP/IP Settings dialog box, select the Options tab and then Properties for TCP/IP filtering.

- Check the Enable TCP/IP Filtering (All adapters) checkbox if it isn't already.
- Under TCP ports, you should only add ports you know are being used: for example, port 21 for FTP, port 80 for HTTP, port 443 for SSL, and port 25 for SMTP. There may of course be others which you should add accordingly
- You should allow no UDP ports.
- You should allow only IPv6. This is a newer version of IP and has more security features.

Depending on what your server uses, the TCP/IP Filtering dialog should look something like this:

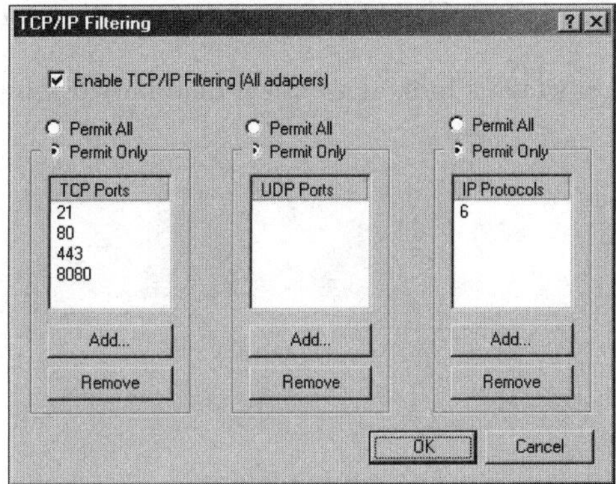

Firewalls and Proxy Servers

Let's stay with the topic of network security for a short while before we continue to develop our security policy. There has been a lot more focus on network security over the past few years than at any time before partially because the Internet has grown at such a phenomenal rate and partially because as a result there has been an increase in hacking activities. We've already looked at some of the measures you can take to protect your server but one of the most widely implemented is to use a firewall or a proxy server to act as a buffer between your servers and the online world.

A firewall is a piece of hardware that creates a secure barrier between two networks – usually the Internet and an internal network. A proxy server is a special type of firewall that will also perform tasks on behalf of a computer that cannot or will not perform the action for itself.

A firewall is often setup with one network interface facing the internal network and another set up to face the Internet but with no direct connection between the two. There's no reason why there shouldn't be more than two network cards but for simplicity's sake, we'll just assume a pair.

The purpose of firewalls and proxy servers is to take non-routable addresses and turn them into routable addresses without the destination or source host ever seeing this transformation take place. In one direction, this means it can help quite a bit to protect your internal network against infringement or intrusion as it can monitor information flowing through it. In the other, this means that firewalls could stop someone on the internal network sending sensitive information out to the Internet.

Most commonly, firewalls work from a basis of two commonly heard phrases:

- That which is not expressly permitted is denied.
- That which is not expressly prohibited is permitted.

You can immediately establish the difference between the two. For a better security choice you would definitely want to pick the firewall that follows the convention that everything is denied until otherwise notified. You would find yourself doing much more work on your server, if you had picked the philosophy of everything being permitted.

Let's take a look at a typical dual network interface set up to see how it works:

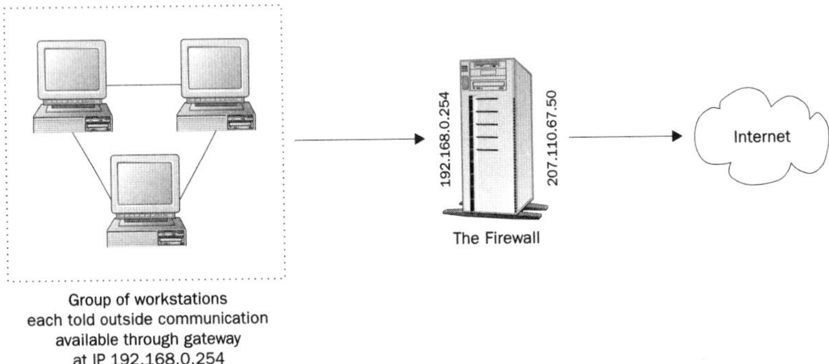

Our setup here has a server with two network cards for a specific purpose. The outside interface is being used to communicate with the (outside) Internet and the inside interface is being used to communicate with the internal network LAN. It's the typical setup I mentioned earlier. The firewall connecting the two would have IP routing disabled. In short, this means that all communications from the inside out would appear to have come either from the firewall itself or from another global address on our external network. This is what separates our internal network from the external public Internet, making the firewall the central security station of our network.

Firewalls can be implemented as software running on an operating system or they can be dedicated hardware like a CISCO PIX firewall. Dedicated OS-independent hardware will always function faster than a software equivalent but is likely to cost a lot more too.

Address Allocation for Private Networks

Your administrator should already have your internal network physically set up so communication with the Internet can only be done through the firewall; possibly by just removing every network card open to the Internet from every non-firewall machine. They can also make sure that the Internet sees only requests which appear to have come from the firewall by assigning those machines on the internal network a **Private Network IP address**.

The Internet Assigned Numbers Authority (IANA) has three blocks of IP address space constrained for internal private networks. These addresses will not be routed to the Internet in their original state. A mediating gateway such as a standard gateway, firewall, or proxy server must route requests from these addresses through itself and transform the source host address into its own IP. So you can still permit full network connectivity between hosts on the private network and the public Internet, but you also protect your private network a bit more too.

The private address blocks are:

- Class A: 10.0.0.0 – 10.255.255.255
- Class B: 172.16.0.0 – 172.31.255.255
- Class C: 192.168.0.0 – 192.168.255.255

For example let's say we have a Web server with the IP 192.168.0.6 we could in no way have this in public Internet address space without some other translation taking place from a firewall without giving it a global outside network address. This is done through what is known as Network Address Translation (NAT), which we will discuss more in the next section.

Before we get to that though, there are some pros and cons of using these private network spaces. The obvious advantage is that our network security increases a goodly amount, allowing us tight control over what few machines we allow direct access to the Internet. This approach is also a bit cheaper to implement as you do not need to register any of the private addresses you're using with your ISP that you would otherwise.

A problem will occur for companys' networks not using the private address space when they decide to connect their LAN to the Internet. In this instance, every machine on the LAN will have been assigned a global IP address to which Internet traffic will be sent directly. It is then almost impossible to route traffic through a single machine acting as the firewall.

Right then, back to the issue of Network Address Translation.

Network Address Translation

The main purpose of network address translation (NAT) is to translate our non-routable addresses into routable addresses. There are two types of NAT – dynamic and static – but we'll only consider the first of the two.

The purpose of dynamic Network Address Translation is to provide an internal host with one or more possible IP addresses to be used as aliases for external communication, as we have seen already. This translation works on a connection basis with the alias IP only being used until the connection is completed. The best way to describe this is through a picture to make it easily understandable:

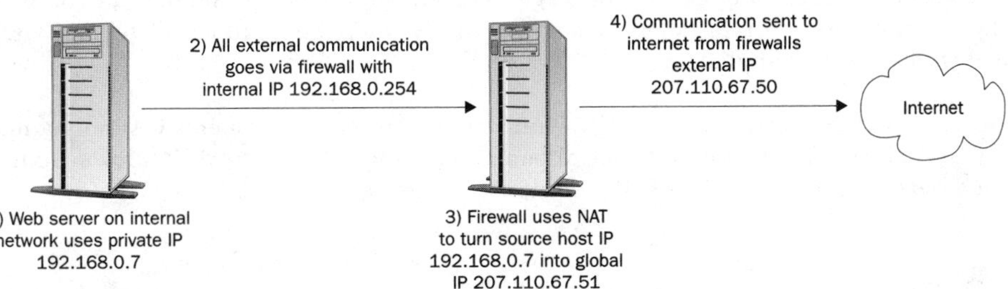
2) All external communication
goes via firewall with
internal IP 192.168.0.254
4) Communication sent to
internet from firewalls
external IP
207.110.67.50
Internet
1) Web server on internal
network uses private IP
192.168.0.7
3) Firewall uses NAT
to turn source host IP
192.168.0.7 into global
IP 207.110.67.51

Using network address translation we can give our internal server a global public address that the rest of the world can get to. The easiest way of looking at this is to think that our internal Web server has two IP addresses. In reality, it does not. The firewall is doing the NAT to translate all packets back and forth to this server through the firewall.

You can set packet-filtering rules on what exactly is allowed to pass through the firewall to the internal server. It would also be in your best interest to only allow port 80 and 443 (if you are using SSL) TCP packets and deny everything else. You can even disable Internet Control Message Protocol (ICMP) packets through the firewall. These are used to check if a machine is still responding to network requests. As you may recall from our discussion of IP Spoofing, by leaving ICMP enabled, your machines may become unwitting volunteers in attacks on other networks.

Problems with IIS and Network Address Translation

Even though the firewall provides an alias for your internal IP as source host, Content-Location references sent in the request (or response) itself by IIS will still contain that internal IP. Obviously, this is not to be desired, but the problem is easily fixed:

1. Open IIS and bring up your Web site's Properties dialog box.
2. Switch to the HTTP Headers tab and click Add in the Custom HTTP Headers area.
3. Set the Custom Header Name box to the actual location of the content (your internal IP)
4. Set the Custom Header Value to the actual global domain of the server (`http://www.example.com`)

This way the header will now give the actual global address of the internal server instead of the internal IP address.

Securing IIS 5.0

Finally we come to the subject that most of you probably surmised would appear at the top of the chapter: how to configure IIS securely. In this section we will discuss how to secure IIS 5.0 and discuss related information for setting up secure Internet sites.

Install as Few Components as Possible

When you install Windows 2000 it will automatically install certain selected items for Internet Information Server 5.0. From a security point of view however, it may well not be in your best interest to install them all. Try and install as few IIS components as possible whilst making sure you still have the functionality required by your Web site. For example, you don't need the Front Page Server Extensions if you're not using FrontPage to create your Web and neither do you need to install SMTP functionality (which *is* installed by default) unless you're going to use CDO or CDONTS to send mail with your ASP applications.

Don't worry if you've already installed IIS. Uninstalling various components is simply a matter of opening the Add/Remove Programs control panel, selecting Add/Remove Windows Components and then deselecting the elements of IIS you don't require.

Create a Logical Securable Directory Structure

A good Web site structure also makes it much simpler to manage the security for the various applications within it. You should be able to define directories such that they contain only one type of file – executables, ASP pages, server-side includes etc. – allowing you to define tight security permissions on a directory rather than a file basis in Windows Explorer.

The example structure below is easy to manage from a security point of view, but leaves a lot to be desired by the Web designer. It does however lay down some useful permissions guidelines to follow:

Directory Name	Contains	File Extensions	Permission Settings
`Webroot\exec`	Executable files	`.exe`, `.dll`, `.pl`	Anonymous Web user (IUSR_MACHINE) (Read and Execute) Administrator (Full Control) System (Full Control)
`Webroot\incs`	Include files	`.inc`, `.shtml`, `.shtm`	
`Webroot\asp`	ASP pages	`.asp`	
`Webroot\html`	HTML \ Client-side script	`.htm`, `.html`	Anonymous Web user (IUSR_MACHINE) (Read Only) Administrator (Full Control) System (Full Control)
`Webroot\imgs`	Image files	`.gif`, `.jpeg`	

Note that if you can avoid putting .exe files in your online applications, you should. They can present several possible security problems of their own.

Keep a Wafer Thin Server

Keeping with our point to remove all unnecessary material from our production server, there are several more items we can remove from our server's sight to keep it fixed on our Web site.

- The sample applications and IIS SDK located in `C:\inetpub\iisamples\` are surplus baggage on a live server.
- Likewise, the Admin Scripts installed at `C:\inetpub\AdminScripts\` can be deleted
- The Default Web Site in IIS is also a candidate for deletion as its physical root is usually on the server's primary boot partition. As explained earlier, should an attacker gain control of the default Web site, he might also gain access to the boot partition, your windows files, the command shell, etc.
- If your online applications do not make use of the scripting runtime library objects (as covered in Chapter 5) or the ASP server components, you can unregister them by choosing Run from the Start menu and typing

```
regsvr32 xxx.dll /u
```

Where `xxx.dll` is the name of the file holding the component. Be aware that some applications require some objects to be available, so be sure to check dependencies before unregistering the components.

Shore Up Your RDS Security

Microsoft has released a security statement for those using the Remote Data Service functionality we looked at in Chapter 10. You can find this at `http://support.microsoft.com/support/kb/articles/Q184/3/75.asp`. RDS has been the basis for denial of service attacks in the past and Microsoft recommends you to either remove RDS from your server or tighten your security around it. Both approaches are covered at the aforementioned Web page.

Don't Index Your Back-End Code

It is not uncommon to see people indexing the underlying code in their application in addition to the information the users will actually see. Even a few `global.asa` files appear from time to time in some sites' search results. Potentially, this mistake could expose a password in a connection string, a username or a directory structure which an attacker could make use of to gain unauthorized access to your site.

The easiest way to prevent this is to separate the back end code from the rest of the site by placing it in one master directory and then configuring index server not to index it. You can then also prevent Internet search engines from indexing it by specifying in your site's `robots.txt` file that the directory should not be touched.

Set Up Your Web Logs and Secure Them

In IIS, all the log configuration options can be accessed by bringing up a Website's Properties dialog and checking the Enable Logging box. Logging is the one of the most important aspects of Web site security. Well-defined logs can provide you with all the information you need to monitor the activity on your site and where that activity originates. In particular, the W3C Extended Log File Format allows you to make note of some key information – Client IP Address, User Name, Server IP, Server Port, Method, URI Stem, and Protocol Status – as you can see from this screenshot.

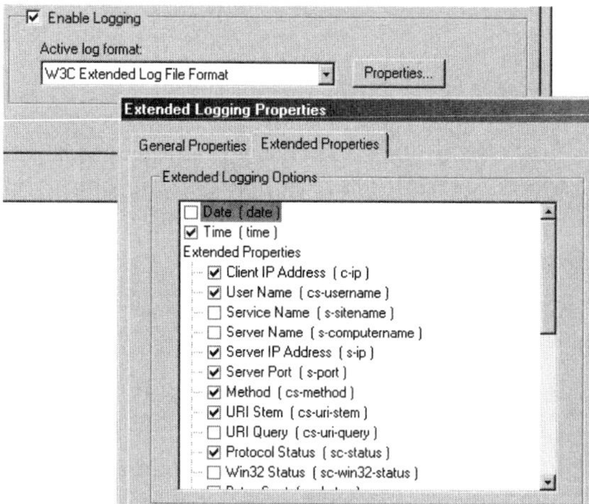

Tempered with the need to know everything, you should of course realize that log files can become very big very quickly as the users begin to flood in, a fact that becomes all the more poignant when you have to download your logs over the Web.

If you do have to download them, then make sure to give only the Administrator and the System account access to the log directory. You might also consider encrypting them or using some Kerberos to make them doubly secure.

On the other hand, if you're generating logs to a local machine, you should do so away from the Web site directory itself. It's then much more unlikely your logs can be accessed by anyone other than yourself.

Restrict Access to the Site by Filtering IP Addresses

One of IIS's security options for a Web site (see the Directory Security tab in your Web site's Properties dialog) is to restrict access to the site based upon the IP address of the client requesting access. This is at least a partial deterrent for the IP spoofing problems we saw at the top of the chapter.

In the event that an address is rejected it returns a custom error page to the client with the key message:

HTTP 403.6 - Forbidden: IP address rejected

You can find this page at `C:\WINNT\help\iisHelp\common\403-6.htm` and should modify it to erase that particular message or perhaps even just blank the screen. Why? Because if clients know that they're being rejected because of their IP, some of them are bound to try to find a way around this. Of course, you can still get the header information but just as an extra precaution it should be modified.

Configure Your Web Application With Care

For each virtual application that you create in IIS, there is a corresponding application configuration box to be aware of and make secure. You can find this by pressing the Configuration button found on the Home/Virtual Directory tab of the application's Properties dialog.

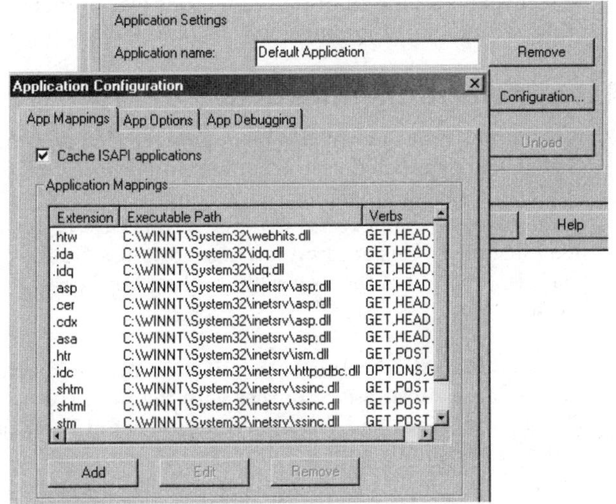

Starting on the App Mappings tab, it's in your best interest to remove any application mappings to file extensions you will not be using. At the time of writing, the latest security hole, detailed at `http://www.eeye.com/database/advisories/ad06081999/ad06081999.html`, used one of these mappings to disable the target server. Simply select an extension you wish to remove and hit the Remove button.

Moving across to the App Options tab, you should consider disabling Parent Paths, so you the client may not use `'..'` to signify a parent directory in his URL requests and possibly step into hidden territory. For example, `http:// www.example.com/'../_vti_bin'`. An alternative solution would be to create a file with the default home page file name in each folder, thus preventing the directory from being browsed.

Authentication Methods

Make sure that each of your Internet/intranet applications uses the strongest user authentication mode possible. The stronger the method, the more confident we can be that a user has correctly identified him (or her)self. As you probably know, IIS supports three types of authentication control – anonymous access, basic authentication and integrated Windows authentication. These can each be configured by selecting the Directory Security tab of the Website properties dialog box in IIS and pressing the top Edit button. You should see the following dialog box.

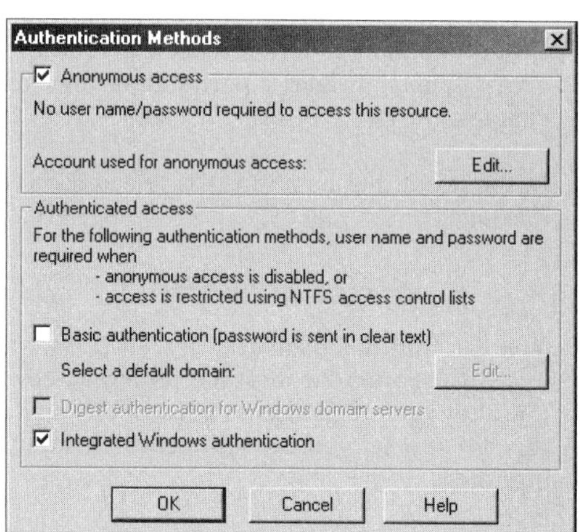

The checkboxes for all of these methods work independently, meaning that it is possible to enable multiple authentication mechanisms, and the appropriate one is then automatically used for a request.

Anonymous Authentication

When anonymous access has been enabled, IIS does not care about the user's identity and simply assigns a pre-specified user account and permissions to anyone accessing the files on the Web server. By default, this anonymous user account is `IUSR_MachineName`, which is created when IIS is installed. Note that `MachineName` in this case is the actual name of the machine on which IIS has been installed. This account is assigned to the Guests account group, given a password that can be changed, and given the user right to 'Log On Locally' which allows it to access the IIS 5.0 WWW services.

Provided that Anonymous authentication has been enabled, users accessing WWW services are allowed access to those resources with the permissions allocated to the `IUSR_MACHINENAME` account. These permissions and the anonymous account itself can be modified by pressing the top Edit button in the dialog shown above.

Note that the IIS 5.0 installation also creates another user account called `IWAM_MACHINENAME`. When we create Web applications that run out of process from IIS, it will create an MTS package that is set to run under the `IWAM_MACHINENAME` account.

Basic Authentication

If a user requests a resource for which the anonymous user account does not have the appropriate permissions, the request will be rejected and a 401 Access Denied message will be returned to the client. If either of the other two authentication methods is enabled, most browsers will then prompt the user for a username and password and then submit both them and the request again to the server for verification.

The difference between basic and integrated Windows authentication lies in how the username and password are transmitted. Under Basic Authentication they are transmitted as unencrypted, clear text. N.B. The user id can either be declared simply, e.g. `Mobius`, fully qualified, e.g. `DomainName/Mobius`, or, new to IIS5.0, in the form `mobius@DomainName.com`.

The transmission of user names and passwords in clear text can be changed by using SSL encryption.

Integrated Windows Authentication

With IWA (formerly known as NTLM or Windows NT Challenge/Response authentication in Windows NT 4.0), the user's password is never sent across the network, and so can never be revealed to an attacker. Instead, when challenged for user information by the server (IIS), the client responds with an encrypted security blob which a server has previously issued it with. The way in which this blob is encrypted and exactly how it is verified is dependent upon which protocol Windows is using.

If both the client and the IIS server have a trusted connection to a Kerberos Key Distribution Center (KDC) and are both Active Directory compatible, then IIS will use the **Kerberos Network Authentication Protocol** to verify the blob. Kerberos is the new security model upon which Windows 2000 authentication is based. You can find more information about it at `http://www.microsoft.com/security/ tech/kerberos`.

If the server, or, more likely, the client is not Kerberos compatible then the server will fall back to the **Windows NT Challenge/Response** protocol. You can find out more about this at `http://www.microsoft.com/NTServer/security`.

The details of these protocols aside, two points must be made clear with respect to IWA:

- The only time IWA is used is when anonymous access is either denied or when an anonymous user has come across a page which forces the user to authenticate before a connection is established to the content.
- IWA is compatible only with Internet Explorer browsers, version 2 and above.

SQL Server 7.0 and ODBC Security

It doesn't matter whether you've got a simple ASP page to display the contents of some SQL database table to screen or you're developing a fully database-integrated an Internet/intranet application; you should take the proper security steps when setting up the ASP to SQL connection.

Securing the sa Account

The first step to take is to secure the `sa` account. This is SQL Server's default systems administrator account which by default has no password. To set one up, you should do the following:

1. Launch SQL Server Enterprise Manager
2. Connect to the SQL Server that holds your database.
3. Open the Security folder.

4. Click on Logins.
5. Right-mouse click on the `sa` account and select Properties.
6. Replace password with a new password in the Password text box.
7. Click on OK.
8. You will be prompted to re-enter the password for verification.

Creating an Alternate Account for Database Access

The next step in securing SQL Server is to create a role that gives the minimum access needed to use your Web site/Web application. In cases where different user accounts perform different tasks you may wish to create several different roles. To create a SQL Database Role in Enterprise Manager:

1. Open the folder for the database your pages work with.
2. Select Roles.
3. Right-mouse click in the open area and select New Database Role.
4. Give the role a name in the text box and select OK.
5. Right mouse click on the newly added role and select Properties.
6. Click on the Permissions button.

The resulting dialog will allow you to specify access permissions for each of the database's related objects. You should be able to figure out what access you'll need to grant for the Web site/Web application to run and configure this role(s) accordingly. For example, if the Web site only reads from a specific table then the role should only have `SELECT` access to that object.

One of the most secure policies is to disallow any direct access to the database tables altogether. Instead, any access to the tables should be through views and stored procedures that provide the functionality and give the roles you've created the proper permissions to use them. Then someone with a valid username/password will still not be able to do anything that they couldn't already do via the ASP code.

You are now ready to add your SQL Account(s) to the database. For security purposes you should never use the `sa` account for your Web site. The systems administrator account has all access to every database and the administrative rights to add users and perform other tasks. If an attacker were able to get control of our ODBC link while we were using the `sa` account, they would have the permissions that it holds. Still in Enterprise Manager then, you can create a new SQL Account to the database like so:

1. Open the Security folder.
2. Select Logins.
3. Right-mouse click in the open white area of the screen and select New Login.
4. Type the user ID in the Name text box.

5. Click **SQL Server Authentication** and enter the password in the **Password** text box.
6. Change the default database to your database.
7. Click on the **Database Access** tab.
8. Permit database access to your database.
9. Permit database role access to the database role that was created for the Web site/Web application.

If you are using SQL in an application environment and want to verify user IDs and passwords by using the SQL database you have two options. On one hand, you could store all your user accounts and passwords in a table and write your own verification routine against the users table. On the other, you could verify the user ID and password as part of the SQL connection string to SQL Server. This would mean creating a user ID for each individual that has access to the system, but it would also mean the ASP database connection will fail if a user enters an invalid user ID and password.

The code to make this work is certainly not difficult. Take, for example, this file `login.html`:

```
<HTML>
<BODY>
  <FORM NAME="login" METHOD="Post" ACTION="verify.asp">
    User: <INPUT TYPE="TEXT" SIZE="10" NAME="USR">
    <BR>
    Pass: <INPUT TYPE="PASSWORD" SIZE="10" NAME="PWD">
    <BR>
    <INPUT TYPE="SUBMIT" VALUE="Login">
  </FORM>
</BODY>
</HTML>
```

This submits a user ID and password to `verify.asp` which inserts them into a connection string and then tries to connect to the database. A message is then displayed based on the success or failure of the connection.

```
<%@ LANGUAGE = VBScript %>
<%
  On Error Resume Next
  Set Conn = Server.CreateObject("ADODB.Connection")

  ' Add user ID and password to connection string
  Connstring = "PROVIDER=SQLOLEDB;" & _
               "SERVER=[name of sql server];" & _
               "DATABASE=[database name];UID=" & Request.Form("USR") & _
               ";pwd=" & Request.Form("PWD") & ";"

  Conn.Open(Connstring)
  If err.number = 0  Then%>
    <HTML>
    <BODY>
        Welcome to our system.
```

```
        </BODY>
        </HTML>

    <%Else%>
        <HTML>
        <BODY>
            Sorry, you have entered invalid account information.
        </BODY>
        </HTML>

    <%End If%>
```

If you're happier using a DSN to connect to your SQL Server database, remember when you set it up to enable SQL Server Authentication with the default login ID and password. The same login procedure above can be used by replacing the database connection string with:

```
Connstring = "DSN=[insert dsn name];UID=" & Request.Form("USR") & _
             ";pwd=" & Request.Form("PWD") & ";"
```

Creating Your Own Security With ASP

Up to this point in the chapter, we've looked solely at the security measures we can take that come as part of the server's hardware and software setup. The one field we have left to look at is the security we can give our applications from within our ASP code. Building our own ASP-based application-level security model lets us define the logic to provide further levels of assurance, better defence mechanisms and custom-made user tracking facilities whilst still giving us a convenient, easy to use and personalised system.

Typical uses of ASP application-level security logic can include:

- Enforcing access controls and restricting Web site access to a closed user group (CUG) .
- Forcing a user to register their personal details before they are allowed to access specific areas of a Web site.
- Making Web access logs more verbose. Such logs can then be used for investigating security breaches, customer billing, capacity planning, and determining the popular/unpopular areas of a Web site.
- Programmatically accessing the data stored in a client digital certificate.

We've already seen how to make our IIS logs more verbose and we'll be looking at digital certificates in much greater detail in the next chapter. For the remainder of this chapter then, we'll address the problem of implementing access controls that restrict certain Web pages to approved members – the Closed User Groups just mentioned.

Feel free to take the following example and bend it to your own requirements. It contains just the skeleton code to handle the user authentication and access controls logic for you to bolt on a front end. You can find all the examples detailed here in the code download for the book, available from `http://www.wrox.com`.

Implementing Closed User Groups / Membership

Our Membership site will involve two separate Web sites:

- **The Members Site** – This is the *Internet* Web application comprising both public Web pages and those that may only be viewed by the Members:

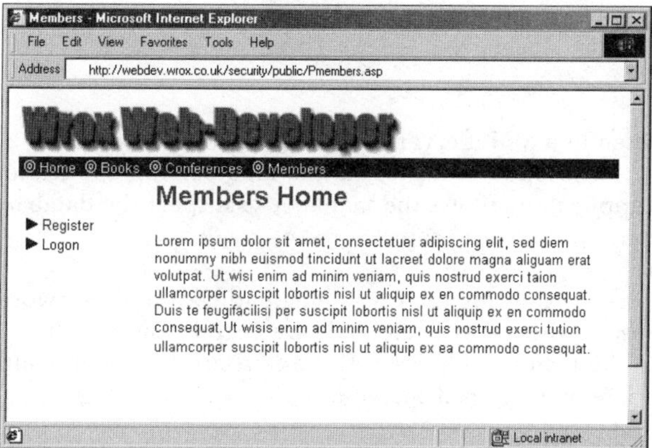

- **The Membership Management Site** – this is the *Intranet* Web application allowing the membership manager to inspect the membership database and approve or reject applicants:

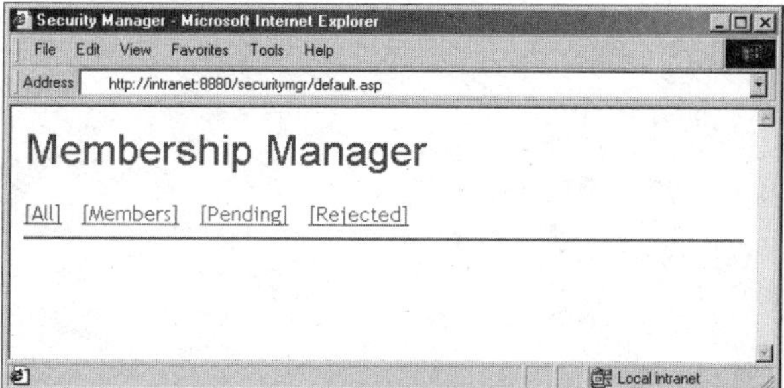

> **Note that the Intranet site is working on TCP/IP port 8880. This assumes that our firewall will only allow access to port 80, so we can be confident that no one outside our corporate network can access this Web application. Furthermore, we'll enable Integrated Windows Authentication on this site to restrict access to specific personnel i.e. the Membership Managers.**

The Members Database

The Members Site includes a facility for a user to register their details and another to logon for entry into the membership area. The fields captured during the user registration are:

- EmailAddress
- Name
- Company
- Password

This information is written to a SQL Server 7.0 database table called Users. In addition, a field in the record called Status is used to indicate that the membership application is Pending. The Membership Manager application allows the manager to inspect the database and alter the status of any entry to either Pending, Rejected or Member.

The logon process involves requesting the user's email address and password, and then verifying them against the database. If the user's credentials are correct and the Status is set to Member, then the user is redirected to the membership area. If the Status is currently either Pending or Rejected, an appropriate message is displayed.

To save you time, you can use the script below to generate the Users table and its fields automatically. Simply open SQL Query Analyzer, select the database you want the table to be created in, type the script into the window and press F5.

```
IF EXISTS (SELECT * FROM sysobjects WHERE id = object_id(N'[dbo].[Users]') AND
OBJECTPROPERTY(id, N'IsUserTable') = 1)
DROP TABLE [dbo].[Users]
GO

CREATE TABLE [dbo].[Users] (
    [EmailAddress] [char] (50) NOT NULL ,
    [Password] [char] (50) NOT NULL ,
    [Name] [char] (50) NOT NULL ,
    [Company] [char] (50) NOT NULL ,
    [Status] [char] (1) NOT NULL
) ON [PRIMARY]
GO
```

The resulting table will look like this:

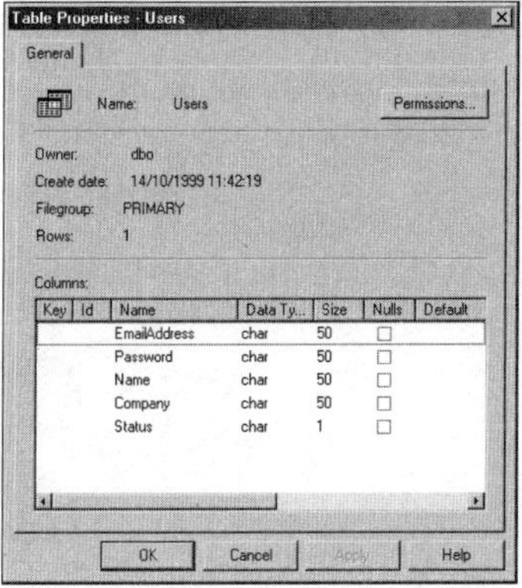

The Members Internet Site

The Members Internet site has a very simple structure as shown below:

The site content is structured into a number of sub-directories; these are:

- `public` – This contains the site content that may be viewed by anyone
- `members` – This contains the site content that may only be viewed by approved members
- `global` – This contains 'common' content that is used across many files
- `images` – This contain any graphics files
- `_private` – This is reserved for use by FrontPage

The contents of the `global`, `images` and `_private` folders should all be self-explanatory, so we'll ignore those and go straight for the meat of the application. It's in the `public` folder that users may register with your site and log on to the restricted parts of the site.

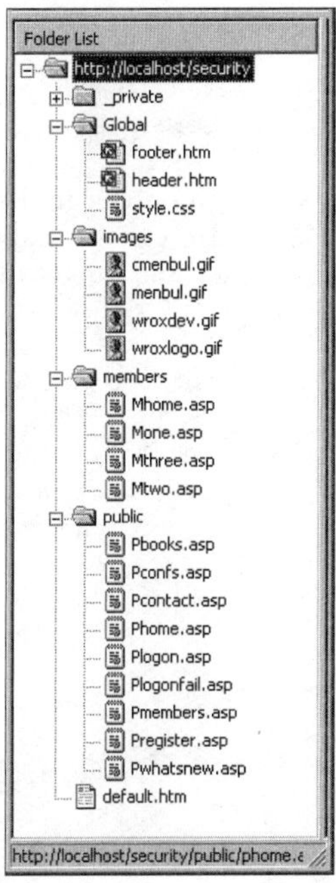

The User Registration Page

In the grand scheme of things, `Pregsiter.asp` is the first page we're interested in as it handles the registration of new users for access to the members' area of the site. It has two tasks (or modes)

- Display the HTML form to capture the user's information.
- Process the user's information once the form is submitted.

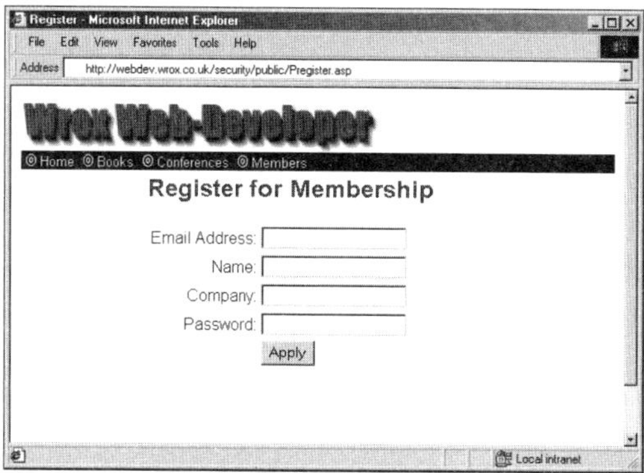

Display Mode

The HTML form submits the information back to the same ASP file but tacks a parameter (`mode=apply`) onto the end of the URL. Thus the ASP logic can easily determine which of the two tasks it is required to perform.

```
<FORM METHOD="POST" ACTION="Pregister.asp?mode=apply">
<TABLE BORDER="0">

    - form fields

</FORM>
```

When the user's information is submitted, in addition to checking for the mode parameter, the ASP logic also checks that none of the form fields have been left blank. If one of more fields have not been set, the logic drops through to redisplay the form.

```
<%
  If Request.QueryString("mode")="apply" And _
     (Trim(Request.Form("txtEmailAddress")) <> "" And _
      Trim(Request.Form("txtName")) <> "" And _
      Trim(Request.Form("txtCompany")) <> "" And _
      Trim(Request.Form("txtPassword")) <> "") Then
%>

        - process the form

<% Else % >

        - display the form

<% End If % >
```

Database Update Mode

The processing of the form involves writing the information to the SQL Server database. This is done using ADO which we met in Chapters 8 - 12 of this book. Note that you will have to add in the connection string to the `Users` table yourself in this and other pages. The contents of the string will of course depend on where you created the table in the first place.

First we must invoke a query to check if the specified email address is already known in our database. If the email address has not been previously recorded, we can then add the information to the Users table. Note that at this stage, the `Status` field is set to 'P' (Pending).

```
<%
  vEmailAddress = LCase(Trim(Request.Form("txtEmailAddress")))
  vPassword = Trim(Request.Form("txtPassword"))
  vName = Trim(Request.Form("txtName"))
  vCompany = Trim(Request.Form("txtCompany"))

  Set objConn = Server.CreateObject("ADODB.Connection")
  objConn.Open [Connection string to Users table]

  vSQL = "SELECT EmailAddress FROM Users WHERE EmailAddress = '" & _
          vEmailAddress & "'"

  Set rsUsers = objConn.Execute (vSQL)

  If rsUsers.Eof Then
    Set rsUsers = Nothing
    Set rsUsers = Server.CreateObject("ADODB.Recordset")
    rsUsers.ActiveConnection = objConn
    rsUsers.CursorType = adOpenKeyset
    rsUsers.LockType = adLockOptimistic
    rsUsers.Source = "Users"
    rsUsers.Open
    rsUsers.AddNew
    rsUsers.fields("EmailAddress") = vEmailAddress
    rsUsers.fields("Password") = vPassword
    rsUsers.fields("Name") = vName
    rsUsers.fields("Company") = vCompany
    rsUsers.fields("Status") = "P"
    rsUsers.Update

    Response.Write "<P>Thank you <B>" & vName & _
        "</B> for your application. " & _
        "<P>Approval will be granted shortly.<P>"
  Else
    Response.Write  "<B>" & vEmailAddress & "</B> is already registered"
  End If
%>
```

The User Log On Page

Having registered with the site, the user needs to wait for his membership request to be approved – we'll leave it to you to decide how this notification is done – and once that arrives, he'll need to log on. We've used `Plogon.asp` to handle this task.

In a similar fashion to `Pregsiter.asp`, this page also has two modes:

- Displaying the HTML form to capture the users credentials.
- Authenticating the user and either providing access to the members area or rejecting the request.

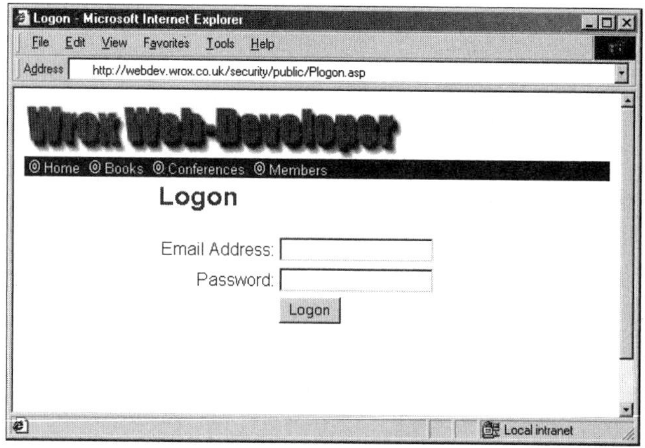

Display Mode

In exactly the same fashion as `Pregister.asp`, the HTML form submits the information back to the same `Plogon.asp` but tacks a parameter (`mode=logon`) onto the end of the URL to make it aware it should be running in authentication mode:

```
<FORM METHOD="POST" ACTION="Plogon.asp?mode=logon">
<TABLE BORDER="0">

    - form fields

</FORM>
```

Authentication Mode

At the top of `Plogon.asp` is a check to see how many times the user has specified invalid credentials and failed to logon. This count is stored in the ASP Session object. After three failures, the user will be redirected back to the site's home page and help thwart any attempt to hack into the site.

```
<%
  If Session("LogonCount") > 2 Then
    Response.Redirect "Plogonfail.asp?reason=1"
  End If
```

That done, we make a check for the mode parameter and that all the form fields were filled in. If this is not the case, we assume that we're still in display mode and output the form:

```
If Request.QueryString("mode")="logon" And _
   (Trim(Request.Form("txtEmailAddress")) <> "" And _
    Trim(Request.Form("txtPassword")) <> "") Then
```

To authenticate the user, the record that matches the specified email address is retrieved from the `Users` table. Again, make sure you fill in the correct connection string for the `Users` table in the code:

```
vEmailAddress = LCase(Trim(Request.Form("txtEmailAddress")))
vPassword = Trim(Request.Form("txtPassword"))

Set objConn = Server.CreateObject("ADODB.Connection")
objConn.Open [Connection string to Users table]

vSQL = "SELECT * FROM Users WHERE EmailAddress = '" & vEmailAddress & "'"

Set rsUsers = objConn.Execute (vSQL)

If Not rsUsers.Eof Then
```

If the record is found the `password` field is then checked. If the password is correct, the logic switches on the `status` field. If the user's application has been rejected or is still pending, the browser is redirected to the `Plogonfail.asp` page to display an appropriate error message:

```
  If vPassword = Trim(rsUsers.Fields("Password")) Then

    Select Case Trim(rsUsers.Fields("Status"))
      Case "P" :
        Response.Redirect "Plogonfail.asp?reason=2"
      Case "R" :
        Response.Redirect "Plogonfail.asp?reason=3"
```

If the user's application has been approved, the user is redirected to the restricted area of the Web site. At the same time, we store some of the user's information from the database in the `Session` object in order to personalize the members' area for the user.

Also notice that we set `Session("Auth") = "Y"`. This flag is to record that we have been through the authentication process. We'll see in a minute why this is important:

```
      Case "M" :
        Session("Auth") = "Y"
        Session("Name") = Trim(rsUsers.Fields("Name"))
        Session("EmailAddress") = Trim(rsUsers.Fields("EmailAddress"))
        Session("Company") = Trim(rsUsers.Fields("Company"))
        Response.Redirect "../members/Mhome.asp"
    End Select

    Response.End
  End If
```

If the password is not correct, the logic drops through and redisplays the HTML form. The failure count is also incremented by 1:

```
Session("LogonCount") =  Session("LogonCount") + 1
```

Failing A User's Log On

As you've already seen, we've used a very simple page, `Plogonfail.asp`, to display the various reasons a user has not been allowed to log on:

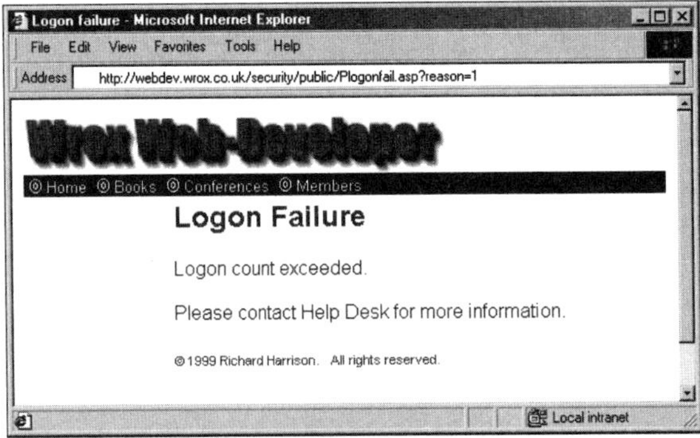

The specific reason for the logon failure to be displayed is dependent upon the `reason` parameter in the URL which is given a value when the user is redirected to this page:

```
<%
  Select Case Request.QueryString("reason")
    Case 1:
      Response.Write "<P>Logon count exceeded."
    Case 2:
      Response.Write "<P>Your application is pending."
    Case 3:
      Response.Write "<P>Your application was rejected."
  End Select
%>
```

Keeping the Members Area Secure

All of the members area restricted content is located in the `Members` subdirectory. As we saw above, once the user has logged on successfully, they are redirected to the file `Mhome.asp`. This file contains links to all restricted content.

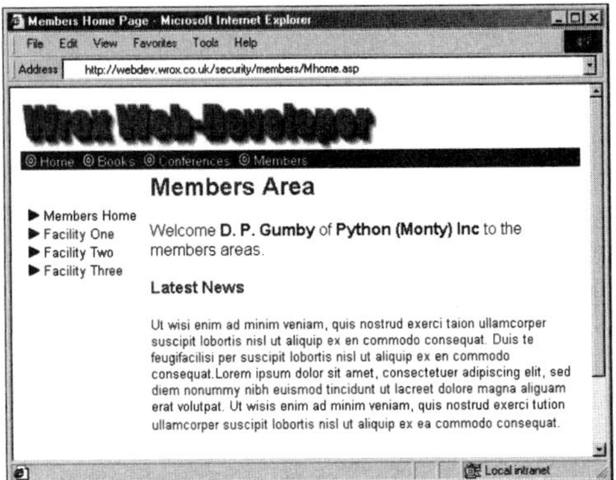

But at this stage you might be asking, 'Why can't anyone just navigate directly to this page and avoid the logon?' Remember that earlier we set `Session("Auth") = "Y"` when we logged on. Every member page must have the following ASP logic to check that the user has been successfully authenticated.

```
<%
  If Not Session("Auth") = "Y" Then
    Response.Redirect "../public/Plogon.asp"
  End if
%>
```

So any attempt to navigate directly and avoid the logon process will just result in the users browser being redirected to the logon screen.

The Membership Managers Intranet Site

In comparison with the Internet site, the intranet-based membership management site is incredibly simple. It contains a menu page (`default.asp`) and the file does all the hard work, `members.asp`:

The Members Administration Page

`Members.asp` is the ASP file that display entries in the membership database. In addition, it allows the status of each record to be amended.

- The file can work in five modes
- Displaying just approved members
- Displaying just applicants pending
- Displaying just rejected applicants
- Displaying all records
- Processing any amendments made by the manager

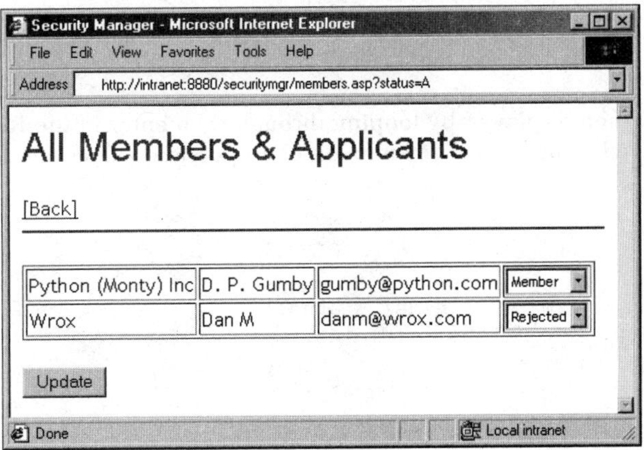

Display mode

The page's particular display mode is chosen by the user from the main menu (`default.asp`) and passed as the `Status` parameter in the URL.

```
<%
  vStatus = Request.QueryString("status")

  Select Case vStatus
    Case "A":
      Response.Write "<H1>All Members & Applicants</H1>"
    Case "R":
      Response.Write "<H1>Rejected Applicants</H1>"
    Case "P":
      Response.Write "<H1>Pending Approval</H1>"
    Case "M":
      Response.Write "<H1>Approved Members</H1>"
  End Select
%>
```

Using simple ADO logic we retrieve a Recordset containing the users' details that match the required `Status`. If the required `Status` is not `A` (All records) then a `Where` clause in the SQL query is specified. The Recordset is ordered on the `Company` field of the table so that this is the order that the records are displayed on the screen. Again, remember to specify the correct connection string to the `Users` table in your code:

```
<%
  Set objConn = Server.CreateObject("ADODB.Connection")
  objConn.Open [Connection string to Users table]

  vSQL = "SELECT * FROM Users"
  If vStatus <> "A" Then
    vSQL = vSQL + " WHERE Status = '" & vStatus & "'"
  End If

  vSQL = vSQL + " ORDER BY users.Company "

  Set rsUsers = objConn.Execute(vSQL)
```

The users' details are then displayed by looping through each entry in the Recordset. The `Status` of each record is displayed using a drop down menu of all possible values and is set to show the correct value:

```
  Do While Not rsUsers.EOF

    vStatus = Trim(rsUsers.Fields("Status"))
    vEmailAddress = Trim(rsUsers.Fields("EmailAddress"))
    vCompany = Trim(rsUsers.Fields("Company"))
    vName = Trim(rsUsers.Fields("Name"))

    Response.Write "<TR>" & _
```

```
            "<TD>" & vCompany & "</TD>" & _
            "<TD>" & vName  & "</TD>" & _
            "<TD>" & vEmailAddress & "</TD><TD>"

        Response.Write "<SELECT SIZE='1' NAME='" & _
            vEmailAddress & "'>"
        Response.Write "<OPTION VALUE='P'"
        If vStatus = "P" Then
            Response.Write " selected "
        End If

        Response.Write ">Pending</OPTION>"
        Response.Write "<OPTION VALUE='R'"
        If vStatus = "R" Then
            Response.Write " selected "
        End If

        Response.Write ">Rejected</OPTION>"
        Response.Write "<OPTION VALUE='M'"
        If vStatus = "M" Then
          Response.Write " selected "
        End If

        Response.Write ">Member</OPTION>" & "</TD></TR>"
        rsUsers.MoveNext

    Loop
```

All the users' details are displayed in an HTML form which can be submitted back to itself to update any member status fields you care to change:

```
<FORM METHOD="POST" ACTION="members.asp?status=<% Request.Form("status") %>" >

    - user details

<INPUT TYPE="SUBMIT" NAME="butSubmit" VALUE="Update">
</FORM>
```

Database Update Mode

At the top of the ASP file is the logic to detect whether or not the `Users` table should be updated. This is done by checking for a value called `butSubmit` in the page request:

```
<%
  If Request.Form("butSubmit") <> "" Then
```

When in update mode, each user record is updated to the `Status` specified in the form:

```
  Set objConn = Server.CreateObject("ADODB.Connection")
  objConn.Open ("DSN=Security;UID=sa;PWD=")

  For Each key In Request.Form
```

```
   If key <> "butSubmit" Then
     vSQL = "UPDATE Users SET Status = '" & _
             Request.Form(key) & "'" & _
             " Where EmailAddress = '" & _
               key & "'"

     objConn.Execute (vSQL)
   End If
   Next
```

Once the database has been updated, the logic then redirects the user back to the main menu:

```
   Response.Redirect "default.asp"
 End If
 %>
```

Summary

By now, you should have a pretty good understanding of most aspects of security that you should be looking at when setting up a secure Web site. There is a lot more information we simply couldn't cover in a single chapter so do keep up to date with the latest technologies available. Don't forget to keep your ears to the ground for any new security holes found in software that you're currently using. Where a hole is found, a patch is soon to follow.

The best way to stay ahead is through research and education. You should get yourself on as many mailing lists as possible related to the security of the products that you are running. Enforce your security policies with your manager to make sure that employees and users of the system are complying with expectations that have been presented to them.

25

Working With Certificates

In the previous chapter, we looked at the different technologies that can be used to provide security for your Web-based applications. These technologies all exist to address the security problems of the Internet, where it is possible, even easy, for determined people to access and manipulate data without any prior authorization. These security systems work by hiding information from unauthorized people and by building virtual private networks over public networks like the Internet.

However, this restriction of access to data is only part of the problem. In scenarios where we deal with the transmission of sensitive data, we need to guarantee that it will arrive safely at its destination and not be altered or partially lost en route. For example, when purchasing a new computer from `Dell.com` the consumer does not want his credit card number to be transmitted in clear text. Information transmitted in this way can be viewed by a network application that knows how to disassemble TCP packets (such as Microsoft's NetMon product). Using a tool such as NetMon, such raw data can easily be read. Rather, it behoves both the retailer and the shopper to transmit data in an encrypted format so that packet sniffers alone are not able to decipher a message between the two parties. The use of **certificates** for communication is one such way that you can ensure that any communication taking place between the client and the server over the Internet is done in a secure manner.

In this chapter we will look at how certificates can verify that users are who they say they are, and how they can ensure that any data transferring over the Internet is not tampered with. We'll cover the basics of certificate technology, how certificates work, and how to incorporate one into your own Web site. Specifically, we'll discuss:

- Basic concepts about identity and authenticity
- Types of certificates and Certificates Authorities
- Information about getting certificates

- Practical examples of getting certificates
- How to use certificates
- How to manage certificates with ASP
- How to set up a Certificate Authority with MS Certificate Services

The material covered in this chapter that deals with server certificate management requires Windows 2000 Server or Advanced Server operating systems. They don't work on the workstation version of Windows 2000 due to the lack of certificate server options.

Security, Identity and Authenticity

Transmission of sensitive data requires a mechanism that guarantees the following three features:

- **Security** – Data cannot be read by extraneous people
- **Identity** – The parties involved in the communication are who they claim to be
- **Authenticity** – The data received is identical with that sent, i.e. nobody has tampered with it

Technologies that provide secure communications have to be based upon a mechanism that guarantees these three features. Usually these technologies rely heavily on encryption algorithms which scramble the data in such a way that it is very difficult and time consuming, and hence practically impossible, for anyone to deduce the original data, given only the encoded data. The current best encryption algorithms are based on a technique known as **asymmetric key encryption**. The way this encryption works seems very simple, but relies on complex mathematical algorithms. However, as we will see, the asymmetric key encryption mechanism is able to guarantee not only security, but also identity and authenticity.

Asymmetric Key Encryption

Let's explain briefly the asymmetric key encryption mechanism.

Two people want to exchange data over a network in a secure way. The receiver has two 'keys' that are mathematically related. A **key** is a piece of data that allows us to encode or decode other data. This pair of keys has a special relationship; if data is encoded by the first key, only the second key is able to decode encrypted data and restore the original information and vice versa. Then the receiver gives one key to the sender and asks him to use this key to encode data. The key that is passed between users is usually known as the **public key** whereas the key that the individual holds on to is the **private key**.

The receiver will never reveal his private key, but can give the public key to anyone he wishes. If a sender wishes to send confidential data to the receiver, he will first encode it using the receiver's public key before sending it across to the receiver. Only the owner of the related private key, i.e. the receiver, will be able to decode the data. The following diagram shows the steps needed to exchange data in a secure way using asymmetric key encryption:

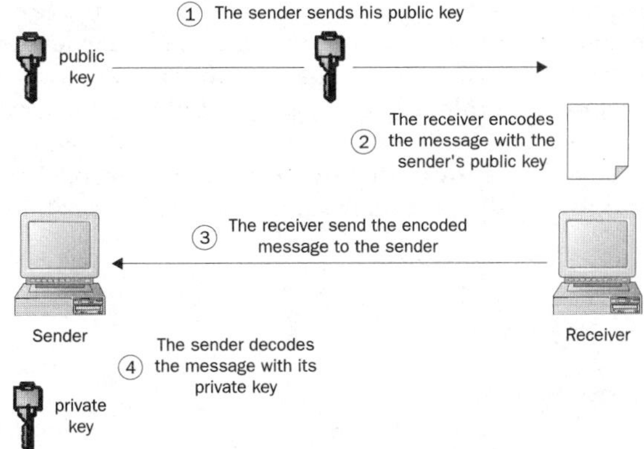

The encryption mechanism, based on the mathematical relationship between public and private keys, is very powerful, and guarantees a high level of security from attack. The mathematical relationship is very complex. To have an idea about its complexity, we can say that a typical relationship between the two keys is based on factoring large numbers. Factoring a 200 digit number requires about 4 billion years of computer time, assuming a computer with 1 μsec instruction time. This gives an idea of the mathematical complexity of the factoring problem and thus the security level of the encryption. The asymmetric key encryption mechanism can be considered the foundation of secure communications over a network, and is used in secure communication protocols such as **Secure Sockets Layer** (**SSL**). The SSL protocol provides a security handshake that is used to initiate a TCP/IP connection. It is used by IIS in establishing a secure connection between the client and the server. In the section called *Using a Server Certificate*, we will see how to enable IIS to use SSL for secure connections.

Asymmetric Key Encryption and Identity

However, in some circumstances, this form of secure communication is not enough to guarantee that the sender is who he says he is. Such situations involve identity verification. Suppose you receive an e-mail message from someone you know well, a friend, for instance. You and your friend can avoid someone else getting access to your private information by encoding the message with the asymmetric key mechanism, described above. This ensures that no third party can read your private message. But are you sure that the message really came from your friend? Your public key can be accessed by anyone, and as such anyone can send you a message pretending to be your friend.

This problem has a fundamental importance in e-commerce applications, where people want to be sure of buying items from the seller they believe they've contacted on the Web, and sellers want to be sure that customers are really who they say they are, and that they have the means to pay for the purchased items. In conclusion, this problem is relevant in every situation where you want to be sure about the **identity** of an individual to whom you are communicating.

In the context of this chapter, **identity** means a mechanism to identify a person or a company. Technically it is a mapping from a real entity, such as a human being or a company, to an Internet entity such as a Web site, a Web browser or an e-mail program.

We can use the same asymmetric key encryption mechanism seen above to verify identity. Remember that what we encode with the public key can be only decoded by the private key. However, the reverse is also true – what we encode with the private key can only be decoded by the public key. So we simply invert the role of the key pair to build a mechanism that verifies identity. The sender sends a message encoded with his private key, and the receiver decodes the message using the sender's public key. This ensures that the message he received came from the owner of the related private key. The following diagram shows how identity verification happens:

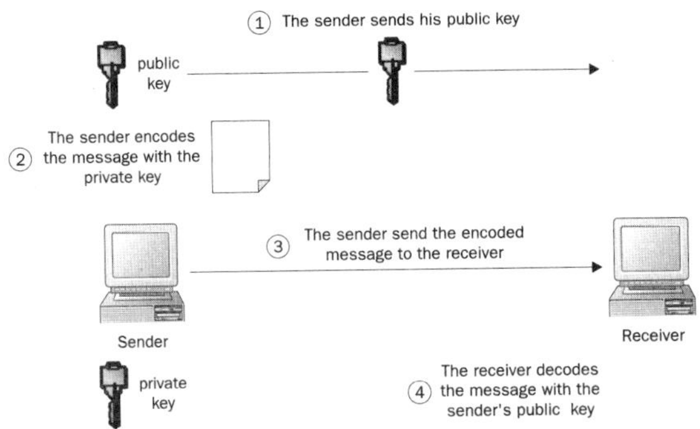

Asymmetric Key Encryption and Authenticity

Identity verification also implies the authenticity of data transmitted – that is the data received is exactly the same as the data that was sent. In fact, the very nature of asymmetric key encryption means that if a message has been tampered with, the receiver will not be able to decode it using the sender's public key. However in some situations, you might want to distribute plain data and also want the receiver to be able to verify that the data came from you and has not been tampered with. For example, a public legal document should be accessible to everyone, but its authenticity should be verifiable. In order to allow people to verify the authenticity of plain data, you can use a **digital signature**.

A digital signature is similar to a person's hand-written signature. It can be used to authenticate a sender's identity and ensure that data (a document, a message, a software component, etc.) is not modified during transit. It is derived from a string, called a **document hash** or **checksum**, that is calculated from the document and then encrypted using the private key of whoever produced the document. The document hash is like a document's fingerprint and is generated by hashing algorithms that take a large amount of data and return a much smaller piece, usually of a fixed size. Hashing algorithms guarantee that it is extremely difficult to obtain an identical document hash for different documents and, in particular, it is especially difficult to get the same hash value by simply altering a few characters.

The digital signature mechanism uniquely binds the hash string to the document and to the owner of the private key. The authenticity of a document can be verified by decoding the signature using the sender's public key (thus proving the identity of the sender), generating the document checksum and comparing it with the received one. The following diagram shows how digital signature generation and verification works:

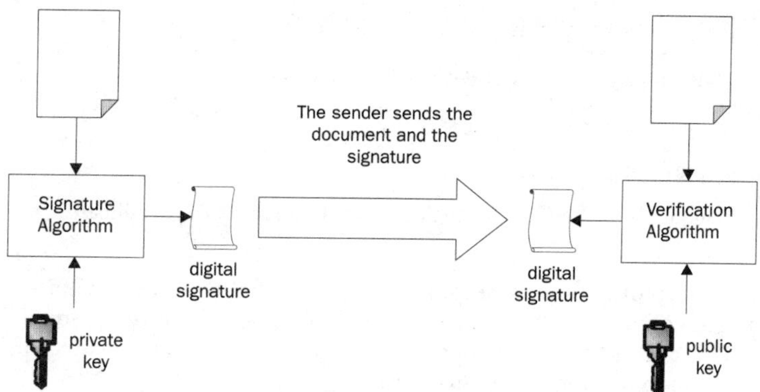

Generating a digital signature for a document is usually known as **signing** the document. Signing a document doesn't alter it. It simply generates a digital signature you can bundle with the document or transmit separately.

Certificates and Certificate Authorities

We have seen how asymmetric key encryption is the basic mechanism that allows us to get security, identity and authenticity verification in data transmission. All these features rely on the distribution of public keys, and the matching of these public keys to the appropriate private keys. In other words, if you want to send an encrypted message to someone, you need to possess his public key, or if you receive a signed document, you need to possess the author's public key to verify its authenticity.

However, if you receive a public key, can you be sure that the individual sending it is whom you would expect or want? It is very conceivable that a public key could be sent to the wrong person by mistake. Remember that asymmetric key encryption guarantees that the key matching mechanism works, not that a public key is in the possession of the intended individual.

Certificates help to solve this matching problem. Certificate technology allows for individuals to be uniquely identified, thus easily authenticated by a trusting application or server if the certificate is valid. However, certificate technology is not restricted to individual user authentication. It can also be used to authenticate documents such as e-mails or any other application that supports certificate encryption.

What is a Certificate?

A **digital certificate** is a unique record that contains the information necessary to verify the identity of an individual or organization. Digital certificates evolved from the X.509 standard format, which conforms to the Public-Key Cryptography Standards (PKCS) proposed by RSA Laboratories. You can find more information about these standards at `http://www.rsa.com/rsalabs/pubs/PKCS/`.

The X.509 standard describes some certificate requirements:

- The format version used by the certificate
- The serial number of the certificate
- The identifier of the algorithm used to sign the certificate

- The Certificate Authority that issued the certificate
- The initial date and the expiration date of the certificate
- The owner's name
- The owner's public key
- The digital signature of the Certificate Authority that issued the certificate

Each of these items of information corresponds to specific fields in the structure of the certificate. Certificates may also contain other information, including postal address, e-mail address, country, age, gender, etc. This additional data is optional and depends on the specific type of certificate. The following table shows a typical example of a certificate's fields:

Version	V3
Serial Number	6F314B0248C6243D2FCD6B7BDC881D83
Sign. Algorithm	RSA (512 bits)
Issuer	VeriSign Inc.
Initial date	07/08/99 0.00.00
Expiration date	07/07/00 23.59.59
Owner's name	John Smith
Owner's public key	304702407E9C8F3EDEC8ADA4C57A46F1C9D07BF0...
Issuer's signature	9BEF54680B4FD3CF9E406465A702030100016A72F1...

The information stored in some of the certificate's fields will be explained in more detail as the chapter progresses. The table above, however, does illustrate the basic structure that a certificate must have. Note that a certificate by itself cannot verify an individual's identity. Anyone can create and issue a certificate following the standard format outlined above. What is needed is a system that issues certificates according to some very strict standards. Only then will certificates be able to provide the security that we want.

Certificate Authorities

Among the information required by the standard certificate format, make a note of the **Certificate Authority**, represented as the **Issuer** in the table above. The Certificate Authority – CA for short – is a trusted third party that is relied upon to verify the matching of public keys to identity, that is to prove that a particular public key is owned by a known user. Certificate Authorities are responsible for issuing, revoking, renewing, and providing directories of digital certificates. CAs must follow rigorous procedures for authenticating the individuals and organizations to whom they issue certificates. Such authentication guarantees the validity of the key matching process for anyone trusting in the CA. We can consider a CA as a notary of the Internet.

The certificate structure shown in the diagram above has two CA-related fields: the *Issuer* and the *Issuer's signature.* The presence of these fields says that the CA guarantees that the public key contained in it belongs to the certificate's owner. Of course this consideration just moves the trust problem from individuals to the CA. In other words, who guarantees that the CA is worthy of trust? There is no simple answer to this question. However, trust is the basis of the CA's existence.

Currently many organizations offer certification services. Their number is growing day by day due to the general great interest in e-commerce opportunities. The following table shows some of the well-known Certificate Authorities along with their Web addresses:

Name	URL
Belsign	`www.belsign.be`
Certisign Certificadora Digital	`www.certisign.com.br`
COST	`www.cost.se`
Entrust Technologies	`www.entrust.com`
EuroSign	`www.eurosign.com`
GTE CyberTrust	`www.cybertrust.gte.com`
InterClear	`www.interclear.co.uk`
Keywitness	`www.keywitness.ca`
SETco	`www.setco.org`
Thawte	`www.thawte.com`
Verisign	`www.verisign.com`
Xcert Software	`www.xcert.com`

When two users or two organizations exchange certificates, both can verify the other's identity, provided that they trust the CA or CAs that issued the certificates. Each certificate contains the owner's public key, so it can be used to encrypt data to be sent to the certificate's owner. The certificate also contains the digital signature of the CA that issued it. This ensures that no one has modified the certificate, and that the information stored in it is correct.

As we seen in the previous section, a digital signature is made by using the private key of the author of the document. So, to verify that a certificate has been signed by a particular CA, you need the public key of this CA. As we will see in the section called *Managing Certificates*, the public keys of most CAs are generally distributed together with browsers, e-mail programs and other software packages. This allows a user to verify that a particular certificate is authentic.

Types of Certificates

There are four kinds of digital certificates used on the Internet, each of which has a particular certification scope:

- **Server Certificates**, also known as **Server IDs**, allow servers that use a secure communication protocols such as SSL to be identified. These certificates allow the user to verify the server or Web site identity before sending confidential information.

- **Personal Certificates** identify individuals. They may be used to authenticate users with a server, or to enable secure e-mail.

- **Software Publisher Certificates** are used to sign software distributed over the Internet. They are meant to solve one of the larger questions facing the software industry today – how users can trust code that is published on the Internet. Packaged software uses branding and shrink-wrapping to assure users of its integrity. The logo implies trust and reputation, while the shrink-wrapping means no one has tampered with the contents since the box was sealed. However, code that has been transmitted over the Internet doesn't include these familiar assurances. To provide them, software publishers need a digital equivalent. Code signing is the Internet equivalent of branding and shrink-wrapping. However, Software Publisher Certificates don't guarantee that signed code is safe to run, or is error free. But, if an error occurs you can quickly identify the producer in order to complain.

- **Certificate Authority Certificates** identify a CA. This type of certificate needs a little more explanation. You can divide CAs into two categories: **Root CAs** and **Intermediate CAs**. The difference between the two is as follows. A Root CA can issue any types of certificate and the identity is certified by itself, whereas an Intermediate CA can issue all types of certificates *except* a certificate for itself. A Root CA Certificate is the only type of certificate where the issuer and the owner of the certificate are the same. A Root CA can issue a certificate to an Intermediate CA, and an Intermediate CA can issue a certificate to another Intermediate CA. The type of certificate issued by one CA to another is a Certificate Authority Certificate. The outcome of this is the creation of a CA hierarchy, where each refers to its issuer for a trust guarantee, right up to the Root CA. This hierarchy is known as the **verification chain**. This hierarchical structure of CAs arises for organizational reasons which depend on the CA itself (its geographical location, the certificate type issued, the ease of administration, etc.).

  The following diagram shows an example of CA hierarchy based on geographical location and certificate type issued:

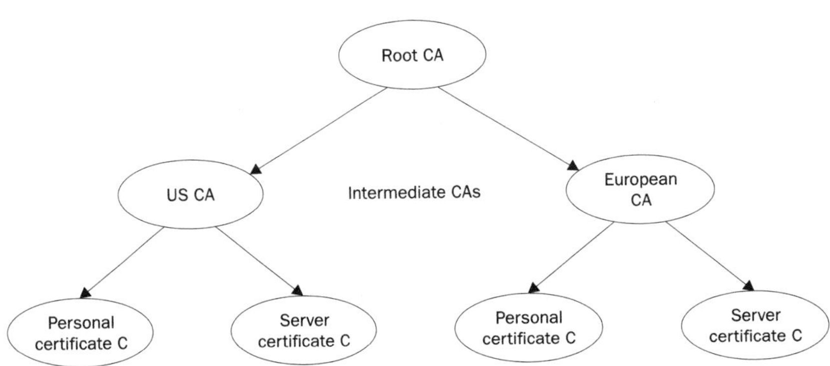

An important advantage of this hierarchical organization is that verification of certificates requires trust in only a relatively small number of Root CAs. In fact, if you can trust the Root CA of a CA hierarchy, you also trust every Intermediate CA it has certified.

Getting a Certificate from a Certificate Authority

If you decide to get a certificate, you have to contact a CA. The process of getting a certificate is commonly know as **enrollment** and is slightly different for each certificate type.

Before starting the enrollment process, you should take time to mull a few things over when choosing a CA. Here are some issues to consider:

- Is the CA a trusted entity operating a certification practice that can both meet your needs and operate efficiently in your region? Clients and other CAs should immediately recognize your CA as a reputable, trustworthy organization. If you choose an authority with questionable reputation, you run the risk of having users reject your certificate.
- Is the CA familiar with your organization's business interests? Look for a CA from whom you can leverage technical, legal and business expertise.
- What type of information will the authority require from you in order to verify your identity? Most Certificate Authorities will require detailed information, such as your identity, your organization's identity, and your official authority to administer the Web server for which you are requesting a certificate. Depending on the level of identification assurance required, a CA may require additional information, such as professional affiliations or financial information and the endorsement of this information by a notary.
- Does the CA have a system for receiving online certificate requests, such as those generated by a key manager server? An online system can speed up the processing of your certificate requests. Most CAs have this feature.

Each CA has its **Certification Practices Statement** (CPS) which publicly states the operating procedures carries out. Usually it is published on the CA's Web site, so you can read it before requesting a certificate.

The following picture shows the home page of the Thawte CA. Notice the links to the CPS and to the certificate enrollment forms:

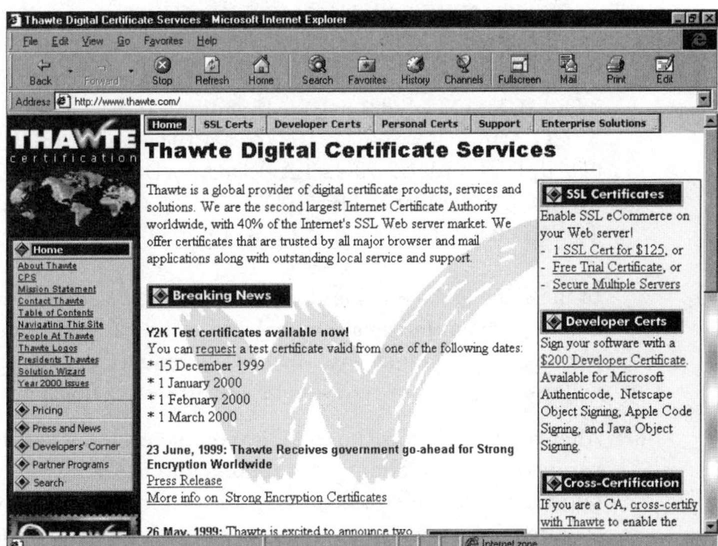

Getting a Server Certificate

We have already seen that a server certificate identifies a server using the SSL protocol for secure communication over the Web. This means that when a browser initiates a communication with a certified Web server through the HTTPS protocol, the secure variant of HTTP, it receives the server's public key along with its certificate. This allows the browser to identify the server's owner securely and use its public key to encrypt data.

In order to enable a Web server to use SSL and certificates, a specific procedure has to be carried out which depends on the particular Web server being used and the chosen CA. However, each of the steps taken to carry out the procedure are general enough to be applied to any server and to most CAs. They are as follows:

1. A server certificate is bound to a registered Internet domain, so make sure that the domain of your Web site is correctly registered. If you have not registered a domain for your Web site, you have to register it before proceeding to request a certificate.
2. Generate a key pair, and a Certificate Signing Request (CSR) using tools that come with your server software. The key generation stage produces the server's private and public key. This first step is important as the CSR that is created includes a copy of the server's public key. During the CSR generation you have to provide some other information such as the URL of your Web site, the name of your company or organization, and your address. The result of this step is an ASCII file containing the certificate request in a standard format known as PKCS#10.
3. At this point you can send the CSR to the CA you have chosen. This task can be accomplished in a number of ways. You can send it by e-mail or using the online enrollment form published on the CA Web site, if there is one. In the latter case you have to perform a cut and paste operation from the CSR file to fill the Web form. The content of your CSR file should look like this:

   -----BEGIN NEW CERTIFICATE REQUEST-----
   MIIBJTCB0AIBADBtMQswCQYDVQQGEwJVUzEQMA4GA1UEChs4lBMHQXJpem9uYT
   ENA1UEBxMETWVzYTEfMB0GA1UEChMWTWVs3XbnzYSBDb21tdW5pdHkgQ29sbGVn
   ZTEA1UEAxMTd3d3Lm1jLm1hcmljb3BhLmVkdTBaMA0GCSqGSIb3DQEBAQUAA0kAM
   EYCQQDRNU6xslWjG41163gArsj/P108sFmjkjzMuUUFYbmtZX4RFxf/U7cZZdMagz4IMmY
   0F9cdpDLTAutULTsZKDcLAgEDoAAwDQYJKoZIhvcNAQEEBQADQQAjIFpTLgfmBVhc9
   SQaip5SFNXtzAmhYzvJkt5JJ4X2r7VJYG3J0vauJ5VkjXz9aevJ8dzx37ir3P4XpZ+NFxK1R=
   -----END NEW CERTIFICATE REQUEST-----

   In the same form you could be asked for other administrative information (such as contact name, payment information,etc.) and technical information (your server software, a challenge phrase, etc.), if you so wish. Most CAs request a challenge phrase, which is a string that you will use to revoke or renew your certificate.
4. After sending the CSR to the CA, you have to wait for the verification process. The CA verifies the information you provided and can ask you for additional information. The information provided to certify your own identity is known as **proof of rights** and can be traditional documentation such as Business License, Articles of Incorporation or a Tax ID number. The policy rules applied during the verification process depend on the CA and on the identity level required.

   When the verification process is complete, the CA creates a certificate with the appropriate information (public key, expiration date, and other data) and signs it using the CA's private key. It then sends it to you or publishes it on its Web site for download. The certificate you receive is an ASCII file containing data in the PKCS#7 standard format. Its content looks like this:

-----BEGIN CERTIFICATE-----
CBHcm91cCBDQS5jcmwwRqBEoEKGQGZpbGU6Ly9cXENFUlRTUlZcQ2VydFNydlxDZ
XJ0RW5yb2xsXE1TIENlcnRTcnYgVGVzdCBHcm91cCBDQS5jcmwwCQYDVR0TBAIwA
DBiBggrBgEFBQcBAQRWMFQwUgYIKwYBBQUHMAKGRmh0dHA6Ly9DRVJUU1JWL0
NlcnRTcnYvQ2VydEVucm9sbC9DRVJUU1JWX01TIENlcnRTcnYgVGVzdCBHcm91cCB
DQS5jcnQwDQYJKoZIhvcNAQEEBQADQQAhq70nRlse0ulPstU+IWdjeNj5p
-----END CERTIFICATE-----

5. Finally you can install your server certificate on your Web server following the instructions of the appropriate documentation. Remember to make a backup copy of the file you received. Note that the CA **never** possesses your private key. If you lose the server certificate you have to submit a new CSR.

Next I will show you how to get a server certificate using MS Internet Information Server, IIS.

Getting A Server Certificate for IIS from Verisign

The steps seen above to get a Server Certificate from a CA were very generic and outlined the procedure valid for most server software and CAs. Here we will see a concrete example of certificate request and installation. I will use IIS 5.0 as Web server and Verisign Inc. as Certificate Authority.

1. **Generate key pair and CSR**

As the first step you have to generate the key pair and the Certificate Signing Request. This step can be accomplished by using the **Internet Service Manager**. Right-click the Web site you want to request the certificate for and select Properties. Then click the Directory Security tab. You should get this window:

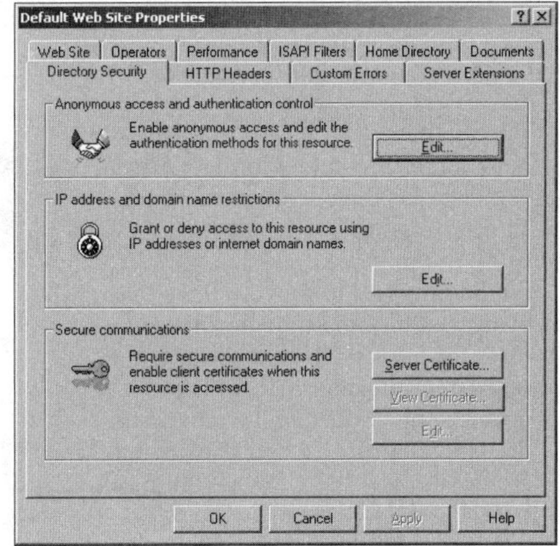

Note that the Edit button in the Secure communications box is not enabled because no server certificate has been installed. By clicking the Server Certificate button you will run the Web Server Certificate Wizard to collect information needed to generate the CSR.

Press Next> and you will get a screen where you specify that you want to Create a New Certificate. On the screen that follows one radio button is checked, which gives you just one option: Prepare the request now, but send it later. Press Next> again and you will be invited to supply the details of your CSR. A sequence of screens will follow where information is entered about your company and your Web site. This information is known as the **Distinguished Name** of your server. In particular, the wizard will ask for details of:

- **Organization** – This should be the organization or company that owns the domain name. The organization name (corporation, university, government agency) must be registered with some authority at the national, state or city level. You have to provide the legal name under which your organization is registered.
- **Organizational Unit** – You can use this optional field to differentiate between divisions within an organization.
- **Common Name** – The common name is the fully qualified domain name used for DNS lookups of your server (such as `www.wrox.com`). This information is used by browsers to identify your Web site. If you change your hostname, you will need to request another certificate. Client browsers connecting to your host will check for a match between your certificate's common name and your URL. You cannot use wildcards (*, ? etc.), IP addresses, or port numbers in this field. Make sure also that you have not included "`http://`" or "`https://`" either.
- **Country/Region** – In this field you will enter the two character ISO format code (e.g. `US` for United States, `IT` for Italy, `GB` for Great Britain).
- **State/Province** – You have to provide the state or province in which the organization is located.
- **City/Locality** – This field denotes the city in which the organization is located.

When you have provided all the needed information, you will be asked to provide the name for the `.txt` file where the CSR will be saved. After a screen that summarizes all the information you provided, the wizard will generate the key pair, create a CSR and save it in the file with the name you just specified. Click the Finish button to complete the process.

2. Request your certificate

Now you can connect to the Verisign Web site for the enrollment process. The address is `http://www.verisign.com`. From the home page, follow the links that bring you to the online enrollment form for Server IDs and provide the requested information. In order to provide the CSR, you have to open the CSR file using a text editor such as Notepad, copy the CSR, including the `BEGIN NEW CERTIFICATE REQUEST` and `END NEW CERTIFICATE REQUEST` lines, and paste it into the form's field:

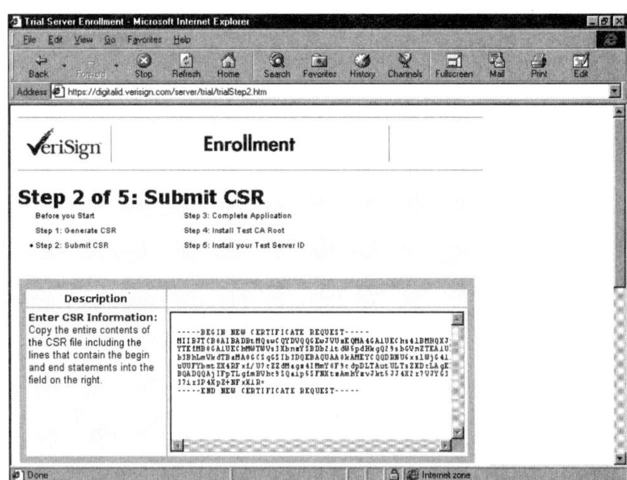

Complete the form providing information about your organization's contacts and payment.

3. Wait for verification process

After submitting the request, you have to wait for a confirmation message. You will receive an e-mail confirming your enrollment. The message will include a PIN (**Personal Identification Number**) and a URL where you can use your PIN to check on the status of your certificate request. Usually this e-mail message is sent within two hours of submitting your request. Then the verification process starts. Verisign will examine the information that you have submitted and possibly can request extra documentation. If no extra documentation is required, you can get your certificate in 3-5 working days.

4. Receive your certificate

Verisign sends the certificate by e-mail. Other CAs, such as Thawte, publish it on their Web server for downloading. Following this example, you should receive your certificate in a file attached to an e-mail. Now you are ready to install it on your Web server.

5. Install your certificate

To install your certificate you have to reopen Internet Service Manager and restart the Web Server Certificate Wizard by clicking the Server Certificate button on the Directory security tab as before. The wizard will show a message saying that you have a pending certificate request. Following the next screen you will be able to process the pending request or delete it. You don't want to do the latter so select the Process the pending request and install the certificate option. You will then be asked to provide the path and file name of the file containing the certificate sent to you by the CA. In the final step, the wizard installs the server certificate.

After installing a certificate, your Web server will be SSL-enabled. However SSL will not be used by the server until you don't explicitly require it on the single IIS resource (HTML page, ASP page or virtual directory). We will see how to enable SSL on an IIS resource in the section called *Using a Server Certificate*. If you need a certificate for the sole purpose of testing your system, free ones are available from Verisign and other CAs.

Getting Personal Certificates

Personal certificates allow people and servers to verify an individual's identity. You can use them with your e-mail program to send encrypted messages. Alternatively, you can use them with your browser to access Web sites requiring client authentication. If you want to get a personal certificate, you have to follow a procedure similar to that already described. Here is a summary:

1. For a personal certificate you don't need to explicitly generate private and public keys – they are generated by your browser during your request. The first step, then, is to access the Web site of the chosen CA and submit a certificate request by filling out the available form. You have to provide your identity information (full name, address, date of birth), your e-mail address and some other data such as gender, passport number, tax number – depending on the CA, and your nationality.

2. After the request has been submitted to the CA, you wait for the verification process to complete. In particular, your e-mail address will be checked by sending instructions for installing the certificate.

3. In the final step, you have to install the certificate in your browser and your e-mail program and use it for client authentication and message encryption. The installation procedure depends on the e-mail program or on the Web browser used. Some CAs provide an online system that automatically installs the certificate on your browser.

Getting a Personal Certificate for IE from Verisign

Getting a personal certificate is slightly different from getting a server certificate. Once you've got a personal certificate you can access Web sites requiring certificate authentication and send authentic or encrypted e-mail messages, or both. In this section I will show you the procedure for obtaining a personal certificate from Verisign using MS Internet Explorer.

1. **Connect to Verisign and request your certificate**

Unlike the server certificate, you don't explicitly generate the key pair. This task is accomplished by an ActiveX control (`Xenroll.dll`) used within the Web page containing the enrollment form. After connecting to the Verisign Web site, you browse for the Digital ID online enrollment form which looks like this:

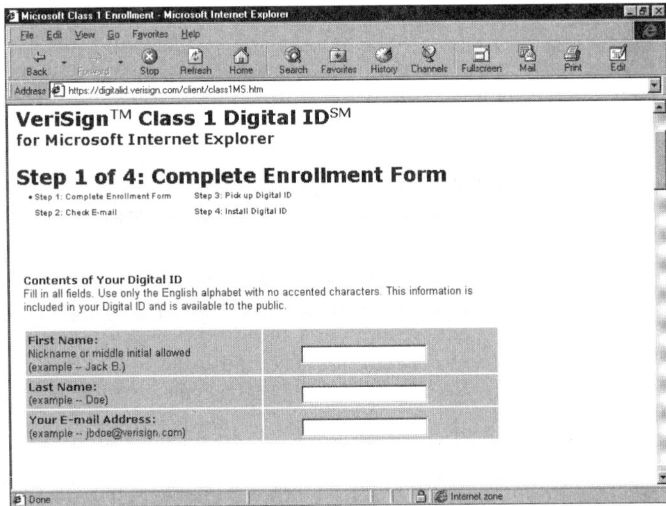

You have to provide the following information: first name, last name and e-mail address. Optionally you can provide more information such as country, date of birth and gender, which can simplify registration at certain Web sites that accepts certificates. Other information you can supply includes a challenge phrase, billing information and protection level for your private key.

When you submit data to the Verisign's server, the ActiveX control generates the key pair and a CSR, and stores your private key in the registry.

Notice that Netscape Communicator 4.0 onwards use a different approach to generate the key pair. Netscape defines the proprietary HTML tag `<KEYGEN>`. This tag has to be used in a form and renders a combo box allowing you to select the size of the key to generate. The following is an example of how to use `<KEYGEN>`:

```
<KEYGEN NAME="mykey">
```

When the submit button is pressed, a key pair of the selected size is generated. The private key is stored in the local key database, a file managed by Communicator, while the public key is embedded in a CSR and sent to the server.

2. Wait for instructions

Now you have to wait for an e-mail message. This message also serves to check the e-mail address you provided in the form. The verification process in this case is very simple. This is due to the class of certificate requested (class 1, in this example). A more accurate verification is made when an higher class certificate is requested.

The message you will receive explains what you have to do. It provides you with a Personal Identification Number (PIN) and asks you to enter it into a form at Verisign's secure Digital ID Center in order to get the certificate. At the time of writing it is located at `https://digitalid.verisign.com/enrollment/mspickup.htm`.

It is important that you complete this step using the same computer and the same browser used to submit the enrollment form.

3. Get and install your certificate

After submitting your PIN, the Verisign server will generate the certificate. This can take several minutes. On completion, you will get a Web page showing the data containing in your new certificate. If data is correct, you can click the Install button and the certificate will be installed on your browser. The same ActiveX control is used to carry out the installation.

You can install the same certificate on MS Outlook Express enabling you to sign and encrypt your e-mail messages. The following instructions guide you in the procedure to associate your personal certificate with your e-mail account in MS Outlook Express.

1. Select Accounts from the Tools menu, then the Mail tab.

2. Select the mail account you want to associate the certificate with, click the Properties button and then select the Security tab. You can then select the certificate you want to use to sign your e-mail messages, in the Signing certificate box, and the certificate you want to use to encrypt e-mail messages, in the Encrypting preferences box. Of course you can select the same certificate for both purposes:

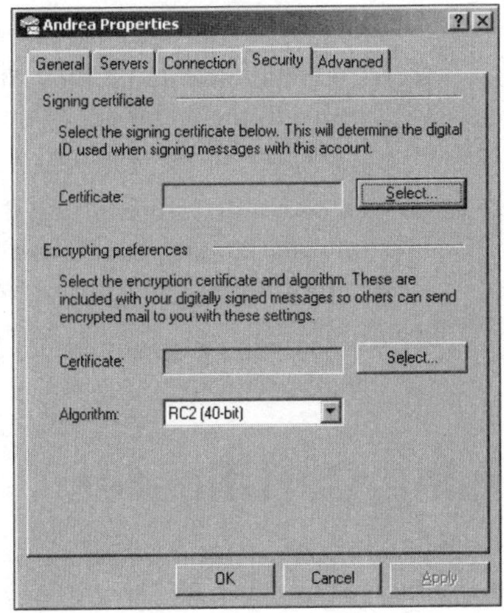

3. Click OK to confirm your selections.

Verisign also provides instructions and other useful information about using personal certificates. As for server certificates, you can get a free test certificate for a limited period of time.

Getting Software Publisher Certificates

Software Publisher Certificates (SPC) identify the producer or the publisher of a software component distributed over the Internet. This kind of certificate allows us to recognize the producer of a signed software and guarantees that the software has not been tampered with. Note however that signing software does not encrypt the software itself.

Before requesting an SPC you have to focus on a couple of points. The first is the technology you want to use to sign your software. The main two technologies currently used to sign software are **Microsoft Authenticode** and **Netscape Object Signing**. These two technologies are incompatible and require different tools and different types of certificates. So you have to request separate certificates to sign software with both technologies.

The second point concerns the type of software producer you are. Many CAs make a distinction between Individual Software Publishers (that is the single programmer) and Commercial Software Publishers (that is a software company). This distinction involves different verification processes and incurs different costs.

When requesting a certificate you have to decide which technology you intend to use and which type of software producer you are.

The process of getting a Software Publisher Certificate consists of the following steps:

1. Before requesting an SPC, be sure to have the right tool to sign software. For Microsoft Authenticode, you need the Internet Explorer Administration Kit (`http://www.microsoft.com/windows/ie/ieak/Webcast.htm`), while for Netscape Object Signing you need the Netscape Object Signing Toolkit (`http://developer.netscape.com/software/signedobj/jarpack.html`).
2. Connect to the CA's Web site and fill out the enrollment form, providing information about yourself, the technology you want to use, the type of software publisher you are, along with other routine administrative information.
3. Once you have completed the application, the CA will take some days to verify your information and issue a certificate. At the end of this process, the CA usually sends instructions to pick up your certificate from its Web site.
4. When you get your certificate and your private key, you can sign your files using the appropriate signing tool.

Using Certificates

After getting a certificate, you can use it to prove your identity in every secure transaction on the Internet. Your certificate assures any other party that the electronic information they receive from you is authentic. But, how do you use your certificate? What do you need to access a Web site requiring authentication? And how can you use authentication on your server? How do you use your certificate on another computer? How can it be used to authenticate an e-mail message? What do you do when your certificate expires?

I'll try to answer all these questions in this section.

Using a Server Certificate

After installing your server certificate on your Web server, you have to enable it to use SSL protocol. With Internet Information Server you can enable SSL on each single resource (HTML page or ASP page) or on a virtual directory. In order to do this, you have to carry out the following steps in Internet Services Manager:

1. Right-click the resource in your Web site on which you want enable SSL and select Properties from the pop up menu.
2. On the Directory Security property page, press the Edit under Secure communications. (Notice that the Edit button has been enabled as if a certificate has been installed for the Web site.)
3. Check the Require Secure Channel (SSL) checkbox and then click OK to accept the changes.

Remember that you have to use HTTPS protocol when you refer to SSL-enabled pages. Then, if you want to link the SSL protected page `mypage.asp`, you will have to write `https://www.myserver.com/mypage.asp` instead of `http://www.myserver.com/mypage.asp`. Notice that you cannot link to a secure page from a non secure page using a relative path, that is to say, you cannot put a link in a non secure Web page to an SSL page using just its relative path and name, such as:

```
<A HREF="securepage.asp">Secure Page</A>
```

You have to provide the absolute path:

```
<A HREF="https://www.myserver.com/securepage.asp">Secure Page</A>
```

A relative path can be used from one secure page to another on the same server. Absolute paths are necessary in order to change protocols.

When a browser requests a page to the Web server through HTTPS, the server sends its certificate (and its public key) to the browser making it able to encode data to send and decode data received. This exchange of information happens automatically.

Most browsers have installed certificates from well-known Certificate Authorities. If your certificate has not been issued by any of the CAs the browser is able to verify, the user will see a warning message prompting him to decide whether to continue to access the Web site or to abort. You can see which CA certificates your browser has already installed by following the instructions provided in the section *Managing Certificates.*

Apart from using HTTPS instead of HTTP when referencing an SSL-enabled resource, there is nothing else you need to do with your Web application.

Using a Personal Certificate

A personal certificate can be used for two purposes: client authentication, and the signing and encryption of e-mail messages. Some Web sites requires certificate authentication before you can access them. This type of authentication is more reliable than the classical login based on user name and password for the following reasons:

- A stolen certificate is useless without the matching private key, while the username and password pair enable anyone to access Web sites as well as you.
- A certificate does not require a user to remember his or her user name and password.
- A certificate definitively associates a user with his transactions, so there cannot be repudiation.

When accessing a Web site that requires certificate authentication, your browser sends your certificate to the Web server allowing it to verify your identity. Most browsers allow you to set some preferences when sending certificates to the server. For instance, they can ask you to confirm before sending the certificate or you can allow it to be sent automatically.

You can use your personal certificate in your e-mail program to sign a message, allowing the receiver to verify that the message has been sent by you and that it has not been tampered with. You can sign a message in MS Outlook Express simply by clicking the envelope with the seal on the toolbar or from the Tools menu by selecting Digitally Sign. This operation adds an attachment to the message containing the signature of the message and your certificate. The receiver can verify the authenticity of your message using this attached data. This verification procedure is usually performed by the e-mail program.

You can also use your private key included in your certificate to encrypt messages. In MS Outlook Express you can do it by clicking the envelope with the key lock on the toolbar or from the Tools menu by selecting Encrypt.

Using a Software Publisher Certificate

A Software Publisher Certificate must be used in combination with some tools to sign your software. These tools depend on the technology you use to sign software. For example, to sign a program file with Authenticode, you have to use the `signcode.exe` utility that comes with the MS Internet Administration Kit, using the following syntax:

```
signcode -n displayname -i http://www.myWeb.com -spc mycertificate.spc
-k myprivatekey.pvk myfilename
```

Where `displayname` is the file description that will be displayed in the certificate, `http://www.myWeb.com` is the Web address where more information about the program can be found, `mycertificate.spc` is your SPC certificate file, `myprivatekey.pvk` is your private key and `myfilename` is the name of the file to sign.

How to use SPC certificates is beyond the scope of this book. However, you can find more information about MS Authenticode from the Microsoft site at `http://msdn.microsoft.com/workshop/security/authcode/authenticode.asp` and for Netscape Object Signing look up `http://developer.netscape.com/library/documentation/signedobj/trust/index.htm`.

When you download software from the Internet, the browser or client-side application calls a function to verify signatures. This function uses the publisher's public key (verified by the certifying authority) to decrypt and check the signature. After the signature is checked, the following may happen, depending on the options selected by the user:

- If the certificate is valid, the user can decide to receive information about each piece of downloaded code, or simply let all signed code execute without first displaying any messages.
- If the code has not been signed, a warning is displayed and the user can decide whether or not to install the code.
- If the signature is invalid, or if the certificate has been revoked or has expired, then a stronger warning appears.

Client Certificate Mapping

In a previous section I discussed client authentication through personal certificates. Here I will explain how to enable IIS to authenticate users by checking the contents of a certificate submitted by the user's Web browser during the logon process. In a following section, we will see how to customize certificate authentication using ASP.

IIS has a client certificate mapping feature that authenticates users who log on with client certificates, without requiring the use of Basic or Windows NT Challenge/Response authentication. A mapping relates the contents of a user's client certificate to a corresponding Windows NT account which defines the rights and access policies of the user. Once you create and enable a mapping, your Web server automatically connects, or maps, that user to an appropriate Windows NT account each time a user logs on with a client certificate.

IIS can be configured to ignore, accept, or require client certificates when a client requests an SSL-enabled Web resource (an HTML page, an ASP page or a virtual directory). It is important to understand how each setting changes how IIS responds to client certificates:

- **Ignore certificates** – IIS doesn't care if a user sends his certificate with a request; it will simply authenticate the user using another method, such as Challenge/Response.
- **Accept certificates** – if a client certificate is sent, IIS will use the information contained in the certificate to authenticate the user. If no certificate is sent, IIS will use another method.
- **Require certificates** – IIS will only fulfill requests from users with valid certificates.

There are two methods that IIS uses to map client certificates to these accounts: many-to-one and one-to-one. The biggest difference between them is that one-to-one uses the actual certificate, whereas many-to-one only uses certain information contained in the certificate, such as who the certificate issuer is. With one-to-one mapping, if a user gets a new certificate, the old mapping will fail and IIS will have to create a new mapping for the new certificate. With many-to-one mapping, if the user gets a new certificate, the mapping will automatically accept it, providing the information that is used by IIS to verify the certificate remains the same.

Many-to-one mapping uses only certain information contained in the certificate. However, you are in control of what information is used for the mapping. You can set wildcard rules, such as, "accept all certificates from such-and-such a certification authority", or you can supply much tighter specifications such as "accept only certificates issued to this particular user". In this way, you can easily and quickly map many certificates to a single user account. Also, there is no need to have a copy of the client certificate on your server. If the user gets a new certificate that has the same information as before, the old mapping will still work. Many-to-one mapping doesn't identify a client, but a group of clients. For instance, this kind of mapping can be used to identify individual employees within a company.

Because one-to-one mapping uses special information that is unique to every certificate, you can be confident about the user's identity. One-to-one mapping uses a cryptographic exchange, much like Challenge/Response, involving the key pair of the client certificate. During this exchange, the server needs to compare the information sent by the user's browser to that of a copy of the client's certificate on the server. Therefore, the server must have a copy of every client certificate used for one-to-one mapping.

As the server uses an actual copy of the client certificate to make this comparison, a copy of that certificate will have to be obtained and a new mapping will have to be made if the client gets another certificate. This is true even if the exact same user information is used to generate the certificate. Remember that the key pair generated for each certificate is absolutely unique.

Unless you enable certificate mapping on your server, it will not be able to use certificates to automatically authenticate users. To enable one-to-one certificate mapping on your server, you have to carry out the following steps:

1. Open Internet Service Manager, right-click the Web site you want to apply certificate mapping on and select Properties.
2. Select the Directory Security tab and click Edit under Secure communications.
3. Check the Require secure channel (SSL) box and select the Require client certificates radio button and then check Enable client certificate mapping.

   Notice that you have to check the Require secure channel box in order to select the Require client certificates option. This option will make IIS to require a client certificate when it tries to access a protected resource in this Web site. If you select the Accept client certificates option, IIS will accept certificates to authenticate clients. If the certificate is not provided or it is not valid, the standard authentication protocol based on user name and password will be enabled.
4. Then click the Edit button on the Secure Communications dialog box. Now you have to choose whether to map certificates on a one-to-one basis or define a rule that will map many certificates to a single user account:

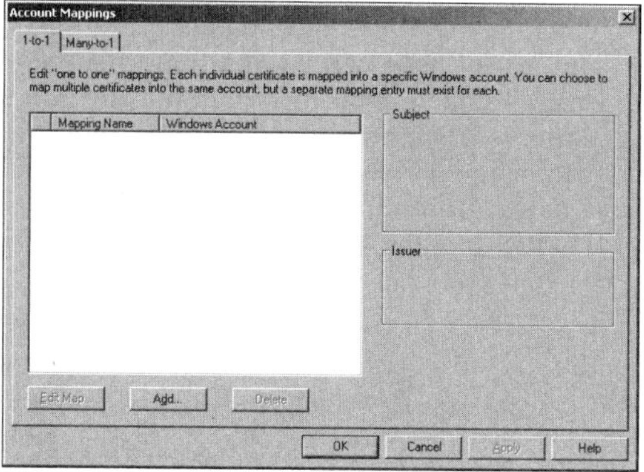

5. Select the 1-to-1 tab and click Add to add a certificate to map. You will be asked to provide the name of the certificate file of the user you want to map to a Windows account. We will discuss certificate file formats in the section *Managing Certificates.*

   After you have selected the certificate file you want to map, you will be prompted to select a Windows user account and password.

6. Click OK to apply the mapping. Whenever the user will access an area of the Web site that requires permissions, he will be automatically logged.

If you want to enable many-to-one certificate mapping, you can apply the steps from 1 to 4 of the previous sequence and carry out the additional steps:

1. Select the Many-to-1 tab.

2. By clicking the Add button a wizard will start to build the rules for the mapping. You will be prompted for a name to assign to the rule set you are creating and you will see the following window:

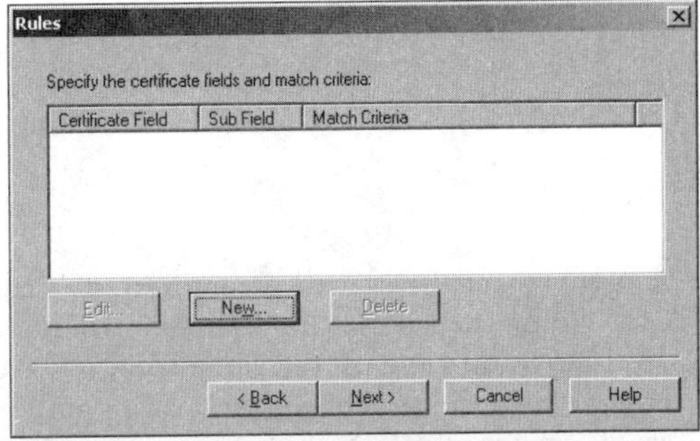

3. In this window you have to define the rules of mapping by entering certificate fields and sub fields and associated match criteria. You can enter as many field as you want by clicking the New button. The following dialog box will be displayed in order to define a rule:

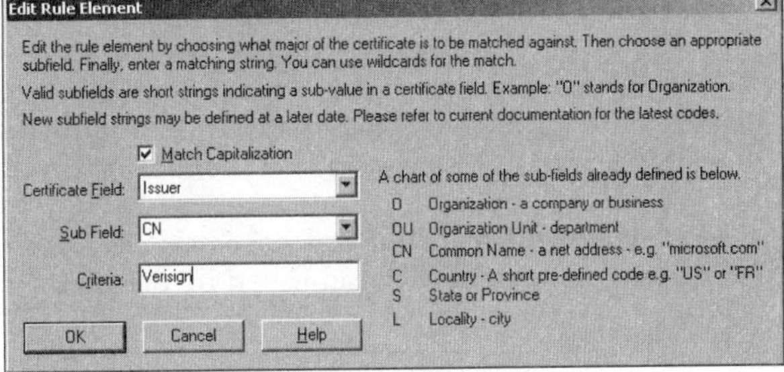

4. In this example, the rule specifies that the issuer common name (CN) of the certificate must be Verisign. You can use wildcards in the criteria field for a less specific match.

5. When you click OK the final dialog box will invite you to specify whether to accept the certificate for logon authentication, which I suggest you do, or refuse access to all users that present certificates matching the specified criteria. By clicking the Finish button you enable many-to-one mapping.

Client certificate mapping is an important feature that greatly simplifies the authentication process when a user accesses a secure Web site. One-to-one and many-to-one methods allow you to define accurate access policies for your Web site. However you might have specific certificate selection criteria that cannot be expressed through these methods. In the section *Certificates and ASP* we will see how to use ASP to manage access to your Web site through certificates in a customized way.

The Life of a Certificate

Certificates have a limited life. They are requested, created, and then, at some point, either expire or are revoked. Expiration is important because advances in computing power, and the potential for the discovery of holes in algorithms or security protocols can make certificates unreliable. Revocation is important if private keys are compromised or if there has been a change in status or policy. For example, a certificate indicating that Jim ABC is an employee of XYZ Corporation should be revoked if he leaves the company. The following diagram shows the steps of the life of a certificate:

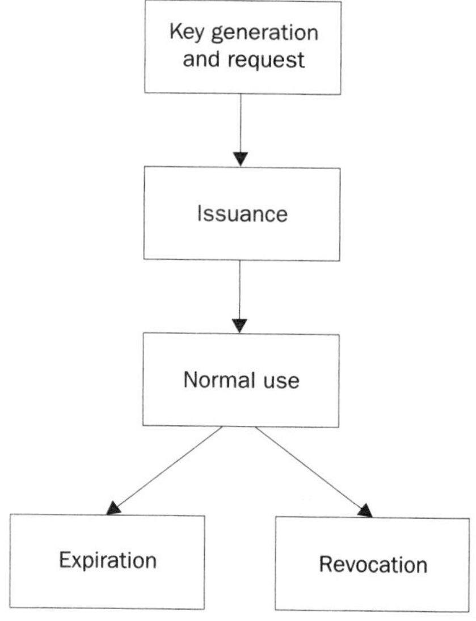

A revoked certificate will be entered on a certificate revocation list (CRL) which is managed by the CA. This is similar to what happens when a credit card is revoked. A bank cannot force people to cut up their credit card. In the same way, a CA cannot force the destruction of all copies of a certificate. However, in the process of requesting authorization for a purchase above some minimum value, a credit card is checked against a card revocation list to make sure that it is still valid. Similarly, a client who is going to use a certificate might want to check it against a CRL to verify its validity.

CAs publish certificate revocation lists containing certificates that have been revoked by the CA, that is they show all the certificates withdrawn after being issued. CRLs are made available for downloading or online viewing by client programs.

To verify a certificate, all that is necessary is to possess the public key of the CA and a check the certificate against the CRL published by that CA.

When a certificate expires, you should quickly renew it. Usually you would renew it well before the expiration date, in order to avoid any security problems that might arise from having no valid certificate at all. From the CA's point of view, renewing a certificate is not the same as requesting a new certificate. You can renew your certificate if none of its information has changed since its original issue.

Managing Certificates

Usually you can manage certificates using the features of the software on which they are installed (Web server, browser, e-mail program). You can back up certificate files or export them for use in another system. For example, if you change your Web site's machine, you should enable the certificate on the new machine. Or if you want to use your certificate with a browser on a different machine, you should export your certificate from your usual browser and import it into the new one. Most programs allow you to display installed certificates, export them to an external file and import new certificates. These three operations can be considered the basic functions to manage certificates from a user's point of view. We will carry out these operations using IIS, Internet Explorer and MS Outlook Express. However the concepts are also valid for other software programs.

The Certificate Store

Before entering in the details of managing certificates with these programs, you should be aware that Windows 2000 has a system area where certificates are kept. This area is known as the **Certificate Store** and it's role is central to much of the certificate functionality in Windows 2000. The Certificate Store contains many certificates issued from a number of different CAs. You can manage certificates installed in the Certificate Store of your system by using the Certificate snap-in for Microsoft Management Console (MMC). To use this snap-in, bring up the MMC window (by typing `mmc.exe` in the Run dialog box from the Start menu), and from the Console menu, select Add/Remove Snap-in. In the window that will be displayed, click the Add button and select the Certificates snap-in, as shown here:

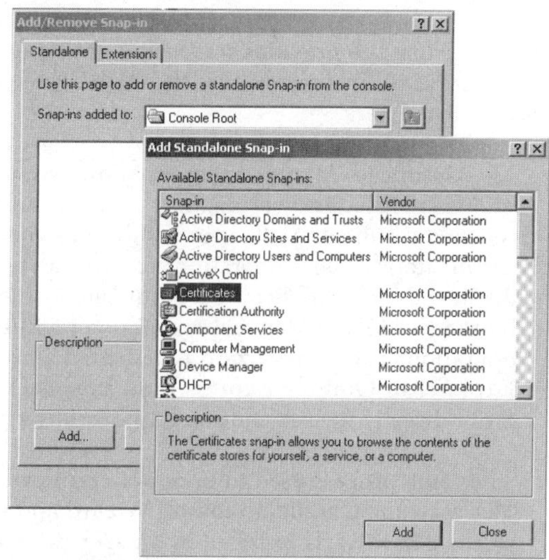

After clicking the Add button, you will be asked to choose which certificates you want to manage for: a user, a computer or a service. When you have selected one of these categories of certificates and have specified the user account, computer name or service name, you can close all the windows and go back to the MMC's main window. If you chose to manage a user account, the MMC windows could look like the following:

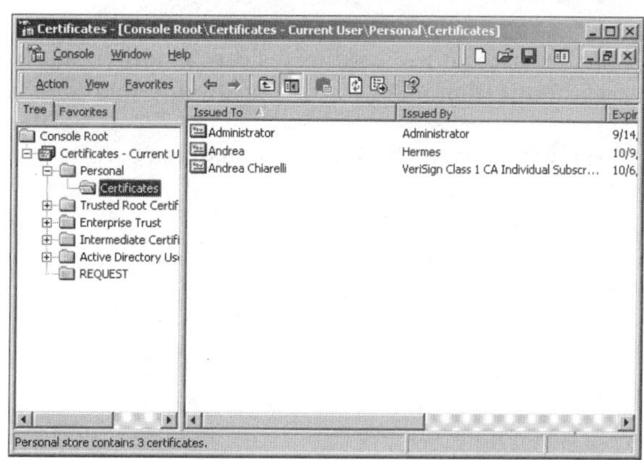

On the other hand, the following picture shows the MMC window if you selected to manage the WWW Publishing Service's certificates:

Notice that the previous screenshot shows the list of the Web server's trusted root Certificate Authorities. This means that the Web server will automatically accept client certificates issued by the CAs listed here.

The Certificate Manager snap-in allows you to perform the most common operations on certificates such as request new certificates, export or import certificates, import certificate revocation lists and renew a certificate. This is in addition to viewing a certificate's details, or copying or deleting a certificate. All these operations can be carried out from the Action menu, or from the popup menu displayed on right-clicking a certificate or the blank panel. On selecting any of the actions provided by the Certificate Manager snap-in you will start the appropriate wizard to perform the requested operation. The same wizard is activated when you request the same operation using IIS, Internet Explorer or Outlook Express. You can also view details or import a certificate into the Certificate Store directly from Windows Explorer, by right-clicking on a certificate file's icon.

The same process used to import a certificate can be used to import a Certificate Revocation List. You start the Certificate Import Wizard and provide the CRL file name instead of a certificate file name. The CRL is installed in the Certificate Store and will be used by all programs that manage certificates.

Programs that use certificates can pick them up from the Certificate Store and use them for server authentication, client authentication, e-mail messages signing etc.

We will now see how you can manage certificates in IIS, Internet Explorer and Outlook Express.

IIS Certificate Management

The Internet Services Manager administration tool allows you to manage certificates in a simple way. You can view, export, import, renew and replace certificates from the Secure communications section of the Directory Security tab in the Web site properties window:

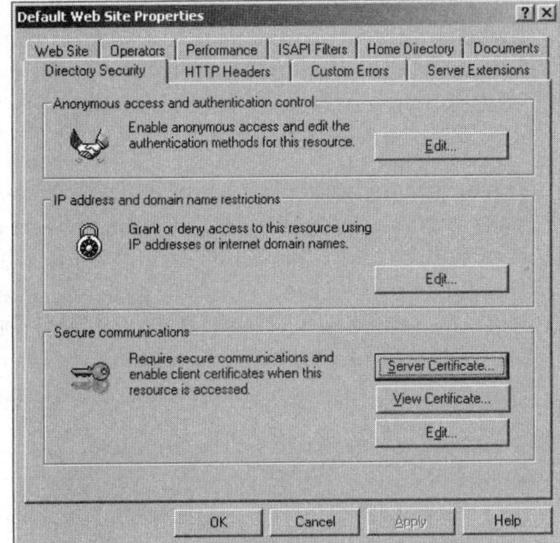

By clicking the View Certificate button you can see the details of the currently installed server certificate, as shown here:

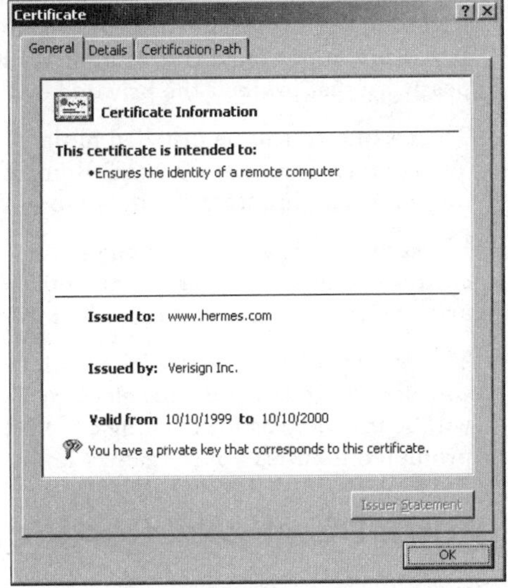

From the Details tab of the certificate window you can see the value of each certificate field and can export the certificate in a file using the Copy to File button.

By clicking the Copy to File button, the **Certificate Export Wizard** starts, which guides you through the process storing your certificate as an export file. Remember that a certificate contains only your public key. If you intend to export your certificate for backup purpose, you should also export your private key in order to recover the key pair. The Certificate Export Wizard asks you whether you want to export your private key with the certificate.

Next you will be allowed to select the file format you want for the exported certificate. If you have chosen to export the private key with your certificate, you will be able to export the certificate only in the **Personal Information Exchange** format, also known as **PKCS#12**. Otherwise you can select among three different formats: DER encoded binary X.509, Base-64 encoded X.509 and PKCS#7. The format you choose to export your certificate depends on which software you will use to import it. Note however that PKCS#7 and PKCS#12 are standard formats – they can be imported by virtually any Web server.

If you have chosen to export your private key with the certificate, the wizard will ask you to supply a password to protect it from unauthorized access. Then you will be prompted for the name of the file that will contain the certificate. Notice that the file name extension will change on the basis of the file format you selected. You will get the `.cer` extension if you selected the DER encoded binary or Base-64 encoded formats. If you selected the PKCS#7 format, your file will have the `.p7b` extension, while it will have the `.pfx` extension if you selected the Personal Information Exchange. A summary screen will present all your choices, then you can click the Finish button to export the certificate.

To import a certificate file for use in IIS, you should first import it in the Certificate Store and then assign it to the Web site. You can import the certificate file by using the Certificate Manager snap-in or by right-clicking the certificate file and selecting Install Certificate. The **Certificate Import Wizard** guides you through the process of importing a certificate. The wizard will ask you to choose a certificate store in which to install it. You can select one of the certificate stores proposed by the wizard or let the wizard to automatically select a certificate store according to the type of certificate. If you are importing a certificate in a PKCS#12 format file, you will be prompted to provide the password that protects the private key.

The certificate will be installed in the Certificate Store and you can use it with IIS by starting the Web Server Certificate Wizard. Remember that this wizard starts by clicking the Server Certificate button in the Directory Security tab of the Properties sheet for the Web site.

If a certificate is already installed, the wizard shows the possible actions you can do with the certificate, i.e. renew, remove or replace. If you want to replace a currently installed certificate with an imported one, the wizard will allow you to select it from the Certificate Store.

The process to renew a server certificate is very simple. Again you will use the Web Server Certificate Wizard and will select the Renew the current certificate option. The rest of the process will be the same as for creating a Certificate Signing Request (CSR) except that you will not be prompted to insert your organization information.

Internet Explorer Certificate Management

To view your personal certificates installed on Internet Explorer, you can click the Certificates button from the Internet Options dialog, as shown here:

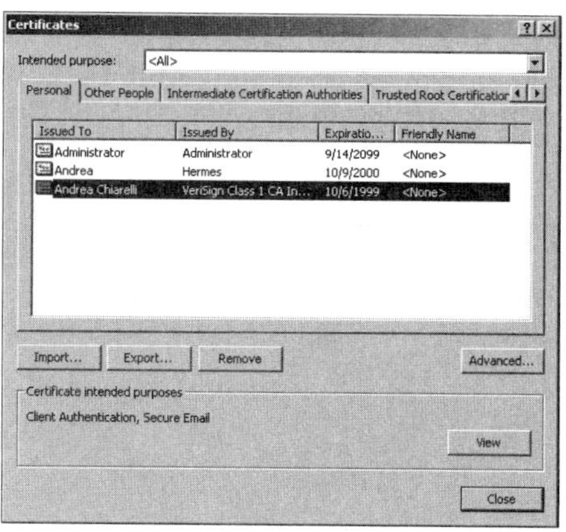

This enables you to export and import certificates, and view details about installed certificates. By clicking the Import and Export buttons you start exactly the same set of wizards that we have already seen. You can also manage Certificate Authorities certificates in order to establish which Web sites you want to trust. The browser will trust all the Web sites presenting certificates issued by the CAs listed in the Trusted Root Certification Authorities and Intermediate Certification Authorities tabs.

Outlook Express Certificate Management

In MS Outlook Express, each certificate is associated with a mail account. You can bind a certificate to an account using the properties of an e-mail account, as this screenshot shows:

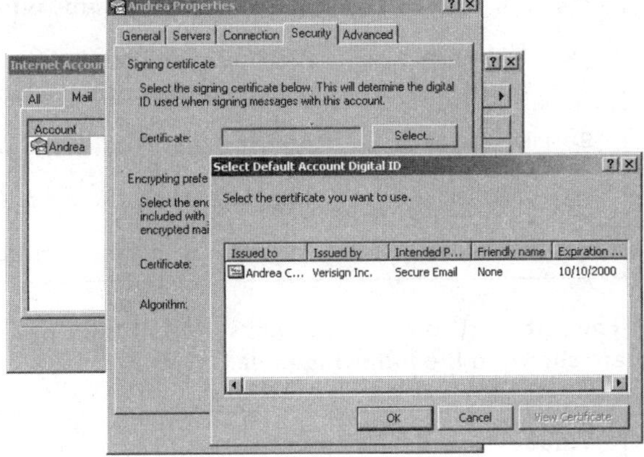

As we've already seen, you can select different certificates for different purposes, i.e. signing and encrypting messages.

Certificates and ASP

You can use certificate authentication enabling client certificate mapping. However, in some situations you would get even better authentication by analyzing the certificate's contents themselves. Suppose you want to apply complex criteria to allow user authentication based on certificates; you could, for example, ensure access to employees of a given company who have a Verisign or a Thawte certificate. Using client certificate mapping, it is very difficult to build a rule matching this criterion. Or, suppose you want to customize your Web pages on the basis of the users that access your Web site; you might, for example, want to present a different home page for each company whose employees access your Web site. You can achieve these things, and more, using ASP. In particular, you can exploit the `ClientCertificate` collection of the Request object.

In order to access a certificate's fields, your Web server must be configured to request a client certificate; otherwise the `ClientCertificate` collection will be empty. By default, Internet Information Server doesn't request certificates. To configure your server to request a certificate refer to the *Client Certificate Mapping* section. Once you have enabled your server to receive certificates from the browser, you can access the information stored in them in order to grant access or perform other actions.

The `ClientCertificate` collection has a number of keys allowing access to the certificate's fields. The following table shows the keys you can use in an ASP script to get certificate information.

Value	Content
`Certificate`	A string containing the binary stream of the entire certificate content.
`Flags`	A set of flags that provide additional client certificate information.
`Issuer`	A string that contains information about the issuer of the certificate.
`SerialNumber`	A string that contains the certificate serial number as an ASCII representation of hexadecimal bytes.
`Subject`	A string that contains information about the subject of the certificate.
`ValidFrom`	The date when the certificate becomes valid.
`ValidUntil`	The date when the certificate expires.

The `Subject` and `Issuer` keys present information structured in subfields. The available subfields are shown in the following table.

Value	Content
`C`	Specifies the identifier of the country of origin.
`CN`	Specifies the common name.
`GN`	Specifies the given name.
`I`	Specifies a set of initials.
`L`	Specifies a locality.
`O`	Specifies the company or organization name.
`OU`	Specifies the name of the organizational unit.
`S`	Specifies the state or province.
`T`	Specifies the title of the person or organization.

Note that not all subfields need to be present in a certificate. You can access a subfield in a certificate by appending the subfield to the key as a suffix. For example, you can access the `Issuer` organization name in the following way:

```
Request.ClientCertificate("IssuerO")
```

Here I will show an example where an ASP script allows access only to employees listed by a company and redirects to a page in the appropriate language:

```
<%
If Date < DateValue(Request.ClientCertificate("ValidUntil")) Then
    'The certificate has expired
    Response.Redirect("error_manager?code=2")
End If

If CheckCompany(Request.ClientCertificate("SubjectO")) <> "WWW Company Inc." _
    Then
      'The company is not the expected one
      Response.Redirect("error_manager?code=3")
End If

Select Case Request.ClientCertificate("SubjectC")
   'Check the country of origin of the user
    Case "IT"
        Response.Redirect("welcome_it.asp")
    Case "FR"
        Response.Redirect("welcome_fr.asp")
    Case "DE"
        Response.Redirect("welcome_de.asp")
    Case "ES"
        Response.Redirect("welcome_es.asp")
    Case Else
        Response.Redirect("welcome.asp")
End Select
%>
```

The script basically checks information stored in certificate's fields and redirects the browser to the appropriate ASP page. It verifies the validity of a certificate and the presence of the company in the list of the authorized ones. The `CheckCompany` function simply searches for the company name in a database. If at least one of these checks fails, the browser is redirected to the error manager ASP page (`error_manager.asp`) along with the appropriate error code. If the values of the certificate fields are accepted, the script tries to get the user's country by testing the `SubjectC` subfield. This causes a redirection to the appropriate welcome page.

This very simple script demonstrates how you can manage certificate fields using ASP in order to perform custom actions based on the user identity. More complex uses of certificates always rely on the simple test of the various fields and subfields of the certificates. In spite of its simplicity, managing certificates with ASP provides simple access for the user, customization of the ASP application and high security.

Becoming your own Certificate Authority

In previous sections, we saw that a Certificate Authority is a third party verifying the identities of people who request a certificate from them. The role of a CA as a neutral party is fundamental to guarantee trust in Internet-based transactions.

However, in some cases you might find the need to issue, revoke and manage certificates for users interacting with you. That is, you would become your own Certificate Authority. This can be true in your intranet or extranet. That is when you need to build your Virtual Private Network, in order to allow your customer to perform orders and other transactions on your Web site in a secure way, or when you want build up a large intranet with secure access to certain areas of the Web site. In this cases you would be able to issue, renew and revoke certificates on your own, without the intervention of an external CA. You want to certify people or entities within your specific context, creating what is also known as **Enterprise CA**.

This offers many advantages over commercial CAs, including total control over certificate management policies and lower costs.

Certificates issued by your CA correspond to corporate identification cards or badges. They are meant to provide identification or access to resources within a particular enterprise or application setting. Under certain circumstances, different enterprise CAs may choose to recognize each other's certificates, a process known as **cross certifying**.

Setting up your own CA requires at least the following extra resources on your system:

- **A Certificate Server**
  This is a server able to issue certificates, manage their content, certificate issuance policy and revocations. There are many products available on the market: GTE's CyberTrust, Verisign OnSite, Netscape Certificate Server, Entrust Web/CA. In the examples shown in this section I will use Microsoft's Certificate Services.

- **A tool to establish trust relationship with the client**
  If your server certificate has been issued by a public CA, the clients that access your Web site will recognize the CA because the CA's certificate is installed. However, if your Web server has a server certificate issued by yourself, the clients will not be able to trust it because they won't necessarily recognize you as a CA. This causes a warning to be displayed to the user or Web site access will be halted, depending on the security level settings of the browser. When setting up your own CA you have to provide means to establish trust between your CA and the clients that will access your Web site. Usually this is accomplished by installing the CA certificate in the browser.

- **A tool to issue client certificates**
  Although you can choose your own way to issue client certificates, an online form for certificate enrollment similar to that of a public CA is the best way to distribute them. Of course you have to perform your verification procedure before issuing certificates.

Certificate Services

Certificate Services provide these tools to set up your own CA. The tools are designed to make certificate management tasks as simple as possible and, at the same time, flexible and highly customizable. In fact, Certificate Services consist of a set of components that can be customized and extended to implement your Enterprise CA. As the following picture shows, the architecture of Certificate Services has a central component, the **server engine**, which is responsible for issuing, renewing and revoking certificates. Around this component are several other components interacting with it for requesting certificates, applying issuing policies and performing other tasks, such as storing certificates in a database:

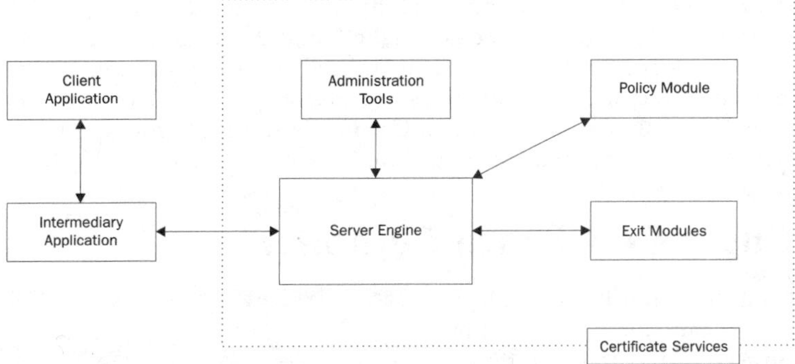

In particular, **client applications** are components that initiate the enrollment process. They can be browsers or other applications that ask an **intermediary application**, typically a Web server, for a client certificate. The intermediary application redirects the request to the server engine that involves the **policy module** and the **exit modules** in order to satisfy the client request. The policy module is a DLL that implements the enterprise's policy rules for issuing certificates. This module can be customized according to your own needs. The exit modules are DLLs that receive notifications from the server engine when some operations occur – a certificate has been issued or revoked, a request is pending etc. The exit modules can be customized to perform specific tasks such as storing certificates in a database.

Customization of Certificate Services is beyond the scope of this chapter. You can find more information at `http://msdn.microsoft.com/workshop/security/client/certsvr.asp` and in the help documentation.

Setting up a Certificate Authority

You can install Certificate Services to create a Certificate Authority for your intranet or extranet. Certificate Services allows you to create two types of CAs: Enterprise CA and Stand-alone CA. An Enterprise CA is intended to be used in a global Windows 2000 environment exploiting Active Directory for information exchange and with an automatic management of issuance policy. A Stand-alone CA is intended to be used when extranets and the Internet are involved. It doesn't use Active Directory nor does it allow more customization of issuance policy.

We will focus on setting up a Stand-alone CA, seeing as it is related to Web services and the Internet. In order to set up a CA you have to log on as Administrator and select the Add/Remove Programs icon in Control Panel. Then click Add/Remove Windows Components and select the Certificates Services check box. The Certificate Services Installation Wizard starts. Select the Stand-alone root CA option box as shown here:

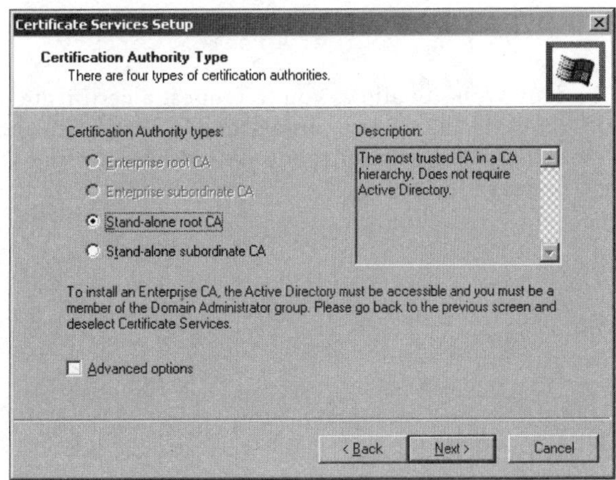

The wizard continues asking information to identify the CA you are setting up. Then you will be prompted to enter the path for the certificate database and the corresponding log. The default path is `\WINNT\System32\CertLog`. During the actual installation step, IIS must be stopped. The wizard automatically detects if it is running and allows you to stop it. After Certificate Services is installed, the wizard restarts IIS. Your system now has a Certificate Authority for issuing, renewing and revoking certificates. Notice that the CA certificate for your CA is automatically created during setup.

Administering a Certificate Authority

Once your Certificate Authority is installed on your system, you can administer it using the Certification Authority administration tool. It is an MMC snap-in that allows you to start or stop the service, issue and revoke certificates, and manage pending requests. The following picture shows the Certification Authority snap-in:

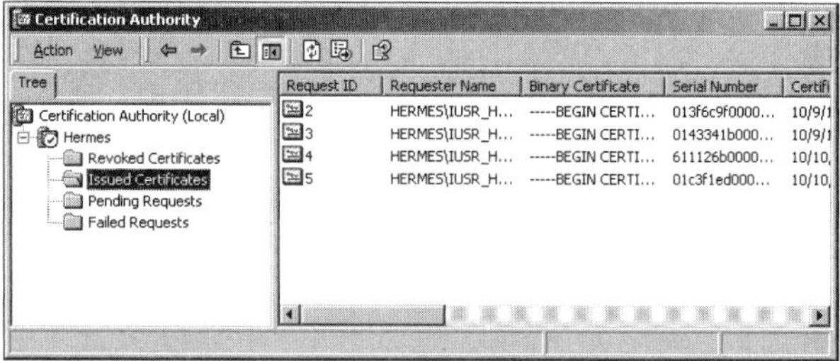

The Certificate manager has four folders, one for each certificate status. When a certificate request is submitted to the service, it is stored in the Pending Requests folder. If the request is accepted, the issued certificate is stored in the Issued Certificates folder. If it is denied, it is stored in the Failed Requests folder. Finally revoked certificates are stored in the Revoked Certificates folder. You can perform operations on certificates using the Action menu or right-clicking the objects in the snap-in.

Revoked certificates need to be published in a Certificate Revocation List in order to make their revocation known. You can publish the CRL by right-clicking the Revoked Certificates folder and selecting Publish in the All Tasks menu. We will see in the following section how the CRL can be accessed by users.

Interacting with your Certificate Authority

When your Certificate Authority is installed on your system, requesting a certificate is an analogous process to that of a public CA. In fact, a Certificate Authority Web site is installed during the Certificate Services setup at the following address:

```
http://<yourservername>/CertSrv
```

This Web site allows you to request a certificate, install a requested certificate, install the CA certificate and download the Certificate Revocation List using your browser:

Since your CA certificate is not installed in the browser used to access your intranet or extranet, you can use your CA Web site to establish the trust relationship with your clients. This can be accomplished by selecting the first task in the option list shown on your CA home page. The page loaded by clicking on the Next button allows you to download the CA certificate and the CRL published by your CA:

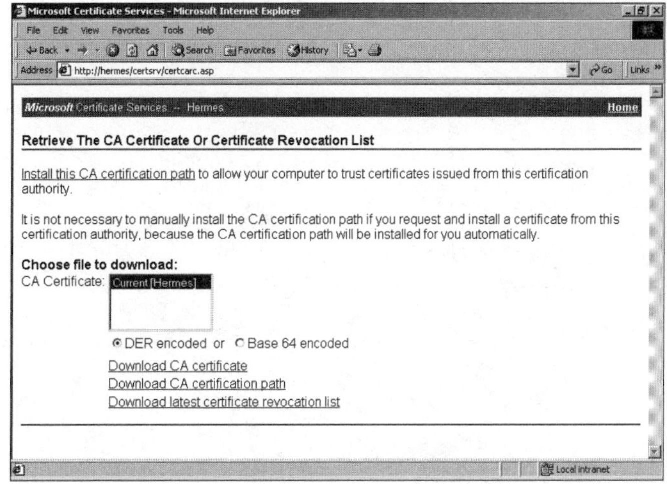

The CA certificate and the CRL can be imported into the Certificate Store as we've already seen.

Summary

When e-commerce becomes an important issue in a Web application, standard security mechanisms may not be enough to guarantee that sensitive information passes across the Internet without trouble. Indeed, secure access is an issue on nearly every Web site that shares the Internet for information exchange, e.g. business to consumer commerce, business to business commerce, document exchanges and so on. Ensuring authentication and authorization in an Internet transaction is very important in some situations. This chapter showed the basic issues of certificate technology, a technology that allows identification and authenticity over the Internet. Types of certificate, Certificate Authorities and the life cycle of a certificate have been discussed as well as practical information about getting server and personal certificates. Also hints about managing certificates with ASP and setting up your own Certificate Authority have been provided.

26

Optimizing ASP Performance

Performance, like correctness, is a quality that's noticed more by its absence. If you've worked hard to fix all the bugs and tune the performance of your Web site, users will seldom comment. If you miss a few bugs or your Web site is slow, they're likely to complain.

This chapter will introduce you to the important concepts relating to ASP performance, and provide you with some guidelines as what to do and what not to do.

We will be covering such diverse subject as:

- The performance metrics of throughput and response time
- Hardware performance
- Script profiling
- Tools such as the Web Application Stress Tool and the NT Performance Monitor
- Session and Application state
- Process isolation, components and threading models

We will end the chapter with a miscellany of tips that we have found useful in our own Web sites and applications to improve performance. First though let us consider what metrics we should be using to measure performance by.

Performance Metrics

Before talking about increasing server performance, we need to understand the two primary metrics, throughput and response time:

- **Throughput** is the rate at which the server can process requests. From a Webmaster's perspective, the higher the achievable throughput, the better. If you can increase the potential throughput, you can deal with increased loads; you can cope with spikes in the load; and you can postpone upgrading your server's hardware.
- **Response Time** measures the time elapsed between a client (browser, Webcrawler, etc.) starting a request and the last byte of the response being received. The lower the response time, the better. Users care greatly about response times, but are seldom interested in the overall system throughput.

Throughput

Throughput is usually measured in *requests per second* or *requests per day*. Sometimes it's more meaningful to think in terms of **page hits** than requests. When a browser requests an HTML page, it typically follows up immediately with separate requests for the images specified by `<IMG>` tags, and for the frames in a frameset. These tightly coupled requests are considered a *single* page hit.

One approximation to throughput is the *number of clients* divided by the *think time*. For example, if you have 100 users, each of whom spends an average of 20 seconds reading a Web page before clicking on a link, your throughput is 100/20, or 5 requests per second. Throughput is not generally related to how long it takes someone to read a Web page; it's a function of how quickly requests arrive at the server and how fast the server can respond to them.

Various factors constrain throughput. One is **bandwidth**, which measures how much data can be transferred each second. If you have an ISDN line connecting your server to the Internet, the relatively low bandwidth will most likely be the limiting factor on your performance, since the ISDN line can easily be saturated. When Web servers are primarily delivering static content, bandwidth is almost always the limiting factor.

Page size also constrains throughput. The bigger the pages you send, the longer each page will take to send, and the fewer the pages you can send each second. If you can reduce your page size (especially the size of embedded images, which are usually the largest files), you not only increase throughput, you can also decrease response time; i.e. the client will see the entire page in less time.

Complex applications decrease throughput. If each request takes a long time to execute, you can process fewer requests per second than a simpler application could. For dynamic content, CPU horsepower is often a constraining factor.

On a fast LAN, HTTP connections are nearly instantaneous, but over a slow WAN, such as the Internet, connections can last for several seconds and the number of **concurrent connections** becomes an important measure, since each connection uses server resources.

There are two ways to measure throughput:

- The first is to use Performance Monitor to read the throughput statistics generated by the Web server. For static files, the NT performance counter is called *Web Service(_Total)\Get Requests/sec*; for ASP, the NT performance counter is *Active Server Pages\Requests/Sec.* These performance counters give you the instantaneous values. We'll be looking at performance counters in more detail later in the chapter.
- The second way is to use a load generation tool such as the **Web Application Stress (WAS)** tool, which will generate a report, listing throughput and many other statistics, after running a particular test.

Response Time

Users prefer *sub-second* response times, but seldom get them. The WWW is often defined, only half-jokingly, as the World-Wide Wait. Response times are determined by the network latency, by the time it takes a request to move through the server request queue, and by the request execution time.

WAS keeps track of TTFB (time-to-first-byte) and TTLB (time-to-last-byte) statistics.

Network **latency** measures how long it takes for a data packet to travel from one point to another, and it is affected by:

- Network congestion
- The quality of the links
- The bandwidth of the links
- The physical distances between links
- The number of hops or stages between the endpoints
- Queuing within routers and switches

Latency affects both the time it takes the request to travel from the client to the server, and the time it takes the subsequent response to travel back from the server. In most environments, the latency is largely beyond the control of both the client and the server.

Low bandwidth devices, such as modems, tend to have high latency, whereas high bandwidth devices usually have low latency, but not always. Consider two systems connected via microwave links to a satellite: megabits of data can be transferred each second but it still takes a long time (by comparison to transfer times on a LAN) for any individual bit of data to go from one endpoint up to the satellite and down to the other system.

Even if there were zero latency between client and server, a request can still spend time in a queue at the server before it is processed. The **request queue time** is determined by the number of outstanding requests (the **queue length**) and the time that it takes the server to process each request. The queue length is usually proportional to the load being seen by the server.

The **request execution time** is the final component of response time and it's the only one that the server has much control over. Long execution times also decrease throughput. Reducing execution time will be a primary focus of this chapter.

Traffic Patterns

Traffic does not arrive evenly throughout the day. A regional newspaper site is likely to receive heavy traffic in the early morning, at lunchtime, and in the evening, but is likely to be very quiet during the middle of the night, when the majority of its readership are asleep. During these heavy traffic periods, a server is probably dealing with three to five times (or more) the volume of traffic it receives on average throughout the 24-hour period. A newspaper site will occasionally experience huge spikes in traffic when a major news story breaks.

Clearly, a Web site must not only be capable of dealing with the average traffic, it must also be able to cope adequately with the expected peaks throughout the day, and ideally it can keep up with even the highest volumes.

Furthermore, the long-term trend is for successful sites to receive ever-increasing amounts of traffic.

Don't run your servers too hot. If your average traffic uses more than 50% of your CPU or your bandwidth, it's unlikely that you'll cope well with spikes in traffic. Use the NT Performance Monitor to keep track of your site's performance. `PerfMon` can record all counters to a log and report alerts in the NT Event Log.

Other Performance Metrics

As we've seen, the primary performance metrics are throughput – the number of requests a server can process each second – and response time – how fast a particular request is processed. As a Webmaster or ASP application developer, you care about *maximizing your throughput*, since it allows you to deal with higher loads and to postpone upgrading your server hardware. Conversely, users prefer that *response times be as low as possible*, since they're tired of the World-Wide Wait.

Other performance metrics can also be of use. These metrics are the megahertz cost, resource utilization, and multiprocessor scalability. Megahertz cost is a way of estimating how "expensive" a dynamic page is to execute and helps you extrapolate the performance you'll get by moving to different hardware. The fewer the resources you use, the more headroom you have to expand and the better citizen you are on multi-purpose servers. Applications developed on a uni-processor system do not automatically scale well on multi-processor systems.

Megahertz Cost

Megahertz cost is expressed in MHz / request / second, or:

```
MHz cost = (Number of CPUs) * (CPU speed in MHz) * (CPU utilization) /
           (Requests/sec)
```

For example, say that you have a dual-processor Pentium II system running at 333 MHz. Your system is able to sustain a steady throughput of 80 pages/second, using 60% of the CPU (as measured by the Task Manager or the Performance Monitor):

```
2 * 333MHz = 666 MHz                    Total MHz capacity
666 * 0.60 = 400 MHz.                   MHz utilization
400 MHz / 80 pages/sec = 5
```

Therefore, your pages will have an MHz cost of 5 MHz per ASP request per second.

The advantage of the MHz cost over other metrics, such as throughput, is that it makes the difficult task of capacity planning a little easier. Generally, a page with a certain MHz cost on System A will have a roughly similar MHz cost on System B, even though System B may have very different hardware. If the two systems have the same number of CPUs, the MHz cost will be quite similar, though a little higher on the faster machine.

However, don't take the MHz cost as gospel; it's only an approximation. Capacity planning for dynamic content is still in its infancy.

Here's an example. The top-level page on your site has a MHz cost of 3, your search page is 25, and your orders page is 15. You want to be able to deal with a sustained rate of 50 users visiting your site each second through the top-level page, 1 user doing a search, 2 users making a purchase on the orders page, and still have some capacity left over for spikes in traffic and users on other pages in the site. Can you do it?

```
(50 * 3) + (2 * 15) + (1 * 25) = 150 + 30 + 25 = 205 MHz.
```

Allowing some extra capacity to cope with spikes in traffic, you should be okay if the total MHz capacity of your system is at least 300 MHz.

However, it's advisable that your average workload consume no more than 50% of your CPU capacity, or you won't be able to cope well with peaks in traffic.

A 400 MHz system would be safer.

Low CPU Utilization

Obviously, the lower the CPU utilization, the better. If we can optimize an ASP page so that it runs faster and uses less CPU, we have more headroom to deal with spikes in traffic. Also, if other services, such as a database or a mail server, are running on the same system, we'd like to be a good citizen and leave as many CPU cycles as possible for their use.

Low Bandwidth Utilization

Even a dedicated Web server has to share the network with other systems. Therefore, it's good to use as little of the network bandwidth as possible. Not only does this leave more bandwidth for the other systems, it generally means that the Web server can achieve higher throughput and provide lower response times to clients. There are three ways to do this.

- The first is to **send less data per request**: trim the HTML; send back portions of a results set instead of the whole thing; send fewer images and make those images that you do send smaller, by cropping them or by using higher compression factors for JPEGs, and fewer colors for GIFs.

- The second way is to **reduce network roundtrips** between client and server. The more work that the server can offload on to the client, the better. Roundtrips are often slow due to network latencies, they add extra load on the server, and they use network bandwidth. Smart clients can validate form data in client-side script; use DHTML to change the appearance of the screen without needing to request fresh HTML or images from the server; manipulate ADO recordsets with RDS; and use XML to transform data.

- The third way to reduce bandwidth utilization is to **buffer data**. Batching data up and sending it in one big block makes much better use of network resources. ASP does not buffer pages by default in IIS 4.0, although it does buffer pages by default in IIS 5.0.

  Every `Response.Write` and every HTML fragment is sent separately to the client. Each send has headers describing the data packet; each send takes time to complete due to network latency; each send adds congestion to the network. It's like making a separate trip to the supermarket for each item on the grocery list instead of buying everything at once. TCP/IP has a slow-start algorithm, where it sends one packet, then two packets together, then four packets together, and so on, until it builds up to the maximum data transfer rate of the link. If a page is sent in multiple small sends, TCP/IP starts the slow-start algorithm afresh for each send, and so never builds up a full head of steam. When the entire page is buffered, TCP/IP becomes much more efficient, especially over high-latency connections.

Multi-Processor Scalability

In an ideal world, adding a second processor to a uni-processor machine would double throughput, and adding two more processors would quadruple throughput. Unfortunately, this is not an ideal world, and it's hard to get applications to scale well on multi-processor systems. IIS 4.0 scales reasonably well going from one processor to two, but does not scale much beyond that point. IIS 5.0 scales quite well to four processors and even up to eight processors:

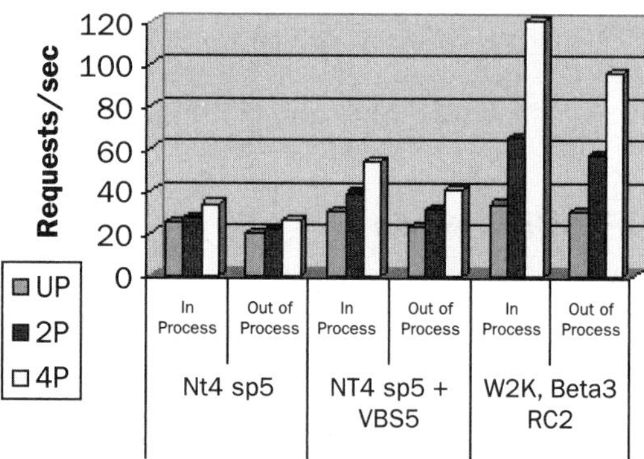

The chart shows the throughput for a moderately complex ASP script – about 1000 lines of code, yielding 25KB of HTML – that makes heavy use of the `LookupTable` component.

The reasons that applications do not scale well are **contention** and **serialization**. Each thread *contends* for shared resources, such as `Application.Lock`, critical sections in components, or the system bus. When a thread does acquire the resource for its exclusive use, the other threads are blocked, waiting for the first one to release the resource. They acquire the resource *serially* and they are not able to work in parallel. These problems tend to show up far less readily on uni-processor systems, since only one thread is actually executing at any one instant. On an *n*-processor system, *n* threads are executing simultaneously.

If there is any chance that your ASP applications will be deployed on a multi-processor system, it's vital to stress-test and performance-test your applications on multi-processor systems.

This will shake out bugs in your components, such as lack of thread-safety or deadlocks, as well as find scaling problems.

Improving Server Hardware Performance

You must have adequate hardware, both to meet the current load and the expected load in the future. A dusty Pentium 133 sitting in a closet might be quite adequate as a small departmental Web server, but it will not do for a busy e-commerce site.

RAM

It's vital that your server has enough physical memory. If you don't have enough RAM, probably the single most effective thing you can do to improve performance is to add more memory. Your server will thrash if it's grossly deficient in memory. The virtual memory subsystem will get an excellent workout, but your throughput will be appalling, as the system will be spending much of its time swapping pages of memory to and from the pagefile on the system disk. Even if you do have enough memory so that you're not thrashing, you may still benefit from additional memory. The IIS core likes plenty of memory for caching static files, and ASP needs memory to cache compiled ASP files and store ASP session data.

Use the NT Performance Monitor to diagnose memory problems. There are articles available on the IIS Technet site, and the MSDN Web Workshop Server Technologies site, that describe this further, as does the IIS Resource Guide from Microsoft Press.

128MB is the minimum amount of memory that I would recommend for a dedicated Web server and 256MB is much better. Heavy-duty e-commerce sites can probably benefit from having 512MB to 1GB of RAM. Additional memory may improve performance further but eventually you will reach the point of diminishing returns. Few Web servers really need 2GB of RAM, for example.

Disks

Disks are used to store static content (HTML and images), programs, scripts, log files, and databases. For many Web sites, standard EIDE or SCSI disks meet their needs. Partitioning system files, databases, log files, temporary files, and the pagefile onto different physical disks can improve disk performance by reducing the amount of time spent in seeking the disk heads across platters. Sites with high disk traffic should investigate using RAID 0, RAID 1, or RAID 5 disk subsystems to improve disk throughput. Be sure to check that the disk traffic is not due to excessive paging.

Network Bandwidth

Make sure that you have enough network bandwidth to keep up with the load placed upon your Web servers. Ensure that you have adequate network cards and switches. Fast Ethernet (100Mbps) should be sufficient for most situations. It's the expensive connection to the Internet that's likely to be the problem.

CPUs

IIS is very efficient at sending static content, but generating dynamic pages can take a lot of CPU horsepower. If your server is regularly running at full CPU utilization, consider upgrading to a faster processor. If you already have a fast CPU, consider adding a second one. If you're running IIS 5.0, consider bringing your system up to 4 or even 8 processors.

Also, make sure that your CPUs have large L2 caches: at least 1MB each. Modern CPU caches are much faster than RAM, and there are harsh penalties for cache misses.

More Servers

Sometimes, one machine just isn't enough. Perhaps it can't keep up with the load. Perhaps you want additional machines for higher availability, so that you won't have a single point of failure and your site will continue to run even if a machine goes down.

You have several options. If you are running a database on the Web server machine, you can offload your database to a backend server to ease the load. This becomes necessary if you move to a Web farm (a collection of machines all acting as one logical Web server).

We will be looking at Web farms in greater detail in the next chapter.

Performance Tuning

In general, few performance problems occur with static content. Those problems that do occur are usually due to inadequate server hardware (especially too little memory), too little bandwidth, or high network latencies. However, IIS and other modern Web servers are all very good at delivering high volumes of static content.

Most performance problems are with *dynamic content.* Unfortunately, these problems can be much harder to solve, since they're open-ended. There are an infinite number of ways to write ASP pages, many of them bad. Even if the frameworks, such as ASP or ISAPI, were perfect, application developers can still write inefficient code.

Fixing Performance Problems

First, you need to set some reasonable goals. For example, you might specify that your Web site must be capable of delivering at least 50 ASP pages per second, using no more than 40% of the CPU, with 95% of requests having a response time of 5 seconds, while under average load.

Then you measure the performance of your Web site under **maximum load** and **average** (or **expected peak load**).

> *By maximum load, I mean that you use a tool such as WAS to generate extremely high load on your server, so high that you saturate the CPU or the network.*

This gives you an upper bound on the throughput that you can sustain. Measuring the performance of your Web site under average load tells you whether you meet your goals or not. Average load should either be derived from your old logs or by your best guess. Measuring under expected peak load tells you how well your site holds up at its busiest.

If the site's performance does not meet your goals, you need to isolate the biggest performance problems and fix them. After finding and fixing a problem, you start the cycle of measurement and tuning again, until you've achieved satisfactory performance or you've wrung the last bit of performance out of the system. If you still can't meet your goals, you have a few options:

- Buy more hardware
- Re-evaluate how realistic your goals are
- Rewrite the key portions of your ASP application as COM components or as an ISAPI

Stress Tools

A key element of performance tuning is an understanding of the behavior of your application. It is important that you establish a controlled environment for doing analysis work, so that you get accurate numbers about the load capabilities. If the application is going to experience significant activity, simulating the anticipated load itself can be part of the challenge. It will be necessary to dedicate several client computers to simulate the behavior of hundreds of concurrent users. An isolated section of network, free from the interference of normal network activity and spikes, is helpful in getting clean results.

The other component that needs to be incorporated as part of your controlled stress environment is the Web server. The stress lab needs to be free from other activities to provide consistency during testing. This allows you to alter settings and scripts and see the effects of these changes clearly. In other words, you need to set up a sort of lab to provide consistency while you conduct performance analysis and tuning. If your test Web server is doubling as a domain controller or mail server, your results will vary based on the machine being called into action for these other responsibilities.

The ideal situation is a test lab with hardware that duplicates what will be in production for the site. However, this is not a requirement. What is important is that the lab be dedicated only to the test procedures for the duration of the testing period.

Once the stress lab is established, there are several options available to you when it comes to picking a stress tool. Many are available, ranging in price from free to very expensive. They cover extremes of functionality, from those questionably in compliance with the HTTP 1.0 specification to fully featured HTTP 1.1 clients with sophisticated reporting and analysis capabilities. My personal favorite is the Web Application Stress Tool, available for free, at the time of writing, from Microsoft.

> *It can be downloaded from* `http://webtool.rte.microsoft.com`*. The site also provides access to a knowledge base devoted to the Stress Tool as well as a comprehensive tutorial. The installation includes online help that is very complete, including samples.*

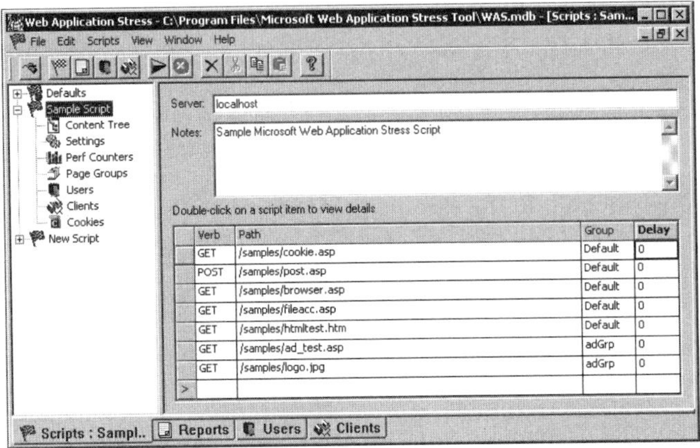

Script Profiling

I like the metaphor about a chain being only as strong as its weakest link. This applies in several ways to Web application performance. You may have identified several scripts that are slower than the rest. However, there may be greater implications than just the lack of performance of these few scripts. There may be a general degradation in the application because these scripts are taking resources away from that being utilized to run other scripts. Increased context switching hurts the entire application. But how do you ascertain the source of the bottleneck? After all, the script may have several includes and a fair amount of code. What you want is the ability to find out where in the script the time is being spent. What is taking too much processing power? A technique I use for script profiling is commonly referred to as '*The Poor Man's Profiler.*'

First, get performance data running stress analysis against just this script. Suppose, for example that a script called `ProcessRequest.asp` is yielding just ten requests per second in your stress run. You have to have a starting point to use as a reference. Next, place a `Response.End` at the mid-point of the script and run the stress analysis again. In this example, if `ProcessRequest.asp` is one hundred lines long, simply insert `Response.End` at line fifty. What does this tell you? The second half of the script will not be executed. By looking at the performance without the second half, you can tell if the bottleneck is in the first half of the script, in the second half, or fairly evenly distributed. Suppose that without the second half of the script, you get one hundred requests per second instead of ten. Now you know that something in the second half is slowing things down disproportionately. If the new metric stays close to the original, you know that the trouble is in the first half.

Now, continue moving the `Response.End` about half way through the part of script that appears to be the culprit and running stress again. We are trying to identify the database call or script that is doing the most damage. In our example, we ended the script at line fifty of one hundred and saw requests per second shoot from ten to one hundred. So, next we would move the `Response.End` to line seventy-five and test again. If performance dropped back down again, we would conclude that the problem must be between lines fifty and seventy-five. Accordingly, we would move the `Response.End` halfway between these two points to line sixty-two and run stress again. You can see how by cutting the suspect part of the script in half with each additional stress run, you should be able to quickly identify the activities that are slowing the script down.

What if the script code seems to scale linearly? It is entirely possible that you will see a script where moving a `Response.End` all through the page and checking the results reveals that there is no specific problem. In this case, you need to look at the operations being performed to determine if what you are doing is just too computationally expensive. Perhaps some of the interpreted script code should be replaced with a call to a custom COM object that can execute more quickly. Refer to the section on *Scripts vs. Components*.

Session and Application State

Active Server Pages provides many conveniences over lesser frameworks, such as ISAPI. Transparent support for **Application** and **Session state** is one of its more noteworthy features. HTTP is a stateless protocol, so state is shared between two different requests from any particular client. This makes HTTP very scalable, because client/server connections do not last for minutes or hours at a time. To maintain Session state, ASP sends out the `ASPSESSIONID` cookie in the headers of every response. Subsequent requests from that client contain that `ASPSESSIONID` cookie in the headers of the request, and ASP uses this cookie to index into its database of Session state.

Session state is especially useful for shopping-basket applications. As the customer moves through the online store, they add items to their shopping basket. When they're ready to buy, the ASP application enumerates all of the items in their shopping basket and calculates the cost and the weight of these items. ASP makes all of this straightforward.

Unfortunately, there are a number of problems associated with Session state. Before we look at the problems, let's look at the advantages of Session state:

- Convenient and easy to use.
- Cache data across requests. Rather than redoing the same expensive calculations or making the same expensive query from a database for every request, calculate the data once and store the data in the Session object. Often a tremendous performance boost.
- No need to build custom infrastructure. You can concentrate on building your applications instead.
- Often good enough for applications that don't require special functionality or massive storage capacity.

Problems with Session State

What are the problems with Session state?

Not all of these problems impair performance, but many of them do.

- **Reliance upon cookies**. Not all browsers support cookies, and even if they do, users may refuse to accept them. Without cookies, Session state just does not work. The Cookie Munger filter can be used as an imperfect workaround for lack of cookies. See below for more details.
- **Session state is fragile**. If you don't consistently use the same case for all URLs, some browsers will believe that you're referring to two different applications and send different cookies. E.g. `<A HREF="/wrox/bar.asp">` will not be considered to be the same as `<A HREF="/Wrox/Quux.asp">`.

- **Session state serializes execution**. In other words, two different requests for the same session will never be executed concurrently. Normally, this is an advantage. It means that the Session object, unlike the Application object, does not need `Lock` and `Unlock` methods, which simplifies the programming model. However, serialized execution causes problems with framesets. The order in which the frames execute is non-deterministic. If one of the frames takes a long time to execute, the other frames may be held up waiting for it to complete. If a frame does not need Session state (it never uses the Session object), it can be disabled for that page by using the `<% @EnableSessionState=False %>` directive at the top of the page.

- **Maintaining Session state consumes memory and slows ASP down**, even when the Session state is unused. If your application does not need Session state at all, disable it in the App options tab in the Properties page for the Application in Internet Service Manager.

- **Session state is not persistent**. If your ASP application crashes, all Session and Application state is lost. If this is unacceptable, you must take care of persisting important data to disk or to a database yourself.

- **Sessions time out**. By default, ASP will delete a Session if no requests have been made to it in the last 20 minutes. If a user goes to lunch in the middle of browsing your site, their Session state will be lost when they comes back.

- **Sessions last a long time**. If a typical user goes through only one or two pages on your site and then leaves, their Session state will endure in memory for another 20 minutes. On a busy site, with hundreds of new visitors every minute, that can add up to a lot of memory.

- **Never have an empty Session_OnEnd procedure in your global.asa**. ASP optimizes Session state by discarding it after a request if the Session object is empty. This can result in considerable memory savings when users don't actually make use of the Session object. However, ASP can't make this optimization if there's a `Session_OnEnd`, as it presumes that custom clean up code may need to be executed.

- **Large arrays should not be stored in the Session or Application objects**. The semantics of VBScript and JScript require that a full, temporary copy of the array be made whenever any element of the array is accessed. For example, if you store a 100,000 element array of strings that map US zip codes to weather stations, then every time you look up the weather station for a particular zip code, the entire 100,000 element array is copied into a temporary array before the particular weather station can be retrieved. Large arrays should be wrapped by custom components that provide special accessor methods.

- **Sessions do not scale well to Web farms**. ASP Session state is confined to one application running on one machine. If you upgrade to a Web farm, either to ensure high availability or to cope with high traffic, you will not be able to share the Session state across the machines in the Web farm. In this case, you have a few choices.

    - **Forgo Session state**. This is the cleanest and most scalable solution.

    - **Build a custom Session state solution**. Persist all state to a shared, back-end database. You need to do this for your important, long-lived data anyway.

  - **Use "sticky sessions"**. Most hardware and software redirectors have a feature that will ensure that all requests from a client at a particular IP address will be addressed to the same server. However, this is less scalable than balancing requests according to the load, since different servers will be working at very different rates. Worse, sticky sessions don't always work. For example, America Online has a huge array of proxy servers with many different IP addresses. There is no guarantee that two successive requests from an AOL client will be routed through the same proxy and end up with the same IP address. Also, many unique users can appear to come from the same IP if they originate at the same proxy.

- **Apartment-threaded components lock a session down to a particular worker thread**. ASP maintains a collection of worker threads. Normally, when a request reaches the head of the request queue, the first available thread services it. If the session has been locked down to a thread, the request must wait for that thread to become available, even though that thread might be busy servicing other requests. It's like going to a supermarket and *always*, *always* going through checkout line number 3, even though other lines might be much shorter. Do not store Apartment-threaded objects in the Session object; store only agile objects (either Neutral-threaded objects or Both-threaded objects that aggregate the Free-threaded marshaler).

- **Connected recordsets should never be stored in the Session or Application objects**. Always disconnect recordsets if they're not going to be destroyed at the end of an ASP page. Leaving the connection to the database open consumes huge amounts of resources.

Now we've covered the fairly large list of problems with using Session state, what can we do to get around them.

Alternatives to Session State

Given these problems of fragility, scalability, and resource consumption, what are the alternatives?

- **Eschew Session state entirely**. This by-passes all the problems with Session state and makes the application more scalable. However, for sites that make heavy use of Session state, this is impractical.

- **Encode the Session state directly in a cookie**, instead of storing the `ASPSESSIONID`. Very effective, especially on a Web farm, but it has a number of shortcomings:

  - The browser must support cookies and cookies must be enabled on the browser.

  - Cookies have size limitations: a browser need store no more than 300 total cookies, with 20 cookies per server, and no more than 4KB per cookie. Most browsers will store more, but these are the lower limits.

  - It's also insecure as the Session state is stored on the user's machine and it travels back and forth across the network with every request.

- **Store a key into a back-end database in a cookie**. Scalable and secure, but it does require a query to the database every time, and it still requires cookie support on the browser. The Active User Object that ships with Site Server does this for you. Third-party component vendors, such as Software Artisans, sell similar components.

- **Store name-value pairs in the Querystring of URLs**; e.g. `<A HREF="wrox.asp?Name=Napoleon&Game=World+Domination">`. This works with all browsers but it exposes the contents of the Session state and it doesn't work well with `POST`s and forms. It also lends itself to being hacked by users.

- **Modify the URLs, so that the Session state is encoded in the URL** (and not the Querystring). `Amazon.com` is an example of a site that does this. Another example of this is the Cookie Munger filter written by George Reilly, which ships as a sample ISAPI filter in the Platform SDK. This filter makes ASP Session state work with browsers that don't support cookies. The filter examines all data sent by the server to browsers, removes the `ASPSESSIONID` cookie from the headers, and modifies all URLs in the body of the page, so that they end up looking like `<A HREF="wrox.asp-ASP=PVZQGHUMEAYAHMFV">`. It also looks at the URLs on all incoming requests and translates ones that match this pattern back into normal URLs and generates a Cookie header. All of this happens transparently; ASP knows nothing about it. There are two problems with the Cookie Munger. Like all raw-data filters, it causes a substantial performance hit. Furthermore, the filter doesn't work with pure HTML pages (pages whose name ends in a `.htm` extension), as the cookie gets lost. See the documentation for details.
- **Forms can contain hidden fields**, which can encode additional state. Works moderately well, but requires every page to be a form (or use Querystrings) and the hidden data tends to get lost if you hit the Back button in a browser. Hidden fields can be seen by the user when viewing the page source, so it is not suitable for private data.

In short, none of these alternatives works well.

Lest you be completely disheartened by the above, let me say that using ASP Session state is an appropriate choice for many applications and that if you can live with the shortcomings, you should use it. However, those shortcomings may cause you severe problems in the future as your site grows in popularity, especially if you migrate to a Web farm, and you may be forced to do some expensive re-engineering.

Application State

Like Session state, Application state has some great advantages and some big disadvantages. Caching data in the Application object can lead to significant performance boosts. Instead of calculating the same data again and again for every session or every request, it can be calculated once and stored in the Application object.

Like the Session object, the Application object's state is not persistent and will not survive a crash. Application state is confined to one machine and does not span a Web farm. This suggests that only read-only data should be cached in Application state, since updating shared data across a Web farm is expensive. The Application object does not rely on cookies, so none of the cookie-related issues arise with the Application object. Large arrays should not be stored in the Application object, as the semantics of VBScript and JScript require that a temporary copy of the entire array be made whenever any element of the array is accessed.

Apartment-threaded objects *should not* be stored in the Application object. Doing so is a serious performance bottleneck. Indeed, to discourage you from attempting to store Apartment-threaded objects, ASP will not allow you to do this with objects created with `Server.CreateObject`. If you really must store Apartment-threaded objects in Application scope, you must use the `<OBJECT>` tag:

```
Application("Wrox") = Server.CreateObject("Apt.Object")             'Doesn't work

<OBJECT SCOPE=APPLICATION RUNAT=SERVER ID=wrox PROGID=Apt.Object>   'Works
```

There are three reasons why storing Apartment-threaded objects in Application scope is bad:

- The object lives in a special STA apartment and all calls to that object must be marshaled from the worker thread's apartment to the object's apartment. This is much, much slower than a direct call to the object.
- All calls to the object are serialized. Only one caller can make use of the object at a time and this can lead to long queues of worker threads waiting to access the shared object. Objects stored at Application scope should be highly concurrent.
- Apartment-threaded objects stored at Application scope never execute in the *security context* of the caller.

Only **agile** objects should be stored in Application scope. Agile objects permit direct calls (so no marshaling) and do not serialize their callers. Agile objects are harder to write, since they must pay particular attention to thread safety, and can be written only in C++/ATL or in Visual J++.

Secure Sockets Layer

SSL (Secure Sockets Layer), which is accessed by the HTTPS protocol, enables secure e-commerce. A secure connection is opened between the browser and the server and all data is encrypted before it's sent across the wire. This makes it safe to transfer sensitive data, such as credit card numbers or medical records, across untrusted networks, like the Internet.

SSL connections are much more expensive than ordinary HTTP connections because implementing the cryptographic protocols requires a great deal of number crunching. It's twenty times more costly to transfer a static file via HTTPS than it is via HTTP. It's less costly to transfer an ASP page via HTTPS than it is to send a static file. Dynamically generating the content with ASP is more expensive than sending a static file; therefore the HTTPS overhead is a smaller fraction of the total cost. It's still huge, however – for a lightweight ASP page, SSL can decrease throughput tenfold.

Since SSL is so costly, it should be used only when it's required. Credit card numbers must be posted to a form via HTTPS; medical records must be displayed on an HTTPS page. Home pages and other pages that do not contain sensitive content should be transferred via HTTP. With the exception of those few images that do have confidential content, no images should be sent via HTTPS. Unfortunately, most browsers will pop-up a message box if an attempt is made to retrieve data via HTTP while connected to an HTTPS page. A slow page is better than a page that forces message boxes to pop-up.

Process Isolation

In IIS 3.0, when ASP was first released, all ASP applications ran in the core IIS process, `inetinfo.exe`. This was fast but fragile. An errant component could crash the entire Web server. IIS 4.0 introduced the notion of process isolation. Applications could either run in-process (in the `inetinfo` process) or out-of-process (hosted by `mtx.exe`). A bad component running out-of-process could crash its host process, but it could not crash the core Web server. However, there is some overhead associated with communicating between `inetinfo` and the out-of-process applications, so out-of-process applications run slower. *Performance is traded off for reliability.*

Processes consume a lot of system resources, so you can't run more than a few dozen out-of-process applications in IIS 4.0. Recognizing this, IIS 5.0 introduces an intermediate level of isolation, pooled-out-of-process applications. High-isolation (out-of-process) applications continue to run in separate processes, which are now hosted by `dllhost.exe`. Medium-isolation (pooled-out-of-process) applications all run together in one process, also hosted by `dllhost`. Low-isolation (in-process) applications run directly in the core IIS process, `inetinfo`.

In IIS 5.0, ASP performance has been greatly improved. Out-of-process performance in IIS 5.0 is better than in-process performance was in IIS 4.0. (In-process performance in IIS 5.0 is even better, of course.) Because of this, we felt comfortable trading off some performance for increased reliability, so new applications run at medium isolation, by default. In IIS 4.0, new applications ran in-process.

If you have a well-trusted application – one that makes use of well-tested components only – you can boost its performance by marking it as a low-isolation application. Be aware that if this application crashes, it will crash the Web server process. As IIS 5.0 includes a new reliable restart feature, controlled by `iisreset.exe`, this is less of a problem than it was in IIS 4.0, but it's still undesirable.

Caching and Dictionaries

Caching is *the* fundamental performance technique. *You trade off space for speed.* Instead of recalculating data from scratch or fetching it slowly from a distant location, you hang on to it and reuse it. Every layer of the computer relies heavily on caching, from the CPU's L1 and L2 caches, to each disk's cache, to the operating system's file cache, to ASP's cache of compiled ASP scripts, and to ODBC's pool of connections.

There are four ways you are likely to make use of caching in ASP:

- The first is to cache some data in a variable and reuse it within a single page; e.g. a String or a recordset.
- The second is to store some data in the Session object that may be reused on other pages visited by the user in this session; e.g. the contents of a shopping basket or the user's name.
- The third is to store some data in the Application object that can be reused by many visitors to the site; e.g. current headlines that are splashed down the right-hand side of every page.
- The last is to use a component to cache global data. When the component is created on a page, its methods access the internal data; e.g. the Browser Capabilities component caches the contents of `browscap.ini`, only updating its cache when the file changes on disk, once every few months.

Dictionaries, which are also known as **associative arrays** or **maps**, are useful for caching name-value pairs. For example, you could map the two-letter country codes to their full names: "FR"•"France", "IE"•"Ireland", etc. Since this data changes only when a new nation is formed, it would be appropriate to cache this dictionary in the Application object.

Another example would be a map of ISBN numbers to full details about a title. Since there are millions of ISBN numbers and thousands of new ones are added every day, this data is too large to store in memory and is best stored in a database, with some provision for updating it regularly. However, it would be appropriate to build a map of ISBNs and details for the contents of a shopping basket at an online bookstore.

ASP comes with a `Dictionary` component, `Scripting.Dictionary`. Unfortunately, `Scripting.Dictionary` is Apartment-threaded and it is *not* suitable for storing in the Session or Application objects. Alas, these are precisely the scenarios for which a Dictionary is most useful.

You have a few alternatives. If you have Commerce Server, you can use the `Commerce.Dictionary`. There are also two freely available dictionaries: `LookupTable`, and `Caprock.Dictionary`.

> `asptoday.com` *has a good tutorial on the* `LookupTable` *dictionary.*

If you want to cache a recordset in the Session or Application objects, be sure to disconnect it first.

> **Maintaining connections across multiple pages is a very bad idea.**

Better still, if the recordset is always going to be transformed into the same HTML (e.g. a table or a list box), cache the HTML text instead and avoid the cost of walking through the recordset every time. If the list box can have different items selected under different circumstances, you can still cache the list box text and use the `Replace` function to generate a new string with the appropriate selection.

Database Performance

To paraphrase a well-known computer company executive, "The database is the Web application". Dynamic sites count on storing, retrieving, and updating data. The performance of the database is oftentimes at the core of the performance of the Web application itself. There are several easy things that can be done to reduce bottlenecks in using a database with the Web application. The effort to tune database performance can be taken much further. Enterprise databases even provide tools for analyzing access patterns and queries to aid the developer and database administrator.

> *Since SQL Server from Microsoft is the database I use with my Web applications, I will refer to it in the following paragraphs. Most, if not all, of the following suggestions will apply to other databases as well.*

The first thing to do is eliminate the use of Microsoft Access from your Web application. Access is a great application when used on the scale for which it was designed. However, it is not appropriate for handling large volumes of data quickly. I'd even go so far as to remove the driver in the Data Sources panel.

By default, ADO is configured as Apartment-threaded. This is probably due to the fact that Access only supports Apartment-threaded access via the ODBC driver. ADO supports the Free-threaded model and using it will result in a performance win. A batch file is provided for making this conversion. On a typical install, it can be found in the `\Program Files\Common Files\System\ado` directory. Run `makefre15.bat` from that directory and ADO will be transformed into a Both-threaded object with support for the Apartment- and Free-threading models. There is also a batch file for restoring it back to the Apartment model if you are so inclined.

> *It is confusing that the batch files and DLLs are named with 15 in their names (referring to ADO 1.5) when we know that the current version of ADO is 2.5. With the improved capabilities of COM in assisting in DLL version control, it appears that the DLL names may remain as a sort of legacy. Although it is less than intuitive, the improved version handling should be much better than having multiple versions of the same components on a system when they are not required.*

Although there are differences between the different enterprise database management systems, they do have one thing very much in common. In order for them to yield high performance, they require significant amounts of memory. IIS also performs much better when it has an adequate memory supply for caching. Because of this, it is a good idea to separate IIS and SQL onto different machines. Most people are immediately concerned about a possible performance degradation in traversing machine boundaries. However, because of the history of large memory requirements for databases and this need for dedicated processing power, the low-level communication methods for accessing a database are quite fast.

There are two scenarios for database use, and both yield better performance for the Web application if the database is on a separate machine:

- First, the application may be almost entirely database-driven. In this case, the database needs the dedicated resources to process queries and cache data effectively.
- The second scenario is the other extreme; the data from a database is rarely used. For this situation, it still makes sense to locate the database on a separate machine. This will allow the Web server, which is handling the majority of the workload, to have resources that would otherwise have to be given to a database on the local machine that was rarely being used. Paying the slight penalty of crossing machine boundaries is more than made up for by the increased efficiency of both the database and the Web server.

A single database resource can usually handle the requirements of several Web servers accessing it simultaneously.

Utilize the features of COM+, formerly included with MTS, to handle some of the data checking. By utilizing referential integrity checks that can be built into the database definition, many error situations can be detected without scripting explicit checks. Utilizing transactions on the Web page can further protect database updates and inserts. Referential integrity checks can execute faster in the databases than they do in script. An example of a referential integrity check would be checking that the zip code provided in a user's postal address is present in a table of zip codes to which you provide service.

Also, make sure that **indexes** exist for the tables that are being accessed. Database engines do a fantastic job of performance self-tuning when they have clues as to how the data will be accessed. These clues are offered through establishing indexes. Take advantage of stored procedures on the database. Routines that are required often can be established as a stored procedure or trigger. These operations are slow and difficult in script. By utilizing table joins, unions and views in the database, the script will be less error prone and much faster. Database administration and tuning is often overlooked in the course of Web application work, but data access is often the single biggest bottleneck for the Web site. When you see the phrase "long-running and blocking processes", the reference is often to a database operation.

Real-Enough Time: MSMQ

You have already seen a section talking about MSMQ, but let's talk about it with respect to performance. Web browsing is a live activity. No one expects to request a page and have it pop up in his or her browser minutes later when they are busy doing something else. However, the actions happening on the server as a result of user input can often happen separately from the execution of the page. In other words, the user doesn't always need to wait for all of the script executing in a Web page to complete to get the next page.

Suppose that an application accepts orders to send out a product sample. This application might need to update a database with the request and send an announcement of the impending arrival of the sample via email. These are examples of tasks that the user might not necessarily need to wait for the server to complete before moving on. And why should they? Rather than complete these operations in the script, we can place the order request in a message queue and complete this page. The Web server continues handling requests and the user continues browsing. The message queue allows the order to be processed and confirmation sent without slowing down the Web application. MSMQ makes it easy to move work from the machine where IIS is running to another back-end server, keeping response times down.

Script vs. Components

Scripts are slower than components because scripts are **interpreted**, while components are **compiled**.

> **You can boost the performance of your ASP pages by replacing chunks of script with calls to components.**

Does this mean that you should rewrite all of your ASP pages as components? No. There are a number of potential problems with components that you should be aware of:

- **Components are harder to debug**, because you can't step into them with the script debugger. You have to use a separate debugger.
- **Components are harder to modify**. With ASP pages, you change the page in your favorite editor, save it, and reload the page with a browser. With a component, you have to stop the ASP application hosting the component, modify the source code, recompile it, restart the ASP application, and only then reload the page with a browser. This makes the edit-run-debug cycle considerably longer.
- **Poorly developed components crash**. A buggy component can bring down the ASP application hosting it. An ASP application comprised entirely of script and system components is very unlikely to crash. If a component is not well-trusted, you should either run the ASP application in a separate process (high or medium isolation) and run the component in the same process as ASP by marking it as a Library package, or you should run the component itself in its own process by marking it as a server application in the COM+ Explorer. I recommend running the ASP application at high isolation and the component as a Library package.
- **Poorly developed components leak memory**. A component that doesn't fastidiously clean up after itself can leak memory, handles, or other resources. If this goes on long enough, it can leave the Web server unusable. Remember, a Web server should have an uptime measured in months: this is not possible if there are leaks.
- **Poorly developed components often do not survive high-stress conditions**. A lot of components are not adequately tested under stress and fail when the Web server is under high load. Deadlocks and access violations are common symptoms, especially on multi-processor systems. ASP applications and components must be stress-tested before they are deployed.
- **Many components have thread affinity** (they are Apartment-threaded) and do not perform well when stored in the Session or Application object. This is true of components written in Visual Basic or with MFC. Session- and Application-scoped components should be agile – Neutral or Both-threaded (and aggregate the free-threaded marshaler) – which can be hard to write well.

- **Components often do not scale to multi-processor systems**. Many components make themselves thread-safe by acquiring locks with merry abandon. This works fairly well on uni-processor systems but leads to considerable contention and serialization on multiprocessor systems. See the section on *Multi-processor Scalability* for further discussion.
- In addition, **many pages are not worth translating into components**, since translating them won't significantly boost the performance of the system. Small pages or pages that are executed infrequently are poor candidates to be reworked as components. Initializing components and calling them takes time – if the component doesn't do much, script could be faster. To find out which pages should be considered, look at the logs. Pages that are visited often and pages that take a long time to execute are candidates. Analyze those pages. Do they use inefficient algorithms? Are there hotspots? Can sections of code be replaced with calls to stock components?

> **Rule of thumb: unless there are at least 100 lines of script and some big loops in that script, it's probably not worth thinking about translating that page into a component.**

Be aware that ASP pages that `#include` functions can contain much more code than is apparent at a casual glance. To find out just how much server-side script is present in `/wrox/bar.asp`, rename it to `/wrox/bar.stm`, visit the new page in a browser, and View Source. (This technique relies on the fact that both ASP and SSI use the same syntax for `#includes`; however, SSI does not interpret the ASP script, so it's sent through to the client.)

What, then, are the reasons why you would consider using components?

- Foremost, for the purposes of this chapter, is **performance**. If you do it right, you might speed up some pages by a factor of twenty or thirty. Usually the speed-ups will be less dramatic, but this can still be enough to save a site from oblivion. Not only do you replace interpreted script with compiled binaries, you replace late-bound calls with early-bound ones. You can by-pass the layers of OLE Automation and make use of more efficient, lower-level interfaces (e.g., use OLE DB instead of ADO). You can make direct calls to the file system instead of using the FileSystem object.
- **Components give you scalability**. If the components use up too much CPU, you can deploy them on back-end servers and connect to them via DCOM; thus you are no longer limited to one machine.
- There are strong arguments to be made for **putting all of your business logic into components**. This isolates the business layer from the presentation layer, and ASP proper is just used as "HTML glue". If you change a few business rules, you just need to modify the components, not every ASP page. It also simplifies translating your site into other languages, if you separate the content from the logic. Furthermore, if one team writes the business logic and another team writes the HTML content, it simplifies integration if the business logic is in separate components.
- **Components also give you better reusability**. You can use the same business logic components behind a richer Win32 user interface as you did behind an ASP HTML interface. You can also reuse the components from many ASP pages within your application and even from many other ASP applications.
- **Components give you strong typing**. VBScript is a weakly typed language: all variables are Variants. This is very convenient for little, quick-and-dirty programs, but for industrial-strength programs, strong typing is a boon.

- **Components allow you to access the full features of the operating system**. For example, you cannot read anything from the registry in ASP. You must use a component. You cannot do anything with files directly from ASP. You have to use the FileSystem object, which ships with ASP.
- Finally, components allow you **to protect your intellectual property**. If you build ASP sites for your customers, those customers can read your source code. If you put the more important code into components, it's safe from prying eyes.

> *Version 5 of the script engines include a script encoding utility. This provides protection against casual scrutiny, but is not cryptographically secure*

Component Threading Models

When writing a COM object for use from within ASP, the choice of a threading model becomes very important. Performance can suffer dramatically because of the complications possible in mixing threading models.

> **Single-threaded objects should never be used with ASP.**

Every use of the object must be marshaled to the COM main thread. Any time that a multi-threaded environment has to wait on the availability of a single thread, performance suffers. The performance typically gets worse under increased load.

> **Free-threaded objects are also not recommended for general-purpose use in ASP applications.**

This type of object does not have the same context available without going through extra steps in registering the object with the COM Services Manager.

Objects utilizing the Single- and Free-threading models both suffer from the problem of running as *System*. Normally the processes of the application run as a designated user, or a default account set up during installation. When running as the Local System Account, typical security checks are by-passed. Running with this level of privilege is not desirable and is a compelling reason in itself not to use the Free and Single models.

The Apartment model is appropriate for page-scoped objects. This means the object should be created using `Server.CreateObject` and should not be assigned to a Session variable. As discussed above in the section on Session state, Apartment-threaded objects cause a session to be "locked down" to a particular thread. It is possible to put an Apartment-threaded object in Application using the `<OBJECT>` tag syntax. However, Apartment-threaded objects should never be run at Application scope. As discussed above in the section on Application state, Apartment-threaded objects perform very poorly at Application scope and they run as System.

Agile objects are the way to go for performance and flexibility. Under IIS 4.0, agile objects were Both-threaded objects that aggregate the Free-threaded marshaler (FTM). Under IIS 5.0, the new COM+ Neutral-threaded objects are also agile. When a Both-threaded object aggregates the FTM, calls between threads can occur without the slow down of marshaling and extra thread switches. If the Both-threaded object does not aggregate the FTM, then it will be treated like an Apartment-threaded object; i.e. it's not suitable for Session or Application scope. This can be worked around by setting `AspTrackThreadingModel` to `True` in the metabase, but this is not recommended, as it violates the semantics of Both-threading.

Neutral-threaded objects are also considered agile. These objects can be called directly from any apartment, so are suitable for storing in Session or Application scope. Neutral objects should not aggregate the FTM.

How do you choose between writing Neutral objects and Both+FTM objects? If the component needs to run on IIS 4.0, you must use Both+FTM objects, as Neutral objects are available only under COM+ in Windows 2000. Objects that aggregate the FTM must take care when caching interface pointers to keep those interface pointers apartment-neutral, or they will run into `RPC_E_WRONGTHREAD` errors. They can either restrict themselves to using interface pointers on objects that themselves aggregate the FTM, or they can store the interface pointers in the Global Interface Table. Neutral components have no such restrictions.

Multi-Processor Scalability

Many people have a naïve expectation that an ASP application written on a uni-processor system will run *n* times better on an *n*-processor system. That certainly wasn't true for IIS 3.0, matters improved somewhat in IIS 4.0 for dual-processor systems, but it wasn't until IIS 5.0 that it became more or less true for four- and eight-processor systems.

The problem is that multi-threaded programs like IIS need to use locks to ensure consistency. Without locks, two or more threads could simultaneously modify shared data, leaving it in a corrupted or inconsistent state. Consider what could happen with the following code in `global.asa`:

```
Sub Session_OnStart

    Application("NumUsers") = Application("NumUsers") + 1

End Sub
```

```
Sub Session_OnEnd

    Application("NumUsers") = Application("NumUsers") - 1

End Sub
```

If there are, say, 200 users and one user's session is starting as another is ending, it's entirely possible (especially on a multi-processor system) that the numbers on the right-hand side of the equals signs are being calculated at the same time (201 and 199). `Session_OnEnd` and `Session_OnStart` will both update `Application("NumUsers")` in some non-deterministic order. The second one to execute will "win", but it's a dubious victory, since in either case the answer is wrong. It should be 200 again, not 201 or 199.

The correct way to make these changes consistent is to use `Application.Lock` and `Application.Unlock` to avoid corrupting the shared data in `Application("NumUsers")`:

```
Sub Session_OnStart

    Application.Lock
        Application("NumUsers") = Application("NumUsers") + 1
    Application.Unlock

End Sub
```

In similar fashion, all of the code that executes under the covers (including third-party components) has to protect shared data with locks. If the shared data is read or modified often, then those locks become hot: threads start contending for the lock and become bottlenecked. The threads become serialized, as only one thread can hold the lock at a time. The threads are all waiting to acquire the lock and none of them can proceed to do useful work until the thread holding the lock releases it. This kind of behavior can result in poor multi-processor scalability: throughput will not be much better than it was on a uni-processor system. If you're particularly unfortunate, throughput will actually go down (negative scalability). One way to tell if this is happening is to monitor the *System|Context Switches/sec* performance counter in the `PerfMon` tool provided as part of Windows. If you are seeing more than a few thousand context switches per second, you have a serious lock contention problem.

A great deal of effort has gone into Windows 2000 and IIS 5.0 to ensure that the system-provided components scale well on multi-processor systems. If you do have multi-processor scalability problems, the most likely cause is poorly written custom components.

Lock contention tends not to be much of a problem on uni-processor systems, whereas it can be a huge problem on multi-processor systems. The reason is that uni-processor systems provide the *illusion* of multiple threads executing simultaneously, whereas on multi-processor systems, multiple threads really *are* executing simultaneously. On a uni-processor system, a thread can execute millions of instructions before the system context switches, letting another thread run. A thread can acquire a lock, do some operations, and release the lock with a high probability that no context switches will occur while it holds the lock, and hence that no other thread would be blocked in trying to acquire the lock. On an *n*-processor system, with *n* threads running at once, the probability that two or more threads will want to acquire a busy lock simultaneously can become very high.

To minimize lock contention in your components, apply the following principles:

- **Don't share data between instances of your component**; i.e. don't have any global data. If it's not shared, it doesn't have to be protected, so there are no locks to bottleneck on. (This only applies if the component itself is not shared.)
- **Don't share an instance of your component between threads** – no global, Application-scoped objects. Application-scoped components must protect their per-instance data from concurrent access as well as their global data. Alas, these two principles are often impractical.
- **Minimize the duration of the lock**. When you must lock data, acquire the lock as late as possible, do as little work as possible while holding the lock, and release the lock as soon as possible. The easiest way to make code thread-safe is to lock the data at the beginning of the code and release the lock at the end of the code, but this leads to lock contention problems.

- **Acquire as few locks as possible.** If you don't need to lock it, don't lock it.
- **Use fine-grained locking.** It's easier to protect all data with one global lock, but this decreases concurrency. For example, if you were building a Dictionary component, you might choose to use a different lock for each letter of the alphabet. This would allow one thread to update an entry that starts with 'h' while another is looking up an entry that starts with 'q'.

Don't go overboard. It's far better to have a somewhat slow, correct program than a fast, unsafe one. Consistency is more important than concurrency.

Thread Gating

When ASP receives an HTTP request, such as a URL ending in `.asp`, it adds this request to the end of a **request queue**. Each low-, medium-, or high-isolation process that hosts ASP has its own request queue. The *Active Server Pages\Requests Queued* performance counter shows the total number of requests in all of the queues. ASP maintains a collection of worker threads in each process to service the request queue. These threads take a request off the head of the queue, compile the ASP page (if it's not already cached), execute the page, and send the results back to the client.

Sometimes, all of the ASP worker threads can be blocked, waiting for external resources to become available (e.g. they're all waiting for responses from databases). The CPU utilization will be low and there may be requests sitting in the queue that could be worked upon while the worker threads are blocked, but there are no more worker threads available to satisfy any more requests. You can tell if this is happening by looking at the *Active Server Pages\Requests Executing*, *Active Server Pages\Requests Queued*, and *Processor(_Total)\% Processor Time* performance counters. In circumstances such as these, it would be appropriate for ASP to have more worker threads. In other circumstances, where all the requests are being executed quickly, having lots of worker threads is a disadvantage; the worker threads consume system resources and add context-switching overhead. Also, if the machine is busy (CPU utilization is high), it's better to have fewer worker threads than many.

In IIS 4.0, if you wanted to tune the number of worker threads, you had to modify the `ProcessorThreadMax` (PTM) setting in the registry and restart IIS. If your Web site had a fairly predictable workload, this was quite effective. However, on many Web sites, the nature of the workload can change dramatically from minute to minute, but it's quite impractical to constantly tune PTM by hand and restart IIS.

> *The PTM setting is not present in the registry by default. Its default value is 10, which means that ASP will create 10 threads per CPU in each ASP process; in other words, a dual-processor system will have 20 ASP worker threads in each ASP process.*

IIS 5.0 attempts to dynamically tune the number of worker threads, in response to changing workloads. This is known as **thread gating**. There are a number of associated settings that reside at the root of the metabase. (The PTM setting is now called `AspProcessorThreadMax` and resides in the metabase; it defaults to 25 threads per CPU, instead of 10.) The `adsutil` script provided with IIS can enumerate the Web service settings. Used in conjunction with `findstr`, we can locate all settings containing the word 'Thread.'

```
C:\> cscript \inetpub\AdminScripts\adsutil.vbs enum w3svc | findstr Thread
AspProcessorThreadMax            : (INTEGER) 25
AspThreadGateEnabled             : (BOOLEAN) True
AspThreadGateTimeSlice           : (INTEGER) 1000
AspThreadGateSleepDelay          : (INTEGER) 100
AspThreadGateSleepMax            : (INTEGER) 50
AspThreadGateLoadLow             : (INTEGER) 50
AspThreadGateLoadHigh            : (INTEGER) 80
```

If thread gating is enabled, the thread gate will look at the CPU utilization (0%–100%) once every `AspThreadGateTimeSlice` milliseconds (defaults to 1000ms) and adjust the thread limit. The thread limit is the maximum number of ASP worker threads that can be active at any time in that ASP process. The lower bound is one thread per CPU; the upper bound is `AspProcessorThreadMax` multiplied by the number of CPUs. If the CPU utilization is below `AspThreadGateLoadLow` (defaults to 50%), then the thread limit is adjusted upwards (i.e. more threads are allowed to run). If the CPU utilization is above `AspThreadGateLoadHigh` (defaults to 80%), the thread limit is adjusted downwards (fewer threads may run). If the CPU utilization lies between these two bounds, the thread limit is not adjusted. Depending upon recent trends in CPU utilization, the thread gate will be more or less aggressive about adjusting the thread limit up or down.

Whenever a worker thread is about to execute a request, it enters the thread gate. If gating is disabled, the thread proceeds through the gate immediately. If gating is enabled, the request can proceed only if the number of active threads is below the thread limit. If the thread limit is exceeded, the thread is put to sleep for (at least) `AspThreadGateSleepDelay` milliseconds (defaults to 100ms). To ensure that the thread doesn't spend too long in the thread gate, it will be put to sleep at most `AspThreadGateSleepMax` times (default: 50) before it's allowed to proceed. Remember also that the thread limit is adjusted once every `AspThreadGateTimeSlice` milliseconds.

In practice, thread gating seems to work a lot more effectively than manually adjusting the registry setting and restarting IIS, since it responds to changes in load as they happen. If you prefer manual control, you need only set `AspThreadGateEnabled` to `False` and modify `AspProcessThreadMax`.

Metabase Settings

Here is a list of the most important metabase settings. These can be retrieved and changed using the ADSI interfaces. There is a simple example script below. There is also a script shipped with IIS that makes manipulating the metabase much easier. Look for `adsutil.vbs` in the `\Inetpub\AdminScripts` directory.

AspAllowSessionState

Changing the value to `FALSE` from the default of `TRUE` in the metabase can have a performance gain. This setting will then have to be explicitly overridden in pages that actually do need to make use of the Session object. It is changed for just the page by using `<% @EnableSessionState=True %>` at the top of the page.

AspProcessorThreadMax

Described in the *Thread Gating* section above.

AspRequestQueueMax

As discussed in the *Performance Counters* section below, the default limit for requests in the queue has been increased for IIS 5.0. Again, the effectiveness of this setting is dependent on the behavior of the application. If the requests execution time is very short and the time in the queue will be short, it is reasonable to increase this limit.

AspQueueConnectionTestTime

This is a new setting for IIS 5.0 and one that aids significantly in the performance of Web applications. In IIS 4.0, execution of a request was always begun when it was removed from the queue. In the next version, if a request has been in the queue longer than the "queue connection test time," the server checks to see that the client is still connected before beginning execution. This feature handles the problem of impatient users filling up the request queue with numerous attempts at the same page. The default value is 3 seconds. Whether to change this value depends on the type of application.

AspSessionMax and AspSessionTimeout

The default behavior is not to limit the number of concurrent sessions, but rather to limit the length of single sessions to twenty minutes. For applications that take advantage of sessions, it may be prudent to reduce the Session Timeout to reduce the overhead required of the server, but, if concurrent sessions increase to unwieldy proportions, it may be necessary to introduce a Session Maximum.

AspScriptEngineCacheMax

The new default for the maximum number of script engines to cache in memory is 125. Adjust this according to the type of content in the application. If there are thousands of unique pages, there is probably some gain associated with increasing the cache size so that the most frequently requested pages could be readily accessed.

Performance Counters: Which Ones Count

Performance counters are at the heart of monitoring and tuning a Web application, but there are so many counters from which to choose. The **Performance Monitor** tool supplied with Windows provides the ability to monitor an abundance of counters. In this section we will look at what can be gained by keeping a watchful eye on some counters while only periodically checking others:

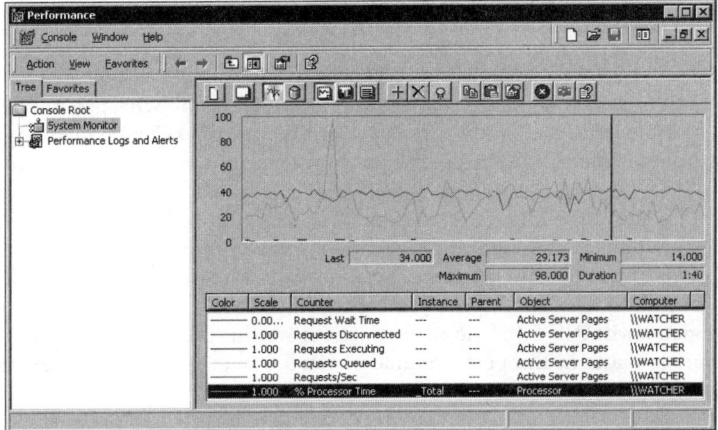

By right-clicking on the main viewing window you can select to Add Counters. This will bring up the Add Counters dialog from which you can select those counter you wish to monitor:

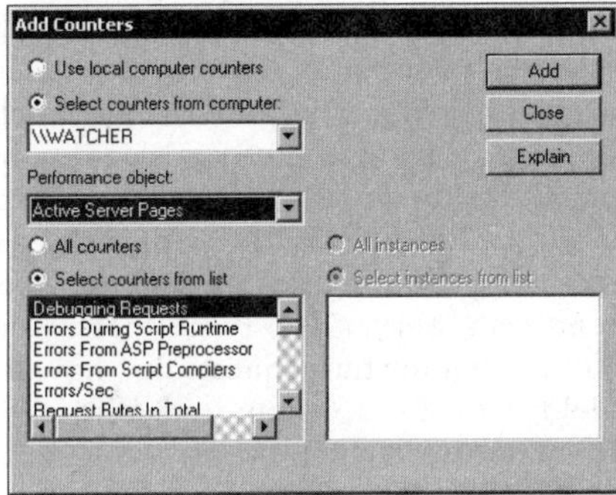

One trick we suggest is to use the Explain button on the Add Counters dialog. This will display a sentence or two about each performance counter:

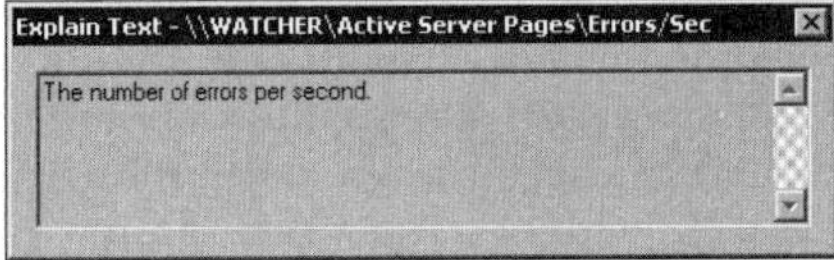

Active Server Pages\Debugging Requests
Active Server Pages\Errors During Script Runtime
Active Server Pages\Errors From ASP Preprocessor
Active Server Pages\Errors From Script Compilers

I learned an important lesson once when doing some benchmarking work. I added a couple of pages to the Web server for testing and unleashed the Web Application Stress Tool. I hadn't added any performance counters to the data collection, so I wasn't looking at these numbers as I worked through some analysis and tuning. I was patting myself on the back at how incredibly well the application was going to do when I requested one of the pages in the browser from the test machine. There was an include file error, so no script code was actually being executed. I was getting great statistics because the server was sending only errors. Periodically, the ASP error counters and debugging counter should be checked to ensure that the application is functioning correctly.

Active Server Pages\Requests Executing
Active Server Pages\Requests Queued

Requests Executing and *Requests Queued* are two counters that everyone who has been involved with administering a heavily loaded Web server has checked many times. Their meaning is straightforward, although different theories on how to interpret them have been widely circulated.

When a request for an ASP page arrives, it is queued for execution. If resources are available for handling the request, whether it be compiling and then executing it, or pulling it from the cache for execution, it is removed from the queue and processed. When the request arrives, it is not placed in the queue until it is verified that the *RequestQueueMax* limit has not been reached. This limit is no longer set in the registry with IIS 5.0. The procedure for modifying it now is to access the Metabase. With the improvements made in the performance of IIS 5.0 over the previous release, the default value has been increased from 500 to 3000.

The interactions and meaning of these two counters have been misunderstood and have differed slightly between IIS 3.0, IIS 4.0 and IIS 5.0. I believe the behavior in IIS 5.0, although only slightly different than that of the previous version, is the most straightforward. In IIS 4.0, the check made prior to placing a script in the queue checked the combined total of *Requests Queued* and *Requests Executing*. This was subtly misleading but marginal in terms of importance. After all, the goal is not to maximize the number of requests waiting in the queue, but to minimize the amount of time that they are forced to wait. With the default values in IIS 4.0 on a single processor machine, with requests incoming at a rate greater than the rate at which they are being completed, the server would start sending a "Server Too Busy" message with just four hundred and ninety requests in the queue. Adding ten for the requests that have been removed from the queue and are in the executing state yields a total of five hundred. With the new release, the value is compared against just those waiting in the queued state.

Although this chapter is not devoted to the metabase and the processes for manipulating it, I have included here the few lines of JScript code necessary to view or set the *RequestQueueMax* value. Reducing this value significantly to test behavior under heavy load can be a valuable experience. Check the performance when returning static files as ASP alternates when the limit has been reached. This little bit of preparation can put you in a good position to answer for the behavior of the application when it receives an unduly large spike in traffic for some unforeseen reason. Don't forget to set the value back. The Windows Script Host can invoke this code by putting it in a file with a `.js` extension and then executing the file:

```
//To view the value
var obj = GetObject("IIS://LocalHost/W3SVC/1/Root");
var RequestQueueMax = obj.AspRequestQueueMax;
WScript.Echo(RequestQueueMax);

//To set the value to something ridiculously low
var obj = GetObject("IIS://LocalHost/W3SVC/1/Root");
obj.AspRequestQueueMax = 50;
obj.SetInfo();
WScript.Echo("Done, don't forget to set RequestQueueMax back");
```

Active Server Pages\Request Execution Time
Active Server Pages\Request Wait Time

These two counters are tracked by sampling the numbers for the most recent request. The Request Execution Time can vary widely according to nature of the last page executed. Observing trends in these two values over time will help you to understand the behavior of the application. A rise in the execution time may indicate increased load being placed on a shared resource (like a database) or may indicate execution of more labor-intensive scripts. Context switches between threads that are competing for Critical Sections can force a request to stay in the executing state longer. If the rate of incoming requests surpasses the rate that scripts are completing execution, the wait time will begin to rise. Monitor these counters to help isolate the source of performance problems.

Active Server Pages\Requests/Sec

Requests per second is the benchmark used most often to get a feel for the overall performance and activity of the Web site. Remember that the numbers displayed for Average, Minimum, and Maximum reflect just the data currently in the viewable area only. To get a better feel for performance over time, take advantage of the logging capabilities of the performance monitor. It can store vast amounts of data, and allows customizing the time on which the numbers are based after the fact. Using this feature allows post-mortem work to be done much more efficiently.

The performance counters provided for Active Server Pages includes an extensive list of totals. Every request is categorized into these categories. It is important to check them periodically to understand the behavior of the application. The cause of an unexpected jump or decline in the performance of the application may be tracked down much more quickly if you see a variation from the typical totals. Additionally, it is important to understand the meanings of these counters, as there is some overlap that can be misleading.

Active Server Pages\Requests Total
Active Server Pages\Requests Succeeded
Active Server Pages\Requests Failed Total

First, there is a record of the total number of requests. This can be broken down into two major subcategories; those that succeeded and those that failed. Obviously, the hope is that almost all of the requests will have succeeded, but that is not always the case. For that reason, the failed total is broken out again into the various reasons that a request can be counted as failed.

Active Server Pages\Requests Disconnected

Some requests fail because of problems in the underlying network communications. There should be a certain amount of tolerance for this, as a global network will have slight mishaps from time to time. Concern about this type of failure comes to the forefront if the number increases dramatically or if the application is operating on an isolated network over which you have control.

Active Server Pages\Requests Rejected

Rejected requests are those that were sent the Server Too Busy message. A Server Too Busy message is almost never a good alternative to returning the dynamic content the user seeks.

Active Server Pages\Requests Timed Out

As discussed before, requests are placed in the queue for execution. By default, they do not time out in the queue, but this can be changed. See the section on manipulating the *Metabase settings*. If a request is timed out while in the queue, or if it exceeds the Script Timeout setting while in the executing state, it will be counted as a failed request. An escalation of this number indicates a performance problem and requires attention.

Active Server Pages\Requests Not Authorized

IIS provides several models for securing access to pages. If the proper credentials are not supplied, a request is counted as failed. A small number of these may be considered normal, but a sudden rise may indicate that access privileges have been changed to an unintended restriction level that denies access to those accustomed to viewing. Alternatively, this might be the result of a deliberate attempt on the part of some user to gain access to secured content to which they have not been granted rights. Either way, it is best to track down the source of these failures if there is a sudden change.

Active Server Pages\Requests Not Found

This is another failure where a few occurrences should probably not be considered as a reason for alarm. Users oftentimes guess at page names resulting in requests failing because the user has guessed incorrectly. Also, various entities have devised algorithms for determining what sites use what Web server software and how they use it. So, a certain number of requests for `default.asp` are to be expected on a public site, even if the server has been configured to look for a different default page. A sudden change in the number of requests received for content that does not exist probably indicates broken links and should be investigated. The log files can provide specifics about the exact document name.

Active Server Pages\Template Cache Hit Rate

The percentage of requests that can be serviced by pulling already compiled scripts from the template cache is important for the performance of the Web site. Web server administrators frustrated as to why they can't get this count to be one hundred percent have asked me about it. The answer is that it is not possible. In order to get a template into the cache, there has to first be a cache miss. There is further discussion about tuning to maximize this number in the section on *Metabase settings*. There is no hard number for which to aim. It is very much a function based on the particular application. Some sites have literally thousands of pages. The efficiency of a cache declines the larger it is allowed to become. Although, for planning purposes, it is important to note here that the cache used for ASP scales phenomenally. Be aware of this number and use it to aid in server tuning, but do not become obsessed by it.

Process(inetinfo)\Private Bytes

If the amount of memory allocated by the process steadily rises over a long period of time, it may indicate the presence of a memory leak. If the server has typically been operating at some steady state of memory after the cache has been filled and then suddenly exhibits a steady upward progression of private bytes, it most likely coincides with the introduction of a new custom COM object to the application. At best, tracking down a memory leak is difficult. The NT Resource Kit includes a tool called `dh.exe` that can aid the developer in this type of work. The easiest way to identify the problem is to stress test using the properties and methods of an object with a stress tool to see if the rise in private bytes corresponds to their use.

System\Context Switches/sec

Discussed in the *Multiprocessor Scalability* section above. Useful in diagnosing lock contention problems.

Miscellaneous Tips

Finally, some tricks that we find useful.

The stm Rename Trick

The `#include` syntax provides an excellent method for encapsulating functionality that is used across multiple pages. It also provides an easy avenue for including functionality in pages that are never used. It is very easy when coding an application for the Web developer to add general-purpose functions to one include file and include that page as needed in other include files. The net effect can be devastating to the performance of a Web application if not managed carefully. The Web server includes a method to help you see the result of using `#includes`. Copy a `.asp` page to a name with a `.stm` extension and issue a request for it in your browser. The Server Side Include processing will bring in all of the `#include` files, but the scripting engine will not be invoked to process the script. Instead, the code will be returned to the browser for viewing. Needless to say, this should not be done on a production machine. Most likely, you don't want to expose the source code for your application to the world. What you will be viewing is the script plus all of the included script exactly as it would be given to the script engine for processing. Look it over. It may be much larger than you anticipated. Even if a function is not called, it still takes up valuable server resources when included in a page. It must be parsed, and if it is in the cache it is taking up memory as well.

Avoid Nested Includes

One common problem you may discover is redundant or nested includes. For example, suppose that some core functions are included in a file called `core.inc`. When writing some error processing code in `error.inc`, the `core.inc` file is `#included`. Later on, when writing some data management routines in `data.inc`, you `#include error.inc` and `core.inc`. Now you have included `core.inc` twice. Furthermore, you might include `core.inc` in a regular ASP page along with `data.inc`. Now you've got three copies of `core.inc` to be parsed when the page is requested, but you don't readily see this without copying the file to a `.stm` extension and looking at the result.

Don't use non-Scriptmapped Extensions

Don't use the `.inc` extension. As a safety precaution against accidentally displaying the contents of include files, a generally good practice is to refrain from naming include files with a different extension. They will still be included correctly. If you want an easy method for distinguishing files that contain only library code, try modifying the file name instead of the extension. If you use a file extension that is not present in the script map (and `.inc` isn't), then IIS will send that file directly to browsers. Consider what could happen if the include file contained SQL Server administrator passwords or connection strings: users will see information that should be hidden from them when the file is sent to the browser instead of being executed on the server.

Turn off Script Debugging

Probably everyone writing an ASP application has done it, and has mentally berated themselves afterwards for neglecting to undo it. At some point it may become useful to use a debugger to step through the execution of an ASP page. The check box labeled Enable ASP server-side script debugging can be found in the App Debugging tab of the Application Configuration Property sheet in the Internet Services Manager. Don't use this on a production machine. The Web server throttles itself back to a single thread of execution for ASP in order to make debugging work as expected. While the debugger is activated, the machine handles no additional ASP requests. This may be a penalty that you are willing to pay when working at some late hour. Invariably when doing this, the option is left checked when the source of the problem is found, and the Web server goes on its way serving pages with just one thread doing all of the work. The reason for the much reduced performance may not be brought to light until some other error condition is reached, days or even weeks later, when that single thread is stopped with the debugger active and waiting for attention.

Minimize Script Block Transitions

Many developers of ASP script write a page with as few blocks of server-side code as possible. They will take great pains to include as little ASP code as possible. This can result in code that is difficult to read and difficult to maintain. Imagine a table that is being populated by data from a database, but does so using as little script code as possible:

```
<TABLE>
<TR><TH><%= header_one %></TH><TH><%= header_two %></TH></TR>
<TR><TD><%= variable_a %></TD><TD><%= variable_b %></TD></TR>
<TR><TD><%= variable_c %></TD><TD><%= variable_d %></TD></TR>
</TABLE>
```

All of this code is converted by the parser into `Response.Write` calls for execution. Imagine the extra work required by the parser to do this. In essence, the code must first be converted internally to something approximating the following:

```
Response.Write("<TABLE><TR><TH>");
Response.Write(header_one);
Response.Write("</TH><TH>");
Response.Write(header_two);
Response.Write("</TH></TR><TR><TD>");
Response.Write(variable_a);
Response.Write("</TD><TD>");
Response.Write(variable_b);
Response.Write("</TD></TR><TR><TD>");
Response.Write(variable_c);
Response.Write("</TD><TD>");
Response.Write(variable_d);
Response.Write("</TD></TR></TABLE>");
```

The performance is slightly better, and the code is much easier to maintain if the HTML that is so heavily interspersed with script is coded as fewer and larger blocks of script code. The original code could be re-written as:

```
Response.Write("<TABLE><TR><TH>" & header_one & "</TH><TH>" & header_two & _
               "</TH><TR>");
Response.Write("<TR><TD>" & variable_a & "</TD><TD>" & variable_b & _
               "</TD></TR>");
Response.Write("<TR><TD>" & variable_c & "</TD><TD>" & variable_d & _
               "</TD></TR></TABLE>");
```

The thirteen lines of intermediary code can easily be reduced to three. This gives a performance boost during execution as well as during compilation. Don't expect huge gains from this sort of change, but adopting it as a standard will pay off in the long run.

Don't Mix Script Engines

JScript versus VBScript has been a question posed and debated for some time now when talking about performance. I have seen demonstrations of one being faster than the other. I have seen counter-examples to the examples. In the past, there were good reasons for using one over the other found in the language features themselves. With VBScript you got `On Error Resume Next`. With JScript you got regular expressions. With the new scripting engines, these much-requested features have been made available from both languages. JScript now supports `try-catch` and VBScript offers a regular expression object.

> **With these new releases of the scripting engines, there is a definite answer to the JScript versus VBScript debate: use either, but *not both*.**

Allow me to explain. Using VBScript for one page, and JScript for another may be a requirement to satisfy the preferences of different developers writing an application. Using JScript and VBScript on the same page introduces a performance cost. The servers must instantiate and attempt to cache two script engines instead of one. When there were gains to be had because of missing features, the performance loss may have seemed acceptable, but, if there is something so compelling in one language that is not available in another, consider switching.

Use Response.IsClientConnected Before Costly Operations

Preventing the server from doing unnecessary work is an easy way to get a performance boost. Using `Response.IsClientConnected` before costly operations is one easy way to reduce the workload on the server. If the client is no longer connected, there is no reason to go on processing. This check should not be used excessively as there is a slight cost associated with it. When a system is underloaded, users may not wait long for a response. Doing long database queries unnecessarily will lengthen wait times.

A standard followed for IIS 4.0 was to place this check at the top of a page. This is redundant in IIS 5.0, as the server will perform this check automatically if the request has been in the queue in excess of three seconds. It may still be useful in the middle of an expensive page.

Use the <OBJECT> Tag

When objects are declared using the `<OBJECT>` tag, they are not created until they are actually used. This can provide significant benefits when objects may only be used if some specific condition comes true. Most applications do not use every object stored at Session and Application on the first session request. Delaying object creation until required for use makes the first request faster and may eliminate unnecessary work if the page where the object is needed is never requested.

Don't Use OnStartPage and OnEndPage

The old model for using objects from within ASP required providing `OnStartPage` and `OnEndPage` methods. This is no longer true. In fact, including empty implementations for these two calls forces the server to do extra unnecessary work. If these methods are provided, they will be called, even if they do nothing useful. Without them, the server will be able to instantiate and release the object more quickly.

Leverage the Client

I was surprised when I discovered, when looking at some ASP code, that it was about ninety percent devoted to validating data sent by clients and checking for errors. For a Web application, many tasks like these can be given to the client to handle. Every round trip to the server for a page costs CPU time, and if the data being submitted is pre-calculated and validated before the request is sent, the Web server doesn't have as much work to do. *Don't misunderstand this tactic*; I am not saying that error checking and validation can be removed from the ASP page. The user experience is better when the browser immediately catches errors. Eliminating round trips between the client and server to report that there is an extra digit in a credit card or no @ in an email address is a win-win situation.

What types of work can the client do? There are algorithms available on the Web for validating postal codes, credit card and telephone numbers. It is simple to introduce a piece of client-side script to perform these tasks. Incorporate the notion of required fields for forms and verify that the user has entered something acceptable before completing the `Submit` action. Most users employ a browser that supports scripting, and those that don't typically downgrade gracefully enough. Fields for inputting names should not allow numeric entries. The major credit card companies have established prefixes and lengths for their credit cards and a formula when creating numbers that makes it easy to verify that an entry is at least potentially capable of guaranteeing an order.

Client capabilities are becoming more robust with each new release. It is fairly simple now to sort and manipulate data inside the browser without requiring lots of client-side code and without involving the server for additional requests. Don't forget to review the established pieces of your ASP application periodically to spot the places where improved client capabilities can relieve the server of some work. These new capabilities include XML, ADO with disconnected recordsets, RDS, and DHTML.

Summary

As you can see, there are many different aspects to consider when working on the performance of a Web-based application. Don't worry about addressing all of these areas at once. First, concentrate on gaining an understanding of how the subject site is used and how it performs. Learn to identify the bottleneck so that you can focus your efforts where they will return the greatest benefit. Going through the effort of turning complicated script logic into components may be disappointing if the slow down is because of resource contention or long running database queries. Tracking performance data from the live servers over time may give you a new understanding of the loads placed on the server as well as how it responds. Sometimes improving the hardware itself can yield the most gains for the least effort.

Web applications are constantly changing and evolving. Their capabilities are constantly advancing and the applications that provide those capabilities are continuously getting larger and more complicated. Don't convince yourself that once you have spent some time working on performance you will be done and won't have to deal with it anymore. If the work has been done so that you always understand the application and know what single item is most responsible for limiting throughput, you will be better able to make the site faster as it continues to change. In almost all circumstances, it does not need to be an all-encompassing endeavor, but performance considerations should be included in all of the Web-application design endeavors.

In the final chapter, we will look in more detail at the concept of Web farms that has been touched upon in the last few chapters.

27

Building Multiple Server Web Sites

For much of this book, the discussion has revolved around the development and optimization of a Web application on a single server. The process of developing and optimizing a Web application with the intention of utilizing multiple servers has some subtle differences compared to that of the single server case. This chapter focuses on multiple server Web sites and how they work.

In particular, we'll look at:

- What a multiple server Web site is, and a discussion of when and if you should build one
- The different methods of implementing a Web farm and their respective advantages / disadvantages
- Architectural considerations for implementing a Web application across several machines

But first, let's take a look at what constitutes a multiple server site.

Multiple Server Web Sites

The typical Web site has a single Web server that responds to HTTP requests. This server may dynamically generate HTML using ASP or it may simply serve up static content. The server may also be linked to a database locally or remotely. Such a configuration is shown below:

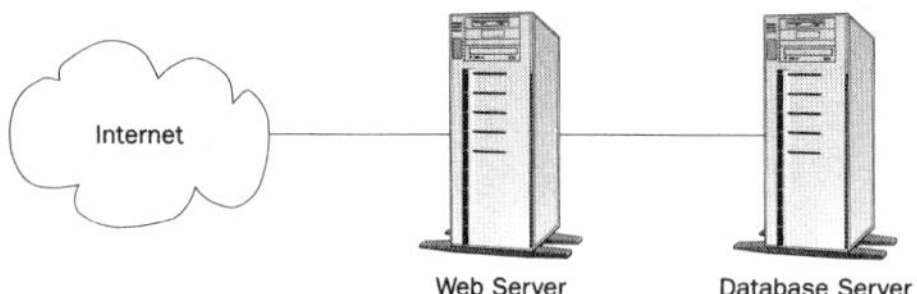

As user volume increases, performance begins to slip. What do you do? As we saw in the previous chapter, typically a period of time is spent analyzing the software architecture and trimming fat from various algorithms. The Web server can also be beefed up by adding processors, additional RAM, and faster hard drives. However, eventually you will reach a point where you cannot improve system performance to an acceptable level. For Internet applications this situation can arise overnight. An obvious solution to improve system performance is to **distribute** or **balance** the **processing load** over *multiple* Web servers.

Even if you don't face large amounts of volume, there are other potential problems with the single server configuration. The underlying assumption of any IT director must be that any one machine will fail. If this one machine is the Web server, users will at best be unable to access the site. At worst, users will lose data in the middle of a transaction. For commercial sites, this can have disastrous implications. Consider the example of an online brokerage. When an online brokerage is inaccessible, clients of that brokerage can conceivably lose large amounts of money while waiting for the site to come back.

In addition, it should be noted that maintenance is a regular part of managing a production environment. There are regular security bulletins that require the application of hot fixes or service patches to the system and to system software. Hardware does need to be replaced. When you only have a single server, you need to bring your entire site down for the most mundane changes. This leads to maintenance done off hours and unhappy IT staff.

Finally, there is the issue of **staging content**. Web application development tends to involve changes to the content of the site on an almost constant basis. It is an extremely good idea to stage new content on a separate server and to allow internal users to verify the correctness of the site. This can avoid many embarrassing problems and phone calls.

The figure opposite shows the configuration of a multiple server Web site:

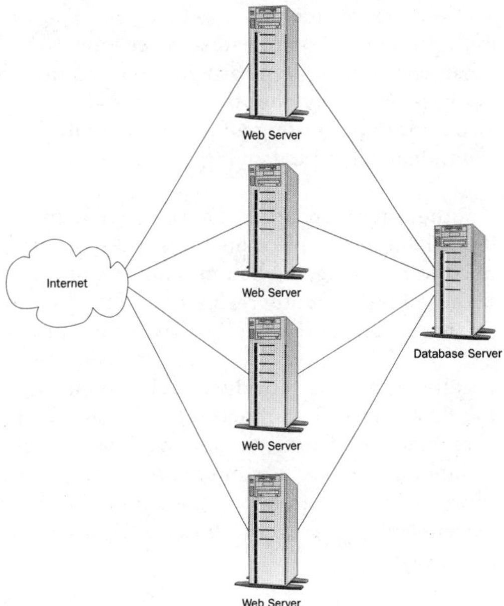

Requests come into one of several Web servers. That server handles the request and, in the process, reads from and/or writes to the database. If a Web server goes down, other Web servers simply handle the additional requests. This configuration provides **load balancing**, in that the processing load is distributed or balanced across multiple servers. The configuration also provides **fault tolerance**, in that any one machine can fail without affecting site availability.

As an aside, notice that we have more Web servers than database servers. Typically, a single database server can handle the load generated by multiple Web servers. This alleviates the need for load balancing the database server. We still need to prevent the failure of any single machine from bringing the site down. For this purpose we configure the database servers in a **redundant configuration**. This means that we have an additional (or redundant) machine that serves only to take over for the primary machine in case of system failure. This is also known as a **fail-over** configuration, for the reason that failures are rolled over to the redundant machine.

In summary, the advantages of using a server farm are:

- Increased transactional throughput
- Larger number of concurrent users allowed
- Redundancy – fault tolerance
- Increased availability – no down time during routine maintenance

Is a Server Farm the Right Solution?

Before we go any further, now is a good time to sit back and ask yourself the question, "Is implementing a server farm a good idea for me?" While we have discussed the advantages of running your Web site with multiple Web servers, we also need to cover the disadvantages of a multiple server Web site.

The obvious disadvantage is that you're adding *complexity* into the system. When you scale across multiple servers, you need some **scheme** (which we'll cover shortly) to distribute the requests across those servers. This typically involves additional software and/or hardware components in your network. Not only does this increase the effort associated with development and administration, it also adds to the testing effort. In order to be sure that the system works as desired, you must test the redundancy, load balancing and fail over aspects of the system.

Another disadvantage is that the change may affect your system architecture. We'll discuss these items later, but some schemes of state management, user management, and resource management will need to be changed when moving to multiple servers. A simple example is managing uploaded files. If those files currently reside in a local directory structure, the system will need to be modified to refer to a central (hopefully also redundant) share.

Finally, when you introduce multiple machines where there used to be one, you add administrative overhead. The IT staff needs to keep track of multiple machines, and monitor the configuration of each machine. Content, code, hot fixes, patches, etc. must be pushed to each server. While the redundancy makes administration a task that can take place during operation, redundancy and fault tolerance does not remove the administrative onus. Additionally, the test environment should mirror (at least to a large extent) the production environment. This means even more machines to administer.

In summary, the disadvantages of using a server farm are:

- Increased complexity
- Impact to system architecture
- Added administration

The impact of these disadvantages should not be discounted. The ability to achieve rapid time to market delivery of software is a strong competitive advantage for Internet businesses. Implementing a server farm will cost more money, take longer (the first time), and has a higher recurring cost than a single Web server site. If your site faces a finite number of users, is not mission critical, and can afford to be down for routine maintenance and the occasional unexpected bugaboo, then you should probably avoid implementing a server farm.

Having said that, if you are developing a Web application and face the potential for high volume in the future, it is best to take the medicine up front. Once you're in a multiple server configuration (even if you don't actually have multiple servers in place) it is very easy to add additional resources to respond to load problems. If you don't take this initial step, your response to slow (and potentially blocking) conditions at your site will take a matter of days or weeks as opposed to a few hours.

Now that we've discussed the pros and cons of server farms, let's take a look at how a farm actually works.

Server Farm Basics

So how does a server farm work? Consider the process of making an HTTP request:

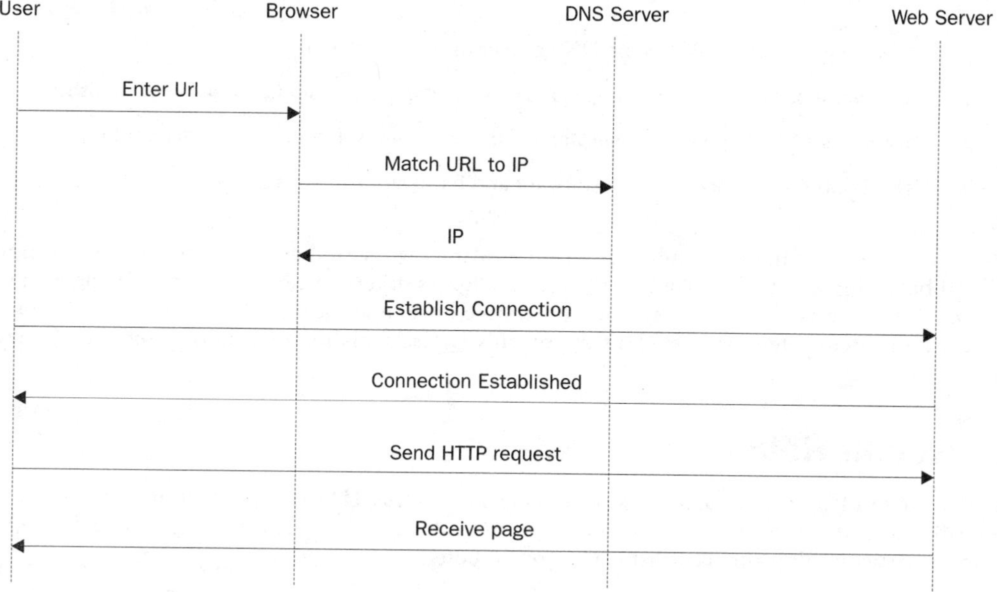

The user enters a URL into the browser. Before the browser can send the TCP/IP request to the server, the browser needs to know the IP address of the site. The browser asks the domain name system (DNS) server to look up the IP address based on the host name entered by the user. This is what your browser is doing when it browser displays "Finding site 127.0.0.0" in the status bar after you've typed in a URL.

DNS Servers contain maps of hostname/IP address pairs. If the hostname/IP address pair is not present on one particular DNS Server, that Server will inquire of a second DNS Server. Eventually, the request will be routed to the DNS Server for the network of the host. That DNS Server will resolve the IP address and return the data to the original DNS Server, which then returns the data to the browser. It should be noted that the actual operation of DNS Servers is more complicated than the simple explanation here. A detailed description of the domain name system utilized by machines on the Internet is beyond the scope of the book.

Once the browser has the IP address, the browser initiates a connection. You'll see something like "Connecting to site 127.0.0.0". Once the connection is established, the browser sends the HTTP request to the server. The server parses the request (or places the request in a queue if the server is overloaded) and sends the HTTP response back to the browser.

When a single server is involved, the same machine always responds to the HTTP request. All of the load balancing schemes involve *routing* each successive HTTP request to (potentially) a different server.

Load Balancing Schemes

There are several viable approaches to load balancing currently in widespread use at Internet and intranet Web sites. They include:

- **DNS round robin**, which uses the DNS Server to balance the load
- **Hardware load balancing**, which uses a hardware component similar to a router to distribute load
- **Microsoft's TCP/IP Network Load Balancing**, a software solution for load distribution
- **Hybrid** approaches that combine software and hardware solutions

We'll look at each of these solutions, describe how they work, and analyze how they perform in terms of load balancing and fault tolerance. We'll also address other concerns related to changes in your system such as impact to the servers, administrative burden and cost. Finally, we'll also take a quick look at associated technologies such as Microsoft's High Availability Clustering and COM+ Dynamic Load Balancing.

DNS Round Robin

A DNS Round Robin approach is a simple means of routing HTTP requests to multiple servers. As described above, a DNS Server maintains a set of hostname/IP address pairings for each machine inside a particular domain. That list can be represented as:

```
wrox.com          xxx.xxx.xxx.2
www.wrox.com      xxx.xxx.xxx.3
```

Where each `xxx` is actually a number between 0 and 255 (the actual numbers have been removed to avoid inadvertently spamming anyone's servers...)

When setting up a DNS Server (a DNS Service is included with Microsoft's Windows 2000 Advanced Server), an additional IP entry (known in the DNS as an **A Record** or **Address Record**) is created for each additional machine. The resulting list looks something like:

```
wrox.com          xxx.xxx.xxx.2
www.wrox.com      xxx.xxx.xxx.3
www.wrox.com      xxx.xxx.xxx.4
www.wrox.com      xxx.xxx.xxx.5
www.wrox.com      xxx.xxx.xxx.6
```

The DNS Server will cycle through all entries in the table when responding to DNS requests. Thus, in our example, for the first request to resolve `www.wrox.com`, the DNS Server would return `xxx.xxx.xxx.3`. For the next request to resolve the host name, the DNS Server would return `xxx.xxx.xxx.4` and so on. This results in an even distribution of all requests across all Web servers.

Load Balancing

HTTP requests are balanced over a number of Web servers, but are only balanced in that each server receives an equal number of requests. This assumes that all servers have equal resources (a workable assumption) and that all transactions require an equal amount of system resources (a significantly less workable assumption). This solution pays no attention at all to the current processor load of the machines on the farm. While we achieve some degree of load distribution, it is in an extremely inefficient manner. Consider a simple Web farm with two servers:

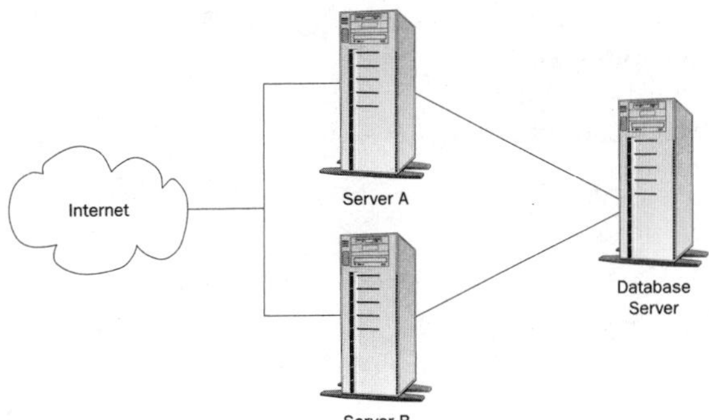

If the processor utilization of Server A is pegged (at 100%) due to the nature of the HTTP requests Server A is responding to, and the processor utilization of Server B is low (say 10-15%), a round robin DNS scheme will send half of the HTTP requests to Server A, which is already overloaded. This is not only inefficient, but it encourages users to hit the Refresh button on their browser when they see slow performance on your site. That is *really bad practice* and can contribute to loading up request queues on servers until the user-friendly "Server too busy" message finds its way to the browser.

Fault Tolerance

The other downside to a DNS round robin approach is that it does not handle system outages well. Again taking our example of a two server farm; if Server A crumbles under its load and crashes, half of all of the HTTP requests will be routed to an unavailable server. This results in the equally friendly message "Server Unavailable" appearing in the user's browser. Machines can be brought down for maintenance, but this requires updates to the DNS table. This is in itself a problem as many DNS Servers cache host name and IP address information and may not update for several days. No doubt by that time your help desk will have received several irate customer calls.

Administration

From an administrative standpoint, a round robin DNS scheme is an administrator's dream. The DNS entries are already being managed; adding entries to the host table takes little time. There is no impact at all on the existing network configuration.

DNS Round Robin Summary

In summary, the DNS round robin approach:

- Distributes requests evenly across all servers by rotating through a list of servers
- Makes no decision about where to distribute requests based on actual load

- Pays no attention to unresponsive or unavailable systems
- Has no impact on the hardware configuration of the Web servers
- Is easy to administer
- Is an inexpensive solution for load balancing

Hardware Load Balancing

A more capable alternative to the DNS round robin approach is hardware load balancing. A sample network configuration is shown below:

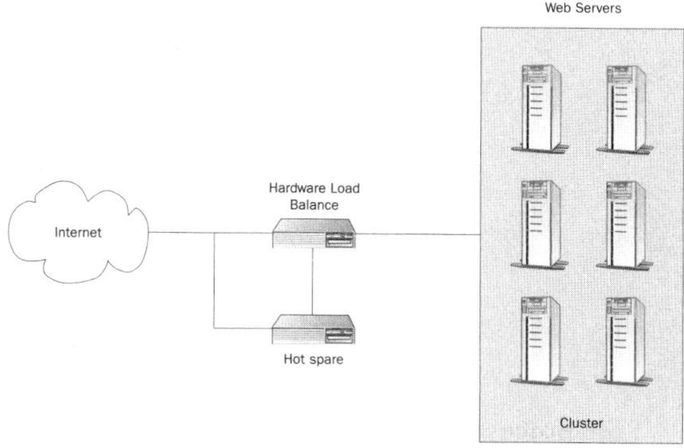

A new piece of hardware, a **Hardware Load Balancer**, is inserted into the network between other network equipment (firewalls, routers, etc.) and the Web servers. User requests coming in for a particular URL are routed through the load balancer. There is a group of Web servers connected to the load balancer that behave as a single server. This configuration is known as a **cluster**. Upon receiving TCP/IP packets destined for the cluster, the load balancer does the following:

- Makes a decision as to which server in the cluster should receive the next TCP/IP request.
- Polls the server and application (TCP/IP port) for availability.
- In some cases, checks the content returned by the server for valid data. This is particularly handy when the server does respond, but due to some problem the response is always "HTTP Error 404".
- Translates the IP header so that the packet points to the selected server. This translation technique is referred to as **Network Address Translation (NAT)**.
- Sends the packet to the server.
- When the server responds to the client, the load balancer performs a similar translation on any packets returning to the client. The result of this second NAT is that the TCP/IP packets the client receives look as if they've come from the IP that represents the cluster.

Load Balancing

So how does the load balancer decide which server to send the request to? This varies with each manufacturer, but the basic algorithm is the same. The load balancer collects a large amount of information by monitoring network activity. This activity includes the volume of traffic traveling to and from each server, the speed of each server's response to TCP/IP requests, the number of connections currently being managed by each server, and the past history of each server's response to load. The load balancer provides the system administrator with a choice of algorithms to use based on the network traffic and typically also including round robin and ratio (or weighted round robin) algorithms.

Network traffic monitoring allows the load balancer to make an intelligent and efficient distribution of the processing load across multiple servers. Let's revisit the two-server example we examined during our discussion on DNS round robin methods:

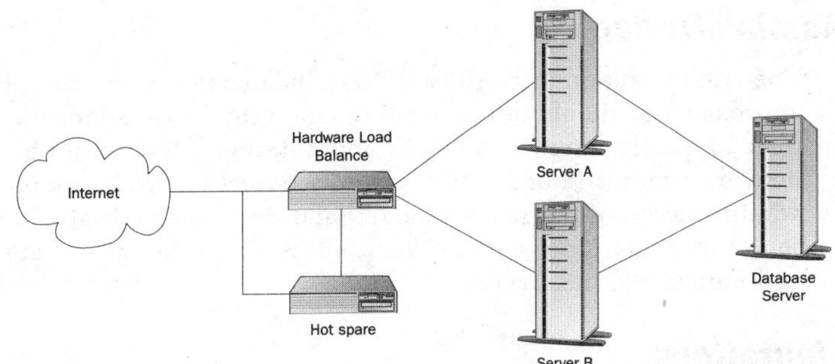

If the processor utilization of Server A is pegged (at 100%), due to the nature of the HTTP request Server A is responding to, and the processor utilization of Server B is low (say 10-15%), the Hardware Load Balancer will notice that the response time for Server A is very slow, and will route successive requests to Server B. This will continue until the load on Server A returns to an acceptable level. This gives a much better result than when using a DNS round robin system.

Fault Tolerance

Taking the example of the two-server farm again, if Server A goes down, the Hardware Load Balancer will not send any TCP/IP traffic to Server A. In fact, the Server itself can be running, but if the Web service fails to respond (say you stop the World Wide Web Publishing Service), the Hardware Load Balancer will remove Server A from the list of available servers and send all traffic to Server B. This too gives a much better result than when using round robin DNS.

One thing to note about our hardware load balanced solution: the load balancer itself can become a central point of failure. In order to address this, typical deployments involve a second load balancer that serves as a **hot spare**. This redundant fail-over configuration is typically very robust. The load balancers are usually connected through some form of serial communications such as an RS-232 cable. Each unit has watchdog processors that constantly communicate with one another. In the event of unit failure or unusual behavior, the watchdog units confer and decide which unit should perform the load balancing.

As a rule, Hardware Load Balancers are production quality components. Common features include the ability to associate a single IP address or an entire class C address space with a single server (known as affinity – which we'll discuss later in this chapter), remote, Web-based administrative capabilities, notification capabilities in case of server failure, and real-time performance monitoring and statistics to name a few.

If you're interested in learning more about hardware load balancing, both Cabletron (`www.cabletron.com`) and Cisco Systems (`www.cisco.com`) have excellent load balancing solutions and have some useful information on their Web sites.

Administration

The administration of Hardware Load Balancers is more complicated than that of a DNS round robin approach, but should not be terribly daunting. Load balancers are not any more difficult to set up than a typical router (if you think about it, these devices are basically a form of a router) and your network administrator has undoubtedly bonded with the router technology at this point. The administration of this network load balancing scheme is also centralized, and has no impact on the server machines themselves. This is a big win in the eyes of the administrators tasked with setting up and monitoring the servers.

Limitations

There are some limitations to the capabilities of hardware load balancing solutions. The most severe limitation is that of **bandwidth**. Due to the step of translating the TCP/IP headers to a new IP address for incoming and outgoing traffic, bandwidth through these devices is limited to about 45-50 Mbps at the time of writing. While this seems like (and is) a huge bandwidth for data, large sites can (and do) exceed this capacity during usage peaks. The additional packets are simply dropped. This is clearly less than optimal, but is also not a likely scenario for most Web sites.

Another downside to a hardware load balanced solution is **cost**. At the time of writing, a redundant configuration using a pair of Hardware Load Balancers starts at US$ 20,000 and goes up from there. This means that you're spending money on load balancing units instead of on additional servers.

Lastly, hardware-based load balancing algorithms base all decisions on data observable from network traffic. It may be that server response time is slow due to the nature of the requests on the server (perhaps the HTTP requests involve a database intensive operation that takes a long time to complete but that does not block the Web service at all). In this case, the Hardware Load Balancer avoids the server in question when that server actually has available resources.

Despite these downsides, hardware load balancing is without a doubt the most tried and true method of effectively achieving load balancing for a Web site. Companies that provide remote hosting services swear by these systems as do many commercial and retail Web sites.

Harware Load Balancing Summary

In summary, Hardware Load Balancers:

- Distribute the load across multiple servers by translating incoming and outgoing TCP/IP traffic to IP addresses within the server cluster.
- Make decisions regarding where to distribute requests based on observations of network traffic within the cluster of servers. This is an effective means of load balancing, but not as effective as looking directly at server resources such as CPU Utilization, HTTP request queue size, number of threads, etc.
- Monitor the availability of each server and (potentially) each application. The load balancer checks the availability prior to sending any packets to that server.
- Have no impact on the hardware configuration of the Web servers.
- Are relatively easy to administer.
- Are an expensive solution for load balancing and fault tolerance.

TCP/IP Network Load Balancing

Microsoft includes a software component called **Network Load Balancing (NLB)** as part of its Windows 2000 Advanced Server offering. NLB was first introduced with the name Windows Load Balancing Service (WLBS) as an add-on to Windows NT Server 4.0 in October 1997. A sample network configuration using NLB is shown below:

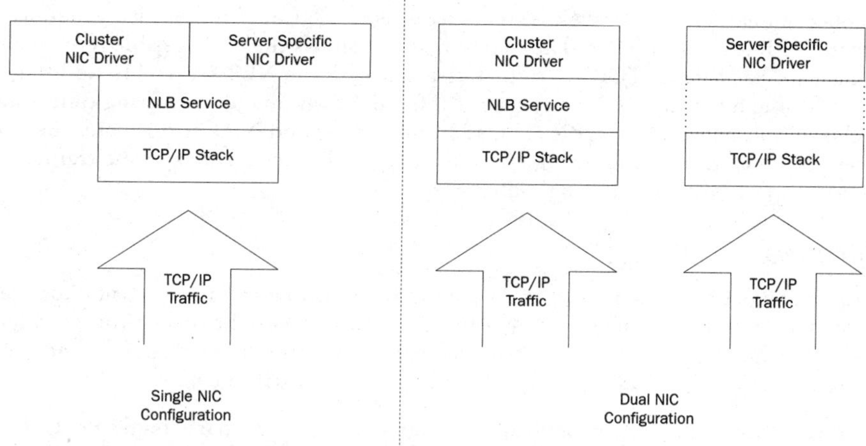

A quick look at the network shows us that the configuration required for NLB differs from the standard network configurations we've seen up to this point. We can see that traffic coming in from the Internet on a specific IP address is seen by all servers in the cluster. This IP address is referred to as the **Cluster IP** and should represent the URL your site serves. Each server also has a unique IP address used for non-cluster traffic. The diagram also implies that there are two separate network connections for each server. NLB does not require this and can function on one Network Interface Card (NIC) thus having no hardware impact on your servers. However, most implementations should use an additional NIC. We'll discuss this in more detail later.

Configuration of each server is straightforward. Once the NLB software is installed, you must specify a cluster IP address, a unique host ID between 1 and 32 (an NLB implementation is limited to a maximum of 32 servers), a weight (not all systems have the same capacity), and a set of rules. Each rule determines which TCP/IP application is load balanced and the affinity of that load balancing (none, single IP, or class C license – we'll discuss affinity shortly). A typical rule for Web-based traffic would be port 80 (standard HTTP port) with no affinity.

Load Balancing

So you must be thinking, there are up to 32 servers all receiving packets for the same IP address, why doesn't the client receive 32 responses to its request? The secret is in what Microsoft calls **parallel filtering**. When the NLB service is installed, it inserts itself between the TCP/IP stack and the NIC driver. All IP traffic specific to the server is passed directly through. For IP traffic directed to the cluster, the NLB software determines which host should process the request. That server allows the traffic to pass up to its cluster NIC driver. All other servers in the cluster filter the IP request so that only the designated server responds to the request.

NLB uses a distributed algorithm to determine which host should respond to each TCP/IP request. This algorithm uses load information gathered by each host and shared through broadcast transmission. Since this is a software implementation, this load information includes details about CPU utilization, available memory, and other metrics. This provides a more accurate and efficient balancing of the load than is possible by monitoring network traffic. Since this only involves filtering of packet traffic instead of modification and retransmission of packet data, NLB does not face the same throughput limitations as hardware load balancing schemes.

It was pointed out earlier that only one NIC is required for NLB. However, it's generally a good idea to implement NLB using two NICs. The diagram above shows the two possible implementations. When using a single NIC, all TCP/IP traffic passes through the NLB service. In addition, non-cluster traffic passes through the same NIC as cluster traffic. Bandwidth and processing time are shared between cluster and non-cluster traffic. The addition of a second NIC card isolates the cluster traffic from the server specific traffic, allowing administrative and other server specific traffic to continue with minimal impact on cluster throughput.

Fault Tolerance

NLB hosts exchange broadcast messages on a periodic basis to allow them to monitor the state of the cluster. When a host enters or leaves the cluster, the NLB software begins a process called **convergence**. During convergence, the hosts assess the new state of the cluster and adjust the mapping algorithm to reflect the new state. This typically takes less than 10 seconds.

One part of the NLB traffic is a "**heartbeat**" message that each host participates in. The interval for this heartbeat is configurable and defaults to a period of one second. A host is considered unavailable if it fails to participate in 5 heartbeats and the remaining NLB hosts will initiate the convergence process.

Administration

Unlike previous solutions we've looked at, NLB has an impact on every server. A rigorous implementation involves the setup and configuration of software on every server and the installation of an additional NIC (which itself implies additional hub or switch ports, cable drops, etc). Additionally, the configuration of each machine is unique due to the host name and potentially the weight assigned to the server.

The good news is that NLB provides excellent administrative capabilities from any networked computer. Once the software is installed on a host, the host can be configured, and added or removed from the cluster remotely.

Network Load Balancing Summary

In summary, an NLB implementation:

- Distributes the load across multiple servers through the process of parallel filtering
- Makes decisions regarding where to distribute requests based on system level load observations
- Handles fault tolerance through a broadcast "heartbeat" process
- Requires installation and configuration of additional software and optionally additional hardware on each server
- Has robust remote administrative capabilities
- Is an inexpensive solution for load balancing and fault tolerance

Hybrid Approaches

An additional option for load balancing is the combination of hardware and software techniques. Consider the following network configuration:

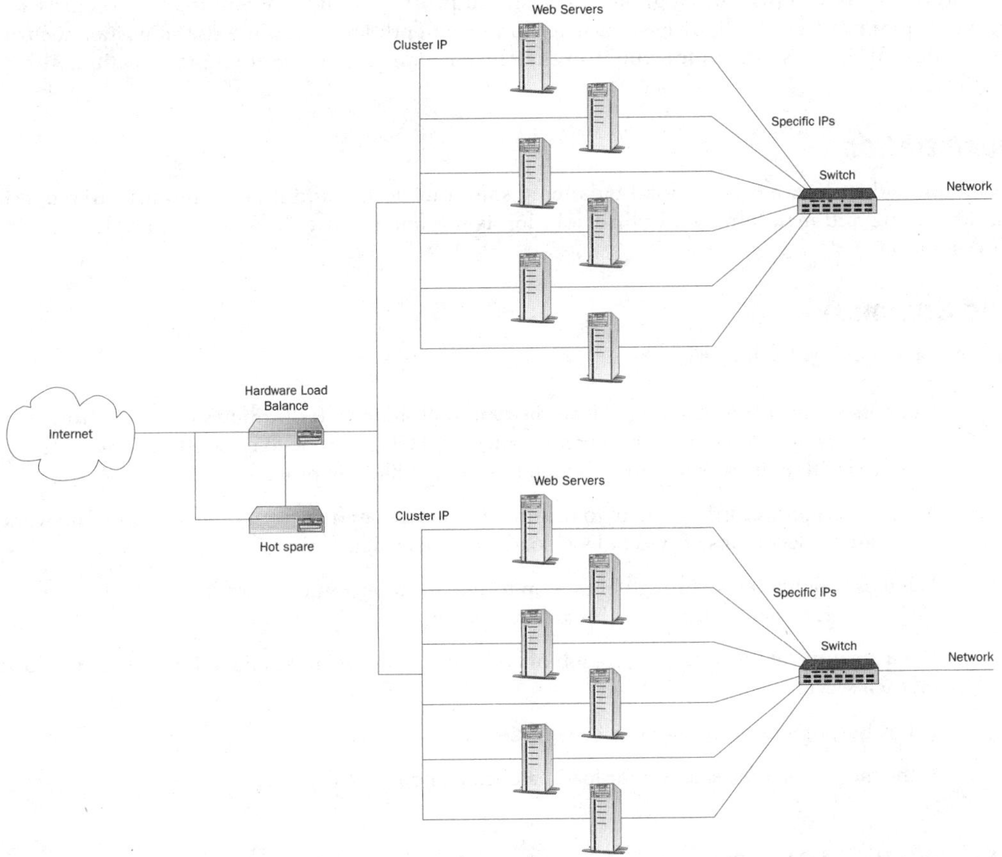

We have a Hardware Load Balancer and two clusters of servers, each using NLB to implement load balancing and fault tolerance. The Hardware Load Balancer has no knowledge that the two IP addresses it is translating to and from are actually a collection of servers. By the same token, each Web farm has no knowledge that the other exists.

Load Balancing

For load balancing, we now can scale past the limit of 32 servers imposed by NLB. In fact, if we assume that the Hardware Load Balancer can distribute load over 256 distinct nodes (an entirely reasonable assumption), we can scale our site up to a ridiculous 8,192 servers.

We also now have the benefit of both network and system monitoring in determining the distribution of load. It may be that network conditions provide more of a bottleneck than processing power. This option allows us to shift the burden of load balancing between the Hardware Load Balancer (network) and each cluster of servers using NLB (system).

Fault Tolerance

With the additional hardware element of the load balancer, we now have more options to choose from when managing fault tolerance. We can completely isolate server farms from each other in both a network and geographic sense. This provides additional measures against environmental (flood, fire, etc.) problems. It also provides a greater measure of protection in the event that the security of any server is compromised. We'll discuss security in more depth later, but one of the nastier security implications of NLB is that all machines in the cluster maintain constant communication with one another.

Administration

As mentioned earlier, hardware load balancing solutions do not add much administrative overhead. Implementing and maintaining a hybrid solution is not much more difficult than implementing an NLB solution.

Hybrid Summary

In summary, a hybrid solution:

- Combines software and hardware load distribution solutions. It distributes the load across multiple server farms by translating incoming and outgoing TCP/IP traffic to cluster IP addresses. Load is managed within the server cluster though the parallel filtering process.
- Makes decisions regarding where to distribute requests based on both observations of network traffic and observations of system level load within each cluster.
- Handles fault tolerance through both monitoring of cluster response and availability and, internal to each cluster, through a broadcast "heartbeat" process.
- Requires installation and configuration of additional software and optionally additional hardware on each server.
- Has robust remote administrative capabilities.
- Is the most expensive solution for load balancing and fault tolerance.

High Availability Clustering Service

Microsoft first introduced its clustering technology as the **Microsoft Clustering Service (MSCS)** with Window NT 4.0 Enterprise Edition in October of 1997. Microsoft has enhanced that clustering ability with Windows 2000 and has changed the name of the service to the **High Availability Clustering Service**. At this time, the clustering service is not meant to be a means of load balancing, but rather as a means of improving availability and fault tolerance.

The clustering service provides a two node fail-over capability for mission critical applications such as your SQL Server database. This is different from NLB, which provides load balancing across a **cluster** of multiple Web servers. Consider the following hardware load balanced network configuration:

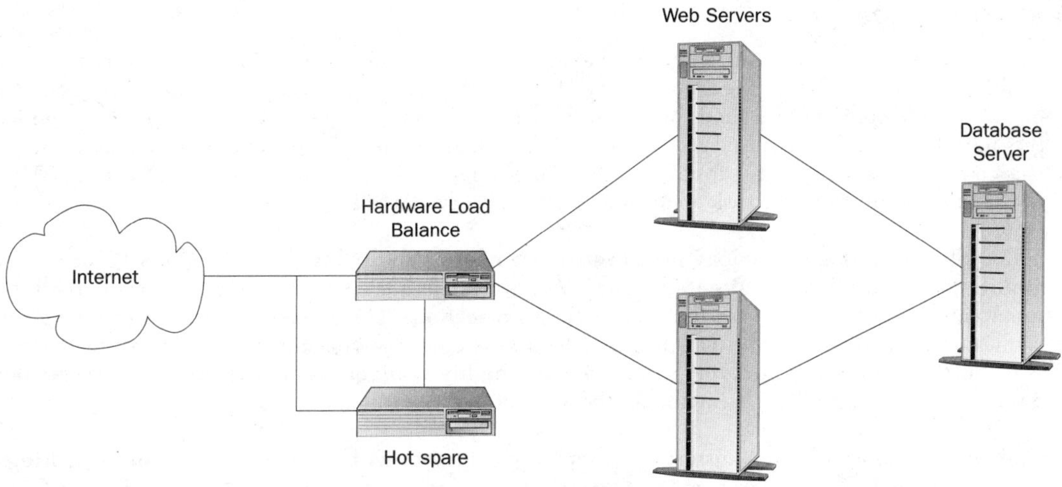

We see our familiar scenario in which two Web servers are handling traffic from the Internet or some network. We've implemented load balancing and fault tolerance using a hardware load balancing approach. However, we still have a single point of failure. If the database server drops, any requests from the Web server that involve the database (probably a large number) will fail.

This is where Microsoft's clustering service helps. Consider the following alternate network configuration utilizing clustering:

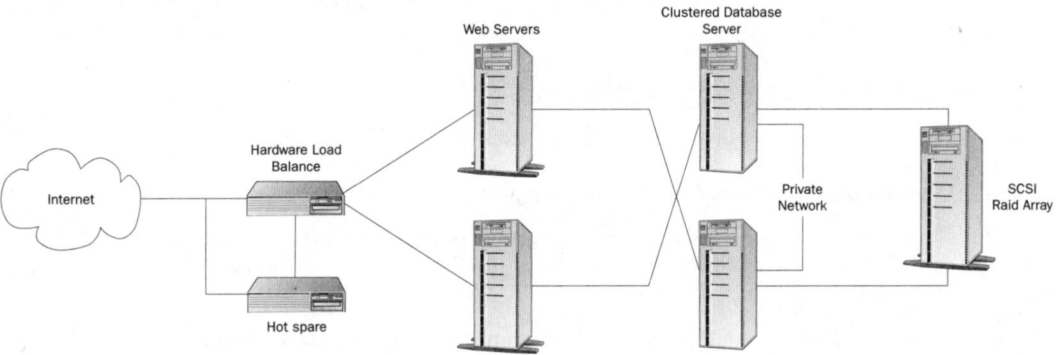

We have removed our single point of failure and now have two database servers acting as a single virtual server. The clustering technology requires an additional NIC for each server, a private network along those additional NICs, and a shared SCSI bus with at least one disk. Additionally, the shared SCSI array must be used only for clustering applications and other resources. System files must reside on a separate SCSI bus for each clustered server.

Load Balancing

Microsoft's clustering technology does not support load balancing at this time. The current clustering solution represents what Microsoft terms as Phase 1 of its clustering strategy. Phase 1 represents the ability to have a fail-over capability with two nodes sharing a common set of data. Phase 2 will combine load balancing and fail-over technology by initially allowing up to 16 servers to share data in real-time, perform load balancing, and provide fail-over support.

Fault Tolerance

You'll notice that the two nodes in the cluster share a private network. All information related to the health of each machine, in the form of "heartbeat" messages is passed along this network. Each server has a software component called the cluster service that monitors the system state and communicates this information to a counterpart on the other node. Cluster-ready applications store data on the shared SCSI disk array. If an application fails, the other node starts the application, recovers the state of the application from the disk array, and begins to service requests.

Microsoft's clustering technology provides an essential capability for availability of a Web application: fault tolerance of stateful data. Web servers in a multiple server site typically do not maintain state locally (we'll discuss state in the next section). This makes it is easy to reroute a user's request to an available server. On the other hand, the database does manage the state of objects – that is its purpose. In order to provide a fault tolerant, highly available system, the database server must have a fail-over capability that manages the state in real time.

The only real alternative to clustering is to **mirror** databases with fail-over upon error. Mirroring does not provide real time synchronization of data, so a system failure will potentially result in lost data. It should also be noted that the clustering service can provide fault tolerance for many resources other than just a database. These resources include file shares, active directory services, and DHCP information to name a few.

Administration

Due to the rigorous hardware requirements and exact system configuration necessary for High Availability Clustering, the administration of such a solution is considerably more involved than that of any of the load balancing schemes we've addressed up to this point. It should be noted that a clustering solution also involves a substantial amount of new hardware, which incurs additional cost.

High Availability Clustering Summary

In summary, a High Availability Clustering solution:

- Does not provide load balancing at this time
- Handles fault tolerance through both monitoring of cluster response and availability and, internal to each cluster, through a broadcast "heartbeat" process. State information is captured on the shared SCSI disk array
- Requires substantial configuration and additional hardware for each server
- Is the only available solution for real time recovery of state data

COM+ Dynamic Load Balancing

Up to this point we've examined adding additional servers for the purpose of load balancing and fault tolerance in two tiers: the presentation tier (Web server) and the database tier. As described in Chapter 13, a common architecture includes components that represent an additional tier – the business logic tier:

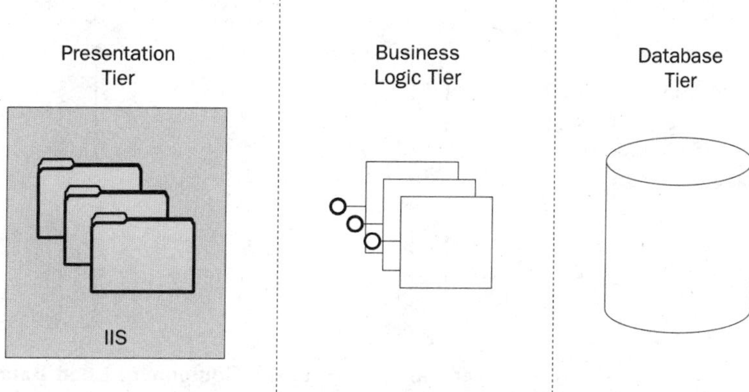

The presentation tier includes the Web server and a series of ASP documents. Server-side script embedded in an ASP document instantiates a COM+ component. This component provides an abstraction from the details of certain business logic and database access and is typically instantiated on the Web server. Given that COM+ already provides us with local/remote transparency, a logical step is to separate the business components out to a separate server.

This results in a network configuration as follows:

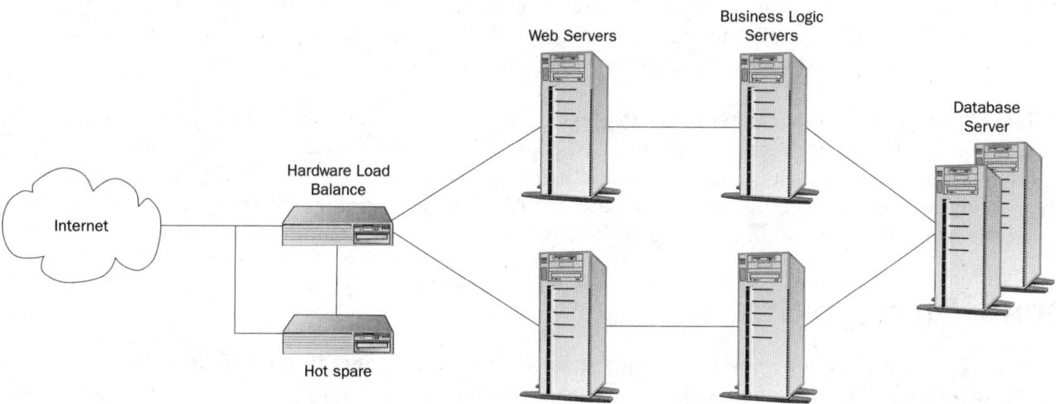

We have now distributed the processing load of the business logic components to another server, freeing the Web server up to spend more time and resources addressing HTTP requests. However, we've now reintroduced a single point of failure. If the business logic server goes down, the load balancer will still send HTTP requests to the Web server, but the Web server will not be able to fill the requests.

Microsoft's solution for scaling the business tier out to a different machine from the presentation tier is **COM+ Dynamic Load Balancing**. This capability, originally scheduled to be part of Windows 2000 Advanced Server, is now scheduled for release with Windows 2000 AppCenter Server at the time of writing. The figure below shows a sample implementation of COM+ Dynamic Load Balancing:

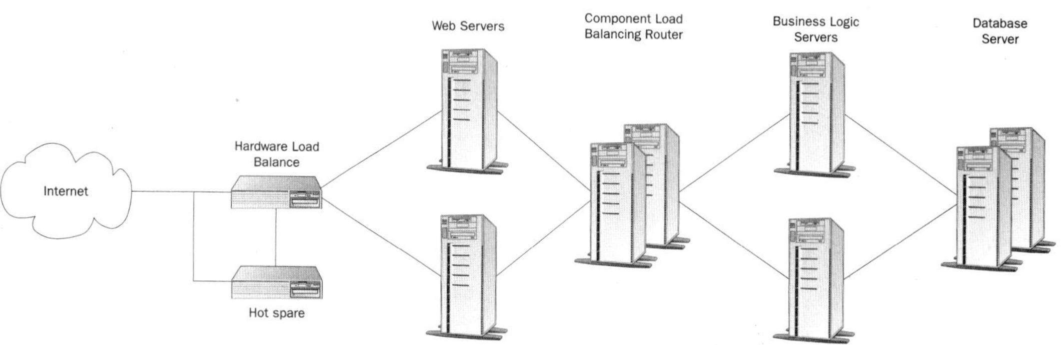

An additional server has been added to the architecture: the **Component Load Balancing Router**. This server (made fault tolerant and highly available through the clustering service) receives requests for components from the Web servers and routes these requests to a farm of business logic servers. This routing is done based on processing load for each application server. Initially, farms of up to eight servers will be supported.

State Management

So far, we've discussed the concepts of a multiple server Web site and investigated a number of means to distribute HTTP requests across a server farm. Unfortunately, getting the requests distributed is only part of the battle – you must also deal with state management.

The HTTP protocol is an inherently stateless protocol. Left to its own means, the server would have no concept of state between HTTP requests. Active Server Pages addresses this problem neatly with the Session object, but the Session object is *machine specific*. There are several solutions to this problem including avoiding the use of state, using client side cookies for state, using affinity to allow for the use of the Session object, and serializing state data into a common repository.

Don't Manage State

Not all Web applications need to manage state from page to page. If you can avoid managing state to begin with, you will save yourself a lot of headaches. This is obviously not a very palatable answer, but one that should not be ignored. State management adds complexity to your Web application.

Client Side Storage

As described in Chapter 2, the Response and Request objects allow for the storage and retrieval of cookies on the client's machine. State may also be stored in hidden forms passed by submission between pages. Client storage approaches are good in the sense that they remove the responsibility of data management completely away from the server. As you scale up in volume, the data stored on the server tends to add up in the form of RAM utilization. As an example, if you store 4K worth of data for each user browsing your site and you have 10000 users with active sessions at one time, you're eating up an extra 40M of RAM space for data that's accessed infrequently. Distributing these storage demands to each client can affect significant improvements in system performance.

On the downside, cookie data is transmitted with every HTTP request. As a result, client storage approaches add additional traffic on the network, increase transmission time, and are less secure than server-side management of state data. There are also limits to the amount of data you can place on the client (i.e. one that is browser dependent), users can remove cookies at any time, and cookies don't work for users with more than one machine.

Affinity

If you want to make use of session variables and use multiple servers, you can use a scaling method that allows for **session affinity**. The dictionary definition of affinity is, "an attraction to a specific item". In the world of server farms, affinity refers to the desire of a Web browser to attach to a single server and to return to that server with each successive request. A browser would first be routed to a particular server in a Web farm. From that point on, for the duration of the user's session, all subsequent requests would be routed to the same server. This is necessary if you make use of the Session object in your application.

Both the hardware routing and NLB solutions can provide for affinity when they determine which server responds to a particular user. However, use of affinity can negate some of the load balancing benefits sought by these solutions. The load balancing solutions base the assignment of a server to a particular request on the load each server is under at the time that the first request is received. The load characteristics of a server may change dramatically during the lifetime of a session. Consider the following example:

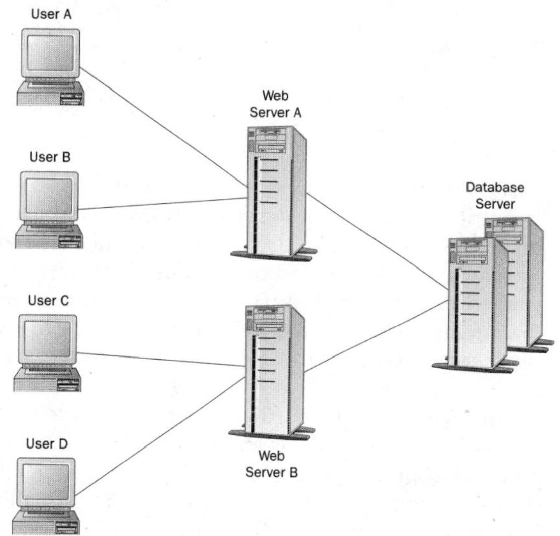

For the sake of simplicity, we've eliminated all networking and load balancing equipment from the diagram.

Assume four users (A-D) connect to the site and their requests are evenly distributed between two Web servers. Now assume that user C and user D disconnect immediately, and user A and user B stay connected for a lengthy period of time and perform many complex calculations. If we're using affinity, all HTTP requests made by user A and user B will be routed to Web server A. Users A and B will see loaded performance while a second server, Web server B, sits idle.

Another problem with the use of affinity is in terms of fault tolerance. The goal for fault tolerance for a Web application is complete recovery of any single failure. If you restrict a user to a single server machine, you've lost all of the benefits of having redundant machines. Consider the same scenario. If Web server A crashes, all transactional and stateful data user A and user B are working with is lost.

Finally, even if you're willing to sacrifice performance and fault tolerance (the two main goals of a server farm) in order to get use of the Session object, the bottom line is that affinity may not work in all cases. Take the following example:

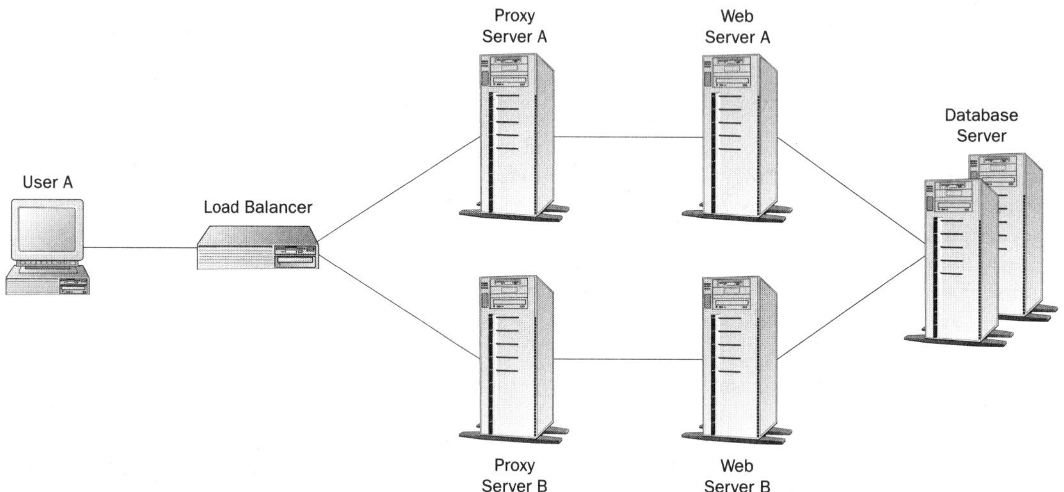

User A is on a network where several proxy servers are load balanced. As user A makes each HTTP request through the browser, the browser in turn passes the request along to a proxy server. In this example, we have two proxy servers. Since we're using single machine affinity, each request from proxy server A is routed to the same Web server – Web server A. All traffic from proxy server B is routed to Web server B. Despite the fact that a single user is accessing our system, we're load balancing the user across two Web servers. This will lead to unpredictable behavior when we attempt to access session data.

Most load balancing hardware and NLB have a solution for this problem. They allow affinity across an entire class C address space, or a total of 256 distinct IP addresses. The rationale is that most clusters of proxy servers should be in the same address space. While this is true, this behavior can have dire implications for the site's ability to balance loads effectively. Proxy servers are often employed to help channel and cache HTTP traffic for large user groups. One such group of users is the membership of America Online (AOL). When you use class C affinity, you run the risk of completely slamming a single server and at the same time leaving a large user community completely unserved.

Storage on a Central Server

The preferred means of storing state data is through persistence on a **central server**. Usually the central server is actually a clustered pair of servers in order to achieve fault tolerance. When the user first authenticates or visits the site, a session ID is generated by a custom server-side component and stored on the browser. Every subsequent HTTP request by the user during that session includes that session ID. The session ID is used as a key along with a text string into a database table that allows us to store and retrieve binary large objects (BLOBS). Despite the name, the BLOBS are generally not that large. Each ASP component that has state information can write itself to this cache table and read itself back in.

At this point, you're probably saying to yourself, this is nuts! Here Microsoft provides a nice solution to the state problem that is then ripped away when we scale out. Furthermore, we're going to a lot of effort to provide a persistable, machine independent state tracking mechanism. There has got to be an easier way.

Commerce Server (formerly Site Server, Commerce Edition) to the rescue! Commerce Server provides personalization services to address exactly this problem. The personalization services are written to a database, but the pain of that is hidden from you through a group of wrapper objects. In addition, the management features of personalization and membership are snap-ins to the MMC and are easy to use.

There is, however, a downside to the Commerce Server solution. Commerce Server weighs in at a whopping 800M of disk space and includes lots of goodies that you may not want or use. Unfortunately, you have no choice but to install the whole package. In addition, the access to the personalization data is through a **lightweight directory access protocol (LDAP)** connection that is considerably slower than a direct connection to the database through ADO or a compiled custom component.

Security

Another issue that must be dealt with when scaling to multiple servers is security. Proper management of security for a multiple server Web site open to the Internet is a subject that could consume an entire book, let alone a section of a chapter. The intention of this section is to touch on a couple of key concepts related to securing multiple server sites. We'll discuss different means of user management and some areas of potential danger when using the NLB service for load balancing.

User Management

The simplest way of tracking users and controlling user access is through the local user registry. Authentication is taken care of with little effort and user management is handled through Windows administrative tools.

The local user registry is of course not sufficient when dealing with multiple sites. If your Web site requires users to login at any point, scaling out to multiple servers may cause you problems. There are two acceptable places to store user credentials for a multiple server site:

- The Windows user registry for a domain
- Encrypted in a central data store

The Windows User Registry

At first glance, the NT domain user registry seems like the ideal place to store user account information. As mentioned earlier, authentication is easy. User passwords are managed for you and stored. You face no encryption worries.

However, there is a downside. The user registry is the same repository used to enable/disable access to all resources in the system. The implication is that every user of your system now has an account across every machine in the domain. It is the responsibility of the person administering these accounts to ensure that the permissions are set up such that machine access will not be compromised.

Furthermore, all machines in the server farm must be members of a domain. At the very least, you need to ensure that production machines run on a separate, isolated domain. Even given this, you can access all server resources from a single machine in the domain. A general goal of a secure system is that any one machine should be capable of being compromised without affecting other machines in the site.

Central Data Store

The preferred alternative to storing user information on the domain is to store the user information in the database. Given that user information is easily inspected from an ASP page or an ISAPI filter, authentication against the database is a relatively easy task. This removes the dependence on connectivity amongst the various Web servers. It also reduces the possibility of compromise due to administrative error, or a worst-case scenario, where someone who should not have access to the Web site gets into the Web application (e.g. a hacker). That's much better than someone having root privileges to the entire domain due to human error.

The one problem with storing password information in the database is that anyone with read query access to the database can retrieve user passwords. The obvious solution to this is to use a commercial encryption scheme to ensure that passwords are not stored in a usable form.

Again we face the same frustration we found with state management. We have a nice solution to the task of user management and authentication that is ripped away when we scale out our system. Implementing our own authentication mechanism with database encryption seems a little drastic. There has got to be an easier way.

Again Commerce Server comes to the rescue. Commerce Server provides user management facilities and allows the Web site authentication to bind to the Commerce Server user database. The same caveat applies as before: Commerce Server is a large install and relies on LDAP for access to user data. This is considerably slower than direct database access. However, it does provide a convenient solution to this problem.

Load Balancing

Finally, let's conclude with a brief word about the security implications of the NLB service. The NLB service manages load balancing through constant communication amongst the cluster servers. This means that given the compromise of one machine, there is the potential for the compromise of the entire server farm. While it is an unlikely scenario, any time many machines pass information amongst themselves, and use that information to adjust system behavior and operation, there is a definite security risk involved.

Summary

In this chapter, we've introduced the concept of multiple server Web sites. We've seen that we scale our applications out past a single server in order to:

- Increase the throughput and load behavior of our site
- Provide redundant, fault tolerant behavior
- Increase the availability of the site

We looked at various schemes to implement multiple server sites and examined the advantages and disadvantages of each scheme. Finally, we ended the chapter with a brief analysis of state management and security for multiple server sites.

Building a robust, scalable Web site that handles large volume seamlessly is a deep topic. Building a site that scales across multiple servers adds complexity and difficulty to your development and testing effort. However, a good deal of the cost associated with creating a multiple server site is nonrecurring. You will only have to solve state issues and security issues one time. If you envision the eventuality of a multiple server site, if you will ever need to handle large volumes or provide high availability, it is *much* easier to build that capability into your system from the start.

N
W

An XML-Driven Newspaper Case Study

As a former journalist, I've been quite fascinated with the prospect of using XML to drive an online version of a newspaper, magazine or other publication. XML is perfect for the task, and while regular HTML does a decent job of formatting articles, it doesn't take advantage of the nifty things you can do with XML.

The online newspaper application was designed to get small-town newspapers up and on the Internet fast, while still giving them powerful tools to enhance the experience of their readers. People generally go to the online version of their favorite local newspaper to get the news early, or to avoid having to pay the cover price altogether.

In either case, publishers generally would like to accommodate their readers as much as possible. It seems like today, as more and more of these small-to-mid size newspapers go online, they're finally trying to introduce better Web site features, and not just continue to throw their content onto the site any old way. On some of the bigger online news sites, such as Fox News Online (`www.foxnews.com`) and `MSNBC.com`, news content is automatically linked to relevant terms or other stories.

However, most of the time, the online newspaper is merely a word-processor-converted rendition of the printed version – that's why the quality of many online publications has been slow to improve. Publishers have had to maintain two separate infrastructures: one for print and one for the Web. As publishers and editors begin to rethink the way they do things, and as advertisers become more willing to spend money on the Internet, reporters will find themselves writing for the Web first and print second.

Publishers of newspapers will be looking for the best way to deliver their content online, and XML is emerging as an obvious choice for the job.

This case study will take you step-by-step through the process of creating the components of an XML-driven online newspaper. Using XML and ASP, we'll create the basic features you might typically find in an online publication, such as:

- A miniature headline listing for easy access to news stories
- An expanded table of contents to give the reader the first paragraph of each story
- A listing of news "briefs" or announcements
- A glossary of background terms that are linked to relevant stories
- A mechanism for administering all these features

The core functionality of the application is encapsulated in several VBScript procedures contained in an ASP page named `headlines.asp`. This file can be inserted via a server-side include into any page that needs to call its procedures. These procedures bear simple names and take only a few parameters, making them easy to use throughout the site.

This library of procedures works in conjunction with an XML "brain" file for the site called `settings.xml`, which controls everything in the site, from the stories that are displayed, down to the site's color scheme.

Anatomy of the Newspaper

My fictitious online newspaper is called The Times-Herald, located in an imaginary town called Southbeach. The look and feel of The Times-Herald is much less important than the code that makes it work. I chose a simple layout with a horizontal navigation bar that covers the major sections of the newspaper, but you could use the techniques and samples examined in this chapter to make your version of our newspaper look completely different. In fact, you could even use the components we'll build in an existing online newspaper – just as long as it resides on Microsoft Windows NT Server 4.0 or Windows 2000 with IIS 4.0 or higher – and insert the code from this chapter with only minor modifications.

> *My focus here is not to instruct you on how to build the exact newspaper you see in the illustrations, but instead to teach you how to leverage XML by creating useful components for insertion into your own Web site. Also note, when I use the term "components" I'm not referring to compiled COM components, but rather to "parts" or "pieces" of a set of tools.*

Everything here can be used pretty much as is, unless you want the navigation for your site to look different to my sample application. It shouldn't be too difficult to alter the code, as long as you're comfortable working with HTML tables and Dynamic HTML. The important thing to remember about the navigation is not how it looks here, but rather how it retrieves the XML data.

In my particular version, News briefs are positioned down the right-hand side, but are replaced by factoids whenever a story is called up. A summary of the current headlines is displayed in the left-hand column for quick access to other stories. It's simple but effective:

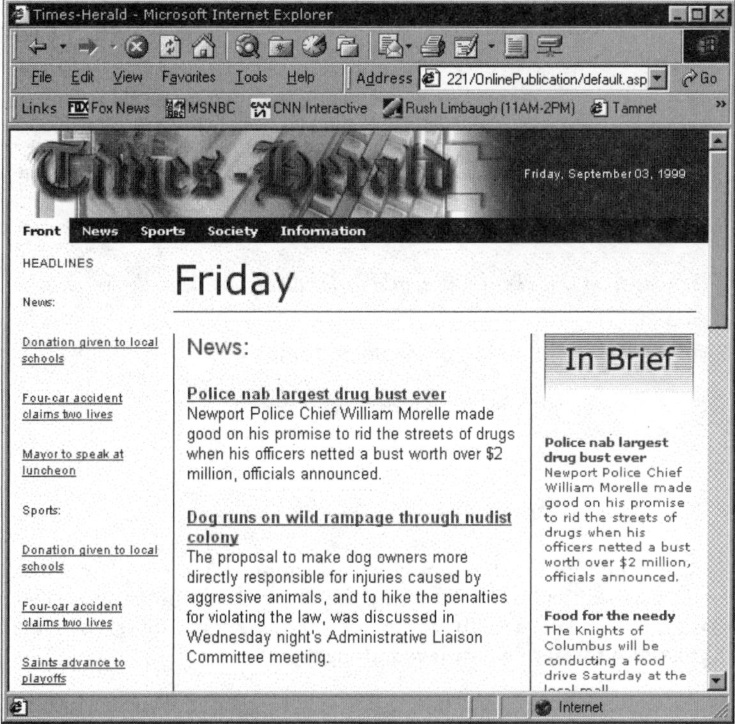
Times-Herald - Microsoft Internet Explorer
File Edit View Favorites Tools Help
Address 221/OnlinePublication/default.asp
Go
Links Fox News MSNBC CNN Interactive Rush Limbaugh (11AM-2PM) Tamnet
Times-Herald
Friday, September 03, 1999
Front News Sports Society Information
HEADLINES
Friday
News:
Donation given to local schools
Four-car accident claims two lives
Mayor to speak at luncheon
Sports:
Donation given to local schools
Four-car accident claims two lives
Saints advance to playoffs
News:
Police nab largest drug bust ever
Newport Police Chief William Morelle made good on his promise to rid the streets of drugs when his officers netted a bust worth over $2 million, officials announced.
Dog runs on wild rampage through nudist colony
The proposal to make dog owners more directly responsible for injuries caused by aggressive animals, and to hike the penalties for violating the law, was discussed in Wednesday night's Administrative Liaison Committee meeting.
In Brief
Police nab largest drug bust ever
Newport Police Chief William Morelle made good on his promise to rid the streets of drugs when his officers netted a bust worth over $2 million, officials announced.
Food for the needy
The Knights of Columbus will be conducting a food drive Saturday at the
Internet

Just about everything in our online newspaper application is centered around one XML file – `settings.xml` – which is the blueprint for the entire Web site. It contains information on the site's color scheme, navigation bar, the story teasers and the glossary of background terms.

Each section of the newspaper is represented by an Active Server Page that extracts the necessary XML data via a set of custom procedures. These procedures are also centralized into one library file, `headlines.asp`, which must be included with any page that needs to access them.

Let's examine the core components of our application and what they will do:

- `settings.xml` – Contains parameter information for the site. Referred to throughout this chapter as the "brains" of the site.
- `headlines.asp` – Used as a server-side include, it contains four basic procedures that collectively generate content for the site from data contained in `settings.xml`.
- `settings_glossary.asp` – Allows the editor to add and delete items from the background glossary, which is contained in `settings.xml`.
- `settings_stories.asp` – Allows the editor to choose which stories are published to the site.

- `storydisplay.asp` – An ASP-powered template that makes calls to procedures contained in `headlines.asp` to display a story, which is also checked for any matching terms from the background glossary in `settings.xml`.
- `[SECTION].asp` – A customizable page for each section that also makes calls to the procedures in `headlines.asp` to display headlines and blurbs from data contained in `settings.xml`. What these pages are named depends on you and the site you design.
- `navbar.asp` – A dynamically generated navigation insert based on data from `settings.xml`. This page generates a horizontal, tabbed navigation bar wherever it is inserted.
- `global.asa` – Several Application variables containing site-related information will be set here using XML.

Remember, all the code from this chapter is available for download from the Wrox Web site.

There are three basic aspects to the online newspaper application:

- Writing
- Editing
- Reading

This application calls for the reporter to comply with a simple XML template when filing stories. The stories are processed by an editor's tool, where the editor or site administrator selects which stories are to be included on the Web site. Finally, the reader can enjoy the news, presented in an easy-to-digest format with related information displayed alongside the story.

Before we get down to the serious coding, let's take a brief overview of how these aspects work.

The Writer Writes

Since everything in an online newspaper revolves around stories, let's start with them. Newspaper reporters have always had to deal with at least a certain amount of formatting when turning in their stories. Even on the old proprietary computer systems from the late 70s and early 80s, reporters were responsible for setting their headline font and size, and any other special formatting the story called for, such as italics or underline.

Those old systems generally used formatting symbols that could be loosely compared to XML. After all, those formatting symbols were nothing more than a custom mark-up language, complete with its own rules of syntax. In the late 80s and early 90s, when newspapers started using desktop publishing systems, reporters, in certain respects, were given less responsibility when it came to formatting. That's because the copy editor could so easily reformat entire stories by pointing-and-clicking the mouse.

Using XML, stories must follow a relatively simple format. In essence, they're just telling the editor which parts of the story are the headline, the byline (author's credit), the filing date, the body, the lead paragraph and the names of any corresponding artwork. A sample news story for our application would look like this:

```
<?xml version="1.0"?>

<story>

   <headline>Headline for the story</headline>

   <byline>By John Doe</byline>

   <dateline>October 21, 1999</dateline>

   <body>
         <blurb>
                <P ALIGN="justify">
                   This is the lead paragraph of our news story.
                </P>
         </blurb>
         <P ALIGN="justify">
            Another paragraph goes here…
         </P>
         <P ALIGN="justify">
            And another paragraph…
         </P>
         <P ALIGN="justify">
            And yet another paragraph…
         </P>
   </body>

   <artset>
          <art>
                <source>somepicture.jpg</source>
                <caption>Caption for the art.</caption>
          </art>
   </artset>

</story>
```

I decided to forego a **Document Type Definition (DTD)** or a Schema for the XML story format, and rely solely on well-formedness. Forcing the XML processor to validate stories against a DTD would not really enhance this particular application. Remember, the XML is being processed on the server and not in the browser. For example, the body text of a story will be retrieved from the XML document, put into a variable, and sent to the browser using `Response.Write`. We don't need the DTD telling us when there's an error, especially at a performance cost. Instead, we'll let ASP detect any general errors in loading the document, and send an appropriate message to the reader should a problem arise.

The `<artset>` element is optional, but you are allowed to have more than one picture with a story. The application will display multiple pictures underneath each other. Each piece of artwork is actually put into a table so that the caption stays positioned with it. In HTML, if a table is right- or left- aligned, text located inside the `<BODY>` element of the page, but outside the `<TABLE>`, itself will wrap around the table. Therefore, by creating a two-row, single-column table – the top cell containing the picture and the lower cell containing the caption text – you're able to keep the caption text underneath the picture, while allowing the text of the page to flow around it.

This application does not provide a means for the reporter to upload stories to the server. It is assumed that the reporter would be working on the same network as the server and would, therefore, have access to drop his stories into the appropriate folder. For remote story filing, one of a number of file upload solutions could be deployed, but because this case study deals primarily with XML, we won't cover it here.

The Editor Edits

After the reporters have turned in their stories, it's up to the editor or site administrator to use the **Editorial Content** management tool to publish the stories he wants to show up on the Web site. This is found in the `admin` folder located in the root directory of the Web site, and it is accessed from a switchboard page, also in the `admin` folder.

It's probably best in an office network environment to let the network administrator handle security for the admin directory, to protect these tools from prying eyes. Only the editor or site administrator should be granted access to them – for obvious reasons.

The editor is free to select the stories they want to appear in the online newspaper, and this selection can be altered at any time. In the Editorial Content tool, each story is displayed with an accompanying check box, grouped by sections (i.e. news, sports, society, etc.).

When the editor first opens the tool, all stories are automatically selected for inclusion. It's up to the editor to deselect the ones he doesn't want in the paper. With this tool, the editor can effectively "hold" certain stories from release until later:

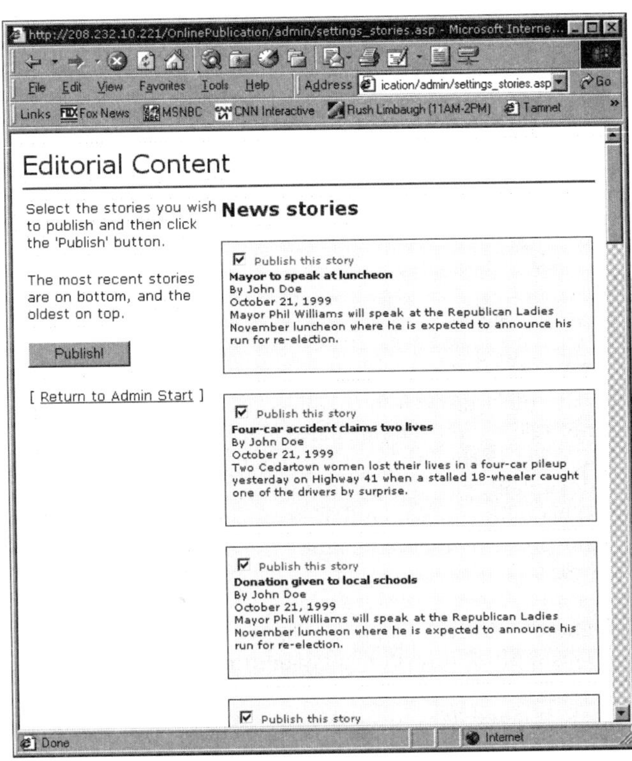

We'll see how to create this page – `settings_stories.asp` *– in the Administrative Tools section later in the chapter.*

The Name Tells the Story

The stories for the application must follow a strict naming convention; one that forces the files to sort by date first, then according to their importance:

```
news19991021001.xml - Filed on October 21, 1999
news19990412011.xml - Filed on April 12, 1999
```

The last three characters before the `.xml` extension represent the rank, or importance, of the story. The more important a story is in each day's batch, the higher this three-digit combination will be. Having three digits to play with means editors are allowed to have up to 1,000 stories per day for each section. We all know that it's highly unlikely that a thousand stories would ever be filed in a single day, so editors have quite a bit of flexibility when assigning file names to stories.

The application displays stories from each directory in reverse order, so the most recent and highest-ranked stories will always appear on top. For this reason, the editor should make certain that whatever his lead story is, it has the highest importance rating among the other stories filed that day.

If he has a reporter writing a hot piece on the local police chief getting canned, and he just knows that story is going to be the lead the next day, he might assign it `news19991104800.xml`. By giving it an importance ranking of `800`, in all probability it will be the lead for that day. The other boring, inconsequential stories would receive ratings like `001`, `002`, etc. However, if a sniper shoots the mayor and two councilmen at the city council meeting that night, the editor is likely to give this new story a name of `news19991104850.xml`. But why not just go ahead and give it an importance ranking of `999` instead of `850`? Well, someone could always shoot the President, right?

The Glossary Manager Tool

Our newspaper site has a glossary, which can contain brief descriptions or definitions of key people, places, organizations etc. that might recur in our stories. The **Glossary Manager** tool allows the editor to create, edit and delete terms from the glossary.

This feature is particularly useful for supplying background information for stories. For example, the name of the mayor might be added to the glossary explaining when they were elected, what political party they belong to, etc.

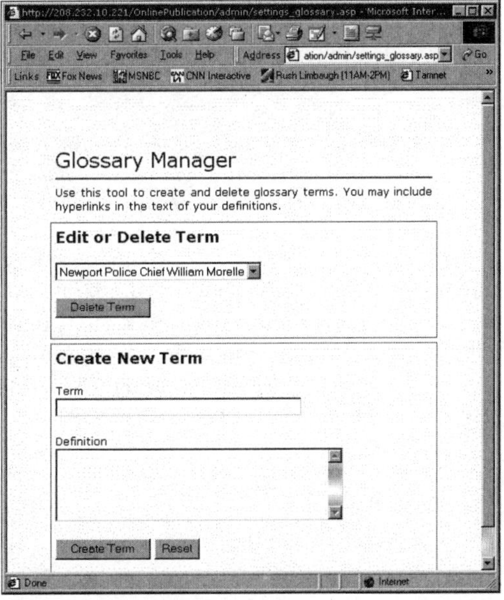

> *Again, we'll look at the code needed to create this page –* `settings_glossary.asp` *– in the Administration Tools section of the chapter.*

Each time a story is displayed for the reader, it is checked for any matching terms from the glossary and the results are shown in the right-hand column of the page. Glossary terms also can contain HTML hyperlinks to other stories, which makes them very useful.

The Reader Reads

The most important thing to the success of an online newspaper is whether or not the reader likes it. The site must be easy to use but powerful. Having all the headlines available from anywhere in the site tends to make things less complicated. The reader doesn't have to go looking for a table of contents – it's always right there on the page.

Clicking on a headline calls up the associated story in a template that is similar in look and feel to the rest of the site, so the reader isn't left with the impression they've been sent to Mars and back just because they wanted to read a story. And the Return link at the bottom of every story makes it extremely simple to return to the previous page, no matter what it was.

Upon selecting a story, the briefs in the right-hand column are replaced by background information related to that particular story. The reader will notice that every related glossary term is underlined upon first reference in the story. As the cursor is passed over that reference, the corresponding definition on the right is highlighted in yellow.

The great thing about the online newspaper application is that it can be heavily customized, bringing the reader more information than just stories or briefs. The components of the application can easily be converted to serve specific needs too.

Structural Requirements

The structure of the site should be kept as simple as possible. You should have a folder for each type of news your site will offer. In the sample application I used **news**, **sports**, **society** and a special folder called **briefs** – these folders are used to store the individual `.xml` story files that belong to these categories.

> *You'll also need a "front page" – probably* `default.asp` *in the root directory – which lists all the headlines, and you might want to have home pages corresponding to each of your news categories to display their items – in the screenshot these are the files* `news.asp`, `sports.asp` *and* `society.asp`.

Of course, you're free to use a completely different naming scheme for your content folders – after all, part of the specification of this site is that it's customizable. Suppose you wanted to create a news site for programmers and have a section for each programming language, or perhaps a sports-only site with a section for each major sport? No problem. Just create section folders to match the content your site will house.

I chose to put settings.xml in the admin folder and headlines.asp in the _ScriptLibrary folder, but you don't have to do this in your site – these are simply the folders that the code in this chapter points to. It's usually a good idea to put administrative type files into one folder – the admin folder. And for consistency, headlines.asp goes into the _ScriptLibrary folder because, after all, it is a library file. You'll see as we build these tools that it's pretty easy to change the locations of these files:

So, now we've explored the logic behind our sample application, let's move on to look at the code that makes it work.

The Brains – settings.xml

First, create a new XML file in the admin folder named settings.xml with the following code:

```
<?xml version="1.0"?>
<site>
      <specifications>
      </specifications>

      <colors>
      </colors>

      <navigation>
      </navigation>

      <content>
      </content>

      <glossary>
      </glossary>
</site>
```

Each of the major elements of this `.xml` file will manage information relating to different aspects of the site. The `specifications`, `colors` and `navigation` elements are pretty much static, while the `content` and `glossary` elements may very well change on a day-to-day basis. For this reason, I've included the Web-based administrative tools for these elements that we've just seen – the Editorial Content and Glossary Managers. We'll return to these later.

The <specifications> Element

Add the following code to the `<specifications>` element, customizing the information for your own Web site:

```
<specifications>
    <Site_Title>Times-Herald</Site_Title>
    <Domain_Name>http://onlinenewspaper.com</Domain_Name>
    <Header_Image>images/header_color.gif</Header_Image>
    <Pref_Font>arial,sans-serif</Pref_Font>
</specifications>
```

You'll notice that you can set a parameter called `domain_name` from here, but it only serves as a reference variable from within the site. There is actually no way to alter the domain name of a Web site from within an Active Server Page. These parameters are stored along with information from the `colors` element in Application variables by the `global.asa`, which we'll examine later.

The <colors> Element

Now add the color information to the `<colors>` element, which will be referenced throughout the site:

```
<colors>
    <Color_Primary>#0043B0</Color_Primary>
    <Color_Secondary>#002277</Color_Secondary>
    <Color_Highlight>#FFFF00</Color_Highlight>
    <Color_Background>#FFFFFF</Color_Background>
    <Color_HeaderText>#7D78AF</Color_HeaderText>
    <Color_BodyText>#222222</Color_BodyText>
</colors>
```

Because these values are stored in Application variables, you simply plug them into the site wherever you want with an implicit write. Remember that an implicit write is merely a shortcut syntax for the Response object's `Write` method:

```
<body bgcolor="<%=Application("Color_Background")%>">
```

Having a set color scheme tends to make the site look more professional, plus it lends itself to making our custom procedures seem a bit more robust, as you'll learn later.

The <navigation> Element

The site's navigation information is maintained in the `<navigation>` element, and is used to populate `navbar.asp`, which is inserted into each page of the site. For each navigation item, three pieces of information are kept: `name`, `url` and `description`. Add the following XML to the `<navigation>` element. Again, feel free to customize these parameters as necessary to fulfill the needs of your site:

```
<navigation>
    <section>
        <name>Front</name>
        <url>default.asp</url>
        <description>Front page - a mixture of all the news.</description>
    </section>
    <section>
        <name>News</name>
        <url>news.asp</url>
        <description>News page - current news for the city.</description>
    </section>
    <section>
        <name>Sports</name>
        <url>sports.asp</url>
        <description>Sports page - sports news from around town.</description>
    </section>
    <section>
        <name>Society</name>
        <url>society.asp</url>
        <description>Society page - gossip and rumors run wild.</description>
    </section>
    <section>
        <name>Information</name>
        <url>info.asp</url>
        <description>Information - who's responsible for the site.</description>
    </section>
</navigation>
```

Preparing global.asa

The `global.asa` plays a role here as well as `navbar.asp`, so let's go ahead and take a look at these two files. Save the changes you've made to `settings.xml`, and open up `global.asa`, adding the following code to the `Application_OnStart` event handler and noting the comments as you do so:

```
Sub Application_OnStart

  Dim strSourceFile, objRootColors, objRootInfo, objRootNav, objNavNames
  Dim objNavURLs, objXML

' Sets the path to settings.xml
  strSourceFile = Server.MapPath("admin") & "\settings.xml"
```

```
' Create an instance of the XML processor
  Set objXML = Server.CreateObject("Microsoft.FreeThreadedXMLDOM")

' Loads settings.xml into memory
  objXML.load(strSourceFile)

' Create a node for each main element of the XML file
  Set objRootColors = objXML.documentElement.selectSingleNode("colors")
  Set objRootInfo = objXML.documentElement.selectSingleNode("specifications")
  Set objRootNav = objXML.documentElement.selectSingleNode("navigation")

' Gets color scheme for the site
  Application.Lock
' Sets an Application object with settings.xml loaded
  Set Application("objXML") = objXML
  Application("Color_Primary")=objRootColors.childNodes.item(0).text
  Application ("Color_Secondary")=objRootColors.childNodes.item(1).text
  Application ("Color_Highlight")=objRootColors.childNodes.item(2).text
  Application ("Color_Background")=objRootColors.childNodes.item(3).text
  Application ("Color_HeaderText")=objRootColors.childNodes.item(4).text
  Application ("Color_BodyText")=objRootColors.childNodes.item(5).text

' Gets technical info for the site
  Application ("Site_Title")=objRootInfo.childNodes.item(0).text
  Application ("Domain_Name")=objRootInfo.childNodes.item(1).text
  Application ("Header_Image")=objRootInfo.childNodes.item(2).text
  Application ("Pref_Font")=objRootInfo.childNodes.item(3).text
  Application.Unlock

' Creates nodes for the navigation parameters
  Set objNavNames = objRootNav.getElementsByTagName("name")
  Set objNavURLs = objRootNav.getElementsByTagName("url")

' Puts the name and url values into a 2-D array
  Dim Navigation(10, 2)
  For navitem=0 To objNavNames.length -1
    Navigation(navitem, 0) = objNavNames.item(navitem).text
    Navigation(navitem, 1) = objNavURLs.item(navitem).text
  Next

  Application.Lock
  Application("Navigation") = Navigation
  Application.Unlock

End Sub

</SCRIPT>
```

Even though a lot of variables are getting plugged here, just two basic things are going on programmatically:

- Locating a specific node with the `selectSingleNode` method and getting the values from its child nodes
- Creating Application level variables for storing navigation bar data, color scheme and other technical information

Note that we used the Free-threaded model of the XML processor:

```
Set objXML = Server.CreateObject("Microsoft.FreeThreadedXMLDOM")
```

An XML document can be parsed using either the Free-threaded or Rental threading model of the processor. The behavior of the two is the same, but with Rental threading you get slightly better performance. However, to store the document element in an Application variable, you must use the Free-threaded model due to concurrent access by multiple users.

Remember, you'll also need to reference the appropriate type library at the top of `global.asa`:

```
<!--METADATA TYPE="typelib" FILE="C:\WINNT\System32\msxml.dll"-->
```

Or:

```
<!--METADATA TYPE="TypeLib" NAME="Microsoft XML, version 2.0" UUID="{D63E0CE2-
A0A2-11D0-9C02-00C04FC99C8E}" VERSION="2.0"-->
```

Making the Navigation Insert

Once the navigation data is in the `Application("Navigation")` array, `navbar.asp` can render the navigation bar.

Create a new page in the root directory named `navbar.asp` and add the following code:

```
<TABLE BORDER=0 BGCOLOR=<%=Color_Secondary%> CELLSPACING=0 CELLPADDING=4>
  <TR>
  <%
  Navigation = Application("Navigation")
' Parses Navigation information from Navigation Array
  For x = 0 To UBound(Navigation, 1) - 1

    If Session("Current_Page")=Navigation(x,0) Then
      Response.Write("<TD BGCOLOR=" & Color_Background & _
                     "><FONT FACE='verdana,sans-serif' SIZE=1 " & _
                     "COLOR=#000000><B>  " & Navigation(x, 0) & _
                     " </FONT></TD>")
    Else
      Response.Write("<TD><FONT FACE=""verdana,sans-serif"" SIZE=1 COLOR=" & _
                     Color_Background & "><B>  <A STYLE="" " & _
                     "text-decoration:none;color:" & Color_Background & _
                     ";"" HREF=" & Navigation(x, 1) & _
                     " ONMOUSEOVER=""this.style.color='" & Color_Highlight & _
                     "'"" ONMOUSEOUT=""this.style.color='" & _
                     Color_Background & "'"">" & Navigation(x, 0) & _
                     "</A> </FONT></TD>")
    End If

Next

  %>
  </TR>
</TABLE>
```

As the For loop is executed, each link's name and URL are retrieved from the two-dimensional array Application("Navigation"), and the rendering HTML is built around those values. The limit of the loop is set by the UBound property of the array.

Notice that the array is in a local variable called Navigation instead of Application("Navigation"). That's because the header section of each page converts all Application variables into locally scoped equivalents. Calling an Application variable uses more system resources than a local variable, and since most of our Application variables will be called multiple times on the same page, this makes the application a little bit more efficient.

Here's the header information that you'll want to include in all your pages:

```
<%
'Color information
Color_Primary = Application("Color_Primary")
Color_Secondary = Application("Color_Secondary")
Color_Highlight = Application("Color_Highlight")
Color_Background = Application("Color_Background")
Color_HeaderText = Application("Color_HeaderText")
Color_BodyText = Application("Color_BodyText")

'Site specifications
Site_Title = Application("Site_Title")
Domain_Name = Application("Domain_Name")
Header_Image = Application("Header_Image")
Pref_Font = Application("Pref_Font")

'Navigation information
Navigation = Application("Navigation")
%>
```

You might want to make life easier on yourself by putting this code into a separate file in the root directory – called getvars.asp – to be included in each page with a server-side include command.

Remember, navbar.asp is where you can do the most customization. Notice the Dynamic HTML we used there to create the onmouseover effects:

```
        Response.Write("<TD><FONT FACE=""verdana,sans-serif"" SIZE=1 COLOR=" & _
                       Color_Background & "><B>  <A STYLE="" " & _
                       "text-decoration:none;color:" & Color_Background & _
                       ";"" HREF=" & Navigation(x, 1) & _
                       " ONMOUSEOVER=""this.style.color='" & Color_Highlight & _
                       "'"" ONMOUSEOUT=""this.style.color='" & _
                       Color_Background & "'"">" & Navigation(x, 0) & _
                       "</A> </FONT></TD>")
```

Additionally, this routine checks to see if the current page matches any of the navigation link names. If so, it displays that name differently than the others, deadening its hyperlink and changing its background to match the document's background. This creates the illusion of raised folder tabs, similar to what's on most of Microsoft's Web sites:

The <content> and <glossary> Elements

Now let's return to `settings.xml`, where we had built the `<specifications>`, `<colors>` and `<navigation>` elements. That leaves the `<content>` element, where the stories and briefs are kept, and the `<glossary>` element, where the background information for stories goes.

All we really need to do for these two elements is put just one story and one glossary term in each. After all, the editor's tools we'll build next will automatically populate these elements for us.

Type the following code into the `<content>` element:

```
<content>
     <story>
          <headline>Some headline here</headline>
          <blurb>The lead paragraph will go here.</blurb>
          <folder>Section Folder</folder>
          <file>filename.xml</file>
     <story>
</content>
```

The information contained in this element will be pulled directly from the equivalent elements in the `.xml` file for each story. If you remember, the story template also has `<headline>` and `<blurb>` elements.

Finally, add this code to the `<glossary>` element:

```
<glossary>
     <term>
         <context>John Doe</context>
         <definition>He is a man.</definition>
     </term>
</glossary>
```

Calling these items "terms" might seem a bit reminiscent of third-grade reading class, but on the other hand that's exactly what they are – very basic terms. The name of the term is stored in the `<context>` tag set, and its matching information in`<definition>`. All sorts of information can be put into the `<definition>`, including HTML tags.

As you'll see later, the story-parsing procedure taps the XML property of the <definition> element rather than the text property. Doing so tells the XML processor to return any XML tags along with the text contained in the element, and because your Web browser will recognize some of that XML from the HTML Document Type Definition (DTD), it will process it accordingly. So if you put a well-formed hyperlink somewhere in the <definition> element, it will function perfectly as HTML.

That pretty much does it for settings.xml, the brains of the site. Save this page, because now we're going to move on to the brawn of the site – headlines.asp.

The Brawn – headlines.asp

The muscle of this application is kept in a single include file called headlines.asp. It has four procedures:

- ShowHeadlines – Displays a summary list of either bulleted or plain headlines with hyperlinks to the related stories based on the <content> element in settings.xml. This routine accepts parameters that tell it what section the stories come from, the style (bulleted or plain) in which to display them, and where in the list of stories to start and stop.
- ShowBlurbs – This routine expands on ShowHeadlines by also displaying the lead paragraph of each story, called the **blurb**. Additionally, the HTML generated for the display is designed to take up more space and play more predominately on the page. It accepts the same parameters as ShowHeadlines.
- ShowBriefs – Here we're only retrieving minor news items that don't take up a whole page. In fact, they are usually only one or two paragraphs long. They're filed in the same XML format as regular stories are, except that the entire body of text is contained within the <blurb> tags. ShowBriefs accepts only one parameter, Limit, which determines how many of the briefs to show.
- ShowStory – The big daddy, ShowStory works the hardest of our four procedures. It retrieves a story, parses its elements into the components of our story format, and then checks the body text against the glossary one item at a time for matching terms. But don't worry; the <glossary> element can handle quite a bit. During testing, I loaded it up with well over a thousand terms and still didn't notice a performance hit.

Go ahead and create a new file in the _ScriptLibrary folder called headlines.asp, and type in the following code:

```
<%

Dim gTermList
gTermList = ""

'Procedures go here

%>
```

Here we basically declare a global variable called `gTermList` for which `ShowStory` will generate content. You must declare this variable outside any procedure so that its value will persist throughout the page. Rather than having `ShowStory` write the contents of `gTermList` as part of its job, we're going to have it only set the value of `gTermList` so that we can use it wherever we want. This gives us greater flexibility in layout.

*Though not necessary, I went ahead and set the variable to a zero-length string. You may decide later to set a default value here, such as "Matching Terms:
" to appear on top of your term list when rendered in the HTML.*

Replace the "'Procedures go here" comment with all four of the procedure declarations like so:

```
<%

Dim gTermList
gTermList = ""

Sub ShowHeadlines(Section, Style, Start, Limit)

End Sub

Sub ShowBlurbs(Section, Style, Start, Limit)

End Sub

Sub ShowBriefs(Limit)

End Sub

ShowStory(Folder, File)

End Sub

%>
```

The ShowHeadlines Procedure

The `ShowHeadlines` procedure produces in the browser a plain-Jane summarized list of the headlines for the specified section. The call to `ShowHeadlines` would look something like:

```
<% Call ShowHeadlines("News", "plain", 1, 5) %>,
```

This retrieves the headlines for the `"News"` section, display them in `"plain"` HTML with no bullets (put `"bullets"` in the Style attribute for bullets), and start on the first headline for that section and end with the fifth. The result of such a call might look something like this.

Dog runs on wild rampage through nudist colony

Donation given to local schools

Four-car accident claims two lives

Local man loves his hobby

Type the following code into the `ShowHeadlines` procedure, noting the comments as you go:

```
Sub ShowHeadlines(Section,Style,Start,Limit)

  Dim strSep, intCount, objXML, objRootHeadlines, intNode, strHeadline
  Dim strFolder, strFile

  If Style = "bullets" Then
    strSep = "<LI>"
  Else
    strSep = "<P>"
  End If

' Checks to see if XML object exists
  If Not IsObject(Application("objXML")) Then
    Response.Write("No data available.")
    Response.End
  End If

' Creates an instance of the XML processor object
  Set objXML = Application("objXML")

' Sets the node 'content' as the root element
  Set objRootHeadlines = objXML.documentElement.selectSingleNode("content")

' Loop through each news item to extract headlines and urls
  For intNode = 0 To (objRootHeadlines.childNodes.length - 1)

    strHeadline = _
          objRootHeadlines.childNodes.item(intNode).childNodes.item(0).text
    strFolder = _
          objRootHeadlines.childNodes.item(intNode).childNodes.item(2).text
    strFile = _
          objRootHeadlines.childNodes.item(intNode).childNodes.item(3).text

    ' Gets only the items from the selected folder and within the proper range
    If Section = strFolder Then
      intCount = intCount + 1
      If intCount >= Start Then
        Response.Write(strSep & "<A HREF='storydisplay.asp?folder=" & _
                       strFolder & "&file=" & strFile & "'>" & _
                       strHeadline & "</A>")
      End If
    End If

   ' Checks to see if at the Limit yet, if so it Exits the loop
    If intCount = Limit Then
       Exit For
    End If

  Next

  Response.Write("<P>")

End Sub
```

Again, just like with `global.asa`, we created an instance of the XML processor object as `objXML` and loaded `settings.xml`. Next, we used the `selectSingleNode` method to retrieve the `<content>` node and filter the headlines that match the `Section` parameter. Each of the first three procedures are doing just that, but for slightly different reasons.

Once the `<content>` element is chosen, the stories are examined one at a time using the `For...Next` loop, and any required information is extracted.

The ShowBlurbs Procedure

`ShowHeadlines` is only concerned with retrieving the headlines and associated hyperlinks, whereas `ShowBlurbs` gets the lead paragraph too.

Go ahead and add the following code to `ShowBlurbs`:

```
Sub ShowBlurbs(Section, Style, Start, Limit)

  Dim strSep, intCount, objXML, objRootHeadlines, intNode, strHeadline
  Dim strBlurb, strFolder, strFile

  If Style = "bullets" Then
    strSep = "<LI>"
  End If

' Checks to see if XML object exists
  If Not IsObject(Application("objXML")) Then
    Response.Write("No data available.")
    Response.End
  End If

' Creates an instance of the XML processor object
  Set objXML = Application("objXML")

' Sets the node 'content' as the root element
  Set objRootHeadlines = objXML.documentElement.selectSingleNode("content")

' Loop through each news item to extract headlines and urls
  For intNode = 0 To (objRootHeadlines.childNodes.length - 1)

    strHeadline = _
          objRootHeadlines.childNodes.item(intNode).childNodes.item(0).text
    strBlurb = _
          objRootHeadlines.childNodes.item(intNode).childNodes.item(1).text
    strFolder = _
          objRootHeadlines.childNodes.item(intNode).childNodes.item(2).text
    strFile = _
          objRootHeadlines.childNodes.item(intNode).childNodes.item(3).text

  ' Gets only the items from the selected folder and within the proper range
    If Section = strFolder Then
      intCount = intCount + 1
      If intCount >= Start Then
```

```
        Response.Write(strSep & "<B><A HREF='storydisplay.asp?folder=" & _
                        strFolder & "&file=" & strFile & "'>" & strHeadline & _
                        "</A></B><BR>")
        Response.Write("<FONT SIZE=2>" & strBlurb & "<P>")
      End If
    End If

    If intCount = Limit Then
      Exit For
    End If

  Next

End Sub
```

There's not much to say here except that the formatting is a little different, in addition to the `<blurb>` element being retrieved. This listing of stories might be described as a detailed table of contents, whereas `ShowHeadlines` produces only a summary table of contents.

The call to `ShowBlurbs` would look almost identical to `ShowHeadlines`:

```
<% Call ShowBlurbs("News", "plain", 1, 5) %>
```

You might even use the two in conjunction with one another on the same page. For instance, use `ShowBlurbs` to display the first five stories and `ShowHeadline` for the remainder.

`ShowBlurbs` generates output to the browser that needs at least 300 pixels in width for it to look right, as you can see here:

Police nab largest drug bust ever
Newport Police Chief William Morelle made good on his promise to rid the streets of drugs when his officers netted a bust worth over $2 million, officials announced.
Dog runs on wild rampage through nudist colony
The proposal to make dog owners more directly responsible for injuries caused by aggressive animals, and to hike the penalties for violating the law, was discussed in Wednesday night's Administrative Liaison Committee meeting.
Times-Herald unveiles new look
Mayor Phil Williams will speak at the Republican Ladies November luncheon where he is expected to announce his run for re-election.
Donation given to local schools
Mayor Phil Williams will speak at the Republican Ladies November luncheon where he is expected to announce his run for re-election.

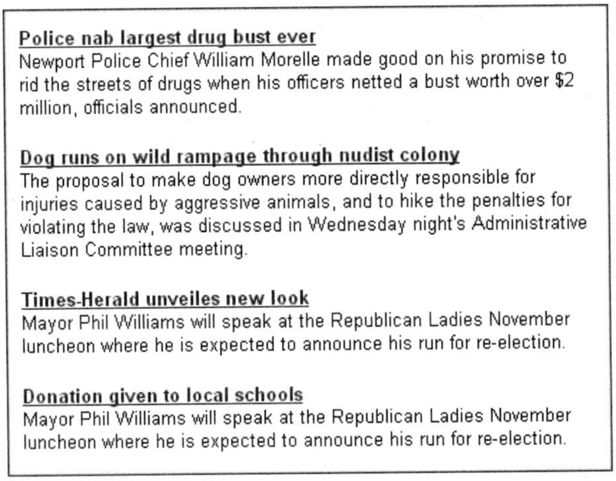

The ShowBriefs Procedure

This subroutine retrieves a list of special stories called "briefs." There's a folder for briefs just like with the other sections, but the difference is the stories stored in the `briefs` folder are very short. All of their `<body>` element content is contained within the `<blurb>` element like so:

```
<body>
      <blurb>
      <P>Here is a very short story.</P>
      </blurb>
</body>
```

Because `ShowBriefs` only displays the content within the `<blurb>` element of the story, regular-size stories from other folders could be copied without modification into the `briefs` folder, allowing them to double as a brief and a regular story at the same time. The extra text outside the blurb element would simply be ignored.

`ShowBriefs` is much simpler to call than the other procedures. The only parameter you're feeding it is the `Limit`:

```
<% Call ShowBriefs(10) %>
```

The output to the browser is best suited for a narrow column, perhaps on the right or left side of a page:

Food for the needy
The Knights of Columbus will be conducting a food drive Saturday at the local mall.

City Council meets Wednesday
This City Council will meet Wednesday of this week due to Labor day. The meeting is set for 7 p.m.

G.W. Bush to make local stop
Presidential candidate George W. Bush will stop to speak to a local Boy Scout troop Thursday at 1 p.m.

Let's add code for the `ShowBriefs` subroutine:

```
Sub ShowBriefs(Limit)

  Dim intCount, objXML, objRootHeadlines, intNode, strHeadline, strBlurb
  Dim strFolder, strFile
```

```
' Checks to see if XML object exists
  If Not IsObject(Application("objXML")) Then
    Response.Write("No data available.")
    Response.End
  End If

  Set objXML = Application("objXML")

  Set objRootHeadlines = objXML.documentElement.selectSingleNode("content")

' Loop through each news item to extract headlines and urls
  For intNode = 0 To (objRootHeadlines.childNodes.length - 1)

    strHeadline = _
          objRootHeadlines.childNodes.item(intNode).childNodes.item(0).text
    strBlurb = _
          objRootHeadlines.childNodes.item(intNode).childNodes.item(1).text
    strFolder = _
          objRootHeadlines.childNodes.item(intNode).childNodes.item(2).text
    strFile = _
          objRootHeadlines.childNodes.item(intNode).childNodes.item(3).text

    If strFolder = "Briefs" Then
      intCount = intCount + 1
      Response.Write(strSep & "<B>" & strHeadline & "</B><BR>")
      Response.Write("<FONT SIZE=1>" & strBlurb & "<P>")
    End If

    If intCount = Limit Then
      Exit For
    End If

  Next

End Sub
```

The ShowStory Procedure

This procedure works a bit differently than the others. Instead of tapping `settings.xml` for story information, it retrieves an actual story, which as you recall will be an XML document. `ShowStory` does call `settings.xml`, but only to retrieve glossary information. Since this procedure is bit more complicated than the others, let's outline what needs to happen before we code it:

- Get the story
- Create an instance of the XML Processor object
- Load the requested story
- Parse main elements into variables
- `<headline>` element
- `<byline>` element

- <dataline> element
- <body> element
- <artwork> element (optional)
- Get whole glossary
- Load settings.xml using existing instance of XML processor
- Select the glossary element as current node
- Collect matching glossary terms
- For...Next loop checking body element for matches in the <glossary> node
- Format each match for HTML display
- Add each formatted match to global string for later use
- Format and write story
- Standard non-font-specific HTML for story
- Response.Write to stream

You'll find that outlining your more complicated procedures before you write them is a good practice, even if your outline is very general like the one here. Outlining forces you to be organized. Once you've completed your outline, all you have to do is fill in the code.

In the ShowStory procedure below, our outline remains intact as all-uppercase comments. (Other comments, appearing in sentence case, are mixed in to provide more details.) Go ahead and enter the following code, using the outline as a guide:

```
Sub ShowStory(Folder, File)

  On Error Resume Next

  Dim strSourceFile, objRootStory, objXML, strHeadline, strByline
  Dim strDateline, strBody, objArtset, strTerm, intNode

  strSourceFile = Server.MapPath(Folder) & "\" & File

' GET THE STORY

' CREATE AN INSTANCE OF THE XML PROCESSOR OBJECT
  Set objXML = Server.CreateObject("Microsoft.XMLDOM")

' LOAD THE REQUESTED STORY
  objXML.load(strSourceFile)

' Sets the document element of the story
  Set objRootStory = objXML.documentElement

' PARSE MAIN ELEMENTS INTO VARIABLES
```

```
' Instead of DTD, check for parsing error in well-formedness
If objXML.parseError = 0 Then

  ' Gets each of the elements of the story, if available
  ' HEADLINE ELEMENT
    strHeadline = objRootStory.childNodes.item(0).text

  ' BYLINE ELEMENT
    strByline = objRootStory.childNodes.item(1).text

  ' DATALINE ELEMENT
    strDateline = objRootStory.ChildNodes.item(2).text

  ' BODY ELEMENT
    strBody = objRootStory.childNodes.item(3).xml

  ' ARTWORK ELEMENT (OPTIONAL)
  ' Puts any artwork into a node
    Set objArtset = objRootStory.selectNodes("artset")

  ' If artwork is in node, then process it and put into HTML table
    If objArtset.length > 0 Then
      artfile = objArtset.item(0).childNodes.item(0).childNodes.item(0).text
      caption = objArtset.item(0).childNodes.item(0).childNodes.item(1).text
      artwork = "<TABLE BORDER=0 BGCOLOR=#CCCCCC ALIGN=RIGHT " & _
                "CELLSPACING=5 WIDTH=150><TR><TD><IMG SRC=""artwork/" & _
                artfile & """ ALIGN=RIGHT BORDER=0></TD></TR>"
      artwork = artwork & "<TR><TD><FONT FACE=""arial,sans-serif""" & _
                "SIZE=1 COLOR=#555555><I>" & caption & _
                "</I></FONT></TD></TR></TABLE>"
    End If

  ' GET WHOLE GLOSSARY
  ' LOAD SETTINGS.XML USING EXISTING INSTANCE OF XML PROCESSOR

    Set objXML = Application("objXML")

  ' SELECT THE GLOSSARY ELEMENT AS CURRENT NODE
    Set objRootTerms = objXML.documentElement.selectSingleNode("glossary")

  'COLLECT MATCHING GLOSSARY TERMS
 ' FOR/NEXT LOOP CHECKING BODY ELEMENT FOR MATCHES IN GLOSSARY NODE
    For intNode = 0 to objRootTerms.childNodes.length - 1
      strTerm = objRootTerms.childNodes(intNode).childNodes(0).text

      If InStr(strBody,strTerm)>0 Then
        If gTermList = "No background information available for this story." _
           Then
              gTermList = ""
        End If
      ' FORMAT EACH MATCH FOR HTML DISPLAY
      ' ADD EACH FORMATTED MATCH TO GLOBAL STRING FOR LATER USE
        gTermList = gTermList & "<DIV ID=""Term" & intNode & """><B>" & _
                    strTerm & ":</B><BR>" & _
                    objRootTerms.childNodes(intNode).childNodes(1).xml & _
                   "</DIV><P>"
```

```
            strBody = Replace(strBody, strTerm, ("<FONT COLOR=#0000BB STYLE=" & _
                           """cursor:hand;"" ONMOUSEOVER=""Term" & intNode & _
                           ".className='selected'"" ONMOUSEOUT=""Term" & intNode & _
                           ".className='plain' ""><U>" & strTerm & _
                           "</U></FONT>"), 1, 1)

          End If
        Next

      ' FORMAT AND WRITE STORY
      ' If one of the elements of the story are missing then don't display it
        If strHeadline="" Or strByline="" Or strDateline="" Or strBody="" Then
          Response.Write("<FONT COLOR=#555555><I>Sorry, the requested " & _
                         "story is not availabe right now.<BR>" & _
                         "Please try again later.</I><P> </P>" & _
                         "<P> </P><P> </P><P> </P>")

        Else
        ' STANDARD NON-FONT-SPECIFIC HTML FOR EACH STORY
        ' RESPONSE.WRITE TO STREAM
          Response.Write("<H2>" & strHeadline & "</H2>")
          Response.Write("<HR Size=1 NOSHADE COLOR=#BBBBBB>")
          Response.Write("<FONT SIZE=1 COLOR=#444444><B>" & strByline & _
                         "</B></FONT><BR>")
          Response.Write("<FONT SIZE=1 COLOR=#444444><I>" & strDateline & _
                         "</I></FONT>")
          Response.Write("<HR SIZE=1 NOSHADE COLOR=#BBBBBB>")
          Response.Write(artwork)
          Response.Write("<FONT SIZE=2>" & strBody & "</FONT>")

        End If

      Else
      ' If there was a well-formedness error, don't display story
        Response.Write("<FONT COLOR=#555555><I>Sorry, the requested story " & _
                       "is not availabe right now.<BR>Please try again " & _
                       "later.</I><P> </P><P> </P><P> </P>" & _
                       "<P> </P>")

    End If

    End Sub
```

The gTermList String

Again I should point out that `gTermList` has global scope because it was declared outside the procedures. As you'll see later in our sample story-display page, you can use `Response.Write gTermList` anywhere you want after the call to `ShowStory`.

`gTermList` is a string containing HTML for displaying the matching glossary terms that `ShowStory` finds in the story. As `gTermList` is being built in the `For...Next` loop, each associated term within the body of the story is also being altered to bring attention to it.

Here's an example of what the HTML for `gTermList` might typically look like:

```
<DIV ID="Term0">
<B>Newport Police Chief William Morelle:</B><BR>
<definition>Newport's fourteenth police chief in its 87-year history. Morelle was
appointed by previous mayor Tommy Toulouse.</definition>
</DIV>
<P>
<DIV Id="Term1">
<B>Southbeach:</B><BR>
<definition>Founded: February 12, 1958<BR/>Mayor: Phil Williams
(R)<BR/>Population: 21,421 (1996)<BR/>Industry: Paper
products<BR/></definition></DIV>
<P>
<DIV ID="Term2">
<B>Highway 41:</B><BR>
<definition>The main artery of traffic running north-south between Southbeach and
Ellington.</definition>
</DIV>
<P>
```

The term "Newport Police Chief William Morelle" can be found somewhere in the body of the story, but without its appearance being altered the reader might not see exactly where. Therefore, `ShowStory` adds the following HTML code around "Newport Police Chief William Morelle:"

```
<FONT COLOR=#0000BB STYLE="cursor:hand;" ONMOUSEOVER="Term0.classname='selected'"
ONMOUSEOUT="Term0.className='plain' ">
<U>Newport Police Chief William Morelle</U></FONT>
```

This extra HTML underlines the term and changes its color to blue. Also, users of Microsoft Internet Explorer 4.0, or higher, get an extra treat. An inline CSS style statement tells the browser to display the pointing hand when users hover over the term, and inline script changes the `className` attribute of the matching definition in `gTermList` to `selected`, which is defined in a `<STYLE>` block in our story-display page.

Police nab largest drug bust ever

By Tommy Fillano
October 23, 1999

Newport Police Chief William Morelle made good on his promise to rid the streets of drugs w[illegible] his officers netted a bust worth over $2 million, officials announced.

Background

Newport Police Chief William Morelle: Newport's fourteenth police chief in its 87-year history. Morelle was appointed by previous mayor Tommy Toulouse.

Using the ShowStory Procedure

It's time we took a look at a sample story-display page, which will be calling our `ShowStory` procedure. I say "sample" because your story display page could look drastically different in your rendition of the online newspaper. It only needs to meet these minimum requirements:

- Contain a server-side include statement for `headlines.asp` (this gives you access to the procedures we created earlier)
- Contain a `<STYLE>` block for the glossary `mouseover` effects, as described earlier
- Contain a server-side include statement for `navbar.asp` (optional)
- Call the `ShowStory` procedure
- `Response.Write` the global `gTermList` string AFTER calling `ShowStory`
- Call `ShowHeadlines` (optional)

The following sample, `storydisplay.asp`, does all of the above. Remember, this could be any ASP in your site. Below, I've highlighted the portions related to our `ShowStory` procedure:

```
<%@ LANGUAGE=VBScript %>

<!--#include file="_ScriptLibrary/headlines.asp"-->

<%Session("Current_Page") = Request.QueryString("Folder")%>

<%
'Color information
Color_Primary = Application("Color_Primary")
Color_Secondary = Application("Color_Secondary")
Color_Highlight = Application("Color_Highlight")
Color_Background = Application("Color_Background")
Color_HeaderText = Application("Color_HeaderText")
Color_BodyText = Application("Color_BodyText")

'Site specifications
Site_Title = Application("Site_Title")
Domain_Name = Application("Domain_Name")
Header_Image = Application("Header_Image")
Pref_Font = Application("Pref_Font")

'Navigation information
Navigation = Application("Navigation")


Select Case WeekDay(Now())

  Case 1
    wd="Sunday"
  Case 2
    wd="Monday"
  Case 3
    wd="Tuesday"
  Case 4
    wd="Wednesday"
```

```
  Case 5
    wd="Thursday"
  Case 6
    wd="Friday"
  Case 7
   wd="Saturday"

End Select

'*****************************************************************

%>

<HTML>
<HEAD>
<TITLE><%=Site_Title%></TITLE>

<STYLE type="text/css">

H1
  {
  font-family:verdana,sans-serif;
  font-size:18pt;
  color:<%=Color_HeaderText%>;
  }

H2
  {
  font-family:verdana,sans-serif;
  font-size:14pt;
  color:<%=Color_HeaderText%>;
  }

H3
  {
  font-family:verdana,sans-serif;
  font-size:10pt;
  color:<%=Color_HeaderText%>;
  }

.selected
  {
  background-Color:#FFFFAA;
  color:<%=Color_BodyText%>;
  }

</STYLE>

</HEAD>
<BODY BGCOLOR="<%=Color_Background%>" LEFTMARGIN="0" TOPMARGIN="0"
MARGINHEIGHT="0" MARGINWIDTH="0" LINK="<%=Color_HeaderText%>"
VLINK="<%=Color_HeaderText%>" ALINK="<%=Color_BodyText%>">

<TABLE BORDER="0" CELLSPACING="0" CELLPADDING="0" WIDTH="100%">
   <TR>
      <TD BGCOLOR="<%=Color_Primary%>" WIDTH="415">
<IMG SRC="<%=Header_Image%>" BORDER="0" VSPACE="0"></td>
```

```
      <TD BGCOLOR="<%=Color_Primary%>" VALIGN="center">
      <FONT FACE="<%=Pref_Font%>" COLOR="<%=Color_Background%>"
      SIZE="1"><%=FormatDateTime(Now(), 1)%></FONT></TD>
    </TR>
    <TR>
      <TD BGCOLOR="<%=Color_Secondary%>" COLSPAN="2">

        <!-- HORIZONTAL NAVIGATION STARTS HERE -->
        <!--#include file="navbar.asp"-->
        <!-- HORIZONTAL NAVIGATION ENDS HERE -->

      </TD>

    </TR>
  </TABLE>

  <TABLE BORDER="0" CELLSPACING="10" CELLPADDING="0">
    <TR>
      <TD WIDTH="150" VALIGN="top" ROWSPAN="2">
        <FONT FACE="<%=Pref_Font%>" SIZE="1" COLOR="<%=Color_HeaderText%>">
        <B>HEADLINES</B><P>
        <!-- START LEFT SIDE NAVIGATION **********************-->

        <%
        Response.Write("News:")
        Call ShowHeadlines("News","plain",1,10)
        Response.Write("Sports:")
        Call ShowHeadlines("Sports","plain",1,10)
        Response.Write("Society:")
        Call ShowHeadlines("Society","plain",1,10)
        %>

        <!-- END LEFT SIDE NAVIGATION ************************-->
      </TD>

      <TD COLSPAN="4" VALIGN="top">
         <FONT FACE="verdana,sans-serif" SIZE="6"
         COLOR="<%=Color_Primary%>"><%=Request.QueryString("Folder")%></FONT>
         <HR SIZE="1" NOSHADE COLOR="<%=Color_Primary%>">
      </TD>

    </TR>

    <TR>

      <TD WIDTH="1" BGCOLOR="<%=Color_Primary%>"><IMG SRC="images/filler.gif"
         WIDTH="1" HEIGHT="22"></TD>

      <TD VALIGN="top" WIDTH="400">
        <!--***** START MAIN PAGE CONTENT HERE ****************-->

 <FONT FACE="<%=Pref_Font%>" SIZE="2" COLOR="<%=Color_BodyText%>">
        <%
        Call ShowStory(Request.QueryString("Folder"), _
                       Request.QueryString("File"))
        %>
         <P>
```

```
            <FONT FACE="<%=Pref_Font%>" SIZE="1" COLOR="<%=Secondary_Primary%>">
               <A HREF="<%=Request.QueryString("HTTP_REFERER")%>">
                [ RETURN TO PREVIOUS PAGE ]</A>
            </FONT>

            <!--***** END MAIN PAGE CONTENT HERE *******************-->
         </TD>

         <TD BGCOLOR="<%=Color_Primary%>" WIDTH="1" VALIGN="top">
            <IMG SRC="images/filler.gif" WIDTH="1" HEIGHT="22"></TD>

         <TD WIDTH="125" VALIGN="top">
             <IMG SRC="images/header_background.gif" WIDTH="122" HEIGHT="62"><P>
             <FONT FACE="<%=Pref_Font%>" SIZE="1" COLOR="#666666">
             <%=gTermList%>
         </TD>
      </TR>
   </TABLE>
   </BODY>
   </HTML>
```

`ShowStory` gets its parameters from the QueryString passed by the hyperlinks from either `ShowHeadlines` or `ShowBlurbs`. The typical headline hyperlink looks like so:

```
<A HREF="storydisplay.asp?Folder=News&File=news19991023001.xml">...</A>
```

And those QueryString values are passed right on to the procedure:

```
Call Showstory(Request.QueryString("Folder"), Request.QueryString("File"))
```

Again, your own version of `storydisplay.asp` doesn't have to look like mine, except for the minimum requirements described earlier. As for the other pages in your online newspaper, you must decide what they'll look like too.

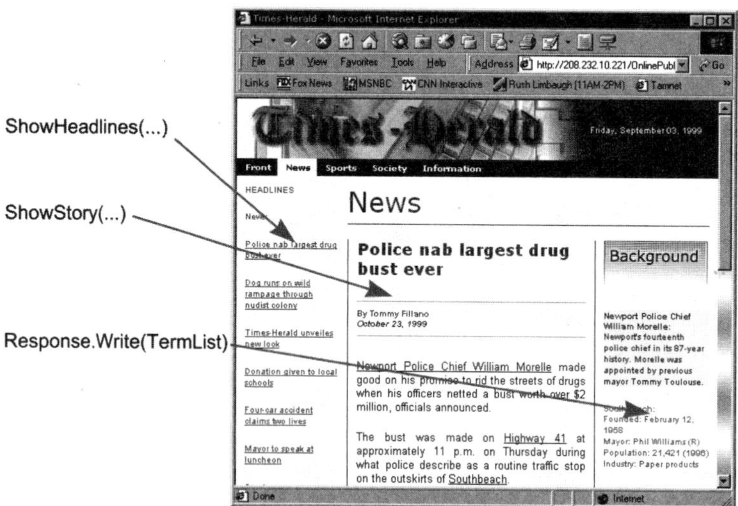

Home Pages

As we said earlier, it's a good idea to have home pages for each of the main content sections of your site (remember, ours were `default.asp`, `news.asp`, etc.). On those pages, you can use `ShowBlurbs` down the main part of the page with perhaps `ShowHeadlines` in the left-hand column and `ShowBriefs` on the right.

So for example, you'd need to change the section of `storydisplay.asp` that displays the main page content:

```
<!--***** START MAIN PAGE CONTENT HERE ****************-->

<FONT FACE="<%=Pref_Font%>" SIZE="2" COLOR="<%=Color_BodyText%>">
<%
Call ShowStory(Request.QueryString("Folder"), _
               Request.QueryString("File"))
%>
 <P>
<FONT FACE="<%=Pref_Font%>" SIZE="1" COLOR="<%=Secondary_Primary%>">
   <A HREF="<%=Request.QueryString("HTTP_REFERER")%>">
    [ RETURN TO PREVIOUS PAGE ]</A>
</FONT>

<!--***** END MAIN PAGE CONTENT HERE *******************-->
```

And replace the call to `ShowStory` with something like:

```
Call ShowBlurbs("News", "plain", 1, 10)
```

Don't forget, `navbar.asp` requires that you tell it what section the current page belongs to. Use a Session variable called `Current_Page` to do this.

```
<% Session("Current_Page") = "News" %>
```

Using a Session variable allows you to add other pages, perhaps with static content, to that section, and as long as you insert `navbar.asp` and set `Current_Page`, it will be able to properly indicate the current section. In the previous figure, the **News** header is determined by this Session variable `Current_Page`.

By now, you've coded these procedures and have seen sample calls to them, as well as their output to the browser. You can use them wherever you like in your site.

Administrative Tools

This application wouldn't be complete without some effective tools for editing the content of `settings.xml` from the Web. Sure, a well-trained editor could access `settings.xml` directly and make the necessary changes each time he wanted to update the site. But that would be excessively laborious considering you could build ASP tools to edit the more frequently accessed settings.

Earlier, we described these tools as settings_stories.asp and settings_glossary.asp. Both of them are included in the admin folder of our application. (As stated earlier, you don't necessarily have to put them in a folder called admin, but you should definitely put them somewhere with restricted access.)

settings_stories.asp

This page performs three main actions that we've divided into three procedures:

- DisplayPublishTool – When the user (the site editor or administrator) first visits the page, all the content from the main section folders of the site is cataloged and displayed so the editor can pick and choose which stories to use.
- GetStories – This procedure is called multiple times by DisplayPublishTool. This guy is doing all the work for DisplayPublishTool.
- PublishStories – This procedure processes the selections made by the editor or administrator using DisplayPublishTool, then displays a confirmation dialogue.

Create a new ASP in the admin directory and name it settings_stories.asp. Add the following code, leaving a place-holder for the procedures, which we'll add later:

```
<%@ LANGUAGE=VBScript %>

<%

Dim intMasterCount
intMasterCount = 0

Sub PublishStories()

...

End Sub

Sub DisplayPublishTool()

...

End Sub

Sub GetStories(Folder)

...

End Sub

%>

<HTML>
<HEAD>
<SCRIPT LANGUAGE=vbscript>
<!--
```

```
Sub HighLight()

  Dim src
  Set src = window.event.srcElement.parentElement.parentElement. _
          parentElement.parentElement.parentElement

  If src.className = "selected" Then
    src.className = ""
  Else
    src.className = "selected"
  End If

End Sub

'-->
</SCRIPT>

<STYLE type="text/css">
.selected
  {
  background-Color:#FFFFBB;
  }
</STYLE>

</HEAD>
<BODY BGCOLOR=#FFFFFF>

<FONT FACE="verdana" SIZE=1>
<%
Select Case Request.Form("Action")

  Case "Publish"
    Call PublishStories()
  Case Else
    Call DisplayPublishTool()

End Select

%>
</FONT>

</BODY>
</HTML>
```

Notice the client-side VBScript and the `<STYLE>` block. They have nothing at all to do with the XML. They work together to highlight each of the story summaries as the editor selects them for use.

The `Select Case` statement calls the appropriate procedure based on what the editor is doing. When he first visits the page, `DisplayPublishTool` is called. However, after he has made his selections, the form variable `Action` is set to `"Publish"`, directing program flow to the `PublishStories` procedure.

Add the following code to the `DisplayPublishTools` and `GetStories` procedures:

```
Sub DisplayPublishTool()

  Dim intNavIndex

  Response.Write("<FORM ACTION=""settings_stories.asp"" METHOD=POST " & _
               "ID=form1 NAME=form1>")
  Response.Write("<INPUT TYPE=HIDDEN NAME=""Action"" VALUE=""Publish"">")
  Response.Write("<FONT FACE=""verdana,sans-serif"" SIZE=5>Editorial " & _
               "Content</FONT><HR SIZE=2 NOSHADE COLOR=#555555>")
  Response.Write("<TABLE BORDER=0><TR><TD VALIGN=TOP>" & _
               "<FONT FACE=""verdana,sans-serif"" " & _
               "SIZE=2>")
  Response.Write("Select the " & Folder & " stories you wish to publish " & _
               "and then click the 'Publish' button.<P>")
  Response.Write("The most recent stories are on bottom, and the oldest on " & _
               "top.<P>")
  Response.Write("<INPUT TYPE=SUBMIT VALUE=""   " & _
               "Publish!   "" NAME=""submit1"">")
  Response.Write("<P>[ <A HREF=""default.asp"">Return to Admin Start</A> " & _
               "]</FONT></TD><TD>")

  Navigation = Application("Navigation")

' Using the Navigation Session variable, we'll get the stories for each section
  For intNavIndex = 0 To UBound(Navigation, 1) - 1

    If Navigation(intNavIndex, 0) <> "Front" And Navigation(intNavIndex, 0) <> _
               "Information" And Navigation(intNavIndex,0) <> "" Then
      Call GetStories(Navigation(intNavIndex,0))
    End If

  Next

' Gets story information for Briefs, a special folder
  Call GetStories("Briefs")

  Response.Write("</TD></TR></TABLE></FORM>")

End Sub

Sub GetStories(Folder)

  Dim objFso, objFolder, objFiles, objFile, strFullPath, strHeadline, strBlurb
  Dim strByline, strDateline, intMasterCount

  strFullPath = Request.ServerVariables("APPL_PHYSICAL_PATH") & "\" & Folder

  Set objFso = Server.CreateObject("Scripting.FileSystemObject")
  If objFso.FolderExists(strFullPath) Then

    Set objFolder = objFso.GetFolder(strFullPath)
    Set objFiles = objFolder.Files

    Response.Write("<H3>" & Folder & " stories</H3>")
```

```
        For Each objFile In objFiles
        intMasterCount = intMasterCount + 1
        Set xmlObj = Server.CreateObject("Microsoft.XMLDOM")
        xmlObj.load(strFullPath & "\" & objFile.Name)
        Set objRootStory = xmlObj.documentElement
        strHeadline = objRootStory.childNodes.item(0).text
        strByline = objRootStory.childNodes.item(1).text
        strDateline = objRootStory.childNodes.item(2).text
        strBlurb = objRootStory.childNodes.item(3).childNodes.item(0).text

        XMLadd = Chr(9) & "<story>" & Chr(13) & Chr(10) & Chr(9) & Chr(9)
        XMLadd = XMLadd & "<headline>" & strHeadline & "</headline>" & _
                 Chr(13) & Chr(10) & Chr(9) & Chr(9)
        XMLadd = XMLadd & "<blurb>" & strBlurb & "</blurb>" & Chr(13) & _
                 Chr(10) & Chr(9) & Chr(9)
        XMLadd = XMLadd & "<folder>" & Folder & "</folder>" & Chr(13) & _
                 Chr(10) & Chr(9) & Chr(9)
        XMLadd = XMLadd & "<file>" & objFile.Name & "</file>" & Chr(13) & _
                 Chr(10) & Chr(9)
        XMLadd = XMLadd & "</story>" & Chr(13) & Chr(10) & Chr(13) & Chr(10)

        Response.Write("<TABLE ID=""blurb" & _
                       intMasterCount & """ class=""selected"" " & _
                       "BORDER=1 CELLPADDING=5 CELLSPACING=0 " & _
                       "BORDERCOLORDARK=#444444 BORDERCOLORLIGHT=#444444>" & _
                       "<TR><TD BORDERCOLORDARK=#FFFFFF " & _
                       "BORDERCOLORLIGHT=#FFFFFF><FONT FACE=""verdana""" & _
                       " SIZE=1>")
        Response.Write("<INPUT NAME=""Blurbs"" TYPE=CheckBox CHECKED " & _
                       "VALUE=""" & XMLadd & """ ONCLICK=""Call " & _
                       "HighLight()""> <FONT COLOR=#444444>" & _
                       "Publish this story</FONT>")
        Response.Write("<BR><B>" & strHeadline & "</B><BR>" & _
                       strByline & "<BR>" & _
                       strDateline & "<BR>")
        Response.Write(strBlurb & "<P>")
        Response.Write("</FONT></TD></TR></TABLE><P>")

      Next

    Else

      Response.Write("<FONT FACE=""verdana"" SIZE=2 COLOR=#FF0000>Error: " & _
                     "The folder " & Folder & " does not exist.</FONT><P>")

    End If

  End Sub
```

DisplayPublishTools relies on the Application("Navigation") variable created in global.asa to know which folders are to be searched for stories. Once it has this information, it calls GetStories, which uses the FileSystemObject object to get the list of files in each folder. It opens each of those XML-based stories and extracts the <headline>, <byline>, <dateline> and <blurb> elements. That information is assembled into an XML-formatted string for each story, which is then used as the value attribute for an associated check box element. Those check box elements are assembled into a <FORM> being generated by DisplayPublishTools.

By putting the collected information from each story into the `value` attribute of a check box form element, we assure ourselves that only the selected information will be processed. By naming all the check boxes `Blurbs`, we've created a collection that can then be processed by `PublishStories`.

Add the following code to `PublishStories`:

```
Sub PublishStories()

   Dim XMLnode, strSourceFile, intElemCount, objXML1, objXML2

   For intElemCount = Request.Form("Blurbs").Count To 1 Step -1
       XMLnode = XMLnode & Request.Form("Blurbs")(intElemCount)
   Next

   XMLnode = "<content>" & Chr(13) & Chr(10) & XMLnode & "</content>" & _
             Chr(13) & Chr(10)

   ' Set the source file location
   strSourceFile = Request.ServerVariables("APPL_PHYSICAL_PATH") & _
                                               "\admin\settings.xml"

   Set objXML1 = Server.CreateObject("Microsoft.XMLDOM")
   objXML1.load(strSourceFile)
   Set rootSettings = objXML1.documentElement

   Set objXML2 = Server.CreateObject("Microsoft.XMLDOM")
   objXML2.loadXML(XMLnode)
   Set rootNewNode = objXML2.documentElement

   ' Replace the old "contents" node with the new one
   rootSettings.replaceChild rootNewNode, rootSettings.childNodes.item(3)

   objXML1.save(strSourceFile)

   Response.Write("<H2>Update Complete</H2>")
   Response.Write("The stories were successfully updated.<P>")
   Response.Write("[ <A HREF=""../default.asp"">Go to publication front" & _
                  "</A> ]<P>")
   Response.Write("[ <A HREF=""settings_stories.asp"">Make changes to " & _
                  "publication</A> ]<P>")

End Sub
```

Because we formatted the values in each of the `Blurbs` check boxes as XML in the `GetStories` procedure, all we have to do is create a new `<content>` node based on those values, and replace the old `<content>` node in `settings.xml`.

The `For…Next` loop assembles the blurbs into one, long string. That string is then sandwiched by `<content>` and `</content>` tags.

> *I also included carriage return and line feed characters to make my XML file easier to decipher for humans – the processor couldn't care less.*

After I'm confident my XMLnode string contains well-formed XML, I load it into the processor using the loadXML method of the DOM. I now have a legitimate node to replace the old node using the replaceChild method.

After the old contents is replaced by the new one, we save our XML using – what else – the save method.

settings_glossary.asp

This little tool allows the editor to create new glossary terms and delete old ones. It's similar in principle to how settings_stories.asp worked, except that we introduce two new methods to our repertoire: removeChild and appendChild.

The functionality of this ASP is distributed among three procedures: DeleteTerm, CreateTerm and ListGlossary.

Create a new ASP in the admin folder and name it settings_glossary.asp. Add the following code, leaving place-holders for the three procedures:

```
<%@ LANGUAGE=VBScript %>

<%

Dim UpdateMessage

Sub DeleteTerm(Term_ID)

...

End Sub

Sub CreateTerm(Term, Definition)

...

End Sub

Function ListGlossary()

...

End Function

Select Case Request.Form("Action")

  Case "Delete_Term"
    Call DeleteTerm(Request.Form("Term_ID"))

  Case "Create_Term"
    Call CreateTerm(Request.Form("Term"),Request.Form("Definition"))

End Select

%>
```

```
<HTML>
<HEAD>
</HEAD>
<BODY BGCOLOR=#FFFFFF>

<P> </P>

<DIV ALIGN="center">

<TABLE BORDER="1" BORDERCOLORDARK=#FFFFFF BORDERCOLORLIGHT=#FFFFFF
 CELLPADDING="5" CELLSPACING="5" WIDTH="473">
  <TR>
    <TD>
      <FONT FACE="verdana,sans-serif" SIZE="2">
      <FONT FACE="verdana,sans-serif" SIZE="5">Glossary Manager</FONT><BR>
      <HR SIZE="2" NOSHADE COLOR="#555555">
      <DIV ALIGN="justify">
         Use this tool to create and delete glossary terms. You may include
         hyperlinks in the text of your definitions.
      </DIV>
      <%=UpdateMessage%>
    </TD>
   </TR>

  <TR>
    <TD BORDERCOLORDARK=#696969 BORDERCOLORLIGHT=#696969>
      <FONT FACE="verdana,sans-serif" SIZE="2">
      <H3>Edit or Delete Term</H3>
      <FORM ACTION="settings_glossary.asp" METHOD=POST ID=form2 NAME="form1">
         <INPUT TYPE="HIDDEN" NAME="Action" VALUE="Delete_Term">
         <SELECT ID="Term_ID" NAME="Term_ID">
            <%=Response.Write(ListGlossary())%>
         </SELECT>
         <P>
         <INPUT TYPE="SUBMIT" VALUE="Delete Term" ID=submit1 NAME=submit1>
      </FORM>
      </FONT>
    </TD>
  </TR>

  <TR>
    <TD BORDERCOLORDARK=#696969 BORDERCOLORLIGHT=#696969>
      <FONT FACE="verdana,sans-serif" SIZE="2">
      <H3>Create New Term</H3>
      <FORM ACTION="settings_glossary.asp" METHOD=POST ID=form2 NAME=form2>
        <INPUT TYPE="HIDDEN" NAME="Action" VALUE="Create_Term">
        Term<BR>
        <INPUT TYPE="TEXT" NAME="Term" SIZE=40><P>
        Definition<BR>
        <TEXTAREA ROWS=5 COLS=40 NAME="Definition"></TEXTAREA><P>
        <INPUT TYPE="SUBMIT" VALUE="Create term" NAME="submit2">
        <INPUT TYPE="RESET" VALUE="Reset" NAME="reset1">
      </FORM>
```

```
          </FONT>
        </TD>
        <TR>
    </TABLE>

    </Body>
    </HTML>
```

This page is displaying two HTML forms: one for deleting glossary terms and the other for creating them. You'll notice that the first form (for deleting terms) makes a call directly to our `ListGlossary` function.

`ListGlossary` does what we've been doing throughout this entire application – it loads an XML document, finds a specific element, and retrieves its content. That content is formatted into the list items for a drop-down menu.

Pay particular attention to how the list items are referenced. `ListGlossary` sets the `value` attribute of each `<OPTION>` element as an integer corresponding to the node from which it was retrieved. It's easier to reference children of a node by their index number as opposed to filtering one of their values or attributes.

Add the code for `ListGlossary`:

```
Function ListGlossary()

  Dim strSourceFile, gTermList

' Creates an instance of the XML processor object
  strSourceFile = Request.ServerVariables("APPL_PHYSICAL_PATH") & _
                                         "\admin\settings.xml"

  Set objXML = Server.CreateObject("Microsoft.XMLDOM")

  objXML.load(strSourceFile)

  Set rootTerms = objXML.documentElement.selectSingleNode("glossary")

  For i = 0 to rootTerms.childNodes.length - 1
    Term = rootTerms.childNodes(i).childNodes(0).text
    Definition =rootTerms.childNodes(i).childNodes(1).xml
    gTermList = gTermList & "<OPTION VALUE=""" & i & """>" & Term & _
                "</OPTION>" & Chr(13) & Chr(10)
  Next

  ListGlossary = gTermList

End Function
```

When the form is processed it calls `DeleteTerm`, which references the term to be deleted by its node index. Add the following code for `DeleteTerm`:

```
Sub DeleteTerm(Term_ID)

   Dim strSourceFile

   strSourceFile = Request.ServerVariables("APPL_PHYSICAL_PATH") & _
                                      "\admin\settings.xml"

   Set objXML = Server.CreateObject("Microsoft.XMLDOM")

   objXML.load(strSourceFile)

   Set rootTerms = objXML.documentElement.selectSingleNode("glossary")

   rootTerms.removeChild(rootTerms.childNodes.item(Term_ID))

   objXML.save(strSourceFile)

   UpdateMessage = "<FONT FACE=""verdana"" SIZE=2 COLOR=#FF000>" & _
                   "LAST ACTION: Term successfully removed.</FONT><P>"

End Sub
```

After the procedure is processed, it sets our global variable `UpdateMessage` with some text to confirm success.

`CreateTerm` is a little simpler than `DeleteTerm`. It collects the form data, puts it into an XML-formatted string, and uses `appendchild` to add it to the `<glossary>` node of `settings.xml`. Type in the `CreateTerm` code:

```
Sub CreateTerm(Term,Definition)

   Dim strSourceFile, XMLnode

   XMLnode = "<term>" & Chr(13) & Chr(10) & Chr(9) & "<context>" & _
             Term & "</context>" & Chr(13) & Chr(10) & Chr(9) & _
             "<definition>" & Definition & "</definition>" & Chr(13) & _
             Chr(10) & "</term>"

   strSourceFile = Request.ServerVariables("APPL_PHYSICAL_PATH") & _
                                          "\admin\settings.xml"

   Set objXML = Server.CreateObject("Microsoft.XMLDOM")

   objXML.load(strSourceFile)

   Set rootTerms = objXML.documentElement.selectSingleNode("glossary")

   Set objXML2 = Server.CreateObject("Microsoft.XMLDOM")
   objXML2.loadXML(XMLnode)
   Set rootNewNode = objXML2.documentElement
```

```
        rootTerms.appendChild(rootNewNode)

        objXML.save(strSourceFile)

        UpdateMessage = "<FONT FACE=""verdana"" SIZE=2 COLOR=#00AA00>LAST " & _
                        "ACTION: Term successfully created.</FONT><P>"

    End Sub
```

Again `UpdateMessage` is used to notify the user of success.

More on the admin folder

You'll find that using these basic techniques you can create your own tools to edit other parts of `settings.xml`. That's not to mention that you can use `settings.xml` to store other types of site-related information.

One thing you will need, of course, is an index page of some type within the `admin` folder, to provide links to your administrative tools.

Putting it all together

Now that we've seen the components that make up the site in more detail, we'll briefly review the sample site structure outline we provided earlier in the chapter, just to clarify how all our pages can fit together:

Place settings.xml, settings_glossary.asp and settings_stories.asp in the admin folder. You should also create another very simple HTML document to act as the index for the folder. It should do nothing more than contain links to the files we just placed in the admin folder (except for settings.xml).

The storydisplay.asp page goes into the root directory of the Web site, along with navbar.asp and getvars.asp (the insert that converts our Application variables to local variables) – and of course, global.asa.

You should also create content pages for each of the sections of your publication you plan to have. Remember, they should match the information contained in the <navigation> element of settings.xml like below:

```
<navigation>
      <section>
            <name>Front</name>
            <url>default.asp</url>
            <description>A mixture of all the news.</description>
      </section>
      <section>
            <name>News</name>
            <url>news.asp</url>
            <description>Current news for the city.</description>
      </section>
      <section>
            <name>Sports</name>
            <url>sports.asp</url>
            <description>Sports news from around town.</description>
      </section>
      <section>
            <name>Society</name>
            <url>society.asp</url>
            <description>Gossip and rumors run wild.</description>
      </section>
      <section>
            <name>Information</name>
            <url>info.asp</url>
            <description>Mission statement.</description>
      </section>
</navigation>
```

Don't forget, you may design your section pages to look however you want, as long as they meet our minimum requirements outlined earlier:

- Contains a server-side include statement for headlines.asp
- Contains a <STYLE> block for the glossary mouseover effects as described earlier
- Contains a server-side include statement for navbar.asp (optional)
- Calls the ShowStory procedure
- Response.Write the global gTermList string AFTER calling ShowStory
- Calls ShowHeadlines (optional)

Each of these section pages (named `news.asp`, `sports.asp`, `society.asp` and `info.asp` in my example) should have a matching folder to contain the XML-formatted stories for that section. You also should create a folder called `artwork` for any pictures that might accompany stories.

Next, you'll need to create several stories based on our XML story template for each section:

```
<?xml version="1.0"?>

<story>

   <headline>December declared Programmer Appreciation Month</headline>

   <byline>By John Doe</byline>

   <dateline>November 15, 1999</dateline>

   <body>
         <blurb>
               <P ALIGN="justify">
                  This is a made-up story with no truth involved.
               </P>
         </blurb>
         <P ALIGN="justify">
            Another paragraph goes here…
         </P>
         <P ALIGN="justify">
            And another paragraph…
         </P>
         <P ALIGN="justify">
            And yet another paragraph…
         </P>
   </body>

   <artset>
           <art>
                <source>somenerdpicture.jpg</source>
                <caption>A caption about the nerd.</caption>
           </art>
   </artset>

</story>
```

Our site's muscle, `headlines.asp`, goes in the `_ScriptLibrary` folder in my example, but you may have other plans for it. Just don't forget to alter your server-side include statement to point to its correct location.

The front of your publication, whether it's named `default.asp` or `index.asp`, doesn't have to be limited to calling `ShowBlurbs`, `ShowHeadlines` and `ShowBriefs`. The front of an online publication typically holds a great deal more information than one of the inside sections. By the way, the minimum requirements to use these procedures are the same as for any of our section pages.

Now that all the key components are in place, you are ready to use `settings_glossary.asp` and `settings_stories.asp` to set the site into motion.

Summary

A lot goes into administering an online news publication, and while the components we built for this application certainly provide a well-grounded conceptual base from which to proceed, they don't nearly go far enough.

From here, you'll be able to apply your own ideas and creativity to the use of XML for an online publication. What about an XML-driven search engine for the site, or the five-day weather forecast? It seem like every news site has one of those. And, of course, what local news site is complete without a classified ad section?

Another thing to remember is that some of the techniques used in this chapter might run into performance problems on higher traffic sites, specifically the navigation bar. When designing this newspaper, I really had smaller to mid-size newspapers in mind, whose readership might generate 400-500 hits on a good day.

As for Extensible Stylesheet Language (XSL), it would have certainly done a nice job displaying stories and other content. It would have only required a couple of lines of code using Microsoft's proposed standard to transform entire XML documents into the desired layout. That's certainly better than scripting entire procedures to accomplish the same thing, like we did in this chapter.

The only problem is, the jury is still out on Microsoft's proposal. In fact, Microsoft's proposal could very well be lost altogether when the W3C better defines the XSL standard. Also, Microsoft's XSL language deserves an entire chapter to itself, certainly a great deal more than a few paragraphs attached to another subject.

All things considered, XML can be very useful when combined with ASP, and I think we're only being to see the practical applications of the marriage of these two technologies.

N
W

The ASP 3.0 Object Model

The ASP object model is made up of six objects. The following diagram shows conceptually how these objects relate to the client and the server, and the requests made by the client and the responses sent back to them from the server:

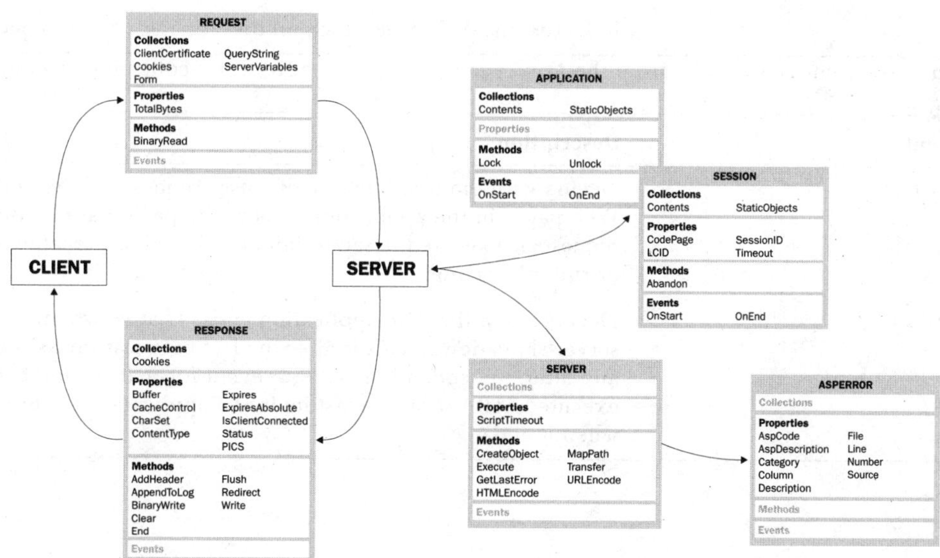

The Application Object

The Application object is created when the ASP DLL is loaded in response to the first request for an ASP page. It provides a repository for storing variables and object references that are available to all the pages that all visitors open.

Collection	Description
`Contents`	A collection of all of the variables and their values that are stored in the Application object, and are not defined using an `<OBJECT>` element. This includes Variant arrays and Variant-type object instance references.
`StaticObjects`	A collection of all of the variables that are stored in the Application object by using an `<OBJECT>` element.

Method	Description
`Contents.Remove ("`*variable_name*`")`	Removes a named variable from the `Application.Contents` collection.
`Contents.RemoveAll()`	Removes all variables from the `Application.Contents` collection.
`Lock()`	Locks the `Application` object so that only the current ASP page has access to the contents. Used to ensure that concurrency issues do not corrupt the contents by allowing two users to simultaneously read and update the values.
`Unlock()`	Releases this ASP page's lock on the `Application` object.

* You *cannot* remove variables from the `Application.StaticObjects` collection at run-time.

Event	Description
`onStart`	Occurs with the first instance of a user requesting one of the Web pages in the application, before the page that the user requests is executed. Used to initialize variables, create objects, or run other code.
`onEnd`	Occurs when the ASP application ends. That is, when the web server shuts down. This is after the last user session has ended, and after any code in the `onEnd` event for that session has executed. All variables existing in the application are destroyed when it ends.

The ASPError Object

The ASPError object is a new object in ASP 3.0, and is available through the `GetLastError` method of the Server object. It provides a range of detailed information about the last error that occurred in ASP.

Property	Description
`ASPCode`	*Integer*. The error number generated by IIS.
`ASPDescription`	*Integer*. A detailed description of the error if it is ASP-related.
`Category`	*String*. Indicates the source of the error. E.g. ASP itself, the scripting language, or an object.
`Column`	*Integer*. The character position within the file that generated the error.
`Description`	*String*. A short description of the error.
`File`	*String*. The name of the file that was being processed when the error occurred.
`Line`	*Integer*. The number of the line within the file that generated the error.
`Number`	*Integer*. A standard COM error code.
`Source`	*String*. The actual code, where available, of the line that caused the error.

The Request Object

The Request object makes available to the script all the information that the client provides when requesting a page, or submitting a form. This includes the HTTP server variables that identify the browser and the user, cookies that are stored on the browser for this domain, and any values appended to the URL as a query string or in HTML controls in a `<FORM>` section of the page. It also provides access to any certificate that may be being used through **Secure Sockets Layer** (SSL) or other encrypted communication protocol, and properties that help to manage the connection.

Collection	Description
`ClientCertificate`	A collection of the values of all the fields or entries in the client certificate that the user presented to our server when accessing a page or resource. Each member is read-only.
`Cookies`	A collection of the values of all the cookies sent from the user's system along with their request. Only cookies valid for the domain containing the resource are sent to the server.

Table Continued on Following Page

Collection	Description
`Form`	A collection of the values of all the HTML control elements in the `<FORM>` section that was submitted as the request, where the value of the `METHOD` attribute is `"POST"`. Each member is read-only.
`QueryString`	A collection of all the name/value pairs appended to the URL in the user's request, or the values of all the HTML control elements in the `<FORM>` section that was submitted as the request where the value of the `METHOD` attribute is `"GET"` or the attribute is omitted. Each member is read-only.
`ServerVariables`	A collection of all the HTTP header values sent from the client with their request, plus the values of several environment variables for the Web server. Each member is read-only.

Property	Description
`TotalBytes`	*Integer.* Read-only value holding the total number of bytes in the body of the request sent by the client.

Method	Description
`BinaryRead(`*count*`)`	Retrieves *count* bytes of data from the client's request when the data is sent to the server as part of a `POST` request. It returns as a `Variant` array (or `SafeArray`). This method *cannot* be used successfully if the ASP code has already referenced the `Request.Form` collection. Likewise, the `Request.Form` collection *cannot* be successfully accessed if you have used the `BinaryRead` method.

The Response Object

The Response object is used to access the response that is being created to send back to the client. It makes available the HTTP variables that identify the server and its capabilities, information about the content being sent to the browser, and any new cookies that will be stored on the browser for this domain. It also provides a series of methods that are used to create the returned page.

Collection	Description
`Cookies`	A collection containing the values of all the cookies that will be sent back to the client in the current response. Each member is write only.

Property	Description
`Buffer = True|False`	*Boolean.* Read/write. Specifies if the output created by an ASP page will be held in the IIS buffer until all of the server scripts in the current page have been processed, or until the `Flush` or `End` method is called. It must be set before any output is sent to IIS, including HTTP header information, so it should be the first line of the `.asp` file after the `<%@LANGUAGE=..%>` statement. Buffering is on (`True`) by default in ASP 3.0, whereas it was off (`False`) by default in earlier versions.
`CacheControl` "*setting*"	*String.* Read/write. Set this property to `"Public"` to allow proxy servers to cache the page, or `"Private"` to prevent proxy caching taking place.
`Charset =` "*value*"	*String.* Read/write. Appends the name of the character set (for example, `ISO-LATIN-7`) to the HTTP Content-Type header created by the server for each response.
`ContentType` "*MIME-type*"	*String.* Read/write. Specifies the HTTP content type for the response, as a standard MIME-type (such as "text/xml" or "image/gif"). If omitted, the MIME-type "text/html" is used. The content type tells the browser what type of content to expect.
`Expires` minutes	*Number.* Read/write. Specifies the length of time in minutes that a page is valid for. If the user returns to the same page before it expires, the cached version is displayed. After that period, it expires and should not be held in a private (user) or public (proxy) cache.
`ExpiresAbsolute` #*date[time]*#	*Date/Time.* Read/write. Specifies the absolute date and time when a page will expire and no longer be valid. If the user returns to the same page before it expires, the cached version is displayed. After that time, it expires and should not be held in a private (user) or public (proxy) cache.
`IsClientConnected`	*Boolean.* Read-only. Returns an indication of whether the client is still connected to and loading the page from the server. Can be used to end processing (with the `Response.End` method) if a client moves to another page before the current one has finished executing.

Table Continued on Following Page

Property	Description
`PICS ("PICS-label-string")`	*String*. Write only. Create a PICS header and adds it to the HTTP headers in the response. PICS headers define the content of the page in terms of violence, sex, bad language, etc.
`Status = "code message"`	*String*. Read/write. Specifies the status value and message that will be sent to the client in the HTTP headers of the response to indicate an error or successful processing of the page. For example `"200 OK"` and `"404 Not Found"`.

Method	Description
`AddHeader ("`*name*`", "`*content*`")`	Creates a custom HTTP header using the *name* and *content* values and adds it to the response. Will *not* replace an existing header of the same name. Once a header has been added, it cannot be removed. Must be used before any page content (i.e. text and HTML) is sent to the client.
`AppendToLog ("`*string*`")`	Adds a string to the end of the Web server log entry for this request when W3C Extended Log File Format is in use. Requires at least the URI Stem value to be selected in the Extended Properties page for the site containing the page.
`BinaryWrite (`*SafeArray*`)`	Writes the content of a `Variant`-type *SafeArray* to the current HTTP output stream without any character conversion. Useful for writing non-string information such as binary data required by a custom application or the bytes to make up an image file.
`Clear()`	Erases any existing buffered page content from the IIS response buffer when `Response.Buffer` is `True`. Does *not* erase HTTP response headers. Can be used to abort a partly completed page.
`End()`	Stops ASP from processing the page script and returns the currently created content, then aborts any further processing of this page.
`Flush()`	Sends all currently buffered page content in the IIS buffer to the client when `Response.Buffer` is `True`. Can be used to send parts of a long page to the client individually.
`Redirect ("`*url*`")`	Instructs the browser to load the page in the string *url* parameter by sending a `"302 Object Moved"` HTTP header in the response.
`Write ("`*string*`")`	Writes the specified *string* to the current HTTP response stream and IIS buffer so that it becomes part of the returned page.

The Server Object

The Server object provides a series of methods and properties that are useful in scripting with ASP. The most obvious is the `Server.CreateObject` method, which properly instantiates other COM objects within the context of the current page or session. There are also methods to translate strings into the correct format for use in URLs and in HTML, by converting non-legal characters to the correct legal equivalent.

Property	Description
`ScriptTimeout`	*Integer*. Has the default value 90. Sets or returns the number of seconds that script in the page can execute for before the server aborts page execution and reports an error. This automatically halts and removes from memory pages that contain errors that may lock execution into a loop or those that stall while waiting for a resource to become available. This prevents the server becoming overloaded with badly behaved pages. You may need to increase this value if your pages take a long time to run.

Method	Description
`CreateObject ("`*identifier*`")`	Creates an instance of the object (a component, application or scripting object) that is identified by "*identifier*", and returns a reference to it that can be used in our code. Can be used in the `global.asa` page of a virtual application to create objects with session-level or application-level scope. The object can be identified by its ClassID (i.e. `"{CLSID:FDC8-...-37A9}"`) value or by a ProgID string such as `"ADODB.Connection"`.
`Execute("`*url*`")`	Stops execution of the current page and transfers control to the page specified in "*url*". The user's current environment (i.e. session state and any current transaction state) is carried over to the new page. After that page has finished execution, control passes back to the original page and execution resumes at the statement after the `Execute` method call.
`GetLastError()`	Returns a reference to an `ASPError` object that holds details of the last error that occurred within the ASP processing, i.e. within `asp.dll`. The information exposed by the `ASPError` object includes the file name, line number, error code, etc.
`HTMLEncode("`*string*`")`	Returns a string that is a copy of the input value "*string*" but with all non-legal HTML characters such as '<', '>', '&' and double quotes converted into the equivalent HTML entity–i.e. <, >, &, ", etc.

Table Continued on Following Page

Method	Description
`MapPath("url")`	Returns the full physical path and filename of the file or resource specified in "*url*".
`Transfer("url")`	Stops execution of the current page and transfers control to the page specified in "*url*". The user's current environment (i.e. session state and any current transaction state) is carried over to the new page. Unlike the `Execute` method, execution *does not* resume in the original page, but ends when the new page has completed executing.
`URLEncode("string")`	Returns a string that is a copy of the input value "*string*" but with all characters that are not valid in a URL, such as '`?`', '`&`' and spaces, converted into the equivalent URL entity–i.e. '`%3F`', '`%26`', and '`+`'.

The Session Object

The Session object is created for each visitor when they first request an ASP page from the site, and remains available until the default timeout period (or the timeout period determined by the script) expires. It provides a repository for storing variables and object references that are available just to the pages that this visitor opens during the lifetime of this session.

Collection	Description
`Contents`	A collection of all the variables and their values that are stored in this particular `Session` object, and are *not* defined using an `<OBJECT>` element. This includes Variant arrays and Variant-type object instance references.
`StaticObjects`	A collection of all of the variables that are stored in this particular `Session` object by using an `<OBJECT>` element.

Property	Description
`CodePage`	*Integer.* Read/write. Defines the code page that will be used to display the page content in the browser. The code page is the numeric value of the character set, and different languages and locales may use different code pages. For example, ANSI code page 1252 is used for American English and most European languages. Code page 932 is used for Japanese Kanji.

Property	Description
LCID	*Integer.* Read/write. Defines the locale identifier (LCID) of the page that is sent to the browser. The LCID is a standard international abbreviation that uniquely identifies the locale; for instance 2057 defines a locale where the currency symbol used is '£'. This LCID can also be used in statements such as `FormatCurrency`, where there is an optional `LCID` argument. The LCID for a page can also be set in the opening `<%@..%>` ASP processing directive and overrides the setting in the `LCID` property of the session.
SessionID	*Long.* Read only. Returns the session identifier for this session, which is generated by the server when the session is created. Unique only for the duration of the parent `Application` object and so may be re-used when a new application is started.
Timeout	*Integer.* Read/write. Defines the timeout period in minutes for this `Session` object. If the user does not refresh or request a page within the timeout period, the session ends. Can be changed in individual pages as required. The default is 20 minutes, and shorter timeouts may be preferred on a high-usage site.

Method	Description
Contents.Remove ("*variable_name*")	Removes a named variable from the `Session.Contents` collection.
Contents.RemoveAll()	Removes all variables from the `Session.Contents` collection.
Abandon()	Ends the current user session and destroys the current `Session` object once execution of this page is complete. You can still access the current session's variables in this page, even after calling the `Abandon` method. However the next ASP page that is requested by this user will start a new session, and create a new `Session` object with only the default values defined in `global.asa` (if any exist).

* You *cannot* remove variables from the `Session.StaticObjects` collection at run-time.

Event	Description
onStart	Occurs when an ASP user session starts, before the first page that the user requests is executed. Used to initialize variables, create objects, or run other code.
onEnd	Occurs when an ASP user session ends. This is when the predetermined session timeout period has elapsed since that user's last page request from the application. All variables existing in the session are destroyed when it ends. It is also possible to end ASP user sessions explicitly in code, and this event occurs when that happens.

N
W

B

The Scripting Run-Time Library Objects

The default scripting languages installed with Windows 2000 and ASP 3.0 provide a scripting run-time library in the file `scrrun.dll`, which implements a series of objects that can be used in ASP on the server and in client-side code running on the client.

The Dictionary Object

The Dictionary object provides a useful storage object that we can use to store values, accessed and referenced by their name rather than by index as would be the case in a normal array. The properties and methods exposed by the Dictionary object are:

Property	Description
`CompareMode`	(*VBScript only*). Sets or returns the string comparison mode for the keys.
`Count`	Read only. Returns the number of key/item pairs in the Dictionary.
`Item(`***key***`)`	Sets or returns the value of the item for the specified key.
`Key(`***key***`)`	Sets or returns the value of a key.

Method	Description
`Add(`*key, item*`)`	Adds the key/item pair to the Dictionary.
`Exists(`*key*`)`	Returns `True` if the specified key exists or `False` if not.
`Items()`	Returns an array containing all the items in a Dictionary object.
`Keys()`	Returns an array containing all the keys in a Dictionary object.
`Remove(`*key*`)`	Removes a single key/item pair specified by *key*.
`RemoveAll()`	Removes all the key/item pairs.

* An error will occur if we try to add a key/item pair when that key already exists, remove a key/item pair that doesn't exist, or change the `CompareMode` of a Dictionary object that already contains data.

The FileSystemObject Object

The FileSystemObject object provides us with access to the underlying file system on the server (or on the client in IE5 when used in conjunction with a special type of page named a **Hypertext Application** or **HTA**). The FileSystemObject object exposes a series of properties and methods of its own, some of which return other objects that are specific to objects within the file system. These subsidiary objects are:

- The Drive object provides access to all the drives available on the machine
- The Folder object provides access to the folders on a drive
- The File object provides access to the files within each folder

While these three objects form a neat hierarchy, the FileSystemObject object also provides methods that can bridge the hierarchy by creating instances of the subsidiary objects directly. The diagram below shows the way that you can navigate the file system of the machine using the various objects:

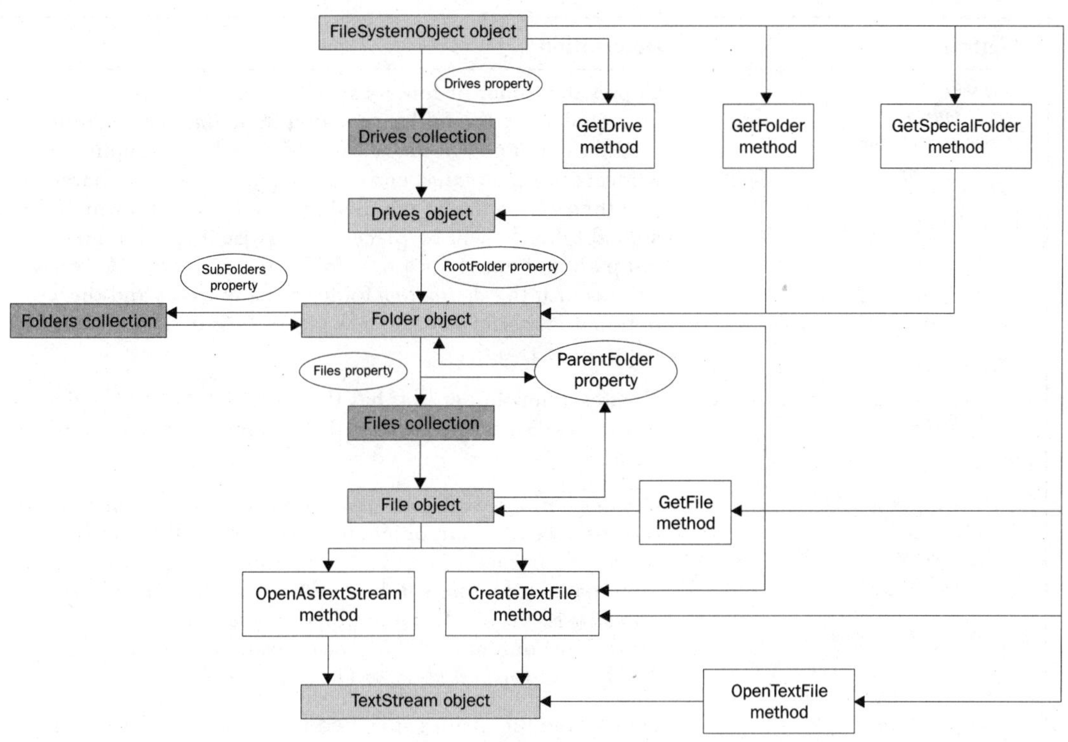

Property	Description
`Drives`	Returns a collection of `Drive` objects that are available from the local machine. This includes network drives that are mapped from this machine.

Method	Description
`BuildPath` (*path*, *name*)	Adds the file or folder specified in *name* to the existing *path*, adding a path separator character ('\') if required.
`CopyFile` (*source*, *destination*, *overwrite*)	Copies the file or files specified in *source* (wildcards can be included) to the folder specified in *destination*. If *source* contains wildcards or *destination* ends with a path separator character ('\') then *destination* is assumed to be a folder, otherwise it is assumed to be a full path and name for the new file. An error will occur if the *destination* file already exists and the optional *overwrite* parameter is set to `False`. The default for *overwrite* is `True`.

Table Continued on Following Page

Method	Description
`CopyFolder` (*source*, *destination*, *overwrite*)	Copies the folder or folders specified in *source* (wildcards can be included) to the folder specified in *destination*, including all the files contained in the *source* folder(s). If *source* contains wildcards or *destination* ends with a path separator character ('\') then *destination* is assumed to be a folder into which the copied folder(s) will be placed, otherwise it is assumed to be a full path and name for a new folder to be created. An error will occur if the *destination* folder already exists and the optional *overwrite* parameter is set to `False`. The default for *overwrite* is `True`.
`CreateFolder` (*foldername*)	Creates a new folder that has the path and name specified in *foldername*. An error occurs if the specified folder already exists.
`CreateTextFile` (*filename*, *overwrite*, *unicode*)	Creates a new text file on disk with the specified *filename* and returns a TextStream object that refers to it. If the optional *overwrite* parameter is set to `True` any existing file with the same path and name will be overwritten. The default for *overwrite* is `False`. If the optional *unicode* parameter is set to `True`, the content of the file will be stored as Unicoded text. The default for *unicode* is `False`.
`DeleteFile` (*filespec*, *force*)	Deletes the file or files specified in *filespec* (wildcards can be included). If the optional *force* parameter is set to `True` the file(s) will be deleted even if its read-only attribute is set. The default for *force* is `False`.
`DeleteFolder` (*folderspec*, *force*)	Deletes the folder or folders specified in *folderspec* (wildcards can be included in the final component of the path) together with all their contents. If the optional *force* parameter is set to `True`, the folders will be deleted even if their, or any contained files', read-only attribute is set. The default for *force* is `False`.
`DriveExists` (*drivespec*)	Returns `True` if the drive specified in *drivespec* exists, or `False` if not. The *drivespec* parameter can be a drive letter as a string or a full absolute path for a folder or file.
`FileExists` (*filespec*)	Returns `True` if the file specified in *filespec* exists, or `False` if not. The *filespec* parameter can contain an absolute or relative path for the file, or just the file name to look in the current folder.
`FolderExists` (*folderspec*)	Returns `True` if the folder specified in *folderspec* exists, or `False` if not. The *folderspec* parameter can contain an absolute or relative path for the folder, or just the folder name to look in the current folder.

Method	Description
`GetAbsolutePathName` (*pathspec*)	Takes a *path* that unambiguously identifies a folder and, taking into account the current folder's path, returns a full path specification for the *pathspec* folder. For example, if the current folder is "`c:\docs\sales\`" and *pathspec* is "`jan`" the returned value is "`c:\docs\sales\jan`". Wildcards and the "`..`" and "`\\`" path operators are accepted.
`GetBaseName` (*filespec*)	Returns just the name of a file specified in *filespec*, i.e. with the path and file extension removed.
`GetDrive` (*drivespec*)	Returns a Drive object corresponding to the drive specified in *drivespec*. The format for *drivespec* can include the colon, path separator or be a network share, i.e. "`c`", "`c:`", "`c:\`" or "`\\machine\sharename`".
`GetDriveName` (*drivespec*)	Returns the name of the drive specified in *drivespec* as a string. The *drivespec* parameter must be an absolute path to a file or folder, or just the drive letter such as "`c:`" or just "`c`".
`GetExtensionName` (*filespec*)	Returns just the file extension of a file specified in *filespec*, i.e. with the path and file name removed.
`GetFile` (*filespec*)	Returns a File object corresponding to the file specified in *filespec*. This can be a relative or absolute path to the required file.
`GetFileName` (*pathspec*)	Returns the name part of the path and filename specified in *pathspec*, or the last folder name of there is no file name. Does not check for existence of the file or folder.
`GetFolder` (*folderspec*)	Returns a Folder object corresponding to the folder specified in *folderspec*. This can be a relative or absolute path to the required folder.
`GetParentFolderName` (*pathspec*)	Returns the name of the parent folder of the file or folder specified in *pathspec*. Does not check for the existence of the folder.
`GetSpecialFolder` (*folderspec*)	Returns a Folder object corresponding to one of the special Windows folders. The permissible values for *folderspec* are `WindowsFolder` (0), `SystemFolder` (1) and `TemporaryFolder` (2).
`GetTempName` ()	Returns a randomly generated file name that can be used for performing operations that require a temporary file or folder.

Table Continued on Following Page

Method	Description
`MoveFile (`*source*`,` *destination*`)`	Moves the file or files specified in *source* to the folder specified in *destination.* Wildcards can be included in *source* but not in *destination.* If *source* contains wildcards or *destination* ends with a path separator character ('\') then *destination* is assumed to be a folder, otherwise it is assumed to be a full path and name for the new file. An error will occur if the *destination* file already exists.
`MoveFolder (`*source*`,` *destination*`)`	Moves the folder or folders specified in *source* to the folder specified in *destination.* Wildcards can be included in *source* but not in *destination.* If *source* contains wildcards or *destination* ends with a path separator character ('\') then *destination* is assumed to be the folder in which to place the moved folders, otherwise it is assumed to be a full path and name for a new folder. An error will occur if the *destination* folder already exists.
`OpenTextFile (`*filename*`,` *iomode*`,` *create*`,` *format*`)`	Creates a file named *filename*, or opens an existing file named *filename*, and returns a `TextStream` object that refers to it. The *filename* parameter can contain an absolute or relative path. The *iomode* parameter specifies the type of access required. The permissible values are `ForReading` (`1` - the default), `ForWriting` (`2`), and `ForAppending` (`8`). If the *create* parameter is set to `True` when writing or appending to a file that does not exist, a new file will be created. The default for *create* is `False`. The *format* parameter specifies the format of the data to be read from or written to the file. Permissible values are `TristateFalse` (`0`, the default) to open it as ASCII, `TristateTrue` (`-1`) to open it as Unicode, and `TristateUseDefault` (`-2`) to open it using the system default format.

The Drive Object

The Drive object provides access to all the drives available on the machine

Property	Description
`AvailableSpace`	Returns the amount of space available to this user on the drive, taking into account quotas and/or other restrictions.
`DriveLetter`	Returns the drive letter of the drive.
`DriveType`	Returns the type of the drive. The values are: `Unknown` (`0`), `Removable` (`1`), `Fixed` (`2`), `Network` (`3`), `CDRom` (`4`), and `RamDisk` (`5`). However, note that the current version of `scrrun.dll` does not include the pre-defined constant for `Network`, so you must use the decimal value `3` instead.

Method	Description
FileSystem	Returns the type of file system for the drive. The values include "FAT", "NTFS" and "CDFS".
FreeSpace	Returns the actual amount of free space available on the drive.
IsReady	Returns a Boolean value indicating if drive is ready (True) or not (False).
Path	Returns the path for the drive as a drive letter and colon, i.e. "C:".
RootFolder	Returns a Folder object representing the root folder of the drive.
SerialNumber	Returns a decimal serial number used to uniquely identify a disk volume.
ShareName	Returns the network share name for the drive if it is a networked drive.
TotalSize	Returns the total size (in bytes) of the drive.
VolumeName	Sets of returns the volume name of the drive if it is a local drive.

The Folder Object

The Folder object provides access to the folders on a drive

Property	Description
Attributes	Returns the attributes of the folder. Can be a combination of any of the values: Normal (0), ReadOnly (1), Hidden (2), System (4), Volume (name) (8), Directory (folder) (16), Archive (32), Alias (64) and Compressed (128).
DateCreated	Returns the date and time that the folder was created.
DateLastAccessed	Returns the date and time that the folder was last accessed.
DateLastModified	Returns the date and time that the folder was last modified.
Drive	Returns the drive letter of the drive on which the folder resides.
Files	Returns a Files collection containing File objects representing all the files within this folder.
IsRootFolder	Returns a Boolean value indicating if the folder is the root folder of the current drive.

Table Continued on Following Page

Property	Description
`Name`	Sets or returns the name of the folder.
`ParentFolder`	Returns the Folder object for the parent folder of this folder.
`Path`	Returns the absolute path of the folder using long file names where appropriate.
`ShortName`	Returns the DOS-style 8.3 version of the folder name.
`ShortPath`	Returns the DOS-style 8.3 version of the absolute path of this folder.
`Size`	Returns the size of all files and subfolders contained in the folder.
`SubFolders`	Returns a `Folders` collection consisting of all folders contained in the folder, including hidden and system folders.
`Type`	Returns a string that is a description of the folder type (such as "Recycle Bin") if available.

Method	Description
`Copy` (*destination*, *overwrite*)	Copies this folder and all its contents to the folder specified in *destination*, including all the files contained in this folder. If *destination* ends with a path separator character ('\') then *destination* is assumed to be a folder into which the copied folder will be placed, otherwise it is assumed to be a full path and name for a new folder to be created. An error will occur if the destination folder already exists and the optional *overwrite* parameter is set to `False`. The default for *overwrite* is `True`.
`CreateTextFile` (*filename*, *overwrite*, *unicode*)	Creates a new text file within this folder with the specified *filename* and returns a TextStream object that refers to it. If the optional *overwrite* parameter is set to `True` any existing file with the same name will be overwritten. The default for *overwrite* is `False`. If the optional *unicode* parameter is set to `True`, the content of the file will be stored as Unicoded text. The default for *unicode* is `False`.
`Delete` (*force*)	Deletes this folder and all its contents. If the optional *force* parameter is set to `True`, the folder will be deleted even if the read-only attribute is set on it or on any contained files. The default for *force* is `False`.
`Move` (*destination*)	Moves this folder and all its contents to the folder specified in destination. If *destination* ends with a path separator character ('\') then *destination* is assumed to be the folder in which to place the moved folder, otherwise it is assumed to be a full path and name for a new folder. An error will occur if the destination folder already exists.

The File Object

The File object provides access to the files within each folder

Property	Description
`Attributes`	Returns the attributes of the file. Can be a combination of any of the values: `Normal` (0), `ReadOnly` (1), `Hidden` (2), `System` (4), `Volume` (name) (8), `Directory` (folder) (16), `Archive` (32), `Alias` (64) and `Compressed` (128).
`DateCreated`	Returns the date and time that the file was created.
`DateLastAccessed`	Returns the date and time that the file was last accessed.
`DateLastModified`	Returns the date and time that the file was last modified.
`Drive`	Returns the drive letter of the drive on which the file resides.
`Name`	Sets or returns the name of the file.
`ParentFolder`	Returns the Folder object for the parent folder of this file.
`Path`	Returns the absolute path of the file using long file names where appropriate.
`ShortName`	Returns the DOS-style 8.3 version of the file name.
`ShortPath`	Returns the DOS-style 8.3 version of the absolute path of this file.
`Size`	Returns the size of the file in bytes
`Type`	Returns a string that is a description of the file type (such as "Text Document" for a `.txt` file) if available.

Method	Description
`Copy` (*destination*, *overwrite*)	Copies this file to the folder specified in *destination*. If *destination* ends with a path separator character ('\') then *destination* is assumed to be a folder into which the copied file will be placed, otherwise it is assumed to be a full path and name for a new file to be created. An error will occur if the destination file already exists and the optional *overwrite* parameter is set to `False`. The default for *overwrite* is `True`.
`CreateTextFile` (*filename*, *overwrite*, *unicode*)	Creates a new text file on disk with the specified *filename* and returns a `TextStream` object that refers to it. If the optional *overwrite* parameter is set to `True`, any existing file with the same path and name will be overwritten. The default for *overwrite* is `False`. If the optional *unicode* parameter is set to `True`, the content of the file will be stored as Unicoded text. The default for *unicode* is `False`.

Table Continued on Following Page

Method	Description
`Delete` (*force*)	Deletes this file. If the optional *force* parameter is set to `True` the file will be deleted even if the Read-only attribute is set. The default for *force* is `False`.
`Move (`*destination*`)`	Moves this file to the folder specified in *destination*. If *destination* ends with a path separator character ('\') then *destination* is assumed to be the folder in which to place the moved file, otherwise it is assumed to be a full path and name for a new file. An error will occur if the destination file already exists.
`OpenAsTextStream` (*iomode*, *format*)	Opens a specified file and returns a TextStream object that can be used to read from, write to, or append to the file. The *iomode* parameter specifies the type of access required. The permissible values are `ForReading` (`1` - the default), `ForWriting` (`2`), and `ForAppending` (`8`). The *format* parameter specifies the format of the data to be read from or written to the file. Permissible values are `TristateFalse` (`0`, the default) to open it as ASCII, `TristateTrue` (`-1`) to open it as Unicode, and `TristateUseDefault` (`-2`) to open it using the system default format.

The TextStream Object

The TextStream object provides access to files stored on disk, and is used in conjunction with the FileSystemObject object.

Property	Description
`AtEndOfLine`	Returns `True` if the file pointer is at the end of a line in the file.
`AtEndOfStream`	Returns `True` if the file pointer is at the end of the file.
`Column`	Returns the column number of the current character in the file starting from `1`.
`Line`	Returns the current line number in the file starting from `1`.

The `AtEndOfLine` and `AtEndOfStream` properties are only available for a file that is opened with `iomode` of `ForReading`. Referring to them otherwise causes an error to occur.

Method	Description
`Close()`	Closes an open file.
`Read(`*numchars*`)`	Reads *numchars* characters from the file.

Method	Description
`ReadAll()`	Reads the entire file as a single string.
`ReadLine()`	Reads a line from the file as a string.
`Skip(`*numchars*`)`	Skips and discards *numchars* characters when reading from the file.
`SkipLine()`	Skips and discards the next line when reading from the file.
`Write(`*string*`)`	Writes *string* to the file.
`WriteLine(`*string*`)`	Writes *string* (optional) and a newline character to the file.
`WriteBlankLines(`*n*`)`	Writes *n* newline characters to the file.

N
W

C

Microsoft Server Components

The AdRotator Component

This component can be found in `adrot.dll`. To create an instance of this component use a ProgID of `MSWC.AdRotator`.

Property	Type	Description
`Border`	SmallInt	Specifies the size of the advertisement border. Read/Write.
`Clickable`	Integer	Specifies whether the advertisement is a link. Read/Write
`TargetFrame`	String	The frame where the advertisement will be displayed. Read/Write

Method	Returns	Description
`GetAdvertisement`	String	Returns the next advertisement. Read-only.

The Content Linking Component

The Content Linker can be found in `nextlink.dll`. To create an instance of it use a ProgID of `MSWC.NextLink`.

Method	Returns	Description
`GetListCount`	Integer	The number of links in the listfile. Read only
`GetListIndex`	Integer	The position in the listfile of the current page. Read only
`GetNextDescription`	String	The description of the next link in the listfile. Read only
`GetNextURL`	String	The URL of the next link in the listfile. Read only
`GetNthDescription`	String	The description of the link at position *n* in the listfile. Read only
`GetNthURL`	String	The URL of the link at position *n* in the listfile. Read only
`GetPreviousDescription`	String	The description of the previous link in the listfile. Read only
`GetPreviousURL`	String	The URL of the previous link in the listfile. Read only

The Content Rotator Component

The Content Rotator can be found in `controt.dll`. To create an instance of it use a ProgID of `IISSample.ContentRotator`

Method	Returns	Description
`ChooseContent`	String	Gets one random entry from the content schedule file.
`GetAllContent`		Gets all entries from the content schedule file.

The Counters Component

The ProgID to create an instance of this component is `MSWC.Counters`. It can be found in `counters.dll`.

Method	Returns	Description
Get	Integer	Returns the value of a counter.
Increment	Integer	Increments the value of a counter by 1.
Remove		Removes a counter.
Set	Integer	Sets the value of a counter.

The Logging Utility Component

The ProgID for this component is MSWC.IISLog. It can be found in Logscrpt.dll.

Method	Returns	Description
AtEndOfLog	Boolean	Reveals if there any more records in the log files unread
CloseLogFiles	Long	All open log files are closed
OpenLogFiles		Open a log file for editing
ReadFilter		Filter records for a time and date
ReadLogRecord		Read the next available record in the log file
WriteLogRecord		Writes a record to the log file

Property	Description
BytesReceived	Returns the number of bytes received during the recorded action
BytesSent	Returns the number of bytes sent in the recorded action
ClientIP	Returns the IP address of the client for the recorded action
Cookie	Returns the client's cookie
CustomFields	Returns any extra HTTP headers included in the recorded operation
DateTime	Returns the date and time for the record
Method	Returns the HTTP operation type recorded
ProtocolStatus	Returns the HTTP protocol status for the HTTP operation recorded
ProtocolVersion	Returns the current record's protocol version string
Referer	Returns the referring URL
ServerIP	Returns the IP address of the server for the recorded action
ServerName	Returns the name of the computer for the recorded action
ServerPort	Returns the port number used in the action recorded
ServiceName	Returns the name of the service for the current record

Property	Description
TimeTaken	Returns the total processing time for the action recorded
URIQuery	Returns any HTTP request parameters passed
URIStem	Returns the target URL of the current record
UserAgent	Returns the browser agent user string
UserName	Returns the user name for non-anonymous clients involved for the current record
Win32Status	Returns theWin32 Status code

The MyInfo Component

The ProgID for this component is `MSWC.MyInfo`. Remember that you won't have to create an instance of it under PWS. The MyInfo component is found in `myinfo.dll`.

Property	Description
PageType	Returns a number corresponding to the value in the "This site is..." pop-up menu in the Personal Web Server control panel.
PersonalName	Returns the owner's name
PersonalAddress	Returns the owner's address
PersonalPhone	Returns the owner's phone number
PersonalMail	Returns the owner's e-mail address
PersonalWords	Returns additional text associated with the owner
CompanyName	Returns the name of the owner's company
CompanyAddress	Returns the address of the owner's company
CompanyPhone	Returns the phone number of the owner's company
CompanyDepartment	Returns the owner's department name
CompanyWords	Returns additional text associated with the owner's company
HomeOccupation	Returns the owner's occupation
HomePeople	Returns text listing the people the owner lives with
HomeWords	Returns additional text associated with the owner
SchoolName	Returns the name of the owner's school
SchoolAddress	Returns the address of the owner's school

Property	Description
`SchoolPhone`	Returns the phone number of the owner's school
`SchoolDepartment`	Returns the owner's department or class
`SchoolWords`	Returns text associated with the owner's school
`OrganizationName`	Returns the name of the organization featured on the site
`OrganizationAddress`	Returns the address of the organization
`OrganizationPhone`	Returns the phone number of the organization
`OrganizationWords`	Returns text describing the organization
`CommunityName`	Returns the name of the community featured on the site
`CommunityLocation`	Returns the location of the community
`CommunityPopulation`	Returns the population of the community
`CommunityWords`	Returns text describing the community
`URL`	Returns the Nth user-defined URL. Corresponds to the Nth link description in `URLWords`
`URLWords`	Returns string containing the Nth user-defined description of a link. Corresponds to the Nth URL in `URL`
`Style`	Returns the relative URL of a style sheet
`Background`	Returns the background for the site
`Title`	Returns the user-defined title for the home page
`Guestbook`	Returns –1 if the guest book should be available on the site. Otherwise returns 0
`Messages`	Returns –1 if the private message form should be available on the site. Otherwise returns 0

The Page Counter Component

The ProgID for this component is `IISSample.PageCounter`. It can be found in `pagecnt.dll`.

Method	Returns	Description
`Hits`	Integer	Returns the number of hits on a URL
`PageHit`	Integer	Increments the counter for a page by one
`Reset`		Resets the number of hits on a URL to 0

The Permission Checker Component

The ProgID for this component is `IISSample.PermissionChecker`. It can be found in `permchk.dll`.

Method	Returns	Description
`HasAccess`	Boolean	Check file access permission

The Tools Component

The ProgID for this component is `MSWC.Tools`. It can be found in `tools.dll`.

Method	Returns	Description
`FileExists`	Boolean	Checks if file exists or not.
`Owner`	Boolean	Checks if the current user is the owner of the site (*Macintosh only*).
`PluginExists`	Boolean	Checks the existence of a server plug-in (*Macintosh only*).
`ProcessForm`		Processes an HTML form.
`Random`	Integer	Generates a random integer.
`Test`	String	No extra description is available.

N
W

D

Error Codes

VBScript Error Codes

Syntax Errors

Syntax errors occur wherever your script contains statements that do not follow the pre-defined rules for that language. Note that this type of error should be caught during development. VBScript contains 53 syntax errors, listed below:

Decimal	Hexadecimal	Description
1001	800A03E9	Out of memory
1002	800A03EA	Syntax error
1003	800A03EB	Expected ':'
1005	800A03ED	Expected '('
1006	800A03EE	Expected ')'
1007	800A03EF	Expected ']'
1010	800A03F2	Expected identifier
1011	800A03F3	Expected '='
1012	800A03F4	Expected 'If'
1013	800A03F5	Expected 'To'

Decimal	Hexadecimal	Description
1014	800A03F6	Expected 'End'
1015	800A03F7	Expected 'Function'
1016	800A03F8	Expected 'Sub'
1017	800A03F9	Expected 'Then'
1018	800A03FA	Expected 'Wend'
1019	800A03FB	Expected 'Loop'
1020	800A03FC	Expected 'Next'
1021	800A03FD	Expected 'Case'
1022	800A03FE	Expected 'Select'
1023	800A03FF	Expected expression
1024	800A0400	Expected statement
1025	800A0401	Expected end of statement
1026	800A0402	Expected integer constant
1027	800A0403	Expected 'While' or 'Until'
1028	800A0404	Expected 'While', 'Until' or end of statement
1029	800A0405	Expected 'With'
1030	800A0406	Identifier too long
1031	800A0407	Invalid number
1032	800A0408	Invalid character
1033	800A0409	Unterminated string constant
1034	800A040A	Unterminated comment
1037	800A040D	Invalid use of 'Me' keyword
1038	800A040E	'loop' without 'do'
1039	800A040F	Invalid 'exit' statement
1040	800A0410	Invalid 'for' loop control variable
1041	800A0411	Name redefined
1042	800A0412	Must be first statement on the line
1043	800A0413	Cannot assign to non-ByVal argument
1044	800A0414	Cannot use parentheses when calling a Sub
1045	800A0415	Expected literal constant

Decimal	Hexadecimal	Description
1046	800A0416	Expected 'In'
1047	800A0417	Expected 'Class'
1048	800A0418	Must be defined inside a Class
1049	800A0419	Expected Let or Set or Get in property declaration
1050	800A041A	Expected 'Property'
1051	800A041B	Number of arguments must be consistent across properties specification
1052	800A041C	Cannot have multiple default property/method in a Class
1053	800A041D	Class initialize or terminate do not have arguments
1054	800A041E	Property set or let must have at least one argument
1055	800A041F	Unexpected 'Next'
1056	800A0420	'Default' can be specified only on 'Property' or 'Function' or 'Sub'
1057	800A0421	'Default' specification must also specify 'Public'
1058	800A0422	'Default' specification can only be on Property Get

Runtime Errors

Runtime errors occur wherever your script attempts to perform an invalid action. Note that the vast majority of these errors should be caught during the debugging and testing stage. VBScript contains 65 runtime errors, listed below:

Decimal	Hexadecimal	Description
5	800A0005	Invalid procedure call or argument
6	800A0006	Overflow
7	800A0007	Out of memory
9	800A0009	Subscript out of range
10	800A000A	This array is fixed or temporarily locked
11	800A000B	Division by zero
13	800A000D	Type mismatch
14	800A000E	Out of string space
17	800A0011	Can't perform requested operation
28	800A001C	Out of stack space

Decimal	Hexadecimal	Description
35	800A0023	Sub or Function not defined
48	800A0030	Error in loading DLL
51	800A0033	Internal error
52	800A0034	Bad file name or number
53	800A0035	File not found
54	800A0036	Bad file mode
55	800A0037	File already open
57	800A0039	Device I/O error
58	800A003A	File already exists
61	800A003D	Disk full
62	800A003E	Input past end of file
67	800A0043	Too many files
68	800A0044	Device unavailable
70	800A0046	Permission denied
71	800A0047	Disk not ready
74	800A004A	Can't rename with different drive
75	800A004B	Path/File access error
76	800A004C	Path not found
91	800A005B	Object variable not set
92	800A005C	For loop not initialized
94	800A005E	Invalid use of Null
322	800A0142	Can't create necessary temporary file
424	800A01A8	Object required
429	800A01AD	ActiveX component can't create object
430	800A01AE	Class doesn't support Automation
432	800A01B0	File name or class name not found during Automation operation
438	800A01B6	Object doesn't support this property or method
440	800A01B8	Automation error
445	800A01BD	Object doesn't support this action
446	800A01BE	Object doesn't support named arguments

Decimal	Hexadecimal	Description
447	800A01BF	Object doesn't support current locale setting
448	800A01C0	Named argument not found
449	800A01C1	Argument not optional
450	800A01C2	Wrong number of arguments or invalid property assignment
451	800A01C3	Object not a collection
453	800A01C5	Specified DLL function not found
455	800A01C7	Code resource lock error
457	800A01C9	This key is already associated with an element of this collection
458	800A01CA	Variable uses an Automation type not supported in VBScript
462	800A01CE	The remote server machine does not exist or is unavailable
481	800A01E1	Invalid picture
500	800A01F4	Variable is undefined
501	800A01F5	Illegal assignment
502	800A01F6	Object not safe for scripting
503	800A01F7	Object not safe for initializing
504	800A01F8	Object not safe for creating
505	800A01F9	Invalid or unqualified reference
506	800A01FA	Class not defined
5016	800A1398	Regular Expression object expected
5017	800A1399	Syntax error in regular expression
5018	800A139A	Unexpected quantifier
5019	800A139B	Expected ']' in regular expression
5020	800A139C	Expected ')' in regular expression
5021	800A139D	Invalid range in character set
32811	800A802B	Element not found

JScript Error Codes

Syntax Errors

Syntax errors occur wherever your script contains statements that do not follow the pre-defined rules for that language. Note that this type of error should be caught during development. JScript contains 32 syntax errors, listed below:

Number	Hexadecimal	Description
1001	800A03E9	Out of memory
1002	800A03EA	Syntax error
1003	800A03EB	Expected ':'
1004	800A03EC	Expected ';'
1005	800A03ED	Expected '('
1006	800A03EE	Expected ')'
1007	800A03EF	Expected ']'
1008	800A03F0	Expected '{'
1009	800A03F1	Expected '}'
1010	800A03F2	Expected identifier
1011	800A03F3	Expected '='
1012	800A03F4	Expected '/'
1013	800A03F5	Invalid number
1014	800A03F6	Invalid character
1015	800A03F7	Unterminated string constant
1016	800A03F8	Unterminated comment
1018	800A03FA	'return' statement outside of function
1019	800A03FB	Can't have 'break' outside of loop
1020	800A03FC	Can't have 'continue' outside of loop
1023	800A03FF	Expected hexadecimal digit
1024	800A0400	Expected 'while'
1025	800A0401	Label redefined
1026	800A0402	Label not found
1027	800A0403	'default' can only appear once in a 'switch' statement

Number	Hexadecimal	Description
1028	800A0404	Expected identifier or string
1029	800A0405	Expected '@end'
1030	800A0406	Conditional compilation is turned off
1031	800A0407	Expected constant
1032	800A0408	Expected '@'
1033	800A0409	Expected 'catch'
1034	800A040A	Expected 'var'
1035	800A040B	throw must be followed by an expression on the same source line

Runtime Errors

Runtime errors occur wherever your script attempts to perform an invalid action. Note that the vast majority of these errors should be caught during the debugging and testing stage. JScript contains 76 runtime errors, listed below:

Number	Hexadecimal	Description
5	800A0005	Invalid procedure call or argument
6	800A0006	Overflow
7	800A0007	Out of memory
9	800A0009	Subscript out of range
10	800A000A	This array is fixed or temporarily locked
11	800A000B	Division by zero
13	800A000D	Type mismatch
14	800A000E	Out of string space
17	800A0011	Can't perform requested operation
28	800A001C	Out of stack space
35	800A0023	Sub or Function not defined
48	800A0030	Error in loading DLL
51	800A0033	Internal error
52	800A0034	Bad file name or number
53	800A0035	File not found
54	800A0036	Bad file mode

Number	Hexadecimal	Description
55	800A0037	File already open
57	800A0039	Device I/O error
58	800A003A	File already exists
61	800A003D	Disk full
62	800A003E	Input past end of file
67	800A0043	Too many files
68	800A0044	Device unavailable
70	800A0046	Permission denied
71	800A0047	Disk not ready
74	800A004A	Can't rename with different drive
75	800A004B	Path/File access error
76	800A004C	Path not found
91	800A005B	Object variable or With block variable not set
92	800A005C	For loop not initialized
94	800A005E	Invalid use of Null
322	800A0142	Can't create necessary temporary file
424	800A01A8	Object required
429	800A01AD	Automation server can't create object
430	800A01AE	Class doesn't support Automation
432	800A01B0	File name or class name not found during Automation operation
438	800A01B6	Object doesn't support this property or method
440	800A01B8	Automation error
445	800A01BD	Object doesn't support this action
446	800A01BE	Object doesn't support named arguments
447	800A01BF	Object doesn't support current locale setting
448	800A01C0	Named argument not found
449	800A01C1	Argument not optional
450	800A01C2	Wrong number of arguments or invalid property assignment
451	800A01C3	Object not a collection
453	800A01C5	Specified DLL function not found

Number	Hexadecimal	Description
458	800A01CA	Variable uses an Automation type not supported in JScript
462	800A01CE	The remote server machine does not exist or is unavailable
501	800A01F5	Cannot assign to variable
502	800A01F6	Object not safe for scripting
503	800A01F7	Object not safe for initializing
504	800A01F8	Object not safe for creating
5000	800A1388	Cannot assign to 'this'
5001	800A1389	Number expected
5002	800A138A	Function expected
5003	800A138B	Cannot assign to a function result
5004	800A138C	Cannot index object
5005	800A138D	String expected
5006	800A138E	Date object expected
5007	800A138F	Object expected
5008	800A1390	Illegal assignment
5009	800A1391	Undefined identifier
5010	800A1392	Boolean expected
5011	800A1393	Can't execute code from a freed script
5012	800A1394	Object member expected
5013	800A1395	VBArray expected
5014	800A1396	JScript object expected
5015	800A1397	Enumerator object expected
5016	800A1398	Regular Expression object expected
5017	800A1399	Syntax error in regular expression
5018	800A139A	Unexpected quantifier
5019	800A139B	Expected ']' in regular expression
5020	800A139C	Expected ')' in regular expression
5021	800A139D	Invalid range in character set
5022	800A139E	Exception thrown and not caught
5023	800A139F	Function does not have a valid prototype object

ASP Error Codes Summary

For errors that involve a failure within the ASP DLL, the following are the common error codes that are returned. These are the codes you'll find in the `ASPCode` property of the ASPError object when an error of this type occurs:

Error Code	Error Message and Extended Information
ASP 0100	Out of memory. (Unable to allocate the required memory.)
ASP 0101	Unexpected error. (The function returned *exception_name.*)
ASP 0102	Expecting string input.
ASP 0103	Expecting numeric input.
ASP 0104	Operation not allowed.
ASP 0105	Index out of range. (An array index is out of range.)
ASP 0106	Type Mismatch. (A data type was encountered that cannot be handled.)
ASP 0107	Stack Overflow. (The quantity of data being processed is above the permitted limit.)
ASP 0115	Unexpected error. (A trappable error *exception_name* occurred in an external object. The script cannot continue running.)
ASP 0177	Server.CreateObject Failed. (Invalid ProgID.)
ASP 0190	Unexpected error. (A trappable error occurred while releasing an external object.)
ASP 0191	Unexpected error. (A trappable error occurred in the `OnStartPage` method of an external object.)
ASP 0192	Unexpected error. (A trappable error occurred in the `OnEndPage` method of an external object.)
ASP 0193	OnStartPage Failed. (An error occurred in the `OnStartPage` method of an external object.)
ASP 0194	OnEndPage Failed. (An error occurred in the `OnEndPage` method of an external object.)
ASP 0240	Script Engine Exception. (A script engine threw exception *exception_name* in *object_name* from *object_name.*)
ASP 0241	CreateObject Exception. (The `CreateObject` of *object_name* caused exception *exception_name.*)
ASP 0242	Query OnStartPage Interface Exception. (The querying object *object_name*'s `OnStartPage` or `OnEndPage` method caused exception *exception_name.*

HTTP 1.1 Header Codes

Code	Reason Phrase
Group 1: Information	
100	Continue
101	Switching Protocols
Group 2: Success	
200	OK
201	Created
202	Accepted
203	Non-Authoritative Information
204	No Content
205	Reset Content
206	Partial Content
Group 3: Redirection	
300	Multiple Choices
301	Moved Permanently
302	Moved Temporarily
303	See Other
304	Not Modified
305	Use Proxy

Code	Reason Phrase
Group 4: Client Error	
400	Bad Request
401	Unauthorized
402	Payment Required
403	Forbidden
404	Not Found
405	Method Not Allowed
406	Not Acceptable
407	Proxy Authentication Required
408	Request Time-out
409	Conflict
410	Gone
411	Length Required
412	Precondition Failed
413	Request Entity Too Large
414	Request-URI Too Large
415	Unsupported Media Type
Group 5: Server Error	
500	Internal Server Error
501	Not Implemented
502	Bad Gateway
503	Service Unavailable
504	Gateway Time-out
505	HTTP Version not supported

Client error and server error codes – with default explanations as provided by Microsoft Internet Information Server – are listed below:

Error Code	Short Text	Explanation
400	Bad Request	Due to malformed syntax, the request could not be understood by the server. The client should not repeat the request without modifications.
401.1	Unauthorized. Logon Failed	This error indicates that the credentials passed to the server do not match the credentials required to log on to the server. Please contact the Web server's administrator to verify that you have permission to access the requested resource.
401.2	Unauthorized: Logon Failed due to server configuration	This error indicates that the credentials passed to the server do not match the credentials required to log on to the server. This is usually caused by not sending the proper WWW-Authenticate header field. Please contact the Web server's administrator to verify that you have permission to access to requested resource.
401.3	Unauthorized: Unauthorized due to ACL on resource	This error indicates that the credentials passed by the client do not have access to the particular resource on the server. This resource could be either the page or file listed in the address line of the client, or it could be another file on the server that is needed to process the file listed on the address line of the client. Please make a note of the entire address you were trying to access and then contact the Web server's administrator to verify that you have permission to access the requested resource.
401.4	Unauthorized: Authorization failed by filter	This error indicates that the Web server has a filter program installed to verify users connecting to the server. The authentication used to connect to the server was denied access by this filter program. Please make a note of the entire address you were trying to access and then contact the Web server's administrator to verify that you have permission to access the requested resource.
401.5	Unauthorized: Authorization failed by ISAPI/CGI app	This error indicates that the address on the Web server you attempted to use has an ISAPI or CGI program installed that verifies user credentials before proceeding. The authentication used to connect to the server was denied access by this program. Please make a note of the entire address you were trying to access and then contact the Web server's administrator to verify that you have permission to access the requested resource.

Error Code	Short Text	Explanation
403.1	Forbidden: Execute Access Forbidden	This error can be caused if you try to execute a CGI, ISAPI, or other executable program from a directory that does not allow programs to be executed. Please contact the Web server's administrator if the problem persists.
403.2	Forbidden: Read Access Forbidden	This error can be caused if there is no default page available and directory browsing has not been enabled for the directory, or if you are trying to display an HTML page that resides in a directory marked for Execute or Script permissions only. Please contact the Web server's administrator if the problem persists.
403.3	Forbidden: Write Access Forbidden	This error can be caused if you attempt to upload to, or modify a file in, a directory that does not allow Write access. Please contact the Web server's administrator if the problem persists.
403.4	Forbidden: SSL required	This error indicates that the page you are trying to access is secured with Secure Sockets Layer (SSL). In order to view it, you need to enable SSL by typing "https://" at the beginning of the address you are attempting to reach. Please contact the Web server's administrator if the problem persists.
403.5	Forbidden: SSL 128 required	This error message indicates that the resource you are trying to access is secured with a 128-bit version of Secure Sockets Layer (SSL). In order to view this resource, you need a browser that supports this level of SSL. Please confirm that your browser supports 128-bit SSL security. If it does, then contact the Web server's administrator and report the problem.
403.6	Forbidden: IP address rejected	This error is caused when the server has a list of IP addresses that are not allowed to access the site, and the IP address you are using is in this list. Please contact the Web server's administrator if the problem persists.
403.7	Forbidden: Client certificate required	This error occurs when the resource you are attempting to access requires your browser to have a client Secure Sockets Layer (SSL) certificate that the server recognizes. This is used for authenticating you as a valid user of the resource. Please contact the Web server's administrator to obtain a valid client certificate.
403.8	Forbidden: Site access denied	This error can be caused if the Web server is not servicing requests, or if you do not have permission to connect to the site. Please contact the Web server's administrator.

Error Code	Short Text	Explanation
403.9	Access Forbidden: Too many users are connected	This error can be caused if the Web server is busy and cannot process your request due to heavy traffic. Please try to connect again later. Please contact the Web server's administrator if the problem persists.
403.10	Access Forbidden: Invalid Configuration	There is a configuration problem on the Web server at this time. Please contact the Web server's administrator if the problem persists.
403.11	Access Forbidden: Password Change	This error can be caused if the user has entered the wrong password during authentication. Please refresh the page and try again. Please contact the Web server's administrator if the problem persists.
403.12	Access Forbidden: Mapper Denied Access	Your client certificate map has been denied access to this Web site. Please contact the site administrator to establish client certificate permissions. You can also change your client certificate and retry, if appropriate.
404	Not Found	The Web server cannot find the file or script you asked for. Please check the URL to ensure that the path is correct. Please contact the server's administrator if this problem persists.
405	Method Not Allowed	The method specified in the Request Line is not allowed for the resource identified by the request. Please ensure that you have the proper MIME type set up for the resource you are requesting. Please contact the server's administrator if this problem persists.
406	Not Acceptable	The resource identified by the request can only generate response entities that have content characteristics that are "not acceptable" according to the Accept headers sent in the request. Please contact the server's administrator if this problem persists.
407	Proxy Authentication Required	You must authenticate with a proxy server before this request can be serviced. Please log on to your proxy server, and then try again. Please contact the Web server's administrator if this problem persists.
412	Precondition Failed	The precondition given in one or more of the Request-header fields evaluated to FALSE when it was tested on the server. The client placed preconditions on the current resource meta-information (header field data) to prevent the requested method from being applied to a resource other than the one intended. Please contact the Web server's administrator if the problem persists.

Error Code	Short Text	Explanation
414	Request-URI Too Long	The server is refusing to service the request because the Request-URI is too long. This rare condition is likely to occur only in the following situations: ❑ A client has improperly converted a POST request to a GET request with long query information. ❑ A client has encountered a redirection problem (for example, a redirected URL prefix that points to a suffix of itself). ❑ The server is under attack by a client attempting to exploit security holes present in some servers using fixed-length buffers for reading or manipulating the Request-URI. Please contact the Web server's administrator if this problem persists.
500	Internal Server Error	The Web server is incapable of performing the request. Please try your request again later. Please contact the Web server's administrator if this problem persists.
501	Not Implemented	The Web server does not support the functionality required to fulfill the request. Please check your URL for errors, and contact the Web server's administrator if the problem persists.
502	Bad Gateway	The server, while acting as a gateway or proxy, received an invalid response from the upstream server it accessed in attempting to fulfill the request. Please contact the Web server's administrator if the problem persists.

Note that Server error message files are placed in `HELP\COMMON` folder of Windows or Windows NT.

ADO Error Codes

The following table lists the standard errors than might get returned from ADO operations.

Constant Name	Number	Description
adErrBoundToCommand	3707	The application cannot change the `ActiveConnection` property of a `Recordset` object with a `Command` object as its source.
adErrCannotComplete	3732	The action could not be completed.
adErrCantChangeConnection	3748	The connection cannot be changed.

Constant Name	Number	Description
adErrCantChangeProvider	3220	The provider cannot be changed.
adErrCantConvertvalue	3724	The value cannot be converted.
adErrCantCreate	3725	The resource cannot be created.
adErrCatalogNotSet	3747	The action could not be completed because the catalog is not set.
adErrColumnNotOnThisRow	3726	The specified column doesn't exist on this row.
adErrDataConversion	3421	The application is using a value of the wrong type for the current application.
adErrDataOverflow	3721	The data was too large for the supplied data type.
adErrDelResOutOfScope	3738	The resource cannot be deleted because it is out of the allowed scope.
adErrDenyNotSupported	3750	You cannot set Deny permissions because the provider does not support them.
adErrDenyTypeNotSupported	3751	The provider does not support the type of Deny requested.
adErrFeatureNotAvailable	3251	The provider does not support the operation requested by the application.
adErrFieldsUpdateFailed	3749	The `Update` method of the Fields collection failed.
adErrIllegalOperation	3219	The operation requested by the application is not allowed in this context.
adErrIntegrityViolation	3719	The action failed due to a violation of data integrity.
adErrInTransaction	3246	The application cannot explicitly close a `Connection` object while in the middle of a transaction.
adErrInvalidArgument	3001	The application is using arguments that are the wrong type, are out of the acceptable range, or are in conflict with one another.
adErrInvalidConnection	3709	The application requested an operation on an object with a reference to a closed or invalid `Connection` object.
adErrInvalidParamInfo	3708	The application has improperly defined a `Parameter` object.
adErrInvalidTransaction	3714	The transaction is invalid.

Constant Name	Number	Description
adErrInvalidURL	3729	The supplied URL is invalid.
adErrItemNotFound	3265	ADO could not find the object in the collection.
adErrNoCurrentRecord	3021	Either `BOF` or `EOF` is `True`, or the current record has been deleted. The operation requested by the application requires a current record.
adErrNotExecuting	3715	The operation is not executing.
adErrNotReentrant	3710	The operation is not reentrant.
adErrObjectClosed	3704	The operation requested by the application is not allowed if the object is closed.
adErrObjectInCollection	3367	Can't append. Object already in collection.
adErrObjectNotSet	3420	The object referenced by the application no longer points to a valid object.
adErrObjectOpen	3705	The operation requested by the application is not allowed if the object is open.
adErrOpeningFile	3002	An error occurred whilst opening the requested file.
adErrOperationCancelled	3712	The operation was cancelled.
adErrOutOfSpace	3734	The operation failed because the server could not obtain enough space to complete the operation.
adErrPermissionDenied	3720	The action failed because you do not have sufficient permission to complete the operation.
adErrPropConflicting	3742	Setting this property caused a conflict with other properties.
adErrPropInvalidColumn	3739	This property is invalid for the selected column.
adErrPropInvalidOption	3740	You have supplied an invalid option for this property.
adErrPropInvalidValue	3741	You have supplied an invalid value for this property.
adErrPropNotAllSettable	3743	Not all properties can be set.
adErrPropNotSet	3744	The property was not set.
adErrPropNotSettable	3745	The property cannot be set.
adErrPropNotSupported	3746	The property is not supported.

Constant Name	Number	Description
adErrProviderFailed	3000	The provider failed to complete the requested action. *
adErrProviderNotFound	3706	ADO could not find the specified provider.
adErrReadFile	3003	There was an error reading from the specified file.
adErrResourceExists	3731	The resource already exists.
adErrResourceLocked	3730	The resource is locked.
adErrResourceOutOfScope	3735	The resource is out of scope.
adErrSchemaViolation	3722	The action caused a violation of the schema.
adErrSignMismatch	3723	The expression contained mismatched signs.
adErrStillConnecting	3713	The operation is still connecting.
adErrStillExecuting	3711	The operation is still executing.
adErrTreePermissionDenied	3728	You do not have permission to view the directory tree.
adErrUnavailable	3736	The command is unavailable.
adErrUnsafeOperation	3716	The operation is unsafe under these circumstances.
adErrURLDoesNotExist	3727	The URL does not exist.
adErrURLNamedRowDoes NotExist	3737	The URL in the named row does not exists.
adErrVolumeNotFound	3733	The file volume was not found.
adErrWriteFile	3004	There was an error whilst writing to the file.
adwrnSecurityDialog	3717	The operation caused a security dialog to appear.
adwrnSecurityDialogHeader	3718	The operation caused a security dialog header to appear.

The following lists the extended ADO errors and their descriptions:

Error Number	Description
-2147483647	Not implemented.
-2147483646	Ran out of memory.
-2147483645	One or more arguments are invalid.

Error Number	Description
-2147483644	No such interface supported.
-2147483643	Invalid pointer.
-2147483642	Invalid handle.
-2147483641	Operation aborted.
-2147483640	Unspecified error.
-2147483639	General access denied error.
-2147483638	The data necessary to complete this operation is not yet available.
-2147467263	Not implemented.
-2147467262	No such interface supported.
-2147467261	Invalid pointer.
-2147467260	Operation aborted.
-2147467259	Unspecified error.
-2147467258	Thread local storage failure.
-2147467257	Get shared memory allocator failure.
-2147467256	Get memory allocator failure.
-2147467255	Unable to initialize class cache.
-2147467254	Unable to initialize RPC services.
-2147467253	Cannot set thread local storage channel control.
-2147467252	Could not allocate thread local storage channel control.
-2147467251	The user supplied memory allocator is unacceptable.
-2147467250	The OLE service mutex already exists.
-2147467249	The OLE service file mapping already exists.
-2147467248	Unable to map view of file for OLE service.
-2147467247	Failure attempting to launch OLE service.
-2147467246	There was an attempt to call `CoInitialize` a second time while single threaded.
-2147467245	A Remote activation was necessary but was not allowed.
-2147467244	A Remote activation was necessary but the server name provided was invalid.
-2147467243	The class is configured to run as a security id different from the caller.
-2147467242	Use of OLE1 services requiring DDE windows is disabled.

Error Number	Description
-2147467241	A `RunAs` specification must be `<domain name>\<user name>` or simply `<user name>`.
-2147467240	The server process could not be started. The pathname may be incorrect.
-2147467239	The server process could not be started as the configured identity. The pathname may be incorrect or unavailable.
-2147467238	The server process could not be started because the configured identity is incorrect. Check the username and password.
-2147467237	The client is not allowed to launch this server.
-2147467236	The service providing this server could not be started.
-2147467235	This computer was unable to communicate with the computer providing the server.
-2147467234	The server did not respond after being launched.
-2147467233	The registration information for this server is inconsistent or incomplete.
-2147467232	The registration information for this interface is inconsistent or incomplete.
-2147467231	The operation attempted is not supported.
-2147418113	Catastrophic failure.
-2147024891	General access denied error.
-2147024890	Invalid handle.
-2147024882	Ran out of memory.
-2147024809	One or more arguments are invalid.

N
W

The ADO 2.5 Object Model

Properties or methods new to version 2.5 are shown *italicized.*

All properties are read/write unless otherwise stated.

The ADO Objects

Name	*Description*
`Command`	A Command object is a definition of a specific command that you intend to execute against a data source.
`Connection`	A Connection object represents an open connection to a data store.
`Error`	An Error object contains the details about data access errors pertaining to a single operation involving the provider.
`Errors`	The Errors collection contains all of the Error objects created in response to a single failure involving the provider.
`Field`	A Field object represents a column of data within a common data type.
`Fields`	A Fields collection contains all of the Field objects of a Recordset object.

Table Continued on Following Page

Name	*Description*
`Parameter`	A Parameter object represents a parameter or argument associated with a Command object based on a parameterized query or stored procedure.
`Parameters`	A Parameters collection contains all the Parameter objects of a Command object.
`Properties`	A Properties collection contains all the Property objects for a specific instance of an object.
`Property`	A Property object represents a dynamic characteristic of an ADO object that is defined by the provider.
`Record`	A Record object represents a row in a recordset, or a file or directory in a file system or Web resource.
`Recordset`	A Recordset object represents the entire set of records from a base table or the results of an executed command. At any time, the Recordset object only refers to a single record within the set as the current record.
Stream	A Stream object represents a stream of text or binary data.

The Command Object

Method	*Returns*	*Description*
`Cancel`		Cancels execution of a pending `Execute` or `Open` call.
`CreateParameter`	Parameter	Creates a new `Parameter` object.
`Execute`	Recordset	Executes the query, SQL statement, or stored procedure specified in the `CommandText` property.

Property	*Returns*	*Description*
`ActiveConnection`	Variant	Indicates to which Connection object the command currently belongs.
`CommandText`	String	Contains the text of a command to be issued against a data provider.
`CommandTimeout`	Long	Indicates how long to wait, in seconds, while executing a command before terminating the command and generating an error. Default is 30.

Property	*Returns*	*Description*
`CommandType`	CommandType Enum	Indicates the type of Command object.
`Name`	String	Indicates the name of the Command object.
`Parameters`	Parameters	Contains all of the Parameter objects for a Command object.
`Prepared`	Boolean	Indicates whether or not to save a compiled version of a command before execution.
`Properties`	Properties	Contains all of the Property objects for a Command object.
`State`	Long	Describes whether the Command object is open or closed. Read only.

The Connection Object

Method	*Returns*	*Description*
`BeginTrans`	Integer	Begins a new transaction.
`Cancel`		Cancels the execution of a pending, asynchronous `Execute` or `Open` operation.
`Close`		Closes an open connection and any dependant objects.
`CommitTrans`		Saves any changes and ends the current transaction.
`Execute`	Recordset	Executes the query, SQL statement, stored procedure, or provider specific text.
`Open`		Opens a connection to a data source, so that commands can be executed against it.
`OpenSchema`	Recordset	Obtains database schema information from the provider.
`RollbackTrans`		Cancels any changes made during the current transaction and ends the transaction.

Property	*Returns*	*Description*
`Attributes`	Long	Indicates one or more characteristics of a Connection object. Default is 0.
`CommandTimeout`	Long	Indicates how long, in seconds, to wait while executing a command before terminating the command and generating an error. The default is 30.
`ConnectionString`	String	Contains the information used to establish a connection to a data source.
`ConnectionTimeout`	Long	Indicates how long, in seconds, to wait while establishing a connection before terminating the attempt and generating an error. Default is 15.
`CursorLocation`	CursorLocation Enum	Sets or returns the location of the cursor engine.
`DefaultDatabase`	String	Indicates the default database for a Connection object.
`Errors`	Errors	Contains all of the Error objects created in response to a single failure involving the provider.
`IsolationLevel`	IsolationLevel Enum	Indicates the level of transaction isolation for a Connection object. Write only.
`Mode`	ConnectMode Enum	Indicates the available permissions for modifying data in a Connection.
`Properties`	Properties	Contains all of the `Property` objects for a Connection object.
`Provider`	String	Indicates the name of the provider for a Connection object.
`State`	Long	Describes whether the Connection object is open or closed. Read only.
`Version`	String	Indicates the ADO version number. Read only.

Event	*Description*
`BeginTransComplete`	Fired after a `BeginTrans` operation finishes executing.
`CommitTransComplete`	Fired after a `CommitTrans` operation finishes executing.

Event	*Description*
`ConnectComplete`	Fired after a connection starts.
`Disconnect`	Fired after a connection ends.
`ExecuteComplete`	Fired after a command has finished executing.
`InfoMessage`	Fired whenever a `ConnectionEvent` operation completes successfully and additional information is returned by the provider.
`RollbackTransComplete`	Fired after a `RollbackTrans` operation finished executing.
`WillConnect`	Fired before a connection starts.
`WillExecute`	Fired before a pending command executes on the connection.

The Error Object

Property	*Returns*	*Description*
`Description`	String	A description string associated with the error. Read only.
`HelpContext`	Integer	Indicates the `ContextID` in the help file for the associated error. Read only.
`HelpFile`	String	Indicates the name of the help file. Read only.
`NativeError`	Long	Indicates the provider-specific error code for the associated error. Read only.
`Number`	Long	Indicates the number that uniquely identifies an `Error` object. Read only.
`Source`	String	Indicates the name of the object or application that originally generated the error. Read only.
`SQLState`	String	Indicates the SQL state for a given Error object. It is a five-character string that follows the ANSI SQL standard. Read only.

The Errors Collection

Method	*Returns*	*Description*
`Clear`		Removes all of the Error objects from the `Errors` collection.
`Refresh`		Updates the Error objects with information from the provider.

Property	*Returns*	*Description*
`Count`	Long	Indicates the number of Error objects in the Errors collection. Read only.
`Item`	Error	Allows indexing into the Errors collection to reference a specific Error object. Read only.

Field Object

Method	*Returns*	*Description*
`AppendChunk`		Appends data to a large or binary Field object.
`GetChunk`	Variant	Returns all or a portion of the contents of a large or binary Field object.

Property	*Returns*	*Description*
`ActualSize`	Long	Indicates the actual length of a field's value. Read only.
`Attributes`	Long	Indicates one or more characteristics of a Field object.
`DataFormat`	Variant	Identifies the format that the data should be display in.
`DefinedSize`	Long	Indicates the defined size of the Field object. Write only.
`Name`	String	Indicates the name of the Field object.
`NumericScale`	Byte	Indicates the scale of numeric values for the Field object. Write only.

Property	Returns	Description
OriginalValue	Variant	Indicates the value of a Field object that existed in the record before any changes were made. Read only.
Precision	Byte	Indicates the degree of precision for numeric values in the Field object. Read only.
Properties	Properties	Contains all of the Property objects for a Field object.
Type	DataType Enum	Indicates the data type of the Field object.
UnderlyingValue	Variant	Indicates a Field object's current value in the database. Read only.
Value	Variant	Indicates the value assigned to the Field object.

The Fields Collection

Method	Returns	Description
Append		Appends a Field object to the Fields collection.
CancelUpdate		Cancels any changes made to the Fields collection.
Delete		Deletes a Field object from the Fields collection.
Refresh		Updates the Field objects in the Fields collection.
Resync		Resynchronizes the data in the Field objects.
Update		Saves any changes made to the Fields collection.

Property	Returns	Description
Count	Long	Indicates the number of Field objects in the Fields collection. Read only.
Item	Field	Allows indexing into the Fields collection to reference a specific Field object. Read only.

The Parameter Object

Methods

Name	*Returns*	*Description*
`AppendChunk`		Appends data to a large or binary Parameter object.

Properties

Name	*Returns*	*Description*
`Attributes`	Long	Indicates one or more characteristics of a Parameter object.
`Direction`	ParameterDirection Enum	Indicates whether the Parameter object represents an input parameter, an output parameter, or both, or if the parameter is a return value from a stored procedure.
`Name`	String	Indicates the name of the Parameter object.
`NumericScale`	Byte	Indicates the scale of numeric values for the Parameter object.
`Precision`	Byte	Indicates the degree of precision for numeric values in the Parameter object.
`Properties`	Properties	Contains all of the Property objects for a Parameter object.
`Size`	Long	Indicates the maximum size, in bytes or characters, of a Parameter object.
`Type`	DataTypeEnum	Indicates the data type of the Parameter object.
`Value`	Variant	Indicates the value assigned to the Parameter object.

The Parameters Collection

Methods

Name	*Returns*	*Description*
`Append`		Appends a Parameter object to the Parameters collection.
`Delete`		Deletes a Parameter object from the Parameters collection.
`Refresh`		Updates the Parameter objects in the Parameters collection.

Property	*Returns*	*Description*
`Count`	Long	Indicates the number of Parameter objects in the Parameters collection. Read only.
`Item`	Parameter	Allows indexing into the Parameters collection to reference a specific Parameter object. Read only.

The Properties Collection

Method	*Returns*	*Description*
`Refresh`		Updates the Property objects in the Properties collection with the details from the provider.

Property	*Returns*	*Description*
`Count`	Long	Indicates the number of Property objects in the Properties collection. Read only.
`Item`	Property	Allows indexing into the Properties collection to reference a specific Property object. Read only.

The Property Object

Property	*Returns*	*Description*
`Attributes`	Long	Indicates one or more characteristics of a Property object.
`Name`	String	Indicates the name of the Property object. Read only.
`Type`	DataType Enum	Indicates the data type of the Property object.
`Value`	Variant	Indicates the value assigned to the Property object.

The Record Object

Method	*Returns*	*Description*
Cancel		Cancels the execution of an asynchronous `Execute` or `Open` operation.
Close		Closes the open record.
CopyRecord	String	Copies the object the Record represents, or a file or directory, from one location to another.
DeleteRecord		Deletes the object the Record represents, or a file or directory.
GetChildren	Recordset	Returns a Recordset containing the files and folders in the directory that the Record represents.
MoveRecord	String	Moves the object the Record represents, or a file or directory, from one location to another.
Open		Creates a new, or opens an existing file or directory.

Property	*Returns*	*Description*
ActiveConnection	Variant	Indicates to which Connection object the specified Recordset object currently belongs.
Fields	Fields	Contains all of the Field objects for the current Recordset object. Read only.
Mode	ConnectMode Enum	Indicates the available permissions for modifying data in a Connection.
ParentURL	String	Indicates the absolute URL of the parent Record of the current Record. Read only.
Properties	Properties	Contains all of the Property objects for the current Recordset object. Read only.
RecordType	RecordType Enum	Indicates whether the record is a simple record, a structured document, or a collection. Read only.
Source	Variant	Indicates what the Record represents – a URL or a reference to an open Recordset.
State	ObjectState Enum	Indicates whether the Record is open or closed, and if open, the state of asynchronous actions. Read only.

The Recordset Object

Method	*Returns*	*Description*
`AddNew`		Creates a new record for an updateable Recordset object.
`Cancel`		Cancels execution of a pending asynchronous `Open` operation.
`CancelBatch`		Cancels a pending batch update.
`CancelUpdate`		Cancels any changes made to the current record, or to a new record prior to calling the `Update` method.
`Clone`	Recordset	Creates a duplicate Recordset object from and existing Recordset object.
`Close`		Closes the Recordset object and any dependent objects.
`CompareBookmarks`	Compare Enum	Compares two bookmarks and returns an indication of the relative values.
`Delete`		Deletes the current record or group of records.
`Find`		Searches the Recordset for a record that matches the specified criteria.
`GetRows`	Variant	Retrieves multiple records of a Recordset object into an array.
`GetString`	String	Returns a Recordset as a string.
`Move`		Moves the recordset cursor to point at a Recordset.
`MoveFirst`		Moves the recordset cursor to point at the first record in the Recordset.
`MoveLast`		Moves the recordset cursor to point at the last record in the Recordset.
`MoveNext`		Moves the recordset cursor to point at the next record in the Recordset.
`MovePrevious`		Moves the recordset cursor to point at the previous record in the Recordset.
`NextRecordset`	Recordset	Clears the current Recordset object and returns the next Recordset by advancing through a series of commands.

Table Continued on Following Page

Method	*Returns*	*Description*
`Open`		Opens a Recordset.
`Requery`		Updates the data in a Recordset object by re-executing the query on which the object is based.
`Resync`		Refreshes the data in the current Recordset object from the underlying database.
`Save`		Saves the Recordset to a file.
`Seek`		Searches the recordset index to locate a value
`Supports`	Boolean	Determines whether a specified Recordset object supports particular functionality.
`Update`		Saves any changes made to the current Recordset object.
`UpdateBatch`		Writes all pending batch updates to disk.

Property	*Returns*	*Description*
`AbsolutePage`	PositionEnum	Specifies in which page the current record resides.
`AbsolutePosition`	PositionEnum	Specifies the ordinal position of a Recordset object's current record.
`ActiveCommand`	Object	Indicates the Command object that created the associated Recordset object. Read only.
`ActiveConnection`	Variant	Indicates to which Connection object the specified Recordset object currently belongs.
`BOF`	Boolean	Indicates whether the current record is before the first record in a Recordset object. Read only.
`Bookmark`	Variant	Returns a bookmark that uniquely identifies the current record in a Recordset object, or sets the current record to the record identified by a valid bookmark.
`CacheSize`	Long	Indicates the number of records from a Recordset object that are cached locally in memory.
`CursorLocation`	CursorLocation Enum	Sets or returns the location of the cursor engine.
`CursorType`	CursorType Enum	Indicates the type of cursor used in a Recordset object.

Property	*Returns*	*Description*
`DataMember`	String	Specifies the name of the data member to retrieve from the object referenced by the DataSource property. Write only.
`DataSource`	Object	Specifies an object containing data to be represented as a Recordset object. Write only.
`EditMode`	EditModeEnum	Indicates the editing status of the current record. Read only.
`EOF`	Boolean	Indicates whether the current record is after the last record in a Recordset object. Read only.
`Fields`	Fields	Contains all of the Field objects for the current Recordset object.
`Filter`	Variant	Indicates a filter for data in the Recordset.
`Index`	String	Identifies the name of the index currently being used.
`LockType`	LockTypeEnum	Indicates the type of locks placed on records during editing.
`MarshalOptions`	MarshalOptions Enum	Indicates which records are to be marshaled back to the server.
`MaxRecords`	Long	Indicates the maximum number of records to return to a Recordset object from a query. Default is zero (no limit).
`PageCount`	Long	Indicates how many pages of data the Recordset object contains. Read only.
`PageSize`	Long	Indicates how many records constitute one page in the Recordset.
`Properties`	Properties	Contains all of the Property objects for the current Recordset object.
`RecordCount`	Long	Indicates the current number of records in the Recordset object. Read only.
`Sort`	String	Specifies one or more field names the Recordset is sorted on, and the direction of the sort.
`Source`	String	Indicates the source for the data in a Recordset object.
`State`	Long	Indicates whether the recordset is open, closed, or whether it is executing an asynchronous operation. Read only.

Table Continued on Following Page

Property	Returns	Description
`Status`	Integer	Indicates the status of the current record with respect to match updates or other bulk operations. Read only.
`StayInSync`	Boolean	Indicates, in a hierarchical Recordset object, whether the parent row should change when the set of underlying child records changes. Read only.

Event	Description
`EndOfRecordset`	Fired when there is an attempt to move to a row past the end of the Recordset.
`FetchComplete`	Fired after all the records in an asynchronous operation have been retrieved into the Recordset.
`FetchProgress`	Fired periodically during a lengthy asynchronous operation, to report how many rows have currently been retrieved.
`FieldChangeComplete`	Fired after the value of one or more Field objects have been changed.
`MoveComplete`	Fired after the current position in the Recordset changes.
`RecordChangeComplete`	Fired after one or more records change.
`RecordsetChangeComplete`	Fired after the Recordset has changed.
`WillChangeField`	Fired before a pending operation changes the value of one or more Field objects.
`WillChangeRecord`	Fired before one or more rows in the Recordset change.
`WillChangeRecordset`	Fired before a pending operation changes the Recordset.
`WillMove`	Fired before a pending operation changes the current position in the Recordset.

The Stream Object

Method	Returns	Description
Cancel		Cancels execution of a pending asynchronous `Open` operation.
Close		Closes an open Stream.

Method	Returns	Description
CopyTo		Copies characters or bytes from one Stream to another.
Flush		Flushes the contents of the Stream to the underlying object.
LoadFromFile		Loads a stream from a file.
Open		Opens a Stream object from a URL or an existing Record, or creates a blank Stream.
Read	Variant	Reads a number of bytes from the Stream.
ReadText	String	Reads a number of characters from a text Stream.
SaveToFile		Saves an open Stream to a file.
SetEOS		Sets the current position to be the end of the Stream.
SkipLine		Skips a line when reading from a text Stream.
Write		Writes binary data to a Stream.
WriteText		Writes text data to a Stream.

Property	Returns	Description
Charset	String	Identifies the character set used by the Stream.
EOS	Boolean	Is set to `True` if the current position is the end of the Stream. Read only.
LineSeparator	LineSeparator Enum	Indicates the character used to separate lines in a text Stream. The default is `vbCrLf`.
Mode	ConnectMode Enum	Indicates the available permissions for modifying data in a Connection.
Position	Long	Specifies the current position in the Stream.
Size	Long	Indicates the length, in bytes, of the Stream. Read only.
State	ObjectState Enum	Indicates whether the Stream is open or closed, and if open the state of asynchronous actions. Read only.
Type	StreamType Enum	Indicates whether the Stream contains text or binary data.

N
W

ADO 2.5 Constants

The following constants are predefined by ADO. For scripting languages these are included in `adovbs.inc` or `adojava.inc`, which can be found in the `\Program Files\Common Files\System\ado` directory. For ASP you can either include the `.inc` file, or set a reference to the type library with a `METADATA` tag:

```
<!-- METADATA TYPE="typelib" uuid="{00000205-0000-0010-8000-00AA006D2EA4}" -->
```

You can include this `METADATA` tag in individual ASP pages or in the `global.asa` page.

For Visual Basic these constants are automatically included when you reference the ADO library.

> **Constants new to ADO 2.5 are shown *italicized*. At the time of writing some of these were undocumented and so we have guessed the descriptions. For these we have added a * character to the end of the description.**

AffectEnum

Name	*Value*	*Description*
adAffectAll	3	Operation affects all records in the recordset.
adAffectAllChapters	4	Operation affects all child (chapter) records.
adAffectCurrent	1	Operation affects only the current record.
adAffectGroup	2	Operation affects records that satisfy the current `Filter` property.

BookmarkEnum

Name	*Value*	*Description*
adBookmarkCurrent	0	Default. Start at the current record.
adBookmarkFirst	1	Start at the first record.
adBookmarkLast	2	Start at the last record.

CEResyncEnum

Name	*Value*	*Description*
adResyncAll	15	Resynchronizes the data for each pending row.
adResyncAutoIncrement	1	Resynchronizes the auto-increment values for all successfully inserted rows. This is the default.
adResyncConflicts	2	Resynchronizes all rows for which an update or delete operation failed due to concurrency conflicts.
adResyncInserts	8	Resynchronizes all successfully inserted rows, including the values of their identity columns.
adResyncNone	0	No resynchronization is performed.
adResyncUpdates	4	Resynchronizes all successfully updated rows.

CommandTypeEnum

Name	*Value*	*Description*
adCmdFile	256	Indicates that the provider should evaluate `CommandText` as a previously persisted file.
adCmdStoredProc	4	Indicates that the provider should evaluate `CommandText` as a stored procedure.
adCmdTable	2	Indicates that the provider should generate a SQL query to return all rows from the table named in `CommandText`.
adCmdTableDirect	512	Indicates that the provider should return all rows from the table named in `CommandText`.
adCmdText	1	Indicates that the provider should evaluate `CommandText` as textual definition of a command, such as a SQL statement.
adCmdUnknown	8	Indicates that the type of command in `CommandText` is unknown.
adCmdUnspecified	-1	The command type is unspecified.

CompareEnum

Name	*Value*	*Description*
adCompareEqual	1	The bookmarks are equal.
adCompareGreaterThan	2	The first bookmark is after the second.
adCompareLessThan	0	The first bookmark is before the second.
adCompareNotComparable	4	The bookmarks cannot be compared.
adCompareNotEqual	3	The bookmarks are not equal and not ordered.

ConnectModeEnum

Name	*Value*	*Description*
adModeRead	1	Indicates read-only permissions.
adModeReadWrite	3	Indicates read/write permissions.
adModeRecursive	32	Used in conjunction with the `ShareDeny` values to propagate sharing restrictions.
adModeShareDenyNone	16	Prevents others from opening a connection with any permissions.
adModeShareDenyRead	4	Prevents others from opening a connection with read permissions.
adModeShareDenyWrite	8	Prevents others from opening a connection with write permissions.
adModeShareExclusive	12	Prevents others from opening a connection.
adModeUnknown	0	Default. Indicates that the permissions have not yet been set or cannot be determined.
adModeWrite	2	Indicates write-only permissions.

ConnectOptionEnum

Name	*Value*	*Description*
adAsyncConnect	16	Open the connection asynchronously.
adConnectUnspecified	-1	The connection mode is unspecified.

ConnectPromptEnum

Name	Value	Description
adPromptAlways	1	Always prompt for connection information.
adPromptComplete	2	Only prompt if not enough information was supplied.
adPromptCompleteRequired	3	Only prompt if not enough information was supplied, but disable any options not directly applicable to the connection.
adPromptNever	4	Default. Never prompt for connection information.

CopyRecordOptionsEnum

Name	Value	Description
adCopyAllowEmulation	4	If the `CopyRecord` method fails, simulate it using a file download and upload mechanism.
adCopyNonRecursive	2	Copy the current directory, but not sub-directories.
adCopyOverWrite	1	Overwrite the existing file or directory.
adCopyUnspecified	-1	No copy behavior specified.

CursorLocationEnum

Name	Value	Description
adUseClient	3	Use client-side cursors supplied by the local cursor library.
adUseClientBatch	3	Use client-side cursors supplied by the local cursor library.
adUseNone	1	No cursor services are used.
adUseServer	2	Default. Uses data provider supplied cursors.

CursorOptionEnum

Name	Value	Description
adAddNew	16778240	You can use the `AddNew` method to add new records.
adApproxPosition	16384	You can read and set the `AbsolutePosition` and `AbsolutePage` properties.
adBookmark	8192	You can use the `Bookmark` property to access specific records.

Name	*Value*	*Description*
adDelete	16779264	You can use the `Delete` method to delete records.
adFind	524288	You can use the `Find` method to find records.
adHoldRecords	256	You can retrieve more records or change the next retrieve position without committing all pending changes.
adIndex	8388608	You can use the `Index` property to set the current index.
adMovePrevious	512	You can use the `MoveFirst`, `MovePrevious`, `Move` and `GetRows` methods.
adNotify	262144	The recordset supports Notifications.
adResync	131072	You can update the cursor with the data visible in the underlying database with the `Resync` method.
adSeek	4194304	You can use the `Seek` method to find records by an index.
adUpdate	16809984	You can use the `Update` method to modify existing records.
adUpdateBatch	65536	You can use the `UpdateBatch` or `CancelBatch` methods to transfer changes to the provider in groups.

CursorTypeEnum

Name	*Value*	*Description*
adOpenDynamic	2	Opens a dynamic type cursor.
adOpenForwardOnly	0	Default. Opens a forward-only type cursor
adOpenKeyset	1	Opens a keyset type cursor.
adOpenStatic	3	Opens a static type cursor.
adOpenUnspecified	-1	Indicates an unspecified value for the cursor type.

DataTypeEnum

Name	*Value*	*Description*
adBigInt	20	An 8-byte signed integer.
adBinary	128	A binary value.
adBoolean	11	A Boolean value.
adBSTR	8	A null-terminated character string.

Table Continued on Following Page

Name	*Value*	*Description*
adChapter	136	A Chapter type, indicating a child recordset.
adChar	129	A string value.
adCurrency	6	A currency value. An 8-byte signed integer scaled by 10,000, with 4 digits to the right of the decimal point.
adDate	7	A Date value. A Double where the whole part is the number of days since December 30 1899, and the fractional part is a fraction of the day.
adDBDate	133	A date value (yyyymmdd).
adDBFileTime	137	A database file time.
adDBTime	134	A time value (hhmmss).
adDBTimeStamp	135	A date-time stamp (yyyymmddhhmmss plus a fraction in billionths).
adDecimal	14	An exact numeric value with fixed precision and scale.
adDouble	5	A double-precision floating point value.
adEmpty	0	No value was specified.
adError	10	A 32-bit error code.
adFileTime	64	A DOS/Win32 file time. The number of 100 nanosecond intervals since Jan 1 1601.
adGUID	72	A globally unique identifier.
adIDispatch	9	A pointer to an `IDispatch` interface on an OLE object.
adInteger	3	A 4-byte signed integer.
adIUnknown	13	A pointer to an `IUnknown` interface on an OLE object.
adLongVarBinary	205	A long binary value.
adLongVarChar	201	A long string value.
adLongVarWChar	203	A long null-terminated string value.
adNumeric	131	An exact numeric value with a fixed precision and scale.
adPropVariant	138	A variant that is not equivalent to an Automation variant.
adSingle	4	A single-precision floating point value.
adSmallInt	2	A 2-byte signed integer.
adTinyInt	16	A 1-byte signed integer.
adUnsignedBigInt	21	An 8-byte unsigned integer.

Name	*Value*	*Description*
adUnsignedInt	19	A 4-byte unsigned integer.
adUnsignedSmallInt	18	A 2-byte unsigned integer.
adUnsignedTinyInt	17	A 1-byte unsigned integer.
adUserDefined	132	A user-defined variable.
adVarBinary	204	A binary value.
adVarChar	200	A String value.
adVariant	12	An Automation Variant.
adVarNumeric	139	A variable width exact numeric, with a signed scale value.
adVarWChar	202	A null-terminated Unicode character string.
adWChar	130	A null-terminated Unicode character string.

EditModeEnum

Name	*Value*	*Description*
adEditAdd	2	Indicates that the `AddNew` method has been invoked and the current record in the buffer is a new record that hasn't been saved to the database.
adEditDelete	4	Indicates that the `Delete` method has been invoked.
adEditInProgress	1	Indicates that data in the current record has been modified but not saved.
adEditNone	0	Indicates that no editing is in progress.

ErrorValueEnum

Name	*Value*	*Description*
adErrBoundToCommand	3707	The application cannot change the `ActiveConnection` property of a `Recordset` object with a `Command` object as its source.
adErrCannotComplete	3732	The action could not be completed.
adErrCantChangeConnection	3748	The connection cannot be changed. *
adErrCantChangeProvider	3220	The provider cannot be changed. *
adErrCantConvertvalue	3724	The value cannot be converted. *

Table Continued on Following Page

Name	Value	Description
adErrCantCreate	3725	The resource cannot be created. *
adErrCatalogNotSet	3747	The action could not be completed because the catalog is not set. *
adErrColumnNotOnThisRow	*3726*	The specified column doesn't exist on this row. *
adErrDataConversion	3421	The application is using a value of the wrong type for the current application.
adErrDataOverflow	3721	The data was too large for the supplied data type. *
adErrDelResOutOfScope	3738	The resource cannot be deleted because it is out of the allowed scope. *
adErrDenyNotSupported	3750	You cannot set Deny permissions because the provider does not support them. *
adErrDenyTypeNotSupported	3751	The provider does not support the type of Deny requested. *
adErrFeatureNotAvailable	3251	The provider does not support the operation requested by the application.
adErrFieldsUpdateFailed	3749	The `Update` method of the Fields collection failed.
adErrIllegalOperation	3219	The operation requested by the application is not allowed in this context.
adErrIntegrityViolation	3719	The action failed due to a violation of data integrity.
adErrInTransaction	3246	The application cannot explicitly close a `Connection` object while in the middle of a transaction.
adErrInvalidArgument	3001	The application is using arguments that are the wrong type, are out of the acceptable range, or are in conflict with one another.
adErrInvalidConnection	3709	The application requested an operation on an object with a reference to a closed or invalid `Connection` object.
adErrInvalidParamInfo	3708	The application has improperly defined a `Parameter` object.
adErrInvalidTransaction	3714	The transaction is invalid.

Name	*Value*	*Description*
adErrInvalidURL	3729	The supplied URL is invalid.
adErrItemNotFound	3265	ADO could not find the object in the collection.
adErrNoCurrentRecord	3021	Either `BOF` or `EOF` is `True`, or the current record has been deleted. The operation requested by the application requires a current record.
adErrNotExecuting	3715	The operation is not executing.
adErrNotReentrant	3710	The operation is not reentrant.
adErrObjectClosed	3704	The operation requested by the application is not allowed if the object is closed.
adErrObjectInCollection	3367	Can't append. Object already in collection.
adErrObjectNotSet	3420	The object referenced by the application no longer points to a valid object.
adErrObjectOpen	3705	The operation requested by the application is not allowed if the object is open.
adErrOpeningFile	3002	An error occurred whilst opening the requested file.
adErrOperationCancelled	3712	The operation was cancelled.
adErrOutOfSpace	3734	The operation failed because the server could not obtain enough space to complete the operation.
adErrPermissionDenied	3720	The action failed because you do not have sufficient permission to complete the operation.
adErrPropConflicting	3742	Setting this property caused a conflict with other properties. *
adErrPropInvalidColumn	3739	This property is invalid for the selected column. *
adErrPropInvalidOption	3740	You have supplied an invalid option for this property. *
adErrPropInvalidValue	3741	You have supplied an invalid value for this property. *
adErrPropNotAllSettable	3743	Not all properties can be set. *

Table Continued on Following Page

Name	*Value*	*Description*
adErrPropNotSet	3744	The property was not set. *
adErrPropNotSettable	3745	The property cannot be set. *
adErrPropNotSupported	3746	The property is not supported. *
adErrProviderFailed	3000	The provider failed to complete the requested action. *
adErrProviderNotFound	3706	ADO could not find the specified provider.
adErrReadFile	3003	There was an error reading from the specified file. *
adErrResourceExists	3731	The resource already exists. *
adErrResourceLocked	3730	The resource is locked. *
adErrResourceOutOfScope	3735	The resource is out of scope. *
adErrSchemaViolation	3722	The action caused a violation of the schema. *
adErrSignMismatch	3723	The expression contained mismatched signs. *
adErrStillConnecting	3713	The operation is still connecting.
adErrStillExecuting	3711	The operation is still executing.
adErrTreePermissionDenied	3728	You do not have permission to view the directory tree. *
adErrUnavailable	3736	The command is unavailable. *
adErrUnsafeOperation	3716	The operation is unsafe under these circumstances.
adErrURLDoesNotExist	3727	The URL does not exist. *
adErrURLNamedRowDoesNotExist	3737	The URL in the named row does not exists. *
adErrVolumeNotFound	3733	The file volume was not found. *
adErrWriteFile	3004	There was an error whilst writing to the file. *
adwrnSecurityDialog	3717	The operation caused a security dialog to appear. *
adwrnSecurityDialogHeader	3718	The operation caused a security dialog header to appear. *

EventReasonEnum

Name	Value	Description
adRsnAddNew	1	A new record is to be added.
adRsnClose	9	The object is being closed.
adRsnDelete	2	The record is being deleted.
adRsnFirstChange	11	The record has been changed for the first time.
adRsnMove	10	A `Move` has been invoked and the current record pointer is being moved.
adRsnMoveFirst	12	A `MoveFirst` has been invoked and the current record pointer is being moved.
adRsnMoveLast	15	A `MoveLast` has been invoked and the current record pointer is being moved.
adRsnMoveNext	13	A `MoveNext` has been invoked and the current record pointer is being moved.
adRsnMovePrevious	14	A `MovePrevious` has been invoked and the current record pointer is being moved.
adRsnRequery	7	The recordset was requeried.
adRsnResynch	8	The recordset was resynchronized.
adRsnUndoAddNew	5	The addition of a new record has been cancelled.
adRsnUndoDelete	6	The deletion of a record has been cancelled.
adRsnUndoUpdate	4	The update of a record has been cancelled.
adRsnUpdate	3	The record is being updated.

EventStatusEnum

Name	Value	Description
adStatusCancel	4	Request cancellation of the operation that is about to occur.
adStatusCantDeny	3	A `Will` event cannot request cancellation of the operation about to occur.
adStatusErrorsOccurred	2	The operation completed unsuccessfully, or a `Will` event cancelled the operation.
adStatusOK	1	The operation completed successfully.
adStatusUnwantedEvent	5	Events for this operation are no longer required.

ExecuteOptionEnum

Name	*Value*	*Description*
adAsyncExecute	16	The operation is executed asynchronously.
adAsyncFetch	32	The records are fetched asynchronously.
adAsyncFetchNonBlocking	64	The records are fetched asynchronously without blocking subsequent operations.
adExecuteNoRecords	128	Indicates `CommandText` is a command or stored procedure that does not return rows. Always combined with `adCmdText` or `adCmdStoreProc`.

FieldAttributeEnum

Name	*Value*	*Description*
adFldCacheDeferred	4096	Indicates that the provider caches field values and that subsequent reads are done from the cache.
adFldFixed	16	Indicates that the field contains fixed-length data.
adFldIsChapter	8192	The field is a chapter field, and contains a rowset.
adFldIsCollection	262144	The field is a collection.
adFldIsDefaultStream	131072	The field is the default Stream.
adFldIsNullable	32	Indicates that the field accepts Null values.
adFldIsRowURL	65536	The field is a URL.
adFldKeyColumn	32768	The field is part of a key column.
adFldLong	128	Indicates that the field is a long binary field, and that the `AppendChunk` and `GetChunk` methods can be used.
adFldMayBeNull	64	Indicates that you can read Null values from the field.
adFldMayDefer	2	Indicates that the field is deferred, that is, the field values are not retrieved from the data source with the whole record, but only when you access them.
adFldNegativeScale	16384	The field has a negative scale.
adFldRowID	256	Indicates that the field has some kind of record ID.
adFldRowVersion	512	Indicates that the field time or date stamp used to track updates.

Name	*Value*	*Description*
adFldUnknownUpdatable	8	Indicates that the provider cannot determine if you can write to the field.
adFldUnspecified	-1	Attributes of the field are unspecified.
adFldUpdatable	4	Indicates that you can write to the field.

FieldEnum

Name	*Value*	*Description*
adDefaultStream	-1	When used as the index into the Fields collection of a record, returns the default Stream for the Record.
adRecordURL	-2	When used as the index into the Fields collection of a record, returns the absolute URL for the Record.

FieldStatusEnum

Name	*Value*	*Description*
adFieldAlreadyExists	26	The field already exists. *
adFieldBadStatus	12	The field has a bad Status value. *
adFieldCannotComplete	20	The action cannot be completed. *
adFieldCannotDeleteSource	23	The field cannot delete the source of the field. *
adFieldCantConvertValue	2	The field cannot convert the value. *
adFieldCantCreate	7	The field cannot be created. *
adFieldDataOverflow	6	The data is too long to fit in the field. *
adFieldDefault	13	The default value has been used. *
adFieldDoesNotExist	16	The field does not exist. *
adFieldIgnore	15	The field has been ignored. *
adFieldIntegrityViolation	10	The field update failed with a data integrity violation. *
adFieldInvalidURL	17	The field contains an invalid URL. *
adFieldIsNull	3	The field is null. *
adFieldOK	0	The field is OK. *

Table Continued on Following Page

Name	Value	Description
adFieldOutOfSpace	22	The field ran out of space for storage. *
adFieldPendingChange	262144	The field has been changed, but the provider has not yet been updated. *
adFieldPendingDelete	131072	The field has been deleted, but the provider has not yet been updated. *
adFieldPendingInsert	65536	The field has been inserted, but the provider has not yet been updated. *
adFieldPendingUnknown	524288	The field has been changed, but it is not known what sort of change it was. *
adFieldPendingUnknownDelete	1048576	The field has been changed, but the field might have been deleted. *
adFieldPermissionDenied	9	Permission to modify the field failed due to access permissions. *
adFieldReadOnly	24	The field is read only. *
adFieldResourceExists	19	The resource specified by the field already exists. *
adFieldResourceLocked	18	The resource specified by the field is locked. *
adFieldResourceOutOfScope	25	The resource specified by the field is out of scope. *
adFieldSchemaViolation	11	The field update failed due to a schema violation. *
adFieldSignMismatch	5	The field contained mismatched signs. *
adFieldTruncated	4	The field value was truncated. *
adFieldUnavailable	8	The field is unavailable. *
adFieldVolumeNotFound	21	The volume specified by the field was not found. *

FilterGroupEnum

Name	Value	Description
adFilterAffectedRecords	2	Allows you to view only records affected by the last `Delete`, `Resync`, `UpdateBatch`, or `CancelBatch` call.

Name	*Value*	*Description*
adFilterConflictingRecords	5	Allows you to view the records that failed the last batch update attempt.
adFilterFetchedRecords	3	Allows you to view records in the current cache.
adFilterNone	0	Removes the current filter and restores all records to view.
adFilterPendingRecords	1	Allows you to view only the records that have changed but have not been sent to the server. Only applicable for batch update mode.
adFilterPredicate	4	Allows you to view records that failed the last batch update attempt.

GetRowsOptionEnum

Name	*Value*	*Description*
adGetRowsRest	-1	Retrieves the remainder of the rows in the recordset.

IsolationLevelEnum

Name	*Value*	*Description*
adXactBrowse	256	Indicates that from one transaction you can view uncommitted changes in other transactions.
adXactChaos	16	Default. Indicates that you cannot overwrite pending changes from more highly isolated transactions.
adXactCursorStability	4096	Default. Indicates that from one transaction you can view changes in other transactions only after they have been committed.
adXactIsolated	1048576	Indicates that transactions are conducted in isolation of other transactions.
adXactReadCommitted	4096	Same as `adXactCursorStability`.
adXactReadUncommitted	256	Same as `adXactBrowse`.
adXactRepeatableRead	65536	Indicates that from one transaction you cannot see changes made in other transactions, but that requerying can bring new recordsets.
adXactSerializable	1048576	Same as `adXactIsolated`.
adXactUnspecified	-1	Indicates that the provider is using a different `IsolationLevel` than specified, but that the level cannot be identified.

LineSeparatorEnum

Name	*Value*	*Description*
adCR	13	The carriage-return character.
adCRLF	-1	The carriage-return and line-feed characters.
adLF	10	The line-feed character.

LockTypeEnum

Name	*Value*	*Description*
adLockBatchOptimistic	4	Optimistic batch updates.
adLockOptimistic	3	Optimistic locking, record-by-record. The provider locks records when `Update` is called.
adLockPessimistic	2	Pessimistic locking, record-by-record. The provider locks the record immediately upon editing.
adLockReadOnly	1	Default. Read only, data cannot be modified.
adLockUnspecified	-1	The clone is created with the same lock type as the original.

MarshalOptionsEnum

Name	*Value*	*Description*
adMarshalAll	0	Default. Indicates that all rows are returned to the server.
adMarshalModifiedOnly	1	Indicates that only modified rows are returned to the server.

MoveRecordOptionsEnum

Name	*Value*	*Description*
adMoveAllowEmulation	4	If the attempt to move the record fails, allow the move to be performed using a download, upload and delete set of operations.
adMoveDontUpdateLinks	2	Do not update hyperlinks of the source Record.
adMoveOverWrite	1	Overwrite the target if it already exists.

ObjectStateEnum

Name	Value	Description
adStateClosed	0	Default. Indicates that the object is closed.
adStateConnecting	2	Indicates that the object is connecting.
adStateExecuting	4	Indicates that the object is executing a command.
adStateFetching	8	Indicates that the rows of the recordset are being fetched.
adStateOpen	1	Indicates that the object is open.

ParameterAttributesEnum

Name	Value	Description
adParamLong	128	Indicates that the parameter accepts long binary data.
adParamNullable	64	Indicates that the parameter accepts Null values.
adParamSigned	16	Default. Indicates that the parameter accepts signed values.

ParameterDirectionEnum

Name	Value	Description
adParamInput	1	Default. Indicates an input parameter.
adParamInputOutput	3	Indicates both an input and output parameter.
adParamOutput	2	Indicates an output parameter.
adParamReturnValue	4	Indicates a return value.
adParamUnknown	0	Indicates parameter direction is unknown.

PersistFormatEnum

Name	Value	Description
adPersistADTG	0	Default. Persist data in Advanced Data TableGram format.
adPersistXML	1	Persist data in XML format.

PositionEnum

Name	*Value*	*Description*
adPosBOF	-2	The current record pointer is at `BOF`.
adPosEOF	-3	The current record pointer is at `EOF`.
adPosUnknown	-1	The Recordset is empty, the current position is unknown, or the provider does not support the `AbsolutePage` property.

PropertyAttributesEnum

Name	*Value*	*Description*
adPropNotSupported	0	Indicates that the property is not supported by the provider.
adPropOptional	2	Indicates that the user does not need to specify a value for this property before the data source is initialized.
adPropRead	512	Indicates that the user can read the property.
adPropRequired	1	Indicates that the user must specify a value for this property before the data source is initialized.
adPropWrite	1024	Indicates that the user can set the property.

RecordCreateOptionsEnum

Name	*Value*	*Description*
adCreateCollection	8192	Create a new collection record (directory) at the specified URL.
adCreateNonCollection	0	Create a new record at the specified URL.
adCreateOverwrite	67108864	Overwrite any existing record at the specified URL.
adCreateStructDoc	-2147483648	Create a new structured document record at the specified URL.
adFailIfNotExists	-1	Fail if the URL does not exist.
adOpenIfExists	33554432	Open the record at the specified URL if it exists.

RecordOpenOptionsEnum

Name	Value	Description
adDelayFetchFields	32768	Delay fetching fields until they are requested.
adDelayFetchStream	16384	Delay fetching the Stream until it is requested.
adOpenAsync	4096	Open the Record asynchronously.
adOpenSource	8388608	Open the source document at the URL, rather than the executed contents.
adOpenURLBind	1024	Indicates the connection string contains a URL.

RecordStatusEnum

Name	Value	Description
adRecCanceled	256	The record was not saved because the operation was cancelled.
adRecCantRelease	1024	The new record was not saved because of existing record locks.
adRecConcurrencyViolation	2048	The record was not saved because optimistic concurrency was in use.
adRecDBDeleted	262144	The record has already been deleted from the data source.
adRecDeleted	4	The record was deleted.
adRecIntegrityViolation	4096	The record was not saved because the user violated integrity constraints.
adRecInvalid	16	The record was not saved because its bookmark is invalid.
adRecMaxChangesExceeded	8192	The record was not saved because there were too many pending changes.
adRecModified	2	The record was modified.
adRecMultipleChanges	64	The record was not saved because it would have affected multiple records.
adRecNew	1	The record is new.
adRecObjectOpen	16384	The record was not saved because of a conflict with an open storage object.
adRecOK	0	The record was successfully updated.

Table Continued on Following Page

Name	Value	Description
adRecOutOfMemory	32768	The record was not saved because the computer has run out of memory.
adRecPendingChanges	128	The record was not saved because it refers to a pending insert.
adRecPermissionDenied	65536	The record was not saved because the user has insufficient permissions.
adRecSchemaViolation	131072	The record was not saved because it violates the structure of the underlying database.
adRecUnmodified	8	The record was not modified.

RecordTypeEnum

Name	Value	Description
adCollectionRecord	1	The record is a collection type (directory).
adSimpleRecord	0	The record is a simple file.
adStructDoc	2	The record is a structured document.

ResyncEnum

Name	Value	Description
adResyncAllValues	2	Default. Data is overwritten and pending updates are cancelled.
adResyncUnderlyingValues	1	Data is not overwritten and pending updates are not cancelled.

SaveOptionsEnum

Name	Value	Description
adSaveCreateNotExist	1	Create a new file if the file does not already exist.
adSaveCreateOverWrite	2	Overwrite any existing file if it exists.

SchemaEnum

Name	Value	Description
adSchemaAsserts	0	Request assert information.
adSchemaCatalogs	1	Request catalog information.
adSchemaCharacterSets	2	Request character set information.
adSchemaCheckConstraints	5	Request check constraint information.
adSchemaCollations	3	Request collation information.
adSchemaColumnPrivileges	13	Request column privilege information.
adSchemaColumns	4	Request column information.
adSchemaColumnsDomainUsage	11	Request column domain usage information.
adSchemaConstraintColumnUsage	6	Request column constraint usage information.
adSchemaConstraintTableUsage	7	Request table constraint usage information.
adSchemaCubes	32	For multi-dimensional data, view the Cubes schema.
adSchemaDBInfoKeywords	30	Request the keywords from the provider.
adSchemaDBInfoLiterals	31	Request the literals from the provider.
adSchemaDimensions	33	For multi-dimensional data, view the Dimensions schema.
adSchemaForeignKeys	27	Request foreign key information.
adSchemaHierarchies	34	For multi-dimensional data, view the Hierarchies schema.
adSchemaIndexes	12	Request index information.
adSchemaKeyColumnUsage	8	Request key column usage information.
adSchemaLevels	35	For multi-dimensional data, view the Levels schema.
adSchemaMeasures	36	For multi-dimensional data, view the Measures schema.
adSchemaMembers	38	For multi-dimensional data, view the Members schema.
adSchemaPrimaryKeys	28	Request primary key information.

Table Continued on Following Page

Name	Value	Description
adSchemaProcedureColumns	29	Request stored procedure column information.
adSchemaProcedureParameters	26	Request stored procedure parameter information.
adSchemaProcedures	16	Request stored procedure information.
adSchemaProperties	37	For multi-dimensional data, view the Properties schema.
adSchemaProviderSpecific	-1	Request provider specific information.
adSchemaProviderTypes	22	Request provider type information.
adSchemaReferentialContraints	9	Request referential constraint information.
adSchemaReferentialConstraints	9	Request referential constraint information.
adSchemaSchemata	17	Request schema information.
adSchemaSQLLanguages	18	Request SQL language support information.
adSchemaStatistics	19	Request statistics information.
adSchemaTableConstraints	10	Request table constraint information.
adSchemaTablePrivileges	14	Request table privilege information.
adSchemaTables	20	Request information about the tables.
adSchemaTranslations	21	Request character set translation information.
adSchemaTrustees	39	Request trustee information.
adSchemaUsagePrivileges	15	Request user privilege information.
adSchemaViewColumnUsage	24	Request column usage in views information.
adSchemaViews	23	Request view information.
adSchemaViewTableUsage	25	Request table usage in views information.

Due to a misspelling in the type library **adSchemaReferentialConstraints** is included twice – once for the original spelling and once for the corrected spelling.

SearchDirectionEnum

Name	Value	Description
adSearchBackward	-1	Search backward from the current record.
adSearchForward	1	Search forward from the current record.

SeekEnum

Name	*Value*	*Description*
adSeekAfter	8	Seek the key just after the match.
adSeekAfterEQ	4	Seek the key equal to or just after the match.
adSeekBefore	32	See the key just before the match.
adSeekBeforeEQ	16	Seek the key equal to or just before the match.
adSeekFirstEQ	1	Seek the first key equal to the match.
adSeekLastEQ	2	Seek the last key equal to the match.

StreamOpenOptionsEnum

Name	*Value*	*Description*
adOpenStreamAsync	1	Opens the Stream asynchronously.
adOpenStreamFromRecord	4	Opens the Stream using an existing Record as the source.
adOpenStreamFromURL	8	Opens the Stream using a URL as the source.

StreamReadEnum

Name	*Value*	*Description*
adReadAll	-1	Reads all bytes from the Stream, from the current position to the end of the stream.
adReadLine	-2	Reads the next line from the Stream. Uses the `LineSeparator` property to identify the end of the line.

StreamTypeEnum

Name	*Value*	*Description*
adTypeBinary	1	The Stream contains binary data.
adTypeText	2	The Stream contains text data.

StreamWriteEnum

Name	*Value*	*Description*
adWriteChar	0	Writes the specified string to the Stream.
adWriteLine	1	Writes the specified string and a line separator to the Stream.
stWriteChar	0	Writes the specified string to the Stream.
stWriteLine	1	Writes the specified string and a line separator to the Stream.

StringFormatEnum

Name	*Value*	*Description*
adClipString	2	Rows are delimited by user-defined values.

XactAttributeEnum

Name	*Value*	*Description*
adXactAbortRetaining	262144	The provider will automatically start a new transaction after a `RollbackTrans` method call.
adXactAsyncPhaseOne	524288	Perform an asynchronous commit.
adXactCommitRetaining	131072	The provider will automatically start a new transaction after a `CommitTrans` method call.
adXactSyncPhaseOne	1048576	Performs a synchronous commit.

N
W

G

Useful Information

Server-Side Include Directives and Utilities

This appendix describes the syntax and parameter values of the Internet Information Server 5.0 **Server Side-Include** directives. It also describes the syntax and use of the `IISRESTART` utility, which can be used to manage the Web services remotely from another computer, from the command line, or from within an SSI directive.

SSI Directives, Attributes and Tokens

Directive	Description
`#include`	Inserts the contents of a specified file into the response stream being sent to the client, replacing the directive. For example: `<!-- #include FILE="usefulbits.inc" -->` See below for a list of the attributes and tokens that can be used in this directive.

`#config`	Specifies the format that will be used for dates, times and file sizes, and the text of the generic SSI error message that is returned to the client. For example:
	`<!-- #config ERRMSG="SSI Processing Error" -->`
	`<!-- #config TIMEFMT ="%A, %B %d %Y %H:%M:%S" -->`
	`<!-- #config SIZEFMT ="BYTES" -->`
	See below for a list of the attributes and tokens that can be used in this directive.

Table Continued on Following Page

Directive	Description
#echo	Inserts the value of an HTTP environment variable into the response stream being sent to the client, replacing the directive. For example: <!-- #echo VAR="SERVER_NAME" --> See below for a list of the attributes and tokens that can be used in this directive.
#exec	Executes a program or a shell command on the server. For example: <!-- #exec CGI="/scripts/myapp.exe?value1=this&value2=that" --> <!-- #exec CMD="cmd.exe /C iisreset /stop" --> <!-- #exec CMD="cmd.exe /C net start cisvc" --> See below for a list of the attributes and tokens that can be used in this directive. You must add the following entry to the Windows Registry to be able to use the CMD attribute: **HKEY_LOCAL_MACHINE** **\SYSTEM** **\CurrentControlSet** **\Services** **\W3SVC** **\Parameters** **\SSIEnableCmdDirective** Set the value to 1 to and restart the WWW service to allow the CMD attribute to be used in the #exec directive. Set it to 0 to disable it and prevent unauthorized use, which could otherwise damage the server installation.
#flastmod	Inserts the date and time that a specified file was last modified into the response stream being sent to the client, replacing the directive. For example: <!-- #flastmod FILE="Default.asp" --> See below for a list of the attributes and tokens that can be used in this directive.
#fsize	Inserts the size of a specified file into the response stream being sent to the client, replacing the directive. For example: <!-- #fsize FILE="Default.asp" --> See below for a list of the attributes and tokens that can be used in this directive.

Command Type Attributes for the #exec Directive

Attribute	Description
CGI	Executes the specified application in the context of the Web server (i.e. with access to the request and response via the ISAPI) and passes the value of any query string to the application. The application runs in a separate memory space from the Web server.
CMD	Starts an instance of the specified operating system command interpreter and executes the specified command.

Path Type Attributes for #include, #flastmod and #fsize

Attribute	Description
FILE	The value of the attribute is a complete or relative physical path plus the name of the file, as would be used at the DOS command prompt, i.e. "\files\web\myfile.txt".
VIRTUAL	The value of the attribute is a complete or relative virtual path plus the name of the file, in relation to the root folder of the current Web site. "/files/web/myfile.txt".

SIZEFMT Tokens for the #config Directive

Token	Description
BYTES	The size of the file will be returned in bytes.
ABBREV	The size of the file will be calculated and returned as the nearest number of kilobytes (KB).

TIMEFMT Tokens for the #config Directive

Token	Description
%a	The day of the week as 'Mon', 'Tue', etc.
%A	The day of the week as 'Monday', Tuesday', etc.
%b	The name of the month as 'Jan', Feb', etc.
%B	The name of the month as 'January', February', etc.
%c	The current date and time formatted appropriately for the server's locale (i.e. 11/06/99 12:51:32).
%d	The day of the month as a number (01 to 31).
%H	The current hour in 24-hour format (00 to 23).
%I	The current hour in 12-hour format (01 to 12).
%j	The day of the year as a number (001 to 366).
%m	The month as a number (01 to 12).
%M	The current minute as a number (00 to 59).
%p	The appropriate 'morning' or 'afternoon' string for the server's locale (i.e. AM or PM).
%S	The current second as a decimal number (00 to 59).
%U	The week of the year as a number with Sunday as the first day of the week (00 to 51).
%w	The day of the week as a number with Sunday as the first day of the week (0 to 6).
%W	The week of the year as a number with Monday as the first day of the week (00 to 51).
%x	The current date formatted appropriately for the server's locale (i.e. 11/06/99).
%X	The current time formatted appropriately for the server's locale (i.e. 12:51:32).
%y	The year number without the century (i.e. 01).
%Y	The year number with the century (i.e. 2001).
%z, %Z	The name or an abbreviation for the server's time zone if known.
%%	A 'percent' character.

VAR Tokens for the #echo Directive

Token	Description
AUTH_TYPE	The type of authentication that the client and server used if this page denied anonymous access, for example 'Basic' or 'NTLM' (i.e. Challenge/Response).
AUTH_PASSWORD	The password provided by the user to the server if this page denied anonymous access and the client authenticated using the Basic method.
AUTH_USER	The username provided by the user to the server if this page denied anonymous access, under both NTLM and Basic (or other) methods.
CONTENT_LENGTH	The number of bytes sent in the body of the request, i.e. the number of bytes sent as a POST to the server.
CONTENT_TYPE	The MIME type of the data sent as a POST in the body of the request.
DOCUMENT_NAME	The full physical path and filename of the document requested by the client.
DOCUMENT_URI	The full virtual path and filename of the document requested by the client, in relation to the root folder of this Web site.
DATE_GMT	The date and time set in the server's operating system, without any adjustment from Greenwich Mean Time.
DATE_LOCAL	The date and time set in the server's operating system after adjustment from Greenwich Mean Time.
GATEWAY_INTERFACE	The type of interface used to handle the request, for example 'CGI/1.1'.
HTTP_ACCEPT	A comma-delimited list of MIME types that the client application has notified the server that it can accept.
LAST_MODIFIED	The date and time when the file or resource requested by the client was last changed.
PATH_INFO	The full virtual path and filename of the document requested by the client, in relation to the root folder of this Web site.
PATH_TRANSLATED	The full physical path and filename of the document requested by the client.
QUERY_STRING	The value of any query string that was appended to the URL of the document or resource the client requested, after translation from the URL-encoded format.
QUERY_STRING_ UNESCAPED	The value of any query string that was appended to the URL of the document or resource the client requested, before translation from the URL-encoded format.
REMOTE_ADDR	The IP address of the client machine that requested the page.
REMOTE_HOST	The host name or IP address of the network from which the client requested the page.
REMOTE_USER	The name (if available) of the client machine that requested the page.
REQUEST_METHOD	The method used when requesting the page, either 'GET' or 'POST'.
SCRIPT_NAME	The full virtual path and filename of the document requested by the client, in relation to the root folder of the Web site.
SERVER_NAME	The network name or URL host name of the server that received the request.
SERVER_PORT	The number of the port on which the request was received, i.e. '80' for normal page requests and '443' for SSL secure requests.
SERVER_PORT_SECURE	The port number if this request was over a secure protocol.
SERVER_PROTOCOL	The HTTP protocol that the request was passed under, i.e. 'HTTP/1.1'.
SERVER_SOFTWARE	The name/version string of the Web server, i.e. 'Microsoft-IIS/5.0'.
URL	The complete URL that the user specified when requesting the document or resource.
ALL_HTTP	All the name/value pairs for HTTP environment variables that are not included in the list above, for example HTTP_COOKIE and HTTP_ACCEPT_LANGUAGE.

The IISRESET Utility and Switches

The iisreset.exe utility can be used to manage the Web services running on any server providing that you have the relevant permissions. It should be used in preference to the NET STOP and NET START commands, as it stops and starts the various integrated services in the correct sequence.

The syntax is iisreset [*computer_name*] /*switch* [/*switch* ...]

Where the available *switch* values are:

Switch	Meaning
RESTART	Stop and then restart all Internet services running on the specified computer.
START	Start all Internet services running on the specified computer.
STOP	Stop all Internet services running on the specified computer.
REBOOT	Reboot the specified computer.
REBOOTONERROR	Reboot the specified computer if an error occurs when starting, stopping, or restarting Internet services.
NOFORCE	Do not force Internet services to terminate if attempting to stop them gracefully fails.
TIMEOUT:*val*	Set the timeout value in seconds for all the Internet services to stop. Default is 20 for RESTART, 60 for STOP, and zero for REBOOT. If the REBOOTONERROR switch is also specified the computer will reboot if the timeout period is exceeded.
STATUS	Displays the status of all Internet services.
ENABLE	Enables restarting of Internet Services on the local system.
DISABLE	Disables restarting of Internet Services on the local system.

This utility can be used in an CMD-type #echo SSI directive, providing that the page has anonymous access removed and the user supplies details of a valid account that has Administrator privileges on the target server. However, in this situation the REBOOT, START and RESTART options will not function correctly.

The NET STOP and NET START Commands

The net.exe utility can be used to manage the services running on a server, either locally or from another machine, providing that you have the relevant permissions. Although not recommended for use with Internet services such as the WWW or FTP service, it is useful for stopping and starting other services (in fact, the NET command can be used to issue a whole range of other network-related commands as well).

The syntax is net [start | stop] *service_name*

So, for example, we can use it to stop and start the Microsoft Indexing Service with the commands: net stop cisvc and net start cisvc. It can be used in a CMD-type #echo SSI directive providing that the page has anonymous access removed and the user supplies details of a valid account that has Administrator privileges on the target server.

A full list of all the options and switches for the NET command can be found in the Windows 2000 Help files. Select Help from the Start menu, and in the Index page of the Help window look for 'net commands'.

Other Useful Information

Wrox Press provides two sites that contain useful information for ASP and Web developers in general:

- **The Wrox Web Developer Site** (`http://webdev.wrox.co.uk/`)
  The main site for sample code for all the Web-developer books we publish. Run the samples on-line or download code to run on your own server. Also contains chapters and extracts from our books, industry news, and a series of useful reference tools and other resources.

- **ASPToday** (`http://www.asptoday.com/`)
  Read focused and useful articles on ASP and other Web programming techniques from a range of experts and industry gurus. A new article is available every day of the week, and you can search the archives for previous ones.

Finding ASP-friendly ISPs

ASP runs on Microsoft Windows servers, while the majority of ISPs still use Unix-based systems or an equivalent. While there are ASP clones that run on Unix or Linux, many people want to use the full spectrum of ASP functions (such as COM components and Windows services) on their sites. This tends to rule out many traditional ISPs.

Two or three years ago, it was very difficult to find an ISP that used Windows NT servers, and would allow you to install your own components or make use of Windows services in your Web applications. Thankfully, the situation is changing fast, and there are now hundreds of ISPs that do support ASP in full on Windows NT servers (predominantly Windows NT 4 at the time of writing, but no doubt this will change fairly quickly as Windows 2000 proves itself) – just check that they allow you to install your *own* components before you sign up.

A search on **InfoSeek** (`http://www.infoseek.com/`) for ASP-enabled Windows NT based ISPs (using the criteria '+asp +Web +hosting') returned 390 matches. Many of these offer ASP on Windows NT Server, plus support for applications such as SQL Server and others. Some of the sites found (at the time of writing) were:

Active Server (`http://www.active-server.com/`)
DataReturn (`http://www.datareturn.com/`)
IMC Online (`http://www.imconline.net/`)
Intermedia (`http://www.intermedia.net/`)
SiteCrafters Internet Services (`http://www.sitecrafters.com/`)
Softcom (`http://www.softcomca.com`)
Technocom plc (`http://www.technocom.net/`)
Virtualscape (`http://www.virtualscape.com/`)

There are also sites that allow you to search for ISPs based of a whole range of criteria, such as **Action Jackson** (`http://www.actionjackson.com/hosts`) and **Top Hosts** (`http://www.tophosts.com`).

Other ASP Web Sites

There are also many other sites that provide ASP, or general Web-oriented information, for developers. This is just a selection of those we know of and recommend:

15 Seconds Free Resources Center (`http://www.15seconds.com/`)
Free resource for developers working with Microsoft Internet Solutions. 15 Seconds proclaims to be the biggest IIS and ASP development resource in the world, with over 2300 pages.

ActionJackson Web Developer Central (`http://www.actionjackson.com`)
A comprehensive resource of news, articles, books and links, including discussion forums, components, IIS hosts, jobs and much more.

Active Server Pages Resources Site (`http://www.activeserverpages.com/`)
This site specializes in Active Server Pages programming issues. Maintained by Charles Carroll, it contains online programming tutorials, references, and links to a wide range of resources and articles.

ASP 101 Resources Site (`http://www.asp101.com/`)
The purpose of this site is to provide both expert and novice developers with useful and timely information on the emerging technology of Active Server Pages.

ASP Forums (`http://www.aspforums.com/`)
This site provides a range of forums and discussion groups for ASP related topics, plus lists of related companies and their software designed for use with ASP.

ASP Hole IIS and ASP Guide (`http://www.asphole.com/`)
Intended to help the Active Server Pages professional locate ASP-related and IIS-related resources quickly and efficiently. A huge range of various resources is available.

ASP Toolbox (`http://www.tcp-ip.com/`)
Here you'll find a range of tutorials and other ASP-related information to help in developing your dynamic Web sites.

The ASP Resource Index (`http://www.aspin.com/`)
Find all the Active Server Pages (ASP) Resources you need in one place. Contains a comprehensive list of ASP components, applications, code snippets, references, and books.

ASPWatch (`http://www.aspwatch.com/`)
Provides real world Active Server Pages solutions and resources. This includes articles, discussions and book lists.

Hangeng (`http://www.haneng.com/`)
Provides content that is free to be used commercially and non-commercially. Dedicated to ASP technology and created and maintained by Alexander Haneng on a hobby basis.

JavaScript Source (`http://javascript.internet.com/`)
An excellent JavaScript resource with tons of cut & paste JavaScript examples for your Web pages. All for free!

Microsoft's NT Server and BackOffice Site (`http://www.microsoft.com/backoffice/`)
This site is the main page for the Microsoft BackOffice products, including NT Server, SQL Server, Exchange, and other components.

PowerASP Active Server Pages (`http://powerasp.com/`)
This site offers code snippets, hints & tips, a discussion board, a chat room and newsletters–all related to ASP and general Web development topics.

Ultimate ASP (`http://www.ultimateasp.com/`)
An ever-expanding wealth of information for building dynamic web pages, including help for beginners.

Website Abstraction (`http://www.wsabstract.com/`)
This site is a webmaster's learning center featuring tutorials on all aspects of JavaScript and Web site construction. It has been featured in many prestigious sources such as the LA Times and Vancouver Province newspapers.

World Wide Web Consortium (`http://www.w3.org/`)
The home of the Web. W3C is the main body that sets and agrees the standards for HTML and Web-related technologies.

Wynkoop BackOffice Pages (`http://www.swynk.com/`)
Maintained by Steve Wynkoop, this site covers all Microsoft BackOffice technologies. Ideal for those who want to combine ASP and corporate databases.

N
W

P2P.WROX.COM

Join the Pro ASP 3 mailing lists for author and peer support. Our unique system provides **programmer to programmer™ support** on mailing lists, forums and newsgroups all in addition to our one-to-one email system. Be confident that your query is not just being examined by a support professional, but by the many Wrox authors and other industry experts present on our mailing lists.

We've extended our commitment to support beyond just while you read the book, to once you start developing applications as well. We'll be there on this crucial second step of your learning. You have the choice of how to receive this information, you can either enroll onto one of several mailing lists, or you can just browse the online forums and newsgroups for an answer. Go to `p2p.wrox.com`. You'll find three different lists, each tailored to a specific support issue:

- **Errata**
  You find something wrong with the book, or you just think something has been badly or misleadingly explained then leave your message here. You'll still receive our customary quick reply, but you'll also have the advantage that every author will be able to see your problem at once and help deal with it.

- **Code Clinic**
  You've read the book, and you're sat at home or work developing your own application, it doesn't work in the way you think it should. Post your code here for advice and supports from our authors and from people in the same position as yourself.

- **How to?**
  Something you think the book should have talked about, something you'd just like to know more about, a completely baffling problem with no solution, then this is your forum. If you're developing an application at work then chances are there's someone out there who's already done the same as you, and has a solution to your problem here.

How To Enroll For Support

Just follow this four-step system:

1. Go to p2p`.wrox.com`
2. Click on the Professional ASP 3.0 cover graphic
3. Click on the type of mailing list you wish to join
4. Fill in your email address and password (of at least 4 digits) and email it to us

Why this system offers the best support

You can choose to join the mailing lists or you can receive them as a weekly digest. If you don't have the time or facility to receive the mailing list, then you can search our online archives. You'll find the ability to search on specific subject areas or keywords. As these lists are moderated, you can be confident of finding good, accurate information quickly. Mails can be edited or moved by the moderator into the correct place, making this a most efficient resource. Junk and spam mail are deleted, and your own email address is protected by the unique Lyris system from web-bots that can automatically hoover up newsgroup mailing list addresses. Any queries about joining, leaving lists or any query about the list should be sent to: `moderatorproasp3@wrox.com`.

N
W

Index

Symbols

A

B

D

E

F

I

J

N

O

Q

S

U

X

N
W

Wrox writes books for you. Any suggestions, or ideas about how you want information given in your ideal book will be studied by our team. Your comments are always valued at Wrox.

Free phone in USA 800-USE-WROX
Fax (312) 893 8001

UK Tel. (0121) 687 4100 Fax (0121) 687 4101

Professional ASP 3.0- Registration Card

Name ______

Address ______

______

______

______

City ______ State/Region ______

Country ______ Postcode/Zip ______

E-mail ______

Occupation ______

How did you hear about this book? ______

- [ ] Book review (name) ______
- [ ] Advertisement (name) ______
- [ ] Recommendation ______
- [ ] Catalog ______
- [ ] Other ______

Where did you buy this book? ______

- [ ] Bookstore (name) ______ City ______
- [ ] Computer Store (name) ______
- [ ] Mail Order ______
- [ ] Other ______

What influenced you in the purchase of this book?

- [ ] Cover Design
- [ ] Contents
- [ ] Other (please specify) ______

How did you rate the overall contents of this book?

- [ ] Excellent
- [ ] Good
- [ ] Average
- [ ] Poor

What did you find most useful about this book? ______

What did you find least useful about this book? ______

Please add any additional comments. ______

What other subjects will you buy a computer book on soon? ______

What is the best computer book you have used this year? ______

Note: This information will only be used to keep you updated about new Wrox Press titles and will not be used for any other purpose or passed to any other third party.

2610 ***Check here if you DO NOT want to receive support for this book*** **2610**

NB. If you post the bounce back card below in the UK, please send it to:
Wrox Press Ltd., Arden House , 1102 Warwick Road,
Acocks Green, Birmingham, B27 6BH

Computer Book Publishers

NO POSTAGE
NECESSARY
IF MAILED
IN THE
UNITED STATES

BUSINESS REPLY MAIL
FIRST CLASS MAIL PERMIT#64 CHICAGO, IL

POSTAGE WILL BE PAID BY ADDRESSEE

WROX PRESS
29 S LASALLE ST
SUITE 520
CHICAGO IL 60603.